TREATISE ON CONSTITUTIONAL LAW

SUBSTANCE AND PROCEDURE

Second Edition

By

RONALD D. ROTUNDA

Professor of Law,
University of Illinois

JOHN E. NOWAK

Professor of Law,
University of Illinois

Volume 4

Sections 20.1 to End

APPENDICES

TABLES

INDEX

ST. PAUL, MINN.
WEST PUBLISHING CO.
1992

Library of Congress Cataloging-in-Publication Data

Rotunda, Ronald D.
 Treatise on constitutional law : substance and procedure / by
Ronald D. Rotunda, John E. Nowak. — 2nd ed.
  p. cm.
 Includes index.
 ISBN 0–314–00803–9 (v. 1). — ISBN 0–314–00804–7 (v. 2). — ISBN
0–314–00805–5 (v. 3). — 0–314–01029–7 (v. 4)
 1. United States—Constitutional law. I. Nowak, John E.
II. Title.
KF4550.R63 1992
342.73'029—dc20
[347.30229]   92–11000
                CIP

ISBN 0–314–01029–7

WESTLAW® Overview

Rotunda & Nowak's *Treatise on Constitutional Law: Substance and Procedure, Second Edition,* offers a detailed and comprehensive treatment of law under the U.S. Constitution. To supplement the information in this hornbook, you can access WESTLAW, a computer-assisted legal research service of West Publishing Company. WESTLAW contains a broad library of constitutional law resources, including case law, statutes, administrative materials, commentary, technical and scientific information and current legal and news developments.

Learning how to use these materials effectively will enhance your legal research. So that you can coordinate your book and WESTLAW research, this volume contains an appendix listing WESTLAW search techniques and sample problems.

THE PUBLISHER

*

SUMMARY OF CONTENTS

Volume 1

Volume 2

Volume 3

Volume 4

SUMMARY OF CONTENTS

Appendices

TABLE OF CONTENTS

Volume 4

TABLE OF CONTENTS

TABLE OF CONTENTS

TABLE OF CONTENTS

TABLE OF CONTENTS

TABLE OF CONTENTS

TABLE OF CONTENTS

TABLE OF CONTENTS

TREATISE ON CONSTITUTIONAL LAW

SUBSTANCE AND PROCEDURE

Second Edition

*

Chapter 20

FREEDOM OF SPEECH

Table of Sections

2

I. INTRODUCTION

§ 20.1 Generally

In this Chapter we focus on the free speech clause of the first amendment. First we begin with an historical summary and philosophical background of some of the important English and American experiences with laws restricting speech, primarily political speech. Then we shall turn to some of the techniques used or attitudes expressed by the Court in reviewing a statute affecting speech.

We will identify the primary techniques used by the Court to balance speech interests against the interests of the state or federal governments in laws alleged to infringe on free speech. The Court often engages in a close analysis of the statute under attack to determine if it is overly broad or too vague; that is, though a narrowly drawn statute could validly restrict certain activity, the fatal flaw in the particular statute may be that it is drafted so that it may be read to restrict valid speech interests. Additionally, the judges will independently determine if the statute alleged to restrict speech can achieve its legitimate goals by less restrictive means.

In the last part of this Chapter, and by far the bulk of it, we consider in the main how the Court has dealt with specific types or categories of speech in concrete situations: subversive speech; obscene speech; the speech of the broadcast media and of the traditional print media; libelous speech; speech affecting associational rights; "fighting words" and speech before hostile audiences; symbolic speech; restrictions on speech that affect the gathering and reporting of news in the context of fair trials and investigative reporting; and speech associated with rights of assembly and petition.

One must bear in mind that these categories are not exhaustive, and they are certainly not airtight. But they are useful in that the Supreme Court oftentimes develops different tests for the permissible scope of restrictions on the various types of speech. This difference in treatment is really to be expected because to the extent there is ever a balancing of interests, the relevant interests of one type of speech, e.g., subversive speech, may vary from those of another, e.g., obscene speech. Moreover, the techniques of reviewing alleged restrictions on speech (overbreadth, vagueness, and so on) may be applied differently to each category, either consciously or unconsciously.

II. HISTORICAL BACKGROUND

§ 20.2 Introduction

Freedom of speech has been recognized as one of the preeminent rights of Western democratic theory, the touchstone of individual liberty.[1] Justice Cardozo characterized it as "... the matrix, the indispensible condition of nearly every other form of freedom."[2] The consequences of an application of this theory, however, has often provoked bitter public controversy. As Justice Holmes has observed, "... it is ... not free thought for those who agree with us, but freedom for the thought that we hate,"[3] which gives the theory its most enduring value.

One can readily appreciate the wisdom of Professor Thomas Emerson's emphasis on the importance as well as the difficulty of arriving at an understanding of the system of freedom of expression as envisioned by the language of the first amendment.

> [T]he theory of freedom of expression is a sophisticated and even complex one. It does not come naturally to the ordinary citizen but needs to be learned. It must be restated and reiterated not only for each generation, but for each new situation.[4]

§ 20.2

1. Dunagin v. City of Oxford, 489 F.Supp. 763, 769 (N.D.Miss.1980) (Keady, D.J., quoting an earlier edition of this Treatise) (per curiam), reversed on other grounds 701 F.2d 335 (5th Cir.1983).

2. Palko v. Connecticut, 302 U.S. 319, 327, 58 S.Ct. 149, 152, 82 L.Ed. 288 (1937).

3. United States v. Schwimmer, 279 U.S. 644, 654–55, 49 S.Ct. 448, 451, 73 L.Ed. 889 (1929) (dissenting opinion).

4. T. Emerson, Toward A General Theory of the First Amendment, 72 Yale L.J. 877, 894 (1963). For an excellent introduction to, and analysis of, the free speech clause, see Van Alstyne, A Graphic Review of the Free Speech Clause, 70 Calif.L.Rev. 107 (1982). The article was "[w]ritten principally for students" and aims "to determine what is at stake among contending interpretations, and to see why great importance tends to be attached to such matters." 70 Calif.L.Rev. at 107.

Consequently, it is necessary to examine the historical and philosophical context out of which the concept of free speech emerged.

§ 20.3   The English Background

(a) Introduction

The intransigence of the developing nation-states toward the idea that speech, regardless of its content, is entitled to a public forum, was a natural outgrowth of the authoritarian nature of those societies following the Middle Ages. Political authority derived its legitimacy from religious authority, where truth was determined by divine revelation. Controversies were, therefore, to be resolved by God through his infallible human agents in the government and churches. Dissent from this authority meant not only to be wrong, but to be damned.

Dissent was no more tolerable when governments became responsive to political, rather than spiritual needs. It was essential, if divine authority were removed, that the popular opinion of the government be preserved in order that the obligations which the government required of the people, primarily taxes and military conscription, were to be efficiently obtained.[1]

In England, the situation was exacerbated by the schism between the English and Roman Catholic Church as well as the protracted struggle for supremacy between the King and Parliament. Thus, in the three centuries prior to the Declaration of Independence, the battle for the hearts and minds of the English people required the suppression of ideas antagonistic to the controlling power. The two primary methods by which this suppression was effectuated were the doctrine of seditious libel and the licensing and regulation of the press.[2]

(b) Seditious Libel

The publication of statements critical of the sovereign or his agents was considered seditious libel. The theory of the action, as developed

---

§ 20.3

1. Thus, Lord Holt in Rex v. Tuchin, Holt 424 (1704) reasoned:

"If men should not be called to account for possessing the people with an ill opinion of the government, no government can subsist; for it is very necessary for every government, that the people should have a good opinion of it. And nothing can be worse to any government, than to endeavor to produce animosities as to the management of it. This has always been looked upon as a crime, and no government can be safe unless it be punished."

Quoted in Z. Chafee, Free Speech In the United States 180 (1941).

2. See generally, C.D. Bowen, The Lion and the Throne: The Life and Times of Sir Edward Coke: 1552–1634 (1956); B. Schwartz, The Roots of Freedom: A Constitutional History of England (1967).

Constructive Treason. A third, but less used, method of suppression was that of conviction for constructive treason. See 1 H. Taylor, The Origin and Growth of the English Constitution 511 (1898); 3 id. 250–51 (1911); C.D. Bowen, The Lion and the Throne: The Life and Times of Sir Edward Coke: 1552–1634 (1956), at 200–203.

in the Court of the Star Chamber and utilized in subsequent common law courts, was that the King, as the originator of justice, was above popular criticism. Publication of opinions which were censurious of the government constituted, therefore, a criminal assault. Truth was not a defense, for "the greater the truth, the greater the libel" against the government.[3] There was no need to prove intent to incite insurrection for if one intended to publish criticism, he acted unlawfully merely by finding "fault with his masters and betters."[4] Prosecution was vigorous.

Eventually Parliament enacted Fox's Libel Act,[5] in 1792, which turned the issue of guilt to the jury, who could bring in a general verdict of guilty or not guilty. No longer could the judge direct the jury to find the defendant guilty merely on proof of the publication. After Fox's Libel Act, seditious prosecutions in England "went on with shameful severity" but the new Act was still a safeguard.[6] This Act was silent as to whether truth should be allowed as a defense.

(c) Prior Restraints

In addition to punishment following the publication of an article, English authors, until 1694, had to contend with an elaborate system of licensing. All writing that was to be published had to be licensed prior to publication; without the license, there could be no lawful publication. "The struggle for the freedom of the press was primarily directed against the power of the licensor."[7]

---

3. Prosser and Keeton, Handbook of the Law of Torts 771–73 (5th ed. 1984); 2 J.S. Stephen, A History of the Criminal Law of England 381 (London 1883); L. Levy, Judgments: Essays on American Constitutional History 119 (1972); Z. Chafee, Free Speech in the United States 500 (1941). See generally, Mayton, Seditious Libel and the Lost Guarantee of a Freedom of Expression, 84 Colum.L.Rev. 91 (1984).

On views regarding the history of English Seditious Libel, see Anderson, The Origin of the Press Clause, 30 U.C.L.A.L.Rev. 455 (1983) (criticizing Levy); Levy, On the Origins of the Free Press Clause, 32 U.C.L.A.L.Rev. 177 (1983) (criticizing Anderson).

4. Z. Chafee, Free Speech in the United States 19 (1941). See generally, Mayton, Seditious Libel and the Lost Guarantee of a Freedom of Expression, 84 Colum.L.Rev. 91 (1984).

5. 32 Geo. 3, c. 60 (1792). See generally, 2 J.S. Stephen, A History of the Criminal Law of England 340–49 (1882).

6. Z. Chafee, Free Speech in the United States 23, 35 (1941).

7. Lovell v. Griffin, 303 U.S. 444, 451, 58 S.Ct. 666, 669, 82 L.Ed. 949 (1938), opinion conformed 57 Ga.App. 901, 197 S.E. 347 (1938).

Regarding the relationship between prior restraints, the punishment of speech, and the role of first amendment values in a democratic system, see generally, Blasi, Towards a Theory of Prior Restraint: The Central Linkage, 66 Minn.L.Rev. 11 (1981); Jeffries, Rethinking Prior Restraint, 92 Yale L.J. 409 (1983); Redish, The Proper Role of the Prior Restraint Doctrine in First Amendment Theory, 70 Virginia L.Rev. 53 (1984).

See also, Mayton, Toward a Theory of First Amendment Process: Injunctions of Speech, Subsequent Punishment, and the Costs of the Prior Restraint Doctrine, 67 Cornell L.Rev. 245 (1982) (The preference for subsequent punishment over injunctive relief diminishes the exercise of free speech. Therefore, a prior restraint model is a better mechanism for protection of speech.); Hunter, Toward a Better Understanding of the Prior Restraint Doctrine: A Reply to Professor Mayton, 67 Cornell L.Rev. 283 (1982).

The history of this censorship is concisely summarized by Justice Story, in his Commentaries on the Constitution:

> The art of printing soon after its introduction, we are told, was looked upon, as well in England as in other countries, as merely a matter of state, and subject to the coercion of the crown. It was, therefore, regulated in England by the King's proclamations, prohibitions, charters of privilege, and licenses, and finally by the decrees of the Court of Star–Chamber, which limited the number of printers and of presses which each should employ, and prohibited new publications, unless previously approved by proper licensers. On the demolition of this odious jurisdiction, in 1641, the Long Parliament of Charles the First, after their rupture with that prince, assumed the same powers which the Star–Chamber exercised with respect to licensing books; and during the Commonwealth (such is human frailty and the love of power even in republics!) they issued their ordinances for that purpose, founded principally upon a Star–Chamber decree in 1637. After the restoration of Charles the Second, a statute on the same subject was passed, copied, with some few alterations, from the parliamentary ordinances. The act expired in 1679, and was revived and continued for a few years after the revolution of 1688. Many attempts were made by the government to keep it in force; but it was so strongly resisted by Parliament that it expired in 1694, and has never since been revived.[8]

§ 20.4   Colonial Background

Although the initial emigration to the New World is credited to the repressive religious policies prevalent in Europe, the colonies exhibited no tendencies to liberalize free communication within their own communities. "Colonial America was an open society dotted with closed enclaves, and one could generally settle with his co-believers in safety and comfort and exercise the right of oppression." [1]

The Trial of John Peter Zenger. The decline in the use of censorship in England no doubt contributed to its relative absence in pre-Revolutionary America. However, the doctrine of seditious libel was in full force on both sides of the Atlantic. Although the last prosecution for seditious libel in the colonies, that of New York printer

---

8. 2 J. Story, Commentaries on the Constitution of the United States, § 1882 (5th ed. 1891) (footnote omitted).

§ 20.4

1. J. Roche, American Liberty: An Examination of the "Tradition" of Freedom, in Shadow and Substance: Essays on the Theory and Structure of Politics 11 (1964), as quoted in L. Levy, Judgments: Essays in American Constitutional History 121 & n. 37 (1972).

John Peter Zenger, occurred in 1735, the threat of prosecution in the ensuing years did not cease.[2]

The trial of Zenger was the first cause célèbre in the name of free speech in America. Zenger had published articles critical of the policies of New York's Governor Cosby, for which the royal governor instituted suit, over the reluctance of the colonial legislature. The defense, organized and argued by a prominent attorney, Andrew Hamilton, centered on the assertion that truth should be a proper defense to the crime. Hamilton recognized that truth, if determined by the jury, would exculpate his client, for the intrusion of the King into colonial affairs was already deeply resented. This position was not the broad libertarian theory of freedom of the press which was being advanced, but merely the right of the press to publish articles in accord with that ephemeral concept known as "popular opinion." The Court rejected Hamilton's argument, but he prevailed by persuading the jury to ignore the law and return a general verdict of acquittal.[3]

Colonial Legislative Practice. At the same time, the popularly elected legislatures were imposing rather draconian punishments, through summary contempt procedures upon printers who criticized their policies.[4] Liberty to speak critically of the government was cherished in the abstract, but manipulated in practice to suit the politics of the time.

Although issues of free speech were by and large subsumed in the general debate over the revolution, the common law view at the time the Constitution was drafted is generally conceded to be that expressed by Blackstone in his Commentaries, first published in 1765. At that time, it will be remembered, the practice of censorship had withered

---

2. Z. Chafee, Free Speech in the United States 21 (1941). See, also the thorough historical discussion in Rabban, The First Amendment in Its Forgotten Years, 90 Yale L.J. 514 (1981).

For a discussion of state court protections of free speech based on state constitutions, see generally, Developments in the Law—The Interpretation of State Constitutional Rights, 95 Harv.L.Rev. 1193, 1398–1428 (1982).

3. Several accounts of the Zenger trial have been published. A bibliography is available in L. Rutherford, John Peter Zenger: His Press, His Trial, and a Bibliography of Zenger Imprints 249–53 (1904). Zenger's counsel argued to the jury: "Men who injure and oppress the people under their administration and provoke them to cry out and complain should not also be allowed to make that very complaint the

foundation for new oppressions and prosecutions." Trial of John Peter Zenger, 17 Howell's State Tr. 675, 721–22 (1735). See also, L. Levy, ed., Liberty of the Press from Zenger to Jefferson (1966); F. Latham, The Trial of John Peter Zenger, August, 1735 (1970).

In England, it was not until 1843 that there was a defense of truth, if publication was for the public benefit. See Lord Campbell's Act, 6 & 7 Vict. (1843), c. 96; T. Plucknett, A Concise History of the Common Law 444 (2d ed. 1936).

4. Leonard Levy provides detailed accounts of the willingness of the colonial legislatures to honor free speech in accord with their political views, but dishonor it when the criticism was directed at them, in his book, Judgments: Essays on American Constitutional History 125–34 (1972).

away, but the law of seditious libel was still viable.[5] As Blackstone noted:

> The liberty of the press is indeed essential to the nature of a free state; but this consists in laying no *previous* restraint upon publications, and not in freedom from censure for criminal matter when published. Every freeman has an undoubted right to lay what sentiments he pleases before the public; to forbid this, is to destroy the freedom of the press; but if he publishes what is improper, mischievous, or illegal, he must take the consequences of his own temerity.... [T]hus, the will of individuals is still left free; the abuse only of that free-will is the object of legal punishment. Neither is any restraint hereby laid upon freedom of thought or enquiry: liberty of private sentiment is still left; the disseminating, or making public, of bad sentiments, destructive of the ends of society, is the crime which society corrects.[6]

§ 20.5   Enactment of the First Amendment

The Framers of the Constitution felt no need to include in the original document a provision expressly upholding a general theory of freedom of speech, undoubtedly holding to the belief that the government they envisioned, limited to the enumerated powers, could not constitutionally enact a law in derogation of the principle of free speech. Popular pressure, however, demanded a more articulate expression of the guarantees of individual rights from governmental interference, which culminated in the adoption of the Bill of Rights in 1791. Thus, the first amendment states:

> Congress shall make no law respecting an establishment of religion, or prohibiting the free exercise thereof; or abridging the freedom of speech, or of the press; or the right of the people peaceably to assemble, and to petition the Government for a redress of grievances.

Little can be drawn from the debates within the House concerning the meaning of the first amendment,[1] nor are there any records of

---

5. There were 70 prosecutions and 50 convictions for seditious libel by the English authorities from 1760 to 1776. 2 T.S. May, Constitutional History of England 9n (2d ed. 1912).

6. Commentaries on the Laws of England, Book IV pp. *151–152 (T. Cooley ed., Chicago: 2d ed., rev. ed. 1872) (emphasis in original).

§ 20.5

1. Constitution of the United States: Analysis & Interpretation, 92d Cong., 2d Sess., Senate Document 92–82 (1973), at p. 936.

See generally, Martin H. Redish, Freedom of Expression: A Critical Analysis (1984); Cole, Creative Misreadings in the First Amendment Tradition, 95 Yale L.J. 857 (1986); James L. Swanson & Christian L. Castle, First Amendment Law Handbook (1990).

debates in the Senate[2] or the states[3] on its ratification. Perhaps the members were following Madison's dictum that they should avoid discussing with particularity "abstract propositions, of which judgment may not be convinced.... If we confine ourselves to an enumeration of simple, acknowledged principles, the ratification will meet with but little difficulty."[4]

Interpretation of the first amendment language has not proved as simple as Madison expected, however. Commentators continually raise the question of the intent of the Framers when considering the meaning of the first amendment, although the significance may be more historical than legal following the expansion of the constitutional guarantee in recent years.

Professor Zachariah Chafee contends that the limited, legalistic view of free speech expounded by Blackstone was supplemented in the New World by a tangible popular meaning: the right of unrestricted discussion of public affairs. Thus, the amendment was intended to serve the dual purpose of eliminating all vestiges of censorship in America and destroying the viability of the doctrine of seditious libel.

Because the practice of censorship was abandoned well before the drafting of the first amendment, Chafee contends that it could not have been intended solely as a prohibition against a non-existent practice. The Zenger trial is, in the Chafee view, not only a repudiation of the legitimacy of seditious libel in the colonies but an expression of the colonists' cherished belief in the principle of free speech.[5]

Leonard Levy, however, maintains that a careful historical study of this period will show that a notion that a broad libertarian approach to freedom of speech was a cherished principle is merely a "sentimental hallucination." There was nothing in the tradition of the colonists to influence them to overthrow seditious libel, and their activities would indicate that free speech in the revolutionary period was accorded only to those who propounded favorable opinions of the struggle for independence.[6]

More recent historical research has tended to support Professor Chafee's broader view of the first amendment. After comparing the

---

2. Id.

3. Id.

4. 1 Annals of Congress, 738 (August 15, 1789).

5. Z. Chafee, Free Speech in the United States (1941) at 19–21.

6. L. Levy, Legacy of Suppression: Freedom of Speech and Press in Early American History, ch. 2 (1960). This book was also published in 1963 as Freedom of Speech and Press in Early American History. See also, Levy, On the Origins of the Free Press Clause, 32 U.C.L.A.L.Rev. 177 (1984).

Levy's "Legacy of Suppression" was revised and republished as L. Levy, Emergence of a Free Press (1985). See, Van Alstyne, Congressional Power and Free Speech: Levy's Legacy Revisited, 99 Harv. L.Rev. 1089 (1986); Mayton, From a Legacy of Suppression to the "Metaphor of the Fourth Estate," 39 Stanford L.Rev. 139 (1986).

relevant language and the history surrounding free speech rights guaranteed in state constitutions that were contemporary to the Bill of Rights, Professor Robert Palmer has concluded that, at the time of the adoption of the Bill of Rights, the meaning of freedom of speech and of the press on the state level as well as on the federal level was "extremely broad." Quite simply, "it meant freedom to speak and publish whatsoever with neither prior restraint nor subsequent punishments," a right similar to a freedom of movement. At the state level, the language and history of the state constitutional provisions indicate that the right of speech and press was qualified by a recognition of right of "communal need." This right of communal need was originally conceived as an actual "right," that is, the right of communal need was placed in the state declaration of rights along with the right to speech and press, with the result that the communal and individual rights were intended to be balanced with each other. "The irreducible effect of that balancing [on the state level] was the absence of prior restraint, but it would have been considered very improper if the effect was that narrow." In contrast, at the federal level, there was no "right of communal need" that was placed in the first amendment, so that the right of free speech and press were not balanced against any alleged right of communal need.[7]

The Alien and Sedition Acts. Whatever the view of the Framers at the time of the drafting of amendment, a broader interpretation of that language was ensured by the controversy surrounding the Alien and Sedition Acts of 1798.[8] Under the Alien Act, the President could order all aliens "as he shall judge dangerous to the peace and safety of the United States. . . ." to leave the country.[9] It was never formally invoked, and expired after two years, but its existence did result in some aliens leaving the country or going into hiding.[10]

The Sedition Act prohibited "publishing any false, scandalous and malicious writing or writings against the government of the United States, or either house of Congress . . . or the President . . . with intent to defame . . . or to bring them . . . into contempt or disrepute. . . ."[11] Truth was a defense and the jury had a right to determine the law and facts under the direction of the court. In this respect the Act was actually a fairly liberal one for its time. England did not establish a

---

7. Palmer, Liberties, 55, 147, in W. Nelson & R. Palmer, Constitutional Rights in the Early American Republic (Institute of Bill of Rights Law Monographs, Number 2, College of William & Mary 1987).

8. J. Smith, Freedom's Fetters—The Alien and Sedition Laws and American Civil Liberties (1956); L. Levy, Legacy of Suppression: Freedom of Speech and Press in Early American History, ch. 6 (1960).

9. 1 Stat. at Large 570.

10. 1 Emerson, Haber, & Dorsen's Political and Civil Rights in the United States 21 (4th ed., Law School ed. 1976). Hereinafter all citations are to the law school edition of this book, not the lawyer's edition.

11. 1 Stat. at Large 596.

defense of truth until 1843,[12] though a general verdict of the jury was allowed in the 1790's.[13]

The Sedition Act was employed by President Adams' Federalist administration against members of Jefferson's Democratic–Republican party for their criticism of his administration. Despite the subsequent retaliation in kind by the Republicans upon Jefferson's election,[14] their attack upon the politically motivated prosecutions and the resulting restriction upon free expression provided the foundation for the modern theory of the first amendment.

Although these Acts were never required to withstand judicial scrutiny under the first amendment in the Supreme Court, the Alien and Sedition Acts remain the epitome of an unconstitutional abridgement of free speech. Justice Brennan later wrote that it was the Sedition Act "which first crystallized a national awareness of the central meaning of the First Amendment." [15] He added:

> Although the Sedition Act was never tested in this Court, the attack upon its validity has carried the day in the court of history. Fines levied in its prosecution were repaid by Act of Congress on the ground that it was unconstitutional.... Calhoun, reporting to the Senate on February 4, 1836, assumed that its invalidity was a matter "which no one now doubts." ... Jefferson, as President, pardoned those who had been convicted and sentenced under the Act.... The invalidity of the Act has also been assumed by Justices of this Court.... These views reflect a broad consensus that the Act, because of the restraint it imposed upon criticism of government and public officials, was inconsistent with the First Amendment.[16]

12. 6 & 7 Vic. c. 96 (1843) (Lord Campbell's Act); 2 J.S. Stephen, A History of the Criminal Law of England 383 (London, 1883).

13. Fox's Libel Act, 32 Geo. 3, c. 60 (1792).

14. L. Levy, Jefferson & Civil Liberties—The Darker Side 58–59 (1963). Levy reports an incident in which Jefferson, in a letter to the Governor of Pennsylvania, noted that the Federalists having failed to destroy the press by their gag law, now appeared to be doing so by encouraging its licentiousness, and that a few well-placed prosecutions might be necessary to restore the integrity of the press.

15. New York Times v. Sullivan, 376 U.S. 254, 273, 84 S.Ct. 710, 722, 11 L.Ed.2d 686 (1964), motion denied 376 U.S. 967, 84 S.Ct. 1130, 12 L.Ed.2d 83 (1964).

16. New York Times v. Sullivan, 376 U.S. 254, 276, 84 S.Ct. 710, 723–24, 11

L.Ed.2d 686 (1964), motion denied 376 U.S. 967, 84 S.Ct. 1130, 12 L.Ed.2d 83 (1964) (footnote omitted).

First Amendment History Prior to World War I. From the time the first amendment was enacted until the World War I era, the Supreme Court and the lower courts did not focus very much at all on free speech issues. One of the few exceptions is the time of the Alien and Sedition Acts, enforced by the lower courts. For a complete and thorough history of the first amendment during this period, see Anderson, The Formative Period of First Amendment Theory, 1870–1915, 24 Am.J.Legal Hist. 56 (1980); Rabban, The First Amendment in its Forgotten Years, 90 Yale L.J. 516 (1981); Rabban, The Emergence of Modern First Amendment Doctrine, 50 U.Chi.L.Rev. 1205 (1983); Hunter, Problems in Search of Principles: The First Amendment in the Supreme

§ 20.6　The Value of Speech and the Function of the First Amendment

Reliance solely on the intent of the founders for an appraisal of the scope of first amendment protections is inadequate for several reasons. First, as we have seen, the tools available to calibrate such intent are imprecise and capable of divergent interpretations. Second, and more importantly, such reliance imposes a narrow view upon the role of the Constitution by ignoring the dynamic nature of its provisions.[1] Justice Holmes, for example, thought that the main purpose of the free speech guarantee of the first amendment "is 'to prevent all such *previous restraints* upon publications as had been practiced by other governments', and they do not prevent the subsequent punishment of such as may be deemed contrary to the public welfare." [2] Yet he also admitted: "There is no constitutional right to have all general propositions of law once adopted remain unchanged." [3] Thus, it is appropriate to note briefly the underlying values of free speech as they have been articulated from time to time in order to ascertain the proper degree of judicial solicitude to be afforded such a concept.

First, it should be recognized, as Professor Meiklejohn has observed, that the first amendment does not forbid the abridging of speech, but abridging the *freedom of speech*.[4] "The First Amendment is not the guardian of unregulated talkativeness." [5] Therefore, the values perceived in a system of free expression will be determinative of whether there exists an inhibition upon that freedom.

John Milton. The initial justification for a system of free speech has long been held to be its value in preventing human error through ignorance. One of the most eloquent defenses of free speech is derived from John Milton's battle with the English censorship laws. In his tract, Areopagitica, Milton said:

> [T]hough all the winds of doctrine were let loose to play upon the earth, so truth be in the field, we do injuriously, by licensing and prohibiting, to misdoubt her strength. Let her and falsehood

Court from 1791–1930, 35 Emory L.J. 59 (1986).

§ 20.6

1. See, e.g., P. Brest, Process of Constitutional Decisionmaking, ch. 2 (1975).

See also, Martin Redish, Freedom of Expression: A Critical Analysis (1984); C. Edwin Baker, Human Liberty and Freedom of Speech (1989); Steven Shiffrin, The First Amendment, Democracy, and Romance (1990); Farber, Free Speech Without Romance: Public Choice and the First

Amendment (1991); Sedler, The First Amendment in Litigation: The "Law of the First Amendment," 48 Wash. & Lee L.Rev. 457 (1991).

2. Patterson v. Colorado, 205 U.S. 454, 462, 27 S.Ct. 556, 558, 51 L.Ed. 879 (1907) (emphasis in original).

3. Patterson v. Colorado, 205 U.S. 454, 461, 27 S.Ct. 556, 557, 51 L.Ed. 879 (1907).

4. A. Meiklejohn, Free Speech and Its Relation to Self Government (1948) p. 19.

5. Id. at 26.

grapple; whoever knew truth put to the worse in a free and open encounter? [6]

John Stuart Mill. John Stuart Mill expanded Milton's arguments two centuries later in his 1859 essay, *On Liberty,* by his recognition of the public good—the public enlightenment—which results from the free exchange of ideas.

First, if any opinion is compelled to silence, that opinion for aught we can certainly know, be true. To deny this is to assume our own infalliability. Secondly, though this silenced opinion be in error, it may, and very commonly does, contain a portion of the truth; and since the generally prevailing opinion on any subject is rarely or never the whole truth, it is only by the collision of adverse opinions that the remainder of the truth had any chance being supplied. Thirdly, even if the received opinion be not only true but the whole truth; unless it is suffered to be, and actually is, vigorously and earnestly contested, it will, by most of those who receive it, be held in the manner of a prejudice, with little comprehension of feeling of its rational grounds. And not only this, but fourthly, the meaning of the doctrine itself will be in danger of being lost or enfeebled....[7]

Holmes and the Marketplace of Ideas. These statements are strongly supportive of Justice Holmes' "marketplace of ideas" theory of free speech.[8] This theory is built upon the premise that the first amendment prohibits government suppression of ideas because the truth of any idea can only be determined in the "marketplace" of competing ideas. There are, of course, other justifications.

Individual Self–Fulfillment. An important function of free speech is to enhance the potential of individual contribution to the social welfare, thus enlarging the prospects for individual self-fulfillment.[9] Another function, a corollary of the first, is that the health of a

---

6. J. Milton, Areopagitica, A Speech for the Liberty of Unlicensed Printing to the Parliament of England (1644). Milton was not as assured of the strength of truth as it appeared, however, for he disavowed any legitimacy for popery, open superstition, impiety, or evil. Id.

7. J.S. Mill, On Liberty (1859), Ch. II.

See also, R. Ladenson, A Philosophy of Free Expression and Its Constitutional Applications (1983), reviewed by Block, 69 Minn.L.Rev. 727 (1985).

See generally, M. Nimmer, Nimmer on Free Speech § 1.02 (1984); J.B. Bury, A History of Freedom of Thought 191–92 (2d ed.); Emerson, Colonial Intentions and Current Realities of the First Amendment, 125 U.Pa.L.Rev. 737 (1977); Scanlon, Free-

dom of Expression and Categories of Expression, 40 U.Pitt.L.Rev. 519 (1979).

8. Abrams v. United States, 250 U.S. 616, 630, 40 S.Ct. 17, 22, 63 L.Ed. 1173 (1919) (dissenting opinion).

See generally, Ingber, The Marketplace of Ideas: A Legitimizing Myth, 1984 Duke L.J. 1. See also, Baker, Scope of the First Amendment Freedom of Speech, 25 U.C.L.A.L.Rev. 964, 967–81 (1978); Blasi, The Checking Value in First Amendment Theory, 1977 A.B.R.Res.J. 523, 551.

9. See Redish, The Value of Free Speech, 130 U.Penn.L.Rev. 591, 593 (1982), emphasizing the value of "individual self-realization." For comment on this thesis, see Baker, Realizing Self-Realization: Corporate Political Expenditures and Redish's

society of self-government is nurtured by the contributions of individuals to its functioning.[10]

Speech is important to self-fulfillment even if the speech is not specifically about politics. Thus, speech with the main purpose of entertaining is protected by the free speech guarantee.[11] It is no accident that Eastern European Communists suppressed art as well as politics and religion. And when the people overturned the Communist dictators of Eastern Europe beginning in late 1989, they regarded freedom of expression as a premier right. The Czech revolution, for example, began in the theatres, and that country's first freely elected president since World War II was a writer and playwright. "[P]eople's spiritual needs, more than their material needs, have driven the commissars from power."[12]

The Value of Free Speech, 130 U.Penn. L.Rev. 646 (1982), and the reply: Redish, Self–Realization, Democracy, and Freedom of Expression: A Reply to Professor Baker, 130 U.Penn.L.Rev. 678 (1982). See also, Steven H. Shiffrin, The First Amendment: Democracy and Romance (1990). Cf. Farber, Free Speech Without Romance: Public Choice and the First Amendment, 105 Harv.L.Rev. 554 (1991).

See Brandeis, J., concurring, in Whitney v. California, 274 U.S. 357, 47 S.Ct. 641, 71 L.Ed. 1095 (1927):

"Those who won our independence believed that *the final end of the state was to make men free to develop their faculties;* and that in its government the deliberative forces should prevail over the arbitrary. They *valued liberty both as an end* and as a means. They believed liberty to be the secret of happiness and courage to be the secret of liberty." 274 U.S. at 375, 47 S.Ct. at 648, 71 L.Ed. at 1105 (emphasis added).

Free Speech and the Nature of Language. Professor Chevigny has argued that a right to free expression may also be derived from and rooted in, the nature of language itself; the necessity of a dialogue in order to understand words at all means that society should allow the dialogue to proceed. Chevigny, Philosophy of Language and Free Expression, 55 N.Y.U.L.Rev. 157 (1980). In reply see, Martin, On a New Argument for Freedom of Speech, 57 N.Y.U.L.Rev. 906 (1982), and Chevigny, A Dialogic Right of Free Expression: A Reply to Michael Martin, 57 N.Y.U.L.Rev. 920 (1982).

See generally, R. Rotunda, The Politics of Language: Liberalism as Word and Symbol (U. of Iowa Press, 1986).

10. See T. Emerson, The System of Freedom of Expression (1970) for an elaboration and integration of these theses in a more complete form. See generally, Bollinger, Free Speech and Intellectual Values, 92 Yale L.J. 438 (1983).

11. Movies as Protected Free Speech. See Joseph Burstyn, Inc. v. Wilson, 343 U.S. 495, 72 S.Ct. 777, 96 L.Ed. 1098 (1952) (motion pictures are protected by the free speech guarantee); Kingsley International Pictures Corp. v. Regents of New York University, 360 U.S. 684, 79 S.Ct. 1362, 2 L.Ed.2d 1512 (1959).

12. Salman Rushdie, Is Nothing Sacred: The Herbert Read Memorial Lecture, Feb. 6, 1990 (Granta, 1990), at 8–9.

Salman Rushdie. Mr. Rushdie was the author of *The Satanic Verses,* published in 1989. In early 1989, the spiritual head of Iran announced to the World that Mr. Rushdie must die because his book was, in the eyes of some Muslims, offensive to Muslim beliefs. Mr. Rushdie, a British subject, went into hiding, protected by the British Government that he often criticized. He described what happened as follows:

"On 14 February 1989, within hours of the dread news from Iran, I received a telephone call from Keith Vaz, M[ember of] P[arliament], during which he vehemently expressed his full support for me and my work, and his horror at the threat against my life. A few weeks later, this same gentleman was to be found addressing a demonstration full of men demanding my death, and of children festooned with murderous placards. By now Mr. Vaz wanted my work

Checking the Government. Once we allow the government any power to restrict the freedom of speech, we may have taken a path that is a "slippery slope," particularly since a central value of the free press, speech, and assembly lies in "checking" the abuse of power by public officials.[13] Linedrawing in such an abstract area is always difficult and especially so when a government's natural inclination is moving the line towards more suppression of criticism and unpopular ideas. Thus, even if one could distinguish between illegitimate and legitimate speech, it may still be necessary to protect all speech in order to afford

banned, and threats against my life seemed not to trouble him any longer....

"And Britain witnessed a brutalization of public debate that seemed hard to believe. Incitement to murder was tolerated on the nation's streets. (In Europe and the United States, swift government action prevented such incitement at a very early stage.) On TV shows, studio audiences were asked for a show of hands on the question of whether I should live or die. A man's murder (mine) became a legitimate subject for a national opinion poll. And slowly, slowly, a point of view grew up, and was given voice by mountebanks and bishops, fundamentalists and Mr. John le Carré, which held that *I knew exactly what I was doing.* I must have known what would happen; therefore, I did it on purpose, to profit by the notoriety that would result. This accusation is, today, in fairly wide circulation, and so I must defend myself against it too.

"I find myself wanting to ask questions: when Osip Mandelstam wrote his poem against Stalin, did he 'know what he was doing' and so deserve his death? When the students filled Tiananmen Square to ask for freedom, were they not also, and knowingly, asking for the murderous repression that resulted?   ... Even if I were to concede (and I do not concede it) that what I did in *The Satanic Verses* was the literary equivalent of flaunting oneself shamelessly before the eyes of aroused men, is that really a justification for being, so to speak, gangbanged? Is any provocation a justification for rape?"

Salman Rushdie, In Good Faith 15–16 (Granta, 1990).

13. Blasi, The Checking Value in First Amendment Theory, 1977 A.B. Foundation Res.J. 521. For a careful analysis of the

greater immunity from government regulation of expression than most other forms of human conduct, see Wellington, On Freedom of Expression, 88 Yale L.J. 1105 (1979). See Coleman, A Free Press: The Need to Ensure an Unfettered Check on Democratic Government Between Elections, 59 Tulane L.Rev. 243 (1984).

See also Blasi, The Pathological Perspective and the First Amendment, 85 Colum.L.Rev. 449, 513 (1985):

"(1) The protection and full realization of the core commitments of the first amendment is an objective that deserves especially high priority in constitutional adjudication. (2) The core commitments of the first amendment tend to be jeopardized most seriously during certain periods that may be regarded as pathological due to their unusual social dynamics regarding the tolerance of dissent. (3) The adjudicative methodologies and doctrines that can best protect the core commitments of the first amendment in pathological periods are those that are consciously designed to counteract the unusual social dynamics that characterize such periods. (4) The strategy of targeting first amendment doctrine for the worst of times in the manner suggested by my thesis does not generate unacceptable costs to the quality of adjudication in periods that are not pathological."

Compare Blasi, The Pathological Perspective and the First Amendment, 85 Colum.L.Rev. 449 (1985), with, Redish, The Role of Pathology in First Amendment Theory: A Skeptical Examination, 38 Case Western Reserve L.Rev. 618 (1988).

On the cyclical nature of suppression, see Frank, United States Supreme Court: 1949–50, 18 U.Chi.L.Rev. 1, 20 (1950); J. Frank, Review and Basic Liberties, in E. Cahn, ed., Supreme Court and Supreme Law 109, 113–39 (1954).

real protection for legitimate speech.[14]

Free Speech as a Safety Valve for Society. Justice Brandeis, in his concurring opinion in *Whitney v. California*,[15] warned that those who won our independence—

> knew that order cannot be secured merely through fear of punishment for its infraction; that it is hazardous to discourage thought, hope and imagination; that fear breeds repression; that repression breeds hate; that hate menaces stable government; that the path of safety lies in the opportunity to discuss freely supposed grievances and proposed remedies; and that the fitting remedy for evil counsels is good ones. . . .

> Fear of serious injury cannot alone justify suppression of free speech and assembly. Men feared witches and burned women.[16]

Thus one of the reasons that Government should not suppress speech is that free speech is a safety valve. Just as the ancient Romans eventually learned that executing Christians did not suppress Christianity, modern Governments should realize that forbidding people to talk about certain topics does not encourage public stability. It only creates martyrs. Punishing people for speech does not discourage the speech; it only drives it underground, and encourages conspiracy. In the battle for public order, free speech is the ally, not the enemy.

As Professor Greenawalt has carefully explained, those societies that prohibit public discussion of certain points of view, pay the price in terms of stability, although the purpose of the suppression is to promote stability:

> Those who are resentful because their interests are not accorded fair weight, and who may be doubly resentful because they have not even had a chance to present those interests, may seek to attain by radical changes in existing institutions what they have failed to get from the institutions themselves. Thus, liberty of expression, though often productive of divisiveness, may contribute to social stability.[17]

---

14. On the other hand, it has been argued that protection should only be afforded to explicitly political speech, and not to scientific, literary or obscene speech. See, Bork, Neutral Principles and Some First Amendment Problems, 47 Ind.L.J. 1 (1971).

For an analysis of how judges may shape their view of the values to be protected by the freedom of speech to conform with their political philosophy regarding the proper role of government in the regulation of relationships between individuals in society see Dorsen & Gora, Free Speech, Property, and the Burger Court: Old Values, New Balances, 1982 Sup.Ct.Rev. 195.

15. 274 U.S. 357, 47 S.Ct. 641, 71 L.Ed. 1095 (1927) (Brandeis, J., concurring).

16. 274 U.S. at 375–76, 47 S.Ct. at 648, 71 L.Ed. at 1106 (Brandeis, J., concurring).

17. Greenawalt, Speech and Crime, 1980 A.B.F.Res.J. 645, 672–73.

Some commentators have argued that the Government should be strictly limited by the First Amendment only when it regulates speech for the purpose of skewing debate on public policy issues. See, Kamenshine, Embargoes on Exports of Ideas and Information: First Amendment Issues, 26 Wm. & Mary L.Rev. 863, 879–81 (1985).

III. SOME BASIC TESTS AND ATTITUDES

§ 20.7 Balancing versus Absolutism

(a) A Preferred Position for Free Speech?

In *United States v. Carolene Products Co.*,[1] the Court upheld the power of Congress to regulate "filled milk" as it endorsed the post–1937 concept of judicial deference to acts of other branches of government in their regulation of economic activities. In the course of the now famous footnote 4 of the opinion, Chief Justice Stone indicated that certain other rights might properly receive more active judicial protection against the democratic process:

> There may be narrower scope for operation of the presumption of constitutionality when legislation appears on its face to be within a specific prohibition of the Constitution, such as those of the first ten amendments, which are deemed equally specific when held to be embraced within the Fourteenth....

> It is unnecessary to consider now whether legislation which restricts those political processes which can ordinarily be expected to bring about repeal of undesirable legislation, is to be subjected to more exacting judicial scrutiny under the general prohibitions of the Fourteenth Amendment than are most other types of legislation....[2]

A few years later this view was made more explicit when the Court asserted: "Freedom of press, freedom of speech, freedom of religion are in a preferred position."[3]

Professor Redish points out the fallacy of this approach in Redish, Limits on Scientific Expression and the Scope of First Amendment Values: A Comment on Professor Kamenshine's Analysis, 26 Wm. & Mary L.Rev. 897 (1985); Solum, Freedom of Communicative Action: A Theory of the First Amendment Freedom of Speech, 83 Northwestern University L.Rev. 54 (1989).

§ 20.7

1. 304 U.S. 144, 58 S.Ct. 778, 82 L.Ed. 1234 (1938).

On balancing of interests, see generally, e.g., T. Emerson, The System of Freedom of Expression 117–18, 181–89 (1970); Note, Of Interests, Fundamental and Compelling: The Emerging Constitutional Balance, 57 B.U.L.Rev. 462 (1977); Aleinikoff, Constitutional Law in the Age of Balancing, 96 Yale L.J. 945 (1987); Gottlieb, Compelling Governmental Interests: An Essential But Unanalyzed Term in Constitutional Adjudication, 68 B.U.L.Rev. 917 (1988).

2. 304 U.S. at 152–53 n. 4, 58 S.Ct. at 783–84 n. 4 (1938).

3. Murdock v. Pennsylvania, 319 U.S. 105, 115, 63 S.Ct. 870, 876, 87 L.Ed. 1292 (1943). See also, Herndon v. Lowry, 301 U.S. 242, 258, 57 S.Ct. 732, 739, 81 L.Ed. 1066 (1937); Thornhill v. Alabama, 310 U.S. 88, 95, 60 S.Ct. 736, 740–41, 84 L.Ed. 1093 (1940); Schneider v. State, 308 U.S. 147, 161, 60 S.Ct. 146, 150–51, 84 L.Ed. 155 (1939); Bridges v. California, 314 U.S. 252, 262–63, 62 S.Ct. 190, 193–94, 86 L.Ed. 192 (1941); Prince v. Massachusetts, 321 U.S. 158, 164, 64 S.Ct. 438, 441, 88 L.Ed. 645 (1944), rehearing denied 321 U.S. 804, 64 S.Ct. 784, 88 L.Ed. 1090 (1944); Follett v. McCormick, 321 U.S. 573, 575, 64 S.Ct. 717, 718, 88 L.Ed. 938 (1944); Marsh v. Alabama, 326 U.S. 501, 509, 66 S.Ct. 276, 280, 90 L.Ed. 265 (1945); Saia v. New York, 334

It should be recognized that the position advanced by footnote 4 is not merely an assertion; it does have a strong rationale. Unlike economic legislation, which is only a product of the political process, and therefore may to some extent be subject to an inner political check, speech is part of the legislative process itself; restriction of speech alters the democratic process and undercuts the basis for deferring to the legislation which emerges. Additionally, the restraint of speech may often be seen as a short range aid to societal programs by insulating the current government from criticism caused by debate. This natural tendency conflicts with the first amendment value of open debate. Thus the judiciary may need to be more active to protect this value against the will of a temporary majority.

Justice Frankfurter and the Preferred Position of Free Speech. Justice Frankfurter strongly criticized the use of the "preferred position" terminology, because of his belief its use might imply "... that any law touching communication is infected with presumptive invalidity ... it radiates a constitutional doctrine without avowing it." [4] Such criticism may be regarded as a warning against unwarranted extension of judicial principle rather than an attack upon established judicial dogma, for in that same opinion, Justice Frankfurter wrote most eloquently of the rationale and meaning of the "preferred position of freedom of speech."

> [S]ociological conclusions are conditioned by time and circumstance. Because of this awareness Mr. Justice Holmes seldom felt justified in opposing his own opinion to economic views which the legislature embodied in law. But since he also realized that the progress of civilization is to a considerable extent the displacement of error which once held sway as official truth by beliefs which in turn have yielded to other beliefs, for him the right to search for truth was of a different order than some transient economic dogma. And without freedom of expression, thought becomes checked and atrophied. Therefore, in considering what interests are so fundamental as to be enshrined in the Due Process Clause, those liberties of the individual which history has attested as the indispensable conditions of an open as against a closed society come to this Court with a momentum for respect lacking when appeal is made to liberties which derive merely from shifting economic arrange-

U.S. 558, 562, 68 S.Ct. 1148, 1150–51, 92 L.Ed. 1574 (1948); West Virginia State Bd. of Education v. Barnette, 319 U.S. 624, 639, 63 S.Ct. 1178, 1186, 87 L.Ed. 1628 (1943); Thomas v. Collins, 323 U.S. 516, 530, 65 S.Ct. 315, 322–23, 89 L.Ed. 430 (1945), rehearing denied 323 U.S. 819, 65 S.Ct. 557, 89 L.Ed. 650 (1945).

The attempt to recognize First Amendment freedoms as being in a "preferred position" was first made by Chief Justice Stone in his dissent in Jones v. Opelika, 316 U.S. 584, 600, 608, 62 S.Ct. 1231, 1240–41, 1244, 86 L.Ed. 1691 (1942) (per curiam), judgment vacated and judgments of the state courts reversed 319 U.S. 103, 63 S.Ct. 890, 87 L.Ed. 1290 (1943).

4. Kovacs v. Cooper, 336 U.S. 77, 90, 69 S.Ct. 448, 455, 93 L.Ed. 513 (1949) (concurring opinion), rehearing denied 336 U.S. 921, 69 S.Ct. 638, 93 L.Ed. 1083 (1949).

ments. Accordingly, Mr. Justice Holmes was far more ready to find legislative invasion where free inquiry was involved than in the debatable area of economics.[5]

Since Frankfurter's sharp attack on the language of "preferred position," the words have been avoided but the substance remains. The preferential treatment of the first amendment is exemplified by the variety of judicial tools utilized by the Court in its review of challenged legislation. As we shall see, the Court has applied a narrowed presumption of constitutionality, strictly construed statutes to avoid limiting first amendment freedoms, restricted prior restraint and subsequent punishment, relaxed general requirements of standing to sue and generally set higher standards of procedural due process in order to give vitality to those freedoms over ordinary governmental functions.[6]

(b) Is Free Speech an Absolute?

The first amendment appears to speak in absolutist terms: "Congress shall make no law ... abridging the freedom of speech...." The strict language is emphasized by a comparison with the fourth amendment's prohibition against "*unreasonable* searches and seizures."

If free speech is an absolute right it is certainly in a preferred position vis-a-vis the majority of rights in the Constitution, which like the fourth amendment, are not expressed in absolute terms. An absolute right, by definition, is not subject to balancing.

Considerable controversy has arisen over the appropriate degree of judicial responsibility in appraising and preserving the rights of free speech. In approaching the significant problem of interpreting the meaning of "free speech", an initial problem must be to determine the strength of first amendment rights in relation to the other individual rights and whether, in light of that, it is appropriate for the judiciary to balance free speech with legitimate governmental objectives. The problem is virtually unique to free speech and its corollaries, freedom of the press and the right to petition the Government for a redress of grievance. Even the freedom of religion is on a slightly different plane, for the first amendment may be read to require some balancing of interests—laws must neither establish a religion nor prohibit its free exercise.

The absolutist view of free speech has been championed and most closely associated with Justices Black and Douglas,[7] but it has never been explicitly adopted by a majority of the Court.

5. Kovacs v. Cooper; 336 U.S. 77, 95, 69 S.Ct. 448, 458, 93 L.Ed. 513 (1949) (concurring opinion), rehearing denied 336 U.S. 921, 69 S.Ct. 638, 93 L.Ed. 1083 (1949).

6. McKay, The Preference for Freedom, 34 N.Y.U.L.Rev. 1182, 1184 (1959); Prygoski, Justice Sanford and Modern Free Speech Analysis: Back to the Future?, 75 Ky.L.J. 45 (1986–1987).

7. Konigsberg v. State Bar of California, 366 U.S. 36, 56, 81 S.Ct. 997, 1010, 6 L.Ed.2d 105 (1961) (dissenting opinion), rehearing denied 368 U.S. 869, 82 S.Ct. 21, 7

As Black himself has summarized his views in *Konigsberg v. State Bar of California:* [8]

> The recognition [that a State] has subjected "speech and association to the deterrence of subsequent disclosure" is, under the First Amendment, sufficient in itself to render the action of the State unconstitutional unless one subscribes to the doctrine that permits constitutionally protected rights to be "balanced" away whenever a majority of this Court thinks that a State might have interest sufficient to justify abridgement of those freedoms.... I do not subscribe to that doctrine for I believe that the First Amendment's unequivocal command that there shall be no abridgement of the rights of free speech and assembly shows that the men who drafted our Bill of Rights did all the "balancing" that was to be done in this field.... [T]he very object of adopting the First Amendment ... was to put the freedoms protected there completely out of the area of any congressional control that may be attempted through the exercise of precisely those powers that are now being used to "balance" the Bill of Rights out of existence.... I fear that the creation of "tests" by which speech is left unprotected under certain circumstances is a standing invitation to abridge it.... [T]he Court's "absolute" statement that there are no "absolutes" under the First Amendment must be an exaggeration of its own views. [9]

L.Ed.2d 69 (1961); Braden v. United States, 365 U.S. 431, 441, 81 S.Ct. 584, 590–91, 5 L.Ed.2d 653 (1961) (dissenting), rehearing denied 365 U.S. 890, 81 S.Ct. 1024, 6 L.Ed.2d 200 (1961); Barenblatt v. United States, 360 U.S. 109, 140–44, 79 S.Ct. 1081, 1100–02, 3 L.Ed.2d 1115 (1959) (dissenting), rehearing denied 361 U.S. 854, 80 S.Ct. 40, 4 L.Ed.2d 93 (1959); Wilkinson v. United States, 365 U.S. 399, 422, 81 S.Ct. 567, 580, 5 L.Ed.2d 633 (1961) (dissenting), rehearing denied 365 U.S. 890, 81 S.Ct. 1024, 6 L.Ed.2d 200 (1961); Uphaus v. Wyman, 364 U.S. 388, 392, 81 S.Ct. 153, 159, 5 L.Ed.2d 148 (1960) (dissenting); American Communications Ass'n v. Douds, 339 U.S. 382, 443, 70 S.Ct. 674, 706, 94 L.Ed. 925 (1950), rehearing denied 339 U.S. 990, 70 S.Ct. 1017, 94 L.Ed. 1391 (1950); Communist Party v. SACB, 367 U.S. 1, 137, 81 S.Ct. 1357, 1431–42, 6 L.Ed.2d 625 (1961) (dissenting), rehearing denied 368 U.S. 871, 82 S.Ct. 20, 7 L.Ed.2d 72 (1961); Beauharnais v. Illinois, 343 U.S. 250, 267, 72 S.Ct. 725, 736, 96 L.Ed. 919 (1952) (dissenting), rehearing denied 343 U.S. 988, 72 S.Ct. 1070, 96 L.Ed. 1375 (1952); New York Times Co. v. Sullivan, 376 U.S. 254, 293, 84 S.Ct. 710, 11 L.Ed.2d 686 (1964) (concurring), motion denied 376 U.S. 967, 84 S.Ct. 1130, 12 L.Ed.2d 83 (1964); New York Times Co. v. United States, 403 U.S. 713, 714, 91 S.Ct. 2140, 2141–42, 29 L.Ed.2d 822 (1971) (concurring); Roth v. United States, 354 U.S. 476, 508, 77 S.Ct. 1304, 1321, 1 L.Ed.2d 1498 (1957) (dissenting), rehearing denied 355 U.S. 852, 78 S.Ct. 8, 2 L.Ed.2d 60 (1957); Brandenburg v. Ohio, 395 U.S. 444, 450, 89 S.Ct. 1827, 1831, 23 L.Ed.2d 430 (1969) (concurring).

See generally, J. Frank, Mr. Justice Black (1949); Frank, The New Court and the New Deal, in S. Strickland, ed., Hugo Black 39 (1967); Frank, Hugo L. Black: Free Speech and the Declaration of Independence, in R. Rotunda, ed., Six Justices on Civil Rights, 11, 31–37 (Oceana Publications, Inc. 1983); Countryman, Justice Douglas and Freedom of Expression, in R. Rotunda, ed., Six Justices on Civil Rights 107 (Oceana Publications, Inc. 1983).

8. 366 U.S. 36, 81 S.Ct. 997, 6 L.Ed.2d 105 (1961), rehearing denied 368 U.S. 869, 82 S.Ct. 21, 7 L.Ed.2d 69 (1961).

9. Konigsberg v. State Bar of California, 366 U.S. 36, 60–61, 63, 68, 81 S.Ct. 997, 1012, 1014, 1016, 6 L.Ed.2d 105 (1961) (Black, J., dissenting, joined by Douglas, J.,

Justice Harlan has often been associated with the "balancing view." In *Konigsberg,* where Black wrote his defense of the absolutist position, Harlan wrote for the Court, and presented his justification for judicial balancing.

> [W]e reject the view that freedom of speech and association ... as protected by the First and Fourteenth Amendments, are "absolutes," not only in the undoubted sense that where the constitutional protection exists it must prevail, but also in the sense that the scope of that protection must be gathered solely from a literal reading of the First Amendment. Throughout its history this Court has consistently recognized at least two ways in which constitutionally protected freedom of speech is narrower than an unlimited license to talk. On the one hand, certain forms of speech, or speech in certain contexts, has been considered outside the scope of constitutional protection.... On the other hand, general regulatory statutes, not intended to control the content of speech but incidentally limiting its unfettered exercise, have not been regarded as the type of law the First or Fourteenth Amendment forbade Congress or the States to pass, when they have been found justified by subordinating valid governmental interests, a pre-requisite to constitutionality which has necessarily involved a weighing of the governmental interest involved....[10]

Stylistically, Harlan's balancing approach is not inconsistent with the language of the first amendment. It is not "speech" which is absolutely protected from restriction but only "free speech." How does the Court decide what speech should be free? Must it balance?

Harlan never advocated an *ad hoc* balancing. The result of his balancing was a rule of law with precedential effect.

Harlan and Black Compared. Harlan's balancing view should not be regarded as necessarily more subservient to state authority than Black's approach. Thus in *Street v. New York,*[11] a flag burning case, Harlan wrote the majority opinion sustaining the first amendment challenge on the facts of that case, while Black dissented. Black believed the prosecution permissible because it did not rest on spoken words; the "talking that was done took place 'as an integral part of

and Chief Justice Warren) (footnote omitted), rehearing denied 368 U.S. 869, 82 S.Ct. 21, 7 L.Ed.2d 69 (1961).

10. Konigsberg v. State Bar of California, 366 U.S. 36, 49–51, 81 S.Ct. 997, 1005–07, 6 L.Ed.2d 105 (1961) (footnote omitted), rehearing denied 368 U.S. 869, 82 S.Ct. 21, 7 L.Ed.2d 69 (1961).

See generally, Farber & Nowak, Justice Harlan and the First Amendment, 2 Const. Commentary 425 (1985).

Compare, Denvir, Justice Brennan, Justice Rehnquist, and Free Speech, 80 Nw. U.L.Rev. 285 (1985).

11. 394 U.S. 576, 89 S.Ct. 1354, 22 L.Ed.2d 572 (1969), on remand 24 N.Y.2d 1026, 302 N.Y.S.2d 848, 250 N.E.2d 250 (1969).

conduct' ".[12] Similarly, Black did not believe that the right of free speech broadly granted "a constitutional right to engage in the conduct of picketing or patrolling, whether on publicly owned streets or on privately owned property." [13]

Black's view may be criticized because, contrary to his assertion, he may be using the balancing test to decide what is speech and what is only expressive conduct. His balancing is more covert and intuitive than Harlan's frank balancing of interests.[14] On the other hand, Harlan's balancing may appear to invite, if not justify, legislative attempts to encroach on the guarantees of free speech.

The Meiklejohn View. Professor Alexander Meiklejohn modified Justice Black's absolute position. Meiklejohn believed that the first amendment is designed to provide unequivocal protection to speech related to self-government while relegating speech that falls outside of this protective zone to the due process safeguards of the fifth and fourteenth amendments.[15]

While it would appear that this analysis offers some middle ground between the "absolutists" and the "balancers" as well as giving some weight to the absolute, unequivocal language of the amendment, there is no strong support for such an interpretation in the history surrounding the amendment, nor does it appear to command much weight with the Court.[16] Moreover, it replaces the question of the scope of protection with the equally perplexing question of the relation of a particular type of speech to "self-government," a phrase which is by no means self-defining.

The difficulty in defining a single standard for judicial review of freedom of expression problems is that the first amendment freedoms play a variety of roles in protecting each individual's interest in intellectual fulfillment as well as the societal interest in robust public

---

12. Street v. New York, 394 U.S. 576, 610, 89 S.Ct. 1354, 1374, 22 L.Ed.2d 572 (1969) (Black, J. dissenting), on remand 24 N.Y.2d 1026, 302 N.Y.S.2d 848, 250 N.E.2d 250 (1969).

Black emphasized: "I would not balance away the First Amendment mandate that speech not be abridged in any fashion whatsoever . . . [But it] is immaterial to me that words are spoken in connection with the burning [of an American flag.]" 394 U.S. at 610, 89 S.Ct. at 1374.

13. Cox v. Louisiana, 379 U.S. 536, 578, 85 S.Ct. 466, 468, 13 L.Ed.2d 487 (1965) (Black, J. dissenting), rehearing denied 380 U.S. 926, 85 S.Ct. 879, 13 L.Ed.2d 814 (1965).

14. See generally, Judge McCurn, citing Treatise in Fox v. The Board of Trustees of State University of New York, 649 F.Supp.

1393, 1397 (N.D.N.Y.1986), judgment reversed and remanded for further findings 841 F.2d 1207 (2d Cir.1988).

See Mendelson, The First Amendment and the Judicial Process: A Reply to Mr. Frantz, 17 Vand.L.Rev. 479, 482 (1964).

15. Meiklejohn, Free Speech and Its Relation to Self Government (1948); Meiklejohn, What Does the First Amendment Mean? 20 U. of Chi.L.Rev. 461 (1953); Meiklejohn, Political Freedom (1960).

See also, Chafee, Book Review, 62 Harv. L.Rev. 891 (1949); Sherry, An Essay Concerning Toleration, 71 Minn.L.Rev. 963 (1987).

16. Chafee, Book Review, 62 Harv. L.Rev. 891, 894 (1949).

debate regarding social issues.[17] Throughout this Chapter, we will see the Supreme Court take a variety of approaches to determining the proper standard of judicial review for various types of free speech problems. When the government tries to suppress speech because of its content, the Court will not permit the prohibition unless the speech to be prohibited falls within one of the limited categories of speech that may be proscribed consistent with first amendment values.[18] When the government regulates speech only within a certain context, or employs only regulations which govern the time, place or manner of speech, the Court may adopt more lenient standards regarding the authority of government to promote important societal interests which are unrelated to the suppression of a specific message.[19]

§ 20.8 The Overbreadth Doctrine

Two closely related doctrines particularly important in dealing with free speech issues are the prohibitions against overbreadth and

---

17. In addition to the other materials cited throughout this chapter regarding first amendment values, readers should also find helpful in considering the various roles of free speech in our society the following publications: F. Schauer, Free Speech: A Philosophical Enquiry (1982); Bollinger, Free Speech and Intellectual Values, 92 Yale L.J. 438 (1983); Greenawalt, Criminal Coercion and Freedom of Speech, 78 Northwestern U.L.Rev. 1081 (1983); Perry, Freedom of Expression: An Essay on Theory and Doctrine, 78 Northwestern U.L.Rev. 1137 (1983); Shiffrin, The First Amendment and Economic Regulation: Away From a General Theory of the First Amendment, 78 Northwestern U.L.Rev. 1212 (1983); Schauer, Must Speech Be Special?, 78 Northwestern U.L.Rev. 1284 (1983); Alexander & Horton, The Impossibility Of A Free Speech Principle, 78 Northwestern U.L.Rev. 1319 (1983); Ingber, The Marketplace of Ideas: A Legitimizing Myth, 1984 Duke L.J. 1. Wellington, On Freedom of Expression, 88 Yale L.J. 1105 (1979) (considers why expression should receive greater immunity from government regulation than other forms of conduct); O'Brien, The First Amendment and the Public's "Right to Know", 7 Hastings Const.L.Q. 579 (1980) (examines constitutional foundations for public's right to know); Baker, Unreasoned Reasonableness: Mandatory Parade Permits and Time, Place, and Manner Regulations, 78 Northwestern U.L.Rev. 937 (1983); Redish, The Warren Court, The Burger Court and the First Amendment Overbreadth Doc-

trine, 78 Northwestern U.L.Rev. 1031 (1983); L. Bollinger, The Tolerant Society: Freedom of Speech and Extremist Speech in America (1986); Farber & Frickey, Practical Reason and the First Amendment, 34 U.C.L.A.L.Rev. 1615 (1987).

18. Examination of the Court's approach to categorizing some types of speech as punishable is examined in various sections throughout this chapter regarding specific topics such as the clear and present danger test, obscenity, and defamation. See generally, Stone, Restrictions of Speech Because of Its Content: The Peculiar Case of Subject–Matter Restrictions, 46 U. Chicago L.Rev. 81 (1978); Farber, Content Regulation and the First Amendment: A Revisionist View, 68 Georgetown L.J. 727 (1980); Schauer, Categories and the First Amendment: A Play In Three Acts, 34 Vanderbilt L.Rev. 265 (1981); Schauer, Codifying The First Amendment: New York v. Ferber, 1982 Sup.Ct.Rev. 285; Stephan, The First Amendment and Content Discrimination, 68 Va.L.Rev. 203 (1982); Stone, Content Regulation and the First Amendment, 25 William and Mary L.Rev. 189 (1983); Farber and Nowak, The Misleading Nature of Public Forum Analysis: Content and Context In First Amendment Adjudication, 70 Va.L.Rev. 1219 (1984); Schlag, An Attack on Categorical Approaches to Freedom of Speech, 30 U.C.L.A.L.Rev. 671 (1983).

19. This subject is examined in § 20.8, infra, regarding the "overbreadth doctrine" and in §§ 20.45–20.47, infra.

vagueness of a statute. Because of the importance of the free speech guarantee, even when the state does have the power to regulate an area, it "must be so exercised as not, in attaining a permissible end, unduly to infringe the protected freedom."[1] In this section we consider the overbreadth doctrine and in the next section we turn to the vagueness doctrine.

An overbroad statute is one that is designed to burden or punish activities which are not constitutionally protected, but the statute includes within its scope activities which are protected by the first amendment.[2] In a case of a statute which is overbroad on its face, the speaker's actions or speech may not be protected by the first amendment and thus the act could have been prohibited under a carefully drawn statute. Nevertheless the Court will strike the overbroad statute because it might apply to others, not before the Court, who may engage in protected activity which the statute appears to outlaw.[3]

As Justice Brennan explained for the Court in *NAACP v. Button:*[4]

> [T]he instant decree may be invalid if it prohibits privileged exercises of First Amendment rights *whether or not* the record discloses that the petitioner has engaged in privileged conduct. For in appraising a statute's inhibitory effect upon such rights, this Court has not hesitated to take into account possible applications of the statute in other factual contexts besides that at bar.

On the other hand, in non first amendment areas, "one to whom application of a statute is constitutional will not be heard to attack the statute on the ground that impliedly it might also be taken as applying to other persons or other situations in which its application might be

---

§ 20.8

1. Cantwell v. Connecticut, 310 U.S. 296, 304, 60 S.Ct. 900, 903, 84 L.Ed. 1213 (1940).

See also, Local 189 International Union of Police Associations v. Barrett, 524 F.Supp. 760, 765 (N.D.Ga.1981) (overbreadth and vagueness are two separate concepts that often go hand in hand), citing an earlier edition of this treatise.

Judge Coffey, dissenting, citing Treatise in City of Watseka v. Illinois Public Action Council and American Civil Liberties Union, 796 F.2d 1547, 1563 n. 1 (7th Cir.1986), affirmed 479 U.S. 1048, 107 S.Ct. 919, 93 L.Ed.2d 972 (1987).

2. Hill v. City of Houston, 764 F.2d 1156, 1161 & n. 16 (5th Cir.1985) (Rubin, J.) (quoting this portion of an earlier edition of this treatise), on rehearing 789 S.W.2d 1103 (1986).

3. People v. Holder, 103 Ill.App.3d 353, 356, 59 Ill.Dec. 142, 145, 431 N.E.2d 427, 430 (2d Dist.1982) (Hopf, J.) (holding intimidation statute not unconstitutionally overbroad), quoting this portion of an earlier edition of this treatise, judgment reversed 96 Ill.2d 444, 71 Ill.Dec. 677, 451 N.E.2d 831 (1983).

4. 371 U.S. 415, 432, 83 S.Ct. 328, 338–39, 9 L.Ed.2d 405 (1963) (emphasis added). See also NAACP v. Alabama, 377 U.S. 288, 307, 84 S.Ct. 1302, 1313–14, 12 L.Ed.2d (1964), on remand 277 Ala. 89, 167 So.2d 171 (1964); Keyishian v. Board of Regents, 385 U.S. 589, 609, 87 S.Ct. 675, 687, 17 L.Ed.2d 629 (1967) (statutes that "seek to bar employment both for association which legitimately may be proscribed and for association which may not be proscribed consistently with First Amendment rights" are struck down and not construed narrowly).

unconstitutional." [5]

Two cases illustrate the power of the overbreadth doctrine as a first amendment test; to those cases we now turn.

The Decision in *Kunz v. New York*. Karl Kunz, a Baptist Minister, was convicted of violating an ordinance which prohibited holding a religious meeting on streets without a permit. The conviction was affirmed by the New York Court of Appeals,[6] and reversed by the Supreme Court, in *Kunz v. New York*.[7] Under the city ordinance those desiring to conduct religious worship meetings on the street had to first obtain a permit from the city police commissioner. Kunz received a one year permit in 1946 which was revoked in November 1946 on the basis of evidence that the appellant had "ridiculed and denounced other religious beliefs in his meeting." [8] No mention was made in the ordinance of grounds for revoking or refusing permits. Kunz reapplied for a permit in 1947 and 1948; his application was rejected in both years. In 1948 he was arrested and convicted for speaking without a permit.[9]

Writing for the Court, Chief Justice Vinson stated, "We are here concerned only with the propriety of the action of the police commissioner in refusing to issue that permit." [10] An administrative official, the police commissioner, was empowered under the ordinance to deny a permit application for conduct he determined, in his discretion, to be condemned by the ordinance. Ordinances giving discretionary power to administrative officials over a citizen's right to speak about religion on the city streets was held to be an invalid prior restraint on a first amendment right.[11] Vinson indicated the decision was in no way an opinion delineating which punitive remedies authorities may implement, but, "New York can not vest restraining control over the right to

5. United States v. Raines, 362 U.S. 17, 21, 80 S.Ct. 519, 522, 4 L.Ed.2d 524 (1960). See also Yazoo & M.V.R. Co. v. Jackson Vinegar Co., 226 U.S. 217, 219–20, 33 S.Ct. 40, 41, 57 L.Ed. 193 (1912).

An excellent example of a conviction for unprotected activity which was nevertheless reversed because the statute affected the first amendment and was overbroad is Kunz v. New York, 340 U.S. 290, 71 S.Ct. 312, 95 L.Ed. 280 (1951).

6. People v. Kunz, 300 N.Y. 273, 90 N.E.2d 455 (1949), motion denied 302 N.Y. 704, 98 N.E.2d 493 (1951).

7. 340 U.S. 290, 71 S.Ct. 312, 95 L.Ed. 280 (1951).

8. 340 U.S. at 292, 71 S.Ct. at 314.

See also, City of Houston v. Hill, 479 U.S. 1079, 107 S.Ct. 1277, 94 L.Ed.2d 137 (1987), invalidating as overbroad a munici- pal ordinance that makes it a crime "to interrupt any policeman in the execution of his duty...." The Court relied on *Broadrick;* the ordinance punished only spoken words and was not limited to "fighting words" or even obscene or opprobrious language. The Court noted that the ordinance's "plain language is admittedly violated scores of times daily, yet only some individuals—those chosen by police in their unguided discretion—are arrested." 482 U.S. at 451, 107 S.Ct. at 2502. The Court added:

"[T]he First Amendment protects a significant amount of verbal criticism and challenge directed at police officers."

482 U.S. at 460, 107 S.Ct. at 2509.

9. 340 U.S. at 293, 71 S.Ct. at 314–15.

10. Id.

11. Id.

speak on religious subjects in an administrative official when there are *no appropriate standards* to guide his action." [12]

In a lengthy dissent Justice Jackson stated that Kunz's speech fell into the inflammatory, insulting or "fighting words" category which traditionally has not been considered to be constitutionally protected.[13] The Court, he urged, should recognize some speech as being outside the first amendment privilege and set up a standard to determine what types of speech should be unprotected.[14]

The majority's analysis however never reached this issue. While a narrowly drawn statute, with appropriate standards, might validly have been used to deny Kunz's permit, the overbroad statute must fail under the first amendment standards. Jackson's argument that one must consider the statute only as applied, while acceptable in a non first amendment context, was not acceptable to the majority because they were dealing with a statute affecting free speech.[15]

The *Lewis* Case. Another interesting example of the application of the overbreadth doctrine is *Lewis v. City of New Orleans*,[16] where the appellant had been convicted for violating a city ordinance making it unlawful "to curse or revile or to use obscene or opprobrious language toward or with reference" to a police officer performing his duties.[17] The Louisiana Supreme Court sustained the appellant's conviction and the Supreme Court reversed.[18]

The Court held that the ordinance as construed by the Louisiana Supreme Court was overbroad and consequently invalid as a violation of the first and fourteenth amendments.[19] Justice Brennan, writing for the Court, indicated the ordinance had gone beyond the bounds of *Chaplinsky v. New Hampshire*[20] and *Gooding v. Wilson*[21] where "fighting words," "which 'by their very utterance inflict injury or tend to incite an immediate breach of the peace,'" were held to be without constitutional protection.[22] The ordinance proscribed the use of "opprobrious language" a term not limited to words which could be categorized as "fighting words."[23]

Earlier, the Louisiana Supreme Court had contended the ordinance's wording was narrow and specific and not in need of refine-

12. 340 U.S. at 295, 71 S.Ct. at 315 (emphasis added).

13. 340 U.S. at 298, 71 S.Ct. at 317 (Jackson, J., dissenting).

14. 340 U.S. at 299, 71 S.Ct. at 317–18 (Jackson, J., dissenting).

15. 340 U.S. at 304–05, 71 S.Ct. at 320 (Jackson, J., dissenting).

16. 415 U.S. 130, 94 S.Ct. 970, 39 L.Ed.2d 214 (1974).

17. 415 U.S. at 132, 94 S.Ct. at 972.

18. 415 U.S. at 130, 94 S.Ct. at 970–71.

19. 415 U.S. at 131–32, 94 S.Ct. at 971–72.

20. 315 U.S. 568, 572, 62 S.Ct. 766, 769, 86 L.Ed. 1031 (1942). See §§ 20.37–20.40 infra.

21. 405 U.S. 518, 522, 92 S.Ct. 1103, 1106, 31 L.Ed.2d 408 (1972).

22. 415 U.S. at 133, 94 S.Ct. at 972.

23. Id.

ment.[24] The Louisiana Supreme Court had emphasized that there would be a damaging effect on the stature of police in the performance of their jobs if it was permissible to address curses and obscenities to officers on duty.[25] Nothing in the Louisiana Supreme Court opinion, noted Brennan, limited the ordinance in accordance with the *Chaplinsky* and *Gooding* decisions.[26]

Brennan, for the majority, concluded that it was immaterial that the appellant's words might have been constitutionally unprotected under a properly drawn statute or ordinance. The ordinance effectively punished all vulgar and offensive speech even though some of this speech may have been protected by the first amendment. Since the ordinance, as construed by the Louisiana Supreme Court, was "susceptible of application to protected speech, the section is constitutionally overbroad and ... facially invalid." [27]

In a separate concurring opinion Justice Powell stated the Louisiana Supreme Court had construed the ordinance as a *per se* rule punishing all obscene language directed at city police.[28] Powell agreed that the ordinance was overbroad and expressed concern that such a regulation:

> confers on police a virtually unrestrained power to arrest and charge persons with a violation.... The opportunity for abuse, especially where a statute has received a virtually open-ended interpretation, is self-evident.[29]

Justices Blackmun and Rehnquist and Chief Justice Burger joined in dissent. Blackmun writing for the dissenters stated the overbreadth and vagueness doctrines had been indiscriminately invoked by the Court without regard to the nature of the speech in question. The Court, said Blackmun, was not just applying constitutional limitations but was invalidating statutes because they might at a future time restrict protected speech.[30] Blackmun relied on and quoted Justice Jackson's dissenting opinion in *Saia v. New York:*[31]

> [T]he issue before us is whether what has been done has deprived this appellant of a constitutional right. It is the law *as applied* that we review, not the abstract academic questions which it might raise in some more doubtful case.[32]

24. New Orleans v. Lewis, 263 La. 809, 269 So.2d 450 (1972), judgment reversed 415 U.S. 130, 94 S.Ct. 970, 39 L.Ed.2d 214 (1974).

25. 415 U.S. at 132, 94 S.Ct. at 972.

26. 415 U.S. at 133, 94 S.Ct. at 972.

27. 415 U.S. at 134, 94 S.Ct. at 973.

28. 415 U.S. at 134–135, 94 S.Ct. at 972–73.

29. 415 U.S. at 135–36, 94 S.Ct. at 973–74.

30. 415 U.S. at 137, 94 S.Ct. at 974.

31. 334 U.S. 558, 68 S.Ct. 1148, 92 L.Ed. 1574 (1948).

32. 334 U.S. at 571, 68 S.Ct. at 1155 (emphasis added).

The appellant's speech had plainly been "fighting words," and should be within the reach of the ordinance, Blackmun concluded.[33]

The Doctrine of Substantial Overbreadth. It is difficult to determine how creative a challenging party must be in conceiving of situations where the language of a statute might be applied to protected speech which is not before the Court. It has been suggested that in all first amendment overbreadth cases, a statute should fall only if it is "substantially overbroad and not readily reconstructed to avoid privileged activity.... [because if it] is not substantially overbroad [it] is unlikely to have a drastic inhibitory impact." [34]

The Supreme Court in *Broadrick v. Oklahoma*,[35] has noted that the overbreadth doctrine is "strong medicine," [36] and consequently has attempted to place some limits on it. By a five to four vote, the Court ruled that substantial overbreadth may be a requirement to invoke the doctrine, particularly when the speech is joined with conduct:

> [The function of the overbreadth doctrine is] a limited one at the outset, [and] attenuates as the otherwise unprotected behavior that it forbids the State to sanction moves from "pure speech" toward conduct and that conduct—even if expressive—falls within the scope of otherwise valid criminal laws that reflect legitimate state interests in maintaining comprehensive controls over harmful, constitutionally unprotected conduct.... To put the matter another way, particularly where conduct and not merely speech is involved, we believe that the overbreadth of a statute must not only be real, but substantial as well, judged in relation to the statute's plainly legitimate sweep.[37]

Such a test is hardly a mechanical one and, perhaps, is most important in showing an attitude of hesitancy to employ the doctrine. Elsewhere in *Broadrick,* the Court offered a more specific test when it stated that it would invalidate statutes for overbreadth "only when the flaw is a substantial concern in the context of the statute as a whole." [38]

Censorial Laws, Inhibitory Laws, and Remedial Laws Compared. A lengthy consideration of the case law suggests that three types of overbreadth statutes may be distinguished for purposes of the overbreadth doctrine: censorial laws, inhibitory laws, and remedial laws. The first type, censorial laws (such as criminal syndicalism laws),

33. 415 U.S. at 141, 94 S.Ct. at 976.

34. Note, The First Amendment Overbreadth Doctrine, 83 Harv.L.Rev. 844, 918 (1970).

35. 413 U.S. 601, 93 S.Ct. 2908, 37 L.Ed.2d 830 (1973).

36. 413 U.S. at 613, 93 S.Ct. at 2916.

37. 413 U.S. at 615, 93 S.Ct. at 2917–18.

38. 413 U.S. at 616 n. 14, 93 S.Ct. at 2918 n. 14. See also Village of Schaumburg v. Citizens for a Better Environment, 444 U.S. 620, 636–38, 100 S.Ct. 826, 835–37, 63 L.Ed.2d 73 (1980), rehearing denied 445 U.S. 972, 100 S.Ct. 1668, 64 L.Ed.2d 250 (1980).

seek to burden the advocacy of matters of public concern.[39] The Court
is less tolerant of overbreadth statutes in this area than it is of
inhibitory laws, "which impinge on expressive and associational conduct but whose impact tends to be neutral as to viewpoints sought to be
advocated....".[40] Libel laws, for example, are inhibitory laws. The
Court is less tolerant of overbreadth in this area of inhibitory laws than
it is of remedial laws, which are laws that "hamper first amendment
activities for the purpose of promoting values which are within the
concern of the amendment." [41] Such remedial laws include, for example, the fairness doctrine of the broadcast media,[42] as well as laws
regulating lobbying, campaign contributions, and union elections.[43]
The law upheld in *Broadrick* fits under this analysis for it was a
remedial law: it regulated partisan political activity of state employees.[44]

Overbreadth and Commercial Speech. Within this framework,
the overbreadth doctrine does not really apply to so-called commercial
speech.[45] In *Ohralik v. Ohio State Bar*,[46] the Supreme Court upheld the
Ohio state bar's discipline of an attorney for in-person solicitation
under the circumstances of that case. In the course of the opinion the
majority opinion stated that such in-person solicitation was commercial
speech and such speech "is not as likely to be deterred as noncommercial speech, and therefore does not require the added protection afforded by the overbreadth doctrine".[47] But the majority immediately went
on to say that "[e]ven if the commercial speaker could mount an
overbreadth attack...." then the requirements of *Broadrick v. Oklahoma* [48] must be met. In the case companion to *Ohralik, In re Primus*,[49]
the Court did in fact apply the overbreadth doctrine,[50] however there
the majority did not find the attorney solicitation to be "commercial"
speech.

Thus, if speech is deemed to be commercial speech, then the
overbreadth analysis is at this point probably inapplicable. "Because
of the special character of commercial speech and the relative novelty

39. E.g., Brandenburg v. Ohio, 395 U.S.
444, 89 S.Ct. 1827, 23 L.Ed.2d 430 (1969)
(per curiam); Herndon v. Lowry, 301 U.S.
242, 57 S.Ct. 732, 81 L.Ed. 1066 (1937); De
Jonge v. Oregon, 299 U.S. 353, 57 S.Ct. 255,
81 L.Ed. 278 (1937).

40. Note, The First Amendment Overbreadth Doctrine, 83 Harv.L.Rev. 844, 918
(1970).

41. Id.

42. See Red Lion Broadcasting Co. v.
FCC, 395 U.S. 367, 89 S.Ct. 1794, 23
L.Ed.2d 371 (1969).

43. Note, The First Amendment Overbreadth Doctrine, 83 Harv.L.Rev. 844, 920
(1970).

44. Broadrick v. Oklahoma, 413 U.S. at
603 n. 1, 93 S.Ct. at 2911–12 n. 1.

45. See §§ 20.26–20.31 infra.

46. 436 U.S. 447, 98 S.Ct. 1912, 56
L.Ed.2d 444 (1978), rehearing denied 439
U.S. 883, 99 S.Ct. 226, 58 L.Ed.2d 198
(1978).

47. 436 U.S. at 462–63, 98 S.Ct. at
1921–22.

48. 413 U.S. 601, 615, 93 S.Ct. 2908,
2917–18, 37 L.Ed.2d 830 (1973).

49. 436 U.S. 412, 98 S.Ct. 1893, 56
L.Ed.2d 417 (1978).

50. 436 U.S. at 433, 438–39, 98 S.Ct. at
1905–06, 1908–09.

of First Amendment protection for such speech, we act with caution in confronting First Amendment challenges to economic legislation that serves legitimate regulatory interests." [51]

Although the Court will not employ overbreadth analysis to invalidate a regulation of commercial speech that is designed to stop false or misleading commercial practices, the Court will require the government to regulate commercial speech in a manner that is "not more extensive than necessary" to serve a substantial government interest.[52]

Overbreadth and Standing Compared. When the Court examines a claim that a statute should be invalidated as being an unconstitutionally overbroad regulation of speech, it is easy to confuse standing and first amendment issues.

Justices who argue against use of the overbreadth doctrine to strike a statute on its face have often asserted that the individuals before the Court lacked standing to raise the rights of hypothetical persons to whom the statute could not be applied without violating the first amendment. However, it is not precise to think of the overbreadth problem as a form of standing or as a justiciability issue. Rather, one should recognize that when the Court is asked to strike a law on its face as being overbroad, the individual is asserting that no one in our society—including persons whose speech is unprotected by the first amendment—can be subjected to punishment under a statute so sweeping that it could include both protected and unprotected speech within its scope.[53] If the Court believes that the statute is so sweeping that it would deter persons from engaging in protected speech, or that the statute may be used on an arbitrary basis against political dissenters, the Court will strike the law as overbroad. If the Court believes that there is little chance that the statute will deter constitutionally protected speech, or will be used in a selective manner to punish dissenters, it will uphold the law and allow it to be applied on a "case-by-case" basis.[54]

51. Friedman v. Rogers, 440 U.S. 1, 11 n. 9, 99 S.Ct. 887, 894 n. 9, 59 L.Ed.2d 100 (1979), rehearing denied 441 U.S. 917, 99 S.Ct. 2018, 60 L.Ed.2d 389 (1979). The Court also noted: "Our decisions dealing with more traditional first amendment problems do not extend automatically to this as yet uncharted area." 440 U.S. at 11 n. 9, 99 S.Ct. at 894, n. 9.

In deferring to commercial regulation, however, the Court should recognize that when this regulation takes the form of restrictions on truthful speech, the first amendment interests should be considered compelling. Cf. Rotunda, The First Amendment Now Protects Commercial Speech, 10 The Center Magazine: A Publi-

cation of the Center for the Study of Democratic Institutions 32, 33 (May/June 1977).

52. Central Hudson Gas & Elec. Corp. v. Public Serv. Com'n, 447 U.S. 557, 571, 100 S.Ct. 2343, 65 L.Ed.2d 341 (1980).

For further discussion of commercial speech regulation, see §§ 20.26–20.31, infra.

53. See generally, Judge Barker, citing Treatise in Indiana Voluntary Fireman's Ass'n, Inc. v. Pearson, 700 F.Supp. 421, 429 (S.D.Ind.1988).

54. A statute that is valid on its face because it does not, by its terms, unconstitutionally restrict free speech must still be examined in its application to the specific

One must be able to separate true jurisdictional or standing issues from substantive first amendment rulings on the overbreadth of statutes in order to understand many Supreme Court decisions. This problem is illustrated in *Secretary of State v. Joseph H. Munson Co., Inc.,*[55] a case which well illustrates some important distinctions.

The Decision in *Secretary of State v. Joseph H. Munson, Inc.* In *Munson,* the Court reviewed a statute that imposed a twenty-five percent limitation on fundraising expenses of charities. The statute was challenged by a professional profit-making fundraiser that entered into contracts with not-for-profit organizations to raise funds for them. This fundraiser regularly charged an amount in excess of twenty-five percent of the gross amount of funds raised through the promotion. The fundraiser had been informed by the governmental administrator charged with enforcing the statute that the fundraiser would be subject to prosecution under the statute by contracting for and accepting more than twenty-five percent of the proceeds from such promotions.

The *Munson* Court invalidated the statute on the basis of earlier decisions finding that restrictions on the amount of money spent by charitable organizations in their fundraising directly limited their first amendment rights to spend money on the dissemination of information and their need for solicited contributions. The statute was not narrowly tailored to promote the governmental interest in protecting the public from fraudulent solicitations by noncharitable organizations.[56]

The majority opinion (by Justice Blackmun) and the dissent (written by Justice Rehnquist and joined by three other members of the

---

speech which the regulatory act at issue restricts. Thus, in Members of City Council v. Taxpayers for Vincent, 466 U.S. 789, 104 S.Ct. 2118, 80 L.Ed.2d 772 (1984), on remand 738 F.2d 353 (9th Cir.1984), the Court found that a statute prohibiting the posting of signs on public property was permissible on its face because it promoted significant governmental interests unrelated to the message conveyed and did not restrict more speech than necessary to accomplish its purpose of eliminating "visual clutter." The Court held this statute to be not only constitutional on its face but constitutional as applied to the individual speakers' expressive activity. The city could thus prohibit the appellees from attaching political signs to utility poles.

The substantive nature of overbreadth rulings and the use of the doctrine in other areas of constitutional analysis is explained in Monaghan, Overbreadth, 1981 Sup.Ct.Rev. 1. The difficulty of developing any formula for use in overbreadth analysis and the relation of that problem to the problem of defining what speech may be made punishable is explained in Redish,

The Warren Court, The Burger Court and the First Amendment Overbreadth Doctrine, 78 Nw.U.L.Rev. 1031 (1984).

55. 467 U.S. 947, 104 S.Ct. 2839, 81 L.Ed.2d 786 (1984).

56. A similar statute was stricken in Village of Schaumburg v. Citizens for a Better Environment, 444 U.S. 620, 100 S.Ct. 826, 63 L.Ed.2d 73 (1980), rehearing denied 445 U.S. 972, 100 S.Ct. 1668, 64 L.Ed.2d 250 (1980). In *Village of Schaumburg,* however, the challenged statute had not allowed for any waiver of the limitation on funds raised through charitable solicitation that could be spent for administrative expenses. The state in *Joseph H. Munson Co.* sought to distinguish its statute from that previously stricken on the basis of its provision allowing for an administrative waiver of the limitation by a showing of economic hardship to specific charities which mitigated its impact on first amendment activity. See § 20.47(d), infra.

Court) disagreed both as to whether the fundraiser should have been allowed to assert the first amendment rights of the charitable organizations and whether the statute should be stricken as overbroad because it constituted an improper restriction on first amendment activity.[57] To have a clear picture of the disagreement between the majority and the dissent in this case, it is important to separate jurisdictional from first amendment issues. This case presented three separate constitutional issues.

First, the Court had to decide whether there was a case or controversy which was ripe for adjudication; because the fundraising company had been threatened with suit and the case had been fully adjudicated by the state courts, there was no doubt that an actual controversy was presented.

Second, the Court had to decide whether to allow the fundraising company to raise the first amendment claims of the charity which wished to spend more than twenty-five percent of the receipts from its promotional events on expenses. This was not a first amendment overbreadth issue but really a third party standing issue.[58] The majority determined that it would allow the fundraiser to have third party standing under the general principle which requires the Court to consider "whether the third party has sufficient injury-in-fact to satisfy the Article III case or controversy requirement, and whether, as a prudential matter, the third party can reasonably be expected properly to frame the issues and present them with the necessary adversarial zeal." The Court noted that, where first amendment rights were at issue, third party standing should be granted to allow persons to challenge the restriction on speech of others "not primarily for the benefit of the litigant but for the benefit of society—to prevent the statute from chilling the First Amendment rights of other parties not before the court." Unfortunately, the Court imprecisely referred to this issue as part of the overbreadth problem, although it recognized the need to separate the standing issue from the question of whether the statute should be considered overbroad and a violation of the first amendment.

Even though a case or controversy was present and even though the Court allowed the fundraiser to assert the constitutional rights of the charities, the Court could still have found that the statute substantively conformed to first amendment principles and was facially valid.

57. Secretary of State v. Joseph H. Munson Co., Inc., 467 U.S. 947, 975, 104 S.Ct. 2839, 2857, 81 L.Ed.2d 786 (1984) (Rehnquist, J., dissenting, joined by Burger, C.J., and Powell and O'Connor, JJ.). Although we refer here to the disagreement between the majority opinion and dissent, this disagreement and the difference between Article III case or controversy issues, Article III standing issues, and the first amendment overbreadth determination was made clear by the concurring opinion of Justice Stevens. Secretary of State v. Joseph H. Munson Co., Inc., 467 U.S. 947, 970, 104 S.Ct. 2839, 2854, 81 L.Ed.2d 786 (1984) (Stevens, J., concurring).

58. See generally § 2.13(f)(3), supra.

The decision to grant standing is unrelated to the substantive first amendment determination of whether the statute is unconstitutionally overbroad.

The third issue in *Joseph H. Munson Co.* was whether the statute limiting fundraising expenses should be stricken on its face and found absolutely void because it restricted speech activity. If the statute was upheld on its face, courts would have to inquire in each case whether the restriction on fundraising expenses was a legitimate limitation on the charges paid to professional fundraisers or whether in the specific case the restriction limited the ability of a charitable organization to disseminate its views. The majority found that the statute should be invalidated on its face even though it included a provision allowing a charity to receive a waiver from the twenty-five percent limitation if that limitation would impose economic hardship on the charitable organization. The majority found that the limitation was not precisely related to a substantial governmental interest in preventing fraud because high solicitation costs or expenses in the dissemination of information are not necessarily correlated to fraudulent activity.

The Court recognized that it normally does not strike a statute on its face but only determines whether a statute may constitutionally be applied to the conduct of a specific individual or organization before the Court. However, in this case, there was no question in the majority's view that the statute was substantially overbroad because "there is no core of easily identifiable and constitutionally proscribable conduct that the statute prohibits." Although some organizations might have high fundraising costs totally unconnected with first amendment activity, the statute operated directly to restrict the expenses of all charitable solicitations, including the dissemination of information, a protected first amendment activity.

The dissenting justices believed that the statute should not be stricken on its face because they saw the statute as only a restriction on the percentage of the receipts of the fundraising events that could be paid to professional fundraisers or spent on other administrative expenses unrelated to true advocacy. The dissenting justices would have upheld the statute on its face, while recognizing that the Court would invalidate the application of the statute to charities which kept their administrative expenses below the twenty-five percent level but wished to spend an additional percentage of their receipts from fundraising on true first amendment activity such as the dissemination of information about their charity.

The disagreement between the majority and dissent regarding whether the statute should be stricken on its face as overbroad, or whether the statute should be applied in a case-by-case manner, was totally unrelated to a determination of whether the individual had standing to raise a first amendment issue in this case.

§ 20.9　The Void-for-Vagueness Doctrine

Closely related to the overbreadth doctrine is the void for vagueness doctrine. The problem of vagueness in statutes regulating speech activities is based on the same rationale as the overbreadth doctrine and the Supreme Court often speaks of them together.[1]

Vagueness and Criminal Laws Generally. The void for vagueness doctrine applies to all criminal laws, not merely those that regulate speech or other fundamental constitutional rights. All such laws must give notice to the populace as to what activity is made criminal so as to provide fair notice to persons before making their activity criminal and also to restrict the authority of police officers to arrest persons for a violation of the law.[2]

Vagueness and the First Amendment. Several rationales require special judicial strictness when reviewing laws that regulate fundamental constitutional rights, such as the freedoms of speech, assembly, or association, to insure that such regulations are not vague. First, the requirement that a law place persons on notice as to precisely what activity is made criminal is of special importance when the activity distinguishes between criminal activity and activity which constitutes a fundamental constitutional right. To the extent that the law is vague and relates to fundamental constitutional rights, it might have an "in terrorem" effect and deter persons from engaging in activities, such as constitutionally protected speech, that are of particular constitutional importance. In other words, an unclear law regulating speech might deter or chill persons from engaging in speech or activity with special protection under the Constitution. On the other

---

§ 20.9

1. E.g. Dombrowski v. Pfister, 380 U.S. 479, 486, 85 S.Ct. 1116, 1120–21, 14 L.Ed.2d 22 (1965); Keyishian v. Board of Regents, 385 U.S. 589, 609, 87 S.Ct. 675, 687, 17 L.Ed.2d 629 (1967); NAACP v. Button, 371 U.S. 415, 433, 83 S.Ct. 328, 338, 9 L.Ed.2d 405 (1963).

See generally, Judge Barker, citing Treatise in Indiana Voluntary Fireman's Ass'n, Inc. v. Pearson, 700 F.Supp. 421, 434 (S.D.Ind.1988).

Commentators also often consider them indistinguishable, e.g., Note, The Void for Vagueness Doctrine in the Supreme Court, 109 U.Pa.L.Rev. 67, 110–13 (1960).

2. The reasons for striking laws for vagueness apply whenever the lack of notice in a law might deter the exercise of a fundamental constitutional right, including rights that are not protected by the first amendment. See, e.g., Colautti v. Franklin, 439 U.S. 379, 99 S.Ct. 675, 58 L.Ed.2d 596 (1979) (holding void for vagueness a state regulation of abortions requiring a doctor to determine if there was "sufficient reason to believe that a fetus may be viable" before determining whether the doctor was permitted to perform the abortion procedure).

When there is no danger that the law will deter lawful speech, the Court is less strict in enforcing the vagueness requirement. See, e.g., Village of Hoffman Estates v. Flipside, 455 U.S. 489, 102 S.Ct. 1186, 71 L.Ed.2d 362 (1982) (upholding statutes requiring a business to obtain a special license if it sells items "designed or marketed for use with illegal drugs" where the Court did not believe the statute deterred constitutionally protected speech), rehearing denied 456 U.S. 950, 102 S.Ct. 2023, 72 L.Ed.2d 476 (1982), on remand 688 F.2d 842 (7th Cir.1982).

See generally, Jeffries, Legality, Vagueness, and the Construction of Penal Statutes, 71 Va.L.Rev. 189 (1985).

hand, an unclear law relating to business property use, such as an unclear zoning statute, would only chill activity without special constitutional significance (until such time as the statute is clarified by appropriate state courts).

A second, and more important, reason for enforcing the void for vagueness doctrine is to require that there be clear guidelines to govern law enforcement. Without such clear guidelines, law enforcement officers have discretion to enforce the statute on a selective basis. This discretion is most dangerous when the law regulates a fundamental right, such as speech or travel, so that the officers might be subjecting persons to arrest and prosecution either because they disagree with the message which the person wishes to convey in his speech or for some other constitutionally suspect reason.[3]

Thirdly, because the first amendment needs breathing space, the governmental regulation that is tolerated must be drawn with "narrow specificity."[4] Such narrow, clear statutes are more likely to reflect the considered judgment of the legislature that certain speech activities must be regulated.[5]

Moreover there is a special danger of tolerating in the first amendment area "the existence of a penal statute susceptible of sweeping and improper application.... These freedoms are delicate and vulnerable, as well as supremely precious in our society. The threat of sanctions may deter their exercise almost as potently as the actual application of sanctions."[6] As a result the doctrine consists of a strict prohibition of statutes which burden speech in terms that are so vague as either to allow including protected speech in the prohibition or leaving an individual without clear guidance as to the nature of speech for which he can be punished.[7]

---

3. See Kolender v. Lawson, 461 U.S. 352, 103 S.Ct. 1855, 75 L.Ed.2d 903 (1983). In *Kolender,* the Court invalidated a state statute requiring persons who loitered or wandered on streets to provide "credible and reliable" identification and to account for their presence when requested to do so by a police officer. The majority opinion by Justice O'Connor noted that the most important aspect of the vagueness doctrine was the imposition of guidelines which prohibited arbitrary, selective enforcement on a constitutionally suspect basis by police officers, and that this rationale for invocation of the doctrine was of special concern in this case because of the potential for arbitrary suppression of first amendment liberties and restrictions on the freedom of movement. 461 U.S. at 357, 103 S.Ct. at 1858–59, 75 L.Ed.2d at 908.

4. NAACP v. Button, 371 U.S. 415, 433, 83 S.Ct. 328, 338, 9 L.Ed.2d 405 (1963),

citing Cantwell v. Connecticut, 310 U.S. 296, 311, 60 S.Ct. 900, 906, 84 L.Ed. 1213 (1940). See generally, Schauer, Fear, Risk and the First Amendment: Unraveling the "Chilling Effect," 58 Boston U.L.Rev. 685 (1978).

5. But cf. NAACP v. Button, 371 U.S. 415, 432–33, 83 S.Ct. 328, 337–38, 9 L.Ed.2d 405 (1963): "The objectionable quality of vagueness and overbreadth does not depend upon absence of fair notice to a criminally accused or upon unchanneled delegation of legislative powers...."

6. NAACP v. Button, 371 U.S. 415, 433, 83 S.Ct. 328, 338, 9 L.Ed.2d 405 (1963) (footnote omitted).

7. State v. Princess Cinema of Milwaukee, Inc., 96 Wis.2d 646, 292 N.W.2d 807, 813 (1980) (Day, J., citing an earlier edition of this treatise); Levine v. United States

Vagueness and Flag–Misuse Statutes. One case illustrating the use of the vagueness doctrine is *Smith v. Goguen,*[8] where appellee had been convicted of violating a state flag-misuse statute for sewing a small United States flag to the seat of his pants.[9] Under the statute an individual who "publicly mutilates, tramples upon, defaces or treats contemptuously the flag of the United States ..." was subject to criminal liability.[10] The Supreme Court held that the statutory language was void for vagueness under the fourteenth amendment due process clause.[11]

Justice Powell, writing the opinion for the Court, explained that the void for vagueness doctrine:

> incorporates the notions of fair notice or warning.... [I]t requires legislatures to set reasonably clear guidelines for law enforcement officials and triers of fact in order to prevent "arbitrary and discriminatory enforcement." Where a statute's literal scope, unaided by a narrowing state court interpretation, is capable of reaching expression sheltered by the First Amendment, the doctrine demands a greater degree of specificity than in other contexts.[12]

The flag-misuse statute was vague because no clear distinction had been made between what type of treatment of the flag was or was not criminal.[13] In addition to the statute's failure to provide any warning or notice, the standard of "contemptuous treatment of the flag" was found to be so ambiguous that police, judges and juries were able to determine what actions were contemptuous on the basis of their personal preferences.[14] This lack of ascertainable standards for defining "treats contemptuously" violated the due process clause.[15]

Powell concluded there was no reason to give police and courts such broad discretion as to what constitutes flag contempt. Flag etiquette changes from generation to generation, he noted, making it necessary for the legislature to specify what behavior has been outlawed.[16]

District Court, 764 F.2d 590, 599 (9th Cir. 1985) (Beezer, J., for plurality, citing earlier edition of this treatise).

8. 415 U.S. 566, 94 S.Ct. 1242, 39 L.Ed.2d 605 (1974). See also, Erznoznik v. City of Jacksonville, 422 U.S. 205, 95 S.Ct. 2268, 45 L.Ed.2d 125 (1975); Hynes v. Mayor and Council of Oradell, 425 U.S. 610, 96 S.Ct. 1755, 48 L.Ed.2d 243 (1976).

9. 415 U.S. at 568–70, 94 S.Ct. at 1244–45.

10. 415 U.S. at 568–69, 94 S.Ct. at 1245.

11. 415 U.S. at 572, 94 S.Ct. at 1246.

On flag-burning, see § 20.49 on Symbolic Speech.

12. 415 U.S. at 572–73, 94 S.Ct. at 1247 (footnotes omitted).

13. 415 U.S. at 574, 94 S.Ct. at 1247–48.

14. 415 U.S. at 575, 94 S.Ct. at 1248.

15. 415 U.S. at 578, 94 S.Ct. at 1250.

16. 415 U.S. at 581–82, 94 S.Ct. at 1251–52.

See also, e.g., City of Mesquite v. Alladin's Castle, Inc., 455 U.S. 283, 291, 102 S.Ct. 1070, 1075–76, 71 L.Ed.2d 152 (1982) (city ordinance directing police chief to consider whether applicant for license to operate coin-operated amusement establishment has any "connections with crimi-

§ 20.10 The Least Restrictive Means Test

Even if the legislative purpose is a legitimate one of substantial governmental interest, "that purpose cannot be pursued by means that broadly stifle fundamental personal liberties when the end can be more narrowly achieved. The breadth of legislative abridgement must be viewed in the light of less drastic means for achieving the same basic purpose."[1] The Court requires that the legislation use means which are the "least restrictive" of free speech. This least restrictive means test has also been applied in nonspeech areas, such as state regulation affecting interstate commerce,[2] but it is particularly important to the free speech area.

Shelton v. Tucker[3] is an important case illustrating the doctrine of least restrictive means. In *Shelton* each Arkansas teacher was required by statute to file an annual affidavit listing all organizations to which he belonged or contributed in the last five years. Petitioner Shelton and others refused to file an affidavit and his teaching contract was not renewed. The trial showed that he was not a member of the

---

nal elements" is not unconstitutionally vague because the applicant's possible connection with criminal elements is merely a subject that the ordinance directs the Police Chief to investigate before he makes his recommendation to the City Manager; the test—"connections with criminal elements"—is not used as the standard by the City Manager for approval or disapproval of the application: "The Federal Constitution does not preclude a city from giving vague or ambiguous directions to officials who are authorized to make investigations and recommendations."), motion to recall judgment denied 464 U.S. 927, 104 S.Ct. 329, 78 L.Ed.2d 300 (1983).

Village of Hoffman Estates v. Flipside, Hoffman Estates, Inc., 455 U.S. 489, 102 S.Ct. 1186, 71 L.Ed.2d 362 (1982) (Court rejected pre-enforcement challenge, on its face, to city ordinance requiring a business to obtain a license if it sells any items "designed or marketed for use with illegal drugs;" the Court rejected challenges based on vagueness, overbreadth, and free speech), rehearing denied 456 U.S. 950, 102 S.Ct. 2023, 72 L.Ed.2d 476 (1982), on remand 688 F.2d 842 (7th Cir.1982).

Contrast Kolender v. Lawson, 461 U.S. 352, 103 S.Ct. 1855, 75 L.Ed.2d 903 (1983) (Court, distinguishing *Flipside,* invalidated, on grounds of vagueness, state statute requiring "credible and reliable" identification of persons found to loiter or wander on the streets; the statute gave too much discretion to the police and thus allowed the

police to interfere with freedom of movement).

§ 20.10

1. Shelton v. Tucker, 364 U.S. 479, 488, 81 S.Ct. 247, 252, 5 L.Ed.2d 231 (1960) (footnotes omitted). See also Schneider v. State, 308 U.S. 147, 161, 165, 60 S.Ct. 146, 150–51, 152, 84 L.Ed. 155 (1939); American Communications Ass'n v. Douds, 339 U.S. 382, 70 S.Ct. 674, 94 L.Ed. 925 (1950), rehearing denied 339 U.S. 990, 70 S.Ct. 1017, 94 L.Ed. 1391 (1950); Louisiana ex rel. Gremillion v. NAACP, 366 U.S. 293, 81 S.Ct. 1333, 6 L.Ed.2d 301 (1961); NAACP v. Alabama ex rel. Flowers, 377 U.S. 288, 307–08, 84 S.Ct. 1302, 1313–14, 12 L.Ed.2d 325 (1964), on remand 277 Ala. 89, 167 So.2d 171 (1964); Talley v. California, 362 U.S. 60, 80 S.Ct. 536, 4 L.Ed.2d 559 (1960).

See generally, Judge Coffey, dissenting, citing Treatise in City of Watseka v. Illinois Public Action Council and American Civil Liberties Union, 796 F.2d 1547, 1563 n. 1 (7th Cir.1986), affirmed 479 U.S. 1048, 107 S.Ct. 919, 93 L.Ed.2d 972 (1987), rehearing denied 480 U.S. 926, 107 S.Ct. 1389, 94 L.Ed.2d 703 (1987); Judge Barker, Treatise in Indiana Voluntary Fireman's Ass'n, Inc. v. Pearson, 700 F.Supp. 421, 439 (S.D.Ind.1988).

2. See, e.g., Dean Milk Co. v. Madison, 340 U.S. 349, 71 S.Ct. 295, 95 L.Ed. 329 (1951).

3. 364 U.S. 479, 81 S.Ct. 247, 5 L.Ed.2d 231 (1960).

Communist Party or any organization advocating the overthrow by force of the Government, but he was a member of the NAACP. The trial court found the information requested in the affidavit relevant.

The Supreme Court readily agreed that the state had an interest in investigating the competence and fitness of its teachers [4] but the Arkansas statute went well beyond its legitimate purposes. The information filed under the statute was not kept confidential, allowing public exposure and risks of offending superiors by belonging to an unpopular group. Moreover the state disclosure requirement was "completely unlimited." [5] The teacher was required to list any associational tie—social, professional, religious, avocational—and his financial support, even though many such relationships had no possible bearing on the teacher's occupational fitness. The "unlimited and indiscriminate sweep of the statute" went "far beyond what might be justified in the exercise of the State's legitimate inquiry into the fitness and competence of its teachers" [6] and thus it was struck down.[7]

§ 20.11 Government Prescribed Speech, Government Subsidies for Speech, Unconstitutional Conditions, and Equal Protection Analysis

Almost all first amendment cases that have reached the United States Supreme Court involve governmental attempts to proscribe speech. In many of these cases the government totally outlawed a message or type of speech, such as obscenity, and the Court was called upon to decide if the government's definition of the category of speech to be banned was consistent with the first amendment. In other proscription cases, the government has regulated the time, place, or manner in which speech or assembly may take place so as to reduce, though not eliminate, the ability of would-be speakers to deliver their message to the public. We examine all of these governmental attempts to proscribe or regulate speech in other sections of this chapter. In this subsection we discuss the more rare problem of a governmental entity entering the first amendment marketplace to advance messages favorable to the government.

Government Speech and Propaganda. The most direct way for government to enter the political marketplace is to have government officials or agencies issue messages or reports designed to convince the public to support governmental positions on domestic or foreign policy. There are not yet any Supreme Court decisions that directly and clearly

4. 364 U.S. at 485, 81 S.Ct. at 250.

5. 364 U.S. at 488, 81 S.Ct. at 252.

6. 364 U.S. at 490, 81 S.Ct. at 253.

7. Another example of a case employing the least restrictive means test is Virginia State Bd. of Pharmacy v. Virginia Citi-

define the limitations that would be placed on such activity.[1] This absence of case law may be considered a strength rather than a weakness of the democratic system, for there has not been a clear need for the Court to intervene to establish precise limits on propaganda efforts by government agencies in the United States. However, with the growing number of reports that are issued by the government and the increasing potential for the governmental use of electronic media (such as the Congressional television network on cable television) there is interest in exploring the limits on government speech.[2]

zens Consumer Council, Inc., 425 U.S. 748, 96 S.Ct. 1817, 48 L.Ed.2d 346 (1976).

§ 20.11

1. Cases, however, have been decided in the lower courts. See Anderson v. City of Boston, 376 Mass. 178, 380 N.E.2d 628 (1978), appeal dismissed 439 U.S. 1060, 99 S.Ct. 822, 59 L.Ed.2d 26 (1979). The Massachusetts Supreme Judicial Court enjoined the city of Boston from using appropriated funds to influence voters to vote for passage of a state constitutional amendment. The city had sought to counteract the corporate expenditures which the Supreme Court had allowed in First National Bank v. Bellotti, 435 U.S. 765, 98 S.Ct. 1407, 55 L.Ed.2d 707 (1978), rehearing denied 438 U.S. 907, 98 S.Ct. 3126, 57 L.Ed.2d 1150 (1978), discussed in § 20.31, infra.

2. See generally, T. Emerson, The System of Freedom of Expression 697–716 (1970) Note, the Constitutionality of Municipal Advocacy in State–Wide Referendum Campaigns, 93 Harv.L.Rev. 535 (1980); Finman & Macaulay, Freedom to Dissent: The Vietnam Protests and the Words of Public Officials, 1966 Wisc.L.Rev. 632; VanAlstyne, The First Amendment and the Suppression of Warmongering Propaganda in the United States: Comments and Footnotes, 31 Law & Contemp.Prob. 530, 531–36 (1966); Black, He Cannot Choose But Hear: The Plight of the Captive Auditor, 53 Colum.L.Rev. 960 (1953). Shriffin, Government Speech, 27 U.C.L.A.L.Rev. 565 (1980). Cf. Goldberg, The Constitutional Status of American Science, 1979 U.Ill.L.F. 1 (recognizes an implied science clause in the Constitution: Congress may legislate the establishment of science, but shall not prohibit the free exercise of scientific speech).

See also, Kamenshine, The First Amendment's Implied Political Establishment Clause, 67 Calif.L.Rev. 1104 (1979); Ziegler, Government Speech and the Constitution: The Limits of Official Partisanship,

21 Bos.C.L.Rev. 578 (1980); Delgado, The Language of the Arms Race: Should the People Limit Government Speech?, 69 Bos. U.L.Rev. 961 (1984); Yudof, Personal Speech and Government Express, 38 Case Western Reserve L.Rev. 673 (1988); Nowak, Using the Press Clause to Limit Government Speech, 30 Arizona L.Rev. 1 (1988); G. Nahitchevansky, Free Speech and Government Funding: Does the Government Have To Fund What It Doesn't Like, 56 Brooklyn L.Rev. 213 (1990); Epstein, Foreword: Unconstitutional Conditions, State Power, and the Limits of Consent, 102 Harv.L.Rev. 5 (1988); Sobel, First Amendment Standards for Government Subsidies of Artistic and Cultural Expression, 41 Vand.L.Rev. 517 (1988).

See M. Yudof, When Government Speaks: Politics, Law, and Government Expression in America (U. of Calif.Press 1983). Professor Yudof concludes:

"The preceding chapters have discussed two constitutional modes of judicial policing of government expression and raised concerns about the institutional competence of the courts to perform this function. The danger that, in attempting to recalibrate communications networks, courts will create more problems than they solve is greatest when judicial intervention is greatest—when the courts rely on the Constitution to provide direct limits on government expression. But the other approach—considering government speech and its impact as additional factors when vindicating traditional private rights—is unduly restrictive. My preferred technique for judicial resolution of government-speech issues is a variation of the 'legislative remand.' When grave issues of government expression and the First Amendment are involved, a court should be especially concerned that legislative bodies authorize the communications activity. This

Undoubtedly there is a valid public interest, and first amendment value, in the government conveyance to the public of information regarding government programs. Governmental activities—from Congressional reports to presidential news conferences, or reports of executive agencies—provide the basis for the discussion and debate of self-governance issues which have been a touchstone value in first amendment analysis. However, if the government were to create publicly funded television stations whose purpose was to present programs favorable to government policies without the possibility of reply, one would assume that the governmental attempt to foreclose opposing views would be seen as a violation of the first amendment.[3] Between the two polar extremes—the provision of information to members of the body politic and attempts to sway public opinion through propaganda that stifles dissent—it will be difficult for the Court to draw a line concerning the permissible scope of government speech or the use of public funds to subsidize speech favorable to the government. Nevertheless, first amendment values should impose some limitation on such governmental activities in this area.

Government officials are expected, as a part of the democratic process, to represent and to espouse the views of a majority of their constituents. In addition, it is certainly appropriate for government officials to seek to sway public opinion. A taxpayer has no constitutional right to stop an official from seeking to persuade his or her constituents. However, the fact that the government and its agents may advocate controversial views, does not give government the right to establish private groups, require individuals to belong to these groups, require these individuals to pay dues to these groups, and allow these groups to use the dues to promote ideas with which some of the members disagree.

essentially statutory approach allows the courts to police government expression, while denying the judiciary the ultimate power to silence executive officers. Courts attempt to rivet legislative attention to alleged abuses and to reach a tentative decision themselves; but, in the end, the power of resolution lies with the legislature. This intermediate method of judicial control ties together the themes of institutional competence, the difficulties of distinguishing constitutional and unconstitutional expression, and the positive and negative implications of government expression."
Yudof, When Government Speaks 301 (1983).

See also, Kmiec, In the Aftermath of *Johnson* and *Eichman:* The Constitution Need Not Be Mutilated to Preserve the Government's Speech and Property Interests in the Flag, 1990 Brigham Young U.L.Rev. 577 (1990), arguing that the flag's design may be statutorily declared to be public property, and this declaration "may permit preservation of the flag and, as an incident to *government* speech, the licensing and control of the flag's use." Id. at 580 (footnote omitted).

3. See Justice Douglas, dissenting in Public Utilities Commission v. Pollak, 343 U.S. 451, 467–69, 72 S.Ct. 813, 823–24, 96 L.Ed. 1068, 1080–81 (1952); Justice Douglas, concurring, in Lehman v. City of Shaker Heights, 418 U.S. 298, 305–08, 94 S.Ct. 2714, 2718–20, 41 L.Ed.2d 770, 778–80 (1974).

Thus, the State Bar of California, to which lawyers in the state are required to belong, may not constitutionally use compulsory dues to finance political and ideological causes (e.g., a nuclear freeze initiative) that the petitioners oppose. The State Bar may only use compulsory due to finance regulation of the legal profession or improve the quality of legal services (for example, bar dues may be used to finance an attorney discipline system). The state bar is not part of the general government of California. Although it is created by state law, it is supposed to represent its members, the attorneys, rather than the state.[4] Similarly, the state may not require a public worker to pay the equivalent of dues to a labor union if the union uses the money collected to finance political campaigns or express political views. The union may only use the mandatory fees or dues collected to finance expenditures for the purpose of collective bargaining, contract administration, and grievance adjustment.[5]

In *Federal Communications Commission v. League of Women Voters,*[6] the Court, by a five to four vote, invalidated a section of the Public Broadcasting Act which prohibited any noncommercial educational broadcasting station receiving a grant from the Corporation for Public Broadcasting from engaging in editorializing or the endorsement of candidates. The four dissenting justices believed that the prohibition on editorializing protected the public from having stations writing editorials favorable to the government so as to increase their prospects for receipt of public funding.[7] The five justices in the majority believed that the ban was not narrowly tailored to provide a balanced presentation of issues to the public, but only suppressed the role of such stations in bringing matters of public concern to the attention of the public.[8]

4. In Keller v. State Bar of California, 496 U.S. 1, 110 S.Ct. 2228, 110 L.Ed.2d 1 (1990), a unanimous opinion. The Court distinguished the State Bar from the State Government: while it is true that government officials are expected, as a part of the democratic process, to represent and to espouse the views of a majority of their constituents, the State Bar of California is not part of the general government of California. Although it is created by state law, it is more analogous, the Court explained, to labor unions representing public and private employees, and that therefore should be subject to the same constitutional rule in order to protect free speech and free association interests.

5. Abood v. Detroit Board of Education, 431 U.S. 209, 97 S.Ct. 1782, 52 L.Ed.2d 261 (1977), rehearing denied 433 U.S. 915, 97 S.Ct. 2989, 53 L.Ed.2d 1102 (1977). See also, Ellis v. Brotherhood of Ry., Airline, & S.S. Clerks, 466 U.S. 435, 104 S.Ct. 1883, 80 L.Ed.2d 428 (1984), on remand 736 F.2d 1340 (9th Cir.1984); Chicago Teachers Union, Local No. 1, AFT, AFL–CIO v. Hudson, 475 U.S. 292, 106 S.Ct. 1066, 89 L.Ed.2d 232 (1986), on remand 117 F.R.D. 413 (N.D.Ill.1987).

6. 468 U.S. 364, 104 S.Ct. 3106, 82 L.Ed.2d 278 (1984).

See § 20.18(a), infra.

7. The dissenters believe that an effective way to avoid the possibility of governmental speech being favored over speech adverse to the government interest is to prevent a subsidized station from all on-the-air editorializing. Therefore, the dissenters saw the statute as a valid means to prevent this occurrence. 468 U.S. at 402, 104 S.Ct. at 3129 (Rehnquist, J., dissenting, joined by Burger, C.J., & White, J.); 468 U.S. at 409, 104 S.Ct. at 3133 (Stevens, J., dissenting).

8. See § 20.18(a), infra, for a more complete examination of this case.

All nine justices, however, recognized that the government was not free to subsidize speech that favored governmental policy on publicly owned stations while refusing to fund speech adverse to governmental interests.

Government Required Speech. The government may not enter the political marketplace by forcing private persons to subscribe to or advance messages favorable to the government. Such activity on the part of the government would be inconsistent with the fundamental freedom of belief that lies at the core of all first amendment guarantees. The government should not be able to force a person who objects to a position to endorse that position absent the most unusual and compelling circumstances, none of which have appeared in the cases to date.

There are at least two clear instances in which the Court has rejected attempts by the government to engage in such activity. In *West Virginia State Board of Education v. Barnette*[9] the Court prohibited states from requiring children to pledge allegiance to the country at the start of the school day. The children who objected to taking the oath were members of a religious sect that objected to such practices, but the majority opinion by Justice Jackson was careful not to limit the decision by basing it on the religion clauses of the first amendment alone. Instead, the opinion made available to all persons a first amendment right to refuse to pledge allegiance to the country or its symbols because of the freedom of thought and belief that is central to all first amendment freedoms.[10]

Similarly, in *Wooley v. Maynard*,[11] the Court prohibited a state from punishing a person for making illegible that portion of the automobile license plate he was required to put on his car which carried the state motto "Live Free or Die." Again, it was a Jehovah's Witness who objected to carrying this message based on his religious belief, but the Court found that no person could be required to carry governmental symbols or to endorse governmental positions absent the most compelling circumstances. Of course, a person will not have the right to deface the numbers on his license plate which identify his vehicle or to mutilate American currency which carries the phrase "In God We Trust." The justices recognize that some "speech" of this type may be necessary to advance societal interests that have nothing to do

---

9. 319 U.S. 624, 63 S.Ct. 1178, 87 L.Ed. 1628 (1943).

10. See also § 21.7, infra, regarding this case and the development of free exercise clause principles.

In Lynch v. Donnelly, 465 U.S. 668, 104 S.Ct. 1355, 79 L.Ed.2d 604 (1984), rehearing denied 466 U.S. 994, 104 S.Ct. 2376, 80 L.Ed.2d 848 (1984), the Court found that the government subsidy for a Christmas display of a creche provided only remote and incidental benefits to any religion and was not an advancement or endorsement of religion. 465 U.S. at 682, 104 S.Ct. at 1364, 79 L.Ed.2d at 616.

11. 430 U.S. 705, 97 S.Ct. 1428, 51 L.Ed.2d 752 (1977).

with censorship or propaganda, such as the identification of vehicles in traffic accidents and the need for an efficient monetary system.[12]

Subsidization and Unconstitutional Conditions. Another way for the government to participate in political expression is to subsidize persons on the condition that they engage in, or refrain from engaging in, a certain type of speech or association. This type of governmental activity is often said to be subject to the principle of "unconstitutional conditions." Some discussions of this type of problem would make it appear that any conditions on the granting of government benefits would be invalid but certainly that is not the case. Courts must in each instance examine the substance of the condition to determine whether it violates constitutional principles.[13] For example, it would be permissible for the federal government to condition a grant to a farmer on a requirement that the farmer not plant more than a specific acreage of a commodity because, under its commerce power, Congress could directly limit agricultural production.[14] However, if the federal government were to condition an agricultural grant on a farmer's promise not to criticize government farm policy, the condition would be invalid. The condition should be viewed as a penalty on a form of speech protected by the first amendment.

Thus, each type of governmental condition must be reviewed by courts to see if its substance violates first amendment principles. The difficulty in assessing the constitutionality of a condition to receiving a government grant which is related to speech may be seen by contrasting the Court's decisions in *Regan v. Taxation with Representation of Washington*[15] and *Federal Communication Commission v. League of Women Voters.*[16]

In *Taxation with Representation,* the Supreme Court unanimously upheld a portion of the Internal Revenue Statute that granted a special

---

12. In *Wooley,* the Court indicated that carrying money with the motto "In God We Trust" is not an endorsement of that message and distinguished this motto from the license plate motto on two grounds. The first is that currency is transferred among people and thus the message is not associated with any one person; the second is that the person carrying the money is not displaying such to the public. 430 U.S. at 715 n. 15, 97 S.Ct. at 1436 n. 15 (1977).

13. Professor Westen has analyzed the concept of "unconstitutional conditions" and the need to examine the substance of any condition in terms of specific constitutional limitations on governmental power in Westen, Incredible Dilemmas: Conditioning One Constitutional Right on the Forfeiture of Another, 66 Iowa L.Rev. 741 (1981); Sullivan, Unconstitutional Condi-

tions, 102 Harvard L.Rev. 1413 (1989); Rosenthal, Conditional Federal Spending and the Constitution, 39 Stanford L.Rev. 1103 (1987).

On subsidization of speech, see generally, M. Yudof, When Government Speaks: Politics, Law, and Government Expression in America 234–45 (U.Calif.Press, 1983).

14. During the period when the Supreme Court believed that the tenth amendment restricted federal power over agriculture, it invalidated such a condition. United States v. Butler, 297 U.S. 1, 56 S.Ct. 312, 80 L.Ed. 477 (1936).

15. 461 U.S. 540, 103 S.Ct. 1997, 76 L.Ed.2d 129 (1983).

16. 468 U.S. 364, 104 S.Ct. 3106, 82 L.Ed.2d 278 (1984).

tax exempt status to organizations which did not use tax deductible contributions for lobbying activity. A pivotal factor in this decision was that a companion section of the Internal Revenue Code granted a slightly different type of tax exempt status to organizations which did use nondeductible contributions for lobbying activities.

If an organization qualifies as a not-for-profit organization which does not use deductible contributions for lobbying activities it is entitled to status as a Section 501(C)(3) organization; in that case, persons who contribute to it may deduct those contributions on their federal income tax returns. A similar not-for-profit organization which desires to use contributions for lobbying activities may receive tax exempt status under Section 501(C)(4). While the 501(C)(4) organization is exempt from taxes, contributions to it are not deductible from individual income tax returns. An organization is allowed to have separate branches, one of which qualifies for deductible contributions and one of which does not. In other words, a single organization, such as the *Taxpayers with Representation of Washington,* may use a section 501(C)(3) organization for nonlobbying activities and receive tax deductible contributions to that branch of its operations while it simultaneously operates a Section 501(C)(4) affiliate to pursue charitable goals through lobbying. Although the Section 501(C)(4) affiliate would be exempt from taxation itself, it would not be eligible to receive tax deductible contributions.

The justices' unanimity in upholding this statutory scheme was based on the fact that the scheme did not penalize persons for engaging in nonpunishable speech, the lobbying of governmental organizations for charitable goals, but only constituted a refusal by Congress to subsidize lobbying activities. Thus, there was no unconstitutional condition in this case in the refusal of Congress to subsidize certain political activities.

In contrast, five justices in *League of Women Voters* believed that Congress was creating an unconstitutional condition to the receipt of federal money when it banned editorials by any noncommercial educational broadcast station which received a grant from the Corporation for Public Broadcasting. The majority opinion by Justice Brennan found that this condition was incompatible with the first amendment because it was not narrowly tailored to further the substantial government interest in insuring adequate and balanced coverage of public issues but was, instead, a penalty on those stations who sought to engage in constitutionally protected analysis of issues of public concern.

The four dissenting justices pointed out that the ban on editorial activity or endorsement of candidates by groups receiving federal money constituted only a refusal to subsidize those activities and was designed to insure that publicly funded stations would not subtly tailor their editorializing so as to please the government agencies that funded them. The majority, however, found that the ban was not precisely tailored to eliminating government influence over editorials; moreover, such unconstitutional influence was protected in other ways in the public broadcasting system.

Also, in the view of the majority, this ban was not merely a refusal by Congress to fund editorializing activities. The majority opinion stated that if Congress were to amend the statutes so as to prohibit noncommercial educational broadcasting stations from using federal funds to subsidize their editorial or candidate endorsement activities, this restriction would be "valid under the reasoning of *Taxation with Representation*." Congress could require such stations to segregate their funds and use only nonfederal funds for activities which Congress did not wish to subsidize. However, Congress could not withdraw all public funding from a station which engaged in editorializing.

Rust v. Sullivan,[17] upheld government regulations prohibiting Title X grant recipients from engaging in abortion related activities, where abortion is a method of family planning. Petitioners challenged the regulations on their face. The funds were to be used only to support preventive family planning services, population research, infertility services, and related activities. The Title X project is expressly prohibited from referring a pregnant woman to an abortion provider. Congress intended that federal funds not be used to "promote or advocate" abortion as a "method of family planning." [18]

The majority emphasized that this case is simply one where the Government is refusing to fund activities, including speech, that are specifically excluded from the scope of the project funded. Petitioners argued that the federal regulations would prohibit a Title X project from referring a woman whose pregnancy placed her life in imminent danger to a provider of abortions, but the Court rejected that interpretation of the regulations. The regulations only prohibit abortion as a "method of family planning;" referring a woman who needs a medically necessitated abortion is not equivalent to a referral in the case where abortion is a method of family planning.

The Court applied the principles in *League of Women Voters* and *Taxation with Representation,* and concluded that there was no viola-

---

17. 500 U.S. ___, 111 S.Ct. 1759, 114 L.Ed.2d 233 (1991).

O'Connor, J., filed a dissenting opinion arguing that the statute in question did not authorize the challenged regulations. Blackmun J, joined by Marshall and Stevens, JJ., filed a dissenting opinion arguing that the statute did not authorize the regulations (he was joined in this portion by O'Connor, J.) and that the regulations were unconstitutional. Stevens, J. also filed a dissenting opinion.

Rodney Smolla, Free Speech In an Open Society 216–18 (1992); Note, The Title X Family Planning Gag Rule: Can the Government Buy Up Constitutional Rights?, 41 Stan.L.Rev. 401 (1989); Leedes, The Discourse Ethics Alternative to *Rust v. Sullivan*, 26 U.Richmond L.Rev. 87 (1991).

18. 500 U.S. at ___ n. 4, 111 S.Ct. at 1773 n. 4.

tion of free speech. The employees in a Title X project remain free to pursue abortion related activities on their own time, when they are not acting under the auspices of the Title X project. It is true that, if there were any inquiries about abortion providers, the regulations suggest, as one permissible response: "the project does not consider abortion an appropriate method of family planning and therefore does not counsel or refer for abortion." [19] However, nothing in the regulations require a doctor or any other employee "to represent as his own any opinion that he does not in fact hold." [20] Nor must the doctor mislead any patient. Nothing in the Title X program provides post-conception care, including abortion (which obviously occurs after conception). The Court acknowledged that the employees' freedom of expression is, in fact, limited during the time that they actually work for the project; "but this limitation is a consequence of their decision to accept employment in a project, the scope of which is permissibly restricted by the funding authority." [21]

Equal Protection. Whenever a statute allows some persons to speak or assemble but not others, or grants a subsidy for some forms of speech but not others, the statute at issue can be analyzed under equal protection as well as first amendment principles. As we explain in Chapter Eighteen [22], the government may classify persons for the receipt of benefits or burdens so long as there is a rational relationship between the classification and a legitimate end of government. However, if the law employs suspect criteria, such as race, to establish the classification, or if the law creates a classification which allocates the ability to exercise a fundamental constitutional right, then the Court will strictly scrutinize the basis for that classification. We have noted elsewhere the difficulty of describing the exact standard of review in these cases, but it is most often said that when a law regulates the ability to engage in a fundamental constitutional right, the courts must determine whether the classification is narrowly tailored to promote a compelling or overriding governmental interest. All first amendment rights are fundamental rights and, therefore, classifications relating to them are subjected to this compelling interest standard.

Whenever the Court finds that a classification violates the first amendment, it alternatively could rule that the classification violated equal protection. For example, if a city ordinance allowed distribution of leaflets by persons who favor the policies of the mayor, but prohibited distribution of leaflets on public streets by persons who opposed the mayor, the law could be stricken under first amendment principles as the suppression of content which did not create a clear and present danger of serious societal harm. Alternatively, if a court did not wish to address the problem in first amendment terms, the statute could be

---

19. 500 U.S. at ___, 111 S.Ct. at 1765.

20. 500 U.S. at ___, 111 S.Ct. at 1776.

21. 500 U.S. at ___, 111 S.Ct. at 1775.

22. See § 18.3, supra.

held invalid under equal protection because the classification regarding who could use the sidewalks to engage in a fundamental constitutional right was not narrowly tailored to promote a compelling governmental interest.[23]

If a statute regulating the use of public places for speech activities does not conflict with first amendment principles, it almost certainly will be held not to violate equal protection because it does not improperly allocate the ability to engage in a fundamental right.[24] For example, in *Minnesota State Board of Colleges v. Knight*,[25] the Court held that a college governing board could be regulated by statute so as to require it to meet only with representatives of a teachers' union to discuss educational issues. The law required the board to exclude nonunion teachers from such discussions.

The majority opinion by Justice O'Connor found that the law violated neither the first amendment nor equal protection principles. The majority first determined that the government was not impairing any first amendment value by creating a mechanism to listen to representatives of the teachers' union but was validly pursuing the interests in efficient labor relations and college governance. The Court then summarily concluded that the law could not violate equal protection since it did not in fact restrict a fundamental constitutional right to freedom of speech or assembly.

Whenever the Court finds that the definition of a subsidy for speech activities, or the refusal to subsidize activities based upon failure to meet certain conditions, is compatible with first amendment principles, it also should find that the subsidy or condition is compatible with equal protection principles. In such cases the Court has analyzed the conditions of the subsidy and determined that they do not improperly allocate the ability to engage in a fundamental first amendment right. By definition, then, the Court should find that the classification is unrelated to a fundamental right and need only be reviewed to determine whether Congress had any reasonable basis for creating the restriction on the subsidy. For example, in *Regan v. Taxation with Representation of Washington*,[26] the justices were unanimous in finding that Congress could allow military veterans' organizations to receive

23. Police Department of the City of Chicago v. Mosley, 408 U.S. 92, 92 S.Ct. 2286, 33 L.Ed.2d 212 (1972); Carey v. Brown, 447 U.S. 455, 100 S.Ct. 2286, 65 L.Ed.2d 263 (1980).

24. Whether a case involves a regulation or subsidy, once the Supreme Court has determined that there is no first amendment violation, it will then determine that the classification does not relate to a fundamental right and, consequently, there is no equal protection violation. See

Perry Educational Association v. Perry Local Educators' Association, 460 U.S. 37, 103 S.Ct. 948, 74 L.Ed.2d 794 (1983), on remand 705 F.2d 462 (7th Cir.1983). (Classification regarding which teacher's union may use school mail system violates neither free speech nor equal protection principles.)

25. 465 U.S. 271, 104 S.Ct. 1058, 79 L.Ed.2d 299 (1984).

26. 461 U.S. 540, 103 S.Ct. 1997, 76 L.Ed.2d 129 (1983).

tax deductible contributions for their lobbying activities to promote the interest of veterans even though no other organization was allowed to use tax deductible contributions for lobbying activities. The Court viewed the regulations at issue as a Congressional decision to subsidize certain types of activity; the subsidy to veterans' organizations was compensation for the veterans' service to their country. The distinction between subsidies for veterans' and nonveterans' organizations was not based on the type of speech they engaged in, but on the permissible decision of the country to compensate persons for military service.[27]

Because this statutory benefit was seen as a compensatory statute to veterans, and not a regulation of the fundamental right to engage in free speech, the statute was not subjected to any judicial scrutiny beyond an inquiry to determine whether the classification had a rational relationship to the legitimate government interest in compensating veterans. If the Court had viewed the restriction on use of tax deductible contributions for lobbying activities as a penalty on constitutionally protected speech, it could have found the law to be either a violation of the first amendment freedom of speech or a classification relating to the freedom of speech which violated the equal protection component of the fifth amendment due process clause.[28]

English as the Official Language. The United States Constitution does not mandate English as the official language, though some state constitutions—e.g., Illinois—do. Other states (Louisiana, New Mexico, and Hawaii) offer state constitutional protection for minority language. During the eighteenth century, Benjamin Franklin expressed concern at the large number of German speaking settlers in Pennsylvania, and Noah Webster urged that "American" and not "English" be the official language. In some instances—Michigan, originally settled by the French; New Mexico, originally settled by Mexicans; Hawaii, originally settled by Hawaiians—Congress has delayed statehood until the territory was settled by English-speaking majorities.

Because of the fever of war, some states during World War I tried to ban the teaching of foreign languages, especially German. In 1919, Nebraska enacted a statute prohibiting the teaching of any subject in any language other than the English language in any school, public or private; it also forbade the teaching of languages other than the English language below the eighth grade. The state supreme court interpreted the statute not to apply to "ancient or dead languages." In

---

27. For another decision based on this veterans' compensation concept, see Johnson v. Robison, 415 U.S. 361, 94 S.Ct. 1160, 39 L.Ed.2d 389 (1974), examined in § 21.9(a), infra; see also Personnel Administrator of Massachusetts v. Feeney, 442 U.S. 256, 99 S.Ct. 2282, 60 L.Ed.2d 870 (1979), on remand 475 F.Supp. 109 (D.Mass.

1979), judgment affirmed 445 U.S. 901, 100 S.Ct. 1075, 63 L.Ed.2d 317 (1980).

28. The Court in *Regan* recognized that the fifth amendment due process clause applies to the federal government to require equal protection in the same manner as the fourteenth amendment applies to state and local government.

Meyer v. Nebraska[29] the Supreme Court, speaking through Justice McReynolds, invalidated the statute as interfering with an aspect of liberty guaranteed by the due process clause of the fourteenth amendment. The Court did not rely on the first amendment (which had not yet been incorporated to apply to the states[30] through the due process clause of the fourteenth amendment); rather, it relied on substantive due process:

> The desire of the Legislature to foster a homogeneous people with American ideals prepared readily to understand current discussions of civil matters is easy to appreciate. Unfortunate experiences during the late war and aversion toward every character of truculent adversaries were certainly enough to quicken that aspiration. But the means adopted, we think, exceed the limitations upon the power of the state and conflict with rights assured to plaintiff in error. The interference is plain enough and no adequate reason therefore in time of peace and domestic tranquility has been shown ...

> As the statute undertakes to interfere only with teaching which involves a modern language, leaving complete freedom as to other matters, there seems no adequate foundation for the suggestion that the purpose was to protect the child's health by limiting his mental activities. It is well known that proficiency in a foreign language seldom comes to one not instructed at an early age, and experience shows that this is not injurious to the health, morals or understanding of the ordinary child.[31]

Justices Holmes and Sutherland dissented without opinion.

Meyer was written during the heyday of substantive due process, but the modern Court has not suggested that it is no longer good law. However, this decision only forbids a state from prohibiting teaching a subject (such as history) in a foreign language or teaching a foreign language. It does not prevent a state or the federal government from encouraging the use of English, or publishing its messages and signs (such as road signs, voting instructions, and so forth) in English.

Meyer does not prevent the state from prohibiting the teaching of foreign language in a *public* as opposed to a *private* school. The defendant in that case was a teacher who taught the subject of reading in the German language in Zion Parochial School. The Court made clear that no "challenge has been made of the state's power to prescribe a curriculum for institutions which it supports."[32] Nor does *Meyer* prevent the state from requiring that English be taught in all schools,

---

29. 262 U.S. 390, 43 S.Ct. 625, 67 L.Ed. 1042 (1923).

30. See, Gitlow v. New York, 268 U.S. 652, 666, 45 S.Ct. 625, 630, 69 L.Ed. 1138 (1925).

31. 262 U.S. at 402–03, 43 S.Ct. at 628.

32. 262 U.S. at 402, 43 S.Ct. at 628.

public or private. The power of the state to "make reasonable regulations for all schools, including a requirement that they shall give instructions in English, is not questioned." [33]

The same year that the Court decided *Meyer,* a Congressman introduced a bill to make "American" the official language, but that bill failed. Since then, some states have made "English" or "American" the official language. During the 1980's there was a renewed effort to make "English" the official language in this country. In 1981, for example, then Senator S.I. Hayakawa, representing California, proposed a federal constitutional amendment making English the official language. Congress did not ratify that amendment. [34]

IV. "CLEAR AND PRESENT DANGER" AND THE ADVOCACY OF VIOLENCE OR OTHER ILLEGAL CONDUCT

§ 20.12 Introduction

First amendment guarantees prohibiting Congress from passing laws abridging speech, press, or peaceful assembly have never been treated as absolute by the Supreme Court. The Court has preferred the view that in certain situations an individual's rights to freely express his or her beliefs must be subordinated to other interests of society. [1] Yet a willingness to balance first amendment rights against other interests has not diminished the importance of the first amendment, for the prevailing view is that the Constitution has placed the burden of reconciling the conflicting interests of the individual and society on the Court. [2] One of the standards the Supreme Court first developed to justify abridgement of freedom of expression for the benefit of society is the "clear and present danger" test.

There are three phases in the development of the "clear and present danger" doctrine. First, the "clear and present danger" test had its genesis in the early part of the twentieth century. The test originated in a number of opinions and dissents written by Justice Holmes and Justice Brandeis dealing primarily with the Espionage and Sedition Acts of World War I.

---

33. 262 U.S. at 402, 43 S.Ct. at 628.

34. See, S.B. Heath, Language and Politics in the United States, in, M. Saville–Troike, ed., Linguistics and Anthropology: Georgetown University Roundtable on Languages and Linguistics (1977); H. Kloss, The American Bilingual Tradition (1977); D. Barron, Grammar and Good Taste: Reforming the English Language (1982); J. Fishman, ed., Language Rights and the English Language Amendment (1986); D. Baron, English Only: The Official Language Question in America (unpublished, 1988).

§ 20.12

1. Whitney v. California, 274 U.S. 357, 375–76, 47 S.Ct. 641, 648, 71 L.Ed. 1095 (1927) (Brandeis, J., concurring).

2. Emerson, Toward a General Theory of the First Amendment, 72 Yale L.J. 877, 905 (1963).

In the second phase, when the Cold War was at its height, a later generation of Supreme Court Justices and federal judges, including Chief Justice Vinson and Judge Learned Hand, applied the "clear and present danger" doctrine in a manner restricting first amendment freedoms more severely than Holmes and Brandeis contemplated. This restrictive approach influenced the Court to develop a "balancing test" for protecting freedom of expression.[3]

Finally, beginning in the 1960's the Supreme Court attempted to breathe new life into the doctrine and, as we shall see in the following sections, has formulated a more strict test, but with strong historical origins in the original clear and present danger standard. This most recent test is more protective of free speech.

§ 20.13 The Holmes–Brandeis "Clear and Present Danger" Test

(a) The Origins and Development

From the time the first amendment was ratified until just prior to World War I the Supreme Court had little exposure to freedom of expression issues. Except for the passage of the 1798 Alien and Sedition Acts[1] Congress generally followed the first amendment directive that "Congress shall make no law" restricting free speech, assembly or press,[2] but Congressional adherence to the literal meaning of the amendment was abandoned when the United States involvement in World War I met with vocal resistance.

Congress, in response to the domestic political unrest, passed the Espionage Act of 1917[3] and the Sedition Act of 1918.[4] This legislation provided the Supreme Court with the opportunity to develop standards for approaching first amendment questions at a time when the climate was not conducive to an expansive reading of the free speech guarantee.

3. For discussions of the balancing test, see generally, Dennis v. United States, 341 U.S. 494, 517, 71 S.Ct. 857, 871, 95 L.Ed. 1137 (1951) (J. Frankfurter concurring), rehearing denied 342 U.S. 842, 72 S.Ct. 20, 96 L.Ed. 636 (1951); Emerson, Toward a General Theory of the First Amendment, 72 Yale L.J. 877, at 912–14 (1963).

§ 20.13

1. Alien Act of June 25, 1798, ch. 58, 1 Stat. 570. Sedition Act of July 14, 1798, ch. 74, 1 Stat. 596.

2. For the early history, see Anderson, The Formative Period of First Amendment Theory, 1870–1915, 24 Am.J.Legal Hist. 56 (1980); L. Levy, Legacy of Suppression (1960); Mayton, Seditious Libel and the Lost Guarantee of a Freedom of Expression, 84 Colum.L.Rev. 91 (1984); Rabban, The Emergence of Modern First Amendment Doctrine, 50 U.Chi.L.Rev. 1205 (1983); Rabban, The First Amendment in its Forgotten Years, 90 Yale L.J. 516 (1981).

3. Espionage Act of June 15, 1917, ch. 30, 40 Stat. 217.

4. Sedition Act of May 16, 1918, ch. 75, 40 Stat. 553.

In 1919, the year that first saw the Palmer raids,[5] the Supreme Court handed down two important decisions involving free speech issues, *Schenck v. United States*[6] and *Abrams v. United States*.[7] In these decisions the Court first discussed "clear and present danger" theory.

During time of war, one of the first casualties is free speech. Yet in ancient Athens, the cradle of democracy, the Greeks widely believed that freedom of speech made their armies more brave. Herodotus, in his history, writes that the Athenians could win victories over the more numerous Persians in the first part of the fifth century B.C. because the Athenians fought as free people, not as slaves. "Thus grew the power of Athens, and it is proved not by one but by many instances that equality is a good thing; seeing that while they were under despotic rulers the Athenians were no better in war than any of their neighbors, yet once they got quit of despots they were far and away the first of all," because "when they were freed each man was zealous to achieve for himself."[8] Aeschylus, in his play *The Persians,* similarly celebrates the victory of the Greeks because: "Of no man are they the slaves or subjects."[9] As one commentator has perceptively noted, "For Aeschylus, and for the Athenians, it was not just a victory of Greeks over Persians but of free men over 'slaves.' The victors at Salamis were men elevated and inspired by the freedom to speak their minds and govern themselves."[10]

Oftentimes we forget this ancient truth. People who are free work more intensely because they work for themselves, not for a master. It is for the same reason that it takes many hunting dogs to catch one fox: the fox works harder because he is self-employed.

5. See, e.g., A. Kelly & W. Harbison, The American Constitution: Its Origins and Development 690 (1970):

"In 1919 a great Red scare began, inspired by Communist successes in Russia and central Europe. This fear was aggravated by the activities of a few bomb-throwing anarchists and of the Industrial Workers of the World.... In January 1919, Attorney–General A. Mitchell Palmer launched a gigantic two-year Red hunt, highlighted by mass arrests without benefit of habeas corpus, by hasty prosecutions, and by mass deportation of Communists and other radicals."

6. 249 U.S. 47, 39 S.Ct. 247, 63 L.Ed. 470 (1919).

7. 250 U.S. 616, 40 S.Ct. 17, 63 L.Ed. 1173 (1919).

8. Herodotus, 4 vols. (Loeb Classical Library, 1922–1931), 5:78 (3:87), quoted in, I.F. Stone, The Trial of Socrates 50 (1988).

Pericles, in his famous funeral oration, commented on the fact that the Athenians were strong because they were free:

"Our city is thrown open to the world, and we never expel a foreigner or prevent him from seeing or learning anything of which the secret if revealed to an enemy might profit him. We rely not upon management or trickery, but upon our own hearts and hands.... The great impediment to action is, in our opinion, not discussion, but the want of knowledge which is gained by discussion preparatory to action."

Pericles, Funeral Oration, in B. Jowett, Thucydides 116, 118–19 (Clarendon Press, 1881).

9. Aeschylus, *Plays,* 2 vols. (Loeb Classical Library, 1922–1926), I:109; I:241*ff.,* quoted in, I.F. Stone, The Trial of Socrates 51 (1988).

10. I.F. Stone, The Trial of Socrates 51 (1988).

The *Schenck* Case. In *Schenck* the appellants' conviction for conspiracy to violate the Espionage Act of 1917 was affirmed. Appellants had mailed leaflets to men eligible for military service asserting that the draft violated the thirteenth amendment.[11] These leaflets, the government argued, were prohibited by provisions in the Espionage Act forbidding obstruction of military recruiting.

Justice Holmes, writing for the Court, upheld the convictions and the restraint on freedom of expression as necessary to prevent grave and immediate threats to national security. Ordinarily, Holmes, believed, the leaflets would have been constitutionally protected but:

> [T]he character of every act depends upon the circumstances in which it is done.... The most stringent protection of free speech would not protect a man in falsely shouting fire in a theater and causing a panic. It does not even protect a man from an injunction against uttering words that may have all the effect of force.... The question in every case is whether the words used are used in such circumstances and are of such a nature as to create a clear and present danger that they will bring about the substantive evils that Congress has a right to prevent. It is a question of proximity and degree.[12]

Holmes concluded that first amendment protection could not be extended during wartime to protect speech hindering the war effort.[13]

---

11. 249 U.S. at 49–51, 39 S.Ct. at 247–49.

12. 249 U.S. at 52, 39 S.Ct. at 249.

See generally, Bogen, The Free Speech Metamorphosis of Mr. Justice Holmes, 11 Hofstra L.Rev. 97 (1982). Cf. Ragan, Justice Oliver Wendell Holmes, Jr., Zachariah Chafee, Jr., and the Clear and Present Danger Test for Free Speech: The First Year, 1919, 58 J.Am.Hist. 24 (1971).

See also, Palmer, The Totalitarianism of Mr. Justice Holmes: Another Chapter in the Controversy, 37 A.B.A.J. 809 (1951); Ragat & O'Fallon, Mr. Justice Holmes: A Dissenting Opinion—The Speech Cases, 36 Stan.L.Rev. 1349 (1984).

Holmes' belief in free speech was a major reason that he was the darling of the liberals of his era. Ironically, Holmes, a lifelong Republican, was a social Darwinist—a cynical believer in the survival of the fittest. "Holmes did not believe in social reform, antitrust or progressive taxation, and despite his abolitionist background, was unmoved by the plight of black people. He was also an atheist, a materialist, a behaviorist and a resolute enemy of natural law." Posner, Star of the Legal Stage, Wall Street Journal, Aug. 9, 1989, at p. A9, cols. 1, 2 (midwest ed.).

Only seven months before the *Schenck* case would be argued before the Supreme Court, Holmes had an interesting train ride with Judge Learned Hand; that ride resulted in correspondence between the two. Thus, on June 24, 1918, Holmes actually said in a letter to Learned Hand: "... free speech stands no differently than freedom of vaccination. The occasions would be rarer when you cared enough to stop it but if for any reason you did care enough you wouldn't care a damn for the suggestion that you were acting on a provisional hypothesis and might be wrong." Kellogg, Learned Hand and the Great Train Ride, The American Scholar 471, 481 (1987). See also, S. Novick, Honorable Justice: The Life of Oliver Wendell Holmes (1989).

13. One week after writing the *Schenck* opinion Holmes wrote two other opinions for the Court affirming convictions in similar cases. In Frohwerk v. United States, 249 U.S. 204, 39 S.Ct. 249, 63 L.Ed. 561 (1919) he stated that: "[T]he First Amendment while prohibiting legislation against free speech as such cannot have been, and obviously was not, intended to give immu-

In a dissenting opinion in *Abrams v. United States*,[14] Holmes further explained his "clear and present danger" test. The appellants were convicted of conspiracy to violate the Espionage Acts amendments which prohibited speech encouraging resistance to the war effort and curtailment of production "with intent to cripple or hinder the United States in the prosecution of the war."[15] They had distributed pamphlets criticizing the United States' involvement in the effort to crush Russia's new Communist Government.

The majority in *Abrams* was unimpressed with Holmes' clear and present danger test. The Court affirmed without being much concerned at all with the free speech interests involved.[16] Because of the "bad tendency" of the defendants' speech, the majority affirmed, even though the defendants' sentences were twenty years.[17] Under the

nity for every possible use of language....
Whatever might be thought of the other counts on the evidence, if it were before us, we have decided in Schenck v. United States, that a person may be convicted of a conspiracy to obstruct recruiting by words of persuasion." 249 U.S. at 206, 39 S.Ct. at 250.

In Debs v. United States, 249 U.S. 211, 39 S.Ct. 252, 63 L.Ed. 566 (1919), Holmes affirmed the conviction of Eugene Debs, a prominent Socialist of the time, for allegedly encouraging listeners to obstruct the recruiting service. Holmes in this case spoke more in common law speech terms which were adopted later by the Court (but not by Holmes) in the *Abrams* and *Gitlow* cases discussed below. Holmes said in the *Debs* case:

"We should add that the jury were most carefully instructed that they could not find the defendant guilty for advocacy of any of his opinions unless the words used had as *their natural tendency and reasonably probable effect* to obstruct the recruiting service, & c., and unless the defendant had the specific intent to do so in his mind."

249 U.S. at 216, 39 S.Ct. at 254 (emphasis added).

See Freund, The *Debs* Case and Freedom of Speech, 19 The New Republic 13 (1919), reprinted in 40 U.Chi.L.Rev. 239 (1973); Kalven, Professor Ernst Freund and Debs v. United States, 40 U.Chi.L.Rev. 235 (1973).

14. 250 U.S. 616, 624, 40 S.Ct. 17, 20, 63 L.Ed. 1173 (1919).

15. Espionage Act of June 15, 1917, ch. 30, 40 Stat. 217, as amended May 16, 1918, 40 Stat. 553.

16. The United States at this time was at war with Germany, not Russia. The actual statute involved forbade conspiracies to interfere with production with the intent to hinder the prosecution of the war. The theory of the trial court and the Supreme Court majority was that to reduce arms production for the Russian fight might aid Germany (with whom the United States was at war) because the United States would have less total arms. The Court did not require any specific intent by defendants. 250 U.S. at 621, 40 S.Ct. at 19: "Men must be held to have intended, and to be accountable for, the effects which their acts were likely to produce." The free speech defense was very briefly dismissed as "sufficiently discussed and is definitely negatived in *Schenck* ..." and other cases. 250 U.S. at 619, 40 S.Ct. at 18.

17. 250 U.S. at 629, 40 S.Ct. at 21–22.

Disquieting echoes of the majority's bad tendency test are found in Haig v. Agee, 453 U.S. 280, 101 S.Ct. 2766, 69 L.Ed.2d 640 (1981). There the majority upheld the power of the Secretary of State to revoke the passport of Agee, a former CIA agent engaged in a policy of exposing clandestine CIA agents abroad. In rejecting Agee's first amendment claims the majority said: "Agee's disclosures, among other things, have the declared purpose of obstructing intelligence operations and the recruiting of intelligence personnel. They are clearly not protected by the Constitution." 453 U.S. at 308–09, 101 S.Ct. at 2783. Note the similarities with Abrams v. United States, 250 U.S. 616, 620–21, 40 S.Ct. 17, 19, 63 L.Ed. 1173 (1919): "The purpose of this [published article] was to persuade the persons to whom it was addressed to turn a

majority's use of the bad tendency test, speech could be prohibited if it was of a type that would tend to bring about harmful results.

Holmes criticized the Court's decision to uphold the conviction arguing that it was ridiculous to assume these pamphlets would actually hinder the government's war efforts in Germany, with which the United States was at war; as a matter of statutory construction Holmes would have reversed the convictions.

But he also quickly moved to consider the constitutional issues. Holmes contended that the government could only restrict freedom of expression when there was "present danger of immediate evil or an intent to bring it about ... Congress certainly cannot forbid all effort to change the mind of the country." [18] Laws regulating free speech, Holmes conceded, would be an effective way for the government to stifle opposition, but he maintained hope that people would realize that—

> the ultimate good desired is better reached by free trade in ideas— that the best test of truth is the power of thought to get itself accepted in the competition of the market.... That ... is the theory of our Constitution. [19]

Holmes warned against overzealous repression of unpopular ideas:

> [W]e should be eternally vigilant against attempts to check the expression of opinions that we loathe and believe to be fraught with death, unless they so imminently threaten immediate interference with the lawful and pressing purposes of the law that an immediate check is required to save the country. [20]

He concluded that the appellants had been unjustly convicted for exercising their first amendment rights.

The *Gitlow* Decision. Six years after *Abrams,* the Court continued to use the bad tendency test and remained reluctant to apply the clear and present danger doctrine in the manner in which Justice Holmes had urged. The appellants in *Gitlow v. New York* [21] were convicted of violating New York's "criminal anarchy statute" which prohibited advocating violent overthrow of the government. They had printed and circulated a radical manifesto encouraging political strikes. There was no evidence that the manifesto had any effect on the individuals who received copies.

The majority of the *Gitlow* Court upheld the conviction and the statute, finding the "clear and present danger test" inapplicable. The Court reasoned that only when a statute prohibits particular acts

---

deaf ear to patriotic appeals in behalf of the Government of the United States, and to cease to render it assistance in the prosecution of the war."

18. 250 U.S. at 628, 40 S.Ct. at 21.

19. 250 U.S. at 630, 40 S.Ct. at 22.

20. 250 U.S. at 630, 40 S.Ct. at 22.

21. 268 U.S. 652, 45 S.Ct. 625, 69 L.Ed. 1138 (1925).

without including any restrictions on language should the "clear and present danger" standard be employed to determine if the particular speech should be constitutionally protected. In such a case the government must prove the defendants' language brought about the statutorily prohibited result.[22] But, in *Gitlow,* the Court noted that the legislature had already determined what utterances would violate the statute. The government's decision that certain words are likely to cause the substantive evil "is not open for consideration." [23] The government must then show only that there is a reasonable basis for the statute. It is irrelevant that the particular words do or do not create a "clear and present danger." [24]

The Holmes' Dissent In *Gitlow*. Holmes, joined by Bradeis, dissented. Holmes wrote that if the "clear and present danger" test was properly applied it would be obvious there was no real danger that the appellants' pamphlets would instigate political revolution. If the manifesto presented an immediate threat to the stability of the governments, then there would be a need for suppression.[25] But in the absence of immediate danger, Holmes concluded, the appellants were entitled to exercise their first amendment rights.

The *Whitney* Case. Two years later, in 1927, the "clear and present danger" test made its appearance once again, but this time at least it was in a concurrence. In *Whitney v. California,*[26] the Court affirmed the conviction of Mrs. Whitney for violating the California Criminal Syndicalism Act by assisting in the organization of the Communist Labor Party of California. The statute defined criminal syndicalism as any doctrine "advocating teaching or aiding and abetting ... crime, sabotage ... or unlawful acts of force and violence" to effect political or economic change.[27]

Whitney contended that she had argued at the organizing convention for political reform through the democratic process. The majority of the convention, however, supported change through violence and terrorism. She maintained that she had not assisted the Communist Party with knowledge of its illegal purpose; her conviction was based on her presence at the convention and consequently she alleged deprivation of liberty without due process.[28]

The Court held the jury had resolved adversely to her the question of fact regarding her participation at the convention, that the united action of the Communist Party threatened the welfare of the state, and

22. 268 U.S. at 670–71, 45 S.Ct. at 631–32.

23. 268 U.S. at 670, 45 S.Ct. at 632.

24. 268 U.S. at 671, 45 S.Ct. at 632. See, Bork, Neutral Principles and Some First Amendment Problems, 47 Ind.L.J. 1, 23 (1971).

25. 268 U.S. at 673, 45 S.Ct. at 632.

26. 274 U.S. 357, 47 S.Ct. 641, 71 L.Ed. 1095 (1927).

27. 274 U.S. at 359–60, 47 S.Ct. at 642.

28. 274 U.S. at 363–67, 47 S.Ct. at 644–45.

Mrs. Whitney was a part of that organization.[29] The conviction was affirmed.

Justice Brandeis' Concurring Opinion in *Whitney*. Holmes joined Brandeis' separate opinion. But while the opinion was labelled a "concurrence" it did not read like one. Brandeis' concurrence was a dissent in all but name, upholding the conviction only on this narrow procedural ground. But calling the opinion a concurrence lent a little more authority to the doctrine that Holmes and Brandeis were unsuccessfully urging. Brandeis specifically objected to any notion, first presented in *Gitlow,* that the enactment of a statute foreclosed the application of the clear and present danger test by the Court. "[T]he enactment of the statute cannot alone establish the facts which are essential to its validity." [30]

Brandeis then proceeded to justify the clear and present danger test. In language perhaps a little more restrained than Holmes had used, he argued that the "state is, *ordinarily,* denied the power to prohibit dissemination of social, economic and political doctrine which a vast majority of its citizens believe to be false and fraught with evil consequence." [31] The framers "valued liberty both as an end and as a means. They believed liberty to be the secret of happiness and courage to be the secret of liberty." [32] Brandeis also argued that public order was secured by free speech. "[R]epression breeds hate; ... hate menaces stable government; ... the path of safety lies in the opportunity to discuss freely supposed grievances and proposed remedies...." [33]

Parts of Brandeis' concurrence appeared to place strong emphasis on the need to show incitement:

29. 274 U.S. at 367–72, 47 S.Ct. at 645–47.

30. 274 U.S. at 374, 47 S.Ct. at 648 (Brandeis, J., concurring). See generally, R. Rotunda, ed., Six Justices on Civil Rights 161–71 (Nathanson, "The Philosophy of Mr. Justice Brandeis and Civil Liberties Today") (Oceana Publications, Inc. 1983).

31. 274 U.S. at 374, 47 S.Ct. at 648. (emphasis added).

32. 274 U.S. at 375, 47 S.Ct. at 648.

These words of Brandeis were portended by the funeral oration of Pericles, who said that we should believe "courage to be freedom and freedom to be happiness...." Pericles, Funeral Oration, in B. Jowett, Thucydides 116, 122 (Clarendon Press, 1881).

33. 274 U.S. at 376–77, 47 S.Ct. at 648–49. Pericles made a similar point in his funeral oration:

"Our city is thrown open to the world, and we never expel a foreigner or prevent him from seeing or learning anything of which the secret if revealed to an enemy might profit him. We rely not upon management or trickery, but upon our own hearts and hands.... We alone regard a man who takes no interest in public affairs, not as a harmless, but as a useless character; and if few of us are originators, we are all sound judges of a policy. The great impediment to action is, in our opinion, not discussion, but the want of that knowledge which is gained by discussion preparatory to action. For we have a peculiar power of thinking before we act and of acting too, whereas other men are courageous from ignorance but hesitate upon reflection."

Pericles, Funeral Oration, in B. Jowett, Thucydides 116, 118, 119 (Clarendon Press, 1881).

But even advocacy of [law] violation however reprehensible morally, is not a justification for denying free speech where the advocacy falls short of incitement and there is nothing to indicate that the advocacy would be immediately acted on.... [N]o danger flowing from speech can be deemed clear and present, unless the incidence of the evil apprehended is so imminent that it may befall before there is opportunity for full discussion.[34]

Only when speech causes unthinking, immediate action is the protection of the first amendment withdrawn.

Brandeis then concluded that in situations where the rights of free speech and assembly were infringed the defendant may contest this suppression alleging that no "clear and present danger" actually existed. Mrs. Whitney should have argued her conviction was void because no "clear and present danger" of a serious evil resulted from the convention activities. Instead, Whitney had challenged her conviction on the basis of denial of due process; therefore, Brandeis said that he was unable to pass on the "clear and present danger" issue.[35] This technicality meant that Brandeis was able to call his opinion a concurrence, thus lending it more authority for future citations.

The *Herdon* Decision. When the Supreme Court, in a few cases during this period, did reverse convictions of speech advocacy, it did not do so under the clear and present danger rationale.[36] Finally, the Holmes doctrine of "clear and present danger" was relied on in a majority opinion in *Herndon v. Lowry*,[37] a five to four decision. The Court reversed a conviction for violating a statute prohibiting attempts to incite insurrection, in effect rejecting the *Gitlow* test. The Court held that a state could not restrict words that only had a "tendency" to

---

34. 274 U.S. at 376–77, 47 S.Ct. at 648–49.

35. 274 U.S. at 379, 47 S.Ct. at 649.

36. In Fiske v. Kansas, 274 U.S. 380, 47 S.Ct. 655, 71 L.Ed. 1108 (1927), decided immediately after the *Whitney* decision, the Court—in a decision written not by Justice Holmes but by Justice Sanford— reversed a conviction of a member of the Industrial Workers of the World under the Kansas Criminal Syndicalism Act. The test of *Whitney* was applied; the State simply did not meet it:

"The result is that the Syndicalism Act has been applied in this case to sustain the conviction of the defendant, without any charge or evidence that the organization in which he secured members advocated any crime, violence or other unlawful acts or methods as a means of effecting industrial or political changes or revolution." 274 U.S. at 387, 47 S.Ct. at 657.

The simple reference in the I.W.W.'s Constitution to a class struggle was insufficient.

Several years later, in Stromberg v. California, 283 U.S. 359, 51 S.Ct. 532, 75 L.Ed. 1117 (1931), the Court, in an opinion by Chief Justice Hughes, reversed, on vagueness grounds, a conviction under California's statute forbidding the display of the red flag for various reasons, including display "as a sign, symbol and emblem of opposition to organized government...." 283 U.S. at 361, 51 S.Ct. at 533.

37. 301 U.S. 242, 57 S.Ct. 732, 81 L.Ed. 1066 (1937). Cf. De Jonge v. Oregon, 299 U.S. 353, 57 S.Ct. 255, 81 L.Ed. 278 (1937) (peaceable assembly for lawful discussion cannot be made a crime; the Court talked of the need to show incitement; 299 U.S. at 359–65, 57 S.Ct. at 739–42).

be dangerous. Power to abridge individual rights to freely express themselves "even of utterances of a defined character must find its justification in a reasonable apprehension of danger to organized government." [38]

Almost immediately after using the doctrine the Court began to expand its application. For a few years, the "clear and present danger" test was employed in a number of cases, not involving sedition, challenging the constitutionality of governmental suppression of free expression.[39] Perhaps the most important of these cases—and the type of speech to which the "clear and present danger" language is still applied to this day—involved a series of contempt-of-court decisions. It is to that issue we now turn. Outside of these contempt of court cases the Court has developed different tests to determine when governmental restraints may be placed on different types of speech.[40]

(b) Present Application in the Contempt of Court Cases

Originally, in contempt of court cases, the Court had held that any spoken or printed criticism of courts obstructed the administration of justice and therefore was not constitutionally protected.[41] In *Bridges v. California*,[42] however, a contempt case, Justice Black writing for the majority applied the "clear and present danger" test stating "the substantive evil must be extremely serious and the degree of imminence extremely high before utterances can be punished." [43] The petitioners' statements criticizing pending court proceedings were not

38. 301 U.S. at 258, 57 S.Ct. at 257.

39. Thornhill v. Alabama, 310 U.S. 88, 60 S.Ct. 736, 84 L.Ed. 1093 (1940) (peaceful picketing); Cantwell v. Connecticut, 310 U.S. 296, 308, 60 S.Ct. 900, 905, 84 L.Ed. 1213 (1940) (power of state to punish clear and present danger of riot); West Virginia State Bd. of Education v. Barnette, 319 U.S. 624, 63 S.Ct. 1178, 87 L.Ed. 1628 (1943) (flag salutes); Terminiello v. Chicago, 337 U.S. 1, 4–5, 69 S.Ct. 894, 895–96, 93 L.Ed. 1131 (1949) (breach of the peace), rehearing denied 337 U.S. 934, 69 S.Ct. 1490, 93 L.Ed. 1740 (1949).

40. For a modern defense of the clear and present danger standard, see Redish, Advocacy of Unlawful Conduct and the First Amendment: In Defense of Clear and Present Danger, 70 Calif.L.Rev. 1159 (1982).

41. Toledo Newspaper Co. v. United States, 247 U.S. 402, 38 S.Ct. 560, 62 L.Ed. 1186 (1918). This history is reflected in Canon 20 ("Newspaper Discussion of Pending Litigation"), American Bar Association, Canons of Professional Ethics (1908, amended), and also in D.R. 7–107 ("Trial Publicity"), American Bar Association, Model Code of Professional Responsibility (1970, as amended). See also, id., D.R. 1–102(A)(5) (a lawyer shall not "engage in conduct that is prejudicial to the administration of justice"). A.B.A., Model Rules of Professional Conduct, Rule 3.6 (1983, as amended).

These broad restrictions have come under constitutional attack. See, e.g., Chicago Council of Lawyers v. Bauer, 522 F.2d 242 (7th Cir.1975), certiorari denied sub nom. Cunningham v. Chicago Council of Lawyers, 427 U.S. 912, 96 S.Ct. 3201, 49 L.Ed.2d 1204 (1976); Hirschkop v. Snead, 594 F.2d 356 (4th Cir.1979) (per curiam). Gentile v. State Bar of Nevada, 501 U.S. ——, 111 S.Ct. 2720, 115 L.Ed.2d 888 (1991).

See generally, T. Morgan & R. Rotunda, Professional Responsibility: Problems and Materials 295–306 (5th ed. 1991); Harry Kalven, Jr., ed. by Jamie Kalven, A Worthy Tradition: Freedom of Speech in America 24–32 (1988).

42. 314 U.S. 252, 62 S.Ct. 190, 86 L.Ed. 192 (1941).

43. 314 U.S. at 263, 62 S.Ct. at 194.

likely, Black reasoned, to bring about a "substantive evil" requiring abridgement of free expression.[44] Justice Douglas later explained that *Bridges* "tightened" the clear and present danger test and "confined" it to this "narrow category" of cases.[45]

The Court struck down another contempt conviction in *Pennekamp v. Florida*[46] holding that the danger to be avoided, interference with the administration of justice, was not a clear and immediate enough danger to justify suppressing public comment. The Court also set aside a contempt citation for publishing inaccurate articles criticizing procedures in a trial, in *Craig v. Harney*,[47] where it held:

> The vehemence of the language used is not alone the measure of the power to punish for contempt. The fires which it kindles must constitute an imminent, and not merely a likely, threat to the administration of justice. The danger must not be remote or even probable; it must immediately imperil.[48]

Later in *Nebraska Press Association v. Stuart*,[49] the Court used the language of "clear and present danger" and reversed a court order restraining reporters from publishing allegedly prejudicial pretrial material.

The application of the test to contempt of court cases perhaps indicated that the Court intended to employ the "clear and present danger" standard as a general test for determining the constitutionality of restrictions on speech.[50] However, outside of the contempt of court cases, different tests had to be developed to evaluate the competing interests where the governmental restraints are placed on different types of speech, such as obscenity or defamation. Even in cases involving the advocacy of violence, breach of the peace, or criminal syndicalism, the "clear and present danger" test was to undergo revision, though the historical debt to Holmes and Brandeis is unmistakable.

---

44. 314 U.S. at 270, 278, 62 S.Ct. at 197, 201.

45. Brandenburg v. Ohio, 395 U.S. 444, 453, 89 S.Ct. 1827, 1832, 23 L.Ed.2d 430 (1969) (Douglas, J., concurring).

46. 328 U.S. 331, 350, 66 S.Ct. 1029, 1039, 90 L.Ed. 1295 (1946).

47. 331 U.S. 367, 67 S.Ct. 1249, 91 L.Ed. 1546 (1947), mandate conformed 150 Tex. Cr. 598, 204 S.W.2d 842 (1947).

48. 331 U.S. at 376, 67 S.Ct. at 1255.

49. 427 U.S. 539, 562–63, 96 S.Ct. 2791, 2804–05, 49 L.Ed.2d 683 (1976), citing United States v. Dennis, 183 F.2d 201, 212 (2d

Cir.1950) (L. Hand, J.), affirmed 341 U.S. 494, 71 S.Ct. 857, 95 L.Ed. 1137 (1951). Cf. 427 U.S. at 569, 96 S.Ct. at 2807–08 (1976).

See Landmark Communications, Inc. v. Virginia, 435 U.S. 829, 844, 98 S.Ct. 1535, 1544, 56 L.Ed.2d 1 (1978), noting that older cases have shown that out of court comments concerning pending cases or grand jury investigations do not constitute a clear and present danger to the administration of justice and cannot be punished by contempt.

50. See Strong, Fifty Years of "Clear and Present Danger": From *Schenck* to *Brandenburg*—And Beyond, 1969 Sup.Ct. Rev. 41, 52.

§ 20.14 Revision of the "Clear and Present Danger" Test

In the early 1950's the Supreme Court decided to reexamine the validity of the Holmes–Brandeis "clear and present danger" doctrine. With the advent of the cold war and the McCarthy paranoia, freedom of expression, especially speech or actions criticizing the government or threatening national security, was severely restricted. The tone of the times was reflected in the Court's opinions, as it managed to avoid direct confrontation with the other branches of government over these issues.

Petitioners in *Dennis v. United States*[1] were convicted of violating the Smith Act by conspiring to organize the Communist Party of the United States. The party's goal allegedly was to overthrow the existing government by force and violence.

There was no majority opinion in this case. Chief Justice Vinson, writing for himself and three other justices, indicated Congress possessed the power to promulgate laws restricting speech. The issue the Court had to decide, thought Vinson, was whether the means Congress employed in suppressing free expression conflicted with first amendment guarantees. He believed the questions would most effectively be resolved by applying the "clear and present danger" test.[2] But that test, as he construed it, meant much less than the original Holmes–Brandeis theory.

The Vinson reformulation of the clear and present danger test contained two steps. First, the Government had to show a substantial interest in limiting the speech. Congress, the Court held, did have a substantial interest here in preventing violent overthrow of the government. Second, the words or actions restricted in the legislation must be shown to constitute a "clear and present danger."

Vinson's theory of "clear and present danger" was decidedly different from that of Holmes and Brandeis:

> [T]he words cannot mean that before the Government may act, it must wait until the *putsch* is about to be executed.... If Government is aware that a group aiming at its overthrow is attempting to indoctrinate its members ... action by the Government is required.... Certainly an attempt to overthrow the Government by force, even though doomed from the outset because of inadequate numbers or power of the revolutionists, is a sufficient evil for Congress to prevent.[3]

Speech which advocates more extreme dangers, such as overthrow of the Government, may be prohibited even though the danger is more

§ 20.14

1. 341 U.S. 494, 71 S.Ct. 857, 95 L.Ed. 1137 (1951), rehearing denied 342 U.S. 842, 72 S.Ct. 20, 96 L.Ed. 636 (1951).

See generally, Marc Rohr, Communists and the First Amendment: The Shaping of Freedom of Advocacy in the Cold War Era, 28 San Diego L.Rev. 1 (1991).

2. 341 U.S. at 501–05, 71 S.Ct. at 863–65.

3. 341 U.S. at 509, 71 S.Ct. at 867.

remote. Vinson contended it was no longer realistic to assert that probability of success should be the basis of determining whether the danger is clear and present.

The Court adopted the lower court's interpretation of the rule, quoting Chief Judge Learned Hand:

> In each case [courts] must ask whether the gravity of the "evil," discounted by its improbability, justifies such invasion of free speech as is necessary to avoid danger.[4]

In other words, the greater the gravity of the act advocated, the less clear and present danger needed to justify governmental intrusion. So rephrased, the clear and present danger test became a disguised balancing test which weighed the seriousness of the danger against competing interest in free speech. Petitioners' conspiracy to advocate revolution, even though it was merely in a preparatory stage, was held to create "clear and present" danger.

> It is the existence of conspiracy which creates the danger.... If the ingredients of the reaction are present, we cannot bind the Government to wait until the catalyst is added.[5]

As one commentator has noted, the Vinson–Hand reformulation of clear and present danger meant that in practice "any radical political doctrine would receive little or no protection, since it would always appear as a threat to the nation and thus as the most serious of all possible evils. This is simply the remote bad tendency test dressed in modern style."[6]

Under traditional criminal conspiracy law the Government could always prosecute a criminal agreement coupled with some overt act. Such an indictment, which places on the Government the burden of proving the elements of a traditional conspiracy, does not require that the "putsch is about to be executed" nor raise substantial free speech problems.[7] But the strategy of the Government approved by the *Dennis* Court was in effect to replace the burden of showing conspiracy with the much lighter burden of showing tendencies and probabilities.

Justice Frankfurter concurred in the affirmance but criticized the clear and present danger test as too inflexible:

> The demands of free speech in a democratic society as well as the interest in national security are better served by candid and

---

4. 341 U.S. at 510, 71 S.Ct. at 868, quoting from, 183 F.2d 201, 212 (2d Cir.1950).

5. 341 U.S. at 511, 71 S.Ct. at 868.

6. Shapiro, Freedom of Speech: The Supreme Court and Judicial Review 65 (1966). The author also notes that the *Dennis* test is even less hospitable to free speech than the bad tendency test because it "considers the gravity of the evil discounted by *its*

improbability—not the improbability that the speech in question will bring the evil about, but that it will occur from any cause." Id. (emphasis in original).

7. Nathanson, The Communist Trial and the Clear-and-Present-Danger Test, 63 Harv.L.Rev. 1167, 1172–73 (1950).

informal weighing of the competing interests, within the confines of the judicial process.[8]

He would have not affirmed the convictions in the *Gitlow* case because the circumstances then did not justify serious concern, but he thought that the conspiracy the Government faced in 1951 justified the legislative judgment that saw a substantial threat to national order and security. He advocated acceptance of a "balancing" test to determine the constitutionality of speech restrictions as a replacement for the now vague clear and present danger theory.

Of course, we should remember that every generation perceives the evils attacking it as serious, while at the same time it views the (unsuccessful) evils attacking prior generations as imagined. Frankfurter's vague balancing test offered little concrete protection for unpopular speech and a right to dissent, for it depended too much on the discretion of whomever weighs the balance and calibrates the scales.

In *Yates v. United States*[9] the Supreme Court strove to retreat from the broad doctrine of the *Dennis* decision. Yates and other Communist party officials were convicted for conspiring to "advocate and teach the necessity of overthrowing the federal government by violence" and organizing the Communist party to carry out this revolution in violation of the Smith Act.[10] The Supreme Court held that the trial court had incorrectly interpreted the *Dennis* precedent.

In the Court's opinion, Justice Harlan indicated the District Court had "apparently thought that *Dennis* obliterated the traditional dividing line between advocacy of abstract doctrine and advocacy of action." [11] Relying on the *Dennis* decision, the trial court had refused to instruct the jury that the statute prohibited advocacy actually inciting violent revolution and actions but not a mere abstract doctrine of forcible overthrow.[12] It was apparent from legislative history that Congress intended the Smith Act to be "aimed at the advocacy and teaching of concrete action for forcible overthrow of the Government, and not at principles divorced from action," the Supreme Court ruled.[13]

The essence of the *Dennis* holding, Harlan stated, was that teaching and preparing a group for immediate or future violent action are not constitutionally protected, if it is reasonable to believe based upon the circumstances, size, and commitment of the group that the action or revolution will occur:

> *Dennis* was ... not concerned with a conspiracy to engage at some future time in seditious advocacy, but rather with a conspiracy to

8. 341 U.S. at 524–25, 71 S.Ct. at 875 (Frankfurter, J., concurring).

9. 354 U.S. 298, 77 S.Ct. 1064, 1 L.Ed.2d 1356 (1957).

10. 18 U.S.C.A. §§ 371, 2385.

11. 354 U.S. at 315–18, 77 S.Ct. at 1075–77.

12. 354 U.S. at 312–13, 77 S.Ct. at 1073–74.

13. 354 U.S. at 319–20, 77 S.Ct. at 1077.

advocate presently the taking of forcible action in the future. It was action not advocacy, that was to be postponed until "circumstances" would "permit." [14]

Harlan concluded the petitioners' statements advocated a philosophy and did not incite action. Without evidence of any actual action or possibility of action the Court would not affirm the convictions.[15]

But the *Yates* decision did not spell the end to Communist membership prosecutions. In *Scales v. United States* [16] the Court affirmed the petitioners' conviction for violating the membership clause of the Smith Act.[17] The trial court found the petitioners were active members of the Communist Party who were aware of the illegality of their teachings and advocated violent revolution and overthrow of the government "as speedily as circumstances would permit."

Justice Harlan, again writing the Court's opinion, upheld the lower court's findings, indicating that its interpretation of the membership clause did not impute "guilt to an individual merely on the basis of his associations and sympathies." [18] This holding limited both the freedom of speech and of association. The freedom of association is implied from the express guarantees of the first amendment and is subject to the same standards as freedom of speech.

Harlan emphasized that the Court's narrowing construction of the membership clause supported the constitutionality of the membership clause of the Smith Act:

> [T]he statute [as interpreted] is found to reach only "active" members having also a guilty knowledge and intent, and which therefore prevents a conviction on what otherwise might be regarded as merely an expression of sympathy with the alleged criminal enterprise, unaccompanied by any significant action in its support or any commitment to undertake such action.[19]

Though the record in *Scales* did not show advocacy of immediate violence, it did show present advocacy of future action for violent overthrow, which satisfied the limited requirements of *Dennis* and *Yates*:

> *Dennis* and *Yates* have definitely laid at rest any doubt that present advocacy of *future* action for violent overthrow satisfies

---

14. 354 U.S. at 324, 77 S.Ct. at 1079–80.

15. *Yates* reversed the conviction of five defendants and remanded for retrial as to the remaining nine; the charges against these nine were dismissed at the request of the Government, which found that it could not meet the tougher evidentiary requirements that *Yates* required on remand. Mollan, Smith Act Prosecutions: The Effect of the Dennis and Yates Decisions, 26 U.Pitt.L.Rev. 705, 732 (1965).

16. 367 U.S. 203, 81 S.Ct. 1469, 6 L.Ed.2d 782 (1961), rehearing denied 366 U.S. 978, 81 S.Ct. 1912, 6 L.Ed.2d 1267 (1961).

17. 18 U.S.C.A. § 2385.

18. 367 U.S. at 220, 81 S.Ct. at 1481–82.

19. 367 U.S. at 228, 81 S.Ct. at 1486.

statutory and constitutional requirements equally with advocacy of *immediate* action to that end. ... [T]his record cannot be considered deficient because it contains no evidence of advocacy for immediate overthrow.[20]

Appellant's advocacy of violent revolution was intended to be a guide for future revolutionary action and consequently violated the Smith Act. If the record did not evidence support for at least advocacy of future action, the Court would dismiss the prosecution for Communist Party membership.[21]

Justice Douglas dissented to this whole theory, arguing that "the essence of the crime ... is merely belief," and the conviction was a "sharp break with traditional concepts of First Amendment rights." [22]

After the *Dennis* and *Yates* decisions the "clear and present danger" doctrine was rejected to a great extent by the Court.[23] The doctrine as defined by Holmes proved no longer to be a viable method for restricting governmental invasion of free expression. To many people at the time, the cold war threat of a communist takeover was a very real possibility. The requirement that the danger resulting from speech or action must be imminent before first amendment protection was denied was unsettling to those living in fear of communism,[24] and as a result the "balancing test" replaced the "clear and present danger" doctrine. The case law was ripe for the third phase of the clear and present danger test, for while the Holmes–Brandeis test was discarded, it had not been forgotten.

§ 20.15 Current Status of the "Clear and Present Danger" Doctrine

The Holmes and Brandeis "clear and present danger" theory was refined during the late 1960's as the Court focused on protecting the advocacy of unpopular ideas. This modification of the Holmes–Brandeis theory was particularly apparent in three cases decided by the Court in the late 1960's: *Bond v. Floyd,*[1] *Watts v. United States,*[2] and

20. 367 U.S. at 251, 81 S.Ct. at 1497 (emphasis in original).

21. E.g. Noto v. United States, 367 U.S. 290, 81 S.Ct. 1517, 6 L.Ed.2d 836 (1961) (conviction reversed).

22. 367 U.S. at 262–65, 81 S.Ct. at 1503–04.

23. Cf. Brennan, The Supreme Court and the Meiklejohn Interpretation of the First Amendment, 79 Harv.L.Rev. 1, 8 (1965).

24. Emerson, Toward a General Theory of the First Amendment, 72 Yale L.J. 877, 911 (1963).

§ 20.15

1. 385 U.S. 116, 87 S.Ct. 339, 17 L.Ed.2d 235 (1966).

See generally, J. Barron and C. Dienes, Handbook of Free Speech and Free Press 11–31 (1979); L. Bollinger, The Tolerant Society: Freedom of Speech and Extremist Speech in America (1986) (seeking to justify America's "remarkable legal principle under which highly subversive and socially harmful speech activity is protected against governmental regulation." Id. at 3); Harry Kalven, Jr., ed. by Jamie Kalven, A Worthy Tradition: Freedom of Speech in America 119–242 (1988).

2. 394 U.S. 705, 89 S.Ct. 1399, 22 L.Ed.2d 664 (1969) (per curiam).

Brandenburg v. Ohio.[3]

The *Julian Bond* Case. Members of the Georgia House, in *Bond v. Floyd*,[4] challenged the right of a duly elected representative, Julian Bond, to be seated. Bond had publicly expressed his support of a statement issued by the Student Nonviolent Coordinating Committee (SNCC) criticizing the United States' involvement in Viet Nam and the operation of the draft laws.[5] The Georgia legislature conducted a special hearing to determine if Bond could in good faith take the mandatory oath to support the Constitution. At the hearing Bond argued that he was willing and able to take his oath of office. He testified that though he supported individuals who burned their draft cards he had not burned his own nor counseled anyone to burn their card.[6] The Georgia House voted not to administer the oath or seat Bond.

The Supreme Court held that the action of the Georgia House violated Bond's right of free expression.[7] Although the oath of office was constitutionally valid, Chief Justice Warren wrote, this requirement did not empower the majority of the representatives to challenge a duly elected legislator's sincerity in swearing allegiance to the Constitution. Such authority could be used to stifle dissents of legislators who disagreed with majority views.[8]

Convicting Bond under the Selective Service Act for counseling or aiding persons to evade or refuse registration, Warren believed would have been unconstitutional. Bond's statements could not be interpreted "as a call to unlawful refusal to be drafted."[9] He actually appeared to have been advocating legal alternatives to the draft, not inciting people to violate the law. The Court, citing *Yates v. United States*,[10] concluded that Bond could not have been convicted for these statements consistently with the first amendment.[11]

The *Watts* Decision. Traces of a modified "clear and present danger" analysis are also evident in *Watts v. United States*.[12] In a per curiam opinion the Supreme Court reversed the appellant's conviction for violating a statute prohibiting persons from "knowingly and willful-

---

3. 395 U.S. 444, 89 S.Ct. 1827, 23 L.Ed.2d 430 (1969) (per curiam).

4. 385 U.S. 116, 87 S.Ct. 339, 17 L.Ed.2d 235 (1966).

5. 385 U.S. at 118–21, 87 S.Ct. at 341–42.

6. 385 U.S. at 123–24, 87 S.Ct. at 343–44. The constitutionality of federal laws punishing draft card burning was subsequently upheld by the Supreme Court. United States v. O'Brien, 391 U.S. 367, 88 S.Ct. 1673, 20 L.Ed.2d 672 (1968), rehearing denied 393 U.S. 900, 89 S.Ct. 63, 21 L.Ed.2d 188 (1968).

7. 385 U.S. at 137, 87 S.Ct. at 350.

8. 385 U.S. at 132, 87 S.Ct. at 347–48.

9. 385 U.S. at 133, 87 S.Ct. at 348.

10. 354 U.S. 298, 77 S.Ct. 1064, 1 L.Ed.2d 1356 (1957).

11. 385 U.S. at 134, 87 S.Ct. at 348–49.

12. 394 U.S. 705, 89 S.Ct. 1399, 22 L.Ed.2d 664 (1969) (per curiam).

ly ... threat[ening] to take the life of or to inflict bodily harm upon the President." Watts, during a public rally in Washington, D.C., stated he would not report for his scheduled draft physical, continuing:

> If they ever make me carry a rifle the first man I want to get in my sights is L.B.J. They are not going to make me kill my black brothers.[13]

On its face the statute was held constitutional: the nation certainly has a valid interest in protecting the President. However, a statute criminalizing certain forms of pure speech must, "be interpreted with the commands of the First Amendment clearly in mind. What is a threat must be distinguished from what is ... protected speech." [14]

Watts' statement was held to be a "political hyperbole" and not a true threat. The Court maintained the nation was committed to unrestrained expression and debate, including criticism of the government and public officials.

> The language of the political arena ... is often vituperative, abusive and inexact. [The petitioner's] ... only offense here was "a kind of very crude offensive method of stating a political opposition to the President." [15]

Considering in context the conditional nature of the remarks and the fact the listeners had laughed at the statement, the words could only be interpreted as an expression of political belief. Had the circumstances of the speech amounted to a literal *incitement* of violence, the Court's decision might have been different.

The influence of the "incitement" prong of the "clear and present danger" doctrine is obvious in both of these cases. The pivotal determination in *Bond* [16] was the fact that the appellant was merely expressing his grievances with the government, not inciting unlawful action. This distinction appeared to be based on the identical distinction made by Brandeis in his concurrence in *Whitney v. California.* [17] The petitioner's conviction in *Watts* [18] was reversed when the Court concluded the statement did not clearly present an imminent threat to the President.

The *Brandenburg* Test. Finally *Brandenburg v. Ohio*[19] signalled a major shift in the Court although the decision was issued as only a per curiam opinion. The Warren Court appeared to be somewhat

13. 394 U.S. at 706, 89 S.Ct. at 1401.

14. 394 U.S. at 707, 89 S.Ct. at 1401.

Contrast, Rankin v. McPherson, 483 U.S. 378, 387, 107 S.Ct. 2891, 2898, 97 L.Ed.2d 315 (1987), rehearing denied 483 U.S. 1056, 108 S.Ct. 31, 97 L.Ed.2d 819 (1987) ("a statement that amounted to a threat to kill the President would not be protected by the First Amendment....").

15. 394 U.S. at 708, 89 S.Ct. at 1401–02.

16. Bond v. Floyd, 385 U.S. 116, 87 S.Ct. 339, 17 L.Ed.2d 235 (1966).

17. 274 U.S. 357, 372–80, 47 S.Ct. 641, 647–50, 71 L.Ed. 1095 (1927) (Brandeis, J., concurring).

18. Watts v. United States, 394 U.S. 705, 89 S.Ct. 1399, 22 L.Ed.2d 664 (1969) (per curiam).

19. 395 U.S. 444, 89 S.Ct. 1827, 23 L.Ed.2d 430 (1969) (per curiam).

influenced by the reasoning of the "clear and present danger" test as Holmes and Brandeis had originally interpreted the test, but with crucial differences in phrasing and emphasis to assure that its protections would not be diluted.

Brandenburg overruled the *Whitney* [20] decision, but without ever explicitly referring to the "clear and present danger" standard. However it completely supported and added new vigor to the reasoning of the Brandeis concurrence in *Whitney,* and eliminated the open-ended use of the test that had prevailed in the "bad tendency" and "balancing" years.

The *Brandenburg* Court's per curiam opinion reversed the conviction of a Ku Klux Klan leader for violating Ohio's Criminal Syndicalism statute. The appellant had been charged with advocating political reform through violence and for assembling with a group formed to teach criminal syndicalism. A man identified as the appellant arranged for a television news crew to attend a Klan rally. During the news film made at the rally, Klan members, allegedly including Brandenburg, discussed the group's plan to march on Congress. [21]

The Court acknowledged that a similar criminal syndicalism statute had been upheld in *Whitney,* but it recognized that later decisions discredited *Whitney.* The Court then held advocacy of violence protected by the First Amendment as long as the advocacy did not incite people to *imminent* action. The key is "incitement."

When a speaker uses speech to cause unthinking, immediate lawless action, one cannot rely on more speech in the market place of ideas to correct the errors of the original speech; there simply is not enough time, because there is an incitement. In addition, the state has a significant interest in, and no other means of preventing, the resulting lawless conduct. The situation is comparable to someone urging the lynch mob to string up the prisoner. Or, to use the Holmes' analogy, it is akin to someone falsely shouting "fire" in a crowded theater. In such circumstances, there is no time for reasoned debate, because both the intent of the speaker and the circumstances in which he harangues the crowd amount to incitement.

Thus, under *Brandenburg,* the Court developed a new test that emphasizes the need for the state to prove incitement. For the state conviction to be valid, the state must prove: (1) the speaker *subjectively intended* incitement; (2) in context, the words used were *likely to produce* imminent, lawless action; and (3) the words used by the speaker *objectively encouraged* and urged and provoked imminent action. This third part of the test, with its focus on the objective words

20. Whitney v. California, 274 U.S. 357,   **21.** 395 U.S. at 446, 89 S.Ct. at 1828–29.
47 S.Ct. 641, 71 L.Ed. 1095 (1927).

used by the speaker, is derived from *Hess v. Indiana*,[22] discussed below.

The Court then formulated the test for speech which advocates unlawful conduct: "[The state may not] forbid or proscribe advocacy of the use of force or of law violation except where such advocacy is directed to inciting or producing imminent lawless action and is likely to incite or produce such action."[23]   Mere teaching of abstract doctrines, the Court noted, was not like leading a group in a violent action. Moreover, the statute must be narrowly drawn, and if it failed to distinguish between advocacy of a theory and advocacy of action, it abridged first amendment freedoms.[24]

Criminal syndicalism as defined in the Ohio statute could not meet the *Brandenburg* test.   The statute forbade teaching of violent political revolution with the intent of spreading such doctrine or assembling with a group advocating this doctrine.   At the appellant's trial no attempt was made to distinguish between incitement and advocacy. The statute consequently was held to be an abridgement of the First and Fourteenth Amendments.   Any law punishing mere advocacy of Ku Klux Klan doctrine and assembly of Klan members to advocate their beliefs was unconstitutional.[25]

Justice Douglas concurred separately entering the caveat that there was no place for the "clear and present danger" test in any cases involving first amendment rights.   He was distrustful of the test, which he believed could be easily manipulated, as it was in *Dennis*, to deny constitutional protection to any speech critical of existing government.[26]

Brandenburg's new formulation offers broad new protection for strong advocacy.   Its major focus is on the inciting language of the speaker, that is, on the *objective* words, in addition to the need to show not only that the speech is directed to produce immediate, unthinking lawless action but that in fact the situation makes this purpose likely to be successful.[27]

The Opinion in *Hess v. Indiana*. A post-Warren Court decision, *Hess v. Indiana*[28] indicates that the Court is serious and literal in its application of the test proposed in *Brandenburg*.   Hess had been arrested and convicted for disorderly conduct when he shouted "we'll take the fucking street later (or again)" during an antiwar demonstration.   Two witnesses testified Hess did not appear to exhort demonstrators to go

---

22. 414 U.S. 105, 94 S.Ct. 326, 38 L.Ed.2d 303 (1973).

23. 395 U.S. at 447, 89 S.Ct. at 1829 (footnote omitted).

24. 395 U.S. at 447–49, 89 S.Ct. at 1829–31.

25. 395 U.S. at 448–49, 89 S.Ct. at 1830–31.

26. 395 U.S. at 450–52, 89 S.Ct. at 1831–32. (Douglas, J., concurring). Jus-

tice Black also concurred separately, and similarly objected to the clear and present danger test as construed in *Dennis*. 395 U.S. at 449–450, 89 S.Ct. at 1831.

27. Gunther, Learned Hand and the Origins of Modern First Amendment Doctrine: Some Fragments of History, 27 Stan.L.Rev. 719 (1975).

28. 414 U.S. 105, 94 S.Ct. 326, 38 L.Ed.2d 303 (1973).

into the street just cleared by the police, that he was facing the crowd, and that his tone of voice was not louder than any of the other demonstrators, although it was loud.[29] The Indiana Supreme Court upheld the trial court's finding that the remarks were in fact intended to incite further riotous behavior and were likely to produce such a result.

But the United States Supreme Court reversed, and in a per curiam opinion the Court stated:

> At best ... the statement could be taken as counsel for present moderation; at worst it amounted to nothing more than advocacy of illegal action at some indefinite future time. This is not sufficient to permit the state to punish Hess' speech. Under our decisions, "the Constitutional guarantees of free speech and free press do not permit a state to forbid or proscribe advocacy of the use of force or of law violation except where such advocacy is directed to inciting or producing *imminent* lawless action and is likely to incite or produce such action." [30]

The Court concluded that since Hess' speech was "not directed to any person or group of persons." Hess had not advocated action which would produce imminent disorder. His statements, therefore, did not violate the disorderly conduct statutes.[31]

Justice Rehnquist, joined by Chief Justice Burger and Justice Blackmun, strongly dissented. The dissent objected to the per curiam opinion's "somewhat antiseptic description of this massing" of people and preferred to rely on the decision of the trial court which was free to reject some testimony and accept other testimony. The majority, Justice Rehnquist claimed, was merely interpreting the evidence differently and thus exceeding the proper scope of review.[32]

The new *Brandenburg* test—a test more vigorously phrased and strictly applied than the older clear and present danger test—now probably appears to be the proper formula for determining when speech which advocates criminal conduct may constitutionally be punished. With its emphasis on incitement, imminent lawless action, and the objective words of the speaker, it should provide a strong measure of first amendment protection.[33]

---

29. 414 U.S. at 106–07, 94 S.Ct. at 327–28.

30. 414 U.S. at 108, 94 S.Ct. at 328 (emphasis in original), citing Brandenburg v. Ohio, 395 U.S. 444, 447, 89 S.Ct. 1827, 1829, 23 L.Ed.2d 430 (1969).

31. 414 U.S. at 108–09, 94 S.Ct. at 328–29.

32. 414 U.S. at 109–12, 94 S.Ct. at 329–30.

33. An examination of the tension between free speech and equality values in the determination of whether the government may be able to restrict "race-I.Q. research" is found in, Delgado et al., Can Science Be Inopportune? Constitutional Validity of Governmental Restrictions on Race-I.Q. Research, 31 U.C.L.A.L.Rev. 128 (1983).

Should the Court confront a situation where a speaker advocates violence through the use of a speech which does not literally advocate action, such as Marc Antony's funeral oration for Caesar,[34] the majority might be urged to abandon the protections of the *Brandenburg* test and instead look for proximity to violence rather than to the literal words of incitement.[35] Only time will tell whether the Court will apply the test in a strict manner or whether a future Court will subject the test to the same periods of vague interpretation as was the old "clear and present danger" test.

V. PRIOR RESTRAINT OF POLITICAL SPEECH

§ 20.16 The Distinction Between Prior Restraint and Subsequent Punishment of Speech

The Common Law Background. Since the expiration of the English licensing system in 1695 under which nothing could be publish-

---

34. For example, the *Brandenburg* test would protect Marc Antony's funeral oration in Shakespeare's *Julius Caesar*, Act III, scene ii.

Tort Claims Against the Media, Because of What They Broadcast. In National Broadcasting Co., Inc. v. Niemi, 434 U.S. 1354, 98 S.Ct. 705, 54 L.Ed.2d 742 (1978) (Rehnquist, Circuit Justice), certiorari denied 435 U.S. 1000, 98 S.Ct. 1657, 56 L.Ed.2d 91 (1978), appeal after remand 126 Cal.App.3d 488, 178 Cal.Rptr. 888 (1981), the respondent sought damages from a television network and publisher for injuries allegedly inflicted upon her by persons acting under the stimulus of observing a scene of brutality broadcast in a television drama. The petitioners sought a stay of the state court order remanding for a trial. While Circuit Justice Rehnquist denied the stay for procedural reasons, he noted that the trial judge had rendered judgment for petitioners because he found that the film "did not advocate or encourage violent and depraved acts and thus did not constitute an incitement." 434 U.S. at 1356, 98 S.Ct. at 706. The *Brandenburg* test should be applicable to determine the free speech defense to plaintiff's tort claim.

See also, Herceg v. Hustler Magazine, Inc., 814 F.2d 1017, 1021 (5th Cir.1987) (overturning of jury verdict against Hustler Magazine arising out of death of adolescent who attempted practice described in a magazine article: "we hold that liability cannot be imposed on Hustler on the basis that the article was an incitement to

attempt a potentially fatal act without impermissibly infringing upon freedom of speech"), cert. denied 485 U.S. 959, 108 S.Ct. 1219, 99 L.Ed.2d 420 (1988).

35. Cf. NAACP v. Claiborne Hardware Co., 458 U.S. 886, 928, 102 S.Ct. 3409, 3433, 73 L.Ed.2d 1215 (1982), rehearing denied 459 U.S. 898, 103 S.Ct. 199, 74 L.Ed.2d 160 (1982):

"The emotionally charged rhetoric of Charles Evers' speeches did not transcend the bounds of protected speech set forth in *Brandenburg*. The lengthy addresses generally contained an impassioned plea for black citizens to unify, to support and respect each other, and to realize the political and economic power available to them. In the course of those pleas, strong language was used. *If that language had been followed by acts of violence, a substantial question would be presented whether Evers could be held liable for the consequences of that unlawful conduct.* In this case, however—with the possible exception of the Cox incident—the acts of violence identified in 1966 occurred weeks or months after the April 1, 1966 speech; the chancellor made no finding of any violence after the challenged 1969 speech. Strong and effective extemporaneous rhetoric cannot be nicely channeled in purely dulcet phrases. An advocate must be free to stimulate his audience with spontaneous and emotional appeals for unity and action in a common cause. When such appeals do not incite lawless action, they must be regarded as protected speech." (emphasis added).

ed without prior approval of the church or state authorities,[1] prior restraint has been considered a more drastic infringement on free speech than subsequent punishment.

Thomas M. Cooley's Treatise on Constitutional Limitations summarized the old law:

> The constitutional liberty of speech and of the press, as we understand it, implies a right to freely utter and publish whatever the citizen may please, and to be protected against any responsibility for so doing, [but after he has done so he is not protected] so far as such publications, from their blasphemy, obscenity, or scandalous character, may be a public offense, or as by their falsehood and malice they may injuriously affect the standing, reputation, or pecuniary interests of individuals.[2]

Cooley's view of prior restraint reflected the prevailing view at the time of the first amendment's adoption.

Blackstone's Commentaries was the harbinger of Cooley's restatement of the law:

> The liberty of the press is indeed essential to the nature of a free state; but this consists in laying no *previous* restraints upon publications, and not in freedom from censure for criminal matter when published.... To subject the press to the restrictive power of a licenser, as was formerly done, both before and since the revolution, is to subject all freedom of sentiment to the prejudices of one man, and to make him the arbitrary and infallible judge of all controverted points in learning, religion and government. But to punish (as the law does at present) any dangerous or offensive writings, which, when published, shall on a fair and impartial trial be adjudged of a pernicious tendency, is necessary for the preservation of peace and good order, of government and religion, the only solid foundations of civil liberty.[3]

§ 20.16

1. Near v. Minnesota, 283 U.S. 697, 713–14, 51 S.Ct. 625, 630, 75 L.Ed. 1357 (1931).

See generally, Emerson, The Doctrine of Prior Restraint, 20 L. & Contemp. Problems 648 (1955); Barnett, The Puzzle of Prior Restraint, 29 Stan.L.Rev. 539 (1977); Blasi, Toward a Theory of Prior Restraint: The Central Linkage, 66 Minn.L.Rev. 11 (1981); Mayton, Toward a Theory of First Amendment Process: Injunctions of Speech, Subsequent Punishment, and the Costs of the Prior Restraint Doctrine, 67 Cornell L.Rev. 245 (1982); Hunter, Toward a Better Understanding of the Prior Restraint Doctrine: A Reply to Professor Mayton, 67 Cornell L.Rev. 283 (1982); Jef-

fries, Rethinking Prior Restraint, 92 Yale L.J. 409 (1983); Redish, The Proper Role of the Prior Restraint Doctrine in First Amendment Theory, 70 Va.L.Rev. 53 (1984); Leonard Levy, Emergence of a Free Press (1985); Scordato, Distinction Without a Difference: A Reappraisal of the Doctrine of Prior Restraint, 68 No.Car.L.Rev. 1 (1989).

2. 2 T. Cooley, A Treatise on the Constitutional Limitations which Rest Upon the Legislative Power of the States of the American Union 886 (8th Ed. by W. Carrington, 1927) (footnote omitted).

3. 4 W. Blackstone, Commentaries on the Laws of England * 151–52 (2d ed. rev. 1872). T. Cooley was the editor. See gen-

While it is no longer true that the first amendment means only freedom from prior restraint of speech, prior restraint is still considered to be more serious than subsequent punishment. As the modern Supreme Court has repeatedly recognized, "liberty of the press ... has meant, principally although not exclusively, immunity from previous restraints or censorship." [4]

The Special Problem of Obscenity. In modern times prior restraint has generally taken the form of court injunctions rather than a system of licensing by a Board of Censors. The only major exception is the case of allegedly obscene speech, where, in practice, there often may be censorship by board review prior to court action.

The courts have generally tolerated more prior restraint in situations involving allegedly obscene materials, because "obscenity" is not protected by the first amendment guarantee of free speech, but even in such cases restraint is still suspect. Another section of this chapter discusses prior restraint of allegedly obscene speech.[5] Here we are primarily concerned with the prior restraint of other types of speech, which often, but not necessarily, occur in a political context.[6]

Prior Restraint and Subsequent Punishment Compared. If a given utterance may be punished, is there any real difference if one is enjoined from making the speech or whether one is punished after having made the speech? In addition to historical distinctions discussed in the beginning of this chapter, the "marketplace" theory of speech supports the distinction between prior restraint and subsequent punishment. While subsequent punishment may deter some speakers, at least the ideas or speech at issue can be placed before the public. Prior restraint limits public debate and knowledge more severely.

erally L. Levy, Legacy of Suppression: Freedom of Speech and Press in Early American History (1960). Also published in 1963 as Freedom of Speech and Press in Early American History. See also, Mayton, Seditious Libel and the Lost Guarantee of a Freedom of Expression, 84 Colum.L.Rev. 91 (1984).

4. Near v. Minnesota, 283 U.S. 697, 716, 51 S.Ct. 625, 631, 75 L.Ed. 1357 (1931). See also, New York Times Co. v. United States, 403 U.S. 713, 714, 91 S.Ct. 2140, 29 L.Ed.2d 822 (1971); Organization for a Better Austin v. Keefe, 402 U.S. 415, 419, 91 S.Ct. 1575, 1577–78, 29 L.Ed.2d 1 (1971); Bantam Books, Inc. v. Sullivan, 372 U.S. 58, 70, 83 S.Ct. 631, 639, 9 L.Ed.2d 584 (1963).

For a well-developed and contrary view, see Mayton, Toward a Theory of First Amendment Process: Injunctions of Speech, Subsequent Punishment, and the

Costs of the Prior Restraint Doctrine, 67 Cornell L.Rev. 245 (1982), concluding: "Because injunctions are necessarily the product of a judicial process, they should be preferred to subsequent punishment." Id. at 281. See also, Hunter, Toward a Better Understanding of the Prior Restraint Doctrine: A Reply to Professor Mayton, 67 Cornell L.Rev. 283 (1982).

No Injunction of Libel Allowed.

See § 20.32.

5. See § 20.61(c), infra.

6. E.g., Southeastern Promotions, Ltd. v. Conrad, 420 U.S. 546, 95 S.Ct. 1239, 43 L.Ed.2d 448 (1975) (denial by city of the use of a municipal theater for showing the musical "Hair"); Blount v. Rizzi, 400 U.S. 410, 91 S.Ct. 423, 27 L.Ed.2d 498 (1971) (postal stop orders); Freedman v. Maryland, 380 U.S. 51, 85 S.Ct. 734, 13 L.Ed.2d 649 (1965) (movies allegedly obscene).

Additionally, some of the procedural aspects of enjoining speech make subsequent punishment a less serious alternative.[7]

Procedural Differences. If the subsequent punishment is criminal, the state prefers the procedural device of a prior restraint because, procedurally, it is easier to initiate a civil injunction action than to start a criminal prosecution. An application for a temporary restraining order is filed in cases where immediate and expeditious relief is needed. Once the court grants a temporary restraining order it sets a hearing, for the earliest possible date, to determine if a preliminary injunction should be issued.[8] In contrast to the rapid disposition of injunctive actions, a criminal prosecution must proceed through indictment or information,[9] arraignment,[10] pleadings, pretrial motions,[11] and jury selection if there is a possibility of imprisonment of six months or more,[12] before the accused is even brought to trial.

The hearing on an application for an injunction, an historically equitable action, is before a judge sitting without a jury.[13] If the injunctive order is violated there is generally no right to a jury at the contempt proceedings[14] except in some cases of criminal contempt.[15]

---

7. See A. Bickel, The Morality of Consent 61 (1975) (A criminal statute "chills," but a prior restraint "freezes.").

If one defines "prior restraint" as including "only those government actions that result in the physical interception and suppression of speech prior to its public expression," then:

> "prior restrains would pose a greater practical deterrent to constitutionally protected speech than do all other speech-related laws [because] (1) actual physical restraint is a far more practically effective form of speech suppression than any scheme of threatened legal sanction that is not imposed until after the public expression of the prohibited speech; (2) every instance of a prior restraint actually will result in the suppression of speech; and (3) every mistake made in the implementation of a prior restraint will involve the actual suppression of constitutionally protected speech."

Scordato, Distinction Without a Difference: A Reappraisal of the Doctrine of Prior Restraint, 68 No.Car.L.Rev. 1, 34 (1989).

8. See Fed.R.Civ.P. 65; see also United States v. United Mine Workers, 330 U.S. 258, 67 S.Ct. 677, 91 L.Ed. 884 (1947); Houghton v. Meyer, 208 U.S. 149, 28 S.Ct. 234, 52 L.Ed. 432 (1908); Moore, Federal Practice and Procedure, § 65.07.

9. Fed.R.Crim.P. 7. Cf. Nebraska Press Ass'n v. Stuart, 427 U.S. 539, 559, 96 S.Ct. 2791, 2802–03, 49 L.Ed.2d 683 (1976).

10. Fed.R.Crim.P. 10.

11. Fed.R.Crim.P. 11.

12. Baldwin v. New York, 399 U.S. 66, 69, 90 S.Ct. 1886, 1888, 26 L.Ed.2d 437 (1970), mandate conformed 27 N.Y.2d 731, 314 N.Y.S.2d 539, 262 N.E.2d 678 (1970).

13. See Ross v. Bernhard, 396 U.S. 531, 90 S.Ct. 733, 24 L.Ed.2d 729 (1970); Beacon Theatres, Inc. v. Westover, 359 U.S. 500, 79 S.Ct. 948, 3 L.Ed.2d 988 (1959); Dairy Queen, Inc. v. Wood, 369 U.S. 469, 82 S.Ct. 894, 8 L.Ed.2d 44 (1962).

14. Shillitani v. United States, 384 U.S. 364, 365, 86 S.Ct. 1531, 1533, 16 L.Ed.2d 622 (1966).

15. See Gompers v. Buck's Stove & Range Co., 221 U.S. 418, 449, 31 S.Ct. 492, 501, 55 L.Ed. 797 (1911); 18 U.S.C.A. § 402.

Jail Time. If the length of the sentence is in the judge's discretion rather than fixed by statute, the Sixth Amendment requires a jury trial in criminal contempt cases if the sentence imposed is in fact more than six months. In contrast, in ordinary criminal cases defendant has a right to a jury trial if the sentence which could be imposed is in excess of six months. Codispoti v. Pennsylvania, 418 U.S. 506, 94 S.Ct. 2687, 41 L.Ed.2d 912 (1974); Muniz v.

The standard of proof in injunctive actions, as in most equitable proceedings, is not the strict criminal requirement of "beyond a reasonable doubt"[16] but the more lenient "clear and convincing proof" standard.[17] Unlike an injunctive case, in criminal prosecutions the government generally has no right of appeal,[18] a limitation imposed by the double jeopardy provision of the fifth amendment.[19] Because injunctive cases are civil proceedings, the Government's right to appeal in civil cases is limited only by the Common law principle of res judicata rather than the constitutional principle of double jeopardy.[20]

The injunctive remedy with its speedier procedural framework is thus more subject to abuse and to indiscriminate application, whereas criminal prosecution entails a more thorough self-selection process resulting in fewer applications and successes. The overall chilling effect on speech is consequently less with criminal prosecution. Also, even if a temporary restraining order is ultimately found to have been improperly granted, the Government may have in fact achieved its end by restraining speech at a crucial time.[21] Although the speech may be subsequently allowed, its impact may then be negligible because of the

Hoffman, 422 U.S. 454, 476, 95 S.Ct. 2178, 2190, 45 L.Ed.2d 319 (1975).

Fines. As for fines, in criminal contempt cases there is no fixed line that determines when the Constitution requires a jury trial. Thus in Muniz v. Hoffman, 422 U.S. 454, 95 S.Ct. 2178, 45 L.Ed.2d 319 (1975) the Court held that the Constitution did not require a jury trial, given the facts of that case, when the fine for criminal contempt was $10,000. If the case had involved an ordinary crime a jury would be required if the fine could exceed $500. 18 U.S.C.A. § 1(3). Subsequently a lower court, in the exercise of its supervisory power, limited fines for criminal contempt to $500. Douglass v. First Nat. Realty Corp., 543 F.2d 894 (D.C.Cir.1976).

See generally, Y. Kamisar, W. LaFave, & J. Israel, Modern Criminal Procedure 1318–20 (5th ed. 1980).

16. In re Winship, 397 U.S. 358, 361, 90 S.Ct. 1068, 1071, 25 L.Ed.2d 368 (1970).

17. McCormick, Evidence, § 340 at 796 (2d ed., E. Clearly, ed. 1972); see, e.g., Fisher v. Miceli, 291 S.W.2d 845, 848 (Mo. 1956); Hyder v. Newcomb, 236 Ark. 231, 365 S.W.2d 271, 274 (1963).

18. Ashe v. Swenson, 397 U.S. 436, 445, 90 S.Ct. 1189, 1195, 25 L.Ed.2d 469 (1970); Benton v. Maryland, 395 U.S. 784, 793–795, 89 S.Ct. 2056, 23 L.Ed.2d 707 (1969), on remand 8 Md.App. 388, 260 A.2d 86 (1969).

19. Ball v. United States, 163 U.S. 662, 668–70, 16 S.Ct. 1192, 1194–95, 41 L.Ed. 300 (1896).

20. Cf. 28 U.S.C.A. § 1292.

In addition, Professor Powe has noted that in national security—prior restraint cases such as the *Pentagon Papers* case, or the efforts to censor ex-CIA agent Victor Marchetti—see, United States v. Marchetti, 466 F.2d 1309 (4th Cir.1972) (Douglas, Brennan, & Stewart, JJ., dissenting to denial of certiorari), cert. denied 409 U.S. 1063, 93 S.Ct. 553, 34 L.Ed.2d 516 (1972)—the appellate court was generous in allowing the government to supplement and add materials on appeal. "Had the case been a criminal one, the government would not have been able to supplement the evidence," Professor Powe explains. Powe, The H–Bomb Injunction, 61 U.Colo.L.Rev. 55, 75 (1990).

21. Cf. Walker v. City of Birmingham, 388 U.S. 307, 336, 87 S.Ct. 1824, 1840, 18 L.Ed.2d 1210 (1967) (Douglas, J., dissenting), rehearing denied 389 U.S. 894, 88 S.Ct. 12, 19 L.Ed.2d 202 (1967).

"For if a person must pursue his judicial remedy [of lifting an injunction] before he may speak, parade, or assemble, the occasion when protest is desired or needed will have become history and any later speech, parade, or assembly will be fruitless or pointless."

time elapsed. If subsequent punishment chills free speech, prior restraint freezes it.

Disobeying Court Orders and Violating Statutes, Compared. Courts treat violations of prior restraint orders as more serious than deliberate refusals to abide by a statute. A significant illustration of this principle is found in a comparison of two Supreme Court cases. In one, the High Court reversed the conviction of civil rights demonstrators who had been convicted of violating an ordinance found to be unconstitutionally vague. The ordinance forbade issuance of a license for a protest march if "the public welfare, peace, safety, health, decency, good order, morals or convenience" require that it be refused.[22] Justice Stewart writing for the Court said that "a person faced with such an unconstitutional licensing law may ignore it and engage with impunity in the exercise of the right of free expression for which the law purports to require a license." [23]

However, in *Walker v. Birmingham* [24] the Court earlier had upheld the conviction of marchers who violated that same statute *after* the statute had been copied verbatim into an ex parte injunction. While the statute could have been violated with impunity, violation of the state court's ex parte injunction was another matter:

> The breadth and vagueness of the injunction itself would also unquestionably be subject to substantial constitutional question. But the way to raise that question was to apply to the Alabama courts to have the injunction modified or dissolved.[25]

In short, while one is free to violate an unconstitutional statute restricting free speech, one is not free to violate the same words when written as a court injunction.

This rule reflects the fact that courts are more adamant in punishing contempts of their orders than in punishing violations of criminal statutes. Because the defendant has violated a specific order of the judge, the judge may interpret a contempt action as an attack on the courts themselves or as a violation of the respect that judges feel is due them; however, this self-interest of the court is not present in criminal cases, where the judge has no personal stake in enforcement of the criminal statute.[26] Because the judge may object more to the violation

22. Shuttlesworth v. Birmingham, 394 U.S. 147, 150–151, 89 S.Ct. 935, 938–39, 22 L.Ed.2d 162 (1969), on remand 45 Ala.App. 723, 222 So.2d 377 (1969).

23. 394 U.S. at 151, 89 S.Ct. at 938–39.

See O. Fiss, The Civil Rights Injunction 68–74 (1978).

24. 388 U.S. 307, 87 S.Ct. 1824, 18 L.Ed.2d 1210 (1967), rehearing denied 389 U.S. 894, 88 S.Ct. 12, 19 L.Ed.2d 202 (1967).

25. Walker v. Birmingham, 388 U.S. 307, 317, 87 S.Ct. 1824, 1830, 18 L.Ed.2d 1210 (1967), rehearing denied 389 U.S. 894, 88 S.Ct. 12, 19 L.Ed.2d 202 (1967).

26. See Walker v. Birmingham, 388 U.S. 307, 87 S.Ct. 1824, 18 L.Ed.2d 1210 (1967), rehearing denied 389 U.S. 894, 88 S.Ct. 12, 19 L.Ed.2d 202 (1967) where the Court held that even though a state injunction forbidding a demonstration was unconstitutional, the subjects of it could be prosecuted for violating it rather than ap-

of his or her own order than to the violation of a state's statute, he or she may correspondingly be more severe in enforcing prior restraints relative to subsequent punishments.

The Court, in deciding that individuals who violate court injunctions do so at their peril, has focused on the principle that individuals in injunction cases have easy access to a neutral determination of the issue; the individual merely has to appeal the judge's order. If the litigant objects to the trial court's ruling, he or she can always appeal. The litigant does not have to violate the court injunction in order to secure an appeal. In contrast, often the best (or only) way to attack the constitutionality of a statute is to violate it. If there were no reasonable review procedures available to the litigant in an injunction case, the *Walker* case should have come to a different conclusion. But so long as there is an outstanding judicial order, and the court that issued it has jurisdiction, the principle in *Walker* does not grant an individual the choice to disregard the order and then claim a right to attack it collaterally.

Judicial Predictions Regarding Effects of Speech on National Security. In the case of prior restraint of controversial political speech touching on national security or similar interests, new problems emerge. In such cases the government may argue that an injunction should issue because publication will cause substantial damage to the United States. In ruling on the application, the Court is really asked to predict the future; that is, will publication in fact cause this vague but substantial damage?

Courts are ill-equipped for such a task. If the Court says no damage will occur and allows publication, there are two possible consequences. The damage may actually occur (or some damage may occur and appear to have been linked with earlier publication) and the Court consequently will share the blame for the damage to the United States' security. If, alternatively, the asserted damage does not occur, the judiciary has still risked its esteem and prestige without noticeable advantage. Thus, courts are encouraged to overpredict the dangers of publication and underprotect the dangers to free speech.

---

pealing it and seeking reversal. Chief Justice Warren in dissent noted:

"It has never been thought that violation of a statute indicated such a disrespect for the legislature that the violator always must be punished even if the statute was unconstitutional.... Indeed it shows no disrespect for law to violate a statute on the ground that it is unconstitutional and then to submit one's case to the courts with the willingness to accept the penalty if the statute is held to be valid.... [But an ex parte] injunction [is] such potent magic that it transformed the command of an unconstitutional statute into an impregnable barrier, challengeable only in what likely would have been protracted legal proceedings and entirely superior in the meantime even to the United States Constitution."

Walker v. Birmingham, 388 U.S. 307, 327, 330, 87 S.Ct. 1824, 1835, 1837, 18 L.Ed.2d 1210 (1967), rehearing denied 389 U.S. 894, 88 S.Ct. 12, 19 L.Ed.2d 202 (1967).

On the other hand, if the Court does not allow publication, the public will probably never know if the Court was wrong, because the allegedly damaging papers may never be published or, if they are printed, may be seized prior to distribution. The public then is never able to judge for itself the importance of the suppressed speech.[27] The Court will never lose esteem or share blame in such cases where it overpredicts danger, and there will be little or no damage to its reputation from nonpublication. Prior restraint, with its emphasis on predicting an unknowable future, encourages courts to overpredict the potential damage from publication. The lack of incentive to engage in underprediction of danger from publication, and the lack of burdens attached to overprediction furnish an important incentive to the Courts, which makes prior restraint a more serious and more effective weapon against free speech.[28]

No Injunctions Against Crimes. For these historical, procedural, and substantive reasons, prior restraint—particularly in the context of political speech attacking governmental policies—has long been suspect. Just as the common law forbade equity from enjoining a crime[29] the overeffectiveness of prior restraint and its strong potential for abuse has made it much more chilling on the exercise of first amendment rights, than subsequent punishments.[30]

Prior Restraints in Other Contexts. It should be generally noted that any governmental order that restricts or prohibits speech prior to its publication constitutes a prior restraint. Such orders may include censorship of movies,[31] denial of mail privileges,[32] refusal of

27. Cf. United States v. Marchetti, 466 F.2d 1309 (4th Cir.1972) (prior restraint of former CIA employee's publication discussing CIA activities; at time of employment the employee contractually agreed to submit such writings to the CIA for approval), certiorari denied 409 U.S. 1063, 93 S.Ct. 553, 34 L.Ed.2d 516 (1972). But cf. Snepp v. United States, 444 U.S. 507, 509 n. 4, 100 S.Ct. 763, 765–66 n. 4, 62 L.Ed.2d 704 (1980) (per curiam) (distinguishing *Marchetti*), rehearing denied 445 U.S. 972, 100 S.Ct. 1668, 64 L.Ed.2d 250 (1980).

Cf. Hollander, Book Review, The New York Times Book Review, May 11, 1986, at 9, col. 3 (an official of the CIA once said: "Remember—the First Amendment *is only an amendment.*").

28. See, Powe, The H–Bomb Injunction, 61 U.Colo.L.Rev. 55, 76 (1990): "Judges, after all, are not editors; they are accustomed to deciding post hoc, and the posture of a national security prior restraint forces guesses about the unknown future."

29. Milliken v. Stone, 16 F.2d 981, 983 (2d Cir.1927), certiorari denied 274 U.S.

748, 47 S.Ct. 764, 71 L.Ed. 1331 (1927); In re Debs, 158 U.S. 564, 593–94, 15 S.Ct. 900, 909–10, 39 L.Ed. 1092 (1895).

30. But see, Mayton, Towards a Theory of First Amendment Process: Injunctions of Speech, Subsequent Punishment, and the Costs of the Prior Restraint Doctrine, 67 Cornell L.Rev. 245 (1982); but compare Hunter, Toward a Better Understanding of the Prior Restraint Doctrine: A Reply to Professor Mayton, 67 Cornell L.Rev. 283 (1982). See also, Jeffries, Rethinking Prior Restraint, 92 Yale L.J. 409 (1983); Redish, The Proper Role of the Prior Restraint Doctrine in First Amendment Theory, 70 Virginia L.Rev. 53 (1984).

31. Freedman v. Maryland, 380 U.S. 51, 85 S.Ct. 734, 13 L.Ed.2d 649 (1965).

For the procedural requirements of prior restraint in obscenity cases see § 20.61(c), infra.

32. Blount v. Rizzi, 400 U.S. 410, 91 S.Ct. 423, 27 L.Ed.2d 498 (1971).

access to a public forum[33] and judicial protective or "gag" orders against the press in criminal cases.[34]

Prior Restraint and Protective Orders and Discovery. The government may impose limited restrictions on the use of information disclosed to individuals by the government, or with government assistance, when the individual does not have a constitutional right of access to the information. Thus in *Seattle Times Co. v. Rhinehart*,[35] the Supreme Court upheld a state trial court order prohibiting a newspaper from publishing information that it had gained through pretrial discovery from an individual suing the newspaper for defamation. The pretrial protective order did not prohibit publication of the information if it was obtained from a source *other than* pretrial discovery. The order only limited the use of the material gained through pretrial discovery to preparation for and use at the trial of the defamation suit.

In the course of upholding this limited protective order, the Court stated that: "A litigant has no First Amendment right of access to information made available only for the purposes of trying his suit.... Thus, continued court control over the discovered information does not raise the same spectre of government censorship that such control might suggest in other situations."[36] This statement should not be taken to indicate that the government is free to condition or control the use of information which it gives to individuals who had no constitutional claim to that information without review under the first amendment or strict review of government prior restraints on speech. With the exception of access to judicial proceedings, the Court has not established a first amendment right of access to programs or information controlled by the government.[37] Nevertheless, a law which conditions disclosure of information to the press or public in terms of an agreement not to use the information to criticize governmental policy should certainly be held to violate the first amendment; a condition on

33. Southeastern Promotions, Ltd. v. Conrad, 420 U.S. 546, 95 S.Ct. 1239, 43 L.Ed.2d 448 (1975).

34. Nebraska Press Ass'n v. Stuart, 427 U.S. 539, 96 S.Ct. 2791, 49 L.Ed.2d 683 (1976). See § 20.25, infra.

35. 467 U.S. 20, 104 S.Ct. 2199, 81 L.Ed.2d 17 (1984). See also, Snepp v. United States, 444 U.S. 507, 100 S.Ct. 763, 62 L.Ed.2d 704 (1980), rehearing denied 445 U.S. 972, 100 S.Ct. 1668, 64 L.Ed.2d 250 (1980).

See generally, Note, The First Amendment Right to Disseminate Discovery Materials: In re Halkin, 92 Harv.L.Rev. 1550 (1979); Note Rule 26(c) Protective Orders and the First Amendment, 80 Colum.L.Rev. 1645 (1980); Comment, Protective Orders Prohibiting Dissemination of Discovery Information: The First Amendment and Good Cause, 1980 Duke L.J. 766; Marcus, Myth and Reality in Protective Order Litigation, 69 Cornell L.Rev. 1 (1983); Post, The Management of Speech: Discretion and Rights, 1984 Supreme Ct. Rev. 169. Note, *Seattle Times:* What Effect on Discovery Sharing?, 1985 Wis. L.Rev. 1055.

36. 467 U.S. at 31, 104 S.Ct. at 2207 (citation omitted).

37. See §§ 20.19, 20.25, infra, for an examination of this issue.

See generally, Casper, Comment: Government Secrecy and the Constitution, 74 Calif.L.Rev. 923 (1986); Sunstein, Government Control of Information, 74 Calif.L.Rev. 889 (1986).

the disclosure of government information to the press and public that the information not be further published or discussed without prior governmental approval should be subject to strict first amendment scrutiny as a prior restraint.

The Court in *Seattle Times* was unanimous in upholding the judicial order because it allowed publication of information identical to that gained through pretrial discovery if it was gained from another source. The limitation on the use of pretrial discovery was found to be a narrow means of promoting the important governmental interest, unrelated to the suppression of expression, in furthering open discovery before trial and protecting privacy interests of individuals in the trial process.[38]

§ 20.17 From *Near* to the Pentagon Papers and Beyond

Near v. Minnesota[1] firmly embedded the prior restraint doctrine in modern jurisprudence, and *New York Times Co. v. United States*[2] applied the principles of *Near* to the special problem of national security.

Near v. Minnesota involved a state statute which permitted enjoining as a nuisance any "malicious, scandalous and defamatory newspaper, magazine or other periodical."[3] Defendant published "The Saturday Press" and had printed articles with strong antisemitic overtones critical of local officials. The trial court issued a permanent injunction against defendant, which was affirmed by the highest state court.

The Supreme Court reversed the conviction on the grounds that it was an infringement of the liberty of the press as guaranteed in the first and fourteenth amendments. In reaching this conclusion, the

38. Justices Brennan and Marshall wrote a brief concurrence but joined in the opinion which Justice Powell wrote for a unanimous Court. Both the concurrence and the majority opinion stated that the protective orders were subject to first amendment scrutiny to determine whether they promoted an important or substantial governmental interest unrelated to the suppression of expression and were no greater than necessary to the protection of such interest.

§ 20.17

1. 283 U.S. 697, 51 S.Ct. 625, 75 L.Ed. 1357 (1931).

On the background of *Near*, see, F. Friendly, Minnesota Rag (1981).

2. 403 U.S. 713, 91 S.Ct. 2140, 29 L.Ed.2d 822 (1971). Organization for a Better Austin v. Keefe, 402 U.S. 415, 91 S.Ct. 1575, 29 L.Ed.2d 1 (1971) was another prior restraint case. Chief Justice Burger,

for the Court, reversed a prior restraint on the OBA which, to encourage integrated housing, had peacefully distributed leaflets objecting to block busting and panic peddling. The leaflets specifically criticized Keefe, a real estate broker.

3. 283 U.S. 697, 701–02, 51 S.Ct. 625, 626, 75 L.Ed. 1357 (1931).

See generally, Symposium: *Near v. Minnesota*, 50th Anniversary, 66 Minn. L.Rev. 1 (1981); Gillmor, Prologue, 66 Minn.L.Rev. 1 (1981); Toward a Theory of Prior Restraint: The Central Linkage, 66 Minn.L.Rev. 11 (1981); Murphy, *Near v. Minnesota* in the Context of Historical Developments, 66 Minn.L.Rev. 95 (1981); Knoll, National Security: The Ultimate Threat to the First Amendment, 66 Minn. L.Rev. 161 (1981); Linde, Courts and Censorship, 66 Minn.L.Rev. 171 (1981).

Court enumerated the gravity of the statute's consequences: (1) In order to obtain an injunction under the statute, one did not need to prove the falsity of the charges made in the publication, as in libel law. The statute only permitted the defense that "truth was published with good motives and for justifiable ends." [4] (2) The statute was directed to publications critical of private citizens and public officers. (3) The object of the statute was not ordinary punishment but suppression. (4) The statute operated not only to suppress the publication but also to effectively place the publisher under censorship.[5]

The Court summarized the working of the statute:

> The operation and effect of the statute in substance is that public authorities may bring the owner or publisher of a newspaper or periodical before a judge upon a charge of conducting a business of publishing scandalous and defamatory matter—in particular that the matter consists of charges against public officers of official dereliction—and unless the owner or publisher is able and disposed to bring competent evidence to satisfy the judge that the charges are true and are published with good motives and for justifiable ends, his newspaper or periodical is suppressed and further publication is made punishable as a contempt. This is the essence of censorship.[6]

A statute that functioned in this way was inconsistent with the historical conception of the freedom of the press guarantee.[7]

---

4. 283 U.S. at 702, 51 S.Ct. at 626.

5. 283 U.S. at 710–12, 51 S.Ct. at 629–30.

6. 283 U.S. at 713, 51 S.Ct. at 630.

7. Id.

Compare Lowe v. SEC, 472 U.S. 181, 105 S.Ct. 2557, 86 L.Ed.2d 130 (1985). After Christopher Lowe was convicted of misappropriating funds of an investment client, of tampering with evidence to cover up fraud of an investment client, of stealing from a bank, and of other similar activities, the Securities and Exchange Commission ordered Lowe not to associate with any investment adviser. About a year later the SEC filed suit to permanently enjoin Lowe and others who were alleged to be violating the 1940 Investment Advisers Act and the earlier SEC order by publishing investment newsletters and soliciting subscriptions for a stockchart service, without being registered as investment advisers or being exempt under the Investment Advisers Act. "There was no evidence that Lowe's criminal convictions were related to the publications; no evidence that Lowe had engaged in any trading activity in any securities that were the subject of advice or

comment in the publications; and no contention that any of the information published in the advisory services had been false or materially misleading." 472 U.S. at 186, 105 S.Ct. at 2561 (footnotes omitted).

The Court, to avoid constitutional problems, interpreted the 1940 Investment Advisers Act to exclude Lowe's newsletters and publications from its definition of "investment adviser." "As long as the communications between petitioners and their subscribers remain entirely impersonal and do not develop into the kind of fiduciary, person-to-person relationships that were discussed at length in the legislative history of the Act and are characteristic of investment adviser-client relationships, we believe the publications are, at least presumptively, within the exclusion and thus not subject to registration under the Act." 472 U.S. at 210, 105 S.Ct. at 2573 (footnote omitted). Thus an unregistered adviser may publish newsletters containing investment advice not specifically tailored to the needs of individual clients.

Justice White, joined by Burger, C.J., and Rehnquist, J., concurred in the result.

In order to reach this conclusion the Court made a major initial presumption: that the chief purpose of the freedom of the press guarantee was to prevent prior restraints on publication.[8] Thus, there could be very few exceptions to the principle of immunity from previous restraint. The Court, in dictum, listed only three "exceptional cases" that *might* justify previous restraint:[9] (1) if it were necessary so that "a government might prevent actual obstruction to its recruiting service or the publication of the sailing dates of transports or the number and location of troops;"[10] (2) the requirements of decency could justify prior restraint on obscene publications; (3) if it were necessary to avoid "incitements to acts of violence and the overthrow by force of orderly government."[11] Because none of these exceptions was applicable to the statute so far as it authorized the proceedings of this action, prior restraint was not constitutionally justified in *Near*.

The Pentagon Papers Case. Forty years later, in 1971, the doctrine of prior restraint of political speech again received special attention in *New York Times Co. v. United States* (The Pentagon Papers Case)[12] when the Court dismissed temporary restraining orders and stays against the *New York Times* and the *Washington Post* and refused to enjoin the newspapers from publishing a classified study on United States policy-making in Viet Nam. The Justice Department had offered to work out a settlement with the newspapers pursuant to which the papers would present the portions of the documents that the

---

They interpreted the Act to include Lowe as an investment adviser, but would hold that the Act could not constitutionally be applied in these circumstances. Justice Powell did not participate in the decision.

8. 283 U.S. at 713, 51 S.Ct. at 630.

9. 283 U.S. at 716, 51 S.Ct. at 631.

10. 283 U.S. at 716, 51 S.Ct. at 631.

The majority relied on this dictum in upholding the power of the Secretary of State to revoke the passport of a former CIA agent who was seeking to expose CIA agents abroad. Haig v. Agee, 453 U.S. 280, 101 S.Ct. 2766, 69 L.Ed.2d 640 (1981). The passport revocation, the majority reasoned, did not violate Agee's first amendment rights because it only inhibited Agee's "*action*", not his "speech." 453 U.S. at 309, 101 S.Ct. at 2783 (emphasis in original). Just as the hypothetical disclosures in *Near* obstruct the government's recruiting services, Agee's disclosures "have the declared purpose of obstructing intelligence operations and the recruiting of intelligence personnel." 453 U.S. at 308–09, 101 S.Ct. at 2782–83.

Brennan, J., in dissent, found *Near* to be an irrelevant and unconvincing precedent and commented that under the majority's speech-action rationale, "a 40 year prison sentence imposed upon a person who criticized the Government's food stamp policy would represent only an 'inhibition of action.' After all, the individual would remain free to criticize the United States Government, albeit from a jail cell." 453 U.S. at 320–21 n. 10, 101 S.Ct. 2788 n. 10.

11. 283 U.S. at 716, 51 S.Ct. at 631.

12. 403 U.S. 713, 91 S.Ct. 2140, 29 L.Ed.2d 822 (1971). The Court therefore reversed the Second Circuit and affirmed the D.C. Circuit. The Court also lifted its own stay. 403 U.S. 943, 91 S.Ct. 2271, 29 L.Ed.2d 853 (1971). The D.C. Circuit had refused to enjoin but still restrained the *Post* pending Supreme Court review.

See J. Barron and C. Dienes, Handbook of Free Speech and Free Press 42–57 (1979). M. Nimmer, Nimmer on Freedom of Speech §§ 4.02–4.06 (1984); S. Ungar, The Papers and the Papers (1972); H. Salisbury, Without Fear or Favor (1981); Abrams, The Pentagon Papers Case a Decade Later, New York Times Magazine, June 7, 1981, at 22.

newspaper proposed to publish and then the Justice Department and the newspaper would negotiate what could be printed. The newspapers rejected the proposal and eventually won before the Supreme Court.[13] The fragmented Court, which decided the case in nine separate opinions by a six to three majority, agreed on only two general themes—any system of prior restraint of expression bears a heavy presumption against its constitutional validity, and the Government carries a "heavy burden" to justify enforcing any system of prior restraint.[14]

The opinions in this case can be grouped in three categories: Justices Black and Douglas, maintained that there can never be prior restraint on the press; Justices Brennan, White, Stewart and Marshall, maintained that there could be prior restraint on the press in some circumstances but not in this case; and Justices Burger, Harlan, and Blackmun, maintained that prior restraint was appropriate in this case.

Justices Black and Douglas argued that no system of prior restraint was ever justified. A holding that the publication of news may sometimes be enjoined, according to Justice Black, would "make a shambles of the First Amendment," and the operation of the injunctions was a "flagrant, indefensible, and continuing violation of the First Amendment."[15]

Black characterized the very purpose of the press as exposing the secrets of government and informing the people; "paramount among the responsibilities of a free press is the duty to prevent any part of the government from deceiving the people and sending them off to distant lands to die of foreign fevers and foreign shot and shell."[16] Rather than be enjoined or condemned for publishing the Pentagon Papers, these newspapers should be "commended for serving the purpose that the Founding Fathers saw so clearly.... The Press was to serve the governed, not the governors."[17]

Justice Douglas deplored governmental restraint on the press and also interpreted the dominant purpose of the First Amendment to be "to prohibit the widespread practice of governmental suppression of embarrassing information."[18] Although Douglas left unanswered the question whether the war power of Congress might change the doctrine of prior restraint, as the doctrine exists now, even serious impact from disclosures of publication cannot justify prior restraint on the press.

Justice Brennan did leave open the possibility of some constitutional prior restraints, but his test was so strict that none might pass any realistic review. Brennan first pointed out the impropriety of granting injunctive relief in the instant case. The basis of the Government's

---

13. Adler & Pollock, Rose Pact is One More Trade–Off, Wall St. Jrl., Aug. 25, 1989, at p. B.1, col. 4 (midwest ed.).

14. 403 U.S. at 714, 91 S.Ct. at 2141.

15. 403 U.S. at 715, 91 S.Ct. at 2142.

16. 403 U.S. at 717, 91 S.Ct. at 2143.

17. Id.

18. 403 U.S. at 723–24, 91 S.Ct. at 2146.

argument was that publication might damage the national interest but, according to Brennan, "the First Amendment tolerates absolutely no prior judicial restraints of the press predicated upon surmise or conjecture that untoward consequences may result." [19]

Brennan did find one situation which would justify an exception to the first amendment ban on prior restraint, cases which may arise when the nation is at war. However, Brennan invoked a high standard for imposition of prior restraint even then. The Government must allege and prove that the publication of information must "inevitably, directly, and immediately" cause the happening of an event such as nuclear holocaust.[20] Thus, although Brennan conceptually allowed the possibility of prior restraint, his test is so strict as to be virtually a prohibition.

19. 403 U.S. at 725–26, 91 S.Ct. at 2147 (footnote omitted).

20. 403 U.S. at 726–27, 91 S.Ct. at 2148.

The H–Bomb Injunction. The hypothetical to which Justice Brennan referred (a hypothetical that Alexander Bickel, defending the New York Times, sought to distinguish during oral argument) was presented in United States v. Progressive, Inc., 467 F.Supp. 990 (W.D.Wis.1979), dismissed on the government's motion in, 610 F.2d 819 (7th Cir.1979) (unpublished opinion).

Professor Powe carefully discusses this case and the issues it raises in, Powe, The H–Bomb Injunction, 61 U.Colo.L.Rev. 55 (1990). The case arose after Erwin Knoll, the editor of *The Progressive* commissioned Howard Morland (a physics dropout and a pacifist who favored unilateral disarmament) to write an article on how the H–Bomb worked. Morland arrived at this information through public sources. He later complained: "I think the government wants to classify the inside of my head." H. Morland, The Secret That Exploded 192 (1981). The district court granted the injunction, 467 F.Supp. 990 (W.D.Wis.1979), and later the government moved to dismiss. Professor Powe concludes: "[E]ven if we assume arguendo that Morland and Knoll were violating the Atomic Energy Act in describing accurately how an H–bomb works, I still believe that they should not have been enjoined." 61 Colo.L.Rev. at 61.

Professor Powe points out that copies of the disputed article were being photocopied and privately distributed all over the place. The injunction would be futile. The lower court order requiring Morland, the author of the disputed article, to retrieve all copies, but "such orders are much like the Utah law forbidding the Great Salt Lake from exceeding set boundaries. They work only in times of tranquility, preferably with an agreed-upon snowfall." Powe, The H–Bomb Injunction, 61 U.Colo.L.Rev. 55, 69–70 (1990). Thus, although the government secured its injunction in the lower court, the government's motion for dismissal is understandable. "Morland's article then became available for comparison with the quite similar discussion in the *Encyclopedia Americana* by Edward Teller, father of the H–bomb." Power, 61 U.Colo. L.Rev. at 70, citing, Teller, Hydrogen Bomb, in 14 Encyclopedia Americana 654–56 (1975).

On this case, see also, Cheh, The Progressive Case and the Atomic Energy Act, 48 Geo.Wash.L.Rev. 163 (1980); Note, United States v. Progressive, Inc.: The Faustian Bargain and the First Amendment, 75 Nw.U.L.Rev. 538 (1980); Knoll, National Security: The Ultimate Threat to the First Amendment, 66 Minn.L.Rev. 161 (1981); H. Morland, The Secret That Exploded (1981); Powe, Espionage Leaks and the First Amendment, 42 Bulletin of the Atomic Scientists 8 (June–July, 1986).

The "Spy Catcher" Case. See, Note, The Spycatcher Cases, 50 Ohio St.L.J. 405 (1989), which discusses British Prime Minister Thatcher's efforts to block publication of the book about M15, a section of the British Secret Service, "Spy Catcher" by Peter Wright. Mr. Wright's book (which alleges, among other things, that there was a counter spy, a "mole," who was the head of M15 for nearly a decade, from 1956 to 1965) was published abroad in 1987 when Ms. Thatcher prevented it from being published in Great Britain.

Justice Stewart argued that prior restraint imposed by the Executive could be justified in order to maintain internal security, because the Executive has a constitutional obligation to preserve the confidentiality required to effectively perform its duties related to national defense and foreign affairs.[21] However, the Executive must show that disclosure of information will result in "direct, immediate, and irreparable damage to our Nation or its people," and the Government did not meet this test for all the documents involved in the instant case.[22]

Even though he was convinced disclosure of the material would do substantial damage to the public interest, Justice White concurred in the Court's judgment also because the Government did not satisfy the "very heavy burden" it must meet to justify prior restraint.[23] White implied that Congressional authorization for prior restraint might lessen this "very heavy burden" and emphasized that the Government could still proceed against the newspapers for criminal publication.

Justice Marshall based his concurrence on the absence of Congressional authorization for prior restraint in this situation. He argued that it would be against the separation of powers concept for the Court, through use of the contempt power, to restrain actions Congress has chosen not to prohibit.[24] Although the power of the Executive could constitutionally justify prior restraint, Congress had clearly refused to give the president the power he sought to exercise here by enjoining publication of these materials. Marshall dismissed the injunction because "[w]hen Congress specifically declines to make conduct unlawful it is not for this Court to redecide those issues—to overrule Congress." [25]

The remaining three justices dissented and found that the injunction was proper in the instant case. Chief Justice Burger did not speak directly to the merits of the case, arguing instead that undue haste in the proceedings removed any possibility of orderly litigation of the proceedings and meant that the justices "literally do not know what we are acting on." [26] He would have upheld the injunction to allow the Court enough time for an orderly hearing on the merits. However, Burger criticized the New York Times as being largely responsible for the "frenetic haste" of the proceedings and his sympathies were apparent in that he "agreed generally" with Harlan's dissent.[27]

Harlan did uphold use of the injunction on the merits, albeit "within the severe limitations imposed by the time constraints." [28] Unlike Justice Marshall, Harlan used the theory of the constitutional separation of powers to justify prior restraint of the Pentagon Papers. Harlan argued that the Executive has "constitutional primacy in the

---

21. 403 U.S. at 729–30, 91 S.Ct. at 2149–50.

22. 403 U.S. at 730, 91 S.Ct. at 2149.

23. 403 U.S. at 731, 91 S.Ct. at 2150.

24. 403 U.S. at 742, 91 S.Ct. at 2155–56.

25. 403 U.S. at 745–46, 91 S.Ct. at 2157.

26. 403 U.S. at 751, 91 S.Ct. at 2160.

27. 403 U.S. at 751–52, 91 S.Ct. at 2161.

28. 403 U.S. at 755, 91 S.Ct. at 2162.

field of foreign affairs" and that the judiciary has only two narrow areas of inquiry over Executive decisions in foreign policy.[29] The Judiciary can (1) insure that the area of dispute actually lies within the scope of the president's foreign relations power; and (2) insure that the decision that disclosure of the subject matter would irreparably impair the national security be made by the head of the executive department concerned, such as the Secretary of State or the Secretary of Defense. But it is not within the power of the Court to redetermine the probable impact of disclosure on national security once this decision has been made by the Executive.[30]

Justice Blackmun added that there was need for developing proper standards between the "broad right of the press to print and ... the very narrow right of the Government to prevent." [31] Representing the opposite extreme from Black's praise for the action of the New York Times, Blackmun included a strong attack on the newspapers and concurring justices who comprised the majority of the Court:

> [I]f, with the Court's action today, these newspapers proceed to publish the critical documents and there results therefrom "the death of soldiers, the destruction of alliances, the greatly increased difficulty of negotiation with our enemies, the inability of our diplomats to negotiate," to which list I might add the factors of prolongation of the war and of further delay in the freeing of United States prisoners, then the Nation's people will know where the responsibility for these sad consequences rests.[32]

The Government lost its injunctive suit and the newspaper proceeded to finish publishing the excerpts of the Pentagon Papers which they had secured by an unauthorized leak from a former government employee, Daniel Ellsberg. The Government neither showed nor claimed that Blackmun's parade of horribles occurred because of the Pentagon Papers publication.[33] Nor did the Government ever prosecute any of

---

29. 403 U.S. at 756, 91 S.Ct. at 2162.

30. 403 U.S. at 757, 91 S.Ct. at 2163.

31. 403 U.S. at 761, 91 S.Ct. at 2165.

32. 403 U.S. at 763, 91 S.Ct. at 2166.

33. While the Pentagon Papers case was being argued before the D.C. Circuit, the Government "filed a top secret supplement to an affidavit of Vice Admiral Noel Gayler, director of the National Security Agency (NSA). He testified that a certain document [of the Pentagon Papers] revealed that the NSA had the ability to intercept North Vietnamese communications and break their code, a serious revelation. But George Wilson, the *Post*'s defense correspondent and the principle technical adviser to the lawyers, recognized the cable as something he had seen before. 'Suddenly it came totally clear to me. I had seen it on page thirty-four of the 1968 Senate Foreign Relations Committee hearings on the Tonkin Gulf. It was on the left side of the page.' Furthermore, Wilson had a copy of those hearings in his pocket which the *Post* attorneys then read to stunned judges and government attorneys. The government's *Washington Post* case had collapsed." Powe, The H–Bomb Injunction, 61 U.Colo.L.Rev. 55, 74–75 (1990), citing, H. Salisbury, Without Fear or Favor 323 (1981), and S. Ungar, The Papers and the Papers 204 (1972).

the newspapers—an option not foreclosed by the Pentagon Papers case [34]—but it did prosecute Daniel Ellsberg. Ellsberg, however, was never convicted. The trial judge directed a verdict of acquittal for Ellsberg because of various prosecution improprieties.

The *Snepp* Case and the CIA. Following the Pentagon Papers case, the Court decided *Snepp v. United States.*[35] *Snepp* was only a brief per curiam opinion, but significantly it held that a former agent of the Central Intelligence Agency breached his fiduciary obligation and his employment contract when he failed to submit for pre-publication review a book concerning the CIA, even though the Government conceded, for the purposes of the case, that the book divulged no classified information. Therefore, the Court put into constructive trust for the Government all the profits from Snepp's book.

The majority explained that the proper procedure that Snepp should have followed, in light of his explicit employment agreement to submit all material to the CIA, for prepublication review, would be to submit the material so that the Agency could determine if it contained harmful disclosures. If Snepp and the CIA failed to agree on this issue, the Agency would have the burden to seek an injunction against

---

34. Cf. Landmark Communications, Inc. v. Virginia, 435 U.S. 829, 98 S.Ct. 1535, 56 L.Ed.2d 1 (1978). The holding in *Landmark*—protecting third party publication of confidential judicial disciplinary proceedings—may not be applicable to a situation like the Pentagon Papers case, where a newspaper might be subject to subsequent punishment for publishing allegedly top secret national security data since the interests of the state in protecting such information is much greater. However, a major issue in such a case would still be whether or not such data was properly classified as top secret, since a "legislature appropriately inquires into and may declare the reasons impelling legislative action but the judicial function commands analysis of whether the specific conduct falls within the reach of the statute...." 435 U.S. at 844, 98 S.Ct. at 1544.

See also, Smith v. Daily Mail Publishing Co., 443 U.S. 97, 104, 99 S.Ct. 2667, 2671, 61 L.Ed.2d 399 (1979) (if a newspaper lawfully obtains truthful information about a matter of public significance "then state officials may not constitutionally punish publication of the information, absent a need to further a state interest of the highest order.")

35. 444 U.S. 507, 100 S.Ct. 763, 62 L.Ed.2d 704 (1980) (per curiam), rehearing denied 445 U.S. 972, 100 S.Ct. 1668, 64 L.Ed.2d 250 (1980). Cf. United States v. Marchetti, 466 F.2d 1309 (4th Cir.1972), certiorari denied 409 U.S. 1063, 93 S.Ct. 553, 34 L.Ed.2d 516 (1972).

When Saigon fell on April 30, 1975, Frank W. Snepp III, a senior analyst for the C.I.A., was one of the last Americans evacuated by helicopter from the roof of the American embassy. He was awarded the C.I.A.'s Medal of Merit when he returned to the United States, but he quit the Agency and wrote *Decent Interval* (1977), which was his version of the final days, and which criticized, inter alia, the C.I.A.'s evacuation planning. See R. Rotunda, Modern Constitutional Law: Cases and Notes 783 (1981).

See generally, Medow, The First Amendment and the Secrecy State: Snepp v. United States, 130 U.Pa.L.Rev. 775 (1982); DuVal, The Occasions of Secrecy, 47 U.Pitts.L.Rev. 579 (1986); Franck & Eisen, Balancing National Security and Free Speech, 14 N.Y.U.J.Internat'l L. & Policy 339 (1982).

For the view of one CIA official on the importance of free speech, see Hollander, Book Review, The New York Times Book Review, May 11, 1986, at 9 col. 3, quoting from L. Ellerbee, And So It Goes: Adventures in Television (1986); a CIA official said: "Remember—the First Amendment is *only an amendment.*"

publication.[36] Without any further discussion the Court appeared to approve of what amounts to prior restraint in those special cases where former CIA employees have been in a position of trust and have agreed to sign employment contracts accepting prepublication review of information dealing with the CIA.[37]

The dissent objected: "the Court seems unaware of the fact that its drastic new remedy [of a constructive trust for failure to abide by prepublication clearance] has been fashioned to enforce a species of prior restraint on a citizen's right to criticize his government."[38]

Properly interpreted, *Snepp* should stand only for the proposition that the government may condition the use of information disclosed to persons who have no constitutional right of access to that information, such as the government's employees: (1) when those persons in fact agree not to discuss or disclose such information; (2) when the governmental interest supporting the condition is significant; (3) when that interest is truly unrelated to the suppression of expression; and (4) when the agreement is a narrow means of promoting governmental interests unrelated to censorship goals.[39]

VI. THE OTHER SIDE OF THE COIN FROM PRIOR RESTRAINT OF THE PRESS— ACCESS TO AND BY THE PRESS

§ 20.18 A Right of Access to the Press

(a) The Fairness Doctrine and the Regulation of the Broadcast Media

Due to the unique nature of electronic media and the present state of the art, there is no comparable right of everyone to broadcast on radio and television what one could speak, write, or publish elsewhere.[1]

---

36. 444 U.S. at 515 n. 8, 100 S.Ct. at 767 n. 8.

37. In the course of congressional testimony, the Central Intelligence Agency has acknowledged that it is more likely to censor with a heavier hand when the material criticizes rather than praises the CIA. Washington Post, April 6, 1980, § A, at 10, col. 1, quoted in Powe, The Constitutional Implications of President Reagan's Censorship Directive '84, 17 The Center Magazine, March–April 1984, at 5.

38. 444 U.S. at 527, 100 S.Ct. at 774 (footnote omitted) (Stevens, J., dissenting, joined by Brennan and Marshall, JJ.).

39. This interpretation is consistent with the approach that the Court took in Seattle Times Co. v. Rhinehart, 467 U.S.

20, 104 S.Ct. 2199, 81 L.Ed.2d 17 (1984) (in which it found that a court order restricting the disclosure of information gained through pretrial discovery should not be examined as a classic prior restraint because it did not constitute government censorship of ideas but only a narrow restriction on the disclosure of information designed to protect a substantial governmental interest in open pretrial discovery and the privacy rights of individuals.) The case is discussed at the end of § 20.16, supra.

§ 20.18

1. While the Supreme Court has often commented on the monopoly nature of broadcasting, e.g., National Broadcasting Co. v. United States, 319 U.S. 190, 226, 63

Frequencies presently available to broadcast are finite, and when some are given the privilege to use them, others must be denied. No particular licensee has a first amendment right to broadcast and his existing privilege may be qualified through reasonable regulation. In general it may be said that the award of a broadcast license may be subjected to reasonable regulation with goals other than the suppression of ideas. Such regulation is permissible because it is the right of the listeners and viewers which is paramount, not the rights of the broadcasters.

In *National Broadcasting Co., Inc. v. United States* [2] the Supreme Court first recognized that, because no one has a first amendment right to a radio license or to monopolize a radio frequency, to deny a station a license on the grounds of public interest is not a denial of free speech. In this action challenging the FCC's regulations of multiple station "chain" broadcasting as an unconstitutional restraint on free speech, the opinion of the Court made much of the fact that broadcasting is a limited media and that an absolute first amendment right of access is not feasible in such circumstances.

Writing for the Court, Justice Frankfurter emphasized that regulation was essential to develop the full potential of radio [3] and that the overriding interest to be served must be "the interest *of the listening public* in 'the larger and more effective use of radio'." [4] To further the public interest in use of this limited resource, government must allocate use of the airways:

> Freedom of utterance is abridged to many who wish to use the limited facilities of radio. Unlike other modes of expression, radio inherently is not available to all. That is its unique characteristic

S.Ct. 997, 1014, 87 L.Ed. 1344 (1943); Red Lion Broadcasting Co. v. FCC, 395 U.S. 367, 376–77, 89 S.Ct. 1794, 1799–1800, 23 L.Ed.2d 371 (1969), this premise has been attacked.

See, e.g., R. Posner, Economic Analysis of Law § 22.3 at 312–13 (1972); Fowler and Brenner, A Marketplace Approach to Broadcast Regulation, 60 Tex.L.Rev. 207 (1982); Powe, "Or of the [Broadcast] Press", 55 Tex.L.Rev. 39, 55–62 (1976); Lively, Fear and the Media: A First Amendment Horror Show, 69 Minn.L.Rev. 1, 1071 (1985); Bollinger, Freedom of the Press and Public Access: Toward a Theory of Partial Regulation of the Mass Media, 75 Mich.L.Rev. 1 (1976); Fiss, Free Speech and Social Structure, 71 Iowa L.Rev. 1405 (1986); Powe, Scholarship and Markets, 56 Geo.Wash.L.Rev. 172 (1987); L. Powe, American Broadcasting and the First Amendment (1987); Ayres, Halfway Home:

On Powe's American Broadcasting and the First Amendment, 13 Law & Social Inquiry 413 (1988); Jonathan W. Emoro, Freedom, Technology, and the First Amendment (1991).

2. 319 U.S. 190, 63 S.Ct. 997, 87 L.Ed. 1344 (1943).

3. 319 U.S. at 217–27, 63 S.Ct. at 1009–14.

4. 319 U.S. at 216, 63 S.Ct. at 1009 (emphasis added).

Cf. Metro Broadcasting Inc. v. F.C.C., 497 U.S. ___, ___, 110 S.Ct. 2997, 3019–27, 111 L.Ed.2d 445 (1990), rehearing denied ___ U.S. ___, 111 S.Ct. 15, 111 L.Ed.2d 829 (1990), Brennan, J., for the Court, upholding an affirmative action program of the Federal Communications Commission, and noting that minority ownership is substantially related to the goal of promoting broadcast diversity.

and that is why, unlike other modes of expression, it is subject to governmental regulation.[5]

The Fairness Doctrine and *Red Lion*. The extent of the right of the government to control the electronic media was not made clear by *NBC*, but it was brought into sharp focus by *Red Lion Broadcasting Co. v. Federal Communications Commission*,[6] which challenged the right of the FCC to require broadcasters to follow a "fairness doctrine." The fairness doctrine required broadcasters to allow reply time to the public in cases involving personal attacks or political editorials. The case was the first time that the Supreme Court ruled on a challenge made to the FCC's fairness doctrine on constitutional grounds.

In *Red Lion*, the petitioner operated a radio station under FCC license. During a broadcast on the station the Reverend Billy James Hargis verbally attacked author Fred J. Cook.[7] Cook demanded free reply time and, upon the station's refusal, filed a formal letter of complaint with the Federal Communications Commission. The Commission deemed the incident a "personal attack" and, citing its *Times–Mirror Broadcasting Co.* doctrine[8] as requiring a station to offer free reply time in such a situation, ordered the station to grant Cook the time requested. Upon appeal by the station the D.C. Circuit Court of Appeals affirmed[9] and the Supreme Court granted certiorari.

After the *Red Lion* litigation had commenced, the FCC issued its Personal Attack Rules, which codified the *Times–Mirror* doctrine and the Commission's ad hoc ruling in *Red Lion* for all personal attacks.[10] The Radio–Television News Directors Association (RTNDA) immediately sought review of the rule-making proceeding in the Court of Appeals for the Seventh Circuit, where the rules were declared unconstitutional abridgments of free speech.[11] The Supreme Court granted certiorari for consideration of the issues together with *Red Lion*.[12]

The broadcasters challenged the fairness doctrine and its specific manifestations in the personal attack and political editorial rules on

---

5. 319 U.S. at 226, 63 S.Ct. at 1014.

6. 395 U.S. 367, 89 S.Ct. 1794, 23 L.Ed.2d 371 (1969).

See Van Alstyne, The Möbius Strip of the First Amendment: Perspectives on Red Lion, 29 So.Car.L.Rev. 539 (1978). See also, Krattenmaker & Powe, The Fairness Doctrine Today: A Constitutional Curiosity and an Impossible Dream, 1985 Duke L.J. 151.

7. During part of a "Christian Crusade" broadcast series, Hargis discussed Cook's book, Goldwater—Extremist on the Right. Hargis claimed that Cook had been fired from a newspaper for leveling false charges at a city official and had subsequently worked for "one of the most scurrilous publications of the left (The Nation)." 395 U.S. at 371–72 n. 2, 89 S.Ct. at 1797 n. 2.

8. 24 P & F Radio Reg. 404 (1962).

9. Red Lion Broadcasting Co. v. FCC, 381 F.2d 908 (D.C.Cir.1967), judgment affirmed 395 U.S. 367, 89 S.Ct. 1794, 23 L.Ed.2d 371 (1969).

10. 47 C.F.R. §§ 73.123, 73.300, 73.598, 73.679.

11. RTNDA v. United States, 400 F.2d 1002 (7th Cir.1968).

12. United States v. Radio Television News Directors Association, 393 U.S. 1014, 89 S.Ct. 631, 21 L.Ed.2d 559 (1969).

conventional first amendment grounds as abridging freedom of speech and press. Their argument was based on the contention that the first amendment protected their desire to use their allotted frequency continuously to broadcast whatever they choose, and to exclude whomever they choose from using that frequency; if no man could be prevented from publishing or saying what he thinks, or from refusing in his speech to give equal weight to the views of his opponents, then broadcasters must have a similar first amendment right it was argued.

The Supreme Court unanimously rejected this contention of a right to free speech for broadcasters identical to published or spoken speech.[13] It emphasized that "differences in the characteristics of news media justify differences in the First Amendment standards applied to them," [14] and stressed that a limited media could not support an absolute right of free speech:

> Where there are substantially more individuals who want to broadcast than there are frequencies to allocate, it is idle to posit an unabridgeable First Amendment right to broadcast comparable to the right of every individual to speak, write, or publish.[15]

The Court reasoned that the fiduciary nature of the relationship between the licensee and the general public put those who hold a license in no more favored position than those to whom licenses are refused. Where the public interest requires, the government could demand that a licensee fulfill his obligation "to present those views and voices which are representative of his community and which would otherwise, by necessity, be barred from the airwaves." [16] Because of this fiduciary role, the rights of the broadcasters must be subordinate to the right of viewers and listeners to suitable access to ideas and information.

It is important to note that while the *Red Lion* case only upheld a Federal Communications Commission rule, parts of the Court's opinion appeared to go much farther and were written as if the fairness doctrine is constitutionally required:

> It is the right of the public to receive suitable access to social, political, esthetic, moral, and other ideas and experiences which is crucial here. That right may not constitutionally be abridged either by Congress or by the [Federal Communications Commission].[17]

Yet other portions were more narrow:

13. Justice Douglas was not present at oral argument and therefore abstained from taking part in the decision.

14. 395 U.S. at 386–87, 89 S.Ct. at 1805, citing Joseph Burstyn, Inc. v. Wilson, 343

U.S. 495, 503, 72 S.Ct. 777, 781, 96 L.Ed. 1098 (1952).

15. 395 U.S. at 388, 89 S.Ct. at 1806.

16. 395 U.S. at 389, 89 S.Ct. at 1806.

17. 395 U.S. at 390, 89 S.Ct. at 1807.

[W]e do hold that the Congress and the Commission do not violate the First Amendment when they require a radio or television station to give reply time to answer personal attacks and political editorials.[18]

While the fairness doctrine regulations do not constitute a prior restraint in the classic sense,[19] they do place a recognizable burden upon broadcaster programming discretion. The *Red Lion* Court, however, spent little time discussing the competing considerations involved in placing this additional burden upon the broadcast industry. The broadcasters' claims that they would be forced into self-censorship and would substantially curtail coverage of controversial issues under a right-to-reply rule were summarily dismissed as "at best speculative." [20]

The Court did admit that if the rules should result in such a reduction of coverage, then "there will be time enough to reconsider the constitutional implications".[21] While as a practical matter, it should be hard to measure a drop in the amount of free speech caused by the fairness doctrine, the Court's acknowledgement of a reconsideration of the fairness rule in such circumstances supports the position that, in spite of the Court's earlier strong language, the fairness doctrine is not constitutionally required.[22]

No General Right of Access. Notwithstanding the Court's suggestion, the generally broad language of *Red Lion* led some commentators to argue that there is a constitutional right of individual access to the airwaves beyond the scope of the fairness doctrine. This right was perceived both in the decision's qualifications on the broadcaster's first amendment rights and in the FCC's power to compel presentation of individual responses to personal attacks and political editorials.[23] Only

18. 395 U.S. at 396, 89 S.Ct. at 1810.

19. See, e.g., Near v. Minnesota, 283 U.S. 697, 51 S.Ct. 625, 75 L.Ed. 1357 (1931).

20. 395 U.S. at 393, 89 S.Ct. at 1808.

21. 395 U.S. at 393, 89 S.Ct. at 1808. Assuming that the broadcaster does indeed have a monopoly, the fairness doctrine as an economic matter might not at all increase the publication of ideas. "On the contrary, it penalizes [the broadcaster] for presenting controversial ideas by requiring him to present all sides of a controversy. The element of penalty lies in the fact that the doctrine comes into play only when the broadcaster's welfare would be maximized by his not presenting all sides." R. Posner, Economic Analysis of Law § 22.3 at 313 (1972).

22. See, FCC v. WNCN Listeners Guild, 450 U.S. 582, 101 S.Ct. 1266, 67 L.Ed.2d 521 (1981), in which the Court held that neither federal statutes nor the U.S. Con-

stitution require the Commission to review past or anticipated changes in a station's entertainment programming when it rules on an application for renewal or transfer of a radio broadcast license. The Commission may rely on market forces to promote diversity and serve the public interest in entertainment programming.

Although *Red Lion* acknowledged that a debate of public issues promotes the public interest it "did not imply that the First Amendment grants individual listeners the right to have the Commission review the abandonment of their favorite entertainment programs." 450 U.S. at 604, 101 S.Ct. at 1279.

23. See, e.g., Note, Freedom of Expression—Violation of First Amendment for Radio and Television Stations to Deny Completely Broadcasting Time to Editorial Advertisers When Time Is Sold to Commercial Advertisers, 85 Harv.L.Rev. 689 (1972);

a slight extension of the *Red Lion* holding would recognize a right of access to electronic media by individuals wishing to make minority views on issues of public importance known. The Democratic National Committee (DNC) and an anti-war group called the Business Executive's Movement for Vietnam Peace (BEM) tried to establish the existence of such a constitutional right in *Columbia Broadcasting System, Inc. v. Democratic National Committee.*[24]

The issue presented in *CBS* was whether "responsible" groups have a constitutional right under the first amendment to purchase air time for the presentation of ads and programs in order to make known their views about controversial issues of public importance. The two groups claiming such a right, DNC and BEM, were challenging separate decisions of the FCC. In the case of BEM, the FCC had held that a radio station acted within its authority in refusing to air BEM's spot advertisement opposed to the Vietnam conflict; in the case of DNC, the FCC had held that as a general matter the DNC did not have a right to purchase time to air its views on controversial public issues.[25]

The Supreme Court deferred to the FCC in both cases and held that there is no such right of access under the Constitution. Though the Court divided on several issues, six justices agreed that the first amendment would not require the sale of time to responsible groups even if state action was involved.[26] The Court of Appeals below had held that "a flat ban on paid public issue announcements is in violation of the First Amendment, at least when other sorts of paid announcements are accepted." [27]

The opinion of the Supreme Court emphasized that a balancing of the first amendment interests involved must be carried out within the framework of the regulatory scheme already imposed by Congress on the broadcast media. It noted that Congress had dealt with, and firmly rejected, the argument "that the broadcast facilities should be open on

Marks, Broadcasting and Censorship: First Amendment Theory After Red Lion, 38 Geo.Wash.L.Rev. 974 (1970); But see, Jaffe, The Editorial Responsibility of the Broadcaster: Reflections on Fairness and Access, 85 Harv.L.Rev. 768 (1972). See generally, Barron, Access to the Press—A New First Amendment Right, 80 Harv.L.Rev. 1641 (1967); Barron, An Emerging First Amendment Right of Access to the Media?, 37 G.W.L.Rev. 487 (1969); J. Barron, Freedom of the Press for Whom? The Right of Access to Mass Media (1973); Lange, The Role of the Access Doctrine in the Regulation of the Mass Media, 52 N.Car.L.Rev. 1 (1973).

24. 412 U.S. 94, 93 S.Ct. 2080, 36 L.Ed.2d 772 (1973).

25. Business Executive's Movement for Vietnam Peace, 25 F.C.C.2d 242 (1970); Democratic National Committee, 25 F.C.C.2d 216 (1970).

26. The majority opinion consisted of Parts I, II, and IV of Chief Justice Burger's opinion, which Justices Rehnquist, White, Blackmun, and Powell joined. The latter three emphasized in their concurring opinion, 412 U.S. at 146–48, 93 S.Ct. at 2108–09, that the state action question had not been decided. For an analysis of the state action issues, see Chapter 16.

27. BEM v. FCC, 450 F.2d 642 (D.C.Cir. 1971).

a nonselective basis to all persons wishing to talk about public issues." [28]

Although a Congressional decision or viewpoint cannot be deemed decisive in an issue of constitutional interpretation, the Court was persuaded that the rationale behind this legislative decision was based on sound principles. The *CBS* decision made it clear that any right of access to the electronic media is very limited and that in balancing the competing interests involved "[o]nly when the interests of the public are found to outweigh the private journalistic interests of the broadcasters will government power be asserted within the framework of the [Federal Communications] Act." [29]

The Court concluded that an unlimited right of access would not best serve the public interest. The views of the affluent could still prevail because they could purchase more time to air their views. Valuable broadcast time might be wasted by groups concerned with trivialities. The Court was reluctant to allow full access by individuals who had no responsibilities or accountability to act in the public interest; complete access rights might exchange "public trustee" broadcasting for "a system of self-appointed editorial commentators." [30] The fairness doctrine was not thought to be applicable to editorial advertisements and the BEM and DNC's argument on this basis was inappropriate. [31]

In a later case the Court held that the Communications Act does not mandate any claimed right of access,[32] and also that neither that Act nor the Constitution authorizes or permits the FCC to require broadcasters to extend a range of public access. The majority relied on the fact that section 3(h) of the Act stipulates that broadcasters shall not be treated as common carriers; and it distinguished the fairness doctrine because that rule contemplates a wide range of licensee discretion and does not mandate access to anyone.

The State Action Question. The Court in *CBS* was strongly split on the question of whether state action was involved but the decision is of little precedential value on this issue. Justice Burger, joined by Justices Stewart and Rehnquist, emphasized that the government was

---

28. 412 U.S. at 105, 93 S.Ct. at 2088.

29. 412 U.S. at 110, 93 S.Ct. at 2090.

30. 412 U.S. at 125, 93 S.Ct. at 2098.

31. 412 U.S. at 124–26, 93 S.Ct. at 2097–98. The Court did not clearly discuss this issue, although some lower courts had already developed a theory that commercial advertising is subject to the fairness doctrine. See, e.g., Friends of Earth v. FCC, 449 F.2d 1164 (D.C.Cir.1971); Retail Store Employees Union v. FCC, 436 F.2d 248 (D.C.Cir.1970).

32. FCC v. Midwest Video Corp., 440 U.S. 689, 705 n. 14, 99 S.Ct. 1435, 1444 n. 14, 59 L.Ed.2d 692 (1979). The Court reserved the question whether it would be constitutional for Congress to give the FCC the power to treat broadcasters as common carriers. Cf. FCC v. WNCN Listeners Guild, 450 U.S. 582, 603–04, 101 S.Ct. 1266, 1279, 67 L.Ed.2d 521 (1981) (FCC may rely on market forces to promote diversity in radio entertainment formats).

not a "partner" nor in a "symbiotic relationship" with the licensee;[33] they saw no governmental action involved here which would invoke the proscriptions of the first amendment. Justices White, Blackmun and Powell on the other hand emphasized in their concurring opinions that the case had been decided on other grounds and that the state action issue had not been reached.[34] Justice Douglas, in his concurrence, argued that "the activities of licensees of the government operating in the public domain are governmental actions, so far as constitutional duties and responsibilities are concerned,"[35] but admitted that this view "has not been accepted."[36] Justice Brennan, joined by Justice Marshall, dissented and argued that there was governmental action and that it was improper to rely on the fairness doctrine as the sole means of presenting controversial ideas; rather citizens should be permitted some opportunity to speak directly for themselves.[37]

Antitrust Considerations, Divestiture, and Free Speech. In *FCC v. National Citizens Committee for Broadcasting*,[38] the Court held that the FCC, consistent with first amendment, may enact a rule prospectively barring the common ownership of a radio or television station and a daily newspaper located in the same community, and retroactively requiring divestiture of such co-located newspaper-broadcast combinations in the "most egregious" cases. Such regulations further both antitrust and first amendment goals and do not violate the first amendment rights of newspapers because—given the physical limitations of the broadcast spectrum—there is no unabridgeable first amendment right to broadcast comparable to the right of persons to speak, write, or publish.

The Court acknowledged that the government may not restrict the speech of some in order to enhance the relative voice of others, but noted that this general rule does not apply to the broadcasting media which poses unique problems justifying special regulations. These FCC regulations are not content related, nor do they unfairly single out newspaper owners, since owners of radio stations, television stations, and newspapers are, by the new rule, treated alike in their ability to acquire licenses for co-located broadcast stations.

The Right of Access of Political Candidates. In *CBS, Inc. v. FCC*[39] the Court upheld, as consistent with the first amendment, the power granted to the FCC under 47 U.S.C.A. § 312(a)(7). This law

33. 412 U.S. at 119, 101 S.Ct. at 2094. See generally Chapter 16.

34. 412 U.S. at 146–48, 101 S.Ct. at 2108–09.

35. 412 U.S. at 150, 101 S.Ct. at 2110.

36. 412 U.S. at 150, 101 S.Ct. at 2110. Because of this admission, Douglas argued that broadcasters are like newspapers, and should be treated no differently. Id. Stewart said that Douglas' views "closely

approach" his own. 412 U.S. at 132, 101 S.Ct. at 2101.

37. 412 U.S. at 180, 189–90, 101 S.Ct. at 2130 (Brennan, J., dissenting).

38. 436 U.S. 775, 98 S.Ct. 2096, 56 L.Ed.2d 697 (1978).

39. 453 U.S. 367, 101 S.Ct. 2813, 69 L.Ed.2d 706 (1981).

offers legally qualified candidates for federal elective office an affirmative, promptly enforceable right of reasonable access, to purchase broadcast time without reference to whether an opponent has secured time. Violation of this section authorizes the FCC to revoke a broadcaster's license. The Court emphasized that it was not approving any "*general* right of access to the media." [40] But section 312(a)(7) is constitutional and properly balances the first amendment rights of the public, the broadcasters, and the candidates because it "creates a *limited* right to 'reasonable' access that pertains only to legally qualified federal candidates and may be invoked by them only for the purpose of advancing their candidates once a campaign has commenced." [41]

Note that in *CBS, Inc. v. Democratic National Committee* [42] the Court refused to create a right of access. In *CBS, Inc. v. FCC,* on the other hand, the Court upheld the constitutionality of a carefully drawn statute providing for limited access. In both cases the Court was deferring to the judgment of Congress and the FCC in their regulation of the broadcast media. Given the complexity of this area it is not unusual that the Court relies so heavily on congressional judgment and administrative expertise. [43]

Constitutional issues in the area of electronic media such as radio and television have presented unique problems to the courts and will continue to do so. While *Red Lion* emphasized that the monopoly nature, which arises from inherent technological restraints on these media, at least permits, implementation of a fairness doctrine to best serve the public interest, later case law has made clear, however, that restriction on access deemed to be reasonable is not prohibited by the Constitution. [44]

Censorship and "Adult" Language. The first amendment rights of free speech in a broadcasting context raise questions not only of access but also of censorship. In *FCC v. Pacifica Foundation* [45] a

40. 453 U.S. at 396, 101 S.Ct. at 2830 (emphasis in original).

41. 453 U.S. at 396, 101 S.Ct. at 2830 (emphasis in original).

42. 412 U.S. 94, 93 S.Ct. 2080, 36 L.Ed.2d 772 (1973).

43. Cf. Radio Corp. of America v. United States, 341 U.S. 412, 420, 71 S.Ct. 806, 810, 95 L.Ed. 1062 (1951): "[C]ourts should not overrule an administrative decision merely because they disagree with its wisdom."

44. See generally, Bollinger, Freedom of the Press and Public Access: Toward a Theory of Partial Regulation of the Mass Media, 75 Mich.L.Rev. 1 (1976). Cf. Kreiss, Deregulation of Cable Television and the Problem of Access Under the First Amendment, 54 So.Calif.L.Rev. 1001 (1981).

45. 438 U.S. 726, 98 S.Ct. 3026, 57 L.Ed.2d 1073 (1978), rehearing denied 439 U.S. 883, 99 S.Ct. 227, 58 L.Ed.2d 198 (1978).

See Krattenmaker and Esterow, Censoring Indecent Cable Programs: The New Morality Meets the New Media, 51 Ford. L.Rev. 606 (1983); Krattenmaker and Powe, Televised Violence: First Amendment Principles and Social Science Theory, 64 Va.L.Rev. 1123 (1978). Content Regulation of Cable Television: "Indecent" Cable Programming and the First Amendment, 41 Record of the Ass'n of Bar of City of N.Y. 71 (Jan./Feb. 1986). Matthew L. Spitzer, Seven Dirty Words and Six Other Sto-

sharply divided Court upheld the power of the FCC to regulate "adult speech" over the radio air waves, at least in some limited circumstances. The Court held that the FCC does have statutory and constitutional power to regulate a radio broadcast that is "indecent" but not "obscene" in the constitutional sense [46] and also does not constitute "fighting words" in the constitutional sense.[47]

In the particular case a radio station broadcast for nearly 12 minutes a record of a George Carlin humorous monologue. This broadcast occurred in the early afternoon when the Court assumed that children were likely to be in the audience. There was no evidence on this point. The Court did not explain why it did not assume that children old enough to understand the Carlin monologue were more likely to be in school during the early afternoon.

During this monologue Carlin repeatedly used various words [48] referring to sexual and excretory activities and organs, and mocked middle class attitudes toward them.

ries: Controlling the Content of Print and Broadcast (1986); Powe, Consistency Over Time: The FCC's Indecency Rerun, 10 Hastings J. Communications & Entertainment L. 571 (1988).

Dial-a-Porn. In Sable Communications of California, Inc. v. FCC, 492 U.S. 115, 109 S.Ct. 2829, 106 L.Ed.2d 93 (1989) the Court held that § 223(b) of the Communications Act of 1934, as amended in 1988, can constitutionally impose an outright ban on "obscene" interstate, pre-recorded, commercial telephone messages ("dial-a-porn"). White, J., for the Court, noted that the Court has "repeatedly held that the protection of the First Amendment does not extend to obscene speech." The Court, however, invalidated the portion of the statute that imposed an outright ban, regardless of age, on "indecent" dial-a-porn messages. "Sexual expression which is indecent but not obscene is protected by the First Amendment; and the government does not submit that the sale of such materials to adults could be criminalized solely because they are indecent." The Government does have a compelling interest in protecting the "physical and psychological well-being of minors," including protecting them from "literature that is not obscene by adult standards." But the means used here—a total legislative ban—are not narrowly tailored to serve that purpose. "The FCC, after lengthy proceedings, determined that its credit card, access code, and scrambling rules were a satisfactory solution to the problem of keeping indecent dial-a-porn messages out of the reach of minors." The

Court found unpersuasive and not supported by the evidence the Government's argument that an outright ban was appropriate because some enterprising youngsters could evade the rules.

The Court carefully distinguished and limited the *Pacifica* case: that was "an emphatically narrow holding;" it did not involve a total ban, for the FCC sought to channel the indecent material to a time of day when children were thought to be less likely to listen; *Pacifica* also relied on the "unique" attributes of broadcasting, not involved in this case; and in the present case there is no "captive audience" or unwilling listener problem as there was in *Pacifica*.

Brennan, J., joined by Marshall & Stevens, JJ., concurred in part and dissented in part, stating: "I have long been convinced that the exaction of criminal penalties for the distribution of obscene materials to consenting adults is constitutionally intolerable."

46. For an analysis of obscenity, see § 20.56–20.61, infra.

47. For an analysis of the "fighting words" doctrine, see § 20.37–20.40, infra.

48. The seven words "that you can't say" were: "shit, piss, fuck, cunt, cocksucker, motherfucker, and tits." Later Carlin added "three more words ... you could never say on television, and they were fart, turd and twat...." 438 U.S. at 751, 755, 98 S.Ct. at 3041, 3043 (appendix).

The entire monologue is reprinted in an appendix to the opinion.

The FCC, after having received only one complaint, from a man who had heard the broadcast with his son on the car radio, issued a "Declaratory Order" against Pacifica. While the FCC did not impose formal sanctions it did add the complaint to the station's license file and noted that if subsequent complaints were received the FCC would then decide whether to utilize any of the sanctions it has, ranging from issuing a cease and desist order or imposing a fine, to revoking the station's license.

First, the justices considered the statutory authority of the FCC to take such actions. One statutory provision forbids the FCC from engaging in "censorship;" [49] another prohibits "obscene, indecent, or profane" broadcasts.[50] Five members of the Court held that the censorship language only prohibits the Commission from engaging in prior censorship. While the Commission cannot excise material in advance, it can review the content of completed broadcasts in fulfilling its regulatory duties.[51] Second, the majority held that the second statutory provision prohibits not only constitutionally "obscene" language but also "indecent" language, defined as "nonconformance with accepted standards of morality." [52]

Next the Court had to decide if the statute as construed by the majority was constitutional. Five members agreed that broadcasting receives "the most limited" free speech protections of all forms of communication because it is "a uniquely pervasive presence in the lives of all Americans" and "is uniquely accessible to children, even those too young to read." [53] But they could not agree any further on the constitutional rationale for their holding.

In one opinion Justice Stevens, joined by Chief Justice Burger and Justice Rehnquist, thought that "indecency is largely a function of context ..." and that "a broadcast of patently offensive words dealing with sex and excretion may be regulated because of its content." [54]

Justice Powell, joined by Justice Blackmun, wrote a separate opinion. They specifically rejected Justice Stevens' view that the Court is

49. 47 U.S.C.A. § 326.

50. 18 U.S.C.A. § 1464.

51. 438 U.S. at 735, 98 S.Ct. at 3033. This five person majority also said: "Respect for that [congressional] intent requires that the censorship language be read as inapplicable to the prohibition on broadcasting obscene, indecent, or profane language." 438 U.S. at 738, 98 S.Ct. at 3034. This language, however, would appear to allow even prior censorship of indecent language. Since the rationale of the opinion does not support this broad language, the majority should not be considered to have embraced it.

52. 438 U.S. at 439–40, 98 S.Ct. at 3035 (footnote omitted).

53. 438 U.S. at 749, 98 S.Ct. at 3040.

54. 438 U.S. at 743, 98 S.Ct. at 3037. (Separate Opinion of Stevens, J., joined by Burger, C.J., and Rehnquist, J.). Another important case in which Justice Stevens has propounded his viewpoint (also not accepted by a majority of the Court) that there can be valid regulations on speech based on the *content* of the communication in his separate opinion in Young v. American Mini Theatres, Inc., 427 U.S. 50, 52, 96 S.Ct. 2440, 2443–44, 49 L.Ed.2d 310 (1976), rehearing denied 429 U.S. 873, 97 S.Ct. 191, 50 L.Ed.2d 155 (1976).

"free generally to decide on the basis of its content which speech protected by the First Amendment is most valuable.... The result turns instead on the unique characteristics of the broadcast media, combined with society's right to protect its children from speech generally agreed to be inappropriate for their years, and with the interest of unwilling adults in not being assaulted by such offensive speech in their homes." [55]

Justices Stewart and White dissented only on statutory grounds and did not read the constitutional issues.[56] Justice Brennan, joined by Justice Marshall, did reach the constitutional issues and strongly dissented.

Brennan and Marshall argued that when an individual turns to a radio station or any transmission broadcast to the public at large, there is no fundamental privacy interest implicated. The listener has, by tuning in, decided to take part in an on-going public discussion. Neither, they believed, is the FCC regulation justified by the need to protect children. While parents have the right to make certain decisions for their children, it is the parents and not the Government who are to make these decisions: "As surprising as it may be to individual members of the Court, some parents may actually find Mr. Carlin's unabashed attitude towards the seven 'dirty words' healthy, and deem it desirable to expose their children to the manner in which Mr. Carlin defuses the taboo surrounding the words." [57] Moreover, the Government, in its efforts to protect children, was denying to adults the right to listen to language that was not constitutionally obscene even as to children. Justice Brennan accused the majority of attempting "to unstitch the warp and woof of First Amendment law...."; and, he added, the majority's "fragile sensibilities" were the result of "an acute ethnocentric myopia." [58]

---

55. 438 U.S. at 761–62, 98 S.Ct. at 3051 (Powell, J., joined by Blackmun, J., concurring).

56. The four in dissent argued that "indecent" means no more than "obscene" in the constitutional sense. A related federal statute, the dissent noted, forbade the mailing of every "obscene, ... indecent, ... or vile article," and the Court had previously construed that language as only referring to obscenity in the constitutional sense. Since Carlin's monologue was conceded to be not obscene, the dissent argued that the FCC had no statutory grounds to regulate it. See 438 U.S. at 779–80, 98 S.Ct. at 3056 (Stewart, J., dissenting, joined by Brennan, White, & Marshall, JJ.).

57. 438 U.S. at 770, 98 S.Ct. at 3051.

58. 438 U.S. at 775, 98 S.Ct. at 3054. Justice Brennan feared that the majority's

various rationales could justify banning from FCC regulated media the Nixon tapes and important literary works, including the Bible, all of which uses one or more of the indecent words of the Carlin monologue. See 438 U.S. at 770–71 & n. 5, 98 S.Ct. at 3051–52 & n. 5 (footnote 5 of Justice Brennan's dissent quotes several passages from the Bible using several of Carlin's indecent words).

The majority thought such examples to be distinguishable: "Even a prime time recitation of Chaucer's Miller's Tale would not be likely to command the attention of many children who are both old enough to understand and young enough to be adversely affected by passages such as, 'And prively he caughte hir by the queynte.' G. Chaucer, The Miller's Tale, 1. 3276 (c. 1386)." 438 U.S. at 750 n. 29, 98 S.Ct. at 3041 n. 29.

The five member majority emphasized that their decision was very narrow, not involving a two-way radio conversation, an Elizabethan comedy, a closed-circuit transmission, or an occasional expletive. The time of day and the content of the program in which the language is used may also be relevant, as well as the type and amount of punishment imposed.[59] But the plurality did not offer a principled way to distinguish these other instances. The three member plurality's willingness to allow government regulation of content, so long as the regulation appears to these justices to promote reasonable ends—in this case, the end of prohibiting "nonconformance" with accepted standards of morality—is a disquieting and a significant departure from traditional first amendment theory, which normally subjects any type of content regulation to very careful and principled judicial review.[60]

In other types of speech, not involving broadcasting, the Court has been much more protective of the first amendment. Thus, the Supreme Court has allowed prohibition of speech that incites illegal conduct within the meaning of *Brandenburg v. Ohio*[61] because when a speaker uses speech to cause unthinking, immediate lawless action and is likely to produce such action, one cannot rely on more speech in the marketplace of ideas to correct the errors of the original speech, and the state has significant interests in (and no other means of preventing) the resulting lawless conduct.[62]

When the Court allowed the prohibition of obscenity, it found, inter alia, that such speech when taken as a whole, lacked any serious literary, artistic, political, or scientific value.[63] It did not judge some types of obscene speech to be more worthy of protection than other types, nor find that obscenity in an Elizabethan comedy is permissible but obscenity in a modern comedy is not. Rather it attempted to fashion a principled means of distinguishing a certain type of speech. But Justice Stevens, by his own admission, would prohibit the use of a word in the Carlin monologue though he would allow the same word to

---

59. 438 U.S. at 750, 98 S.Ct. at 3041.

60. In April of 1987 the F.C.C. announced that it would no longer rely on the "seven dirty words" standard to determine whether programming was "indecent." In November of 1987, the F.C.C. announced that radio and television stations could broadcast "indecent" (but non-obscene) material between midnight and 6 a.m., a time when children are unlikely to be in the listening or viewing audience. Though the definition of what is "indecent" is not clear, to say the least, the F.C.C., in effect, sought to channel "indecent" speech by carving out a safe harbor for when broadcasters can air "adult" entertainment. Davis, FCC Limits Shows of Raunchy Nature to After Midnight, Wall St. Jrl., Nov. 25, 1987, at 36, col. 4–6.

61. 395 U.S. 444, 89 S.Ct. 1827, 23 L.Ed.2d 430 (1969) (per curiam).

62. Brandenburg v. Ohio, 395 U.S. 444, 89 S.Ct. 1827, 23 L.Ed.2d 430 (1969) (per curiam). See § 20.15, supra.

63. Note also that the zoning of adult movies allowed in Young v. American Mini Theatres, Inc., 427 U.S. 50, 96 S.Ct. 2440, 49 L.Ed.2d 310 (1976), involved valid goals other than the regulation of speech, 427 U.S. at 71 n. 34, 96 S.Ct. at 2453 n. 34 (Stevens, J.) & 427 U.S. at 80, 96 S.Ct. at 2457 (Powell, J.). See also 438 U.S. at 774, 98 S.Ct. at 3053 (Brennan, J., dissenting).

be used in a reading of Chaucer's Miller's Tale,[64] or an Elizabethan comedy,[65] apparently because he feels the latter types of speech are more valuable than the Carlin satire. Similarly, he would allow the same words to be used if he thought the monologue to have political content.[66] Stevens is engaging in result-oriented jurisprudence by using a very personal, subjective evaluation of the content of speech.

The four member dissent, as well as Justices Powell and Blackmun in their concurring opinion, specifically disavowed the theory that the degree of protection of speech varies with the ad hoc view of five members of the Court as to its social value, but the latter two justices did agree that the FCC action was constitutional. With this decision, then, one is left in doubt as to the strictness with which the Court will review content regulation—at least as regards the electronic media—in the future.

It appears that the permissibility of this type of regulation may depend on the personal notions of at least five justices concerning the worth of the regulated speech. As Justice Stevens concluded in a portion of his opinion joined by four justices:

> We simply hold that when the Commission finds that a pig has entered the parlor [instead of the barnyard], the exercise of its regulatory power does not depend on proof that the pig is obscene.[67]

This "pig in the parlor" test will not be too helpful to lower courts.

Individual Tort Claims Against the Media. In any event, although a fragmented Court in *FCC v. Pacifica* upheld the FCC's declaratory order aginst Pacifica Foundation, that case does not imply that the individual who filed a complaint with the FCC would have any tort claim against the radio station that aired the George Carlin monologue. Individual tort claims against the media because of what they broadcast should be governed by the strict standard of *Brandenburg v. Ohio,*[68] discussed above.[69]

---

64. See 438 U.S. at 775, 98 S.Ct. at 3054.

65. See 438 U.S. at 770–71 & n. 5, 98 S.Ct. at 3051–52 & n. 5.

66. 438 U.S. at 746, 98 S.Ct. at 3038–39.

67. 438 U.S. at 750–51, 98 S.Ct. at 3041.

68. 395 U.S. 444, 89 S.Ct. 1827, 23 L.Ed.2d 430 (1969) (per curiam).

69. See generally, § 20.15.

In National Broadcasting Co., Inc. v. Niemi, 434 U.S. 1354, 98 S.Ct. 705, 54 L.Ed.2d 742 (1978) (Rehnquist, Circuit Justice), certiorari denied 435 U.S. 1000, 98 S.Ct. 1657, 56 L.Ed.2d 91 (1978), appeal after remand 126 Cal.App.3d 488, 178 Cal. Rptr. 888 (1981), the respondent sought damages from a television network and publisher for injuries allegedly inflicted upon her by persons acting under the stimulus of observing a scene of brutality broadcast in a television drama. The petitioners sought a stay of the state court order remanding for a trial. While Circuit Justice Rehnquist denied the stay for procedural reasons, he noted that the trial judge had rendered judgment for petitioners because he found that the film "did not advocate or encourage violent and depraved acts and thus did not constitute an incitement." 434 U.S. at 1356, 98 S.Ct. at 706. The *Brandenburg* test should be applicable to determine the free speech defense to plaintiff's tort claim.

Censorship and Bans on Editorials by Public Broadcast Stations. The concept of frequency scarcity and the special impact of the electronic media on listeners or viewers have provided the basis for judicial approval of government regulation of electronic media beyond the permissible scope of regulatory control of nonbroadcast media. However, the Supreme Court must not adopt the position of total deference to the Congress or its executive agencies in the regulation of the electronic media lest it allow those branches of government to impair first amendment values.

In *Federal Communications Commission v. League of Women Voters* [70] the Court, by a five to four vote, invalidated a section of the Public Broadcasting Act that forbade any nonprofit educational broadcasting station which receives a grant from the Corporation for Public Broadcasting to engage in editorializing or endorsing candidates for political office. Writing for the majority, Justice Brennan reviewed the Court's earlier decisions regarding electronic media regulation and concluded that restrictions on the electronic media "have been upheld only when we were satisfied that the restriction is narrowly tailored to further a substantial governmental interest, such as ensuring adequate and balanced coverage of public issues." [71] This standard had been developed in earlier cases, according to the majority, on the basis of several "fundamental principles:" that Congress, acting pursuant to its commerce clause power, has the right to regulate the use of this scarce national resource; that in the exercise of this power Congress could assure that the public received a balanced presentation of information; and that the first amendment interest of listeners and broadcasters in broadcast stations performing independent communicative activity must shape Congress' exercise of its regulatory powers. [72]

The dissenting justices in *League of Women Voters* pointed out that the statute at issue appeared to further first amendment values in that the restriction on editorializing was designed to achieve the twin goals of (1) avoiding a station's tailoring of editorials or endorsements to gain favor with the governmental entities which funded them, and (2) reducing the government's role in putting forth or funding messages in

---

70. 468 U.S. 364, 104 S.Ct. 3106, 82 L.Ed.2d 278 (1984).

See generally, Spitzer, Controlling the Content of Print and Broadcast, 58 So.Calif.L.Rev. 1349 (1985); Note, FFC v. League of Women Voters: Conditions on Federal Funding that Inhibit Speech, 71 Cornell L.Rev. 477 (1986); Note, Broadcasters' First Amendment Rights: A New Approach?, 39 Vanderbilt L.Rev. 323 (1986).

71. 468 U.S. at 380, 104 S.Ct. at 3118. The Court found that even the decision in FCC v. Pacifica Foundation, 438 U.S. 726,

98 S.Ct. 3026, 57 L.Ed.2d 1073 (1978), rehearing denied 439 U.S. 883, 99 S.Ct. 227, 58 L.Ed.2d 198 (1978), discussed above, was consistent with this standard in that the reduction of the risks of unwilling listeners being offended by indecent language and the access to that material by children were of sufficient importance to justify the regulation. 468 U.S. at 380 n. 13, 104 S.Ct. at 3117 n. 13.

72. 468 U.S. at 377, 104 S.Ct. at 3116.

the political marketplace.[73] The majority, however, found the restriction to be invalid because it suppressed a form of speech "that lies at the heart of first amendment protection;" the Restriction banned speech related to self-governance issues solely because of the content of the suppressed speech. Even though the statute banned all editorials or endorsements, rather than merely those that objected to the official views of the government or the views held by incumbent office holders, this statute was still censorial because it prohibited discussion of an entire topic and thereby shaped and reduced the agenda for public debate.[74]

The statute at issue in *League of Women Voters* was invalid under the test previously set forth by Justice Brennan because it was not narrowly tailored to further the substantial interest in presenting balanced information to the public. The interest in providing balanced coverage could be advanced by other less restrictive means such as the requirement that opposing viewpoints be broadcast free of charge. Indeed, the majority found that the structure of the system for financing public broadcasting already operated to insulate local stations from governmental interference. The majority did agree with the dissenters that Congress could avoid funding that portion of a noncommercial educational broadcasting station's budget which was used for editorials or candidate endorsements. Although Congress could refuse to fund speech activities of this type, it could not punish a station that engaged in editorializing by terminating all federal funding for the station.[75]

Cable Television. In *City of Los Angeles v. Preferred Communications, Inc.*[76] the Court rejected a city's claim that its refusal to grant a franchise to a cable television company raised no First Amendment concerns. Though the applicant had not participated in an auction for a single franchise, the city did not dispute that there was excess physical capacity to allow more than one cable television. The city did claim that multiple cable systems would cause visual blight, traffic delays and traffic hazards. The cable operator responded that the

---

73. FCC v. League of Women Voters, 468 U.S. 364, 402, 104 S.Ct. 3106, 3129, 82 L.Ed.2d 278, 306 (1984) (Rehnquist, J., dissenting, joined by Burger, C.J., and White, J.); 468 U.S. at 408, 104 S.Ct. at 3132, 82 L.Ed.2d at 310 (opinion of White, J.); 468 U.S. at 410, 104 S.Ct. at 3133, 82 L.Ed.2d at 310 (Stevens, J., dissenting).

74. 468 U.S. at 384, 104 S.Ct. at 3120, 82 L.Ed.2d at 294. The Court here referred to its opinion in Consolidated Edison Co. v. Public Service Commission, 447 U.S. 530, 100 S.Ct. 2326, 65 L.Ed.2d 319 (1980), prohibiting Public Service Commission from banning all advertising for certain

products or power uses. See §§ 20.26–20.31, infra.

75. 468 U.S. at 398, 104 S.Ct. at 3127, 82 L.Ed.2d at 303.

76. 476 U.S. 488, 106 S.Ct. 2034, 90 L.Ed.2d 480 (1986).

Devins, Affirmative Action After Reagan, 68 Texas L.Rev. 353 (1989); Devins, Metro Broadcasting, Inc. v. FCC: Requiem for a Heavyweight, 69 Texas L.Rev. 125 (1990); Sedler, The Constitution, Racial Preference, and the Supreme Court's Institutional Ambivalence: Reflections on Metro Broadcasting, 36 Wayne L.Rev. 1187 (1990).

city's concerns, even if valid, could easily be satisfied without limiting free speech rights to a single speaker.

The Court readily concluded that the cable operator's claims raised valid First Amendment issues that could not be resolved solely on the basis of the complaint, so it remanded for further pleadings and a resolution of the factual disputes. Because the cable operator's speech (its communication of messages) and its conduct (its use of telephone poles, and so forth) are joined together in a single course of action, the trial court on remand must balance the First Amendment values against competing societal interests, after a full development of the disputed issues. Beyond that, *Preferred Communications* offered no hint of the ultimate resolution of the controversy except to emphasize that the city ordinance will not be saved merely because it is rational. The city's burden, given the First Amendment, is certainly higher than that.

Affirmative Action, and FCC License Preferences for Women and Minority Groups. In order to broadcast on the radio or television airwaves, the broadcaster must first secure a license, either by purchasing it from an existing license holder or receiving it directly from the Federal Communications Commission. Periodically these licenses are subject to renewal.[77] In recent years, the FCC, when it grants or transfers a broadcast license, considers minority and female ownership of the license as a preference, in order to increase diversity of ownership of the airwaves, which is assumed to (and intended to) lead to greater diversity in programming content. The FCC, in creating its minority and female preference policy, reacted to several decisions in the District of Columbia Circuit as well as to a Joint Resolution of Congress directing the FCC to use racial and gender preferences.[78] In *Metro Broadcasting, Inc. v. Federal Communications Commission,*[79] a five to four majority of the Court held that certain minority preference policies did not violate the equal protection component of the fifth amendment's due process clause.

---

77. See generally, Radio Formats by Administrative Choice, 47 U.Chi.L.Rev. 647 (1980).

78. See, TV 9, Inc. v. FCC, 495 F.2d 929 (D.C.Cir.1973) (minority preferences), cert. denied 419 U.S. 986, 95 S.Ct. 245, 42 L.Ed.2d 194 (1974); West Michigan Broadcasting Co. v. FCC, 735 F.2d 601 (D.C.Cir. 1984) (minority preference upheld), cert. denied 470 U.S. 1027, 105 S.Ct. 1392, 84 L.Ed.2d 782 (1985); Steele v. FCC, 770 F.2d

1192 (D.C.Cir.1985) (female preferences rejected).

See generally, Leiby, The Female Merit Policy in Steele v. FCC: "A Whim Leading to a Better World?", 37 Am.U.L.Rev. 379 (1988).

79. 497 U.S. ___, 110 S.Ct. 2997, 111 L.Ed.2d 445 (1990), rehearing denied ___ U.S. ___, 111 S.Ct. 15, 111 L.Ed.2d 829 (1990).

(b) The Fairness Doctrine and the Regulation of Traditional Print Media

Traditional media, particularly newspapers, have come under pressure from those advocating a first amendment right of access to make their views on public issues known, similar to the restrictions placed on the electronic media.[80] In general, some commentators have argued that the right of free speech guaranteed by the Constitution is meaningless if the speakers are not also given access to the media necessary to present these views to the general public [81] because of the monopolistic nature of modern newspapers. Others are concerned that any government regulation of access to the print media is fraught with danger. Once the camel gets its nose under the tent, the rest of the camel is not far behind.

No Right of Access to Newspapers. The Supreme Court has strongly rejected the notion that a government guaranteed right of access or a fairness doctrine can apply to the press. In *Miami Herald Publishing Co. v. Tornillo,*[82] a unanimous Court struck down, as violative of the first amendment, a Florida statute that required newspapers to give free reply space to political candidates whom they had attacked in their columns. The Court based its holding on the premise that a statute which told a newspaper what it must print in fact was exacting a penalty on the basis of the content of the newspaper; this, the Court felt, was unconstitutional censorship.[83]

Although not subject to the same finite limitations of the broadcast media which were deemed so important in the electronic media cases [84]

80. Cf. Red Lion Broadcasting Co. v. FCC, 395 U.S. 367, 89 S.Ct. 1794, 23 L.Ed.2d 371 (1969) (fairness doctrine upheld); CBS, Inc. v. Democratic National Committee, 412 U.S. 94, 93 S.Ct. 2080, 36 L.Ed.2d 772 (1973) (no right of access to broadcast media is constitutionally required for groups seeking to place editorial advertisements).

81. E.g., Barron, Access to the Press—A New First Amendment Right, 80 Harv. L.Rev. 1641 (1967); Cf. T. Emerson, The System of Freedom of Expression 671 (1970).

82. 418 U.S. 241, 94 S.Ct. 2831, 41 L.Ed.2d 730 (1974), on remand 303 So.2d 21 (Fla.1974).

See also, Pacific Gas & Electric Co. v. Public Utilities Commission, 475 U.S. 1, 106 S.Ct. 903, 89 L.Ed.2d 1 (1986) (order of public utility requiring utility to insert third-party newsletters in billing envelopes violated free speech rights of the utility), rehearing denied 475 U.S. 1133, 106 S.Ct. 1667, 90 L.Ed.2d 208 (1986).

For a thoughtful discussion and analysis of *Tornillo,* see, Powe, Tornillo, 1987 Supreme Ct.Rev. 345.

See generally, Bollinger, Freedom of the Press and Public Access: Toward a Theory of Partial Regulation of the Mass Media, 75 Mich.L.Rev. 1 (1976); Lewis, A Preferred Position for Journalism, 7 Hofstra L.Rev. 595 (1979); Nimmer, Is Freedom of the Press a Redundancy?—What Does It Add to Freedom of Speech, 26 Hast.L.J. (1975); Canby, The First Amendment and the State as Editor, 52 Tex.L.Rev. 1123 (1974). Spitzer, Controlling the Content of Print and Broadcast, 58 So.Calif.L.Rev. 1349 (1985).

83. In discussing precedent, the Court noted that "[T]he clear implication has been that any such a compulsion to publish that which 'reason' tells them [newspaper publishers] should not be published is unconstitutional." And it went on to say "The Florida statute exacts a penalty on the basis of the content of a newspaper." 418 U.S. at 256, 94 S.Ct. at 2839.

84. See, e.g., National Broadcasting Co. v. United States, 319 U.S. 190, 63 S.Ct. 997, 87 L.Ed. 1344 (1943); Red Lion Broadcasting Co. v. FCC, 395 U.S. 367, 89 S.Ct. 1794, 23 L.Ed.2d 371 (1969); Columbia Broadcasting System v. Democratic National

the opinion of the Court recognizes that newspapers are also subject to space limitations which must be considered in balancing the public interest in access against the rights of the publishers.[85]   But such physical limitations were not seen to be the primary concern in denying reply space in newspapers, an issue which in fact was only briefly discussed.[86]   Even if a compulsory law did not create economic problems or cause the newspaper to have to forego printing something else to give space to a reply, the reply law's great evil was that it intruded on the rights and functions of the newspaper and its editors and reporters:

> It has yet to be demonstrated how governmental regulation of this crucial process can be exercised consistent with First Amendment guarantees of a free press as they have evolved to this time.[87]

Miami Herald firmly established that the right of newspaper editors to choose what they wish to print or not to print cannot be abridged to allow the public access to the newspaper media.   The "virtually insurmountable barrier"[88] which freedom of the press erects between governmental regulation and the print media stands firm.

An important distinction between the fairness doctrine as applied to electronic media and the fairness doctrine which cannot be applied to the print media is that the former enjoys a legal monopoly, which justifies FCC regulations requiring "fairness."[89]   There is no legal monopoly of newspapers.   While some local towns may be served by only one paper, yet other print media—nationwide newspapers such as the New York Times, weekly newsmagazines, or so-called underground newspapers—are not legally barred from these same "channels."   If someone is not satisfied that the local newspaper is printing his views he may publish his pamphlets, posters, or leaflets—all without securing a Government license and opening up his channels of communication to others of opposing views.   Moreover if a newspaper is sufficiently

Committee, 412 U.S. 94, 93 S.Ct. 2080, 36 L.Ed.2d 772 (1973).

85.   "It is correct, as appellee contends, that a newspaper is not subject to the finite technological limitations of time that confront a broadcaster but it is not correct to say, that, as an economic reality, a newspaper can proceed to infinite expansion of column space to accommodate the replies that a government agency determines or a statute commands the readers should have available."   418 U.S. at 256–57, 94 S.Ct. at 2839.   (Footnote omitted).

86.   418 U.S. at 256–57, 94 S.Ct. at 2838–39.

87.   418 U.S. at 258, 94 S.Ct. at 2840.

Accord, 2 Z. Chafee, Government and Mass Communications 709–10 (1947) ("If

officials can tell newspapers what to put into their editorial pages, ... [the next] step [is] to tell them what to leave out.").

88.   418 U.S. at 259, 94 S.Ct. at 2840 (White, J., concurring opinion).   However, the right of the press to make the editorial judgment to print or not print does not protect the press from appropriate libel actions and, in such libel actions, the press has no immunity from a libel plaintiff inquiring about the editorial process.   Herbert v. Lando, 441 U.S. 153, 166–69, 99 S.Ct. 1635, 1644–45, 60 L.Ed.2d 115 (1979).

89.   Red Lion Broadcasting Co. v. FCC, 395 U.S. 367, 89 S.Ct. 1794, 23 L.Ed.2d 371 (1969).

insensitive to the needs of its readers, the economic system will develop competitors who are.[90]

Finally, if we assume that the problem of lack of access is as serious as those arguing for government regulation of the print media assert, the solution of access overestimates its effectiveness:

> To say that the media have great decision-making powers without defined legal responsibilities or any formal duties of public accountability is both to overestimate their power and to put forth a meaningless formula for reform. How shall we make the *New York Times* "accountable" for its anti-Vietnam policy? Require it to print letters to the editor in support of the war? If the situation is as grave as stated, the remedy is fantastically inadequate. But the situation is not that grave. The *New York Times,* the *Chicago Tribune,* NBC, ABC, and CBS play a role in policy formation, but clearly they were not alone responsible, for example, for Johnson's decision not to run for reelection, Nixon's refusal to withdraw the troops from Vietnam, the rejection of the two billion dollar New York bond issue, the defeat of Carswell and Haynsworth, or the Supreme Court's segregation, reappointment and prayer decisions. The implication that the people of this country—except the proponents of the theory—are mere unthinking automatons manipulated by the media, without interests, conflicts, or prejudices is an assumption which I find quite maddening. The development of constitutional doctrine should not be based on such hysterical overestimation of media power and underestimation of the good sense of the American public.[91]

No Right of Equal Access to City–Owned Billboards. In the same term with *Miami Herald* the Court considered another access case, this time not involving the private press but rather the use of billboard space on a city-owned public transportation system. In *Lehman v. Shaker Heights,*[92] a divided Court held, five to four,[93] that a city which operates a public rapid transit system does not violate the first or fourteenth amendments by selling commercial advertising space for cigarette companies, banks, liquor companies, churches, and public service groups on its vehicles while refusing to accept any political advertising on behalf of candidates for public office or public issue

---

90. Cf. R. Posner, Economic Analysis of Law § 22.3 at 314 (1972).

91. Jaffe, The Editorial Responsibility of the Broadcaster: Reflections on Fairness and Access, 85 Harv.L.Rev. 768, 786–87 (1972). See also, Abrams, Book Review, 86 Yale L.J. 361, 363–64 (1976). But see, B. Schmidt, Freedom of the Press vs. Public Access 13, 227–29 (1976).

92. 418 U.S. 298, 94 S.Ct. 2714, 41 L.Ed.2d 770 (1974).

93. Justice Blackmun's opinion was joined in by three other Justices; Justice Douglas, the fifth vote, wrote his own concurrence, relying heavily on the idea that the audience of a bus is captive. 418 U.S. at 305–08, 94 S.Ct. at 2718–20.

advertising.[94]

The essential problem in *Lehman* was not a pure right to access, but rather a right of equal access. Plaintiffs argued that by making the advertising space available for some uses, the city had created a public forum and could not now censor the content of speech in that forum by banning political advertisements. The majority of the Court firmly rejected the contention that card space on a city transit system is to be deemed a public forum for a variety of reasons, to minimize chances of abuse, the appearance of favoritism, and the risk of imposing upon a captive audience.[95]

Justice Douglas' concurring opinion emphasized the distinctions between this claimed forum and the situations which had previously given rise to the concept of a "public forum."

> But a streetcar or bus is plainly not a park or sidewalk or other meeting place for discussion, any more than is a highway. It is only a way to get to work or back home. The fact that it is owned and operated by the city does not without more make it a forum.... And if we are to turn a bus or streetcar into either a newspaper or a park, we take great liberties with people who because of necessity become commuters and at the same time captive viewers or listeners.[96]

The Court noted that the city, like a newspaper or the electronic media, could exercise its discretion concerning the types of advertising it accepted,[97] although because of the state action involved, policies

94. 418 U.S. at 300–01, 94 S.Ct. at 2716. See also, United States Postal Service v. Council of Greenburgh Civic Associations, 453 U.S. 114, 101 S.Ct. 2676, 69 L.Ed.2d 517 (1981) (18 U.S.C.A. § 1725, prohibiting the deposit of unstamped, "mailable matter" in a letter box approved by the U.S. Postal Service is constitutional; mail boxes are not public forums, and section 1725 does not regulate on the basis of content).

95. 418 U.S. at 304, 94 S.Ct. at 2717–18. "These are reasonable legislative objectives advanced by the city in a proprietary capacity. In these circumstances, there is no First or Fourteenth Amendment violation." 418 U.S. at 304, 94 S.Ct. at 2718.

Contrast Metromedia, Inc. v. San Diego, 453 U.S. 490, 101 S.Ct. 2882, 69 L.Ed.2d 800 (1981), on remand 32 Cal.3d 180, 185 Cal.Rptr. 260, 649 P.2d 902 (1982). There a fragmented Court invalidated laws restricting the display of billboards. The zoning laws, inter alia, drew a distinction between on-site commercial advertising (allowed) and on-site noncommercial advertis-

ing (not allowed). The Court found this distinction unconstitutional. In this case, however, the city could not advance adequate justification for the distinction; moreover it was not acting in a proprietary capacity.

96. 418 U.S. at 306–07, 94 S.Ct. at 2718–19 (concurring opinion). See also 418 U.S. at 304, 94 S.Ct. at 2717–18 (Blackmun, J.) Cf., Hague v. CIO, 307 U.S. 496, 515–16, 59 S.Ct. 954, 964, 83 L.Ed. 1423 (1939), where Justice Roberts argued parks and streets are public forums whose use "may be regulated in the interest of all ... but it must not, in the guise of regulation, be abridged or denied". While a majority of the Court at this time did not join in this view, the Court has now adopted it. E.g., Schneider v. New Jersey, 308 U.S. 147, 163, 60 S.Ct. 146, 151–52, 84 L.Ed. 155 (1939); Kunz v. New York, 340 U.S. 290, 293, 71 S.Ct. 312, 314–15, 95 L.Ed. 280 (1951).

97. 418 U.S. at 303, 94 S.Ct. at 2717. Cf. Public Utilities Com'n v. Pollak, 343 U.S. 451, 72 S.Ct. 813, 96 L.Ed. 1068 (1952).

governing access by advertisers must not be "arbitrary, capricious, or invidious." [98]

The four dissenters [99] were seemingly not as concerned with the rights of the commuter because they felt that a public forum had been created:

> [T]he city created a forum for the dissemination of information and expression of ideas when it accepted and displayed commercial and public service advertisements on its rapid transit vehicles.[100]

Having once created a public forum, the dissent argued, the city could not discriminate on the basis of message content between types of advertising,[101] and the fact that entire classes of advertising were banned, rather than particular ads, did not make the city's choice any less censorship.[102]

Although later cases have extended the public forum concept to go beyond parks and streets, to include a public auditorium,[103] the Court in *Lehman* refused to expand the doctrine to include public transportation facilities. "If a bus is a forum it is more akin to a newspaper than to a park," and newspapers cannot be forced to include items "which outsiders may desire but which the owner abhors." [104]

No Right of Access to Utility Company's Billing Envelopes. In *Pacific Gas & Electric Co. v. Public Utilities Commission*,[105] a fragmented Court, with no majority opinion, held that the California Public Utilities Commission may not require a privately owned utility company to include, in its billing envelopes, the speech of a third party (in this case, a private group called TURN, "Toward Utility Rate Normalization") with which the utility disagreed.[106] Justice Powell's

---

98. 418 U.S. at 303, 94 S.Ct. at 2717.

99. Brennan, J., filed a lengthy dissenting opinion, in which Stewart, Marshall, and Powell, JJ., joined. 418 U.S. at 308–22, 94 S.Ct. at 2719–26.

100. 418 U.S. at 310, 94 S.Ct. at 2721 (Brennan, J., dissenting opinion).

101. 418 U.S. at 310, 94 S.Ct. at 2721 (Brennan, J., dissenting opinion).

102. 418 U.S. at 316, 94 S.Ct. at 2724 (Brennan, J., dissenting opinion).

103. See, e.g., Southeastern Promotions, Ltd. v. Conrad, 420 U.S. 546, 95 S.Ct. 1239, 43 L.Ed.2d 448 (1975). Here the Court evidenced willingness to apply public forum analysis whenever use of a public facility is denied those who wish to exercise their free speech rights; held: a municipal auditorium is a public forum.

See generally, § 20.47.

See also, Note, Constitutional Law—Southeastern Promotions, Ltd. v. Conrad:

A Contemporary Concept of the Public Forum, 54 N. Carolina L.Rev. 439 (1976).

104. Lehman v. Shaker Heights, 418 U.S. 298, 306, 94 S.Ct. 2714, 2719, 41 L.Ed.2d 770 (1974) (Douglas, J., concurring); Miami Herald Publishing Co. v. Tornillo, 418 U.S. 241, 94 S.Ct. 2831, 41 L.Ed.2d 730 (1974), on remand 303 So.2d 21 (Fla.1974).

105. 475 U.S. 1, 106 S.Ct. 903, 89 L.Ed.2d 1 (1986), rehearing denied 475 U.S. 1133, 106 S.Ct. 1667, 90 L.Ed.2d 208 (1986).

106. Cf. Wooley v. Maynard, 430 U.S. 705, 97 S.Ct. 1428, 51 L.Ed.2d 752 (1977). (New Hampshire may not require persons to display slogan on their license plates and thus use their private property as a mobile billboard for the state). In *Pacific Gas & Electric* the plurality said of *Wooley:* "The 'private property' that was used to spread the unwelcome message was the automobile, not the license plates." 475 U.S. at 17, 106 S.Ct. at 912.

plurality opinion, joined by Chief Justice Burger, and Justices Brennan and O'Connor, concluded that the utility's newsletter is "no different from a small newspaper." Its stories ranged from energy-savings tips to wildlife conservation to billings to recipes. The Utility Commission may not force the utility to grant TURN access to the utility's newsletter. Because the Utility Commission concluded that the public would benefit "more from exposure to a variety of views," it had concluded that TURN should be allowed to use the "extra space" in the billing envelope four times a year. The "extra space" was defined as the space remaining in the billing envelope after the monthly bill and required legal notices up to the total envelope weight so as not to result in any additional postage. The Commission had ruled that the ratepayers owned this extra space, but "expressly declined to hold that under California law appellant's customers own the entire billing envelopes and everything contained therein." The "Commission's access order thus clearly requires appellant to use *its* property as a vehicle for spreading a message with which it disagrees." [107]

§ 20.19 A Right of Access by the Press—Speech in a Restricted Environment

Speech and Press Clauses Compared. Does the press generally, or the institutional press in particular, have any preferred rights under the first amendment? Does the press clause guarantee the press any rights of access which is different from the rights which any individual might have under the free speech clause? Thus far, when the Court has guaranteed a right of access—as the right of access to a criminal trial, the right of a public trial [1]—this right has been granted to all; it

---

107. 475 U.S. at 17, 106 S.Ct. at 912.

In PruneYard Shopping Center v. Robins, 447 U.S. 74, 100 S.Ct. 2035, 64 L.Ed.2d 741 (1980) the Court upheld a provision of the state constitution preventing a shopping center owner from excluding pamphleteers from the area in the shopping center open to the public at large. In *PruneYard,* though, the right of access was not content-based, and granting such access would not affect the shopping center owner's own right to speak. See 475 U.S. at 12, 106 S.Ct. at 910. The shopping center in *PruneYard* was not like a newspaper as the utility's newsletter in *Pacific Gas & Electric* was.

§ 20.19

1. E.g., Richmond Newspapers, Inc. v. Virginia, 448 U.S. 555, 100 S.Ct. 2814, 65 L.Ed.2d 973 (1980).

See also, F. Siebert, T. Peterson, & W. Schramm, Four Theories of the Press (1963); Note, Resolving the Free Speech—

Free Press Dichotomy: Access to the Press Through Advertising, 22 U.Fla.L.Rev. 292 (1969); Note, First Amendment Protections Against Libel Actions: Distinguishing Media and Non–Media Defendants, 47 So.Cal. L.Rev. 902 (1974); Stewart, "Or of the Press," 26 Hastings L.J. 761 (1975); Nimmer, Speech and Press: A Brief Reply to Professor Lange, 23 U.C.L.A.L.Rev. 120 (1975); Note, Problems in Defining the Institutional Status of the Press, 11 U.Richmond L.Rev. 177 (1976); Van Alstyne, Comment: The Hazards to the Press of Claiming a "Preferred Position," 28 Hastings L.J. 761 (1977).

Original Intent. See generally, L. Levy, Legacy of Suppression: Freedom of Speech and Press in Early American History (1960); Anderson, The Origins of the Press Clause, 30 U.C.L.A.L.Rev. 455 (1983); Levy, On the Origins of the Press Clause, 32 U.C.L.A.L.Rev. 177 (1984); L. Levy, Emergence of a Free Press (1985); Van

is not limited to the institutional press.[2] The Court has refused to draw any constitutional distinction between speech and "the press," or between speech and the "institutional press," or between speech and the "organized media." The reason for the judicial unwillingness to make such a differentiation lies, in part, in the fact that there is no principled way of doing so. In addition, the first amendment, itself, makes no such distinction, offering its umbrella of coverage to "speech, or the press."

Prison cases. In the companion cases of *Pell v. Procunier*[3] and *Saxbe v. Washington Post Co.,*[4] the Supreme Court rejected claims by prisoners and the press that the first amendment guaranteed a right of access to the newspapers to interview individual prisoners; California and federal prison regulations which prohibited face-to-face interviews between prisoners and members of the news media were upheld.[5]

The constitutional right of inmates to seek individual interviews with members of the press was not explored in *Saxbe* because inmates were not a party to the litigation.[6] In *Pell v. Procunier,*[7] however, the Court explored this aspect of the first amendment in light of the prisoners' unique position in society. Justice Stewart, writing for the

Alstyne, Congressional Power and Free Speech: Levy's Legacy Revisited, 99 Harv. L.Rev. 1089 (1986).

2. Chief Justice Burger analyzed these issues in his concurring opinion in First National Bank v. Bellotti, 435 U.S. 765, 795, 98 S.Ct. 1407, 1426, 55 L.Ed.2d 707, 730 (1978), rehearing denied 438 U.S. 907, 98 S.Ct. 3126, 57 L.Ed.2d 1150 (1978) and concluded that the Press Clause did not confer special or extraordinary privileges on the "institutional press." On the question of whether the press should have preferred rights under the first amendment, see generally, Anderson, The Origins of the Press Clause, 30 U.C.L.A.L.Rev. 455 (1983); Bezanson, The New Free Press Guarantee, 63 Va.L.Rev. 731 (1977); Lange, The Speech and Press Clauses, 23 U.C.L.A.L.Rev. 77 (1975); Nimmer, Introduction—Is Freedom of the Press a Redundancy: What Does It Add to Freedom of Speech?, 26 Hastings L.J. 639 (1975); Lewis, A Preferred Position for Journalism, 7 Hofstra L.Rev. 595 (1979); LeBel, The Good, The Bad, And The Press, 1986 Duke L.J. 1074.

3. 417 U.S. 817, 94 S.Ct. 2800, 41 L.Ed.2d 495 (1974).

See generally, Note, Press Passes and Trespasses: Newsgathering on Private Property, 84 Colum.L.Rev. 1298 (1984).

4. 417 U.S. 843, 94 S.Ct. 2811, 41 L.Ed.2d 514 (1974).

5. *Pell* challenged regulation section 415.071 of the California Department of Corrections Manual (Aug. 23, 1971) which reads as follows: "Press and other media interviews with specific individual inmates will not be permitted." 417 U.S. at 819, 94 S.Ct. at 2802. In *Saxbe,* the Washington Post and one of its reporters challenged Policy Statement 1220 1A para. 4b(6) of the Federal Bureau of Prisons (February 11, 1972), which reads as follows:

"Press representatives will not be permitted to interview individual inmates. This rule shall apply even where the inmate requests or seeks an interview. However, conversation may be permitted with inmates whose identity is not to be made public, if it is limited to the discussion of institutional facilities, programs and activities." 417 U.S. at 844 n. 1, 94 S.Ct. at 2812 n. 1.

6. Only the newspaper involved, the Washington Post, and one of its reporters brought suit against the Attorney General to challenge the regulation.

7. 417 U.S. 817, 94 S.Ct. 2800, 41 L.Ed.2d 495 (1974).

majority,[8] began by noting that while an absolute ban on interviews applied to the public at large would clearly involve a freedom of speech issue, the right to hold a press conference does not necessarily survive incarceration. Starting from the proposition that "[l]awful incarceration brings about the necessary withdrawal or limitation of many privileges and rights, a retraction justified by the considerations underlying our penal system",[9] the Court proceeded to balance the rights of inmates against the state's legitimate interests in security and rehabilitation of prisoners.[10]

Great emphasis was placed on the fact that the prisoners had alternative means of communication with the press, including uncensored mailing privileges and a visitation policy allowing face-to-face conversation with family, attorneys, the clergy and longstanding friends. Determining that these alternative channels were sufficient to ensure that reasonable and effective means of communication with the outside remain open to the prisoner, the Court refused to find that a restriction of one manner of communication was sufficient to violate a prisoner's first amendment rights.[11]

8. Justice Powell concurred in the majority opinion holding that the prison regulations did not abridge the inmates' freedom of the press' right. 417 U.S. at 835–36, 94 S.Ct. at 2810–11 (1974). Justice Douglas, joined by Justices Brennan and Marshall, dissented in both Pell v. Procunier and Saxbe v. Washington Post Co. See 417 U.S. at 836, 94 S.Ct. at 2827. Cf. Jones v. North Carolina Prisoners' Labor Union, Inc., 433 U.S. 119, 97 S.Ct. 2532, 53 L.Ed.2d 629 (1977).

9. 417 U.S. at 822, 94 S.Ct. at 2804, quoting Price v. Johnston, 334 U.S. 266, 285, 68 S.Ct. 1049, 1060, 92 L.Ed. 1356 (1948). See also, Cruz v. Beto, 405 U.S. 319, 321, 92 S.Ct. 1079, 1081, 31 L.Ed.2d 263 (1972), appeal after remand 497 F.2d 496 (5th Cir.1974). Cf. Jones v. North Carolina Prisoners' Labor Union, Inc., 433 U.S. 119, 97 S.Ct. 2532, 53 L.Ed.2d 629 (1977).

The principle that a convicted prisoner does not possess the full range of freedoms of an unincarcerated person "applies equally" to lawfully incarcerated pretrial detainees, although the detainers have not yet been convicted beyond a reasonable doubt. Bell v. Wolfish, 441 U.S. 520, 545–547, 553, 99 S.Ct. 1861, 1877–78 1881–82, 60 L.Ed.2d 447 (1979).

10. 417 U.S. at 822–24, 94 S.Ct. at 2804–05. It is interesting to note that at the time that these regulations were adopted, prison officials were very concerned that press attention to individual inmates was fostering a "big wheel" syndrome and causing certain prisoners to gain prestige and undue influence over the other inmates. The California regulation had been enacted two days after one of these "big wheels" had engineered an escape attempt which resulted in the deaths of three staff members and two inmates.

11. 417 U.S. at 824–28, 94 S.Ct. at 2805–07.

Incoming versus Outgoing Mail. It should be noted that some forms of prisoner communication are protected, but based on the right of the non-prisoner correspondent, not on the rights of prisoners. Procunier v. Martinez, 416 U.S. 396, 412–13, 94 S.Ct. 1800, 1810–11, 40 L.Ed.2d 224 (1974). Thus, prison officials cannot censor mail *from* prisoners "simply to eliminate unflattering or unwelcome opinions or factually inaccurate statements." 416 U.S. at 413, 94 S.Ct. at 1811. Cf. Procunier v. Navarette, 434 U.S. 555, 563–66, 98 S.Ct. 855, 860–62, 55 L.Ed.2d 24 (1978), on remand 581 F.2d 202 (9th Cir.1978). See also, Woods v. Aldworth, 561 F.Supp. 891 (N.D.Ill.1983).

Consistent with the first amendment, prison authorities may prohibit the *receipt*, by prisoners, of hardcover books unless they are mailed directly from publishers, book stores, or book clubs. That restriction is a limited one and a "rational re-

While the Court admitted "we would find the availability of such alternatives unimpressive if they were submitted as justification for governmental restriction of personal communication among members of the general public," [12] it went on to recognize that prisoners are in a closer relationship with their wardens than the average person is with the state and "[s]o long as reasonable and effective means of communication remain open and no discrimination in terms of content is involved, we believe that in drawing such lines, 'prison officials must be accorded latitude'." [13]

Both *Pell* and *Saxbe* considered the issue of whether this limitation on press interviews violates freedom of the press as guaranteed by the Constitution. The press contended that, irrespective of any first amendment rights of the prisoners, members of the press have a constitutional right of access to interview any willing inmate. This right, they claimed, could only be abridged if the prison authorities made an individualized determination that interviewing a particular inmate would constitute a clear and present danger to prison security or another substantial interest of the prison system. The press did not claim a violation or restriction of their right to publish, only of their right to gather news.

The Court rejected this argument in both cases, stating in *Pell* that: "[N]ewsmen have no constitutional right of access to prisons or their inmates beyond that afforded the general public." [14] While agreeing that a journalist is free to seek out sources of information, the Court

sponse by prison officials to an obvious security problem" because hardback books are especially serviceable for smuggling contraband, and it is difficult and time consuming to search them effectively. Bell v. Wolfish, 441 U.S. 520, 548–51, 99 S.Ct. 1861, 1879–81, 60 L.Ed.2d 447 (1979).

In Turner v. Safley, 482 U.S. 78, 107 S.Ct. 2254, 96 L.Ed.2d 64 (1987) the Court rejected a strict scrutiny test and upheld prison regulations that, in effect, prohibited prison inmates from writing to nonfamily inmates. Later Thornburgh v. Abbott, 490 U.S. 401, 109 S.Ct. 1874, 104 L.Ed.2d 459 (1989) rejected a facial attack on prison regulations that authorized prison officials to reject outside publications, such as magazines, sent to prisoners if the prison officials find the publications to be "detrimental to security, good order, or discipline of the institution or if it might facilitate criminal activity." The prison warden, under the regulations, had to review each issue of the magazine separately. The Court applied the deferential standard of *Turner*: the regulations are valid if they are reasonably related to legitimate penological interests. The Court rejected the stricter standard of Procunier v. Martinez,

416 U.S. 396, 94 S.Ct. 1800, 40 L.Ed.2d 224 (1974) and limited that case to the situation where the prison regulations concern *outgoing* correspondence.

The Court in *Thornburgh v. Abbott* explained that there is an important difference between *outgoing* correspondence and *incoming* materials. *Martinez* is limited to outgoing correspondence because the prison securities implications for outgoing correspondence are of a categorically lesser magnitude. To the extent that *Martinez* might suggest that more than the *reasonableness* standard of *Turner* should apply to incoming correspondence from nonprisoners, "we today overrule that case; the Court accomplished much of this step when it decided *Turner.*" Thornburgh v. Abbott, 490 U.S. 401, 413, 109 S.Ct. 1874, 1881, 104 L.Ed.2d 459 (1989).

12. 417 U.S. at 825, 94 S.Ct. at 2805.

13. 417 U.S. at 826, 94 S.Ct. at 2806, citing Cruz v. Beto, 405 U.S. at 321, 92 S.Ct. at 1081.

14. 417 U.S. at 834, 94 S.Ct. at 2810.

pointed out that this was a far cry from saying that the Constitution places upon the State "the affirmative duty to make available to journalists sources of information not available to members of the public generally." [15]

The majority of the Court found *Saxbe* to be "constitutionally indistinguishable" from *Pell* on these issues.[16] In *Saxbe,* the Court pointed out that the record revealed that the press had actually been given more access to the prisoners than the general public had,[17] noting that newsmen could tour, take pictures, and even conduct on-the-spot interviews with inmates they ran into. Justice Powell, dissenting in *Saxbe,*[18] felt that testimony had shown that personal interviews are crucial to effective reporting in a prison context and rejected the idea of alternative means of communication as adequate.[19]

Pell and *Saxbe* may not have much precedential value outside the restricted environment of a prison, for they do not apply usual first amendment standards. However, the cases do firmly reject a right of access by the press greater than that of the general public, a holding which appears to go beyond prison cases, although *Pell* acknowledged that "news gathering is not without its First Amendment protections." [20]

A few years later, in another prison case, *Houchins v. KQED, Inc.*[21] the Supreme Court, in a four to three vote, with two justices not participating, reversed a lower court injunction ordering prison officials to grant access to the press to certain prison facilities; however, the fragmented court produced no majority opinion. Chief Justice Burger, joined by Justices White and Rehnquist, found that there is no first or

15. 417 U.S. at 834, 94 S.Ct. at 2810.

16. 417 U.S. at 850, 94 S.Ct. at 2815.

17. 417 U.S. at 849, 94 S.Ct. at 2814–15.

18. Powell was joined by Brennan and Marshall, 417 U.S. at 850, 94 S.Ct. at 2815. Douglas dissented from both *Pell* and *Saxbe* in the same opinion, 417 U.S. at 836, 94 S.Ct. at 2811.

19. 417 U.S. at 853–54, 94 S.Ct. at 2816–17.

20. 417 U.S. at 833, 94 S.Ct. at 2809, quoting Branzburg v. Hayes, 408 U.S. 665, 707, 92 S.Ct. 2646, 2670, 33 L.Ed.2d 626 (1972).

See also, Burger, C.J., concurring in First Nat. Bank v. Bellotti, 435 U.S. 765, 795, 798, 98 S.Ct. 1407, 1426, 1427, 55 L.Ed.2d 707 (1978), rehearing denied 438 U.S. 907, 98 S.Ct. 3126, 57 L.Ed.2d 1150 (1978), where the Chief Justice noted that the "Court has not yet resolved whether the Press Clause confers upon the 'institutional press' any freedom from government

restraint not enjoyed by all others"; however, after a careful and powerful analysis he concluded that there is no difference in rights guaranteed by the speech vs. press clauses.

See generally, Halle, The News–Gathering/Publication Dichotomy and Government Expression, 1982 Duke L.J. 1.

21. 438 U.S. 1, 98 S.Ct. 2588, 57 L.Ed.2d 553 (1978).

See also Gannett Co., Inc. v. DePasquale, 443 U.S. 368, 391–93, 99 S.Ct. 2898, 2911–12, 61 L.Ed.2d 608 (1979) (assuming that members of the press and public have a constitutional right of access to pretrial hearings, this alleged right was given appropriate deference by the state trial court when it closed a pretrial hearing; the press did not object immediately to defendant's closure motion and any denial of access was not absolute but only temporary because a transcript of the suppression hearing was made available after the dangers of pretrial prejudice dissipated).

fourteenth amendment right of access to government information or sources of information within the government's control. Further, the press has no greater right of access than that of the public generally.

Justice Stewart concurred in the judgment, but on much narrower grounds. He agreed the press has no right of access "superior to that of the public generally," but that the concept of equal access must be flexibly applied "to accommodate the practical distinctions between the press and the general public." [22] In the context of this case, he believed that flexibility could require reasonable use of camera and sound equipment to members of the press in the areas open to both press and public, because the fact that "the First Amendment speaks separately of freedom of speech and of the press is no constitutional accident, but an acknowledgement of the critical role played by the press in American society." [23] Because the lower court injunction was overbroad and had granted the press greater access to prison areas than the public generally, he agreed with the reversal, but would not prohibit more carefully tailored relief on remand.

Justice Stevens, joined by Justices Brennan and Powell, dissented. They distinguished *Pell* and *Saxbe* [24] as limited to the case where there already was substantial press and public access to the prison. The dissent would grant a right of public and press access to prisons, while allowing the prison officials only a right to regulate reasonably the time and manner of that access. The dissent agreed that the press has "no greater right of access to information than that possessed by the public at large" but would not have reversed the lower court injunction granting a greater access to the press because the public generally had not requested separate relief and it was proper for the lower court to fashion relief to the needs of the litigant before it.

Because there was no majority opinion and two justices—Marshall and Blackmun—did not participate, the *Houchins* decision probably will not end litigation over public access to prisons in cases where there is only limited access to parts of the jail.[25] However, the seven justices did agree that there the press has no greater right of access to prisons than the public generally.

---

22. 438 U.S. at 16, 98 S.Ct. at 2597–98 (Stewart, J., concurring). Contra, Burger, C.J., concurring in First Nat. Bank v. Bellotti, 435 U.S. 765, 795, 98 S.Ct. 1407, 1426, 55 L.Ed.2d 707 (1978).

23. 438 U.S. at 17, 98 S.Ct. at 2598 (Stewart, J., concurring).

24. Pell v. Procunier, 417 U.S. 817, 94 S.Ct. 2800, 41 L.Ed.2d 495 (1974); Saxbe v. Washington Post Co., 417 U.S. 843, 94 S.Ct. 2811, 41 L.Ed.2d 514 (1974).

25. Cf. Philadelphia Newspapers, Inc. v. Jerome, 434 U.S. 241, 98 S.Ct. 546, 54 L.Ed.2d 506 (1978) (per curiam) (raising issue of press and public access to pretrial suppression hearings; state court judgment vacated to clarify the record), on remand 478 Pa. 484, 387 A.2d 425 (1978), appeal dismissed 443 U.S. 913, 99 S.Ct. 3104, 61 L.Ed.2d 877 (1979).

Open School Board Meetings. The Supreme Court has invalidated a state employment commission's order requiring a school board to prohibit teachers who are not union representatives from speaking at open meetings at which public participation is permitted, even if the speech is addressed to the subject of pending collective bargaining negotiations,[26] thus giving the press and the public a similar right of access to such speech.

The Right of Publicity. The state's power to restrict the use which the press makes of its access in a *nonprison* setting was approved in the facts of *Zacchini v. Scripps–Howard Broadcasting Co.*[27] There the Court held the right of a state to grant a "right of publicity" to an individual, such as a performer (a person with a name having commercial value) by protecting the proprietary interest in his act, in part to encourage such entertainment. The freedom of speech protections do not immunize the news media from a damage action by the performer when it broadcasts the performer's entire act (in this case a 15 second act) for which he normally gets paid. "The Constitution no more prevents a state from requiring respondent to compensate petitioner for broadcasting his act on television than it would privilege respondent to film and broadcast a copyrighted dramatic work without liability to the copyright owner." [28]

Access to Trials. The press has no constitutional right to access to evidence given at trials greater than that of the general public. In *Nixon v. Warner Communications, Inc.,*[29] the Court held that neither the first amendment guarantee of free speech and press nor the sixth amendment guarantee of a public trial gives the press the right to copy evidence given at trial. News organizations sought to copy several Watergate tapes that had been introduced at the trial of several defendants, but the Court held that the opportunity to listen to the tapes at trial and to receive transcripts of them had satisfied both constitutional guarantees. The Court held that, within the courtroom, the press enjoys no greater rights than does the public, but that the press is free, within broad limits, to report what its representatives have seen at the proceeding.[30]

---

26. City of Madison v. Wisconsin Employment Relations Com'n, 429 U.S. 167, 97 S.Ct. 421, 50 L.Ed.2d 376 (1976).

27. 433 U.S. 562, 97 S.Ct. 2849, 53 L.Ed.2d 965 (1977), on remand 54 Ohio St.2d 286, 376 N.E.2d 582 (1978).

28. 433 U.S. at 575, 97 S.Ct. at 2857. The Court specifically distinguished Time, Inc. v. Hill, 385 U.S. 374, 87 S.Ct. 534, 17 L.Ed.2d 456 (1967), as a false light privacy case not involving an appropriation of a name or likeness for purposes of trade. For further discussion of the *Zacchini* case, see § 20.36, infra.

29. 435 U.S. 589, 98 S.Ct. 1306, 55 L.Ed.2d 570 (1978).

30. 435 U.S. at 608–09, 98 S.Ct. at 1317–18. The Court also held that the common law right of access to judicial records does not authorize release of the tapes, in light of the Presidential Recordings Act. Justices Marshall and Stevens dissented, each writing a separate opinion, and Justice White dissented in part, joined by Justice Brennan.

Press Access to Report News Regarding Wars. Does the institutional press have a special constitutional right of access to require the military to allow the press access to the battle grounds or theater of war in order to report war activities? This issue is to be distinguished from the question whether the Government may ever enjoin the press from reporting information judged to be harmful to the war effort.[31]

Although reporters have claimed a special right to be at the scene of the fighting and to report without regard to military efforts to censor, these claims have not won support in the courts.[32] Courts have been unwilling to grant any special right of access or interfere with military judgment as to the conditions the military will place on newsgathering.[33] For example, the military may allow the press to interview soldiers at the front, but only on the condition that the reporters not include the exact position of the soldiers, or the number of troops in the immediate area.

Reporters covering foreign theaters of war often will need the permission of the host country to even enter the country. For example, if the host-foreign country (Saudi Arabia, during the war with Iraq in early 1991) does not grant a visa, the American reporter will have difficulty entering the country. Similarly, during this war against Iraq, Israel allowed American and other journalists to report Iraqi Scud missile attacks, but the journalists were not allowed to report exactly where the missiles hit (so that Iraq could not use that information in order to better target civilian areas). If the host country grants a visa subject to various conditions that the reporters must accept as a condition of securing the visa, one should not be surprised if the foreign country expels the journalist who agrees to the conditions but then does not abide by them.

Exit Polls. As part of their election eve news coverage, the various television networks often engage in exit polls, i.e., asking voters leaving the polling booth how they have voted. Voters have no obligation to answer (or to answer truthfully), but they usually do answer, and their responses tend to be accurate predictions of how the election will turn out. Various politicians have often proposed laws to limit the effect of exit polls. It is often argued that exit polls decrease voter

---

31. See, Rodney Smolla, Free Speech In an Open Society 291–320 (1992).

On this question, see also §§ 20.16–20.17.

32. See generally, Cassell, Restrictions on Press Coverage of Access, Grenada and "Off-the-Record Wars," 73 Georgetown L.J. 931 (1985). Cf. Zillman, Free Speech and Military Command, 1977 Utah L.Rev. 423; Dienes, When the First Amendment Is Not Preferred: The Military and Other "Special Contexts," 56 U.Cinn.L.Rev. 779 (1988).

See also, id., 56 U.Cinn.L.Rev. at 801 n. 73: "The concept of the military as a 'specialized society' has had extensive historical recognition. The founding fathers originally viewed the military as subject to a different set of constraints and protections from the rest of society."

33. See, e.g., The Nation Magazine v. Department of Defense, 762 F.Supp. 1558 (S.D.N.Y.1991) (court rejects media's objection to regulations limiting media access to Gulf War battlefield as too abstract).

turnout,[34] though this conclusion is far from a given.[35]

A law requiring networks to delay election night predictions should violate the First Amendment, for it would prevent the networks from broadcasting a truthful poll result. If prospective voters decide not to cast their votes because of the prediction, the decision not to vote is freely made by the voter.[36] The Government, though, should be able to enact a nationwide uniform poll closing time without restricting free speech.[37]

VII. OTHER REGULATION OF THE PRESS— ANTITRUST, LABOR RELATIONS, AND TAXATION

§ 20.20 The Antitrust Laws

The Court has clearly established that the first amendment does not bestow antitrust immunity on newspapers, broadcasters, and other news media even though enforcement of the antitrust laws might cause a newspaper to go bankrupt.[1] The principle underlying the Court's position was described by Justice Black in *Associated Press v. United States.*[2]

> Freedom to publish means freedom for all and not for some. Freedom to publish is guaranteed by the Constitution, but freedom to combine to keep others from publishing is not. Freedom of the press from governmental interference under the First Amendment does not sanction repression of that freedom by private interests [through conspiracies in restraint of trade]. The First Amendment affords not the slightest support for the contention that a combination to restrain trade in news and views has any constitutional

---

34. See, e.g., Jackson, Election Night Reporting and Voter Turnout, 27 Am. J.Pol.Sci. 615, 629 (1983).

35. Epstein & Strom, Election Night Projections and West Coast Turnout, 9 Am. Pol.Q. 479, 486, 489 (1981) (concluding that no evidence demonstrates lower voter turnout related to voter projections). See also, Note, Elections, Computers and the First Amendment, 2 Colum.J.L. & Soc.Probs. 17, 25 (1966); Dubois, Election Night Projections and Voter Turnout in the West: A Note on the Hazards of Aggregate Data Analysis, 11 Am.Pol.Q. 349, 358 (1983).

36. Note, The Rights of the Public and the Press to Gather Information, 87 Harv. L.Rev. 1505, 1533 (1974) (newsgathering from a willing source is a constitutional right.).

37. See U.S. Const. art. III, § 4, cl. 1.

See generally, Note, Exit Polls and the First Amendment, 98 Harv.L.Rev. 1927 (1985).

§ 20.20

1. Citizen Publishing Co. v. United States, 394 U.S. 131, 89 S.Ct. 927, 22 L.Ed.2d 148 (1969). See also Lorain Journal Co. v. United States, 342 U.S. 143, 72 S.Ct. 181, 96 L.Ed. 162 (1951); United States v. Radio Corp. of America, 358 U.S. 334, 79 S.Ct. 457, 3 L.Ed.2d 354 (1959).

2. 326 U.S. 1, 65 S.Ct. 1416, 89 L.Ed. 2013 (1945), rehearing denied 326 U.S. 802, 66 S.Ct. 6, 90 L.Ed. 489 (1945).

immunity.[3]

The test in such cases should be that the applicable antitrust laws should be evenhanded, nondiscriminatory and neutral on their face and in effect.   A state antitrust law that was written only to apply to the dissemination of news should be unconstitutional, and would raise more substantial first amendment issues.[4]

§ 20.21   Labor Laws

On a theory similar to that used in the antitrust area, the Court held that the first amendment does not bar nondiscriminatory application of the National Labor Relations Act to the news media in *Associated Press v. NLRB*.[1]   The law in question did not affect the impartial distribution of news.[2]

§ 20.22   Tax Laws

The Government may not impose flat taxes that serve to single out and impose a tax on the exercise of a privilege guaranteed by the Bill of Rights.[1]   Thus, in *Follett v. McCormick*,[2] the Court struck down a flat license tax as applied to one who earns his livelihood as an evangelist

3.   326 U.S. at 20, 65 S.Ct. at 1425 (footnote omitted).

4.   Cf. Grosjean v. American Press Co., 297 U.S. 233, 250–51, 56 S.Ct. 444, 449, 80 L.Ed. 660 (1936).

§ 20.21

1.   301 U.S. 103, 57 S.Ct. 650, 81 L.Ed. 953 (1937).

Flat License Taxes and Sales and Use Taxes Compared.   Compare, Jimmy Swaggart Ministries v. Board of Equalization, 493 U.S. 378, 110 S.Ct. 688, 107 L.Ed.2d 796 (1990), where a unanimous Court held that the religion clauses of the First Amendment do not prevent a state from imposing generally applicable sales and use taxes, with such taxes also applying to sales of books, tapes, and other religious and nonreligious merchandise by religious organizations.   Such sales and use taxes are to be distinguished from *flat* license taxes: because such taxes are fixed in amount and unrelated to the scope of the activities or to revenues received, they operate as preconditions or prior restraints on the exercise of religious freedom.

2.   Associated Press v. NLRB, 301 U.S. at 132, 57 S.Ct. at 655–56 (1937). See also Oklahoma Press Publishing Co. v. Walling, 327 U.S. 186, 66 S.Ct. 494, 90 L.Ed. 614 (1946) (Wage and hour laws).

§ 20.22

1.   Murdock v. Pennsylvania, 319 U.S. 105, 113, 63 S.Ct. 870, 875, 87 L.Ed. 1292 (1943).

2.   321 U.S. 573, 64 S.Ct. 717, 88 L.Ed. 938 (1944).

As to the constitutionality of a license tax in a nonreligious context, see Corona v. Corona Daily Independent, 115 Cal.App.2d 382, 252 P.2d 56 (1953), certiorari denied 346 U.S. 833, 74 S.Ct. 2, 98 L.Ed. 356 (1953).   Justice Douglas, joined by Justice Black, dissented from the denial of certiorari.   He summarized the case as follows:

"Petitioners publish a newspaper in Corona, California.   The city has by ordinance imposed a license tax for the privilege of engaging in any business in the city, including the business of publishing a newspaper.   Petitioners refused to pay the license fee, and the California courts have held that they may be compelled to do so."   (346 U.S. at 833, 74 S.Ct. at 3).

Justice Douglas unsuccessfully argued that such a license tax violates the First Amendment because "No government can exact a price for the exercise of a privilege which the Constitution guarantees."   346 U.S. at 834, 74 S.Ct. at 3.   Note that this tax was nondiscriminatory.

or preacher. Those who preach, "like other citizens, may be subject to general taxation [but that] does not mean that they can be required to pay a tax for the exercise of that which the First Amendment has made a high constitutional privilege." [3]

The Court has also invalidated discriminatory taxes on the dissemination of news. The leading case is *Grosjean v. American Press Co.*[4] where the Court struck down a state tax (which was in addition to other taxes of general applicability) on 2% of the gross receipts of advertising in those newspapers with circulation of more than 20,000 copies per week. The Court explained:

> It is not intended by anything we have said to suggest that the owners of newspapers are immune from any of the ordinary forms of taxation for support of the government. But this is not an ordinary form of tax .... It is bad because, in the light of its history and of its present setting, it is seen to be a deliberate and calculated device *in the guise of a tax* to limit the circulation of information to which the public is entitled in virtue of the constitutional guaranties. ...

> The form in which the tax is imposed is in itself suspicious. It is not measured or limited by the volume of advertisements. It is measured alone by the extent of the circulation of the publication in which the advertisements are carried, with the plain purpose of penalizing the publishers and curtailing the circulation of a selected group of newspapers.[5]

Though the state may apply general business taxes without violating the first amendment, even though some of these business activities relate to free speech,[6] it may not enact laws, in the guise of a tax, designed to limit the circulation of newspapers.

In *Minneapolis Star and Tribune Co. v. Minnesota Com'r of Revenue*[7] the Court interpreted *Grosjean* as dependent on the legislature having improper censorial goals or motive.[8] However, even without such improper goals a tax may be invalid. In Minnesota, periodic publications were exempt from the state's general sales and use taxes. But Minnesota had a special "use" tax on the cost of paper and ink products consumed in the production of periodic publications after the first $100,000 worth of ink and paper consumed in a calendar year.

---

3. 321 U.S. at 578, 64 S.Ct. at 719.

4. 297 U.S. 233, 56 S.Ct. 444, 80 L.Ed. 660 (1936).

5. 297 U.S. at 250–51, 56 S.Ct. at 449 (emphasis added).

6. Cf. Cammarano v. United States, 358 U.S. 498, 79 S.Ct. 524, 3 L.Ed.2d 462 (1959)

(Government may forbid as a business deduction, money spent on lobbying activities).

7. 460 U.S. 575, 103 S.Ct. 1365, 75 L.Ed.2d 295 (1983), on remand 332 N.W.2d 914 (Minn.1983).

8. 460 U.S. at 580, 103 S.Ct. at 1369.

The Court correctly invalidated this tax, which singled out the press for special tax burdens. The state's interest in revenue "cannot justify the special treatment of the press" because the state could "raise the revenue by taxing businesses generally ...."[9] The Court emphasized this point by noting that a nondiscriminatory sales tax, which also taxed the sale of newspapers would be constitutional.[10] Finally, the Court found the Minnesota use tax improper because it targeted a small group within the press, those who would exceed the $100,000 exemption. Singling out only the larger publishers had a strong potential for abuse.[11] Similarly, a state may not constitutionally levy a sales tax on certain types of magazines based on the content of those magazines—the state sales tax in question applied to general interest magazines but exempted newspapers and certain types of magazines (any religious, professional, trade or sports periodical was exempted, but not a general interest magazine).[12]

9. 460 U.S. at 586, 103 S.Ct. at 1372 (footnote omitted).

10. 460 U.S. at 586–87 n. 9, 103 S.Ct. at 1373 n. 9. The Court rejected a rule which would allow the state to single out the press for a different method of taxation so long as the effective tax burden was no greater, because differential treatment threatens the press and "courts as institutions are poorly equipped to evaluate with precision the relative burdens of various methods of taxation." 460 U.S. at 589, 103 S.Ct. at 1374 (footnote omitted).

11. 460 U.S. at 591–92, 103 S.Ct. at 1375.

Contrast Matter of Assessment of Additional North Carolina and Orange County Use Taxes Against Village Pub. Corp. for Period from April 1, 1972 through March 31, 1978, 312 N.C. 211, 322 S.E.2d 155 (1984) (constitutionality of North Carolina Sales and Use Tax exemption upheld; the law exempts sales of newspapers "by resident newspaper street vendors and by newsboys making house-to-house deliveries and sales of magazines by resident magazine vendors making house-to-house sales."), appeal dismissed for want of a substantial federal question, sub nom., Village Publishing Corp. v. North Carolina Department of Revenue, 472 U.S. 1001, 105 S.Ct. 2693, 86 L.Ed.2d 710 (1985).

Justice White, joined by Justice Brennan dissented, in view of the *Minneapolis Star* case. The state law offers newspapers using a certain means of delivery a tax benefit denied other members of the press, thus raising free speech and equal protection problems in the view of these two justices.

In Rust v. Sullivan, 500 U.S. ___, 111 S.Ct. 1759, 114 L.Ed.2d 233 (1991), the Court upheld government regulations prohibiting Title X grant recipients from engaging in abortion related activities, where abortion is a method of family planning. The funds were to be used only to support preventive family planning services, population research, infertility services, and related activities. The Title X project is expressly prohibited from referring a pregnant woman to an abortion provider. Indeed, the Title X project does not provide any post-conception medical care. Congress intended that federal funds not be used to "promote or advocate" abortion as a "method of family planning." 500 U.S. at ___ n. 4, 111 S.Ct. at 1773 n. 4.

The petitioners argued that *Arkansas Writers' Project* and *Minneapolis Star & Tribune Co.* prohibited the strings attached to the Title X grants, but a majority of the Court disagreed. The Title X regulations did not single out a disfavored group on the basis of the content of the speech; rather, the Government's regulations were designed to assure that it would not fund activities, including speech, that were specifically excluded from the scope of the project funded.

12. Arkansas Writers' Project, Inc. v. Ragland, 481 U.S. 221, 107 S.Ct. 1722, 95 L.Ed.2d 209 (1987), on remand 293 Ark. 395, 738 S.W.2d 402 (1987). The Court did not decide whether a distinction between different types of periodicals—e.g., newspapers versus all magazines—would also be invalid. 481 U.S. at 233, 107 S.Ct. at 1729. It is important to appreciate that such a distinction is not content-based.

Texas Monthly, Inc. v. Bullock,[13] raised the question whether a Texas statute was constitutional when it exempted from its sales tax, "[p]eriodicals that are published or distributed by a religious faith and that consist wholly of writings promulgating the teaching of the faith and books that consist wholly of writings sacred to a religious faith." The Court (6 to 3), with no majority opinion, invalidated this tax.

13. 489 U.S. 1, 109 S.Ct. 890, 103 L.Ed.2d 1 (1989). Brennan, J., announced the judgment of the Court and delivered an opinion joined by Marshall and Stevens, JJ. He based his decision on the Establishment Clause of the first amendment.

Brennan argued that, "when confined exclusively to publications advancing the tenets of a religious faith, the exemption runs afoul of the Establishment Clause...." Brennan said that the "breadth of New York's property tax exemption was essential to our holding" in Walz v. Tax Commission of City of New York, 397 U.S. 664, 90 S.Ct. 1409, 25 L.Ed.2d 697 (1970). In *Walz*, said Brennan, New York had granted a property tax exemption to all houses of worship within a broad class of property owned by non-profit corporations such as hospitals, libraries, and playgrounds. In contrast, "Texas' sales tax exemption for periodicals published or distributed by a religious faith and consisting wholly of writings promulgating the teaching of the faith lacks sufficient breadth to pass scrutiny under the Establishment clause.... This is particularly true where, as here, the subsidy is targeted as writings that *promulgate* the teachings of religious faiths." 489 U.S. at 13–15, 109 S.Ct. at 899 (emphasis in original). He added: "If the State chose to subsidize, by means of a tax exemption, all groups that contributed to the community's cultural, intellectual, and moral betterment, then the exemption for religious publications could be retained, provided that the exemption swept as widely as the property tax exemption we upheld in *Walz*." 489 U.S. at 15–17, 109 S.Ct. at 900. The Brennan plurality explicitly did not reach the question whether the Texas sales tax exemption also violated the free press guarantee as interpreted in Arkansas Writers' Project, Inc. v. Ragland, 481 U.S. 221, 107 S.Ct. 1722, 95 L.Ed.2d 209 (1987).

White, J., concurred in the judgment, and explicitly relied on *Arkansas Writers' Project*. He argued that the law violated the press clause of the first amendment because Texas discriminates on the basis of the content of the publications [periodicals "that consist wholly of writings promulgating the teachings of the faith"] in determining whether to grant the exemption. 489 U.S. at 24–26, 109 S.Ct. at 905.

Blackmun, J., joined by O'Connor, J., concurred in the judgment. They would issue a more narrow ruling, that "a tax exemption *limited to* the sale of religious literature by religious organizations violates the Establishment Clause." (emphasis in original). 489 U.S. at 28–30, 109 S.Ct. at 907. Texas engaged in "preferential support for the communication of religious messages."

Scalia, J., joined by Rehnquist, C.J. and Kennedy, J., filed a vigorous dissent. The opinions of Brennan and Blackmun, JJ., he said, are based on the bold assertion that "government may not 'convey a message of endorsement of religion,'" an assertion which is unsupported given such realities as the text of the Declaration of Independence, the inscriptions on our coins, and the invocation with which sessions of our Court are opened. 489 U.S. at 28–30, 109 S.Ct. at 907. Justice Scalia accused Justice Brennan of rewriting *Walz*. That case, Scalia said, rested "upon the more direct proposition that 'exemption constitutes a reasonable and balanced attempt to guard against' the 'latent dangers' of governmental hostility towards religion 'inherent in the imposition of property taxes.'" 489 U.S. at 35–37, 109 S.Ct. at 911, quoting *Walz*. He noted that *Walz* specifically found "it unnecessary to justify the tax exemption on the social welfare services of 'good works' that some churches perform for parishioners and others...." 489 U.S. at 35–37, 109 S.Ct. at 911. As for *Arkansas Writers' Project*, Justice Scalia concluded that it also does not apply to invalidate the tax exemption: the Constitution "sometimes *permits* accommodation despite" the establishment clause, the press clause, and the speech clause of the Constitution. 489 U.S. at 43–45, 109 S.Ct. at 915 (emphasis in original).

Leathers v. Medlock[14] rejected a first amendment challenge to an Arkansas sales tax that excluded or exempted the print media but not cable television, or cable and satellite services. It is important to note that the challenged tax was of general applicability, covering all tangible personal property and a broad range of services. The tax did not single out the press and did not threaten to suppress the expression of particular ideas and viewpoints. Nor did the Arkansas tax target a small group of speakers. And there was no evidence of improper motive: Arkansas did not target cable television in a purposeful attempt to interfere with free speech. Finally, the tax did not discriminate on the basis of the content of the taxpayer's speech. The disputed tax, in short, was not directed against a portion of the press, and created no danger that it would suppress particular ideas.

In short, when there is a complaint that a tax discriminates among the media, or within a medium, the first amendment is not implicated unless the tax is directed at, or presents the danger of, suppressing particular ideas.

VIII. THE PRESS AND THE CRIMINAL JUSTICE SYSTEM

§ 20.23 Introduction

It has been said that the press and the government are natural adversaries. An appreciation of the conflicting functions with which each is endowed will aid in an understanding of their adversarial roles in the area of criminal justice. The Supreme Court has observed:

> A responsible press has always been regarded as the handmaiden of effective judicial administration, especially in the criminal field. Its function in this regard is documented by an impressive record of service over several centuries. The press does not simply publish information about trials but guards against the miscarriage of justice by subjecting the police, prosecutors, and judicial processes to extensive public scrutiny and criticism.[1]

It is not surprising that this relationship is accompanied by a certain degree of rancor as well as suspicion that each is attempting to stunt the effectiveness of the other by intruding unnecessarily into the other's respective sphere of responsibility. The courts have been

---

14. 499 U.S. ___, 111 S.Ct. 1438, 113 L.Ed.2d 494 (1991), on remand 305 Ark. 610, 808 S.W.2d 785 (1991). Marshall, J., joined by Blackmun, J., dissented because the tax placed heavier tax burdens on cable television while excluding print media, which was, in the view of the dissent, a like-situated media.

§ 20.23

1. Sheppard v. Maxwell, 384 U.S. 333, 350, 86 S.Ct. 1507, 1515, 16 L.Ed.2d 600 (1966).

charged with the duty of maintaining this dynamic tension without diminishing the independence of either.

The central question which confronts the judiciary in this area is whether there exists any order of pre-eminence among the conflicting rights and duties with constitutional recognition? This question has been assessed in several contexts concerning the press and the criminal justice system. Does the first amendment provide for the protection of confidential sources when such information is relevant to a criminal investigation or prosecution? Are there any constitutional limitations on laws that the states might enact that shield the press from subpoenas? Are there limits on the power of the Government to execute search warrants on newspaper offices? Does there exist any power in the government to restrain the publication of information that may jeopardize a defendant's rights to a fair trial? To what extent may the Government allow television to broadcast trials? Does it make a difference if the trial is criminal or civil? It is to those issues that we now turn.

§ 20.24 The Protection of Confidential Sources

Branzburg v. Hayes **and a Reporter's Privilege.** In *Branzburg v. Hayes,*[1] the Supreme Court, by a five to four majority, rejected a reporter's claim that, because the flow of information available to the press would be impeded if newsmen were compelled to release the names of confidential sources for use in a government investigation, the first amendment must be held to embrace a privilege to constitutionally refuse to divulge such information in order to protect the reporter's channels to the community.

Though the issue before the Court and the *Branzburg* decision itself has far-reaching implications, Justice White in speaking for the majority phrased the question and his holding narrowly: "The issue in these cases is whether requiring newsmen to appear and testify before state or federal grand juries abridges the freedom of speech and press guaranteed by the First Amendment. We hold that it does not." [2] Left undecided was the scope of a newsman's privilege, if any, in testimony before administrative hearings, legislative hearings, and in civil suits.

The issue of the existence of such a constitutional privilege was initially raised in 1958 before the Second Circuit in *Garland v. Torre,*[3]

§ 20.24

1. 408 U.S. 665, 92 S.Ct. 2646, 33 L.Ed.2d 626 (1972).

See generally, V. Blasi, Press Subpoenas: An Empirical and Legal Analysis (1972). See also, Murasky, The Journalist's Privilege: Branzburg and Its Aftermath, 52 Tex.L.Rev. 829 (1974); Stewart, "Or of the Press," 26 Hast.L.J. 631 (1975).

2. 408 U.S. at 667, 92 S.Ct. at 2649–50.

3. 259 F.2d 545 (2d Cir.1958), certiorari denied 358 U.S. 910, 79 S.Ct. 237, 3 L.Ed.2d 231 (1958). Prior to *Garland,* newsmen had attempted, generally unsuccessfully, to establish a common law privilege in the federal courts, see e.g., Brewster v. Boston Herald–Traveler Corp., 20 F.R.D. 416 (D.Mass.1957).

but had generally been rejected by the lower courts. *Branzburg* was the first time the Supreme Court had granted certiorari to review the issue.

Although *Branzburg* acknowledged that some protection of news sources was necessary to prevent the information-gathering process from being totally eviscerated, petitioners had not established that such a result would occur unless greater protection than that traditionally afforded the press was made available.

> Only where news sources themselves are implicated in crime or possess information relevant to the grand jury's task need they or the reporter be concerned about grand jury subpoenas. Nothing before us indicates that a large number or percentage of *all* confidential news sources falls into either category and would in any way be deterred by our holding that the Constitution does not, as it never has, exempt the newsman from performing the citizen's normal duty of appearing and furnishing information relevant to the grand jury's task.[4]

Even if it were assumed that the flow of news would be greatly diminished by sources who were not subject to a grand jury subpoena, the public interest in the investigation and prosecution of crimes outweighs that public interest in the availability of sources for future use, the Court concluded.

Moreover, the opinion emphasized that the difficulties of administering such a privilege would be enormous. It would eventually be necessary to categorize the various individuals and organizations participating in the distribution of information to determine those qualified to exercise the privilege. This would be a most "questionable procedure in light of the traditional doctrine that liberty of the press is the right of the lonely pamphleteer ... as much as of the large metropolitan publisher...."[5] In addition, because the privilege claimed was only conditional, each assertion would require a judicial determination that it was properly invoked; i.e., there existed alternative methods to obtain this information, that it was not relevant to the subject of the investigation, or that such information is not intrinsic to a successful prosecution.[6]

In spite of these arguments the Court did leave open an avenue of redress for reporters who feel they are being harassed by government officials.

---

4. Branzburg v. Hayes, 408 U.S. 665, 691, 92 S.Ct. 2646, 2661–62, 33 L.Ed.2d 626 (1972) (emphasis in original).

5. 408 U.S. at 704, 92 S.Ct. at 2668.

6. 408 U.S. at 705, 92 S.Ct. at 2668–69. Petitioner did not assert an absolute privi- lege, but one where information could be compelled only upon a showing of exhaustion of alternative sources and under strict guidelines as to relevance, see 408 U.S. at 630, 92 S.Ct. at 2644–45.

[G]rand jury investigations if instituted or conducted other than in good faith, would pose wholly different issues for resolution under the First Amendment. Official harassment of the press undertaken not for purposes of law enforcement but to disrupt a reporter's relationship with his news sources would have no justification. Grand juries are subject to judicial control and subpoenas to motions to quash.[7]

Justice Powell, who cast the crucial fifth vote, strikes a somewhat problematical note for future litigation relying upon *Branzburg*. Believing that the "state and federal authorities are not free to 'annex' the news media as 'an investigative arm of government,'" he indicated in his concurrence a broader test than mere "good faith" for assessing the need to disclose confidential sources. In his view:

[I]f the newsman is called upon to give information bearing only a remote and tenuous relationship to the subject of the investigation, or if he has some other reason to believe that his testimony implicates confidential source relationships without a legitimate need of law enforcement, he will have access to the Court on a motion to quash and an appropriate protective order may be entered.[8]

The ambiguity surrounding "a legitimate need of law enforcement" arguably suggests an approach not too dissimilar to that rejected in the majority opinion due to inherent administrative difficulties.[9] Indeed, Justice Stewart's dissent interpreted this ambiguity as offering "some hope of a more flexible view in the future."[10] Since *Branzburg*, there have been numerous appeals from contempt citations against newsmen in the wake of *Branzburg*.[11]

State Shield Laws. Despite intensive lobbying efforts, there has not yet been any federal bill enacted which would provide a statutory privilege for newsmen.[12] However, several states have enacted "state shield" laws which vary in the range of protection, depending upon the statute and the interpretation it has received from the state court.[13] Of course, under the supremacy clause of the Constitution such state shield laws could not apply to limit the power of federal courts exercising jurisdiction over federal questions.

---

7. 408 U.S. at 707–08, 92 S.Ct. at 2670 (footnote omitted).

8. 408 U.S. at 710, 92 S.Ct. at 2671. See Stewart, "Or of the Press," 26 Hast. L.J. 631, 635 (1975).

9. See Note, The Supreme Court, 1971 Term, 86 Harv.L.Rev. 1, 144 (1972).

10. Branzburg v. Hayes, 408 U.S. 665, 725, 92 S.Ct. 2646, 2671, 33 L.Ed.2d 626 (1972).

11. Citation of cases in which the Supreme Court has denied certiorari may be found at e.g., 1, Dorsen, Bender, and Newborne, Emerson, Haber, and Dorsen's Political and Civil Rights in the United States, p. 309, n. 1 (4th ed. Law School 1976).

12. Id. at 311.

13. Id. at 314. See also, Marcus, The Reporter's Privilege: An Analysis of the Common Law, Branzburg v. Hayes, and Recent Statutory Developments, 25 Ariz. L.Rev. 815 (1984).

The *Farber* **Case.** State shield laws may vary greatly in how they are applied in state cases to prevent a state court from subpoenaing information from a newsreporter when such information may be helpful to a criminal defendant. For example, the New Jersey Supreme Court has declared that its seemingly strong shield law must yield to sixth amendment rights and the state constitutional provisions relating to the rights of criminal defendants. The state court said: "[W]hen faced with the shield law, [the criminal defendant] invokes the rather elementary but entirely sound proposition that where the Constitution and statute collide, the latter must yield. Subject to what is said below, we find this argument unassailable." [14] The state court held, in this decision, *In re Farber,*[15] that the press would have a right to a preliminary determination (before being required to submit materials to the trial judge for *in camera* inspection) that there was a reasonable likelihood that the information sought was material and relevant, that it could not be secured from any less intrusive source, and that the defendant had a legitimate need to see and use it.

The U.S. Supreme Court denied certiorari but two justices suggested their views on the merits when they both earlier refused to stay an order of the New Jersey Superior Court holding the reporter, Myron Farber, and the New York Times Co. in civil contempt. Justice White, sitting as a circuit justice, noted that even if four or more justices of the full Court would hold that a reporter's obligation to comply with a subpoena is subject to some special showing of materiality not applicable to ordinary third party witnesses, the Court would not likely accept review "at this time." "The order at issue directs submission of the documents and other materials for only an *in camera* inspection; it anticipates a full hearing on all issues of federal and state law; and it is based on the trial court's evident views that the documents sought are sufficiently material to warrant at least *in camera* inspection." [16]

Justice Marshall also denied a stay because he did not believe it likely that four justices would vote to grant certiorari, but he explicitly differed with Justice White as to the merits of the constitutional issue involved because even a judge's *in camera* inspection might burden the ability of the news media to gather information.[17] The issue thus

---

14. In re Farber, 78 N.J. 259, 394 A.2d 330 (1978) certiorari denied 439 U.S. 997, 99 S.Ct. 598, 58 L.Ed.2d 670 (1978).

15. 78 N.J. 259, 394 A.2d 330 (1978), certiorari denied, 439 U.S. 997, 99 S.Ct. 598, 58 L.Ed.2d 670 (1978).

See generally, Note, 32 Rutgers L.Rev. 545 (1979); Goodale, Courts Begin Limiting Scope of Various State Shield Laws, 1 Natl.L.Journal 28 (Dec. 11, 1978).

16. New York Times Co. (and Myron Farber) v. Jascalevich, 439 U.S. 1317, 1322,

1323, 99 S.Ct. 6, 10, 58 L.Ed.2d 25 (1978), (White, Circuit Justice), reapplication denied 439 U.S. 1331, 99 S.Ct. 11, 58 L.Ed.2d 38 (1978) (Marshall, Circuit Justice).

17. New York Times Co. (and Myron Farber) v. Jascalevich, 439 U.S. 1331, 1334, 99 S.Ct. 11, 14, 58 L.Ed.2d 38 (1978) (Marshall, Circuit Justice). See also, New York Times Co. v. New Jersey, 439 U.S. 886, 99 S.Ct. 241, 58 L.Ed.2d 233 (1978) (motion to vacate stay granted) (Marshall, J., dissenting).

remains unresolved, though several state courts have shown hostility to state shield laws both on federal and state constitutional law grounds.[18]

Branzburg v. Hayes[19] specifically recognized that Congress has the freedom to fashion a statutory reporter's privilege "as narrow or broad as deemed necessary...." Moreover, the state legislatures are also free "within First Amendment limits, to fashion" their own shield laws, and state courts could construe their state constitutions "so as to recognize a newsman's privilege, either qualified or absolute."[20]

One should also note that many statutory or judge-made laws create a host of privileges that serve to deprive the accused or the prosecutor of relevant evidence. The attorney-client privilege, the doctor-patient privilege, the husband-wife privilege—all serve certain important social policies and none of them has been found to violate the accused's rights. To illustrate, if a client confesses to a particular crime to his attorney, the attorney may not (without the client's consent) breach the wall of secrecy, even to offer the evidence in order to help acquit an innocent man wrongfully accused of that same crime. If that "shield" law is constitutional, may one logically treat the reporter-source privilege any differently?

A Reporter's Privilege and Civil Cases. Assertion of a reporter's privilege in civil cases has met with a qualified success, the lower courts distinguishing *Branzburg* on the grounds that a civil action does not present as significant a countervailing interest as a criminal prosecution, particularly where the plaintiffs seeking access to a reporter's notes are not parties to a pending criminal action, but merely prospective witnesses. Thus, in one district court case where the privilege has been sustained, the standard required the party seeking discovery to exhaust alternative sources and to show that the information requested is central to the party's claim.[21] Such a claim may well be present in libel suits brought by public officials and figures against the media, because the plaintiff needs to establish "malice" or *New York Times* scienter in publishing the defamatory information in order to be successful.[22] If the story is purportedly based on the information obtained from a confidential source, scienter can be proven by a showing that the source is non-existent.[23]

---

18. See generally, e.g., Goodale, Courts Begin Limiting Scope of Various State Shield Laws, 1 Nat'l.L.Journal 28 (Dec. 11, 1978).

19. 408 U.S. 665, 92 S.Ct. 2646, 33 L.Ed.2d 626 (1972).

20. 408 U.S. at 706, 92 S.Ct. 2669.

21. Democratic Nat. Committee v. McCord, 356 F.Supp. 1394 (D.D.C.1973).

22. New York Times Co. v. Sullivan, 376 U.S. 254, 84 S.Ct. 710, 11 L.Ed.2d 686

(1964), motion denied 376 U.S. 967, 84 S.Ct. 1130, 12 L.Ed.2d 83 (1964). See § 20.33, infra.

23. See, e.g., Carey v. Hume, 492 F.2d 631 (D.C.Cir.1974), application denied 417 U.S. 905, 94 S.Ct. 2636, 41 L.Ed.2d 231 (1974), certiorari dismissed 417 U.S. 938, 94 S.Ct. 2654, 41 L.Ed.2d 661 (1974). Cf. Herbert v. Lando, 441 U.S. 153, 99 S.Ct. 1635, 60 L.Ed.2d 115 (1979).

Newspaper's Breach of a Promise of Confidentiality. In *Cohen v. Cowles Media Co.*[24] the Court held that the first amendment does not prohibit a plaintiff from recovering damages, under state promissory estoppel law, if the newspaper breaches its promise of confidentiality given to the plaintiff in exchange for information. Cohen, associated with one party's campaign, gave court records concerning another party's candidate for Lieutenant Governor to news reporters after receiving a promise of confidentiality.[25] The newspapers did not keep this promise and published Cohen's name. Because Cohen was then fired from his job, he sued for damages in state court on a breach of promise theory. He won, but the state supreme court reversed, ruling that the First Amendment barred the cause of action.

Justice White, for the Court, reversed the state court and held that the First Amendment did not bar this type of cause of action. It was permissible for the state to apply a law of general applicability, such as a law of promissory estoppel. The majority then remanded for further state proceedings.

The ironic result of this case is that *Branzburg* refused to create a reporter's privilege. But if the reporter reveals the information that *Branzburg* refuses to protect, then the reporter can be held liable under *Cowles*. Presumably the Court would apply *Cowles* only when the reporter *voluntarily* breaches the confidentiality, not when the reporter is forced to comply with a subpoena.

Search Warrants of Newsrooms. In *Zurcher v. The Stanford Daily,*[26] the Supreme Court refused to create any special protections for newspapers that might be searched by government authorities pursuant to a search warrant which had been based on probable cause to look for evidence of a crime in the newspaper office. The majority opinion quickly dismissed arguments based on the need to protect confidential sources:

> Nor are we convinced, anymore than we were in *Branzburg v. Hayes,* 408 U.S. 665, 92 S.Ct. 2646, 33 L.Ed.2d 626 (1972), that confidential sources will disappear and that the press will suppress news because of fears of warranted searches. Whatever incremental effect there may be in this regard if search warrants, as well as

24. 501 U.S. ___, 111 S.Ct. 2513, 115 L.Ed.2d 586 (1991), on remand ___ N.W.2d ___ (Minn.1992). Justice Blackmun, joined by Marshall and Souter, dissented, arguing this fact situation did not involve holding the press to a law of general applicability involving commercial activities, but rather a law making the press liable based on the content of the publication. Justice Souter, joined by Marshall, Blackmun, and O'Connor, also dissented, but distinguished other cases where liability might be more appro-

priate, such as where the injured party is a more private party.

25. The court records showed that the candidate, in 1969, was charged with three counts of unlawful assembly, and in 1970 was convicted of petit theft (later vacated).

26. 436 U.S. 547, 98 S.Ct. 1970, 56 L.Ed.2d 525 (1978), rehearing denied 439 U.S. 885, 99 S.Ct. 231, 58 L.Ed.2d 200 (1978).

subpoenas, are permissible in proper circumstances, it does not make a constitutional difference in our judgment.[27]

Thus there are no special privileges for the press to refrain from responding to either subpoenas or search warrants for evidence of a crime.

In *Zurcher* the police had probable cause to believe that the files of the student newspaper at Stanford University would contain photographs of persons who had assaulted police officers during a sit-in demonstration. On this basis they secured a search warrant to search for and seize such photographs in the newspaper office. Though locked drawers and rooms were not opened, the police did have an opportunity to read the newspaper's notes and correspondence, and the police did search the newspaper's photographic laboratories, filing cabinets, desks and waste paper baskets. No materials were removed from the newspaper offices. The newspaper later sued in federal court seeking, among other things, a declaratory judgment that the search violated the first and fourth amendments, as applied to the states through the fourteenth amendment. The district granted the declaratory judgment but the Supreme Court reversed.

First, the majority rejected any argument that the fourth amendment establishes different requirements for search warrants that are issued to search for material in possession of one not suspected of a crime, such as the student newspaper which only was thought to have evidence of a crime committed by others. The Supreme Court held that the fourth amendment is not a barrier to search for property on which there is probable cause to believe that the fruits, instrumentalities, or evidence of a crime is located, whether or not the owner or possessor of the premises covered by the warrant is reasonably suspected of involvement in the crime being investigated.

Secondly, the majority rejected any rule based on the first amendment that would require the use of subpoenas, rather than the more intrusive search procedure, when the premises to be searched are a newspaper's offices. The Supreme Court, however, did emphasize that where "the materials sought to be seized may be protected by the First Amendment, the requirements of the Fourth Amendment must be applied with 'scrupulous exactitude.' "[28] Thus in prior cases the Court has invalidated a search warrant authorizing a search of a private home for all books, records, and other materials relating to the Communist Party. The warrant in that context was the functional equivalent of a general warrant, which was prohibited by the fourth amendment.[29]

27. 436 U.S. at 566, 98 S.Ct. at 1982.
28. 436 U.S. at 564, 98 S.Ct. at 1981, citing Stanford v. Texas, 379 U.S. 476, 485, 85 S.Ct. 506, 511, 13 L.Ed.2d 431 (1965),

rehearing denied 380 U.S. 926, 85 S.Ct. 879, 13 L.Ed.2d 813 (1965).

29. Id.

Similarly, before a warrant may be issued for the seizure of allegedly obscene material, there must be an opportunity for the judicial officer to " 'focus searchingly on the question of obscenity; ' ".[30] Because of first amendment concerns, the police officer is not allowed to rely on merely his own judgment of what is obscene either in securing the warrant or seizing material without a warrant incident to an arrest.[31]

The majority in *Zurcher* did not believe that its ruling would result in a rash of incidents of police rummaging through newspaper files. First, there have been only a few instances since 1971 that search warrants have been issued to apply to newspaper premises,[32] and search warrants themselves—which are only issued by the judiciary upon proof of probable cause—are more difficult to obtain than subpoenas.[33] In addition, the local prosecutor would not likely choose the more difficult procedure unless he or she had a special reason. The prosecutor may wish to utilize the warrant procedure because of fear that the evidence might be destroyed if the less intrusive subpoena method were used. In *Zurcher,* the student newspaper had an announced policy of destroying photographs that could aid in the prosecution of protestors.[34]

Finally, while a subpoena is less intrusive, it is also much less satisfactory for prosecutorial purpose than a search warrant because the fifth amendment privilege against self incrimination is not available to one resisting a search warrant.[35] Thus, there are practical reasons supporting the majority's holding and past practices do not suggest that the warrant powers applied to newspaper premises will be abused.

Congress' Response to *Zurcher*. Nevertheless, Congress re-

30. 436 U.S. at 565, 98 S.Ct. at 1981, citing Marcus v. Search Warrants, 367 U.S. 717, 732, 81 S.Ct. 1708, 1716, 6 L.Ed.2d 1127 (1961); A Quantity of Copies of Books v. Kansas, 378 U.S. 205, 210, 84 S.Ct. 1723, 1725, 12 L.Ed.2d 809 (1964); Lee Art Theatre, Inc. v. Virginia, 392 U.S. 636, 637, 88 S.Ct. 2103, 2104, 20 L.Ed.2d 1313 (1968), on remand 209 Va. 354, 164 S.E.2d 665 (1968); Roaden v. Kentucky, 413 U.S. 496, 502, 93 S.Ct. 2796, 2800, 37 L.Ed.2d 757 (1973); and Heller v. New York, 413 U.S. 483, 489, 93 S.Ct. 2789, 2793, 37 L.Ed.2d 745 (1973), on remand 33 N.Y.2d 314, 352 N.Y.S.2d 601, 307 N.E.2d 805 (1973), certiorari denied 418 U.S. 944, 94 S.Ct. 3231, 41 L.Ed.2d 1175 (1974).

31. The Court, however, has upheld the use of a search warrant to search a law office for business records of criminal activity. Andresen v. Maryland, 427 U.S. 463, 96 S.Ct. 2737, 49 L.Ed.2d 627 (1976).

32. 436 U.S. at 566, 98 S.Ct. at 1982. However, the problem raised by *Zurcher* would not have arisen prior to 1967 when the Supreme Court finally rejected the "mere evidence" rule and thus allowed search warrants for mere evidence of a crime. Warden v. Hayden, 387 U.S. 294, 87 S.Ct. 1642, 18 L.Ed.2d 782 (1967). After that case, the focus of a special reporter's privilege was on the question of subpoenas, the issue dealt with in Branzburg v. Hayes, 408 U.S. 665, 92 S.Ct. 2646, 33 L.Ed.2d 626 (1972).

33. 436 U.S. at 562–63, 98 S.Ct. at 1980.

34. 436 U.S. at 568 n. 1, 98 S.Ct. at 1983 n. 1 (Powell, J., concurring).

35. Maness v. Meyers, 419 U.S. 449, 95 S.Ct. 584, 42 L.Ed.2d 574 (1975). Both Justice Stevens' dissent in *Zurcher,* and Justice Stewart's dissent (joined by Justice Marshall) did not answer this point.

sponded to *Zurcher* by enacting the Privacy Protection Act;[36] this law applies to state as well as federal law enforcement personnel. It limits their power to secure evidence from the news media by search warrant, and requires in many circumstances that they prefer a subpoena.

Comparison With Academic Freedom and Confidentiality of Tenure Review Process. The Court has long recognized that the first amendment protects academic freedom. In *Keyishian v. Board of Regents,*[37] for example, the Court explained: "Our Nation is deeply committed to safeguarding academic freedom, which is of transcendent value to all of us and not merely to the teachers concerned." [38]

However, while the government may not dictate or punish the "content" of the speech in which the university and those affiliated with it engage,[39] the government may prevent universities from discriminating on the basis of race, sex, and national origin in hiring decisions. The first amendment right of academic freedom does not give the university any privilege to avoid disclosure of its confidential peer review materials in a university professor's Title VII race and sex discrimination case; and the Equal Employment Opportunity Commission is not required to demonstrate any special justification to sustain the constitutionality of Title VII as applied to a subpoena requesting the university to produce tenure peer review materials.[40] The university, like the reporter in *Branzburg,* has no special immunity to refuse to comply with a subpoena, but, like the reporter in *Branzburg,* a "bad faith" exercise of the subpoena powers "might raise First Amendment concerns." [41]

§ 20.25   Judicial Protective Orders and the Press

The compatibility of a commitment to an "uninhibited, robust, and

36. Pub.L. 96–440, 94 Stat. 1879, codified at 42 U.S.C.A. §§ 2000aa–2000aa–12.

37. Importance of Academic Freedom. Keyishian v. Board of Regents of University of New York, 385 U.S. 589, 87 S.Ct. 675, 17 L.Ed.2d 629 (1967). See also, e.g., Adler v. Board of Education, 342 U.S. 485, 511, 72 S.Ct. 380, 394, 96 L.Ed. 517 (1952), noting that academic freedom is necessary to the "pursuit of truth which the First Amendment is designed to protect." See also, Regents of University of Michigan v. Ewing, 474 U.S. 214, 225, 106 S.Ct. 507, 513, 88 L.Ed.2d 523 (1985), warning that judges who are asked to review the substance of a "genuinely academic decision" should "show great respect for the faculty's professional judgement."

38. 385 U.S. at 603, 87 S.Ct. at 683.

39. E.g., Sweezy v. New Hampshire, 354 U.S. 234, 77 S.Ct. 1203, 1 L.Ed.2d 1311 (1957), rehearing denied 355 U.S. 852, 78 S.Ct. 7, 2 L.Ed.2d 61 (1957), where the Court overturned the contempt conviction of a person who refused to answer questions about the content of a lecture that he had presented at a state university.

40. University of Pennsylvania v. Equal Employment Opportunity Commission, 493 U.S. 182, 110 S.Ct. 577, 107 L.Ed.2d 571 (1990).

41. 493 U.S. at 201 & n. 8, 110 S.Ct. at 588 & n. 8, citing Branzburg v. Hayes, 408 U.S. 665, 92 S.Ct. 2646, 33 L.Ed.2d 626 (1972).

wide-open" discussion of public issues in a free press[1] with a commitment to a criminal process in which the "conclusions to be reached in a case will be induced only by evidence and argument in open court"[2] has been a subject of long standing debate.[3] The problem becomes more acute with the growth of national news coverage and the electronic media. The prominent issue within this area is the extent to which a trial judge may insulate his courtroom procedures from the intrusion of outside prejudice caused by publicity surrounding the case. In this area the rights of the press often conflict with the rights of the accused. The Supreme Court offered a qualified response to this question when it invalidated a Nebraska district court "gag order" which prohibited the press from the publication of certain implicative evidence pertaining to a murder suspect until the jury selection process was completed.[4]

Pre-trial Publicity, Cameras in the Courts, and Court Orders Against the Press. Well before the Nebraska decision the danger to the sixth amendment guarantee of a fair trial posed by inflammatory publicity had become apparent following a series of cases in which the Court reversed state convictions upon a finding that pre-trial publicity had so infected the trial atmosphere to amount to a denial of due process. The first reversal of a state conviction due to prejudicial pre-trial publicity occurred in 1961[5] in *Irvin v. Dowd.*[6]

In that case, ninety percent of the venire and eight of the twelve members of the petit jury admitted that they had formed opinions based on the publicity surrounding the murder, and this result was obtained *after* a change of venue to an adjoining county. The unanimous opinion of the Court, by Justice Clark, stated:

> To hold that the mere existence of any preconceived notion as to the guilt or innocence of an accused, without more, is sufficient to rebut the presumption of a prospective juror's impartiality would be to establish an impossible standard. It is sufficient if the juror can lay aside his impression or opinion and render a verdict based on the evidence presented in court.... With his life at stake, it is not requiring too much that petitioner be tried in an atmosphere undisturbed by so huge a wave of public passion and by a jury

§ 20.25

1. New York Times Co. v. Sullivan, 376 U.S. 254, 84 S.Ct. 710, 11 L.Ed.2d 686 (1964), motion denied 376 U.S. 967, 84 S.Ct. 1130, 12 L.Ed.2d 83 (1964).

See generally, Harry Kalven, Jr., ed. by Jamie Kalven, A Worthy Tradition: Freedom of Speech in America 24–32 (1988).

2. Patterson v. Colorado, 205 U.S. 454, 27 S.Ct. 556, 51 L.Ed. 879 (1907).

3. See Chief Justice Burger's discussion of the history of this conflict in Nebraska Press Ass'n v. Stuart, 427 U.S. 539, 547–51, 96 S.Ct. 2791, 2797–99, 49 L.Ed.2d 683 (1976).

4. Nebraska Press Ass'n v. Stuart, 427 U.S. 539, 96 S.Ct. 2791, 49 L.Ed.2d 683 (1976).

5. Federal convictions had previously been overturned in the exercise of the federal supervisory power, see Marshall v. United States, 360 U.S. 310, 79 S.Ct. 1171, 3 L.Ed.2d 1250 (1959).

6. 366 U.S. 717, 81 S.Ct. 1639, 6 L.Ed.2d 751 (1961).

other than one in which two-thirds of the members admit, before hearing any testimony, to possessing a belief in his guilt.[7]

Although concurring in the judgment of the Court, Justice Frankfurter portended the future by acerbically noting the omission of any discussion of the responsibilities of the press in protecting the fair trial guarantee:

> The Court has not yet decided that, while convictions must be reversed and miscarriages of justice result because the minds of jurors or potential jurors were poisoned, the poisoner is constitutionally protected in plying his trade.[8]

Nevertheless, the Court continued to avoid this issue as the appeals mounted following *Irvin*. In *Rideau v. Louisiana*,[9] the Court found that a denial of a request for change in venue offended due process when a local television had broadcast a film of the defendant confessing to the crimes in response to leading questions by the sheriff. The opinion indicates that the Court's reaction may be attributable to the coercive and pervasive nature of the television medium and the apparent complicity of the state in the broadcast.[10]

This view of the case is buttressed by the result in *Estes v. Texas*,[11] in which the presence of television cameras recording the trial proceedings for rebroadcast over the defendant's objections was found to be so inherently intrusive that a violation of due process was inevitable. As the majority opinion of Justice Clark observed,

> It is true that in most cases involving claims of due process deprivations we require a showing of identifiable prejudice to the accused. Nevertheless, at times a procedure employed by the state involves such a probability that prejudice will result that it is deemed inherently lacking in due process.[12]

The Court believed that the incremental value of television reporting over traditional print reporting in serving the press function of providing the public with information on the operation of the criminal justice system was negligible and could justifiably be sacrificed in light of the impact that television cameras had upon the judicial process. However Justice Harlan's concurring opinion left open the possibility

---

7. 366 U.S. at 723, 728, 81 S.Ct. at 1643, 1645.

8. 366 U.S. at 730, 81 S.Ct. at 1646.

9. 373 U.S. 723, 83 S.Ct. 1417, 10 L.Ed.2d 663 (1963), on remand 246 La. 451, 165 So.2d 282 (1964). Clark and Harlan, JJ., dissented.

10. Justice Clark's dissent found this conduct reprehensible, but argued that, as state officials, they violated no constitutional mandate and remedies were proper-

ly left to the states. 373 U.S. at 727–33, 83 S.Ct. at 1419–23.

11. 381 U.S. 532, 85 S.Ct. 1628, 14 L.Ed.2d 543 (1965), rehearing denied 382 U.S. 875, 86 S.Ct. 18, 15 L.Ed.2d 118 (1965), on remand 396 S.W.2d 123 (Tex.Crim.App. 1965). Justices Black, Brennan, Stewart and White dissented.

12. 381 U.S. at 542–43, 85 S.Ct. at 1632–33.

that future experimentation with the television might produce different results.[13]

Nearly two decades later the Supreme Court retreated from the broad implications of Justice Clark's opinion in *Estes* and instead followed the direction of Justice Harlan's *Estes'* concurring opinion.[14] *Chandler v. Florida*[15] held that there is no per se constitutional prohibition against Florida providing for radio, television, and still photographic coverage of a criminal trial for public broadcast, notwithstanding the objection of the accused.

In *Chandler,* Chief Justice Burger speaking for the Court, first concluded that *Estes* did not establish a per se rule. The Court then noted that many of the negative factors relating to television coverage that existed in 1962, when Estes was tried—"cumbersome equipment, cables, distracting lighting, numerous camera technicians—are less substantial factors today than they were at that time."[16]

In addition, the Florida program avoided many of the most egregious problems that had concerned the justices in *Estes.* Under the program the Florida courts are admonished to protect certain witnesses (e.g., children, victims of sex crimes, some informants, the very timid) from the tensions of being televised. If the accused objects to broadcast coverage, the trial judge may define the steps necessary to eliminate the risks of prejudice to the accused.[17] The Florida guidelines also provided for other safeguards, such as the use of only one television camera in a fixed position, only one technician, no artificial lighting, no changing of film, videotape and lenses while court is in session, and no filming of the jury.[18]

The Court concluded that due process did not require any per se prohibition against broadcasting of criminal trials. Since the defendants did not demonstrate with "specificity that the presence of cameras impaired the ability of jurors to decide the case on only the evidence before them or that the trial was affected adversely by the impact on any of the participants of the presence of cameras and the prospect of broadcast," the convictions were affirmed.[19]

The Sam Sheppard Case and the Role of Protective Orders. In addition to problems related to the general topic discussed above and often called "cameras in the courts," the Supreme Court has had to lay guidelines governing judicial power to restrict prejudicial pretrial pub-

13. Justice Harlan limited the majority holding to merely stating that no requirement existed that television be allowed in a courtroom over the defendant's objections, particularly on a case of great notoriety, 381 U.S. at 587, 85 S.Ct. at 1662.

14. 381 U.S. at 587, 85 S.Ct. at 1662.

15. 449 U.S. 560, 101 S.Ct. 802, 66 L.Ed.2d 740 (1981).

See generally, Note, Cameras in the Criminal Courtroom: A Sixth Amendment Analysis, 85 Column.L.Rev. 1546 (1985).

16. 449 U.S. at 575, 101 S.Ct. at 810.

17. 449 U.S. at 577, 101 S.Ct. at 811.

18. 449 U.S. at 565, 101 S.Ct. at 804–05.

19. 449 U.S. at 582, 101 S.Ct. at 813.

licity. *Sheppard v. Maxwell*,[20] the appeal from the celebrated Dr. Sam Sheppard murder trial, found the Court again concerning itself with the manner in which conduct of the press offended defendant's due process rights to a fair trial. The Court held that the trial judge had failed to properly protect the defendant, jurors, and witnesses from the firestorm of publicity, much of which was erroneous and prejudicial. The Court reversed the conviction, noting that there were more than adequate procedures at the judge's disposal to prevent a murder trial from being converted into a "carnival." In particular, the Court emphasized stricter control over the activities of the press within the courtroom and provision for the insulation of witnesses.[21] Moreover, when it is apparent that the crime has already attracted massive publicity, the trial judge must take pre-trial steps to remove the prejudice inherent in such publicity from the trial itself.[22]

Initially, the Court said, the judge has the duty of intensive voir dire examination of prospective jurors to assure himself that excessive pre-trial publicity has not clouded the juror's presumed impartiality. Once a jury is selected, sequestration will protect its members from being subjected to the opinions and possible intimidations of an aroused community. Should the judge determine that such procedures have already been rendered inadequate by press accounts of the crime and its investigation, the alternatives of a continuance or a change of venue should be considered.

The opinion in *Sheppard* also stressed the responsibilities of the parties to the case, i.e. defense and prosecution counsel, police officers, and witnesses, not to release information to the press. Should they evidence an inclination to abdicate this responsibility, the judge should re-impose it by court order.

> Had the judge, the other officers of the court, and the police placed the interest of justice first, the news media would have soon learned to be content with the task of reporting the case as it unfolded in the courtroom—not pieced together from extrajudicial statements.[23]

And, in a highly significant passage, the Court concluded,

> From the cases coming here we note that unfair and prejudicial news comment on pending trials has become increasingly prevalent ... [T]here is nothing that proscribes the press from reporting events that transpire in the courtroom.... But we must remember that reversals are but palliatives; the cure lies in those remedial measures that will prevent the prejudice at its inception. The

---

20. 384 U.S. 333, 86 S.Ct. 1507, 16 L.Ed.2d 600 (1966).

21. 384 U.S. at 358, 86 S.Ct. at 1519–20.

22. 384 U.S. at 358–59, 86 S.Ct. at 1519–20.

23. 384 U.S. at 362, 86 S.Ct. at 1522.

courts must take such steps by rule and regulation that will protect their processes from prejudicial outside interferences.[24]

Within those words lay the genesis of future controversy.

Faced with increasing claims of prejudice following *Sheppard*,[25] trial courts began increasing utilization of protective orders to prevent the publication of inflammatory material, at least until a jury was impaneled. The dilemma confronting the courts and law enforcement officials was a real one, because the most heinous crimes attracted the greatest publicity, some of which was irresponsible, and were thus the most prone to be prejudicially affected by that publicity.[26] Protective orders provided a method of controlling this possibility.

However a judicial protecture order was neither the least restrictive nor the most efficacious method of resolving the dilemma, as early recognized by Justice Powell, speaking in his capacity as Circuit Judge for the Fifth Circuit, in *Times–Picayune Publishing Corp. v. Schulingkamp*.[27] He stayed a protective order promulgated by a criminal court judge in New Orleans which banned the publication of information on a murder trial until a jury had been selected, because there had been no showing of an imminent threat to a fair trial or that the alternative measures outlined in *Sheppard* would be insufficient to protect the accused's rights.[28]

The *Nebraska Press* Decision and Protective Orders. The full Court did not get an opportunity to hear arguments on this basic issue until two years later, in another case, *Nebraska Press Association v. Stuart*,[29] an appeal by members of the state press association challenging a restraining order prohibiting them from publishing confessions by an accused in a murder trial (except those made directly to members of

24. 384 U.S. at 362–65, 86 S.Ct. at 1522.

25. E.g., Doggett v. Yeager, 472 F.2d 229 (3d Cir.1973).

26. See Report of the President's Commission on the Assassination of President Kennedy, 94–99 (Assoc. Press ed. 1964) for the publicity of the Lee Harvey Oswald case.

27. 419 U.S. 1301, 95 S.Ct. 1, 42 L.Ed.2d 17 (1974).

28. While attention has focused on the extent of a court's power to issue restraining orders in criminal cases, the first amendment implications of such orders in civil cases is also not to be forgotten. In Gulf Oil Co. v. Bernard, 452 U.S. 89, 101 S.Ct. 2193, 68 L.Ed.2d 693 (1981), for example, the Court, speaking through Justice Powell, restricted the scope of a federal district court's authority to limit communications from named plaintiffs and their counsel to prospective class members during the pendency of class action. Although the Court based its ruling on its interpretation of the Federal Rules of Civil Procedure, particularly Rule 23, it acknowledged the first amendment interests and ruled that any order limiting communications between parties and potential class members should be based on a clear record and specific findings that reflect a weighing of the need for a limitation and the potential interference with the right of the parties.

29. 427 U.S. 539, 96 S.Ct. 2791, 49 L.Ed.2d 683 (1976).

See Marcus, The Media in the Courtroom, Attending, Reporting, Televising Criminal Cases, 57 Ind.L.J. 235 (1982), arguing for less judicial deference to the media.

the press) as well as other facts "strongly implicative" of the accused.[30] In this posture, the case is removed from the due process cases previously discussed by its direct challenge, by the press, to the validity of such an order in light of the hostility of the first amendment toward prior restraints.[31] The Court unanimously held the order invalid, but there were five separate opinions.

The opinion of the Court, written by Chief Justice Burger, was subscribed to by four other members.[32] The Chief Justice, after narrating the history of those cases invalidating prior restraints, characterized them as follows:

> Prior restraints on speech are the most serious and least tolerable infringement on First Amendment rights.... A prior restraint ... has an immediate and irreversible sanction. If it can be said that a threat of criminal or civil sanctions after publication "chills" speech, prior restraint "freezes" it at least for the time.[33]

By contrast, deprivations of due process do not inevitably result from unregulated publicity surrounding notorious crimes. Rather, it was only in a rare circumstance that publicity could be regarded as fatally infecting the judicial process.[34]

This view does not indicate that the rights of an accused awaiting trial are always subordinated to those of the press as embodied in the first amendment. While the barriers to the validity of prior restraints remain high, they are not insuperable, as the Chief Justice took pains to point out.

> If the authors of these guarantees, fully aware of the potential conflicts between them, were unwilling or unable to resolve the issue by assigning to one priority over the other, it is not for us to rewrite the Constitution by undertaking what they declined to do.[35]

The opinion of the Court concluded that the state, before it could suppress commentary by the press on evidentiary matters, must demonstrate that "further publicity, unchecked, would so distort the views of potential jurors that 12 could not be found who would, under proper instructions, fulfill their sworn duty to render a just verdict exclusively on the evidence presented in open court."[36] The Court adopted this very strict test because of the historical antipathy towards prior re-

---

30. 427 U.S. at 541, 96 S.Ct. at 2794.

31. See Near v. Minnesota, 283 U.S. 697, 51 S.Ct. 625, 75 L.Ed. 1357 (1931); New York Times v. United States, 403 U.S. 713, 91 S.Ct. 2140, 29 L.Ed.2d 822 (1971).

32. Justices White, Blackmun, Powell, and Rehnquist joined in the majority opinion. Justice Brennan (with Justices Stewart and Marshall joining) and Justices White, Powell, and Stevens all wrote separate concurring opinions.

33. Nebraska Press Ass'n v. Stuart, 427 U.S. 539, 559, 96 S.Ct. 2791, 2803, 49 L.Ed.2d 683 (1976).

34. 427 U.S. at 560–61, 96 S.Ct. at 2803–04.

35. 427 U.S. at 561, 96 S.Ct. at 2803–04.

36. Nebraska Press Association v. Stuart, 427 U.S. 539, 569, 96 S.Ct. 2791, 2807, 49 L.Ed.2d 683 (1976).

straint. In addition, the press—unlike the litigants or their lawyers,—is not a party to the law suit.

However, despite the fact that pretrial press coverage posed a severe danger to the neutrality of the trial, the trial court in *Nebraska Press* had not made a showing that the entire panoply of procedures outlined in *Sheppard* would be insufficient to forestall this occurrence; for example, continuance, change of venue, intensive voir dire examination, sequestration of the jurors, instruction on the duty of each juror to decide the issues on the evidence, and restraining orders on the parties involved and their attorneys in discussing issues with the press. In the absence of such a showing, the imposition of a protective order could never overcome the heavy presumption against constitutionality which inevitably attaches to prior restraints.

Further, there existed no assurance that such an order would even have served to eliminate the offending danger. Jurisdictional difficulties exist, because the editors of some of the publications might well lie beyond the reach of the *in personam* jurisdiction of the court while their publications are distributed throughout the country or district from which the jurors are drawn. Moreover, the speculative nature of a protective order created problems in drafting since it appeared to prohibit the publication of material which would not possess a prejudicial effect while not encompassing seemingly innocent information which would later develop into very damaging evidence.

Finally, the Court emphasized that that portion of the order which prohibited the publication of information obtained in open court could under no circumstances prevail. As was said in *Sheppard*, "there is nothing which proscribes the press from reporting events that transpire in the courtroom".[37] The judge may in his discretion, if the relevant statutes allow, and subject to constitutional limitations discussed below, close the courtroom during portions of the proceedings, but if that alternative is bypassed, it cannot be effectuated retroactively by a protective order. If the information is lawfully obtained from an open hearing in court, its republication by the press cannot be restrained.[38]

37. Sheppard v. Maxwell, 384 U.S. 333, 86 S.Ct. 1507, 16 L.Ed.2d 600 (1966); cf. Cox Broadcasting Corp. v. Cohn, 420 U.S. 469, 95 S.Ct. 1029, 43 L.Ed.2d 328 (1975), on remand 234 Ga. 67, 214 S.E.2d 530 (1975).

38. Cf. Cox Broadcasting Corp. v. Cohn, 420 U.S. 469, 95 S.Ct. 1029, 43 L.Ed.2d 328 (1975), on remand 234 Ga. 67, 214 S.E.2d 530 (1975); Virginia State Bd. of Pharmacy v. Virginia Citizens Consumer Council, Inc., 425 U.S. 748, 96 S.Ct. 1817, 48 L.Ed.2d 346 (1976). See also, Oklahoma Publishing Co. v. District Court, 430 U.S. 308, 97 S.Ct. 1045, 51 L.Ed.2d 355 (1977) (per curiam).

In Landmark Communications, Inc. v. Virginia, 435 U.S. 829, 98 S.Ct. 1535, 56 L.Ed.2d 1 (1978) the Court held that a state cannot punish a newspaper or other third party who is neither an employee nor participant of a judicial disciplinary commission for publishing truthful information about a confidential investigation in progress. The Court noted that such publication lies "near the core" of the First Amendment and that criminally punishing was not justified by the interests advanced by the state, the Supreme Court found the state's justifications insufficient, noting that New York Times v. Sullivan, 376 U.S.

Justice Brennan in his separate opinion argued that the only instance in which the presumption against prior restraints is rebuttable is in crises affecting national security. In all other situations, the protections of the first amendment must remain preeminent. The defendant's rights to a fair trial must rest upon those procedures which had traditionally been within the province of the trial judge.[39]

254, 272–73, 84 S.Ct. 710, 722, 11 L.Ed.2d 686 (1964), motion denied 376 U.S. 967, 84 S.Ct. 1130, 12 L.Ed.2d 83 (1964), had "firmly established" that injury to official reputation was insufficient reason "for repressing speech that would otherwise be free." There was no support for the claim that without criminal sanctions against nonparticipants the objectives of the statutory scheme would be seriously undermined, since the advantages of confidentiality may still be served without such sanctions.

See also Smith v. Daily Mail Publishing Co., 443 U.S. 97, 99 S.Ct. 2667, 61 L.Ed.2d 399 (1979) (state may not punish a newspaper's truthful publication of an alleged juvenile delinquent's name lawfully obtained by a newspaper).

39. 427 U.S. at 572–613, 96 S.Ct. at 2809–29, Justices Stewart and Marshall joining.

The Noriega Tapes. In Cable News Network, Inc. v. Noriega, ___ U.S. ___, 111 S.Ct. 451, 112 L.Ed.2d 432 (1990), the Supreme Court (7 to 2) refused to stay a district court order restraining the television broadcast of tapes of conversations Manuel Noriega had with his attorneys while in prison. The Supreme Court issued no opinion to accompany its decision, but Justice Marshall, joined by Justice O'Connor, wrote a short dissent. Manuel Noriega had been the dictator of Panama, who was deposed after American forces invaded Panama and was arrested for illegal drug dealings.

Cable News Network, Inc. v. Noriega involves a battle between the press's First Amendment right to be free from prior restraints on speech and a criminal defendant's Sixth Amendment rights to a fair trial and effective legal counsel as well as his right to privacy under the Fourth Amendment. Citing the well-known Pentagon Papers decision, New York Times Co. v. United States, 403 U.S. 713, 91 S.Ct. 2140, 29 L.Ed.2d 822 (1971), Justice Marshall, joined by O'Connor, supported a stay of the lower court's order prohibiting the broadcast of the tapes because, he argued, a criminal defendant should be required to make at least a threshold showing that the

information sought to be enjoined will threaten his right to a fair trial and that suppression (i.e., the prior restraint) is the only means of averting that harm. The lower court, in contrast, had ruled that no such showing was necessary until the tapes were first surrendered to the court for inspection. See United States v. Noriega, 752 F.Supp. 1032, 18 Media L.Rep. 1348 (S.D.Fla.1990) The Cable News Network ("CNN") had refused such a surrender at the time of the initial order. United States v. Noriega, 752 F.Supp. 1045, 1047, 18 Media L.Rep. 1537 (S.D.Fla.1990).

In defiance of the District Court's temporary restraining order of November 8, 1990 prohibiting the television broadcast of the privileged attorney-client conversations, CNN aired segments containing these conversations on November 9 and 10. United States v. Noriega, 752 F.Supp. at 1047. CNN's legal staff believed that either Noriega or his attorney had waived any alleged attorney-client privilege and that the lower court's restraining order was erroneous. Los Angeles Times, Part A, p. 36, Col. 1, Nov. 22, 1990. Nonetheless, on November 10, the 11th Circuit upheld the lower court's restraining order and the Supreme Court denied a stay of the temporary restraining order on November 18, 1990.

It was not until November 26, 1990, that CNN complied with the District Court's order to produce the tapes. After the denial of certiorari, the same trial court judge who had issued the temporary restraining order then examined the tapes, and decided that the CNN broadcast of the tapes did not and would not threaten Noriega's right to a fair trial; consequently, the judge lifted the order on December 6, 1990. The judge, however, reserved the right to file criminal contempt charges against CNN for its broadcast of the tapes in flagrant disobedience to the original order.

The controversial portion of the tapes contained a conversation between Noriega and an employee of Mr. Rubino, who was Noriega's attorney. The United States Prison Bureau randomly monitors and

However, five of the justices thought that it was unnecessary to formulate such a broad rule on the basis of the facts. Because the state courts had made no finding as to the efficacy of these alternative procedures, it might, in theory, still be permitted to argue that, in highly unusual circumstances, a fair trial will be impossible to obtain without a limitation upon the information that the press can publish.[40] Such a position might possibly be acceptable to only some of the justices, and then, only as a last resort.

The *Gentile* Case—Controlling Lawyers and the "Substantial Likelihood of Material Prejudice" Test. Perhaps the most important practical result of the *Nebraska Press Association* case may be the increase of restraining orders on those parties who are under the court's control: the litigants and their attorneys, and the agents of either the litigants or their attorneys. Such orders may be more effective in light of the holding in *Branzburg v. Hayes,* which supports the power of the court to compel reporters to reveal their sources of information.[41] The courts, in short, can control pretrial publicity by enforcing attorney ethics rules governing pretrial and trial publicity.

But such "silence orders" issues against the attorneys for the litigants will not usually be upheld unless there is a substantial likelihood of material prejudice to a fair trial. The "substantial likelihood of material prejudice" test is the rule after *Gentile v. State Bar of Nevada.*[42]

tapes all prisoners telephone lines as a routine security measure. This monitoring was not covert: a sticker affixed to Noriega's phone alerted him to the fact that his conversations were so monitored. To exclude a privileged conversation from such monitoring a prisoner had to request permission to use a different phone, which Noriega had not done. United States v. Noriega, 764 F.Supp. 1480 (S.D.Fla.1991). The prosecution obtained the tapes through a subpoena, gave copies of a few of them to the Panamanian government, and from there they were leaked to a Panamanian-based CNN reporter. The Washington Post, § 1, at p. A1, Nov. 25, 1990.

The conversation that caused all of the controversy was, in fact, insignificant. Noriega had read about the arrest of two Panamanians in the Miami Herald and in the conversation inquired of his lawyer's employee if that employee knew whether the two were going to be government witnesses in the case against him. United States v. Noriega, 752 F.Supp. at 1053. This conversation was the basis for the original court order. See generally, Rodney Smolla, Free Speech In an Open Society

ty 243–90 (1992) (discussing the Noriega Tapes).

40. See United States v. Abbott Laboratories, 369 F.Supp. 1396 (E.D.N.C.1973), judgment reversed 505 F.2d 565 (4th Cir. 1974), certiorari denied 420 U.S. 990, 95 S.Ct. 1424, 43 L.Ed.2d 671 (1975). This was an unusual case, in which the trial court dismissed the indictment for introduction of adulterated drugs into interstate commerce on the grounds that alternative procedures were insufficient to ensure a fair trial. This ruling of the trial court cannot be justified, for its logical conclusion is that if a crime is heinous enough—perhaps even was committed on television—the resulting publicity (created by the crime itself) should be enough to prevent a trial. The appellate court appropriately reversed.

41. 408 U.S. 665, 92 S.Ct. 2646, 33 L.Ed.2d 626 (1972).

42. 501 U.S. ___, 111 S.Ct. 2720, 115 L.Ed.2d 888 (1991).

See also, Chicago Council of Lawyers v. Bauer, 522 F.2d 242 (7th Cir.1975), certiorari denied sub nom., Cunningham v. Chicago Council of Lawyers, 427 U.S. 912, 96

143

This test is not as strict as that applied in *Nebraska Press Association v. Stuart.* Recall that in that case, discussed above, the state, before it could suppress press commentary on evidentiary matters, must demonstrate that "further publicity, unchecked, would so distort the views of potential jurors that 12 could not be found who would, under proper instructions, fulfill their sworn duty to render a just verdict exclusively on the evidence presented in open court."[43] In contrast, *Gentile* applies a less strict test because the judicial order is not against the press, a nonparty to the proceeding, but is against the lawyers who represent the parties to the proceeding.

In this case, Attorney Gentile held a press conference a few hours after Nevada had indicted his client. Gentile made a brief statement but declined to answer reporters' questions seeking more detailed comments. Six months later a jury acquitted Gentile's client of all counts. Then the State Bar of Nevada filed a complaint against Gentile for allegedly violating Nevada's Supreme Court Rule 177, governing pretrial publicity. This ethics rule is almost identical to ABA Model Rule 3.6, ABA Model Rules of Professional Conduct.[44] The Nevada Disciplinary Board recommended a private reprimand for Mr. Gentile and the State Supreme Court agreed. But on appeal, a very divided U.S. Supreme Court reversed.[45]

Nevada Rule 177(1) prohibits an attorney from making "an extrajudicial statement that a reasonable person would expect to be disseminated by means of public communication if the lawyer knows or reasonably should know that it will have a substantial likelihood of materially prejudicing an adjudicative proceeding." The next subsection of this rule, Rule 177(2), then lists a number of statements (e.g., the expected testimony of a witness, or the credibility, reputation, or criminal record of a party) that are "ordinarily ... likely" to result in material prejudice. Then, Rule 177(3) purports to provide a "safe harbor," listing statements that can be made (e.g., the general nature of the claim or defense, information contained in a public record, etc.) "notwithstanding" the previous two sections.

S.Ct. 3201, 40 L.Ed.2d 1204 (1976); Hirschkop v. Snead, 594 F.2d 356 (4th Cir.1979) (per curiam).

See generally, T. Morgan & R. Rotunda, Problems and Materials on Professional Responsibility 295–306 (5th ed. 1991).

43. Nebraska Press Association v. Stuart, 427 U.S. 539, 569, 96 S.Ct. 2791, 2807, 49 L.Ed.2d 683 (1976).

44. Reprinted, e.g., in T. Morgan & R. Rotunda, 1991 Selected Standards on Professional Responsibility 71–72 (Foundation Press, 1991).

45. Kennedy, J., announced the judgment of the Court, and delivered the opinion of the Court with respect to Parts III and VI. Marshall, Blackmun, Stevens, & O'Connor, JJ., joined that opinion. Kennedy, J. (joined by Marshall, Blackmun, & Stevens, JJ.) also delivered a separate opinion as to Parts I, II, IV, & V.

Rehnquist, C.J. delivered the opinion of the Court with respect to Parts I & II. White, O'Connor, Scalia, and Souter, JJ., joined that opinion. Rehnquist, C.J. also delivered a dissenting opinion with respect to Part III; White, O'Connor, & Souter, JJ. joined that dissenting opinion. Finally, O'Connor, J. also filed a concurring opinion.

Justice Kennedy, for the Court, in Part III, held that Rule 177, as interpreted by the State Court, was unconstitutionally vague: the safe harbor provision of Rule 177(3), by the use of the word "notwithstanding," misled Gentile into thinking that he could give his press conference without fear of discipline, as long as he complied with Rule 177(3), even if he should have reasonably known that his statements would have a substantial likelihood of materially prejudicing an adjudicative proceeding.

A review of the press conference supported Gentile's claim that he thought that Rule 177(3) protected his statements. Gentile gave only a brief opening statement. On numerous occasions he decline to answer a reporter's questions seeking more information. Even though Gentile studied the ethics rules and made "a conscious effort" to comply with them, he was still found to be in violation, demonstrating that "Rule 177 creates a trap for the wary as well as the unwary." [46]

Part I of Justice Kennedy's separate Opinion [47] emphasized that it was important to realize what this case was about:

> [O]ne central point must dominate the analysis: this case involves classic political speech. The State Bar of Nevada reprimanded petitioner for his assertion, supported by a brief sketch of his client's defense, that the State sought the indictment and conviction of an innocent man as a "scapegoat," and had not "been honest enough to indict the people who did it; the police department, crooked cops." At issue here is the constitutionality of a ban on political speech critical of the government and its officials. [48]

Even though Mr. Gentile won—given the specific facts of his case and given the ambiguity created by Nevada's "safe harbor" provision— Chief Justice Rehnquist, who authored another portion of the Opinion of the Court, [49] approved of the "substantial likelihood" test found in Nevada Rule 177. This portion of the Opinion concluded that the "substantial likelihood of material prejudice" test satisfies the first amendment interests when used to restrict the speech of lawyers representing clients in pending cases, even though it is admittedly less protective of speech interests than the *Nebraska Press Association* test, which is used to regulate the speech of a nonparty, the press, during pending proceedings. [50] Rehnquist, for the Court, specifically rejected

46. 501 U.S. at ___, 111 S.Ct. at 2732 (Kennedy, J., Part III, Opinion for the Court). In Part II, Kennedy J., joined by Marshall, Blackmun, & Stevens, JJ. noted that neither "the disciplinary board nor the reviewing court explain any sense in which petitioner's statements had a substantial likelihood of causing material prejudice." 501 U.S. at ___, 111 S.Ct. at 2726.

47. Only Marshall, Blackmun, & Stevens, JJ. joined this part.

48. 501 U.S. at ___, 111 S.Ct. at 2720 (Opinion of Kennedy, J., joined by Marshall, Blackmun, & Stevens, JJ.).

49. He was joined by White, O'Connor, Scalia, & Souter, JJ. as to his portions of the opinion labelled Parts I and II.

50. At the time that *Gentile* was decided, most jurisdictions, had adopted the "substantial likelihood of material preju-

the argument that Nevada must demonstrate a "clear and present danger" or "actual prejudice of imminent threat" before discipline can be imposed on a lawyer. Rehnquist noted that this restraint on lawyers' speech is narrowly tailored because it applies only to speech that is substantially likely to have a materially prejudicial effect, is neutral as to points of view, and does not forbid the lawyer from speaking but merely postpones it until after the trial.[51]

The Right to a Public Trial and the _Gannett_ Case. To cope with problems of pretrial publicity, courts at times have sought to close portions of the proceedings to the public, because where the press lawfully obtains information the court cannot thereafter prohibit the press from publishing it.[52] In _Gannett Co., Inc. v. DePasquale_,[53] the Supreme Court upheld this practice under the narrow circumstances of that case. The Court held, by a five to four vote, that neither the public nor the press has an independent constitutional right to insist upon access to a _pretrial_ suppression hearing, _if_ the accused, the prosecutor, and the trial judge all agree that the proceeding should be closed in order to assure a fair trial.

The majority first noted that to safeguard the due process rights of the accused a trial judge may take "protective measures [to minimize the effects of prejudicial pretrial publicity] even when they are not strictly and inescapably necessary."[54] Publicity as to pretrial suppression hearings is particularly unfair because the purpose of such hearings is to screen out unreliable or illegally obtained evidence and insure that the prospective jury does not learn of such evidence. After the trial has begun and the jury chosen, on the other hand, the trial court has a variety of other means to keep information from the jury.

Second, the majority emphasized that the sixth amendment guarantee of a public trial is a right personal to the accused.[55] Although

dice" test. 501 U.S. at ___, 111 S.Ct. at 2741 (Rehnquist, C.J., for the Court).

Cf. Sheppard v. Maxwell, 384 U.S. 333, 363, 86 S.Ct. 1507, 1522, 16 L.Ed.2d 600 (1966): "Collaboration between counsel and the press as to information affecting the fairness of a criminal trial is not only subject to regulation, but is highly censurable and worthy of disciplinary measures."

51. 501 U.S. at ___, 111 S.Ct. at 2745 (Part II of Opinion of Rehnquist, C.J., for the Court).

52. Landmark Communications, Inc. v. Virginia, 435 U.S. 829, 98 S.Ct. 1535, 56 L.Ed.2d 1 (1978); Smith v. Daily Mail Pub. Co., 443 U.S. 97, 99 S.Ct. 2667, 61 L.Ed.2d 399 (1979).

53. 443 U.S. 368, 99 S.Ct. 2898, 61 L.Ed.2d 608 (1979).

54. 443 U.S. at 377–78, 99 S.Ct. at 2904 (1979).

55. 443 U.S. at 380, 99 S.Ct. at 2905, quoting Blackmun, J., dissenting in Faretta v. California, 422 U.S. 806, 846, 95 S.Ct. 2525, 2546, 45 L.Ed.2d 562 (1975): "[T]he specific guarantees of the Sixth Amendment are personal to the accused." Justice Blackmun, joined by Brennan, White, and Marshall, JJ., dissented in _Gannett_ on all issues except in the majority's holding that the case was not moot. Justice Blackmun thought it "clear" from the prior cases that "the fact that the Sixth Amendment casts the right to a public trial in terms of the right of the accused is not sufficient to permit the inference that the accused may compel a private proceeding simply by waiving the right." 443 U.S. at 418, 99 S.Ct. at 2925. On the facts of this case

the majority conceded that "there is a strong societal interest in public trials" it held that interest does not involve a constitutional right on the part of the public.[56] Yet the *Gannett* Court would not grant defendant a right to insist on a closed hearing since the five member-majority emphasized that the waiver of the defendant was joined with the consent of the prosecutor and the approval of the court. To these participants is delegated the duty to protect the public interest.[57] Also, the majority phrased the issue narrowly: "whether the Constitution *requires* that a pretrial proceeding such as this one be opened to the public even though the participants in the litigation agree that it should be closed to protect the defendant's right to a fair trial." [58] The majority answered this question in the negative, but also stated that a court's failure to close a pretrial hearing does not necessarily require reversal of a subsequent conviction.[59] Thus it would appear that the defendant does not have an absolute right to close a hearing over the objection of the judge and prosecutor.

There were various suggestions in *Gannett* indicating that the opinion should be read narrowly. The majority emphasized that any denial of public access was only temporary, because once the danger of prejudice had dissipated the court made available a transcript of the suppression hearing.[60] The majority also discussed the dangers of pretrial publicity in this particular case.

In addition, the decision was a five to four opinion, so a shift of even one vote would change the result. Three of the five member majority wrote separate concurrences. Chief Justice Burger emphasized that what was involved in their case was "not a *trial;* it is a *pre-trial hearing*." [61] Justice Powell concurring, stated that he would have held that the press, as an agent of the public, does have a first amendment right to be present at the pretrial suppression hearing but that on balance this nonabsolute right was adequately respected in the present case.[62] Only Justice Rehnquist, concurring, argued that if the parties agreed to a closed proceeding, the trial court need not advance any reason whatsoever for declining to open a pretrial hearing "or trial" to the public.[63]

The four member dissent would have held that pretrial hearings could be closed only upon a showing of "strict and inescapable necessi-

Justice Blackmun concluded that there was an insufficient showing to establish "the strict and inescapable necessity that supports a suppression order." 443 U.S. at 447, 99 S.Ct. at 2940.

56. 443 U.S. at 382, 99 S.Ct. at 2907.

57. 443 U.S. at 384 & n. 12, 99 S.Ct. at 2907–08 & n. 12.

58. 443 U.S. at 384, 99 S.Ct. at 2908 (emphasis in original) (footnote omitted).

59. 443 U.S. at 379 n. 6, 99 S.Ct. at 2905 n. 6.

60. 443 U.S. at 392, 99 S.Ct. at 2911–12.

61. 443 U.S. at 394, 99 S.Ct. at 2913 (Burger, C.J., concurring) (emphasis in original).

62. 443 U.S. at 403, 99 S.Ct. at 2917.

63. 443 U.S. at 404, 99 S.Ct. at 2918.

ty...." [64]

The *Richmond* Case. A narrow interpretation of *Gannett* limited to pretrial hearings is supported by the decision shortly thereafter in *Richmond Newspapers, Inc. v. Virginia.*[65] The fragmented Court, with only Justice Rehnquist dissenting (and Justice Powell not participating), rejected the asserted power of a state trial judge to close a criminal trial. The state judge had relied on a state statute granting broad discretion in such matters.

Chief Justice Burger, joined by Justices White and Stevens, concluded that the first and fourteenth amendments give the public the right of access to criminal trials. There is a "presumption of openness," [66] and that "[a]bsent an overriding interest articulated in findings, the trial of a criminal case must be open to the public." [67]

Justice Brennan, joined by Justice Marshall, concurred in the judgment; though they did not appear to disagree with the substance of Chief Justice Burger's opinion, they did not join his opinion. They also noted that mere agreement of the trial judge and parties cannot constitutionally close a trial to the public in light of the first amendment guarantees. And, because the state statute in this case authorized the trial judge and parties to engage in trial closures with unfettered discretion, "[w]hat countervailing interest might be sufficiently compelling to reverse this presumption of openness need not concern us now...." [68]

Justice Stewart, concurring in the judgment, also relied on a first amendment right of access. Justice Blackmun, also concurring in the judgment, relied principally on the sixth amendment, but also acknowledged the secondary role of the first amendment as a source of this right to access.

The *Globe Newspaper* Decision. In *Globe Newspapers Co. v. Superior Court* [69] the Court produced a majority opinion, elaborated on the meaning of *Richmond Newspapers,* and invalidated a state statute, unique to Massachusetts, which *required* trial judges to exclude the press and general public from the courtroom during the testimony of the victim in cases involving certain specified sexual offenses. Al-

---

64. 443 U.S. at 447–48, 99 S.Ct. at 2940 (Blackmun, J., dissenting and concurring, joined by Brennan, White, and Marshall, JJ.).

65. 448 U.S. 555, 100 S.Ct. 2814, 65 L.Ed.2d 973 (1980).

See generally, Note, Confusion in the Courthouse: The Legacy of the Gannett and Richmond Newspapers Public Right of Access Cases, 59 So.Calif.L.Rev. 603 (1986).

66. 448 U.S. at 576, 100 S.Ct. at 2826–27. As Justice Stevens noted in a concurring opinion, this case is the first ever to find constitutional protection for a right of access, a right to acquire newsworthy information. 448 U.S. at 583, 100 S.Ct. at 2830–31.

67. 448 U.S. at 587, 100 S.Ct. at 2833 (footnote omitted).

68. 448 U.S. at 600, 100 S.Ct. at 2840 (footnote omitted).

69. 457 U.S. 596, 102 S.Ct. 2613, 73 L.Ed.2d 248 (1982).

though the Court invalidated the mandatory state law (which required no particularized determinations in individual cases), it left open the possibility that under appropriate circumstances and in individual cases the trial court could exclude the press and public during the testimony of minor victims of sex crimes.

Justice Brennan, for the Court, explained that under *Richmond Newspapers* the first amendment, as applied to the states, grants to the press and general public "a right of access to *criminal trials*" [70] under the first amendment because historically such trials have been open and such openness aids in the functioning of the judicial process and the government of the whole.[71] Thus states may deny access only if denial serves "a compelling governmental interest, and is narrowly tailored to serve that interest." [72]

The statute was said to serve two basic state interests: first, protecting minor victims of sex crimes from further trauma and embarrassment and, second, encouraging victims to come forward and testify truthfully. Though this first interest was compelling, it did "not justify a *mandatory*-closure rule, for it is clear that the circumstances of the particular case may affect the significance of the interest." [73] The judge should consider the minor victim's wishes regarding disclosure, as well as the victim's age and maturity, the interests of relatives, the nature of the crime, and so on. In the present case the defendant objected to closure, the state made no motion for closure, and the victims may have been willing to testify without closure.

The second interest—to encourage witnesses to come forward—was speculative, and, given the nature of the statute, illogical: the statute did not deny the press access to the transcript or other possible sources that could provide an account of the testimony; the press could still publish the victim's identity and the substance of the testimony. Finally, the state's interest is not compelling. The asserted state interest would justify too many types of closure because "minor victims of sex crimes are [not] the *only* crime victims who, because of publicity attendant to criminal trials, are reluctant to come forward." [74]

---

70. 457 U.S. at 604–05, 102 S.Ct. at 2619 (emphasis in original).

71. 457 U.S. at 604–07, 102 S.Ct. at 2619–20.

72. 457 U.S. at 607, 102 S.Ct. at 2620.

73. 457 U.S. at 608, 102 S.Ct. at 2621.

74. 457 U.S. at 610, 102 S.Ct. at 2622 (emphasis in original).

O'Connor, J., concurred in the judgment and emphasized her view that neither *Richmond Newspapers* nor this case carried implications outside of criminal trials. Burger, C.J., joined by Rehnquist, J., dissented and objected to the paradox that the

Court decision "denies the victim the kind of protection routinely given to juveniles who commit crimes." 457 U.S. at 620, 102 S.Ct. at 2627.

Stevens, J., dissented because he believed that the case was moot, because, as presently construed, it had never been applied in a live controversy: the trial court had interpreted the statute to require closure of the entire trial; after the defendant had been acquitted the Massachusetts Supreme Judicial Court interpreted the statute to require closure only of the portions of the trial when the minor sex victim testified. All the Justices except for Stevens thought

Voir Dire Proceedings: The *Press–Enterprise* Test. In *Press–Enterprise Co. v. Superior Court*,[75] the Court attempted to clarify the standard for closure of trial proceedings when it held that the first amendment protected a right of access to voir dire proceedings for the screening of potential jurors. Chief Justice Burger, who wrote the majority opinion, found that the history of open jury selection and first amendment values justified the conclusion that these pretrial proceedings should come within the presumption of openness that had been established in the *Richmond Newspapers* and *Globe Newspaper* cases. The Chief Justice then set out a standard to be followed by lower courts when determining whether a portion of the trial process should be closed: "The presumption of openness may be overcome only by an overriding interest based on findings that closure is essential to preserve higher values and is narrowly tailored to serve that interest. The interest is to be articulated along with findings specific enough that a reviewing court can determine whether the closure order was properly entered." [76]

that the issue was "capable of repetition, yet evading review."

75. 464 U.S. 501, 104 S.Ct. 819, 78 L.Ed.2d 629 (1984).

76. 464 U.S. at 510, 104 S.Ct. at 824, 78 L.Ed.2d at 638. The quoted passage appears to establish a two step method of analysis. First, a court must find that the interest asserted is overriding or compelling and outweighs the first amendment right of access of the press and the public to attend trial proceedings. Second, the court must then make specific findings determining that the closure was essential to preserve those compelling or overriding interests by determining that alternative procedures would not adequately protect those interests.

Sixth Amendment Right to Public Trial. It must be remembered that a defendant has a sixth amendment right to a trial which is applicable to the states through the fourteenth amendment. The right of the defendant to a public trial applies to pretrial proceedings as well as to the trial itself. The Court has found that the *defendant's* sixth amendment right is no less protective of a public trial than the *public's* first amendment right established in these cases.

In Waller v. Georgia, 467 U.S. 39, 104 S.Ct. 2210, 81 L.Ed.2d 31 (1984), on remand 253 Ga. 146, 319 S.E.2d 11 (1984), the Court found that when a defendant requests pretrial proceedings to be open to the public there can be a closure of the proceedings

only if the trial court makes findings sufficient to "meet the tests set out in *Press–Enterprise* and its predecessors." Thus, the trial court must make specific findings as to the interest that would justify closure of any portion of the pretrial proceedings. Where the proceedings would disclose information about persons not involved in the litigation, their privacy interest or the interest in guaranteeing them a fair trial (if those persons may face separate criminal charges relating to the evidence), might justify some type of closure order. However, a trial court may not justify closure of the entire hearing based upon such generalized interest; the trial court must make specific findings regarding the nature of the closure that is required to promote those interests.

Press–Enterprise Co. v. Superior Court, 478 U.S. 1, 106 S.Ct. 2735, 92 L.Ed.2d 1 (1986) (*Press–Enterprise II*). The Court, per Burger, C.J., held that there was a First Amendment right of access to transcripts of a preliminary hearing of the type conducted in California. The State, later joined by the Press–Enterprise Company, moved to release a preliminary hearing transcript, but the trial court denied the motion. Unlike a Grand Jury proceeding, there has been "a tradition of accessibility" to this type of public hearing, and this hearing "is often the final and most important step in the criminal proceeding." Therefore, the court cannot close these proceedings "unless specific, on the record findings are made demonstrating that 'clo-

Witnesses' Disclosure of His Own Testimony Before the Grand Jury. In *Butterworth v. Smith*,[77] the Court invalidated a Florida statute that, with certain limited exceptions, prohibited a grand jury witness from ever disclosing testimony that he gave before the grand jury. A reporter for a Florida newspaper had written a series of articles about alleged improprieties committed by his county's State Attorney's Office and Sheriff's Department, and later testified before a grand jury that was called to investigate the alleged improprieties. After the grand jury had terminated its investigation, he sought a declaration of the statute's invalidity because he wanted to publish a series of articles (or perhaps a book) about the investigation and his experiences in dealing with the grand jury. A unanimous Court held that insofar as the Florida law prohibits a grand jury witness from disclosing his own testimony after the term of the grand jury has ended, it violates the First Amendment. The state's interest in preserving grand jury secrecy is either not served by, or insufficient to warrant, proscription of truthful speech on matters of public concern.

In the *Press–Enterprise* case, the Court found that the lower courts were not justified in closing all but a few days of a six week jury selection process. However, the Chief Justice's opinion for the Court stated that "the jury selection process may, in some circumstances, give rise to a compelling interest of a prospective juror when interrogation touches upon deeply personal matters...."[78] The lower court, however, had not articulated findings showing that no alternative procedure less intrusive on first amendment rights would have protected the privacy rights of jurors in this case. The Chief Justice indicated that courts should require potential jurors to affirmatively request that some portion of the selection process be closed to protect their privacy interest and that the trial court should determine both that the individual privacy interest asserted outweighed the first amendment right of access and that no other alternative to closure would adequately protect that interest.

Discovery in Civil Cases. Although the Supreme Court has consistently invalidated judicial protective orders which prohibited newspapers from publishing information about trial proceedings, in *Seattle Times Co. v. Rhinehart*,[79] the Court upheld a protective order

sure is essential to preserve higher values and is narrowly tailored to serve that interest,'" citing *Press–Enterprise I*, 478 U.S. at 13–14, 106 S.Ct. at 2742–43.

77. 494 U.S. 624, 110 S.Ct. 1376, 108 L.Ed.2d 572 (1990). Scalia, J., concurring, thought that "there is considerable doubt whether a witness can be prohibited, even while the grand jury is sitting, from making public what he knew before he entered

the grand-jury room. Quite a different question is presented, however, by a witness's disclosure of the grand-jury proceedings, which is knowledge he acquires not 'on his own' but only by virtue of being made a witness."

78. 464 U.S. at 511, 104 S.Ct. at 825, 79 L.Ed.2d at 639.

79. 467 U.S. 20, 104 S.Ct. 2199, 81 L.Ed.2d 17 (1984).

restricting the use of information gained through pretrial civil discovery by a newspaper which was a party to the litigation.

Federal trial courts and many state trial courts have the power to order parties to civil litigation to disclose a wide range of information to opposing parties that is of possible relevance to the preparation for trial of the lawsuit. This power to order wide-ranging discovery in virtually every jurisdiction also involves court authority to issue a protective order requiring the parties to whom the information is disclosed not to publish or disclose the information for any purpose other than the limited purposes of preparing for and trying the lawsuit if disclosure of the information would cause demonstrable harm to the disclosing party.[80]

In *Seattle Times,* the Court examined a trial court order restricting a newspaper, which was a defendant in a defamation action, from publishing information gained from the plaintiff; the newspaper was allowed to publish identical information if it could show that it had received that information from a source independent of the pretrial discovery proceedings. The Supreme Court found that this did not constitute a true prior restraint of speech nor an impermissible suppression of speech because the newspaper was a *party* to the lawsuit. This protective order placed the *Seattle Times* in no worse position than any other newspaper. The purpose of the order was to make sure that it was not in a better position than other newspapers, by publishing material that it had secured solely as a litigant, by the use of the discovery process.

The justices were unanimous in finding that the order should be upheld only if it could be said to be narrowly tailored to promote an important or substantial governmental interest unrelated to the suppression of expression.[81] The government's interest in protecting the

---

80. For a description of the scope of modern discovery and the need for protective orders in relation to the discovery process, see Marcus, Myth and Reality in Protective Order Litigation, 69 Cornell L.Rev. 1 (1983). This article was cited in the text of the majority opinion in *Seattle Times Co. v. Rhinehart* for the description of the nature of the process and the need for protective orders, and also for the proposition that pretrial discovery proceedings normally are conducted in private so there could be no analogy to a public right of access to this information similar to that established by the Court in the cases previously noted in this section regarding access to trials.

See also, Note, The First Amendment Right to Disseminate Discovery Materials: In re Halkin, 92 Harv.L.Rev. 1550 (1979); Note Rule 26(c) Protective Orders and the First Amendment, 80 Colum.L.Rev. 1645 (1980); Comment, Protective Orders Prohibiting Dissemination of Discovery Information: The First Amendment and Good Cause, 1980 Duke L.J. 766; Note, Access to Pretrial Documents Under the First Amendment, 84 Colum.L.Rev. 1813 (1984); Post, The Management of Speech: Discretion and Rights, 1984 Supreme Ct.Rev. 169; Note, Seattle Times: What Effect on Discovery Sharing?, 1985 Wis.L.Rev. 1055.

81. Justice Powell wrote for a unanimous Court in *Seattle Times.* Justices Brennan and Marshall concurred in the opinion but noted separately their belief that the most important aspect of the case was that all of the Justices recognized that pretrial protective orders were subject to scrutiny under the first amendment to assure that the order was necessary to pro-

privacy rights of parties to litigation and operating a system of truly open pretrial discovery that would facilitate the adjudicatory process were both substantial and unrelated to any governmental interest in suppressing or punishing speech. Because the order would allow publication of the information if it were gained from an independent source, it was not unnecessarily restrictive of the newspaper's rights.[82]

Suppression of the Records in Civil Cases. In *Richmond Newspapers* Chief Justice Burger noted that while the question of the public's right to attend trials in *civil* was not before it, "we note that historically both civil and criminal trials have been presumptively open." [83] Notwithstanding this legal fact, some judges claim an inherent power to close civil trials, or to seal the records produced in such trial, in order, it is alleged, to protect "privacy." In fact, empirical evidence shows that judges are more likely to close civil trials in order to protect the establishment (and the sons and daughters of the wealthy) from public scrutiny.[84]

IX. REGULATION OF COMMERCIAL SPEECH

§ 20.26 Introduction

Commercial speech, for purposes of our discussion, may be understood as speech of any form that advertises a product or service for

mote an important or substantial governmental interest unrelated to the suppression of expression.

82. The majority opinion stated that: "A litigant has no First Amendment right of access to information made available only for purposes of trying his suit ... Thus, continued court control over the discovered information does not raise the same spectre of government censorship that such control might suggest in other situations." 467 U.S. at 31, 104 S.Ct. at 2207. This statement should not be taken too broadly. It does not mean that all trial court protective orders, no matter how broad or unnecessary to the promotion of a significant governmental interest unrelated to censorship goals, should be upheld. Rather, the statement seems only to suggest that a limited order, which is reasonably tailored to promote the interest in protecting the personal or commercial privacy of the litigants or in promoting wide-ranging discovery, may be upheld. Some findings should be made by the court issuing the protective order as to the nature of interests that are to be protected by the order so that it could be reviewed on appeal to determine whether it in fact was necessary or at least reasonably related to

the protection of governmental interests unrelated to the suppression of expression. See Seattle Times Co. v. Rhinehart, 467 U.S. 20, 37, 104 S.Ct. 2199, 2210, 81 L.Ed.2d 17 (1984) (Brennan and Marshall, JJ., concurring). See Marcus, Myth and Reality in Protective Order Litigation, 69 Cornell L.Rev. 1 (1983), regarding the need for specific findings when issuing a protective order.

83. Richmond Newspapers, Inc. v. Virginia, 448 U.S. 555, 581 n. 17, 100 S.Ct. 2814, 2829 n. 17, 65 L.Ed.2d 973 (1980) (plurality opinion of Burger, C.J., joined by White & Stevens, JJ.).

84. See, Rooney, Sealed Court Files a Growing Concern, 136 Chicago Daily Law Bulletin, at 1, col. 1–3 & 7, col. 1–4 (April, 1990), showing that many judges routinely seal court files to protect well-known people. For example, Illinois courts impounded two lawsuits involving a well-known Chicago divorce lawyer accused of improperly coaxing a client into having sexual relations with him. In at least one of these cases, entitled "Suppressed v. Suppressed" (Circuit Court), Il. 88 L 22434 (Appellate Court) No. 1–89–2950, the plaintiff's lawyer opposed the impoundment order, but the trial judge issued it anyway.

profit or for business purpose. This definition is not precise, nor consistently applied by the courts. Neither is it self-evident why this category of speech should be treated differently from other types of speech. Flawed as this definition is, it is at least helpful in understanding the earlier cases.

Commercial speech, such as advertising, has always been subject to substantial governmental regulation. If all commercial speech, even truthful advertising, is excluded from the coverage of the First Amendment, the extent and nature of such regulation will create no free speech problems. And until relatively recently it has commonly been assumed that such is the case. Under the most recent case law, commercial speech appears now to be vested with substantial first amendment protection. The state can issue reasonable time, place, or manner regulations of such speech, and it also appears that the state has a broader power to regulate misleading commercial speech than its power to regulate misleading or libelous speech directed against public officials or public figures.

§ 20.27   Origins of the Commercial Speech Doctrine

In *Valentine v. Chrestensen,*[1] an entrepreneur in New York City distributed a leaflet containing on one side an advertisement for a commercial exhibition of a former Navy submarine and on the other side a message protesting the City's denial of wharfage facilities for the exhibition. The entrepreneur was convicted of violating a sanitary code provision forbidding the distribution of advertising matter in the streets.

The Supreme Court upheld the conviction unanimously. Three years earlier, the Court had struck down several municipal ordinances applied to severely restrict the distribution of political or religious handbills in the streets or in house-to-house canvassing.[2] The Court

---

§ 20.27

1. 316 U.S. 52, 62 S.Ct. 920, 86 L.Ed. 1262 (1942).

See generally, Rotunda, The Commercial Speech Doctrine in the Supreme Court, 1976 U.Ill.L.Forum 1080. Jackson & Jeffries, Commercial Speech: Economic Due Process and the First Amendment, 65 Va. L.Rev. 1 (1979); Alexander, Commercial Speech and First Amendment Theory: A Critical Exchange, 75 Nw.U.L.Rev. 307 (1980); Baker, Commercial Speech: A Problem in the Theory of Freedom, 62 Iowa L.Rev. 1 (1976); Farber, Commercial Speech and First Amendment Theory, 74 Nw.U.L.Rev. 372 (1979); Redish, The First

Amendment in the Marketplace: Commercial Speech and the Values of Free Expression, 39 Geo.Wash.U.L.Rev. 429 (1971); Schauer, Commercial Speech and the Architecture of the First Amendment, 56 U. of Cincinnati L.Rev. 1181 (1988); Rotunda, Commercial Speech and the Platonic Ideal: Libre Expression et Libre Enterprise, in David Schneiderman, ed., Freedom of Expression and the Charter 319 (Carswell, Canada, 1991).

2. Schneider v. State (Town of Irvington), 308 U.S. 147, 60 S.Ct. 146, 84 L.Ed. 155 (1939); see also Lovell v. Griffin, 303 U.S. 444, 58 S.Ct. 666, 82 L.Ed. 949 (1938), opinion conformed 57 Ga.App. 901, 197

---

had stated that "the public convenience in respect of cleanliness of the streets does not justify an exertion of the police power which invades the free communication of information and opinion secured by the Constitution."[3] But the Court had carefully noted that it did not hold "that commercial soliciting and canvassing may not be subjected to such regulation as the ordinance requires."[4] In *Chrestensen,* the Court took this proviso and expanded it into what has become known as the "commercial speech" doctrine:

> This court has unequivocally held that the streets are proper places for the exercise of the freedom of communicating information and disseminating opinion and that, though the states and municipalities may appropriately regulate the privilege in the public interest, they may not unduly burden or proscribe its employment in these public thoroughfares. We are equally clear that the Constitution imposes *no such restraint on government as respects purely commercial advertising.*[5]

This casual pronouncement, as we shall see, was long read to completely exclude so-called "commercial speech" from any protection of the First Amendment.[6]

In distributing his leaflet, the entrepreneur in *Chrestensen* was, in the Court's view, attempting to "pursue a gainful occupation in the streets,"[7] and his right to do so was purely a matter for "legislative judgment."[8] By implication, this judgment need not have been justified by an overriding or compelling state interest, or balanced against any inherent right to employ advertising as a business technique. The Court reasoned that if speech is "purely commercial," it is subject to regulation to the same extent and for the same reasons as other forms of commercial activity. As commentators have since noted, the *Chrestensen* Court, "without citing precedent, historical evidence, or policy considerations, ... effectively read commercial speech out of the first amendment."[9] Commercial speech, under this ruling, is not subject to

S.E. 347 (1938). In both cases the ordinances were held unconstitutional, apparently for reasons of overbreadth.

3. Schneider v. State (Town of Irvington), 308 U.S. 147, 163, 60 S.Ct. 146, 151, 84 L.Ed. 155 (1939).

4. 308 U.S. at 165, 60 S.Ct. at 152.

5. 316 U.S. at 54, 62 S.Ct. at 921 (emphasis added).

6. This broad holding of *Chrestensen* has occasionally been attacked in several strong dissents in the high court. E.g., Lehman v. Shaker Heights, 418 U.S. 298, 314–15, 94 S.Ct. 2714, 2722–23, 41 L.Ed.2d 770 (1974) (Brennan, J., dissenting); Pittsburgh Press Co. v. Pittsburgh Commission on Human Relations, 413 U.S. 376, 398, 93

S.Ct. 2553, 2564–65, 37 L.Ed.2d 669 (1973) (Douglas, J., dissenting), rehearing denied 414 U.S. 881, 94 S.Ct. 30, 38 L.Ed.2d 128 (1973), and 413 U.S. at 401 & n. 6, 93 S.Ct. at 2566 & n. 6 (Stewart, J., dissenting); Dun & Bradstreet, Inc. v. Grove, 404 U.S. 898, 904–06, 92 S.Ct. 204, 208–09, 30 L.Ed.2d 175 (1971) (Douglas, J., dissenting from denial of certiorari).

7. Valentine v. Chrestensen, 316 U.S. 52, 54, 62 S.Ct. 920, 921, 86 L.Ed. 1262 (1942).

8. Id.

9. Redish, The First Amendment in the Marketplace: Commercial Speech and the Values of Free Expression, 39 Geo.Wash. L.Rev. 429, 450 (1971).

less first amendment protection; rather it is subject to no first amendment protection.

As to the political protest message the entrepreneur had placed on the back of his advertising leaflet, the Court said it was "enough" that the message had admittedly been designed "with the intent, and for the purpose, of evading the prohibition of the ordinance." [10] Thus, although the Court declined to "indulge nice appraisals based upon subtle distinctions," [11] it did point to the primary purpose of the protest message. The Court might have issued a narrower ruling, by simply approving the regulation as a reasonable one under the circumstances. Instead it fashioned a more general approach for future cases: when the primary purpose of the speech is "commercial," it falls within a category of speech that is not within the protection of the First Amendment.

Apparently it was the "speech-on-the-handbill" which was considered "commercial" and thus not within the First Amendment. It is not clear that even the *Chrestensen* Court would have allowed the entrepreneur to be enjoined from merely telling someone about his submarine. If the *Chrestensen* Court would indeed have made a distinction between the "speech" versus the "speech-on-the-handbill" then the difficulty of defining "commercial" speech with any precision is emphasized.

§ 20.28 Subsequent Development of the Commercial Speech Doctrine

The significant reach of *Chrestensen* and its primary purpose test was clarified in *Murdock v. Pennsylvania* [1] and *Breard v. Alexandria.* [2] In *Murdock,* the Court overturned the convictions of several Jehovah's Witnesses who had violated an ordinance by selling religious books without paying a license tax. The Court stated flatly that a "state may not impose a charge for the enjoyment of a right guaranteed by the Federal Constitution" and equated the power to impose the license tax with "the power of censorship which this Court has repeatedly struck down." [3] The Court stressed that the fact that the books had been sold did not automatically bring the books within the Commercial Speech doctrine nor diminish the petitioners' first amendment privileges; the sales had been "merely *incidental* and collateral" to a principal purpose of disseminating religious beliefs. [4]

10. 316 U.S. at 55, 62 S.Ct. at 921–22.

11. Id.

§ 20.28

1. 319 U.S. 105, 63 S.Ct. 870, 87 L.Ed. 1292 (1943).

2. 341 U.S. 622, 71 S.Ct. 920, 95 L.Ed. 1233 (1951), rehearing denied 342 U.S. 843, 72 S.Ct. 21, 96 L.Ed. 637 (1951).

3. 319 U.S. at 113, 63 S.Ct. at 875.

4. 319 U.S. at 112, 63 S.Ct. at 874 (emphasis added).

It should be added that the petitioners had not attempted to profit from the sales, and indeed there is some suggestion in the Court's opinion that this fact influenced the Court nearly as much as the petitioners' religious motives.[5] At one point the Court stated in dictum that the "constitutional rights of those spreading their religious beliefs through the spoken and printed word are not to be gauged by standards governing retailers or wholesalers of books."[6] In its holding, however, *Murdock* is authority for the more limited principle that the exercise of an established first amendment right cannot be circumscribed merely because it contains an incidental commercial aspect. Apparently, however, if the profit in the sales had been the primary purpose of the speech, *Chrestensen* would have applied.[7]

This view is supported by *Breard,* where the Court faced the profit motive squarely in upholding an ordinance prohibiting unsolicited door-to-door magazine subscription sales. Earlier, in *Martin v. Struthers,*[8] the Court, pointing to the freedoms of speech and religion, had voided a similar ordinance applied to prevent Jehovah's Witnesses from distributing free religious tracts door-to-door. The Court in *Breard* agreed that "the fact that periodicals are sold does not put them beyond" the first amendment, but it reasoned that in *Martin* "no element of the commercial" had entered into the distribution, and here, the "selling ... brings into the transaction a commercial feature."[9] The Court found that the appellant's sales pitch was not itself protected speech: "Only the press or oral advocates of ideas could urge this point. It was not open to the solicitors for gadgets or brushes."[10] The Court did not hold, of course, that the first amendment does not extend to any speech possessing a commercial feature,[11] but the *profit motive* underlying magazine sales was sufficient in *Breard* to deprive those sales of at least some first amendment protection.

However, *Breard* reached this result not by a subjective, factual inquiry into motive but by "balancing ... the conveniences between some householders' desire for privacy and the publisher's right to distribute publications in the precise way that those soliciting for him think brings the best results."[12]

At first glance, the Court's reliance on this balancing process would appear to have been a rather severe departure from the categorizing

5. The Court noted that the Witnesses' "main object ... was to preach and publicize the doctrines of their order". 319 U.S. at 112, 63 S.Ct. at 874.

6. 319 U.S. at 111, 63 S.Ct. at 874.

7. Although *Murdock* did limit somewhat the reach of the *Chrestensen* doctrine it left unclear how a court should determine the "primary purpose" of a communication.

8. 319 U.S. 141, 63 S.Ct. 862, 87 L.Ed. 1313 (1943).

9. Breard v. Alexandria, 341 U.S. 622, 642–43, 71 S.Ct. 920, 932–33, 95 L.Ed. 1233 (1951), rehearing denied 342 U.S. 843, 72 S.Ct. 21, 96 L.Ed. 637 (1951).

10. 341 U.S. at 641, 71 S.Ct. at 932.

11. 341 U.S. at 642, 71 S.Ct. at 932–33.

12. 341 U.S. at 644, 71 S.Ct. at 933.

approach in *Chrestensen.* In *Chrestensen* once speech fell into the category of commercial speech, it became mere commercial activity, held to be a matter for legislative judgment; suddenly in *Breard* it was a "right" to be balanced against that of privacy. But the two cases are not really inconsistent. In *Breard* the Court did not directly hold that door-to-door magazine subscription solicitation is "purely commercial" in the sense contemplated by *Chrestensen.* While the Court did not dwell on the extent to which effective competition is necessary to a free press, a factor discussed at length in the dissent,[13] it was undoubtedly aware that if subscription solicitation were deemed purely commercial, logically the state arguably could ban all such solicitation without regard to the inevitable effects of such a ban on the content of magazines. Viewed conversely, *Breard* might be interpreted to stand for the concept that the first amendment does not automatically extend to profit-making aspects of otherwise protected activity. As such *Breard* is consistent with the line of decisions upholding the neutral application of the antitrust, labor, and tax laws to newspapers and other communications media.[14]

§ 20.29 What Is "Commercial" Speech?

For many years, the extent to which *Chrestensen* and its progeny have been controlling beyond their own facts was unclear. If speech is labeled "commercial," it loses, under this line of cases, all first amendment protection. But when is speech "commercial"?

Shortly after *Breard* was decided, for example, the Court, in rejecting the argument that motion pictures are unprotected because they are made and exhibited for profit, stated that the fact that "books, newspapers, and magazines are published and sold for profit does not prevent them from being a form of expression whose liberty is safeguarded by the First Amendment. We fail to see why operation for profit should have any different effect in the case of motion pictures."[1]

Later, in *New York Times Co. v. Sullivan,*[2] the Court declined to apply *Chrestensen* to sustain a libel action against a newspaper which had published an allegedly offensive paid political advertisement. The advertisement in *New York Times,* said the Court,

---

13. 341 U.S. at 646–48, 71 S.Ct. at 934–35.

14. Citizen Publishing Co. v. United States, 394 U.S. 131, 89 S.Ct. 927, 22 L.Ed.2d 148 (1969) (antitrust); Associated Press v. NLRB, 301 U.S. 103, 57 S.Ct. 650, 81 L.Ed. 953 (1937) (labor laws); Oklahoma Press Publishing Co. v. Walling, 327 U.S. 186, 66 S.Ct. 494, 90 L.Ed. 614 (1946) (wage and hour laws). Cf. Cammarano v. United States, 358 U.S. 498, 79 S.Ct. 524, 3 L.Ed.2d 462 (1959) (business deduction on federal income tax of sums spent for lobbying activities disallowed).

See generally, §§ 20.20–20.22 supra.

§ 20.29

1. Joseph Burstyn, Inc. v. Wilson, 343 U.S. 495, 501–502, 72 S.Ct. 777, 780, 96 L.Ed. 1098 (1952) (footnote omitted).

2. 376 U.S. 254, 84 S.Ct. 710, 11 L.Ed.2d 686 (1964), motion denied 376 U.S. 967, 84 S.Ct. 1130, 12 L.Ed.2d 83 (1964).

was not a "commercial" advertisement in the sense in which the word was used in *Chrestensen*. It communicated information, expressed opinion, recited grievances, protested claimed abuses, and sought financial support on behalf of a movement whose existence and objectives are matters of the highest public interest and concern.[3]

If nothing else, *New York Times* suggests in this context that the primary purpose test for determining commercial speech, to the extent it had been adopted in the past, was laid to rest. The newspaper's commercial motives in publishing the advertisement were irrelevant; it was the advertisement's content that swayed the Court to apply First Amendment protection.

The "purely commercial advertising" which appeared to have been carved out from protected speech in the case law following *Chrestensen* and *New York Times* was—to say the least—confused. While financial motive is not enough to make speech "commercial," [4] where product sales are the so-called "primary purpose" of the speech, inclusion of political comment or other material which itself could be protected will not suffice to pull the speech within the ambit of the amendment.[5] This primary purpose test apparently looks, not to the form, but to the function of the publication. First, under this primary purpose test, a book or other expression which itself could fall within the guarantee of free speech can be the subject of otherwise prohibited regulation if either the book is promoted by advertising, in which case the advertising may be regulated,[6] or the book itself is used to advertise or promote

---

3. 376 U.S. at 266, 84 S.Ct. at 718.

4. See, e.g., New York Times Co. v. Sullivan, 376 U.S. 254, 84 S.Ct. 710, 11 L.Ed.2d 686 (1964) (protection of publication of public political advertisement is not diminished by the fact that newspaper was paid to carry the ad), motion denied 376 U.S. 967, 84 S.Ct. 1130, 12 L.Ed.2d 83 (1964); Cammarano v. United States, 358 U.S. 498, 514, 79 S.Ct. 524, 534, 3 L.Ed.2d 462 (1959) ("The profit motive should make no difference."); Thornhill v. Alabama, 310 U.S. 88, 102, 60 S.Ct. 736, 744, 84 L.Ed. 1093 (1940) (purely informational union picketing is protected); Grosjean v. American Press Co., 297 U.S. 233, 56 S.Ct. 444, 80 L.Ed. 660 (1936) (newspaper successfully challenges discriminatory tax on its publication). Indeed, even selling is not itself enough to make speech unprotected where the sale activity is "merely incidental and collateral." Murdock v. Pennsylvania, 319 U.S. 105, 112, 63 S.Ct. 870, 874–75, 87 L.Ed. 1292 (1943) (holding unconstitutional a tax on the sale of religious material where the "main object [was] to preach and publicize

the doctrines."); see also Jamison v. Texas, 318 U.S. 413, 63 S.Ct. 669, 87 L.Ed. 869 (1943); Cantwell v. Connecticut, 310 U.S. 296, 60 S.Ct. 900, 84 L.Ed. 1213 (1940); Hannan v. Haverhill, 120 F.2d 87 (1st Cir. 1941), certiorari denied 314 U.S. 641, 62 S.Ct. 81, 86 L.Ed. 514 (1941).

5. Valentine v. Chrestensen, 316 U.S. 52, 55, 62 S.Ct. 920, 922, 86 L.Ed. 1262 (1942) (advertising handbill not protected where political statement was included "with the intent, and for the purpose, of evading the prohibition" on commercial handbills).

6. See Bantam Books, Inc. v. F.T.C., 275 F.2d 680 (2d Cir.1960) (F.T.C. regulation of book labeling upheld without discussion of First Amendment), certiorari denied 364 U.S. 819, 81 S.Ct. 51, 5 L.Ed.2d 49 (1960); Witkower Press, Inc., 57 F.T.C. 145 (1960); cf., M.B. Waterman & Co., 46 F.T.C. 133 (1949) (deceptive advertising of religious objects).

the sale of another product.[7] Second, statements which might be considered non-commercial if made by persons not materially interested in the affected trade apparently can take on a different character when made by one involved in trade.[8]

§ 20.30   Rationales for, and Criticisms of, the Commercial Speech Doctrine

The validity of *Chrestensen's* Commercial Speech doctrine was subject to much dispute, a dispute encouraged by the uncertain and confusing tests used to determine the types of speech that are commercial. In 1959, Justice Douglas stated that the "ruling [in *Chrestensen*] was casual, almost offhand. And it has not survived reflection."[1] But this view was expressed in a concurring opinion and not embraced by the full Court. Other justices have on occasion agreed with Justice Douglas,[2] and commentators have also criticized the doctrine as inflexible and insensitive to the informational value of commercial advertising;[3] *Breard* has similarly been attacked as demonstrative of "the Court's general lack of enthusiasm for the commercial element in first amendment questions."[4]

One obvious logical problem in distinguishing commercial speech from political expression is the simple fact that inherent in every speech labeled as "commercial" is at least some noncommercial message: the expression of ideas and values such as materialism or capitalism. There is no such thing as "pure" commercial speech.[5] Certainly

---

7. Compare United States v. 8 Cartons, etc., 103 F.Supp. 626, 628 (W.D.N.Y.1951) ("The seizure relates not to books offered for bona fide sale but to copies of the book claimed to be offending against the Act by being associated with the article ... in a distribution plan in such a way as to misbrand the product.") and United States v. Articles of Drug, 32 F.R.D. 32, 35 (S.D.Ill. 1963), with Koch v. FTC, 206 F.2d 311, 317–18 (6th Cir.1953).

8. Compare, Scientific Manufacturing Co. v. FTC, 124 F.2d 640, 644 (3d Cir.1941), with Perma–Maid Co. v. FTC, 121 F.2d 282 (6th Cir.1941).

§ 20.30

1. Cammarano v. United States, 358 U.S. 498, 514, 79 S.Ct. 524, 534, 3 L.Ed.2d 462 (1959) (Douglas, J., concurring). See also, Pittsburgh Press Co. v. Pittsburgh Commission on Human Relations, 413 U.S. 376, 393, 93 S.Ct. 2553, 2562, 37 L.Ed.2d 669 (1973) (Burger, C.J., dissenting), rehearing denied 414 U.S. 881, 94 S.Ct. 30, 38 L.Ed.2d 128 (1973); 413 U.S. at 401, 93 S.Ct. at 2566 (Stewart, J., dissenting).

2. Lehman v. Shaker Heights, 418 U.S. 298, 314–15 n. 6, 94 S.Ct. 2714, 2723 n. 6, 41 L.Ed.2d 770 (1974) (Brennan, J., dissenting); Pittsburgh Press Co. v. Pittsburgh Com'n on Human Relations, 413 U.S. 376, 401 & n. 6, 93 S.Ct. 2553, 2566 & n. 6, 37 L.Ed.2d 669 (Stewart, J., dissenting), rehearing denied 414 U.S. 881, 94 S.Ct. 30, 38 L.Ed.2d 128 (1973).

3. See Note, Deceptive Advertising, 80 Harv.L.Rev. 1005, 1029–34 (1967); see also Redish, The First Amendment in the Marketplace: Commercial Speech and the Value of Free Expression, 39 Geo.Wash.L.Rev. 429, 432–38 (1971); Rotunda, The Commercial Speech Doctrine in the Supreme Court, 1976 U.Ill.L.Forum 1080.

4. Redish, The First Amendment in the Marketplace: Commercial Speech and the Value of Free Expression, 39 Geo.Wash. L.Rev. 429, at 454 (1971).

5. E.g., Black, He Cannot Choose But Hear: The Plight of the Captive Auditor, 53 Colum.L.Rev. 960 (1953):

"One Article of Faith in this [advertising] Gospel emerges as a matter of

the first amendment makes no obvious distinction between commercial and non-commercial speech, and the difficulty of the Court over the years in defining commercial speech at least suggests that the distinction does not really exist.

In an attempt to rationalize the doctrine, some have argued that since "state and federal governments enjoy wide powers of regulation" over "the economic welfare of business enterprises", therefore the "possibly desirable objectives furthered by advertising would not seem to require its protection by the first amendment...."[6] That argument, however, appears to assume the point in dispute: how wide should the government's power over advertising be? And when the form of the regulation over business is not a direct economic matter (such as taxes, subsidies, minimum wages), but direct control over speech, should there be some role for the Court in reviewing the reasonableness of the restrictions on speech?

Unlike straightforward economic regulation, speech is preservative of other rights. While regulatory legislation affecting ordinary commercial transactions is usually presumed constitutionally valid, regulation restricting or forbidding speech restricts the public process of debate and exchange of ideas which can ordinarily be expected to bring about repeal of undesirable legislation.[7] The regulation of speech, including commercial speech, inhibits public debate and evaluation of proposed regulatory measures.

Others still justify the doctrine on the grounds that only minimal protection of commercial advertising is necessary because there is little risk that its regulation will exist "for political purposes or even that its regulation will hamper the workings of democracy."[8] But this empirical assertion certainly cannot be assumed. Moreover, as a constitutional matter, the Court implicitly has rejected this justification by its refusal to construe the antitrust laws to prohibit anticompetitive activities which are sheltered by the first amendment.[9]

soundest induction, commercial by commercial: Prices were never so reasonable, products never so fine.... We know another Article well, for it is the easily tallied integral sum of all advertising, and its deepest philosophic wellspring: material possessions produce happiness.... The adman has every right to preach his Gospel." (53 Colum.L.Rev. at 968).

See also, R. Posner, Economic Analysis of Law § 22.4 at 316 (1973).

6. Note, Freedom of Expression in a Commercial Context, 78 Harv.L.Rev. 1191, 1195 (1965).

7. United States v. Carolene Products Co., 304 U.S. 144, 152–153 n. 4, 58 S.Ct.

778, 783–84 n. 4, 82 L.Ed. 1234 (1938) (Stone, J.); cf. Wright, Professor Bickel, the Scholarly Tradition, and the Supreme Court, 84 Harv.L.Rev. 769, 787–89 (1971).

8. Cooper, The Tax Treatment of Business Grassroots Lobbying: Defining and Attaining the Public Policy Objectives, 68 Colum.L.Rev. 801, 832 (1968).

9. **The *Noerr–Pennington* Cases.** In two related cases, Eastern R.R. Presidents Conference v. Noerr Motor Freight, Inc., 365 U.S. 127, 81 S.Ct. 523, 5 L.Ed.2d 464 (1961), rehearing denied 365 U.S. 875, 81 S.Ct. 899, 5 L.Ed.2d 864 (1961) and United Mine Workers of America v. Pennington, 381 U.S. 657, 85 S.Ct. 1585, 14 L.Ed.2d 626 (1965), on remand 257 F.Supp. 815

If a political candidate is selling himself, the first amendment applies; yet if he sells peanuts, the commercial speech doctrine asserts that there is *no* first amendment protection. Rationalizing these results is more than a little difficult. Certainly this commercial speech doctrine cannot be based on a realistic belief that the dangers of falsehood are less likely when the speech is political.

One commentator has asserted that the "government is more likely to be impartial in censoring speech influencing commercial decisions than in regulating speech affecting its own policies and composition." [10] This assertion is not supported by any authority and it is difficult to believe that it could be. Commercial regulation usually is enacted to benefit one economic group (businessmen, a certain class of businessmen, consumers, a certain class of consumers) and impose a burden on other classes. The government merely responds to these pressures. Why we would always expect the result of these conflicting pressures to be impartial is a mystery.

Perhaps because neither the states nor the federal government have until recently had much interest in prohibiting truthful advertising, the older cases concerned either control of false or misleading speech or regulations, like those in *Valentine* and *Breard,* or those affecting the time and manner of the communication.[11] But now government is asserting broader prohibiting regulations on speech affected by a commercial interest, and some of the most recent cases have illustrated some of the possible dangers of the commercial speech doctrine. It is to those cases we now turn.

§ 20.31   The Modern Commercial Speech Doctrine

In *Capital Broadcasting Co. v. Mitchell,*[1] the commercial speech doctrine was given its most far-reaching interpretation by a three-judge

(D.Tenn.1966), judgment affirmed in part, reversed in part 400 F.2d 806 (6th Cir. 1968), certiorari denied 393 U.S. 983, 89 S.Ct. 450, 21 L.Ed.2d 444 (1968), rehearing denied 393 U.S. 1045, 89 S.Ct. 616, 21 L.Ed.2d 599 (1969), the Court held, on first amendment grounds, that the Sherman and Clayton Acts do not extend to exercises of the right to petition the government in either a legislative or administrative setting, despite anticompetitive effects. Compare, National Society of Professional Engineers v. United States, 435 U.S. 679, 98 S.Ct. 1355, 55 L.Ed.2d 637 (1978).

See generally, Fische, Antitrust Liability for Attempts to Influence Government Action: The Basis and Limits of the *Noerr–Pennington* Doctrine, 45 U.Chi.L.Rev. 80 (1977).

10. Note, Freedom of Expression in a Commercial Context, 78 Harv.L.Rev. 1191, 1195 (1965).

11. One important exception may be Williamson v. Lee Optical Co., 348 U.S. 483, 489–90, 75 S.Ct. 461, 465–66, 99 L.Ed. 563 (1955), rehearing denied 349 U.S. 925, 75 S.Ct. 657, 99 L.Ed. 1256 (1955), where the Court upheld a state law prohibiting solicitations for the sale of optical appliances. However, the First Amendment issues were not discussed; the Court relied on the state's asserted special interest in the underlying health related conduct.

§ 20.31

1. 333 F.Supp. 582 (D.D.C.1971), affirmed without opinion sub nom. Capital Broadcasting Co. v. Acting Attorney Gener-

district court, which the Supreme Court affirmed without opinion. This decision upheld a flat statutory ban on the advertising of cigarettes over any medium of electronic communications subject to F.C.C. jurisdiction. The district court mechanically applied the old case law. It noted that "advertising is less vigorously protected than other forms of speech" and, thus, that "Congress has the power to prohibit the advertising of cigarettes in any media" as an exercise of its power to regulate commerce. The district court's analysis belies any effort to limit its approval of Congressional regulation either to cigarettes (on the theory that they are uniquely hazardous) or to electronic media (which are necessarily subject to regulation).

The dissent argued, to no avail, that because cigarette advertising has been held to express a position on a matter of public controversy,[2] it is not merely commercial speech but comes "within the core protection of the First Amendment." The dissent did not expressly dispute the proposition that commercial speech may be regulated by Congress, but it did implicitly reject the primary purpose test in favor of a content-analysis test, though it may be read to implicitly reject the commercial speech doctrine. The Supreme Court affirmed the majority position of the district court without opinion.

Capital Broadcasting is a troublesome case. If Congress may forbid truthful advertising urging the purchase of a legal, validly offered item, it is hard to see a way to establish a principled limitation in its power to restrict advertisements for anything it chooses to consider "harmful." May Congress prohibit the advertising of movies which are not obscene,[3] or of political pamphlets which do not constitute advocacy directed "to inciting or producing imminent lawless action and [are] likely to incite or produce such actions?"[4] These were serious questions following *Capital Broadcasting*.

In a series of three decisions—*Pittsburgh Press Co. v. Pittsburgh Commission on Human Rights*,[5] *Bigelow v. Virginia*,[6] and *Virginia State Board of Pharmacy v. Virginia Citizens Council, Inc.*[7]—the Supreme Court recognized these problems and rejected the commercial speech doctrine. Yet the Court, in the bitterly divided five to four opinion in

---

al Kleindienst, 405 U.S. 1000, 92 S.Ct. 1290, 31 L.Ed.2d 472 (1972).

See generally, Note, The First Amendment and Legislative Bans of Liquor and Cigarette Advertisements, 85 Colum.L.Rev. 632 (1985).

2. Banzhaf v. FCC, 405 F.2d 1082 (D.C.Cir.1968), certiorari denied 396 U.S. 842, 90 S.Ct. 50, 24 L.Ed.2d 93 (1969).

3. See Miller v. California, 413 U.S. 15, 93 S.Ct. 2607, 37 L.Ed.2d 419 (1973), rehearing denied 414 U.S. 881, 94 S.Ct. 26, 38 L.Ed.2d 128 (1973).

4. Brandenburg v. Ohio, 395 U.S. 444, 447, 89 S.Ct. 1827, 1829, 23 L.Ed.2d 430 (1969) (footnote omitted) (per curiam).

5. 413 U.S. 376, 93 S.Ct. 2553, 37 L.Ed.2d 669 (1973), rehearing denied 414 U.S. 881, 94 S.Ct. 30, 38 L.Ed.2d 128 (1973).

6. 421 U.S. 809, 95 S.Ct. 2222, 44 L.Ed.2d 600 (1975).

7. 425 U.S. 748, 96 S.Ct. 1817, 48 L.Ed.2d 346 (1976).

Posadas De Puerto Rico Associates v. Tourism Company,[8] approved of limited restrictions on advertising of casino gambling, in what may be a unique fact situation. In that case, the Court upheld a law that restricted advertising of legal casino gambling when that advertising was directed at residents of Puerto Rico. The legislators wanted the tourists (but not residents) to flock to the casinos to gamble.

Advertising of Illegal Activities. In *Pittsburgh Press,* a newspaper had been charged with violating an ordinance prohibiting sex-designated help-wanted advertisements except where the employer or advertiser would be free to make hiring decisions on the basis of sex. The newspaper argued that the advertisements involved the exercise of editorial judgment, as to where to place the advertisement, rather than its commercial context. Therefore the advertisements, it was argued, were sufficiently noncommercial to fall within the ambit of the first amendment. The Supreme Court disagreed.

The Court conceded that the newspaper does make a judgment as to whether or not to allow the advertiser to select the column in which the want-ad should be placed. And, also, the newspaper's profit motive alone could not be determinative because then all aspects of the newspaper business—"from selection of news stories to choice of editorial position"—would come under the commercial speech doctrine. But relying heavily on *New York Times,* the Court found that the advertisements constituted "in practical effect an integrated commercial statement"[9] devoid of any truly editorial expression on matters of public interest or social policy. "The advertisements are thus classic examples of commercial speech" of the sort left unprotected in *Chrestensen.*[10]

Once again, the Court appeared to examine the content rather than the primary purpose underlying the advertisements in reaching its decision. Yet this factual conclusion in *Pittsburgh Press* illustrates that a determination of commercial speech is a fruitless task: what if the want-ad had been placed to protest the laws relating to sex discrimination? Chief Justice Burger in dissent attempted to point out the problem of having judges make page by page determinations of what parts of a newspaper were commercial speech.[11]

If *Pittsburgh Press* had stopped here in its analysis, it would have merely given further support to a broad reading of the *Capital Broadcasting* case. But significantly, the Court noted the argument that "the exchange of information is as important in the commercial realm as in any other,"[12] a view which is a common basis for criticism of the

---

8. 478 U.S. 328, 106 S.Ct. 2968, 92 L.Ed.2d 266 (1986).

9. 413 U.S. at 388, 93 S.Ct. at 2560.

10. 413 U.S. at 385, 93 S.Ct. at 2559.

11. 413 U.S. at 393, 93 S.Ct. at 2562 (Burger, C.J., dissenting).

12. 413 U.S. at 388, 93 S.Ct. at 2560.

rationale in *Chrestensen*. And, the Court did not reject that argument, but said, in response to the urging of the newspaper that the justices abrogate the distinction between commercial and other speech:

> Whatever the merits of this contention may be in other contexts, it is unpersuasive in this case. Discrimination in employment is not only commercial activity, it is *illegal* commercial activity under the Ordinance. We have no doubt that a newspaper constitutionally could be forbidden to publish a want ad proposing a sale of narcotics or solicting prostitutes. Nor would the result be different if the nature of the transaction were indicated by placement under columns captioned "Narcotics for Sale" and "Prostitutes Wanted" rather than stated within the four corners of the advertisement.[13]

Even more importantly, after emphasizing the illegal nature of this activity, the opinion cited in a footnote the dissent in *Capital Broadcasting*.[14] The Court, while not yet rejecting *Chrestensen*, relied on a much narrower and more concrete test: if an activity is illegal, the state may prohibit the advertising or touting of that activity. The negative implication of this reasoning is that if the activity is legal, the state may not prohibit truthful advertising of the activity. The Court's reasoning follows a traditional balance of interests:

> Any First Amendment interest which might be served by advertising an ordinary commercial proposal and which might arguably outweigh the governmental interest supporting the regulation is altogether absent when the commercial activity itself is illegal and the restriction on advertising is incidental to a valid limitation on

13. 413 U.S. at 388, 93 S.Ct. at 2560 (emphasis in original) (footnote omitted).

See also, Village of Hoffman Estates v. Flipside, Hoffman Estates, Inc., 455 U.S. 489, 102 S.Ct. 1186, 71 L.Ed.2d 362 (1982), rehearing denied 456 U.S. 950, 102 S.Ct. 2023, 72 L.Ed.2d 476 (1982), on remand 688 F.2d 842 (7th Cir.1982). In that case a city ordinance required a business to obtain a license if it sells any items "designed or marketed for use with illegal drugs." The Court, in rejecting a preenforcement challenge on its face to the ordinance on the grounds of vagueness and overbreadth, turned to the free speech claims. The ordinance did not infringe noncommercial speech interests of drug paraphernalia stores, or "head shops" ("head" is slang for frequent user of drugs), even though the city guidelines treated the proximity of drug related literature to paraphernalia as evidence that the paraphernalia was marketed for use with illegal drugs: the ordinance did not prohibit the sale of the literature itself but "simply regulates the commercial marketing of items that the labels reveal may be used for an illicit purpose." As far as commercial speech is concerned, the ordinance's restriction on the manner of marketing does not significantly limit the store's communication of information with the exception of "commercial activity promoting or encouraging illegal drug use. If that activity is 'speech,' then it is speech proposing an illegal transaction, which a government may regulate or ban entirely." 455 U.S. at 496, 102 S.Ct. at 1192.

14. Pittsburgh Press Co. v. Pittsburgh Commission on Human Relations, 413 U.S. 376, 388 n. 12, 93 S.Ct. 2553, 2560 n. 12, 37 L.Ed.2d 669 (1973), rehearing denied 414 U.S. 881, 94 S.Ct. 30, 38 L.Ed.2d 128 (1973), citing Wright, J., dissenting, in Capital Broadcasting Co. v. Mitchell, 333 F.Supp. 582, 593 n. 42 (D.D.C.1971), judgment affirmed 405 U.S. 1000, 92 S.Ct. 1289, 31 L.Ed.2d 472 (1972).

economic activity.[15]

Advertising Legal Activities

Advertisements for Abortions. In *Bigelow v. Virginia*[16] the Court began to establish a corollary principle (implicit in *Pittsburgh Press*): If an activity is legal, the state cannot prohibit advertising it. In *Bigelow* a newspaper publisher had been convicted of violating a state statute outlawing advertisements that "encourage or prompt the procuring of abortion."[17] The advertisement in question had been placed by a profit-making organization in New York which had offered to arrange for legal abortions in New York.

The Court stated that—

Viewed in its entirety, the advertisement conveyed information of potential interest and value to a diverse audience—not only to readers possibly in need of the services offered, but also to those with a general curiosity about, or genuine interest in, the subject matter or the law of another State and its development, and to readers seeking reform in Virginia. [Also], the activity advertised pertained to constitutional interests.... Thus, in this case, appellant's First Amendment interests coincided with the constitutional interests of the general public.[18]

With this, however, the Court did not rule that the advertisement was sufficiently editorial or noncommercial in nature to fall outside the ambit of *Chrestensen*. Instead, *Bigelow* proceeded with a reinterpretation of *Chrestensen*:

the holding [in *Chrestensen*] is distinctly a limited one: the ordinance was upheld as a reasonable regulation of the manner in which commercial advertising could be distributed. The fact that

---

15. 413 U.S. at 389, 93 S.Ct. at 2561. See also, National Society of Professional Engineers v. United States, 435 U.S. 679, 697–98 & nn. 26–27, 98 S.Ct. 1355, 1368–69 & nn. 26–27, 55 L.Ed.2d 637 (1978). In that case the Court held that the Professional Society's canon of ethics prohibiting competitive bidding violates section 1 of the Sherman Act. Hence, the district court could enjoin the Society from adopting any official opinion, policy statement, or guideline stating or implying that competitive pricing is unethical, even though the Society can seek to influence governmental action. "While the resulting order may curtail the exercise of liberties that the Society might otherwise enjoy, that is a necessary and, in cases such as this, unavoidable consequence of the violation. Just as an injunction against price fixing abridges the freedom of businessmen to talk to one another about prices, so too the

injunction in this case must restrict the Society's range of expression on the ethics of competitive bidding." 435 U.S. at 697, 98 S.Ct. at 1368 (footnote omitted).

On the relationship between professional ethics, the antitrust laws, and free speech, see, e.g., Morgan, The Evolving Concept of Professional Responsibility, 90 Harv.L.Rev. 702 (1977); Rotunda, The Word "Profession" Is Only a Label—And Not a Very Useful One, 4 Learning and the Law 16 (No. 2, Summer, 1977); Rotunda, The First Amendment Now Protects Commercial Speech, 10 The Center Magazine: A Publication of the Center for the Study of Democratic Institutions 33 (May/June 1977).

16. 421 U.S. 809, 95 S.Ct. 2222, 44 L.Ed.2d 600 (1975).

17. 421 U.S. at 812–13, 95 S.Ct. at 2228.

18. 421 U.S. at 822, 95 S.Ct. at 2232–33.

it had the effect of banning a particular handbill does not mean that *Chrestensen* is authority for the proposition that all statutes regulating commercial advertising are immune from constitutional challenge.[19]

This view of *Chrestensen* was a new one, to say the least. As Justice Rehnquist argued in his dissent, *Chrestensen* had been considered authority for the proposition that the first amendment cannot be used to attack a statute regulating commercial advertising, assuming, as Justice Rehnquist did, that "[w]hatever slight factual content the advertisement may contain and whatever expression of opinion may be laboriously drawn from it does not alter its predominantly commercial content."[20] Thus *Bigelow,* by reducing *Chrestensen* to an exercise in a generalized balancing process, might well have interpreted the commercial speech doctrine out of existence.

One might have argued that, in spite of the language of *Bigelow,* its facts allow a very narrow interpretation: the state may not prohibit one from advertising an activity which is a constitutional right. In this case, the right is that very special right created in *Roe v. Wade,*[21] the right to obtain an abortion, particularly during the first trimester. Under *Pittsburgh Press,* the state may prohibit advertisements of *illegal* commercial activity; under *Bigelow,* the state may not prohibit advertisements of activity which enjoys special constitutional protection. However, a later decision, *Virginia State Board of Pharmacy v. Virginia Citizens Consumer Council, Inc.*[22] indicates that a narrow view of *Bigelow* is inappropriate and that commercial speech is now within the protection of the first amendment.

Advertising Prescription Drug Prices. In *Virginia State Board of Pharmacy,* a consumer group claimed that the first amendment prohibited a statute making illegal the advertisement of prescription drug prices as unprofessional conduct. The statute was defended on the grounds that it was a permissible regulation of commercial speech that had the effect of maintaining professional standards of pharmacy.

Justice Blackmun, writing for the majority, phrased the issue simply:

Our pharmacist does not wish to editorialize on any subject, cultural, philosophical, or political. He does not wish to report any particularly newsworthy fact, or to make generalized observations even about commercial matters. The "idea" he wishes to commu-

---

19. 421 U.S. at 819–20, 95 S.Ct. at 2231.

20. 421 U.S. at 831–32, 95 S.Ct. at 2237 (Rehnquist, J., dissenting).

21. 410 U.S. 113, 93 S.Ct. 705, 35 L.Ed.2d 147 (1973), rehearing denied 410 U.S. 959, 93 S.Ct. 1409, 35 L.Ed.2d 694 (1973).

22. 425 U.S. 748, 96 S.Ct. 1817, 48 L.Ed.2d 346 (1976).

See generally, Rotunda, The First Amendment Now Protects Commercial Speech, 10 The Center Magazine: A Publication of the Center for the Study of Democratic Institutions 32–33 (May/June 1977).

nicate is simply this: "I will sell you the X prescription drug at the Y price." Our question, then, is whether this communication is wholly outside the protection of the First Amendment.[23]

The Court held that the consuming public had a protected first amendment interest in the free flow of truthful information concerning lawful activity.[24]

At the same time, the *Virginia State Board of Pharmacy* opinion reaffirmed the states' authority to issue regulations of the time, place, and manner of speech, if such restrictions are justified without reference to the content of the speech, serve a significant governmental interest and leave open other channels of communication.[25] Also untruthful speech, "commercial or otherwise, has never been protected for its own sake." [26] Thus the state may continue to regulate so as to prohibit false or even misleading speech.

In disposing of the claim that the advertising prohibition protected professional standards, the Court rejected the rationale that banning advertising was justified by the alleged salutary results—more small pharmacies, less demand for potentially dangerous drug consumption, and high public esteem for the pharmaceutical profession. Conceding the desirability of those results, the Court rejected the advertising ban as a paternalistic means of securing them. In essence, the state was taking away the consumer's ability to choose among economic decisions (where to shop, what prescription to request, and so on) by depriving him of the information needed to make these decisions intelligently. Such pre-emption of individual decision-making is deemed by the Court to be objectionable in a free-market economy.

But the Court did not use neoclassical, laissez-faire economic thinking to restrict the government's ability to regulate industry, only to show that it could not accomplish these ends by suppression of first amendment freedoms. It clearly allowed Virginia to subject its pharmacists to "close regulation", to adopt other professional standards or

23. 425 U.S. at 761, 96 S.Ct. at 1825. To emphasize the lack of any nice distinction between commercial and noncommercial speech, the Court noted that "[o]ur pharmacist, for example, could cast himself as a commentator on store-to-store disparities in drug prices, giving his own and those of a competitor as proof. We see little point in requiring him to do so, and little difference if he does not." 425 U.S. at 764–65, 96 S.Ct. at 1827.

24. 425 U.S. at 773, 96 S.Ct. at 1831.

25. 425 U.S. at 771, 96 S.Ct. at 1830.

26. Id. Justice Stewart, in his concurrence, elaborates on this issue. Unlike libel actions, where the First Amendment offers some protection in appropriate cases even for false factual assertions, New York Times Co. v. Sullivan, 376 U.S. 254, 84 S.Ct. 710, 11 L.Ed.2d 686 (1964), motion denied 376 U.S. 967, 84 S.Ct. 1130, 12 L.Ed.2d 83 (1964), the commercial advertiser generally is not under the deadline pressures of the press, generally knows the product or service he seeks to sell and is in a position to verify the accuracy of his factual assertions, and consequently there is little danger that state regulation of false or misleading price or product advertising will chill nondeceptive commercial expression. 425 U.S. at 777–78, 96 S.Ct. at 1833–34 (Stewart, J., concurring).

to "subsidize them or protect them from competition in other ways." [27] What the state cannot do is to completely suppress dissemination of concededly truthful information about entirely lawful activity.

The advertising prohibition in this case was really being used to implement hidden policy decisions that were better left to be decided by free and open debate. For example, the statute allegedly protected the small, high service pharmacy by keeping the consumer uninformed as to the cost he pays for such services. The Court suggested the desired results of the statute may yet be attained in a non-paternalistic fashion by *encouraging* dissemination of information, rather than restricting it.

Presumably, if there is value to individual service from pharmacists, a fully informed consumer (or a sufficient number of them) will choose to bear the cost of such service. Alternatively, the government may choose to subsidize low-volume, high-service pharmacies by free individual choice, through tax advantages, or outright subsidies, and this decision itself may be the subject of public debate. Similarly, if it is socially desirable to discourage the indiscriminate consumption of drugs, warnings of the hazards of consumption may prevent abuses; if not, an informed public may choose to discourage consumption by taxing or prohibiting certain drugs.

After *Virginia State Board of Pharmacy* the state may reach the same policy goals as it chose to reach before, but it may not use the means of prohibiting the dissemination of truthful information about lawful activity. The purpose of this holding is not merely to tidy-up the interpretation of the first amendment; rather it is to encourage more rational majority decision-making and a more open weighing of the advantages and disadvantages of policy alternatives by preventing the use of the "commercial speech" concept to deny entirely first amendment protection to an important area of speech.

Truthful Advertising of Harmful Substances, Such as Cigarettes, on the Electronic Media.

Two additional aspects of *Virginia State Board of Pharmacy* should be noted. First, the decision by implication raises anew the question of the constitutionality of restrictions on the advertising of cigarettes in the electronic media. Despite Justice Blackmun's offhand dismissal of the point as having been based on the "special problem of the electronic broadcast media" not present in this case,[28] we have already seen that

27. 425 U.S. at 770, 96 S.Ct. at 1829. Cf. Parker v. Brown, 317 U.S. 341, 63 S.Ct. 307, 87 L.Ed. 315 (1943).

28. 425 U.S. at 773, 96 S.Ct. at 1831. See Lamar Outdoor Advertising, Inc. v. Mississippi State Tax Com'n, 701 F.2d 314 (5th Cir.1983), on rehearing 718 F.2d 738 (1983), certiorari denied 467 U.S. 1259, 104 S.Ct. 3553, 82 L.Ed.2d 855 (1984) (citing an earlier edition of this treatise). The *Lamar* fifth circuit panel, in an opinion by Judge Gee, invalidated, as a violation of free speech, certain statutes and regulations of Mississippi which effectively banned liquor advertising on billboards and in printed and electronic media originating within the state.

the *Capital Broadcasting* decision was not based upon any special aspects of the broadcast media; rather it was squarely based on a view of the commercial speech doctrine promulgated in *Chrestensen,* that so-called commercial speech is completely outside the protections of the first amendment.

Justice Rehnquist's conclusion in his dissent that television ciga-rette ads may no longer be completely prohibited is probably correct. The state, of course, may tax cigarettes to discourage their use and the federal government may place a nationwide tax on cigarettes, or prohibit their production and sale entirely. To prevent misleading advertisements the FCC may require warnings to be placed in the commercials, as well as requiring anticigarette ads under the fairness doctrine. But unless Congress outlaws cigarettes, it should not be able to prohibit "concededly truthful information"—e.g., brand X cigarettes offer less tar and nicotine than any other cigarette—about "entirely lawful activity"—the smoking of cigarettes. Any other conclusion would allow Virginia to prohibit the advertising of drug prices on radio or television.

Perhaps the Court may one day fashion some special constitutional rules dealing with this problem in the still formative area of the first

The en banc fifth circuit reversed *Lamar* and affirmed a companion decision in a case entitled Dunagin v. Oxford, 718 F.2d 738 (5th Cir.1983) (en banc), the Supreme Court denied certiorari in 467 U.S. 1259, 104 S.Ct. 3553, 82 L.Ed.2d 855 (1984). The Supreme Court cited *Dunagin* with approval in Posadas De Puerto Rico v. Tourism Company, 478 U.S. 328, 343, 344 n. 9, 106 S.Ct. 2968, 2978, 2979 n. 9, 92 L.Ed.2d 266 (1986).

The Supreme Court avoided ruling on whether a state law prohibiting cable tele-vision systems from retransmitting out-of-state signals containing alcoholic beverage commercials violated the first amendment because the Court found that the state law conflicted with, and was preempted by, fed-eral regulation of the cable television in-dustry in Capital Cities Cable, Inc. v. Crisp, 467 U.S. 691, 104 S.Ct. 2694, 81 L.Ed.2d 580 (1984). *Capital Cities Cable* held that an invalidation of the state law on this basis was consistent with the twenty-first amendment because the limited restriction on advertising was not closely related to "exercising control over whether to permit importation or sale of liquor and to struc-ture the liquor distribution system," 467 U.S. at 716, 104 S.Ct. at 2709, 81 L.Ed.2d at 599 (internal quotation and citation omit-ted). But see, Capital Broadcasting Co. v. Mitchell, 333 F.Supp. 582 (D.D.C.1971), af-

firmed without opinion sub nom. Capital Broadcasting Co. v. Acting Attorney Gener-al Kleindienst, 405 U.S. 1000, 92 S.Ct. 1290, 31 L.Ed.2d 472 (1972).

See generally, Note, The First Amend-ment and Legislative Bans of Liquor and Cigarette Advertisements, 85 Colum.L.Rev. 632 (1985).

Welkowitz, Smoke in the Air: Commer-cial Speech and Broadcasting, 7 Cardozo L.Rev. 47 (1985). Professor Welkowitz con-cludes:

"The Court's treatment of both commer-cial speech and broadcasting has been fraught with the substitution of instinct for analysis. A reasoned approach yields the conclusion that the goals of the Court are better served by an approach that scrutinizes viewpoint-based restric-tions on commercial speech of *all* media with extreme skepticism.... Indeed, Congress' unwillingness to act [to bar cigarettes] may reflect a public accept-ance of smoking that makes governmen-tal intervention in the form of speech suppression even more intolerable." 7 Cardozo L.Rev. at 89, 91 (emphasis in original).

See, Redish, Product Health Claims and the First Amendment: Scientific Expres-sion and the Twilight Zone of Commercial Speech, 43 Vanderbilt L.Rev. 1433 (1990).

amendment and the broadcast media.[29]   But the Court has not yet done so; certainly Justice Blackmun's brief, inaccurate reference to the *Capital Broadcasting* decision banning cigarette advertising on television hardly qualifies as a legal distinction of constitutional proportions.   Moreover, Chief Justice Burger's attempt, in his concurrence, to distinguish between advertisements by "true professionals" (doctors and lawyers) and advertisements by pseudo-professionals (pharmacists)[30] creates a distinction as unworkable as that inherent in the *Chrestensen* doctrine itself, and since rejected in *Bates v. State Bar*,[31] discussed below.

The *Posadas* Case.   In *Posadas De Puerto Rico Associates v. Tourism Company*,[32] Justice Rehnquist, for a bare five Justice majority, upheld the constitutionality of a Puerto Rican statute that restricted local advertising inviting the residents of Puerto Rico to patronize gambling casinos but that did not restrict local advertising targeted at tourists, even though the local advertising aimed at the tourists may incidentally reach the hands of a resident.   In fact, during oral argument before the Supreme Court, counsel for Puerto Rico said that a casino advertising in a Spanish Language Daily, with ninety-nine percent local circulation would be permitted, so long as the advertising "is addressed to tourists and not to residents."   The plaintiffs attacked the statute on its face and the court rejected this facial attack.

The Court said that it applied the general principles identified in *Central Hudson*.[33]   The commercial speech in *Posadas* "concerns a lawful activity and is not misleading or fraudulent," hence, it met the first prong of the four part test of *Central Hudson*.   The governmental interest in reducing the demand for casino gambling by Puerto Rican residents because of the legislature's apparent belief that excessive casino gambling would seriously harm the health, safety, and welfare of

29.   Compare Red Lion Broadcasting Co. v. FCC, 395 U.S. 367, 89 S.Ct. 1794, 23 L.Ed.2d 371 (1969), with Columbia Broadcasting System, Inc. v. Democratic Nat. Committee, 412 U.S. 94, 93 S.Ct. 2080, 36 L.Ed.2d 772 (1973).

30.   425 U.S. at 774, 96 S.Ct. at 1831–32 (Burger, C.J., concurring).

31.   433 U.S. 350, 97 S.Ct. 2691, 53 L.Ed.2d 810 (1977), rehearing denied 434 U.S. 881, 98 S.Ct. 242, 54 L.Ed.2d 164 (1977).

It should be noted that the scope of attorney advertising when restricted by professional association rather than by the state also raises important issues of antitrust law. The Justice Department for example sued the American Bar Association claiming its advertising restrictions in the Code of Professional Responsibility violate the antitrust laws. See Bar News, A Special

Report on the Justice Department Antitrust Suit Against the ABA (Summer 1976); see generally T. Morgan & R. Rotunda, Problems and Materials on Professional Responsibility 95–132 (1976), and its 1978 Supplement, ch. 4. This suit was later settled.

32.   478 U.S. 328, 106 S.Ct. 2968, 92 L.Ed.2d 266 (1986).

See generally, Rotunda, The Constitutional Future of the Bill of Rights: A Closer Look at Commercial Speech and State Aid to Religiously Affiliated Schools, 65 No.Car.L.Rev. 917, 921–29 (1987).

33.   Central Hudson Gas & Electric Corp. v. Public Service Commission, 447 U.S. 557, 100 S.Ct. 2343, 65 L.Ed.2d 341 (1980).

Puerto Rican citizens is "substantial," however, and the majority believed that the challenged restrictions "directly advance" Puerto Rico's asserted interest because "the legislature's belief is a reasonable one." [34]

The majority was unpersuaded that the challenged advertising was underinclusive merely because other kinds of gambling (such as horse racing, cockfighting, and the lottery) may be advertised to residents of Puerto Rico. First, the advertising restrictions " 'directly advance' the legislature's interest in reducing demand for games for chance," and second, the legislative interest "is not necessarily to reduce demand for all games of chance, but to reduce demand for casino gambling." That is, the majority thought that the legislature must have felt that the risks associated with casino gambling are greater because these other forms of gambling " 'have been traditionally part of the Puerto Rican's roots.' " [35] The majority did not otherwise elaborate on why casino gambling may be different in kind from other games of chance. Thus, the law, in the view of the majority, met the second and third prongs of the *Central Hudson* test.

Then, the Court turned to the fourth prong: are the restrictions no more extensive than necessary to serve the state's interest? The Court concluded that the fit between the legislature's ends and its means was close enough. The restriction, limited to advertising aimed at residents of Puerto Rico, was no more extensive than necessary to serve the governmental interest.

The majority cited with approval lower court cases approving of advertising restrictions on smoking and alcohol, and sought to distinguish *Carey v. Population Services International,* [36] (advertising of contraceptives is protected speech), and *Bigelow v. Virginia* [37] (advertising of abortion clinic is protected speech) as cases where underlying conduct that was the subject of the advertising restrictions was constitutionally protected. "Here, on the other hand, the Puerto Rico Legislature surely could have prohibited casino gambling by the residents of

34. Does a Ban on Advertising Necessarily Dampen Demand for a Product: the Case of Cigarettes. The Court's easy assumption that a ban on advertising of legal casino gambling will dampen demand by Puerto Rican citizens appears reasonable enough—but the empirical evidence suggests otherwise. Take, for example, the case of tobacco advertising. A cross-national study by London's INFO-TAB and Children's Research Unit showed that 36% of 15–year–old children smoke in Norway, where tobacco advertising is banned! But in Hong Kong, where there are very few restrictions on tobacco advertising, only 11% of 15–year–olds smoke. Wall Street Journal, Dec. 12, 1989, at B1, col. 2 (midwest ed.) (information complied

by American Demographics Magazine for the Wall Street Journal).

Advertising may shift demand (from one brand to another) but may be substantially less effective in increasing total demand; indeed, a well-known and well-publicized ban on advertising may be more effective in increasing total demand, because the ban gives tobacco the air of forbidden fruit.

35. 478 U.S. at 343 & n. 8, 106 S.Ct. at 2977–78 & n. 8.

36. 431 U.S. 678, 97 S.Ct. 2010, 52 L.Ed.2d 675 (1977).

37. 421 U.S. 809, 95 S.Ct. 2222, 44 L.Ed.2d 600 (1975).

Puerto Rico altogether. In our view the greater power to completely ban casino gambling necessarily includes the lesser power to ban advertising of casino gambling, and *Carey* and *Bigelow* are hence inapposite." [38]

Dictum in the majority may (but need not) be read to suggest that legislatures could similarly engage in a limited restriction of advertising of other subjects which the Court views as harmful, even though the activity itself may not be illegal in the particular jurisdiction, such as advertising of cigarettes, alcohol, and legal prostitution. [39] However, the extent to which this dictum is valid is unclear.

"[T]he greater power ... includes the lesser power...." It is unclear to what extent the Court's statement in *Posadas*—that "the greater power ... includes the lesser power...."—represents any real principle of law. For example, the power to ban casinos does not imply the power to allow casinos and to ban all political discussions within the casinos. Nor does the power to ban casinos in their entirety imply the power to allow casinos, but ban within them, any discussions of the merits of the Puerto Rico restriction of casino advertising inviting the residents of Puerto Rico to patronize the casinos.

In an earlier case, the Court rejected entirely the suggestion that the state's power to directly ban the use of products which waste electricity implies the power to completely ban an electrical utility from engaging in promotional advertising encouraging the use (including the wasteful use) of electricity. [40] And in a later case, the Court made clear that whatever this statement means—the greater power includes the lesser—it, at most, only applies in the commercial speech context. [41]

38. 478 U.S. at 345–46, 106 S.Ct. at 2979.

39. 478 U.S. at 350 & n. 10, 106 S.Ct. at 2979–80 & n. 10.

See, e.g., Nevada Revised Statutes §§ 201.430, 201.440 (1986) (prohibiting advertising of houses of prostitution in certain instances even though prostitution legal in counties with less than 250,000 people). Nev.Rev.Stat. §§ 244, 345(1), (8).

40. Central Hudson Gas & Elec. Corp. v. Public Service Commission, 447 U.S. 557, 100 S.Ct. 2343, 65 L.Ed.2d 341 (1980). Compare: City of Lakewood v. Plain Dealer Publishing Co., 486 U.S. 750, 763, 108 S.Ct. 2138, 2147, 100 L.Ed.2d 771 (1988): "[The] 'greater-includes-lesser' syllogism ... is blind to the radically different constitutional harms inherent in the 'greater' and 'lesser' restrictions. Presumably in the case of an ordinance that completely prohibits a particular manner of expression, the law on its face is both content and viewpoint neutral. In analyzing such a hypothetical ordinance, the Court would apply the well-settled time, place, and manner test. The danger giving rise to the First Amendment inquiry is that the government is silencing a channel of speech.... Therefore, even if the government may constitutionally impose content-neutral prohibitions on a particular manner of speech, it may not *condition* that speech on obtaining a license or permit from a government official in that official's boundless discretion." (footnote and internal citations omitted; emphasis in original).

41. Meyer v. Grant, 486 U.S. 414, 424–25, 108 S.Ct. 1886, 1893–94, 100 L.Ed.2d 425 (1988).

It is often the case that a partial ban—or a ban on speech advertising a product—is not a lesser power but a greater one, for it allows the state to avoid the hard choices that come with a decision to engage in a complete ban. A complete ban has within it an inner political check that restricts the excesses of state power. For example, in *Posadas,* in order for Puerto Rico to engage in a complete ban of casinos, it must give up tax revenue and tourist income associated with legalized casino gambling. The "lesser" power to prohibit speech allows the state to avoid the inner political check that the first amendment provides.

The *Posadas* Dissent. Justice Brennan, joined by Justices Marshall and Blackmun, dissented. They noted that the justices have "consistently invalidated restrictions designed to deprive consumers of accurate information about products and services legally offered for sale," [42] citing cases where the underlying conduct was *not* constitutionally protected including *Linmark Associates, Inc. v. Willingboro,*[43] (ban on for-sale signs in front of houses invalidated); *Virginia Pharmacy Board v. Virginia Citizens Consumer Council,*[44] (ban on advertising of prescription drug prices by pharmacists invalidated); *Bates v. State Bar,*[45] (ban on advertising of lawyer's services invalidated). The Brennan dissent objected to the "relaxed standards" used by the majority, because, when the state "seeks to suppress the dissemination of nonmisleading commercial speech relating to legal activities for fear that recipients will act on the information provided, such regulation should be subject to strict judicial scrutiny." [46] The Government should not be allowed "to manipulate private behavior by depriving citizens of truthful information concerning lawful activities." [47]

The dissent also noted that the Puerto Rican legislature had never "actually asserted" that advertising of casino gambling aimed at Puerto Rican residents will cause serious harmful effects.[48] Moreover, Puerto Rico allows its residents to legally patronize casinos, and residents of Puerto Rico are permitted to gamble at horse and dog racing, cockfighting, and the Puerto Rican lottery, "all of which are allowed to advertise freely to residents." [49] Perhaps, suggested Brennan, the state legislature was not really concerned with the evils of casino gambling; it

42. 478 U.S. at 350, 106 S.Ct. at 2981 (Brennan, J., dissenting, joined by Marshall & Blackmun, JJ.).

43. 431 U.S. 85, 97 S.Ct. 1614, 52 L.Ed.2d 155 (1977).

44. 425 U.S. 748, 96 S.Ct. 1817, 48 L.Ed.2d 346 (1976).

45. 433 U.S. 350, 97 S.Ct. 2691, 53 L.Ed.2d 810 (1977), rehearing denied 434 U.S. 881, 98 S.Ct. 242, 54 L.Ed.2d 164 (1977). Note that in Central Hudson Gas & Elec. Corp. v. Public Service Commis-

sion, 447 U.S. 557, 100 S.Ct. 2343, 65 L.Ed.2d 341 (1980), the Court invalidated a state regulation which *completely* banned promotional advertising by an electrical utility, even though the state could have directly banned wasteful use of electricity.

46. 478 U.S. at 351, 106 S.Ct. at 2982.

47. 478 U.S. at 351, 106 S.Ct. at 2982.

48. 478 U.S. at 354, 106 S.Ct. at 2984.

49. 478 U.S. at 353, 106 S.Ct. at 2983 (footnote omitted).

simply wanted the residents to spend their gambling dollars on the government run lottery.[50] Brennan also objected to the new principle which Justice Rehnquist tried to advance, that the state may ban truthful advertising if the state could ban the activity directly. "[A] ban on casino advertising is [not] 'less intrusive' than an outright ban on such activity. [T]he 'constitutional doctrine' which bans Puerto Rico from banning advertisements concerning lawful casino gambling is not so strange a restraint—it is called the First Amendment." [51]

Justice Stevens noted that "Puerto Rico blatantly discriminates in its punishment of speech depending on the publication, audience, and words employed." And the prohibition is based on a "standard that is hopelessly vague and unpredictable." [52]

In *Virginia Pharmacy Board*, Justice Blackmun for the Court had said that the choice "between the dangers of suppressing information and the dangers of its misuse if it is freely available" is a choice "that the First Amendment makes for us." [53] He added:

> Virginia is free to require whatever professional standards it wishes of its pharmacists; it may subsidize them or protect them from competition in other ways. But it may not do so by keeping the public in ignorance of the entirely lawful terms that competing pharmacists are offering. In this sense, the justifications Virginia has offered for suppressing the flow of prescription drug price information, far from persuading us that the flow is not protected by the First Amendment, have reinforced our view that it is. We so hold.[54]

Justice Rehnquist was the only dissenter in *Virginia Pharmacy Board.* That case is still good law (the *Posadas* majority cited it with approval).

Attempts to Ban For Sale Signs. The Court has continued the principle of *Virginia Board of Pharmacy* in *Linmark Associates, Inc. v. Township of Willingboro.*[55] There the unanimous Court ruled that the first amendment did not permit a municipality to prohibit by ordinance the posting of "For Sale" or "Sold" signs even though the town acted to stem what it perceived as the flight of white homeowners from a racially integrated community.

The respondent argued that the first amendment concerns were less because the ordinance only restricted one form of communication. The Court decided, however, that the other forms of advertising—mainly by newspapers and realtor listings—were more costly and less effective. Also, the Court emphasized that the Township's ordinance,

50. 478 U.S. at 354, 106 S.Ct. at 2983.

51. 478 U.S. at 354–55 n. 4, 106 S.Ct. at 2984 n. 4.

52. 478 U.S. at 359, 106 S.Ct. at 2986 (Stevens, J., dissenting, joined by Blackmun & Marshall, JJ.).

53. 425 U.S. at 77, 96 S.Ct. at 1829.

54. 425 U.S. at 77, 96 S.Ct. at 1829 (internal citation omitted).

55. 431 U.S. 85, 97 S.Ct. 1614, 52 L.Ed.2d 155 (1977).

by its own terms, made clear that it was not concerned with the time, place, or manner of the speech but its content. It did not prohibit all lawn signs, or all lawn signs of a particular size, in order, perhaps, to promote aesthetic values or other goals unrelated to the suppression of free expression. In addition, the "respondents have not demonstrated that the place or manner of speech produces a detrimental 'secondary effect' on society. . . . Rather, Willingboro has proscribed particular types of signs based on their content because it fears their 'primary' effect—that they will cause those receiving the information to act upon it." [56]

Finally, the *Linmark* Court was unwilling to regard the governmental objective of assuring that Willingboro remains an integrated community as sufficient to justify the ordinance. The Court rejected this rationale on two grounds, one very narrow and one much broader. First, the Court concluded that the record before it did not support the township's fears that it was experiencing panic selling by white home-owners because of a belief the township was changing from a white to a black community.[57] More broadly, the Court found the defect in the ordinance "more basic" because if "dissemination of this information can be restricted, then every locality in the country can suppress any facts that reflect poorly on the locality, so long as a plausible claim can be made that disclosure would cause the recipients of the information to act 'irrationally.' " [58]

Bans on Contraceptives. In *Carey v. Population Services International*,[59] the Court invalidated a prohibition of any advertisement or display of contraceptives, a product which was not only legal but constitutionally protected. The arguments that such a prohibition was necessary because advertisements would be offensive or embarrassing to some or would legitimize sexual activities were rejected as "classically not justifications. . . ." [60]

Problems Related to Lawyer Advertising.

In 1977, in *Bates v. State Bar* [61] the Court struck down state limitations on attorney advertising. The majority noted that the case

---

56. 431 U.S. at 94, 97 S.Ct. at 1619, citing Young v. American Mini Theatres, Inc., 427 U.S. 50, 71 n. 34, 96 S.Ct. 2440, 2452 n. 34, 49 L.Ed.2d 310 (1976), rehearing denied 429 U.S. 873, 97 S.Ct. 191, 50 L.Ed.2d 155 (1976).

57. The Court specifically cast doubt on Barrick Realty, Inc. v. Gary, 491 F.2d 161 (7th Cir.1974) which upheld Gary, Indiana's prohibition of "For Sale" signs on a record which showed that whites were fleeing en masse. "We express no view as to whether *Barrick Realty* can survive *Bigelow* and *Virginia Pharmacy*." 431 U.S. 85 at 95 n. 9, 97 S.Ct. 1614 at 1620 n. 9.

58. 431 U.S. 85 at 96, 97 S.Ct. 1614 at 1620.

59. 431 U.S. 678, 97 S.Ct. 2010, 52 L.Ed.2d 675 (1977).

60. 431 U.S. at 701, 97 S.Ct. at 2024. See also Bolger v. Youngs Drug Products Corp., 463 U.S. 60, 103 S.Ct. 2875, 77 L.Ed.2d 469 (1983) (law prohibiting mailing of unsolicited advertisements for contraceptives invalid).

61. 433 U.S. 350, 97 S.Ct. 2691, 53 L.Ed.2d 810 (1977), rehearing denied 434 U.S. 881, 98 S.Ct. 242, 54 L.Ed.2d 164 (1977).

did not involve person-to-person solicitation nor advertising as to the quality of legal services, but only the question of whether lawyers may constitutionally advertise the prices of routine services, such as uncontested divorces, uncontested adoptions, simple personal bankruptcies, and changes of name.[62] Such advertising is constitutionally protected.

At this point in the development of the case law the *Bates* Court left open the extent to which certain types of advertising may be misleading, though it found appellants' particular advertisement not misleading. The Court also raised the question of whether advertising claims as to the quality of services "may be so likely to be misleading as to warrant restriction. . . .   And the special problems of advertising on the electronic broadcast media will [also] warrant special consideration." [63]

Later, in *In re R.M.J.*,[64] a unanimous Supreme Court, in an opinion by Justice Powell, applied *Bates* and invalidated various restrictions on lawyer advertising. The state supreme court had reprimanded R.M.J. because he had deviated from the precise listing of areas of practice included in the state's Rule 4 governing lawyer advertising; for example, his advertisement listed "real estate" instead of "property," and he listed "contracts," although Rule 4 did not list that latter term at all.

Because the state did not show that R.M.J.'s listing was deceptive and because the state could show no substantial interest which its restriction on advertising promoted, the Court invalidated it. Similarly the Court invalidated a part of Rule 4 prohibiting a lawyer from identifying the jurisdictions in which he is licensed to practice law.[65] The Court also struck a prohibition against the lawyer widely mailing announcement cards to persons other than lawyers, former clients, personal friends, and relatives. These cards announced the opening of

---

See generally, e.g., Andrews, Lawyer Advertising and the First Amendment, 1981 A.B.Found.Res.J. 967 (1981). Cf. Canby & Gellhorn, Physician Advertising: The First Amendment and the Sherman Act, 1978 Duke L.J. 543; McChesney, Commercial Speech in the Professions: The Supreme Court's Unanswered Questions and Questionable Answers, 134 U.Pa.L.Rev. 45 (1985).

62. 433 U.S. at 366, 97 S.Ct. at 2700.

63. 433 U.S. at 383–84, 97 S.Ct. at 2709.

After this case the American Bar Association's Model Code of Professional Responsibility was amended to allow radio and television advertising subject to certain restrictions. See, e.g., D.R. 2–101(D): "If the advertisement is communicated to the public over television or radio, it shall be prerecorded, approved for broadcast by the

lawyer, and a recording of the actual transmission shall be retained by the lawyer."

64. 455 U.S. 191, 102 S.Ct. 929, 71 L.Ed.2d 64 (1982).

See Blackmar, the Missouri Supreme Court and Lawyer Advertising: *RMJ* and its Aftermath, 47 Mo.L.Rev. 621 (1982).

65. 455 U.S. at 205, 102 S.Ct. at 938.

R.M.J. also emphasized in large boldface type that he was a member of the U.S. Supreme Court bar, a "relatively uninformative fact" but the record did not show that it was misleading. Rule 4 did not specifically identify this information as misleading, nor place a limitation on the type size, nor require any explanation of the significance of admission to the U.S. Supreme Court bar. 455 U.S. at 205–06, 102 S.Ct. at 938–39.

his law office. The state produced no evidence justifying such a restrictive prohibition.

Targeted Direct Mail–Advertising. *Shapero v. Kentucky Bar Association* [66] invalidated, as a violation of free speech, state prohibitions against attorneys sending truthful, non-deceptive letters to potential clients known to face particular legal problems (i.e., targeted, direct-mail advertising). The state rule was based on the American Bar Association's Model Rule of Professional Conduct, Rule 7.3. The Court relied primarily on *Zauderer v. Office of Disciplinary Counsel,* and noted that the Supreme Court's lawyer advertising cases have never distinguished among various modes of written advertising to the general public. For example, *In re R.M.J.* treated mailed announcement cards the same as newspaper and telephone directory advertisements.[67]

Mass mailing is a form of advertising and therefore also constitutionally protected. Given that attorneys may engage in mass mailing, it makes little sense for the state to prohibit targeted mailing, which is only a more efficient form of advertising than mass mailing. It is quite reasonable for an attorney to mail a letter only to those who are more likely to find it of interest.

Advertising That a Lawyer Is a "Specialist" or "Certified." The Illinois Supreme Court promulgated ethical rules governing lawyers. These rules did not permit an attorney to hold himself out as "certified" or a "specialist" except for patent, trademark, and admiralty lawyers. Therefore the Illinois Supreme Court publicly censured Peel, an Illinois attorney, because his letterhead stated that he is

---

66. 486 U.S. 466, 108 S.Ct. 1916, 100 L.Ed.2d 475 (1988), on remand 763 S.W.2d 126 (Ky.1989).

See generally, Andrews, Lawyer Advertising and the First Amendment, 1981 Am. Bar Foundation Res.J. 967; Note, Direct–Mail Solicitation by Attorneys: Bates to R.M.J., 33 Syracuse L.Rev. 1041 (1982); Maute, Scrutinizing Lawyer Advertising and Solicitation Rules Under Commercial Speech and Antitrust Doctrine, 13 Hastings Const. L.Q. 487 (1986); Hill, Solicitation by Lawyers: Piercing the First Amendment Veil, 42 Maine L.Rev. 369 (1990).

67. Brennan, J., in a plurality opinion went on to conclude that petitioner's particular letter was not misleading merely because it engaged in the liberal use of underscored, upper case letters—e.g., "Call NOW, don't wait"; "it is FREE, there is NO charge for calling." Nor was the letter misleading because it contained assertions that state no objective fact ("It may surprise you what I may be able to do for you"). The plurality said that a "truthful and nondeceptive letter, no matter how big

its type and how much it speculates can never 'shou[t] at the recipient' or 'gras[p] him by the lapels,' as can a lawyer engaging in face-to-face solicitation. The letter simply presents no comparable risk of overreaching."

White and Stevens, JJ., dissented from this plurality opinion because they believed that the issue of whether the petitioner's particular letter was misleading should be decided by the state courts in the first instance.

O'Connor, J., joined by Rehnquist, C.J. and Scalia, J., filed a dissenting opinion. They agreed that the reasoning of *Zauderer* supported the majority's conclusion, but the dissenters wanted to reexamine the entire line of cases. "The roots of the error in our attorney advertising cases are a defective analogy between professional services and standardized consumer products and a correspondingly inappropriate skepticism about the States' justification for their regulations."

certified as a civil trial specialist by the National Board of Trial Advocacy (NBTA), a bona fide private group that developed a set of objective and demanding standards and procedures for periodic certification of lawyers with experience and competence in trial work.   In *Peel v. Attorney Registration and Disciplinary Commission of Illinois* [68] the U.S. Supreme Court (five to four, with no majority opinion) reversed.

The facts on Peel's letterhead were both verifiable and true.   The issue before the Court was whether a lawyer has a constitutional right, under the standards applicable to commercial speech, to advertise his or her certification as a trial specialist by NBTA.   Though Peel's claim was facially accurate, Illinois argued that Peel's letterhead implied a higher quality or ability, than noncertified lawyers.   Justice Stevens' plurality opinion explained that Illinois had confused "the distinction between statements of opinion or quality and statements of objective facts that may support an inference of quality." [69]

Peel's statement of certification by a private group, the NBTA, has no more potential to mislead than an attorney advertising that he is admitted to practice before the U.S. Supreme Court, a statement the Supreme Court approved in, *In re R.M.J.*   Thus, Peel's letterhead was neither actually nor inherently nor potentially misleading.   If the state believes that statements of private certification might be potentially misleading, the state might be able to require a disclaimer about the certifying organization or the standards of a specialty. [70]   To require more disclosure is better than a total prohibition.

The Illinois Supreme Court claimed that Peel's statement that he was certified was misleading because, that court said, everyone knows that "certified" means that he was certified by the state, because a certificate is—and here the Illinois Supreme Court, in an effort to gather support for its claim, quoted from Webster's Dictionary—

> [A] document issued by ... a state agency, ... certifying that one has satisfactorily ... attained professional standing in a given field and may officially practice or hold a position in that field.   Webster's Third New International Dictionary 367 (1986 ed.) [71]

---

68. 496 U.S. 91, 110 S.Ct. 2281, 110 L.Ed.2d 83 (1990).

69. 496 U.S. at 101, 110 S.Ct. at 2288. (Stevens, J., joined by Brennan, Blackmun, & Kennedy, JJ.).

Marshall, J., joined by Brennan, J., concurred in the judgment, arguing that the letterhead was potentially misleading and that Illinois could enact regulations other than a total ban in order to protect the public.   White, J., dissented and agreed that the letterhead was potentially misleading.   O'Connor, J., joined by Rehn-

quist, C.J. & Scalia, J., also dissented and objected that the Court's "[f]ailure to accord States considerable latitude in this area embroils this Court in the micromanagement of the State's inherent authority to police the ethical standards of the profession within its borders."   496 U.S. at 119, 110 S.Ct. at 2297.

70. 496 U.S. at 110 n. 17, 110 S.Ct. at 2292 n. 17.

71. In re Peel, 126 Ill.2d 397, 405, 128 Ill.Dec. 535, 534 N.E.2d 980, 984 (1989), reversed 496 U.S. 91, 110 S.Ct. 2281, 110

It is ironic, to say the least, that the Illinois Supreme Court criticized Peel for being misleading while the Illinois Supreme Court itself was misleading, for the full quotation to which the Illinois court referred, *without* the ellipses, is quite different. A certificate is—

> [A] document issued by *a school,* a state agency, *or a professional organization* certifying that one has satisfactorily *completed a course of studies, has passed a qualifying examination, or has* attained professional standing in a given field and may officially practice or hold a position in that field. Webster's Third New International Dictionary 367 (1986 ed.)

The portions that the Illinois Supreme Court deleted are in italics.

As the Stevens' plurality noted, the consuming public knows that states routinely issue licenses for a host of activities—such as licenses to sell liquor, or drive a car—all the time. Similarly, private groups issue certificates to commemorate a solo flight or a hole in one. It is hardly uncommon for people to claim that they are foreign car "specialists" or air conditioning "specialists" without the public automatically believing that the state has formally recognized these claims. Justice Stevens rejected the paternalistic assumption that the reader of Mr. Peel's stationery was no more discriminating or sophisticated than those who watch children's television. The state's rule was overbroad: one does not burn down the house to roast the pig.[72]

Disclosure Requirements. In *Zauderer v. Office of Disciplinary Counsel,*[73] Justice White for the Court held that the state may not discipline an attorney who solicits business by running newspaper advertisements containing nondeceptive illustrations and legal advice. The attorney in question placed an advertisement offering to represent women who had suffered injury from the Dalkon Shield Intrauterine Device. This advertisement included a drawing of the Shield and offered legal advice, such as the advice that claims may not yet be time barred. Though the legal advice regarded a specific legal problem, it was neither false not deceptive, and did not involve face-to-face solicitation.

L.Ed.2d 83 (1990). After this case, the Illinois Supreme Court promptly modified its rules and required lawyers who used the words "certified," "specialist," "expert," or "any other, similar terms", to state, *inter alia,* that "the Supreme Court of Illinois does not recognize certifications of specialists in the practice of law and that the certificate, award or recognition is not a requirement to practice law in Illinois." See, Illinois Amended Rule 7.4 (July 16, 1990), reprinted in, T. Morgan & R. Rotunda, Problems and Materials on Professional Responsibility 446 (5th ed. 1991).

72. 496 U.S. at 105–06, 110 S.Ct. at 2290. Cf. Bolger v. Youngs Drug Products Corp., 463 U.S. 60, 74, 103 S.Ct. 2875, 2884, 77 L.Ed.2d 469 (1983), where the Court invalidated a federal statute prohibiting unsolicited mailings of contraceptive advertisements. *Bolger* rejected the argument that the statute aided parents' efforts to discuss birth control with their parents. To purge all mailboxes of material suitable for adults because some children may see it is more extensive regulation than the first amendment allows.

73. 471 U.S. 626, 105 S.Ct. 2265, 85 L.Ed.2d 652 (1985).

However, the Court held that the state could discipline an attorney for failure to include in his advertisements some information reasonably necessary to make his advertisement not misleading. The lawyer advertised that he was available to represent clients on a contingent fee basis and that "if there is no recovery, no legal fees are owed by our clients." Thus, the advertisement failed to disclose that the clients might be liable for significant litigation costs even though their lawsuits were unsuccessful.

The Court first carefully distinguished between disclosure requirements and outright prohibitions of speech. A disclosure requirement prohibits no speech and the lawyer's "constitutionally protected interest in *not* providing any particular factual information in his advertising is minimal." [74] As long as the disclosure requirements (1) are reasonably related to the state's interest in preventing deception of consumers, and, (2) there is no problem of vagueness,[75] and, (3) they are not "unjustified or unduly burdensome,"[76] there is no first amendment violation. This "unduly burdensome" caveat is an important one. The Supreme Court did not give regulatory authorities a blank check to make every advertisement look like a securities prospectus.

But if the disclosure requirements meet this three-part test, it is not necessary for the state to demonstrate that they are the least restrictive means to serve the state's purposes. Nor is a disclosure requirement invalid if it is underinclusive, i.e., if it does not get at all facets of the problem it is designed to ameliorate. As a general matter, governments are entitled to attack problems piecemeal, unless their policies implicate rights that are so fundamental that strict scrutiny must be applied.

Applying these principles the Court concluded:

Appellant's advertisement informed the public that "if there is no recovery, no legal fees are owed by our clients." The advertisement makes no mention of the distinction between "legal fees" and "costs," and to a layman not aware of the meaning of these terms of art, the advertisement would suggest that employing appellant would be a no-lose proposition in that his representation in a losing cause would come entirely free of charge. The assumption that substantial numbers of potential clients would be so misled is hardly a speculative one: it is a commonplace that members of the public are often unaware of the technical meanings of such terms as "fees" and "costs"—terms that, in ordinary usage, might well be virtually interchangeable. When the possibility of deception is as self-evident as it is in this case, we need not require the State to

---

74. 471 U.S. at 651, 105 S.Ct. at 2282 (emphasis in original).

75. 471 U.S. at 653 n. 15, 105 S.Ct. at 2283 n. 15.

76. 471 U.S. at 651, 105 S.Ct. at 2282.

"conduct a survey of the ... public before it [may] determine that the [advertisement] had a tendency to mislead." [77]

Solicitation of Legal Business. In the year following the *Bates* decision, the Court began to define the limits of state regulation of attorney solicitation of clients in two cases decided the same day, *Ohralik v. Ohio State Bar* [78] and *In re Primus*.[79] In so doing the majority, speaking through Justice Powell, appeared to resurrect some elements of the "commercial" speech distinction that had been discredited by the earlier cases. Justice Powell said in *Ohralik* that the distinction between other types of speech and commercial speech is a "commonsense" one, though later he stated in *Primus* that the line between commercial and noncommercial speech "will not always be easy to draw," [80] an admission that suggests the distinction is not so commonsensical.

It is difficult to derive any specific principle of law from *Ohralik* and *Primus* because language in each case suggests both broad and

---

77. 471 U.S. at 652, 105 S.Ct. at 2282. Powell, J., took no part in the consideration or decision of this case. Brennan, J., joined by Marshall, J., concurred in part and dissented in part. They did not dispute the Court's basic disclosure principles, but did not believe, inter alia, that Ohio's "vaguely expressed disclosure requirements" were permissible. O'Connor, J., joined by Rehnquist, J., also concurred in part and dissented in part. They would have upheld Ohio's rule prohibiting the use of unsolicited legal advice in printed advertisements in order to attract clients.

78. 436 U.S. 447, 98 S.Ct. 1912, 56 L.Ed.2d 444 (1978).

79. 436 U.S. 412, 98 S.Ct. 1893, 56 L.Ed.2d 417 (1978).

Doctors' Advertising. Closely related to the issue of advertising and solicitation by lawyers is the question of similar activities by physicians. See generally, Canby & Gellhorn, Physician Advertising: The First Amendment and the Sherman Act, 1978 Duke L.J. 543.

80. 436 U.S. at 455–56, 438 n. 32, 98 S.Ct. at 1918, 1908 n. 32. Justice Powell said that the line is "based in part on the motive of the speaker and the character of the expressive activity...." Id. Justice Rehnquist, dissenting, noted that to the extent this " 'commonsense' distinction focuses on the content of the speech, it is at least suspect under many of the Court's First Amendment cases ... and to the extent it focuses upon the motive of the speaker, it is subject to manipulation by

clever practitioners." 436 U.S. at 441–42, 98 S.Ct. at 1910.

Moreover, Justice Powell's tortured discussion of attorney's fees—in which he sought to demonstrate that there are differences in counsel fees awarded by the court and counsel fees awarded in a "traditional" manner—demonstrates that distinguishing between commercial and noncommercial speech is a fruitless endeavor. Justice Powell said, inter alia, that:

"Counsel fees [here] are awarded in the discretion of the court; awards are not drawn from the plaintiff's recovery, and are usually premised on a successful outcome; and the amounts awarded may not correspond to fees generally obtainable in private litigation." 436 U.S. at 430, 98 S.Ct. at 1903–04.

All of these characteristics, even the last one supposedly unique to the ACLU litigation, apply to many private securities lawsuits where the attorneys secure a benefit for shareholders but create no res. Similar types of fees may be generated by truth in lending cases. See, e.g., Mills v. Electric Auto–Lite Co., 396 U.S. 375, 389–97, 90 S.Ct. 616, 624–28, 24 L.Ed.2d 593 (1970), appeal after remand 552 F.2d 1239 (7th Cir.1977), certiorari denied 434 U.S. 922, 98 S.Ct. 398, 54 L.Ed.2d 279 (1977), rehearing denied 434 U.S. 1002, 98 S.Ct. 649, 54 L.Ed.2d 499 (1977); Mirabal v. General Motors Acceptance Corp., 576 F.2d 729 (7th Cir.1978), certiorari denied 439 U.S. 1039, 99 S.Ct. 642, 58 L.Ed.2d 699 (1978).

narrow holdings.[81] The decisions in the two cases, taken together, indicate that the state may regulate lawyer solicitation in order to protect the public from false or deceptive commercial practices, so long as the regulations are reasonable and are not applied to speech that does not clearly present such dangers to the public.[82]

The Court recognized in *Ohralik* that the state has an interest in protecting the "unsophisticated, injured, or distressed lay person" from "those aspects of solicitation that involve fraud, undue influence, intimidation, overreaching, and other forms of 'vexatious conduct.' "[83] This rule is justified in part because of the special nature of "in-person" solicitation. In general advertising the recipient may simply turn away, but in-person solicitation may exert pressure and seek an immediate response from the prospective client, who then has less opportunity for reflection. The Bar and supervisory authorities have less opportunity to engage in counter education in such circumstances. And there is less opportunity for public scrutiny because the in-person solicitation often takes place in private, with no witness other than the lawyer and the prospective client.[84]

However, even these distinctions apparently do not justify a broad, per se rule against in-person solicitation, for the *Ohralik* majority seemed careful to limit its holding to the facts before the Court. The opinion emphasized that the issue was whether the antisolicitation rule could constitutionally be applied to the appellant,[85] and that "the appropriate focus is on appellant's conduct."[86]

---

81. For example, in *Ohralik*, Justice Powell for the majority summarized *Primus* as follows:

"We hold today in *Primus* that a lawyer who engaged in solicitation as a form of protected political association may not be disciplined without proof of actual wrongdoing that the State constitutionally may proscribe." 436 U.S. at 462–63 n. 20, 98 S.Ct. at 1922 n. 20.

Yet in *Primus* itself, Justice Powell for the majority spoke more hesitantly, stating, for example, that "[w]e express no opinion whether an analysis of this case [*Primus*] would be different [if the ACLU had shared court awarded fees between the state chapter and the private attorney cooperating with the ACLU]." 436 U.S. at 430 n. 24, 98 S.Ct. at 1904 n. 24.

82. The distinction between this type of regulation and unjustified prohibition of lawyer advertising is evidenced by the fact that the majority in *Ohralik* accepted reasons for regulating attorney solicitation that would not be sufficient to ban attorney advertising. Thus in *Ohralik* the Court emphasized that law is a "profession," that the transaction in question was commercial in nature, and that a strong prophylactic rule was necessary to protect the unsophisticated, even though there is no explicit proof or finding of harm. Such rationales were rejected in Bates v. State Bar, 433 U.S. 350, 97 S.Ct. 2691, 53 L.Ed.2d 810 (1977), rehearing denied 434 U.S. 881, 98 S.Ct. 242, 54 L.Ed.2d 164 (1977), when they were used to prohibit attorney advertising.

83. 436 U.S. at 462, 98 S.Ct. at 1921 (footnote omitted). See Reich, Preventing Deception in Commercial Speech, 54 N.Y.U.L.Rev. 775 (1979).

84. 436 U.S. at 466, 98 S.Ct. at 1923–24.

85. 436 U.S. at 462–63 n. 20, 98 S.Ct. at 1922 n. 20.

86. 436 U.S. at 463, 98 S.Ct. at 1922. The attorney who argued the *Ohralik* case on behalf of the state bar also believes that the case should be limited to its facts. (June 13, 1978) (Report of A.B.A. Disciplinary Workshop, in 46 U.S.L.W. 2662).

Justice Powell began the opinion by summarizing in detail the appellant's outrageous in-person solicitation, and concluded by restating the factual context:

On the basis of the undisputed facts of record, we conclude that the disciplinary rules constitutionally could be applied to appellant. He approached two young accident victims at a time when they were especially incapable of making informed judgments or of assessing and protecting their own interests. He solicited Carol McClintock in a hospital room where she lay in traction and sought out Wanda Lou Holbert on the day she came home from the hospital, knowing from his prior inquiries that she had just been released. Appellant urged his services upon the young women and used the information he had obtained from the McClintocks, and the fact of his agreement with Carol, to induce Wanda to say "O.K." in response to his solicitation. He employed a concealed tape recorder, seemingly to insure that he would have evidence of Wanda's oral assent to the representation. He emphasized that his fee would come out of the recovery, thereby tempting the young women with what sounded like a cost-free and therefore irresistible offer. He refused to withdraw when Mrs. Holbert requested him to do so only a day after the initial meeting between appellant and Wanda Lou and continued to represent himself to the insurance company as Wanda Holbert's lawyer.[87]

Justice Marshall's thoughtful concurring opinion specifically would allow "benign" commercial solicitation, that is "solicitation by advice and information that is truthful and that is presented in a noncoercive, nondeceitful and dignified manner to a potential client who is emotionally and physically capable of making a rational decision either to accept or reject the representation with respect to a legal claim or matter that is not frivolous."[88] Nothing in the majority opinion rejects Justice Marshall's conclusions.

In the companion case, *In re Primus*,[89] a lawyer whose firm was cooperating with the American Civil Liberties Union (ACLU) wrote to a woman who had been sterilized as a condition of receiving public medical assistance. The lawyer offered the ACLU's services to represent her. The state had disciplined the attorney for this action but the Supreme Court of the United States reversed that decision.

The Court distinguished *Ohralik* because of the nature of the interests involved. Solicitation for private gain under the circumstances of *Ohralik* could be proscribed without showing harm in a given case because the circumstances were likely to result in the misleading, deceptive, and overbearing conduct, but solicitation on behalf of non-

---

87. 436 U.S. at 467, 98 S.Ct. at 1924.
88. 436 U.S. at 472 n. 3, 98 S.Ct. 1927 n. 3 (Marshall, J., concurring).

89. 436 U.S. 412, 98 S.Ct. 1893, 56 L.Ed.2d 417 (1978).

profit organizations which litigate as a form of political expression may be regulated only when actual harm is shown in the particular case.[90] The Court reviewed the record in *Primus* and found nothing indicating fraud, overreaching or other regulable behavior; consequently, it held the solicitation within the zone of political speech and association protected in *NAACP v. Button*.[91]

Under *Ohralik*, the states are free to proscribe in-person solicitation for gain in circumstances where it is likely to be fraudulent, misleading, or overreaching, but under *Primus* they may only proscribe solicitation on behalf of nonprofit political organizations if it is in fact misleading, and then regulations must be "carefully tailored" so as not to "abridge unnecessarily the associational freedom of nonprofit organizations, or their members, having characteristics like those of the NAACP or the ACLU."[92]

Justice Powell's opinion for the Court seems to emphasize two factors distinguishing *Primus* from *Ohralik:* the absence of misrepresentation and pressure tactics, and the lack of major pecuniary award. Yet a careful reading of the *Primus* opinion indicates a third, equally important factor: the form of the solicitation. In *Ohralik* the solicitation was "in-person," *face-to-face*.[93] In *Primus,* the attorney first was invited to address a gathering of women and then sent a letter to one of them offering free representation after being advised that the woman wished to sue the doctor who had sterilized her. This "act of solicitation took the form of a letter.... This was not *in-person* solicitation for pecuniary gain."[94]

Later the Court was more specific in recognizing that a letter is not face-to-face solicitation but is more like the advertising protected in *Bates:*

> The transmittal of this letter—as contrasted with in-person solicitation—involved no appreciable invasion of privacy; nor did it afford any significant opportunity for overreaching or coercion. Moreover, the fact that there was a written communication lessens substantially the difficulty of policing solicitation practices that do offend valid rules of professional conduct.[95]

90. 436 U.S. at 435, 98 S.Ct. at 1906–07. The Court noted that in *Primus* the lawyer did not attempt to "pressure" the prospective client into filing the suit. 436 U.S. at 417 n. 7, 98 S.Ct. at 1897 n. 7. "[A]ppellant's letter cannot be characterized as a pressure tactic." 436 U.S. at 435 n. 28, 98 S.Ct. at 1906 n. 28.

91. 371 U.S. 415, 83 S.Ct. 328, 9 L.Ed.2d 405 (1963).

92. 436 U.S. at 439, 98 S.Ct. at 1908.

93. It does not matter whether the face-to-face solicitation was by the lawyer himself or one of his agents or "runners." 436 U.S. at 464 n. 22, 98 S.Ct. at 1923 n. 22. Accord, D.R. 1–102(A)(2), A.B.A. Model Code of Professional Responsibility (1970, as amended).

94. 436 U.S. at 422, 98 S.Ct. at 1899 (emphasis added).

95. 436 U.S. at 435–36, 98 S.Ct. at 1906–07 (footnote omitted) (emphasis added).

As Justice Powell himself had earlier recognized in his separate opinion in *Bates:* "No distinction can be drawn between newspapers and a rather broad spectrum of other means—for example, magazines, signs in buses and subways, posters, handbills, and mail circulations." [96] The letter in *Primus* seems identical to the "mail circulations" referred to in *Bates*.

In a later case a unanimous Court, in an opinion by Justice Powell, invalidated a state rule that prohibited mailing cards (which announced the opening of his office) to persons other than "lawyers, former clients, personal friends and relatives." The silent record did not justify the reason for the absolute prohibition. Even if a reason existed, the state could use less restrictive means, such as requiring that a copy of any mailings be filed with the state, if the state wished to supervise mailings. "[A]lthough the states may regulate commercial speech, the First and Fourteenth Amendments require that they do so with care and in a manner no more extensive than reasonably necessary to further substantial interests." [97] Later, the Court approved of targeted, direct mail advertising.[98] Thus, letters and other non-face-to-face solicitation are "in-person" solicitation for purposes of *Ohralik,* even if the lawyer seeks pecuniary gain.

Separate treatment of face-to-face solicitation by the state can be justified by the greater public need to guard against possible deceptive or coercive advertising practices. Of course, actual misrepresentation and overreaching can always be prohibited. As Justice Marshall's concurrence emphasized, "[w]hat is objectionable about Ohralik's behavior here is not so much that he solicited business for himself, but rather the circumstances in which he performed that solicitation and the means by which he accomplished it." [99]

96. Bates v. State Bar, 433 U.S. 350, 402 n. 12, 97 S.Ct. 2691, 2718 n. 12, 53 L.Ed.2d 810 (1977), rehearing denied 434 U.S. 881, 98 S.Ct. 242, 54 L.Ed.2d 164 (1977). See also, Koffler v. Joint Bar Ass'n, 51 N.Y.2d 140, 432 N.Y.S.2d 872, 412 N.E.2d 927 (1980), certiorari denied 450 U.S. 1026, 101 S.Ct. 1733, 68 L.Ed.2d 221 (1981) (direct mail communications are not "in-person" solicitation within the meaning of *Ohralik* and therefore protected under *Bates*); Kentucky Bar Ass'n v. Stuart, 568 S.W.2d 933 (Ky.1978) (same). Contra, Allison v. Louisiana State Bar Ass'n, 362 So.2d 489 (La.1978).

See generally, T. Morgan and R. Rotunda, Problems and Materials on Professional Responsibility 204–06 (2d ed. 1981).

97. In re R.M.J., 455 U.S. 191, 207, 102 S.Ct. 929, 939, 71 L.Ed.2d 64 (1982).

98. Shapero v. Kentucky Bar Association, 486 U.S. 466, 108 S.Ct. 1916, 100 L.Ed.2d 475 (1988), discussed above.

99. 436 U.S. at 470, 98 S.Ct. at 1926 (Marshall, J., concurring).

At the end of *Primus,* Justice Powell for the majority stated in dictum:

"And a State may insist that lawyers not solicit on behalf of lay organizations that exert control over the actual conduct of any ensuing litigation."

436 U.S. at 439, 98 S.Ct. at 1908.

The only authority for that assertion was dictum by Justice White concurring and dissenting in NAACP v. Button, 371 U.S. 415, 447, 83 S.Ct. 328, 345, 9 L.Ed.2d 405 (1963). Justice Powell's dictum—at least in its broad form—is not even supported by the American Bar Association. See A.B.A. Formal Opinion 334 (Aug. 10, 1974) (dealing with restrictions on lawyers' activities

The Noncommercial, Political Speech of Corporations. The Supreme Court in *First National Bank v. Bellotti*,[100] held that states cannot prohibit corporations from spending money to express their views on referendum questions even if such issues are not directly related to their business interests.[101] The Court characterized its recent commercial speech decisions as illustrating that the first amendment prohibits government from limiting the stock of information from which the public may draw, and noted that the state's argument that it could not regulate commercial speech of corporations but could ban

by legal services offices as they affect independence of professional judgment).

Justice Marshall specifically disassociated himself from Justice Powell's dictum and noted that it "is by no means self-evident, has never been the actual holding of this Court and is not put in issue by the facts presently before us." 436 U.S. at 471, 98 S.Ct. at 1927. See also 436 U.S. at 439, 98 S.Ct. at 1908 (Blackmun, J., concurring).

100. 435 U.S. 765, 98 S.Ct. 1407, 55 L.Ed.2d 707 (1978), rehearing denied 438 U.S. 907, 98 S.Ct. 3126, 57 L.Ed.2d 1150 (1978).

See generally, Note, The Corporation and the Constitution: Economic Due Process and Corporate Speech, 90 Yale L.J. 1833 (1981); Patton and Bartlett, Corporate "Persons" and Freedom of Speech: The Political Impact of Legal Mythology, 1981 Wisc.L.Rev. 494. Alderman, Commercial Entities' Noncommercial Speech: A Contradiction in Terms, 1982 Utah L.Rev. 731; Brudney, Business Corporations and Stockholders' Rights Under the First Amendment, 91 Yale L.J. 325 (1981); Prentice, Consolidated Edison and Bellotti: First Amendment Protection of Corporate Political Speech, 16 Tulsa L.J. 599 (1981); O'Kelly, The Constitutional Rights of Corporation Revisited: Social and Political Expression and the Corporation after First National Bank v. Bellotti, 67 Georgetown L.J. 1347 (1979).

See, Lowenstein, Campaign Spending and Ballot Propositions: Recent Experience, Public Choice Theory and the First Amendment, 29 U.C.L.A.L.Rev. 505 (1982) (offers a study which demonstrates that the power of some groups to raise large sums of money to oppose ballot propositions without regard to popular feeling seriously interferes with the ability of other groups to use the institutions of democracy for their intended purpose); Brudney, Business Corporations and Stockholders' Rights Under the First Amendment, 91 Yale L.J. 235 (1981) (examines and criticizes first amendment protection recently extended to political utterances of business corporations).

101. 435 U.S. at 783–84 & n. 20, 98 S.Ct. at 1419–20 & n. 20. The Court did caution that "our consideration of a corporation's right to speak on issues of general public interest implies no comparable right in the quite different context of participation in a political campaign for election to public office. Congress might well be able to demonstrate the existence of a danger of real or apparent corruption in independent expenditures by corporations to influence candidate elections." 435 U.S. at 788 n. 26, 98 S.Ct. at 1422 n. 26.

Justice Rehnquist, dissenting, argued that corporations as creatures of the state, have only those rights granted them and those necessarily incident to their business purposes. 435 U.S. at 822–28, 98 S.Ct. at 1439–43. Justice White, joined by Justices Brennan and Marshall, also dissented.

In Federal Election Commission v. Massachusetts Citizens for Life, Inc., 479 U.S. 238, 107 S.Ct. 616, 93 L.Ed.2d 539 (1986) the Court explained that in First National Bank of Boston v. Bellotti, 435 U.S. 765, 98 S.Ct. 1407, 55 L.Ed.2d 707 (1978), rehearing denied 438 U.S. 907, 98 S.Ct. 3126, 57 L.Ed.2d 1150 (1978) the state law was invalid because it provided for "complete foreclosure of any opportunity for political speech...." 479 U.S. at 259 n. 12, 107 S.Ct. at 628 n. 12. In contrast, as recognized in FEC v. Massachusetts Citizens for Life, Inc., it is different when the state regulates the corporate form of a commercial enterprise because of unfair deployment of wealth for political purposes: "Direct corporate spending on political activity raises the prospect that resources amassed in the economic marketplace may be used to provide an unfair advantage in the political marketplace." 479 U.S. at 257, 107 S.Ct. at 628.

their political speech, would reverse the traditional constitutional values attaching to political and commercial speech.[102]

Commercial Speech and Trade Names. *Friedman v. Rogers,*[103] may have signaled a shift, or at least a detour, in the direction of the Supreme Court. In this case the Court held that Texas constitutionally could prohibit the practice of optometry under a trade name, assumed name, or corporate name.

It now appears that the Court, encouraged by Justice Powell in this area, will engage in a series of *ad hoc* decisions as to the permissible scope of regulation of commercial speech. In so doing, the majority appears to shift away from Justice Blackmun's principled position that the state may not regulate commercial speech so long as the underlying activity advertised is legal, and the speech itself is not actually misleading. While Justice Blackmun had authored the most of the majority opinions in the initial round of modern commercial speech cases,[104] more recently it has been Justice Powell who has authored the majority opinions.[105]

In upholding the ban on trade names the majority refrained from establishing rigid rules for the regulation of commercial speech, but it established some guidelines that tie together the earlier cases and help provide a framework for the future determination of the permissibility of particular regulations of commercial practices involving speech.

Powell's majority opinion in *Friedman* differentiated "commercially motivated" speech, which appears entitled to full first amendment

---

102. In Consolidated Edison Co. of New York, Inc. v. Public Service Com'n, 447 U.S. 530, 100 S.Ct. 2326, 65 L.Ed.2d 319 (1980), the Court, applying a similar analysis, invalidated a state public utility commission order which prohibited a utility from inserting in monthly electric bills inserts discussing controversial issues of public policy. In this case the utility advocated nuclear power. See also, Central Hudson Gas & Elec. Corp. v. Public Service Com'n, 447 U.S. 557, 100 S.Ct. 2343, 65 L.Ed.2d 341 (1980).

See Comment, Public Utility Bill Inserts, Political Speech, and the First Amendment: A Constitutionally Mandated Right to Reply, 70 Calif.L.Rev. 1221 (1982), arguing that the first amendment requires opposing groups a right to reply to billing envelope inserts which voice opinions on controversial subjects.

103. 440 U.S. 1, 99 S.Ct. 887, 59 L.Ed.2d 100 (1979), rehearing denied 441 U.S. 917, 99 S.Ct. 2018, 60 L.Ed.2d 389 (1979).

The Court also upheld regulations in this case that required four of the six members of an optometrist regulatory board to be members of a specific professional organization. Because this regulation governed general and economic welfare matters, the Court applied only the minimum rationality test to this law. 440 U.S. at 17, 99 S.Ct. at 898. The Court also refused to consider whether or not a board composed of members of a particular trade association could fairly judge disciplinary proceedings brought against a non member. 440 U.S. at 17, 99 S.Ct. at 898.

104. Bates v. State Bar, 433 U.S. 350, 97 S.Ct. 2691, 53 L.Ed.2d 810 (1977), rehearing denied 434 U.S. 881, 98 S.Ct. 242, 54 L.Ed.2d 164 (1977); Virginia State Bd. of Pharmacy v. Virginia Citizens Consumer Council, Inc., 425 U.S. 748, 96 S.Ct. 1817, 48 L.Ed.2d 346 (1976); Bigelow v. Virginia, 421 U.S. 809, 95 S.Ct. 2222, 44 L.Ed.2d 600 (1975).

105. Ohralik v. Ohio State Bar, 436 U.S. 447, 98 S.Ct. 1912, 56 L.Ed.2d 444 (1978); In re Primus, 436 U.S. 412, 98 S.Ct. 1893, 56 L.Ed.2d 417 (1978). Justice Blackmun wrote a concurring opinion in these two cases.

protection, from "commercial speech," which is subject to the *ad hoc* approach.[106] It is now clear that cases such as *New York Times Co. v. Sullivan*[107] and *First Nat. Bank of Boston v. Bellotti*[108] did not involve "commercial speech" in the sense of speech designed to sell a product or solicit patronage for profit. Instead, as was suggested in each of those decisions, those cases involved speech concerning non-commercial issues, even though the speech might have been motivated by commercial and monetary desires of the speakers. This commercially motivated speech is not "commercial speech" and it is protected by all first amendment principles.[109]

The majority opinion in *Friedman* indicated that commercial speech is speech connected to the selling of a product or service. Such speech has more limited first amendment protection than does non commercial speech. Justice Powell noted that principles relating to "more traditional first amendment problems" are not to be applied automatically to commercial speech regulations in a "yet uncharted area."[110]

For example, the *Friedman* majority treated *Bigelow v. Virginia*[111]—which invalidated a law forbidding a profit making organization's advertisement offering to arrange for legal abortions out of state—as "more than" a commercial speech case because it "did more than simply propose a commercial transaction."[112] By way of contrast, *Virginia State Board of Pharmacy v. Virginia Citizens Consumer Council*[113]—invalidating a law forbidding advertisements offering prescrip-

---

106. 440 U.S. at 11 n. 10, 99 S.Ct. at 895 n. 10.

107. 376 U.S. 254, 84 S.Ct. 710, 11 L.Ed.2d 686 (1964), motion denied 376 U.S. 967, 84 S.Ct. 1130, 12 L.Ed.2d 83 (1964). See §§ 20.32–20.36, infra.

108. 435 U.S. 765, 98 S.Ct. 1407, 55 L.Ed.2d 707 (1978), rehearing denied 438 U.S. 907, 98 S.Ct. 3126, 57 L.Ed.2d 1150 (1978), discussed above.

109. See also, Village of Schaumburg v. Citizens for a Better Environment, 444 U.S. 620, 636, 100 S.Ct. 826, 835–36, 63 L.Ed.2d 73 (1980), rehearing denied 445 U.S. 972, 100 S.Ct. 1668, 64 L.Ed.2d 250 (1980): "[B]ecause charitable solicitation does more than inform private economic decisions and is not primarily concerned with providing information about the characteristics and costs of goods and services, it has not been dealt with in our cases as a variety of purely commercial speech." (footnote omitted). Secretary of State of Maryland v. Joseph H. Munson Co., Inc., 467 U.S. 947, 104 S.Ct. 2839, 81 L.Ed.2d 786 (1984) (statute placing twenty-five per-cent limit on charitable fund raising expenses invalidated as a violation of the first amendment right of charities to engage in first amendment activity in connection with economic solicitation).

110. 440 U.S. at 10 n. 9, 99 S.Ct. at 895 n. 9.

111. 421 U.S. 809, 95 S.Ct. 2222, 44 L.Ed.2d 600 (1975).

112. Friedman v. Rogers, 440 U.S. at 11 n. 10, 99 S.Ct. at 895 n. 10 quoting Bigelow v. Virginia, 421 U.S. at 822, 95 S.Ct. at 2232. In re Von Wiegen, 63 N.Y.2d 163, 481 N.Y.S.2d 40, 470 N.E.2d 838, 842 (1984) (Simons, J.) (citing an earlier edition of this treatise), on remand 108 A.D.2d 1012, 485 N.Y.S.2d 399 (1985), certiorari denied 472 U.S. 1007, 105 S.Ct. 2701, 86 L.Ed.2d 717 (1985).

113. 425 U.S. 748, 96 S.Ct. 1817, 48 L.Ed.2d 346 (1976).

The majority's efforts to distinguish commercial from noncommercial speech made no effort to explain why movies exhibited purely for profit and advertisements of such movies—"a mere solicitation of pa-

tion drugs for sale at certain prices—was, in the view of the majority, only commercial speech because the advertisements simply offered to make an economic exchange for profit. Yet the law was still invalidated because of "the other interests in the advertisements...." For example, information about prices at competing pharmacies would enable consumers to enjoy, at a lesser cost, the "basic necessities." [114]

Once the speech is found to be commercial speech, the majority opinion found, first, that the government could place more general restrictions on the time, place, or manner of commercial speech than on noncommercial speech and, second, that the government would be given greater latitude in forming regulations of the content of commercial speech to avoid potentially false, deceptive, or misleading commercial practices.

The government was given greater powers in controlling this type of speech for several reasons: commercial speech is more verifiable because it relates to a particular product or service; the communicative value of this speech is less likely to be inhibited or deterred by regulations due to the economic incentive to engage in alternative forms of commercial communication; effective rules to prevent false, deceptive or misleading practices may not be too precise.

Although the Court did not establish rigid categories of commercial speech, the *Friedman* majority indicated that there would be a distinction in the degree of permissible government regulation related to the types of commercial speech. For regulations of commercial speech that contain explicit product, price, or service information the state must demonstrate a clear relationship between the regulation and the avoidance of false, deceptive, or misleading practices. If it cannot do so, the state must demonstrate that the regulation of this commercial speech is a demonstrably reasonable restriction of the time, place, or physical manner of the commercial expression. However when the "commercial speech" conveys less substantive information the government has great-

tronage...." 440 U.S. at 11 n. 10, 99 S.Ct. at 895 n. 10 is nonetheless apparently entitled to full first amendment protection under the prior case law. See, e.g., Joseph Burstyn, Inc. v. Wilson, 343 U.S. 495, 501–02, 72 S.Ct. 777, 780–81, 96 L.Ed. 1098 (1952). Perhaps, under Justice Powell's theories, such advertisements are entitled to lessened first amendment protection. He has joined in cases offering lessened first amendment protection for nonobscene but "adult" movies. Young v. American Mini Theatres, Inc., 427 U.S. 50, 73, 96 S.Ct. 2440, 2453, 49 L.Ed.2d 310 (1976) (Powell, J., concurring), rehearing denied 429 U.S. 873, 97 S.Ct. 191, 50 L.Ed.2d 155 (1976). Cf. FCC v. Pacifica Foundation, 438 U.S. 726, 759–763, 98 S.Ct. 3026, 3045–3048, 57 L.Ed.2d 1073 (1978) (Powell, J., concurring) (FCC may regulate radio broadcast which is not obscene in a constitutional sense but is "indecent"), rehearing denied 439 U.S. 883, 99 S.Ct. 227, 58 L.Ed.2d 198 (1978).

See also, Hospital & Service Employees Union, Local 399 v. N.L.R.B., 743 F.2d 1417, 1428 n. 8 (9th Cir.1984) (Choy, J.) (citing Treatise and recognizing that the Supreme Court's definition of commercial speech is difficult to apply).

114. 440 U.S. at 8, 99 S.Ct. at 893.

See generally, De Vier, Justice Powell and the First Amendment's "Societal Function": A Preliminary Analysis, 68 Va. L.Rev. 177 (1982).

er latitude in regulating the speech. The majority deemed such speech to have little first amendment value because it does not (in the view of the majority) clearly communicate information. In so holding, the majority stated that there was no requirement that states tolerate practices with little or no communicative content that might be used in a deceptive or misleading manner, even though the possible deception could also be cured by less drastic means, for example, if the state were to require the publication of additional information to clarify or offset the effects of the spurious communication.[115]

Based upon these assumptions, Powell found it easy to allow the prohibition of the use of trade names by optometrists. The opinion noted that the use of these trade names had a purpose which was "strictly business" and was "a form of commercial speech and nothing more."[116] This point differentiated the case from the commercially motivated speech cases in which the speaker desires more than simply an offer to sell goods or solicit patronage.

Justice Powell also sought to distinguish this prohibition from the earlier prohibitions on advertising service and price information that had been overturned in *Virginia Pharmacy,* and *Bates.* While both of those cases simply proposed a commercial transaction—an offer to sell prescription drugs for a price in the former case, and an offer to sell legal services for a price in the latter—those messages contained useful information, which inherently has meaning. Trade names, on the other hand, do not have any inherent meaning.

The majority did concede that trade names might acquire some meaning over a period of time, and become a valuable property right. But such a property interest in the trade name only meant that such property could not be taken without due process of law. The fact of a property interest neither enlarged nor diminished first amendment rights.[117]

In both the *Virginia Pharmacy*[118] case, involving pharmacists, and the *Bates*[119] case, involving lawyers, the Court was not moved by the argument that these occupations were "professions," a title which was supposed to justify lessened first amendment protection. But in *Friedman* the majority, without explanation, found it important to emphasize that the Texas legislature considered optometry to be a profession.[120]

115. 440 U.S. at 12 n. 11, 99 S.Ct. at 895 n. 11.

116. 440 U.S. at 11, 99 S.Ct. at 895 (footnote omitted).

117. 440 U.S. at 12 n. 11, 99 S.Ct. at 895 n. 11.

118. Virginia State Bd. of Pharmacy v. Virginia Citizens Consumer Council, Inc., 425 U.S. 748, 96 S.Ct. 1817, 48 L.Ed.2d 346 (1976).

119. Bates v. State Bar, 433 U.S. 350, 97 S.Ct. 2691, 53 L.Ed.2d 810 (1977), rehearing denied 434 U.S. 881, 98 S.Ct. 242, 54 L.Ed.2d 164 (1977).

120. 440 U.S. at 5 n. 7, 99 S.Ct. at 892 n. 7.

Because this use of trade names, or any commercial speech practice, has the potentiality of conveying information, the majority indicated that the state had to assert some reasonable basis for the prohibition. But the majority readily accepted the state's assertion that some optometrists in the past had used trade names in a misleading manner and that this history justified the general prohibition of trade names even if the particular plaintiff in this case had never engaged in a misleading practice.

Thus it appears that the Court will not exercise active review and will use a test approaching the traditional "rational basis" test when reviewing statutes which regulate speech in circumstances where the speech is found to be commercial speech, *and* that speech does not explicitly convey product, service, or price information.

Yet, the scope of *Friedman* remains unclear. For example, may the state prohibit lawyers from practicing under a trade name even though the state allows lawyers to use the name of one or more deceased or retired partners as the firm name? [121] May the state consistently contend that trade names are inherently misleading while at the same time maintaining that a firm named after lawyers who died and left the firm years ago is not in reality a trade name?

Justice Blackmun wrote a vigorous dissent, joined by Justice Marshall.[122] Justice Blackmun noted that the use of trade names would allow for more efficient advertisement of eye glasses and therefore a lowering in the price of such items, which he described as one of the basic necessities of life. He found, as he had indicated in some of his earlier opinions, that the increase in informational transaction costs was prohibited unless the state could demonstrate an overriding reason for the speech prohibition.

Justice Blackmun, who had written the majority opinion in *Virginia Pharmacy,* readily agreed with Justice Powell that misleading speech can be regulated, but denied trade names are inherently misleading. But while Justice Powell thought that "because a trade name has no intrinsic meaning it can cause deception," the dissent countered that "[b]ecause a trade name has no intrinsic meaning, it cannot by itself be deceptive. A trade name will deceive only if it is used in a

---

121. Compare, Police Dept. of Chicago v. Mosley, 408 U.S. 92, 92 S.Ct. 2286, 33 L.Ed.2d 212 (1972); see A.B.A. Code of Professional Responsibility, D.R. 2–102(B): "A lawyer in private practice shall not practice under a trade name, a name that is misleading ... or a firm name containing names other than those of one or more of the lawyers in the firm, *except* ... a firm may use as, or continue to include in its name, the name or names of one or more deceased or retired members of the firm or of a predecessor firm in a continuing line of succession." (emphasis added).

122. 440 U.S. at 19, 99 S.Ct. at 899 (Blackmun, J., concurring and dissenting joined by Marshall, J.). Justice Blackmun joined in part III of the Court's opinion which validated the composition of the optometry board.

misleading context." [123]   Justice Blackmun thus would have required the state to tolerate the use of trade names and only to prosecute those who in fact used them in a misleading manner.

While Justice Blackmun's approach is a principled one, the majority of the justices do not seem ready to follow Justice Blackmun's active review of all commercial speech cases, perhaps in part because of fears of returning to the discredited substantive economic due process rulings of the pre 1937 Court.[124]   Instead the Court has granted only limited protection to commercial speech.

It appears that the justices will prohibit states from banning the truthful conveyance of commercial information but that they will allow the state a much greater leeway in protecting against false, deceptive or misleading practices.   The lower the informational content of the regulated speech, the greater latitude the Court will give the government in drafting such regulations.   Thus it appears that future rulings will of necessity have an *ad hoc* quality in determining the degree of informational content of a regulated commercial speech practice and the reasonableness of the regulation, but there will not be an absolute prohibition of regulating any speech activity that might increase information or transaction costs in the marketplace.

The Four–Part Test of *Central Hudson*.   This analysis is supported by *Central Hudson Gas & Electric Corporation v. Public Service Commission*.[125]   The Court invalidated a regulation of the state Public Service Commission which completely banned all public utility advertising which promoted the use of electricity.   The Commission argued that all such promotional advertising was contrary to the national policy of conserving energy.   The Court, per Justice Powell, applied a four-part analysis to the question:

> At the outset we must determine whether the expression is protected by the First Amendment.   For commercial speech to come within that provision, it at least must concern lawful activity and

123. 440 U.S. at 24, 99 S.Ct. at 901 (Blackmun, J., joined by Marshall, J., dissenting and concurring in part).

124. See Jackson and Jeffries, Commercial Speech: Economic Due Process and the First Amendment, 65 Va.L.Rev. 1 (1979). Farber, Commercial Speech and First Amendment Theory, 74 Nw.U.L.Rev. 372 (1979), concluding that while the informative function of speech deserves traditional first amendment protection, "commercial speech also serves a contractual function which does not directly implicate first amendment interests. Regulations aimed at this contractual function, though they relate to the meaning of the speech, should not be tested under the stricter scrutiny reserved for 'content related' reg-

ulation. Most traditional consumer protection legislation is based on the contractual nature of the speech. Misrepresentation, duress, overreaching, and unconscionability are well-known contract doctrines. When the state attacks these problems with modern regulatory tools, it can legitimately claim an interest quite distinct from the suppression of free expression." Id. at 407–08. See generally, Rotunda, The Commercial Speech Doctrine in the Supreme Court, 1976 U.Ill.L.Forum 1080.

125. 447 U.S. 557, 100 S.Ct. 2343, 65 L.Ed.2d 341 (1980).

See Note, Constitutional Protection of Commercial Speech, 82 Colum.L.Rev. 720 (1982).

not be misleading. Next we ask whether the asserted governmental interest is substantial. If both inquiries yield positive answers, we must determine whether the regulation directly advances the governmental interest asserted, and whether it is not more extensive than is necessary to serve that interest.[126]

Applying this test the *Central Hudson* Court invalidated the New York regulation. Promotional advertising is lawful commercial speech;[127] the state interests in conservation are substantial; the ban on promotional advertising advances this ban; but the state's complete suppression of speech was more extensive than necessary to further energy conservation.[128] For example, some promotional advertising would cause no net increase in energy use. Also more limited restrictions might promote conservation sufficiently. The state could "require that the advertisements include information about the relative efficiency and expense of the offered service, both under current conditions and for the foreseeable future."[129]

The four-part test of *Central Hudson* is based on a two step method of analysis synthesized from the modern commercial speech cases. First, a court must determine whether the speech is truthful, nonmisleading speech concerning a lawful commercial activity. Promotion of illegal activity therefore is not protected advertising.[130] If the government is attempting to deter or punish false or misleading advertising it will not be subjected to overbreadth analysis and therefore will not be required to demonstrate that its law is no more extensive than necessary to achieve that goal.[131] Second, after finding that the government regulation restricts nonmisleading commercial communications, a court must determine whether the government regulation directly advances a substantial government interest without unnecessary restrictions on the freedom of speech. The government regulation will fail if the interest is not sufficiently substantial to justify a restriction on speech or if the means used to advance a substantial interest either do not

---

126. 447 U.S. at 566, 100 S.Ct. at 2351.

127. Accord, Consolidated Edison Co. of New York, Inc. v. Public Service Com'n, 447 U.S. 530, 100 S.Ct. 2326, 65 L.Ed.2d 319 (1980). See also Bolger v. Youngs Drug Products Corp., 463 U.S. 60, 103 S.Ct. 2875, 77 L.Ed.2d 469 (1983) (law prohibiting mailing of unsolicited advertisements for contraceptives invalid).

128. Cf. N.L.R.B. v. Retail Store Employees Union, Local 1001, 447 U.S. 607, 618, 100 S.Ct. 2372, 2379, 65 L.Ed.2d 377 (1980) (Powell, J., joined by Burger, C.J., Stewart, and Rehnquist, JJ.) (Congress, consistent with first amendment, may prohibit secondary picketing calculated "to persuade the customers of the secondary employer to cease trading with him in order to force him to cease dealing with, or

put pressure upon, the primary employer;" such picketing spreads labor discord by coercing neutral party to join the dispute and furthers an unlawful objective).

129. 447 U.S. at 571, 100 S.Ct. at 2354.

130. See Pittsburgh Press Co. v. Pittsburgh Commission on Human Relations, 413 U.S. 376, 93 S.Ct. 2553, 37 L.Ed.2d 669 (1973), rehearing denied 414 U.S. 881, 94 S.Ct. 30, 38 L.Ed.2d 128 (1973); National Society of Professional Engineers v. United States, 435 U.S. 679, 697–98 nn. 26, 27, 98 S.Ct. 1355, 1368–69 nn. 26, 27, 55 L.Ed.2d 637, 654 nn. 26, 27 (1978).

131. See Ohralik v. Ohio State Bar, 436 U.S. 447, 462–63, 98 S.Ct. 1912, 1921–22, 56 L.Ed.2d 444, 457–58 (1978).

directly advance the government interest or do so with an unnecessary burden on the ability to communicate the commercial message.[132]

The "Least Restrictive Means" Test

In *Board of Trustees of the State University of New York v. Fox,*[133] the Court ruled that it was error to apply the "least restrictive means" test to commercial speech cases. Cases like *Central Hudson* do not require that government restrictions on commercial speech be "absolutely the least severe that will achieve the desired end." Rather, there must be only a "reasonable" fit—a "fit that is not necessarily perfect"—between the governmental ends and the means chosen to accomplish those ends. So long as the means are "narrowly tailored" to achieve the desired objectives, it is for the government decisionmakers to judge what manner of regulation may best be employed. The government, however, has the burden to show that its goal is "substantial" and that "the cost [has been] carefully calculated." The "least

---

132. In Bolger v. Youngs Drug Products Corp., 463 U.S. 60, 103 S.Ct. 2875, 77 L.Ed.2d 469 (1983), the justices were unanimous in striking down a federal statute prohibiting the unsolicited mailing of contraceptive advertisements. The majority opinion by Justice Marshall found that the interest in shielding mail recipients from offensive materials was not sufficiently substantial to burden speech, and that the regulation did not directly and narrowly promote a substantial interest in aiding parents' efforts to discuss birth control methods with their children. Justice Brennan took no part in the decision of this case.

Justices Rehnquist and O'Connor, 463 U.S. at 75, 103 S.Ct. at 2885, 77 L.Ed.2d at 483 (concurring), and Justice Stevens, 463 U.S. at 80, 103 S.Ct. at 2888, 77 L.Ed.2d at 486 (concurring), would have considered a government interest in protecting persons from receiving material they find offensive in their homes to be substantial. However these justices believed that the law did not sufficiently promote that interest. All justices appeared to agree with the two step methodology inherent in the four-part test put forth in *Central Hudson.*

133. 492 U.S. 469, 109 S.Ct. 3028, 106 L.Ed.2d 388 (1989), on remand 764 F.Supp. 747 (N.D.N.Y.1991). In that case, the State University of New York (SUNY) had a rule (Resolution 66–156) prohibiting private commercial enterprises from operating in SUNY facilities. The Resolution was applied to prohibit students in their dormitories from hosting Tupperware-type parties demonstrating and selling house-

wares of the American Future System, Inc. (AFS). Justice Scalia, for the Court, concluded that the student AFS parties were commercial speech because they " 'propose a commercial transaction,' which is the test for identifying commercial speech." Although these Tupperware-type parties touch on other subjects, such as how to run an efficient home, that fact does not put them in the category of fully protected speech. It is incorrect to conclude that pure speech and commercial speech are "inextricably intertwined" because nothing in state law or the Resolution requires the noncommercial and commercial messages to be combined: "No law or man or nature makes it impossible to sell housewares without teaching home economics...." 492 U.S. at 473, 109 S.Ct. at 3031.

The Court then remanded to consider respondents' other challenges to Resolution 156. The Court noted that the Resolution reaches other conduct that consists of speech for profit (such as private tutoring, legal advice, and medical consultation). The Court then said simply: "While these examples consist of speech for a profit, they do not consist of speech that *proposes* a commercial transaction, which is what defines commercial speech." 492 U.S. at 482, 109 S.Ct. at 3036 (emphasis in original). Thus, on remand, the lower court should decide whether the Resolution, as applied to such speech, is constitutional; and then, if it is, the court should decide whether the Resolution is overbroad. Blackmun, J., joined by Brennan & Marshall, JJ., dissented.

restrictive means" test does not apply to commercial speech cases.[134]

X. LIBEL AND INVASION OF PRIVACY

§ 20.32 Introduction

(a) The Problem of Values in Conflict

The modern era has not witnessed a dearth of libel suits. Indeed, libel suits are now brought against the press and broadcast media with greater and greater frequency. A Beverly Hills doctor filed suit for $20 million against Bob Woodward for claiming in Woodward's biography of John Belushi that the doctor had prescribed drugs to Belushi and others without sufficient medical reasons; Senator Paul Laxalt sued *The Sacramento Bee* for a quarter of a billion dollars for writing stories linking him to a criminal investigation of Nevada casino operations; Lillian Hellman sued Mary McCarthy for $2¼ million because McCarthy—while being interviewed on the Dick Cavett Show—said that Hellman was "terribly overrated, a bad writer and a dishonest writer;" former Governor King of Massachusetts sued *The Boston Globe* for over $3½ million because the *Globe* had published a series of articles, editorials, and political cartoons charging that King was an unfit Governor; actress Shirley Jones sued *The National Enquirer* for $20 million after it published a story alleging that she had a bad drinking problem; the former American ambassador to Chile sued the producers of the 1982 movie, *MISSING,* for $150 million alleging that the movie implied that the U.S. embassy was somehow linked to the death of an American writer; the former mayor of Philadelphia sued a CBS TV station for over $5 million when it reported that he was subject to a federal criminal investigation; and several justices of the Pennsylvania Supreme Court sued the *Philadelphia Inquirer* because it ran a series of stories criticizing the judicial conduct of the justices.[1]

Juries today are also much more likely to award million or multimillion dollar verdicts in libel cases. Commentators have expressed concern about the "libel litigation explosion." It should be no great surprise that jurors often side with the plaintiff and against the media defendant. Public opinion polls routinely show that people just do not trust the media. A 1984 survey, for example, showed that 70% of the people think that most influential newspapers are biased; while 58% of Americans have confidence in the military, only 20% have confidence

---

134. 492 U.S. at 477–81, 109 S.Ct. at 3033–35. See also, San Francisco Arts & Athletics, Inc. v. United States Olympic Committee, 483 U.S. 522, 537 n. 16, 107 S.Ct. 2971, 2981 n. 16, 97 L.Ed.2d 427 (1987).

§ 20.32

1. Rodney Smolla, Suing the Press 5–7 (1986). Symposium: Offensive and Libelous Speech, 47 Wash. & Lee L.Rev. 105 (1990); Rodney Smolla, Law of Defamation (1986).

in broadcast journalists. Indeed, journalists ranked *behind* Congress, big business, and organized labor.[2]

The law of libel was born in medieval times in an era that did not believe in free speech. Until 1964, when the Supreme Court constitutionalized the law of libel in *New York Times Co. v. Sullivan*,[3] courts were not sympathetic to the plights of libel defendants. But that decision, discussed in the next section, has not made the law of libel simpler. If anything, it has become more complex and confusing. Libel cases have also gotten to be very expensive. A newspaper or private individual who wins often finds victory is Pyrrhic because attorneys fees are debilitating.

By the end of 1988, a study of libel verdicts indicated that in only 20% of the cases do the courts leave the jury verdict intact. In the other cases the reward is reduced or simply thrown out. The average award that the appellate courts have affirmed is for about $145,000, a sum that is often less than the cost of bringing the libel action.[4]

Libel issues represent an inherent problem of values in conflict. On the one hand, we have the right of free speech, the right to information, the concern about chilling speech. On the other hand, we have the concern about reputation. Even though our Constitution creates a right of free speech and does not create a right to vindicate one's reputation, commentators often speak of a "right" to reputation. In any event, reputation is something we value.

New York Times v. Sullivan and its progeny represent an effort to draw balance between these conflicting values—free speech and reputation. It is because of these inherently conflicting values that the Supreme Court, no less than society generally, has found it difficult to draw a satisfactory line. When we think of the value of reputation, we often quote Shakespeare's *Othello* where the character Iago says:

Who steals my purse steals trash—tis something, nothing;

'Twas mine, 'tis his, and has been slave to thousands;

But he that flinches from me my good name

Robs me of that which not enriches him

And makes me poor indeed.[5]

Yes, we quote those lines and we believe in the importance of reputation. But let us put things in perspective; Shakespeare did. The same character, Iago, also says to Cassio—when Cassio complained that he had lost his reputation—

2. See, The Media on Trial, Newsweek, Oct. 22, 1984.

3. 376 U.S. 254, 84 S.Ct. 710, 11 L.Ed.2d 686 (1964).

4. Wong, In the Wake of Westmorland, Sharon Cases, Libel Suits Against the Media Decline, Wall St.Jrl., Oct. 17, 1988, at B5, cols. 1, 2 (midwest ed.).

5. Othello, III, iii, lines 155–62.

As I am an honest man, I thought you had received some bodily wound. There is more sense in that than in reputation. Reputation is an idle and most false imposition; off'got without merit and lost without deserving. You have lost no reputation at all unless you repute yourself such a loser.[6]

(b) The Problem of Group Libel

The Supreme Court upheld the constitutionality of a state criminal statute prohibiting libel of a class of citizens in *Beauharnais v. Illinois.*[7] Petitioner had distributed a leaflet calling for white unity against further "encroachment ... by the Negro" and urging "the need to prevent the white race from becoming mongrelized by the negro [sic]...."[8] The Court could have reached a decision based on the narrow facts of the case, avoiding the issue of the constitutionality of the statute and holding that the particular pamphlet did not violate the terms of the Illinois group libel law.[9] However, Justice Frankfurter affirmed the conviction in a broad holding that libelous, insulting, or fighting words are not within the realm of constitutionally protected speech.[10] State statutes that curtail group libel do not raise a constitutional problem, he said, unless they are a "wilful and purposeless restriction unrelated to the peace and well being of the state."[11] Frankfurter pointed out that the judiciary should not interfere with the state legislature's choice of policy. He emphasized that state libel laws were not within a constitutionally protected category of speech.

6. Othello, II, iii, lines 256–61.

See generally, Bellah, The Meaning of Reputation in American Society, 74 Calif.L.Rev. 743 (1986), Post, The Social Foundations of Defamation Law: Reputation and the Constitution, 74 Calif.L.Rev. 691 (1986), Skolnick, Foreword: The Sociological Tort of Defamation, 74 Calif.L.Rev. 677 (1986); Reston, Reputation and the Modern Journalistic Imperative, 74 Calif.L.Rev. 753 (1986); LeBel, Reforming the Tort of Defamation: An Accommodation Of The Competing Interests Within The Current Constitutional Framework, 66 Neb.L.Rev. 249 (1987); Denniston, The Burger Court and the Press, in H. Schwartz, ed., The Burger Years: Rights and Wrongs in the Supreme Court, 1969–1986 (1987), at 23–44.

7. 343 U.S. 250, 72 S.Ct. 725, 96 L.Ed. 919 (1952), rehearing denied 343 U.S. 998, 72 S.Ct. 1070, 96 L.Ed. 1375 (1952). See, Levine v. CMP Publications, Inc., 738 F.2d 660, 678–79 (5th Cir.1984) (Tate, J., dissenting) (citing an earlier edition of this Treatise), rehearing denied 753 F.2d 1341 (1985).

See generally, J. Barron and C. Dienes, Handbook of Free Speech and Free Press, ch. 6, "The Rise of the Public Law of Defamation," pp. 222–361 (1979); S. Halpern, The Law of Defamation, Privacy, Publicity and "Moral Rights" 25–36 (1988); W. Van Alstyne, First Amendment: Cases and Materials 155–223 (1991).

8. 343 U.S. at 252, 72 S.Ct. at 728.

9. The law proscribed "any lithograph, moving picture, play, drama, or sketch," that was libelous to a class of citizens. The Court called Beauharnais' leaflet, a "lithograph," but to avoid the broad constitutional issue it could have held that as a requirement of fair warning, the statute would be unduly vague if so construed, and thus the statute by its term did not forbid libelous pamphlets.

10. 343 U.S. at 256–57, 72 S.Ct. at 730–31.

11. 343 U.S. at 258, 72 S.Ct. at 731.

The dissenting views in *Beauharnais* were a precursor to the future direction of the law of libel. Justice Douglas argued that the expansion of individual and criminal libel to include group libel constituted an invasion of free expression that should occur only in circumstances wherein the "peril of speech must be clear and present ... raising no doubts as to the necessity of curbing speech in order to prevent disaster." [12] The balancing between private vindication of reputation and free expression should be in favor of free expression, Justice Black argued, because of the "unequivocal First Amendment command that its defined freedoms shall not be abridged."[13] Black noted as especially restrictive the potential that under the Illinois statute one could proceed against a book publisher, newspaper, radio or television station. Any danger in public discussion was outweighed "by the danger incident to the stifling of thought and speech." [14]

As we shall see it has been the views of Justices Black and Douglas that, to a great extent, have prevailed in later cases. And while *Beauharnais* has not been expressly overruled, it should be impossible to reach its results under the modern cases.[15] Vague laws that seek to ban hate speech, but which are not narrowly tailored, and are not based on the limited fighting words doctrine,[16] or the incitement to imminent lawless conduct doctrine [17] will not survive constitutional attack.

12. 343 U.S. at 285, 72 S.Ct. at 745.

13. 343 U.S. at 269, 72 S.Ct. at 737.

14. 343 U.S. at 275, 72 S.Ct. at 740.

Enjoining Defamation. It has long been established that courts simply cannot enjoin a libel. Such an injunction would be contrary to equitable principles, American Malting Co. v. Keitel, 209 Fed. 351 (2d Cir.1913), and would violate the first amendment, Parker v. Columbia Broadcasting System, Inc., 320 F.2d 937 (2d Cir. 1963); Konigsberg v. Time, Inc., 288 F.Supp. 989 (S.D.N.Y.1968).

See also, M. Nimmer, Nimmer on Freedom of Speech § 4.06[D] at p. 4–32, n. 30 (1984).

15. See, Collin v. Smith, 578 F.2d 1197, 1205 (7th Cir.1978), certiorari denied 439 U.S. 916, 99 S.Ct. 291, 58 L.Ed.2d 264 (1978).

Group Libel and Hate Speech. Various lower courts have recognized that because the purpose of defamation "is to protect *individuals;* a group may be sufficiently large that a statement concerning it cannot defame individual group members." Khalid Abdullah Tariq Al Mansour Faissal Fahd Al Talal v. Fanning, 506 F.Supp. 186 (N.D.Cal.1980) (emphasis in original). See also, Fowler v. Curtis Publishing Co., 182 F.2d 377 (D.C.Cir.1950). In Michigan United Conservation Clubs v. CBS News, 485 F.Supp. 893 (W.D.Mich. 1980), affirmed 665 F.2d 110 (6th Cir.1981), the court—also prohibiting group libel— noted obvious first amendment concerns:

16. See § 20.40, infra.

17. See § 20.15, supra.

"If plaintiffs were allowed to proceed with this claim, it could invite any number of vexatious lawsuits and seriously interfere with public discussion of issues, or groups, which are in the public eye. Statements about a religious, ethnic, or political group could invite thousands of lawsuits from disgruntled members of these groups claiming that the portrayal was inaccurate and thus libelous. Such suits would be especially damaging to the media, and could result in the public receiving less information about topics of general concern."

485 F.Supp. at 900.

The Court of Appeals for the Seventh Circuit has held invalid local ordinances designed to prevent a march of a Nazi organization. That court found that the *Beauharnais* rationale would not justify prohibition of a peaceful march based on its implied message of racial animosity or

§ 20.33 *New York Times v. Sullivan* and Libel of a Public Official

(a) The Case

Although *Beauharnais v. Illinois* has never been explicitly rejected, it should not represent present law in light of *New York Times Co. v. Sullivan*,[1] decided in 1964. The Court there held for the first time that constitutional protections for speech and press do limit state powers to award damages in libel actions brought by public officials against critics of official conduct.

Sullivan, one of three elected commissioners of Montgomery, Alabama, brought the action against four individuals and the *New York Times,* claiming he had been libeled in two paragraphs of a full page advertisement. Even though he was not mentioned by name in the advertisement, Sullivan recovered $500,000 damages against the *New York Times,* based on a state legal doctrine whereby criticism of the Montgomery Police Department was transmuted to criticism of him as the official in charge. The state court instructed the jury that such criticism was libel per se. Under such instruction Sullivan need only prove that the statement was false and that it referred to him.

The Supreme Court reversed in a holding broader than was strictly necessary given the facts of the case. The Court might have reversed by creating a narrower constitutionally based theory: no defamation on its face existed in the ad because Sullivan was not mentioned; alternatively, it might have held that the only amount of damages was

---

the racial beliefs of the marchers. Collin & National Socialist Party v. Smith, 578 F.2d 1197 (7th Cir.1978) (Blackmun, J., joined by White, J., dissented), certiorari denied 439 U.S. 916, 99 S.Ct. 291, 58 L.Ed.2d 264 (1978).

Cf. Delgado et al., Can Science Be Inopportune? Constitutional Validity of Governmental Restrictions on Race—I.Q. Research, 31 U.C.L.A.L.Rev. 128 (1983).

See also, A. Neier, Defending My Enemy: American Nazis, the Skokie Case, and the Risks of Freedom (1979); Bollinger, Book Review, 80 Mich.L.Rev. 617 (1982); Shiffrin, Defamatory Non–Media Speech and First Amendment Methodology, 25 U.C.L.A.L.Rev. 915 (1978); Arkes, Civility and the Restriction of Speech: Rediscovering the Defamation of Groups, 1974 Sup.Ct. Rev. 281; Delgado, Words that Wound: A Tort Action for Racial Insults, Epithets, and Name–Calling, 17 Harv.Civ.Rts.–Civ. Lib.L.Rev. 133 (1982); Note, Group Defamation: Five Guiding Factors, 64 Tex. L.Rev. 591 (1985); S. Halpern, The Law of Defamation, Privacy, Publicity and "Moral

Rights": Cases and Materials on Protection of Personality Interests (1988); Harry Kalven, Jr., ed. by Jamie Kalven, A Worthy Tradition: Freedom of Speech in America 60–73 (1988); Reisman, Democracy and Defamation: Control of Group Libel, 42 Colum.L.Rev. 727 (1942); Shapiro, Libel Regulatory Analysis, 74 Calif.L.Rev. 883 (1986); Rodney Smolla, Free Speech In an Open Society 167 (1992).

§ 20.33

1. 376 U.S. 254, 84 S.Ct. 710, 11 L.Ed.2d 686 (1964), motion denied 376 U.S. 967, 84 S.Ct. 1130, 12 L.Ed.2d 83 (1964). See Collin & Nat. Socialist Party v. Smith, 578 F.2d 1197 (7th Cir.1978), certiorari denied 439 U.S. 916, 99 S.Ct. 291, 58 L.Ed.2d 264 (1978). See also, Levine v. CMP Publications, Inc., 738 F.2d 660, 678–79 (5th Cir. 1984) (Tate, J., dissenting) (citing an earlier edition of this Treatise), rehearing denied 753 F.2d 1341 (1985).

For a fascinating study of this case, see, Anthony Lewis, Make No Law: The *Sullivan* Case and the First Amendment (1991).

constitutionally regulated and that only actual damages (out-of-pocket loss) would be allowed; or, it could have held that a newspaper which merely republished an advertisement drawn up by others should have some constitutional protection; it also might have created a defense that the statements alleged in the advertisement were substantially true. Instead, the majority opinion by Justice Brennan expounded a much more dramatic change in state libel law, which now must be measured against the first amendment.

The Court reasoned that a state must safeguard freedom of speech and press in its libel laws as required by the first amendment as applied to the states through the fourteenth amendment. This first amendment protection exists against the background of "profound national commitment to the principle that debate on public issues should be uninhibited, robust, and wide-open, and that it may well include vehement, caustic, and sometimes unpleasantly sharp attacks on government and public officials." [2] Neither erroneous statement nor injury to official reputation forfeits the first amendment protection, which should provide "breathing space" for freedom of expression.

The Test Under *New York Times*. The Court drew an analogy to the Sedition Act of 1798,[3] an early attempt to prohibit criticism of the government. The Court noted that state statutes punishing libel of public officials must likewise be restricted by the first amendment, for a broad libel law serving to protect public officials from criticism is closely analogous to the Sedition Laws. The Alabama statute did provide for a defense of truth, but given the importance of safeguarding the "breathing space" necessary so as not to discourage valid criticism of public officials, a "defense for erroneous statements honestly made" was essential.[4]

Given this general and basic policy, the Court laid out the standard for recovery of any alleged defamatory falsehood relating to a public official's conduct. First, the defamatory statement would have to relate to the individual plaintiff-government official;[5] no generalized criticism of government policy could be punished, for that would constitute a sedition action. The plaintiff-government official would also have the burden of proving that the statement was false. Citizens are certainly free to disclose truthful information about their officials. Finally, and most significantly, for there to be a defamation action, the plaintiff must allege and prove that the defendant had made the defamatory statements with "malice."

Group Libel. See § 20.32(b).

2. 376 U.S. at 270, 84 S.Ct. at 721.

3. 376 U.S. at 273–77, 84 S.Ct. at 722–24. See § 20.40, supra.

4. 376 U.S. at 278, 84 S.Ct. at 725.

5. The *New York Times* Court also held unconstitutional the Alabama proposition that criticism of a government agency is transmuted to criticism of the official in charge, a practice which strikes at the center of constitutionally protected area of free expression by expanding the law of libel beyond the requirement of scienter.

See also Rosenblatt v. Baer, 383 U.S. 75, 86 S.Ct. 669, 15 L.Ed.2d 597 (1966).

The Requirement of *New York Times* "Malice." On this point—the question of "malice"—the Court said:

> The constitutional guarantees require, we think, a federal rule that prohibits a *public official* from recovering damages for a defamatory falsehood relating to his official conduct unless he proves that the statement was made with *"actual malice"*....[6]

The Court defined "actual malice" as "knowledge that [the defamation that was published] was false or with reckless disregard of whether it was false or not."[7] While the Court used the word "malice," it was not referring to the old, common law libel meaning of "malice" as hatefulness or ill will;[8] rather, from its definition, the Court meant *"scienter."*[9]

(b) New York Times Scienter

This scienter requirement was clearly applied in *Garrison v. Louisiana.*[10] There the Supreme Court struck down a Louisiana statute

6. 376 U.S. at 279–80, 84 S.Ct. at 726 (emphasis added).

7. 376 U.S. at 280, 84 S.Ct. at 726.

8. W. Prosser, Torts 771–72 (4th ed. 1971). See also, Cantrell v. Forest City Publishing Co., 419 U.S. 245, 251–52, 95 S.Ct. 465, 469–70, 42 L.Ed.2d 419 (1974).

9. Cf. Herbert v. Lando, 441 U.S. 153, 199, 99 S.Ct. 1635, 1660–61, 60 L.Ed.2d 115 (1979) (Stewart, J., dissenting): "Although I joined the Court's opinion in *New York Times,* I have come greatly to regret the use in that opinion of the phrase 'actual malice.' ... In common understanding, malice means ill will or hostility. ... [but *New York Times* malice] has nothing to do with hostility or ill will...."

10. 379 U.S. 64, 78, 85 S.Ct. 209, 217–18, 13 L.Ed.2d 125, 135 (1964).

Criminal Libel. *Garrison* applied the *New York Times* scienter rule and invalidated the conviction of Garrison, who was charged with criminal libel under Louisiana law. The Court held that the Louisiana criminal law was unconstitutional as interpreted because it punished true statements made with ill will. 379 U.S. at 77–78, 85 S.Ct. at 217, 13 L.Ed.2d at 134–35. The Court also held that the statute was not narrowly drawn:

"... Louisiana's rejection of the clear-and-present danger standard as irrelevant to the application of its statute, coupled with the absence of any limitation in the statute itself calculated to

cause breaches of the peace, leads us to conclude that the Louisiana statute is not this sort of narrowly drawn statute."

379 U.S. at 70, 85 S.Ct. at 213, 13 L.Ed.2d at 130.

Thus, a statute called a criminal libel statute would be unconstitutional unless it was narrowly drawn and incorporated *both* the *New York Times* scienter requirement *and* also was likely to cause a breach of the peace (so called "fighting words"), see Chaplinsky v. New Hampshire, 315 U.S. 568, 62 S.Ct. 766, 86 L.Ed. 1031 (1942), or incited the listeners to violence within the meaning of *Brandenburg v. Ohio*, 395 U.S. 444, 89 S.Ct. 1827, 23 L.Ed.2d 430 (1969) (per curiam). Unless a criminal libel statute met these strict requirements, it would be unconstitutional.

See Emerson, Toward a General Theory of the First Amendment, 72 Yale L.J. 877, 924 (1963): "[I]t can hardly be urged that maintenance of peace requires a criminal prosecution for private defamation."

See also, Model Penal Code, Tentative Draft No. 13, § 250.7, Comments at 44 (A.L.I.1961): "It goes without saying that penal sanctions cannot be justified merely by the fact that defamation is evil or damaging to a person in ways that entitle him to maintain a civil suit. [P]ersonal calumny ... is therefore inappropriate for penal control...."

See generally, Kelly, Criminal Libel and Free Speech, 6 Kan.L.Rev. 295 (1958).

which permitted liability for true statements about public officials made negligently, "not made in the reasonable belief of its truth," or made with "actual malice" in the common law sense. The Court reiterated that only the knowing or reckless falsehood could be subject to civil or criminal sanction.

Defining "Reckless Disregard." Four years after *Garrison,* the Court made clear that "reckless disregard" could not be shown by proof of mere negligence; for "reckless disregard" there must be "serious doubts as to the truth of [the] publication." [11] The standard is that of the knowing lie—at the time of publication defendant must have known that the statement was false, or must have had serious doubts as to the statement's truth and have published it despite these doubts.

Thus, where one defendant had relied solely on a union member's affidavit charging a public official with criminal conduct and did not verify the charges with other union members, the Court would not allow plaintiff to go to the jury with a charge of reckless falsity.[12] There was not enough evidence of *New York Times* scienter to go to the jury. Similarly, the Court has not found "reckless falsity" when defendant has failed to conduct an affirmative investigation,[13] or for

---

[11]. St. Amant v. Thompson, 390 U.S. 727, 730–33, 88 S.Ct. 1323, 1325–27, 20 L.Ed.2d 262 (1968).

Defining "Reckless Disregard for the Truth." In Harte–Hanks Communications, Inc. v. Connaughton, 491 U.S. 657, 109 S.Ct. 2678, 105 L.Ed.2d 562 (1989), the Court, with no dissents, upheld a $200,000 libel verdict ($5,000 compensatory and $195,000 punitive damages) in favor of an unsuccessful candidate for judge and against a local newspaper that supported the reelection of the incumbent. This case was the first in 22 years where the Supreme Court upheld a damage award against the news media in a case filed by a public figure.

Respondent alleged that the newspaper published a defamatory, false story, with *New York Times* "malice," i.e., with scienter. This *New York Times* "malice" is not satisfied "merely through a showing of ill will...." 491 U.S. at 667 & n. 7, 109 S.Ct. at 2686 & n. 7. Stevens, J., for the Court, ruled that "a public figure plaintiff must prove more than an extreme departure from professional standards and that a newspaper's motive in publishing a story— whether to promote an opponent's candidacy or to increase its circulation—cannot provide a sufficient basis for finding actual malice." 491 U.S. at 664, 109 S.Ct. at 2684.

"Reckless disregard" means that the defendant has a "high degree of awareness of ... probably falsity" or has "entertained serious doubts as to the truth of his publication." 491 U.S. at 666–69, 109 S.Ct. at 2685–86.

The Court then carefully examined the testimony and concluded that there was "clear and convincing proof" supporting the jury's finding of "actual malice." The Court said that the reviewing court "must consider the factual record in full," although "credibility determinations are reviewed under the clearly erroneous standard" because the fact finders could observe the demeanor of the witnesses. The Court considered the trial court's instructions, the jury's answers to three special interrogatories, and the facts not in dispute in reaching its conclusion.

[12]. Id.

See generally, R. Adler, Reckless Disregard (1986); Westmoreland, A Case for Press Responsibility, 38 Mercer L.Rev. 771 (1987); Rodney Smolla, Suing the Press: Libel, the Media, and Power (1986).

[13]. Beckley Newspaper Corp. v. Hanks, 389 U.S. 81, 88 S.Ct. 197, 19 L.Ed.2d 248 (1967).

203

omissions which could constitute merely an error of judgment.[14]

In subsequent cases, the Supreme Court also clarified other issues first raised in *New York Times v. Sullivan*—the burden of proof requirement and the definition of "public official."

(c) Burden of Proof

Convincing Clarity. According to *New York Times v. Sullivan*, plaintiff bears the burden of proving actual malice with "convincing clarity."[15] This standard is apparently somewhere between "preponderance of the evidence" and "beyond a reasonable doubt," because later the Court uses the term "clear and convincing,"[16] a standard of proof which historically has required plaintiff in a civil case to bear more of a burden than a bare "preponderance."

The "clear and convincing" standard has its origins in the standards used by the chancellors finding facts in equity cases. It has now been expanded in many states to include other classes of cases such as charges of fraud. In general this standard is used "where there is thought to be special danger of deception, or where the court considers that the particular type of claim should be disfavored on policy grounds."[17]

The "clear and convincing" standard is not only applied on review to determine if there was a sufficient basis for the verdict or whether the jury must be instructed in these terms. To be a meaningful restriction, the jury should be instructed to apply the "clear and convincing" standard.

Summary Judgment and Directed Verdicts. In a *New York Times* libel action, a court, when ruling on defendant's summary judgment motion, must determine whether the evidence presented

---

14. St. Amant v. Thompson, 390 U.S. 727, 88 S.Ct. 1323, 20 L.Ed.2d 262 (1968).

The Petition Clause. McDonald v. Smith, 472 U.S. 479, 105 S.Ct. 2787, 86 L.Ed.2d 384 (1985) held that the petition clause of the first amendment does not give a defendant in a libel action absolute immunity. The plaintiff had charged defendant with knowingly sending false and libelous letters to President Reagan and others in order to undermine the chances of his being appointed U.S. Attorney. The petition clause does not require state libel law to expand the qualified privilege already afforded by *New York Times v. Sullivan.*

15. 376 U.S. 254 at 285–86, 84 S.Ct. 710 at 729.

16. Gertz v. Robert Welch, Inc., 418 U.S. 323, 331–32, 94 S.Ct. 2997, 3003, 41 L.Ed.2d 789 (1974), appeal after remand 680 F.2d 527 (7th Cir.1982), cert. denied 459 U.S. 1226, 103 S.Ct. 1233, 75 L.Ed.2d 407 (1983); see also Beckley Newspapers Corp. v. Hanks, 389 U.S. 81, 83, 88 S.Ct. 197, 199, 19 L.Ed.2d 248 (1967) (per curiam).

17. E. Cleary, et al., McCormick's Handbook of the Law of Evidence § 340, at 798 (2d ed. 1972). For an analysis of the constitutional problems in defining and applying the burden of proof in defamation cases see Franklin & Bussel, The Plaintiff's Burden In Defamation: Awareness and Falsity, 25 William and Mary L.Rev. 825 (Special Issue, 1983–84); and the commentary regarding their analysis by Professor Sunstein in Sunstein, Hard Defamation Cases, 25 William and Mary L.Rev. 891 (Special Issue, 1983–84); Bloom, Proof of Fault in Media Defamation Litigation, 38 Vanderbilt L.Rev. 247 (1985).

could support a reasonable jury finding that plaintiff has demonstrated *New York Times* scienter with "convincing clarity." Thus, *Anderson v. Liberty Lobby, Inc.*[18] held that a district court acted properly when it granted summary judgment to Jack Anderson and others who were sued because they published articles describing various respondents (including Willis Carto, the founder of Liberty, Lobby, Inc., a self-styled citizens lobby) as neo-Nazi, anti-semitic, and racist. If the affidavits *after full discovery* show no genuine issue for the jury, the defendant should not be put through the burden of a full trial.

In *Liberty Lobby,* Anderson submitted an affidavit by the author of the two articles in question. This affidavit said that the reporter had spent a substantial amount of time researching the articles and that the facts were obtained from a wide variety of sources. He detailed the sources for the statements alleged to be libelous. The reporter said he believed and still believes the truth of the statements made. The respondents argued that several sources were patently unreliable and that the petitioners had failed to adequately verify their information. Because a summary judgment motion is similar to a directed verdict motion, plaintiff must show more than a mere "scintilla" of evidence: "whether the evidence presented is such that a reasonable jury might find that actual malice [i.e., scienter] had been shown with convincing clarity."[19] While the defendant has the burden of showing no genuine issue of fact, the plaintiff, in order to survive the summary judgment motion, must present affirmative evidence to support a jury verdict. This principle remains true if the evidence is likely to be within the possession of the defendant, so long as the plaintiff has had full opportunity to conduct discovery.[20]

Appellate Review. Appellate courts must independently review a trial court finding of actual malice to determine whether the finding that the defendant acted with actual malice in publishing a knowing or reckless falsehood was established by clear and convincing evidence.[21]

Discovery of Editorial Thought Processes. In meeting his or her burden of proof, plaintiff may directly depose the defendants about

---

18. 477 U.S. 242, 106 S.Ct. 2505, 91 L.Ed.2d 202 (1986). Brennan, J., filed a dissenting opinion. Rehnquist, J., joined by Burger, C.J., also filed a dissenting opinion.

19. 477 U.S. at 257, 106 S.Ct. at 2515.

20. 477 U.S. at 257, 106 S.Ct. at 2514.

21. Bose Corp. v. Consumers Union of United States, Inc., 466 U.S. 485, 104 S.Ct. 1949, 80 L.Ed.2d 502 (1984), rehearing denied 467 U.S. 1267, 104 S.Ct. 3561, 82 L.Ed.2d 863 (1984). The Court found that where the actual "malice" standard of New York Times v. Sullivan is applicable, "[a]ppellate judges in such a case must exercise independent judgment and determine whether the record establishes actual malice with convincing clarity." 466 U.S. at 514, 104 S.Ct. at 1967.

In a footnote, the Court commented that in a defamation case there might be many other questions of fact that are irrelevant to the constitutional standard of New York Times v. Sullivan and to which a "clearly erroneous" standard of appellate review, such as was established by the Federal Rules of Civil Procedure, might be used in reviewing trial court findings. 466 U.S. at 514 n. 31, 104 S.Ct. at 1967 n. 31, 80 L.Ed.2d at 526 n. 31.

their thought processes and state of mind. In *Herbert v. Lando*,[22] the press urged the Supreme Court to create a privilege based on the first amendment that would bar a plaintiff suing for libel to inquire into the editorial processes of those responsible for the publication. The majority refused.

Plaintiffs are not limited to proving intent by inferences from objective circumstances; they may also ask the defendant (including the media defendant) about the ultimate fact directly. The rationale of *New York Times* contemplates such an inquiry. "*New York Times* and its progeny made it essential to proving liability that plaintiffs focus on the conduct and state of mind of the defendant.... Inevitably, unless liability is to be completely foreclosed, the thoughts and editorial processes of the alleged defamer would be open to examination."[23]

The majority noted that in past cases plaintiffs had asked direct questions about the editorial processes, with no one objecting to plaintiffs treading on allegedly forbidden areas, and in other cases libel defendants have offered such evidence to show good faith.[24] Similarly, there is no privilege for collegiate conversations or exchanges with fellow editors or damaging admissions to third persons;[25] nor must plaintiff first prove a prima facie case of falsity before asking about such questions.[26]

However, there may be some first amendment protection from discovery in other circumstances. The case should be different if plaintiff claimed libel for a false statement of pure opinion rather than a false assertion of fact. The majority specifically stated that: "There is no law that subjects the editorial process to private or official examination merely to satisfy curiosity or to serve some general end such as the public interest; and if there were, it would not survive constitutional scrutiny as the First Amendment is presently construed. No such problem exists here, however, where there is a specific claim of

---

22. 441 U.S. 153, 99 S.Ct. 1635, 60 L.Ed.2d 115 (1979).

See generally, Bezanson, Herbert v. Lando, Editorial Judgment, and Freedom of the Press: An Essay, 1978 U.Ill.L.Forum 605. Barron, The Rise and Fall of a Doctrine of Editorial Privilege: Reflections on Herbert v. Lando, 47 Geo.Wash.L.Rev. 1002 (1979) (considers first amendment-based editorial privilege with respect to story on TV show "60 Minutes" on Colonel Anthony Herbert).

See, Louis, Summary Judgment and the Actual Malice Controversy in Constitutional Defamation Cases, 57 So.Calif.L.Rev. 707 (1984).

Professor Smolla has examined the relationship of legal and social developments that appear to have resulted in a more permissive judicial attitude toward defamation suits in recent years. Smolla, Let the Author Beware: The Rejuvenation of the American Law of Libel, 132 U.Pa. L.Rev. 1 (1983).

23. 441 U.S. at 160, 99 S.Ct. at 1640.

24. 441 U.S. at 160 & n. 6, 165 & n. 15, 99 S.Ct. at 1641 & n. 6, 1643 & n. 15.

25. 441 U.S. at 169–71, 99 S.Ct. at 1645–46.

26. Justice Brennan, dissenting, took that position, 441 U.S. at 180, 99 S.Ct. at 1650, but the majority specifically rejected such a bifurcated approach. 441 U.S. at 174 n. 23, 99 S.Ct. at 1648 n. 23.

injury arising from a publication that is alleged to have been knowingly or recklessly false." [27]

Assertions of Fact versus Statements of Opinion. In *Milkovich v. Lorain Journal Co.,*[28] the Court, speaking through Chief Justice Rehnquist, recognized the distinction between "fact" and "opinion," but rejected any artificial dichotomy between the two. There is no wholesale exemption for defamation just because it might be labeled "opinion." [29]

27. 441 U.S. at 174, 99 S.Ct. at 1648 (footnote omitted). Justice Powell joined in the six member majority, but also wrote a concurring opinion to emphasize that the trial judge has some discretion to control discovery to protect the parties from undue burden or expense. Justice Brennan dissented in part. Justices Stewart and Marshall each wrote separate dissenting opinions.

Labor Disputes and Defamation. When labor and management make charges and countercharges alleging improper conduct during labor disputes, there may be some residual state power (not preempted by federal labor laws) to punish defamatory statements made during labor disputes. But state courts must employ the *New York Times* scienter standard and a libel action cannot be brought merely because the defendant used opinions or epithets. Old Dominion Branch No. 496 v. Austin, 418 U.S. 264, 94 S.Ct. 2770, 41 L.Ed.2d 745 (1974) (under federal law the use of the epithet "scab" in a union newsletter cannot be made the basis of a state libel judgment); Linn v. United Plant Guard Workers, 383 U.S. 53, 58, 86 S.Ct. 657, 660–61, 15 L.Ed.2d 582 (1966) (NLRA did not completely preempt state defamation actions, but it offered much protection because labor campaigns frequently are characterized by "bitter and extreme charges, countercharges, unfounded rumors, vituperations, personal accusations, misrepresentation and distortions). See also 383 U.S. at 60–61, 86 S.Ct. at 662 (epithets such as "scab," "unfair," and "liar," even if erroneous, are not subject to a defamation suit).

28. 497 U.S. ___, 110 S.Ct. 2695, 111 L.Ed.2d 1 (1990), on remand ___ Ohio App. ___, ___ N.E.2d ___ (1990).

See generally, Rodney Smolla, Law of Defamation § 6.12 (1990).

29. Libel for Assertions of Fact versus Statements of Opinion. A plaintiff should not be able to bring a libel action merely when he is complaining that someone defamed him by publicizing an unflattering opinion. Assertions of fact may be actionable; assertions of opinion (if the statement really is an opinion) are in a different category. Speech often uses epithet, hyperbole, charges and countercharges. This issue had been much debated in the lower courts prior to the *Milkovich* decision. Most lower courts had ruled that allegedly defamatory expression of opinion are absolutely protected—the question of whether plaintiff can prove *New York Times* scienter is never reached. These courts hold that only assertions of fact may be made the subject of libel actions. See, e.g., Ollman v. Evans, 750 F.2d 970 (D.C.Cir.1984) (D.C. Circuit holds that various statements in an Evans and Novak newspaper column about plaintiff Ollman—including that his principal scholarly work in "a ponderous tone in adoration of [Karl Marx] the master," and that an unnamed source said that "Ollman has no status within the profession, but is a pure and simple activist"—is a nonactionable statement of opinion), certiorari denied 471 U.S. 1127, 105 S.Ct. 2662, 86 L.Ed.2d 278 (1985).

See also, McBride v. Merrell Dow and Pharmaceuticals Inc., 717 F.2d 1460, 1464 & n. 7 (D.C.Cir.1983), on remand 613 F.Supp. 1349 (D.D.C.1985); Bose Corp. v. Consumers Union, Inc., 692 F.2d 189, 192–94 (1st Cir.1982), affirmed on other grounds 466 U.S. 485, 104 S.Ct. 1949, 80 L.Ed.2d 502 (1984), rehearing denied 467 U.S. 1267, 104 S.Ct. 3561, 82 L.Ed.2d 863 (1984); Hammerhead Enterprises, Inc. v. Brezenoff, 707 F.2d 33, 40 (2d Cir.1983), certiorari denied 464 U.S. 892, 104 S.Ct. 237, 78 L.Ed.2d 228 (1983); Avins v. White, 627 F.2d 637, 642 (3d Cir.1980), certiorari denied 449 U.S. 982, 101 S.Ct. 398, 66 L.Ed.2d 244 (1980); Church of Scientology v. Cazares, 638 F.2d 1272, 1286 (5th Cir. 1981); Orr v. Argus–Press Co., 586 F.2d 1108, 1114 (6th Cir.1978), certiorari denied

440 U.S. 960, 99 S.Ct. 1502, 59 L.Ed.2d 773 (1979); Lewis v. Time Inc., 710 F.2d 549, 552–53 (9th Cir.1983); Rinsley v. Brandt, 700 F.2d 1304, 1307 (10th Cir.1983).

See also National Foundation for Cancer Research, Inc. v. Council of Better Business Bureaus, Inc., 705 F.2d 98 (4th Cir.1983) (finding that statement that charity was not "spending a reasonable percentage of total income on program services" was constitutionally protected opinion based on the authority of Greenbelt Cooperative Publishing Association v. Bresler, 398 U.S. 6, 90 S.Ct. 1537, 26 L.Ed.2d 6 (1970)), certiorari denied 464 U.S. 830, 104 S.Ct. 108, 78 L.Ed.2d 110 (1983). *Greenbelt* found that a newspaper could not be held liable for reporting statements made by citizens at a city council meeting, which statements described the conduct of a local real estate developer and builder as "blackmail." The developer created "substantial local controversy" when he simultaneously negotiated both a sale of land to the city for use as a school site and zoning variance for other properties he owned in the area. The Court found that characterizing the bargaining tactics as blackmail could not fairly be understood as charging him with a criminal act and therefore the words could not be punished.

Cf. Rosenblatt v. Baer, 383 U.S. 75, 86 S.Ct. 669, 15 L.Ed.2d 597 (1966) (a newspaper column's questions as to why a ski resort owned by the government had not produced significant revenues while it was operated by the plaintiff could not be understood as a specific accusation of wrongdoing on the part of plaintiff; nor could they serve as the basis of a defamation action; for the statements merely constituted fair comment on governmental activity). Givhan v. Western Line Consolidated School District, 439 U.S. 410, 99 S.Ct. 693, 58 L.Ed.2d 619 (1979) (governmental employees who do not hold positions with highly discretionary authority—which makes them subject to dismissal for any reason, political or otherwise—cannot be fired simply for making statements critical of governmental policy), on remand 592 F.2d 280 (5th Cir.1979), appeal after remand 691 F.2d 766 (1982). Pickering v. Board of Education, 391 U.S. 563, 88 S.Ct. 1731, 20 L.Ed.2d 811 (1968) (same). Procunier v. Martinez, 416 U.S. 396, 413, 94 S.Ct. 1800, 1811, 40 L.Ed.2d 224, 240 (1974) ("Prison officials may not censor inmate correspondence simply to eliminate unflattering or unwelcome opinions or factually inaccurate statements."). Cantwell v. Connecticut, 310 U.S. 296, 310, 60 S.Ct. 900, 906, 84 L.Ed. 1213, 1221 (1940) ("To persuade others to his own point of view, the pleader, as we know, at times, resorts to exaggeration, to vilification of men who have been, or are, prominent in church or state, and even to falsehood. But the people of this nation have ordained in the light of history, that, in spite of the probability of excesses and abuses, these liberties are, in the long view, essential to enlightened opinion and right conduct on the part of the citizens of a democracy."). Watts v. United States, 394 U.S. 705, 707–08, 89 S.Ct. 1399, 1401–02, 22 L.Ed.2d 664 (1969) (per curiam) (political hyperbole cannot be punished). In re Snyder, 472 U.S. 634, 105 S.Ct. 2874, 86 L.Ed.2d 504 (1985) (in order to avoid first amendment problems, the Court interpreted a federal rule of appellate procedure prohibiting "conduct unbecoming a member of the bar" not to allow judge to suspend an attorney because he wrote a letter to a court employee criticizing the administration of the Criminal Justice Act—even if the letter was harsh, ill-mannered, and rude), on remand 770 F.2d 743 (8th Cir.1985).

The fact versus opinion dichotomy had its origins, in part, on reasoning in Gertz v. Robert Welch, Inc., 418 U.S. 323, 339–40, 94 S.Ct. 2997, 3007, 41 L.Ed.2d 789 (1974), appeal after remand 680 F.2d 527 (7th Cir. 1982), certiorari denied 459 U.S. 1226, 103 S.Ct. 1233, 75 L.Ed.2d 467 (1983), quoting New York Times Co. v. Sullivan, 376 U.S. 254, 270, 84 S.Ct. 710, 720, 11 L.Ed.2d 686 (1964):

"Under the First Amendment there is no such thing as a false idea. However pernicious an opinion may seem, we depend for its correction not on the conscience of judges and juries but on the competition of other ideas. But there is no constitutional value in false statements of fact. Neither the intentional lie nor the careless error materially advances society's interest in uninhibited, robust, and wide-open debate on the public issues."

The *Gertz* dictum was quoted by the Supreme Court with approval in Bose Corp. v. Consumers Union, Inc., 466 U.S. 485, 503, 104 S.Ct. 1949, 1961, 80 L.Ed.2d 502 (1984), rehearing denied 467 U.S. 1267, 104 S.Ct. 3561, 82 L.Ed.2d 863 (1984). However, two justices have suggested that they would not apply the *Gertz* dictum in this way. See Ollman v. Evans, 471 U.S. 1127, 105 S.Ct. 2662, 86 L.Ed.2d 278 (1985) (Rehnquist, J.,

In this case a newspaper columnist wrote an article implying that a local high school wrestling coach lied under oath in a judicial proceeding about an altercation involving his team at a home wrestling match. The article, for example, said that "Anyone who attended the meet ... knows in his heart that Milkovich and Scott lied at the hearing after each having given his solemn oath to tell the truth."

After *Milkovich,* if a statement is [1] an opinion, and [2] relates to matters of public concern, and [3] does not contain a provable false factual connotation,[30] then it will receive full constitutional protection.[31] For example, the statement—"I think that Mayor Jones lied"—is really no different than the statement—"Jones is a liar." Both statements may be proved to be false because the speaker did not really think that Jones lied, but published the statement anyway or, because Jones had not really lied. On the other hand, the statement—"In my opinion Mayor Jones shows his abysmal ignorance by accepting the teachings of Marx and Lenin"—is not actionable because it is a statement of opinion relating to matters of public concern and does not contain a provable false factual connotation.[32] The issue of falsity relates to "the *defamatory* facts implied by a statement." [33] Similarly, mere vigorous epithet (to label a real estate developer's negotiating position as "blackmail") is not actionable when the reasonable reader perceived the words as mere rhetorical hyperbole.

Milkovich summed up the law of fact versus opinion with respect to public figures and officials, private individuals, and matters of public concern as follows:

> [W]here a statement of "opinion" on a matter of public concern reasonably implies false and defamatory facts regarding public figures or officials, those individuals must show that such statements were made with knowledge of their false implications or with reckless disregard of their truth. Similarly, where such a statement involves a private figure on a matter of public concern, a plaintiff must show that the false connotations were made with some level of fault as required by *Gertz.* Finally, the enhanced appellate review required [in such cases] provides assurance that

joined by Burger, C.J., dissenting to denial of certiorari).

See generally, Note, Fact and Opinion after Gertz v. Robert Welch, Inc.: The Evolution of a Privilege, 34 Rutgers L.Rev. 81 (1981); Keeton, Defamation and Freedom of the Press, 54 Tex.L.Rev. 1221 (1976); Wade, The Communicative Torts and the First Amendment, 48 Miss.L.J. 671 (1980).

30. In Hustler Magazine v. Falwell, 485 U.S. 46, 55, 108 S.Ct. 876, 882, 99 L.Ed.2d 41 (1988), it is significant to note that Rehnquist, C.J., for the Court, held that public figures and public officials "may not recover for the tort of intentional infliction of emotional distress by reason of publications such as the one here at issue without showing in addition that the publication contains a false statement *of fact* which was made with 'actual malice,' i.e. with knowledge that the statement was false or with reckless disregard as to whether or not it was true." (emphasis added).

31. 497 U.S. at ___, 110 S.Ct. at 2706.

32. 497 U.S. at ___, 110 S.Ct. at 2706.

33. 497 U.S. at ___ n. 7, 110 S.Ct. at 2706 n. 7 (emphasis in original).

the foregoing determinations will be made in a manner so as not to "constitute a forbidden intrusion of the field of free expression."[34]

Justice Brennan, joined by Justice Marshall, filed a dissenting opinion. They agreed with the majority that only defamatory statements that are capable of being proved false are subject to liability under state libel law, and that plaintiff must prove that what is false is not the literal phrase published but what a reasonable reader would have understood the author to have said. In the view of the dissent, the statements at issue in this case "cannot reasonably be interpreted as stating or implying defamatory facts about petitioner" because, read in context, the columnist's assumption that the petitioner lied at the court hearing is patently conjecture.[35]

The Single Publication Rule. Both public figures and private persons who suffer injury from the publication of false statements about them may have a choice of bringing suit against the publisher in any one of several states. Various state statutes of limitations, statutory definitions of damages or privilege, state systems of pretrial discovery and other procedural rules that vary by state may influence a plaintiff's choice of jurisdiction. A publication which is broadcast or distributed in several states, such as a magazine with nationwide distribution, may be shown to cause harm to an individual by damaging his or her reputation in each state in which the defamatory statement was broadcast or published.

A state jurisdictional statute may allow a plaintiff who resides in another state to use the state courts to sue a publisher from a third state because of the damage done to the individual's reputation in the forum state. Such a state may allow the plaintiff to bring action against the publisher not only for the damage done to the plaintiff's reputation in the forum state but also, under a "single publication rule," for the damage done to the plaintiff's reputation throughout the nation. In other words, a plaintiff who resides in state A may sue the publisher, editor, or reporter of a magazine published in state B in the courts of state C if some copies of the magazine were distributed in state C. State C's jurisdictional statutes or rules may allow the plaintiff to bring suit in state C not only for the damage done by the distribution of the magazine in state C but also for the damages caused the plaintiff by the distribution of the magazine in various states throughout the nation.[36]

---

34. 497 U.S. at ___, 110 S.Ct. at 2706–07.

35. 497 U.S. at ___, 110 S.Ct. at 2709.

36. **Jurisdiction.** Courts are to judge the extension of jurisdiction over magazines in defamation suits solely by due process standards as to whether the defendant magazine has sufficient minimum contacts with the forum state. Courts are not to consider the fact that the plaintiff has virtually no previous contact with the state other than the injury caused by the distribution of the magazine in that state. Keeton v. Hustler Magazine, Inc., 465 U.S. 770, 104 S.Ct. 1473, 79 L.Ed.2d 790 (1984); Calder v. Jones, 465 U.S. 783, 104 S.Ct.

Fabricated Quotations. In *Masson v. New Yorker Magazine, Inc.,*[37] a public figure sued for libel, claiming that an author, in the course of writing a very unflattering portrait of him, used quotation marks, with knowledge of their inaccuracy, to attribute to him comments that he had not made. Justice Kennedy, for the Court, reversed the Ninth Circuit and ruled that the attributed quotations in this case had the degrees of falsity required to prove a state of mind of deliberate or reckless falsification (that is, scienter, or *New York Times* "malice"), so that the plaintiff could defeat a motion for summary judgment and go to trial on the merits. The Court considered six purported quotations, yet in each instance no identical statement appeared in the more than 40 hours of taped interviews. The plaintiff claimed that defendant Malcolm fabricated five passages, and omitted a crucial portion of the sixth, rendering it misleading.

Justice Kennedy noted that, "[i]n general, quotation marks around a passage indicate to the reader that the passage reproduces the speaker's words verbatim."[38] However, quotations do not always convey that the speaker actually said or wrote the quoted material. For example, "an acknowledgement that the work is so-called docudrama or historical diction, or that it recreates conversations from memory, not from recordings, might indicate that the quotations should not be interpreted as the actual statements of the speaker to whom they are attributed."[39]

However, the Court rejected the Ninth Circuit's view that an altered quotation is protected so long as it is a "rational interpretation" of an actual statement. The Court also rejected plaintiff's argument that any alteration beyond correction of grammar or syntax by itself proves falsity for *New York Times* scienter or "malice." The majority concluded: "If an author alters a speaker's words but effects no material change in meaning, including any meaning conveyed by the manner or fact of expression, the speaker suffers no injury to reputation that is

---

1482, 79 L.Ed.2d 804 (1984). The Supreme Court has rejected the claim that the first amendment should restrict state jurisdiction over the publishers or editors of a magazine in such a situation. All first amendment values involved in protecting broadcasters or publishers of allegedly libelous statements were accommodated through the substantive law limitations established by *New York Times v. Sullivan* and its progeny. Thus, there is no first amendment barrier to a state exercising jurisdiction and allowing the plaintiff to sue the publisher in its courts for the damages caused the plaintiff throughout the nation by the publication and distribution of the statement.

Cf. Cray, Choice of Law in Right of Publicity, 31 U.C.L.A.L.Rev. 640 (1984).

See, Pielemeir, Constitutional Limitations on Choice of Law: The Special Case of Multistate Defamation, 133 U.Pa.L.Rev. 381 (1985) (This article is "a guide to choice of law defamation law problems in the wake of *Keeton*'s validation of expansive jurisdiction over the multistate media," id. at 383). See also 133 U.Pa.L.Rev. at 439, arguing that "superficial reliance on precedent enunciating constitutional limitations on choice of law will not adequately protect important constitutional values in the context of defamation law."

37. 501 U.S. ___, 111 S.Ct. 2419, 115 L.Ed.2d 447 (1991).

38. 501 U.S. at ___, 111 S.Ct. at 2430.

39. 501 U.S. at ___, 111 S.Ct. at 2431.

compensable as a defamation. [A] deliberate alteration of the words uttered by a plaintiff does not equate with knowledge of falsity for purposes of *New York Times Co. v. Sullivan* and *Gertz v. Robert Welch, Inc.*, unless the alteration results in a material change in the meaning of the words conveyed by the statement. The use of quotations to attribute words not in fact spoken bears in a most important way on that inquiry, but it is not dispositive in every case." [40]

Justice White, joined by Justice Scalia, concurred in part and dissented to this portion of the opinion and would prefer a rule that is much less protective of speech and the press. "The Court states that deliberate misquotation does not amount to New York Times malice unless it results in a material change in the meaning conveyed by the statement. This ignores the fact that under *New York Times*, reporting a known falsehood—here the knowingly false attribution—is sufficient proof of malice. The falsehood, apparently, must be substantial; the reporter may lie a little, but not too much." [41] Justice White argued that plaintiff alleged "knowing falsehood" because he alleged that reporter, Malcolm, wrote that Masson said certain things that she knew Masson did not say.

(d) Public Officials

Candidates for Public Office and Nonelected Public Officials as "Public Officials." A special reason for the constitutional restriction on libel laws is that threat of libel lawsuits might deter criticism of official conduct. As we have seen, the requirement of *New York Times* scienter was initially limited to elected public officials. Sullivan himself was an elected official in Montgomery, Alabama, and some commentators at first speculated that the definition of "public official" would be limited to elected officials. However, the Court later extended the *New York Times* privilege by expanding the definition of "public official" to include those who were candidates for public office and to statements that did not relate to official conduct but did relate to fitness for office. [42] The Court also included certain non-elected persons in the expanded definition of "public official." [43]

The Test for Public Official. The breadth of the concept of "public official" is illustrated in *Rosenblatt v. Baer*, [44] where the Court applied the *New York Times* privilege to the discharged supervisor of a

40. 501 U.S. at ___, ___, 111 S.Ct. at 2432, 2433.

41. 501 U.S. at ___, 111 S.Ct. at 2438.

42. Monitor Patriot Co. v. Roy, 401 U.S. 265, 91 S.Ct. 621, 28 L.Ed.2d 35 (1971), on remand 112 N.H. 80, 290 A.2d 207 (1972).

43. Rosenblatt v. Baer, 383 U.S. 75, 86 S.Ct. 669, 15 L.Ed.2d 597 (1966).

44. 383 U.S. 75, 86 S.Ct. 669, 15 L.Ed.2d 597 (1966).

See Christie, Underlying Contradictions in the Supreme Court's Classification of Defamation 1981 Duke L.J. 811. See also, Elder, Defamation, Public Officialdom, and the Rosenblatt v. Baer Criteria—A Proposal for Revivification Two Decades After New York Times Co. v. Sullivan, 33 Buffalo L.Rev. 579 (1985).

county-owned ski resort. The Court held that in order to encourage criticism of government, the "public official" designation must apply "at the very least to those among the hierarchy of government employees who have, or appear to the public to have, substantial responsibility for or control over the conduct of governmental affairs." [45]

The *New York Times* privilege exists for criticism of any government position of such "apparent importance that the public has an independent interest in the qualifications and performance of the person who holds it." [46] Thus, while persons occupying low level technical positions might not be included in this category, any government employee with discretionary power in matters of public interest should be considered a public official.

As the Court explained in *Rosenblatt:*

> Where a position in government has such an apparent importance that the public has an independent interest in the qualifications and performance of the person who holds it, beyond the general public interest in the qualifications and performance of all government employees, ... [then] the *New York Times* malice standards apply.[47]

Thus, a public employee may be a "public official" even though the employee is not at the top of the bureaucratic hierarchy. For example, a public grade school teacher should be a "public official" for purposes of *New York Times* malice because he or she performs a task going "to the heart of representative government." [48]

(e) Actual Damages, Punitive Damages, and a Right of Retraction

Punitive Damages. If the plaintiff in a libel action is a *private* individual—that is, one not a public official within the doctrine of *New York Times v. Sullivan,* nor even a public figure within the meaning of later case law that has extended *New York Times v. Sullivan* to those who assume "roles of especial prominence in the affairs of society" [49]—

45. 383 U.S. at 85, 86 S.Ct. at 676 (footnote omitted).

46. 383 U.S. at 86, 86 S.Ct. at 676. See also, Hutchinson v. Proxmire, 443 U.S. 111, 119 n. 8, 99 S.Ct. 2675, 2680 n. 8, 61 L.Ed.2d 411 (1979) ("public official" cannot "be thought to include all public employees....").

47. Rosenblatt v. Baer, 383 U.S. 75, 85, 86 S.Ct. 669, 676, 15 L.Ed.2d 597 (1966).

48. Ambach v. Norwick, 441 U.S. 68, 75–76, 99 S.Ct. 1589, 1593–94, 60 L.Ed.2d 49 (1979). See also, Johnston v. Corinthian Television Corp., 583 P.2d 1101 (Okl.1978) (grade school wrestling coach is public official). Lower courts have gone all over the lot on this issue. See Lorain Journal Co. v. Milkovich, 474 U.S. 953, 959 & n. 3, 106 S.Ct. 322, 327 & n. 3, 88 L.Ed.2d 305 (1985) (Brennan, J., joined by Marshall, J., dissenting from denial of certiorari).

49. Gertz v. Robert Welch, Inc., 418 U.S. 323, 345, 94 S.Ct. 2997, 3009, 41 L.Ed.2d 789, 811 (1974), appeal after remand 680 F.2d 527 (7th Cir.1982), certiorari denied 459 U.S. 1226, 103 S.Ct. 1233, 75 L.Ed.2d 467 (1983).

See generally § 20.34, infra, on Libel of Public Figures.

then that plaintiff (suing on a matter of public concern) can collect actual damages only on proof of negligence, and can collect punitive damages or damages not supported by the evidence (i.e., presumed damages) *only if* the plaintiff can prove *New York Times* "malice."[50] By analogy, then, if the plaintiff is a public official or public figure, this type of plaintiff could not collect punitive or presumed damages because such a plaintiff must prove *New York Times* "malice" (i.e., scienter) in order to make out a prima facie case, merely to get actual damages. If the private person must prove more than *New York Times* "malice" to go beyond actual damages, then the public official or public person (who must prove scienter just to get actual damages) should have to prove *more than* scienter to get punitive damages. But there is nothing more than scienter.

The Court has not explicitly ruled that a public official or public figure cannot collect punitive damages, but a contrary conclusion is troubling.[51] The Court has condemned the inhibiting effect of damage awards in excess of any actual injury,[52] so one should expect it to hold that any punitive damage awards for libels against public officials or public persons interfere with the "breathing space" required in the exercise of robust first amendment debate.

Actual Damages. A libel plaintiff, whether or not he is a public official, can collect actual damages, which the Court has defined broadly to include out-of-pocket losses, and also "impairment of reputation and standing in the community, personal humiliation, and mental anguish and suffering."[53] There is no need for evidence which assigns "an actual dollar value to the injury."[54] Thus, under present law, defamation is an oddity of the law of torts, "the only tort that allows substantial recovery without proof of injury."[55]

---

50. Gertz v. Robert Welch, Inc., 418 U.S. 323, 350, 94 S.Ct. 2997, 3012, 41 L.Ed.2d 789, 811 (1974), appeal after remand 680 F.2d 527 (7th Cir.1982), certiorari denied 459 U.S. 1226, 103 S.Ct. 1233, 75 L.Ed.2d 467 (1983).

51. Cf. 418 U.S. at 350, 94 S.Ct. at 3012. See Comment, Punitive Damages and Libel Law, 98 Harv.L.Rev. 847 (1985). But see Smolla, Let the Author Beware: The Rejuvenation of the American Law of Libel, 132 U.Pa.L.Rev. 1, 91 (1983).

52. Gertz v. Robert Welch, Inc., 418 U.S. 323, 94 S.Ct. 2997, 41 L.Ed.2d 789 (1974), appeal after remand 680 F.2d 527 (7th Cir.1982), certiorari denied 459 U.S. 1226, 103 S.Ct. 1233, 75 L.Ed.2d 467 (1983).

53. 418 U.S. at 350, 94 S.Ct. at 3012, 41 L.Ed.2d at 811 (1974).

54. 418 U.S. at 350, 94 S.Ct. at 3012, 41 L.Ed.2d at 811.

55. Anderson, Reputation, Compensation, and Proof, 25 Wm. & Mary L.Rev. 747, 748 (1984). Professor Anderson concludes that "compensating individuals for actual harm to reputation is the only legitimate purpose of defamation law today.... By actual harm, I mean provable injury to reputation. Nonpecuniary reputational losses would qualify, but mental anguish alone would not." Id. at 749. Cf. Van Alstyne, First Amendment Limitations on Recovery from the Press—An Extended Comment on "The Anderson Solution," 25 Wm. & Mary L.Rev. 793 (1984); LeBel, Defamation and the First Amendment: The End of the Affair, 25 Wm. & Mary L.Rev. 779 (1984); Barron, Punitive Damages in Libel Cases—First Amendment Equalizer?, 47 Wash. & Lee L.Rev. 105 (1990).

The Libel–Proof Plaintiff. Various courts have held that some plaintiffs for some purposes are libel-proof. Thus *Cardillo v. Doubleday & Co., Inc.*[56] held, as a matter of law, that a particular libel plaintiff who sued for libel because defendant had charged that the plaintiff had engaged in various specific crimes, was "libel-proof, *i.e.,* so unlikely by virtue of his life as a habitual criminal to be able to recover anything other than nominal damages as to warrant dismissal of the case, involving, as it does First Amendment considerations."[57]

Rights of Reply. The Supreme Court has held that it is unconstitutional for a state to force a newspaper to give a political candidate a right to equal space in order to reply to attacks on his record.[58] But the Supreme Court has never ruled out the possibility that a court could order a retraction statement from a person who is found (under the proper standard for the case) to have defamed another.[59] Members of the Court covering the ideological spectrum from Justice Brennan to Justice Rehnquist have noted that the constitutional prohibition on "right of reply" statutes does not suggest that a right of retraction statute would be forbidden.[60] Empirical evidence shows that most libel plaintiffs are mainly interested in correcting false statements rather than in money damages.[61]

(f) Emotional Distress

In *Hustler Magazine v. Falwell*[62], the Court considered a parody that *Hustler Magazine* had published. The parody involved a Compari Liqueur advertisement and Reverend Jerry Falwell. The parody was entitled, "Jerry Falwell talks about his first time." The actual Compari advertisements included interviews with famous personalities about the "first time" they tried Compari. The advertisements focused on the sexual double entendre of the "first time." The *Hustler* parody

---

56. 518 F.2d 638 (2d Cir.1975). See generally, Note, The Libel–Proof Plaintiff Doctrine, 98 Harv.L.Rev. 1909 (1985).

57. 518 F.2d at 639.

58. Miami Herald Pub. Co. v. Tornillo, 418 U.S. 241, 94 S.Ct. 2831, 41 L.Ed.2d 730 (1974), on remand 303 So.2d 1 (Fla.1974). See § 20.18(b), supra.

59. See generally, Note, Vindication of the Reputation of a Public Official, 80 Harv.L.Rev. 1730 (1967).

60. 418 U.S. at 258, 94 S.Ct. at 2839–40, 41 L.Ed.2d at 741–42 (1979) (Brennan, J., joined by Rehnquist, J., concurring).

See generally, Barrett, Declaratory Judgments for Libel: A Better Alternative, 74 Calif.L.Rev. 847 (1986). Franklin, Declaratory Judgment Alternative to Current Libel Law, 74 Calif.L.Rev. 809 (1986); Powe, Tornillo, 1987 S.Ct.Rev. 345.

61. See generally, R. Bezanson, G. Cranberg & J. Soloski, Libel Law and the Press: Myth and Reality (1987); Bezanson, The Libel Suit in Retrospect: What Plaintiffs Want and What Plaintiffs Get, 74 Calif.L.Rev. 789 (1986). Libel cases are expensive for both plaintiffs and defendants. The average libel case takes nearly four years of litigation.

62. 485 U.S. 46, 108 S.Ct. 876, 99 L.Ed.2d 41 (1988).

See, Post, The Constitutional Concept of Public Discourse: Outrageous Opinion, Democratic Deliberation, and Hustler Magazine v. Falwell, 103 Harv.L.Rev. 603 (1990); Rodney Smolla, Jerry Falwell v. Larry Flynt: The First Amendment on Trial (1988).

resembled a Compari advertisement and included an alleged interview with Jerry Falwell, a nationally known minister, host of a nationally syndicated television show, and commentator on public affairs. Neither party disputed that Jerry Falwell is a "public figure" [63] and therefore should be treated as a "public figure" for libel purposes. In the *Hustler* parody, Jerry Falwell states that his "first time" was during a drunken incestuous meeting with his mother in an outhouse. The bottom of the page contained the disclaimer: "Fiction; Ad and Personality Parody." Jerry Falwell filed suit and, while that case was pending, *Hustler* reprinted the parody. The jury awarded $100,000 in actual damages and $50,000 in punitive damages.

The Court held that a public figure or public official may not recover for the tort of intentional infliction of emotional distress without showing that the publication at issue contains a "false statement of fact which was made with 'actual malice,' i.e., with knowledge that the statement was false or with reckless disregard as to whether or not it was true." [64] The plaintiff did not meet this test because the jury found that the *Hustler* parody could not reasonably be understood as describing actual facts about the plaintiff or actual events in which he participated. "Were we to hold otherwise, there can be little doubt that political cartoonists and satirists would be subjected to damages awards without any showing that their work falsely defamed its subject." [65] The Court noted, for example, that early political cartoons portrayed George Washington as an ass, and that Thomas Nast engaged in a graphic vendetta against Boss Tweed.

There were no dissents. Justice White concurred in the judgment with the comment that "*New York Times v. Sullivan* has little to do with this case, for here the jury found that the ad contained no assertion of fact." [66]

§ 20.34 Libel of Public Figures

The Supreme Court extended the *New York Times v. Sullivan* doctrine when it held that the standard of "actual malice," that is, scienter, applied to alleged defamations against people who did not fit into the definition of "public official" but who were nonetheless "public figures."

---

63. See § 20.34, infra.

64. 485 U.S. at 55, 108 S.Ct. at 882. Rehnquist, C.J., wrote the opinion for the Court. White, J., concurred in the judgment. Kennedy, J., took no part in the consideration or decision of this case.

65. 485 U.S. at 54, 108 S.Ct. at 881.

See, e.g., Long, The Political Cartoon: Journalism's Strongest Weapon, The Quill, 56, 57 (Nov. 1962):

"The political cartoon is a weapon of attack, of scorn and ridicule and satire; it is least effective when it tries to pat some politician on the back. It is usually as welcome as a bee sting and is always controversial in some quarters."

66. 485 U.S. at 57, 108 S.Ct. at 883.

In *Curtis Publishing Co. v. Butts* and its companion case, *Associated Press v. Walker*,[1] Chief Justice Warren's concurring opinion noted that the distinction between government and the private sector was increasingly blurred. He therefore created a new category within the *New York Times* rule beyond that of public official. He called this category "public figure" and defined such figures as those who are "intimately involved in the resolution of important public questions or, by reason of their fame, shape events in areas of concern to society at large."[2] Warren reasoned that the *New York Times v. Sullivan* standard should apply to these people precisely because they are not subject to the restraints of the political process—"public opinion may be the only instrument by which society can attempt to influence their conduct."[3] The broad range of those whom the Court intended to classify as "public figures" is evident in that in *Associated Press*, Walker was a retired army general, while in *Curtis Publishing Co.*, Butts was athletic director of the University of Georgia.[4]

More recently, the Court has explained:

§ 20.34

1. 388 U.S. 130, 87 S.Ct. 1975, 18 L.Ed.2d 1094 (1967), mandate conformed 418 S.W.2d 379 (Tex.Civ.App.1967), certiorari denied 391 U.S. 966, 88 S.Ct. 2036, 20 L.Ed.2d 880 (1968).

See also, Levine v. CMP Publications, Inc., 738 F.2d 660, 678–79 (5th Cir.1984) (Tate, J., dissenting) (citing an earlier edition of this Treatise), rehearing denied 753 F.2d 1341 (1985).

2. 388 U.S. at 164, 87 S.Ct. at 1996 (Warren, C.J., concurring). There was no majority opinion.

See generally, Christie, Underlying Contradictions in the Supreme Court's Classification of Defamation, 1981 Duke L.J. 811 (exposes the undermining of the public figure/private person dichotomy); Schauer, Public Figures, 25 Wm. & Mary L.Rev. 905 (Special Issue, 1983–84); Ashdown, Of Public Figures and Public Interest—The Libel Law Conundrum, 25 Wm. & Mary L.Rev. 937 (Special Issue, 1983–1984); Daniels, Public Figures Revisited, 25 Wm. & Mary L.Rev. 957 (Special Issue, 1983–1984). Professor Schauer is quite unsympathetic to First Amendment concerns in his article, Public Figures, 25 Wm. & Mary L.Rev. 905 (Special Issue, 1983–84). Professor Redish responds that, when Schauer "compares legislative regulation [of public figure libel] to regulation of the manufacture of pharmaceuticals, [he is] in total disregard of the fact that the former is protected by the first amendment while the latter is not." Redish, Limits on Scientific Expression and the Scope of First Amendment Analysis: A Comment on Professor Kamenshine's Analysis, 26 Wm. & Mary L.Rev. 897, 903 n. 18 (1985).

3. 388 U.S. at 164, 87 S.Ct. at 1996.

4. In a nine to zero decision, the Supreme Court reversed a Mississippi jury award of $500,000 compensatory and $300,000 punitive damages for the eyewitness news report which stated that Walker had personally taken command of a violent crowd's charge against federal marshalls who were enforcing a court decree ordering the University of Mississippi to enroll a Black student. According to the Court, the situation involved reporting "hot" news by a trustworthy and competent reporter. The evidence was insufficient to support even a finding of negligence.

In a five to four decision, however, the Court affirmed Butts' damage award for an article in the Saturday Evening Post which accused him of conspiring to fix a football game by divulging information on Georgia plays. Four justices held that the Post had met Harlan's negligence test of "highly unreasonable conduct" and Chief Justice Warren joined them to create a majority by holding that the Post had met the *New York Times v. Sullivan* standard of "reckless disregard" and that the jury had been properly instructed.

For the most part [public figures are] those who attain this status [by assuming] roles of especial prominence in the affairs of society. Some occupy positions of such persuasive power and influence that they are deemed public figures for all purposes. More commonly, those classed as public figures have thrust themselves to the forefront of particular public controversies in order to influence the resolution of the issues involved.[5]

Thus, a research scientist who is the recipient of a government grant, the award of which a U.S. Senator attacked as wasteful in allegedly defamatory statements, is not a "public figure" even for the limited purpose of comment on his receipt of public funds.[6] The mere receipt of public funds did not confer public figure status; nor could it be said in this case that the scientist-libel plaintiff assumed any role of public prominence in the broad question of public expenditures. The scientist's limited access to the media for the purpose of responding to the Senator's charges did not establish the regular and continuing access to the media that is a sign of a public figure.[7]

§ 20.35   Private Individuals

(a) Time, Inc. v. Hill

Because of their general fame and notoriety both Walker and Butts could be considered public figures for all purposes. However, in *Time, Inc. v. Hill*[1] the Supreme Court faced the issue of a private individual being thrust into the limelight for the purpose of one particular event. In 1952, the Hill family had been the subject of national news coverage when three escaped convicts held them hostage in their home. The incident was fictionalized in a play, and in 1955 Life Magazine published a picture story which showed the play's cast re-enacting scenes from the play in the former Hill house.

---

5. Gertz v. Robert Welch, Inc., 418 U.S. 323, 345, 94 S.Ct. 2997, 3009, 41 L.Ed.2d 789 (1974), appeal after remand 680 F.2d 527 (7th Cir.1982), certiorari denied 459 U.S. 1226, 103 S.Ct. 1233, 75 L.Ed.2d 467 (1983).

6. Hutchinson v. Proxmire, 443 U.S. 111, 99 S.Ct. 2675, 61 L.Ed.2d 411 (1979). See also Wolston v. Reader's Digest Ass'n, Inc., 443 U.S. 157, 99 S.Ct. 2701, 61 L.Ed.2d 450 (1979) (court rejects the argument that any person who engages in criminal conduct automatically becomes a public figure for purposes of a limited range of issues relating to his conviction).

7. It is interesting to note that after the death of Robert Maxwell, the British media king, his media empire crashed and his financial misdeeds came to light. The

British press was unable to publish relevant allegations earlier because Maxwell used Britain's tough libel laws to silence critics. Hayes, Britain's Libel Laws Helped Maxwell Keep Charges of Misdeeds From Public, Wall St. Jrl., Dec. 9, 1991, at B2, col. 3–4 (Midwest ed.).

§ 20.35

1. 385 U.S. 374, 87 S.Ct. 534, 17 L.Ed.2d 456 (1967). See Levine v. CMP Publications, Inc., 738 F.2d 660, 678–79 (5th Cir. 1984) (Tate, J., dissenting) (citing an earlier edition of this Treatise), rehearing denied 753 F.2d 1341 (1985).

See generally Felcher & Ruhin, Privacy, Publicity, and the Portrayal of Real People by the Media, 88 Yale L.J. 1577 (1979).

The Hills sued on the basis of a New York state privacy statute which made truth a complete defense but allowed a privacy action to "newsworthy people" or "events" in case of "[m]aterial and substantial falsification."[2] However, the Supreme Court applied the *New York Times* standard of "knowing or reckless falsity" to alleged defamations concerning false reports of matters of public interest.[3]

In determining the standard of liability for private individuals, the Court looked to whether these individuals were involved in a matter of public interest. If they were so involved, the Court held the more stringent standard of recovery defined in *New York Times v. Sullivan* to be applicable, even in the circumstances like that of the Hills, who were thrust into the limelight by events not of their own doing.

Although the Court applied the *New York Times* standard to the Hill's privacy action, it left open the question of whether the same standard of liability should be applicable in a libel action to persons voluntarily and involuntarily thrust into the public limelight.[4] Four years later the Court offered a tentative answer to this question in *Rosenbloom v. Metromedia, Inc.,*[5] a fragmented plurality decision containing five separate opinions. The Court held, in a decision which did not attract even a bare majority of the justices, that the *New York Times v. Sullivan* standard must apply to private citizens caught up in events of public interest—whether voluntarily or involuntarily so involved. But this concept ended as abruptly as it appeared.

(b) Gertz v. Robert Welch, Inc.

Private Figures Who are Public Figures for Certain Purposes. The *Rosenbloom* issue was still open and three years later the Court, in a five to four decision, rejected the extension of the *New York Times v. Sullivan* doctrine to publication of all matters of public interest. Instead, in *Gertz v. Robert Welch, Inc.,*[6] the Court created a third category within which the *New York Times v. Sullivan* doctrine applied: private citizens who obviously are not public officials and who are not public enough to be public figures for all purposes, may be public figures with respect to a particular controversy. Now, clarifying the issues in *Hill* and in similar cases, the Court decided that the important question was not whether the alleged defamation was a matter of public interest but

---

2. 385 U.S. at 383, 386, 87 S.Ct. at 539, 541.

3. 385 U.S. at 387–88, 87 S.Ct. at 542.

4. 385 U.S. at 390–91, 87 S.Ct. at 543–44.

5. 403 U.S. 29, 91 S.Ct. 1811, 29 L.Ed.2d 296 (1971).

6. 418 U.S. 323, 94 S.Ct. 2997, 41 L.Ed.2d 789 (1974), appeal after remand 680 F.2d 527 (7th Cir.1982), certiorari de-

nied 459 U.S. 1226, 103 S.Ct. 1233, 75 L.Ed.2d 467 (1983).

See generally, Christie, Injury to Reputation and the Constitution: Confusion Amid Conflicting Approaches, 75 Mich.L.Rev. 431 (1976); Shiffrin, Defamatory Non–Media Speech and First Amendment Methodology, 25 U.C.L.A.L.Rev. 915 (1978); Christie, Underlying Contradictions in the Supreme Court's Classification of Defamation, 1981 Duke L.J. 811.

whether the individual defamed was a private citizen for purposes of that activity.

The Court stated that a person is not to be considered a public figure for the purpose of libel actions absent clear evidence of general fame and notoriety in the community or the assumption of roles of special prominence in the affairs of society. But even though one is not a public figure for all purposes, one may be a public figure for a particular incident. The Court suggested this view by explaining that an individual's status as "public figure" can be determined by looking specifically to his participation in the "*particular* controversy giving rise to the defamation;"[7] that is, he may be a public figure for some purpose but not for others. According to the Court, private individuals may be "public figures" for purposes of *New York Times* if they have "thrust themselves to the forefront of particular public controversies in order to influence the resolution of the issues involved."[8] The truly involuntary public figure is considered rare.

Under this newly defined category, Gertz was an example of a private citizen who was not public enough to be a public figure for all purposes and who was not a public figure with respect to the particular controversy giving rise to the defamation. In the facts of that case a Chicago policeman, Richard Nuccio, shot and killed a young man, Nelson. Nuccio was ultimately convicted of murder in the second degree. Gertz filed his libel action after a 1969 article in American Opinion Magazine, a monthly outlet for the views of the John Birch Society, alleged that he had been the architect of a Communist frameup which led to Nuccio's murder conviction.

Gertz, a reputable Chicago lawyer, had acted as counsel for the Nelson family in civil litigation and had attended the coroner's inquest, but Gertz did not discuss Nuccio with the press and was not involved in the criminal proceedings against Nuccio.[9] Although Gertz had been active in community affairs, according to the Court he was not a "public figure" for all purposes of libel law. In making this determination, the Court relied on the fact that Gertz seemingly did nothing to thrust himself into the public eye nor did he attempt to engage the public's attention during the period in which the controversy arose.

Because Gertz was not sufficiently public to be a public figure, nor was he "public" with respect to the particular controversy, the Court had to determine the standard of libel recovery for such private individuals. It held that the standard was a matter for the States to determine: "[S]o long as they do not impose liability without fault, the States may define for themselves the appropriate standard of liability for a publisher or broadcaster of defamatory falsehood injurious to a

---

7. 418 U.S. at 352, 94 S.Ct. at 3013 (emphasis added); see also 418 U.S. at 345, 94 S.Ct. at 3009–10.

8. 418 U.S. at 345, 94 S.Ct. at 3009–10; see also 418 U.S. at 352, 94 S.Ct. at 3013.

9. 418 U.S. at 352, 94 S.Ct. at 3013.

private individual." [10]   The Court found this solution to be an equitable balance for the competing interests. "It recognizes the strength of the legitimate state interest in compensating private individuals for wrongful injury to reputation, yet shields the press and broadcast media from the rigors of strict liability for defamation." [11]

The Burden of Proof Standard Against Private Persons. If the plaintiff is a truly private person in a libel action, the plaintiff can collect actual money damages on the basis of defendant's negligence, if state law so provides. State law could require a tougher standard for plaintiffs, but *Gertz* provides that under the Constitution a state could not provide a more favorable standard for libel plaintiffs: strict liability

---

10. 418 U.S. at 347, 94 S.Ct. at 3010.

11. 418 U.S. at 348, 94 S.Ct. at 3011.

Gertz **Applied to the Nonmedia Defendant.** Because of language (such as that quoted in the text) in *Gertz* referring to the broadcast media defendant, some lower courts have tried to draw a distinction between media and non-media defendants, with the protections of *Gertz* being afforded only the media defendant. See, e.g., Denny v. Mertz, 106 Wis.2d 636, 318 N.W.2d 141 (1982), certiorari denied 459 U.S. 883, 103 S.Ct. 179, 74 L.Ed.2d 147 (1982); Stuempges v. Parke, Davis & Co., 297 N.W.2d 252 (Minn.1980); Rowe v. Metz, 195 Colo. 424, 579 P.2d 83 (1978); Harley–Davidson Motorsports, Inc. v. Markley, 279 Or. 361, 568 P.2d 1359 (1977).

Other courts have properly rejected this attempted distinction. Jacron Sales Co. v. Sindorf, 276 Md. 580, 350 A.2d 688 (1976); Antwerp Diamond Exchange v. Better Business Bureau, 130 Ariz. 523, 637 P.2d 733 (1981).

The purported distinction finds no support in the Supreme Court case law that has routinely applied the protection of *New York Times v. Sullivan* to the nonmedia defendant. See, e.g., New York Times v. Sullivan, 376 U.S. 254, 286 n. *, 84 S.Ct. 710, 729 n. *, 11 L.Ed.2d 686, 710 n. * (1964) (noting that *New York Times* was decided together with Abernathy et al. v. Sullivan, and that the Court applied the *New York Times* rule to protect the "individual petitioners" as well as the Newspaper). See also, Henry v. Collins, 380 U.S. 356, 85 S.Ct. 992, 13 L.Ed.2d 892 (1965), on remand 176 So.2d 891 (Miss.1965); Garrison v. Louisiana, 379 U.S. 64, 85 S.Ct. 209, 13 L.Ed.2d 125 (1964).

In other contexts the Court has clearly rejected the argument that the "media" (assuming such a term even has a constitu-

tional definition) has any special first amendment rights. See First National Bank v. Bellotti, 435 U.S. 765, 782, 98 S.Ct. 1407, 1418, 55 L.Ed.2d 707 (1978), rehearing denied 438 U.S. 907, 98 S.Ct. 3126, 57 L.Ed.2d 1150 (1978). See also 435 U.S. at 795, 802, 98 S.Ct. at 1426, 1429 (Burger, C.J., concurring).

As Justice White explained in Dun & Bradstreet, Inc. v. Greenmoss Builders, Inc., 472 U.S. 749, 773–74, 105 S.Ct. 2939, 2952–53, 86 L.Ed.2d 593 (1985) (White, J., concurring in the judgment), the attempted distinction between media and nonmedia defendants is also bad policy; it is a perverse rule, for it gives more protection to those who can cause the most damage:

"... I agree with Justice Brennan [and Marshall, Blackmun, & Stevens, JJ., who joined the Brennan opinion] that the First Amendment gives no more protection to the press in defamation suits than it does to others exercising their freedom of speech. None of our cases affords such a distinction; to the contrary, the Court has rejected it at every turn. [I]t makes no sense to give the most protection to those publishers who reach the most readers and therefore pollute the channels of communication with the most misinformation and do the most damage to private reputation."

472 U.S. at 773, 105 S.Ct. at 2952–53 (footnote omitted).

But some members of the Court have intimated that the question is open. See Philadelphia Newspapers, Inc. v. Hepps, 475 U.S. 767, 779 n. 4, 106 S.Ct. 1558, 1565 n. 4, 89 L.Ed.2d 783 (1986): "[We need not consider what standards would apply] if the plaintiff sues a nonmedia defendant." Contrast 475 U.S. at 779, 106 S.Ct. at 1565 (Brennan, J., joined by Blackmun, J., concurring, and objecting to any distinction between media and nonmedia defendants).

for defamatory speech would not be tolerated.[12]   Any reward which a jury would grant a plaintiff would have to be supported by competent evidence, "although there need be no evidence which assigns an actual dollar value to the injury." [13]   Such plaintiffs—suing truly private defendants—would not (as a Constitutional requirement) have to prove *New York Times* "malice" *unless* the plaintiff sought to collect punitive damages or damages not supported by the evidence (i.e., presumed damages).

The plaintiff must not only prove negligence; the plaintiff, in general, has the burden of proving falsity.   Because of the need to encourage debate on public issues, it is unconstitutional for the state to shift this burden to the defendant.   As the Court explained in *Philadelphia Newspapers, Inc. v. Hepps*,[14] in a five to four opinion, which was narrowly written, "We hold that at least where a newspaper publishes speech of public concern, a private-figure plaintiff cannot recover damages without also showing that the statements at issue are false." [15] There can be no common law presumption that defamatory speech is false.   Thus, in order to tip the balance in favor of protecting true speech, the private-figure plaintiff must show not only fault on the part of defendant but also that the speech was false.

Even if the media defendant relied on a shield law (allowing media employees to refuse to divulge their sources), the plaintiff must still prove falsity.[16]   If the plaintiff is not a public figure and if the matter is "exclusively private concern," then the Court said, enigmatically, "the constitutional requirements do not necessarily force any change in at least some of the features of the common-law landscape." [17]

Actual Damages and Punitive Damages.   Although *Gertz* held that a private individual must prove actual damages in order to recover under a standard requiring less than knowing or reckless falsity in a libel action, the Court defined actual damages quite broadly to include not only out-of-pocket loss but also "impairment of reputation and standing in the community, personal humiliation, and mental anguish and suffering." [18]   This broad definition has been subject to well taken

12. 418 U.S. at 350, 94 S.Ct. at 3012.

13. 418 U.S. at 350, 94 S.Ct. at 3012. The appellate courts must independently review findings of "actual malice" in defamation cases. Bose Corp. v. Consumers Union of United States, 466 U.S. 485, 104 S.Ct. 1949, 80 L.Ed.2d 502 (1984), rehearing denied 467 U.S. 1267, 104 S.Ct. 3561, 82 L.Ed.2d 863 (1984). See, Levine v. CMP Publications, Inc., 738 F.2d 660, 678–79 (5th Cir.1984) (Tate, J., dissenting) (citing earlier edition of this Treatise), rehearing denied 753 F.2d 1341 (1985).

See generally, Monaghan, Constitutional Fact Review, 85 Colum.L.Rev. 229 (1985); Note, Making Sense of Bose Corp. v. Consumers Union of United States, Inc., 71 Cornell L.Rev. 477 (1986).

14. 475 U.S. 767, 106 S.Ct. 1558, 89 L.Ed.2d 783 (1986).

15. 475 U.S. at 768, 106 S.Ct. at 1559. Justice O'Connor wrote the opinion for the Court.

16. 475 U.S. at 778, 106 S.Ct. at 1565.

17. 475 U.S. at 775, 106 S.Ct. at 1563.

18. 418 U.S. at 350, 94 S.Ct. at 3012.

scholarly criticism.[19]   *Gertz* thus may be an invitation to convert defamation suits to a new remedy for mental distress.[20]

In order for a private individual who has been libeled to collect punitive damages, the Constitution requires that such a plaintiff prove that the defendant engaged in *New York Times* "malice." Under the first amendment, "State may not permit recovery of presumed or punitive damages, at least when liability is not based on a showing of knowledge of falsity or reckless disregard for the truth." [21]

While the *Gertz* Court did leave open the possibility that a private person could recover punitive damages if knowing or reckless falsity were proven, it left unresolved the question of whether a *public* figure or *public* official could recover punitive damages at all. The *Gertz* Court in fact condemned the inhibiting effect of damage awards in excess of any actual injury, so it should not be surprising if it were held that any punitive damage awards for libels directed against public figures or officials impinge upon the "breathing space" required in the exercise of first amendment freedoms.[22]

(c) Time, Inc. v. Firestone

Two years after its decision in *Gertz v. Robert Welch, Inc.,*[23] the Court re-emphasized the narrow applicability of the *New York Times* scienter test when one moves outside the category of "public official" into the "public figure" domain of *Gertz.* In *Time, Inc. v. Firestone,*[24] a libel action was brought after Time Magazine reported that plaintiff's husband divorced her "on grounds of extreme cruelty and adultery." [25] The state court had actually granted the divorce on the grounds that "neither party is domesticated, within the meaning of that term as used by the Supreme Court of Florida." [26]

The Court decided that *New York Times* scienter should not be the standard of recovery in the case; plaintiff's role in Palm Beach society

19. See, Anderson, Reputation, Compensation, and Proof, 25 Wm. & Mary L.Rev. 747, 749 (1984): "[C]ompensating individuals for actual harm to reputation is the only legitimate purpose of defamation law today. Proof of such harm, therefore, should be required in every libel or slander case. By actual harm, I mean provable injury to reputation. Nonpecuniary reputational losses would qualify, but mental anguish alone would not."

20. Ashdown, *Gertz* and *Firestone:* A Study in Constitutional Policy–Making, 61 Minn.L.Rev. 645, 670–71 (1977): "Any plaintiff who can persuade a jury that defamation caused him anguish apparently can satisfy the [*Gertz*] standard." See also, Anderson, Reputation, Compensation, and Proof, 25 Wm. & Mary L.Rev. 747, 757 (1984).

21. 418 U.S. at 349, 94 S.Ct. at 3011.

22. See § 20.33(e), supra.

23. 418 U.S. 323, 94 S.Ct. 2997, 41 L.Ed.2d 789 (1974), appeal after remand 680 F.2d 527 (7th Cir.1982), certiorari denied 459 U.S. 1226, 103 S.Ct. 1233, 75 L.Ed.2d 467 (1983). See Ashdown, *Gertz* and *Firestone:* A Study in Constitutional Policy–Making, 61 Minn.L.Rev. 645 (1977).

24. 424 U.S. 448, 96 S.Ct. 958, 47 L.Ed.2d 154 (1976), on remand 332 So.2d 68 (Fla.1976).

25. 424 U.S. at 452, 96 S.Ct. at 964.

26. 424 U.S. at 450–51, 96 S.Ct. at 963–64.

did not make her a "public figure" for the purpose of the libel action, nor did plaintiff "thrust herself to the forefront of any particular public controversy in order to influence the resolution of the issues involved in it." [27] The Court said that a "public controversy" is not *any* controversy of interest to the public—it had rejected that definition of "public controversy" when it repudiated *Rosenbloom v. Metromedia* in *Gertz.*[28] Firestone had no choice but to go to court in order to dissolve her marriage, the Court reasoned, and by this action she did not freely choose to publicize her marital problems nor did she assume "special prominence in the resolution of public questions." [29]

Significantly the Court also said that Firestone's several press conferences during divorce proceedings did not convert her into a "public figure." The press conferences were not an attempt to influence the outcome of the divorce proceedings nor were they an attempt to influence the outcome of some unrelated controversy, according to the Court.[30]

The Court thus limited the media's ability to make an issue a "public controversy" and then claim the *New York Times* standard of recovery in libel actions arising therefrom. Mere existence or generation of public interest is not sufficient to define someone as a "public figure" for the purpose of libel law. *Firestone* therefore applied the *Gertz* standard.

The rationale of *Firestone* should indicate that *Time v. Hill* no longer governs the standard for "false light" privacy suits which cause the plaintiff mental anguish and humiliation. Such suits are based on a theory that the disclosure of private facts is made in a way that casts the individual in a false and unflattering light before the public. Unless the Court were to resurrect the *Rosenbloom* plurality opinion, the *Gertz* standard should apply to these cases where the plaintiff is a private person.[31]

While it is possible that the Court will preserve *Hill* and instead rely on one element of the *Rosenbloom* public issues concept for people caught up in public issues by finding such people to be involuntary public figures, we must remember that the Court in *Firestone* emphasized that Mrs. Firestone had not voluntarily placed herself in the public domain. *Hill,* discussed above, involved the opening of a new play linked to an actual incident that had been a matter of public interest; the Hill family was involuntarily a part of this actual inci-

27. 424 U.S. at 453, 96 S.Ct. at 965.

28. 424 U.S. at 454, 96 S.Ct. at 965.

29. 424 U.S. at 454–55, 96 S.Ct. at 965.

30. 424 U.S. at 454–55 n. 3, 96 S.Ct. at 965 n. 3.

31. See Wood v. Hustler Magazine, Inc., 736 F.2d 1084, 1092 (5th Cir.1984) (Reavley, J., for a unanimous court, citing this Treatise), rehearing denied 744 F.2d 94 (1984), certiorari denied 469 U.S. 1107, 105 S.Ct. 783, 83 L.Ed.2d 777 (1985).

dent, and, like Mrs. Firestone, the Hills did not voluntarily place themselves in the public domain.[32]

(d) Dun & Bradstreet, Inc. v. Greenmoss Builders, Inc.

Those who thought that the constitutional law of libel could not be made more complex must be few in number after the fragmented Supreme Court decision in *Dun & Bradstreet, Inc. v. Greenmoss Builders, Inc.*[33] Justice Powell, joined by Justices Rehnquist and O'Connor, wrote a plurality opinion. Chief Justice Burger and Justice White each wrote separate opinions concurring in the judgment, and Justice Brennan, joined by Justices Blackmun, Marshall, and Stevens, dissented.

In this case plaintiff was a construction contractor who discovered that Dun & Bradstreet, a credit reporting agency had, on July 26, 1976, sent a report to five of its subscribers. This report mistakenly indicated that the contractor had filed a petition for voluntary bankruptcy. The contractor learned of this error on the same day, when the president of the contracting company talked to its bank about financing. The contractor called Dun & Bradstreet's regional office, explained the error, asked for a correction, and asked for the names of the firms which had received the false credit report. Dun & Bradstreet promised to look into the matter but refused to divulge the names of the recipients of the credit report. About one week after Dun & Bradstreet released the incorrect credit report to the five subscribers, it issued a corrective notice on or about August 3, 1976. It reported that one of the contractor's former employees, not the contractor, had filed for bankruptcy, and that the contractor "continued in business as usual." The contractor again asked for the list of subscribers and Dun & Bradstreet refused.

The contractor then sued in Vermont state court for defamation. The trial established that Dun & Bradstreet's error was caused when one of its employees (a 17 year old high school student) inadvertently misattributed the bankruptcy filing of the contractor's former employee to the contractor. Dun & Bradstreet did not check the accuracy of this report, though it was routine to do so.

The trial judge gave the jury instructions that failed to define many of the crucial terms. The trial judge did tell the jury that the credit report was libelous per se and that the plaintiff was not required to prove actual damages "since damage and loss [are] conclusively presumed."[34] The trial court also permitted the jury to award pre-

---

32. See Fitzgerald v. Penthouse International, Ltd., 525 F.Supp. 585, 602 (D.Md. 1981) (Miller, D.J.), citing an earlier edition of this treatise; affirmed in part, reversed in part 691 F.2d 666 (4th Cir.1982), certiorari denied 460 U.S. 1024, 103 S.Ct. 1277, 75 L.Ed.2d 497 (1983).

33. 472 U.S. 749, 105 S.Ct. 2939, 86 L.Ed.2d 593 (1985).

34. 472 U.S. at 755, 105 S.Ct. at 2943.

sumed and punitive damages without proof of scienter.[35] The jury awarded $50,000 in so-called "compensatory" or presumed damages and $300,000 in punitive damages.[36] The Supreme Court, with no majority opinion, affirmed this award.

The Powell Plurality: Speech Involving Matters of Public Concern. Justice Powell's opinion, joined only by Justices Rehnquist and O'Connor, concluded that in all of the previous cases in which the Court found constitutional limits to state libel laws the speech involved expression "on a matter of public concern," or "*public speech.*"[37] These justices concluded that because speech on matters of "purely private" concern[38] is of less first amendment concern, "the state's interest [in reputation] adequately supports awards of presumed and punitive damages—even absent a showing of 'actual malice.'"[39] They reasoned the plaintiff could collect "presumed" damages because proof of actual damage is often impossible and yet plaintiff's reputation has been tarnished. So a jury should be allowed to presume damages. Unfortunately, the test, "matter of public concern," is hardly self-defining, and the Powell plurality offered no further guidance to the lower courts.

Justices Powell, Rehnquist and O'Connor clearly concluded that plaintiffs could collect punitive and presumed damages without any showing of "actual malice" (*i.e., New York Times* scienter) if the alleged defamation did not involve a matter of "public concern." They did not discuss whether a plaintiff in such circumstances could collect presumed or punitive damages in the absence of even negligence on the part of the defendant. *Gertz*[40] had required proof of negligence before a private person could collect damages for defamation, but Justices Powell, Rehnquist, and O'Connor stated explicitly that *Gertz* "involved expression on a matter of undoubted public concern."[41] Thus, for these three justices, it may well be the case that if the speech did not involve a matter of public concern, they would allow plaintiff to collect presumed or punitive damages without proof of any kind of fault on the part of the defendant. Justice White's separate opinion concurring in the judgment so concluded.[42]

35. 472 U.S. at 755, 105 S.Ct. at 2943. These instructions thus did not satisfy the requirements of Gertz v. Robert Welch, Inc., 418 U.S. 323, 94 S.Ct. 2997, 41 L.Ed.2d 789 (1974), appeal after remand 680 F.2d 527 (7th Cir.1982), certiorari denied 459 U.S. 1226, 103 S.Ct. 1233, 75 L.Ed.2d 467 (1983).

36. 472 U.S. at 753, 105 S.Ct. at 2942.

37. 472 U.S. at 757 & n. 4, 105 S.Ct. at 2494 & n. 4 (emphasis on original).

38. 472 U.S. at 760, 105 S.Ct. at 2946.

39. 472 U.S. at 760, 105 S.Ct. at 2946 (footnote omitted). When these justices

use the term "actual malice" they mean "scienter."

40. Gertz v. Robert Welch, Inc., 418 U.S. 323, 94 S.Ct. 2997, 41 L.Ed.2d 789 (1974), appeal after remand 680 F.2d 527 (7th Cir.1982), cert. denied 459 U.S. 1226, 103 S.Ct. 1233, 75 L.Ed.2d 467 (1983).

41. 472 U.S. at 756, 105 S.Ct. at 2944.

42. 472 U.S. at 773, 105 S.Ct. at 2953 (White, J.):

"Although Justice Powell speaks only of the inapplicability of the *Gertz* rule with respect to presumed and punitive damages, it must be that the *Gertz* require-

Public Officials and Matters Not of Public Concern. There is nothing in the Powell plurality which would limit its application to cases where the plaintiff is a private person. That is, for the three justices who make up the Powell plurality, it may well be the case that a public official or public figure could also collect presumed or punitive damages without even showing any negligence on the part of the defendant if the alleged defamation does not involve a matter of "public concern." Such a rule would greatly deflate protection for the news media and others.

The major question for the Powell plurality was whether the credit report involved a matter of public concern. The Powell plurality concluded that it did not. First, the Powell plurality announced that the credit report concerned "no public issue. It was speech solely in the individual interest of the speaker and its specific business audience." [43] From this statement one might be tempted to conclude that all credit reports or all commercial speech are in the category of reduced free speech protection as involving matters not of "public concern." But the Powell plurality, without discussion, specifically rejected that conclusion. Some credit reports are of public concern; some are not. "The protection to be accorded a particular credit report depends on whether the report's 'content, form, and context' indicate that it concerns a public matter." [44] If the "public concern" test is like a raft, Powell refuses to supply any rudder to guide its use.

Secondly the Powell plurality relied on the fact that the credit report was made available only to five subscribers who were under contract not to disseminate it further: the confidential nature of the communication is evidence that it does not involve a matter of public concern. However, the perverse anomaly created by Justice Powell's argument is that to the extent that the defendant's alleged libel is not treated confidentially, it is more likely to be protected by *Gertz* and *New York Times v. Sullivan;* to the extent that the defendant takes care not to spread the alleged defamatory remarks, he is more likely subject to liability.

Finally, the Powell plurality believed that speech involving credit reporting is likely not to be chilled by libel laws because the free market already provides many incentives to be accurate "since false credit reporting is of no use to creditors." [45] However, this argument can easily be turned around: the free market incentive to provide accurate credit reports lessens the need for the Court to add libel law protection.

ment of some kind of fault on the part of the defendant is also inapplicable in cases such as this."

43. 472 U.S. at 762, 105 S.Ct. at 2947 (footnote omitted).

44. 472 U.S. at 762 n. 8, 105 S.Ct. at 2947 n. 8.

45. 472 U.S. at 762, 105 S.Ct. at 2947.

The Burger and White Opinions. Chief Justice Burger concurred in the judgment. He had dissented in *Gertz* and now would overrule it. He also argued that *New York Times* should be reexamined.[46]

Justice White also concurred in the judgment. Like Burger, he had dissented in *Gertz* and still believed that decision was wrong. He had joined the Court in *New York Times v. Sullivan* but he "came to have increasing doubts about the soundness of the Court's approach and about some of the assumptions underlying it." [47] He suggested "that the press would be no worse off financially if the common-law rules were to apply and if the judiciary was careful to insist that damage awards be kept within bounds." [48]

The Dissent. Justice Brennan's dissent would have applied *Gertz* to the facts of this case. And he criticized the five members of the Court who, in three different opinions, affirmed the damage award but "have provided almost no guidance as to what constitutes a protected 'matter of public concern.' " [49]

The Future of the "Public Concern" Doctrine. Nearly a decade and a half before the Supreme Court plurality decision in *Dun & Bradstreet* another plurality of the Court in *Rosenbloom v. Metromedia, Inc.*[50] tried to offer *New York Times* protection for defendants who made defamatory statements about private individuals when those statements were related to matters of "public concern." In that case Justices Marshall, Stewart and Harlan in dissent warned that courts are ill-equipped for such an ill-defined task inevitably involving ad hoc balancing.[51] Courts "will be required to somehow pass on the legitimacy of interest in a particular event or subject; what information is relevant to self-government. The danger such a doctrine portends for freedom of the press seems apparent." [52] Judges are not able to determine what is "public concern" without examining the contents of the speech and then applying their subjective judgments.

It may well be that the road the Powell plurality in *Dun & Bradstreet* seeks to travel will end in a dead end, as it did the last time the Court travelled on it.[53] What is clear from *Dun & Bradstreet* is that

---

46. 472 U.S. at 764, 105 S.Ct. at 2948.

47. 472 U.S. at 769, 105 S.Ct. at 2950.

48. 472 U.S. at 773, 105 S.Ct. at 2953.

49. 472 U.S. at 787, 105 S.Ct. at 2960.

50. 403 U.S. 29, 30, 91 S.Ct. 1811, 1813, 29 L.Ed.2d 296 (1971) (plurality opinion of Brennan, J., joined by Burger, C.J., and Blackmun, J.).

51. 403 U.S. at 78–81, 91 S.Ct. at 1836–38, 29 L.Ed.2d at 331–33 (dissent of Marshall, J., joined by Stewart, J.). Justice Harlan's separate dissent agreed with

this analysis. 403 U.S. at 62, 91 S.Ct. at 1829, 29 L.Ed.2d at 323.

52. 403 U.S. at 79, 91 S.Ct. at 1837, 29 L.Ed.2d at 332 (Marshall, L., dissenting, joined by Stewart, J.).

53. Gertz v. Robert Welch, Inc., 418 U.S. 323, 94 S.Ct. 2997, 41 L.Ed.2d 789 (1974), appeal after remand 680 F.2d 527 (7th Cir.1982), certiorari denied 459 U.S. 1226, 103 S.Ct. 1233, 75 L.Ed.2d 467 (1983) rejected the *Rosenbloom* plurality because, inter alia, it forced state and federal judges to decide on "an ad hoc basis" when publi-

a majority of the Court is unhappy with the constitutional law of libel as formulated in *New York Times* and *Gertz*. And this unhappiness goes well beyond complaints about the entire system of credit reporting.[54] The future should witness new efforts to modify or even overhaul present doctrine.

In *Philadelphia Newspaper, Inc. v. Hepps*,[55] Justice O'Connor for the majority, shed little light on the meaning of the definition of a "matter of public concern." In this case, a series of newspaper articles contained the theme that the appellees had links to organized crime

cations address issues of "general or public interest." 418 U.S. at 346, 94 S.Ct. at 3010, 41 L.Ed.2d at 809.

"Matters of Public Concern" in the Government Employment Area Distinguished. In the government employment area, nontenured (typically low-level) government employees cannot be fired solely because of their political beliefs. See, e.g., Pickering v. Board of Education, 391 U.S. 563, 88 S.Ct. 1731, 20 L.Ed.2d 811 (1968) (school board prohibited from firing teacher because she wrote a letter to the editor, published in the local paper, and the letter criticized School Board policies); Givhan v. Western Line Consolidated School District, 439 U.S. 410, 99 S.Ct. 693, 58 L.Ed.2d 619 (1979) (school board prohibited from firing teacher because she privately objected to allegedly racially discriminatory school policies), on remand 592 F.2d 280 (5th Cir.1979), appeal after remand 691 F.2d 766 (1982); Branti v. Finkel, 445 U.S. 507, 100 S.Ct. 1287, 63 L.Ed.2d 574 (1980) (assistant public defender cannot be discharged solely because he is Republican).

Rankin v. McPherson, 483 U.S. 378, 107 S.Ct. 2891, 97 L.Ed.2d 315 (1987) (discharge of county employee because she said, in a private conversation to coemployee, that she hoped any future attempt to assassinate the President would be successful, is unconstitutional), rehearing denied 483 U.S. 1056, 108 S.Ct. 31, 97 L.Ed.2d 819 (1987).

Compare McCormick v. Edwards, 646 F.2d 173, 177–79 (5th Cir.1981) (noncivil service state employee who had no policy-making or confidential duties may be constitutionally fired for becoming actively involved in a partisan election campaign), rehearing denied 651 F.2d 776 (1981), certiorari denied 454 U.S. 1017, 102 S.Ct. 552, 70 L.Ed.2d 415 (1981), rehearing denied 454 U.S. 1165, 102 S.Ct. 1042, 71 L.Ed.2d 323 (1982).

The Court has had to create some test to limit the applicability of the first amendment protection from discharge in order to prevent nontenured public employees from securing de facto tenure by deciding to criticize their superior and disrupt office morale. The public employer need not accept action which he or she reasonably believes disrupts the office, undermines authority, and destroys close working relationships. Connick v. Myers, 461 U.S. 138, 103 S.Ct. 1684, 75 L.Ed.2d 708 (1983). The Court distinguishes between the type of speech which protects the public employee from discharge and the type of speech which does not, and labels the former a "matter of public concern."

It is one thing to decide what is a matter of public concern for the purpose of protecting a government employee from discharge—where the Court must tie in the type of speech engaged in to the effective functioning of the office—and quite another thing for the Court to engage in the much more open-ended task of trying to decide what is a "matter of public concern" in the *Dun & Bradstreet* sense.

54. See Shiffrin, The First Amendment and Economic Regulation: Away from a General Theory of the First Amendment, 78 Nw.U.L.Rev. 1212, 1268 (1983) ("If the first amendment requirements outlined in *Gertz* apply [to the credit report that defames], there is something clearly wrong with the first amendment or with *Gertz*."). R. Smolla, Suing the Press: Libel, Media, & Power (1986). In this book Professor Smolla presents a thorough analysis of various case studies of libel actions. He suggests that the Supreme Court will cut back on First Amendment protections for the press, in part, because the justices are "politically sensitive persons who rose to prominence in political and legal circles where image was a precious commodity...." Id. at 252.

55. 475 U.S. 767, 106 S.Ct. 1558, 89 L.Ed.2d 783 (1986).

and that those links influenced the state's governmental processes. Speech concerning the political process, the Court simply announced, without elaboration, is of public concern.[56]

§ 20.36 Rights of Privacy and Rights of Publicity

Publication of "Private" Truthful Details. In addition to the categories of public officials, public figures, and *Gertz*-public figures, we have true privacy cases: the accurate description of private facts. May the state, to protect an individual's privacy, prohibit the publication of information which is true but which admittedly relates to and infringes on private matters? This general issue was raised in *Cox Broadcasting Corp. v. Cohn*[1] but the Court decided the case on narrow grounds.

Cohn, father of a deceased rape victim, brought suit against an Atlanta, Georgia, television station after a news broadcast reported the name of his victim-daughter. The name had been obtained from judicial records open to public inspection which were maintained in connection with public prosecution.

The Supreme Court held that a state may not impose right of privacy liability for public dissemination of true information derived from official court records open to public inspection. Because the state allowed the court records to be public, it could not forbid the republication of the information by the press. The Court reasoned that the strong interest of the public to know about governmental operations and the strong interest in a free press not subject to self-censorship outweighed the individual's interest in privacy concerning information already appearing in public records. The public interest was presumedly being served, the Court continued, when the information was placed

---

56. See generally, David A. Anderson, Is Libel Law Worth Reforming?, 140 U.Penn.L.Rev. 487 (1991).

§ 20.36

1. 420 U.S. 469, 95 S.Ct. 1029, 43 L.Ed.2d 328 (1975), on remand 234 Ga. 67, 214 S.E.2d 530 (1975).

See generally, Warren and Brandeis, The Right to Privacy, 4 Harv.L.Rev. 193, 196 (1890). See also, Kalven, Privacy in Tort Law—Were Warren and Brandeis Wrong?, 31 Law & Contemp.Prob. 326 (1966); Zimmerman, Requiem for a Heavyweight: A Farewell to Warren & Brandeis' Privacy Tort, 68 Cornell L.Rev. 291 (1983). Felcher & Rubin, Privacy, Publicity, and the Portrayal of Real People by the Media, 88 Yale L.J. 1577 (1979) (considers the case of unauthorized media portrayals and concludes that traditional privacy and publicity analysis should be replaced with explicit

recognition of new principles); Gavison, Privacy and the Limits of the Law, 89 Yale L.J. 421 (1980) (to be useful the concept of privacy must be neutral and coherent). Cf. Smith, Constitutional Privacy in Psychotherapy, 49 Geo.Wash.L.Rev. 1 (1980) (suggests that the constitutional right of privacy should include the protection of the confidential communications of therapy); The Tension Between the First Amendment and the "Right of Publicity," 39 Record Ass'n Bar of City of N.Y. 368 (1984); Cray, Choice of Law in Right of Publicity, 31 U.C.L.A.L.Rev. 640 (1984); J. Barron and C. Dienes, Handbook of Free Speech and Free Press, ch. 7, "The New Public Law of Privacy," pp. 363–406 (1979); George Turbow, ed., Privacy Law and Practice (1987) (looseleaf updating); S. Halpern, The Law of Defamation, Privacy, Publicity and "Moral Rights": Cases and Materials on Protection of Personality Interests (1988).

in the public domain on official court records. Privacy interests must be protected by means which avoid public documentation or other disclosure of private information, concluded the Court, not by limiting the press.

The Supreme Court confined its holding to the narrow facts of the case—information in court records lawfully available to the public which was accurately republished. Explicitly left unresolved was the constitutional question of a state policy which denies access to the public and press of certain kinds of official records which are not public information and normally cannot be lawfully obtained by the press, such as juvenile court proceedings.[2]

The Court in *Cox Broadcasting* also reserved the question of whether truth must be recognized as a defense in a defamation action brought by a truly private person (as distinguished from a public official or public figure) and noted that *Time, Inc. v. Hill*,[3] had reserved the question of whether truthful publication of private matters could ever be constitutionally proscribed.

However, in light of later constitutional cases, and given the general rationale articulated by the Supreme Court over the years, the state should always recognize that truth is a defense in a defamation or right of privacy action—unless the plaintiff publishes confidential information that he has stolen. And even in such cases, the right of action is not really based on defamation but on publishing and attempting to benefit from knowingly stolen materials.

Thus, in *Landmark Communications, Inc. v. Virginia*,[4] the Supreme Court answered one of the questions reserved in *Cox Broadcasting Corp.* when it held that the first amendment prohibits the criminal punishment of persons who are not participants to a judicial disciplinary inquiry, including newspapers, from divulging or publishing truthful information regarding confidential proceedings of the judicial inquiry board. The Court found it unnecessary to hold broadly that truthful reporting about public officials in connection with their official duties is always insulated from criminal punishment by the first amendment, nor did the Court consider any special right of access to the press or the applicability of the state confidentiality statutes to one who secures the information by illegal means and thereafter divulges it.[5]

2. 420 U.S. at 496 n. 26, 95 S.Ct. at 1047 n. 26. See Oklahoma Publishing Co. v. District Court, 430 U.S. 308, 97 S.Ct. 1045, 51 L.Ed.2d 355 (1977) (per curiam).

3. 385 U.S. 374, 87 S.Ct. 534, 17 L.Ed.2d 456 (1967). See 420 U.S. at 490–91, 95 S.Ct. at 1043–44. Justice Powell, concurring in Cox, thought that Gertz v. Robert Welch, Inc., 418 U.S. 323, 94 S.Ct. 2997, 41 L.Ed.2d 789 (1974), appeal after remand 680 F.2d 527 (7th Cir.1982), certiorari de-

nied 459 U.S. 1226, 103 S.Ct. 1233, 75 L.Ed.2d 467 (1983) "largely resolves this issue" and makes truth a complete defense. 420 U.S. at 498, 95 S.Ct. at 1047.

4. 435 U.S. 829, 98 S.Ct. 1535, 56 L.Ed.2d 1 (1978).

5. 435 U.S. at 837–38, 98 S.Ct. at 1540–41. See also Smith v. Daily Mail Publishing Co., 443 U.S. 97, 99 S.Ct. 2667, 61 L.Ed.2d 399 (1979) (state may not punish a newspaper's truthful publication of an alleged juvenile delinquent's name lawfully obtained by a newspaper).

Publication of the Names of Rape Victims. In Florida Star v. B.J.F., 491 U.S. 524, 109 S.Ct. 2603, 105 L.Ed.2d 443 (1989), Marshall, J., for the Court, held that, in light of the First Amendment, a Florida statute (§ 794.03) could not make a newspaper civilly liable for publishing the name of a rape victim, a name that the newspaper had obtained from a publicly released police report. The Florida Star violated its own internal policy of not publishing the names of sexual offense victims. The victim then sued the newspaper for negligently violating the statute, and was awarded $75,000 in compensatory damages and $25,000 in punitive damages.

The Court distinguished *Cox Broadcasting* as a case where the name of the rape victim "was obtained from courthouse records open to public inspection;" the press, emphasized the Court, plays "an important role" in "subjecting trials to public scrutiny" and in reporting accurately "*judicial* proceedings." However, the Court still reversed, stating: "Applied to the instant case, the [*Smith v.*] *Daily Mail* principle [443 U.S. 97, 99 S.Ct. 2667, 61 L.Ed.2d 399 (1979)] clearly commands reversal." The Court, however, did not "accept appellant's invitation to hold broadly that truthful publication may never be punished consistent with the First Amendment. Our cases have carefully eschewed reaching this ultimate question, mindful that the future may bring scenarios which prudence counsels our not resolving anticipatorily." The Court concluded that it was only holding that "where a newspaper publishes truthful information which it has lawfully obtained, punishment may lawfully be imposed, if at all, only when narrowly tailored to a state interest of the highest order, and that no such interest is satisfactorily served by imposing liability under § 794.03 to appellant under the facts of this case."

Scalia, J., concurring in part and concurring in the judgement, noted the inconsistencies in the law:

"In the present case, I would anticipate that the rape victim's discomfort at the dissemination of news of her misfortune among friends and acquaintances would be at least as great as her discomfort at its publication by the media to people to whom she is only a name. Yet the law in question does not prohibit the former in either in oral or written form. Nor is

it at all clear, as I think it must be to validate this statute, that Florida's general privacy law would prohibit such gossip. Nor, finally, is it credible that the interest meant to be served by the statute is the protection of the victim against a rapist still at large—an interest that arguably would extend only to mass publication. There would be little reason to limit a statute with that objective to rape alone; or to extend it to all rapes, whether or not the felon has been apprehended and confined. In any case, the instructions here did not require the jury to find that the rapist was at large.

"*This law has every appearance of a prohibition that society is prepared to impose upon the press but not upon itself.* Such a prohibition does not protect an interest 'of the highest order.'"

491 U.S. at 540–44, 109 S.Ct. at 2613–14 (Scalia, J., concurring in part and concurring in the judgment) (emphasis added). In other words, the institutional press, under the first amendment, has no more rights than any ordinary individual exercising freedom of speech. But the institutional press also has *no fewer rights* than those enjoyed by ordinary persons. The Florida law really discriminated against the institutional press by placing on the press a burden that society was quite unwilling to place on itself.

White, J., joined by Rehnquist, C.J. and O'Connor, J., filed a dissenting opinion:

"[T]he violation [B.J.F.] suffered at a rapist's knifepoint marked only the beginning of her ordeal. A week later, while her assailant was still at large, an account of this assault—identifying by name B.J.F. as the victim—was published by The Florida Star. As a result, B.J.F. received harassing phone calls, required mental health counseling, was forced to move from her home, and was even threatened with being raped again. Yet today, the Court holds that a jury award of $75,000 to compensate B.J.F. for the harm she suffered due to the Star's negligence is at odds with the First Amendment. I do not accept this result."

491 U.S. at 542, 109 S.Ct. at 2614 (White, J., dissenting, joined by Rehnquist, C.J. & O'Connor, J.).

The attempt of the Florida legislature to impose a gag rule on the publication of the names of rape victims by newspapers is an attempt not unique to Florida. However,

The Right of Publicity. In *Zacchini v. Scripps–Howard Broadcasting Co.*[6] the Court upheld, in a five to four decision, the power of the state to allow a damage action brought by a performer against the operator of a television broadcasting station when it telecast a videotape of the plaintiff's entire 15 second act. The majority stressed that it was the entire act that was telecast. Plaintiff was a "human cannonball" who was shot from a cannon into a net at a county fairgrounds. The videotaping was done after Zacchini had asked the freelance reporter not to do it.

Relying on Dean Prosser, the majority divided privacy into four branches. (1) *Time, Inc. v. Hill* was a "false-light" privacy case; there also are cases; (2) involving an "appropriation" of a name or likeness for the purposes of trade; or (3) publicizing "private details" about a nonnewsworthy person or event; or (4) involving a performer, a person with a name having commercial value with a claim to a "right of publicity."[7]

The plaintiff, Zacchini, fell into the fourth category of a person with a right to publicity, and the majority found that the unauthorized telecast of his entire performance (even though accompanied by favorable commentary) injured his propriety interest. Without violating free speech guarantees, the state need not, but may, protect this interest, which the Court found analogous to the goals of the copyright and patent laws.

this effort to keep private the names of rape victims is coming under increasing attack. The editor of the *Des Moines Register,* Ms. Geneva Overholser, published an essay in that paper (on July 11, 1989) arguing that newspapers (including her own) should reconsider this policy because it harmed women who had been raped. The "sour blight of prejudice is best subjected to strong sunlight." When papers refuse to publish the names of rape victims, but routinely print the names of burglary victims, robbery victims, attempted murder victims, etc., the newspapers attach a stigma to rape victims that will not go away until names are routinely published. Failure to publish the names suggests that the rape victim was somehow to blame for the crime done to her: "I urge women who have suffered this awful crime and attendant injustice to speak out.... As long as rape is deemed unspeakable—and is therefore not fully and honestly spoken of—the public outrage will be muted as well."

In response to Ms. Overholser's essay, an Iowa rape victim discussed her story in a five-part newspaper series that led to many letters to the editor from women and men applauding the decision to go public, so that the rape victim will lose the stigma that somehow she did something wrong and, somehow, must be shunned because she was raped. Gartner, The Scarlet Letter of Rape: A Courageous Victim Fights Back, Wall St. Jrl., Mar. 15, 1990, at p. A15, cols. 3–6 (midwest ed.).

See, Rotunda, Eschewing Bright Lines, 25 TRIAL Magazine 52, 54–55 (Dec. 1989) (discussing *Florida Star v. B.J.F.*).

6. 433 U.S. 562, 97 S.Ct. 2849, 53 L.Ed.2d 965 (1977), on remand 56 Ohio St.2d 286, 376 N.E.2d 582 (1978).

See generally, Samuelson, Reviving *Zacchini:* Analyzing First Amendment Defenses in Right of Publicity and Copyright Cases, 57 Tulane L.Rev. 836 (1983).

7. 433 U.S. at 571–72 & nn. 7 & 8, 97 S.Ct. at 2855–56 & nn. 7 & 8.

Cf. Nimmer, Does Copyright Abridge the First Amendment Guarantees of Free Speech and Press?, 17 U.C.L.A.L.Rev. 1180 (1970); cf. also, Maggs, New Directions in US–USSR Copyright Relations, 68 Am.J. Internat'l L. 391 (1974). See Gordon, Right of Property in Name, Likeness, Personality and History, 55 Nw.U.L.Rev. 553 (1960) for an analysis of the early cases.

It is unclear, given the majority's emphasis on the telecast of the "entire" performance, whether *Zacchini* has any application to cases where the videotaping is less than the entire act. Even in Zacchini's case, Justice Powell's dissent noted that the plaintiff, Zacchini, might not be able to bring himself within the Court's holding because it is unlikely that the "entire" act took only 15 seconds. It was likely to have been accompanied by some fanfare.[8]

Also unclear is the measure of damages in the case. The majority said that Zacchini had to prove his damages, which apparently could be eliminated if the "respondent's newsbroadcast increased the value of petitioner's performance by stimulating the public's interest in seeing the act live."[9]

Free Speech and Copyright Laws

There is an inevitable tension between copyright protection and free speech. One cannot consider in detail and resolve all of this tension, for that would require a careful consideration of the entire statutory law of copyright.[10] Yet the subject demands discussion, even if only broad principles can be outlined.

To some extent, of course, copyright protects free speech, because it protects the value in speech created by authors. Copyright law adds a stick to that bundle of rights we call "property." Copyright law protects "the creations of authors from exploitation by others...."[11] Yet, as the Court has also recognized, to suppress particular words runs "a substantial risk of suppressing ideas in the process."[12] As Justice

---

8. 433 U.S. at 579 n. 1, 97 S.Ct. at 2859 n. 1 (Powell, J., dissenting, joined by Brennan & Marshall, JJ.).

9. 433 U.S. at 575 n. 12, 97 S.Ct. at 2857 n. 12.

See generally, Shipley, Publicity Never Dies; It Just Fades Away: The Right of Publicity and Federal Preemption, 66 Cornell L.Rev. 673 (1981).

10. See generally, e.g., Section 3.8, of this Treatise, supra; Nimmer, Does Copyright Abridge the First Amendment Guarantees of Free Speech and Press?, 17 U.C.L.A.L.Rev. 1180 (1970); Breyer, The Uneasy Case for Copyright in Books, Photocopies, and Computer Programs, 84 Harv.L.Rev. 281 (1970); Comment, Copyright and the First Amendment: Where Lies the Public Interest?, 59 Tulane L.Rev. 135 (1984); M. Nimmer, Nimmer on Freedom of Speech § 2.05[c][2] (1984).

11. Dallas Cowboys Cheerleaders, Inc. v. Scoreboard Posters, Inc., 600 F.2d 1184, 1187 (5th Cir.1979).

See also, Hemingway's Estate v. Random House, Inc., 23 N.Y.2d 341, 348, 296 N.Y.S.2d 771, 778, 244 N.E.2d 250, 255 (1968) (purpose of copyright is to protect "intellectual labor," copyright protects the author's right not to speak); Schnapper v. Foley, 667 F.2d 102, 114 (D.C.Cir.1981) (the first amendment interests are based on "the author's freedom to speak or remain silent as an end in itself."), cert. denied 455 U.S. 948, 102 S.Ct. 1448, 71 L.Ed.2d 661 (1982).

12. Cohen v. California, 403 U.S. 15, 26, 91 S.Ct. 1780, 1788, 29 L.Ed.2d 284 (1971) (state cannot punish person for wearing a jacket with the words "Fuck the Draft" written on it), rehearing denied 404 U.S. 876, 92 S.Ct. 26, 30 L.Ed.2d 124 (1971).

Some words have acquired meanings and "a life and force of their own. They cannot be replaced with definitions...." J.B. White, When Words Lose Their Meaning 11 (1984). See also, R. Rotunda, The Politics of Language: Liberalism as Word and Symbol (1986) (certain words "reflect and mold the way we think and act.").

Douglas noted: "Serious First Amendment questions would be raised if Congress' power over copyrights were construed to include the power to grant monopolies over certain ideas." [13]   Copyright law thus only protects the form of expression, not the facts or ideas expressed.[14]   Nonetheless, still tensions remain between free speech and copyright protection. The line is not as bright as we might wish.   In one case, for example, a court held photographs of the assassination of President John Kennedy did not have full copyright protection because of the "public interest in having the fullest information available...." [15]

The Supreme Court turned its attention to these problems in *Harper & Row Publishers, Inc. v. Nation Enterprises.*[16]   The Court held that *The Nation* Magazine violated the copyright laws when it published, without permission, extensive quotations from a purloined copy of former President Ford's then unpublished memoirs, "A Time to Heal." *The Nation* excerpt focused on Ford's pardon of former President Nixon.

The article in *The Nation* was "composed of quotes, paraphrases and facts drawn exclusively from the manuscript."   The verbatim quotes of Ford's original language totaled between 300 and 400 words, and constituted about 13% of *The Nation* article.   *The Nation* piece was designed to scoop an article based on Ford's memoirs which *Time* Magazine had earlier contracted to publish.   Because of *The Nation's* publication, *Time* cancelled its plans to publish its own article.

The Court held that *The Nation's* "generous verbatim excerpts" were, under the circumstances, a copyright infringement which was not sanctioned as a "fair use" under the Copyright Act.   *The Nation* Magazine's "*intended purpose*" was to interfere with the copyright holder's valuable right of first publication.[17]   The Court then rejected the argument that the first amendment required a different standard simply because the information conveyed is of high public concern:

> [C]opyright assures those who write and publish factual narratives such as "A Time to Heal" that they may at least enjoy the right to market the original expression contained therein as just compensation for their investment....   "[T]o propose that fair use be imposed whenever the 'social value [of dissemination] ... outweighs

13. Lee v. Runge, 404 S.Ct. 887, 892, 92 S.Ct. 197, 202, 30 L.Ed.2d 169 (1971) (Douglas, J., dissenting to denial of certiorari).

14. E.g., International News Service v. Associated Press, 248 U.S. 215, 234, 39 S.Ct. 68, 71, 63 L.Ed. 211 (1918); New York Times Co. v. United States, 403 U.S. 713, 726 n.*, 91 S.Ct. 2140, 2147 n.*, 29 L.Ed.2d 822 (1971) (Brennan, J., concurring).

15. Time, Inc. v. Bernard Geis Associates, 293 F.Supp. 130, 146 (S.D.N.Y.1968). Oddly enough, the court then relied on the copyright doctrine of "fair use" to allow the defendant to make and publish a copy of the "Zapruder film" of the Kennedy assassination.

16. 471 U.S. 539, 105 S.Ct. 2218, 85 L.Ed.2d 588 (1985).   Justice Brennan, joined by White and Marshall, JJ., dissented.

17. 471 U.S. at 562, 105 S.Ct. at 2232 (emphasis in original).

any detriment to the artist,' would be to propose depriving copyright owners of their right in the property precisely when they encounter those users who could afford to pay for it." ... In view of the First Amendment protections already embodied in the Copyright Act's distinction between copyrightable expression and uncopyrightable facts and ideas, and the latitude for scholarship and comment traditionally afforded by fair use, we see no warrant for expanding the doctrine of fair use to create what amounts to a public figure exception to copyright.[18]

In *San Francisco Arts & Athletics, Inc. v. United States Olympic Committee*,[19] a divided Court offered surprisingly broad protection for the United States Olympic Committee (USOC) and the International Olympic Committee in their use of the word "Olympics." Section 110 of the Amateur Sports Act of 1978 grants to the USOC the right to prohibit (without its consent), inter alia, any person from using the word "Olympic" for the "purpose of trade, to induce the sale of any goods or services, or to promote any theatrical exhibition, athletic performance, or competition." San Francisco Arts & Athletics, Inc. (SFAA), a nonprofit corporation, sought to promote the "Gay Olympic Games" in 1982 and every four years thereafter. The Gay Games were touted as opening with a ceremony "which will rival the traditional Olympic Games." Over 2000 relay runners starting from New York would carry the "Gay Olympic Torch" and light the "Gay Olympic Flame." The winners of the various contests would receive gold, silver, and bronze medals. The SFAA proposed to sell T-shirts, buttons and other items, all showing the title "Gay Olympic Games."

At the request of the USOC the district court enjoined the use of the word "Olympic" in the description of the planned games (which were then held under the name "Gay Games I," in 1982, and "Gay Games II" in 1986). The Supreme Court, in a divided opinion, affirmed.[20]

Justice Powell, for the Court, concluded that Congress intended to provide the USOC with protection broader than normal trademark protection in that the USOC has "exclusive control of the use of the

18. 471 U.S. at 556–60, 105 S.Ct. at 2229–30, citing Zacchini v. Scripps–Howard Broadcasting Co., 433 U.S. 562, 575, 97 S.Ct. 2849, 2857, 53 L.Ed.2d 965 (1977), on remand 54 Ohio St.2d 286, 376 N.E.2d 582 (1978).

19. 483 U.S. 522, 107 S.Ct. 2971, 97 L.Ed.2d 427 (1987).

20. Justice O'Connor, joined by Justice Blackmun, concurring in part and dissenting in part, agreed with the first amendment issue but would have found that the USOC was a state actor and remand for a

determination of discriminatory enforcement.

Justice Brennan, joined by Justice Marshall, dissenting, argued that there was state action and that § 110 violated the first amendment because it was overbroad, because it is susceptible to substantial amount of noncommercial speech, and because the law discriminates on the basis of content. Justice Brennan noted that there are over 200 organizations listed in just the Los Angeles and Manhattan telephone directories whose names start with the word "Olympic."

word 'Olympic' without regard to whether an unauthorized use of the word tends to cause confusion." In addition, an unauthorized user of "Olympic" would not have the normal statutory trademark defenses.[21] Nonetheless, the Court noted that given that the SFAA sought to sell T-shirts, bumper stickers, etc., all emblazoned with "Gay Olympic Games," the "possibility of confusion as to sponsorship is obvious." [22] The Court said that section 110 "extends to promotional uses of 'Olympic' even if the promotion is not used to induce the sale of goods." [23] The Court then added language which narrowed its holding: Under section 110, "the USOC may prohibit surely promotional uses of the word *only* when the promotion relates to an athletic or theatrical event. The USOC created the value of the word by using it in connection with an athletic event." [24]

The Court said that there was no need to decide whether Congress could ever grant a private entity exclusive use of a generic word, because the Court found that "Olympic" was not generic. Quoting *Zacchini*, the Court said that "Congress reasonably could conclude that the commercial and promotional value of the word 'Olympic' was the product of the USOC's 'own talents and energy, the end result of much time, effort, and expense.' " [25] The USOC and the International Olympic Committee "have used the word 'Olympic' at least since 1896, when the modern Olympic Games began." [26] Congress could reasonably conclude that the word has acquired a special "secondary meaning." [27] Thus, Congress could grant the USOC a "limited property right" in the word "Olympic." [28]

In addition, Congress acted reasonably when it did not require the USOC to prove that an unauthorized use of "Olympic" is likely to confuse the public. To the extent that the law applies to the use of "Olympic" for "the purpose of trade [or] to induce the sale of any goods or services," it applies only to commercial speech which receives less first amendment protection than political speech.[29] While Justice Brennan in dissent found the law overbroad, the majority responded that the application of the overbreadth doctrine to commercial speech is "highly questionable." The Congressional prohibition neither prevented the SFAA from holding its athletic event in its planned format, "[n]or is it clear that § 110 restricts purely expressive uses of the word 'Olympic'." [30] The Congressional restrictions on the use of "Olympic"

---

21. 483 U.S. at 530, 107 S.Ct. at 2978.

22. 483 U.S. at 539, 107 S.Ct. at 2982. The Court emphasized this point. See, e.g., 483 U.S. at 534 & n. 12, 107 S.Ct. at 2980 & n. 12.

23. 483 U.S. at 540, 107 S.Ct. at 2983.

24. 483 U.S. at 540, 107 S.Ct. at 2983 (emphasis added).

25. 483 U.S. at 532, 107 S.Ct. at 2979.

26. 483 U.S. at 532, 107 S.Ct. at 2979.

27. 483 U.S. at 534, 107 S.Ct. at 2980.

28. 483 U.S. at 534, 107 S.Ct. at 2980.

29. 483 U.S. at 534, 107 S.Ct. at 2980.

30. See 483 U.S. at 535 & n. 15, 107 S.Ct. at 2981 & n. 15. At this point the Court cited with approval a lower court decision, Stop the Olympic Prison v. United States Olympic Committee, 489 F.Supp.

are incidental to the primary Congressional purpose of encouraging and rewarding the USOC's activities.[31]

Finally the Court rejected the argument that the USOC enforced its right to the word "Olympic" in a discriminatory manner, in violation of the Fifth Amendment. The USOC is a private corporation with a federal corporate charter, but that federal charter does not make the USOC's actions state action, for all corporations have a government (usually state government) charter. The Government granted the USOC the exclusive use of "Olympic," but all trademarks are created by Government act or law. Congress has given the USOC some funding (though much of its funding is private), but such funding does not necessarily create state action.[32] And nothing in the corporate charter gives the Federal Government any right to control the USOC or its officers.

Commercial Performances and Defamation. The Supreme Court has not yet held that first amendment principles should restrict defamation or privacy actions when the subject matter of the action is a commercial performance or commercial information. Invasion of an individual's right of publicity for commercial purposes may be subjected to greater state regulation than publication of information regarding a person's private life or activity when that publication is unrelated to a commercial venture.[33]

False Light Privacy Cases. In *Cantrell v. Forest City Publishing Co.*[34] the Court upheld a jury verdict for compensatory damages in a "false light" privacy case brought by a mother and son against a

---

1112, 1118–21 (S.D.N.Y.1980), which upheld the use of the Olympic logo of five interacting rings and the Olympic torch on a poster opposing the planned conversion of the Olympic Village at Lake Placid: the lower court "found that the use of the symbols did not fit the commercial or promotional definition of uses in § 110." 483 U.S. at 537 n. 14, 107 S.Ct. at 2981 n. 14.

31. 483 U.S. at 535, 107 S.Ct. at 2981 (footnote omitted).

32. 483 U.S. at 543–47, 107 S.Ct. at 2984–86.

33. In Bose Corp. v. Consumers Union of United States, Inc., 466 U.S. 485, 104 S.Ct. 1949, 80 L.Ed.2d 502 (1984), rehearing denied 467 U.S. 1267, 104 S.Ct. 3561, 82 L.Ed.2d 863 (1984), the Supreme Court ruled that appellate courts must independently review findings of actual "malice" in defamation cases. The subject matter of this case was a claim for "product disparagement" by the manufacturer of a product which had been falsely described in a derogatory manner by a magazine review-

ing the product. The lower courts had believed that the *New York Times v. Sullivan* standards should apply in this case because the producer of the product was the equivalent of a public figure. The Supreme Court accepted for the purpose of this case the lower court's assumption that the *New York Times* standard should be applied in this situation but noted that it was not ruling on that issue. 466 U.S. at 512–15, 104 S.Ct. at 1966–67, 80 L.Ed.2d at 525.

34. 419 U.S. 245, 95 S.Ct. 465, 42 L.Ed.2d 419 (1974).

See generally, Restatement (Second) of Torts, § 652E (A.L.I.1976); Prosser, Privacy, 48 Calif.L.Rev. 383, 422 (1960); Wade, Defamation and the Right of Privacy, 15 Vand.L.Rev. 1093 (1962); Wade, The Communicative Torts and the First Amendment, 48 Miss.L.J. 671 (1977); Hill, Defamation and Privacy Under the First Amendment, 76 Colum.L.Rev. 1205 (1976); Note, Right to Privacy—Availability of Injunctive Relief for Invasions of Privacy, 39 Mo.L.Rev. 647 (1974).

newspaper publisher and reporter. The article discussed the impact on the family of the death of the father in a bridge collapse. The story contained several inaccuracies regarding the description of the poverty in which the plaintiffs were living and the dilapidated conditions of their home. The plaintiffs' cause of action was based on the argument that the defendants, by publishing the false feature story, made the plaintiffs the object of pity and ridicule, causing them to suffer outrage, mental distress, shame and humiliation.

In this diversity case the *Cantrell* Court implicitly acknowledged that a false light privacy case, where the publication is inaccurate *and* causes mental anguish and humiliation, is constitutional.[35]

Regarding the question of the burden of proof, the *Cantrell* Court carefully left this issue open. The trial court had instructed the jury that liability could be imposed only if the false statements were made with *New York Times* scienter.[36] The Court reversed the appellate court and affirmed the trial verdict, but made clear that it was not ruling that as a constitutional matter the plaintiff in a false light privacy case must prove *New York Times* scienter. No party had made any objection to the jury instruction and the issue was not before the Supreme Court.[37] Thus the Court left open the question of whether a more relaxed standard should apply.

Several years before, in *Time, Inc. v. Hill*,[38] discussed earlier,[39] the Court had held that the plaintiff must prove *New York Times* scienter given the facts of that case. However, subsequent Supreme Court cases indicate that *Time, Inc. v. Hill* should no longer govern the burden of proof standard for false light privacy torts which cause the plaintiff to suffer mental anguish and humiliation. The *Gertz*[40] standard should apply in such cases where the plaintiff is a private person.

Thus in *Wood v. Hustler Magazine, Inc.*[41] the fifth circuit applied the *Gertz* standard when the plaintiff sued Hustler Magazine because it published a stolen photograph depicting her in the nude. Plaintiff was awarded actual damages of $150,000 for negligence because Hustler Magazine had placed her in an offensive false light. The photographs were submitted by the thief with a forged consent form. This form also included false information regarding plaintiff's sexual fantasies. Hus-

---

35. Cf. 419 U.S. at 248–50, 95 S.Ct. at 468–69.

36. 419 U.S. at 250, 95 S.Ct. at 469.

37. 419 U.S. at 249–50 & n. 3, 95 S.Ct. at 469 & n. 3.

38. 385 U.S. 374, 87 S.Ct. 534, 17 L.Ed.2d 456 (1967).

39. See § 20.35(a).

40. Gertz v. Robert Welch, Inc., 418 U.S. 323, 94 S.Ct. 2997, 41 L.Ed.2d 789 (1974), appeal after remand 680 F.2d 527 (7th Cir.1982), certiorari denied 459 U.S. 1226, 103 S.Ct. 1233, 75 L.Ed.2d 467 (1983).

See § 20.35(b).

41. 736 F.2d 1084, 1092 (5th Cir.1984) (Reavley, J., for a unanimous court) (citing Treatise), rehearing denied 744 F.2d 94 (1984), certiorari denied 469 U.S. 1107, 105 S.Ct. 783, 83 L.Ed.2d 777 (1985).

tler Magazine had been negligent in determining the authenticity of the consent form.

XI. FIGHTING WORDS AND HOSTILE AUDIENCES

§ 20.37 Introduction

Government regulation of speech has been allowed when the purpose of the statute was to proscribe "fighting words." While the definition of this phrase is best left to case analysis below, it is helpful in understanding the underlying rationale to reconsider the dichotomy between action and speech traditionally illustrated by the hypothetical situation of the individual shouting "fire" in a crowded theater.

In an absolutist sense, convictions for fighting words are a regulation of speech. Yet it is the better analysis to regard fighting words as within the ambit of action rather than speech because there is no intellectual content to be conveyed to the listener, but merely a provocative, emotional message intended and likely to incite an *immediate*, violent response. Thus, the state's interest in order overshadows the minimal protection to be afforded the "slight social value as a step to truth"[1] of the speech. The theory of the regulation of "fighting words" is not contrary to the theory of the free marketplace of ideas because

§ 20.37

1. Chaplinsky v. New Hampshire, 315 U.S. 568, 572, 62 S.Ct. 766, 769, 86 L.Ed. 1031 (1942).

See, Doe v. University of Michigan, 721 F.Supp. 852 (E.D.Mich.1989), which used the first amendment to strike down the University of Michigan's regulations against hate and offensive speech.

Hate Speech and Group Libel. Riesman, Democracy and Defamation: Control of Group Libel, 42 Colum.L.Rev. 727 (1942); J. Barron & C.T. Dienes, Handbook of Free Speech and Free Press 63–93 (1979); Gard, Fighting Words as Free Speech, 58 Wash. U.L.Q. 531 (1980); Delgado, Words that Wound: A Tort Action for Racial Insults, Epithets, and Name–Calling, 17 Harv.Civ. Rts.–Civ.Lib.L.Rev. 133 (1982); Wright, Racist Speech and the First Amendment, 9 Miss. College L.Rev. 1 (1988); Matsuda, Public Response to Racist Speech: Considering the Victim's Story, 87 Mich.L.Rev. 2320 (1989); Lawrence, If He Hollers Let Him Go: Regulating Racist Speech on Campus, 1990 Duke L.J. 431 (1990); Bartlett & O'Barr, The Chilly Climate on College Campuses: An Expansion of the "Hate Speech" Debate, 1990 Duke L.J. 574 (1990); Strossen, Regulating Racist Speech on Campus: A Modest Proposal?, 1990 Duke L.J. 484 (1990); Note, Closing the Campus Gates to Free Expression: The Regulation of Offensive Speech at Colleges and Universities, 39 Emory L.J. 1351 (1990); Love, Discriminatory Speech and the Tort of Intentional Infliction of Emotional Distress, 47 Wash. & Lee L.Rev. 123 (1990); Smolla, Rethinking First Amendment Assumptions about Racist and Sexist Speech, 47 Wash. & Lee L.Rev. 171 (1990); Delgado, Campus Antiracism Rules: Constitutional Narratives in Collision, 85 Nw. U.L.Rev. 343 (1991); Linzer, White Liberal Looks at Racist Speech, 65 St. John's L.Rev. 187 (1991); Post, Racist Speech, Democracy, and the First Amendment, 32 Wm. & Mary L.Rev. 267 (1991); Paust, Rereading the First Amendment in Light of Treaties Proscribing Incitement to Racial Discrimination or Hostility, 43 Rutgers L.Rev. 565 (1991); Wolfson, Free Speech and Hateful Words, 60 U.Cinn.L.Rev. 1 (1991); Sedler, Doe v. University of Michigan and Campus Bans on "Racist Speech": the View from Within, 37 Wayne L.Rev. 1325 (1991).

this speech triggers an automatic, unthinking reaction, rather than a consideration of an idea.

§ 20.38   The Doctrine Emerges

In 1942, the United States Supreme Court in *Chaplinsky v. New Hampshire*[1] unanimously upheld a statute which had previously been construed by the state court to ban "face-to-face words plainly likely to cause a breach of the peace by the addressee."[2] Chaplinsky's conviction was based on his encounter with the City Marshal of Rochester whom he described as a "God damned racketeer and a damned fascist"[3] as a policeman was leading Chaplinsky away from a public sidewalk because of fear that his distribution of religious literature was causing a public disturbance. It is important to remember that Chaplinsky was not convicted for his distribution of religious literature or because of the policeman's fear of a public disturbance, but for his denunciations made directly to the fire marshal.

The Court argued that Chaplinsky's epithet was without communicative value, since "[a]rgument is unnecessary to demonstrate that the appellations ... are epithets likely to provoke the average person to retaliation, and thereby cause a breach of the peace."[4] Justice Murphy stated in dictum that " 'fighting' words—those which by their very utterance inflict injury or *tend to incite* an *immediate* breach of the peace"—are not constitutionally protected because their "slight social value as a step to truth ... is clearly outweighed by the social interest in order and morality."[5]

The Court indicated that breach of the peace convictions can be upheld when there is merely a danger the listener will be incited to violence. There was no need to prove actual violence between the fire marshal and Chaplinsky. Neither was it error for the state court to refuse "to admit evidence of provocation and evidence bearing on the truth or falsity of the utterances...."[6] The rationale of the Court, as noted above, was that in the balance, the state's interest outweighed the slight value of communication demonstrated by the appellant's remark.

Chaplinsky may be read to stand for the broad proposition that breach of the peace convictions can be upheld when there is merely a danger the listener will be *incited* to violence, for the Court in that case

§ 20.38

1. 315 U.S. 568, 62 S.Ct. 766, 86 L.Ed. 1031 (1942).

See generally, Harry Kalven, Jr., ed. by Jamie Kalven, A Worthy Tradition: Freedom of Speech in America 77–118 (1988).

2. 315 U.S. at 573, 62 S.Ct. at 770. The state statute forbade a person to address "any offensive, derisive or annoying word

to any other person who is lawfully in any street or other public place." 315 U.S. at 569, 62 S.Ct. at 768.

3. 315 U.S. at 569, 62 S.Ct. at 768.

4. 315 U.S. at 574, 62 S.Ct. at 770.

5. 315 U.S. at 572, 62 S.Ct. at 769 (footnotes omitted) (emphasis added).

6. 315 U.S. at 574, 62 S.Ct. at 770.

was presuming fighting words would produce an "uncontrollable impulse" to violence and thus their harm easily outweighed their social value.[7] The test outlined in *Chaplinsky* was whether or not men of common intelligence would understand the words as likely to cause the average addressee to fight, "words and expressions which by general consent are 'fighting words' when said without a disarming smile...."[8] There was no consideration as to whether fire marshals or policemen could be (or should be) expected to resist epithets which would produce violent responses in the average citizen who has not been trained to prevent breaches of the peace.[9]

§ 20.39 Subsequent Modifications

Decisions following *Chaplinsky* reflect the Court's desire to limit the broad implications of the doctrine outlined there and the recognition of the potential social value in statements that might come under the initial definition of "fighting words."

In *Terminiello v. Chicago*,[1] the Supreme Court overturned a municipal ordinance prohibiting breaches of the peace. The trial court's instruction to the jury construed the statute as prohibiting conduct which "stirs the public to anger, invites dispute, brings about a condition of unrest or creates a disturbance."[2] Terminiello's address was a denunciation of Jews and blacks. Outside of the auditorium where he spoke, a "howling" crowd gathered in protest and he denounced them as well.

The majority opinion of Justice Douglas analyzed the purpose of free speech and found it contradictory to the jury instruction

> [A] function of free speech ... is to invite dispute. It may indeed best serve its high purpose when it induces a condition of unrest, creates dissatisfaction with conditions as they are, or even stirs people to anger. Speech is often provocative and challenging. It may strike at prejudices and preconceptions and have profound unsettling effects as it presses for acceptance of an idea ... the alternative would lead to standardization of ideas either by legislatures, courts, or dominant political or community groups.[3]

---

7. Rutzick, Offensive Language and the Evolution of First Amendment Protection, 9 Harv.Civ.Rts.–Civ.Lib.L.Rev. 1, 8 n. 36 (1974).

8. 315 U.S. at 573, 62 S.Ct. at 770. See also 315 U.S. at 572, 62 S.Ct. at 769.

9. Rutzick, Offensive Language and the Evolution of First Amendment Protection, 9 Harv.Civ.Rts.–Civ.Lib.L.Rev. 1, 10.

§ 20.39

1. 337 U.S. 1, 69 S.Ct. 894, 93 L.Ed. 1131 (1949), rehearing denied 337 U.S. 934, 69 S.Ct. 1490, 93 L.Ed. 1740 (1949).

2. 337 U.S. at 3, 69 S.Ct. at 895. Four justices dissented on the grounds that the instructions issue was not properly preserved for review.

3. Terminiello v. Chicago, 337 U.S. 1, 4, 69 S.Ct. 894, 896, 93 L.Ed. 1131 (1949), rehearing denied 337 U.S. 934, 69 S.Ct. 1490, 93 L.Ed. 1740 (1949).

The Court's invalidation of the statute as vague and overbroad allowed it to avoid the more difficult question of whether the speech was protected under the First Amendment. The strong language of the majority opinion does, however, indicate a retreat from the *Chaplinsky* "uncontrollable impulse" test by recognizing that a certain amount of provocative and challenging speech is protected.[4]

Two years after *Terminiello,* in *Feiner v. New York,*[5] the Court upheld the conviction of petitioner under a state disorderly conduct statute. *Feiner* directly raised the question of the hostile audience. Feiner's address included descriptions of President Truman as a "bum", the mayor of Syracuse as a "champagne sipping bum", the American Legion as a "Nazi Gestapo" and the need for blacks to "rise up in arms and fight for equal rights."[6] The speaker's racial statements " 'stirred up a little excitement.' Some of the onlookers made remarks to the police about their inability to handle the crowd and at least one threatened violence if the police did not act. There were others who appeared to be favoring petitioner's arguments."[7] The police asked Feiner to stop, but he refused. After their request, the officer arrested Feiner, who had been speaking for over a half hour.[8]

The majority opinion of Chief Justice Vinson stressed that the arrest was not an attempt to censor the content of the speech, but an effort to protect the peace before the threatened violent reaction took place.

> It is one thing to say that the police cannot be used as an instrument for the suppression of unpopular views, and another to say that, when as here the speaker passes the bounds of argument or persuasion and undertakes incitement to riot, they are powerless to prevent a breach of the peace.[9]

Feiner's claim differed from Terminiello's in that he did not assert that the statute was unconstitutionally broad or vague, but that the police had abused their discretion and were motivated by a desire to suppress the content of his speech, an assertion which the majority found unsupported by evidence.

In *Feiner,* Justices Douglas and Black dissented vigorously, arguing that the minimal threat of violence was insufficient to justify this suppression. Moreover, both Douglas and Black emphasized that the first duty of the police is to protect the speaker's rights by dissuading those threatening violence, an attempt not evidenced in this case. By

4. Rutzick, Offensive Language and the Evolution of First Amendment Protection, 9 Harv.Civ.Rts.–Civ.Lib.L.Rev. 1, 12–13; Kaufman, The Medium, The Message, and the First Amendment, 45 N.Y.U.L.Rev. 761, 767 (1970).

5. 340 U.S. 315, 71 S.Ct. 303, 95 L.Ed. 295 (1951).

6. 340 U.S. at 330, 71 S.Ct. at 311–12 (Douglas, J., dissenting).

7. 340 U.S. at 317, 71 S.Ct. at 305.

8. 340 U.S. at 318, 71 S.Ct. at 305.

9. 340 U.S. at 321, 71 S.Ct. at 306.

immediately acquiescing in the face of a single threat by one individual, the police had acted merely as conduits for the desires of suppression and denied the provocation value attributed to speech in *Terminiello*,[10] regardless of the impetus which motivated the policemen. Thus, the dissent raised the ultimate question in "fighting words" cases: whose rights are pre-eminent in a *Feiner* situation, the audience voluntarily listening, or the speaker? [11]

The authority of *Feiner* has been undercut significantly in subsequent cases where the Court applied the language of *Terminiello* and distinguished *Feiner* on the factual situation, although at times it may appear to be a distinction without a difference. *Edwards v. South Carolina*,[12] for example, involved a civil rights demonstration on the grounds of the state legislature. Although the state officials and lower courts found that the crowd observing the demonstration was growing increasingly restive, and the demonstrators refused to leave when requested, the Court (in 1963) refused to consider the conduct of the demonstrators—the singing of religious and patriotic hymns and a "religious harangue" urging them to go to segregated lunch counters— to constitute "fighting words." Neither did the "hostile audience" doctrine apply.

Although the situation in *Edwards* might have been potentially more dangerous than that of *Feiner* (a 1951 "hostile audience" case) the Court was appreciative of the ability of an expansive *Feiner* doctrine to serve effectively as a vehicle for the suppression of civil rights demonstrations by persons falsely claiming that their emotions were uncontrollably aroused. The discretion to halt the demonstration of those "sufficiently opposed to the views of the majority" [13] was lodged in individuals while the Courts had no effective measure to determine whether the motivation was to preserve peace or suppress content of the speech. As a factual matter the Court found the situation in *Edwards* a "far cry" from the hostile audience problem in *Feiner*.[14] Recall that the Court had found that Mr. Feiner was seeking to incite a riot.

It is important to distinguish the *Terminiello, Feiner,* and *Edwards* cases from that of *Chaplinsky*. The latter case involved *face-to-face* confrontation where insults were delivered which were likely to provoke violence by the listeners. The harangues delivered in the former

10. 340 U.S. at 326–27, 71 S.Ct. at 309–10 (Black, J., dissenting) and 340 U.S. at 331, 71 S.Ct. at 312 (Douglas, J., dissenting).

11. The better view is that hecklers would be arrested rather than speakers when the former arrived with preconceived intent to commit violence. Sellers v. Johnson, 163 F.2d 877 (8th Cir.1947), certiorari

denied 332 U.S. 851, 68 S.Ct. 356, 92 L.Ed. 421 (1948).

12. 372 U.S. 229, 83 S.Ct. 680, 9 L.Ed.2d 697 (1963); see also Cox v. Louisiana, 379 U.S. 536, 85 S.Ct. 453, 13 L.Ed.2d 471 (1965).

13. 372 U.S. at 237, 83 S.Ct. at 684.

14. 372 U.S. at 236, 83 S.Ct. at 684.

cases were not anger which focused on the audience—"fighting words" directed at particular members of the audience—nor was the audience even compelled to listen. While such speech may have offended the listeners' sensibilities, the Court has generally emphasized that regulation of speech needs more compelling justification in this context to avoid the censorship of ideas which are unpopular.

Cohen v. California,[15] decided in 1971, provides important support for this distinction and leaves the authority of *Feiner* in a very questionable state. *Cohen* was appealing his conviction for breach of the peace based on his presence in a Los Angeles courthouse wearing a jacket bearing the clearly printed words "Fuck the Draft."

The Court recognized that, in the nature of things, people in public places must be subject to some objectionable speech, and the Court stated that they could simply avert their eyes. The Court, in the majority opinion of Justice Harlan, stated that—

> [T]he ability of government, consonant with the Constitution, to shut off discourse solely to protect others from hearing it is . . . dependent upon a showing that substantial privacy interests are being invaded in an essentially intolerable manner.[16]

The fact that an offensive expletive was utilized does not detract from the protection afforded the speech, because, in Justice Harlan's phrase, "one man's vulgarity is another's lyric."[17] Moreover, the offensive words were not "a direct personal insult" specifically directed at the hearer; neither was the state exercising its police power (as in *Feiner*) "to prevent a speaker from intentionally provoking a given group to a hostile reaction."[18] There was no in-person, face-to-face verbal assault directed to a particular individual.

It remains to be considered whether, after the *Cohen* limitations, *Chaplinsky* remains a viable precedent allowing the States to proscribe these words "likely to provoke the average person to retaliation." *Cohen* favored a more critical examination of the audience, the results of the speech, the length of the speech, the actual results of the speech, and the wording of the statute:

> [W]e do not think the fact that some unwilling "listeners" in a public building may have been briefly exposed to [the offensive speech] can serve to justify this breach of the peace conviction where, as here, there was no evidence that persons powerless to

15. 403 U.S. 15, 91 S.Ct. 1780, 29 L.Ed.2d 284 (1971), rehearing denied 404 U.S. 876, 92 S.Ct. 26, 30 L.Ed.2d 124 (1971).

For a different and interesting analysis of this case, and possible limits on its holding, see Farber, Civilizing Public Discourse: An Essay on Professor Bickel, Justice Harlan, and the Enduring Significance of Cohen v. California, 1980 Duke L.J. 283.

16. 403 U.S. at 21, 91 S.Ct. at 1786.

17. 403 U.S. at 25, 91 S.Ct. at 1788.

18. 403 U.S. at 20, 91 S.Ct. at 1786.

avoid appellant's conduct did in fact object to it, and where that portion of the statute upon which Cohen's conviction rests evinces no concern, either on its face or as construed ... with the special plight of the captive auditor....[19]

§ 20.40 The Present Status of the "Fighting Words" and "Hostile Audience" Doctrines

In addition to the explicit limitations on *Chaplinsky* created by *Cohen,* more recent cases have illustrated that the Court does not look with favor on prosecutions for "fighting words." However, to avoid a direct overruling of *Chaplinsky,* the Court has employed the vagueness and overbreadth standards to avoid upholding convictions. Thus, in *Gooding v. Wilson,*[1] a 1972 case, the defendant addressed a policeman, "you son of a bitch I'll choke you to death." Similarly, in *Lewis v. City of New Orleans,*[2] the defendant said "you goddamn motherfucking police." Both convictions were overturned because the statutes were held vague and overbroad.

Though the Court in *Gooding* noted that when the statute is narrowly drawn or construed, such convictions may be upheld under

---

19. Cohen v. California, 403 U.S. 15, 22, 91 S.Ct. 1780, 1786, 29 L.Ed.2d 284 (1971), rehearing denied 404 U.S. 876, 92 S.Ct. 26, 30 L.Ed.2d 124 (1971).

§ 20.40

1. 405 U.S. 518, 92 S.Ct. 1103, 31 L.Ed.2d 408 (1972).

On vagueness and overbreadth, see §§ 20.8, 20.9, supra.

Tort Liability for Words Intended to Inflict Severe Emotional Distress

See, Note, First Amendment Limits on Tort Liability for Words Intended to Inflict Severe Emotional Distress, 85 Colum.L.Rev. 1749, 1749–50 (1985):

"[E]xtreme and outrageous language can be the object of tort liability but only when the use of such language constitutes 'fighting' words or invades an area of recognized spatial privacy of the plaintiff, such as his home. [And even then] tort liability should not be permitted if the plaintiff is either a public official or a public figure, unless the defendant made it impossible for the public official or figure to avert his attention."

Sexual Harassment and the Hostile Environment. Title VII of the Civil Rights Act of 1964 prohibits sexual harassment in the workplace. Efforts to prevent statements—such as "Women do not be-

long in the medical profession; they should stay home and make babies!"—raise first amendment issues. As Professor Kingsley Browne notes: "Is such a statement occurring in the workplace a constitutionally protected expression of a currently unfashionable social view, or is it sexual harassment in violation of title VII of the Civil Rights Act of 1964?" Browne, Title VII as Censorship: Hostile–Environment Harassment and the First Amendment, 52 Ohio State L.J. 481 (1991). Professor Browne concluded:

"The only effective method of altering a world view that is deemed pernicious is to provide a persuasive response—that is, 'more speech.' 'Shut up!' is not a persuasive response." Id. at 550.

See also, Strauss, Sexist Speech in the Workplace, 25 Harv.Civ.–Rts.–Civ.Lib. L.Rev. 1 (1990).

See, Doe v. University of Michigan, 721 F.Supp. 852 (E.D.Mich.1989), which invalidated, under the first amendment, the efforts of the University of Michigan to ban "offensive speech." See also, Sedler, Doe v. University of Michigan and Campus Bans on "Racist Speech": The View from Within, 37 Wayne L.Rev. 1325 (1991).

2. 415 U.S. 130, 94 S.Ct. 970, 39 L.Ed.2d 214 (1974).

the *Chaplinsky* standard,[3] it also conducted its own examination of state case law and held that the state decisions did not limit the statute "to words that 'have a direct tendency to cause acts of violence by the person to whom individually, the remark is addressed.' "[4] And in *Lewis* the Court made clear that words conveying or intended to convey disgrace are not "fighting words."[5]

In *Norwell v. City of Cincinnati,*[6] the Court refused to uphold the conviction of one "verbally and negatively" protesting his arrest, finding no fighting words. Also, in *Hess v. Indiana*[7] the Court held the speaker's statement during an antiwar protest that "We'll take the fucking street later" was constitutionally protected, for, as in *Cohen,* the words were not aimed at anyone in particular.

The result of these cases appears to be that the "fighting words" doctrine is still alive, but the Court will carefully scrutinize any convictions under it. Alternatively, Justice Blackmun may be correct when he complained in his dissent in *Gooding v. Wilson,*[8] that "the Court, despite its protestations to the contrary, is merely paying lip service to *Chaplinsky.*"[9] Similarly, while *Feiner* has never been overruled, the Court has distinguished it on its facts and not allowed the state to justify the prosecution of speakers for breach of the peace on the grounds that the speech invites dispute by hostile audiences.[10]

In a "fighting words" case we really have a situation like *Brandenburg/Hess*[11] but on an individual, *face-to-face level* rather than a mob level. The state may forbid such speech because it is calculated to cause violence in a situation where there is a studied effort to "incite" a particular individual to fight, and therefore there is no time to avert the problem by discussion of the falsehood and fallacies. Words are "fighting words" when they are an offer to exchange fisticuffs. But the state should not punish a person because others (who don't like his

3. Gooding v. Wilson, 405 U.S. 518, 523, 92 S.Ct. 1103, 1106–07, 31 L.Ed.2d 408 (1972).

4. Gooding v. Wilson, 405 U.S. 518, 524, 92 S.Ct. 1103, 1107, 31 L.Ed.2d 408 (1972).

5. Lewis v. New Orleans, 415 U.S. 130, 133, 94 S.Ct. 970, 972, 39 L.Ed.2d 214 (1974).

6. 414 U.S. 14, 94 S.Ct. 187, 38 L.Ed.2d 170 (1973).

7. 414 U.S. 105, 94 S.Ct. 326, 38 L.Ed.2d 303 (1973).

8. 405 U.S. 518, 92 S.Ct. 1103, 31 L.Ed.2d 408 (1972).

9. 405 U.S. at 537, 92 S.Ct. at 1113 (Blackmun, J., dissenting).

10. E.g., Gregory v. City of Chicago, 394 U.S. 111, 89 S.Ct. 946, 22 L.Ed.2d 134 (1969) (civil rights demonstration); see also, Cox v. Louisiana, 379 U.S. 536, 551, 85 S.Ct. 453, 462, 13 L.Ed.2d 471 (1965) (citing *Feiner* but distinguishing it as a "far cry" from the civil rights demonstration involved in the instant case); Bachellar v. Maryland, 397 U.S. 564, 567, 90 S.Ct. 1312, 1314, 25 L.Ed.2d 570 (1970) (antiwar demonstration); Edwards v. South Carolina, 372 U.S. 229, 236, 83 S.Ct. 680, 684, 9 L.Ed.2d 697 (1963) (civil rights demonstration; a "far cry from the situation . . ." in *Feiner*).

11. Brandenburg v. Ohio, 395 U.S. 444, 89 S.Ct. 1827, 23 L.Ed.2d 430 (1969) (per curiam); Hess v. Indiana, 414 U.S. 105, 94 S.Ct. 326, 38 L.Ed.2d 303 (1973).

See generally, § 20.15.

mental attitude) engage in violence against him. As Professor Chaffee has pointed out:

> This breach of the peace theory is peculiarly liable to abuse when applied against unpopular expressions and practices. It makes a man a criminal simply because his neighbors have no self-control and cannot refrain from violence. The *reductio ad absurdum* of this theory was the imprisonment of Joseph Palmer, one of Bronson Alcott's fellow-settlers at "Fruitlands," not because he was a communist, but because he persisted in wearing such a long beard that people kept mobbing him, until law and order were maintained by shutting him up. A man does not become a criminal because someone else assaults him, unless his own conduct is in itself illegal or may be reasonably considered a direct provocation to violence.[12]

XII. FREEDOM OF ASSOCIATION

§ 20.41 Introduction—The Freedom to Associate and Not to Associate

The Right of Association as Derived From Freedom of Speech and Assembly. In *NAACP v. Alabama ex rel. Patterson*,[1] a unanimous Court, speaking through Justice Harlan, clearly articulated a right of association. The Court held that the state of Alabama could not compel the National Association for the Advancement of Colored People to reveal to the state's Attorney General the names and addresses of all of its Alabama members without regard to their positions and functions in the association. The NAACP made a showing that compelled disclosure of its rank and file members on past occasions exposed them to economic reprisal, loss of employment, threat of physical coercion, and general public hostility. Unlike an organization with illegal ends [2] the NAACP's nondisclosure interest was directly related to the right of the members to pursue their lawful interests privately.

---

12. Z. Chaffee, Free Speech in the United States 151–52 (1942).

§ 20.41

1. 357 U.S. 449, 78 S.Ct. 1163, 2 L.Ed.2d 1488 (1958), on remand 268 Ala. 531, 109 So.2d 138 (1959); see also Bates v. City of Little Rock, 361 U.S. 516, 80 S.Ct. 412, 4 L.Ed.2d 480 (1960); Louisiana ex rel. Gremillion v. NAACP, 366 U.S. 293, 81 S.Ct. 1333, 6 L.Ed.2d 301 (1961); Brown v. Socialist Workers '74 Campaign Committee, 459 U.S. 87, 103 S.Ct. 416, 74 L.Ed.2d 250 (1982).

See generally, Harry Kalven, Jr., ed. by Jamie Kalven, A Worthy Tradition: Freedom of Speech in America 241–587 (1988); Torke, What Price Belonging: An Essay on Groups, Community, and the Constitution, 24 Ind.L.Rev. 1 (1990).

2. The Court so distinguished Bryant v. Zimmerman, 278 U.S. 63, 49 S.Ct. 61, 73 L.Ed. 184 (1928) where the Court upheld a New York State requirement of disclosure of the roster of membership of all unincorporated associations which required an oath as a condition to membership, as applied to the Ku Klux Klan. See 357 U.S. at 465, 78 S.Ct. at 1173.

See Note, The First Amendment and Law Enforcement Infiltration of Political Groups, 56 So.Cal.L.Rev. 207 (1982) argu-

In reaching this conclusion, the Court announced in clearest form the right of association:

> Effective advocacy of both public and private points of view, particularly controversial ones, is undeniably enhanced by group association, as this Court has more than once recognized by remarking upon the close nexus between the freedoms of speech and assembly. It is beyond debate that freedom to engage in association for the advancement of beliefs and ideas is an inseparable aspect of the "liberty" assured by the Due Process Clause of the Fourteenth Amendment, which embraces freedom of speech. Of course, it is immaterial whether the beliefs sought to be advanced by association pertain to political, economic, religious or cultural matters, and state action which may have the effect of curtailing the freedom to associate is subject to the closest scrutiny.[3]

The Three Separate Aspects of the Right of Association. Since *NAACP v. Alabama ex rel. Patterson,*[4] the Supreme Court has examined at least three separate aspects of the right to associate or to refuse to associate, though later case development may reveal a wide variety of other types or variations of associational rights beyond these three categories.

First, individuals might associate to achieve economic or other goals that are unconnected to any fundamental constitutional right. For example, individuals may join together in labor unions or trade associations. This ability to control one's economic associations is a part of the liberty protected by due process, but the Court has refused to substitute its judgment for the legislature's as to the legitimate basis for restricting such types of association. So long as the legislature is rationally promoting an arguably legitimate government goal by restricting the activities of a business association, the Court will not invalidate this legislation.[5]

A second type of freedom to associate is protected by the concept of liberty in the due process clauses and as an implicit part of the Bill of Rights guarantees; this right is connected to the fundamental right to privacy. The type of association declared to be a fundamental right

---

ing for first amendment limits on such infiltration.

3. 357 U.S. at 460–61, 78 S.Ct. at 1171 (internal citations omitted).

4. 357 U.S. 449, 78 S.Ct. 1163, 2 L.Ed.2d 1488 (1958).

5. Railway Mail Ass'n v. Corsi, 326 U.S. 88, 93–94, 65 S.Ct. 1483, 1487, 89 L.Ed. 2072 (1945) (upholding state law prohibiting labor organization from denying membership to persons because of their race).

The Supreme Court stated: "the Constitution undoubtedly imposes constraints on the State's power to control the selection of one's spouse that would not apply to regulations affecting the choice of one's fellow employees. Compare, Loving v. Virginia, 388 U.S. 1, 12, 87 S.Ct. 1817, 1823, 18 L.Ed.2d 1010 (1967) with Railway Mail Ass'n v. Corsi. ..." Roberts v. United States Jaycees, 468 U.S. 609, 620, 104 S.Ct. 3244, 3251, 82 L.Ed.2d 462 (1984).

See generally, Garet, Communality and Existence: The Rights of Groups, 56 So.Calif.L.Rev. 1001 (1983).

connected to the concept of privacy includes the freedom to choose one's spouse [6] and to maintain a relationship with members of one's family. The rationale for protecting these relationships could provide a basis for active judicial review of laws restricting the ability of persons to enter into other highly personal associations.[7]

Third, the Court has recognized a right to associate for the purpose of engaging in types of activity expressly protected by the first amendment.[8] For example, the ability to associate for religious purposes clearly cannot be restricted by the state unless the state is pursuing a compelling interest and acting in conformity with the Court's definition of religious freedom.[9] The exercise of other first amendment rights, such as speech or assembly, of necessity involves association with other persons either physically or in organizations designed to promote expressive activity.

The Court has found that the right to associate for expressive activity is justifiably implied from the expressed first amendment rights. This right cannot be limited by the government unless the limitation serves a compelling governmental interest unrelated to the suppression of ideas and this governmental interest cannot be furthered through means which are significantly less restrictive of the associational or expressive freedom. In other words, the regulation of association must be narrowly tailored to promote an end that is unrelated to suppressing the message which will be advanced by the association and is unrelated to suppressing the association because of government disapproval of its purposes.[10]

The _Roberts_ Decision. In some instances the precise type of associational right that is asserted in a case may not be easily categorized, but the Court must consider the nature of the right in order to determine the validity of governmental restrictions at issue. The Court's diagnosis of the type of associational freedom at issue will dictate the position it should take in determining how much, if any, deference it owes the legislative or executive branches of government in the particular case. An example of the difficulty that may confront the

6. Loving v. Virginia, 388 U.S. 1, 87 S.Ct. 1817, 18 L.Ed.2d 1010 (1967).

7. Moore v. City of East Cleveland, 431 U.S. 494, 97 S.Ct. 1932, 52 L.Ed.2d 531 (1977) (plurality opinion) (constitutional protection of family relationships extends beyond nuclear family); see §§ 18.26, 18.30(b), supra.

Prisons

See generally, Note, Punishing the Innocent: Unconstitutional Restrictions on Prison Marriage and Visitation, 60 N.Y.U.L.Rev. 275 (1985).

8. See generally, Judge Doty, citing Treatise in Cornerstone Bible Church v. City of Hastings, Minn., 740 F.Supp. 654, 663 (D.Minn.1990), affirmed in part, reversed in part 948 F.2d 464 (8th Cir.1991).

9. See generally § 21.8, infra.

10. See §§ 20.1–20.15, supra. In the remainder of this subsection we will refer to the cases establishing this first amendment right of freedom of association.

courts in this area is *Roberts v. United States Jaycees*.[11]

In *Roberts* the Supreme Court was reviewing a state law and state administrative action which prohibited a state branch of a national nonprofit corporation from refusing to grant full membership rights to women solely because of their gender. The seven justices who voted in this case were unanimous in upholding the state's ability to restrict this right of association, but there was some difficulty in identifying the correct standard of review which should be employed in this case.

Justice Brennan, who wrote the majority opinion, noted that "our decisions have referred to constitutionally protected 'freedom of association' in two distinct senses."[12] First, he noted that "[t]he Court has long recognized that, because the Bill of Rights is designed to secure individual liberty, it must afford the formation and preservation of certain kinds of highly personal relationships a substantial measure of sanctuary from unjustified interference by the State."[13] This type of freedom of association was related to the fundamental right of privacy which protects family relationships and personal decisions regarding such matters as childbirth and abortion.[14] Brennan noted that such

---

11. 468 U.S. 609, 104 S.Ct. 3244, 82 L.Ed.2d 462 (1984) (Chief Justice Burger and Justice Blackmun did not participate in this decision).

In Board of Directors of Rotary International v. Rotary Club of Duarte, 481 U.S. 537, 107 S.Ct. 1940, 95 L.Ed.2d 474 (1987), the Court, without dissent, upheld the constitutionality of a California law that required California Rotary Clubs to admit women members. Relying on *Roberts v. United States Jaycees,* the Court concluded that the evidence showed that Rotary Club membership is not the kind of "intimate or private relation" that warrants constitutional protection, and that admitting women will not "affect in any significant way the existing members' ability to carry out their various purposes." Also, any "slight infringement" on the Rotary members' freedom of expressive association was justified because of the State's "compelling interest" in the elimination of discrimination against women. See also, New York State Club Association, Inc. v. City of New York, 487 U.S. 1, 108 S.Ct. 2225, 101 L.Ed.2d 1 (1988), where the Court, without dissent, rejected the facial constitutional challenge to a city law (enacted in 1984), that forbids discrimination on the basis of race, creed, color, national origin or sex of any private club, defined as "any institution, club or place of accommodation [that] has more than four hundred members, provides regular meal service and regularly receives

payment for dues, fees, use of space, facilities, services, meals or beverages directly or indirectly from or on behalf of nonmembers for the furtherance of trade or business." The law exempted benevolent orders (e.g., the American Legion, the Loyal Order of Moose, the Nobles of the Mystic Shrine, etc.) and religious corporations. The Court, speaking through Justice Kennedy, also found no equal protection violation with these exceptions because it was rational for the city to conclude that the exempted organizations were different in relevant respects. The city council explained that "small clubs, benevolent orders and religious corporations have not been identified as places where business activity is prevalent...." The purpose of the law was to offer all persons, without discrimination, "a fair and equal opportunity to participate in the business and professional life of the city...."

See, Marshall, Discrimination And The Right Of Association, 81 Nw.U.L.Rev. 68 (1986).

See generally, Linder, Freedom of Association After Roberts v. United States v. Jaycees, 82 Mich.L.Rev. 1878 (1984).

12. 468 U.S. at 617, 104 S.Ct. at 3249.

13. 468 U.S. at 619, 104 S.Ct. at 3250.

14. See, e.g., Pierce v. Society of Sisters of the Holy Names of Jesus and Mary, 268 U.S. 510, 534–35, 45 S.Ct. 571, 573, 69 L.Ed.

associations would be relatively small, highly selective, and in their nature almost exclusive because they concern highly personal relationships. "Conversely, an association lacking these qualities—such as a large business enterprise—seems remote from the concerns giving rise to this constitutional protection. Accordingly, the Constitution undoubtedly imposes constraints on the State's power to control the selection of one's spouse that would not apply to regulations affecting the choice of one's fellow employees." [15] He noted that there would be a range of relationships between the most intimate, which would relate to the fundamental right to privacy, and those economic associations for which there would be very little constitutional protection. The Jaycees were found to be "outside of the category of relationships worthy of this kind of constitutional protection" because the organization was a "large and basically unselective" organization designed to promote commercial activity, community programs, and award ceremonies.[16]

Another type of freedom of association which came into play in *Roberts v. United States Jaycees* is the freedom to choose membership. Limitations on the organization's ability to choose its membership would be subjected to significant review under the first amendment because the Jaycees were organized in part for the purpose of expressive activity. "An individual's freedom to speak, to worship, and to petition the Government for the redress of grievances could not be vigorously protected from interference by the State unless a correlative freedom to engage in group effort toward those ends were not also guaranteed. ... Consequently, we have long understood as implicit in the right to engage in activities protected by the First Amendment a corresponding right to associate with others in pursuit of a wide variety of political, social, economic, educational, religious, and cultural ends." [17]

1070 (1925) (child rearing and education); Moore v. City of East Cleveland, Ohio, 431 U.S. 494, 503–04, 97 S.Ct. 1932, 1937–38, 52 L.Ed.2d 531 (1977) (cohabitation with relatives); Carey v. Population Services International, 431 U.S. 678, 684–86, 97 S.Ct. 2010, 2015–16, 52 L.Ed.2d 675 (1977) (begetting children); Zablocki v. Redhail, 434 U.S. 374, 383–86, 98 S.Ct. 673, 679–81, 54 L.Ed.2d 618 (1978) (marriage).

15. 468 U.S. at 620, 104 S.Ct. at 3251.

Cf. Runyon v. McCrary, 427 U.S. 160, 187–89, 96 S.Ct. 2586, 2602–03, 49 L.Ed.2d 415 (1976) (Powell, J., concurring), appeal after remand 569 F.2d 1294 (4th Cir.1978), cert. denied 439 U.S. 927, 99 S.Ct. 311, 58 L.Ed.2d 320 (1978).

In Board of Directors of Rotary International v. Rotary Club of Duarte, 481 U.S. 537, 107 S.Ct. 1940, 95 L.Ed.2d 474 (1987), the Court, without dissent, upheld the constitutionality of a California law that required California Rotary Clubs to admit women members. Relying on *Roberts v. United States Jaycees,* the Court concluded that the evidence showed that "the relationship among Rotary Club members is not the kind of intimate or private relation that warrants constitutional protection," and that admitting women will not "affect in any significant way the existing members' ability to carry out their various purposes." Also, any "slight infringement" on the Rotary members' freedom of expressive association was justified because of the State's "compelling interest in eliminating discrimination against women."

16. 468 U.S. at 620, 104 S.Ct. at 3251.

17. 468 U.S. at 622, 104 S.Ct. at 3252.

The Court found that this right of association was not absolute and that "[i]nfringements on that right may be justified by regulations adopted to serve compelling state interests, unrelated to the suppression of ideas, that cannot be achieved through means significantly less restrictive of associational freedoms." [18] The Court upheld the state law requiring the Jaycees to admit women to full membership because the state interest in guaranteeing equal access to publicly available goods and services without racial or gender discrimination was among "compelling state interests of the highest order.[19] In addition to advancing a compelling state interest, the state demonstrated that its regulation was the least restrictive means of achieving its end because it did not impose serious burdens on the male members' freedom of expressive association." [20]

To be sure, the determination of who would be a member in the association was a significant restriction on the Jaycees' associational freedom, but the state law "requires no change in the Jaycees' creed of promoting the interests of young men, and it imposes no restrictions on the organization's ability to exclude individuals with ideologies or philosophies different from those of its existing members." [21] Any incidental abridgement of the speech of the organization was "no greater than is necessary to accomplish the State's legitimate purposes" [22] of eliminating gender or racial discrimination in the distribution of public services. In this way, the Court appeared to indicate that an organization whose basic expressive purpose might be destroyed by a statute requiring it to refrain from discriminating in its membership selection on the basis of gender might present a more substantial first amendment claim.

Justice O'Connor wrote a very astute concurring opinion in *Roberts*. She believed that the Court must determine whether the organization was significantly dedicated to first amendment activity or whether it was primarily a commercial organization that only inciden-

---

18. 468 U.S. at 622, 104 S.Ct. at 3252.

19. 468 U.S. at 624, 104 S.Ct. at 3253.

The Supreme Court also has upheld Title IX of the Education Amendments of 1972, which prohibits sex discrimination in "any education program or activity receiving Federal financial assistance." Grove City College v. Bell, 465 U.S. 555, 104 S.Ct. 1211, 79 L.Ed.2d 516 (1984).

The majority opinion in *Grove City College* found that this condition on the receipt of federal funds did not violate the first amendment rights of the College or students, who were free to pursue discriminatory activity without federal funds. "Congress is free to attach reasonable conditions to federal financial assistance that

educational institutions are not obligated to accept." 465 U.S. at 576, 104 S.Ct. at 1223. In *Grove City College*, as in *Roberts*, the government action was promoting an interest that outweighed the minimal burden it imposed on associational freedom.

Some conditions to the receipt of financial assistance from the government could violate the first amendment or other constitutional provisions. See generally, § 20.11, supra.

20. 468 U.S. at 625, 104 S.Ct. at 3254.

21. 468 U.S. at 625, 104 S.Ct. at 3254.

22. 468 U.S. at 627, 104 S.Ct. at 3255.

tally exercised first amendment [23] rights. She realized that "[m]any associations cannot readily be described as purely expressive or purely commercial"; she was much more insightful than the majority in realizing that the key decision to be made in such cases is whether the state need have more than a rational basis for regulating an association's membership practices.

Justice O'Connor was correct in noting that subjecting every regulation of organizational activity to a meaningful form of review under the first amendment, even under a sliding scale of first amendment associational interests, presented an unnecessary judicial hurdle for a legislature to clear in order to demand an end to discrimination in the membership practices of commercial organizations. A sliding scale has a very *ad hoc,* unprincipled quality. It invites unreviewable discretion. The Court, O'Connor noted, should establish a strong presumption of validity for regulations of commercial organizations even though the Court also should "give substance to the ideal of complete protection for purely expressive association, even while it readily permits state regulation of commercial affairs." She would allow regulation of the association's membership practices under a due process, rational basis standard "when, and only when, the association's activities are not predominantly of the type protected by the First Amendment." [24]

The Continuum of Associational Rights. Perhaps it is best to think of associational rights as proceeding on a continuum. This continuum ranges from the least protected form of association (for example, the associational rights related to commercial activities) to the most protected forms of association (for example, the associational rights related to political or religious speech or associations existing for highly personal reasons, such as family relationships). The association of persons for law practice may thus be regulated to prohibit discrimination on the basis of sex or race. [25] Regulations of law practice which relate to the ability of persons to associate for the advancement of social goals, however, may be protected to a greater extent from governmental regulation. [26] A boycott for political purposes may re-

23. She admitted: "Many associations cannot readily be described as purely expressive or purely commercial." 468 U.S. at 635, 104 S.Ct. at 3259 (O'Connor, J., concurring in part and concurring in the judgment).

24. 468 U.S. at 635, 104 S.Ct. at 3259.

25. Hishon v. King & Spalding, 467 U.S. 69, 104 S.Ct. 2229, 81 L.Ed.2d 59 (1984).

26. See, e.g., NAACP v. Button, 371 U.S. 415, 83 S.Ct. 328, 9 L.Ed.2d 405 (1963) (holding ban on solicitation of legal business invalid as applied to NAACP activity in financing desegregation litigation).

Group activity regarding commercial litigation is also protected by the freedom of association. See Brotherhood of R.R. Trainmen v. Virginia, 377 U.S. 1, 84 S.Ct. 1113, 12 L.Ed.2d 89 (1964), rehearing denied 377 U.S. 960, 84 S.Ct. 1625, 12 L.Ed.2d 505 (1964), on remand 207 Va. 182, 149 S.E.2d 265 (1966), certiorari denied 385 U.S. 1027, 87 S.Ct. 754, 17 L.Ed.2d 675 (1967); United Mine Workers, Dist. 12 v. Illinois State Bar Ass'n, 389 U.S. 217, 88 S.Ct. 353, 19 L.Ed.2d 426 (1967); United Transp. Union v. Michigan State Bar, 401 U.S. 576, 91 S.Ct. 1076, 28 L.Ed.2d 339 (1971).

ceive significant first amendment protection, although a similar boycott for the purposes of maintaining a preferred economic position for one's business or union may receive very little protection.[27] A prohibition of race or gender discrimination in the employment practices of commercial enterprises or in the admissions practices of schools open to a wide segment of the public may not present significant freedom of association problems.[28] A similar restriction on the membership practices of a religious organization that was highly selective in its membership and dedicated to goals totally inconsistent with the acceptance of members of a particular race or gender might present a more significant freedom of associational problem even if the Court were to find that the goal of ending that form of discrimination would override associational rights.[29]

This right of association takes many forms, as the *Roberts* opinion recognized. These forms are considered elsewhere in this Chapter.[30]

Student Organizations. A state college cannot deny official recognition (and the loss of privilege to distribute literature on campus and other such privileges which such denial entails) to a student organization because of its parent organization's history.[31]

Group Activity to Obtain Counsel. Under the freedom of association the Court has also struck down laws which prevented the NAACP from assisting individuals[32] and which prevented a labor union from

Regulations of the practice of law carefully designed to protect the public will be upheld although the Court must be careful to invalidate regulations that would suppress first amendment rights. Compare, Ohralik v. Ohio State Bar Ass'n, 436 U.S. 447, 98 S.Ct. 1912, 56 L.Ed.2d 444 (1978) (state may prohibit face-to-face solicitation of clients by attorney soliciting case for contingent fee), with In re Primus, 436 U.S. 412, 98 S.Ct. 1893, 56 L.Ed.2d 417 (1978) (prohibition of in-person solicitation of clients could not be applied, without violating the first amendment, to an A.C.L.U. attorney who informed potential litigants of the availability of A.C.L.U. representation).

27. Compare NAACP v. Claiborne Hardware Co., 458 U.S. 886, 102 S.Ct. 3409, 73 L.Ed.2d 1215 (1982) (boycott of stores organized to influence government practices held to be activity protected by the first amendment), rehearing denied 459 U.S. 898, 103 S.Ct. 199, 74 L.Ed.2d 160 (1982), with NLRB v. Retail Store Employees Local 1001, 447 U.S. 607, 100 S.Ct. 2372, 65 L.Ed.2d 377 (1980) (labor union picket line advocating boycott of secondary employer is prohibited).

28. See Runyon v. McCrary, 427 U.S. 160, 96 S.Ct. 2586, 49 L.Ed.2d 415 (1976), appeal after remand 569 F.2d 1294 (4th Cir.1978), certiorari denied 439 U.S. 927, 99 S.Ct. 311, 58 L.Ed.2d 320 (1978).

29. See Runyon v. McCrary, 427 U.S. 160, 188–89, 96 S.Ct. 2586, 2603, 49 L.Ed.2d 415 (1976) (Powell, J., concurring), appeal after remand 569 F.2d 1294 (4th Cir.1978), certiorari denied 439 U.S. 927, 99 S.Ct. 311, 58 L.Ed.2d 320 (1978); see also § 21.4, infra.

30. See §§ 20.50–20.55, infra.

31. Healy v. James, 408 U.S. 169, 92 S.Ct. 2338, 33 L.Ed.2d 266 (1972).

32. NAACP v. Button, 371 U.S. 415, 429–30, 83 S.Ct. 328, 336–37, 9 L.Ed.2d 405 (1963).

Simon, Fee Sharing Between Lawyers and Public Interest Groups, 98 Yale L.J. 1069, 1116–33 (1989) (concluding that "a fee-sharing rule that prohibits all fee sharing between lawyers and all nonlawyer public interest organizations is unconstitutionally imprecise and hence unenforceable." Id. at 1131).

assisting its members [33] in retaining lawyers to assert the legal rights of these individuals.

Political Parties. The freedom of association allows political parties, within certain bounds, to regulate the selection of delegates to their national conventions even when such regulations are contrary to state law [34] because there must be a limit on the extraterritorial effect of *state* laws which seek to impose conflicting delegate selection rules on *national* conventions.[35]

There is a broader power of states to regulate political parties within their jurisdiction, though even here, the Supreme Court has placed some limits based on the freedom of association. The leading case is *Tashjian v. Republican Party of Connecticut.*[36]

In that case a strongly divided Court (five to four), invalidated a state law to the extent that it conflicted with a Connecticut Republican

33. Brotherhood of R.R. Trainmen v. Virginia, 377 U.S. 1, 84 S.Ct. 1113, 12 L.Ed.2d 89 (1964), rehearing denied 377 U.S. 960, 84 S.Ct. 1625, 12 L.Ed.2d 505 (1964), on remand 207 Va. 182, 149 S.E.2d 265 (1966), certiorari denied 385 U.S. 1027, 87 S.Ct. 754, 17 L.Ed.2d 675 (1967); United Mine Workers v. Illinois State Bar Ass'n, 389 U.S. 217, 88 S.Ct. 353, 19 L.Ed.2d 426 (1967); United Transp. Union v. State Bar of Michigan, 401 U.S. 576, 91 S.Ct. 1076, 28 L.Ed.2d 339 (1971).

See also Ohralik v. State Bar, 436 U.S. 447, 98 S.Ct. 1912, 56 L.Ed.2d 444 (1978); In re Primus, 436 U.S. 412, 98 S.Ct. 1893, 56 L.Ed.2d 417 (1978).

See § 20.54.

34. See, Democratic Party v. LaFollette, 450 U.S. 107, 101 S.Ct. 1010, 67 L.Ed.2d 82 (1981).

See generally, McCleskey, Parties at the Bar: Equal Protection, Freedom of Association, and the Rights of Political Organizations, 46 Jrl. of Politics 347 (1984); Gottlieb, Rebuilding the Right to Association: The Right to Hold a Convention as a Test Case, 11 Hofstra L.Rev. 191 (1982). Note, Freedom of Association and State Regulation of Delegate Selection: Potential for Conflict at the 1984 Democratic National Convention, 36 Vanderbilt L.Rev. 105 (1983); Weisburd, Candidate–Making and the Constitution: Constitutional Restraints on and Protections of Party Nominating Methods, 57 So.Calif.L.Rev. 213 (1984).

See also, Anderson v. Celebrezze, 460 U.S. 780, 103 S.Ct. 1564, 75 L.Ed.2d 547 (1983), invalidating Ohio's excessive restrictions on ballot eligibility for independent presidential candidates because of the voter's freedom of choice and freedom of association.

35. Democratic Party v. LaFollette, 450 U.S. 107, 101 S.Ct. 1010, 67 L.Ed.2d 82 (1981).

There remain questions regarding when a state may dictate the terms under which a political party must accept someone for a position on a party primary ballot in a *state* election in contravention of party rules. See Bellotti v. Connolly, 460 U.S. 1057, 103 S.Ct. 1510, 75 L.Ed.2d 938 (1983) (dismissing appeal for want of jurisdiction and denying certiorari). In that case the Supreme Court refused to consider a case in which a state court had ruled that a person who had qualified for a position on a party primary ballot by meeting statutory terms of eligibility (including the submission of 10,000 certified signatures) was nonetheless barred from the ballot because he failed to meet a party rule. The party required a person to receive 15% of the votes on any ballot at the state party convention in order to be eligible for the state primary ballot. Although it appeared that the state court had required the person to meet the party primary rule, as well as the terms of the state statutes, on the belief that failure to honor the party rule would violate the party's first and fourteenth amendment rights of freedom of association, the Supreme Court refused to consider this issue. 460 U.S. at 1058, 103 S.Ct. at 1511, 75 L.Ed.2d at 939 (Stevens, Rehnquist, and O'Connor, JJ., dissenting from dismissal of appeal).

36. 479 U.S. 208, 107 S.Ct. 544, 93 L.Ed.2d 514 (1986).

Party rule which permitted *independent* voters to vote in Republican primaries for federal and state-wide offices. The state law provided for a closed primary; the Republican Party rules provided for an open primary for federal and state-wide offices but a closed primary for other offices (e.g., state legislator, mayor). State law provided that any previously unaffiliated voter may become eligible to vote in the Party's primary simply *by enrolling as a Party member* as late as noon on the last business day preceding the primary. The Court never cited *Roberts v. United States Jaycees*,[37] but said that the Connecticut law violated freedom of association.

In 1976 a three judge court had upheld the Connecticut law when an independent voter sought a declaratory judgment that he had a right to vote in the Republican primary. The Supreme Court summarily affirmed that decision in *Nader v. Schaffer*.[38] Several years later the Republican state convention adopted new rules allowing independents to vote in the Republican Party so long as their ballots were limited to federal and state-wide offices (but not other offices, such as mayor, or state representative).[39] The State of Connecticut refused to change its primary laws, so the Party sued.

The Supreme Court specifically approved of its 1976 decision upholding the closed primary, but Justice Marshall, for the Court, distinguished the earlier case because it was brought by independent voters, not by the Republican Party itself. In the *Nader* case "the nonmember's desire to participate in the party's affairs is overborne by the countervailing and legitimate right of the party to determine its own membership." [40] In the *Tashjian* case the majority reasoned that there is no conflict between the associational interests of members of the Republican Party and nonmembers because the Republican Party wants to "provide enhanced opportunities for participation by willing nonmembers." [41] The Republican Party itself objects to the state law, which it contends "impermissibly burdens the rights of the members to determine for themselves with whom they will associate, and whose support they will seek, in their quest for political success. The Party's attempt to broaden the base of public participation in and support for

37. 468 U.S. 609, 104 S.Ct. 3244, 82 L.Ed.2d 462 (1984).

38. 429 U.S. 989, 97 S.Ct. 516, 50 L.Ed.2d 602 (1976), summarily affirming 417 F.Supp. 837 (D.Conn.1976).

39. The motivation behind this change was grounded in the fact that U.S. Senator Weicker from Connecticut, in a reelection bid, was concerned that he could not win a primary without an influx of non-Republican voters. (Plaintiffs' admissions, in Joint Appendix at 124–127). Other Repub-

lican candidates did not want independents voting in their primary, and so a compromise was reached with independents limited to voting for *state-wide* offices.

Weicker later won the primary but lost in his reelection bid. Later, he was elected Governor of Connecticut as an independent.

40. 479 U.S. at 215 n. 6, 107 S.Ct. at 549 n. 6.

41. Id.

its activities is conduct undeniably central to the exercise of the right of association." [42]

Justice Marshall concluded that the state statute was unconstitutional because it did not advance any "compelling" State interests. For example, the state law did not prevent raiding of the Republican Party, because "a raid on the Republican Party primary by independent voters [is] a curious concept," and if such a raid were to occur, the challenged state law would not really stop it, for the state law did not prevent independents from registering as Republicans on the business day before the primary. [43]

The Court concluded: "the Party's determination of the boundaries of its own association, and of the structure which best allows it to pursue its political goals, is protected by the Constitution." [44] Then it added a significant narrowing footnote:

> Our holding today does not establish that state regulation of primary voting qualifications may never withstand challenge by a political party or its membership. A party seeking, for example, to open its primary to all voters, including members of other parties, would raise a different combination of considerations. Under such circumstances, the effect of one party's broadening of participation would threaten other parties with the disorganization effects which the statutes were designed to prevent. We have observed on several occasions that a State may adopt a "policy of confining each voter to a single nominating act," a policy decision which is not involved in the present case. The analysis of these situations derives much from the particular facts involved. . . . [45]

Justice Scalia, joined by Chief Justice Rehnquist, and Justice O'Connor, dissented and objected to the majority's freedom of association rationale: "Appellees' only complaint is that the Party cannot leave the selection of its candidates to persons who are *not* members of the Party, and are unwilling to become members. It seems to me fanciful to refer to this as an interest in freedom of association between the members of the Republican Party and the putative independent voters." [46] This "associational" interest is based on only casual contact between Republicans and nonRepublicans. These nonRepublicans do not even wish to be called "Republicans." Moreover—"*even if* it were the fact that the majority of the Party's members wanted its candidates to be determined by outsiders, there is no reason why the State is bound to honor that desire—any more than it would be bound to honor

---

42. 479 U.S. at 215, 107 S.Ct. at 549.

43. 479 U.S. at 219, 107 S.Ct. at 551. The Court, however, also argued (somewhat inconsistently) that the act of registering as a Republican is a significant public act of affiliation. 479 U.S. at 226 n. 7, 107 S.Ct. at 550 n. 7.

44. 479 U.S. at 224, 107 S.Ct. at 554.

45. 479 U.S. at 224 n. 13, 107 S.Ct. at 554 n. 13.

46. 479 U.S. at 235, 107 S.Ct. at 559 (emphasis in original).

a party's democratically expressed desire that its candidates henceforth be selected by convention rather than by primary, or by the party's executive committee in a smoke-filled room.... Connecticut may lawfully require that significant elements of the democratic election process be democratic—whether the Party wants that or not. It is beyond my understanding why the Republican Party's delegation of its democratic choice to a Republican Convention can be proscribed, but its delegation of that choice to non-members for the Party cannot." [47]

Subsequently, in *Eu v. San Francisco County Democratic Central Committee,*[48] a unanimous Court invalidated provisions of the California Election Code that prohibited official governing bodies of political parties from endorsing candidates in party primaries, and dictated the organization and composition of political parties. For example, California law controlled the size and composition of the state central committees, set forth the rules governing the selection and removal of committee members, set the maximum term of office for the chair of the state central committee, required that the chair rotate between residents of northern and southern California, and so forth. Violation of the California law could be punished by fine and imprisonment.

Relying on *Tashjian* the Court said that if "the challenged law burdens the rights of political parties and their members, it can survive constitutional scrutiny only if the State shows that it advances a compelling state interest, and is narrowly tailored to serve that interest." [49] Applying this test, the Court invalidated the law.

The California law did, in fact, burden associational rights of the political parties and their members. The endorsement prohibition, for example, hamstrings the ability of the party to spread its message and the ability of voters to inform themselves about the candidates. With the ban on official party endorsements (a ban not applicable to other groups such as labor organizations, newspapers, and political action committees) it is easier for a candidate with views antithetical to the

---

47. 479 U.S. at 236–37, 107 S.Ct. at 560–61 (emphasis in original).

The Qualifications Clause of the Seventeenth Amendment. The majority also held that the implementation of Party rules—which established qualifications for voting for congressional elections that differ from the voting qualifications in elections for the more numerous house of the state legislature—did not violate the Qualifications Clause, art. I, § 2, cl. 1, and the Seventeenth Amendment. Primaries are subject to these clauses, the Court said, but the purpose of those clauses are satisfied "if all those qualified to participate in the selection of members of the more numerous branch of the state legislature are also qualified to participate in the election of

Senators and Members of the House of Representatives." There is no need for "perfect symmetry." 479 U.S. at 226–29, 107 S.Ct. at 555–56. Justice Stevens, joined by Scalia, J., dissented: "The Court nevertheless separates the federal qualifications from their state counterparts, inexplicably treating the mandatory 'shall have' language of the clauses as though it means only that the federal voters 'may but need not have' the qualifications of state voters." 479 U.S. at 230, 107 S.Ct. at 557.

48. 489 U.S. 214, 109 S.Ct. 1013, 103 L.Ed.2d 271 (1989).

49. 489 U.S. at 221–24, 109 S.Ct. at 1019–20.

party to win its primary. And the statutory restrictions on organization prevents the parties from governing themselves as they think best: "by specifying who shall be the members of the parties' official governing bodies, California interferes with the parties' choice of leaders. A party might decide, for example that it will be more effective if a greater number of its official leaders are local activists rather than Washington-based elected officials." [50] The California law also serves no compelling state interest. The "State has not shown that its regulation of internal party governance is necessary to the integrity of the electoral process." [51] The state's intervention in this case is not necessary to "prevent the derogation of the civil rights of party adherents." [52]

State–Imposed Age Limits on Entrance to Dance Halls. In *Dallas v. Stranglin,* [53] the Court, with no dissents, held that a city ordinance limiting the use of certain dance halls to persons between 14 and 18 did not violate any associational rights. The activity of dance hall patrons "qualifies as neither a form of 'intimate association' nor as a form of 'expressive association' as those terms were described in

---

50. 489 U.S. at 221–31, 109 S.Ct. at 1019–24.

The state may, of course, enact laws when necessary to regulate a party's internal affairs when it is necessary to ensure that elections are fair. E.g., Storer v. Brown, 415 U.S. 724, 730, 94 S.Ct. 1274, 1279, 39 L.Ed.2d 714 (1974), rehearing denied 417 U.S. 926, 94 S.Ct. 2635, 41 L.Ed.2d 230 (1974). However, that is quite different than the *Eu* case where the state laws placed direct regulation of the party's leaders.

The *Eu* Court distinguished Marchioro v. Chaney, 442 U.S. 191, 99 S.Ct. 2243, 60 L.Ed.2d 816 (1979). In *Marchioro* the Court upheld a Washington State law requiring that political parties create a state central committee. The state law required this central committee to engage in certain, quite limited functions, such as filling vacancies that might occur on the party ticket; nominating presidential electors and national convention delegates, and calling state-wide conventions. However, the Democratic Party—not the state—decided to assign to that central committee important responsibilities regarding the administration of the party, the raising and distribution of party funds, and the setting of party policy. The party members did not object to the state-imposed (i.e., the statutory) requirements, and so the Supreme Court did not rule on their constitutionality. When the central committee performed its state-assigned elector-al functions, it complied with the one person, one vote principle. 442 U.S. at 197, n. 12, 99 S.Ct. at 2247 n. 12.

See generally, Note, Equal Representation of Party Members on Political Party Central Committees, 88 Yale L.J. 167 (1978).

51. 489 U.S. at 231–33, 109 S.Ct. at 1025.

52. 489 U.S. at 233–33, 109 S.Ct. at 1025.

Stevens, J., concurring, warned that phrases such as "compelling state interest" and "least restrictive means" are "really not very helpful for constitutional analysis. They are too convenient and result oriented, and I must endeavor to disassociate myself from them." 489 U.S. at 233–34, 109 S.Ct. at 1026, quoting Blackmun, J., concurring, in Illinois State Board of Elections v. Socialist Workers Party, 440 U.S. 173, 188–89, 99 S.Ct. 983, 992, 59 L.Ed.2d 230 (1979).

53. 490 U.S. 19, 109 S.Ct. 1591, 104 L.Ed.2d 18 (1989).

Cf. Prince v. Massachusetts, 321 U.S. 158, 64 S.Ct. 438, 88 L.Ed. 645 (1944), rehearing denied 321 U.S. 804, 64 S.Ct. 784, 88 L.Ed. 1090 (1944), where the Court rejected equal protection and freedom of religion claims to a statute that prohibited children under 12 years of age from selling newspapers on the street corners.

Roberts." [54] Chief Justice Rehnquist, for the Court, added: "[W]e do not think the Constitution recognizes a generalized right of 'social association' that includes chance encounters in dance halls." [55] Nor does the ordinance violate equal protection, for it implicates no suspect class and impinges on no constitutionally protected right. It is "rational" for the city to impose a rule that separates 14 to 18–year–olds from what may be the "corrupting influences of older teenagers and young adults." [56]

Governmental Refusal to Subsidize Associational Interests. The first amendment right of association does not require the Government to subsidize activities or choices that have associational interests. Thus, in *Lyng v. International Union, United Automobile, Aerospace and Agricultural Implement Workers of America, UAW,*[57] the Court upheld a provision in the Food Stamp Act that states that no household shall become eligible to participate in the food stamp program during the time that any member of the household is on strike or shall increase the allotment of food stamps that it was receiving already because the income of the striking member has decreased. The Court found no violation of either the first or fifth amendments.

The Court in *Lyng* noted that the federal statute does not forbid people from associating together in order to conduct a strike, or for any other purpose. The only real impact on associational rights results from the fact that the Government refuses to extend food stamp benefits to those on strike, who (because of the strike) are not without their wage income. But "the strikers' right of association does not require the Government to furnish funds to maximize the exercise of their rights." [58] The legislative decision not to subsidize the exercise of a fundamental constitutional right does not infringe on that right.[59] And that legislative decision was certainly rational. It served the purpose of reducing federal expenditures; limiting the expenditure of federal funds to people Congress concluded had the greatest need; and removing the perception and criticism that the food stamp program provided one-sided support for labor strikes.

54. 490 U.S. at 24–26, 109 S.Ct. at 1595.

55. 490 U.S. at 24–26, 109 S.Ct. at 1595.

56. 490 U.S. at 24–26, 109 S.Ct. at 1595.

Stevens, J., joined by Blackmun, J., concurred in the judgment. They argued that the "opportunity to make friends and enjoy the company of other people—in a dance hall or elsewhere—is an aspect of liberty" protected by the substantive due process clause of the fourteenth amendment, but that the city's justification "adequately justified the ordinance's modest impairment of the liberty of teenagers." 490 U.S. at 28–29, 109 S.Ct. at 1597.

57. 485 U.S. 360, 108 S.Ct. 1184, 99 L.Ed.2d 380 (1988).

58. 485 U.S. at 366, 108 S.Ct. at 1190.

59. Cf., Ohio Bureau of Employment Services v. Hodory, 431 U.S. 471, 97 S.Ct. 1898, 52 L.Ed.2d 513 (1977); Regan v. Taxation with Representation of Washington, 461 U.S. 540, 103 S.Ct. 1997, 76 L.Ed.2d 129 (1983); Bob Jones University v. United States, 461 U.S. 574, 103 S.Ct. 2017, 76 L.Ed.2d 157 (1983).

The Right Not to Associate. The right of association raises a corollary issue: the right not to associate. If the state requires individuals to join—for example a union, as a requirement to work, or a state bar, as a requirement in some states to practice law—the union or state bar may, consistent with the freedom of association, use the dues required of its members to advance causes not favored by all of the members.[60]

In *Abood v. Detroit Board of Education*,[61] the Court held that the state may require a public worker to pay dues or a service fee equal to dues insofar as the money is used to finance expenditures by the union

60. International Ass'n of Machinists v. Street, 367 U.S. 740, 81 S.Ct. 1784, 6 L.Ed.2d 1141 (1961) (statute construed to avoid association issue by holding that union dues money could only be used, under the statute, to support collective bargaining and not to support political causes), on remand 217 Ga. 351, 122 S.E.2d 220 (1961); Lathrop v. Donohue, 367 U.S. 820, 81 S.Ct. 1826, 6 L.Ed.2d 1191 (1961) (integrated bar; issue of whether dues money could constitutionally be used to support causes opposed by a member not reached by the Court), rehearing denied 368 U.S. 871, 82 S.Ct. 23, 7 L.Ed.2d 72 (1961). In both of these cases Justices Harlan and Frankfurter would have reached the issue and allowed the compelled dues money to be spent for causes not approved by the involuntary members. Justices Douglas and Black also would have reached the issue and both would have found the use of dues money in this way unconstitutional.

In First Nat. Bank v. Bellotti, 435 U.S. 765, 98 S.Ct. 1407, 55 L.Ed.2d 707 (1978), rehearing denied 438 U.S. 907, 98 S.Ct. 3126, 57 L.Ed.2d 1150 (1978), the Court held that states cannot prevent corporations from spending money to influence referendum questions, even if such referenda do not affect business interests. The state asserted as one interest to support the restriction on corporate speech the protection of shareholders by preventing waste of corporate resources to further views with which some shareholders disagreed. The Court noted that the statute was over-inclusive because it precluded corporations all of whose shareholders voted to allow the expenditure to engage in public debate.

The Court dismissed *Street* and *Abood* as "irrelevant," because in those cases the employees were required either by state law or union agreement to pay dues or a service fee to the union. The shareholder

was free to withdraw his investment, but the union member could disassociate himself from the debate only at the cost of his job. 435 U.S. at 792–94 & n. 34, 98 S.Ct. at 1424–25 & n. 34.

Justices White, Brennan, and Marshall, dissenting, argued that the state interests in protecting stockholders from waste of corporate assets, in preventing corporations from dominating political debate, and in promoting economically efficient corporate decisionmaking overrode the first amendment restriction. 435 U.S. at 802–22, 98 S.Ct. at 1429–39.

The majority did not decide whether it may be possible for the state to place greater restrictions on corporate expenditures to influence candidate elections. 435 U.S. at 788 n. 26, 98 S.Ct. at 1422 n. 26.

See also, Communications Workers of America v. Beck, 487 U.S. 735, 108 S.Ct. 2641, 101 L.Ed.2d 634 (1988). In this case, employees who were not union members objected to the union's use of their agency fee for purposes other than collective bargaining, contract administration, or grievance adjustment. The Court held that the courts had jurisdiction over the claim that the union exactions violated a duty of fair representation and the nonunion members' free speech rights; and that the section of the National Labor Relations Act that permitted the employer and the exclusive bargaining representative to enter into an agreement requiring all employees to pay union dues and initiation fees as a condition of continued employment, does not also permit the union, over the objection of the dues-paying, nonunion employees, to spend funds collected from them on activities unrelated to collective-bargaining activities.

61. 431 U.S. 209, 97 S.Ct. 1782, 52 L.Ed.2d 261 (1977), rehearing denied 433 U.S. 915, 97 S.Ct. 2989, 53 L.Ed.2d 1102 (1977).

for the purposes of collective bargaining, contract administration, and grievance adjustment. But under the first amendment, the workers may not be compelled to contribute to political candidates, and the workers may constitutionally prevent the union's spending a part of its required fees to contribute to political candidates and to express political views unrelated to its duties as exclusive bargaining representative.[62]

62. The principles as set forth in this paragraph and accompanying footnotes were applied in Ellis v. Brotherhood of Ry., Airline and S.S. Clerks, 466 U.S. 435, 104 S.Ct. 1883, 80 L.Ed.2d 428 (1984), on remand 736 F.2d 1340 (9th Cir.1984). In this case the Supreme Court reviewed the statutory and constitutional limitations on the collection of fees from nonmembers by a union which had been elected by employees of a private sector airline company to be their exclusive bargaining agent. The union had negotiated a contract with the employer requiring all employees to be union members or pay dues to the union.

The Court found that the governmental interest in "industrial peace" justified the interference with first amendment rights of employees to the extent that they could be required to pay fees to a union so that the majority of employees, through a certified union, could negotiate for a "union shop." The government may require public or private sector employees to pay such dues. First amendment rights are not infringed beyond the degree required to allow for union shop agreements by requiring the payment of dues from nonmembers for costs related to the union's function as the bargaining representative of the workers.

The nonunion or objecting employee can be compelled to pay a share of not only the direct costs of negotiating and administering collective bargaining agreements and settling disputes arising under those agreements but also the expenses of activities normally or reasonably related to effectuating the duties of the union as the exclusive bargaining representative. Incidental costs of union activity that can be imposed upon nonmembers include some speech activities such as union publications and convention costs but not the costs of supporting political candidates or political positions. To the extent that a union can collect dues from nonmembers, its dues collection scheme cannot require the nonmembers to pay dues or fees for all purposes, and then offer a rebate upon objection to improper use of dues. It must

instead use a dues or fee collection system that does not involve requiring even temporary contributions of dissenting employees to improper uses.

In Ellis, the Court interpreted federal statutes to allow charging nonmembers fees for costs of conventions, social activities, and many union publications, but not for costs of organizing unionization efforts or the expenses of litigation not having a clear connection to the functions of the bargaining unit. The Court's rulings involve a mixture of first amendment interpretation and statutory interpretation undertaken to avoid first amendment problems.

The Court expressly stated that the first amendment did not prohibit requiring the nonunion (dissenting) employees to pay a fair share of the costs of the union activities that were germane to its collective bargaining function for the employees.

See also, Chicago Teachers Union, Local No. 1, AFL–CIO v. Hudson, 475 U.S. 292, 106 S.Ct. 1066, 89 L.Ed.2d 232 (1986), on remand 117 F.R.D. 413 (N.D.Ill.1987), which applied Abood and Ellis to determine the constitutionality of the procedures adopted by the Chicago Teachers Union with the approval of the Chicago Board of Education. The Court held that the union procedure for determining the proportionate share that nonunion employees were required to contribute to support the union as collective bargaining agent was constitutionally inadequate because it failed to minimize the risk that the contribution of the nonunion employees might temporarily be used for impermissible purposes, because it failed to provide adequate justification for the advance deduction of dues, and because it also failed to provide a reasonably prompt opportunity to challenge the amount of the fee before an impartial decision-maker.

For a thoughtful examination of the constitutional values at stake whenever the government assigns important functions to private sector organizations in a way that requires persons to join or support those

Similarly, in *Keller v. State Bar of California*,[63] the Court unanimously held that the State Bar of California (an "integrated bar," that is, an association created by state law, to which lawyers must join and pay dues as a condition of practicing law), may not constitutionally use *compulsory* dues to finance political and ideological causes that the petitioners oppose. The State Bar may only use compulsory dues to finance regulation of the legal profession or improve the quality of legal services (for example, Bar dues may be used to propose ethical codes or discipline Bar members), not to promote political or ideological activities (for example, to endorse gun control or nuclear freeze initiatives).

While it is true that government officials are expected, as a part of the democratic process, to represent and to espouse the views of a majority of their constituents, the State Bar of California is not part of the general government of California. It is more analogous to labor unions representing public and private employees, and therefore should be subject to the same constitutional rule in order to protect free speech and free association interests.

In *Lehnert v. Ferris Faculty Association*,[64] a fragmented court, with an opinion of the Court on some issues and only a plurality on other issues, did muster a majority to conclude that a union may impose dues on its members if the activities so funded are: (1) germane to collective bargaining activities; (2) justified by the government's vital policy interest in labor peace and in avoiding "free rider" problems; and (3) do not significantly add to the burden of free speech that is already inherent in allowing a union shop or an agency shop.

In the following sections we shall examine some of the basic issues of freedom of association by focusing on the major cases dealing with loyalty and security requirements.

§ 20.42 Public Employment Restrictions

(a) Political Affiliation

The Courts have developed over the years guidelines that affect the legislature's ability to impose restrictions upon public employment. The emergence of the doctrine of unconstitutional conditions, discussed below, gave impetus to this development in the law. As a result, denial

organizations see Cantor, Forced Payments to Service Institutions and Constitutional Interests in Ideological Non–Association, 36 Rutgers L.Rev. 3 (1983).

63. 496 U.S. 1, 110 S.Ct. 2228, 110 L.Ed.2d 1 (1990).

64. 500 U.S. ___, 111 S.Ct. 1950, 114 L.Ed.2d 572 (1991), rehearing denied ___ U.S. ___, 111 S.Ct. 2878, 115 L.Ed.2d 1044 (1991). Thus a plurality of the Court in *Lehnert* concluded that the state cannot compel public employees who were not members of the union to pay union dues to subsidize legislative lobbying or other political union activities outside of the limited scope of contract ratification or implementation. A majority of the Court also concluded that it is not necessary that the union charge be required to be incurred in performance of the union's statutory duties in order for the charge to be constitutional.

of public employment on the basis of political affiliation is in violation
of the first amendment, unless the proscribed organization is one
legitimately designated as "subversive," that is, dedicated to the use of
illegal means to effectuate its political or social objectives, and the
prospective employee is one who is aware of those objectives and
intends specifically to further those objectives.[1] The development of
these standards and the rationale for their implementation is left for
consideration within the factual situations in which they developed.

Adler v. Board of Education,[2] the first significant venture of the
Court into loyalty programs, involved an appeal from the dismissal of a
teacher pursuant to a New York statute which disqualified from civil
service and public school employment any person advocating, advising,
or teaching governmental overthrow by force or violence.[3]

Appellant's claim that his freedom of speech and association had
been infringed by the statutes was not persuasive because the Court, at
this point in the development of the law, did not consider employment
to be constitutionally a "right," thus removing it from the spectrum of
constitutional protection. As the majority opinion phrased it—

> They [appellants] may work for the school system upon the reason-
> able terms laid down by the proper authorities of New York. If
> they do not choose to work on such terms, they are at liberty to
> retain their beliefs and associations and go elsewhere.[4]

Thus, the Court employed the then traditional view that public
employment was a privilege rather than a right, illustrated by Justice
Holmes' famous dictum, ". . . petitioner may have a constitutional right
to talk politics, but he has no constitutional right to be a policeman."[5]
However, the subsequent erosion of the doctrine that public employment, as a mere privilege, could be conditioned upon a surrender of
constitutional rights,[6] forced a re-examination of the basic tenets of
Adler and eventually removed *Adler's* constitutional underpinnings.

Loyalty Oaths. *Wieman v. Updegraff,*[7] decided the same term as
Adler, demonstrated that the Court would not allow even a privilege to

---

§ 20.42

1. For more detailed and interpretive
analyses, see T. Emerson, The System of
Freedom of Expression (1970); and Developments In the Law—The National Security Interest and Civil Liberties, 85 Harv.
L.Rev. 1130 (1972); Developments in the
Law—Public Employment, 97 Harv.L.Rev.
1611, 1738–1800 (1984); Harry Kalven, Jr.,
ed. by Jamie Kalven, A Worthy Tradition:
Freedom of Speech in America 340–67
(1988).

2. 342 U.S. 485, 72 S.Ct. 380, 96 L.Ed.
517 (1952) (Justices Black, Douglas, &

Frankfurter dissented), affirmed 342 U.S.
951, 72 S.Ct. 624, 96 L.Ed. 707 (1952).

3. 342 U.S. at 487–89 n. 3, 72 S.Ct. at
382–83 n. 3.

4. 342 U.S. at 492, 72 S.Ct. at 385.

5. McAuliffe v. New Bedford, 155 Mass.
216, 220, 29 N.E. 517, 517 (1892).

6. See Van Alstyne, The Demise of the
Right–Privilege Distinction in Constitutional Law, 81 Harv.L.Rev. 1439 (1968);
see § 17.5(d), supra.

7. 344 U.S. 183, 73 S.Ct. 215, 97 L.Ed.
216 (1952).

be withdrawn on the basis of certain broad classifications. Oklahoma required that its state employees take what is often called a negative oath—that is, an oath requiring an individual to swear that he or she had not done something in the past. (An affirmative oath, in contrast, requires the prospective employee to swear support in the future to the constitutional processes of government.) The Oklahoma oath required state employees to swear that they were not members of the Communist Party, or—

> any agency, party, organization, association or group whatever which has been officially determined ... to be a communist front or subversive organization ... that advocated the overthrow of the Government of the United States or of the State of Oklahoma by force or violence or other unlawful means.[8]

Reacting to the Oklahoma Supreme Court's interpretation of that language as including within the proscription persons "solely on the basis of organizational membership, regardless of their knowledge" [9] concerning the activities of such organizations, the Court determined that the oath offended due process.[10] The majority found that the denial of public employment for subversive association stigmatizes the individual and is unjustified when the member is innocent of the group's illegal and subversive goals:

> [U]nder the Oklahoma Act, the fact of association alone determines disloyalty and disqualification; it matters not whether association existed innocently or knowingly. To thus inhibit individual freedom of movement is to stifle the flow of democratic expression and controversy at one of its chief sources ... Indiscriminate classification of innocent with knowing activity must fall as an assertion of arbitrary power.[11]

Following *Wieman,* the Supreme Court at first chose to deal with loyalty qualifications primarily by the use of the vagueness and overbreadth doctrines. Thus, *Shelton v. Tucker,*[12] invalidated an Arkansas statute requiring teachers to file an affidavit listing all the organizations to which they had belonged or contributed within the past five years. The state's legitimate interest in investigating the loyalty of its teachers did not justify the "unlimited and indiscriminate sweep" of the statute when less restrictive alternatives, offering less impingement upon the teachers' freedom of association, were available.

8. 344 U.S. at 184–85 n. 1, 73 S.Ct. at 215–16 n. 1.

9. 344 U.S. at 190, 73 S.Ct. at 218.

10. See Garner v. Board of Public Works, 341 U.S. 716, 71 S.Ct. 909, 95 L.Ed. 1317 (1951), rehearing denied 342 U.S. 843, 72 S.Ct. 21, 96 L.Ed. 637 (1951).

11. 344 U.S. at 191, 73 S.Ct. at 219.

12. 364 U.S. 479, 81 S.Ct. 247, 5 L.Ed.2d 231 (1960) (Frankfurter, Harlan, Clark, & Whittaker, JJ., dissented).

In *Cramp v. Board of Public Instruction,*[13] the Court unanimously invalidated a Florida statute requiring employees to swear, "I have not and will not lend my aid, support, advice, counsel or influence to the Communist Party."[14] The consequences of such vague and ambiguous wording would not only inhibit legitimate activity by those whose "conscientious scruples were the most sensitive," but would increase the likelihood of prosecution for ideas antithetical to those held by the general community.

Employing a similar rationale in *Baggett v. Bullitt,*[15] the Court invalidated two Washington loyalty oath requirements. The first required the affiant to promote, by teaching and example, "respect for the flag and the institutions of the United States of America and the State of Washington" and the second, to swear that he was not a member of a "subversive organization." Once again, the language was found susceptible of an interpretation applying to a broad spectrum of behavior with which the State could not interfere. Moreover, the lack of any criminal sanction for its future violation did not prevent the oath from being stricken since this would not avoid the prohibited deterrent effect upon those who will only swear to that which they can obey.

The Leading Case of *Elfbrandt v. Russell.* The Court eventually found that the *Wieman* standard—mere knowledge of illegal aims of the organization—was insufficient to terminate an individual's employment. *Elfbrandt v. Russell*[16] involved a challenge to an Arizona statute imposing an oath upon the prospective employee that he had not knowingly and willfully become or remained a member of an organization dedicated to the overthrow by force or violence of the government with knowledge of its illegal aims.

The majority opinion found this oath to prohibit "knowing, but guiltless" behavior because the oath did not require the individual to have participated in, or subscribed to the unlawful activities in order for employment to be terminated and prosecution for perjury to be instituted. The Court relied on previous decisions involving criminal prosecutions under the Smith Act[17] and held that the same standards were applicable to employment discrimination; "knowing membership" coupled with a specific intent to further the illegal aims of the organizations would be required because "quasi-political parties or other groups

13. 368 U.S. 278, 82 S.Ct. 275, 7 L.Ed.2d 285 (1961), on remand 137 So.2d 828 (Fla. 1962).

14. 368 U.S. at 279 n. 1, and 286–87, 82 S.Ct. at 276 n. 1 and 280–81.

15. 377 U.S. 360, 84 S.Ct. 1316, 12 L.Ed.2d 377 (1964).

16. 384 U.S. 11, 86 S.Ct. 1238, 16 L.Ed.2d 321 (1966).

See generally Israel, Elfbrandt v. Russell, The Demise of The Oath?, 1966 Sup. Ct.Rev. 193.

17. Scales v. United States, 367 U.S. 203, 81 S.Ct. 1469, 6 L.Ed.2d 782 (1961), rehearing denied 366 U.S. 978, 81 S.Ct. 1912, 6 L.Ed.2d 1267 (1961) and Noto v. United States, 367 U.S. 290, 81 S.Ct. 1517, 6 L.Ed.2d 836 (1961).

... may embrace both legal and illegal aims."[18] Following *Elfbrandt* the Court focused its attention to substantive loyalty-security restrictions on public employment. We shall now consider these decisions, and their contribution to the development of the law, and then revisit the loyalty oath cases when the Court in the next decade turned its sights once again on the loyalty oath.

Substantive Loyalty–Security Employment Restrictions. In *Keyishian v. Board of Regents,*[19] the Court finally came full circle and invalidated the Feinberg Law which had been upheld in *Adler* fifteen years before. Noting the pertinent constitutional doctrines which had arisen in the interim, and the absence of any claim of vagueness in *Adler,* the Court determined *Adler* to be no longer controlling. Examining the complex interdependence of the various provisions of the New York law, Justice Brennan, speaking for the Court, found them unconstitutionally vague.

> The very intricacy of the plan and the uncertainty as to the scope of its proscriptions make it a highly efficient *in terrorem* mechanism. It would be a bold teacher who would not stay as far as possible from utterances or acts which might jeopardize his living by enmeshing him in this intricate machinery.... The result must be to stifle that free play of the spirit which all teachers ought especially to cultivate and practice.[20]

Further, a provision added to the statute since the *Adler* decision stated that mere membership in a prohibited organization, as determined by the State Board of Regents, created *prima facie* evidence of disqualification for employment which could be rebutted by appellant only in one of three ways: denial of membership, denial that the organization advocated overthrow, or denial that appellant had knowledge of such advocacy. The provision was invalidated as overbroad relying on *Elfbrandt,* because the New York law did not allow the presumption to be rebutted by denial of specific intent to further the unlawful aims of the organization or denial of active membership.[21]

In the same year, the Court, in *United States v. Robel,*[22] dealt with employment restrictions in federal legislation. The majority opinion of Chief Justice Warren determined that § 5(a)(1)(D) of the Subversive

---

18. 384 U.S. at 15, 86 S.Ct. at 1240, quoting Scales v. United States, 367 U.S. 203, 229, 81 S.Ct. 1469, 1486, 6 L.Ed.2d 782 (1961), rehearing denied 366 U.S. 978, 81 S.Ct. 1912, 6 L.Ed.2d 1267 (1961).

See also, Cole v. Richardson, 405 U.S. 676, 92 S.Ct. 1332, 31 L.Ed.2d 593 (1972), discussed below.

19. 385 U.S. 589, 87 S.Ct. 675, 17 L.Ed.2d 629 (1967).

20. 385 U.S. at 601, 87 S.Ct. at 683 citing Wieman v. Updegraff, 344 U.S. 183,

195, 73 S.Ct. 215, 221, 97 L.Ed. 216 (1952) (Frankfurter, J. concurring).

21. In light of Speiser v. Randall, 357 U.S. 513, 78 S.Ct. 1332, 2 L.Ed.2d 1460 (1958), it is doubtful that the addition of those requirements would save the statute because the burden remains on the affiant to establish his innocent connection with the organization.

22. 389 U.S. 258, 88 S.Ct. 419, 19 L.Ed.2d 508 (1967).

Activities Control Act was unconstitutionally overbroad by denying to members of designated "communist-action" groups employment in any defense facility.

The Court refused to narrow the application of the statutory prohibition to bring it within constitutional standards, as had been done in *Scales*,[23] noting—

> the clarity and preciseness of the provision in question make it impossible to narrow its indiscriminately cast and overly broad scope without substantial rewriting.[24]

The statutory language made irrelevant the active or passive status of the individual's membership, his knowledge of the illegal aims of the organization or lack of it, the degree of his agreement or disagreement with those aims, and the sensitive nature of his position of employment as it affected national security. The Court held that the statute literally established guilt by association and inhibited the exercise of first amendment rights while less restrictive means of achieving the legislative objective were at hand.

Thus, the constitutional requirements involving loyalty-security qualifications for employment by either federal or state governments parallel each other quite closely. An individual may not be punished or deprived of public employment for political association unless: (1) he is an active member of a subversive organization; (2) such membership is with knowledge of the illegal aims of the organization; *and* (3) the individual has a specific intent to further those illegal ends, as opposed to the general support of the general objectives of an organization.

Robel does leave an indication, however, that the federal government's interest in national security may on occasion override individual rights of association, depending upon the sensitivity of the proffered employment. Denial of a position with a demonstrable relationship to important national security interests might be justified on a finding that the person's status is nothing more than active, knowing membership in a subversive organization, because the potential conversion of such an individual to the adoption of illegal means to achieve the organization's political objectives would not offer the government an adequate opportunity to forestall the implementation of those means.[25]

Loyalty Oaths Revisited. The subsequent decisions have had little impact on the prior law governing the ability of the government to discharge workers for their associational or speech activities. In

23. Scales v. United States, 367 U.S. 203, 81 S.Ct. 1469, 6 L.Ed.2d 782 (1961), rehearing denied 366 U.S. 978, 81 S.Ct. 1912, 6 L.Ed.2d 1267 (1961).

24. 389 U.S. at 262, 88 S.Ct. at 422 quoting Aptheker v. Secretary of State, 378 U.S. 500, 515, 84 S.Ct. 1659, 1669, 12 L.Ed.2d 992 (1964).

25. See 389 U.S. at 266–68, 88 S.Ct. at 424–26.

Connell v. Higginbotham,[26] the Court, in a per curiam opinion, invalidated a section of a Florida loyalty oath requiring the affiant to disclaim belief in the overthrow of the federal or state government by force or violence. The statute's requirement of dismissal without notice or hearing for failure to take the oath was violative of due process because the appellant was afforded no opportunity to explain his refusal, thus potentially allowing dismissal for possible protected activity.

The Court applied similar standards to access to the ballot in unanimously invalidating an Indiana oath requiring political parties to disclaim *any* advocacy of overthrow of the government by force.[27]

Loyalty Oaths and the Decision in *Cole v. Richardson.* The Court decision in *Cole v. Richardson,*[28] represents an opinion of significant impact upon statutory oaths as opposed to substantive legislative restrictions. The Court in *Cole* indicated a greater willingness to construe arguably overbroad or vague oath requirements so as to comport with constitutional guidelines.

The analysis in *Cole* began by acknowledging that previous decisions of the Court had established a distinction between oaths which require individuals to swear to the appropriateness of their past conduct, so-called negative oaths, and oaths which merely require the individual to swear his support in the future to the constitutional processes of government, so-called affirmative oaths.[29] Unlike negative oaths, affirmative oaths have traditionally been viewed as constitutionally permissible despite the inherent vagueness of the terms employed. The primary justification for overlooking the inability of the wording to distinguish between protected and unprotected activity (which must be defended against by the affiant) is the presence of such wording in the body of the Constitution for the presidential oath [30] and the oath for federal and state officials.[31] The purpose motivating the enactment of such affirmative oaths is looked upon as merely "to assure that those in positions of public trust were willing to commit themselves to live by the constitutional processes." [32] The effect is substantially equated with that of a vow of allegiance.[33]

26. 403 U.S. 207, 91 S.Ct. 1772, 29 L.Ed.2d 418 (1971) (per curiam).

27. Communist Party of Indiana v. Whitcomb, 414 U.S. 441, 94 S.Ct. 656, 38 L.Ed.2d 635 (1974), rehearing denied 415 U.S. 952, 94 S.Ct. 1476, 39 L.Ed.2d 568 (1974).

28. 405 U.S. 676, 92 S.Ct. 1332, 31 L.Ed.2d 593 (1972).

29. See Bond v. Floyd, 385 U.S. 116, 135, 87 S.Ct. 339, 349, 17 L.Ed.2d 235 (1966); Knight v. Board of Regents, 269 F.Supp. 339 (S.D.N.Y.1967), affirmed per curiam 390 U.S. 36, 88 S.Ct. 816, 19 L.Ed.2d 812 (1968).

30. Art. II, § 1, cl. 8.

31. Art. VI, cl. 3.

32. 405 U.S. at 684, 92 S.Ct. at 1337.

33. Knight v. Board of Regents, 269 F.Supp. 339, 341 (S.D.N.Y.1967), affirmed 390 U.S. 36, 88 S.Ct. 816, 19 L.Ed.2d 812 (1968). See Ohlson v. Phillips, 397 U.S. 317, 90 S.Ct. 1124, 25 L.Ed.2d 337 (1970), rehearing denied 397 U.S. 1081, 90 S.Ct. 1520, 25 L.Ed.2d 819 (1970).

The challenged oath in *Cole,* which Massachusetts required of its state employees, read as follows:

> I do solemnly swear (or affirm) that I will uphold and defend the Constitution of the United States ... and the Constitution of the Commonwealth of Massachusetts and that I will oppose the overthrow of the government of the United States of America or of this Commonwealth by force, violence or by any illegal or unconstitutional method.[34]

Chief Justice Burger, writing for a four to three majority, read the first portion of the oath, swearing to "uphold and defend", as a permissible "affirmative oath." This result allowed the Court to conclude that a literal reading of the second part, requiring opposition to attempted overthrow, was unnecessary. The second part of this oath was not unduly vague; it did not raise the specter of some undefinable responsibility to actively combat a potential revolution. Rather, it should be read as merely a negative restatement of the "support" oath:

> [A] commitment not to use illegal and constitutionally unprotected force to change the constitutional system. The second clause does not expand the obligation of the first; it simply makes clear the application of the first clause to a particular issue. Such repetition, whether for emphasis or cadence, seems to be the wont of authors of oaths. That the second clause may be redundant is no ground to strike it down; we are not charged with correcting grammar but with enforcing a constitution.[35]

The dissenters, Justices Douglas, Marshall, and Brennan, ignored the nebulous nature of the positive portion of the oath, but argued that the vagueness of "oppose" left the affiant in a quandary concerning when and by what method he must demonstrate his opposition. As Justice Douglas put the dilemma, the oath "requires that appellee 'oppose' that which she has an indisputable right to advocate." [36]

Thus, after *Cole* and *Elfbrandt* [37] it is now clear that they must be clear, concise, and narrow in scope, although affirmative oaths, relating only to allegiance to constitutional processes of government, are accorded a wider range of permissibility. The Court is more likely to construe arguably vague requirements so as to avoid constitutional requirements. Negative oaths cannot require a disclaimer of past conduct or belief other than that for which the employee may be constitutionally denied employment pursuant to an investigation, i.e. the two step standard of *Elfbrandt.*

---

34. 405 U.S. at 677–78, 92 S.Ct. at 1334 (footnote omitted).

35. 405 U.S. at 684, 92 S.Ct. at 1337.

36. 405 U.S. at 689, 92 S.Ct. at 1339 (dissenting opinion).

37. Elfbrandt v. Russell, 384 U.S. 11, 86 S.Ct. 1238, 16 L.Ed.2d 321 (1966), discussed supra.

Political Patronage Dismissals. The *Cole* decision has not signaled any diluting of the basic proposition that one may not be excluded from public employment on the basis of political affiliation unless the proscribed organization is truly subversive. The Court emphasized this constitutional rule in *Elrod v. Burns*,[38] where it invalidated political patronage dismissals by the Democratic Sheriff of Cook County. Respondents' discharge was unrelated to membership in any subversive organization. They were Republicans who were discharged or threatened with discharge because they were Republicans.

While individuals affiliated with subversive organizations may be denied public employment pursuant to the safeguards outlined in *Keyishian* and *Robel*, dismissal merely for membership in an opposing political party which poses no illegal threat to the democratic process falls squarely within the overarching principle of those cases: the imposition of burdens based solely upon political association is forbidden. The Court in *Elrod* did entertain arguments alleging the existence of a significant state interest in political patronage, primarily the preservation of the two party system and promotion of interest in lower echelon elections, but such interests were unpersuasive when weighed against the restraint such practices placed upon the freedoms of belief and association.

It is important to note that, while the broad language of the plurality opinion of Justice Brennan questioned the validity of patronage practices at all levels of government, the pivotal concurrences of Justices Stewart and Blackmun narrowed the effect of the case. In their view, *Elrod* held only that the dismissal of a non-policy making, non-confidential government employee could not be constitutionally justified by the alleged benefits of political patronage.[39] Different considerations, attend those higher-echelon government employees because they are principally responsible for promulgating and implementing the goals of the party attaining office in the election.

The Court reaffirmed the *Elrod* protection against political patronage dismissals in *Branti v. Finkel*,[40] an opinion that, unlike *Elrod*, attracted a majority. The proper test, said the majority, to determine

---

38. 427 U.S. 347, 96 S.Ct. 2673, 49 L.Ed.2d 547 (1976), appeal after remand 757 F.2d 151 (7th Cir.1985).

See generally, Johnson, Successful Reform Litigation: The *Shakman* Patronage Case, 64 Chicago–Kent L.Rev. 479 (1988); Strauss, Legality, Activism and the Patronage Case, 64 Chicago–Kent L.Rev. 585 (1988).

39. Elrod v. Burns, 427 U.S. 347, 374–75, 96 S.Ct. 2673, 2690–91, 49 L.Ed.2d 547 (1976), appeal after remand 757 F.2d 151 (7th Cir.1985).

40. 445 U.S. 507, 100 S.Ct. 1287, 63 L.Ed.2d 574 (1980). See also, McCormick v. Edwards, 646 F.2d 173 (5th Cir.1981), rehearing denied 651 F.2d 776 (5th Cir. 1981), certiorari denied 454 U.S. 1017, 102 S.Ct. 552, 70 L.Ed.2d 415 (1981), rehearing denied 454 U.S. 1165, 102 S.Ct. 1042, 71 L.Ed.2d 323 (1982).

See generally, Note, First Amendment Limitations on Patronage Employment Practices, 49 U.Chi.L.Rev. 181 (1982).

whether political affiliation is a legitimate factor to consider in government employment "is not whether the label 'policymakers' or 'confidential' fits a particular position; rather, the question is whether the hiring authority can demonstrate that party affiliation is an appropriate requirement for the effective performance of the public office involved." [41] Thus *Branti* reasoned that a state's election laws could require that there be two election judges each representing one of the two main parties, even though the job of election supervision does not involve policy making or access to confidential information. Similarly, the state could not fire a state university football coach because of his political affiliation, even though his job involves some policy making. In *Branti* the Court prohibited the Democratic Public Defender from firing the Republican Assistant Public Defenders solely because of their political beliefs.

Branti thus ruled that a state official may not terminate the employment of a public defender for purely political grounds because any policy making role he might have should not relate to partisan political interests; his confidential information based on the attorney client relationship has no relation to partisan political concerns; and making his tenure depend on his political affiliation would not advance the effective performance of his duties. However, a public employee cannot secure tenure by the simple expedient of undermining and criticizing her superiors and disrupting office morale. In the usual case it is only when the public employee speaks on "matters of public concern" that the first amendment prohibits a retaliatory discharge. [42]

---

41. 445 U.S. at 521, 100 S.Ct. at 1296. Stewart, J., dissented because he disagreed with the standard created by the majority; he found the professional and confidential nature of employment to be determinative. Justice Stewart relied on the distinction that he had drawn in his concurrence in *Elrod* (a concurrence joined by Justice Blackmun), in which he argued that *Elrod* only ruled that the dismissal of a nonpolicy making, nonconfidential governmental employee could not be constitutionally justified by the alleged benefits of political patronage. 427 U.S. at 374–75, 96 S.Ct. at 2690–91.

Powell, J., joined by Rehnquist, J., objected to the majority creating a first amendment protection in the first place.

42. **Matters of Public Concern.** See Connick v. Myers, 461 U.S. 138, 103 S.Ct. 1684, 75 L.Ed.2d 708 (1983), where the Court, in a five to four decision, upheld the firing of an assistant district attorney for circulating a questionnaire regarding office policies. The questionnaire did not touch upon matters of public concern in any real

sense. The employer need not tolerate action which he reasonably believed would disrupt the office, undermine his authority, and destroy close working relationships. "We hold only that when a public employee speaks not as a citizen upon matters of public concern, but instead as an employee upon matters of personal interest, absent the most unusual circumstances, a federal court is not the appropriate forum in which to review the wisdom of a personnel decision taken by a public agency allegedly in reaction to the employee's behavior." 461 U.S. at 147, 103 S.Ct. at 1690.

See also, Schmidt v. Fremont County School District, 558 F.2d 982, 984 (10th Cir.1977).

An employee may speak out on a matter of public concern even though she arranges to speak privately. Givhan v. Western Line Consolidated School District, 439 U.S. 410, 415–16, 99 S.Ct. 693, 696–97, 58 L.Ed.2d 619 (1979).

Rankin v. McPherson, 483 U.S. 378, 107 S.Ct. 2891, 97 L.Ed.2d 315 (1987) (it is un-

Elrod and *Branti* serve to silhouette the basic legislative goals that may serve as a constitutional basis for denial or termination of public employment. The initial focus must be on the character of the organization; unless it is one posing a threat to democratic government not only in terms of its advocacy but also its ultimate goals there is little chance that there can be found to be significant state interest in prohibiting its members *qua* members from the public payroll. Moreover, even if the organization is one which may constitutionally be guarded against, only those members who have knowledge of its illegal goals and have a specific intent to further those goals may be precluded from public employment.[43]

Rutan v. Republican Party of Illinois,[44] extended *Branti* in a five to four decision. Justice Brennan, for the Court, held that not only the patronage practice of discharging public employees on the basis of their political affiliation violates the First Amendment, but related patronage practices "involving low-level public employees"—such as hiring, promotion, transfer, and recall after layoff—also may not constitutionally be based on party affiliation and support. "Employees who do not compromise their beliefs stand to lose the considerable increases in pay and job satisfaction attendant to promotions, the hours and maintenance expenses that are consumed by long daily commutes, and even their jobs if they are not rehired after a 'temporary' layoff.... Unless these patronage practices are narrowly tailored to further vital government interests, we must conclude that they impermissibly encroach on First Amendment freedoms."[45] In a footnote the Court said that the First Amendment protects state employees not only from patronage dismissals but " 'even an act of retaliation as trivial as failing to hold a birthday party for a public employee ... when intended to punish her for exercising her free speech rights.' "[46] In short, it violates the first amendment for the Government to determine promotions, transfers, or recalls after layoffs based on the political affiliation of low-level Government employees.

The majority emphasized that the first amendment does not give

constitutional to discharge a county employee because she said, in a private conversation to coemployee, that she hoped any future attempt to assassinate the President would be successful), rehearing denied 483 U.S. 1056, 108 S.Ct. 31, 97 L.Ed.2d 819 (1987).

Note, *Connick v. Myers:* New Restrictions on the Free Speech Rights of Government Employees, 60 Indiana L.J. 339 (1985).

43. As discussed above, *Robel* offers a potential exception for individuals in highly sensitive governmental jobs who are

knowing members, as they may adopt, subsequent to their employment, the illegal aims of the organization. See Robel v. United States, 389 U.S. 258, 266–68, 88 S.Ct. 419, 424–26, 19 L.Ed.2d 508 (1967).

44. 497 U.S. ___, 110 S.Ct. 2729, 111 L.Ed.2d 52 (1990), rehearing denied ___ U.S. ___, 111 S.Ct. 13, 111 L.Ed.2d 828 (1990).

45. 497 U.S. at ___, 110 S.Ct. at 2736.

46. 497 U.S. at ___, 110 S.Ct. at 2738 n. 8.

Government workers tenure.[47] The Government has an interest in having effective employees, so it certainly can discharge, demote, or transfer staff members whose work is deficient.[48] The Government also has an interest in securing employees who will loyally implement its policies, but this interest can be "adequately served by choosing or dismissing certain high-level employees on the basis of their political views." [49]

(b) Exercise of the Fifth Amendment

Questions occasionally arise as to the legitimacy of sanctions applied against a public employee who has asserted the fifth amendment privilege against self-incrimination when questioned as to his political associations. In *Slochower v. Board of Higher Education of New York City*,[50] the Court considered a summary dismissal of a teacher following his refusal to answer such questions. A provision in the New York municipal charter required the dismissal—without any notice or hearing—of any city employee who pled the fifth amendment in order to refuse to answer questions related to his official conduct. The city law in effect treated the questions asked as confessed and made the basis of the discharge because the city employee (in this case an associate professor at Brooklyn College) pled the fifth amendment. The Court held that the dismissal in these circumstances was unconstitutional. Without further evidence, independent of the assertion of the privilege, such a dismissal violated due process.

Use Immunity. However, the fifth amendment does not serve as an impenetrable barrier which will protect the identity of one's political affiliations. The Court has held that if "use immunity" [51] is granted the employee, he or she can no longer assert the privilege, and may be compelled to answer.[52] However, if no immunity is offered, the employee cannot be forced to choose between forfeiture of his public employ-

---

47. 497 U.S. at ___, 110 S.Ct. at 2737–78.

48. 497 U.S. at ___, 110 S.Ct. at 2737.

49. 497 U.S. ___, 110 S.Ct. at 2737. The Court did not discuss this issue further, but in another footnote stated that the scope of the exception in *Branti*—where "party affiliation is an appropriate requirement for the effective performance of the public office involved"—"does not concern us here as respondents concede that the five employees who brought this suit are not within it." 497 U.S. at ___ n. 5, 110 S.Ct. at 2735 n. 5. The Court remanded so that the petitioners could have their trial.

Justice Scalia, joined by Rehnquist, C.J., Kennedy, J., and (in part), O'Connor, J., dissented, arguing that *Branti* should be overruled. Stevens, J., filed a concurring opinion.

50. 350 U.S. 551, 76 S.Ct. 637, 100 L.Ed. 692 (1956), rehearing denied 351 U.S. 944, 76 S.Ct. 843, 100 L.Ed. 1470 (1956); see also Konigsberg v. State Bar of California, 353 U.S. 252, 77 S.Ct. 722, 1 L.Ed.2d 810 (1957), rehearing denied 354 U.S. 927, 77 S.Ct. 1374, 1 L.Ed.2d 1441 (1957) discussed below.

51. Use immunity, as defined in 18 U.S.C.A. § 6002, provides immunity from the use of the compelled testimony and evidence derived therefrom.

52. Kastigar v. United States, 406 U.S. 441, 92 S.Ct. 1653, 32 L.Ed.2d 212 (1972), rehearing denied 408 U.S. 931, 92 S.Ct. 2478, 33 L.Ed.2d 345 (1972).

ment or self-incrimination.[53] Under the narrow use immunity, his answers may be used against him in a decision to terminate his employment because use immunity only bars use of the testimony in a criminal case.[54]

(c) National Security Restrictions

The Supreme Court has justified various first amendment restrictions on the activities of present or former government employees on the basis of the employees contract of employment. In the leading case the litigant against whom the Court upheld restraints was a former employee of the Central Intelligence Agency. In *Snepp v. United States*,[55] a former CIA agent, Frank W. Snepp, III, published a book concerning CIA involvement in South Vietnam, without seeking or securing the Agency's prepublication approval, in violation of his employment contract. Snepp, in this contract had promised that he would "not ... publish ... any information or material relating to the Agency, its activities or intelligence activities generally, either during or after the term of [his] employment ... without specific prior approval of the Agency."[56] He also agreed not to disclose any classified material without proper authorization.

Because Snepp published his book without submitting it for prepublication review, the CIA sued for an order enjoining him to submit future writings for prepublication review, a declaration that he had breached his contract, and a constructive trust for the Government of

---

53. Garrity v. New Jersey, 385 U.S. 493, 87 S.Ct. 616, 17 L.Ed.2d 562 (1967).

Lefkowitz v. Cunningham, 431 U.S. 801, 97 S.Ct. 2132, 53 L.Ed.2d 1 (1977) (state statute which provided that if an officer of a political party subpoenaed by a grand jury or other authorized tribunal to testify concerning the conduct of his office refuses to testify or refuses to waive immunity from later prosecution from the use of his testimony, then the statute immediately terminates his party office and prohibits him from holding any other party or public office for a period of five years, held unconstitutional as a violation of the self incrimination clause of the fifth amendment as applied to the states through the fourteenth amendment).

If the employee is given "use immunity" and forced to testify that testimony cannot be used in a later criminal prosecution. In New Jersey v. Portash, 440 U.S. 450, 99 S.Ct. 1292, 59 L.Ed.2d 501 (1979) that grand jury testimony given under such immunity cannot be used even for impeachment purposes at trial. The Court found use of a balancing approach to be impermissible because testimony given under im-

munity is compulsory self-incrimination in its most "pristine" form.

54. Kastigar v. United States, 406 U.S. 441, 453, 92 S.Ct. 1653, 1661, 32 L.Ed.2d 212 (1972), rehearing denied 408 U.S. 931, 92 S.Ct. 2478, 33 L.Ed.2d 345 (1972). Cf. In re Schwarz, 51 Ill.2d 334, 282 N.E.2d 689 (1972), certiorari denied 409 U.S. 1047, 93 S.Ct. 527, 34 L.Ed.2d 499 (1972), rehearing denied 410 U.S. 917, 93 S.Ct. 959, 35 L.Ed.2d 281 (1973).

55. 444 U.S. 507, 100 S.Ct. 763, 62 L.Ed.2d 704 (1980), rehearing denied 445 U.S. 972, 100 S.Ct. 1668, 64 L.Ed.2d 250 (1980) (per curiam).

L. Ellerbee, And So It Goes: Adventures in Television (1986) reports that one CIA official said of free speech, "Remember— the First Amendment is only *an amendment*." (Quoted in Hollander, Book Review, The New York Times Book Review, May 11, 1986, at 9, col. 3).

See generally, Medow, The First Amendment and the Secrecy State: Snepp v. United States, 130 U.Penn.L.Rev. 775 (1982). See also § 20.17, supra.

56. 444 U.S. at 508, 100 S.Ct. at 765.

all profits earned from the publication of the book. For purposes of this litigation the Government conceded that Snepp's book disclosed *no* classified intelligence.

The Supreme Court, in a short per curiam opinion, delivered without benefit of oral arguments or full briefing, granted all of the Government's requested relief. In a footnote the majority dismissed Snepp's first amendment claims: "[E]ven in the absence of an express agreement—the CIA could have acted to protect substantial government interests by imposing reasonable restrictions on employee activities that in other contexts might be protected by the First Amendment. The Government has a compelling interest in protecting both the secrecy of information important to our national security and the appearance of confidentiality so essential to the effective operation of our foreign intelligence service. The agreement that Snepp signed is a reasonable means for protecting this vital interest." [57]

The majority contended that because Snepp's employment involved a high degree of trust and his explicit obligation to submit for prepublication review all material, whether classified or not, Snepp's violation impaired the CIA's statutory functions by limiting the CIA's ability to guarantee the security of information and protect intelligence sources. What Snepp should have done, rather than flout his preclearance obligation, said the majority, was to submit the book for prepublication review. This Agency clearance would be subject to judicial review. Thus if the CIA claimed that the book contained harmful classified disclosures and Snepp disagreed, the CIA then would have the burden of seeking an injunction against publication. [58]

The strong dissent of Justice Stevens, joined by Brennan and Marshall argued that because the Government had stipulated that the book contained no classified nonpublic material, the interest in confidentiality that Snepp's employment agreement was designed to protect had not been affected. Moreover there was no precedent to authorize a constructive trust because his book did not use, or profit from, confidential information as the Government stipulated. [59]

(d) Restrictions on Extra-Judicial Speech of Judges

Many states have based their rules governing judges on the American Bar Association's Model Code of Judicial Conduct. [60] This Model Code, and hence the codes of the states that derive their law from the ABA Judicial Code, have various (and often vague) restrictions on the

57. 444 U.S. at 511 n. 3, 100 S.Ct. at 765 n. 3 (citations omitted).

58. 444 U.S. at 513 n. 8, 100 S.Ct. at 767 n. 8.

59. 444 U.S. at 516–26, 100 S.Ct. at 768–74.

60. (1972, as amended), reprinted, e.g., in, T. Morgan & R. Rotunda, 1989 Selected Standards on Professional Responsibility (1989). See also, ABA Model Code of Judicial Conduct (1990), reprinted, e.g., in, T. Morgan & R. Rotunda, 1991 Selected Standards on Professional Responsibility (1991).

extra-judicial conduct of judges. Thus, Canon 3A(6) provides that a judge "should abstain from public comment about a pending or impending proceeding in *any* court...." (emphasis added). Canon 4 states that a judge may engage in certain "quasi-judicial activities" (such as speaking, writing, lecturing, and teaching "concerning the law, the legal system, and the administration of justice") "*if* in doing so he does not cast doubt on his capacity to decide impartially any issue that may come before him...." (emphasis added). Canon 7 places various other restrictions on political activities of judges. For example, Canon 7(A)(1)(b) prohibits a candidate for judicial office—some states still have select judges in partisan elections—from making "speeches for a political organization or candidate or publicly endorsing a candidate for public office."

A survey of the state cases and lower federal court cases suggests that some lower court judges do not carefully balance—or do not even attempt to balance—societal interests in placing some limits on the speech of judges with free speech concerns.[61] Indeed, it is not unusual for a judge subject to discipline not to raise any first amendment challenge to the restrictions as they are applied in a given case.

In re Bonin,[62] for example, is a case where the court was insensitive to free speech concerns. The court there held that a judge violated a Judicial Code when he attended a public meeting that included a lecture by Gore Vidal on "Sex and Politics in Massachusetts." At this meeting the judge was exposed to comments about a case pending in the superior court. That case was *not* before this judge but this judge was chief judge of the superior court. The defendants in the criminal case had been indicted for alleged sexual acts between men and boys. The Court said that this judge should have known that the purpose of

---

61. See generally, Anderson, Ethical Problems of Lawyers and Judge in Election Campaigns, 50 A.B.A.J. 819 (1964); Gary, Ethical Conduct in a Judicial Campaign: Is Campaigning an Ethical Activity?, 57 Wash.L.Rev. 119 (1981); S. Lubet, Beyond Reproach: Ethical Restrictions on the Extrajudicial Activities of State and Federal Judges (American Judicature Society 1984); Lubet, Judicial Ethics and Private Lives, 79 Nw.U.L.Rev. 983 (1985); Gross, Judicial Speech: Discipline and the First Amendment, 36 Syracuse L.Rev. 1181 (1986); Lubet, Judicial Impropriety: Love, Friendship, Free Speech and Other Intemperate Conduct, 1986 Ariz.St.L.J. 379 (1986); D'Alemberte, Searching for the Limits of Judicial Free Speech, 61 Tulane L.Rev. 611 (1987); Lubet, The Search for Analysis in Judicial Ethics or Easy Cases Don't Make Much Law, 66 Neb.L.Rev. 430 (1987); Snyder, The Constitutionality and

Consequences of Restrictions on Campaign Speech by Candidates for Judicial Office, 35 U.C.L.A.L.Rev. 207 (1987); Ross, The Questioning of Supreme Court Nominees at Senate Confirmation Hearings: Proposals for Accommodating the Needs of the Senate and Ameliorating the Fears of the Nominees, 62 Tulane L.Rev. 109 (1987); Copple, From the Cloister to the Street, 64 Denver U.L.Rev. 549 (1988); Ross, Extrajudicial Speech: Charting the Boundaries of Propriety, 2 Georgetown J. Legal Ethics 589 (1989); Lubet, Professor Polonius Advises Judge Laertes: Rules, Good Taste and the Scope of Public Comment, 2 Georgetown J. Legal Ethics 665 (1989); Jeffrey Shaman, Steven Lubet & James Alfini, Judicial Conduct and Ethics, §§ 6.01–6.08, 10.30 (1990).

62. 375 Mass. 680, 378 N.E.2d 669 (1978).

the public meeting was to raise money for the criminal defendants. In addition, by attending this public meeting, Judge Bonin "not only exposed himself to *ex parte* or one sided statements and argumentation on matters before his court, but further compromised his position by seeming to favor or have particular sympathy with the views of the partisan group which sponsored the affair." [63]   The Massachusetts Supreme Judicial Court acknowledged that normally "any judge would be entirely free to attend a public lecture about sex and politics whether or not sponsored by a 'gay' group." [64]   Yet that court unanimously held that Judge Bonin's actions were improper and justified his suspension and censure.

However, Judge Bonin had not been assigned to hear the criminal case at issue and would make no ruling regarding it, so the reference to hearing "one sided argumentation" was not particularly relevant. When Judge Bonin was sitting on the bench, he made no comments regarding the case, which was not before him.   And when Judge Bonin was off the bench (at the large public meeting) he made no remarks or comments about the case.   "While it is true that his attendance at the meeting might cause some to infer his support for the cause, it is at least equally likely that it would be interpreted as being motivated by curiosity or interest in the remarks of the well-known featured speaker." [65]

In contrast, in the case of *In re Gridley* [66] the Supreme Court of Florida refused to discipline a trial judge who had written letters to the editor and an article in his church newsletter expressing his opposition to capital punishment (though the judge did state that he would follow the law as written).   However, it is disquieting to note that the opinion refusing to discipline the judge did have a dissent, and even the majority said that Judge's Gridley's statements on the death penalty were "close to the dividing line." [67]

§ 20.43 Regulation of Labor Organizations

The Court has on several occasions dealt with federal legislation attempting to limit subversive influence in the labor hierarchy.   Because the decisions are quite dissimilar in both approach and result, it is difficult, if not impossible, to draw any thread of uniformity.   The easy answer may be simply that the difference in the membership of the Court as well as the political climate in each decision best explains the philosophical disparity.   Moreover, the major labor cases delineat-

---

63. 378 N.E.2d at 683.

64. 378 N.E.2d at 683.

65. S. Lubet, Beyond Reproach: Ethical Restrictions on the Extrajudicial Activities of State and Federal Judges 44 (American Judicature Society 1984). R. Rotunda, Pro-

fessional Responsibility 207–08 (West Black Letter Series, 2d ed. 1988).

66. 417 So.2d 950 (Fla.1982).

67. 417 So.2d at 954.

ing the protections afforded political association were not decided until after these opinions were handed down, leaving the possibility that wholly new considerations may apply to any future attempts by Congress to control subversives in the labor movement.

The first case, *American Communications Association v. Douds,*[1] decided in 1950, considered a challenge to § 9(h) the "non-Communist affidavit" provision of the Taft–Hartley Act of 1947.[2] Pursuant to that provision, any labor organization which desired the benefits of the National Labor Relations Act (N.L.R.A.) was required to have its officers file annually with the National Labor Relations Board affidavits disavowing membership in or support of the Communist Party as well as disclaiming membership, support, or belief in any organization which advocates or believes in the overthrow of the federal government by force or any illegal or unconstitutional means.[3] Legislative findings of fact supporting this statute determined that strikes called to achieve political rather than economic goals posed a severe threat to the flow of interstate commerce. The past beliefs and associations of the individuals designated by the provision would serve as a reasonable method to identify them as potential instigators of such strikes and the presence of such individuals in positions of influence in labor unions would greatly increase their potential.

The Court found that there existed a reasonable relationship between the evil and the means implemented to avoid that evil, because past beliefs and associations are sufficient criterion to infer future conduct consistent with those beliefs.[4] However, further analysis was required because the means employed discouraged the lawful exercise of first amendment freedoms.

The Court rejected appellant's claim that whenever rights of free speech and association are impaired the clear and present danger test is the appropriate adjudicative standard. In the Court's view, Congress had focused the thrust of its prohibition at preventing conduct and the subsequent effect on speech was merely incidental. The government's interest was—

> not in preventing the dissemination of Communist doctrine ... because it is feared that unlawful action will result ... such strikes

§ 20.43

1. 339 U.S. 382, 70 S.Ct. 674, 94 L.Ed. 925 (1950), rehearing denied 339 U.S. 990, 70 S.Ct. 1017, 94 L.Ed. 1391 (1950).

2. Officially known as the Labor–Management Relations Act; 61 Stat. 136, 146, 29 U.S.C.A. §§ 141, 159(h). Section 159(h) was later repealed by the Labor–Management Reporting and Disclosure Act

of 1959, 73 Stat. 519, 525, 29 U.S.C.A. § 201(d).

3. 339 U.S. at 385–86, 70 S.Ct. at 677–78.

4. American Communications Ass'n v. Douds, 339 U.S. 382, 391, 70 S.Ct. 674, 680, 94 L.Ed. 925 (1950), rehearing denied 339 U.S. 990, 70 S.Ct. 1017, 94 L.Ed. 1391 (1950).

are called by persons who, so Congress has found, have the will and power to do so *without* advocacy or persuasion that seeks acceptance in the competition of the market.[5]

Because the effect upon the first amendment was minimal and the public interest in an untrammelled flow of commerce great, the Court felt that a requirement of showing imminent national peril to invoke prophylactic measures would be an absurdity.[6] Rather, the competing values of free speech and the public interest in a responsible exercise of the power vested in labor by the N.L.R.A. must be weighed and the appropriate balance struck.[7]

In view of the great public interest in protecting the flow of commerce and the relative handful of individuals whose beliefs may actually be restrained by their desire for union office, as well as the fact that those individuals who were affected were not required to forego their beliefs because they could resign their position with the union with their beliefs intact, the Court found that Congress had not contravened the purposes of the first amendment.[8] Moreover, the Court construed the portions of the Act prohibiting mere belief to encompass only those union officials who held the belief in violent overthrow of the Government to be an objective, as opposed to a prophecy.[9]

Following *Douds,* there were 18 prosecutions instituted by the Government for the filing of false affidavits.[10] In only one of these cases did the appeal reach the Supreme Court, *Killian v. United States.*[11] The Court reversed petitioner's conviction on procedural grounds, but in the course of this decision it approved a broad interpretation of the requirement of "membership or affiliation" as related to the Communist Party. Emphasizing that no criminal sanctions applied to membership in or affiliation with the Communist Party under the terms of the Act, the Court rejected petitioner's claim that membership could only be determined by factual phenomena, such as a "specific formal act of joining."[12] The instruction to the jury which was approved allowed membership to be shown by state of mind; "the desire on the part of the individual to belong to the Communist Party and a

---

5. 339 U.S. at 396, 70 S.Ct. at 682–83 (emphasis in original; footnote omitted).

6. 339 U.S. at 397, 70 S.Ct. at 683.

7. 339 U.S. at 400, 70 S.Ct. at 684–85.

8. 339 U.S. at 404, 70 S.Ct. at 686–87.

9. 339 U.S. at 407, 70 S.Ct. at 688. Justice Jackson, although concurring in the decision as it related to the prohibition upon members of the Communist Party, dissented as to the prohibition upon those for mere belief. 339 U.S. at 437–43, 70 S.Ct. at 703–06; Justice Black dissented, stating that the statute should have out-

lawed political strikes and avoided the unnecessary impairment of First Amendment freedoms. 339 U.S. at 445, 70 S.Ct. at 707; Justices Douglas, Clark, and Minton did not participate.

10. 1 N. Dorsen, P. Bender, B. Newborne, Emerson, Haber, & Dorsen's Political and Civil Rights in the United States, 111 (4th ed. 1976).

11. 368 U.S. 231, 82 S.Ct. 302, 7 L.Ed.2d 256 (1961), rehearing denied 368 U.S. 979, 82 S.Ct. 476, 7 L.Ed.2d 441 (1962).

12. 368 U.S. at 247, 82 S.Ct. at 312.

recognition by that Party that it considers him as a member." [13]

In 1959, Congress repealed § 9(h) and provided, in its stead, § 504 of the Landrum–Griffin Act [14] which provided:

> No person who is or has been a member of the Communist Party ... shall serve ... as an officer, director, trustee, member of any executive board or similar governing body, business agent, manager, organizer, or other employee ... of any labor organization. [15]

United States v. Brown,[16] invalidated this provision as a bill of attainder.[17] The Court did not deny the legislative power to prevent political strikes by rationally related means, but a blanket decree that all individuals on the membership rolls of the Communist Party was unjustifiable in that it determined guilt by legislative fiat.

In language casting doubt on the reasoning in *Douds,* Chief Justice Warren's majority opinion declared:

> The designation of Communists as those persons likely to cause political strikes ... rests, as the Court in *Douds* explicitly recognized ... upon an empirical investigation by Congress of the acts, characteristics, and propensities of Communist Party members. In a number of decisions, this Court has pointed out the fallacy of the suggestion that membership in the Communist Party, or any other political organization, can be regarded as an alternative, but equivalent expression for a list of undesirable characteristics. [18]

However, since § 9(h) of the Taft–Hartley Act had permitted Communists to resign their membership in the Party if they wished to remain in their position as union officials, *Douds* was not explicitly overruled. While the decision may have blurred the lines between a bill of attainder and an *ex post facto* law, the Court in *Brown* held that, because former Communists could not serve as union officials for five years after their resignation, the statute served as prohibited legislative punishment,[19] regardless of the argument that the function of the statute was preventive rather than retributive:

> It would be archaic to limit the definition of "punishment" to "retribution." Punishment serves several purposes: retributive, rehabilitative, deterrent—and preventive. [20]

---

13. 368 U.S. at 247 n. 5, 82 S.Ct. at 312 n. 5.

14. Officially, the Labor–Management Reporting and Disclosure Act, 73 Stat. 536, 29 U.S.C.A. § 504.

15. 368 U.S. at 247 n. 5, 82 S.Ct. at 312 n. 5.

16. 381 U.S. 437, 85 S.Ct. 1707, 14 L.Ed.2d 484 (1965).

17. For an extensive analysis of bills of attainder, see Note, The Bounds of Legisla-

tive Specification: A Suggested Approach to the Bill of Attainder Clause, 72 Yale L.J. 330 (1962).

18. 381 U.S. at 455, 85 S.Ct. at 1718.

19. The statute must impose punishment to be voided as a bill of attainder; Cummings v. Missouri, 71 U.S. (4 Wall.) 277, 18 L.Ed. 356 (1867).

20. 381 U.S. at 458, 85 S.Ct. at 1720.

The authority of *Douds* in the wake of the language quoted above is nebulous, although *Brown* has not been relied on as precedent to overturn any further restrictions banning Communists or other political groups.

Moreover, the rise of the doctrine of unconstitutional conditions in the public employment area [21] seems to conflict with the *Douds* reasoning that § 9(h) imposed no unreasonable restraint on beliefs as the official had the option of resigning his position. However, *United States v. Robel*,[22] as discussed above, leaves the implication that mere beliefs may be restrained without a specific intent to further illegal goals if the individual occupies a sensitive position, which is precisely the rationale which motivated Congress to enact the provision.[23]

In the absence of federal regulation,[24] many unions have provided for limitation of subversive influence in their constitutions or have excluded subversives without the benefit of a constitutional provision.[25] The courts have declined to interfere in such intra-union activities.[26]

§ 20.44 Restrictions on Entry Into the Bar

States routinely require that applicants for membership to the bar possess certain attributes of character which are consistent with the practice of law. A significant component of this character, as a prospective member of a "profession dedicated to the peaceful and reasoned settlement of disputes between men, and between a man and his government,"[1] is loyalty to that system of government fostered by the Constitution and a devotion to "the law in its broadest sense, including not only its substantive provision, but also its procedures for orderly change."[2]

---

21. See § 20.42(a), supra. On employment restrictions.

22. 389 U.S. 258, 88 S.Ct. 419, 19 L.Ed.2d 508 (1967).

23. See, § 20.42(a), supra. However, see Osman v. Douds, 339 U.S. 846, 70 S.Ct. 901, 94 L.Ed. 1328 (1950), rehearing denied 340 U.S. 846, 71 S.Ct. 12, 95 L.Ed. 620 (1950), where the Court evenly split on the belief provisions of § 9(h), Justice Clark not participating.

24. Note that § 703(f), Civil Rights Act of 1964, 42 U.S.C.A. § 2000e–2(f), denies to Communist Party members and members of other subversive groups the benefits of the fair employment practices provision of that statute.

25. See Summers, The Right to Join a Union, 47 Colum.L.Rev. 33 (1947); Paschell and Theodore, Anti–Communist Provisions in Union Constitutions, 77 Monthly Lab. Rev. 1097 (1954).

26. N. Dorsen, P. Bender, B. Newborne, Emerson, Haber and Dorsen's Political and Civil Rights in the United States, 114 (4th ed. 1976), vol. I.

§ 20.44

1. Law Students Civil Rights Research Council, Inc. v. Wadmond, 401 U.S. 154, 166, 91 S.Ct. 720, 728, 27 L.Ed.2d 749 (1971).

See generally, Harry Kalven, Jr., ed. by Jamie Kalven, A Worthy Tradition: Freedom of Speech in America 548–87 (1988).

2. Konigsberg v. State Bar of California, 366 U.S. 36, 52, 81 S.Ct. 997, 1008, 6 L.Ed.2d 105 (1961) (Konigsberg II), rehearing denied 368 U.S. 869, 82 S.Ct. 21, 7 L.Ed.2d 69 (1961).

Not surprisingly, denials of admission to the bar on grounds of disloyalty have produced a spate of litigation alleging that such requirements restrict the applicant's rights of belief and association. Such cases have generally been presented in two basic contexts: the legitimacy of a denial based upon inferences of disloyalty due to specific incidents or circumstances in the applicant's past or the legitimacy of a denial due to a refusal to answer questions delving into the applicant's past political associations.[3]

Ex parte Garland,[4] the initial case dealing with loyalty oaths for attorneys, invalidated as a bill of attainder and an ex post facto law an oath that the individual had never supported or expressed sympathy for the enemies of the United States, foreign or domestic. Although *Garland* did not rest on the first amendment, which was not applicable to the states at that time, the modern cases make it clear that the statute would be invalid under present first amendment theory.

Political association cannot be construed as evidence of disloyalty unless the standard for criminally punishable political affiliation delineated in *Scales v. United States*[5] is satisfied.[6] The rationale is also much the same. Disabilities imposed by the legislatures upon an organization's ability to attract members cannot be justified unless the goals of such an organization encompass violent overthrow of the constitutionally established governments. Therefore, a member cannot be punished for his political affiliations unless he has knowledge of those illegal goals and has evidenced a specific intent to aid in the implementation of those goals.

The question of whether active membership status is required to infer disloyalty as a character trait was the issue in *Schware v. Board of Bar Examiners.*[7] In that case the New Mexico Board of Bar Examiners disqualified the petitioner on the grounds of membership in the Communist Party fifteen years prior to his application for admission to the bar.

The Supreme Court was unanimous in reversing this decision. As Justice Black noted in his majority opinion, membership in the Communist Party had not even been illegal at the time of Schware's membership. Moreover, the affirmative evidence produced by the petitioner as to his loyalty during the intervening fifteen years had demonstrated that his affiliation with the Party was sufficiently attenuated from his

---

3. The early cases are collected in Note, 18 A.L.R.2d 268, 283–91, 335–36 (1951).

4. 71 U.S. (4 Wall.) 333, 18 L.Ed. 366 (1867).

5. 367 U.S. 203, 81 S.Ct. 1469, 6 L.Ed.2d 782 (1961), rehearing denied 366 U.S. 978, 81 S.Ct. 1912, 6 L.Ed.2d 1267 (1961). See § 20.42(a), supra.

6. T. Emerson, The System of Freedom of Expression 240–41 (1970); and Note, Developments in the Law—The National Security Interest and Civil Liberties, 85 Harv.L.Rev. 1130, 1137–38, 1172–76 (1972).

7. 353 U.S. 232, 77 S.Ct. 752, 1 L.Ed.2d 796 (1957).

present life so as to remove any justification for relying on it as grounds for disloyalty.

There may be no general rule to be gleaned from the cases. At the least, it may be stated that past membership in a subversive organization cannot create an irrebuttable presumption of unfitness for the bar; also the first amendment will not protect an active, knowing member of the Communist Party with specific intent to aid in its illegal goals. The area between these extremes necessarily rests with the equities inherent in the particular fact situation.[8]

Following *Schware,* the Supreme Court was confronted with a series of cases in which there was no claim that past incidents in the applicant's life had revealed characteristics incompatible with the practice of law. Rather, the applicants had asserted a privilege in refusing to answer questions which they believed intruded unnecessarily into their first amendment freedoms.

The first case of this posture, *Konigsberg v. State Bar of California*[9] *(Konigsberg I),* decided the same term as *Schware,* dealt with the range of inferences which could properly be drawn from the applicant's refusal to answer questions relating to his past political affiliations. The California Bar had determined that petitioner's refusal to respond to inquiries into his membership in the Communist Party, coupled with other characteristics, required it to deny admission on the grounds that the petitioner had failed to establish his good moral character as well as his non-advocacy of illegal overthrow of the government.

The Supreme Court found such a conclusion unjustified based upon the evidence presented to the bar examiners. There must exist some authentic, affirmative evidence of disloyalty to deny admission to an applicant, not a conclusion of disloyalty based upon suspicions deduced from a refusal to answer questions. The majority opinion of Justice Black noted:

> We recognize the importance of leaving States free to select their own bars, but it is equally important that the State not exercise this power in an arbitrary or discriminatory manner nor in such way as to impinge on the freedom of political expression or association.... A lifetime of good citizenship is worth very little if it is so frail that it cannot withstand the suspicions which apparently were the basis for the Committee's action.[10]

Konigsberg (I) expressed no opinion as to the propriety of denying admission to the bar solely on the basis of an applicant's refusal to

8. See also In re Summers, 325 U.S. 561, 65 S.Ct. 1307, 89 L.Ed. 1795 (1945), rehearing denied 326 U.S. 807, 66 S.Ct. 94, 90 L.Ed. 491 (1945).

9. 353 U.S. 252, 77 S.Ct. 722, 1 L.Ed.2d 810 (1957) (Frankfurter, Harlan and Clark,

JJ., dissented), rehearing denied 354 U.S. 927, 77 S.Ct. 1374, 1 L.Ed.2d 1441 (1957).

10. 353 U.S. at 273–74, 77 S.Ct. at 733–34.

answer, because it did not consider that issue before it. Four years later the same parties appeared before the Court to litigate that question.[11] On rehearing for Konigsberg's application for admission to the bar of California, the applicant introduced further evidence of his good character and reiterated that he did not believe in or advocate violent overthrow of the government. Further he stated that he had never knowingly been a member of any organization with such objectives. Nevertheless, he steadfastly refused to answer questions concerning possible membership in the Communist Party. Relying solely on this refusal as an obstruction to a legitimate investigation, the bar examiners again denied him certification to practice law in that State.

In *Konigsberg (II)* the majority opinion of Justice Harlan rejected the claim that the state had placed upon Konigsberg the burden of establishing his loyalty, which would contravene the holding of *Speiser v. Randall.*[12] The denial had not been based upon any inference as to Konigsberg's character, but simply on his obstruction of the investigation. Because the state had the burden of producing evidence as to disloyalty, an applicant could not be allowed to frustrate that burden by refusing to submit relevant information.

This conclusion was dictated by the majority's view that, because the regulatory statute imposed only an incidental infringement upon speech, the state's interest in such regulation must be weighed against the appellant's interest in remaining silent. The balance was struck in favor of the state; the rationale for this conclusion was implicit in the Court's characterization of the competing values:

> [W]e regard the State's interest in having lawyers who are devoted to the law in its broadest sense, including not only its substantive provisions, but also its procedures for orderly change, as clearly sufficient to outweigh the minimal effect upon free association occasioned by compulsory disclosure in the circumstances here presented.[13]

Nor did the petitioner's voluntary disclosure of his general beliefs and associations moot the issue or make the question irrelevant, for the Committee is entitled to conduct its investigation in the manner it deems best suited to its purposes. Thus, although a denial of admission to the bar may not be premised on arbitrary or irrelevant information, there exists no privilege to refuse to provide legitimate information and denial of the application to practice is an appropriate device to prevent such frustrations of the investigative purpose.[14]

---

11. Konigsberg v. State Bar of California, 366 U.S. 36, 38, 81 S.Ct. 997, 1000, 6 L.Ed.2d 105 (1961) (Konigsberg II), rehearing denied 368 U.S. 869, 82 S.Ct. 21, 7 L.Ed.2d 69 (1961).

12. 357 U.S. 513, 78 S.Ct. 1332, 2 L.Ed.2d 1460 (1958).

13. 366 U.S. at 52, 81 S.Ct. at 1008.

14. See also In re Anastaplo, 366 U.S. 82, 81 S.Ct. 978, 6 L.Ed.2d 135 (1961), rehearing denied 368 U.S. 869, 82 S.Ct. 21, 7 L.Ed.2d 69 (1961).

Justice Black, in dissent, wrote one of his most celebrated attacks upon the theory of "balancing" in the first amendment area. Although he disagreed with the majority's characterization of this scheme as an "incidental" abridgement of speech,[15] the brunt of his attack was focused upon his philosophical antipathy towards balancing.

> I fear that the creation of "tests" by which speech is left unprotected under certain circumstances is a standing invitation to abridge it.... The Court suggests that a "literal reading of the First Amendment" would be totally unreasonable because it would invalidate many widely accepted laws ... it certainly would invalidate all laws that abridge the right of the people to discuss matters of religious or public interest, in the broadest meaning of those terms, for it is clear that a desire to protect this right was the primary purpose of the First Amendment.[16]

Balancing, in Black's view, is inherently dangerous and wholly lacking in judicial integrity because "... the application of such a test is necessarily tied to the emphasis particular judges give to competing societal values." [17] As if to illustrate this dictum, he stated that the appropriate characterization of these values would give emphasis to the social value of maintaining unimpaired freedoms of association and belief over a bar committee's curiosity concerning the applicant's possible membership in the Communist Party.

The validity of *Konigsberg (II)* was reemphasized and amplified by a trio of cases decided by the Court in 1971. The primary case, *Law Students Civil Rights Research Council, Inc. v. Wadmond*,[18] involved an attack upon the manner in which New York screened its applicants for the bar. The appellants had challenged, inter alia, that the appellees' use of a questionnaire, which bifurcated inquiry between knowing membership and membership with intent to further illegal goals, unnecessarily intruded into rights of association by requiring applicants to divulge knowing membership although there could be no inference of disloyalty based on such information. The Court, however, held that it was within reasonable legislative boundaries to inquire into knowing membership as a preliminary inquiry upon which to base further investigation.

Thus, an applicant to the bar may be required to answer a question concerning only his knowing membership on pain of denial of certification. If the applicant responds affirmatively, the examiners may probe more deeply into the nature of that association to determine if it is appropriate to deny admission. Judicial review is available to remedy

---

15. 366 U.S. at 71, 81 S.Ct. at 1017 (Black, J., dissenting joined by Warren, C.J., and Douglas, J.).

16. 366 U.S. at 63–64, 81 S.Ct. at 1014 (Black, J., dissenting).

17. 366 U.S. at 75, 81 S.Ct. at 1019.

18. 401 U.S. 154, 91 S.Ct. 720, 27 L.Ed.2d 749 (1971). (Justices Black, Douglas, Brennan and Marshall dissented).

any abuses resulting from solely an admission of knowing membership. Moreover, *Wadmond* found that there was no constitutional infirmity in inquiring into the applicant's ability to take the oath required of attorneys without any mental reservations,[19] as such inquiry is incorporated into the federal oath for uniformed and civil service personnel.

In the two accompanying decisions also handed down in 1971, *Baird v. State Bar of Arizona*[20] and *In re Stolar*,[21] the Court reaffirmed the rationale of *Wadmond* by invalidating denials of admission to the bar based on the petitioners' refusal to answer questions which were not limited to ascertaining "knowing" membership. Because the questions were overbroad and beyond the legitimate interest of the state in the affiliations of its attorneys, the sanction of denial of admission to the bar was improper.

Thus, at present, the first amendment does not provide an unlimited sanctuary for a bar applicant who does not desire to disclose his political affiliations. The state has an interest in informing itself of the philosophical context of the bar, particularly since it has the burden of establishing affirmative evidence of disloyalty. Frustration of a legitimate inquiry is subject to a denial of application for membership in the bar. However, the state's interest does not extend beyond interrogation concerning knowing membership, and a question beyond that permissible spectrum may be refused without penalty.

XIII. REGULATION OF THE TIME, PLACE, AND MANNER OF SPEECH IN PUBLIC PLACES AND THE PUBLIC FORUM

§ 20.45 Introduction

Justice Roberts, in his concurring opinion in *Hague v. CIO*,[1] expressed a narrow view of the Government's power to control speech that takes place on public property: "Wherever the title of streets and parks may rest, they have immemorially been held in trust for the use of the public and, time out of mind, have been used for purposes of assembly, communicating thoughts between citizens, and discussing public questions." [2] Yet other justices have inserted language in later

---

19. See also In re Summers, 325 U.S. 561, 65 S.Ct. 1307, 89 L.Ed. 1795 (1945), rehearing denied 326 U.S. 807, 66 S.Ct. 94, 90 L.Ed. 491 (1945).

20. 401 U.S. 1, 91 S.Ct. 702, 27 L.Ed.2d 639 (1971).

21. 401 U.S. 23, 91 S.Ct. 713, 27 L.Ed.2d 657 (1971).

§ 20.45

1. 307 U.S. 496, 59 S.Ct. 954, 83 L.Ed. 1423 (1939).

2. 307 U.S. at 515, 59 S.Ct. at 964 (Roberts, J., concurring, joined by Black, J.). Note that subsequently Justice Black appeared to retreat from this narrow view. E.g., Cox v. Louisiana, 379 U.S. 559, 578, 85 S.Ct. 476, 468–69, 13 L.Ed.2d 487 (1965) (Black, J., concurring and dissenting in part), rehearing denied 380 U.S. 926, 85 S.Ct. 879, 13 L.Ed.2d 814 (1965); Adderley v. Florida, 385 U.S. 39, 47–48, 87 S.Ct. 242, 247, 17 L.Ed.2d 149 (1966) (Black, J.), re-

opinions which treats public property as if it were private property for free speech purposes. Thus Justice Black, who had concurred with Roberts, later stated that he did not think the first and fourteenth amendments granted "a constitutional right to engage in the conduct of picketing or patrolling, whether on publicly owned streets or on privately owned property." [3] Justice Black's position, if taken literally, is an echo of Justice Holmes' view when he was a state court judge. Holmes said: "For the legislature absolutely or conditionally to forbid public speaking in a highway or public park is no more an infringement of the rights of a member of the public than for the owner of a private house to forbid it in his house." [4]

One's judgments between these competing viewpoints should be a function of how one weighs the interests at stake, that is, "the right to disseminate ideas in public places as against claims of an effective power in government to keep the peace and to protect other interests of a civilized community." [5] To this balance some would add claims of a special right of access by the public to commandeer such public places so that they can become a Public Forum.[6] Subsequent sections will examine some of the leading cases in this area in order to illustrate the major rules which have developed.[7]

§ 20.46 Licensing Schemes Implemented by Administrators and Injunctions Issued by the Courts

Often the state seeks to exercise time, place, or manner restrictions on speech in public places by use of licensing schemes. Justice Frankfurter has warned that the administrator's "net of control must not be cast too broadly." [1] Thus, a "licensing standard which gives an official authority to censor the content of a speech differs *toto caelo* from one limited by its terms, or by nondiscriminatory practice, to considerations of public safety and the like." [2] This rule may be illustrated by briefly

hearing denied 385 U.S. 1020, 87 S.Ct. 698, 17 L.Ed.2d 559 (1967).

3. Cox v. Louisiana, 379 U.S. 559, 578, 85 S.Ct. 476, 468, 13 L.Ed.2d 487 (1965), rehearing denied 380 U.S. 926, 85 S.Ct. 879, 13 L.Ed.2d 814 (1965) (Black, J. concurring and dissenting in part).

4. Commonwealth v. Davis, 162 Mass. 510, 511, 39 N.E. 113, 113 (1895), aff'd sub nom., Davis v. Massachusetts, 167 U.S. 43, 17 S.Ct. 731, 42 L.Ed. 71 (1897).

5. Niemotko v. Maryland, 340 U.S. 268, 273–274, 71 S.Ct. 328, 328–29, 95 L.Ed. 280 (1951) (Frankfurter, J., concurring).

6. See Kalven, The Concept of the Public Forum: Cox v. Louisiana, 1965 S.Ct. Rev. 1.

7. Other commentators have taken broader or narrower views of the concept of the "Public Forum." For a broad view, see 1 N. Dorsen, P. Bender, & B. Newborne, Political and Civil Rights in the United States, 236–302 (4th ed. 1976) which includes within the topic of the Public Forum other questions, such as advocacy of criminal activity and picketing in private shopping centers, all considered elsewhere in this Treatise.

§ 20.46

1. Niemotko v. Maryland, 340 U.S. 268, 282, 71 S.Ct. 328, 333, 95 L.Ed. 280 (1951) (concurring).

2. 340 U.S. at 282, 71 S.Ct. at 333.

reviewing some of the important cases.[3]

When an Administrator Has Excessive Discretion to Deny a License. In *Lovell v. Griffin*,[4] a member of the Jehovah's Witnesses[5] was prosecuted for disobeying a city ordinance which forbade the distribution of circulars, advertising matter, and similar material unless one secured a permit from the city manager. The city argued that its sanitary and litter problems made "apparent" the reasons for the ordinance.[6]

In *Lovell* the defendant was convicted for distributing religious tracts. Because she had not secured a license nor even applied for it, the city argued that in such a case she was not in the "position of having suffered from the exercise of the arbitrary and unlimited power of which she complains."[7] If she had applied and then been denied, the city argued, then she would have suffered loss of constitutional right; in other words, only then would she have standing to complain.

The Supreme Court, in a unanimous opinion, was unpersuaded. The vague ordinance—which prohibited the distribution of literature of any kind under every sort of circulation, at any time, at any place, and in any manner, without a permit from the City Manager—was held to be invalid on its face, as a prior restraint of free speech.[8] Because the ordinance was void on its face, it was not necessary for the defendant to apply for a permit under it before she could contest it.

Other decisions, when faced with similar fact situations, have followed this basic principle.[9] As the Court articulated most clearly in

3. For an analysis of cases regarding permits to engage in expressive conduct and a theory that would justify judicial intervention against most governmental attempts to use such regulations to restrict expressive activity see Baker, Unreasoned Reasonableness: Mandatory Parade Permits and Time, Place, and Manner Regulations, 78 Northwestern U.L.Rev. 937 (1983).

4. 303 U.S. 444, 58 S.Ct. 666, 82 L.Ed. 949 (1938).

5. In the approximately three decades following *Lovell,* there were more than thirty cases in the Supreme Court raising issues of the regulation of speech in the public forum. A large majority of these cases involved the Jehovah's Witnesses. Kalven, The Concept of the Public Forum: Cox v. Louisiana, 1965 S.Ct.Rev. 1 n. 2.

6. 303 U.S. at 445, 58 S.Ct. at 667 (argument for appellee).

7. 303 U.S. at 446, 58 S.Ct. at 667.

8. 303 U.S. at 451, 58 S.Ct. at 669.

9. E.g., Thornhill v. Alabama, 310 U.S. 88, 60 S.Ct. 736, 84 L.Ed. 1093 (1940); Cantwell v. Connecticut, 310 U.S. 296, 304–05, 60 S.Ct. 900, 903–04, 84 L.Ed. 1213 (1940); Thomas v. Collins, 323 U.S. 516, 65 S.Ct. 315, 89 L.Ed. 430 (1945), rehearing denied 323 U.S. 819, 65 S.Ct. 557, 89 L.Ed. 650 (1945); Niemotko v. Maryland, 340 U.S. 268, 71 S.Ct. 328, 95 L.Ed. 280 (1951); Kunz v. New York, 340 U.S. 290, 71 S.Ct. 312, 95 L.Ed. 280 (1951); Staub v. Baxley, 355 U.S. 313, 78 S.Ct. 277, 2 L.Ed.2d 302 (1958); Shuttlesworth v. Birmingham, 394 U.S. 147, 89 S.Ct. 935, 22 L.Ed.2d 162 (1969), on remand 45 Ala.App. 723, 222 So.2d 377 (1969).

In City of Lakewood v. Plain Dealer Publishing Co., 486 U.S. 750, 108 S.Ct. 2138, 100 L.Ed.2d 771 (1988) the Court (4 to 3) invalidated a city ordinance authorizing the Mayor to grant or to deny applications for annual permits to publishers to place their newsracks on public property. If the Mayor denies the application, he must then state the reasons for the denial. If he grants the application, he may place any

Thornhill v. Alabama: [10] "One who might have had a license for the asking may therefore call into question the whole scheme of licensing when he is prosecuted for failure to procure it." [11]

To be distinguished from the *Lovell* case and its progeny is the line

terms and conditions he deems necessary and reasonable. Justice Brennan, for the Court, ruled that the newspaper had standing to challenge the statute on the ground that it delegates overly broad licensing discretion to the Mayor; it was not necessary for the newspaper to apply for a license. The broad discretion served to invalidate the ordinance even if a properly drawn statute could proscribe all use of newsracks on public property. The majority ruled that a facial challenge to the licensing law lies "whenever a licensing law gives a government official or agency substantial power to discriminate based on the content or viewpoint of speech by suppressing disfavored speech or disliked speakers. This is not to say that the press or a speaker may challenge as censorship any law involving discretion to which it is subject. The law must have a close enough nexus to expression, or to conduct commonly associated with expression, to pose a real and substantial threat of the identified censorship risks."

The City asked the Court to "presume that the Mayor will deny a permit application only for reasons related to the health, safety, or welfare of Lakewood citizens, and that additional terms and conditions will be imposed only for similar reasons. This presumes the Mayor will act in good faith and adhere to standards absent from the statute's face. But this is the very presumption that the doctrine forbidding unbridled discretion disallows." The Court specifically noted that "we do not pass on [the dissent's] view that a city may constitutionally prohibit [entirely] the placement of newsracks on public property."

White, J., joined by Stevens & O'Connor, JJ., dissented. Justice White argued that the dispute with the majority was over what he termed a "technical" question: "What is the scope of the peculiar doctrine that governs facial challenges to local laws in the First Amendment area?" 486 U.S. at 772, 108 S.Ct. at 2152. White objected to the breadth of the majority's test—"a close enough nexus to expression, or to conduct commonly associated with expression"—as to when a facial challenge is appropriate. "The doctrine, as I see it, applies only when the specific conduct

which the locality seeks to license is protected by the First Amendment. Because the placement of newsracks on city property is not so protected (as opposed to the circulation of newspapers as a general matter), the exception to our usual facial challenge doctrine does not apply here." The newspaper has no right, said the dissent, to take city property (which is part of the public forum) for its exclusive use. Unlike the newsboy hawking papers on the city streets, newsracks are semi-permanent structures, often bolted to city sidewalks.

Rehnquist, C.J., and Kennedy, J., took no part in the consideration or discussion of the case of *City of Lakewood.*

10. Thornhill v. Alabama, 310 U.S. 88, 60 S.Ct. 736, 84 L.Ed. 1093 (1940).

11. 310 U.S. at 97, 60 S.Ct. at 742.

In *Thornhill* the Court also held, inter alia, "the dissemination of information concerning the facts of a labor dispute must be regarded as within that area of free discussion that is guaranteed by the Constitution." 310 U.S. at 102, 60 S.Ct. at 744. But the modern view does not grant full first amendment protection to all forms of peaceful labor picketing. Thus, "a State, in enforcing some public policy, whether of its criminal or its civil law, and whether announced by its legislature or its courts, could constitutionally enjoin peaceful picketing aimed at preventing effectuation of that policy." International Brotherhood of Teamsters v. Vogt, Inc., 354 U.S. 284, 293, 77 S.Ct. 1166, 1171, 1 L.Ed.2d 1347 (1957), rehearing denied 354 U.S. 945, 77 S.Ct. 1423, 1 L.Ed.2d 1558 (1957).

See also, e.g., Giboney v. Empire Storage & Ice Co., 336 U.S. 490, 69 S.Ct. 684, 93 L.Ed. 834 (1949) (state court injunction of peaceful labor picketing upheld where state court found purpose of violating state statute forbidding agreements in restraint of trade); Local Union No. 10, United Ass'n of Journeymen Plumbers and Steamfitters v. Graham, 345 U.S. 192, 73 S.Ct. 585, 97 L.Ed. 946 (1953) (injunction against peaceful labor picketing upheld where picketing carried on for purposes in conflict with state statute). But cf. Youngdahl v. Rainfair, Inc., 355 U.S. 131, 139–140, 78 S.Ct. 206, 211–12, 2 L.Ed.2d 151 (1957).

of cases illustrated by *Poulos v. New Hampshire*,[12] another Jehovah's Witness case. In *Poulos* the defendant was convicted for conducting a religious service in a public park without a proper license. Unlike *Lovell*, the defendant did apply for the license. He was denied the license but did not appeal that denial in the state court system. And, one would think it equally important, his defense in the criminal charge was not that the licensing statute was so vague or overbroad as to be void on its face but rather that the City Council arbitrarily and unreasonably refused his application for a license.

The state trial court held that, on its face, the ordinance in question was constitutional, as a reasonable restriction of the time, place, and manner of speech in public places.[13] The court also found that the refusal of the City Council to grant the requested license was arbitrary and unreasonable. Nonetheless the trial court upheld the criminal prosecution, and the state supreme court affirmed because, since "the ordinance was valid on its face the state court determined the [defendant's] remedy was by certiorari to review the unlawful refusal of the [city] Council to grant the license, not by holding public religious services in the park without a license, and then defending because the refusal of the license was arbitrary." [14]

The Supreme Court affirmed the conviction, with Justice Frankfurter concurring in the result and only Justices Black and Douglas dissenting. First, the Supreme Court majority found that the licensing statute, as construed by the state court to require uniform, nondiscriminatory, and consistent treatment of the granting of licenses for public meetings on public streets and parks, was constitutional on its face.[15] The ordinance provided only a ministerial role for the police.[16]

Secondly, the defendant could be convicted for holding his religious meeting without a license, even though it had wrongly been denied to him by the city. The defendant should have sought judicial review of the license denial rather than use the public park without a proper license. The Court recognized that—

> It must be admitted that judicial correction of arbitrary refusal by administrators to perform official duties under valid laws is exulcerating and costly. But to allow applicants to proceed without the required permits to ... hold public meetings without prior

12. 345 U.S. 395, 73 S.Ct. 760, 97 L.Ed. 1105 (1953), rehearing denied 345 U.S. 978, 73 S.Ct. 1119, 97 L.Ed. 1392 (1953).

13. The state trial court relied on the reasoning and holding of an earlier U.S. Supreme Court decision upholding the constitutionality of another section of the same New Hampshire statute. Cox v. New Hampshire, 312 U.S. 569, 61 S.Ct. 762, 85 L.Ed. 1049 (1941). See 345 U.S. at 399–400, 73 S.Ct. at 763.

See generally, Goldberger, A Reconsideration of Cox v. New Hampshire: Can Demonstrators be Required to Pay the Costs of Using America's Public Forums?, 62 Tex. L.Rev. 403 (1983).

14. 345 U.S. at 400, 73 S.Ct. at 763–64.

15. 345 U.S. at 402–03, 73 S.Ct. at 764–66.

16. 345 U.S. at 403, 404, 73 S.Ct. at 765, 766.

safety arrangements or take other unauthorized action is apt to cause breaches of the peace or create public dangers.... Delay is unfortunate, but the expense and annoyance of litigation is a price citizens must pay for life in an orderly society where the rights of the First Amendment have a real and abiding meaning.[17]

There are some exceptions to the *Poulos* rule regarding the failure to obtain a license where the relevant licensing statute is not void on its face. The *Poulos* majority noted that a state may always, if it chooses, make an unlawful refusal a defense to a licensing statute.[18] But it also said that if the statute is valid on its face, a defense of failure to apply for a license on the ground that such application would be unavailing is not allowed.[19]

Justice Frankfurter's concurrence explained that nothing in the record even suggested that the judicial remedy in the state court that Poulos must utilize was a procedural pretense or even would effectively frustrate by delay his right to speech. Poulos did not show the unavailability of a prompt judicial remedy, particularly given the fact that Poulos was denied his license on May 4 for meetings that were not to be held until June 25 and July 2.[20] If there were no prompt judicial remedy in the state court system, *Poulos* should probably have come out differently.

Finally, we must remember that the *Poulos* Court upheld the statute as construed by the state court. This power of a state court to save the constitutionality of one of the state's statutes by narrow interpretation has some limits, for it can deprive a litigant of fair warning if a statute that appears void on its face is later upheld in the very case in which the litigant is protesting the application. Therefore, even though the state court may authoritatively construe a statute for its future application, when the interpretation is "a remarkable job of plastic surgery" [21] and it would have taken "extraordinary clairvoyance" to anticipate the decision,[22] a conviction under the statute, when one could not know its limited construction, could not stand.

When a Court Enjoins Speech in the Public Forum. To be distinguished from the *Lovell* and *Poulos* line of cases—where the application for the license is made to an administrator—is the fact situation when the speaker is prevented from speaking, not by the denial of a license, but by a court injunction or temporary restraining order. Although one may collaterally attack a licensing ordinance that

17. 345 U.S. at 409, 73 S.Ct. at 768.

18. 345 U.S. at 409 n. 13, 73 S.Ct. at 769 n. 13.

19. 345 U.S. at 410 n. 13, 73 S.Ct. at 769 n. 13.

20. 345 U.S. at 420, 73 S.Ct. at 773–74 (Frankfurter, J., concurring).

21. Shuttlesworth v. Birmingham, 394 U.S. 147, 153, 89 S.Ct. 935, 940, 22 L.Ed.2d 162 (1969), on remand 45 Ala.App. 723, 222 So.2d 377 (1969).

22. Shuttlesworth v. Birmingham, 394 U.S. 147, 156, 89 S.Ct. 935, 941, 22 L.Ed.2d 162 (1969), on remand 45 Ala.App. 723, 222 So.2d 377 (1969).

is invalid on its face, under the doctrine of *Lovell v. Griffin*,[23] one may not disregard a court injunction or temporary restraining order issued by a court with jurisdiction (even though the court order repeats the language of the invalid licensing order) in the hope of having the injunction overturned in a later proceeding. The proper procedure to attack the court order is to appeal it. Therefore the individual may be barred in a collateral proceeding from contesting the validity of the injunction, if he is prosecuted for violating it.[24]

Walker v. Birmingham[25] illustrates this principle. In that case the Court upheld the contempt of court convictions of Martin Luther King Jr. and other black ministers who participated in civil rights marches and parades in violation of an *ex parte* temporary injunction issued by a state circuit court.[26]

The Supreme Court found that the state court had jurisdiction over the petitioners and over the subject matter of the controversy. Moreover the injunction was not "transparently invalid" nor did it have "only a frivolous pretense to validity."[27] The majority did not define those terms, but it should be understood that it would be the most atypical injunctive order that could probably meet this test, for the *Walker* order, as the majority admitted, was written in terms of such "breadth and vagueness" as to "unquestionably" raise a "substantial constitutional question."[28] In fact, two terms later, the Supreme Court held that marchers in the same events involved in *Walker* did not have to comply with the same Birmingham licensing ordinance, because it was invalid on its face and could not be saved even by judicial construction applied to the parties before the state court.[29] Thus, an *ex parte* court order is not "transparently invalid" simply because it "recites the words of the invalid statute."[30] In other words, the marchers could ignore an ordinance that was invalid on its face (pursuant to the *Lovell*

---

23. 303 U.S. 444, 58 S.Ct. 666, 82 L.Ed. 949 (1938).

24. Compare Walker v. Birmingham, 388 U.S. 307, 87 S.Ct. 1824, 18 L.Ed.2d 1210 (1967), rehearing denied 389 U.S. 894, 88 S.Ct. 12, 19 L.Ed.2d 202 (1967), with Shuttlesworth v. Birmingham, 394 U.S. 147, 89 S.Ct. 935, 22 L.Ed.2d 162 (1969), on remand 45 Ala.App. 723, 222 So.2d 377 (1969).

25. 388 U.S. 307, 87 S.Ct. 1824, 18 L.Ed.2d 1210 (1967), rehearing denied 389 U.S. 894, 88 S.Ct. 12, 19 L.Ed.2d 202 (1967).

26. Petitioners were each sentenced to five days in jail and $50 fine. 388 U.S. at 312, 87 S.Ct. at 1827.

27. 388 U.S. at 315, 87 S.Ct. at 1829.

28. 388 U.S. at 317, 87 S.Ct. at 1830. The order was reprinted in 388 U.S. at 321–22, 87 S.Ct. at 1832–33.

29. Shuttlesworth v. Birmingham, 394 U.S. 147, 89 S.Ct. 935, 22 L.Ed.2d 162 (1969), on remand 45 Ala.App. 723, 222 So.2d 377 (1969). The Court noted that: "a person faced with such an unconstitutional licensing law may ignore it, and engage with impunity in the exercise of the right of free expression for which the law purports to require a license." 394 U.S. at 151, 89 S.Ct. at 939 (footnote omitted). The Court also acknowledged that the "petitioner here was one of the petitioners in the *Walker* case. . . ." 394 U.S. at 157, 89 S.Ct. at 942.

30. Walker v. Birmingham, 388 U.S. 307, 346, 87 S.Ct. 1824, 1845, 18 L.Ed.2d 1210 (1967) (Brennan, J., dissenting, joined by Warren, C.J., and Douglas and Fortas, JJ.), rehearing denied 389 U.S. 894, 88 S.Ct. 12, 19 L.Ed.2d 202 (1967).

doctrine), but they had to obey a court order that merely repeated the words of the invalid ordinance.

The *Walker* majority was concerned that the petitioners did not even attempt to appeal within the Alabama court system the lower court's order. The proper procedure was to apply to the Alabama courts to have the injunction modified or dissolved.[31] If petitioners had done so and had been met with delay or frustration of their constitutional claims the case "would arise in quite a different constitutional posture." [32] Finally, the majority concluded:

> This Court cannot hold that the petitioners were constitutionally free to ignore all the procedures of the law and carry their battle to the streets. One may sympathize with the petitioners' impatient commitment to their cause. But respect for judicial process is a small price to pay for the civilizing hand of law, which alone can give abiding meaning to constitutional freedom.[33]

Chief Justice Warren, Justices Douglas, Brennan, and Fortas all dissented vigorously.[34] Chief Justice Warren argued in his dissent that the petitioners should be treated the same as persons who challenge the constitutionality of a statute and then defend themselves on the grounds that the statute is unconstitutional. "It has never been thought that violation of a statute indicated such a disrespect for the legislature that the violator always must be punished even if the statute was unconstitutional." [35]

Several years later the Supreme Court held unconstitutional the *ex parte* procedure in free speech cases such as *Walker*, where officials obtain an *ex parte* court order restraining the holding of meetings or rallies. An order in such cases is defective if it is issued *ex parte*, without notice to the subjects of the order, and without any effort, even an informal one, to invite or permit their participation, unless a showing is made that it is impossible to serve or to notify the opposing parties and give them an opportunity to respond.[36] In the case in

31. 388 U.S. at 317, 87 S.Ct. at 1830.

32. 388 U.S. at 318, 87 S.Ct. at 1831.

Cf. National Socialist Party v. Village of Skokie, 432 U.S. 43, 97 S.Ct. 2205, 53 L.Ed.2d 96 (1977) (per curiam), on remand 51 Ill.App.3d 279, 9 Ill.Dec. 90, 366 N.E.2d 347 (1977) (per curiam).

See also, National Socialist Party v. Village of Skokie, 434 U.S. 1327, 98 S.Ct. 14, 54 L.Ed.2d 38 (1977) (Stevens, Circuit Justice) (refusing to allow a stay of lower court injunction of march of Nazi group where there was no showing that the state supreme court would not review the decision promptly), on remand 69 Ill.2d 605, 14 Ill. Dec. 890, 373 N.E.2d 21 (1978); Collin & Nat. Socialist Party v. Smith, 578 F.2d 1197 (7th Cir.1978) (holding unconstitutional village ordinances designed to stop the same march by the Nazi group), certiorari denied 439 U.S. 916, 99 S.Ct. 291, 58 L.Ed.2d 264 (1978).

33. 388 U.S. at 321, 87 S.Ct. at 1832.

34. 388 U.S. at 324–49, 87 S.Ct. at 1833–47.

35. 388 U.S. at 327, 87 S.Ct. at 1835 (Warren, C.J., dissenting, joined by Brennan and Fortas, JJ.).

36. Carroll v. President and Com'rs of Princess Anne, 393 U.S. 175, 89 S.Ct. 347, 21 L.Ed.2d 325 (1968); cf. A Quantity of Books v. Kansas, 378 U.S. 205, 84 S.Ct. 1723, 12 L.Ed.2d 809 (1964).

which this holding was announced the petitioners obeyed the order and then appealed it rather than disobeying it and attacking it collaterally; thus the *Walker* rule did not apply.

§ 20.47   Reasonable Time, Place, and Manner Restrictions on Speech, Without Regard to Content

(a) Introduction

In general it may be said that the state may place reasonable time, place, or manner restrictions on speech that takes place in the public forum, but these regulations must be implemented without regard to the content of the speech.[1] Otherwise the state would be able to cloak restrictions on speech itself in the guise of regulations of the mode of speech or the place—the streets, the parks, public buildings—that is used for the speech. To prevent abuse of the power to exercise such reasonable regulations, and to help assure that the regulations are in fact reasonable, the Court will independently determine if the regulation is a narrow means of protecting important interests unrelated to content.

The Court has stated its analytical method of review of time, place, or manner restrictions in two slightly different forms. First, there is a general principle that "government regulation is sufficiently justified if it is within the constitutional power of the Government; if it furthers an important or substantial governmental interest; if the governmental interest is unrelated to the suppression of free expression; and if the incidental restriction on alleged First Amendment freedoms is no greater than is essential to the furtherance of that interest."[2] The

---

§ 20.47

1. E.g., Madison School District v. Wisconsin Employment Relations Comm'n, 429 U.S. 167, 176, 97 S.Ct. 421, 426, 50 L.Ed.2d 376 (1976) ("when the board sits in public meetings to conduct public business and hear the views of citizens, it may not be required to discriminate between speakers on the basis of their employment, or the content of their speech."); Linmark Associates, Inc. v. Township of Willingboro, 431 U.S. 85, 97 S.Ct. 1614, 52 L.Ed.2d 155 (1977) (ordinance banning "for sale" and "sold" signs for the purpose of stemming the flight of white homeowners from racially integrated town invalidated; ordinance concerned with content of speech).

But cf. Young v. American Mini Theatres, Inc., 427 U.S. 50, 96 S.Ct. 2440, 49 L.Ed.2d 310 (1976), rehearing denied 429 U.S. 873, 97 S.Ct. 191, 50 L.Ed.2d 155 (1976) (zoning of "adult" theatres upheld); FCC v. Pacifica Foundation, 438 U.S. 726,

98 S.Ct. 3026, 57 L.Ed.2d 1073 (1978) (FCC may regulate radio broadcast which is "indecent" but not "obscene").

See also, Farber, Content Regulation and the First Amendment: A Revisionist View, 68 Georgetown L.J. 727 (1980); Redish, The Content Distinction in First Amendment Analysis, 34 Stan.L.Rev. 113 (1981). See generally, Stephan, The First Amendment and Content Discrimination, 68 Va. L.Rev. 203 (1982). Stone, Restrictions of Speech Because of Its Content: The Peculiar Case of Subject–Matter Restrictions, 46 U.Chi.L.Rev. 81 (1978); Content Regulation and the Dimensions of Free Expression, 96 Harv.L.Rev. 1854 (1983); Stone, Content Regulation and the First Amendment, 25 Wm. & Mary L.Rev. 189 (1983); Stone, Content–Neutral Restrictions, 54 U.Chi. L.Rev. 46 (1987).

2. United States v. O'Brien, 391 U.S. 367, 377, 88 S.Ct. 1673, 1679, 20 L.Ed.2d

second method of analysis merely clarifies the general principle by stating it in terms of a three-part test under which the Court will uphold time, place, or manner restrictions as long as the restrictions "are content-neutral, are narrowly tailored to serve a significant government interest, and leave open ample alternative channels of communication." [3]

Regardless of whether the Court states its analytical framework in terms of the general principle or the three-part test, when the Court reviews time, place, or manner restrictions, it really is engaging in a two-step form of analysis. First, it seeks to determine whether the regulation is in fact an attempt to suppress content because of its message. A content-based restriction of this type will be upheld only if the Court can find that the content fits within a category of speech unprotected by the first amendment.[4] If the regulation is not an

---

672 (1968), rehearing denied 393 U.S. 900, 89 S.Ct. 63, 21 L.Ed.2d 188 (1968).

O'Brien was quoted with approval as the standard used by the Court in Members of City Council v. Taxpayers for Vincent, 466 U.S. 789, 104 S.Ct. 2118, 80 L.Ed.2d 772 (1984), on remand 738 F.2d 353 (9th Cir. 1984), in which the Court upheld an ordinance prohibiting the posting of signs on public property. The *Vincent* Court found that the statute prohibited no more speech than was necessary to effectuate the governmental interest in eliminating "visual clutter" and promoting esthetic interests. While the statute may not have been absolutely necessary to promote the esthetic interest, it was reasonably tailored to do so and did not restrict significantly more speech than was justified by promotion of these content neutral ends. "Given our analysis of the legitimate interest served by the ordinance, its viewpoint neutrality, and the availability of alternative channels of communication, the ordinance is certainly constitutional...." 466 U.S. at 815, 104 S.Ct. at 2134, 80 L.Ed.2d at 793–94.

3. United States v. Grace, 461 U.S. 171, 177, 103 S.Ct. 1702, 1707, 75 L.Ed.2d 736 (1983), quoting Perry Educ. Ass'n v. Perry Local Educators' Ass'n, 460 U.S. 37, 45, 103 S.Ct. 948, 955, 74 L.Ed.2d 794 (1983), on remand 705 F.2d 462 (7th Cir.1983). The cases which set out the standard are examined in § 20.47(c), infra.

In Clark v. Community for Creative Non–Violence, 468 U.S. 288, 104 S.Ct. 3065, 82 L.Ed.2d 221 (1984), the justices used this three-part test when they upheld, by a 7–2 vote, a National Park Service regulation prohibiting around-the-clock use of parks in the center of Washington, D.C.; they also upheld the Park Service's refusal to allow demonstrators to make a public statement by sleeping in "tent cities" in those parks. The regulation was content neutral, promoted the government's substantial interest in maintaining the parks, and left open alternative means for communication of the speakers' message.

4. The strictness with which the Court examines content-based restrictions was demonstrated in Regan v. Time, Inc., 468 U.S. 641, 104 S.Ct. 3262, 82 L.Ed.2d 487 (1984). At issue in that case were government statutes which prohibited photographing or reproducing photographs of government currency. An original statute had completely banned photographic reproductions of currency; the later statute permitted the "printing, publishing or importation ... of illustrations of ... any ... obligation or other security of the United States ... for philatelic, numismatic, educational, historical, or newsworthy purposes in articles, books, journals, newspapers or albums...." Exemptions to the ban not only had to meet one of the purposes approved by Congress but also had to be in black-and-white, and of a size different from the actual size of the currency; the negatives and plates used in making permitted illustrations had to be destroyed after their authorized use.

Eight justices of the Court agreed that the portion of the statute exempting publications from the ban based on the purpose of the reproduction and publication was impermissible because the exemption was content based and therefore could not be upheld as a content neutral time, place, or manner regulation. However, there was

attempt to censor content, the Court will go on to determine whether the incidental restriction on speech is outweighed by the promotion of significant governmental interests. Although this method of analysis is sometimes stated as a least restrictive means test when phrased in terms of a general principle, the analysis really assesses whether the regulation leaves open ample means for communication of the message and thus is not an unnecessary or gratuitous suppression of communication.[5]

no majority opinion regarding whether the statute could be upheld after striking down the part of the exemption that related to purpose of publication.

Justice White wrote for four justices in finding that the statutory restriction on the color and size of the photographs could be interpreted to stand independently from the purpose requirement; the statute could be treated as if it prohibited all publications or reproductions of the currency except those that were in black-and-white and of a size different than that of the actual currency. These four justices found that the resulting color and size limitations could be upheld as reasonable manner regulations because they were content neutral (after the Court had eliminated the purpose requirement), and they "effectively serve the Government's concededly compelling interest in preventing counterfeiting." These justices stated that "the less-restrictive-alternative analysis invoked by [the magazine company which objected to the regulation] has never been a part of the inquiry into the validity of a time, place, and manner regulation. It is enough that the color restriction substantially serves the Government's legitimate ends."

In some instances, the Court has discussed time, place, or manner restrictions in terms of a less-restrictive-alternatives form of analysis. However, the Court more commonly is concerned with whether the time, place, or manner regulation leaves open adequate alternative channels of communication. Certainly, the restriction on the color and size of photographic reproductions of currency promotes important content neutral ends and allows persons to convey messages regarding the currency or issues dealing with currency in any manner other than with an exact size and color reproduction of currency.

Justice Stevens joined with the four-justice plurality to uphold the restrictions on size and color but did not join to form a majority opinion. He believed that the purpose requirements did no more than determine that all reproductions of the currency that met the color and size requirements were permissible unless the productions were connected to an attempt to counterfeit currency.

Justices Powell and Blackmun agreed that color and size restrictions would be constitutional limitations on the manner of such publications. However, as a matter of statutory interpretation, Justices Powell and Blackmun found that the entire exemption system had to be stricken once the purpose element of the exemption was found to be unconstitutional.

Justices Brennan and Marshall would have invalidated the entire statute and required Congress to draft a statute that was narrowly tailored to prohibit counterfeiting without unnecessarily restricting speech which posed no danger of aiding counterfeiting activity.

5. It may be that once a court has determined that a statute is truly content neutral the court can do nothing except balance the extent to which the regulation promotes a legitimate interest unrelated to the suppression of ideas against the degree to which society is deprived of communications by the regulation.

See generally, Farber and Nowak, The Misleading Nature of Public Forum Analysis: Content and Context in First Amendment Adjudication, 70 Va.L.Rev. 1219 (1984); Ely, Flag Desecration: A Case Study in the Roles of Categorization and Balancing in First Amendment Analysis, 88 Harv.L.Rev. 1482 (1975).

(b) Regulation of Sound and Noise

In *Saia v. New York* [6] the Court, in a five to four decision, invalidated a city ordinance which forbade the use of sound amplification devices such as loudspeakers on trucks, except with permission of the Chief of Police. The ordinance was unconstitutional on its face because of the uncontrolled discretion of the Chief of Police. The abuses of loudspeakers can be controlled, the majority agreed, if the control is pursuant to a narrowly-drawn statute. [7]

In *Kovacs v. Cooper* [8] the Court upheld such a statute, though the fragmented Court could not agree on the reasons. [9] Justice Reed's plurality opinion found the city ordinance in *Kovacs* not overbroad nor vague. It prohibited sound trucks and similar devices from emitting "loud and raucous noises." These words were found not to be too vague. Moreover the New Jersey courts by construction had narrowed the ordinance's applicability only to vehicles containing a sound amplifier or any other instrument emitting loud and raucous noises, when operated or standing in the public streets, alleys or thoroughfares of the city. [10] Justice Reed added that just as unrestrained use of all sound amplifying devices in a city would be intolerable, "[a]bsolute prohibition within municipal limits of all sound amplification, even though reasonably regulated in place, time and volume, is undesirable and probably unconstitutional as an unreasonable interference with normal activities." [11]

---

6. 334 U.S. 558, 68 S.Ct. 1148, 92 L.Ed. 1574 (1948). See, Bovey v. City of Lafayette, 586 F.Supp. 1460, 1468 (N.D.Ind.1984) (Sharp, J.) (citing Treatise); Mesarosh v. State, 459 N.E.2d 426, 427 (Ind.App.1984) (Conover, J.) (citing Treatise).

7. 334 U.S. at 562, 68 S.Ct. at 1150–51.

8. 336 U.S. 77, 69 S.Ct. 448, 93 L.Ed. 513 (1949), rehearing denied 336 U.S. 921, 69 S.Ct. 638, 93 L.Ed. 1083 (1949).

9. Justice Reed announced the judgment of the Court, in an opinion by Vinson, C.J., and Burton, J.; Murphy, J. dissented without opinion. Frankfurter, J. concurred. Jackson, J. also concurred, but in a separate opinion. Black, J., dissented in an opinion joined by Douglas and Rutledge, JJ. Rutledge, J., also wrote a separate dissent.

10. 336 U.S. at 83, 69 S.Ct. at 451 (opinion of Reed, J.).

11. 336 U.S. at 81–82, 69 S.Ct. at 450–51 (opinion of Reed, J.). Examples of more recent loudspeaker cases include Phillips v. Township, 305 F.Supp. 763 (E.D.Pa.1969); Phillips v. Borough of Folcroft, 305 F.Supp. 766 (E.D.Pa.1969); Maldonado v. County, 330 F.Supp. 1282 (N.D.Cal.1971).

See also Grayned v. Rockford, 408 U.S. 104, 107–121, 92 S.Ct. 2294, 2298–2306, 33 L.Ed.2d 222 (1972) (antinoise ordinance prohibiting a person while on grounds adjacent to a building in which school is in session from making a noise or diversion that disturbs the peace and good order of the school session is not unconstitutionally vague or overbroad).

Cf. Ward v. Rock Against Racism, 491 U.S. 781, 109 S.Ct. 2746, 105 L.Ed.2d 661 (1989), where the Court upheld city regulations designed to regulate the volume of excessively amplified music at the Naumberg Acoustic Bandshell in New York City's Central Park in order not to intrude on those who use a quiet, passive recreational area of the Park called the Sheep Meadow and also not to intrude on apartments and residences in the Central Park West area. In the past, the city, in response to numerous complaints, would monitor the volume and request that it be lowered when volume limits were exceeded. After two citations were issued to Rock Against Racism (an unincorporated association dedicated to promote "antiracist views") the city eventually turned off the power during one of their concerts, but then the audience became "abusive and

Somewhat related is the class of cases in which recipients of information claim a right not to hear a message. A leading case in this area is *Public Utilities Commission v. Pollak*,[12] where the majority found no deprivation of either the first or fifth amendment because a city-regulated bus company broadcast FM music, news, and commer-

disruptive." Then the city considered establishing a fixed decibel limit, but abandoned that idea when it learned that the impact on listeners varies in response to factors like change in air temperature, audience size, and so forth. Next the city considered employing a sound technician to operate the equipment of whomever was using the Bandshell but rejected that idea as well because the city technician might have difficulty satisfying the needs of the musicians while operating unfamiliar and perhaps inadequate equipment. Instead, the city concluded that the most effective way to achieve adequate (but not excessive) sound amplification would be for the city to furnish high quality sound equipment and retain an independent, experienced sound technician for all performances at the Bandshell. The respondents then sued seeking damages and a declaration that the guidelines were invalid on their face.

The district court, after hearing testimony, upheld the sound-amplification guidelines, finding that the city's technician "does all he can to accommodate the sponsor's desires" regarding the sound mix, balancing treble with bass, and so on. The hearings showed that the performers who used the city's sound system (ranging from opera to salsa to reggae) "were uniformly pleased with the quality of the sound provided."

The Court of Appeals reversed, holding that the guideline was not the "least intrusive upon the freedom of expression as is reasonably necessary to achieve a legitimate purpose of the regulation." 848 F.2d 367, 370. The Second Circuit concluded that there were alternative methods of controlling volume without also intruding on the respondent's ability to control the sound mix. For example, the city could order the respondent's sound technician to keep the volume below specified levels, or, "the plug can be pulled on the sound to enforce the volume limit."

The Supreme Court, per Kennedy, J., rejected the facial challenge to these city noise regulations. First, the sound amplification rules do not authorize the city to vary the sound quality "based on the mes-

sage being delivered by performers." In addition, the Second Circuit erred "in sifting through all the available or imagined alternative means of regulating sound volume in order to determine whether the city's solution was the 'least intrusive means' of achieving the desired end. [R]estrictions on the time, place, or manner of protected speech are not invalid 'simply because there is some imaginable alternative that might be less burdensome on speech.'" The Court reaffirmed that time, place, and manner regulations "must be narrowly tailored to serve the government's legitimate content-neutral interests but that it need not be the least-restrictive means of doing so. Rather, the requirement of narrow tailoring is satisfied 'so long as the ... regulation promotes a substantial government interest that would be achieved less effectively absent the regulation.'"

Blackmun, J., wrote no opinion and concurred in the result. Marshall, J., joined by Brennan & Stevens, JJ., dissented because, in their view, New York City's sound amplification guidelines are not narrowly tailored to serve its interest in regulating loud noise. The government's interest in avoiding loud sounds "cannot justify giving government total control over sound equipment, any more than its interest in avoiding litter could justify a ban on handbill distribution. In both cases, government's legitimate goals can be effectively and less intrusively served by directly punishing the evil—the persons responsible for excessive sounds and the persons who litter." The dissent also claimed that the city's "exclusive control of sound equipment" was a "quintessential prior restraint." Whether the city "denies a performer a Bandshell permit or grants the permit and then silences or distorts the performer's music, the result is the same—the city censors speech."

12. 343 U.S. 451, 72 S.Ct. 813, 96 L.Ed. 1068 (1952).

See generally, Black, He Cannot Choose But Hear: The Plight of the Captive Auditor, 53 Colum.L.Rev. 960 (1953).

cials to buses and streetcars, in return for money payments.[13] The Court refused to upset the ruling of the Public Utilities Commission allowing the practice.[14]

Pollak, however, does not forbid the state from deciding to protect those who do not wish to be recipients. Thus, it is constitutional for a statute to provide that any addressee of mail may request the post office to prohibit all future mailings from any particular sender. The law was upheld because the government made no decision on the basis of the content of the speech but only allowed the addressee to act in his sole discretion.[15] If the addressee requested that certain types of mail not be forwarded, the post office should respect that decision. However, it would burden first amendment rights if the post office would require the addressee to specifically request certain types of mail. Such a statute would chill the addressee by requiring him or her to specifically request mailings that the Government determined that he or she should not receive. Thus, it would be unconstitutional for the post office to censor mail by refusing to deliver, for example, communist propaganda unless the addressee specifically requested it. Such a law would put a burden on the addressee and would be a violation of the addressee's unfettered right to receive mail that is not constitutionally obscene or otherwise constitutionally illegal.

But the statute at issue did not do that; it did not affect the mail but the mailer. The law that the Court approved gives the addressee unfettered discretion to take his or her name off the mailer's mailing list. The statute implements the desire of the addressee to be left alone. If the addressee can turn the television dial and not view a program, he or she should have the equal right to inform the post office that he or she wishes to receive no more mail from any given source. Congress, in short, may permit individuals to erect a metaphorical wall around their homes.[16]

---

13. The majority was "assuming that the action of Capital Transit in operating the radio service, together with the action of the Commission in permitting such operation, amounts to sufficient Federal Government action to make the First and Fifth Amendments applicable thereto." 343 U.S. at 462–463, 72 S.Ct. at 820–21.

14. Justice Black issued a separate opinion dissenting insofar as the majority allowed the passengers of Capital Transit to be subjected to news, public speeches, views, or propaganda of any kind. He would only allow musical programs. Douglas also dissented in a separate opinion. And Justice Frankfurter disqualified himself for the following reasons:

"My feelings are so strongly engaged as a victim of the practice in controversy that I had better not participate in judicial judgment upon it. I am explicit as to the reasons for my non-participation in this case because I have for some time been of the view that it is desirable to state why one takes himself out of a case." (343 U.S. at 467, 72 S.Ct. at 823.)

15. Rowan v. U.S. Post Office Dept., 397 U.S. 728, 90 S.Ct. 1484, 25 L.Ed.2d 736 (1970). Cf. United States v. Ramsey, 431 U.S. 606, 97 S.Ct. 1972, 52 L.Ed.2d 617 (1977) (border searches of foreign mail upheld over fourth amendment and first amendment objections; the letters were not read and there was no "chill".)

16. Lamont v. Postmaster General, 381 U.S. 301, 85 S.Ct. 1493, 14 L.Ed.2d 398 (1965).

Similarly, a city may protect householders from unwanted solicitors knocking on their doors, but the means selected must not be unreasonably harsh: thus, a city ordinance may prohibit the business practice of soliciting magazine subscriptions door-to-door without prior invitation of the homeowner.[17]

The balance of interests was struck differently, however, in *Martin v. Struthers*,[18] where the Court was confronted with a far broader ordinance. There the city of Struthers enacted an ordinance which forbade any person to knock on doors, ring doorbells, or otherwise summon any residents to the door for the purpose of receiving handbills or other distributions. The Court was particularly concerned that the *Struthers* ordinance made one a criminal trespasser if he entered the property of another for an innocent purpose and without an explicit command from the owners to stay away.[19] Moreover the Court was aware that door to door distribution of circulars is "essential to the poorly financed causes of little people." [20] The defendant in *Struthers* was a Jehovah's Witness who sought to distribute to households a free leaflet advertising a religious meeting. Thus:

> A city can punish those who call at a home in defiance of the previously expressed will of the occupant and, in addition, can by identification devices control the abuse of the privilege by criminals posing as canvassers. ... [W]e conclude that the [*Struthers*] ordinance is invalid because in conflict with the freedom of speech and press.[21]

Under analogous reasoning, a city cannot forbid all leaflet distribution in order to prevent littering, fraud, or disorder, because the state can less drastically prohibit only the actual littering, fraud, or disorder.[22]

(c) Where the Speech Takes Place—The Degrees of Public Forum

The substantive rules for public demonstrations and other such speech activities in the public forum are in part a function of where the speech takes place.[23] In *Police Department of Chicago v. Mosley* [24] the

---

17. Breard v. Alexandria, 341 U.S. 622, 71 S.Ct. 920, 95 L.Ed. 1233 (1951), rehearing denied 342 U.S. 843, 72 S.Ct. 21, 96 L.Ed. 637 (1951). The Court specifically relied on the commercial nature of the transactions in question. One should compare this case with the modern view of the commercial speech doctrine. See §§ 20.26–20.31, supra.

18. 319 U.S. 141, 63 S.Ct. 862, 87 L.Ed. 1313 (1943).

19. 319 U.S. at 148, 63 S.Ct. at 865–66.

20. 319 U.S. at 146, 63 S.Ct. at 865.

21. 319 U.S. at 148–49, 63 S.Ct. at 866 (footnote omitted).

22. Schneider v. Irvington, 308 U.S. 147, 60 S.Ct. 146, 84 L.Ed. 155 (1939).

23. Cf. Niemotko v. Maryland, 340 U.S. 268, 282–283, 71 S.Ct. 328, 333, 95 L.Ed. 280 (1951) (Frankfurter, J., concurring):

> "Where does the speaking which is regulated take place? Not only the general classifications—streets, parks, private buildings—are relevant. The location and size of a park; its customary use for the recreational, esthetic and

24. See note 24 on page 303.

Court considered the constitutionality of a city ordinance that prohibited picketing on a public way within 150 feet of a grade or high school from one-half hour before the school was in session until one-half hour after the school session had been concluded. Exempted from this prohibition was peaceful labor picketing. The ordinance was invalidated.

While it purported to regulate the time, place, and manner of speech activities in the public forum, it did so with regard to the content of the speech, and that content regulation was the fatal flaw in the ordinance:

> The central problem with Chicago's ordinance is that it describes permissible picketing in terms of its subject matter. Peaceful picketing on the subject of a school's labor-management dispute is permitted, but all other peaceful picketing is prohibited. The operative distinction is the message on a picket sign. But, above all else, the First Amendment means that government has no power to restrict expression because of its message, its ideas, its subject matter, or its content. .... Necessarily, then, under the Equal Protection Clause, not to mention the First Amendment itself, government may not grant the use of a forum to people whose views it finds acceptable, but deny use to those wishing to express less favored or more controversial views. ... Once a forum is opened up to assembly or speaking by some groups, government may not prohibit others from assembling or speaking on the basis of what they intend to say.[25]

In *Cary v. Brown*[26] the Court invalidated an Illinois statute which prohibited all picketing of residences or dwellings except for the peaceful picketing of a place of employment involved in a labor dispute. The majority relied on the earlier analysis in *Mosley* and concluded that the residential picketing statute accorded preferential treatment to the expression of views on one particular subject and thus allowed only

contemplative needs of a community; the facilities, other than a park or street corner, readily available in a community for airing views, are all pertinent considerations in assessing the limitations [of] the Fourteenth Amendment...."

See generally, Dienes, The Trashing of the Public Forum: Problems in First Amendment Analysis, 55 Geo.Wash.L.Rev. 109 (1986); Post, Between Governance and Management: The History and Theory of the Public Forum, 34 U.C.L.A.L.Rev. 1713 (1987); Farber & Nowak, The Misleading Nature of Public Forum Analysis: Content and Context in First Amendment Adjudication, 70 Va.L.Rev. 1219 (1984).

24. 408 U.S. 92, 92 S.Ct. 2286, 33 L.Ed.2d 212 (1972).

25. 408 U.S. at 95–96, 92 S.Ct. at 2290. Accord Grayned v. Rockford, 408 U.S. 104, 105–107, 92 S.Ct. 2294, 2297–98, 33 L.Ed.2d 222 (1972). See also, Niemotko v. Maryland, 340 U.S. 268, 71 S.Ct. 328, 95 L.Ed. 280 (1951) (Jehovah's Witnesses cannot be denied permit to use a city park for Bible talks when other religious and political groups had been allowed to use the park for similar purposes); Fowler v. Rhode Island, 345 U.S. 67, 73 S.Ct. 526, 97 L.Ed. 828 (1953) (same).

26. 447 U.S. 455, 100 S.Ct. 2286, 65 L.Ed.2d 263 (1980). Rehnquist, J., joined by Burger, C.J., and Blackmun, J., dissented.

certain types of residential picketing based on the content of the message. The state cannot ban speech based on its content. The state's goal of protecting privacy may not be advanced in such a constitutionally impermissible manner; nor was the statute narrowly drawn to protect residential privacy in light of the fact it allowed all labor picketing regardless of how disruptive that was. The majority, however, made clear that it was not implying that the first amendment would prohibit an antiresidential picketing statute that was uniform and nondiscriminatory in its regulation.

If a statute is sufficiently narrow in scope, and applied without regard to content, it can apply to remove certain public areas from the public forum. *Adderley v. Florida* [27] illustrates this principle. In *Adderley,* 32 students were convicted of a statutory crime of "trespass with malicious and mischievous intent" on the grounds of a county jail. The students had demonstrated at the jail to protest the earlier arrests of other protesting students and to protest the state's segregated practices, including the policy of racial segregation of the jail. The local sheriff tried to persuade the students to leave and when that failed, he warned them that he would charge them with trespassing.

The Supreme Court affirmed the convictions and distinguished earlier protest cases where the convictions had been reversed. [28] Unlike one of the earlier cases, where the Court reversed the trespass convictions of demonstrators on the state capitol grounds, the *Adderley* demonstrators were on jailhouse grounds. While state capitol grounds are traditionally open to the public, jails, "built for security purposes, are not." [29] Moreover, unlike the breach-of-the-peace statutes involved in the earlier cases the trespass statute in *Adderley* was not unnecessarily vague or overbroad. [30]

The majority was apparently not concerned that the state convicted the defendants under the statute which did not apply specifically to jails or even to public property but seemed to be limited to private property. [31] The majority appeared to simply treat jailhouse property as private property. [32]

Adderley stands out as one of the few cases in this period involving demonstrations on public property where the Supreme Court affirmed

27. 385 U.S. 39, 87 S.Ct. 242, 17 L.Ed.2d 149 (1966).

28. 385 U.S. at 41–42, 87 S.Ct. at 244–45, distinguishing Edwards v. South Carolina, 372 U.S. 229, 83 S.Ct. 680, 9 L.Ed.2d 697 (1963), and Cox v. Louisiana, 379 U.S. 536, 85 S.Ct. 453, 13 L.Ed.2d 471 (1965).

29. 385 U.S. at 41, 87 S.Ct. at 244.

30. 385 U.S. at 42, 87 S.Ct. at 244–45.

31. The Florida statute spoke of "[e]very trespass upon the property of another...." 385 U.S. at 40 n. 1, 87 S.Ct. at 243 n. 1.

32. Justice Douglas, joined by Chief Justice Warren and Justices Brennan and Fortas. 385 U.S. at 48–56, 87 S.Ct. at 248–52.

the conviction. Normally the Supreme Court reversed, sometimes on narrow or unusual grounds.[33]

Later, the Supreme Court upheld military regulations of Fort Dix, New Jersey, which banned speeches and demonstrations of a partisan political nature.[34] The Court found, inter alia, that this regulation had been rigidly and neutrally enforced and that civilians were freely permitted to visit unrestricted areas of the military reservation. The Court ruled that federal military reservations are not like municipal streets and parks because only the latter have traditionally served as a public forum; the business of a military installation is to train soldiers, not to provide a public area for debate.

The Fort Dix policy of keeping official military activities wholly free of entanglement with any partisan political campaigns was reasonable. Thus, while individual soldiers could attend military political rallies, out of uniform and off-base, "the military as such is insulated from both the reality and the appearance of acting as a handmaiden for partisan political causes or candidates."[35]

The Court also upheld a regulation authorizing the Fort Dix commander to prohibit the distribution of literature that he finds constitutes a clear danger to military loyalty, discipline, or morale; he was not to prohibit distribution of a publication because he does not like it or even because it unfairly criticized the governmental policy or governmental officials. The Court found no evidence the authorities had applied this regulation arbitrarily.

Similarly the Court later upheld Air Force regulations prohibiting members of the service from circulating petitions on Air Force bases unless they first secured the approval of their commanders. A commander could deny permission only if he found that distribution of the material would cause "a clear danger to the loyalty, discipline, or morale of the Air Force, or material interference with the accomplishment of a military mission." The regulations were not invalid on their

---

33. E.g., Gregory v. Chicago, 394 U.S. 111, 89 S.Ct. 946, 22 L.Ed.2d 134 (1969) (disorderly conduct conviction reversed; protest to press claim for desegregated schools); Edwards v. South Carolina, 372 U.S. 229, 83 S.Ct. 680, 9 L.Ed.2d 697 (1963) (breach of the peace conviction reversed; demonstration against racial segregation); Cox v. Louisiana, 379 U.S. 536, 85 S.Ct. 453, 13 L.Ed.2d 471 (1965) (breach of the peace conviction, obstructing of public passages conviction, and picketing near courthouse conviction all reversed; demonstration against racial segregation), cf. the anti-racial discrimination "sit-in" cases,

e.g. Peterson v. Greenville, 373 U.S. 244, 83 S.Ct. 1119, 10 L.Ed.2d 323 (1963); Lombard v. Louisiana, 373 U.S. 267, 83 S.Ct. 1122, 10 L.Ed.2d 338 (1963); Garner v. Louisiana, 368 U.S. 157, 184, 82 S.Ct. 248, 262, 7 L.Ed.2d 207 (1961); Bell v. Maryland, 378 U.S. 226, 84 S.Ct. 1814, 12 L.Ed.2d 822 (1964), on remand 238 Md. 356, 204 A.2d 54 (1964); Hamm v. City of Rock Hill, 379 U.S. 306, 85 S.Ct. 384, 13 L.Ed.2d 300 (1964), rehearing denied 379 U.S. 995, 85 S.Ct. 698, 13 L.Ed.2d 614 (1965).

34. Greer v. Spock, 424 U.S. 828, 96 S.Ct. 1211, 47 L.Ed.2d 505 (1976).

35. 424 U.S. at 839, 96 S.Ct. at 1218.

305

face.[36]

To be distinguished is the case where a street, technically within the jurisdiction of a military fort, had in fact been treated by the military as a public thoroughfare of the city, with the military abandoning any special interest and any right to exclude civilian vehicular and foot traffic. The military authorities could not then order a person to leave the public street because he was distributing leaflets any more than a city policeman could order someone off a city street.[37]

The Three Categories of Public Forum: The Analysis in *Perry*. The Supreme Court made the first major effort to recognize and classify the types of public forums involved in the previous cases in *Perry Educational Ass'n v. Perry Local Educators' Ass'n*.[38] In that case

36. Brown v. Glines, 444 U.S. 348, & 354 n. 2, 100 S.Ct. 594, 597 n. 2, 62 L.Ed.2d 540 (1980), on remand 618 F.2d 623 (9th Cir.1980).

See also United States Postal Service v. Council of Greenburgh Civic Associations, 453 U.S. 114, 101 S.Ct. 2676, 69 L.Ed.2d 517 (1981), appeal dismissed, certiorari denied 453 U.S. 917, 101 S.Ct. 3150, 69 L.Ed.2d 999 (1981), where the Court upheld the constitutionality of 18 U.S.C.A. § 1725 prohibiting the deposit of unstamped "mailable matter" in a letter box approved by the U.S. Postal Service, although the appellees had argued that the law violated the first amendment. The Postal Service justified the law as protecting mail revenues; facilitating the efficient and secure delivery of mail; preventing overcrowding of the mailboxes; and promoting the privacy of mail patrons. Testimony also showed that the statute aided in the investigation of mail theft by restricting access to mailboxes, thus allowing postal inspectors to assume that anyone who opens a mailbox other than a mailman or householder may be engaged in a violation of law. About 10% of the arrests made under the external theft statute resulted from surveillance operations aided by the enforcement of 18 U.S.C.A. § 1725.

The Court majority reasoned that mailboxes, unlike streets or parks, are not public forums but more like prisons, as in Adderley v. Florida, 385 U.S. 39, 87 S.Ct. 242, 17 L.Ed.2d 149 (1966), rehearing denied 385 U.S. 1020, 87 S.Ct. 698, 17 L.Ed.2d 559 (1967). Nor does section 1725 regulate speech on the basis of content.

Brennan, J., concurred in the judgment, concluding that a mailbox is a public forum but that § 1725 was a reasonable time, place, and manner regulation that was content neutral and the burden on expression advanced a significant governmental interest: preventing loss of mail revenue. White, J., also concurred in the judgment, relying on the Government's interest in defraying its operating expenses: "stuffing the mailbox with unstamped materials is a burden on the system."

Marshall, J., dissenting, argued that mailboxes are public forums. Stevens, J., also dissenting, did not accept the public forum argument but concluded that the Government's justifications for § 1725 were inadequate and less restrictive alternatives would meet its interests. For example, the Government could require that if the homeowner opted to receive unstamped mail in his mailbox, an overstuffed box must be replaced with a larger one.

See also, Consolidated Edison Co. of New York, Inc. v. Public Service Com'n, 447 U.S. 530, 100 S.Ct. 2326, 65 L.Ed.2d 319 (1980) (Public Service Commission order banning public utilities from inserting in monthly electric bills inserts discussing controversial issues of policy constitutes invalid attempt to regulate speech based on content).

37. Flower v. United States, 407 U.S. 197, 198, 92 S.Ct. 1842, 1843, 32 L.Ed.2d 653 (1972) (per curiam), mandate conformed 462 F.2d 1133 (5th Cir.1972).

38. 460 U.S. 37, 103 S.Ct. 948, 74 L.Ed.2d 794 (1983), on remand 705 F.2d 462 (7th Cir.1983).

See generally, Schmedemann, Of Meetings and Mailboxes: The First Amendment and Exclusive Representation in Public Sector Labor Relations, 72 Va.L.Rev. 91 (1986).

a teachers' union, the Perry Education Association (PEA), was the duly elected exclusive bargaining representative of the teachers in a certain school district. A collective bargaining agreement granted this union, and no other union, the right to access to the interschool mail system and teacher mailboxes in that school system. The rival union, the Perry Local Educators' Association (PLEA), sought similar access. In a five to four opinion the Supreme Court, in an opinion by Justice White, found that the school's denial of access to the rival union of the mailboxes and interschool mail system was no violation of free speech.

Of significance is the majority's reasoning. The Court first recognized that there were degrees of public forums. Along the spectrum, three major distinctions exist. First, the public streets and parks:

> In places which by long tradition or by government fiat have been devoted to assembly and debate, the rights of the state to limit expressive activity are sharply circumscribed. At one end of the spectrum are streets and parks which "have immemorially been held in trust for the use of the public, and, time out of mind, have been used for purposes of assembly, communicating thoughts between citizens, and discussing public questions." In these quintessential public forums, the government may not prohibit all communicative activity. For the state to enforce a content-based exclusion it must show that its regulation is necessary to serve a compelling state interest and that it is narrowly drawn to achieve that end. The state may also enforce regulations of the time, place, and manner of expression which are content-neutral, are narrowly tailored to serve a significant government interest, and leave open ample alternative channels of communication.[39]

The restrictions on residential picketing on the public streets—which the Court invalidated in *Carey v. Brown*[40]—fall in this first category, where the Court is most likely to invalidate regulation.

The Court then turned to the second category:

> A second category consists of public property which the state has opened for use by the public as a place for expressive activity. The Constitution forbids a state to enforce certain exclusions from a forum generally open to the public even if it was not required to create the forum in the first place. Although a state is not required to indefinitely retain the open character of the facility, as long as it does so it is bound by the same standards as apply in a traditional public forum. Reasonable time, place and manner

39. 103 S.Ct. at 954–55 (internal citations omitted without indication).

See generally, Farber & Nowak, The Misleading Nature of Public Forum Analysis; Content and Context in First Amendment Adjudication, 70 Va.L.Rev. 1219 (1984).

40. 447 U.S. 455, 100 S.Ct. 2286, 65 L.Ed.2d 263 (1980).

regulations are permissible, and a content-based prohibition must be narrowly drawn to effectuate a compelling state interest.[41]

Thus in *Widmar v. Vincent*[42] a state university made its facilities generally available for the activities of registered student groups. Having done so, it could not discriminate among those groups on the basis of content without a compelling justification. In that case the Court therefore held that the state university could not close its facilities to a registered student group desiring to use its facilities for religious worship and discussion because the university created the forum, it had to justify its discriminations and exclusions.

Finally the Court turned to the third category:

> Public property which is not by tradition or designation a forum for public communication is governed by different standards. We have recognized that the "First Amendment does not guarantee access to property simply because it is owned or controlled by the government." In addition to time, place, and manner regulations, the state *may reserve the forum for its intended purposes, communicative or otherwise, as long as the regulation on speech is reasonable* and not an effort to suppress expression merely because public officials oppose the speaker's view. As we have stated on several occasions, "the State, no less than a private owner of property, has power to preserve the property under its control for the use to which it is lawfully dedicated."[43]

A few years earlier the Supreme Court had held that a U.S. mailbox was not a public forum, and that therefore it was constitution-

---

41. 460 U.S. at 45–46, 103 S.Ct. at 955 (internal citations omitted without indication).

42. 454 U.S. 263, 102 S.Ct. 269, 70 L.Ed.2d 440 (1981).

See also, Flower v. United States, 407 U.S. 197, 198, 92 S.Ct. 1842, 1843, 32 L.Ed.2d 653 (1972) (per curiam), mandate conformed, 462 F.2d 1133 (5th Cir.1972) (street technically within the jurisdiction of a military fort is treated by the military as a public thoroughfare of the city; hence, the military authorities could not then order a person to leave the street merely because he was distributing leaflets, any more than a city policeman could order someone off the streets).

Compare, Board of Education v. Mergens, 496 U.S. 226, 110 S.Ct. 2356, 110 L.Ed.2d 191 (1990). The Court, in this case, held that the Equal Access Act, 20 U.S.C.A. §§ 4071–74, did not violate the establishment clause of the first amendment. The Equal Access Act prohibits public secondary schools that receive federal assistance and that maintain a "limited open forum" from denying equal access to students who wish to meet within the forum on the bases of the content of the speech at such meetings. The students in this case wished to have their Christian Club meet on school premises during noninstructional time. The school allowed other noncurriculum related student groups, such as the scuba club and chess club, to meet on school property during noninstructional time.

See generally, Strossen, A Framework for Evaluating Equal Access Claims by Student Religious Groups: Is There a Window for Free Speech in the Wall Separating Church and State?, 71 Cornell L.Rev. 143 (1985).

43. 460 U.S. at 46, 103 S.Ct. at 955 (emphasis added) (internal citations omitted without indication). See also, Adderley v. Florida, 385 U.S. 39, 87 S.Ct. 242, 17 L.Ed.2d 149 (1966) (jail grounds not public forum).

al to prohibit the deposit of unstamped, "mailable matter" in a mailbox approved by the U.S. Postal Service.[44] Now the Court ruled that the school mail facilities also fell in this third class.

After *Perry* it is clear that it is very important into which category the alleged public forum falls; what is much less clear from *Perry* is what test the courts should use to decide whether—for example, a school classroom, a school mail system—is in the second category or the third category. The first category—the streets and parks—may be self-defining for most purposes, but the latter two categories are not. The *Perry* majority really offered no precise test to distinguish between the second category (public property opened for use by the public as a place for expressive activity) and the third category (public property not by designation or tradition a forum for public communication). The school internal mail system in *Perry* is placed in the third category, even though the mail system was open to nonschool groups like the Cub Scouts; and the school classroom in *Widmar* is in the second category, although the school officials in that case probably believed that its classrooms should fall into the third category because its state-owned classrooms were not dedicated to being used for religious worship.

The Court believed that it was obvious that the school's internal mail system was not a traditional public forum like a street or park. All of the parties agreed that the school board could close its mail system to all but official business. Presumably the board could also simply close down the system entirely.

While the internal mail system was not open to the public generally, the PLEA argued that the school at times allowed private, nonschool groups to use the mail system. Also, prior to the certification of the PEA, the PLEA and the PEA both had unrestricted access. Had the school, by permitting such access, converted the internal mail system to the second category of public forum? The majority ruled that the fact that groups like the Cub Scouts and YMCA had access did not convert the mailboxes to a public forum. Such users had to secure permission, which would not be granted to all; the access was selective. Also, the Court announced, even if the permission granted to such groups created a limited public forum, the constitutional right of access would only extend to other entities of similar character.[45]

44. United States Postal Serv. v. Council of Greenburgh Civic Associations, 453 U.S. 114, 101 S.Ct. 2676, 69 L.Ed.2d 517 (1981), appeal dismissed, certiorari denied 453 U.S. 917, 101 S.Ct. 3150, 69 L.Ed.2d 999 (1981).

45. "While the school mail facilities thus might be a forum generally open for use by the Girl Scouts, the local boys' club and other organizations that engage in activities of interest and educational rele-

vance to students, they would not as a consequence be open to an organization such as PLEA, which is concerned with the terms and conditions of teacher employment." 460 U.S. at 48, 103 S.Ct. at 956. See also, Greer v. Spock, 424 U.S. 828, 838 n. 10, 96 S.Ct. 1211, 1217–18 n. 10, 47 L.Ed.2d 505 (1976).

Greer upheld certain military regulations of Fort Dix, in New Jersey. The regulations banned speeches and demon-

When the school did decide to preclude the PLEA, the school did not discriminate against the content of the speech of the PLEA; the PEA Union, however, did object to the viewpoint expressed by the PLEA Union. The Court did not address that point directly, but concluded: "We believe it more accurate to characterize the access policy as based on the *status* of the respective unions rather than their views. Implicit in the concept of the nonpublic forum is the right to make distinctions in access on the basis of subject matter and speaker identity."[46]

The PLEA, in short, could say what it wanted and communicate with teachers on school property, post notices on school bulletin boards, and make announcements on the public address system.[47] It simply could not use the mailboxes. The school's policies were quite reasonable in this regard, and consistent with preserving the property for the use to which it was lawfully dedicated. The school allowed the PEA to use the mailboxes, which facilitated its obligations to represent all of the teachers. In contrast, the PLEA had no official responsibility.[48] "[W]hen government property is not dedicated to open communication the government may—without further justification—restrict use to those who participate in the forum's official business."[49]

Applying the *Perry* Analysis

The General Rule. When the government regulates speech in a traditional public forum it may only base its restrictions on the content of the speech being regulated (1) if that content falls within a category of speech that the Supreme Court has found unprotected by the first amendment, or (2) if the government can demonstrate a compelling interest in suppressing the speech. However, the government may employ a reasonable time, place, or manner regulation to regulate speech in a traditional public forum so long as the regulation promotes an important interest unrelated to the suppression of a particular message and does not unnecessarily restrict the ability to communicate the message. The regulation should allow adequate alternative channels of communication.[50]

strations of a partisan political nature. The military authorities did not treat the Fort as a public forum, and there was no viewpoint discrimination in the regulations. Brown v. Glines, 444 U.S. 348, 354 n. 2, 100 S.Ct. 594, 597 n. 2, 62 L.Ed.2d 540 (1980), on remand 618 F.2d 623 (9th Cir. 1980).

46. 460 U.S. at 49, 103 S.Ct. at 957 (emphasis in original).

47. 460 U.S. at 41, 103 S.Ct. at 952.

48. 460 U.S. at 51, 103 S.Ct. at 958.

49. 460 U.S. at 53, 103 S.Ct. at 959 (footnote omitted). Brennan, J., joined by Marshall, Powell, and Stevens, JJ., dissented, arguing that the exclusive access provision in the collective bargaining agreement was viewpoint discrimination and violated the first amendment.

50. See generally, Post, Between Governance and Management: The History and Theory of the Public Forum, 34 U.C.L.A.L.Rev. 1713 (1987).

If the government opens public property to the public as a place for expressive activity, even though it is not a traditional public forum, the government is subject to the same restrictions of its actions in this forum as would be applicable to regulations of speech in a traditional public forum. It will be able to employ only reasonable time, place, or manner regulations; any content based prohibition of speech in this forum must relate to a compelling government interest. However, the government may choose to close the forum to the public and expressive activities. It does not have to keep this type of forum open indefinitely.

If the public property is not a public forum, the Government may not only impose time, place or manner restrictions, it also may reserve the place for its intended purposes if the speech regulation is: (1) reasonable, and (2) not an effort to suppress speech merely because the public officials oppose the speaker's viewpoint.

Public Sidewalks and Parks. Two months after its decision in *Perry,* the Supreme Court in *United States v. Grace*[51] applied the *Perry* analysis and invalidated a portion of a federal statute prohibiting picketing on the public sidewalks surrounding the United States Supreme Court building.

The public sidewalks are in the first category under *Perry* and the Government could not present the strong justification needed to allow such a restriction on the public forum. There was no evidence, for example, that the picketing obstructed access to the Supreme Court building. The suppression of all speech of this type in a public forum was seen as a total suppression of the ability to communicate messages in a public place; it was not a permissible time, place, or manner regulation. The state, or a state-owned entity such as a public university, may regulate picketing on the sidewalk so that the noise level would not be so high that nearby classroom instruction was made impossible.[52] The state university may also limit the number of people on a sidewalk so that the picketers did not obstruct passage. But it has no *carte blanche* power to simply prohibit pickets on the public sidewalks.

Grace stated the test for time, place, or manner regulations of speech in a public forum as follows: "[t]he government may enforce reasonable time, place, and manner regulations as long as the restrictions are content neutral, are narrowly tailored to serve a significant government interest, and leave open ample alternative channels of communication."[53] The Court later employed this test to uphold a

---

51. United States v. Grace, 461 U.S. 171, 103 S.Ct. 1702, 75 L.Ed.2d 736 (1983), remanded 717 F.2d 1480 (D.C.Cir.1983). Marshall, J., and Stevens, J., each filed separate opinions concurring in part and dissenting in part. However, neither these justices nor any other objected to the majority's reliance on the *Perry* analysis.

52. E.g. Kovacs v. Cooper, 336 U.S. 77, 69 S.Ct. 448, 93 L.Ed. 513 (1949), rehearing denied 336 U.S. 921, 60 S.Ct. 638, 93 L.Ed. 1083 (1949).

53. 461 U.S. at 177, 103 S.Ct. at 1707 (internal quotations and citations omitted).

National Park Service refusal to allow an around-the-clock demonstration in a park in Washington, D.C. In *Clark v. Community for Creative Non–Violence,*[54] the Court upheld a regulation limiting the time when a public park could be used, even though the limitation restricted the ability of the would be demonstrators to bring their message to the attention of the public by sleeping in symbolic "tent cities" in the park. The refusal to allow such a demonstration was a valid time, place, or manner regulation because it was a content neutral means of promoting the government interest in preserving parks and the regulation allowed adequate alternative channels of communication.[55]   These parks were not meant to be used as camp grounds, and the tent-cities obstructed the use of the parks by the nonprotestors.

Residential Picketing.   The Court has been quite strict in reviewing laws that purport to regulate residential picketing.   Even before the decision in *Perry,* the Court made clear that the sidewalks and streets are traditionally an open public forum.   Thus, in *Police Department v. Mosley*[56] the Court invalidated a city ordinance that prohibited picketing on a public way within 150 feet of a grade or high school during the school day.   The ordinance, however, allowed labor picketing, and that, said the Court, was a fatal flaw, for it showed that it was regulating speech based on content: was the message of the picketers related to labor conditions, or something else, such as school desegregation?   "Once a forum is opened up to assembly or speaking by some groups, government may not prohibit others from assembling or speaking on the basis of what they intend to say."[57]

Subsequently, the Court invalidated a more narrowly drawn residential picketing statute in *Carey v. Brown.*[58]   However, that statute— while purporting to prohibit picketing of all residences or dwellings— also did allow the peaceful picketing of a place of employment involved in a labor dispute.

In 1988 the Court did finally approve of a residential picketing statute—but the Court did so only after interpreting it in an unusually narrow fashion, based on a strained construction.   And even then, the

---

54.   468 U.S. 288, 104 S.Ct. 3065, 82 L.Ed.2d 221 (1984).

55.   The review of time, place, or manner regulations is designed to determine whether they are content based or a truly unnecessary restriction of the ability to communicate.   Courts must still accord deference to the other branches of government in determining the reasonableness of regulations.   In Clark v. Community for Creative Non–Violence, 468 U.S. 288, 299, 104 S.Ct. 3065, 3072, 82 L.Ed.2d 221, 231 (1984), the Court stated: "We do not believe, [contrary to the Court of Appeals] however, that either *United States v.*

O'Brien, or the time, place, and manner decisions assign to the judiciary the authority to replace the Park Service as manager of the Nation's parks or endowed the judiciary with the competence to judge how much protection of the park lands is wise and how that level of conservation is to be attained."

56.   408 U.S. 92, 92 S.Ct. 2286, 33 L.Ed.2d 212 (1972).

57.   408 U.S. at 95–96, 92 S.Ct. at 2290.

58.   447 U.S. 455, 100 S.Ct. 2286, 65 L.Ed.2d 263 (1980).

opinion drew several dissents. In *Frisby v. Schultz*[59] a majority of the Court rejected a facial challenge to a statute which it interpreted to ban only "focused" picketing, that is, picketing that would take place solely in front of a particular residence. The Court majority found that, as construed, the statute was not valid on its face and served the interest in residential privacy.

In *Frisby* Justice O'Connor, for the Court, rejected a facial challenge to an ordinance that completely bans picketing "before or about" any residence. The appellees, individuals strongly opposed to abortion, picketed on a public street before the residence of a doctor who performed abortions at clinics in neighboring towns. Though the picketing was generally orderly and peaceful, it generated controversy and the town responded, in 1985, by enacting an ordinance banning all picketing in neighborhoods except labor picketing. The town attorney advised the town that the labor picketing exception in the ordinance probably made it unconstitutional because it distinguished between classes of speech based on content. The town then repealed that ordinance and enacted a flat ban: "It is unlawful for any person to engage in picketing before or about the residence of dwelling of any individual in the Town of Brookfield."[60]

The plaintiffs obtained declaratory and injunctive relief, and the Supreme Court reversed. It interpreted the ordinance as prohibiting "only picketing focused on," and taking place "solely in front of a particular residence;" in contrast, marching through residential neighborhoods "or even walking a route in front of an entire block of houses, is not prohibited by this ordinance," the Court said.[61]

Though the Court readily agreed that a public street, even in a residential neighborhood, is "the archetype of a traditional public forum," it rejected the facial attack on the ordinance because of the state's interest in protecting residential privacy and the unwilling listener. "The type of focused picketing prohibited by the Brookfield ordinance is fundamentally different from more generally directed means of communication that may not be completely banned in residential areas," such as handbilling, solicitation, or marching. "Here, in contrast, the picketing is narrowly directed at the household, not the public." Such picketers "generally do not seek to disseminate a message to the general public, but to intrude upon the targeted resident, and to do so in an especially offensive way. Moreover, even if some such picketers have a broader communicative purpose, their activity nonetheless inherently and offensively intrudes on residential privacy."[62]

59. 487 U.S. 474, 108 S.Ct. 2495, 101 L.Ed.2d 420 (1988), on remand 857 F.2d 1175 (7th Cir.1988).

60. 487 U.S. at 476, 108 S.Ct. at 2498.

61. 487 U.S. at 482, 108 S.Ct. at 2501.

62. 487 U.S. at 486, 108 S.Ct. at 2503.

At the end of the majority opinion, Justice O'Connor emphasized that the Court was only rejecting a facial challenge to the law. Specific applications of the law—"for example, a particular resident's use of his or her home as a place of business or public meeting, or to picketers present at a particular home by invitation of the resident—may present somewhat different questions." [63] Justice White, concurring in the judgment, emphasized this point and his reluctance to challenge the ordinance as overbroad, at this point in time, in light of the Town counsel's representation at oral argument that the ordinance forbids only single-residence picketing. [64]

Justice Brennan, joined by Justice Marshall, dissented. [65] They would allow the Government to regulate the number of residential picketers, the hours during which the picketing could take place, and the noise level of the picketing, but they would not allow the Government to ban residential picketing in its entirety.

Justice Stevens also dissented. He believed that the ordinance was overbroad: its plain language covered picketing to willing and indifferent recipients. For example, the ordinance would literally prohibit a fifth grader from carrying a sign in front of a residence that simply said, "Get well Charlie—Our team needs you." Thus, he concluded, the ordinance as written gives too much discretion to law enforcement officials, requiring picketers to picket at their peril. [66]

On the other hand, if the ordinance was written to exclude the case that Justice Stevens proposed—that is, the statute would allow focused picketing *except* focused picketing if the recipient was willing or indifferent—then the statute would run up against the problem that the Court had raised in *Mosley* and *Carey;* the statute would regulate speech based on content. Such a statute would, in effect, provide, that the focused picketeer could have a sign that announced—"Get well, Charlie" (where Charlie is the willing recipient), but not—"Get sick, Charlie" (where Charlie is less willing to embrace that message).

Public Street Posts. Recall that the third category of public forum analysis under *Perry* is public property not open to the public either by designation or by tradition. The government may operate property that is dedicated to the promotion of a specific governmental purpose. As stated in *Perry,* the government may reserve this type of property for its intended purpose, and regulate expressive activity therein, "as long as the regulation on speech is reasonable and not an effort to supress expression merely because public officials oppose the speaker's view." [67]

63. 487 U.S. at 488, 108 S.Ct. at 2504.

64. 487 U.S. at 488, 108 S.Ct. at 2504 (White, J., concurring in the judgment).

65. 487 U.S. at 491, 108 S.Ct. at 2506 (Brennan, J., joined by Marshall, J., dissenting).

66. 487 U.S. at 495, 108 S.Ct. at 2508 (Stevens, J., dissenting).

67. 460 U.S. at 46, 103 S.Ct. at 955.

Boos v. Barry, 485 U.S. 312, 108 S.Ct. 1157, 99 L.Ed.2d 333 (1988) ruled on the

The decision in *Members of the City Council of Los Angeles v. Taxpayers for Vincent,*[68] illustrates this third category under public forum analysis. The Court upheld a city ordinance that prohibited the posting of signs on public property and upheld the application of that ordinance to prohibit the placing of campaign signs on street light posts in the city. The majority opinion by Justice Stevens noted that light posts are not a type of government property traditionally designated for public communication and did not constitute a public forum. The prohibition of speech was permissible because it promoted important government interests in aesthetic values and the environment which were unrelated to the suppression of a particular viewpoint.

Postal Property. In *United States v. Kokinda,*[69] the Court, with no majority opinion, upheld the constitutionality of a federal law that

constitutionality of a District of Columbia statute enacted by Congress. The first part of the statute, called the "display clause," prohibited the display of any sign within 500 feet of a foreign embassy if that sign tends to bring the foreign government into "public odium" or "public disrepute." It applied only to signs, not the spoken word. The Court invalidated that provision as a content-based restriction on political speech in the public forum. The Government argued that the law served a compelling state interest—our international law obligation to shield diplomats from speech that offends their dignity. The Court said that even assuming that such an interest was compelling—and the Court said that it was "not persuaded" that differences between American citizens (who must tolerate "insulting and even outrageous speech") and foreign officials "require us to deviate from these principles here"—the law was not "narrowly tailored" to serve that interest. A significantly less restrictive alternative would be a statute prohibiting anyone who attempts to intimidate, obstruct, harass a foreign official. Indeed, Congress had already enacted such a statute for the rest of the country.

The Court upheld the second portion of the statute, the "congregation clause," which prohibited three or more people from congregating within 500 feet of the embassy if the congregation is directed at the embassy and if the people refuse to disperse after having been ordered to do so by the police. The lower court had narrowly interpreted the statute to allow the police to order dispersal "only when the police reasonably believe that a threat to the security or peace of the embassy is present." As interpreted, the statute was

constitutional and not impermissibly vague. The statute reached only groups posing a security threat.

Nor was there any violation of equal protection because another statute excluded labor picketing from the reach of the congregation clause. Because that clause only prohibits congregations that threaten the peace or security of an embassy, the clause allows all peaceful congregations, including "peaceful" labor congregations. If the labor picketing statute was interpreted to allow "violent" labor picketing (but not violent nonlabor picketing), the statute (which would be prohibiting speech based on content—whether it related to labor disputes) would run afoul of equal protection guarantee, said the Court. But the Court declined to so interpret the statute.

68. 466 U.S. 789, 104 S.Ct. 2118, 80 L.Ed.2d 772 (1984), on remand 738 F.2d 353 (9th Cir.1984).

69. ___ U.S. ___, 110 S.Ct. 3115, 111 L.Ed.2d 571 (1990). O'Connor, J., joined by Rehnquist, C.J., and White & Scalia, JJ., concluded that the post office sidewalk was not a traditional public forum open to the public, because it was not a public passageway and was constructed solely to provide for the passage of customers engaged in postal business. The postal authorities did not dedicate this property to First Amendment activity, but only to the posting of public notices on designated bulletin boards. These justices concluded that the practice of allowing persons to leaflet, speak, and picket on postal premises (together with a regulation forbidding disruptive conduct) does not mean that the property is dedicated to all First Amendment

315

prohibits solicitation on postal property. The respondents in this case were members of a political advocacy group who set up a table on a sidewalk near the entrance to a United States Post Office in order to solicit contributions, sell books and subscriptions, and distribute literature. The sidewalk, which lies entirely on Postal Service property, was the only way that customers could travel from the post office to the parking lot. The solicitors impeded the normal flow of traffic, and it is intrusive for the postal customers to confront people, face-to-face, soliciting contributions.

Private Meetings. Similarly, in *Minnesota State Board for Community Colleges v. Knight,*[70] the Court upheld a state law which required academic administrators to "meet and confer" with teachers regarding questions of policy and governance but limited these discussions to representatives of the teachers selected by a union which had been elected to be the exclusive bargaining representative of the teachers. Justice O'Connor, writing for the majority, found that the meet and confer sessions were not a forum of any type and could be reserved for discussions between administrators and representatives of the exclusive bargaining agent of the teachers even though the issues to be discussed at these meetings were outside of the scope of contract negotiations. The majority assumed the regulation did not significantly restrict the ability of nonunion employees to communicate their views on policy issues to college administrators. This was not a public meeting; it could be reserved for communication between the administration and union representatives.[71]

Military Bar Letters. *United States v. Albertini*[72] illustrates another application of, and lack of clarity of, the *Perry* public forum

activity. Confronting a person soliciting money is more intimidating than meeting a person who is merely giving out information. Even if this postal sidewalk is not a purely nonpublic forum and is dedicated to some First Amendment uses, the postal regulation is reasonable because the Postal Service's experience is that solicitation is intrusive, interferes with the work of the postal officials, and impedes the normal flow of traffic.

Kennedy, J., concurring in the judgment, concluded that the postal regulation was constitutional even if the sidewalk is a public forum because it is a reasonable time, place, and manner regulation. Pursuant to the disputed regulation everyone may engage in political speech and distribute literature soliciting money, provided that there is no in-person solicitation for immediate payments on the premises. This regulation is proper given the special nature of in-person solicitation and the Postal Service's past experience.

Brennan, J., joined by Marshall, Stevens, JJ. (and by Blackmun, J., in part), dissented.

70. 465 U.S. 271, 104 S.Ct. 1058, 79 L.Ed.2d 299 (1984).

71. Although the government can create a special purpose public forum and limit access to it, the government could not use a similar classification to restrict speech in the public forum. Thus, the government could not totally prohibit teacher access to a school board meeting open to the public because that would be a content based restriction on speech in a public forum. See City of Madison Joint School Dist. No. 8 v. Wisconsin Employment Relations Commission, 429 U.S. 167, 97 S.Ct. 421, 50 L.Ed.2d 376 (1976).

72. 472 U.S. 675, 105 S.Ct. 2897, 86 L.Ed.2d 536 (1985).

categorizing analysis. Section 1382 of title 18 makes it a crime to reenter a military base after having been barred by the commanding officer. In 1972 Albertini received a letter (a "bar letter") from the commanding officer of Hickam Air Force Base ("Hickman") barring him from reentering without the written permission of the Commander or his designee. Albertini received the bar letter because he and a companion had entered Hickam and destroyed secret Air Force documents by pouring animal blood on them. For these acts he was convicted of conspiracy to destroy Government property.

Nearly a decade later, in 1981, Hickam advertised that while it "is normally a closed base, the gates will be open to the public for this 32nd Annual Armed Forces Day Open House." Radio advertisements stated that "the public is invited and it's all free." Albertini and four friends attended, passed out leaflets, and, in front of a B–52 bomber display, unfurled a banner reading "Carnival of Death." Albertini did not disrupt the Open House activities. After he and his friends were escorted off the base, he was convicted of violating § 1382.

Justice O'Connor, in a six to three decision, upheld the conviction. First, the Court relied heavily on the bar letter. The original bar order was valid and had not been issued in response to activity which was protected by the First Amendment. Thus the Court distinguished this case from *Flower v. United States.*[73] In *Flower* the defendant had received a bar letter because he tried to distribute unauthorized publications on a military base which was always open to the public. Such activity—the distribution of publications—was protected by the first amendment, the Court said. But in contrast to *Flower,* Albertini's act of vandalism in 1972 was not protected expression. And he was not prosecuted for his 1981 peaceful demonstration; rather, he was prosecuted for reentering the base in violation of the 1972 bar letter.

Second, even if Hickam was temporarily transformed into a public forum on the day of the open house, Albertini's position was different from that of the general public because he had previously received a valid bar letter. "Where a bar letter is issued on valid grounds, a person may not claim immunity from its prohibition on entry merely because the military has temporarily opened a military facility to the public. Section 1382 is content-neutral and serves a significant Government interest in barring entry to a military base by persons whose previous conduct demonstrates that they are a threat to security."[74] The majority also rejected as "implausible" Albertini's claim that he lacked notice that his entry was prohibited. "The bar letter in no way indicated that it applied only when public access to Hickam was

73. 407 U.S. 197, 92 S.Ct. 1842, 32 L.Ed.2d 653 (1972) (per curiam).   **74.** 472 U.S. at 688, 105 S.Ct. at 2906.

restricted." [75] If Albertini was uncertain, he should have requested permission to reenter, the majority argued.

Charitable Solicitation on Government Property. Shortly after *Albertini*, the Court, in a four to three opinion, upheld an Executive Order limiting charitable solicitation of federal employees during working hours in *Cornelius v. NAACP Legal Defense and Educational Fund, Inc.*[76] The federal government participates in the Combined Federal Campaign (CFC), which is a charity drive directed at federal employees during working hours. An Executive Order limited participation to tax-exempt, nonprofit charitable agencies which provide direct health and welfare services to individuals or their families. The Order specifically excluded legal defense and political advocacy organizations. The Court, applying *Perry*, upheld the constitutionality of the Executive Order.

The Court, again speaking through Justice O'Connor, readily agreed that charitable solicitation is a form of speech protected by the first amendment. This speech did not lose protection merely because the participating organizations did not engage in face to face solicitation but instead each submitted 30–word statements which would be included in the CFC literature.

Then the Court turned to the question of what was the relevant forum. The relevant forum, said the Court, is the CFC, not the federal workplace, because the respondents only seek access to a particular means of communication, the CFC. Respondents did not claim any general right of access to the federal workplace. In determining what is the relevant forum, the focus should be on the type of access sought, not merely on the physical Government property at issue.

Then the Court concluded that the CFC is a nonpublic forum. Neither the Government's practice nor policy suggests any intent to convert the CFC into a public forum open to all tax-exempt organizations. The charitable organizations have to seek permission to solicit. Although the record did not show how many organizations have been denied permission throughout the 24–year history of CFC, the Court was satisfied with the fact that there was no evidence suggesting that the granting of the requisite permission was merely ministerial.[77]

75. 472 U.S. at 684, 105 S.Ct. at 2904. Justice Stevens, joined by Brennan and Marshall, JJ., dissented: "respondent's visit to the open house in this case in response to a general invitation to the public extended nine years after he was removed from the base and ordered not to reenter does not involve the kind of reentry that Congress intended to prohibit when it enacted the 1909 statute." 472 U.S. at 694, 105 S.Ct. at 2909.

76. 473 U.S. 788, 804–06, 105 S.Ct. 3439, 3450–51, 87 L.Ed.2d 567 (1985). Marshall and Powell, JJ., did not participate. Blackmun, J., joined by Brennan, J., filed a dissenting opinion. Stevens, J., also filed a dissenting opinion.

77. 473 U.S. at 804–06, 105 S.Ct. at 3450–51. Cf. *Perry*, 460 U.S. at 47, 103 S.Ct. at 956.

The Court, relying on *Perry,* concluded that control "over access to a nonpublic forum can be based on subject matter and speaker identity so long as the distinctions drawn are reasonable in light of the purpose served by the forum and are viewpoint neutral." [78] Turning to the first issue, the Court found that the restrictions were reasonable. It was reasonable for the Government to conclude that money given directly for food and shelter to the needy is more beneficial than money given for litigation. Second, the restrictions on access avoided the appearance of government favoritism or entanglement with particular viewpoints. Also, the record was adequate enough to support an inference that the respondents' participation in the CFC jeopardized its success and the federal workplace. The evidence was in the form of correspondence and telephone calls from federal workers "expressing concern" about the inclusion of political groups in the CFC.

As for the need to avoid workplace disruption, the Court assumed this point and analogized to *Perry,* where exclusion of the rival union was thought necessary to insure labor peace.[79] The first amendment does not forbid a viewpoint neutral exclusion of speakers who would disrupt a nonpublic forum and hinder its effectiveness for its intended purpose. Because this is a nonpublic forum, there is no requirement that the Government's restrictions on access be "narrowly tailored," or that its interests in exclusion be "compelling." The Court added: "Although the avoidance of controversy is not a valid ground for restricting speech in a public forum, a nonpublic forum by definition is not dedicated to general debate or the free exchange of ideas." [80]

The Court then remanded to determine whether the Government impermissibly excluded the respondents from the CFC because it disagreed with their viewpoints.

Justice Blackmun, joined by Justice Brennan dissented. They accepted *Perry* but argued, inter alia:

> Rather than recognize that a nonpublic forum is a place where expressive activity would be incompatible with the purposes the property is intended to serve, the Court states that a nonpublic forum is a place where we need not even be concerned about whether expressive activity is incompatible with the purposes of the property. Rather than taking the nature of the property into account in balancing the First Amendment interests of the speaker and society's interest in freedom of speech against the interests served by reserving the property to its normal use, the Court simply labels the property and dispenses with the balancing.[81]

78.   473 U.S. at 806, 105 S.Ct. at 3451. See also *Perry,* 460 U.S. at 49, 103 S.Ct. at 957.

79.   473 U.S. at 810, 105 S.Ct. at 3453. Compare *Perry,* 460 U.S. at 52, 103 S.Ct. at 959.

80.   473 U.S. at 812, 105 S.Ct. at 3454.

81.   473 U.S. at 821, 105 S.Ct. at 3459.

Justice Stevens also filed a dissenting opinion in which he questioned the *Perry* analysis as not "particularly helpful." [82] He emphasized that none of the advocacy organizations would receive any CFC donations unless the employees specifically designated such an organization; thus he believed that the arguments in favor of excluding such organizations from the CFC "are so plainly without merit that they actually lend support to an inference of bias." [83]

School Assemblies

In *Bethel School District No. 403 v. Fraser,*[84] the Court upheld a broad power of school authorities to discipline a student for delivering, at a school assembly, a speech which promoted another student as a candidate for student government by using "persuasive sexual innuendo." Fraser promoted his candidate in a speech describing him as "a man who is firm—he's firm in his pants, he's firm in his shirt, his character is firm—but most of all, his belief in you, the students of Bethel, is firm." The student added that his candidate was also "a man who takes his point and pounds it in;" "a man who will go to the very end—even to the climax, for each and every one of you." The majority opinion described this speech as "lewd and obscene" [85] and refused to even quote it. One must turn to the separate opinion of Justice Brennan to find out exactly what Mr. Fraser said.[86]

The school suspended the 17 year old student for two days.[87] The audience of about 600 students included students 14 years old or older. Some responded to the speech with hooting and yelling.

Chief Justice Burger, for the Court, said "Surely it is a highly appropriate function of public school education to prohibit the use of vulgar and offensive terms in public discourse." School officials must have broad power to punish what they conclude is "inappropriate" speech in classrooms and assemblies. Schools "must teach by example the shared values of a civilized social order." [88] Burger also called the speech "obscene," claimed that it included "graphic, and explicit sexual metaphor," [89] and said that it "was plainly offensive to both teachers and students," "was acutely insulting to teen-age girl students," and "could well be seriously damaging to its less mature audience, many of

82. 473 U.S. at 835, 105 S.Ct. at 3466.

83. 473 U.S. at 836, 105 S.Ct. at 3467 (footnote omitted).

84. 478 U.S. 675, 106 S.Ct. 3159, 92 L.Ed.2d 549 (1986), on remand 800 F.2d 222 (9th Cir.1986).

85. 478 U.S. at 679, 106 S.Ct. at 3163 (Burger, C.J., for the Court).

86. 478 U.S. at 687, 106 S.Ct. at 3167 (Brennan, J., concurring in the judgment).

87. Initially, Fraser was suspended for three days and his name was removed from the list of candidates for graduation speakers at the school's commencement activities. But the school allowed Fraser to return after only two days of suspension, 478 U.S. at 677, 106 S.Ct. at 3162–63, and, although he was removed from the list of speaker candidates, the student body chose him to speak at the graduation ceremonies anyway. 478 U.S. at 691, 106 S.Ct. at 3169 (Stevens, J., dissenting).

88. 478 U.S. at 684, 106 S.Ct. at 3165.

89. 478 U.S. at 677, 106 S.Ct. at 3162.

whom were only 14 years old and on the threshold of awareness of human sexuality." [90] Burger asserted, "The determination of what manner of speech in the classroom or in school assembly is inappropriate properly rests with the school board." [91] Thus, this case is probably limited to its facts that is, to speech in school or the school assembly.

Justice Brennan concurred in the result. He said that the speech was no more obscene or lewd "than the bulk of programs currently on prime-time television or in the local cinema." Yet, he would uphold the school board action because this speech may be punished as "disruptive" in the school environment.[92]

Justice Marshall, dissenting, said that the speech was not even disruptive. In fact, both lower courts found no evidence of disruption at all.[93] Justice Stevens, also dissenting, said that the student "should not be disciplined for speaking frankly in a school assembly if he had no reason to anticipate punitive consequences." The student had discussed his proposed speech with three teachers beforehand, and had not been warned that he risked discipline.[94] Moreover, said Stevens, Fraser's contemporaries did not appear upset by his speech: they shortly thereafter elected him to be their graduation speaker. Fraser was in a better position to judge his audience of contemporaries than is "a group of judges who are at least two generations and 3,000 miles away from the scene of the crime." [95]

School Newspapers

In *Hazelwood School District v. Kuhlmeier*,[96] the Court held (five to three) that educators may exercise broad editorial control over the contents of a *high school* newspaper produced as part of the school's journalism curriculum. The majority found no first amendment violation when the principal did not allow the school-sponsored newspaper to publish two articles, one dealing with student pregnancy and the other dealing with the impact of divorce on students. The principal was concerned that it might be easy to identify the identity of the pregnant students from the story and that the references to sexual activity and birth control were inappropriate for some of the younger students. He also believed that the second article should not be

90. 478 U.S. at 683, 106 S.Ct. at 3165.

91. 478 U.S. at 683, 106 S.Ct. at 3165.

92. 478 U.S. at 687, 106 S.Ct. at 3166 (Brennan, J., concurring in the judgment).

93. 478 U.S. at 690, 106 S.Ct. at 3169 (Marshall, J., dissenting); 478 U.S. at 691 n. 2, 106 S.Ct. at 3169 n. 2 (Stevens, J., dissenting, quoting the Court of Appeals opinion at 755 F.2d 1356, 1361 n. 4 (9th Cir.1985)).

94. 478 U.S. at 691–96, 106 S.Ct. at 3169–72 (Stevens, J., dissenting).

95. 478 U.S. at 691, 106 S.Ct. at 3169 (Stevens, J., dissenting) (footnote omitted). Blackmun, J., concurred in the result, without opinion. 478 U.S. at 687, 106 S.Ct. at 3167.

96. 484 U.S. 260, 108 S.Ct. 562, 98 L.Ed.2d 592 (1988). Brennan, J., joined by Marshall & Blackmun, J., filed a dissenting opinion. At this point, there were only eight members on the Court, for the Senate had not yet confirmed a replacement.

published unless the person criticized in it has the opportunity to defend himself.

The majority decided that under *Perry*, the school newspaper was not a public forum because the school authorities did not open it for indiscriminate use by the general public: the students publishing the newspaper received grades and academic credit; the newspaper was produced as part of a class taught by a faculty member during regular class hours; this journalism teacher exercised a great deal of authority over the school newspaper, such as the power to select editors, assign story ideas, edit stories, and select and edit the letters to the editor; the school principal reviewed each issue prior to publication; and the school subsidized the school newspaper's annual budget.[97]

Under the first amendment, educators may exercise editorial control over the style and content of student speech "in school-sponsored activities so long as their actions are reasonably related to legitimate pedagogical concerns." There is a violation of the first amendment only when the censorship of the school-sponsored activity "has no valid educational purpose".

In a footnote the Court stated: "We need not now decide whether the same degree of deference is appropriate with respect to school-sponsored expressive activities at the college and university level."[98]

Prisons

In *Turner v. Safley*,[99] the Court upheld prison regulations which, in effect, prohibited prison inmates from writing to non-family inmates.

---

97. Under these circumstances the Court also held that Tinker v. Des Moines Independent Community School District, 393 U.S. 503, 89 S.Ct. 733, 21 L.Ed.2d 731 (1969) is inapplicable. *Tinker* dealt with the extent to which a school must tolerate student speech; in *Hazelwood*, however, the issue is the extent to which a school must affirmatively promote particular student speech. "The latter question concerns educators' authority over school-sponsored publications, theatrical productions, and other expressive activities that students, parents, and members of the public might reasonably perceive to bear the imprimatur of the school." These activities may fairly be considered part of the school curriculum, even if they do not occur in a traditional classroom setting, "so long as they are supervised by faculty members and designed to impart particular knowledge or skills to student participants and audiences." Therefore a school, in its capacity as publisher of a school newspaper or producer of a school play, may "disassociate itself" from speech which is "ungrammatical, poorly written,

inadequately researched, biased or prejudiced, vulgar or profane, or unsuitable for immature audiences."

98. 484 U.S. at 273 n. 7, 108 S.Ct. at 571 n. 7.

99. 482 U.S. 78, 107 S.Ct. 2254, 96 L.Ed.2d 64 (1987). For analysis of the prison cases where the press or the public seek access to inmates, or where prisoners seek access to the press, see § 20.19.

In Thornburgh v. Abbott, 490 U.S. 401, 109 S.Ct. 1874, 104 L.Ed.2d 459 (1989), the Court upheld, as facially valid, federal prison regulations that permit federal prisoners to receive publications such as magazines from the outside, but authorized prison officials to reject such incoming publications if they find them to be "detrimental to security, good order, or discipline of the institution or if it might facilitate criminal activity." The regulations do not allow the warden to establish an excluded list of publications; he must review each issue separately. The Court applied the standard articulated in *Turner:* the regulations

---

322

The Court rejected the argument that the ban on inmate-to-inmate correspondence violated the first amendment. It also rejected a strict scrutiny test. The ban was upheld because it "reasonably related to legitimate penalogical interests." [100] The evidence showed that the prison adopted the correspondence rule primarily for security reasons. Inmate mail between prisons can compromise protective custody offered to inmates from other institutions; such correspondence facilitates communications between gang members who had been transferred to other prisons in an effort to break up the gang; and such correspondence aids in the communication of escape plans and assault efforts. The correspondence rule "is content-neutral, it logically advances the goals of institutional security and safety," and "it is not an exaggerated response to those objectives." [101]

Airports

The Board of Airport Commissioner's of Los Angeles International Airport adopted a Resolution that baldly provided, in part, that "the Central Terminal Area at Los Angeles International Airport is not open for First Amendment activities by any individual and/or entity." Jews for Jesus, Inc., a nonprofit religious corporation, challenged the Resolution and a unanimous Court invalidated it in, *Board of Airport Commis-*

---

are "valid if [they are] reasonably related to legitimate penological interests." The Court rejected the stricter standard used in Procunier v. Martinez, 416 U.S. 396, 94 S.Ct. 1800, 40 L.Ed.2d 224 (1974), a case invalidating broad prison regulations over outgoing inmate correspondence to noninmates. The majority said that *Martinez* must be limited to regulations concerning outgoing correspondence because the "implications of outgoing correspondence for prison security are of a categorically lesser magnitude than the implications of incoming materials." Moreover, to the extent that *Martinez* might suggest a distinction between incoming correspondence from prisoners and incoming correspondence from nonprisoners, "we today overrule that case.... [W]e prefer the express flexibility of the *Turner* reasonableness standard." Stevens, J., joined by Brennan and Marshall, JJ., concurred in part and dissented in part.

100. 482 U.S. at 87, 107 S.Ct. at 2261.

101. 482 U.S. at 93, 107 S.Ct. at 2264. In another portion of this opinion, the Court invalidated an inmate marriage regulation that prohibited inmates from marrying inmates unless the prison superintendent determined that there were compelling reasons for marriage.

Cf. Kentucky Department of Corrections v. Thompson, 490 U.S. 454, 109 S.Ct. 1904, 104 L.Ed.2d 506 (1989), where Justice Blackmun for the Court held that Kentucky prison regulations do not give state inmates a liberty interest in receiving certain visitors. If the due process clause itself does not directly guarantee the liberty, then the state may create a protected liberty interest "by placing substantive limitations on official discretion." Normally the state reaches this result by limiting official decisionmaking and "by mandating the outcome to be reached upon a finding that the relevant criteria have been met." If the administrator has "unfettered" discretion, there is no state-created liberty interest. The Court then concluded that the regulations in this case lack "the requisite relevant mandatory language." The regulations, for example, provide that the "administrative staff reserves the right to allow or disallow visits". The Court said: "This language is not mandatory. Visitors *may* be excluded if they fall within one of the described categories, but they need not be. Nor need visitors fall within one of the described categories in order to be excluded." Consequently the regulations did not establish a liberty interest. Kennedy, J., filed a concurring opinion, and Marshall, J. (joined by Brennan & Stevens, J.) filed a dissenting opinion.

sioners of City of Los Angeles v. Jews for Jesus, Inc.[102] The Airport board claimed that the Airport is a nonpublic forum but the Court ruled that, even if that were true, the Resolution is still unconstitutionally overbroad.[103]

(d) Regulation to Prevent Fraud

Anonymity. A state statute banning anonymous handbills was struck down as invalid on its face in *Talley v. California*,[104] where the Court recognized that throughout history some persecuted groups have been able to criticize oppressive practices either anonymously or not at all. This right to anonymity is a function of the freedom of association,[105] for identification and the subsequent fear of reprisal could well effectively chill legitimate discussions of public interest. The *Talley* Court specifically did not pass on the validity of an ordinance limited to prevent the evils of identifying those responsible for fraud, false advertising, or libel.[106]

Fraud. If a city seeks to regulate to prevent fraud, its law must be carefully tailored to achieve this purpose without unduly limiting speech. In *Village of Schaumburg v. Citizens for a Better Environment*[107] the Court invalidated as overbroad a local ordinance which prohibited the solicitation of contributions by charitable organizations which do not use at least 75% of their receipts directly for "charitable purposes," which the law defined as excluding the expenses of solicitation, salaries, overhead, and other administrative expenses.

The Village justified its regulation primarily as a prevention of fraud. It argued that if an organization spends more than one quarter of its fundraising receipts on overhead, it really is engaged in a profit enterprise benefiting itself. But the Court said that this reasoning cannot hold as to those organizations "that are primarily engaged in research, advocacy, or public education and that use their own paid

---

102. 482 U.S. 569, 107 S.Ct. 2568, 96 L.Ed.2d 500 (1987).

103. Justice White, joined by Rehnquist, C.J., concurred, but said that the Court's opinion "should not be taken as indicating that a majority of the Court considers the Los Angeles International Airport to be a traditional public forum." 482 U.S. at 112, 107 S.Ct. at 2573.

104. 362 U.S. 60, 80 S.Ct. 536, 4 L.Ed.2d 559 (1960).

See generally, Note, The Interest in Limited Disclosure of Personal Information: A Constitutional Analysis, 36 Vanderbilt L.Rev. 139 (1983).

105. See, e.g., Gibson v. Florida Legislative Investigation Committee, 372 U.S. 539, 83 S.Ct. 889, 9 L.Ed.2d 929 (1963); Louisi-

ana ex rel. Gremillion v. NAACP, 366 U.S. 293, 81 S.Ct. 1333, 6 L.Ed.2d 301 (1961); NAACP v. Alabama, 357 U.S. 449, 78 S.Ct. 1163, 2 L.Ed.2d 1488 (1958), on remand 268 Ala. 531, 109 So.2d 138 (1959), judgment reversed 360 U.S. 240, 79 S.Ct. 1001, 3 L.Ed.2d 1205 (1959); Thomas v. Collins, 323 U.S. 516, 65 S.Ct. 315, 89 L.Ed. 430 (1945), rehearing denied 323 U.S. 819, 65 S.Ct. 557, 89 L.Ed. 650 (1945).

Cf. Note, The First Amendment and Law Enforcement Infiltration of Political Groups, 56 So.Calif.L.Rev. 207 (1982).

106. 362 U.S. at 64, 80 S.Ct. at 538–39.

107. 444 U.S. 620, 100 S.Ct. 826, 63 L.Ed.2d 73 (1980), rehearing denied 445 U.S. 972, 100 S.Ct. 1668, 64 L.Ed.2d 250 (1980).

staff to carry out these functions as well as to solicit financial support." [108]

The Village could protect its antifraud interests by more narrowly drawn regulations which would directly prohibit fraudulent misrepresentations, or require that charitable organizations inform the public how their moneys are spent. Nor did the law serve to protect privacy because it could hardly be maintained that solicitors covered by the 75 percent rule were somehow more intrusive than solicitors not within the ordinance's prohibition. Because the ordinance did not serve a "strong, subordinating interest that the Village is entitled to protect" and is a "direct and substantial limitation on protected activity" the Court invalidated it under the first and fourteenth amendments. [109]

In *Secretary of State v. Joseph H. Munson Co., Inc.,* [110] the Court examined a statute which placed a twenty-five percent limitation on charitable fund raising expenses. The statute was slightly different from that examined in *Citizens for a Better Environment* because the statute at issue in *Joseph H. Munson* allowed for an administrative waiver of the limitation based on a demonstration of financial necessity by a charity. The Court concluded that a waiver provision would not save the statute from being stricken as unconstitutionally overbroad.

The *Munson* statute imposed a "direct restriction on protected first amendment activity" by limiting the amount of expenses that could be earmarked for speech activity in terms of disseminating information about an organization or its position in connection with its fund raising activities. Although the statute might generally be said to be designed to guard the public against fraudulent activities there was "no core of easily identifiable and constitutionally proscribable conduct" prohibited by the statute. The statute therefore was not really aimed at fraud or misrepresentation but placed only a ceiling on the percentage of receipts that might be used for all fund raising activities including speech. Waiver of the limitation for a charity that faced economic hardship did not significantly decrease the restriction on protected first amendment activity because the waiver did not exempt from the spending ceiling the money spent on the dissemination of information by the organization. Because this statute involved a direct restriction on speech and the means chosen to prevent the public from being defrauded were "imprecise," the Court found that "the statute creates an unnecessary risk of chilling free speech" and should be invalidated on its face. [111]

---

108.   444 U.S. at 639, 100 S.Ct. at 837.

109.   444 U.S. at 639, 100 S.Ct. at 837. Justice Rehnquist was the sole dissent.

110.   467 U.S. 947, 104 S.Ct. 2839, 81 L.Ed.2d 786 (1984).

111.   See also, Riley v. National Federation of the Blind of North Carolina, Inc., 487 U.S. 781, 108 S.Ct. 2667, 101 L.Ed.2d 669 (1988), where the Court invalidated the North Carolina Charitable Solicitations Act. The state law set up a three tier schedule to define a prima facie reasonable

One should not underestimate the problem with fraudulent charities. There exist a number of self-described charities that purport to raise money for supposed health purposes, and yet "virtually none" of the donated money goes to the cause in question, such as cancer research. Such mail solicitations often imply, falsely, that the recipient has already won, or has a very good chance of winning, a prize and only has to send in a donation to collect. The problem is not aided by a change in the accounting profession's rules; a change adopted in 1987 permits some fundraising expenses to be allocated to "public education," making it difficult to determine what percentage of donations actually goes to fund raising. For example, a fraudulent sweepstakes "charitable" solicitation letter might have a line in it telling readers to "maintain ideal weight," and then, that "charity" might allocate the

fee which a professional fund raiser may charge: (1) a fee of up to 20% of the receipts is deemed reasonable; (2) a fee from 20% to 35% is deemed unreasonable if it is shown that the solicitation did not involve the dissemination of information, discussion, or advocacy related to public issues as directed by the charity. A fee in excess is presumed unreasonable unless solicitor can show that the solicitation involves dissemination or advocacy on public issues directed by the charity or because otherwise the charity's ability to raise money or communicate would be significantly diminished. The Court invalidated this three tier system burdening free speech and not narrowly tailored to prevent fraud, even with its flexibility.

The North Carolina law also required professional fund raisers to disclose to potential donors the percentage of charitable funds, collected during the previous 12 months, that actually gave to the charity. The Court invalidated this provision as well. The majority said that it was a content based regulation because mandating speech necessarily alters the speech's content. Freedom of speech includes the freedom of what not to say. And, even if the mandated speech is, in the abstract, "commercial speech," it loses its commercial character when inextricably intertwined with the fully protected speech involved in charitable solicitations. The state's interest in forming donors is not weighty enough, said the majority, nor narrowly tailored.

Finally, the majority also invalidated North Carolina's licensing requirement for professional fund raisers. The majority said that even assuming that North Carolina could license professional fund raisers, the regulation must provide that the

licensor, in a brief period, will either issue the license or go to court. The North Carolina law at issue here permits a delay with no limit.

Justice Brennan wrote the opinion for the Court, joined by White, Marshall, Blackmun, and Kennedy, JJ. Justice Scalia joined in all of the opinion except for footnote 11, where the majority had said: "However, nothing in this opinion should be taken to suggest that the State may not require a fund raiser to disclose unambiguously his or her professional status." Scalia argued that where "core First Amendment speech is at issue, the State can assess liability for specific instances of deliberate deception, but it cannot impose a prophylactic rule requiring disclosure even when deliberate statements are not made."

Justice Stevens concurred in part and dissented in part. He agreed with the portion of Chief Justice Rehnquist's dissent which would have upheld the licensing requirement because there was no evidence to suggest that North Carolina would be dilatory in processing the applications.

Chief Justice Rehnquist's dissent, joined by O'Connor, J. noted that North Carolina had revised the statute in an attempt to comply with *Munson*, "[y]et the Court obdurately refuses to allow the various States which have legislated in this area to distinguish between ... incidental fund raising ... and the entirely commercial activities of people whose job is, simply put, figuring out how to raise money for charities."

expense of that mailing to "educational expenses." [112]   For example, in 1989, the Doris Day Animal League raised more than $7 million, but about 90 cents of every dollar went to sending out more mail, asking for more money.   Most of the income of the nonprofit Animal League went to National Direct Marketing, which does make a profit. [113]

Allegedly Pejorative Labeling Requirements and Disclosure of Foreign Origin

The Government may require labeling or disclosure requirements in order to protect or offer information to recipients so long as these requirements do not unduly burden the free speech of the disseminators and are not based on content.   For example, it is constitutional for a statute to provide that the addressee of mail may instruct the post office not to deliver all future mailings from any given sender. [114]   The government, in such a case, itself places no restrictions on speech on the basis of content.   The government merely respects the wishes of the intended recipient.

However a statute could not prohibit the post office from delivering mail determined by the Secretary of the Treasury to be "communist political propaganda" unless the addressee returns a reply card indicating a desire to receive such mail. [115]   Such a law violates the first amendment, because the Post Office may not regulate the flow of mail based on its content.   It was the government's physical detention of the materials, not the fact that a government official merely labeled them as "communist political propaganda" that offended the first amendment. [116]

This point is made clear in *Meese v. Keene*. [117]   In that case the Court upheld certain provisions of the Foreign Agents Registration Act. That Act defines the term "political propaganda" to include any communication which is reasonably adapted to, or intended to influence the recipient within the United States with reference to "the policies of a foreign country or foreign political party." [118]   When the agent of a foreign principal disseminates this "political propaganda" the law requires that he or she must make a disclosure statement to the recipients; this disclosure includes the agent's identity, the identity of the

112. Rundle, A Crackdown on "Charity" Sweepstakes, Wall St. Jrl., Mar. 6, 1989, at B1, cols. 3–6 (midwest ed.).

113. Crossen, Imperfect Pitch: Organized Charities Pass Off Mailing Costs as "Public Education," Wall St.Jrl., Oct. 29, 1990, at A1, Col. 1 (midwest ed.).

114. Rowan v. United States Post Office Dept., 397 U.S. 728, 90 S.Ct. 1484, 25 L.Ed.2d 736 (1970).

115. Lamont v. Postmaster General of U.S., 381 U.S. 301, 85 S.Ct. 1493, 14 L.Ed.2d 398 (1965).

116. See 381 U.S. at 306, 85 S.Ct. at 1496: "The Act sets administrative officials astride the flow of mail to inspect it, appraise it, write the addressee about it, and await a response before dispatching the mail.... [F]ederal agencies regulate the flow of mail."

117. 481 U.S. 465, 107 S.Ct. 1862, 95 L.Ed.2d 415 (1987).

118. 481 U.S. at 472, 107 S.Ct. at 1866.

principle for whom the agent acts, a statement that a report describing the extent of the material is registered with the Department of Justice, and that such registration "does not indicate approval of the contents of this material by the United States Government." The term "political propaganda" does *not* appear in the disclosure form which must be filed, but it is used in the Act.[119] This registration requirement "is comprehensive, *applied equally* to agents of friendly, neutral, and unfriendly governments." [120] As defined in the Act, "propaganda" includes all advocacy materials, even those which are completely accurate.[121]

Barry Keene, a member of the California State Senate, wanted to exhibit three Canadian films, distributed by the National Film Board of Canada, a registered agent of the Government of Canada. Keene did "not want the Department of Justice and the public to regard him as the disseminator of foreign political propaganda, but wishes to exhibit three Canadian motion picture films that have been so identified." [122] The films discussed acid rain and nuclear war. The district court ruled "that Congress violated the First Amendment by using the term 'political propaganda' as the statutory name for the regulated category of expression"; [123] the Supreme Court reversed.

The Court although recognizing that "political propaganda" may mean completely accurate advocacy materials, but also has a pejorative meaning of slanted, misleading advocacy—concluded that "it is our duty to construe legislation as it is written, not as it might be read by a layman, or as it might be understood by someone who has not even read it." [124] The purpose of the statute, as written, and as the district court acknowledged, was to inform recipients of the source of advocacy materials produced by or under the aegis of a foreign government. The statute did not prohibit, edit, or restrain the distribution of the foreign advocacy materials. "To the contrary, Congress simply required the disseminators of such material to make additional disclosures that would better enable the public to evaluate the import of the propaganda." [125] Congress simply required disclosure, the labeling of information to disclose its foreign origin. The law did not prohibit Keene or others from explaining to prospective viewers (before, during, or after the film's viewing, or in a separate context) "that Canada's interest in

119. 481 U.S. at 472, 107 S.Ct. at 1866.

120. 481 U.S. at 469, 107 S.Ct. at 1865 (emphasis added). See also, 481 U.S. at 483 n. 17, 107 S.Ct. at 1872 n. 17 (the Act's definition of propaganda is "neutrally applied" and includes allies as well as adversaries).

121. See 22 U.S.C.A. § 611(j); 481 U.S. at 477, 107 S.Ct. at 1869.

122. 481 U.S. at 467, 107 S.Ct. at 1864.

123. 481 U.S. at 467, 469, 107 S.Ct. at 1865, 1864. The constitutionality of the underlying registration requirements of the Foreign Agents Registration Act were not at issue. 481 U.S. at 467, 107 S.Ct. at 1864.

124. 481 U.S. at 485, 107 S.Ct. at 1873.

125. 481 U.S. at 481, 107 S.Ct. at 1871. See also, Viereck v. United States, 318 U.S. 236, 244, 63 S.Ct. 561, 564, 87 L.Ed.2d 734 (1943).

the consequences of nuclear war and acid rain does not necessarily undermine the integrity or the persuasiveness of its advocacy." Ironically, the district court injunction suppressed information from the public: that information is "the fact that the films fall within the category of materials that Congress has judged to be 'political propaganda.' " [126]

(e) Zoning Regulations

In recent years the Court has scrutinized with particular care state zoning laws which have the effect of restricting speech. In addition to *Carey v. Brown*,[127] dealing with state restrictions on residential picketing, other cases include *Heffron v. International Society for Krishna Consciousness, Inc.*,[128] governing state "zoning" restrictions on solicitation of donations at a state fair; *Metromedia, Inc. v. City of San Diego*,[129] and similar cases governing zoning restrictions on billboards; and *Schad v. Mount Ephraim*,[130] governing zoning restrictions on live entertainment.

In *Schad v. Borough of Mount Ephraim*[131] a zoning ordinance banned *all* live entertainment in a commercial zone. But an adult bookstore operating in the commercial zone wished to introduce a special type of coin operated machine whereby a customer, having inserted a coin, could then watch a live nude dancer performing behind a glass panel. The Court invalidated the ordinance under the first amendment as overbroad. The Borough argued that it was a reasonable time, place and manner restriction, yet it did not "identify the municipal interests making it reasonable to exclude all commercial live entertainment but to allow a variety of other commercial uses in the Borough." [132] The Borough presented no evidence that the manner of expression—live entertainment—is basically incompatible with the normal activities allowed in the commercial zone.

Secondly, "[t]o be reasonable, time, place and manner restrictions not only must serve significant state interests but also leave open adequate alternative channels of communication." The Borough did not leave open alternative channels because it totally banned live

---

126. 481 U.S. at 481, 107 S.Ct. at 1871. Justice Blackmun, joined by Brennan and Marshall, JJ., dissented based on their views of Congress' motives: "The Act mandates disclosure, not direct censorship, but the underlying goal was to control the spread of propaganda by foreign agents." They also believed that it "strains credulity" to believe that the term "propaganda" is neutral. 481 U.S. at 486, 107 S.Ct. at 1874.

127. 447 U.S. 455, 100 S.Ct. 2286, 65 L.Ed.2d 263 (1980), discussed in text at § 20.47(c), supra.

128. 452 U.S. 640, 101 S.Ct. 2559, 69 L.Ed.2d 298 (1981), on remand 311 N.W.2d 843 (Minn.1981).

129. 453 U.S. 490, 101 S.Ct. 2882, 69 L.Ed.2d 800 (1981), on remand 32 Cal.3d 180, 185 Cal.Rptr. 260, 649 P.2d 902 (1982).

130. 452 U.S. 61, 101 S.Ct. 2176, 68 L.Ed.2d 671 (1981). See also § 20.61(d), infra.

131. 452 U.S. 61, 101 S.Ct. 2176, 68 L.Ed.2d 671 (1981).

132. 452 U.S. at 74–75, 101 S.Ct. at 2186 (footnote omitted).

entertainment. Unlike *Young v. American Mini Theatres, Inc.*[133] where the Court had upheld a zoning law which had dispersed but not completely banned theatres showing nonobscene "adult films," the zoning law in *Schad* completely excluded live entertainment.

The Borough argued that live entertainment, including nude dancing, was available in nearby areas. This "position suggests the argument that if there were countywide zoning, it would be quite legal to allow live entertainment in only selected areas of the county and to exclude it from primarily residential communities, such as the Borough of Mount Ephraim." The Court said that this argument "may well be true" but it was of no help to Mount Ephraim.[134] There was no countywide zoning and, the record did not show that such entertainment was available in reasonably nearby areas.

Finally—and somewhat incongruously, in light of its earlier apparent emphasis that the ordinance should have left open alternative channels of speech—the Court stated: " '[O]ne is not to have the exercise of his liberty of expression in appropriate places abridged on the plea that it may be exercised in some other place.' " [135]

In *Heffron v. International Society for Krishna Consciousness, Inc.*[136] the Court held that a state may require a religious organization which desired to distribute and sell religious literature and to solicit donations at a state fair to do so only at an assigned booth within the fairgrounds. These booths were rented to anyone on a first come, first serve basis. This Minnesota state fair rule applied to all enterprises, whether nonprofit, charitable, or commercial. It also allowed anyone to engage in face to face discussions with fair visitors anywhere on the fairgrounds.

The Krishna Society argued that one of its religious rituals, called "Sankirtan," required its members to distribute and sell religious literature and solicit donations. The Court, however, upheld the rule as reasonable time, place, and manner regulation, not violative of the first and fourteenth amendments. First, the rule was not based on the content or subject matter of the speech. Second, the method of allocating rental space was nondiscriminatory and not open to arbitrary application. Third, the rule served a significant government interest because of the state's special need to maintain the orderly movement of the crowd, given the large number of exhibitors and visitors attending the fair. Unlike a city street which is "continually open, often congested, and constitutes not only a necessary conduit in the daily affairs of a

---

133. 427 U.S. 50, 96 S.Ct. 2440, 49 L.Ed.2d 310 (1976), rehearing denied 429 U.S. 873, 97 S.Ct. 191, 50 L.Ed.2d 155 (1976).

134. 452 U.S. at 76, 101 S.Ct. at 2187.

135. 452 U.S. at 76–77, 101 S.Ct. at 2187 quoting Schneider v. State, 308 U.S.

147, 163, 60 S.Ct. 146, 151, 84 L.Ed. 155 (1939).

136. 452 U.S. 640, 101 S.Ct. 2559, 69 L.Ed.2d 298 (1981), on remand 311 N.W.2d 843 (Minn.1981).

locality's citizens, but also a place where people may enjoy the open air or the company of friends and neighbors in a relaxed environment," a state fair "is a temporary event attracting great numbers of visitors who come to the event for a short period to see and experience the host of exhibits and attractions at the fair. The flow of the crowd and demands of safety are more pressing in the context of the fair." [137]

Finally, less restrictive alternatives, such as directly penalizing disorder and disruption, would probably not be effective, because any exemption that applied to the Krishna Society would also have to apply to a large number of other groups. These other groups would include religious, social, political, charitable, and perhaps even commercial organizations. The Court stated that none of its previous cases suggest that the Krishna Society and the ritual of Sankirtan have any "special claim to First Amendment protection as compared to that of other religions who also distribute literature and solicit funds ... but do not purport to ritualize the process. Nor for present purposes do religious organizations enjoy rights to communicate, distribute, and solicit on the fairgrounds superior to those of other organizations having social, political, or other ideological messages to proselytize." [138] A decision favoring the Krishna Society would also raise the question whether commercial organizations have a similar right under the first amendment, [139] a question avoided by the majority's disposition of this case. [140]

Restrictions on Billboards. The question of the constitutionality of zoning laws restricting billboards severely fragmented the Supreme Court in *Metromedia, Inc. v. City of San Diego*, [141] a case producing five separate opinions. [142] San Diego, in an attempt to eliminate the hazards caused by "distracting sign displays" and to "improve the appearance of the City," enacted a comprehensive zoning ordinance prohibiting outdoor display signs, subject to several important restrictions.

These exceptions fell into two main categories. First, the law allowed "on-site signs." On-site signs are those "designating the name

---

137. 452 U.S. at 651, 101 S.Ct. at 2566.

138. 452 U.S. at 652, 101 S.Ct. at 2566.

139. 452 U.S. at 653, 101 S.Ct. at 2566–67: "The question would also inevitably arise as to what extent the First Amendment also gives commercial organizations a right to move among the crowd to distribute information about or to sell their wares as respondents claim they may do."

140. Brennan, J., joined by Marshall and Stevens, JJ., concurred in part and dissented in part. 452 U.S. at 656, 101 S.Ct. at 2568. They would not allow the state to prohibit the distribution of literature because they did not find the crowd control justification applicable. But they would allow the state to ban the sale of

literature and solicitation of funds. Blackmun, J., in a separate opinion, also concurring in part and dissenting in part, agreed with Justice Brennan's conclusions. 452 U.S. at 663, 101 S.Ct. at 2572.

141. 453 U.S. 490, 101 S.Ct. 2882, 69 L.Ed.2d 800 (1981), on remand 32 Cal.3d 180, 185 Cal.Rptr. 260, 649 P.2d 902 (1982).

142. White, J., announced the judgment of the Court and delivered an opinion joined by Stewart, Marshall, and Powell, JJ. Brennan, J., joined by Blackmun, J., concurred in the judgment. 453 U.S. at 521, 101 S.Ct. at 2900. Stevens, J., Burger, C.J., and Rehnquist, J., each wrote dissenting opinions. 453 U.S. at 540, 555, 569, 101 S.Ct. at 2909, 2917, 2924.

of the owner or occupant of the premises upon which such signs are placed, or identifying such premises; or signs advertising goods manufactured or produced or services rendered on the premises upon which such signs are placed." The second category of exemptions were really twelve specified exemptions: "government signs; signs located at public bus stops; signs manufactured, transported or stored within the city, if not used for advertising purposes; commemorative historical plaques; religious symbols; signs within shopping malls; for-sale and for-lease signs; signs on public and commercial vehicles; signs depicting time, temperature, and news; approved temporary, off-premises, subdivision directional signs; and 'temporary political campaign signs.' " [143] Companies in the outdoor advertising business sued, claiming a violation of their first amendment rights in that enforcement of the ordinance would in effect destroy their business.

The plurality opinion of Justice White first turned to the zoning law insofar as it regulated commercial speech and found that portion of the ordinance constitutional.[144] However the plurality was less tolerant of the distinctions the city drew as to noncommercial advertising. Because the city allowed on-site commercial advertising it had to allow on-site *non*commercial advertising so that an occupant could display its own ideas or the ideas of others. The noncommercial billboard would not be any more distracting or nonaesthetic than a permitted, on-site commercial billboard.[145] Nor was the ordinance a time, place, or

---

143. 453 U.S. at 494–95, 101 S.Ct. at 2886. See also, 453 U.S. at 495 n. 3, 101 S.Ct. at 2886 n. 3.

144. Because the outdoor advertising was concerned with lawful activity and was not misleading, it was protected as commercial speech. But the governmental regulations in this case were valid restrictions on commercial speech, meeting the four part test of Central Hudson Gas & Electric Corp. v. Public Service Com'n, 447 U.S. 557, 100 S.Ct. 2343, 65 L.Ed.2d 341 (1980). That is, the two goals that the ordinance furthered were substantial: traffic safety and the city's esthetic interests. The ordinance directly advanced those interests and regulated no further than necessary.

Although the law did permit on-site commercial advertising while prohibiting off-site billboards, it was permissible for the city to conclude that off-site advertising, with "periodically changing content, presents a more acute problem than does on-site advertising." 453 U.S. at 511, 101 S.Ct. at 2894, citing Railway Express Agency v. New York, 336 U.S. 106, 110, 69 S.Ct. 463, 465, 93 L.Ed. 533 (1949).

145. 453 U.S. at 513, 101 S.Ct. at 2895. See also, 453 U.S. at 515, 101 S.Ct. at 2896:

"Because some noncommercial messages may be conveyed on billboards throughout the commercial and industrial zones [e.g., commemorative plaques of recognized historical societies; signs telling time or temperature; signs erected in discharge of a governmental function; temporary political campaign signs] San Diego must similarly allow billboards conveying other noncommercial messages throughout those zones." (footnote omitted)

The Court had earlier allowed a city to ban noncommercial speech but to allow commercial speech in the use of billboard space on a city-owned public transportation system. Lehman v. City of Shaker Heights, 418 U.S. 298, 94 S.Ct. 2714, 41 L.Ed.2d 770 (1974). In that case, however, the Court was persuaded that the commercial space available on city buses, etc., was not a public forum. The city could limit noncommercial speech in order to limit chances of abuse, the appearance of favoritism, and the risk of imposing on a captive audience. 418 U.S. at 304, 94 S.Ct. at 2718. See § 20.18(b), supra.

manner restriction because it completely banned on-site noncommercial billboards based on content, i.e., that their content was noncommercial. The plurality then concluded that because the ordinance reached "too far into the realm of protected speech," it was "unconstitutional on its face"; on remand the state court could decide if the unconstitutional portions of the ordinance could be severed from the constitutional parts.[146]

Justice Brennan, joined by Justice Blackmun, concurred in the judgment. However they analyzed the case quite differently; gave much less deference to the legislative judgment; and found the entire ordinance unconstitutional. They reasoned that the practical effect of the ordinance was to ban totally all billboards and that such a ban was unconstitutional because the city had not provided "adequate justification" for its assertion that billboards actually impair traffic safety in San Diego.[147] Similarly these justices believed that the city's interests in aesthetics was not "sufficiently substantial in the commercial and industrial areas of San Diego," which might already be so blighted that the removal of billboards would have a negligible impact.[148]

The three dissenters all would have upheld the billboard ordinance in its entirety. Justice Stevens would have upheld the ordinance and uphold as constitutional a law entirely banning billboards, but he would not reach the question of whether the ordinance could ban on-site noncommercial signs. He had no trouble with "the content neutral exception" of the ordinance.[149]

Justice Rehnquist believed that the aesthetic justification for the ordinance was sufficient to sustain the law. He did not believe that judges were better qualified than local planning commissions to decide whether removal of billboards "would have more than a negligible impact on aesthetics." [150]

Chief Justice Burger also wrote a very strong dissent. He rejected the view of the plurality which apparently gave the city a choice of banning all signs (a choice that the plurality might not allow if actually faced with deciding that issue) or permitting all noncommercial signs without any restriction. "This is the long arm and voracious appetite

---

146. 453 U.S. at 521 & n. 26, 101 S.Ct. at 2899–2900 & n. 26.

147. 453 U.S. at 528, 101 S.Ct. at 2903. These justices analogized the case to Schad v. Borough of Mt. Ephraim, 452 U.S. 61, 72, 101 S.Ct. 2176, 2184–85, 68 L.Ed.2d 671 (1981).

148. 453 U.S. at 530–31, 101 S.Ct. at 2904–05. At one point Brennan suggested that "San Diego could demonstrate its interest in creating an aesthetically pleasing environment is genuine and substantial" by "showing a comprehensive commitment to making its physical environment in

commercial and industrial areas more attractive and by allowing only narrowly tailored exceptions if any...." 453 U.S. at 532, 101 S.Ct. at 2905–06 (footnotes omitted). Yet at another point Brennan suggested that San Diego might never meet this burden: "I express no view on whether San Diego or other large urban areas will be able to meet the burden." 453 U.S. at 534, 101 S.Ct. at 2906 (footnote omitted).

149. 453 U.S. at 542, 101 S.Ct. at 2910.

150. 453 U.S. at 570, 101 S.Ct. at 2925.

of federal power—this time judicial power—with a vengeance, reaching and absorbing traditional concepts of local authority." [151] The distinctions and exceptions in the City's ordinance—"the presence of which is the plurality's sole ground for invalidating the ordinance—are few in number, are narrowly tailored to peculiar public needs, and do not remotely endanger freedom of speech." The ordinance "has not preferred any viewpoint and, aside from these limited exceptions, has not allowed some subjects while forbidding others. [I]n no instance is the exempted topic controversial...."

Burger also believed that the distinctions that the City made were reasonable. For example, "on-site signs, by identifying the premises (even if in the process of advertising), [could] actually promote traffic safety [because prohibiting] them would require motorists to pay more attention to street numbers and less to traffic." [152]

The *Metromedia* case and its babel of opinions raise more questions than the case settles. It is likely that if a city enacts a law that restricts billboards only to the extent that they convey commercial speech, a majority of the Court (composed of the White plurality and the three dissenters) would uphold the ordinance. If litigants attacked the constitutionality of the federal Highway Beautification Act of 1965,[153] it is unclear how the Court would respond. The three dissenters would no doubt uphold this law, but the other six justices specifically refused to reach this question, though the White plurality, at least, hinted that the federal law might be distinguishable.[154]

In *Members of the City Council of Los Angeles v. Taxpayers for Vincent*,[155] the Court upheld an ordinance prohibiting the posting of signs on public property; this ordinance also prohibited posting political signs on light posts. The majority opinion by Justice Stevens stated that "the appropriate framework for reviewing a viewpoint neutral regulation of this kind" involved determining whether the statute promoted an important or substantial government interest unrelated to the suppression of expression and whether the "incidental restriction on alleged first amendment freedoms is no greater than is essential to

151. 453 U.S. at 556, 101 S.Ct. at 2917. He added: "The Court today unleashes a novel principle, unnecessary and, indeed, alien to First Amendment doctrine announced in our earlier cases." 453 U.S. at 569, 101 S.Ct. at 2924.

152. 453 U.S. at 564–65 & n. 6, 101 S.Ct. at 2921–22 & n. 6.

153. 23 U.S.C.A. § 131. That law also regulates billboards and permits on-site commercial billboards in certain circumstances where it forbids billboards carrying noncommercial messages.

154. 453 U.S. at 515 n. 20, 101 S.Ct. at 2896 n. 20: "[U]nlike the San Diego ordi-

nance, which prohibits billboards conveying noncommercial messages throughout the city, the federal law does not contain a total prohibition of such billboards in areas adjacent to the Interstate and primary highway systems." (White, J.) See also 453 U.S. at 534 n. 11, 101 S.Ct. at 2906 n. 11: "I express no opinion on the constitutionality of the Highway Beautification Act...." (Brennan, J.).

155. 466 U.S. 789, 104 S.Ct. 2118, 80 L.Ed.2d 772 (1984), on remand 738 F.2d 353 (9th Cir.1984).

the furtherance of that interest." [156]   In finding that the city's interest in protecting the aesthetic quality of the community as well as its property justified the prohibition, the Court found that its previous decision in *Metromedia* justified this conclusion.   "There the Court considered the city's interest in avoiding visual clutter, and seven Justices explicitly concluded that this interest was sufficient to justify a prohibition of billboards. . . .   We reaffirm the conclusion of the majority in *Metromedia*." [157]

The *Vincent* regulation, although it prohibited one form of communication, was narrowly tailored to promote this interest because it did not restrict any individual's freedom to speak or distribute literature in the same place where the posting of signs on public property was prohibited.   The ordinance only eliminated the ability to create visual clutter by posting material on public property which has never been converted into a public forum for speech. [158]   The aesthetic interest in the elimination of signs on public property justified this content neutral restriction on the posting of signs on such property.   This ordinance was not a content based restriction merely because the government did not prohibit similar signs on private property. [159]

(f) User Fees and Hold Harmless Agreements

It is not unusual for cities to require those who wish to hold demonstrations or parades, or rock concerts, to "obtain insurance, sign hold-harmless agreements, pay police and other public service fees, and post cleanup deposits, in addition to paying traditional permit application fees." [160]   Flat taxes for local solicitation are not permissible [161] but

156.   466 U.S. at 805, 104 S.Ct. at 2129, quoting United States v. O'Brien, 391 U.S. 367, 377, 88 S.Ct. 1673, 1679, 20 L.Ed.2d 672 (1968), rehearing denied 393 U.S. 900, 89 S.Ct. 63, 21 L.Ed.2d 188 (1968).   For a more complete discussion regarding the *O'Brien* standard and its interpretation in this case, see §§ 20.48, 20.49, infra.

157.   466 U.S. at 806–07, 104 S.Ct. at 2130.

158.   On this basis, the Court distinguished cases such as Schneider v. State, 308 U.S. 147, 60 S.Ct. 146, 84 L.Ed. 155 (1939), which held that the interest in preventing litter in the streets could not justify a total prohibition of the ability to distribute handbills and leaflets in public places.   Regarding regulations of speech activities in various types of public fora see § 20.47(c), supra.

159.   466 U.S. at 811, 104 S.Ct. at 2132.

160.   Neisser, Charging for Free Speech: User Fees and Insurance in the Marketplace of Ideas, 74 Georgetown L.J. 257, 258

(1985).   (footnote omitted).   This article is a thorough examination of these issues.

See also, Note, Conditioning Access to the Public Forum on the Purchase of Insurance, 17 Georgia L.Rev. 815 (1983); Goldberger, A Reconsideration of Cox v. New Hampshire: Can Demonstrators Be Required to Pay the Costs of Using America's Public Forums?, 62 Tex.L.Rev. 403 (1983).

161.   Murdock v. Pennsylvania, 319 U.S. 105, 113–14, 63 S.Ct. 870, 875, 87 L.Ed. 1292 (1943) (footnote omitted): "And the license tax is fixed in amount and unrelated to the scope of activities of petitioners or to their realized revenues.   It is not a nominal fee imposed as a regulatory measure to defray the expenses of policing the activities in question."   Follett v. McCormick, 321 U.S. 573, 576–77, 64 S.Ct. 717, 719, 88 L.Ed. 938 (1944) (flat license fee of $1 per day or $15 per year in order to sell books as applied to evangelist is unconstitutional).

a reasonable sliding scale of fees to pay for reasonable administrative costs is constitutional.[162]

XIV. SYMBOLIC SPEECH

§ 20.48 Introduction

The notion that speech may be nonverbal had been recognized by the Supreme Court as far back as 1931.[1] In *Stromberg v. California*,[2] the Court provided first amendment protection to certain forms of symbolic expression. A state statute which prohibited the displaying of a red flag "as a sign, symbol or emblem of opposition to organized government" was found to be unconstitutional on first amendment grounds because it was so vague as to allow punishment for the fair use of "the opportunity for free political discussion."[3]

Twelve years later, in *West Virginia State Board of Education v. Barnette*,[4] another form of symbolic speech was given first amendment

---

162. Cox v. New Hampshire, 312 U.S. 569, 61 S.Ct. 762, 85 L.Ed. 1049 (1941). In this case, the statute provided for license fees ranging from a nominal amount to $300. The purpose of the fee was "not a revenue tax, but one to meet the expense incident to the administration of the act and to the maintenance of public order in the matter licensed." A "less expansive and attractive parade or procession" is less expensive to police than a more expansive one. The Court upheld the tax:

"There is nothing contrary to the Constitution in the charge of a fee limited to the purpose stated. The suggestion that a flat fee tax should have been charged fails to take account of the difficulty of framing a fair schedule to meet all circumstances, and we perceive no constitutional ground for denying to local governments that flexibility of adjustment of fees which in light of varying conditions would tend to conserve rather than impair the liberty sought." 312 U.S. at 577, 61 S.Ct. at 766.

§ 20.48

1. Stromberg v. California, 283 U.S. 359, 51 S.Ct. 532, 75 L.Ed. 1117 (1931).

See generally, J. Barron and C. Dienes, Handbook of Free Speech and Free Press 189–219 (1979); Nimmer, The Meaning of Symbolic Speech Under the First Amendment, 21 U.C.L.A.L.Rev. 27 (1973); Note, Symbolic Conduct, 68 Colum.L.Rev. 1091 (1968); Nahmod, Artistic Expression and Aesthetic Theory: The Beautiful, The Sub-

lime and The First Amendment, 1987 Wisconsin L.Rev. 221 (1987).

2. 283 U.S. 359, 51 S.Ct. 532, 75 L.Ed. 1117 (1931).

3. 283 U.S. at 369, 51 S.Ct. at 535.

On the importance of symbolic speech, see, e.g., F. Haiman, Speech and Law in a Free Society 6 (U.Chi.Press 1981): "Symbolic behavior is one of the most fundamental ways in which human beings express and fulfill themselves. Its exercise thus lies at the core of a free society." See, R. Rotunda, The Politics of Language: Liberalism as Word and Symbol (U. of Iowa Press, 1986); B. Whorf, Language, Thought, and Reality 251 (Carroll, ed. 1956): "Natural man, whether simpleton or scientist, knows no more of the linguistic forces that bear upon him than the savage knows of gravitational forces."

4. 319 U.S. 624, 63 S.Ct. 1178, 87 L.Ed. 1628 (1943). The remedy in this case was to allow the Jehovah Witness children to refuse to salute the flag. This remedy itself indicates that the case is a free-speech case and not an establishment of religion case, for if it were the latter, the remedy should have been to enjoin all flag salutes. Cf. Engel v. Vitale, 370 U.S. 421, 82 S.Ct. 1261, 8 L.Ed.2d 601 (1962) and, School District of Abington Township v. Schempp, 374 U.S. 203, 83 S.Ct. 1560, 10 L.Ed.2d 844 (1963) (Establishment of Religion clause bars school prayer whether or not the laws establishing prayer operate directly to coerce nonobserving individuals).

protection: Public school children could not be compelled to salute the flag in violation of their religious beliefs. The Court recognized the expressive nature of certain actions in this decision:

"[N]o official ... can prescribe what shall be orthodox in politics, nationalism, religion or other matters of opinion or force citizens to confess by word or *act* their faith therein." [5]

The Court has not retreated from the position that certain actions may be entitled to first amendment protection. Thus, in *Brown v. Louisiana*,[6] a 1966 decision that involved a peaceful sit-in at a segregated public library, the opinion of Justice Fortas (there was no opinion of the Court), reemphasized that first amendment rights "are not confined to verbal expression [but] embrace appropriate types of action which certainly include the right in a peaceable and orderly manner to protest ... unconstitutional segregation of public facilities." [7]

§ 20.49   Fashioning a Test for First Amendment Protection for Symbolic Speech and the Role of Improper Legislative and Administrative Motivation

Although the Court has long accepted the premise that certain "expressive" acts are entitled to first amendment protection, presumably not all activity with an expressive component will be afforded first amendment protection; and these early cases did not create a test for defining what kinds of actions, in what circumstances, fall within the speech orbit of the first amendment. The Court finally began to set boundaries for the extent of first amendment protection afforded to symbolic speech in 1968, in *United States v. O'Brien*.[1] This case, in effect, applied the "time, place, or manner restrictions, without regard to content"—the public forum rules—to symbolic speech.

O'Brien burned his selective service registration certificate on the steps of the South Boston Courthouse and was convicted in federal court for violating section 462(b) of the Universal Military Training and Service Act of 1948. As amended by Congress in 1965, section 462(b) made it an offense for any person who "forges, alters, knowingly

---

5. 319 U.S. at 642, 63 S.Ct. at 1187 (emphasis added).

See generally, Danzig, Justice Frankfurter's Opinions in the Flag Salute Cases; Blending Logic and Psychologic in Constitutional Decision-making, 36 Stand.L.Rev. 675 (1984).

6. 383 U.S. 131, 86 S.Ct. 719, 15 L.Ed.2d 637 (1966).

7. 383 U.S. at 142, 86 S.Ct. at 724 (footnote omitted).

§ 20.49

1. 391 U.S. 367, 88 S.Ct. 1673, 20 L.Ed.2d 672 (1968), rehearing denied 393 U.S. 900, 89 S.Ct. 63, 21 L.Ed.2d 188 (1968).

See generally, Ely, Flag Desecration: A Case Study in the Roles of Categorization and Balancing in First Amendment Analysis, 88 Harv.L.Rev. 1482 (1975).

Cf. Sullwan, First Amendment Protection of Artistic Entertainment: Toward Reasonable Municipal Regulation of Video Games, 36 Vanderbilt L.Rev. 1223 (1983).

destroys, knowingly mutilates...." [2] or changes such certificate in any manner.

O'Brien argued that the 1965 Amendment was unconstitutional as applied to him because it restricted his freedom of expression. The Court rejected this contention: "We cannot accept the view that an apparently limitless variety of conduct can be labeled 'speech' whenever the person engaging in the conduct intends thereby to express an idea." [3]

The Court likewise rejected the contention that an action with a clearly noncommunicative aspect is outside any first amendment consideration. Rather, the Court presumed that O'Brien's action had a "communicative element ... sufficient to bring into play the First Amendment." [4] However, this presumption does not mean that the conduct automatically receives full first amendment protection. The government may prohibit such conduct in certain circumstances: "[W]hen 'speech' and 'non-speech' elements are combined in the same course of conduct, a sufficiently important governmental interest in regulating the non-speech element can justify incidental limitations on First Amendment freedoms." [5]

The *O'Brien* Court set out a four-part test for determining when a government interest sufficiently justifies the regulation of expressive conduct:

> [A] government regulation is sufficiently justified [1] if it is within the constitutional power of the Government; [2] if it furthers an important or substantial governmental interest; [3] if the governmental interest is unrelated to the suppression of free expression; and [4] if the incidental restriction on alleged First Amendment freedoms is no greater than is essential to the furtherance of that interest. [6]

The 1965 Amendment of the Universal Military Training and Service Act met the requirements of the above test, according to the Court, and "consequently ... O'Brien can be constitutionally convicted for violating it." [7] The 1965 Amendment met the requirements of the first part of the test because it is within the constitutional power of the Government "to raise and support armies and to make all laws necessary to that end...." [8]

---

2. 391 U.S. at 370, 88 S.Ct. at 1675 (emphasis eliminated).

3. 391 U.S. at 376, 88 S.Ct. at 1678.

4. Id.

5. Id.

6. 391 U.S. at 377, 88 S.Ct. at 1679.

7. Id.

8. Id.

Wearing of Ku Klux Klan Masks. In State v. Miller, 260 Ga. 669, 398 S.E.2d 547 (1990), the Georgia Supreme Court upheld the constitutionality of a state statute that forbids the wearing of the traditional face mask worn by Ku Klux Klan members. The effect of the mask is to hide the identity of the wearer. The purpose of the law, as reflected in the legislature's "Statement of Public Policy," is that, given "the Gener-

Part two of the test was also fulfilled because the Selective Service certificate served a number of purposes in addition to initial notification. These purposes include quick determination of those registrants delinquent in Selective Service obligations; facilitation of quick induction in time of national crisis; facilitation of communication between registrants and local boards; reminders of notification of changes in status; deterrence for deceptive use of certificates.

These important governmental interests met the requirements of part three of the test because they were unrelated to the suppression of free expression. The Court noted a distinction between the case at bar and one where "the communication allegedly integral to the conduct is itself thought to be harmful." [9] For example, the 1965 Amendment did not bar only *contemptuous* destruction; if the act had been written in the former terms, it would have indicated that its purpose was to punish the publication of certain opinions, in violation of part three of the *O'Brien* test.[10]

al Assembly's awareness of and concern over the dangers to society posed by anonymous vigilante organizations," the law is designed to protect people "not only against actual physical violence, but also against threats and intimidations from any person or group of persons,". The defendant, Shade Miller, Jr., was arrested for violating a Georgia law, known as the "Anti–Mask Act," § 6–11–38, that states:

"(a) A person is guilty of a misdemeanor when he wears a mask, hood, or device by which any portion of his face is so hidden, concealed, or covered as to conceal the identity of the wearer and is upon any public way or public property or upon the private property of another without the written permission of the owner or occupier of the property to do so."

Subsection (b) of the law listed various exceptions where the wearing of masks is allowed: traditional holiday costumes on the occasion of the holiday; trade or sporting activities where the mask is worn for safety; theatrical productions, Mardi Gras celebrations; masquerade balls; and gas masks during emergencies and drills.

Miller argued that the prohibition against the KKK mask violated, inter alia, his right to symbolic speech. The Georgia Court rejected that argument as well as all of the others raised and then upheld the law.

Note that the law does not forbid Miller from marching in this Klan garb; nor does it regulate what Miller may say. It only restricts Miller with respect to his desire for *anonymous* speech. Miller can march in Klan parades, but he (and the other Klan members) must march without masks.

9. 391 U.S. at 382, 88 S.Ct. at 1682.

10. Nude Dancing. Thus, the Supreme Court upheld an Indiana statute forbidding anyone to "knowingly or intentionally" appear nude in a "public place." Barnes v. Glen Theatre, Inc., 501 U.S. ___, 111 S.Ct. 2456, 115 L.Ed.2d 504 (1991), on remand 941 F.2d 1212 (7th Cir.1991). Rehnquist, C.J., announced the judgment of the Court and delivered an opinion in which O'Connor & Kennedy, JJ., joined. Scalia, J., filed an opinion concurring in the judgment. Souter, J., filed another opinion concurring in the judgment. White, J., joined by Marshall, Blackmun, & Stevens, JJ., filed a dissenting opinion.

The plaintiffs wanted to perform or show live, totally nude, nonobscene dances. The Rehnquist plurality relied on the symbolic speech analysis of *O'Brien*. The state law forbade public nudity, whether or not the nudity is combined with expressive activity. The law did not ban only nudity that conveys an erotic message; it banned all nudity. Nor did the law ban erotic dances; the dancers were permitted to present erotic dances so long as they wore a scant amount of clothing, that is, G-strings and pasties.

Finally, the Court concluded that the 1965 amendment was sufficiently limited to insure the smooth functioning of the Selective Service System towards the purposes enumerated, meeting the requirements of part four of the *O'Brien* test.

At this point in the development of the law, the Court, under "settled principles," [11] refused to examine subjective legislative motive in deciding a statute's constitutionality. Thus, after *O'Brien* it seemed that so long as a statute on its face serves one "important governmental interest," unrelated to the regulation or suppression of speech, with only incidental restrictions on free speech no greater than necessary, there is an opportunity for the legislature to regulate symbolic speech without further review by the Court. The Court found that O'Brien was convicted because "he willfully frustrated this governmental interest. For this noncommunicative impact of his conduct, and for nothing else, he was convicted." [12]

School Armbands. One year after *United States v. O'Brien,* [13] the Court decided a case involving a similar form of expressive conduct, the wearing of black armbands to show objection to the Vietnam War. [14] In *Tinker v. Des Moines Independent Community School District,* [15] petitioners were high school and junior high school students who had been suspended and sent home for refusing to remove the armbands pursuant to a school policy adopted two days earlier in anticipation of the protest. Petitioners were denied injunctive relief from the federal courts on the grounds that school authorities acted reasonably in order to prevent disturbance, but the Supreme Court upheld petitioners' right to wear the armbands by characterizing the act as one "closely akin" to "pure speech." [16]

The Court characterized the wearing of armbands in the circumstances of *Tinker v. Des Moines Independent Community School District* [17] as an action which involved "direct, primary First Amendment rights," [18] entitling the participants to comprehensive protection under the first amendment. Although the wearing of armbands was symbolic

---

11. 391 U.S. at 383, 88 S.Ct. at 1682. But see the discussion of Board of Education, Island Trees Union Free School District No. 26 v. Pico, 457 U.S. 853, 102 S.Ct. 2799, 73 L.Ed.2d 435 (1982), discussed in this section, infra.

12. 391 U.S. at 382, 88 S.Ct. at 1681–82.

Some commentators criticized the *O'Brien* Court for not disposing of O'Brien's action in terms of a more traditional first amendment balancing of speech and nonspeech interests. They claimed that the Court should have discussed the constitutional impact of the *speech* element of O'Brien's action rather than the nonspeech regulatory aspects of the statute. See Alfange, Free Speech and Symbolic

Conduct: The Draft–Card Burning Case, 1968 Sup.Ct.Rev. 1.

13. 391 U.S. 367, 88 S.Ct. 1673, 20 L.Ed.2d 672 (1968), rehearing denied 393 U.S. 900, 89 S.Ct. 63, 21 L.Ed.2d 188 (1968).

14. See generally, Note, Symbolic Conduct, 68 Colum.L.Rev. 1091 (1968).

15. 393 U.S. 503, 89 S.Ct. 733, 21 L.Ed.2d 731 (1969).

16. 393 U.S. at 505, 89 S.Ct. at 736. See also 393 U.S. at 508, 89 S.Ct. at 737.

17. 393 U.S. 503, 89 S.Ct. 733, 21 L.Ed.2d 731 (1969).

18. 393 U.S. at 508, 89 S.Ct. at 737.

speech, the school regulation which forbade the action clearly failed the third part of the *O'Brien* test: the regulation was *not* unrelated to the suppression of free expression.

Unlike the statute in *O'Brien,* which banned all draft card destruction, the school authorities did not ban all political symbols—students were even allowed to wear the Iron Cross, and some did. "Instead, a particular symbol—black armbands worn to exhibit opposition to this Nation's involvement in Vietnam—was singled out for prohibition." [19] This governmental interest is definitely related to the suppression of free expression. The prohibition of these symbols would relate to the regulation of ideas rather than conduct.[20]

Having failed the *O'Brien* test, the regulation must be analyzed within general first amendment principles. Thus, according to the Court, the problem in *Tinker* was really one of balancing the students' exercise of first amendment rights against the conflicting rules of school authorities. To resolve this conflict, the Court adopted and quoted the standard used by the Fifth Circuit in *Burnside v. Byars:* [21] such conduct cannot be prohibited unless it " 'materially and substantially interfere[s] with the requirements of appropriate discipline in the operation of the school.' " [22] There was no such showing in the instant case. Petitioners' action was a "silent, passive expression of opinion" and there was "no indication that the work of the schools or any class was disrupted." [23]

The Court made two further points in concluding that the facts of the instant case did not meet the requirements of *Burnside* for prohibiting expression in schools. First, the school officials' ban of the armbands was not based on disruptive effect on school work or impingement on other students' rights. Rather, the purpose of the prohibition was to avoid legitimate controversy: the ban on armbands did "not concern aggressive, disruptive action or even group demonstrations ... [but only] silent, passive expression of opinion...." [24] The "undifferentiated fear" stemming from this silent expression of political opinion was not enough "to overcome the right to freedom of expression." [25]

Second, the Court emphasized that the prohibition of one particular opinion was not constitutionally permissible. The regulation failed the *O'Brien* test for symbolic speech and failed the *Burnside* test for

---

19. 393 U.S. at 510–11, 89 S.Ct. at 739.

20. Cf. Ho Ah Kow v. Nunan, 12 Fed. Cas. 252 (No. 6,546) (C.C.D.Cal.1879) (Justice Field). In this case Justice Field invalidated the "queue ordinance," a law that required male prisoners in the county jail to have their hair cut to "a uniform length of one inch from the scalp." The Chinese at the time felt that they would "lose face" if their queues would be cut. Field allowed the alien Chinese to recover damages against the sheriff pursuant to the Civil Rights Act. The purpose of the law was to discriminate against the Chinese, to make them lose face.

21. 363 F.2d 744, 749 (5th Cir.1966).

22. 393 U.S. at 509, 89 S.Ct. at 738.

23. 393 U.S. at 508, 89 S.Ct. at 737.

24. Id.

25. Id.

prohibiting expression in schools. The wearing of armbands in the instant case was thus permitted under the strong first amendment protections for speech:

> [I]n our system, undifferentiated fear or apprehension of disturbance is not enough to overcome the right to freedom of expression.... Any word spoken, in class, in the lunchroom, or on the campus that deviates from the views of another person may start an argument or cause a disturbance. But our Constitution says we must take this risk ... and our history says that it is this sort of hazardous freedom—this kind of openness—that is the basis of our national strength and of the independence and vigor of Americans who grow up and live in this relatively permissive, often disputatious society.[26]

Tinker raised, but does not decide, the issue of whether the protections for symbolic speech encompass other school regulations, such as hair or shirt length or style or types of clothing.[27] The lower courts have split on such issues.[28]

Later, the Court allowed a school to discipline a student for giving a speech at a school assembly when the speech included sexual innuendo.[29] The Court emphasized the deference it would give to the conclu-

---

26. 393 U.S. at 508–09, 89 S.Ct. at 737–38.

27. 393 U.S. at 507–08, 89 S.Ct. at 736–37.

On hairlength, consider Professor Z. Chaffee's discussion in his book, Free Speech in the United States (1942):

"This breach of the peace theory is peculiarly liable to abuse when applied against unpopular expressions and practices. It makes a man a criminal simply because his neighbors have no self-control and cannot refrain from violence. The *reductio ad absurdum* of this theory was the imprisonment of Joseph Palmer, one of Bronson Alcott's fellow-settlers at 'Fruitlands,' not because he was a communist, but because he persisted in wearing such a long beard that people kept mobbing him, until law and order were maintained by shutting him up. A man does not become a criminal because someone else assaults him, unless his own conduct is in itself illegal or may be reasonably considered a direct provocation to violence."

Id. at 151–52.

28. See generally, Casenote, 84 Harv. L.Rev. 1702 (1971); see also, New Rider v. Board of Education, 414 U.S. 1097, 94 S.Ct. 733, 38 L.Ed.2d 556 (1973) (Douglas, J.,

joined by Marshall, J., dissenting from denial of certiorari), rehearing denied 415 U.S. 939, 94 S.Ct. 1456, 39 L.Ed.2d 497 (1974). Cf. Kelley v. Johnson, 425 U.S. 238, 96 S.Ct. 1440, 47 L.Ed.2d 708 (1976) (county regulation of police hair length upheld based on fact that policeman is not an ordinary citizen), on remand 543 F.2d 465 (2d Cir.1976).

See also, J. Barron and C. Dienes, Handbook of Free Speech and Free Press 212–19 (1979).

29. Bethel School District No. 403 v. Fraser, 478 U.S. 675, 106 S.Ct. 3159, 92 L.Ed.2d 549 (1986), on remand 800 F.2d 222 (9th Cir.1986).

School Newspapers.

In Hazelwood School District v. Kuhlmeier, 484 U.S. 260, 108 S.Ct. 562, 98 L.Ed.2d 592 (1988), on remand 840 F.2d 596 (8th Cir.1988), the Court held (5–3) that high school educators, consistent with the first amendment, may exercise broad editorial control over the contents of a high school newspaper produced as part of the school's journalism curriculum. (The majority stated in a footnote, 484 U.S. at 273 n. 7, 108 S.Ct. at 571 n. 7: "We need not now decide whether the same degree of deference is appropriate with respect to school-sponsored expressive activities at

sion of the school authorities that the speech disrupted the school assembly. Lewd speech delivered to a captive audience at a school assembly is not like the nondisruptive, passive expression of political viewpoint involved in *Tinker*.

Flag Desecration Statutes. Another area in which the Supreme Court has been called upon to elaborate the test it set out in *O'Brien* is in litigation surrounding flag desecration statutes. The first case was *Street v. New York*.[30] In response to the slaying of a civil rights leader, Street burned his personally-owned flag on a street corner in New York while "talking out loud" to a group of approximately thirty people.[31] The arresting officer testified that he heard Street say, *inter alia*, " 'We don't need no damn flag.' "[32] Street was convicted under a statute making it a misdemeanor "publicly [to] mutilate, deface, defile or defy, trample upon, or cast contempt upon either by *words* or *act* [any flag of the United States]...."[33]

The Court overturned Street's conviction in a narrow holding which avoided the issue of the constitutionality of a statute prohibiting flag desecration by action. The case was decided in terms of the first amendment protection afforded verbal expression. On the basis of the record, it was possible that Street's words alone or his words and actions together were the basis of his conviction. According to the

the college and university level.") In *Hazelwood*, the principal did not allow the school-sponsored newspaper to publish two articles, one dealing with student pregnancy and the other dealing with the impact of divorce on students. The principal was concerned that it might be easy to identify the identity of the pregnant students from the story and that the references to sexual activity and birth control were inappropriate for some of the younger students. He also believed that the second article should not be published unless the person criticized in it has the opportunity to defend himself.

Under these circumstances the Court found that *Tinker* is inapplicable. *Tinker* dealt with the extent to which a school must tolerate student speech; in this case, however, the issue is the extent to which a school must affirmatively promote particular student speech. "The latter question concerns educators' authority over school-sponsored publications, theatrical productions, and other expressive activities that students, parents, and members of the public might reasonably perceive to bear the imprimatur of the school." These activities may fairly be considered part of the school curriculum, even if they do not occur in a traditional classroom setting, "so long as they are supervised by faculty

members and designed to impart particular knowledge or skills to student participants and audiences." Therefore a school, in its capacity as publisher of a school newspaper or producer of a school play, may "disassociate itself" from speech which is "ungrammatical, poorly written, inadequately researched, biased or prejudiced, vulgar or profane, or unsuitable for immature audiences."

Under the first amendment, educators may exercise editorial control over the style and content of student speech "in school-sponsored activities so long as their actions are reasonably related to legitimate pedagogical concerns." There is a violation of the first amendment only when the censorship of the school-sponsored activity "has no valid educational purpose". 484 U.S. at 271–74, 108 S.Ct. at 570–71 (footnote omitted).

30. 394 U.S. 576, 89 S.Ct. 1354, 22 L.Ed.2d 572 (1969), on remand 24 N.Y.2d 1026, 302 N.Y.S.2d 848, 250 N.E.2d 250 (1969).

31. 394 U.S. at 578, 89 S.Ct. at 1358.

32. 394 U.S. at 579, 89 S.Ct. at 1359.

33. 394 U.S. at 578, 89 S.Ct. at 1358 (emphasis added).

Court, a conviction based on Street's words—totally or in part—would be unconstitutional.

The Court did not prohibit outright on first amendment grounds the desecration of the flag by words. Rather, there were four possible governmental interests which could justify Street's conviction for defiling the flag by words, none of which existed in this case, so Street's conviction had to be overturned. The Court first rejected the argument that there was a government interest in preventing incitement, because Street's words "did not urge anyone to do anything unlawful"—they amounted only to "excited public advocacy of [an] idea." [34] The Court next rejected the possibility that Street's remarks were "fighting words," sufficient to provoke violent retaliation. [35] Nor could Street be punished for his words because they might shock passersby because "[i]t is firmly settled that under our Constitution the public expression of ideas may not be prohibited merely because the ideas are themselves offensive to some of their hearers." [36] Finally, the Court rejected the governmental interest in demanding that every citizen show certain respect for the national symbol, citing Justice Jackson's opinion in *Board of Education v. Barnette* [37] that it is " '. . . the right to differ as to things that touch the heart of the existing order.' " [38] This right to "differ" includes the right to make publicly defiant or contemptuous statements about the flag. [39]

It is interesting that the *Street* Court focused not on the first amendment protection for expressive action discussed in *Barnette,* but rather on general first amendment protection for speech. While citing *Barnette,* one of the early cases in symbolic speech, the *Street* Court would not consider two of Street's contentions: that the statute "is vague and imprecise because it does not clearly define the conduct which it forbids;" and that publicly destroying or damaging an American flag as a means of protest is constitutionally protected expression. [40]

The Court held that an individual's alteration of a flag under specific circumstances was protected by the first amendment in *Spence v. Washington.* [41] Appellant had affixed to both surfaces of a personally-owned flag peace symbols made from black masking tape and had displayed the flag upside down in the window of his apartment. He was convicted under the state's "improper use" statute which prohibited placing a figure, design or mark on a United States flag or exposing any such flag to view. [42]

---

34. 394 U.S. at 591, 89 S.Ct. at 1365.

35. 394 U.S. at 592, 89 S.Ct. at 1365.

36. Id.

37. 319 U.S. 624, 63 S.Ct. 1178, 87 L.Ed. 1628 (1943).

38. Street v. New York, 394 U.S. 576, 593, 89 S.Ct. 1354, 1366, 22 L.Ed.2d 572 (1969), on remand 24 N.Y.2d 1026, 302 N.Y.S.2d 848, 250 N.E.2d 250 (1969).

39. Id.

40. 394 U.S. at 580–81, 89 S.Ct. at 1360.

41. 418 U.S. 405, 94 S.Ct. 2727, 41 L.Ed.2d 842 (1974) (per curiam).

42. 418 U.S. at 407, 94 S.Ct. at 2728–29.

In a narrow holding, the Court overturned appellant's conviction because he had engaged in a form of constitutionally protected first amendment activity. The Court enumerated several facts important in its decision: the flag was privately owned; the flag was displayed on private property; there was no evidence of any risk of breach of the peace. Absent the specific circumstances of this case, the general applicability of this decision could thus be extremely limited.

Another fact important to the Court was that the state had conceded that appellant had engaged in a form of communication. The framework set out in *United States v. O'Brien* [43] for determining when a governmental interest sufficiently justifies expressive conduct was thereby applicable. However, the Court considered not only the nature of appellant's activity (as in *O'Brien*), but also "the factual context and environment in which it was undertaken." [44] The context was important because it helped define the communicative component of the symbol:

> [A]ppellant's activity was roughly simultaneous with ... the Cambodian incursion and the Kent State tragedy.... A flag bearing a peace symbol and displayed upside down by a student today might be interpreted as nothing more than bizarre behavior, but it would have been difficult for the great majority of citizens to miss the drift of appellant's point at the time that he made it. [45]

With this reasoning the Court departed from several assumptions in *O'Brien,* where it had refused to consider appellant's *motivation* to communicate and the clearly communicative nature of the draft card burning. The Court. openly discussed both these considerations in *Spence v. Washington.* [46] A subtle shift seems to have occurred from the speech/conduct distinction relied upon in *O'Brien* to a more general balancing of first amendment interests against other governmental interests.

This shift became more apparent when the *Spence* Court went on to apply an analysis similar to the one employed in *Street v. New York.* [47] Only now the *Street* framework of governmental interests was balanced against expressive *activity* rather than against words. The Court concluded that none of the four possible governmental interests was compelling enough to uphold Spence's challenged conviction, according to the facts of the case. However, the Court did leave open the possibility that there could be a legitimate state interest in preserving

---

43. 391 U.S. 367, 88 S.Ct. 1673, 20 L.Ed.2d 672 (1968), rehearing denied 393 U.S. 900, 89 S.Ct. 63, 21 L.Ed.2d 188 (1968).

44. 418 U.S. at 410, 94 S.Ct. at 2730.

45. Id.

46. 418 U.S. 405, 410–11, 94 S.Ct. 2727, 2730–31, 41 L.Ed.2d 842 (1974).

47. 394 U.S. 576, 89 S.Ct. 1354, 22 L.Ed.2d 572 (1969), on remand 24 N.Y.2d 1026, 302 N.Y.S.2d 848, 250 N.E.2d 250 (1969).

the flag as an "unalloyed symbol of our country." [48]

The Court concluded that even if there were a legitimate governmental interest here, it would be unconstitutional as applied to Spence's activity. The Court did not conclude, on the other hand, that there was no government interest in preserving the flag as a national symbol strong enough to outweigh first amendment considerations. This state interest yet to be found may fulfill the requirements of the first two parts of the four-part test of *O'Brien*.

Another case involving flag desecration was *Smith v. Goguen*,[49] where the defendant wore a small flag sewn to the seat of his trousers and was convicted under a Massachusetts flag misuse statute which made it a crime if one "publicly ... treats contemptuously" the United States flag.[50] Justice Powell, for the Court, avoided an analysis based on symbolic speech and instead overturned defendant's conviction on the basis that the statute was "void for vagueness." [51]

According to Justice Powell, the statute failed to give fair notice by not providing clear guidelines as to what treatment of the flag was criminal. Although the Court did not rely on the *O'Brien* test, the "treats contemptuously" language would appear to fall within the prohibition of part three: the governmental interest is, as expressed in the statute in *Goguen*, related to the suppression of free expression. However, given the apparent recognition by the Supreme Court of the state interest in somehow protecting the flag as a symbol of the Nation, the failure of such statutes under the *O'Brien* test may not be fatal to their constitutionality.

License Plate Desecration. In *Wooley v. Maynard*,[52] the Court applied settled symbolic speech principles and held that a motorist has a free speech right not to be prosecuted for obscuring on his own license plates the state's motto, "Live Free or Die." The individual (who was a Jehovah's Witness) claimed political, moral, and religious objections to the views expressed by the motto.

The Court held that the state cannot force an individual to be an instrument of an ideological point of view with which he disagrees. The state's claimed interests of facilitating identification of passenger vehicles and promoting state pride and an appreciation of history and individualism were insufficient to justify the restriction on free speech.

---

48. 418 U.S. at 412–14, 94 S.Ct. at 2731–32.

49. 415 U.S. 566, 94 S.Ct. 1242, 39 L.Ed.2d 605 (1974).

50. 415 U.S. at 568, 94 S.Ct. at 1245.

51. 415 U.S. at 582, 94 S.Ct. at 1252.

52. 430 U.S. 705, 97 S.Ct. 1428, 51 L.Ed.2d 752 (1977).

Flag Burning

In *Texas v. Johnson*,[53] the Court applied settled symbolic speech law and held that a Texas law—making it a crime to "desecrate" or otherwise "mistreat" the American flag in a way that the "actor knows will seriously offend one or more persons likely to observe or discover his action"—was unconstitutional as applied[54] to one Gregory Lee Johnson. Mr. Johnson was sentenced to one year in jail and a $2,000 fine because he unfurled an American flag, doused it with kerosene, and set it afire while protestors chanted, "America, the red, white, and blue, we spit on you."[55] No one was physically injured or even threatened with injury, but several witnesses testified that they were "seriously offended by the flag burning."[56] The flag burning was part of a demonstration that coincided with the Republican National Convention and its renomination of President Reagan.

As the majority pointed out, Mr. Johnson was *not* charged with stealing an American flag, or burning or destroying someone else's property. Nor was he charged with trespass, disorderly conduct, or arson. He was *"only"* prosecuted for flag desecration, that is, flag burning with an improper motive.[57] If Johnson had burned the flag because it was dirty or worn out, he could not have been convicted of flag "desecration" because, as the majority pointed out, federal law provides that burning the flag is the preferred means of disposing of it "when it is in such a condition that it is no longer a fitting emblem for display."[58] In short, Johnson was prosecuted because of what he thought and what he intended to convey while burning the flag. He was prosecuted for his expressive conduct.

This decision does not venture into uncharted waters. As contemporary commentators pointed out, the "majority opinion is a relatively

53. 491 U.S. 397, 109 S.Ct. 2533, 105 L.Ed.2d 342 (1989).

See, Stone, Flag Burning and the Constitution, 75 Iowa L.Rev. 111 (1989); Kmiec, In the Aftermath of *Johnson* and *Eichman:* The Constitution Need Not Be Mutilated to Preserve the Government's Speech and Property Interests in the Flag, 1990 Brigham Young U.L.Rev. 577 (1990); Bloom, Barnette and Johnson: A Tale of Two Opinions, 75 Iowa L.Rev. 417 (1990); Nahmod, The Sacred Flag and the First Amendment, 66 Ind.L.J. 511 (1991).

Historical Origins of the Flag. For a study of the historical origins of the American flag, see, D. Eggenberger, Flags of the U.S.A. (1964).

54. 491 U.S. at 404 n. 3, 109 S.Ct. at 2539 n. 3:

"A tired person might, for example, drag a flag through the mud, knowing that this conduct is likely to offend others, and yet have no thought of expressing any idea; neither the language nor the Texas courts' interpretations of the statute precludes the possibility that such a person would be prosecuted for flag desecration. Because the prosecution of a person who had not engaged in expressive conduct would pose a different case, and because we are capable of disposing of this case on narrower grounds, we address only Johnson's claim that § 42.09 [of the Texas law] as applied to political expression like his violates the First Amendment."

55. 491 U.S. at 398, 109 S.Ct. at 2536.

56. 491 U.S. at 393, 109 S.Ct. at 2532.

57. 491 U.S. at 412 n. 8, 109 S.Ct. at 2544 n. 8 (emphasis in original).

58. 36 U.S.C.A. § 176(k), quoted in 491 U.S. at 411, 109 S.Ct. at 2543.

straightforward application of traditional first amendment jurisprudence...." [59] Indeed, the Supreme Court merely affirmed the Texas Court of Appeals, which had held that the conviction was a violation of the first amendment.[60] Nearly two decades earlier, in *Schacht v. United States*,[61] the Court (with no dissents) invalidated a federal statute permitting an actor portraying a member of one of our Armed Forces to "wear the uniform of that armed force if the portrayal does not tend to *discredit* that armed force." [62] What is surprising about *Texas v. Johnson* is that the decision was the result of a bare majority of five to four. This bare majority reflected the emotionally charged issue of burning the flag, the symbol of our country. Justice Brennan, joined by Marshall, Blackmun, Scalia, and Kennedy, delivered the opinion of the Court.

Chief Justice Rehnquist, joined by White and O'Connor filed a blistering dissent, that included long excerpts from Ralph Waldo Emerson's "Concord Hymn" ("By the rude bridge that arched the flood/Their flag to April's breeze unfurled,/Here once the embattled farmers stood/And fired the shot heard round the world."); Francis Scott Key's poem that became our National Anthem; and John Greenleaf Whittier's poem, "Barbara Frietchie" (" 'Shoot if you must, this old grey head,/But spare your country's flag,' she said.") [63]

Justice Stevens also filed a strong dissent. He spoke of the flag as a "unique symbol" and compared the majority's decision to the "creation of a federal right to post bulletin boards and graffiti on the Washington Monument...." [64] However, that argument ignores a basic point of the majority: the United States Government owns the Washington Monument and can thus prosecute, as ordinary trespass and vandalism, any graffiti on the Washington Monument. But Texas did not prosecute Johnson for trespass, vandalism, disorderly conduct, or arson. He was "convicted for engaging in expressive conduct." [65]

Justice Kennedy filed a thoughtful concurring opinion in which he explained that he joined the opinion of the majority "without reservation"; he added: "It is poignant but fundamental that the flag protects

59. Note, The Supreme Court, 1988 Term, 103 Harv.L.Rev. 40, 253 (1989). See also, 103 Harv.L.Rev. at 249–50: the case is "relatively straightforward from a doctrinal perspective...." Even the State of Texas conceded at oral argument that Johnson's conduct was "expressive." Transcript of Oral Argument at 4.

60. Johnson v. State, 755 S.W.2d 92 (Tex.Crim.App.1988), affirmed sub nom., Texas v. Johnson, 491 U.S. 397, 109 S.Ct. 2533, 105 L.Ed.2d 342 (1989).

61. 398 U.S. 58, 90 S.Ct. 1555, 26 L.Ed.2d 44 (1970).

62. 398 U.S. at 60, 90 S.Ct. at 1557 (emphasis added).

63. 491 U.S. at 420–35, 109 S.Ct. at 2548–55 (Rehnquist, C.J., dissenting, joined by White & O'Connor, JJ.).

64. 491 U.S. at 436, 109 S.Ct. at 2556 (Stevens, J., dissenting).

65. 491 U.S. at 420, 109 S.Ct. at 2548 (Brennan, J., for the Court).

those who hold it in contempt.... [The defendant's] acts were speech, in both the technical and the fundamental meaning of the Constitution. So I agree with the Court that he must go free." [66]

Strong public opposition greeted the Court's decision.[67] President Bush proposed a constitutional amendment designed to overturn the result, but Congress refused to propose such an amendment to the Constitution. Instead, Congress enacted a new statute purportedly designed to ban flag burning without regard to the contemptuousness of the act.[68] This new statute also faced constitutional difficulty because purportedly it seeks to prevent the defacement of the flag without regard to intent. This Act allows someone to burn the flag when it becomes "worn or soiled." Yet it is a crime to "physically defile[ ]" that same flag if one acts "knowingly." The flag-burner's "intent" is relevant for purposes of this statute.

66. 491 U.S. at 420, 109 S.Ct. at 2548 (Kennedy, J., concurring). See also, 491 U.S. at 418–21, 109 S.Ct. at 2547–48: "We do not consecrate the flag by punishing its desecration, for in doing so we dilute the freedom that this cherished emblem represents." (Brennan, J., for the Court).

67. See, e.g., Van Alstyne, Stars and Stripes and Silliness Forever, Legal Times of Washington, D.C., Oct. 2, 1989, at 34; R. Rotunda, 1989 Supplement to Modern Constitutional Law: Cases & Notes 93 (1989).

68. Flag Protection Act of 1989, H.R. 2978, 101st Cong., 1st Sess., 135 Cong.Rec. H5500 (daily ed., Sept. 12, 1989), Pub.L. 101–131, to be codified at 18 U.S.C.A. § 700.

The law provided:

PL 101–131 (HR 2978)

October 28, 1989

FLAG PROTECTION ACT OF 1989

An Act to amend section 700 of title 18, United States Code, to protect the physical integrity of the flag.

Be it enacted by the Senate and House of Representatives of the United States of America in Congress assembled,

SECTION 1. SHORT TITLE.

This Act may be cited as the "Flag Protection Act of 1989".

SEC. 2. CRIMINAL PENALTIES WITH RESPECT TO THE PHYSICAL INTEGRITY OF THE UNITED STATES FLAG.

(a) IN GENERAL.—Subsection (a) of section 700 of title 18, United States Code, is amended to read as follows:

"(a)(1) Whoever knowingly mutilates, defaces, physically defiles, burns, maintains on the floor or ground, or tramples upon any flag of the United States shall be fined under this title or imprisoned for not more than one year, or both.

"(2) This subsection does not prohibit any conduct consisting of the disposal of a flag when it has become worn or soiled.".

(b) DEFINITION.—Section 700(b) of title 18, United States Code, is amended to read as follows:

"(b) As used in this section, the term 'flag of the United States' means any flag of the United States, or any part thereof, made of any substance, of any size, in a form that is commonly displayed.".

SEC. 3. EXPEDITED REVIEW OF CONSTITUTIONAL ISSUES.

Section 700 of title 18, United States Code, is amended by adding at the end the following:

"(d)(1) An appeal may be taken directly to the Supreme Court of the United States from any interlocutory or final judgment, decree, or order issued by a United States district court ruling upon the constitutionality of subsection (a).

"(2) The Supreme Court shall, if it has not previously ruled on the question, accept jurisdiction over the appeal and advance on the docket and expedite to the greatest extent possible.".

The statute appears to make it a crime for someone to burn, in the privacy of the bedroom, his or her privately owned flag. The Government must justify what interest it has that gives it the power to ban such a burning. Could the Government also ban a burning of a copy of the United States Constitution?

Moreover, if the statute is based on the argument that the flag is a "unique" symbol, there will be future problems defining what is a flag. Will it be a crime for someone to burn a flag with only 49 stars on it? What about burning a photograph of a flag? Or burning fireworks in the shape of an American flag? May a movie director (filming Francis Scott Key watching Fort McHenry) order that the American flag of 1812 be shot at and otherwise defaced? Will it be a crime for the post office to cancel (*i.e.*, deface) a stamp that has on it a copy of the American flag? If a flag design is on a birthday cake, will it be a federal crime to light the birthday candles on the cake? Will cutting the cake deface it? Is it defacing the flag to display it upside down? It is one thing for the Government to forbid destruction of an endangered fish; it is quite another for the Government to forbid someone from destroying or defacing his or her own copy of an American flag. To illustrate that point, the cartoonist Garry Trudeau printed a copy of the American flag in his Sunday comic strip, and then notified the reader that it would be defacing the flag to use that section of the Sunday funnies to line a bird-cage, start a fire in the fireplace, or train a puppy. Would it even be illegal flag desecration to throw that page of the Sunday funnies in the garbage? He called this comic strip, "Konundrum Korner." [69]

Congress' new flag-burning statute claimed to be content neutral, but it really had the same fatal flaw as the statute invalidated in *Texas v. Johnson,* for the statute did not prohibit "any conduct consisting of the disposal of a flag when it has become worn or soiled." [70] Thus the next term, the Supreme Court, by the same five to four majority,

---

Approved October 28, 1989.

69. Garry Trudeau, "Doonesbury," reprinted in Chicago Tribune, Nov. 5, 1989, at § 9, p. 2.

See also, Van Alstyne, Stars and Stripes and Silliness Forever, Legal Times of Washington, D.C., Oct. 2, 1989, at 34.

Well known liberal commentators argued that the new federal statute was somehow consistent with the Supreme Court decision in *Texas v. Johnson.* See, e.g., Hearings on Statutory and Constitutional Responses to the Supreme Court Decision in *Texas v. Johnson,* Hearings Before the Subcommittee on Civil and Constitutional Rights of the House Committee on the Judiciary, 101st Cong., 1st Sess. (1989), at 48 (testimony of Professor Walter Del-

linger); at 99 (testimony of Professor Laurence Tribe). See also, Hearings Before the Committee of the Judiciary, United States Senate, 101st Cong., 1st Sess. (1989), at 140 (testimony of L. Tribe, arguing that the Administration's position, that a mere statute could not make flag burning a crime in light of *Texas v. Johnson,* is "a bizarre constitutional theory"). On the other hand, L. Tribe, American Constitutional Law 801–02 (2d ed. 1988), earlier argued that it would be improper to make it even a misdemeanor to destroy or mutilate any object bearing the pattern of the U.S. flag; there is no government interest in preventing private flag burnings: "the symbol is degraded, if at all, only to the degree that people learn of the act."

70. 18 U.S.C.A. § 700(a)(2).

overturned convictions brought under that statute as well, in *United States v. Eichman.*[71]

The *Eichman* majority agreed that Congress has the right to protect the flag (even a privately owned flag) at least as much as it can protect a "trademark" like "Smokey the Bear" or the name "Olympics."[72] Congress and the states can protect the flag from being "diluted" or misused just like it can protect other "trademarks" like "Smokey the Bear" from dilution.[73]

Hate Crimes. In addition, the flag-burning cases should allow Congress or the states to protect its property (the tomb of the Unknown Soldier) or other people's property (a house of worship or a graveyard) from "hate-crimes": that is, Congress or the states may constitutionally make it a crime to commit a hate-crime (spraying a Nazi emblem on a synagogue, or burning a cross in someone's yard) and punish that type of crime more severely and vigorously than a simple act of vandalism (spray-painting a nonsense word on a subway train). The hate or terrorism element of the crime allows Congress or the states to punish that element more severely because the hate aspect of the crime affects both the harm by the act and the likelihood of recidivism by the perpetrator. The Court in *Eichman* is not saying that a "political" act of vandalism—vandalism coupled with an intent to broadcast hate or terrorize—cannot be punished (or cannot be punished more severely) than a nonpolitical act of vandalism. The first amendment does not

---

71. 496 U.S. 310, 110 S.Ct. 2404, 110 L.Ed.2d 287 (1990). The Court noted that some of the appellees were charged with causing wilful injury to federal property in violation of another statute. The Court explained that nothing in *Eichman* affects the constitutionality of that prosecution. 496 U.S. at ___ n. 1, 110 S.Ct. at 2406 n. 1. Similarly, the government has an interest in protecting the flags that *it owns* (its property) and may enact special measures to protect that interest. 496 U.S. at ___ n. 5, 110 S.Ct. at 2408 n. 5.

72. See, San Francisco Arts & Athletics, Inc. v. United States Olympics Committee, 483 U.S. 522, 107 S.Ct. 2971, 97 L.Ed.2d 427 (1987), holding that Congress may protect the name "Olympics" from being used, without consent from the United States Olympic Committee, for purpose of trade, to induce sales of goods or services, or to promote any theatrical exhibition, athletic event, or competition.

See, Kmiec, In the Aftermath of *Johnson* and *Eichman*: The Constitution Need Not Be Mutilated to Preserve the Government's Speech and Property Interests in

the Flag, 1990 Brigham Young U.L.Rev. 577 (1990), skillfully elaborating on the argument that the "flag's design may be statutorily declared to be public property, and that this declaration may not only permit preservation of the flag, but also, as an incident of *government* speech, the licensing and control of the flag's use." 1990 Brigham Young L.Rev. at 580 (footnote omitted).

73. 496 U.S. at ___ n. 4, 110 S.Ct. at 2408 n. 4, citing Halter v. Nebraska, 205 U.S. 34, 27 S.Ct. 419, 51 L.Ed. 696 (1907). In *Halter*, Justice Harlan, for the Court, upheld a Nebraska statute that made it a misdemeanor to sell merchandise that had printed or placed on it, for purposes of advertisement, a representation of the flag of the United States. The state law expressly excepted from its operation any newspaper, periodical, or book on which there was a representation of a flag "disconnected from any advertisement." The defendants had offered for sale a bottle of beer on which, for purposes of advertisement, there was printed a representation of the American flag. Only Justice Peckham dissented, without opinion.

offer protection for criminal acts committed with a political motive. If that were the law, then *United States v. O'Brien* is wrong and Martin Luther King's assassin—who claimed that his murder of King was a political crime—could not have been convicted.

Comparison With Soviet Legislation on "Discrediting" a Public Official. It is interesting to compare *Texas v. Johnson* with a situation that arose in the U.S.S.R. at virtually the same time. On April 8, 1989, the Presidium of the Supreme Soviet of the U.S.S.R. adopted legislation making it a criminal offense to "discredit" a public official. Soviet liberals immediately attacked the statute. In the legislation's defense, Soviet conservatives published an article in "Nedelya," the Sunday supplement to *Izvestia*, which has a circulation of millions.[74] This article listed dozens of foreign laws punishing disrespect for public officials or public symbols. In particular it relied on section 700 of title 18 of the United States Code, which prohibits "desecration of the flag of the United States." The Texas law in *Texas v. Johnson* was similar to this section 700.

Dissident Andrei Sakharov, speaking to the Congress of People's Deputies, attacked this and other April 8th legislation limiting free speech:

> In my opinion, [this Edict of the Presidium of the Supreme Soviet] contradicts the principles of democracy. There is a most important principle, which is formulated in the Universal Declaration of Human Rights, adopted in 1948, and by such an international organization as Amnesty International. This is the principle that no actions connected with persuasion, unless they are connected with violence or with a call to violence, can be the subject of criminal prosecution. This is the key principle lying at the base of a democratic political system. And this key word "violence" is lacking in the language of the Edict of April 8.[75]

On June 8, the Soviet Congress responded to the criticism of Sakharov and other Soviet liberals by repealing the Edict.[76]

Book Banning in Public Schools and the Problem of Motivation. Though *Wooley* raised no difficult problem of the motivation of the legislative or administrative decision-maker, and the judicial use of that motivation in order to invalidate state action restricting speech, the Court certainly did return to that issue and elaborate on the uses of motivation and the implications of *Tinker v. Des Moines Independent Community School District*[77] in the case of *Board of Education, Island*

---

74. *Nedelya*, 1989, No. 15, p. 19.

75. *Izvestia*, May 29, 1989, at p. 6.

76. See, Rotunda & Maggs, Meanwhile Back in Mother Russia, Legal Times of Washington, D.C., Oct. 2, 1989, at 35.

77. 393 U.S. 503, 89 S.Ct. 733, 21

Trees Union Free School District No. 26 v. Pico.[78] The Court was asked to decide what were the first amendment restrictions on a decision of a local school board to remove certain books from high school and junior high school libraries.

The books were not obscene in a constitutional sense but the board had concluded that the books were "anti-American, anti-Christian, anti-Semitic, and just plain filthy." [79] The Court could produce no majority opinion and returned the case to the lower courts for a trial on the merits, in order to determine the motivation of the school board.

Justice Brennan, in an opinion joined by Justices Marshall and Stevens, and in part by Justice Blackmun, emphasized that the Court was dealing with a case that did not involve any textbooks or required reading; nor did the case involve judicial intrusion on the Board's discretion to prescribe curricula. "[T]he only books at issue are *library* books, books that by their nature are optional rather than required reading." [80] And even as to these books, Brennan noted, the Court's ruling would not affect the discretion of the local school board to decide which books to add. "Rather, the only action challenged in this case is the *removal* from school libraries of books originally placed there by the school authorities, or without objection from them." [81] Because this case is concerned with the suppression of ideas, "our holding today

---

L.Ed.2d 731 (1969).

78. 457 U.S. 853, 102 S.Ct. 2799, 73 L.Ed.2d 435 (1982).

Note, Judicial Clairvoyance and the First Amendment; The Role of Motivation in Judicial Review of Book Banning in Public Schools, 1983 U.Ill.L.Rev. 731. See also Finkin, On "Institutional Academic Freedom," 61 Tex.L.Rev. 817 (1983) (argues that the justifications for academic freedom do not always justify institutional freedom from governmental regulation); Diamond, The First Amendment and Public Schools: The Case Against Judicial Intervention, 59 Tex.L.Rev. 477 (1981) (argues that courts should apply only a limited standard of review to local school administration); Gottlieb, In the Name of Patriotism: The Constitutionality of "Bending" History in Public Secondary Schools, 62 N.Y.U.L.Rev. 497 (1987).

79. 457 U.S. at 857–58, 102 S.Ct. at 2803. See the lower court decision at Pico v. Board of Education, 474 F.Supp. 387, 390 (E.D.N.Y.1979), reversed 638 F.2d 404 (2d Cir.1980), rehearing denied 646 F.2d 714

(1980), affirmed 457 U.S. 853, 102 S.Ct. 2799, 73 L.Ed.2d 435 (1982).

The Board, after objections were raised by a parents group, decided (contrary to the recommendations of a Book Review Committee which it had appointed) that the book, *Black Boy,* by Richard Wright, should be made available in the high school library subject to parental approval and that nine other books should be removed from elementary and secondary libraries and from use in the curriculum. These books were: *Slaughter House Five,* by Kurt Vonnegut, Jr.; *The Naked Ape,* by Desmond Morris; *Down These Mean Streets,* by Piri Thomas; *Best Short Stories of Negro Writers,* edited by Langston Hughes; *Go Ask Alice,* of anonymous authorship; *A Hero Ain't Nothin' But a Sandwich,* by Alice Childress; *Soul on Ice,* by Eldridge Cleaver; *A Reader for Writers,* edited by Jerome Archer; and *The Fixer,* by Bernard Malamud.

80. 457 U.S. at 861–62, 102 S.Ct. at 2805 (emphasis in original).

81. 457 U.S. at 865–66, 102 S.Ct. at 2807 (emphasis in original).

affects only the discretion to *remove* books." [82]   Brennan then focused heavily on the subjective motivations of the decision-makers.

Students have a "right to receive ideas." [83]   Although first amendment rights must be interpreted in light of the special characteristics of the school environment, under *Tinker* the school library, said Brennan, is a special locus of first amendment freedoms.   Justice Brennan, in a far cry from *O'Brien*, focused on the motivation of the school board. Thus—

> Petitioners rightly possess significant discretion to determine the content of their school libraries.   But that discretion may not be exercised in a narrowly partisan or political manner.   If a Democratic school board, motivated by party affiliation, ordered the removal of all books written by or in favor of Republicans, few would doubt that the order violated the constitutional rights of the students denied access to those books....   Our Constitution does not permit the official suppression of *ideas.*   Thus whether petitioners' removal of books from their school libraries denied respondents their First Amendment rights depends upon the motivation behind petitioners' actions.   If petitioners *intended* by their removal decision to deny respondents access to ideas with which petitioners disagreed, and if this intent was the decisive factor in petitioners' decision, then petitioners have exercised their discretion in violation of the Constitution....   On the other hand, respondents implicitly concede that an unconstitutional motivation would *not* be demonstrated if it were shown that petitioners had decided to remove the books at issue because those books were pervasively vulgar.   And again, respondents concede that if it were demonstrated that the removal decision was based solely upon the "educational suitability" of the books in question, then their removal would be "perfectly permissible."   In other words, in respondents' view such motivations, if decisive of petitioners' actions, would not carry the danger of an official suppression of ideas, and thus would not violate respondents' First Amendment rights.   In brief, we hold that local school boards may not remove books from school library shelves simply because they dislike the ideas contained in those books and seek by their removal to "prescribe what shall be orthodox in politics, nationalism, religion, or other matters of opinion."   Such purposes stand inescapably condemned by our precedents. [84]

82. 457 U.S. at 870–72, 102 S.Ct. at 2810 (emphasis in original).

83. 457 U.S. at 866–68, 102 S.Ct. at 2808, citing, inter alia, Martin v. Struthers, 319 U.S. 141, 143, 63 S.Ct. 862, 863, 87 L.Ed. 1313 (1943); Stanley v. Georgia, 394 U.S. 557, 564, 89 S.Ct. 1243, 1247–48, 22 L.Ed.2d 542 (1969), on remand 225 Ga. 273, 167 S.E.2d 756 (1969); Kleindienst v. Mandel, 408 U.S. 753, 762–63, 92 S.Ct. 2576, 2581–82, 33 L.Ed.2d 683 (1972).

84. 457 U.S. at 870–72, 102 S.Ct. at 2810 (emphasis in original).

Justice Blackmun concurred in part and in the judgment; he emphasized that school officials may not remove books "for the *purpose* of restricting access to the political ideas or social perspectives discussed in them, when that action is motivated simply by the officials' disapproval of the ideas involved." [85] For example, "removing a learned treatise criticizing American foreign policy from an elementary school library because the students would not understand it is an action unrelated to the *purpose* of suppressing ideas. In my view, however, removing the same treatise because it is 'anti-American' raises a far more difficult issue." [86]

Justice Blackmun was dubious that the distinction between removing and failing to acquire a book was analytically sound, but he did recognize that there was a practical and evidentiary distinction because removal of a book (more than a mere failure to acquire it) suggests an impermissible motive. Many justifications, including finite resources, could explain why a book was not purchased, but it is more difficult to explain why it would be removed from a library not filled to capacity. [87]

Justice White, concurring in the judgment, abstained from issuing what he called a "dissertation" on the Constitutional issues involved until after a full trial as to why the Board removed the books. [88]

Chief Justice Burger, joined by Powell, Rehnquist, and O'Connor, dissented. They reasoned that the Board placed no restraints of any kind on the students. They could read the books, available from public libraries, bookstores, or elsewhere; they could discuss the books in class. [89] But the school library need not be the conduit; there is no " 'right' to have the government provide continuing access to certain books," to be made "a slavish currier of the materials of third parties." [90] The plurality's test allowing the books to be withdrawn if "educationally unsuitable" is standardless, argued the dissent. Why also must a book be "pervasively vulgar" before it is offensive; would not "random" vulgarity be enough to make the book inappropriate? [91]

The Burger dissent also found no principled distinction between *removing* unwanted books and *acquiring* books. Books do not have any constitutional tenure, argued the dissent. [92]

Justice Rehnquist's dissent, joined by Burger, and Powell, stated that it could agree with the plurality that a Democratic school board could not order the removal of all books written by Republicans, but

85. 457 U.S. at 878–80, 102 S.Ct. at 2814 (emphasis in original).

86. 457 U.S. at 880–82, 102 S.Ct. at 2815 (emphasis in original).

87. 457 U.S. at 879 n. 1, 102 S.Ct. at 2814 n. 1.

88. 457 U.S. at 882–84, 102 S.Ct. at 2816.

89. 457 U.S. at 886–87, 102 S.Ct. at 2818.

90. 457 U.S. at 888–89, 102 S.Ct. at 2819.

91. 457 U.S. at 890–91, 102 S.Ct. at 2820.

92. 457 U.S. at 892 & n. 8, 102 S.Ct. at 2821 & n. 8 (emphasis in original).

"would save for another day" such extreme examples because the books here were removed because of their vulgarity and profanity.[93] Moreover, if Justice Brennan "truly has found a 'right to receive ideas,' " his "distinction between acquisition and removal makes little sense." [94]

Student Speech at School Assemblies. In *Bethel School District No. 403 v. Fraser,*[95] the Court, seven to two, upheld a broad power of school authorities to discipline a student for delivering, at a school assembly, a speech which promoted another student as a candidate for student government by using "persuasive sexual innuendo," describing the candidate as "a man who is firm—he's firm in his pants, he's firm in his shirt, his character is firm—but most of all, his belief in you, the students of Bethel, is firm." The student added that his candidate was also "a man who takes his point and pounds it in" ... "a man who will go to the very end—even to the climax, for each and every one of you." [96] The school suspended the 17 year old student for two days.[97] The audience of about 600 students included students 14 years old or older. Some responded to the speech with hooting and yelling. Others responded "by gestures [which] graphically simulated the sexual activities pointedly alluded to in respondent's speech." [98]

Chief Justice Burger, for the Court, said that this speech, which he never quoted in his majority opinion, was "an elaborate, graphic, and explicit sexual metaphor." [99] He added, "Surely it is a highly appropriate function of public school education to prohibit the use of vulgar and offensive terms in public discourse." [100] School officials must have broad power to punish what they conclude is "inappropriate" speech in classrooms and assemblies. Schools "must teach by example the shared values of a civilized social order." [101] Burger also called the speech "offensively lewd," "indecent," "vulgar," "sexually explicit," and

93. 457 U.S. at 907–09, 102 S.Ct. at 2829.

94. 457 U.S. at 909–11, 102 S.Ct. at 2830. O'Connor and Powell, JJ., each also wrote dissenting opinions. 457 U.S. at 894–95, 102 S.Ct. at 2822 (Powell, J.), 457 U.S. at 919–21, 102 S.Ct. at 2835 (O'Connor, J.).

95. 478 U.S. 675, 106 S.Ct. 3159, 92 L.Ed.2d 549 (1986), on remand 800 F.2d 222 (9th Cir.1986).

See generally, Note, Tinker Revisited: Fraser v. Bethel School District and the Regulation of Speech in Public Schools, 1986 Duke L.J. 1169.

96. 478 U.S. at 687, 106 S.Ct. at 3167 (Brennan, J., concurring in the judgment).

97. Initially the school suspended Fraser for three days for his "obscene" speech,

478 U.S. at 678, 106 S.Ct. at 3162, but then allowed him to return after serving two days of his suspension. 478 U.S. at 678, 106 S.Ct. at 3163.

The school also decided that Fraser's name would be removed from the list of candidates for graduation speaker at the school's commencement exercises, 478 U.S. at 677, 106 S.Ct. at 3162; 478 U.S. at 689 n. 3, 106 S.Ct. at 3168 n. 2 (Brennan, J., concurring in the judgment). Fraser was nonetheless "chosen by the student body to speak at the school's commencement exercises...." 478 U.S. at 692, 106 S.Ct. at 3169 (Stevens, J., dissenting).

98. 478 U.S. at 677, 106 S.Ct. at 3162.

99. 478 U.S. at 677, 106 S.Ct. at 3162.

100. 478 U.S. at 683, 106 S.Ct. at 3165.

101. 478 U.S. at 683, 106 S.Ct. at 3165.

"obscene." [102] He said that it "was plainly offensive to both teachers and students," "was acutely insulting to teen-age girl students," and "could well be seriously damaging to its less mature audience, many of whom were only 14 years old and on the threshold of awareness of human sexuality." [103] The Court distinguished *Tinker v. Des Moines Independent Community School District.*[104] "Unlike the sanctions imposed by the students wearing armbands in *Tinker,* the penalties imposed in this case were unrelated to any political viewpoint." [105] The school officials could conclude "that to permit a vulgar and lewd speech such as respondent's would undermine the school's basic educational mission. A high school assembly or classroom is no place for a sexually explicit monologue directed towards an unsuspecting audience of teenage students." [106]

Justice Brennan concurred in the judgment. He said that the speech was no more obscene or lewd "than the bulk of programs currently on prime-time television or in the local cinema," [107] but that this speech may be punished as "disruptive." He added, "the Court's holding concerns only the authority that school officials have to restrict a high school student's use of disruptive language in a speech given to a high school audience." [108]

Justice Marshall, dissenting, argued that the speech was not even disruptive. The district court and court of appeals concluded that the Board of Education has not shown any disruption of the educational process.[109] Justice Stevens, also dissenting, said that the student "should not be disciplined for speaking frankly in a school assembly if he had no reason to anticipate punitive consequences." The student had discussed his proposed speech with some teachers beforehand, and while he had been told that the speech would "raise eyebrows," he had no "fair notice" that he risked discipline.[110] The speaker was in a better position to determine whether his audience would be offended by

102. 478 U.S. at 686, 106 S.Ct. at 3166; 478 U.S. at 680, 106 S.Ct. at 3163.

103. 478 U.S. at 683, 106 S.Ct. at 3165.

104. 393 U.S. 503, 89 S.Ct. 733, 21 L.Ed.2d 731 (1969).

105. 478 U.S. at 686, 106 S.Ct. at 3166.

Burger added, "The determination of what manner of speech in the classroom or in school assembly is inappropriate properly rests with the school board." 478 U.S. at 683, 106 S.Ct. at 3165.

106. 478 U.S. at 686, 106 S.Ct. at 3166. Burger called the plaintiff a "confused boy." 478 U.S. at 683, 106 S.Ct. at 3165.

107. 478 U.S. at 689 n. 2, 106 S.Ct. at 3168 n. 2 (Brennan, J., concurring in the judgment).

108. 478 U.S. at 689, 106 S.Ct. at 3168 (Brennan, J., concurring in the judgment).

109. 478 U.S. at 690, 106 S.Ct. at 3168–69 (Marshall, J., dissenting). Indeed, the Ninth Circuit had ruled that there "is no evidence in the record indicating that any students found the speech to be offensive." Fraser v. Bethel School District No. 403, 755 F.2d 1356, 1361 n. 4 (9th Cir.1985), reversed 478 U.S. 675, 106 S.Ct. 3159, 92 L.Ed.2d 549 (1986). See also 755 F.2d at 1360–61.

110. 478 U.S. at 691, 106 S.Ct. at 3169, 3171 (Stevens, J., dissenting).

the use of sexual metaphor "than is a group of judges who are at least two generations, and 3,000 miles away from the scene of the crime." [111]

Selective Enforcement. The decision to violate the law may be considered symbolic speech if the violation is engaged in as a form of protest. Yet it is clear that a person who violates a criminal law as a form of protest does not thereby acquire immunity from prosecution. The Government does not engage in selective prosecution in violation of the first amendment unless its enforcement policy is discriminatory against the first amendment on its face, or has a discriminatory effect *and* was motivated by a discriminatory purpose. The Government's mere knowledge of the discriminatory effect does not call into question an otherwise valid enforcement scheme; the Government must actually have a discriminatory intent.

A passive criminal enforcement scheme neither constitutes selective enforcement nor violates the *O'Brien* test. A passive enforcement scheme may be justified for various reasons which are unrelated to the suppression of free speech, such as the need to conserve prosecutorial resources and the need to promote deterrence by prosecuting the most vocal and visible violators.

These principles are well illustrated in the case of *Wayte v. United States*,[112] where the Court upheld the constitutionality of the Government's passive enforcement policy in cases where individuals refuse to register with the Selective Service System. The Government made the decision to prosecute only those who reported themselves as having violated the law or who were reported by others. The Government would send these reported violators a letter requesting that the alleged violator either comply with the law or explain why he was not subject to registration. Petitioner Wayte received such a letter but did not respond. Thus his name, along with others, was sent to the Department of Justice, which sent to each of the nonregistrants a letter and an FBI agent who encouraged them to change their minds and register. This procedure was called the "beg policy." Then the Department of Justice, after its grace period had ended and its beg policy had been ignored, began to prosecute, although it acknowledged, in an internal memorandum, that those prosecuted were "liable to be vocal proponents of nonregistration" or holding "religious or moral objections," and that such prosecutions would "undoubtedly result in allegations

---

111. 478 U.S. at 691, 106 S.Ct. at 3169 (footnote omitted) (Stevens, J., dissenting).

112. 470 U.S. 598, 105 S.Ct. 1524, 84 L.Ed.2d 547 (1985).

See generally, Note, Rethinking Selective Enforcement in the First Amendment Context, 84 Colum.L.Rev. 144 (1984); Comment, Equal Protection and the Passive Enforcement System of Draft Registration: Selective Service or Selective Prosecution—United States v. Wayte, 12 Hastings Const.L.Q. 149 (1984); Shane, Equal Protection, Free Speech, and the Selective Prosecution of Draft Nonregistrants, 72 Iowa L.Rev. 359 (1987).

that the [case was] brought in retribution for the nonregistrant's exercise of his first amendment rights." [113] Wayte claimed that he and other vocal opponents of registration—16 had been indicted out of 674,000 nonregistrants—were targeted because of their first amendment beliefs.[114]

First the Court held that the passive enforcement policy did not constitute unconstitutional selective enforcement. The decision to prosecute may not be "deliberately based upon an unjustifiable standard such as race, religion, or other arbitrary classification." [115] Because the passive enforcement scheme did not discriminate on its face, Wayte had to demonstrate not only that the passive enforcement scheme had a discriminatory effect but also that it was motivated by a discriminatory purpose.[116] Wayte could not show that the passive enforcement scheme selected nonregistrants on the basis of their speech, because of the way the "beg policy" was implemented. The Government did not prosecute those who reported themselves but later registered; it did not prosecute those who protested registration but did not report themselves or were not reported by others; it did not even investigate those who wrote letters criticizing Selective Service but who did not state that they were not complying with the law; it did prosecute those who reported themselves or who were reported by others even though they never engaged in any public protest.

Moreover, Wayte never could show that the Government intended any discriminatory effect, only that the Government was aware of the likely effect of its program and the claims of vocal protestors. Wayte could not prove "that the Government prosecuted *him because of* his protest activities." [117]

Then the Court turned to the petitioner's argument that the Government's passive enforcement policy constituted content-based regulation. The Court noted, first, that the Government's "beg policy" removed "most, if not all, of any burden passive enforcement placed on free expression." [118] Nonregistrants have no right to refuse to register, and yet no matter how strong their protest, registration would immunize them from prosecution.[119] Passive enforcement punished nonregistration, not speech.

---

113. 470 U.S. at 604, 105 S.Ct. at 1529.

114. 470 U.S. at 604, 105 S.Ct. at 1529 & n. 3.

115. Bordenkircher v. Hayes, 434 U.S. 357, 364, 98 S.Ct. 663, 668, 54 L.Ed.2d 604 (1978), rehearing denied 435 U.S. 918, 98 S.Ct. 1477, 55 L.Ed.2d 511 (1978), quoting Oyler v. Boles, 368 U.S. 448, 456, 82 S.Ct. 501, 505, 7 L.Ed.2d 446 (1962). See also, United States v. Goodwin, 457 U.S. 368, 372, 102 S.Ct. 2485, 2488, 73 L.Ed.2d 74 (1982), on remand 687 F.2d 44 (4th Cir. 1982).

116. 470 U.S. at 610 & n. 10, 105 S.Ct. at 1532 & n. 10.

117. 470 U.S. at 610, 105 S.Ct. at 1532 (emphasis in original).

118. 470 U.S. at 611 n. 12, 105 S.Ct. at 1532 n. 12.

119. 470 U.S. at 611 n. 12, 105 S.Ct. at 1532 n. 12.

The Court applied the four part test of *United States v. O'Brien*,[120] and found that the passive enforcement scheme passed constitutional muster. First, it was undisputed that the registration system is within the constitutional power of the Government. Second, the passive enforcement scheme furthered the important governmental interest in military security. The Government justified this particular enforcement policy because it conserved resources, for an active enforcement scheme would have been very costly. Also, the letters admitting noncompliance were strong evidence of intent not to register. And prosecuting visible nonregistrants would promote general deterrence. Third, it was undisputed—in light of the earlier analysis in this case— that the governmental interest is unrelated to the suppression of free expression. And the fourth prong of the *O'Brien* test was met as well: the incidental restrictions on first amendment freedoms caused by this interim enforcement system were no greater than necessary to ensure registration for the national defense.

Finally the Court found petitioner's arguments proved too much, and were equally applicable to an active enforcement system as applied to a nonregistrant who reported himself. Such a view "would allow any criminal to obtain immunity from prosecution simply by reporting himself and claiming that he did so in order to 'protest' the law." [121]

Group Boycotts. In *FTC v. Superior Court Trial Lawyers Association*,[122] various individual lawyers in Washington, D.C. agreed not to represent indigent criminal defendants in the Superior Court unless the District increased their statutory rate of compensation, which the District eventually did. The lawyers were not employees of any employer; their group action was therefore not a union strike. Then the Federal Trade Commission issued a cease-and-desist order against future boycotts, and the respondents claimed, *inter alia*, that the boycott was protected symbolic speech. The Supreme Court, after noting that the respondents' concerted action was a "plain violation of the antitrust laws," disagreed.

First, the lower court exaggerated the expressive portion of the group boycott. "Every concerted refusal to do business with a potential customer or supplier has an expressive component." [123] The lower court had ruled that courts must apply the antitrust laws "prudently and with sensitivity" whenever an economic boycott has an "expressive component" but such a proposed rule would create a gaping hole in the fabric of those laws." [124]

---

120. 391 U.S. 367, 376, 88 S.Ct. 1673, 1678, 20 L.Ed.2d 672 (1968), rehearing denied 393 U.S. 900, 89 S.Ct. 63, 21 L.Ed.2d 188 (1968).

121. 470 U.S. at 613, 105 S.Ct. at 1534.

122. 493 U.S. 411, 110 S.Ct. 768, 107 L.Ed.2d 851 (1990), on remand 897 F.2d 1168 (D.C.Cir.1990).

123. 493 U.S. at 430, 110 S.Ct. at 779.

124. 493 U.S. at 432, 110 S.Ct. at 780.

Secondly, the lower court denigrated the importance of the antitrust price fixing rules. The *per se* rules against price fixing and boycotts are justified by administrative convenience and reflect "a longstanding judgment" that the prohibited practices have a substantial impact on competition. Every horizontal price fixing agreement among competitors poses a threat to the free market even if the conspirators do not have the power to control market prices.[125]

In contrast, when black citizens engage in a boycott against white merchants for political and economic reasons, the first amendment applies. In *NAACP v. Claiborne Hardware Co.,*[126] the Court ruled that Mississippi's right to regulate economic activity cannot justify "a complete prohibition against a nonviolent, politically motivated boycott designed to force governmental and economic change and to effectuate rights guaranteed by the Constitution itself." [127] In contrast to *Superior Court Trial Lawyers Association,* those who joined the boycott in *Claiborne Hardware* did not desire to destroy legitimate competition and sought no special advantage for themselves.[128] They would not profit from any lessening of competition in the boycotted market, but the lawyers in *Superior Court Trial Lawyers Association* would profit financially from any lessening of competition in the boycotted market.

Conclusion. Symbolic speech cases really present no issues different from those in other types of speech cases, once the court has determined that the activity being regulated or prohibited should be considered speech. It is this decision—to determine that an activity is speech—which may not always appear easy. Individuals may take actions which other persons do not recognize as communicating a message. For example, an individual might wish to make a symbolic statement of his opposition to an ordinance prohibiting the burning of leaves or garbage by burning such materials on the driveway of his residential property. However, a court, in considering whether he may be convicted for violating this ordinance need only apply the *O'Brien* test, without having to decide whether leaf-burning is communicative or not. A city ordinance prohibiting leaf-burning, for example, would easily meet parts one, two, and four of the four-part *O'Brien* test. If the ordinance only prohibits leaf burning by socialists, it would fail part

---

125. 493 U.S. at 434–37, 110 S.Ct. at 781–82. Brennan, J., joined by Marshall, J., concurred in part but dissented to this portion of the majority opinion. The dissent argued that the court should inquire whether "expressive political boycotts" actually "cause any of the harms that the antitrust laws are designed to prevent." Blackmun, J. also wrote a separate opinion concurring in part and dissenting to this portion of the majority opinion. He argued that the market was "unique" because the District's courts and city council could have required lawyers (as officers of

the court) to represent indigents *pro bono;* thus, he concluded, the "Trial Lawyers lacked any market power and their boycott could have succeeded only through political persuasion." 493 U.S. at 454, 110 S.Ct. at 792.

126. 458 U.S. 866, 102 S.Ct. 3409, 73 L.Ed.2d 1215 (1982), rehearing denied 459 U.S. 898, 103 S.Ct. 199, 74 L.Ed.2d 160 (1982).

127. 458 U.S. at 914, 102 S.Ct. at 3426.

128. 493 U.S. at 426, 110 S.Ct. at 777.

three of the *O'Brien* test because the governmental interest is *not* unrelated to the suppression of free expression. If the city ordinance prohibited leaf burning only if done in a contemptuous manner, or if done for the purpose of protesting the city's environmental policy, it likewise fails part three of *O'Brien.* But if the city ordinance is a typical one, it prohibits all leaf burning. Then, like the statute in *O'Brien* (which prohibited knowing destruction of a draft card—it did not prohibit only contemptuous destruction of a draft card, or destruction with intent to hinder the war effort), the leaf burning ordinance would be constitutional.

In *O'Brien* the Court assumed that draft card burning was a form of speech. However, the Court stated, "[w]e cannot accept the view that an apparently limitless variety of conduct can be labeled 'speech' whenever the person engaging in the conduct intends thereby to express an idea." [129] But the real question is not the motive of the speaker so much as it is the purpose of the governmental regulation: in the words of *O'Brien,* is the governmental interest "unrelated to the suppression of free expression"?

If conduct is treated as symbolic speech, it can still be regulated, if the pure speech could be regulated. Even if government regulation of symbolic speech fails the *O'Brien* test, the regulation may be valid. Pure speech or symbolic conduct can be regulated in two distinct ways. First, the expressive activity, whether symbolic or express, may be prohibited because of its message, if that message fits one of the categories of speech, such as obscenity, which the Court has found punishable consistently with the first amendment. If the content of the speech does not fit within such a category, the content cannot be proscribed unless the Court finds that the government has a compelling interest in prohibiting such messages so as to create a new category of punishable content.[130]

Second, the time, place, or manner aspects of speech, whether express or symbolic, may be regulated through laws or administrative actions narrowly tailored to promote an important or substantial governmental interest unrelated to suppressing the message. Time, place,

129. 391 U.S. at 376, 88 S.Ct. at 1678, 20 L.Ed.2d at 679.

130. Farber and Nowak, The Misleading Nature of Public Forum Analysis: Content and Context in First Amendment Adjudication, 70 Va.L.Rev. 1219 (1984); Ely, Flag Desecration: A Case Study in the Roles of Categorization and Balancing in First Amendment Analysis, 88 Harv.L.Rev. 1482 (1975); F. Schauer, Free Speech: A Philosophical Enquiry (1982).

This principle was established in United States v. O'Brien, 391 U.S. 367, 88 S.Ct. 1673, 20 L.Ed.2d 672 (1968), rehearing denied 393 U.S. 900, 89 S.Ct. 63, 21 L.Ed.2d 188 (1968) discussed in the text. The principle was endorsed and applied in Members of City Council v. Taxpayers for Vincent, 466 U.S. 789, 104 S.Ct. 2118, 80 L.Ed.2d 772 (1984), on remand 738 F.2d 353 (9th Cir.1984) in which the Court upheld a regulation that prohibited placing signs, including political campaign signs, on public property because the government had an important interest in protecting esthetic values and the restriction was narrowly tailored to promote those esthetic values.

or manner regulations must be content neutral because if they are not unrelated to the content of the speech the Court must determine whether the content fits within a category of punishable speech. These regulations must be narrowly tailored to serve an important or substantial governmental interest and leave open ample alternative channels of communication to assure the Court that channels of communication in society have not been eliminated for insubstantial or content-based reasons.[131]

XV.   REGULATION OF THE ELECTORAL PROCESS BY RESTRICTIONS ON CAMPAIGN FINANCING AND BY LIMITATIONS OF POLITICAL ACTIVITY OF GOVERNMENT EMPLOYEES

§ 20.50 Introduction

There can be little question now that political expression lies at the core of first amendment values.[1] Nonetheless, political expression is subject to government regulation provided the state can show a substantial interest in such regulation. The transcendent legislative objective in this field is the elimination of corruption as well as the appearance of corruption in order that public participation in the electoral process is not dampened by cynicism or alienation. As a result, reasonable legislative proscriptions upon political activity by government employees are consistently upheld,[2] as well as regulation of

131. In United States v. Grace, 461 U.S. 171, 177, 103 S.Ct. 1702, 1707, 75 L.Ed.2d 736 (1983), on remand 717 F.2d 1480 (D.C.Cir.1983), the Court stated the test as it had been established in earlier cases as a three-part test: "the government may enforce reasonable time, place, and manner regulations as long as the restrictions are content-neutral, are narrowly tailored to serve a significant government interest, and leave open ample alternative channels of communication." (internal quotations and citation omitted).

In Clark v. Community for Creative Non–Violence, 468 U.S. 288, 104 S.Ct. 3065, 82 L.Ed.2d 221 (1984), the Court, by a seven to two vote, applied the three-part test used for time, place, and manner restrictions and upheld the National Park Service's refusal to allow demonstrators to make a public statement by sleeping in parks in the center of Washington, D.C. Park Service regulations prohibited around-the-clock use of the parks. The regulation at issue was content neutral, promoted the government's substantial interest in maintaining the parks, and left

open alternative means for communicating the demonstrators' message. In the course of upholding the legislation, the majority opinion stated that the justices would "assume for present purposes, but do not decide" that overnight sleeping in the park to demonstrate plight of the homeless was expressive conduct. The Court noted that "[e]xpression, whether oral or written or symbolized by conduct, is subject to reasonable time, place, and manner restrictions."

§ 20.50

1. Buckley v. Valeo, 424 U.S. 1, 96 S.Ct. 612, 46 L.Ed.2d 659 (1976) (per curiam), mandate conformed 532 F.2d 187 (D.C.Cir. 1976); Williams v. Rhodes, 393 U.S. 23, 89 S.Ct. 5, 21 L.Ed.2d 24 (1968); Cf. United States v. O'Brien, 391 U.S. 367, 88 S.Ct. 1673, 20 L.Ed.2d 672 (1968), rehearing denied 393 U.S. 900, 89 S.Ct. 63, 21 L.Ed.2d 188 (1968).

2. United Public Workers v. Mitchell, 330 U.S. 75, 67 S.Ct. 556, 91 L.Ed. 754 (1947); United States Civil Service Commission v. National Ass'n of Letter Carri-

the conduct of, and contributions to, political campaigns.[3]

On the other hand, as the Supreme Court noted without dissent in *Brown v. Hartlage*[4] a state may not punish a political candidate because he made a campaign statement that he intended, if elected, to serve at a salary less than that "fixed by law." The state claimed that such statements violated a statute prohibiting candidates from offering material benefits to voters in consideration for their votes, but the Court held that the statute could not constitutionally be applied in such circumstances; the promise hardly fitted into the category of a private, politically corrupt arrangement. The state can prohibit bribes, but it

ers, 413 U.S. 548, 93 S.Ct. 2880, 37 L.Ed.2d 796 (1973); Broadrick v. Oklahoma, 413 U.S. 601, 93 S.Ct. 2908, 37 L.Ed.2d 830 (1973); Keyishian v. Board of Regents, 385 U.S. 589, 605–06, 87 S.Ct. 675, 684–85, 17 L.Ed.2d 629 (1967); Pickering v. Board of Education, 391 U.S. 563, 88 S.Ct. 1731, 20 L.Ed.2d 811 (1968).

3. Buckley v. Valeo, 424 U.S. 1, 96 S.Ct. 612, 46 L.Ed.2d 659 (1976) (per curiam), mandate conformed 532 F.2d 187 (D.C.Cir. 1976).

4. 456 U.S. 45, 102 S.Ct. 1523, 71 L.Ed.2d 732 (1982). In this case, the Kentucky Corrupt Practices Act prohibited a candidate from making an expenditure, loan, or promise as to action to be taken when elected, in consideration for a vote or support of any person. Carl Brown, a candidate for the office of County Commissioner, promised the voters in a press conference that if elected he would lower his salary $3,000 per year. Because the salary had been "fixed by law" the Kentucky Court of Appeals held that the Corrupt Practices Act prohibited Brown's promise. Since Brown had been elected the state court declared the election void and found that free speech guarantees were inapplicable. After the press conference Brown retracted his pledge when he discovered that it might be illegal. Instead he promised to seek corrective legislation. The Kentucky appellate court found that the retraction was irrelevant.

The U.S. Supreme Court readily agreed that the state could prohibit bribes or agreements to buy votes. While there might be some borderline cases between such corrupt arrangements and normal, open, candidate promises (e.g., to lower taxes, to provide some group with public services), this case lies far from the border. Brown's promise, even though if it could

not legally be kept, was not a private, politically corrupt arrangement. Brown's "generalized" commitment "scarcely contemplated a particularized acceptance;" it "was conditioned not on any particular vote or votes, but entirely on the *majority's* vote." 456 U.S. at 58, 102 S.Ct. at 1531 (emphasis in original). A "candidate's promise to confer some ultimate benefit on the voter, *qua* taxpayer, citizen, or member of the general public, does not lie beyond the pale of the First Amendment protection." 456 U.S. at 58–59, 102 S.Ct. at 1531. Nor does the state's fear that voters might make an ill-advised choice provide any compelling justification for such a limitation on speech.

Finally, even the state's interest in protecting voters from falsehoods did not offer any compelling justification for the law. Under the state law the candidate's liability for error is absolute: "His election victory must be voided even if the offending statement was made in good faith and was quickly repudiated. The chilling effect of such absolute accountability for factual misstatements in the course of political debate is incompatible with the atmosphere of free discussion contemplated by the First Amendment in the context of political campaigns. Although the state interest in protecting the political process from distortions caused by untrue and inaccurate speech is somewhat different from the state interest in protecting individuals from defamatory falsehoods, the principles underlying the First Amendment remain paramount.... In a political campaign, a candidate's factual blunder is unlikely to escape the notice of, and correction by, the erring candidate's political opponent. The preferred First Amendment remedy [is] 'more speech, not enforced silence'...." 456 U.S. at 61, 102 S.Ct. at 1533. The

cannot constitutionally prohibit open promises made to voters generally.

§ 20.51 Regulation of Campaign Financing

(a) Introduction

Due to the disclosures concerning the scandals in financing surrounding recent elections as well as concern for the possible effects upon democratic government of the spiraling costs of election campaigns, Congress enacted the Federal Election Campaign Act of 1971 and added more stringent amendments with the Federal Election Campaign Act Amendments of 1974.[1] These statutes involved the federal government in the regulation of much of the day-to-day operation of political campaigns for federal office. There are four primary regulations: (1) regulating the amounts contributed to or expended by the candidate or his campaign committee; (2) forbidding "dirty tricks" by creating penalties for the "fraudulent misrepresentation of campaign authority"; (3) requiring public disclosure of contributions to and expenditures by a candidate, his campaign committee or individual expenditures on behalf of a candidate; (4) providing for public financing of all phases of presidential elections.

The Supreme Court heard a comprehensive challenge to this statute in *Buckley v. Valeo,*[2] in which significant first amendment issues were raised relating to central provisions of the Act. Distinguishing between the speech interest inherent in campaign contributions and campaign expenditures, the Court, per curiam, upheld the limitations imposed on contributions, but invalidated those related to expenditures. The disclosure and reporting requirements were sustained as necessary for the enforcement of the Act.[3]

state, in short, offered no compelling justification for its restriction on free speech.

§ 20.51

1. Federal Election Campaign Act of 1971, Pub.L. No. 92–225, 86 Stat. 3, as amended by Federal Election Campaign Act Amendments of 1974, Pub.L. No. 93–443, 88 Stat. 1263.

2. 424 U.S. 1, 96 S.Ct. 612, 46 L.Ed.2d 659 (1976) (per curiam), mandate conformed 532 F.2d 187 (D.C.Cir.1976).

Blum, The Divisible First Amendment: A Critical Functionalist Approach to Freedom of Speech and Electoral Campaign Spending, 58 N.Y.U.L.Rev. 1273 (1983); Nicholson, Buckley v. Valeo: The Constitutionality of the Federal Election Campaign Act of 1974, 1977 Wisc.L.Rev. 323; Polsby, Buckley v. Valeo: The Special Nature of Political Speech, 1976 Sup.Ct.Rev. 1;

Wright, Politics and the Constitution: Is Money Speech, 85 Yale L.J. 1001 (1976); Clagett & Bolton, Buckley v. Valeo, Its Aftermath and Its Prospects, 29 Vanderbilt L.Rev. 1327 (1976); Federal Campaign Financing—New Approaches, 39 Record of the Association of the Bar of the City of N.Y. 501 (1984); BeVier, Money and Politics: A Perspective on the First Amendment and Campaign Finance Reform, 73 Calif.L.Rev. 1045 (1985). Gottlieb, Fleshing Out the Right of Association: The Problem of the Contribution Limits of the Federal Election Campaign Act, 49 Alb. L.Rev. 825 (1985); Stephen E. Gottlieb, Election Reform and Democratic Objectives—Match or Mismatch, 9 Yale L. & Policy Rev. (1991).

3. In holdings unrelated to first amendment considerations, the Court invalidated the provisions of the Act creating a Feder-

Initially, it is important to note the underlying rationale for the result in *Buckley*. Employing Justice White's observation, the Court has granted constitutional recognition to the maxim "money talks,"[4] for the opinion rests on the foundation that campaign contributions and expenditures are speech or are so intrinsically related to speech that any regulation of such funding must be constrained by the prohibitions of the first amendment.[5]

(b) Campaign Contributions and Expenditures

The primary importance of the *Buckley* decision lies in the Court's distinction between campaign contributions and expenditures.[6]

Contributions. The Court found that the speech interests in campaign contributions are marginal, because they convey only an undifferentiated expression of support rather than the specific values which motivate that support.[7] Such a tangential relationship to first amendment values cannot be successfully balanced against the primary purpose and effect of the limitation on those contributions—a reduction in the probability of corruption and the concomitant reduction in the appearance of corruption. Because the limitations imposed on *contributions* do not have a substantial effect on the ability of a candidate to obtain funding (they require only that a broader base of contributors be drawn upon rather than lessening the total funds used), such contribution limitations were within the power of the legislature to control.[8]

Buckley grants to the legislature a power to limit large contributions to a *candidate* because of the perception of undue influence flowing from such contributions. "To the extent that large contributions are given to secure a political *quid pro quo* from current and potential office holders, the integrity of our system of representative democracy is undermined."[9] But *Buckley* does not support limitations on contributions to committees to favor or oppose *issues* such as ballot

al Election Commission appointed by the Congress; public financing of campaigns was upheld as a legitimate exercise of the taxing and spending power.

4. 424 U.S. at 262, 96 S.Ct. at 747 (White, J. concurring in part and dissenting in part).

5. 424 U.S. at 18–23, 96 S.Ct. at 634–37 (per curiam). Cf. United States v. O'Brien, 391 U.S. 367, 88 S.Ct. 1673, 20 L.Ed.2d 672 (1968), rehearing denied 393 U.S. 900, 89 S.Ct. 63, 21 L.Ed.2d 188 (1968); Tinker v. Des Moines Independent Community School District, 393 U.S. 503, 89 S.Ct. 733, 21 L.Ed.2d 731 (1969); West Virginia State Bd. of Education v. Barnette, 319 U.S. 624, 63 S.Ct. 1178, 87 L.Ed. 1628 (1943); Stromberg v. California, 283 U.S. 359, 51 S.Ct. 532, 75 L.Ed. 1117 (1931).

6. Congress had defined contributions to include not only funds given directly to the campaign, but also money spent in support of a candidate which was within the candidate's control and coordination.

7. 424 U.S. at 19, 20, 96 S.Ct. at 634, 635.

8. 424 U.S. at 21–22, 96 S.Ct. at 635–36.

See generally, BeVier, Money and Politics: A Perspective on the First Amendment and Campaign Finance Reform, 73 Calif.L.Rev. 1045 (1985). Gottlieb, Fleshing Out the Right of Association: The Problem of the Contribution Limits of the Federal Election Campaign Act, 49 Alb. L.Rev. 825 (1985).

9. Buckley v. Valeo, 424 U.S. 1, 26–27, 96 S.Ct. 612, 638, 46 L.Ed.2d 659 (1976) (per

measures.[10] Thus, in *Citizens Against Rent Control/Coalition for Fair Housing v. Berkeley*[11] the Court invalidated a city ordinance that limited to $250 contributions committees formed to support or oppose ballot measures submitted to popular vote. The committees accepted the contributions to advance their views on the ballot measures. The Court explained that it violated the freedom of association to place any limit on persons wishing to band together to make known their views on ballot measures while placing none on persons acting alone. The Court added:

> Whatever may be the state interest or degree of that interest in regulating and limiting contributions to or expenditures of a candidate to a candidate's committees there is no significant state or public interest in curtailing debate and discussion of a ballot measure. Placing limits on contributions which in turn limit expenditures plainly impairs freedom of expression.[12]

Expenditures. The *Buckley* Court also ruled that *expenditures* for candidates, as directly related to the expression of political views, are on a higher plane of constitutional values; thus justifications for such legislative intrusion into protected speech require a more exacting scrutiny.

> A restriction on the amount of money a person or group can spend on political communication during a campaign necessarily reduces the quantity of expression by restricting the number of issues discussed, the depth of their exploration, and the size of the audience reached. This is because virtually every means of communicating in today's mass society requires the expenditure of money.[13]

The effectiveness of such limitations to reduce corruption diminishes as the value of the communication increases. Because there exists little relationship between the campaign expenditures in bulk and the corruptive influence upon the electoral process, particularly in light of the limitations on the amount an individual may contribute, the Court held that the amount of money an individual can spend to advocate either his own candidacy or that of another is a matter within his own discretion.

Nor could expenditure limitations be saved by the ancillary justification of limiting the escalating costs of political campaigns, thus increasing the possibilities for those candidates less able to attract

---

curiam), mandate conformed 532 F.2d 187 (D.C.Cir.1976).

10. Cf. First National Bank v. Bellotti, 435 U.S. 765, 98 S.Ct. 1407, 55 L.Ed.2d 707 (1978), rehearing denied 438 U.S. 907, 98 S.Ct. 3126, 57 L.Ed.2d 1150 (1978), holding that a state may not constitutionally prohibit corporations from making contributions or expenditures advocating views on ballot measures, on issues.

11. 454 U.S. 290, 102 S.Ct. 434, 70 L.Ed.2d 492 (1981).

12. 454 U.S. at 300, 102 S.Ct. at 439.

13. 424 U.S. at 19, 96 S.Ct. at 634–35 (footnote omitted).

massive amounts of capital. Such a justification necessarily implies that the regulation must impinge upon the operation of the political marketplace by restricting the effectiveness of a candidate's most salable commodity, his appeal to the voters, to the benefit of those whose attraction is less. If money talks, more money talks louder, and more effectively. Just as the Government cannot still some voices in order to enhance the persuasiveness of others, it cannot still political expenditures.

The Court found nothing "invidious, improper, or unhealthy" [14] in allowing a political campaign to turn on the ability of a candidate to attract a broad base of financial support, because the law limiting the amount of contributions allowed served to reduce or eliminate the possibility that *quid pro quos* would be offered for large contributions.

The Political Speech of Commercial and Other Entities. In *First National Bank v. Bellotti,*[15] the Court, in a five to four decision, found unconstitutional a Massachusetts law which prohibited corporate expenditures for the purpose of influencing the vote on any referendum submitted to the voters other than one materially affecting the property, business, or assets of the corporation. The statute was applied to corporations which had sought to spend money to publicize their view in opposition to a proposed progressive income tax on corporations.

The majority first rejected the argument that corporate speech is protected only when it pertains directly to the corporation's business interests. No precedent supported this arbitrary distinction. Then the Court considered the question of whether the state statute, which restricted corporate speech, could "survive the exacting scrutiny necessitated by a state-imposed restriction on freedom of expression." [16] Measured by this test, the state did not show a compelling, subordinating interest.

There was no showing that corporate participation would exert an undue influence on the outcome of a referendum. More importantly, "the fact that advocacy may persuade the electorate is hardly a reason to suppress it." [17] Finally, the purpose of allegedly protecting corporate

14. 424 U.S. at 44, 96 S.Ct. at 646–47.

15. 435 U.S. 765, 98 S.Ct. 1407, 55 L.Ed.2d 707 (1978), rehearing denied 438 U.S. 907, 98 S.Ct. 3126, 57 L.Ed.2d 1150 (1978).

See generally, Lowenstein, Campaign Spending and Ballot Propositions: Recent Experience, Public Choice Theory and the First Amendment, 29 U.C.L.A.L.Rev. 505 (1982), for a thorough empirical study.

See also, Wright, Money and the Pollution of Politics: Is the First Amendment an Obstacle to Political Equality, 82 Colum.L.Rev. 609 (1982) (attacking both

Buckley and *Bellotti*); Note, Regulation of Campaign Contributions: Maintaining the Integrity of the Political Process Through an Appearance of Fairness, 56 So.Calif.L.Rev. 669 (1983), discussing limitations on contributions to local officials responsible for single issues, e.g., land use decisions affecting land developers. Ribstein, Corporate Political Speech, 49 Washington & Lee L.Rev. 109 (1992).

See also § 20.31, supra.

16. 435 U.S. at 786, 98 S.Ct. at 1421.

17. 435 U.S. at 790, 98 S.Ct. at 1423.

shareholders was contradicted by the over- and under-inclusiveness of the statute. Thus, the statute did not prohibit the use of corporate funds for lobbying nor allow the prohibited expenditures if all the shareholders would unanimously authorize the spending.

The dissent noted that the majority holding calls into question federal law barring corporate contributions to political campaigns.[18] However the Court distinguished corporate contributions to referenda from corporate contributions to political candidates on the grounds that the latter raises more clearly problems of corruption through the creation of political debt. The government has an important interest in regulating such corruption.

The majority also emphasized that laws prohibiting corporate gifts to candidates were not before the Court, and that "Congress might well be able to demonstrate the existence of a danger of real or apparent corruption in independent expenditures by corporations to influence candidate elections."[19] Nonetheless, *Bellotti*, in connection with the *Buckley* decision,[20] raised questions about the constitutionality of federal limitations on corporate political expenditures. The two situations should be contrasted.

Bellotti involved a complete suppression of corporate political speech, and that speech related to a political issue; it did not involve giving a corporate campaign contribution to a political candidate. In other cases the Court has distinguished between funds accumulated in the economic marketplace versus funds accumulated in the political marketplace. Congress thus may protect an individual (who invests in a commercial, corporate enterprise) so that the commercial enterprise does not use those funds (invested for economic gain) for political candidates that the investor does not support.[21] The moneys that a commercial enterprise collects from investors does not reflect the investors' support for the political ideas favored by the corporation's management. "Direct corporate spending on political activity raises the prospect that resources amassed in the economic marketplace may

---

18. 435 U.S. at 811, 98 S.Ct. at 1434 (White, J., dissenting, joined by Brennan and Marshall, JJ.). Justice Rehnquist filed a separate dissent.

19. 435 U.S. at 788 n. 20, 98 S.Ct. at 422 n. 20.

20. Buckley v. Valeo, 424 U.S. 1, 96 S.Ct. 612, 46 L.Ed.2d 659 (1976) (per curiam), mandate conformed in 532 F.2d 187 (D.C.Cir.1976).

21. See, Pipefitters Local Union No. 562 v. United States, 407 U.S. 385, 414–15, 92 S.Ct. 2247, 2264, 33 L.Ed.2d 11 (1972);

Federal Election Commission v. National Right to Work Committee, 459 U.S. 197, 208, 103 S.Ct. 552, 559, 74 L.Ed.2d 364 (1984), on remand 716 F.2d 1401 (D.C.Cir. 1983).

Congress, historically, has had broad authority to regulate political activities by commercial corporations. See, United States v. International Union, United Automobile, Aircraft and Agr. Implement Workers of America, 352 U.S. 567, 570–84, 77 S.Ct. 529, 530–37, 1 L.Ed.2d 563 (1957), rehearing denied 353 U.S. 943, 77 S.Ct. 808, 1 L.Ed.2d 763 (1957).

be used to provide an unfair advantage in the political marketplace." [22] Thus, it should be proper for Congress to require commercial corporations that make expenditures "in connection with any election to any public office" to finance those expenditures by "voluntary" contributions to a separate, segregated fund, although such a requirement would be unconstitutional as applied to voluntary political associations that happen to be incorporated but that cannot engage in business activities, have no shareholders on others who have a claim on its assets or earnings, and are not a conduit for a business corporation or a union. [23]

In *California Medical Association v. Federal Election Commission,* [24] a fragmented Court rejected new challenges to the Federal Election Campaign Act of 1971. The California Medical Association (CMA), an unincorporated association of doctors, formed a political committee, the California Medical Political Action Committee (CALPAC), which was registered with the Federal Election Commission. The Federal Election Commission charged CMA with making contributions in excess of $5000 to CALPAC and also charged CALPAC with knowingly accepting such contributions in violation of the Act, which prohibits individuals and unincorporated associations from contributing more than $5000 per year to any multicandidate political committee such as CALPAC. The Act similarly prohibits political committees such as CALPAC from knowingly accepting contributions in excess of this limit.

The Court formed a majority on this issue, and ruled that, although a corporation or labor union's contributions to a segregated political fund are unlimited under the Act, the limitation on the unincorporated association's contributions did not violate the equal protection aspects of the fifth amendment. "Appellants' claim of unfair treatment ignores the plain fact that the statute as a whole imposes far *fewer* restrictions on individuals and unincorporated associations than it does on corporations and unions." [25] For example, individuals and unincorporated associations may contribute to candidates, and their committees, and to all other political committees while corporations and unions are absolutely barred from making any such contributions. The different restrictions "reflect a judgment by Congress that these entities have differing structures and purposes, and that they therefore

22. Federal Election Commission v. Massachusetts Citizens for Life, Inc., 479 U.S. 238, 257, 107 S.Ct. 616, 628, 93 L.Ed.2d 539 (1986).

23. Though the Court did say that that particular question is "not before us," its reasoning would allow regulations on commercial enterprises in the corporate form which would be unconstitutional as applied to political organizations which happen to be in the corporate form. Federal Election Commission v. Massachusetts Citizens for Life, Inc., 479 U.S. 238, 259, 107 S.Ct. 616,

629, 93 L.Ed.2d 539 (1986). Government regulation of corporate political activity reflects concern "not about the use of the corporate form *per se,* but about the potential for unfair deployment of wealth for political purposes." 479 U.S. at 258, 107 S.Ct. at 628 (footnote omitted).

24. 453 U.S. 182, 101 S.Ct. 2712, 69 L.Ed.2d 567 (1981).

25. 453 U.S. at 200, 101 S.Ct. at 2724 (emphasis in original).

may require different forms of regulations in order to protect the integrity of the electoral process." [26]

Nor did the law violate the first amendment. Marshall's plurality opinion on this issue, joined by Brennan, White, and Stevens, found that the statute did not limit the amount that CMA or its members may independently spend to advocate political views. Rather the law only limits the amount that CMA may contribute to CALPAC. The analysis in *Buckley v. Valeo* [27] allows this limitation:

> If the First Amendment rights of a contributor are not infringed by limitations on the amount he may contribute to a campaign organization which advocates the views and candidacy of a particular candidate, the rights of a contributor are similarly not impaired by limits on the amount he may give to a multicandidate political committee, such as CALPAC, which advocates the views and candidacies of a number of candidates. [28]

Justice Blackmun, concurred in part and in the judgment. He rejected the contribution-expenditure distinction that gives less protection to contributions; he nonetheless concluded that the contribution limit to multicandidate political committees was valid in order to prevent evasion of the Act's contribution limitations upheld in *Buckley*. He analogized it to the $25,000 limitations on total annual contributions upheld in *Buckley*. [29]

Independent Expenditures by Political Committees. Subsequently, in *Federal Election Commission v. National Conservative Political Action Committee*, [30] the Court, in a five to four opinion, invalidated a section of the Presidential Election Campaign Fund Act which makes it a criminal offense for an *independent* political committee to spend more than $1,000 to further the election of a presidential candidate who elects public funding. In this case the National Conservative Political Action Committee (NCPAC) and the Fund for a Conservative Majority (FCM), two political action committees or PAC's, solicited funds in support of President Reagan's 1980 presidential campaign. They spent these funds on radio and television advertising in support of

26. 453 U.S. at 201, 101 S.Ct. at 2724.

27. 424 U.S. 1; 96 S.Ct. 612, 46 L.Ed.2d 659 (1976) (per curiam), mandate conformed 532 F.2d 187 (D.C.Cir.1976).

28. 453 U.S. at 197, 101 S.Ct. at 2722 (footnote omitted).

See also the unanimous opinion in Federal Election Com'n v. National Right to Work Committee, 459 U.S. 197, 103 S.Ct. 552, 74 L.Ed.2d 364 (1982), on remand 716 F.2d 1401 (D.C.Cir.1983), per Rehnquist, J., holding that a provision of the Federal Election Campaign Act of 1971, 2 U.S.C.A. § 441b(b)(4)(C), is constitutional and does not violate any first amendment associa-

tion rights because of the important interests which Congress has sought to protect. The section provided that a nonstock corporation cannot solicit contributions from persons other than its "members" when the nonstock corporation uses these funds for certain designated political federal election purposes.

29. 453 U.S. at 203, 101 S.Ct. at 2725. Stewart, J., joined by Burger, C.J., and Powell and Rehnquist, JJ., dissented on jurisdictional grounds.

30. 470 U.S. 480, 105 S.Ct. 1459, 84 L.Ed.2d 455 (1985).

President Reagan. These expenditures were "independent"; that is, these political committees did not make any expenditures at the request of, or in coordination with, the Reagan Election Committee.

The Court—relying on *Buckley v. Valeo* and the distinction it drew between expenditures and contributions—held that the political committee's *independent* expenditures were constitutionally protected, for they "produce speech at the core of the First Amendment." [31] The Court then added:

> The PACs in this case, of course, are not lone pamphleteers or street corner orators in the Tom Paine mold; they spend substantial amounts of money in order to communicate their political ideas through sophisticated media advertisements. And of course the criminal sanction in question is applied to the expenditure of money to propagate political views, rather than to the propagation of those views unaccompanied by the expenditure of money. But for purposes of presenting political views in connection with a nationwide Presidential election, allowing the presentation of views while forbidding the expenditure of more than $1,000 to present them is much like allowing a speaker in a public hall to express his views while denying him the use of an amplifying system.[32]

The Court distinguished the *California Medical Association v. Federal Election Commission* [33] decision because that case upheld regulations on *contributions* to political action committees, not regulations on their *expenditures.*

Then the Court (using the same analysis used in *Buckley v. Valeo*) found that no countervailing governmental interest was sufficiently strong enough to justify the limitation on the independent expenditures by political action committees.

However, the Court explicitly did not decide whether it would be constitutional to restrict a *corporation* in making independent expenditures to support or influence elections for public office. The Court invalidated the statute before it because it was not limited in its application just to corporations.[34]

---

31. 470 U.S. at 493, 105 S.Ct. at 1467.

32. 470 U.S. at 493, 105 S.Ct. at 1467.

33. 453 U.S. 182, 101 S.Ct. 2712, 69 L.Ed.2d 567 (1981).

34. The Court also distinguished Federal Election Committee v. National Right to Work Committee (NRWC), 459 U.S. 197, 103 S.Ct. 552, 74 L.Ed.2d 364 (1982), on remand 716 F.2d 1401 (D.C.Cir.1983). The Court said:

"Our decision in FEC v. National Right to Work Committee (*NRWC*), 459 U.S. 197, 103 S.Ct. 552, 74 L.Ed.2d 364

(1982), is not to the contrary. That case turned on the special treatment historically accorded corporations. In return for the special advantages that the State confers on the corporate form, individuals acting jointly through corporations forgo some of the rights they have as individuals. 459 U.S., at 209–210, 103 S.Ct., at 560–561. We held in *NRWC* that a rather intricate provision of the Federal Election Campaign Act dealing with the prohibition of corporate campaign contributions to political candidates did not violate the First Amend-

In *Federal Election Commission v. Massachusetts Citizens for Life, Inc.,* [35] the Court invalidated, *as applied,* Section 441b of title 2, a provision of the Federal Election Campaign Act which prohibits corporations from using treasury funds to make an expenditure "in connection with any election to any public office." [36] The election law requires that such expenditures must be financed, instead, by voluntary contributions to a separate segregated fund. The Massachusetts Citizens for Life, Inc. (MCFL) is a nonprofit, nonstock corporation dedicated to fostering respect for human life, "born and unborn." It raises money through garage sales, raffles, etc., and receives voluntary donations from interested people but does not accept contributions from business corporations or unions.

The Federal Election Commission claimed that the MCFL violated Section 441b when it used its corporate funds to widely distribute a "Special Election Edition" newsletter distributed prior to the September 1978 primary elections. This newsletter urged people to support pro-life candidates and listed the candidates' views on MCFL legislation.

ment. The prohibition excepted corporate solicitation of contributions to a segregated fund established for the purpose of contributing to candidates, but in turn limited such solicitations to stockholders or members of a corporation without capital stock. We upheld *this limitation on solicitation of contributions* as applied to the National Right to Work Committee, a corporation without capital stock, in view of the well-established constitutional validity of legislative regulation of corporate contributions to candidates for public office. *NRWC* is consistent with this Court's earlier holding that a corporation's *expenditures* to propagate its views on issues of general public interest are of a different constitutional stature than corporate *contributions* to candidates. First National Bank of Boston v. Bellotti, 435 U.S. 765, 789–790, 98 S.Ct. 1407, 1422–1423, 55 L.Ed.2d 707 (1978)."

470 U.S. at 495, 105 S.Ct. at 1468 (emphasis added).

Note that the Court did not emphasize the distinction between the statute in the instant case, which limited expenditures and was invalidated, and the law in the *NRWC* case, which regulated contributions and was upheld. Rather, the Court seemed to focus on the corporate form, a distinction which appears metaphysical to say the least. Apparently the point of this focus on the corporate form is that the Court wished to leave open the question of whether it is constitutional for the Government to restrict a corporation in making independent expenditures to support particular candidates for public office. The Court explained:

"In *Bellotti*, of course, we did not reach, nor do we need to reach in this case, the question whether a corporation can constitutionally be restricted in making independent expenditures to influence elections for public office. 435 U.S., at 788, n. 26, 98 S.Ct., at 1422, n. 26.

"Like the National Right to Work Committee, NCPAC and FCM are also formally incorporated; however, this is not a 'corporations' case because § 9012(f) applies not just to corporations but to any 'committee, association, or organization (whether or not incorporated)' that accepts contributions or makes expenditures in connection with electoral campaigns. The terms of § 9012(f)'s prohibition apply equally to an informal neighborhood group that solicits contributions and spends money on a Presidential election as to the wealthy and professionally managed PAC's involved in this case."

470 U.S. at 495, 105 S.Ct. at 1468.

35. 479 U.S. 238, 107 S.Ct. 616, 93 L.Ed.2d 539 (1986).

36. Fed. Election Campaign Act § 316, 2 U.S.C.A. § 441b.

Justice Brennan, for the Court, explained that direct "corporate spending on political activity raises the prospect that resources amassed in the economic marketplace may be used to provide an unfair advantage in the political marketplace." [37]   Relying on *Federal Election Commission v. National Conservative Political Action Committee*,[38] the Court agreed that normally it was constitutional for Congress "to restrict 'the influence of political war chests funneled through the corporate form ...'." [39]   While the relative availability of funds is a rough barometer of support, the resources in the treasury of a *business* corporation "are not an indication of popular support for the corporation's political ideas." [40]   Thus, Section 441b requires that the corporation establish political committees in order to engage in campaign spending.   But MCFL is not a *business* corporation.   "Groups such as MCFL, however, do not pose that danger of corruption.   MCFL was formed to disseminate political ideas, not to amass capital." [41]

MCFL has three features which the Courts said are essential to the holding that it may not constitutionally be bound by Section 441b. First, MCFL was formed for the express purpose of promoting political ideas and cannot engage in business activities.   Second, it has no shareholders who have a claim to its assets.   Third, MCFL was not established by a business corporation or labor union and accepts no contributions from such entities so it will not be their conduit.[42]   Thus, section 441b was unconstitutional as applied to MCFL, a noncommercial enterprise.   Such noncommercial corporations (which are more like voluntary political associations) should not have to bear the independent spending limitations imposed solely because they happen to be incorporated.   The Government may regulate commercial corporations because of concern over unfair deployment of economic wealth for political purposes; but noncommercial enterprises like MCFL, which merely use the corporate form, cannot be so regulated.[43]

---

37.   479 U.S. at 257, 107 S.Ct. at 628.

38.   470 U.S. 480, 501, 105 S.Ct. 1459, 1471, 84 L.Ed.2d 455 (1985).

39.   479 U.S. at 256, 107 S.Ct. at 627.

40.   479 U.S. at 257, 107 S.Ct. at 628.

41.   479 U.S. at 257, 107 S.Ct. at 628. See also, Federal Election Commission v. National Right to Work Committee, 459 U.S. 197, 204, 209–10, 103 S.Ct. 552, 557, 560, 74 L.Ed.2d 364 (1982), on remand 716 F.2d 1401 (D.C.Cir.1983); Pipefitters Local Union No. 562 v. United States, 407 U.S. 385, 416, 92 S.Ct. 2247, 2264, 33 L.Ed.2d 11 (1972).

The Court did say that the particular question is "not before us," but its reasoning would allow regulations on commercial enterprises in the corporate form that would be unconstitutional as applied to

political organizations that simply happen to be in the corporate form.   Federal Election Commission v. Massachusetts Citizens for Life, Inc., 479 U.S. 238, 260, 107 S.Ct. 616, 629, 93 L.Ed.2d 539 (1986).   The majority reasoned that government regulation of corporate political activity reflects concern "not about the use of the corporate form *per se*, but about the potential for unfair deployment of wealth for political purposes."   479 U.S. at 259, 107 S.Ct. at 628 (footnote omitted).

42.   479 U.S. at 265, 107 S.Ct. at 631.

43.   However, even in the case of commercial corporate political activity, the state cannot impose "complete foreclosure of any opportunity for political speech...."   479 U.S. at 259 n. 12, 107 S.Ct. at 628 n. 12, citing First Nat. Bank of

Austin. In *Austin v. Michigan Chamber of Commerce* [44] the Court (six to three) upheld provisions of the Michigan Campaign Finance Act that prohibits corporations—excluding media corporations—from using corporate treasury funds for independent expenditures in support of, or in opposition to, any candidate in elections for state office. The law, however, did allow corporations to make expenditures from segregated funds used solely for political purposes. The law in question however, did not regulate independent expenditures of media corporations or unincorporated labor unions.

The Michigan State Chamber of Commerce challenged the law. The Chamber's bylaws provide that it is a nonprofit corporation with both political and nonpolitical purposes. It funds its activities through annual dues from its members, three-quarters of whom are for-profit corporations. The Chamber wanted to run an advertisement, in a local newspaper, in support of a particular candidate for state office. It sought to enjoin the Michigan statute as unconstitutional but the Court upheld the provision, reversing the Court of Appeals.

The Chamber, said the Court, is not a voluntary political association like *Massachusetts Citizens for Life (MCFL)*. *MCFL*'s narrow focus on promoting particular political ideas served to assure that its resources reflected its political support. It was formed for an express political purpose and could not engage in any business activities. *MCFL*, unlike the Chamber, also had no shareholders or other persons with a claim on its assets or earnings. If any of *MCFL*'s members disagreed with its political activities, they could disassociate themselves without suffering any economic disincentive. In contrast, many of the Chamber's activities are "politically neutral" and focus on economic and business issues; it provides its members with, for example, group insurance and educational seminars. While the Chamber also has no shareholders, its members have economic disincentives that discourage them from disassociating themselves with the Chamber; the members, for example, might wish to enjoy the Chamber's nonpolitical programs and the contacts with the other members of the business community acquired through membership in the Chamber.

Unlike the Chamber, *MCFL* took no contributions from business corporations. The Chamber, in contrast, receives three-quarters of its contributions from for-profit corporations, who (by paying dues to the Chamber) would be able to circumvent the state restrictions on cam-

Boston v. Bellotti, 435 U.S. 765, 98 S.Ct. 1407, 55 L.Ed.2d 707 (1978), rehearing denied 438 U.S. 907, 98 S.Ct. 3126, 57 L.Ed.2d 1150 (1978).

44. 494 U.S. 652, 110 S.Ct. 1391, 108 L.Ed.2d 652 (1990), on remand 937 F.2d 608 (6th Cir.1991). Marshall, J., was joined by Rehnquist, C.J., and Brennan, White, Blackmun, & Stevens, JJ. Brennan, J. and

Stevens, J. also filed concurring opinions. Scalia, J., filed a dissenting opinion. Kennedy, J., also filed a dissenting opinion in which O'Connor & Scalia, JJ. joined.

Eule, Promoting Speaker Diversity: Austin and Metro Broadcasting, 1990 Supreme Ct.Rev. 105 (1990); Ribstein, Corporate Political Speech, 49 Washington & Lee L.Rev. 109 (1992).

paign contributions and expenditures. *Buckley v. Valeo* allows the state to regulate the campaign contributions and expenditures of these for-profit corporations. Thus for-profit business corporations could use the Chamber as a conduit.

The Court also concluded that the state's decision to regulate only corporations—not unincorporated labor unions, and not media corporations, such as broadcasting stations, newspapers, magazines, or other commentary in the "regular course of publication or broadcasting"—did not violate the equal protection clause of the Fourteenth Amendment. Michigan's decision to regulate only non-media corporations is "precisely tailored to serve the compelling state interest of eliminating from the political process the corrosive effect of political 'war chests' amassed with the aid of the legal advantages given to corporations." [45]

Justice Scalia issued a strong dissent, calling the majority's opinion "Orwellian." What Michigan has done, and what the Court has endorsed, said Scalia, is to restrict speech on the ground that too much speech is an evil. It was as if the state had said: "Attention all citizens. To assure the fairness of elections by preventing disproportionate expression of the view of any single powerful group, your Government has decided that the following associations of persons shall be prohibited from speaking in support of any candidate: ___." [46]

Justice Scalia also noted that the Court only concluded that Michigan's exemption for media corporations was constitutional.[47] The Court did not compel the state to grant the exemption. But, said Scalia, Michigan might change its mind and forbid newspapers or other media corporations from making candidate endorsements. Michigan might decide that media corporations should be regulated: "Amassed corporate wealth that regularly sits astride the ordinary channels of information is much more likely to produce the New Corruption (too much of one point of view) than amassed corporate wealth that is busy making money elsewhere." [48]

However, the issue before the Court in *Austin* was only the constitutionality of the state's ban on corporations making independent expenditures in connection with state candidate elections. The Court upheld the ban. The law did not prohibit corporations from endorsing candidates, only from making independent expenditures on their behalf. If a newspaper published an editorial in favor of a candidate, the marginal cost to the newspaper in publishing that editorial would be zero, for if the newspaper did not publish the editorial on one subject, it

---

45. 494 U.S. at 666, 110 S.Ct. at 1401.

46. 494 U.S. at 679, 110 S.Ct. at 1408 (Scalia, J., dissenting).

47. See, Marshall, J., for the Court, 494 U.S. at 668, 110 S.Ct. at 1402: "Although the press' unique societal role may not entitle the press to greater protection un-

der the Constitution, it does provide a compelling reason for the State to exempt media corporations from the scope of political expenditure limitations."

48. 494 U.S. at 691, 110 S.Ct. at 1414 (Scalia, J., dissenting).

would publish it on another. Consequently, the fact that the *Austin* majority approved the state law at issue in that case offers no support for a state law that would purport to ban newspapers from writing editorials endorsing or opposing candidates. In other words, *Austin* does not suggest that a state could restrict newspapers from endorsing candidates.

Justice Kennedy also dissented. He objected to two forms of censorship: first, Michigan's content-based law makes it a crime for a nonprofit corporate speaker to endorse or oppose a candidate for Michigan public office; and second, the "value-laden, content-based" speech suppression that allows some nonprofit corporations to engage in political speech but not others.[49]

(c) Disclosure and Reporting Requirements

The statutes challenged in *Buckley*,[50] also required the campaign committees to disclose a list of their contributors as well as requiring individual contributors to report contributions to a candidate or expenditures in support of a candidate.[51] In the only previous case challenging the disclosure of campaign finances, decided in 1934, the Court had upheld the requirement over claims that such a disclosure impaired the individuals' right of association.[52] Following that decision, the Court recognized that compelled disclosure of membership lists may constitute a restraint upon the associational rights of the members, because there may often exist an interest in maintaining the privacy of such associations.[53]

In *NAACP v. Alabama*,[54] the Court had also denied the State the right to compel the disclosure of the NAACP's members for the purpose of ferreting out subversives within the association. Such an interest was only tenuously related to the request and was overborne by the

49. 494 U.S. at 695–96, 110 S.Ct. at 1416 (Kennedy, J., dissenting, joined by O'Connor & Scalia, JJ.)

50. Buckley v. Valeo, 424 U.S. 1, 96 S.Ct. 612, 46 L.Ed.2d 659 (1976) (per curiam), mandate conformed 532 F.2d 187 (D.C.Cir.1976).

51. 2 U.S.C.A. § 431 et seq.

52. Burroughs and Cannon v. United States, 290 U.S. 534, 54 S.Ct. 287, 78 L.Ed. 484 (1934).

53. E.g., United States v. Rumely, 345 U.S. 41, 73 S.Ct. 543, 97 L.Ed. 770 (1953); NAACP v. Alabama, 357 U.S. 449, 78 S.Ct. 1163, 2 L.Ed.2d 1488 (1958), on remand 268 Ala. 531, 109 So.2d 138 (1959), judgment reversed 360 U.S. 240, 79 S.Ct. 1001, 3 L.Ed.2d 1205 (1959) (per curiam), rehearing denied 361 U.S. 856, 80 S.Ct. 43, 4 L.Ed.2d

96 (1959); Bates v. Little Rock, 361 U.S. 516, 80 S.Ct. 412, 4 L.Ed.2d 480 (1960); Talley v. California, 362 U.S. 60, 80 S.Ct. 536, 4 L.Ed.2d 559 (1960); Louisiana ex rel. Gremillion v. NAACP, 366 U.S. 293, 81 S.Ct. 1333, 6 L.Ed.2d 301 (1961); Gibson v. Florida Legislative Investigation Committee, 372 U.S. 539, 83 S.Ct. 889, 9 L.Ed.2d 929 (1963), mandate conformed 153 So.2d 301 (Fla.1963); DeGregory v. Attorney General of New Hampshire, 383 U.S. 825, 86 S.Ct. 1148, 16 L.Ed.2d 292 (1966).

54. 357 U.S. 449, 78 S.Ct. 1163, 2 L.Ed.2d 1488 (1958), on remand 268 Ala. 531, 109 So.2d 138 (1959), judgment reversed 360 U.S. 240, 79 S.Ct. 1001, 3 L.Ed.2d 1205 (1959) (per curiam), rehearing denied 361 U.S. 856, 80 S.Ct. 43, 4 L.Ed.2d 96 (1959); see also Talley v. California, 362 U.S. 60, 80 S.Ct. 536, 4 L.Ed.2d 559 (1960).

fears of the members that they would be subject to harassment and intimidation if their associational ties were made public, regardless of the presence of any subversive connection.

The appellant in *Buckley* relied on this case as precedent to argue that such disclosure in campaign financing would violate those interests in private political associations. The *Buckley* Court distinguished *NAACP v. Alabama*[55] because, unlike that case, the countervailing interests of the state, to be served by such disclosure—providing information in order to allow the voter a more informed judgment as to the candidates future performance in office; deterring corruption by providing notice that contributions and expenditures would be exposed; and establishing machinery for the enforcement of the Act—were directly related to the purposes in requiring the disclosure.[56]

Moreover, the Court emphasized that there had been no showing in *Buckley* that potential contributors were deterred by fear of humiliation or public ridicule if their identities were linked to a particular candidate.[57] Although such fears were not unreasonable when related to the funding of minority parties, there also existed no evidence that legitimate associational activity would necessarily be dampened in all minority parties by disclosure. Therefore, only if a party could show a reasonable probability that compelled disclosure of the list of its contributors—or the recipients of campaign disbursements—would subject those contributors or recipients to threats, harassment, or reprisals from either government officials or private parties, an exemption from the disclosure provisions for that organization will be granted.[58] The creation of a blanket exemption, for all minority parties, irrespective of the inherent administrative difficulties, was simply not shown to be necessary to protect the individual member's rights of association.[59]

55. 357 U.S. 449, 78 S.Ct. 1163, 2 L.Ed.2d 1488 (1958), on remand 268 Ala. 531, 109 So.2d 138 (1959), judgment reversed 360 U.S. 240, 79 S.Ct. 1001, 3 L.Ed.2d 1205 (1959), rehearing denied 361 U.S. 856, 80 S.Ct. 43, 4 L.Ed.2d 96 (1959).

56. 424 U.S. at 66, 67, 96 S.Ct. at 657, 658.

57. 424 U.S. at 72–73, 96 S.Ct. at 660–61.

58. 424 U.S. at 74, 96 S.Ct. at 661. *Buckley* actually referred only to "a party's contributors' names ..." but in a later case the Court made clear that the *Buckley* dictum sets forth the correct test to determine when the first amendment protects minor parties from compelled disclosure and that test applies not only to contributors but also to the recipients of campaign

disbursements. Brown v. Socialist Workers '74 Campaign Committee, 459 U.S. 87, 103 S.Ct. 416, 74 L.Ed.2d 250 (1982) (holding that an Ohio statute was unconstitutional as applied to the Socialist Workers Party, given the evidence of threats, harassment, and reprisals).

For an analysis of these issues, see Stone & Marshall, Brown v. Socialist Workers: Inequality as a Command of the First Amendment, 1983 Sup.Ct.Rev. 583.

59. See also, Citizens Against Rent Control/Coalition for Fair Housing v. Berkeley, 454 U.S. 290, 300–01, 102 S.Ct. 434, 439, 70 L.Ed.2d 492 (1981), holding that the state could protect public integrity simply by identifying contributors in a public filing revealing the amounts contributed; the legislators can even outlaw anonymous contributions.

§ 20.52   Regulation of Political Activity of Government Employees

The Court has on several occasions held that a governmental interest in fair and effective operation of the federal government justified regulation of partisan political activities of government employees.[1] The statute in question in both cases was § 9(a) of the Hatch Act[2] which forbids government employees from taking "an active part in political management or political campaigns. All such persons shall retain the right to vote as they may choose and to express their opinions on all political subjects."

In *United States Civil Service Commission v. National Association of Letter Carriers*,[3] the Court reaffirmed its 26 year old holding in *United Public Workers v. Mitchell*[4] that such restrictions upon public employment were valid, since they served an overriding state interest which only restricts certain methods of political expression, and does not deny governmental employees the right to hold political views or express those views outside the context of a political campaign.

The Court has recognized that the government's interest in regulating the speech and conduct of its employees differs from its interest in such regulation of general citizens for several reasons.[5] First, government employees by virtue of their position exert a great deal of influence as the growth of government increasingly affects the daily life of private citizens. To allow that employee to reap political dividends by virtue of his employment demeans the government and induces disrespect for its functionaries.[6] Second, political participation by public employees may threaten the effective operation of government. It is essential that employees implement the will of Congress, unswayed by the directives of a political party.[7]

The prohibitions on political activity also serve the related concern of insuring that government employees are not required to engage in partisan political support in order to retain their positions, not only so that governmental employees avoid engaging in "political justice" but also that they "appear to the public to be avoiding it. . . ."[8] Because

---

§ 20.52

1. United Public Workers v. Mitchell, 330 U.S. 75, 67 S.Ct. 556, 91 L.Ed. 754 (1947) and United States Civil Service Com'n v. National Ass'n of Letter Carriers, 413 U.S. 548, 93 S.Ct. 2880, 37 L.Ed.2d 796 (1973); see also Broadrick v. Oklahoma, 413 U.S. 601, 93 S.Ct. 2908, 37 L.Ed.2d 830 (1973) applying the same principles to a state restriction on political activities of public employees.

2. 5 U.S.C.A. § 7324. See United States Civil Service Com'n v. National Ass'n of Letter Carriers, 413 U.S. 548, 560–61, 93 S.Ct. 2880, 2887–88, 37 L.Ed.2d 796 (1973).

3. 413 U.S. 548, 93 S.Ct. 2880, 37 L.Ed.2d 796 (1973).

4. 330 U.S. 75, 67 S.Ct. 556, 91 L.Ed. 754 (1947).

5. See Pickering v. Board of Education, 391 U.S. 563, 88 S.Ct. 1731, 20 L.Ed.2d 811 (1968).

6. 413 U.S. at 565, 93 S.Ct. at 2890.

7. Id.

8. 413 U.S. at 565, 93 S.Ct. at 2890.

the interest of the employee in the right to political association is not dampened, but only his right to participate in political campaigns, the overwhelming governmental interest must prevail.

Thus, in *Letter Carriers* the Court held that federal employees can be prevented from engaging in "plainly identifiable acts of political management and political campaigning" [9] such as holding a party office, working at the polls, acting as a party paymaster for other party workers, organizing a political party or club, actively participating in fund-raising activities for a partisan candidate, becoming a partisan candidate or campaigning for an elective political office, initiating or circulating a partisan nominating petition, soliciting votes for a partisan candidate for political office, or serving as a delegate to a political party convention.[10]

Union Rules and Public and Private Criticism on Matters of Public Concern by Government Employees. Governmental interests in regulating the controversial speech of its employees are not boundless. Rather, the regulations must be narrowly drawn to serve the objectives of effective government without intruding unnecessarily into the private associations and beliefs of its employees. As the Court noted in *Pickering v. Board of Education*,[11]

> The problem in any case is to arrive at a balance between the interests of the [employee], as a citizen, in commenting upon matters of public concern and the interest of the [government], as an employer in promoting the efficiency of the public services it performs through its employees.[12]

Thus the Board of Education was prohibited from firing a teacher who wrote and published in a newspaper a letter criticizing the Board's budgetary policies and public information methods.

9. 413 U.S. at 567, 93 S.Ct. at 2891.

10. 413 U.S. at 554–67, 93 S.Ct. at 2885–91.

See also, Clements v. Fashing, 457 U.S. 957, 102 S.Ct. 2836, 73 L.Ed.2d 508 (1982), rehearing denied 458 U.S. 1133, 103 S.Ct. 20, 73 L.Ed.2d 1404 (1982), on remand 689 F.2d 593 (5th Cir.1982). The Court found no first amendment defect in two provisions of the Texas Constitution. The first, § 19, insofar as it was before the Court, prohibited state judges from being eligible to serve in the Texas legislature until the judge had completed his term of judicial office. The second, § 65, provided that holders of certain state and county offices, if they become candidates for any other state or federal office, automatically resigned their positions unless the unexpired portion of their current terms were less than one year. Neither provision violated the first amendment (nor also the equal protection clause). First, state interests justified the *de minimis* interference with one's interest in candidacy. Second, "§ 19 and § 65 are in reality no different than the provisions we upheld in" *Letter Carriers* and similar cases. "Appellees are *elected* state officeholders who contest restrictions on partisan political activity. Section 19 and § 65 represent a far more limited restriction on political activity than this Court has upheld with regard to civil *servants*." 457 U.S. at 971–73, 102 S.Ct. at 2848 (emphasis in original).

11. 391 U.S. 563, 88 S.Ct. 1731, 20 L.Ed.2d 811 (1968).

12. 391 U.S. at 568, 88 S.Ct. at 1734–35.

As to those charges by the teacher which were substantially correct, they were also matters of "public concern" and presented no issues of faculty discipline or harmony; hence they did not justify dismissal. The charges which were false were also concerned with issues of public concern and similarly were not shown to have interfered with the teacher's job or with the school's general operation.   In the absence of the scienter required in *New York Times Co. v. Sullivan* [13] of a knowing or reckless falsehood, the Board could not fire the teacher from his public employment.

Similarly, in *Elrod v. Burns,* [14] the Court struck down a system of political patronage in determining eligibility for government employment.   Such a program delved into beliefs and associations of the employees without a significant countervailing interest.

Givhan v. Western Line Consolidated School District [15] made clear that the first amendment protection of public employees is not limited by any requirement that the speech must be public, when the statements involve matters of public concern.[16]   The Court explained that no

13. 376 U.S. 254, 84 S.Ct. 710, 11 L.Ed.2d 686 (1964), motion denied 376 U.S. 967, 84 S.Ct. 1130, 12 L.Ed.2d 83 (1964).

14. 427 U.S. 347, 96 S.Ct. 2673, 49 L.Ed.2d 547 (1976), appeal after remand 757 F.2d 151 (7th Cir.1985).   Accord, Branti v. Finkel, 445 U.S. 507, 100 S.Ct. 1287, 63 L.Ed.2d 574 (1980).

15. 439 U.S. 410, 99 S.Ct. 693, 58 L.Ed.2d 619 (1979), on remand 592 F.2d 280 (5th Cir.1979), appeal after remand 691 F.2d 766 (1982).

16. See also, Givhan v. Western Line Consolidated School District, 439 U.S. 410, 99 S.Ct. 693, 58 L.Ed.2d 619 (1979), on remand 592 F.2d 280 (5th Cir.1979), appeal after remand 691 F.2d 766 (1982) where the Court unanimously held that the teacher could not be discharged for privately communicating her grievances about allegedly racially discriminatory policies or her opinion concerning other public issues, to her employer.   The opinion reaffirmed the principle established in *Mt. Healthy* that when an employee has shown that constitutionally protected conduct played a role in the government's decision not to retain him or her in their job that the employer is required to and entitled to demonstrate "by a preponderance of the evidence that it would have reached the same decision as to [the employee's] reemployment even in the absence of the protected conduct."   439 U.S. at 416, 99 S.Ct. at 697, quoting Mt. Healthy City School Bd. of Education v. Doyle, 429 U.S. 274,

287, 97 S.Ct. 568, 576, 50 L.Ed.2d 471 (1977), appeal after remand 670 F.2d 59 (6th Cir.1982).

In *Givhan* the statements were a matter of public concern: the school's district's allegedly racially discriminatory policies were the subject of the conversation.

Contrast Connick v. Myers, 461 U.S. 138, 103 S.Ct. 1684, 75 L.Ed.2d 708 (1983) where the Court, in a five to four decision, upheld the firing of an assistant district attorney for circulating a questionnaire regarding office policies; the questionnaire did not touch upon matters of public concern.   A federal court is not the appropriate forum to review the wisdom of such personnel decisions.   The employer need not tolerate action which he reasonably believes would disrupt the office, undermine his authority, and destroy close working relationships.

Note, Connick v. Myers: New Restrictions on the Free Speech Rights of Government Employees, 60 Indiana L.J. 339 (1985).

See generally, Finkin, Intramural Speech, Academic Freedom, and the First Amendment, 66 Texas L.Rev. 1323 (1988).

In Rankin v. McPherson, 483 U.S. 378, 107 S.Ct. 2891, 97 L.Ed.2d 315 (1987), rehearing denied 483 U.S. 1056, 108 S.Ct. 31, 97 L.Ed.2d 819 (1987) the Court (5 to 4) held that it was unconstitutional for a constable to fire a data-entry employee for privately remarking to a co-worker (who

first amendment freedom "is lost to the public employee who arranges to communicate privately with his employee rather than to spread his views before the public." [17]

Thus, while *Letter Carriers* indicates that certain modes of actively expressing partisan political belief may be banned in the interest of preserving a non-partisan government work force, *Pickering* and *Burns* establish that political beliefs themselves and their reasonable expression are not subject to the dictates of the government employer. This principle was reaffirmed in *Madison School District v. Wisconsin Employment Relations Committee,*[18] where the Court held that the state employment commission could not bar a public school board from allowing a teacher to address it at a public meeting; the teacher addressed the board on pending labor negotiations and the employment commission had sought to bar this speech because the teacher was not a union representative and in fact was not even a union member. However the meeting was *public,* and *public participation* was generally permitted.

Although the state cannot punish a public employee because of his associations or because he speaks freely, the state has no obligation to listen, to recognize the association, and bargain with it. Thus, *Smith v. Arkansas State Highway Employees, Local 1315*[19] held that a state

happened to be her boyfriend), after hearing of an attempt on President Reagan's life, "If they go for him again, I hope they get him." The Court, per Marshall, J., held that the statement constituted "a matter of public concern" and was protected by the first amendment. (In contrast, an actual threat to kill the President would not be protected, the Court said.) It is irrelevant that the statement made was inappropriate and controversial, the majority said. In this case the constable did not demonstrate that the state's interest justified firing the data-entry employee: she had purely clerical duties; she had no law enforcement duties; the statement was made privately in a room not readily accessible to the public; and there was no evidence that the employee's statement had discredited her office or interfered with its efficient functioning.

In Rowland v. Mad River Local School District, 730 F.2d 444 (6th Cir.1984), certiorari denied 470 U.S. 1009, 105 S.Ct. 1373, 84 L.Ed.2d 392 (1985), rehearing denied 471 U.S. 1062, 105 S.Ct. 2127, 85 L.Ed.2d 491 (1985), the Court of Appeals ruled that the decision to discharge a bisexual non-tenured high school guidance counselor based on her workplace statements about her bisexuality was permissible under the first amendment because the guidance counselor's speech was not about "a matter of public concern." 730 F.2d at 451. In dissenting from the denial of certiorari, Justice Brennan, joined by Justice Marshall, did not accept this ruling or the Sixth Circuit's reliance on *Connick* because, first, the speech did touch a matter of public concern, and second, the speech—even if private speech—did not interfere with the employer's business.

Cf. National Gay Task Force v. Board of Education, 729 F.2d 1270 (10th Cir.1984) (portion of statute which permits teacher to be discharged for engaging in "public homosexual activity" is valid, but portion of statute which provides punishment for mere advocacy of homosexual activities is overbroad) (per curiam) (Powell, J., did not participate), affirmed by an equally divided Court, 470 U.S. 903, 105 S.Ct. 1858, 84 L.Ed.2d 776 (1985).

17. 439 U.S. at 415, 99 S.Ct. at 696–97.

18. 429 U.S. 167, 97 S.Ct. 421, 50 L.Ed.2d 376 (1976).

19. 441 U.S. 463, 99 S.Ct. 1826, 60 L.Ed.2d 360 (1979) (per curiam). Accord, Babbitt v. United Farm Workers Nat. Union, 442 U.S. 289, 99 S.Ct. 2301, 60 L.Ed.2d 895 (1979).

agency can refuse to consider or act upon grievances when filed by the union rather than by the employee directly.

The converse is also true. If the state does recognize a union as an exclusive representative, the state has no first amendment obligation to confer with its public employees who are not members of the bargaining unit. In *Minnesota State Board for Community Colleges v. Knight*[20] a state law provided that if a particular group of professional employees had formed an appropriate bargaining unit and selected an exclusive representative for mandatory bargaining, then the public employer must meet only with that exclusive representative when engaging in an "official exchange" of views on policy questions which relate to employment, but which are *outside* the scope of mandatory bargaining. The Court majority opinion phrased the issue in the case as: "whether this restriction on participation in the nonmandatory-subject exchange process violates the constitutional rights of professional employees within the bargaining unit who are not members of the exclusive representative and who may disagree with his views."[21] Justice O'Connor, writing for the majority, upheld the law, for she found that there was no constitutional right to "participate directly in government policy making" and that these special "meet and confer" sessions could be restricted to those persons with whom the government wished to communicate.

In the particular case, the Minnesota statute had the effect of excluding nonunion teachers from participating in these "meet and confer" sessions in which educational policy issues were discussed. However, all faculty members would be free to attempt to communicate their views on educational policy issues to educational administrators; they were only excluded from participating in these "meet and confer" sessions.[22] These "meet and confer" sessions did not constitute any type of first amendment public forum.[23]

Thus there are no significant constitutional restraints when the government sets up special purpose meetings to receive in a structured way the views of its employees. "It is doubtless true that the unique status of the exclusive representative in the 'meet and confer' process amplifies its voice in the policymaking process. But that amplification no more impairs individual instructors' constitutional freedom to speak than the amplification of individual voices impaired the union freedom to speak in *Smith v. Arkansas State Highway Employees, Local 1315*."[24]

20. 465 U.S. 271, 104 S.Ct. 1058, 79 L.Ed.2d 299 (1984). See also, Bi–Metallic Investment Co. v. State Board of Equalization, 239 U.S. 441, 445, 36 S.Ct. 141, 142, 60 L.Ed. 372 (1915).

21. 465 U.S. at 273, 104 S.Ct. at 1060, 79 L.Ed.2d at 305.

22. 465 U.S. at 277 & n. 3, 104 S.Ct. at 1062 & n. 3, 79 L.Ed.2d at 307 & n. 3.

23. "A 'meet and confer' session is obviously not a public forum." 465 U.S. at 280, 104 S.Ct. at 1064, 79 L.Ed.2d at 309.

24. 465 U.S. at 288, 104 S.Ct. at 1068, 79 L.Ed.2d at 314, citing Smith v. Arkansas State Highway Employees, Local 1315, 441

However it is significant that the nonunion teachers in *Knight* still had the complete freedom to communicate their views on policy issues; they simply had no constitutional right to attend a private, special purpose "meet and confer" meeting.[25]

XVI. ASSEMBLY AND PETITION

§ 20.53 Introduction

The Magna Carta. When King John signed the Magna Carta in 1215, he established a base to which our modern right of petition for redress of grievances can, to some extent, be traced. The right to petition the Crown for redress of grievances originally given to both houses of the English Parliament, and to Commons in particular, was gradually taken over by the House of Commons. As Commons became more important, petitions for redress grievances began to be directed to it, instead of the Crown. The right to petition the House of Commons, as an extension of the original Magna Carta provision was later guaranteed to every commoner.[1]

John Quincy Adams and Petitioning the Government. The last clause of the first amendment provides: "Congress shall make no law ... abridging ... the right of the people peaceably to assemble and to petition the Government for a redress of grievances." The first clear test under this clause took place in 1836.

The United States House of Representatives, having found itself inundated with abolitionist petitions, adopted in 1836 a gag rule that limited acceptance of those petitions. The rule had the effect of tabling, without discussion, petitions concerned with slavery or the abolition of slavery received by the House of Representatives. John Quincy Adams of Massachusetts, who had opposed adoption of the gag rule as a direct violation of the Constitution of the United States, was even more strongly opposed when the House strengthened of that rule in 1840 in order to prohibit the receipt of any petition on the subject of slavery. The former President was finally successful in obtaining repeal of the rule in 1844, when the strength of antislavery views in the

U.S. 463, 99 S.Ct. 1826, 60 L.Ed.2d 360 (1979) (per curiam).

25. 465 U.S. at 277 & n. 3, 104 S.Ct. at 1062 & n. 3, 79 L.Ed.2d at 307 & n. 3.

§ 20.53

1. C. Stephenson & F. Marcham, Sources of English Constitutional History 125 (2d ed. 1972).

In the 1790's, Parliament forbade public meetings held in order to petition the King if more than 50 persons were present, unless the meeting was held in the presence of a magistrate with authority to arrest everybody present. Parliament reacted to a gathering of 150,000 people petitioning because of various grievances. I. Brant, The Bill of Rights 245 (1965).

See Sherrard v. Hull, 53 Md.App. 553, 456 A.2d 59, 64 (1983), affirmed 296 Md. 189, 460 A.2d 601 (1983), citing an earlier edition of this treatise.

North intensified.[2]

It was not until 1876 that the first major United States Supreme Court interpretation of the rights of assembly and petition took place in *United States v. Cruikshank*.[3] The majority opinion by Chief Justice Waite narrowly interpreted the right of assembly as an attribute of national citizenship.[4] That is, the Court held that in order to claim the protection of the first amendment, it must have been asserted that a peaceful assembly existed in order to petition the *national* government for redress of a grievance connected with the powers and duties of the national government. It must be alleged that this right had been violated or in some way restricted.[5] Because the defendants in *Cruikshank* had been indicted only in general language of having prevented an assembly for a lawful purpose, the Supreme Court found the indictment insufficient, for the case was only within the domain of the states.[6]

Incorporation Into the Fourteenth Amendment. It was not until *Hague v. C.I.O.*,[7] that protection against state abridgment of the rights of assembly and petition was recognized when the Supreme Court found the first amendment rights applicable to the states through the fourteenth amendment. A majority of the Court used two different lines of reasoning in striking down a Jersey City, New Jersey ordinance.

Justice Roberts, with Chief Justice Hughes and Justice Black concurring, found protection for the right of assembly as a privilege and immunity of a United States citizen, within the meaning of the fourteenth amendment.[8]

The opinion of Justice Stone, with Justice Reed concurring, while agreeing that the ordinance was in violation of the fourteenth amendment, found protection for the right of assembly in the due process clause.[9] The due process viewpoint has prevailed and it is into that

---

2. A.H. Kelly & W.H. Harbison, The American Constitution: Its Origins and Development, 357–58 (4th ed. 1970).

3. United States v. Cruikshank, 92 U.S. (2 Otto) 542, 23 L.Ed. 588 (1876).

The Right to Petition and the Law of Libel. McDonald v. Smith, 472 U.S. 479, 105 S.Ct. 2787, 86 L.Ed.2d 384 (1985) held that the petition clause of the first amendment does not give a defendant in a libel action absolute immunity. The plaintiff had charged defendant with knowingly sending false and libelous letters to President Reagan and others in order to undermine the chances of his being appointed U.S. Attorney. The petition clause does not require state libel law to expand the qualified privilege already afforded by New York Times Co. v. Sullivan, 376 U.S. 254, 84 S.Ct. 710, 11 L.Ed.2d 686 (1964).

See also White v. Nicholls, 44 U.S. (3 How.) 266, 11 L.Ed. 591 (1845).

4. 92 U.S. (2 Otto) at 552, 23 L.Ed. at 591.

5. 92 U.S. (2 Otto) at 553, 23 L.Ed. at 591–92.

6. 92 U.S. (2 Otto) at 552, 23 L.Ed. at 591.

7. 307 U.S. 496, 59 S.Ct. 954, 83 L.Ed. 1423 (1939).

8. 307 U.S. at 512, 59 S.Ct. at 962–63.

9. 307 U.S. at 525, 59 S.Ct. at 968–69.

broad clause that the Supreme Court has breathed an expansive interpretation of civil rights.[10]

In *Schneider v. Smith*,[11] the Supreme Court reaffirmed the importance and central meaning of the rights to peacefully assemble and petition. In striking down regulations dealing with "the reading habits, political philosophy, beliefs, and attitudes on social and economic issues of prospective seamen" on United States merchant vessels,[12] the Court, through Justice Douglas, explained:

> The purpose of the Constitution and Bill of Rights, unlike more recent models promoting a welfare state, was to take government off the backs of the people. The First Amendment's ban against Congress "abridging" freedom of speech, the right peaceably to assemble and to petition, and the "associational freedom" ... that goes with those rights create a preserve where the views of the individual are made inviolate. This is the philosophy of Jefferson, that "the opinions of men are not the object of civil government, nor under its jurisdiction...." [13]

Later cases indicate that it is not significant whether one is engaged in speech, association, assembly, or petition. All four rights are now considered to be elements of a broad right to freedom of expression.[14] Nonetheless, some specific cases particularly related to assembly and petition are worthy of mention.

§ 20.54 The Basic Legal Principles

The first amendment allows a peaceful gathering of persons for almost any lawful purpose.[1] The Supreme Court had early recognized that it could not be made a crime to participate in a peaceful assembly.[2] Thus, participation in a Communist Party political meeting cannot be a

---

10. E.g., De Jonge v. Oregon, 299 U.S. 353, 364, 57 S.Ct. 255, 259–60, 81 L.Ed. 278 (1937); Thomas v. Collins, 323 U.S. 516, 532, 65 S.Ct. 315, 323–24, 89 L.Ed. 430 (1945), rehearing denied 323 U.S. 819, 65 S.Ct. 557, 89 L.Ed. 650 (1945); Douglas v. Jeannette, 319 U.S. 157, 162, 63 S.Ct. 877, 880, 87 L.Ed. 1324 (1943); Shelton v. Tucker, 364 U.S. 479, 493, 81 S.Ct. 247, 254–55, 5 L.Ed.2d 231 (1960).

11. 390 U.S. 17, 88 S.Ct. 682, 19 L.Ed.2d 799 (1968).

12. 390 U.S. at 24, 88 S.Ct. at 686.

13. 390 U.S. at 25, 88 S.Ct. at 687. (footnote omitted).

14. E.g., De Jonge v. Oregon, 299 U.S. 353, 364, 57 S.Ct. 255, 259–60, 81 L.Ed. 278 (1937); Thomas v. Collins, 323 U.S. 516, 65 S.Ct. 315, 89 L.Ed. 430 (1945), rehearing denied 323 U.S. 819, 65 S.Ct. 557, 89 L.Ed.

650 (1945); Schneider v. Smith, 390 U.S. 17, 88 S.Ct. 682, 19 L.Ed.2d 799 (1968); United Mine Workers v. Illinois State Bar Ass'n, 389 U.S. 217, 88 S.Ct. 353, 19 L.Ed.2d 426 (1967).

§ 20.54

1. Griswold v. Connecticut, 381 U.S. 479, 482, 85 S.Ct. 1678, 1680–81, 14 L.Ed.2d 510 (1965). But cf. Jones v. North Carolina Prisoners' Labor Union, Inc., 433 U.S. 119, 97 S.Ct. 2532, 53 L.Ed.2d 629 (1977) where the Court upheld prison regulations which made more difficult the organizing efforts of a prisoners' union. The restrictive environment of a penal institution was emphasized. While the prison authorities had forbade union solicitation, the union itself was allowed.

2. De Jonge v. Oregon, 299 U.S. 353, 57 S.Ct. 255, 81 L.Ed. 278 (1937).

crime unless violence is advocated,[3] and under the broad category of civil rights, assembly for marches, demonstrations, and picketing have been protected as lawful assemblages.[4] Labor organizing meetings have also been found lawful exercises of the first amendment right of assembly.[5]

Anonymous Membership. Implicit in the right of assembly is the right of association which is implied from the expressly listed rights concerning free expression in the first amendment. Association is more than the right to attend a meeting: "it includes the right to express one's attitudes or philosophies by membership in a group, or affiliation with it or by other lawful means."[6] The Supreme Court, in *Bates v. Little Rock*,[7] recognized that a corollary of this right is the right of an association to conceal from the state the names of the individual members if it is likely that a deprivation of the personal liberty of the individuals would result which was not balanced by the state demonstrating a "controlling justification" for the information.[8]

Securing Legal Advice and Suing. The right to petition the government for redress of grievances has been before the Supreme Court in civil suits against state and federal governmental units. One group of these cases involve the efforts of several different groups and associations to refer their members to lawyers after having first advised their members of their legal rights.[9] The Court upheld that practice

---

3. 299 U.S. at 363–65, 57 S.Ct. at 259–60.

4. Hague v. CIO, 307 U.S. 496, 59 S.Ct. 954, 83 L.Ed. 1423 (1939).

5. Thomas v. Collins, 323 U.S. 516, 65 S.Ct. 315, 89 L.Ed. 430 (1945), rehearing denied 323 U.S. 819, 65 S.Ct. 557, 89 L.Ed. 650 (1945).

6. Griswold v. Connecticut, 381 U.S. 479, 483, 85 S.Ct. 1678, 1681, 14 L.Ed.2d 510 (1965); see also Bates v. Little Rock, 361 U.S. 516, 523, 80 S.Ct. 412, 416–17, 4 L.Ed.2d 480 (1960).

7. 361 U.S. 516, 80 S.Ct. 412, 4 L.Ed.2d 480 (1960); see also, NAACP v. Alabama, 357 U.S. 449, 78 S.Ct. 1163, 2 L.Ed.2d 1488 (1958), on remand 268 Ala. 531, 109 So.2d 138 (1959), judgment reversed 360 U.S. 240, 79 S.Ct. 1001, 3 L.Ed.2d 1205 (1959), rehearing denied 361 U.S. 856, 80 S.Ct. 43, 4 L.Ed.2d 96 (1959); Shelton v. Tucker, 364 U.S. 479, 81 S.Ct. 247, 5 L.Ed.2d 231 (1960).

8. 361 U.S. at 527, 80 S.Ct. at 418–19.

See also, Brown v. Socialist Workers '74 Campaign Committee, 459 U.S. 87, 103 S.Ct. 416, 74 L.Ed.2d 250 (1982), holding that certain disclosure requirements of the Ohio Expense Reporting Law cannot constitutionally be applied to the Socialist Workers Party, a minor political party which historically both government officials and private parties have harassed. The Court applied the test of Buckley v. Valeo, 424 U.S. 1, 74, 96 S.Ct. 612, 661, 46 L.Ed.2d 659 (1976) (per curiam), mandate conformed 532 F.2d 187 (D.C.Cir.1976), that the state cannot compel such disclosures from minor parties which can demonstrate a "reasonable probability" that such disclosures will subject those identified to "threats, harassment, or reprisals."

9. United Transp. Union v. State Bar of Michigan, 401 U.S. 576, 91 S.Ct. 1076, 28 L.Ed.2d 339 (1971); United Mine Workers v. Illinois State Bar Ass'n, 389 U.S. 217, 88 S.Ct. 353, 19 L.Ed.2d 426 (1967); Brotherhood of R.R. Trainmen v. Virginia, 377 U.S. 1, 84 S.Ct. 1113, 12 L.Ed.2d 89 (1964), rehearing denied 377 U.S. 960, 84 S.Ct. 1625, 12 L.Ed.2d 505 (1964), on remand 207 Va. 182, 149 S.E.2d 265 (1966), certiorari denied 385 U.S. 1027, 87 S.Ct. 754, 17 L.Ed.2d 675 (1967); NAACP v. Button, 371 U.S. 415, 83 S.Ct. 328, 9 L.Ed.2d 405 (1963). See also Ohralik v. State Bar, 436 U.S. 447, 98 S.Ct. 1912, 56 L.Ed.2d 444 (1978); In re Primus, 436 U.S. 412, 98 S.Ct. 1893, 56 L.Ed.2d 417 (1978).

based in part on the first amendment right of every person to petition for redress of grievances. In many situations, litigation is the only practical method open to a minority for redress of their grievances.[10] As to the union workers, the Court recognized a similar broad justification. The Court has found that a "common thread" of cases in this area is that "collective activity undertaken to obtain meaningful access to the courts is a fundamental right within the protection of the First Amendment." [11]

The Court has also held that the right is not limited solely to religious or political causes, but is applicable to any field of human endeavor including business or other economic activity.[12] Thus in the context of labor unions, a state statute cannot require labor union organizers to register with a state official before urging workers to join a union, for such a statute imposes a prior restraint on free speech and free assembly.[13]

Prohibitions on the Use of Paid Personnel to Circulate Initiative Petitions. In *Meyer v. Grant*,[14] the Court invalidated, pursuant to the first amendment, a Colorado statute that made it a crime to pay persons to circulate initiative petitions. The petition circulators sought to collect enough qualified signatures in order to have the initiative placed on the ballot. The Court rejected the state's argument that

10. 371 U.S. at 429–30, 83 S.Ct. at 335–36.

11. 401 U.S. at 585, 91 S.Ct. at 1082.

In Walters v. National Association of Radiation Survivors, 473 U.S. 305, 105 S.Ct. 3180, 87 L.Ed.2d 220 (1985), on remand 111 F.R.D. 595 (N.D.Cal.1986), the Court, in a six to three vote, upheld the constitutionality of 38 U.S.C.A. § 3404(c), which limits to only $10 the fee which may be paid to an attorney or agent who represents a claimant seeking Veterans Administration benefits for a service-connected death or disability. The Court held that the veterans suffered no due process violation because the Court gave "great weight" to the governmental interest in administering benefits in an informal, nonadversarial way, so that the claimant could receive the award without dividing it with the attorney. "It would take an extraordinarily strong showing of probability of error under the present system—and the probability that the presence of attorneys would sharply diminish that possibility—to warrant a holding that the fee limitation denies claimants due process of law."

Then the Court turned to first amendment claims of a meaningful right of access to the courts. Given the due process analysis, the first amendment claim had no independent significance. And cases like United Mine Workers v. Illinois State Bar Ass'n, 389 U.S. 217, 88 S.Ct. 353, 19 L.Ed.2d 426 (1967) and Brotherhood of Ry. Trainmen v. Virginia ex rel. Va. State Bar, 377 U.S. 1, 84 S.Ct. 1113, 12 L.Ed.2d 89 (1964) are distinguishable for they involved group efforts to retain or recommend counsel "where counsel were allowed to appear, and the First Amendment interest at stake was primarily the right to associate collectively for the common good." 473 U.S. at 338, 105 S.Ct. at 3198.

12. Thomas v. Collins, 323 U.S. 516, 65 S.Ct. 315, 89 L.Ed. 430 (1945), rehearing denied 323 U.S. 819, 65 S.Ct. 557, 89 L.Ed. 650 (1945).

13. 323 U.S. at 532, 65 S.Ct. at 323–24.

14. 486 U.S. 414, 108 S.Ct. 1886, 100 L.Ed.2d 425 (1988). The Court was unanimous.

See also, Urevich v. Woodard, 667 P.2d 760, 763 (Colo.1983), holding that when a state provides for an initiative, statutes that limit the power of the people to initiate legislation "are to be closely scrutinized and narrowly construed." *Urevich* took judicial notice of the obvious fact that "it is often more difficult to get people to work without compensation than it is to get them to work for pay."

because the initiative is a state-created right, the state could place any restrictions on that right. Indeed, the prohibition of paid circulators "trenches upon an area in which the importance of First Amendment protections is 'at its zenith.' " [15]

The *Noerr–Pennington* Doctrine. The principle called *"The Noerr–Pennington Doctrine,"* after the leading cases,[16] provides that, business interests may combine and lobby to influence the legislative, executive, or judicial branches of government or the administrative agencies without violating the antitrust laws, for such activities are protected by the right of petition.[17]

Even if the result of such activity is the enactment of laws that restrict competition, there is no violation of federal antitrust laws. The Sherman Act does not apply to anticompetitive restraints imposed by states as an act of government. This principle is called *"The Parker Doctrine,"* after the leading case.[18] A private entity, such as a corporation or individual, who obeys a state law that limits competition is not conspiring; one does not "conspire" with the state.

Thus, there is no conspiracy exception to the *Parker* doctrine. Government *regulatory* action is not private action and is therefore not

15. 486 U.S. at 425, 108 S.Ct. at 1894.

16. Eastern R.R. Presidents Conference v. Noerr Motor Freight, Inc., 365 U.S. 127, 81 S.Ct. 523, 5 L.Ed.2d 464 (1961), rehearing denied 365 U.S. 875, 81 S.Ct. 899, 5 L.Ed.2d 864 (1961); United Mine Workers v. Pennington, 381 U.S. 657, 85 S.Ct. 1585, 14 L.Ed.2d 626 (1965), on remand 257 F.Supp. 815 (E.D.Tenn.1966), affirmed in part, reversed in part 400 F.2d 806 (6th Cir.1968), certiorari denied 393 U.S. 983, 89 S.Ct. 450, 21 L.Ed.2d 444 (1968), rehearing denied 393 U.S. 1045, 89 S.Ct. 616, 21 L.Ed.2d 599 (1969); California Motor Transport Co. v. Trucking Unlimited, 404 U.S. 508, 92 S.Ct. 609, 30 L.Ed.2d 642 (1972).

Allied Tube & Conduit Corp. v. Indian Head, Inc., 486 U.S. 492, 108 S.Ct. 1931, 100 L.Ed.2d 497 (1988). In this case the Court holds that the efforts to influence the product standard-setting process of a private association is not immune from antitrust liability under the *Noerr–Pennington* Doctrine even though the standards are then routinely incorporated into state and local statutes.

See generally, Fische, Antitrust Liability for Attempts to Influence Government Action: The Basis and Limits of the *Noerr–Pennington* Doctrine, 45 U.Chi.L.Rev. 80 (1977). See also, Kennedy, Political Boycotts, the Sherman Act, and the First

Amendment: An Accommodation of Competing Interests, 55 So.Calif.L.Rev. 983 (1982) (arguing that political boycotts can be regulated by the Sherman Act without violating the first amendment); Note, The Misapplication of the *Noerr–Pennington* Doctrine in Non-Antitrust Right to Petition Cases, 36 Stand.L.Rev. 1243 (1984); Hurwitz, Abuse of Governmental Processes, the First Amendment, and the Boundaries of *Noerr*, 74 Georgetown L.J. 65 (1985); Note, A Standard for Tailoring Noerr–Pennington Immunity More Closely to the First Amendment Mandate, 95 Yale L.J. 832 (1986).

17. California Motor Transport Co. v. Trucking Unlimited, 404 U.S. 508, 92 S.Ct. 609, 30 L.Ed.2d 642 (1972).

Cf. Citizens Against Rent Control/Coalition for Fair Housing v. Berkeley, 454 U.S. 290, 294, 102 S.Ct. 434, 436, 70 L.Ed.2d 492 (1981): "[T]he practice of persons sharing common views banding together to achieve a common end is deeply embedded in the American political process. The 18th-century Committees of Correspondence and the pamphleteers were early examples of this phenomena and the Federalist Papers were perhaps the most significant and lasting example."

18. Parker v. Brown, 317 U.S. 341, 352, 63 S.Ct. 307, 314, 87 L.Ed. 315 (1943).

subject to antitrust liability, even if the regulatory action was taken pursuant to a conspiracy between the governmental unit and private parties. Public officials often agree to do what one or another group of private citizens urge them to do. There is no loss of *Parker* immunity even if the governmental action in question was the result of bribery or some other violation of state or federal law.[19]

If the action complained of is that of the State itself, the action is exempt from antitrust liability regardless of the State's motives in taking the action.[20] To the extent that the Sherman Act "sets up a code of ethics at all, it is a code that condemns trade restraints, not political activity." [21]

Sham Actions. Just as there is no conspiracy exception to the *Parker* doctrine, there is no conspiracy exception to the *Noerr–Pennington* doctrine. The *Parker* doctrine does not subject the states' act of governing to the federal antitrust laws, and the *Noerr–Pennington* doctrine does not subject the citizenry to the antitrust laws when they participate in government.

The "sham" exception to the *Noerr–Pennington* doctrine covers cases where persons use the process of government itself, rather than the outcome of that process, to reduce competition. Thus, if an individual files frivolous objections to a competitor's license applications, not in a good faith effort to defeat the license application, but merely in an effort to impose added expense and delay, there is a misuse of the process of government.[22] But there is no violation of the antitrust laws simply because an outdoor advertising company lobbied city officials to enact zoning ordinances that would restrict additional billboard construction.[23]

This immunity from antitrust liability also does not extend to litigation which is merely a "sham." "Sham" litigation is somewhat similar to abuse of process.[24] The line between protected and unpro-

---

19. City of Columbia v. Omni Outdoor Advertising, Inc., 499 U.S. ___, 111 S.Ct. 1344, 113 L.Ed.2d 382 (1991).

See, Elhauge, The Scope of Antitrust Process, 104 Harv.L.Rev. 667, 704–05 (1991).

20. Hoover v. Ronwin, 466 U.S. 558, 579–80, 104 S.Ct. 1989, 2001, 80 L.Ed.2d 590 (1984), rehearing denied 467 U.S. 1268, 104 S.Ct. 3564, 82 L.Ed.2d 865 (1984).

21. Eastern Railroad Presidents Conference v. Noerr Motor Freight, Inc., 365 U.S. 127, 140, 81 S.Ct. 523, 531, 5 L.Ed.2d 464 (1961), rehearing denied 365 U.S. 875, 81 S.Ct. 899, 5 L.Ed.2d 864 (1961).

22. California Motor Transport Co. v. Trucking Unlimited, 404 U.S. 508, 92 S.Ct. 609, 30 L.Ed.2d 642 (1972).

23. City of Columbia v. Omni Outdoor Advertising, Inc., 499 U.S. ___, 111 S.Ct. 1344, 113 L.Ed.2d 382 (1991).

24. California Motor Transport Co. v. Trucking Unlimited, 404 U.S. 508, 513, 92 S.Ct. 609, 613, 30 L.Ed.2d 642 (1972):

"One claim, which a court or agency may think baseless, may go unnoticed; but a pattern of baseless, repetitive claims may emerge which leads the factfinder to conclude that the administrative and judicial processes have been abused. That may be a difficult line to discern and draw. But once it is drawn, the case is established that *abuse of those processes* produced an illegal result, *vis.* effectively barring respondents from access to the agencies and courts. Inso-

tected litigation is crossed when the party's purpose is not to win a favorable judgment against a competitor but to harass him, and deter others, by the process itself—regardless of outcome—of litigating.[25] Motive is important, but the motive or scienter that is necessary is the intent to harm merely by instituting litigation, without regard to its outcome

> is *not* sufficient to make litigation … a sham. That anticompetitive motive is the very matter protected under *Noerr–Pennington*. Rather, the prerequisite motive for the sham exception is the intent to harm one's competitors not by the *result* of the litigation but by the simple fact of the *institution* of the litigation.[26]

The right to petition for redress of grievances is a defense to criminal actions brought for violation of various assembly laws.[27] As long as the assembly to petition for redress of grievances is peaceful, and no violence is advocated, it may not be restricted.[28]

However, to say that parties may act in concert in order to persuade the Government to enact a policy that will result in a restraint of trade is not to say that parties may act in concert in order to restrain trade. In other words, the first amendment protects group action seeking to persuade the Government to impose rules that may restrain trade; but the first amendment offers no constitutional protection to parties who engage in a restraint of trade even though they use

far as the administrative or judicial processes are involved, actions of that kind cannot acquire immunity by seeking refuge under the umbrella of 'political expression.' " (emphasis added)
See also, 404 U.S. at 515, 92 S.Ct. at 614:
"First Amendment rights may not be used as the means or the pretext for achieving 'substantive evils' which the legislature has the power to control.... A combination of entrepreneurs to harass and deter their competitors from having 'free and unlimited access' to the agencies and courts, to defeat that right by massive, concerted, and purposeful activities of the group are ways of building up one empire and destroying another."

25. Grip–Pak, Inc. v. Illinois Tool Works, Inc., 694 F.2d 466, 472 (7th Cir. 1982), cert. denied 461 U.S. 958, 103 S.Ct. 2430, 77 L.Ed.2d 1317 (1983).

26. Winterland Concessions Co. v. Trela, 735 F.2d 257, 263–64 (7th Cir.1984), quoting Gainesville v. Florida Power & Light Co., 488 F.Supp. 1258, 1265–66 (S.D.Fla.1980) (emphasis in original).

Cf. ABA, Model Code of Professional Responsibility, D.R. 2–109(A); D.R.

7–102(A)(1)(2); ABA, Model Rules of Professional Conduct, Rule 3.1.

See also, LaSalle National Bank v. DuPage County, 777 F.2d 377 (7th Cir.1985), cert. denied 476 U.S. 1170, 106 S.Ct. 2892, 90 L.Ed.2d 979 (1986).

27. De Jonge v. Oregon, 299 U.S. 353, 57 S.Ct. 255, 81 L.Ed. 278 (1937); Thomas v. Collins, 323 U.S. 516, 65 S.Ct. 315, 89 L.Ed. 430 (1945), rehearing denied 323 U.S. 819, 65 S.Ct. 557, 89 L.Ed. 650 (1945); Edwards v. South Carolina, 372 U.S. 229, 83 S.Ct. 680, 9 L.Ed.2d 697 (1963); Bridges v. California, 314 U.S. 252, 62 S.Ct. 190, 86 L.Ed. 192 (1941).

28. De Jonge v. Oregon, 299 U.S. 353, 364, 57 S.Ct. 255, 259–60, 81 L.Ed. 278 (1937); Thomas v. Collins, 323 U.S. 516, 532, 65 S.Ct. 315, 323–24, 89 L.Ed. 430 (1945), rehearing denied 323 U.S. 819, 65 S.Ct. 557, 89 L.Ed. 650 (1945); Douglas v. Jeannette, 319 U.S. 157, 162, 63 S.Ct. 877, 880, 87 L.Ed. 1324 (1943); Shelton v. Tucker, 364 U.S. 479, 493, 81 S.Ct. 247, 254–55, 5 L.Ed.2d 231 (1960); Edwards v. South Carolina, 372 U.S. 229, 83 S.Ct. 680, 9 L.Ed.2d 697 (1963).

that restraint to obtain favorable legislation. As the Court explained in *F.T.C. v. Superior Court Trial Lawyers Association,*[29] the alleged restraint of trade in *Noerr* was the intended *consequence* of public action; but that does not allow a group to engage in a restraint of trade, such as a boycott, as the *means* to obtain favorable legislation.

In *Superior Court Trial Lawyers Association,* individual lawyers in private practice—not members of a union, not employees of any one employer—engaged in a group boycott. These lawyers, who were often court-appointed counsel for indigents in criminal cases in the District of Columbia Superior Court, believed that their statutory fees in such cases were too low. They agreed to stop providing representation until the District of Columbia Government agreed to increase their compensation, which was then from $20 to $30 per hour. The resulting boycott had a severe impact on the District's criminal justice system. The Court agreed that their group boycott violated section 5 of the Federal Trade Commission Act and that this boycott was not protected under the first amendment.

The *Noerr–Pennington* doctrine does not extend to horizontal boycotts designed to extract higher prices from the Government simply because the members of the boycott, the conspirators, genuinely intend to influence the Government to agree to their terms.[30]

Liability of Member of an Association for the Torts of the Association. Even if violence is advocated, the first amendment rights require that the state may not impose tort liability for business losses caused by violence or the threat of violence, if such conduct occurs in the context of constitutionally protected activity, unless there is "precision of regulation." [31] Thus in *NAACP v. Claiborne Hardware Co.,*[32] the Court, without a single dissent, overturned a Mississippi state court judgment of over one and one quarter million dollars against the NAACP and certain individuals for business losses suffered by several white merchants because of an economic boycott against them. On October 31, 1969, after black citizens in Clairborne County failed to achieve their demands met for racial equality and integration several hundred blacks at a local NAACP meeting voted to boycott white merchants. Although some boycott supporters engaged in acts of

29. 493 U.S. 411, 110 S.Ct. 768, 107 L.Ed.2d 851 (1990), on remand 897 F.2d 1168 (D.C.Cir.1990).

30. Allied Tube & Conduit Corp. v. Indian Head, Inc., 486 U.S. 492, 503, 108 S.Ct. 1931, 1938, 100 L.Ed.2d 497 (1988); F.T.C. v. Superior Court Trial Lawyers Association, 493 U.S. 411, 110 S.Ct. 768, 107 L.Ed.2d 851 (1990), on remand 897 F.2d 1168 (D.C.Cir.1990).

31. 371 U.S. at 438, 83 S.Ct. at 340–41.

32. 458 U.S. 886, 102 S.Ct. 3409, 73 L.Ed.2d 1215 (1982), rehearing denied 459 U.S. 898, 103 S.Ct. 199, 74 L.Ed.2d 160 (1982). Rehnquist, J., concurred in the result, without opinion. Marshall, J., took no part in the consideration or decision of the case.

See generally, Harper, The Consumer's Emerging Right to Boycott: NAACP v. Claiborne Hardware and Its Implications for American Labor Law, 93 Yale L.J. 409 (1984).

violence, most of the practices used to encourage support for the boycott were peaceful, orderly, and protected by the first amendment. All of the marches were carefully controlled.

The Court first held that the state could constitutionally impose liability for "the consequences of violent conduct [but] it may not award compensation for the consequences of nonviolent, protected activity. Only those losses proximately caused by unlawful conduct may be recovered." [33] Nor can a member of a group be liable simply because another member of the same group proximately caused damage by violence:

> Civil liability may not be imposed merely because an individual belonged to a group, some members of which committed acts of violence. For liability to be imposed by reason of association alone, it is necessary to establish that the group itself possessed unlawful goals and that the individual held a specific intent to further those illegal goals.[34]

Thus mere association cannot make one liable, but those persons who actually engaged in violence or other illegal activity can be held liable for the injuries that they caused.[35]

The Court then turned to the NAACP and ruled that the lower court findings were also not adequate to support the judgment against it. "To impose liability without a finding that the NAACP authorized—either actually or apparently—or ratified unlawful conduct would impermissibly burden the rights of political association that are protected by the First Amendment." [36]

---

33. 458 U.S. at 918, 102 S.Ct. at 3429.

34. 458 U.S. at 920, 102 S.Ct. at 3430 (footnote omitted).

35. 458 U.S. at 926–28, 102 S.Ct. at 3433.

Contrast, F.T.C. v. Superior Court Trial Lawyers Association, 493 U.S. 411, 110 S.Ct. 768, 107 L.Ed.2d 851 (1990). The Court applied the antitrust laws to various self-employed individual lawyers (not employees of any employer) in Washington, D.C. These lawyers agreed among themselves not to represent indigent criminal defendants in the Superior Court unless the District increased their compensation. The District eventually responded by raising the Criminal Justice Act rates. Later, the Federal Trade Commission ruled that the lawyers' conduct violated § 5 of the FTC Act, and issued a cease-and-desist order against future such boycotts. The lawyers claimed that their concerted action was protected speech, but the Court held that it was a "plain violation" of the antitrust laws. The *per se* rules against price

fixing and boycotts are justified by administrative convenience and reflect the long-standing judgment that the prohibited practices adversely affect competition.

The Supreme Court ruled that *Claiborne Hardware*, did not immunize this boycott from the antitrust laws. In *Claiborne*, the boycott supporters sought no special advantage for themselves; *Claiborne* does not apply to a boycott conducted by business competitors who "stand to profit financially from a lessening of competition in the boycotted market." In contract, the immediate objective of the respondents in *Superior Court Trial Lawyers Association* was to increase the price that they would be paid for their services.

36. 458 U.S. at 931, 102 S.Ct. at 3435. See also, Douglas, J., dissenting from a dismissal of a writ of certiorari, in NAACP v. Overstreet, 384 U.S. 118, 86 S.Ct. 1306, 16 L.Ed.2d 409 (1966), rehearing denied 384 U.S. 981, 86 S.Ct. 1857, 16 L.Ed.2d 692 (1966). Douglas, J., in his opinion, was

Conspiracy Laws and the *Noerr–Pennington* Doctrine. Protection for the actions of groups or individuals is not unlimited under the first amendment rights of assembly and petition. In several instances, courts have justified limitations on those rights. The initial broad limitation on these rights is that they must be enjoyed in a law abiding manner.[37] Courts have stated that the rights may not be used as a shield to violate valid statutes,[38] nor may they be used as the means or pretext for achieving substantive evil.[39]

Thus the antitrust laws may be applied to groups that conspire to bar competitors from meaningful access to the agencies and the courts.[40] Similarly, a conspiracy with a licensing authority to eliminate a competitor may be prosecuted under the antitrust laws.[41] And of course criminal conspiracy laws deserve no first amendment protection if the conspiracy is to achieve a criminal end in the immediate future rather than merely a combination to advocate ideas (even violent ideas) to promote future change.[42] Correspondingly, there is no free speech protection for sham litigation, that is, litigation designed not to win a favorable judgment but to harass a competitor and deter others by the process of litigation itself, regardless of its outcome.

However, the *Noerr–Pennington* doctrine recognizes that business interests have the first amendment right to combine and lobby to influence the legislative, executive, or judicial branches of government, or the administrative agencies. Such activities do not violate the antitrust laws,[43] and are protected by the right of petition.[44]

joined by Warren, C.J., and Brennan & Fortas, JJ.

37. Cox v. Louisiana, 379 U.S. 559, 85 S.Ct. 476, 13 L.Ed.2d 487 (1965), rehearing denied 380 U.S. 926, 85 S.Ct. 879, 13 L.Ed.2d 814 (1965).

38. California Motor Transport Co. v. Trucking Unlimited, 404 U.S. 508, 92 S.Ct. 609, 30 L.Ed.2d 642 (1972).

39. NAACP v. Button, 371 U.S. 415, 438, 83 S.Ct. 328, 340–41, 9 L.Ed.2d 405 (1963).

40. California Motor Transport Co. v. Trucking Unlimited, 404 U.S. 508, 512, 92 S.Ct. 609, 612–13, 30 L.Ed.2d 642 (1972).

41. Walker Process Equipment, Inc. v. Food Machinery & Chemical Corp., 382 U.S. 172, 175–77, 86 S.Ct. 347, 349–50, 15 L.Ed.2d 247 (1965).

42. Brandenburg v. Ohio, 395 U.S. 444, 89 S.Ct. 1827, 23 L.Ed.2d 430 (1969). See also, NAACP v. Claiborne Hardware Co., 458 U.S. 886, 928–29, 102 S.Ct. 3409, 3434, 73 L.Ed.2d 1215 (1982), rehearing denied 459 U.S. 898, 103 S.Ct. 199, 74 L.Ed.2d 160 (1982).

43. Eastern R.R. Presidents Conference v. Noerr Motor Freight, Inc., 365 U.S. 127, 81 S.Ct. 523, 5 L.Ed.2d 464 (1961), rehearing denied 365 U.S. 875, 81 S.Ct. 899, 5 L.Ed.2d 864 (1961); United Mine Workers v. Pennington, 381 U.S. 657, 85 S.Ct. 1585, 14 L.Ed.2d 626 (1965), on remand 257 F.Supp. 815 (E.D.Tenn.1966), affirmed in part, reversed in part 400 F.2d 806 (6th Cir.1968), certiorari denied 393 U.S. 983, 89 S.Ct. 450, 21 L.Ed.2d 444 (1968), rehearing denied 393 U.S. 1045, 89 S.Ct. 616, 21 L.Ed.2d 599 (1969); California Motor Transport Co. v. Trucking Unlimited, 404 U.S. 508, 92 S.Ct. 609, 30 L.Ed.2d 642 (1972).

44. California Motor Transport Co. v. Trucking Unlimited, 404 U.S. 508, 92 S.Ct. 609, 30 L.Ed.2d 642 (1972).

Cf. Citizens Against Rent Control/Coalition for Fair Housing v. Berkeley, 454 U.S. 290, 294, 102 S.Ct. 434, 436, 70 L.Ed.2d 492 (1981): "[T]he practice of persons sharing common views banding together to achieve a common end is deeply embedded in the American political process. The 18th-century Committees of Correspondence and

In general, when the rights of assembly and petition are limited, the state must demonstrate a compelling interest in an area in which it can otherwise lawfully regulate.[45]

Speech and Assembly Compared. When the government limits the rights of persons to communicate in public, it is most common for courts to examine the governmental action in terms of the freedom of speech rather than the freedom of assembly. Acts of assembly, whether or not for purposes of "petitioning," involve questions of whether the values that underlie the principles developed under the free speech clause will allow restriction of the activity. If the governmental regulation complies with the principles and standards used to determine the freedom of speech, it will also withstand scrutiny under the freedom of assembly clause. If a governmental action regulating speech in public places would violate the freedom of speech, that governmental action might also be stricken as a violation of the freedom of assembly.[46]

In order to determine whether government restrictions of public speech constitute a violation of the freedoms of speech and assembly, one must first determine whether the governmental action is a time, place, or manner regulation, a content based restriction, or a regulation of speech within a limited situation or special context.[47]

Time, Place and Manner Restrictions. When the government seeks to regulate only the time, place, or manner of speech, the courts will seek to ensure that the government is not using the regulation as a device to mask the prohibition of unpopular views and that the government is not unnecessarily restricting the channels of communication. A time, place, or manner regulation will only be upheld as such if it meets a three part test. First, the regulation must be content neutral; it must apply with equal force to all speech or assembly regardless of

the pamphleteers were early examples of this phenomena and the Federalist Papers were perhaps the most significant and lasting example."

45. Williams v. Rhodes, 393 U.S. 23, 31, 89 S.Ct. 5, 10–11, 21 L.Ed.2d 24 (1968); American Party of Texas v. White, 415 U.S. 767, 94 S.Ct. 1296, 39 L.Ed.2d 744 (1974), rehearing denied 416 U.S. 1000, 94 S.Ct. 2414, 40 L.Ed.2d 777 (1974).

Access to the Ballot.

In general, the state does not need to make any particularized showing of voter confusion, ballot crowding, or the presence of frivolous candidates in order to impose reasonable restrictions on access to the ballot. If such were the case, all demonstrated support requirements (e.g., 1% of the voters who had not participated in another party's primary must sign petition in order for minor party to get on the ballot) would

be followed by lengthy litigation. It is reasonable for the state to condition access to the ballot on a showing of a modicum of support. E.g., Anderson v. Celebrezze, 460 U.S. 780, 788–89 n. 9, 103 S.Ct. 1564, 1569–70 n. 9, 75 L.Ed.2d 547 (1983); Munro v. Socialist Workers Party, 479 U.S. 189, 107 S.Ct. 533, 93 L.Ed.2d 499 (1986).

46. Such actions in some circumstances might also be found to be violations of equal protection. See Police Department of Chicago v. Mosley, 408 U.S. 92, 92 S.Ct. 2286, 33 L.Ed.2d 212 (1972); Carey v. Brown, 447 U.S. 455, 100 S.Ct. 2286, 65 L.Ed.2d 263 (1980); and §§ 20.45–20.47, supra.

47. See §§ 20.45–20.47, supra, for a more detailed discussion of these principles.

the message conveyed. Second, the government action must be narrowly tailored to serve a significant government interest. Insubstantial interests will not support the restriction of speech; the government must not unnecessarily burden the ability to communicate. Third, a time, place, or manner regulation must leave open ample alternative channels of communication so that the regulation does not effectively stifle the ability of those who would express the message to bring that message to the attention of the citizenry.[48]

Content Regulation. Government restrictions of speech or assembly based on the content of the message being conveyed in the speech or assembly will be invalid under the first amendment unless the message to be proscribed falls within a category of speech which the Supreme Court has found to be unprotected by the first amendment. Thus, a public speech or assembly which involves incitement to imminent lawless action might be punished, but the government has the burden of showing that the assembly or speech falls within a category of communication unprotected by the first amendment.[49]

Assemblies in Special Situations. The government may sometimes regulate speech or assembly due to the context in which the speech is to take place and the impact of the speech or assembly upon its environment. When the government operates a facility or area that is not traditionally open to the public and, therefore, is not a "public forum," it may limit access to that area or facility to those persons, including would-be speakers, who have business within the restricted area.[50] Thus, the government may prohibit the distribution of leaflets inside a courthouse (which is not a public forum) even though it could not prohibit the distribution of such material on the sidewalks surrounding the courthouse, though the government could enact reasonable time, place, or manner regulation.[51] The government may sometimes be able to restrict speech or assembly near a government facility which itself is not a public forum if the speech or assembly would interfere with the operation of that government facility. Thus, the Court has allowed the government to prohibit demonstrations and assemblies on the grounds surrounding a jail and to prohibit all speech on the sidewalk surrounding a school building that might disturb classes in progress within the school.[52] And it is permissible for the

---

48. See United States v. Grace, 461 U.S. 171, 103 S.Ct. 1702, 75 L.Ed.2d 736 (1983), on remand 717 F.2d 1480 (D.C.Cir.1983). See also §§ 20.45–20.47, supra.

49. See NAACP v. Claiborne Hardware Co., 458 U.S. 886, 102 S.Ct. 3409, 73 L.Ed.2d 1215 (1982), rehearing denied 459 U.S. 898, 103 S.Ct. 199, 74 L.Ed.2d 160 (1982). See also §§ 20.15, 20.40, supra.

50. See Perry Educational Association v. Perry Local Educators' Association, 460

U.S. 37, 103 S.Ct. 948, 74 L.Ed.2d 794 (1983), on remand 705 F.2d 462 (7th Cir. 1983). See also §§ 20.45–20.47, supra.

51. See United States v. Grace, 461 U.S. 171, 178, 103 S.Ct. 1702, 1707–8, 75 L.Ed.2d 736 (1983), on remand 717 F.2d 1480 (D.C.Cir.1983).

52. See Adderley v. Florida, 385 U.S. 39, 87 S.Ct. 242, 17 L.Ed.2d 149 (1966), rehearing denied 385 U.S. 1020, 87 S.Ct. 698, 17 L.Ed.2d 559 (1967); Grayned v. City

government to prohibit demonstrations within a defined area near a courthouse when the purpose of the demonstration or speech was to influence judicial proceedings.[53] The government could not distinguish between speech which was favorable or unfavorable to the government. Nevertheless, the government could restrict speech designed to apply pressure to judges and juries regarding the outcome of litigation. The government must make some demonstration, however, that the speech will interfere with the operation of the facility.[54] Thus, the government could not prohibit the distribution of leaflets around the Supreme Court building when such activity would not interfere with the functioning of the Court.[55]

§ 20.55 The Special Case of Assemblies Related to Labor Disputes

It is sometimes questioned whether the freedoms of speech and assembly apply with equal force to the activities of persons who engage in picketing, leafleting or other public speech relating to labor organization and labor disputes. Although the Supreme Court has allowed both state and federal courts and legislatures to control such activities the Court has attempted to fit its rulings within the previously described principles regarding these first amendment freedoms. Of course, those who picket, distribute literature, or speak in public regarding labor issues are subject to content neutral time, place, and manner restrictions, as would be any other person in a public place.[1]

If a group of workers engages in a strike which is illegal under state or federal law, and they form a picket line or distribute literature outside of an employer's premises with the intent to cause other workers to join in their illegal strike, their activities may be punished

of Rockford, 408 U.S. 104, 92 S.Ct. 2294, 33 L.Ed.2d 222 (1972).

The government may not use an impermissible content based classification which would give a preference to some speech over others when the nature of the speech does not relate to the ability of the government to use the facility for its intended purpose. Police Department of Chicago v. Mosley, 408 U.S. 92, 92 S.Ct. 2286, 33 L.Ed.2d 212 (1972); Carey v. Brown, 447 U.S. 455, 100 S.Ct. 2286, 65 L.Ed.2d 263 (1980).

53. Cox v. Louisiana, 379 U.S. 559, 85 S.Ct. 476, 13 L.Ed.2d 487 (1965), rehearing denied 380 U.S. 926, 85 S.Ct. 879, 13 L.Ed.2d 814 (1965).

54. For a further explanation of the ability of government to regulate speech within a limited context or environment, see Farber and Nowak, The Misleading Nature of Public Forum Analysis: Content

and Context in First Amendment Adjudication, 70 Va.L.Rev. 1219 (1984).

55. See United States v. Grace, 461 U.S. 171, 103 S.Ct. 1702, 75 L.Ed.2d 736 (1983), on remand 717 F.2d 1480 (D.C.Cir.1983).

§ 20.55

1. In United States v. Grace, 461 U.S. 171, 103 S.Ct. 1702, 75 L.Ed.2d 736 (1983), on remand 717 F.2d 1480 (D.C.Cir.1983), the Supreme Court noted that any type of leafletter could be restricted by legitimate time, place, or manner regulations. A time, place, or manner regulation that gave a preference to labor pickets was found to violate equal protection in Police Department of Chicago v. Mosley, 408 U.S. 92, 92 S.Ct. 2286, 33 L.Ed.2d 212 (1972), and Carey v. Brown, 447 U.S. 455, 100 S.Ct. 2286, 65 L.Ed.2d 263 (1980).

or enjoined.[2] The theory in these cases is that such picketing is only a call to illegal action by encouraging others to help the picketers engage in applying coercive pressure on an employer in a manner that violates state or federal law. Therefore, the picketing is enjoinable as an invitation to engage in illegal activity.

In other contexts, the Court has upheld lower court actions prohibiting organizations from engaging in agreements and other speech/action which constituted a violation of antitrust laws.[3] In earlier decades the Court was quite lenient in upholding laws or court actions which restrained labor organization activities, such as the distribution of literature or the picketing of businesses, whenever these activities could be said to transgress state or federal policies regarding the proper conduct of labor disputes.[4] But the Court has always attempted to define a principle that the government could not prohibit or enjoin labor picketing unless there was some valid government policy regarding the control of labor organizations or labor disputes that was jeopardized by such picketing.[5] Where a labor organization is engaging in a strike or organizational activities that are clearly illegal under

2. See generally International Brotherhood of Teamsters v. Vogt, Inc., 354 U.S. 284, 77 S.Ct. 1166, 1 L.Ed.2d 1347 (1957) (state injunction against picketing upheld when picketing was for the purpose of "coercing" employers to induce employees to join union and had caused drivers of several trucks to refuse to transport goods to employer's plant), rehearing denied 354 U.S. 945, 77 S.Ct. 1423, 1 L.Ed.2d 1558 (1957).

3. See National Society of Professional Engineers v. United States, 435 U.S. 679, 697–98 nn. 26, 27, 98 S.Ct. 1355, 1368–69 nn. 26, 27, 55 L.Ed.2d 637 (1978) (prohibition of professional society's use of canon of ethics to restrain competitive bidding).

4. Giboney v. Empire Storage & Ice Co., 336 U.S. 490, 69 S.Ct. 684, 93 L.Ed. 834 (1949) (Supreme Court upholds state court injunction of labor picketing that would be violation of state anti-trust laws); Hughes v. Superior Court, 339 U.S. 460, 70 S.Ct. 718, 94 L.Ed. 985 (1950) (Court upholds injunction prohibiting picketing of business to secure compliance with demand that employees be hired in percentage with racial origin of customers); International Brotherhood of Teamsters v. Hanke, 339 U.S. 470, 70 S.Ct. 773, 94 L.Ed. 995 (1950) (upholding injunction of picketing demanding that small business become a union shop), rehearing denied 339 U.S. 991, 70 S.Ct. 1018, 94 L.Ed. 1391 (1950); Building Service Employees Intern. Union v. Gaz-

zam, 339 U.S. 532, 70 S.Ct. 784, 94 L.Ed. 1045 (1950) (upholding injunction of picketing based on state's statutory policy against employer coercion of employees' choice of bargaining representative), rehearing denied 339 U.S. 991, 70 S.Ct. 1019, 94 L.Ed. 1391 (1950); Local Union No. 10, United Association of Journeymen Plumbers, and Steamfitters v. Graham, 345 U.S. 192, 73 S.Ct. 585, 97 L.Ed. 946 (1953) (upholding injunction against peaceful labor picketing in conflict with state statutes).

5. Compare A.F.L. v. Swing, 312 U.S. 321, 61 S.Ct. 568, 85 L.Ed. 855 (1941) (holding unconstitutional injunction against picketing where there is no immediate dispute between employer and employee), rehearing denied 312 U.S. 715, 61 S.Ct. 735, 85 L.Ed. 1145 (1941), with Milk Wagon Drivers Union v. Meadowmoor Dairies, 312 U.S. 287, 294, 61 S.Ct. 552, 555, 85 L.Ed. 836, 841 (1941) (injunction against picketing upheld on the basis that injunction was reasonably necessary to avoid violence), rehearing denied 312 U.S. 715, 61 S.Ct. 803, 85 L.Ed. 1145 (1941).

The Court's first pronouncements of principles restraining vague and overbroad laws were made in the context of holding impermissible a statute that prohibited all picketing, including peaceful labor picketing, that did not transgress legitimate state policies in labor regulation. See Thornhill v. Alabama, 310 U.S. 88, 60 S.Ct. 736, 84 L.Ed. 1093 (1940).

valid state or federal statutes, then laws restricting picketing or the distribution of information regarding such strike, even though the activity is called only "informational," may be compatible with first amendment theory on the rationale that the government can force persons in a labor dispute to resolve their grievance through legally established channels rather than seeking to secure the support of others, through illegal strikes or other illegal activities.[6]

Secondary Boycotts. The Supreme Court has upheld prohibitions of union activities that constitute "secondary boycotts" even though those activities might be seen as only the distribution of information. In a secondary boycott case, union members picket or distribute information outside of a business asking persons not to deal with that business because the business uses the products of or otherwise deals with a second business with which the union has a dispute. Federal labor laws, with exceptions, require the union to picket only the primary business with whom it has a dispute and not seek to coerce the persons with whom that business deals to side with the union.[7]

The Court has held that such activity may be prohibited or enjoined because it constitutes coercion of persons (the boycotted enterprise) to aid the union in its attempt to violate federal law.[8] However, the giving of information to the public, whether through picketing or other means, regarding the nature of a labor organization's dispute with a business (business # 1) at the site of a second business (business

---

6. See International Longshoremen's Ass'n, AFL–CIO v. Allied International, Inc., 456 U.S. 212, 102 S.Ct. 1656, 72 L.Ed.2d 21 (1982), on remand 554 F.Supp. 32 (D.Mass.1982), finding illegal a refusal of a longshoremen's union to load or unload ships engaged in trade with the Soviet Union as a protest against the Soviet Union's invasion of Afghanistan. The Union activity was found to be a "secondary boycott" in that it was a refusal to deal with the shippers on the basis of the actions of another party. The application of the antisecondary boycott provision was found not to violate the first amendment rights of the union or its members.

Labor Strikes for Political Purposes
Cf. Eastex, Inc. v. N.L.R.B., 437 U.S. 556, 98 S.Ct. 2505, 57 L.Ed.2d 428 (1978) (employer's refusal to allow union distribution of various political leaflets in nonworking areas of employer's property during nonworking time violates N.L.R.A.).

Compare International Longshoremen's Association, AFL–CIO v. Allied International, Inc., 456 U.S. 212, 102 S.Ct. 1656, 72 L.Ed.2d 21 (1982) (union refusal to load and unload ships engaged in trade with U.S.S.R. in order to protest Russian invasion of Afghanistan was illegal secondary

boycott, application of antisecondary boycott rule held not to violate free speech), on remand 554 F.Supp. 32 (D.Mass.1982), with Jacksonville Bulk Terminals, Inc. v. International Longshoremen's Association, 457 U.S. 702, 102 S.Ct. 2672, 73 L.Ed.2d 327 (1982) (Norris–LaGuardia Act prohibits employer suit to enjoin union refusal to load certain ships bound for U.S.S.R. in order to protest Russian invasion of Afghanistan).

See generally, Kupferberg, Political Strikes, Labor Law, and Democratic Rights, 71 Va.L.Rev. 685 (1985).

7. See generally Robert A. Gorman, Basic Text on Labor Law, 257–61 (1976).

8. See International Longshoremen's Association, AFL–CIO v. Allied International, Inc., 456 U.S. 212, 102 S.Ct. 1656, 72 L.Ed.2d 21 (1982), on remand 554 F.Supp. 32 (D.Mass.1982); NLRB v. Retail Store Employees Union, 447 U.S. 607, 616, 100 S.Ct. 2372, 2378, 65 L.Ed.2d 377, 385–86 (1980); American Radio Association v. Mobile S.S. Association, Inc., 419 U.S. 215, 229–31, 95 S.Ct. 409, 417–18, 42 L.Ed.2d 399, 409–11 (1974).

2) which engages in trade with business # 1 (with whom the organization has a dispute) may be considered only the peaceful conveyance of information and protected by the first amendment. Although the Court has not yet defined the exact nature of the informational activity which would be protected by the first amendment, it appears to be attempting to make some accommodation between proscribable and nonproscribable labor organization speech through its interpretation of federal labor relations laws.[9]

Initially it may appear easy for the Court to justify the punishment of labor picketing which only coerces or "signals" others to aid the union in engaging in activity that violates valid labor statutes.[10] But it is difficult to distinguish the area of informational activity by labor organizations that could be made punishable (because it relates to a labor dispute) from the constitutionally protected activities of persons who organize boycotts of businesses for the purpose of coercing those businesses to help them influence government action.[11] Thus, there may be some type of speech by labor organizations or employers that cannot be prohibited because it relates to public issues or the need to influence government action.[12] However, all that is clear is that the Supreme Court will allow the injunction or punishment of speech by employers or organizations when that speech would undercut the

9. See Edward J. DeBartolo Corp. v. National Labor Relations Board, 463 U.S. 147, 103 S.Ct. 2926, 77 L.Ed.2d 535 (1983) (avoiding constitutional issue regarding "publicity proviso" exemption from secondary boycott provision because it had not been ruled on by the labor relations board although the Court narrowly construes the nature of the exemption for such activities), appeal after remand 796 F.2d 1328 (11th Cir.1986), rehearing denied 806 F.2d 1070 (1986); National Labor Relations Board v. Retail Store Employees Union, Local 1001, 447 U.S. 607, 100 S.Ct. 2372, 65 L.Ed.2d 377 (1980) (in a plurality opinion on this issue, four justices find that picketing encouraging a secondary boycott is not constitutionally protected); National Labor Relations Board v. Fruit and Vegetable Packers and Warehousemen, 377 U.S. 58, 84 S.Ct. 1063, 12 L.Ed.2d 129 (1964) (National Labor Relations Act held not to prohibit all peaceful consumer picketing at secondary sites).

10. Justice Stevens has based his vote to uphold restrictions on picketing on this basis. See National Labor Relations Board v. Retail Store Employees Union, Local 1001, 447 U.S. 607, 618–19, 100 S.Ct. 2372, 2379–80, 65 L.Ed.2d 377, 387–88 (1980) (Stevens, J., concurring in part and concurring in the result).

The distinction between this type of illegal signal picketing and picketing that should be protected by the first amendment has previously been made by constitutional theorists. See generally, T. Emerson, The System of Freedom of Expression 445–49 (1971); Cox, Strikes, Picketing and the Constitution, 4 Vand.L.Rev. 574, 592–602 (1951).

11. See NAACP v. Claiborne Hardware Co., 458 U.S. 886, 913, 102 S.Ct. 3409, 3426, 73 L.Ed.2d 1215, 1236 (1982) (holding that organization could not be punished for organizing boycott to cause economic injury to merchants so as to influence the merchants to aid the organization in changing government policies regarding race discrimination), rehearing denied 459 U.S. 898, 103 S.Ct. 199, 74 L.Ed.2d 160 (1982). "The right of states to regulate economic activity could not justify a complete prohibition against a nonviolent, politically-motivated boycott designed to force governmental and economic change and to effectuate rights guaranteed by the Constitution itself." Id. (footnote omitted).

12. See Eastern Railroad Presidents Conference v. Noerr Motor Freight, Inc., 365 U.S. 127, 81 S.Ct. 523, 5 L.Ed.2d 464 (1961), rehearing denied 365 U.S. 875, 81 S.Ct. 899, 5 L.Ed.2d 864 (1961).

legitimate governmental regulation of the manner in which labor disputes must be resolved.

XVII. OBSCENITY

§ 20.56 Introduction

Edmund Wilson was, without question, one of the most influential literary critics of the twentieth century. A conservative and exacting man, he was to F. Scott Fitzgerald "my artistic conscience,"[1] an admission that in all honesty might well have been made by many of the American novelists of the 1920's and 1930's whose work, taken together, is now an indelible part of the American self-image.

Wilson was also a novelist himself. In 1946, at the peak of his reputation, he published his second novel, *Memoirs of Hecate County,* in which he related two rather spiritless passages describing sexual intercourse. Upon complaint of the New York Society for the Suppression of Vice, the novel's publisher, Doubleday & Co., was charged under a state criminal obscenity statute. Despite the testimony of Columbia University Professor Lionel Trilling, who said that the allegedly-ob-

---

§ 20.56

1. F.S. Fitzgerald, Pasting It Together, in The Fitzgerald Reader 415 (A. Mizener ed. 1963).

See generally, Harry Kalven, Jr., ed. by Jamie Kalven, A Worthy Tradition: Freedom of Speech in America 33–53 (1988).

Causation and the Attorney General's Commission on Pornography. The Final Report of the Attorney General's Commission on Pornography stated:

"[S]ubstantial exposure to sexually violent materials as described here bears a causal relationship to antisocial acts of sexual violence and, for some subgroups, to unlawful acts of sexual violence."

U.S. Department of Justice, Final Report: Attorney General's Commission on Pornography 326 (Gov't Printing Office 1986).

That conclusion, among others, has been the subject of a great deal of criticism. See, e.g., Linz, Penrod, & Donnerstein, The Attorney General's Commission on Pornography: The Gaps Between "Findings" and Facts, 1987 A.B.F.Res.J. 713, 713–14 (1987) (emphasis in original):

"[W]hile several of the Commission's findings appear to be sound extrapolations from the empirical studies conducted by social scientists, many of its recommendations are incongruent with the re-

search findings.... First, much of the research has demonstrated that it is sexually *violent* material, rather than *explicit* material, that results in harmful effects. Given these findings, the Commission's focus on harsher legal restrictions on all forms of pornography is misguided. Second, while laboratory investigations of the psychological and behavioral effects of violent pornography have the advantage of tight experimental control and thus permit the researcher to draw causal inference, they also have certain built-in methodological limitations. Most prominent among these is the use of artificial measures of aggression that prohibit direct extrapolation of experimental findings to situations outside the laboratory. The Commission seemed unable or perhaps unwilling to acknowledge these limitations."

See generally, Downs, The Attorney General's Commission and the New Politics of Pornography, 1987 A.B.F.Res.J. 641 (1987); West, The Feminist–Conservative Anti–Pornography Alliance and the 1986 Attorney General's Commission on Pornography Report, 1987 A.B.F.Res.J. 681 (1987); Schauer, Causation Theory and the Causes of Sexual Violence, 1987 A.B.F.Res.J. 737 (1987); D'Amato, A New Political Truth: Exposure to Sexually Violent Materials Causes Sexual Violence, 31 Wm. & Mary L.Rev. 575 (1990).

scene passages were inextricably related to the novel's literary merit, a three-judge trial panel found Doubleday guilty. This verdict was upheld by the Appellate Division and the New York Court of Appeals,[2] and the United States Supreme Court, in one of the first major obscenity cases to reach it, affirmed without opinion in a four-to-four vote.[3]

The Court's affirmation came down in 1948. A year later, in Philadelphia, several booksellers were charged with violating a Pennsylvania criminal statute that outlawed the sale of "any obscene, lewd, lascivious, filthy, indecent or disgusting book...."[4] Among the books to which the Commonwealth applied these adjectives were James T. Farrell's *Studs Lonigan* trilogy, William Faulkner's *Sanctuary* and *The Wild Palms,* and Erskine Caldwell's *God's Little Acre,* books which are now familiar items on a college English major's required-reading list. In this case, however, the prosecution failed.

In his trial opinion, Judge Curtis Bok granted the "several general dicta by the Supreme Court to the effect that obscenity is indictable just because it is obscenity,"[5] but he reasoned that constitutionally, conviction under a criminal obscenity statute requires a "causal connection"[6] beyond a reasonable doubt between the allegedly-obscene activity— here, the sale of the books—and actual or imminent criminal behavior in individuals exposed to the activity. On this basis, Judge Bok found the booksellers not guilty.

Among the "several general dicta" to which Judge Bok referred was Justice Murphy's statement in *Chaplinsky v. New Hampshire*[7] that the "lewd and obscene" are among "certain well-defined and narrowly limited classes of speech, the prevention and punishment of which have

2. People v. Doubleday & Co., 272 App. Div. 799, 71 N.Y.S.2d 736 (1947), affirmed 297 N.Y. 687, 77 N.E.2d 6 (1947), affirmed by an equally divided Court, sub nom. 335 U.S. 848, 69 S.Ct. 79, 93 L.Ed. 398 (1948).

3. Doubleday & Co. v. New York, 335 U.S. 848, 69 S.Ct. 79, 93 L.Ed. 398 (1948) (Justice Frankfurter not participating).

For a more detailed discussion of the *Doubleday* case, see M. Konvitz, Fundamental Liberties of a Free People 159 (1957).

Sacrilege.

A few years later the Court did strike down a New York statute banning motion pictures on the ground that they were "sacrilegious." The Court held that motion pictures are not precluded from First Amendment protection even though they are sold for profit. The statute was then struck down as too vague. Joseph Burstyn, Inc. v. Wilson, 343 U.S. 495, 72 S.Ct.

777, 96 L.Ed. 1098 (1952). This case thus does have important implications for obscenity legislation, although the Court did not specifically decide it on such grounds. See also, Kingsley International Pictures Corp. v. Regents of New York, 360 U.S. 684, 79 S.Ct. 1362, 3 L.Ed.2d 1512 (1959) (denial of license to show the film "Lady Chatterley's Lover" is reversed; decision not on obscenity grounds).

4. As cited in M. Konvitz, Fundamental Liberties of a Free People 160 (1957).

5. Commonwealth v. Gordon, 66 Pa.D. & C. 101, 146 (1949) (per curiam), affirmed sub nom. Commonwealth v. Feigenbaum, 166 Pa.Super. 120, 70 A.2d 389 (1950).

6. 66 Pa.D. & C. at 156.

7. 315 U.S. 568, 62 S.Ct. 766, 86 L.Ed. 1031 (1942).

never been thought to raise any Constitutional problem."[8] The dicta continued after Judge Bok's decision.

In *Beauharnais v. Illinois,*[9] decided in 1952, Justice Frankfurter equated obscenity with group libel as being beyond "the area of constitutionally protected speech."[10] Frankfurter did not elaborate his point; neither, for that matter, had Murphy, whose inclusion of obscenity with libel and "fighting words" in a single, undifferentiated constitutional classification seemed offhand, almost peremptory. To Justice Murphy, the "lewd and obscene" were among the utterances about which "[i]t has been well observed that [they] are no essential part of any exposition of ideas, and are of such slight social value as a step to truth that any benefit that may be derived from them is clearly outweighed by the social interest in order and morality."[11]

In making this statement, Justice Murphy cited and paraphrased the work of Professor Zachariah Chafee, Jr.[12] It is to Chafee, then, that we must turn for a fuller explication of the legal principle emerging at that time which argued that "obscenity is indictable just because it is obscenity."

To Chafee, "profanity and indecent talk and pictures" were inherently void of "any exposition of ideas, ... The harm is done as soon as they are communicated, or is liable to follow almost immediately in the form of retaliatory violence. The only sound explanation of the punishment of obscenity and profanity is that the words are criminal, not because of the ideas they communicate, but like acts because of their immediate consequences to the five senses."[13] As Professor Konvitz pointed out, Chafee's treatment of obscenity as verbal "acts" comported with legal analogy drawn by Justices Murphy and Frankfurter between obscenity, libel, and "fighting words," and further justified the Court's reluctance to confer first amendment protection.[14]

On the other hand, two years before he discussed obscenity in the *Chaplinsky* case, Justice Murphy himself delivered the Court's opinion in *Thornhill v. Alabama,*[15] a case dealing with labor picketing in a rural company town. In *Thornhill,* Justice Murphy did not deny that picketing is an "act" in any meaningful sense of the word. But he stated that picketing and similar activities "may enlighten the public on the nature and causes of a labor dispute," and that "[t]he safeguarding of these means is essential to the securing of an informed and

---

8. 315 U.S. at 571–72, 62 S.Ct. at 769.

9. 343 U.S. 250, 72 S.Ct. 725, 96 L.Ed. 919 (1952), rehearing denied 343 U.S. 988, 72 S.Ct. 1070, 96 L.Ed. 1375 (1952).

10. 343 U.S. at 266, 72 S.Ct. at 735.

11. Chaplinsky v. New Hampshire, 315 U.S. 568, 572, 62 S.Ct. 766, 769, 86 L.Ed. 1031 (1942).

12. Z. Chafee, Free Speech in the United States (1941).

13. Z. Chafee, Free Speech in the United States 150 (1942).

14. M. Konvitz, Fundamental Liberties of a Free People 158 (1957).

15. 310 U.S. 88, 60 S.Ct. 736, 84 L.Ed. 1093 (1940).

educated public opinion with respect to a matter which is of public concern." [16]   In *Thornhill*, then Justice Murphy allowed that a verbal "act" may, under certain circumstances, be deemed "speech" within the meaning of the first amendment.

So Justice Murphy created a definitional dilemma for the Court. This dilemma was obvious in the prosecutions involving Edmund Wilson, James T. Farrell, and William Faulkner. If Faulkner, whose work brought him a Nobel Prize, played an "essential part" in the "exposition of ideas," if his Snopes trilogy, for example, may be taken as "a step to truth," then under the dictum in *Chaplinsky*, Faulkner's work could not have been obscene to Justice Murphy. But according to Professor Chafee, upon whom Justice Murphy so heavily relied, the more enticing passages in some of Faulkner's novels were by definition unrelated to the useful exposition of ideas, and were thus as a matter of law of "such slight social value" as to be beyond the protection of the first amendment.

Yet Faulkner surely addressed himself to matters "of social concern"; while under *Chaplinsky* his use of obscenity constituted a verbal "act," under *Thornhill* it surely constituted a literary device, "essential to the securing of an informed and educated public opinion ..." under the first amendment. It may be easy to draw a distinction between labor picketing and 50-cent peep shows, but can the distinction be drawn where the "obscenity" at issue takes the form of a paragraph in *Sanctuary?*

In 1946, Justice Douglas noted in passing in *Hannegan v. Esquire, Inc.*,[17] that:

> [u]nder our system of government there is an accommodation for the widest varieties of tastes and ideas. What is good literature, what has educational value, what is refined public information, what is good art, varies with individuals as it does from one generation to another. There doubtless would be a contrariety of views concerning Cervantes' *Don Quixote*, Shakespeare's *Venus and Adonis*, or Zola's *Nana*. But a requirement that literature or art conform to some norm prescribed by an official smacks of an ideology foreign to our system.[18]

Nonetheless, when Judge Bok observed in 1949 that to the Supreme Court, "obscenity is indictable just because it is obscenity," he was alluding to an accurate contemporary legal principle. He was also alluding to the core problem of this area of first amendment law: What is obscenity?

16. 310 U.S. at 104, 60 S.Ct. at 745.

17. 327 U.S. 146, 66 S.Ct. 456, 90 L.Ed. 586 (1946).

18. 327 U.S. at 157–58, 66 S.Ct. at 462.

§ 20.57   Obscenity—The *Roth* Case

The dicta on obscenity in *Chaplinsky v. New Hampshire*[1] and *Beauharnais v. Illinois*[2] raised the obvious question of how the Court would treat the issue when it rendered its first decision on the subject. That decision, *Roth v. United States,*[3] was handed down in 1957. In *Roth,* two state criminal statutes were invoked against the publication and sale of obscene matter.

After stating in a footnote that "[n]o issue is presented [here] concerning the obscenity of the material involved,"[4] Justice Brennan, writing for the Court, stated that: "The dispositive question is whether obscenity is utterance within the area of protected speech and press."[5] On the basis of a series of earlier cases in which obscenity had been discussed in dictum, including *Chaplinsky* and *Beauharnais,* it had always been "assumed" that obscenity was not protected by the first amendment.[6] The Court thereupon discussed several historical elements underlying the phrasing of the first amendment, and concluded: "All ideas having even the slightest redeeming social importance— unorthodox ideas, controversial ideas, even ideas hateful to the prevailing climate of opinion—have the full protection of the guaranties [of the first amendment], unless excludable because they encroach upon the limited area of more important interests. But implicit in the history of the first amendment is the rejection of obscenity as utterly without redeeming social importance."[7] Then, after quoting the *Chaplinsky* dictum at some length, the Court converted its traditional assumption into a rule of law, and held that "obscenity is not within the area of constitutionally protected speech or press."[8]

At this point the Court attempted to dispose of two lingering issues. First, it rejected the contention that there is a burden on the state to prove that a given piece of obscene material must be related to antisocial conduct. The Court adopted Justice Frankfurter's comment in *Beauharnais* and held that if obscenity is without constitutional protection, it may be proscribed by statute without further justification.[9]

Second, the Court drew a distinction between sex and obscenity. "Obscene material," said the Court, "is material which deals with sex

---

§ 20.57

1. 315 U.S. 568, 571–72, 62 S.Ct. 766, 768–69, 86 L.Ed. 1031 (1942).

2. 343 U.S. 250, 266, 72 S.Ct. 725, 735, 96 L.Ed. 919 (1952), rehearing denied 343 U.S. 988, 72 S.Ct. 1070, 96 L.Ed. 1375 (1952).

3. 354 U.S. 476, 77 S.Ct. 1304, 1 L.Ed.2d 1498 (1957), rehearing denied 355 U.S. 852, 78 S.Ct. 8, 2 L.Ed.2d 60 (1957). *Roth* was consolidated with Alberts v. California, and all references herein to *Roth* shall include *Alberts.*

4. 354 U.S. at 481 n. 8, 77 S.Ct. at 1307 n. 8.

5. 354 U.S. at 481, 77 S.Ct. at 1307 (footnote omitted).

6. 354 U.S. at 481, 77 S.Ct. at 1307.

7. 354 U.S. at 484, 77 S.Ct. at 1309.

8. 354 U.S. at 485, 77 S.Ct. at 1309.

9. 354 U.S. at 486–87, 77 S.Ct. at 1309–10.

in a manner appealing to prurient interest," while the mere portrayal of sex in art, literature, scientific works, and similar forms "is not itself sufficient reason to deny material the constitutional protection of freedom of speech and press." [10]   In fleshing out this distinction, the Court adopted the standard of whether "to the average person, applying contemporary community standards, the dominant theme of the material taken as a whole appeals to prurient interest." [11]

The Court closed its opinion with the observation that in accordance with *United States v. Petrillo*,[12] a statute outlawing obscenity will not violate due process by a mere lack of precision.   Except in marginal cases, the Court suggested that the language of such a statute will be sufficient if it gives "adequate warning of the conduct proscribed" and enables the law to be administered fairly.[13]

Thus when reduced to a formula, *Roth* provided that material may be deemed obscene, and therefore wholly without constitutional protection, if it (a) appeals to a prurient interest in sex, (b) has no redeeming social value, and (c) is, on the whole, offensive to the average person under contemporary community standards.

There are two elements in *Roth* that deserve special attention. First, there is the problem with the word "prurient."   This single word was quite clearly the touchstone of Justice Brennan's analysis of the case.   Its application spelled the difference between sex and obscenity, between applicable community standards and mere community prejudice, between material that is sanctioned by the Constitution and material that may be subject to criminal penalty.   To the Court, prurient material was that which has "a tendency to excite lustful thoughts." [14]   This definition deserved some further explication, and the Court provided it with excerpts from Webster's Second New International Dictionary, i.e., that "prurient" is ". . . [i]tching; longing; uneasy with desire or longing; of persons, having itching, morbid, or lascivious longings; of desire, curiosity, or propensity, lewd. . . ." [15]

It is obviously possible that material can be prurient and political; that it can be possessed of a tendency to excite lustful thoughts and contain profound social commentary; or that it can create in an individual morbid and lascivious desires and constitute poetry of the highest order.   It was with this in mind, perhaps, that Chief Justice Warren stated in concurrence that the "conduct of the defendant is the central issue, not the obscenity of a book or picture.   The nature of the

---

10.   354 U.S. at 487, 77 S.Ct. at 1310.

11.   354 U.S. at 489, 77 S.Ct. at 1311. The Court explicitly rejected the leading English case holding that obscenity is to be judged merely by the effect of an isolated passage upon particularly susceptible persons. Regina v. Hicklin, [1868] L.R. 3 Q.B. 360.

12.   332 U.S. 1, 7–8, 67 S.Ct. 1538, 1542, 91 L.Ed. 1877 (1947).

13.   *Roth,* 354 U.S. at 491, 77 S.Ct. at 1313.

14.   354 U.S. at 487 n. 20, 77 S.Ct. at 1310 n. 20.

15.   Id.

materials is, of course, relevant as an attribute of the defendant's conduct, but the materials are thus placed in context from which they draw color and character. A wholly different result might be reached in a different setting." [16]

In a separate opinion, Justice Harlan, concurring and dissenting, carried Chief Justice Warren's observation further and objected to the very concept of reducing a constitutional question to a "distinct, recognizable and classifiable ... poison ivy" under the term "prurient." [17] To Justice Harlan, obscenity was by its nature an abstraction; and under the Constitution it presents a problem that "cannot be solved in such a generalized fashion." [18]

Justice Harlan preferred a case-by-case approach in which a reviewing court could take into account the fact that "[e]very communication has an individuality and 'value' of its own": [19]

The suppression of a particular writing or other tangible form of expression is, therefore, an *individual* matter, and in the nature of things every such suppression raises an individual constitutional problem, in which a reviewing court must determine for *itself* whether the attacked expression is suppressable within constitutional standards. Since those standards do not readily lend themselves to generalized definitions, the constitutional problem in the last analysis becomes one of particularized judgments which appellate courts must make for themselves.[20]

The second element in *Roth* to which one might pay special attention is the now-famous dissent of Justice Douglas and Black. This short dissent, which is often cited as evidence of its authors' "absolutist" approach to speech and press issues under the first amendment, should be read in its entirety. It contains a direct challenge to Justice Harlan's view that "in the last analysis [obscenity] becomes one of particularized judgments which appellate courts must make for themselves." Justice Harlan assumed these judgments would be made under the applicable constitutional standard; but to Justices Douglas and Black the appropriate standard should not in any event give "the censor free range over a vast domain. To allow the State to step in and punish mere speech or publication that the judge or jury thinks has an *undesirable* impact on thoughts but that is not shown to be a part of unlawful action is drastically to curtail the First Amendment...." [21]

They concluded that obscenity, under any definition in any environment, is a form of expression, and as such "can be suppressed if, and

---

16. 354 U.S. at 495, 77 S.Ct. at 1314–15 (concurring opinion).

17. 354 U.S. at 497, 77 S.Ct. at 1315 (concurring in the result in *Alberts*—the state case—and dissenting in *Roth*—the federal case).

18. Id.

19. Id.

20. 354 U.S. at 497, 77 S.Ct. at 1315 (emphasis in original).

21. 354 U.S. at 509, 77 S.Ct. at 1322 (dissenting opinion) (emphasis in original).

to the extent that, it is so closely brigaded with illegal action as to be an inseparable part of it.... As a people, we cannot afford to relax that standard." [22] Thus Justices Douglas and Black adopted Judge Curtis Bok's approach in *Commonwealth v. Gordon*,[23] and argued that there must be a causal connection between the allegedly-obscene expression— which at all times must, for analytical purposes, be deemed to be within the protection of the first amendment—and illegal conduct, which, under long-established principle, could be sufficient to render the expression unlawful.

§ 20.58 The Implications of *Roth*

There is a small curiosity in the *Roth* opinion that, in some respects, symbolizes the nature and import of the opinion as a whole. As we have noted, Justice Brennan placed this prefatory footnote at the beginning of his majority opinion: "No issue is presented [here] concerning the obscenity of the material involved." [1] Apparently, the purpose of this footnote was to clarify the Court's limited task on review, which was to determine the facial validity of two state criminal obscenity statutes rather than the validity of those statutes in light of the circumstances under which they were invoked.

This disclaimer points to a broad technical problem in the case. Because the Court dealt only with the facial validity of two typically-comprehensive anti-obscenity statutes, the Court was able to treat obscenity as an abstract proposition and to formulate a definitional standard for obscenity in terms of abstract Constitutional principle. While in a limited technical sense, there was nothing "advisory" about *Roth*, and while the *Roth* test was not dictum, the opinion came perilously close to a loose theoretical exercise in Constitutional law. Unburdened by the factual circumstances that triggered the case in the first place, the Court in *Roth* rendered a decision that was framed in terms that would not easily address themselves to the plethora of varying factual circumstances that would burden the Court in obscenity cases in the years to come.

Shortly after *Roth* was handed down, Dean William B. Lockhart and Professor Robert C. McClure of the University of Minnesota Law School wrote two often noted law review articles [2] which have "greatly influenced" the "struggle for a fair and realistic definition of obscenity

22. 354 U.S. at 514, 77 S.Ct. at 1324 (dissenting opinion).

23. 66 Pa.D. & C. 101 (1949), affirmed sub nom. Commonwealth v. Feigenbaum, 166 Pa.Super. 120, 70 A.2d 389 (1950).

§ 20.58

1. Roth v. United States, 354 U.S. 476, 481 n. 8, 77 S.Ct. 1304, 1307 n. 8, 1 L.Ed.2d

1498 (1957), rehearing denied 355 U.S. 852, 78 S.Ct. 8, 2 L.Ed.2d 60 (1957).

2. Lockhart and McClure, Censorship of Obscenity: The Developing Constitutional Standards, 45 Minn.L.Rev. 5 (1960); Lockhart and McClure, Obscenity Censorship: The Core Constitutional Issue—What is Obscene?, 7 Utah L.Rev. 289 (1961).

in the wake of *Roth*...."[3] In these articles Lockhart and McClure proposed two alternative approaches to an understanding of *Roth*.

First, they suggested that the case settled only two aspects of the obscenity question:[4] (1) that the material in question must be considered as a whole, and cannot be condemned on the basis of isolated passages; and (2) that the material, taken as a whole, must be examined in light of the average person whose attitudes reflect a common community standard, not in terms of the material's impact on the exceptional individual who is particularly susceptible to the material's prurient aspects.[5] Second, Lockhart and McClure argued that the attention paid by the Court in *Roth* to the possibly redeeming social importance of allegedly-obscene material indicated an implied acceptance of a concept they termed "variable obscenity." Under this concept the pivotal word "prurient" can be understood only in a relative sense; its meaning and application would vary according to the tastes and sophistication of the audience at which the material is directed.[6]

An example of the application of the "variable obscenity" approach might be litigation over the obscenity of some of the later drawings of Aubrey Beardsley, the late-nineteenth century English illustrator and art editor of the somewhat infamous *Yellow Book*. To an average audience, Beardsley's elaborate, neo-Baroque renditions of homosexual and lesbian sexual activity would perforce be prurient, and thus obscene; but to an audience of art historians or aficionados of Victorian social psychology, the drawings, while doubtless titillating, would carry a social importance that would override a prosecutor's objections to their sexual content.

It was this sort of situation, perhaps, that Chief Justice Warren had in mind when he stated in his concurrence in *Roth* that the central issue in obscenity is the conduct of the defendant himself, and thus the "context from which [the materials] draw color and character." This situation certainly lends support to Justice Harlan's objections to a rigid, undifferentiating approach to obscenity under the term "prurient." In any event the Court did move in the direction of "variable obscenity" in *Ginzburg v. United States*[7] and *Ginsberg v. New York*,[8] which are discussed below.

The value of Lockhart and McClure's scholarship, however, must be balanced against the inherently insoluble enigma of *Roth* that renders virtually any theoretical attempt to "explain" the case into an

3. J. Barron & C. Dienes, Constitutional Law: Principles and Policy 905 (1975).

4. W. Lockhart & R. McClure, Censorship of Obscenity: The Developing Constitutional Standards, 45 Minn.L.Rev. 5, 53 (1960).

5. Id.

6. Id. at 68–70.

7. 383 U.S. 463, 86 S.Ct. 942, 16 L.Ed.2d 31 (1966), rehearing denied 384 U.S. 934, 86 S.Ct. 1440, 16 L.Ed.2d 536 (1966).

8. 390 U.S. 629, 88 S.Ct. 1274, 20 L.Ed.2d 195 (1968), rehearing denied 391 U.S. 971, 88 S.Ct. 2029, 20 L.Ed.2d 887 (1968).

exercise in apologetics. The enigma was perhaps best described by Justice Stewart in his short concurring opinion in *Jacobellis v. Ohio,*[9] one of a series of cases in which the Court applied *Roth* to an allegedly obscene motion picture. Justice Stewart's concurrence, in its entirety, with only citations omitted, is as follows:

> It is possible to read the Court's opinion in *Roth v. United States* and *Alberts v. California* . . . in a variety of ways. In saying this, I imply no criticism of the Court, which in those cases was faced with the task of trying to define what may be indefinable. I have reached the conclusion, which I think is confirmed at least by negative implication in the Court's decisions since *Roth* and *Alberts,* that under the First and Fourteenth Amendments criminal laws in this area are constitutionally limited to hard-core pornography. I shall not today attempt further to define the kinds of material I understand to be embraced within that shorthand description; and perhaps I could never succeed in intelligibly doing so. But I know it when I see it, and the motion picture involved in this case is not that.[10]

Perhaps, when all else is said, that is the best that any judge can do; he cannot define obscenity, but he can admit that "I know it when I see it."

It is worth noting that Edmund Wilson, whose novel *Memoirs of Hecate County* was the subject of the Court's first decision of record on obscenity, somewhat accidentally stumbled into an "art" movie house in Utica, New York in the summer of 1968. He found himself watching a movie consisting largely of an actress manipulating her genitals, which, he said, "close up and magnified, had the thoroughly repellant appearance of the pieces of raw meat in a butcher's shop."[11] The great critic concluded with little explanation that "I do not think that such films should be allowed."[12] Perhaps he thought that the subject did not deserve detailed discussion, that his judgment required no justification. He, too, knew it when he saw it; and for him that was the beginning and the end of the matter.

§ 20.59   The Development of the Case Law Under *Roth*

Two years after *Roth* the Court held that the state could not eliminate the need to prove *scienter* in an obscenity prosecution, in a case where it reversed the conviction of a bookseller under a statute which dispensed with any requirement of knowledge of the contents of

---

9. 378 U.S. 184, 84 S.Ct. 1676, 12 L.Ed.2d 793 (1964).

10. 378 U.S. at 197, 84 S.Ct. at 1683 (concurring opinion) (citations omitted).

11. E. Wilson, Upstate: Records and Recollections of Northern New York 311 (1971).

12. Id.

the books on the part of the seller.[1]

Then, in *Jacobellis v. Ohio*,[2] the Court held, *inter alia*, "that, in 'obscenity' cases as in all others involving rights derived from the First Amendment guarantees of free expression, this Court cannot avoid making an independent constitutional judgment on the facts of the case as to whether the material involved is constitutionally protected." In short, a trial court's findings as to the obscenity of the material at issue is not binding on review—if the appellate court takes the case, it will have to watch the movie or read the book itself.

Thus, the import of *Roth* would unfold as the Supreme Court was forced to reconsider the implications of the *Roth* test in terms of the problems of specific areas. As one might expect, the applications of *Roth* eventually subverted some of the major analytical elements of the opinion itself; it also revealed the failure of the Supreme Court to agree on any real tests to apply in practice to allegedly obscene material.

Two examples illustrating this problem may be found in the decisions of the Court's 1966 term. First, a fragmented Supreme Court used the "social value" test to overturn a conviction under the Massachusetts obscenity statute that held the book *Fanny Hill* to be obscene, in *A Book Named "John Cleland's Memoirs of a Woman of Pleasure" v. Attorney General of Massachusetts*.[3] Justice Brennan announced the judgment of the Court reversing the state court's finding of obscenity, but Brennan's opinion was only joined by Chief Justice Warren and Justice Fortas.

Brennan argued that each of the three elements of the *Roth* test must be applied independently,[4] and thus that material cannot be adjudged obscene if it passes muster under any of them. Justice Brennan reasoned that *Fanny Hill*, which has long been a classic of ribald literature, could not properly be deemed to be "*utterly* without redeeming social value,"[5] and thus is sheltered by the First Amendment. By applying the elements of the *Roth* test independently, Justice Brennan stepped away from the strict definitional approach employed in *Roth*. *Fanny Hill* may or may not have appealed to prurient interests under any definition or under any set of community standards, but this was now irrelevant; the book contained at least a modicum of literary value, and that was enough to save it from

---

§ 20.59

1. Smith v. California, 361 U.S. 147, 80 S.Ct. 215, 4 L.Ed.2d 205 (1959), rehearing denied 361 U.S. 950, 80 S.Ct. 399, 4 L.Ed.2d 383 (1960). See generally, Kalven, The Metaphysics of the Law of Obscenity, 1960 Sup.Ct.Rev. 1; Magrath, The Obscenity Cases: Grapes of Roth, 1966 Sup.Ct.Rev. 7; Henkin, Morals and the Constitution: The Sin of Obscenity, 63 Colum.L.Rev. 391 (1963).

2. 378 U.S. 184, 190, 84 S.Ct. 1676, 1679, 12 L.Ed.2d 793 (1964) (footnote omitted).

3. 383 U.S. 413, 86 S.Ct. 975, 16 L.Ed.2d 1 (1966).

4. 383 U.S. at 419, 86 S.Ct. at 977–78.

5. Id. (emphasis in original).

suppression by the Attorney General of Massachusetts. Suddenly "pruriency" was no longer the pivotal element of obscenity under the first amendment.

Justice Stewart concurred in the reversal for a different reason: he felt that the material was not hard core pornography. Justice Black in his separate concurrence emphasized that the Court's opinions in this area agreed only on results and not on reasons, offering no useful tests or guidance for lower courts or laymen. Justice Douglas, composing the sixth vote, concurred because he believed that the first amendment forbade censorship of any expression not intertwined with illegal conduct. And the three remaining Justices (Clark, Harlan, and White) dissented, each writing separate opinions.

Far more important, however, was Justice Brennan's opinion for the Court in *Ginzburg v. United States.*[6] In *Ginzburg,* the Court was faced with three professionally produced publications devoted to sex, including EROS, which the Court described as "a hard-cover magazine of expensive format."[7] The Court found the publications to be obscene because they represented "commercial exploitation of erotica solely for the sake of their prurient appeal." In reaching this conclusion, the Court stated that the "leer of the sensualist" had "permeate[d]" the manner in which the publications had been distributed and advertised:[8] mailing privileges had been sought from Intercourse and Blue Ball, Pennsylvania, and Middlesex, New Jersey; and the advertising circulars describing the publications "stressed the sexual candor of the respective publications, and openly boasted that the publishers would take full advantage of what they regarded as an unrestricted license allowed by law in the expression of sex and sexual matters."[9] The Court reasoned that the "brazenness"[10] of the defendant's marketing tactics unveiled his intent in distributing the materials, and that this intent was the heart of the matter: "Where the purveyor's sole emphasis is on the sexually provocative aspects of his publications, that fact may be decisive in the determination of obscenity."[11] If the defendant had earlier claimed, even boasted, that his publication was obscene, that "admission" can be used against him.

In the *Memoirs* case, Justice Brennan emphasized that "the social value of the book can neither be weighed against nor cancelled by its prurient appeal or patent offensiveness."[12] But in *Ginzburg,* the Court,

---

6. 383 U.S. 463, 86 S.Ct. 942, 16 L.Ed.2d 31 (1966), rehearing denied 384 U.S. 934, 86 S.Ct. 1440, 16 L.Ed.2d 536 (1966).

7. 383 U.S. at 466, 86 S.Ct. at 945.

8. 383 U.S. at 468, 86 S.Ct. at 946. Later pandering cases include Splawn v. California, 431 U.S. 595, 97 S.Ct. 1987, 52 L.Ed.2d 606 (1977), and Hamling v. United States, 418 U.S. 87, 130, 94 S.Ct. 2887,

2914, 41 L.Ed.2d 590 (1974), rehearing denied 419 U.S. 885, 95 S.Ct. 157, 42 L.Ed.2d 129 (1974).

9. 383 U.S. at 468, 86 S.Ct. at 946.

10. 383 U.S. at 470, 86 S.Ct. at 947.

11. Id.

12. A Book Named "John Cleland's Memoirs of a Woman of Pleasure" v. Attorney General of Massachusetts, 383 U.S.

per Justice Brennan, did not even address the question of the social value of the three publications—its decision rested solely on the defendant's intent, his pandering. Thus an intent to appeal "solely" to prurient interests *can* outweigh the social value of the materials in question while the prurient appeal of the materials, of itself, cannot.

In a series of obscenity decisions the rationales of the individual members became more, rather than less, divergent. There was never majority agreement concerning the "contemporary community standards" aspect of the *Memoirs* plurality, with some justices favoring a national community standard;[13] others favoring a national standard for federal prosecutions;[14] still others favoring local community or flexibility for state standards.[15]

As to the "prurient interest" aspect, some justices held that if the material was designed for and primarily disseminated to a clearly defined deviant sexual group rather than the public at large, the prurient-appeal requirement is satisfied by looking to that group and not to the "average" or "normal" person referred to in *Roth*.[16] Other cases emphasized the element of "pandering" in close cases [17] or defined obscenity in terms of the juvenile audience.[18] And various justices also had differing views of the tests used to determine the "social value" aspect of the *Memoirs* test.[19]

The *Redrup* Approach. As Justice Brennan later openly acknowledged:

413, 419, 86 S.Ct. 975, 978, 16 L.Ed.2d 1 (1966).

13. Jacobellis v. Ohio, 378 U.S. 184, 192–95, 84 S.Ct. 1676, 1680–82, 12 L.Ed.2d 793 (1964) (Brennan, J., joined by Goldberg, J.).

14. Manual Enterprises v. Day, 370 U.S. 478, 488, 82 S.Ct. 1432, 1437–38, 8 L.Ed.2d 639 (1962) (Harlan, J., joined by Stewart, J.).

15. Jacobellis v. Ohio, 378 U.S. 184, 200–201, 84 S.Ct. 1676, 1684–85, 12 L.Ed.2d 793 (1964) (Warren, C.J., joined by Clark, J., dissenting) (local community standards); Hoyt v. Minnesota, 399 U.S. 524, 90 S.Ct. 2241, 26 L.Ed.2d 782 (1970) (Blackmun, J., joined by Burger, C.J., and Harlan J., dissenting) (flexibility of state standards).

16. Mishkin v. New York, 383 U.S. 502, 508, 86 S.Ct. 958, 963, 16 L.Ed.2d 56 (1966) (Brennan, J., for the Court, with Douglas, Black, and Stewart, JJ., dissenting, and Harlan, J., concurring), rehearing denied 384 U.S. 934, 86 S.Ct. 1440, 16 L.Ed.2d 535 (1966).

17. Ginzburg v. United States, 383 U.S. 463, 86 S.Ct. 942, 16 L.Ed.2d 31 (1966)

(Brennan, J., for the Court, with Black, Douglas, Stewart, and Harlan, JJ., each dissenting separately), rehearing denied 384 U.S. 934, 86 S.Ct. 1440, 16 L.Ed.2d 536 (1966).

18. Ginsberg v. New York, 390 U.S. 629, 88 S.Ct. 1274, 20 L.Ed.2d 195 (1968) (Brennan, J., for the Court, with Stewart, J., concurring in the result; Fortas, J., dissenting; and Harlan, J., concurring), rehearing denied 391 U.S. 971, 88 S.Ct. 2029, 20 L.Ed.2d 887 (1968).

19. E.g., A Book Named "John Cleland's Memoirs of a Woman of Pleasure" v. Attorney General of Massachusetts, 383 U.S. 413, 445, 86 S.Ct. 975, 991, 16 L.Ed.2d 1 (1966) (Clark, J., dissenting) (consider "social importance" together with evidence that the material in question "appeals to prurient interest and is patently offensive"); Id. at 462, 86 S.Ct. at 999 (social importance not an independent test of obscenity but "relevant only to determin[e] the predominant prurient interest of the material ...").

In the face of this divergence of opinion the Court began the practice in *Redrup v. New York,* 386 U.S. 767, 87 S.Ct. 1414, 18 L.Ed.2d 515 (1967), rehearing denied 388 U.S. 924, 87 S.Ct. 2091, 18 L.Ed.2d 515 (1967) of *per curiam* reversals of convictions for the dissemination of materials that at least five members of the Court, applying their separate tests, deemed not to be obscene. This approach capped the attempt in *Roth* to separate all forms of sexual oriented expression into two categories—the one subject to full governmental suppression and the other beyond the reach of governmental regulation to the same extent as any other protected form of speech or press.[20]

No fewer than 31 cases had followed this *Redrup* approach.[21]

§ 20.60 The *Miller* Decision

Finally, in *Miller v. California,*[1] the Court decided to abandon the *Memoirs* approach entirely, and for the first time since *Roth* a majority of the justices agreed to the proper test for obscenity:

> While *Roth* presumed "obscenity" to be "utterly without redeeming social importance," *Memoirs* [the *Fanny Hill* case] required that to prove obscenity it must be affirmatively established that the material is "*utterly* without redeeming social value." Thus, even as they repeated the words of *Roth,* the *Memoirs* plurality produced a drastically altered test that called on the prosecution to prove a negative, *i.e.,* that the material was "*utterly* without redeeming social value"—a burden virtually impossible to discharge under our criminal standards of proof. Such considerations caused Mr. Justice Harlan to wonder if the "*utterly* without redeeming social value" test had any meaning at all.[2]

The *Miller* Court might well have been correct in pointing to the difficulties the *Memoirs* approach imposed on the practicalities of meeting the burden of proof where the state is asked, in effect, to prove a negative. But in *Memoirs* the Brennan plurality emphasized the adjective "utterly" in order to give the word an independent significance, not to give it an overriding meaning as suggested in *Miller.*

In any event, in rejecting the *Memoirs* approach, the Court in *Miller* had to return to the problems that the *Memoirs* plurality had tried to resolve. The Court in *Miller* carefully noted that "in the area of freedom of speech and press the courts must always remain sensitive

---

20. Paris Adult Theatre I v. Slaton, 413 U.S. 49, 82–83, 93 S.Ct. 2628, 2646–47, 37 L.Ed.2d 446 (1973) (Brennan, J., dissenting) (footnote omitted), rehearing denied 414 U.S. 881, 94 S.Ct. 27, 38 L.Ed.2d 128 (1973).

21. 413 U.S. at 82 n. 8, 93 S.Ct. at 2647 n. 8.

§ 20.60

1. 413 U.S. 15, 93 S.Ct. 2607, 37 L.Ed.2d 419 (1973), rehearing denied 414 U.S. 881, 94 S.Ct. 26, 38 L.Ed.2d 128 (1973).

2. 413 U.S. at 21–22, 93 S.Ct. at 2613. (emphasis in original).

to any infringement on genuinely serious literary, artistic, political, or scientific expression. This is an area in which there are few eternal verities."[3] On this basis the Court stated that "State statutes designed to regulate obscene materials must be carefully limited";[4] and thus the Court held that "we now confine the permissible scope of [state] regulation [of obscenity] to works which depict or describe sexual conduct."

The actual test for obscenity set forth in *Miller* is as follows:

The basic guidelines for the trier of fact must be: (a) whether "the average person, applying contemporary community standards" would find that the work, taken as a whole, appeals to the prurient interest, (b) whether the work depicts or describes, in a patently offensive way, sexual conduct specifically defined by the applicable state law, and (c) whether the work, taken as a whole, lacks serious literary, artistic, political, or scientific value.[5]

It is easiest to consider the three elements of the *Miller* test in reverse order. Therefore let us now examine the third element.

The Third Element of the *Miller* Test. The third element of the *Miller* test—"whether the work, taken as a whole, lacks serious literary, artistic, political, or scientific value"—appears on its face considerably more restrictive than the "utterly without redeeming social value" test in *Roth* given independent significance in *Memoirs* through the emphasis on the word "utterly." The shift from "utterly" to "serious" indicates that juries may be given greater leeway under this standard. In addition, the Court eliminated the concept of "social value" and replaced it with "literary, artistic, political, or scientific value"—a distinction without a difference, perhaps, unless one believes that material can contain "social" value without being literary, artistic, political, or scientific. However, to the extent that the Court requires judicial supervision of these issues and the directing of verdicts when the evidence shows the speech to be "serious" or nonpornographic in nature, there may be little practical difference.[6]

In deciding this "value" question, the third prong of the *Miller* test, is *not* to be determined by reference to community standards. The first two prongs of *Miller* (patent offensiveness and prurient appeal) are discussed in terms of "contemporary community standards" but the

---

3. 413 U.S. at 22–23, 93 S.Ct. at 2614.

4. 413 U.S. at 23–24, 93 S.Ct. at 2614.

5. 413 U.S. at 24, 93 S.Ct. at 2615.

6. See Jenkins v. Georgia, 418 U.S. 153, 94 S.Ct. 2750, 41 L.Ed.2d 642 (1974), on remand 232 Ga. 797, 209 S.E.2d 151 (1974).

Brockett v. Spokane Arcades, Inc., 472 U.S. 491, 497 n. 7, 105 S.Ct. 2794, 2798 n. 7, 86 L.Ed.2d 394 (1985) noted:

"The basic difference between the *Memoirs* test and the *Miller* test was the *Memoirs* requirement that in order to be

third element is not.[7] The value of the work does not vary from community to community based on the degree of local acceptance it has won.[8] The test is whether a reasonable person (not an ordinary member of any given community) would find value in the material taken as a whole.[9]

The Second Element of the *Miller* Test. With respect to the second part of the *Miller* test, the Court offered "a few plain examples of what a state statute could define for regulation under part (b) of the standard announced in this opinion...." [10]

These examples were:

(a) Patently offensive representations or descriptions of ultimate sexual acts, normal or perverted, actual or simulated.

(b) Patently offensive representations or descriptions of masturbation, excretory functions, and lewd exhibition of the genitals.[11]

The Court explicitly acknowledged that under *Miller,* "no one [may] be subject to prosecution for the sale or exposure of obscene materials unless these materials depict or describe patently offensive 'hard core' sexual conduct specifically defined by the regulating state law, as written or construed." [12]

This portion of the test might have served as a basis for improving the ability of individuals to engage in publishing or film-making by offering them clear notice of what is prohibited by statute. But the Court has allowed state courts to save their statutes by construction and in so doing expand the Court's list of examples. Thus sadomasochistic materials may be constitutionally prohibited even though not listed in *Miller:* the *Miller* specifics "were offered merely as 'examples' ..., they 'were not intended to be exhaustive.' " [13]

The First Element of the *Miller* Test. The most controversial aspect of the *Miller* decision, however, may be the first part of its test

judged obscene, a work must be 'utterly without redeeming social value.' ..."

7. Smith v. United States, 431 U.S. 291, 301, 97 S.Ct. 1756, 1763, 52 L.Ed.2d 324 (1977).

8. Pope v. Illinois, 481 U.S. 497, 501, 107 S.Ct. 1918, 1921, 95 L.Ed.2d 439 (1987), on remand 162 Ill.App.2d 299, 113 Ill.Dec. 547, 515 N.E.2d 356 (1987), appeal denied 118 Ill.2d 549, 117 Ill.Dec. 229, 520 N.E.2d 390 (1988).

9. 481 U.S. at 501 & n. 3, 107 S.Ct. at 1921 & n. 3.

10. 413 U.S. at 25, 93 S.Ct. at 2615.

11. 413 U.S. at 25, 93 S.Ct. at 2615.

12. 413 U.S. at 27, 93 S.Ct. at 2616.

Material which provokes only normal, healthy sexual desires cannot be character-ized as obscene. Brockett v. Spokane Arcades, Inc., 472 U.S. 491, 105 S.Ct. 2794, 86 L.Ed.2d 394 (1985).

13. Ward v. Illinois, 431 U.S. 767, 773, 97 S.Ct. 2085, 2089, 52 L.Ed.2d 738 (1977), quoting Hamling v. United States, 418 U.S. 87, 114, 94 S.Ct. 2887, 2906, 41 L.Ed.2d 590 (1974), rehearing denied 419 U.S. 885, 95 S.Ct. 157, 42 L.Ed.2d 129 (1974). Cf. Mishkin v. New York, 383 U.S. 502, 86 S.Ct. 958, 16 L.Ed.2d 56 (1966), rehearing denied 384 U.S. 934, 86 S.Ct. 1440, 16 L.Ed.2d 535 (1966).

See Brockett v. Spokane Arcades, Inc., 472 U.S. 491, 105 S.Ct. 2794, 86 L.Ed.2d 394 (1985) (facial invalidation of obscenity statute was improper).

with its rejection of the national standards test. The national standards concept had never been adopted by a majority of the Court.[14] It was only the most restrictive concept that could get a working majority of five justices to suppress an item as obscene. Now a majority finally agreed on the national standards test—and they rejected it.

In *Miller,* the Court decided to give the "community standards" aspect of the *Roth* test a more literal meaning, and it held that trial courts may draw upon actual community standards in determining whether the material at issue is factually obscene. As *Miller* explicitly stated: "In resolving the inevitable sensitive questions of fact and law, we must continue to rely on the jury system, accompanied by the safeguards that judges, rules of evidence, presumption of innocence, and other protective features provide...." [15]

Curiously, in *Miller* the Court reiterated the notion that had provided the basis for the plurality *Jacobellis* national-standards test in the first place, that "fundamental First Amendment limitations on the powers of the States do not vary from community to community." [16] Thus the Constitutional source for the *Miller* "community standards" test is difficult to locate. Any implication in *Miller* of a broader role for the jury, as we shall see in the next section below, has not proven correct. It may be that the Court only meant that the trier of fact should not be required to guess at some hypothetical "median" standard.

Justice Brennan, in a dissent in another case filed the same day as *Miller,* expressed deep concern with the vagueness of the obscenity tests as developed from *Roth* to *Miller.* He felt that the differences between *Miller* and his plurality opinion in *Memoirs* "are, for the most part, academic," [17] but he nonetheless felt compelled to reject it as well as his earlier *Roth* opinion.[18] After considering and rejecting a wide variety of tests for the validity of obscenity legislation he offered his own brightline approach:

> In short, while I cannot say that the interests of the State—apart from the question of juveniles and unconsenting adults—are trivial or nonexistent, I am compelled to conclude that these interests cannot justify the substantial damage to constitutional rights and to this Nation's judicial machinery that inevitably results from state efforts to bar the distribution even of unprotected material to consenting adults.... I would hold, therefore, that at least in the

---

14. See Jacobellis v. Ohio, 378 U.S. 184, 84 S.Ct. 1676, 12 L.Ed.2d 793 (1964) (no opinion of the Court).

15. 413 U.S. at 26, 93 S.Ct. at 2616.

16. 413 U.S. at 30, 93 S.Ct. at 2618.

17. Paris Adult Theatre I v. Slaton, 413 U.S. 49, 95, 93 S.Ct. 2628, 2653, 37 L.Ed.2d 446 (1973) (Brennan, J., dissenting) (foot-note omitted), rehearing denied 414 U.S. 881, 94 S.Ct. 27, 38 L.Ed.2d 128 (1973), on remand 231 Ga. 312, 201 S.E.2d 456 (1973), certiorari denied 418 U.S. 939, 94 S.Ct. 3227, 41 L.Ed.2d 1173 (1974), rehearing denied 419 U.S. 887, 95 S.Ct. 163, 42 L.Ed.2d 133 (1974).

18. 413 U.S. at 98, 93 S.Ct. at 2655.

absence of distribution to juveniles or obtrusive exposure to unconsenting adults, ... the First and Fourteenth Amendments prohibit
the State and Federal Governments from attempting wholly to
suppress sexually oriented materials on the basis of their allegedly
'obscene' contents. Nothing in this approach precludes those
governments from taking action to serve what may be strong and
legitimate interests through regulation of the manner of distribution of sexually oriented material.[19]

Justice Brennan's position has not persuaded his colleagues, who
have followed *Miller*. But then a majority has always held that some
speech known as "hard core" pornography can be banned. Indeed for
fifteen years Justice Brennan had espoused this view.

The *Jenkins* Decision. Only one year after *Miller*, the Court
decided *Jenkins v. Georgia*.[20] The Court, speaking through Justice
Rehnquist, reversed the obscenity conviction of defendant, who was
charged with showing the film "Carnal Knowledge" in a theatre. The
movie had appeared on several "Ten Best" lists for the year in which it
was released, 1971. The Court explained that *Miller* did not mandate
that the jurors be instructed to apply a hypothetical statewide community standard; the Court said that *Miller* only made clear that "state
juries need not be instructed to apply 'national standards.'" The Court
also approved of the trial instruction to apply "community standards"
even though the trial judge had not specified which community.[21]

The Court then turned to the film itself. "Our *own viewing* of the
film satisfies us that 'Carnal Knowledge' could not be found under the
Miller standard to depict sexual conduct in a patently offensive way."[22]
The nudity alone does not make the film obscene, and "it would be a
serious misreading of *Miller* to conclude that the juries have unbridled
discretion in determining what is 'patently offensive.'"[23]

Justice Brennan, joined by Justices Stewart and Marshall, concurred in the result and noted the irony that the new *Miller* test did
not eliminate the need for case by case decision making—a task that is
inherent in any decision that does not leave regulation of obscenity to
the free marketplace and yet desires to protect literature and art.
"After the Court's decision today," said Brennan, "there can be no
doubt that *Miller* requires appellate courts—including this Court—to
review independently the constitutional fact of obscenity."[24] Thus
"one cannot say with certainty that material is obscene until at least

---

19. 413 U.S. at 112–13, 93 S.Ct. at 2662.
20. 418 U.S. 153, 94 S.Ct. 2750, 41
L.Ed.2d 642 (1974), on remand 232 Ga. 797,
209 S.E.2d 151 (1974).
21. 418 U.S. at 157, 94 S.Ct. at 2753.

22. 418 U.S. at 161, 94 S.Ct. at 2755
(emphasis added).

23. 418 U.S. at 160, 94 S.Ct. at 2755.
24. 418 U.S. at 163, 94 S.Ct. at 2756.

five members of this Court, applying inevitably obscure standards, have pronounced it so."[25]

§ 20.61　Special Considerations in Light of the *Miller* Case

(a) Private Possession

In *Stanley v. Georgia*,[1] the Court, relying on the first and fourteenth amendments, held that "mere private possession of obscene matter"[2] is not a crime. *Stanley*, however, must be read quite narrowly. The crucial fifth vote in *Stanley* was Justice Harlan's; thus, in spite of the broad language of the opinion, the *Stanley* Court's own summary of its decision emphasized that while "the States retain broad power to regulate obscenity; that power simply does not extend to mere possession by the individual in the privacy of his own home."[3] The Court itself had previously emphasized, in other contexts, the privacy of the home[4] and Justice Harlan in particular had been concerned with the sanctity of the home,[5] although he repeatedly has emphasized the broad power of the state over obscenity outside of the home.[6]

While the Court has refused to expand *Stanley* it has also not explained why a seller of obscenity may not raise the third party right of persons to keep the obscenity in the home. In other contexts the Supreme Court has allowed such derivative rights.[7] Thus under *Stanley* one may enjoy obscene material in one's own home, but the state may nonetheless prohibit an individual from transporting the material for private use,[8] and may also prohibit the individual from receiving the materials through the mails,[9] or from importing them from foreign countries.[10] The state, in short, may regulate obscene materials even if

---

25. 418 U.S. at 164–65, 94 S.Ct. at 2757.

§ 20.61

1. 394 U.S. 557, 89 S.Ct. 1243, 22 L.Ed.2d 542 (1969), on remand 225 Ga. 273, 167 S.E.2d 756 (1969).

2. 394 U.S. at 568, 89 S.Ct. at 1249.

3. 394 U.S. at 568, 89 S.Ct. at 1250.

4. E.g., Griswold v. Connecticut, 381 U.S. 479, 85 S.Ct. 1678, 14 L.Ed.2d 510 (1965).

5. E.g., Griswold v. Connecticut, 381 U.S. 479, 499, 85 S.Ct. 1678, 1689–90, 14 L.Ed.2d 510 (1965) (concurring opinion); Poe v. Ullman, 367 U.S. 497, 550, 81 S.Ct. 1752, 1790, 6 L.Ed.2d 989 (1961) (dissenting opinion), rehearing denied 368 U.S. 869, 82 S.Ct. 21, 7 L.Ed.2d 69 (1961).

6. E.g., Smith v. California, 361 U.S. 147, 169, 80 S.Ct. 215, 227, 4 L.Ed.2d 205

(1959) (concurring opinion), rehearing denied 361 U.S. 950, 80 S.Ct. 399, 4 L.Ed.2d 383 (1960).

7. Griswold v. Connecticut, 381 U.S. 479, 85 S.Ct. 1678, 14 L.Ed.2d 510 (1965); Carey v. Population Services International, 431 U.S. 678, 97 S.Ct. 2010, 52 L.Ed.2d 675 (1977) (third party standing and right to distribute contraceptives).

8. United States v. Orito, 413 U.S. 139, 93 S.Ct. 2674, 37 L.Ed.2d 513 (1973).

9. United States v. Reidel, 402 U.S. 351, 91 S.Ct. 1410, 28 L.Ed.2d 813 (1971).

10. United States v. 12 200 Foot Reels of Film, 413 U.S. 123, 93 S.Ct. 2665, 37 L.Ed.2d 500 (1973); see also United States v. 37 Photographs, 402 U.S. 363, 91 S.Ct. 1400, 28 L.Ed.2d 822 (1971).

those using them voluntarily sought them out.[11]   Though the private possession of obscene materials in the home is protected activity, virtually any process that leads to such possession may be declared illegal.

(b) Protection of Minors

In *Ginsberg v. New York*,[12] the Court adopted the "variable obscenity" approach suggested by Professors Lockhart and McClure and held that a statute defining obscenity in terms of an appeal to the prurient interest of minors was constitutional.   As such, *Ginsberg* represents a departure from a pure or neutral concept of "pruriency" as explicated in *Roth;* it is also a departure from the "average man" standard.   In light of the Court's revision of the *Roth* test in *Miller,* however, *Ginsberg* may be theoretically reconcilable within the "community standards" test currently in operation.

Such statutes for the protection of children must be narrowly drawn in two respects.   First, the statute must not be overbroad; the state cannot prevent the general public from reading or having access to materials on the grounds that the materials would be objectionable if read or seen by children.   Second, the statute must not be vague.

Thus in *Butler v. Michigan*[13] the Court reversed a conviction under a statute which made it an offense to make available to the general public materials found to have a potentially deleterious influence on minors.   The state argued that by "quarantining the general reading public against books not too rugged for grown men and women in order to shield juvenile innocence, it is exercising its power to promote the general welfare."[14]   The unanimous Court answered: "Surely, this is to burn the house to roast the pig."[15]   This law was overbroad.

11.   Paris Adult Theatre I v. Slaton, 413 U.S. 49, 93 S.Ct. 2628, 37 L.Ed.2d 446 (1973), rehearing denied 414 U.S. 881, 94 S.Ct. 27, 38 L.Ed.2d 128 (1973), on remand 231 Ga. 312, 201 S.E.2d 456 (1973), certiorari denied 418 U.S. 939, 94 S.Ct. 3227, 41 L.Ed.2d 1173 (1974), rehearing denied 419 U.S. 887, 95 S.Ct. 163, 42 L.Ed.2d 133 (1974).

12.   390 U.S. 629, 88 S.Ct. 1274, 20 L.Ed.2d 195 (1968), rehearing denied 391 U.S. 971, 88 S.Ct. 2029, 20 L.Ed.2d 887 (1968).

See generally, e.g., Krislov, From Ginzburg to Ginsberg: The Unhurried Children's Hour in Obscenity Litigation, 1968 Sup.Ct.Rev. 153; F. Schauer, The Law of Obscenity 77–95 (1976); Harry Kalven, Jr., ed. by Jamie Kalven, A Worthy Tradition: Freedom of Speech in America 54–59 (1988).

13.   352 U.S. 380, 77 S.Ct. 524, 1 L.Ed.2d 412 (1957).   Cf. FCC v. Pacifica Foundation, 438 U.S. 726, 98 S.Ct. 3026, 57 L.Ed.2d 1073 (1978) (FCC has power to regulate radio broadcast which is "indecent" but not "obscene" because, in part, of the presence of children in the early afternoon audience), rehearing denied 439 U.S. 883, 99 S.Ct. 227, 58 L.Ed.2d 198 (1978).

14.   352 U.S. at 383, 77 S.Ct. at 526.

15.   Id.

Dial-a-Porn.   In Sable Communications of California, Inc. v. FCC, 492 U.S. 115, 109 S.Ct. 2829, 106 L.Ed.2d 93 (1989) the Court held that § 223(b) of the Communications Act of 1934, as amended in 1988, can constitutionally impose an outright ban on "obscene" interstate, pre-recorded, commercial telephone messages ("dial-a-porn"). White, J., for the Court, noted that the Court has "repeatedly held that the protec-

Second, the statute was also too vague. The problem of vagueness is "not rendered less objectionable because the regulation is one of classification rather than direct suppression. . . . Nor is it an answer to an argument that a particular regulation of expression is vague to say that it was adopted for the salutary purpose of protecting children." [16]

Child Abuse. A law which met both of these requirements of vagueness and overbreadth and was designed to prevent the abuse of children was a state statute which the Court upheld, without a dissent, in *New York v. Ferber.*[17] New York statutes made it a crime for a person knowingly to promote sexual performances by children under the age of 16 by distributing material which depicts such performances[18] even though the materials themselves were not necessarily

tion of the First Amendment does not extend to obscene speech." The Court, however, invalidated the portion of the statute that imposed an outright ban, regardless of age, on "indecent" dial-a-porn messages. "Sexual expression which is indecent but not obscene is protected by the First Amendment; and the government does not submit that the sale of such materials to adults could be criminalized solely because they are indecent." The Government does have a compelling interest in protecting the "physical and psychological well-being of minors," including protecting them from "literature that is not obscene by adult standards." But the means used here—a total legislative ban—are not narrowly tailored to serve that purpose. "The FCC, after lengthy proceedings, determined that its credit card, access code, and scrambling rules were a satisfactory solution to the problem of keeping indecent dial-a-porn messages out of the reach of minors." The Court found unpersuasive and not supported by the evidence the Government's argument that an outright ban was appropriate because some enterprising youngsters could evade the rules. And the Court distinguished FCC v. Pacifica Foundation, 438 U.S. 726, 98 S.Ct. 3026, 57 L.Ed.2d 1073 (1978), rehearing denied 439 U.S. 883, 99 S.Ct. 227, 58 L.Ed.2d 198 (1978): that was "an emphatically narrow holding;" it did not involve a total ban, for the FCC sought to channel the indecent material to a time of day when children were thought to be less likely to listen; *Pacifica* also relied on the "unique" attributes of broadcasting, not involved in this case; and in the present case there is no "captive audience" or unwilling listener problem as there was in *Pacifica*.

Brennan, J., joined by Marshall & Stevens, JJ., concurred in part and dissented

in part, stating: "I have long been convinced that the exaction of criminal penalties for the distribution of obscene materials to consenting adults is constitutionally intolerable."

16. Interstate Circuit, Inc. v. Dallas, 390 U.S. 676, 688–89, 88 S.Ct. 1298, 1306, 20 L.Ed.2d 225 (1968) (footnote omitted); see also, Erznoznik v. Jacksonville, 422 U.S. 205, 95 S.Ct. 2268, 45 L.Ed.2d 125 (1975) (ordinance prohibiting drive-in movie theatre from showing nudity invalid on its face; the broad nudity ban exceeds the permissible restraints on obscenity and thus applies to protected speech; assuming that the law is aimed at youths, it is still not sufficiently limited—the law would seek to bar even a baby's buttocks from being shown on the drive-in movie screen).

17. 458 U.S. 747, 102 S.Ct. 3348, 73 L.Ed.2d 1113 (1982), on remand 57 N.Y.2d 256, 455 N.Y.S.2d 582, 441 N.E.2d 1100 (1982). Blackmun, J., concurred in the result without opinion. O'Connor, J., filed a concurring opinion. Brennan, J., joined by Marshall, J., filed an opinion and concurred in the judgment. Stevens, J., wrote a separate opinion also concurring in the judgment. White, J., wrote the opinion of the Court.

18. The Supreme Court described the New York statutory framework:

In 1977, the New York legislature enacted Article 263 of its Penal Law. Section 263.05 criminalizes as a class C felony the use of a child in a sexual performance:

"A person is guilty of the use of a child in a sexual performance if knowing the character and content thereof he employs, authorizes or induces a

"obscene" in a constitutional sense.[19]

The Court articulated five basic premises. First, the state's interests in protecting the physical and psychological well being of minors was compelling. Second, prohibiting the distribution of films and photos depicting such activities was closely related to this compelling governmental interest in two ways: the permanent record of the child's activity and its circulation exacerbates the harm to the minor, and also the distribution encourages the sexual exploitation of the children and the production of the material. Third, the advertising and selling of the material encourages the evil by supplying an economic motive. Fourth, the value of allowing live performances and photographic reproduction of children engaged in lewd sexual conduct is *de minimis*. The Court noted, for example, that the person who put together the material depicting the sexual performance could always use a model who was over the statutory age but looked younger. And, fifth, the classification of child pornography as outside of first amendment protection is consistent with earlier precedent and justified by the need to protect the welfare of the children.

The Court cautioned that there were limits to the extent to which child pornography is unprotected speech. The conduct prohibited must be adequately defined and described. And, the circumstances of this case require that the crime "be limited to works that *visually* depict conduct by children below a specified age." [20]

child less than sixteen years of age to engage in a sexual performance or being a parent, legal guardian or custodian of such child, he consents to the participation by such child in a sexual performance."

A "sexual performance is defined as 'any performance or part thereof which includes sexual conduct by a child less than sixteen years of age,'" § 263.1. "Sexual conduct" is in turn defined in § 263.3:

"'Sexual conduct' means actual or simulated sexual intercourse, deviate sexual intercourse, sexual bestiality, masturbation, sado-masochistic abuse, or lewd exhibition of the genitals."

A performance is defined as "any play, motion picture, photograph or dance" or "any other visual presentation exhibited before an audience." § 263.4.

At issue in this case is § 263.15, defining a class D felony:

"A person is guilty of promoting a sexual performance by a child when, knowing the character and content thereof, he produces, directs or promotes any performance which includes sexual conduct by a child less than sixteen years of age."

To "promote" is also defined:

"'Promote' means to procure, manufacture, issue, sell, give, provide, lend, mail, deliver, transfer, transmute, publish, distribute, circulate, disseminate, present, exhibit or advertise, or to offer or agree to do the same."

A companion provision bans only the knowing dissemination of obscene material. § 263.10.

458 U.S. at 751, 102 S.Ct. at 3351–52 (footnote omitted).

19. The films in this case primarily depicted young boys masturbating. 458 U.S. at 752, 102 S.Ct. at 3352.

20. 458 U.S. at 764, 102 S.Ct. at 3358 (emphasis in original) (footnote omitted). For an examination of the Court's approach to defining punishable categories of speech which is exemplified by its decision in *Ferber,* see Schauer, Codifying The First Amendment: New York v. Ferber, 1982 S.Ct.Rev. 285.

The Court then explained how the test of *Miller*[21] must be modified when dealing with child pornography:

> The *Miller* formulation is adjusted in the following respects: A trier of fact need not find that the material appeals to the prurient interest of the average person; it is not required that sexual conduct portrayed be done so in a patently offensive manner; and the material at issue need not be considered as a whole. We note that the distribution of descriptions or other depictions of sexual conduct, not otherwise obscene, which do not involve live performance or photographic or other visual reproduction of live performances, retains First Amendment protection. As with obscenity laws, criminal responsibility may not be imposed without some element of scienter on the part of the defendant.[22]

Although the Court dealt with the New York law as if it were a special type of obscenity legislation, the *Ferber* statute is really quite different. The prime purpose of the New York law is to protect young children from being used and abused as performers in a sexual performance. This performance may also be published and republished. The purpose of typical obscenity legislation is to protect people, the viewers, from looking at the performance. In contrast, the New York law focuses on the need to protect the *juvenile performers*. Thus, it should be easy to uphold.

Ferber also rejected the argument that the New York statute was overbroad within the meaning of *Broadrick v. Oklahoma*.[23] Because the facts of *Ferber* involved conduct plus speech, the Court held that *Broadrick* required substantial overbreadth.[24] Under this test, section 263.15[25] was not substantially overbroad. True, the statute might be applied to pictures in medical textbooks or National Geographic pictorials, but "we seriously doubt, and it has not been suggested, that the *arguably impermissible applications* of the statute amount to more than a tiny fraction of the materials within the statute's reach."[26]

Justice O'Connor, in her separate concurring opinion, argued that it may well be the case that it would be constitutional to ban clinical pictures in medical textbooks.[27] In contrast, Justice Brennan's opinion, concurring in the judgment, concluded that application of the New York statute to depictions of children when those depictions have serious literary, artistic, scientific, or medical value would violate free

21. Miller v. California, 413 U.S. 15, 93 S.Ct. 2607, 37 L.Ed.2d 419 (1973), rehearing denied 414 U.S. 881, 94 S.Ct. 26, 38 L.Ed.2d 128 (1973).

22. 458 U.S. at 764–65 102 S.Ct. at 3358.

23. 413 U.S. 601, 93 S.Ct. 2908, 37 L.Ed.2d 830 (1973). See Section III, B, supra.

24. 458 U.S. at 771, 102 S.Ct. at 3362.

25. See n. 18, supra.

26. 458 U.S. at 773, 102 S.Ct. at 3363 (emphasis added).

27. 458 U.S. at 775, 102 S.Ct. at 3364 (O'Connor, J., concurring).

speech.[28] Justice Stevens would have avoided the overbreadth analysis in this case because, for him, the question of whether a specific act of communication is protected as free speech involves a consideration not only of content but context.[29]

Although the Court appeared to deal with the New York law as if it were a type of typical obscenity legislation, the *Ferber* statute was really quite different. The prime purpose of the New York law was to protect young children from being used and abused as performers in a sexual performance. The purpose of obscenity legislation is to prevent people from viewing the performance. Because the New York law focuses on protecting the *juvenile performers* (rather than the adult viewers) it should be easy to uphold.

28. 458 U.S. at 776, 102 S.Ct. at 3365 (Brennan, J., joined by Marshall, J., concurring in the judgment).

29. 458 U.S. at 778, 102 S.Ct. at 3366 (Stevens, J., concurring in the judgment).

Overbreadth. In Massachusetts v. Oakes, 491 U.S. 576, 109 S.Ct. 2633, 105 L.Ed.2d 493 (1989), on remand 407 Mass. 92, 551 N.E.2d 910 (1990), a state statute made it a crime to take photographs of a child under 18 years of age in a state of nudity. The statute excluded from its coverage photos for a "bona fide scientific or medical purpose, or for an educational or cultural purpose for a bono fide school, museum or library." In 1984, the respondent had taken about 10 color photographs of his partially nude, bare-breasted, physically mature 14 year old stepdaughter who was then attending modeling school. He was convicted and sentenced to 10 years imprisonment. A divided Massachusetts Supreme Judicial Court invalidated, on First Amendment grounds, the respondent's conviction. The majority concluded that the statute was substantially overbroad in that it would make "a criminal of a parent who takes a frontal view picture of his or her naked one-year old running on a beach or romping in a wading pool." The state court dissent responded: "Soliciting, causing, or encouraging, or permitting a minor to pose for photographs is no more speech than is setting a house afire in order to photograph a burning house."

The U.S. Supreme Court then granted certiorari. After that, the state legislature amended the statute to add a "lascivious intent" requirement to portion of the statute applied to respondent and to repeal the exemption for bona fide scientific, medical, educational, or cultural purposes.

O'Connor, J., joined by Rehnquist, C.J. and White & Kennedy, JJ., refused to reach the overbreadth question. In their view, in light of the statutory changes it had become moot: "Because the special concern that animates the overbreadth doctrine is no longer present after the amendment or repeal of the challenged statute, we need not extend the benefits of the doctrine to a defendant whose conduct is not protected.... [W]e took the case to decide the overbreadth question alone." 491 U.S. at 583, 585, 109 S.Ct. at 2638, 2639. The Court then vacated the judgment below and remanded so that the state court could decide whether the former version of the state statute at issue could constitutionally be applied to the respondent.

Scalia, J., joined by Brennan, Marshall & Stevens, JJ., concurred in the judgment in part and dissented in part: "It seems to me strange judicial theory that a conviction initially invalid can be resuscitated by postconviction alteration of the statute under which it was obtained." 491 U.S. at 585, 109 S.Ct. at 2639.

Brennan, J., joined by Marshall & Stevens, JJ., filed a dissenting opinion arguing that the first amendment "blocks the prohibition of nude posing by minors in connection with the production of works of art not depicting lewd behavior and not specifically prepared, in accordance with [the state statute's] exclusion, for museums or libraries." The state statute, in the view of these justices, was overbroad. 491 U.S. at 592–95, 109 S.Ct. at 2643–44.

In *Osborne v. Ohio* [30] the Court made this point clear when it held that the state may constitutionally prohibit the possession and viewing of child pornography at home. The distinction with *Stanley v. Georgia*,[31] the Court concluded, was "obvious." Unlike *Stanley* the state here does not rely on a paternalistic interest in regulating Osborne's mind. Rather, the purpose of the law is to protect the children, victims of child pornography. The state hopes to destroy a market for the exploitative use of children by prohibiting the possession of child pornography.

Osborne went on to conclude that the statute was not overbroad. The law prohibited any person from possessing or viewing any material or performance showing a minor (who is not his child or ward) in a state of nudity unless (a), the material or performance is presented for a bona fide purpose by or to a person having a proper interest therein, or (b) the possessor knows that the minor's parents or guardian has consented in writing to such photographing or use of the minor. As construed by the Ohio Supreme Court the law requires proof of scienter and is limited to depictions of nudity that involve lewd exhibition or involve graphic focus of the minor's genitals.[32]

(c) *Prior Restraint*

The Court has often stated that "Any system of prior restraints of expression comes to this Court bearing a heavy presumption against its constitutional validity."[33] Obscenity, however, is one of a few areas of the law in which prior restraint has been upheld.

There are, however, certain fifth and fourteenth amendment safeguards that the Court has imposed on the procedures employed in the prior restraint of allegedly-obscene materials. In *Freedman v. Maryland*,[34] the Court held that a local censorship board authorized to

---

30. 495 U.S. 103, 110 S.Ct. 1691, 109 L.Ed.2d 98 (1990), rehearing denied __ U.S. __, 110 S.Ct. 2605, 110 L.Ed.2d 285 (1990).

31. 394 U.S. 557, 89 S.Ct. 1243, 22 L.Ed.2d 542 (1969), on remand 225 Ga. 273, 167 S.E.2d 756 (1969).

32. However the Court remanded for a new trial because of the trial court's failure to instruct the jury on the state's obligation to prove lewdness. Brennan, J., joined by Marshall & Stevens, JJ., dissented, arguing that "our decision in *Stanley v. Georgia* prevents the State from criminalizing appellant's possession of the photographs at issue in this case." 495 U.S. at 126, 110 S.Ct. at 1705 (Brennan, J., dissenting).

33. Bantam Books, Inc. v. Sullivan, 372 U.S. 58, 70, 83 S.Ct. 631, 639, 9 L.Ed.2d 584 (1963). See §§ 20.3(c), 20.16, 20.17, supra.

34. 380 U.S. 51, 85 S.Ct. 734, 13 L.Ed.2d 649 (1965); see also, e.g., Carroll v. President and Com'rs of Princess Anne, 393 U.S. 175, 89 S.Ct. 347, 21 L.Ed.2d 325 (1968). It is unlikely that the *Freedman* rule of prior restraints would apply if the allegedly obscene material were not films but only books.

In an injunctive proceeding, which is civil, there is no federal constitutional requirement that proof be beyond a reasonable doubt, Cooper v. Mitchell Bros.' Santa Ana Theater, 454 U.S. 90, 102 S.Ct. 172, 70 L.Ed.2d 262 (1981) (per curiam), on remand 128 Cal.App.3d 937, 180 Cal.Rptr. 728 (1982), certiorari denied 459 U.S. 944, 103 S.Ct. 259, 74 L.Ed.2d 202 (1982), rehearing denied 459 U.S. 1093, 103 S.Ct. 581, 74 L.Ed.2d 940 (1982). Nor is there a federal constitutional requirement of a jury. Al-

revoke a book or motion-picture distributor's license for the sale or display of obscene materials, or otherwise authorized to engage in the prior restraint of allegedly-obscene materials, (1) must afford the accused party a prompt hearing; (2) has the burden of showing that the material is, in fact, obscene; (3) must defer to a judicial proceeding for the imposition of a valid final restraint on the material; and (4) must either refrain from making a finding of obscenity or, as a requirement of law under the board's enabling statute or clear judicial mandate, take action on its own behalf in a court of law to seek an affirmation of its initial finding of obscenity. In the court proceeding the distributor or retailer may contest the issue of obscenity even though the book or film has been found to be obscene in other cases to which he was not a party.[35] Even if a judge rather than an administrative tribunal initially enters the prior restraint, the procedural safeguards of *Freedman* must be followed, in order to mitigate the unconstitutional consequences if the restraint were erroneously entered.[36]

Search Warrants. If materials that are the subject of a search warrant may be protected by the first amendment—"when the 'things' are books, and the basis for their seizure is the ideas which they contain"—then the requirements of the fourth amendment must be applied with "the most scrupulous exactitude." [37] Thus the search warrant must be particularized and should not be issued only on the police officer's conclusory assertion in order that there be an opportunity for the judicial officer to "focus searchingly on the question of obscenity." [38] There is no higher standard of probable cause, however. The Court should use the same standard of probable cause used to review warrant applications generally, but the police cannot rely on the

exander v. Virginia, 413 U.S. 836, 93 S.Ct. 2803, 37 L.Ed.2d 993 (1973) (per curiam), rehearing denied 414 U.S. 881, 94 S.Ct. 29, 38 L.Ed.2d 128 (1973), mandate conformed 214 Va. 539, 203 S.E.2d 441 (1974).

35. McKinney v. Alabama, 424 U.S. 669, 96 S.Ct. 1189, 47 L.Ed.2d 387 (1976) (in rem proceeding not bar to litigation of the obscenity issue of the material as to a distributor not party to the in rem proceeding).

36. Vance v. Universal Amusement Co., Inc., 445 U.S. 308, 100 S.Ct. 1156, 63 L.Ed.2d 413 (1980) (per curiam), rehearing denied 446 U.S. 947, 100 S.Ct. 2177, 64 L.Ed.2d 804 (1980).

37. Stanford v. Texas, 379 U.S. 476, 485, 85 S.Ct. 506, 511–12, 13 L.Ed.2d 431 (1965) (5 hour search and seizure of 2000 books, pamphlets, and papers invalidated), rehearing denied 380 U.S. 926, 85 S.Ct. 879, 13 L.Ed.2d 813 (1965).

See also, Wilkey v. Wood, 19 How.St.Tr. 1153 (1763); Entick v. Carrington, 19 How. St.Tr. 1029 (1765).

See generally, Z. Chafee, Government and Mass Communications 200–18 (1947).

38. Marcus v. Search Warrants, 367 U.S. 717, 732, 81 S.Ct. 1708, 1716, 6 L.Ed.2d 1127 (1961).

See also, Quantity of Books v. Kansas, 378 U.S. 205, 210, 84 S.Ct. 1723, 1725–26, 12 L.Ed.2d 809 (1964); Lee Art Theatre, Inc. v. Virginia, 392 U.S. 636, 637, 88 S.Ct. 2103, 2104, 20 L.Ed.2d 1313 (1968) (per curiam), on remand 209 Va. 354, 164 S.E.2d 665 (1968); Roaden v. Kentucky, 413 U.S. 496, 502, 93 S.Ct. 2796, 2800, 37 L.Ed.2d 757 (1973); Heller v. New York, 413 U.S. 483, 489, 93 S.Ct. 2789, 2793, 37 L.Ed.2d 745 (1973), on remand 33 N.Y.2d 314, 352 N.Y.2d 601, 307 N.E.2d 805 (1973), cert. denied 418 U.S. 944, 94 S.Ct. 3231, 41 L.Ed.2d 1175 (1974).

"exigency" exception to the fourth amendment warrant requirement.[39] In addition, the police may not seize allegedly obscene material without a warrant even though the seizure is contemporaneous with, and incident to, an arrest.[40]

However, when an undercover police officer enters a bookstore where the public was invited to enter and transact business, and then examines materials openly offered for sale, that is not a "search" within the meaning of the fourth amendment. Nor was there any "seizure" within the meaning of the fourth amendment when the undercover officer purchased several magazines. The store attendant voluntarily transferred any possessory interest he might have in the magazines in exchange for the money. This nonseizure also was not later transferred into a fourth amendment seizure simply because the police officer seized the marked $50 bill which he used to purchase the magazines, and neglected to return the change. "The risk of prior restraint, which is the underlying basis for the special Fourth Amendment protections accorded searches for and seizures of First Amendment materials, does not come into play in such cases, and the purchase is analogous to purchases of other unlawful substances previously found not to violate the Fourth Amendment." [41]

Where the censorship board or other state body confiscates a single piece of allegedly obscene material (while others are available for exhibition) for the purpose of preserving it as evidence, the board need not provide a hearing so long as the confiscation is made pursuant to a warrant issued upon a showing of probable cause. Even here, though, a prompt judicial hearing is required to determine whether the material is obscene. If a showing is made to the trial court that other copies of the film are not available for exhibition, the trial court should permit the seized film to be copied so that the exhibition can be continued until the obscenity issue is resolved in an adversary hearing. Otherwise the film must be returned.[42]

Before a search warrant may be issued for the seizure of allegedly obscene material, there must be an opportunity for a neutral and detached judicial officer to focus searchingly on the question of obscenity. Such neutrality and detachment did not exist when the Town Justice signed an open-ended warrant and then joined the law enforce-

---

39. New York v. P.J. Video, Inc., 475 U.S. 868, 875 & n. 6, 106 S.Ct. 1610, 1615 & n. 6, 89 L.Ed.2d 871 (1986), on remand 68 N.Y.2d 296, 508 N.Y.S.2d 907, 501 N.E.2d 556 (1986), cert. denied 479 U.S. 1091, 107 S.Ct. 1301, 94 L.Ed.2d 156 (1987).

40. Roaden v. Kentucky, 413 U.S. 496, 497–98, 504, 93 S.Ct. 2796, 2798–2801, 37 L.Ed.2d 757 (1973).

41. Maryland v. Macon, 472 U.S. 463, 470, 105 S.Ct. 2778, 2783, 86 L.Ed.2d 370 (1985). Cf. Roaden v. Kentucky, 413 U.S. 496, 504, 93 S.Ct. 2796, 2801, 37 L.Ed.2d 757 (1973).

42. Heller v. New York, 413 U.S. 483, 93 S.Ct. 2789, 37 L.Ed.2d 745 (1973), on remand 33 N.Y.2d 314, 352 N.Y.S.2d 601, 307 N.E.2d 805 (1973), certiorari denied 418 U.S. 944, 94 S.Ct. 3231, 41 L.Ed.2d 1175 (1974).

ment officials in conducting a search of the book store lasting nearly six hours and examining and seizing numerous films and magazines. The judicial officer in effect conducted a prohibited generalized search and seizure and became "a member, if not, the leader of the search party which was essentially a police operation." [43]

Licensing of Sexually Oriented Businesses. In *FW/PBS, Inc. v. City of Dallas*,[44] a fragmented Court affirmed in part, reversed in part, vacated in part, and remanded a case where the Fifth Circuit had upheld an ordinance that licensed sexually oriented businesses, such as adult book stores, adult cabarets, and escort agencies. Petitioners challenged the ordinance on its face. There was no issue whether the entertainment, books, videos, etc. were obscene. Justice O'Connor, joined by Justices Stevens & Kennedy, invalidated the licensing scheme as an invalid prior restraint under *Freedman*. The city licensing system required that premises to be used for "sexually oriented businesses" must be first approved by the health and fire departments and the building official before the chief of police issued a license.

Because the ordinance, first, did not provide for an effective limitation on the time within which the licensor's decision must be made, and, second, it also failed to provide for prompt judicial review, it was invalid as to those businesses engaged in first amendment activity (as determined by the Court on remand). However, Justice O'Connor did not require that the ordinance meet the third requirement of *Freedman*—that is, the first amendment does not require that the city bear the burden of going to court to effect the denial of the license; nor must the city bear the burden of proof once in court. Justice O'Connor reasoned that "the city does not exercise discretion by passing judgment on the content of any protected speech. Rather, the city reviews the general qualifications of each license applicant, a ministerial action that is not presumptively invalid." [45] While the movie distributor in *Freedman* might be deterred from challenging the licensing decision of a particular movie, the license applicants here have much more at stake, because the license is the key to the applicant's obtaining and maintaining a business and hence there is every incentive to pursue a license denial through the courts.[46]

Justice Brennan, joined by Justices Marshall and Blackmun, concurred in the judgment and would have applied all three of the procedural safeguards discussed in *Freedman*.[47]

43. Lo–Ji Sales, Inc. v. New York, 442 U.S. 319, 325–27, 99 S.Ct. 2319, 2323–25, 60 L.Ed.2d 920 (1979), distinguishing Heller v. New York, 413 U.S. 483, 93 S.Ct. 2789, 37 L.Ed.2d 745 (1973), on remand 33 N.Y.2d 314, 352 N.Y.S.2d 601, 307 N.E.2d 805 (1973), cert. denied 418 U.S. 944, 94 S.Ct. 3231, 41 L.Ed.2d 1175 (1974).

44. 493 U.S. 215, 110 S.Ct. 596, 107 L.Ed.2d 603 (1990), on remand 896 F.2d 864 (5th Cir.1990).

45. 493 U.S. at 229, 110 S.Ct. at 607.

46. 493 U.S. at 229, 110 S.Ct. at 607.

47. 493 U.S. at 237, 110 S.Ct. at 611.

Scalia, J., concurred in part and dissented in part, as did Stevens, J. White, J.,

(d) Zoning Laws and Public Exhibition of "Adult" Non-obscene Material

Paris Adult Theatre I v. Slaton,[48] decided by the Court on the same day as *Miller,* held that the state may prohibit public exhibitions or displays of obscenity even if access to the exhibitions is limited to consenting adults. The Court carried *Paris Adult Theatre* a step further in *Young v. American Mini Theatres, Inc.*,[49] in which it held that an appropriately definite zoning ordinance prohibiting the location of an "adult movie theatre" within 1000 feet of any two other "regulated uses," including 10 different kinds of establishments in addition to adult theatres, is constitutionally permissible *even* if the theatre is not displaying obscene material.

While the ordinance in question characterized an adult theatre as one presenting certain specified "sexual activities" or "anatomical areas," the Court reasoned that the ordinance did not constitute an exercise in prior restraint, but rather a valid use of the city's zoning power to regulate the location of commercial establishments. The Court specifically held that this zoning power overrides the first amendment element in the display of the material at any locality the distributor chooses. However the Court placed great emphasis on the continual availability of these movies and the fact that the restrictions were unrelated to the suppression of ideas.

It was true that a concentration of these theatres brought certain physical changes to the neighborhoods where they were located. These changes were due not only to the advertisements and posters associated with the theatres but also to the size and type of crowd they attracted. The zoning of a reasonable amount of space between such theatres avoided the concentration of this physical effect on a neighborhood. Nevertheless the regulation describes the theatres in terms of the content of their films.

joined by Rehnquist, C.J., concurred in part and dissented in part. O'Connor, for the Court, also ruled that no petitioner had standing to challenge other portions of the law, such as the portion prohibiting the licensing of an applicant who has resided with an individual whose license application has been revoked. The Court also concluded that the ordinance's provision requiring that motels that rent rooms for fewer than 10 hours must be specially licensed is not a violation of the Due Process clause.

48. 413 U.S. 49, 93 S.Ct. 2628, 37 L.Ed.2d 446 (1973), rehearing denied 414 U.S. 881, 94 S.Ct. 27, 38 L.Ed.2d 128 (1973), on remand 231 Ga. 312, 201 L.Ed.2d 456 (1973), certiorari denied 418 U.S. 939, 94 S.Ct. 3227, 41 L.Ed.2d 1173 (1974), rehearing denied 419 U.S. 887, 95 S.Ct. 163, 42 L.Ed.2d 133 (1974). The Court thus restricted Stanley v. Georgia, 394 U.S. 557, 89 S.Ct. 1243, 22 L.Ed.2d 542 (1969), on remand 225 Ga. 273, 167 S.E.2d 756 (1969).

49. 427 U.S. 50, 96 S.Ct. 2440, 49 L.Ed.2d 310 (1976), rehearing denied 429 U.S. 873, 97 S.Ct. 191, 50 L.Ed.2d 155 (1976). See also, Bellanca v. New York State Liquor Authority, 54 N.Y.2d 228, 241, 445 N.Y.S.2d 87, 93, 429 N.E.2d 765, 771 (1981) (Gabrielli, J., dissenting), citing an earlier edition of this treatise, certiorari denied 456 U.S. 1006, 102 S.Ct. 2296, 73 L.Ed.2d 1300 (1982).

Whether this doctrine will be expanded to other types of speech will have to await future cases, though the language of Justice Stevens' plurality opinion in *American Mini Theatres* appears to allow the doctrine to be confined:

> [E]ven though we recognize that the First Amendment will not tolerate the total suppression of erotic materials that have some arguably artistic value, it is manifest that society's interest in protecting this type of expression is of a wholly different, and lesser, magnitude than the interest in untrammeled political debate.... But few of us would march our sons and daughters off to war to preserve the citizen's right to see "Specified Sexual Activities" exhibited in the theaters of our choice. Even though the First Amendment protects communication in this area from total suppression, we hold that the State may legitimately use the content of these materials as the basis for placing them in a different classification from other motion pictures.
>
> . . .
>
> Since what is ultimately at stake is nothing more than a limitation on the place where adult films may be exhibited, even though the determination of whether a particular film fits that characterization turns on the nature of its content, we conclude that the city's interest in the present and future character of its neighborhoods adequately supports its classification of motion pictures.[50]

Thus the Court held that *non*-obscene motion pictures involving the display of sexual activities are entitled to a lesser degree of protection under the first amendment than other forms of protected expression, at least in the context of the otherwise valid purposes of a zoning ordinance. In so doing, the Court made it clear that the artistic value of a non-obscene display of sexual activity is of less value to society than political expression, and implied that a zoning ordinance based upon the latter would not pass constitutional muster. The implications of this distinction has stirred up a great deal of controversy, for the Court in this case allowed time, place or manner restrictions on speech based on the content of the speech.

---

50. 427 U.S. at 70–72, 96 S.Ct. at 2452–53 (footnote omitted) (opinion of Stevens, J., joined by Burger, C.J., and White & Rehnquist, JJ.).

Justice Stevens has been the prime force in encouraging the Court to allow restrictions (in some circumstances) to be placed on speech because of its content. See also, e.g., FCC v. Pacifica Foundation, 438 U.S. 726, 98 S.Ct. 3026, 57 L.Ed.2d 1073 (1978) (FCC has power—in order to protect children—to regulate radio broadcast which is "indecent" but not "obscene"), rehearing denied 439 U.S. 883, 99 S.Ct. 227, 58 L.Ed.2d 198 (1978). Note that Justice Stevens' separate opinion, joined by Chief Justice Burger and Justice Rehnquist, specifically relied on a power to regulate speech based on its content, but the other two

In *Schad v. Borough of Mount Ephraim* [51] the Court distinguished *American Mini Theatres* and invalidated a zoning ordinance that, as construed by the state courts, forbade *all* "live entertainment," including non-obscene nude dancing, in a commercial zone. "[N]o property in the Borough may be principally used for the commercial production of plays, concerts, musicals, dance, or any other form of live entertainment." [52] An adult book store, operating in a commercial zone in the Borough of Mount Ephraim, introduced a coin operated device: a customer, after inserting a coin, would be able to watch a live dancer, usually nude, perform behind a glass panel; the store was therefore found guilty of violating the ordinance.

Justice White, for the Court, reasoned, first, that nude dancing is entitled to some first amendment protection.[53] The Court also allowed the appellants to raise an overbreadth challenge to the ordinance. The ordinance on its face did not even seek to justify the exclusion of such a broad category of protected expression—all live entertainment.

Before the Supreme Court, counsel for Mount Ephraim presented some justifications, but none of these were persuasive and none had been articulated by the state courts. The Borough argued that it could allow a broad range of commercial uses but nonetheless exclude live entertainment because that use led to special problems such as increased need for parking, trash pick-up, police protection, and medical facilities. However the Borough presented no evidence to support this assertion, and the Court did not find it "self-evident that a theatre, for example, would create greater parking problems than would a restaurant." [54] Assuming that live entertainment would create special problems not associated with other commercial uses, the Borough had not narrowly tailored a zoning law to address any unique problems. The Borough's claim that its zoning restriction was an attempt to create a commercial area catering only to the residents' "immediate needs" also did not survive scrutiny. The Borough introduced no evidence to support this assertion and the face of the ordinance contradicted it, for the ordinance permitted car showrooms, hardware stores, offices, etc.

Nor did the *American Mini Theatres* analysis support the constitutionality of the ordinance, for the restriction in *American Mini Theatres* did not ban all adult theatres or even affect the number of adult movie theatres in the city; "it merely dispersed them." [55] And in *American*

members of the majority rejected this analysis.

51. 452 U.S. 61, 101 S.Ct. 2176, 68 L.Ed.2d 671 (1981). See § 20.47(e), supra.

52. 452 U.S. at 66, 101 S.Ct. at 2181 (footnote omitted).

53. 452 U.S. at 66, 101 S.Ct. at 2181, citing Doran v. Salem Inn, Inc., 422 U.S. 922, 95 S.Ct. 2561, 45 L.Ed.2d 648 (1975),

and Southeastern Promotions, Ltd. v. Conrad, 420 U.S. 546, 95 S.Ct. 1239, 43 L.Ed.2d 448 (1975).

54. 452 U.S. at 74, 101 S.Ct. at 2185 (footnote omitted).

55. 452 U.S. at 71, 101 S.Ct. at 2184. Later in the opinion the Court rejected Mount Ephraim's argument that residents could view nude dancing in nearby areas

Mini Theatres the city had presented evidence that a concentration of adult theatres led to a deterioration of surrounding neighborhoods.

Finally, the Court could not accept the ordinance as a reasonable "time, place, and manner" restriction. The Borough presented no evidence that the manner of expression—live entertainment—is basically incompatible with the normal activity in a commercial zone. Thus the Court invalidated the ordinance with only two justices dissenting.[56]

While *American Mini Theatres* allowed a city to disperse adult theatres, *City of Renton v. Playtime Theatres, Inc.*[57] allowed a city to concentrate them. Justice Rehnquist for the Court (with only Brennan and Marshall dissenting) upheld a zoning ordinance that prohibited "adult" motion picture theatres from locating within 1,000 feet of any residential zone, single- or multiple-family dwelling, church, park, or school. The district court found that the city council's "*predominate* concerns" were with the secondary effects of adult theatres—e.g., to prevent crime, protect the city's *retail trade*, maintain property values, and preserve the quality of life—and not with the content of adult films themselves.[58] This finding was "more than adequate to establish that the city's pursuit of its zoning interests here was unrelated to the suppression of free expression." The ordinance was a "content-neutral" speech regulation because it was "*justified* without reference to the content of the regulated speech."[59] The Court then upheld the ordinance because it served a substantial governmental interest (preserving the quality of life), and allowed reasonable alternative avenues of communication as, more than five percent of the entire land area of Renton was allowed to be used by adult theatres. "Cities may regulate adult theatres by dispersing them, as in Detroit [in *American Mini Theatres*], or by effectively concentrating them, as in Renton."[60] And unlike *Schad*, the Renton ordinance was "narrowly tailored" to those theatres producing the unwanted secondary effects.[61]

outside of the limits of the Borough. Since there was no countywide zoning, the Borough could not argue that the county wished to exclude live entertainment only from residential areas within the county. Further, no evidence supported the assertion that nearby areas offered nude dancing as a form of entertainment. Finally, one " 'is not to have the exercise of his liberty of expression in appropriate places abridged on the plea that it may be exercised in some other place.' " 452 U.S. at 76–77, 101 S.Ct. at 2187, quoting Schneider v. Irvington, 308 U.S. 147, 163, 60 S.Ct. 146, 151, 84 L.Ed. 155 (1939).

56. Burger, C.J., joined by Rehnquist, J., dissented. 452 U.S. at 85, 101 S.Ct. at 2191.

See § 20.47(e), supra, on zoning regulations and time, place, and manner restrictions.

57. 475 U.S. 41, 106 S.Ct. 925, 89 L.Ed.2d 29 (1986), rehearing denied 475 U.S. 1132, 106 S.Ct. 1663, 90 L.Ed.2d 205 (1986).

58. 475 U.S. at 47, 106 S.Ct. at 929 (emphasis in original).

59. 475 U.S. at 48, 106 S.Ct. at 929 (emphasis in original).

60. 475 U.S. at 52, 106 S.Ct. at 931.

61. 475 U.S. at 52, 106 S.Ct. at 931, contrasting Schad v. Mount Ephraim, 452 U.S. 61, 101 S.Ct. 2176, 68 L.Ed.2d 671 (1981). Compare also, Erznoznik v. Jack-

Closures of Businesses Used as Places of Prostitution. In *Arcara v. Cloud Books, Inc.,*[62] the Court held that there is no first amendment bar to the enforcement of a state law that authorized the closure of any premises used as a place for prostitution. The defendant claimed an exception because the place was an adult bookstore, but the Court found no constitutional problem in the state's closure order. *O'Brien* did not protect the bookstore because the law did not single out bookstores at all. The law applied to any premises and the case raised no issue regarding the contents of the materials sold at the bookstore, whether these materials were constitutionally "obscene" or protected expression. Though Justice Blackmun's dissent objected to the fact that the closure order was triggered by the conduct of patrons rather than by the defendant's sale of books,[63] the majority pointed out that the management of the bookstore was fully aware of the explicit sexual activity engaged in and solicited on the premises,[64] and the closure order did not preclude the defendants from selling their same material at another location.[65] In addition, there was no evidence in the record that the closure order was a mere pretext to close the store because it sold adult books. The state's closure order, in this case, was not directed against speech or the nonexpressive effect of speech; it was directed at illegal sexual activities.

(e) Obscenity and the Twenty–First Amendment

Related to the state's power to use the zoning laws to restrict "adult" speech which is not constitutionally obscene is the state's power, under the twenty-first amendment, to regulate "adult" speech in establishments licensed by the state to serve liquor. As the Court stated in *New York State Liquor Authority v. Bellanca:* [66]

---

sonville, 422 U.S. 205, 95 S.Ct. 2268, 45 L.Ed.2d 125 (1975) (law too vague).

62. 478 U.S. 697, 106 S.Ct. 3172, 92 L.Ed.2d 568 (1986), on remand 68 N.Y.2d 553, 510 N.Y.S.2d 844, 503 N.E.2d 492 (1986).

63. 478 U.S. at 708, 106 S.Ct. at 3179 (Blackmun, J., joined by Brennan & Marshall, JJ., dissenting).

64. 478 U.S. at 698, 106 S.Ct. at 3173.

65. 478 U.S. at 706, 106 S.Ct. at 3177.

66. 452 U.S. 714, 101 S.Ct. 2599, 69 L.Ed.2d 357 (1981) (per curiam), on remand 54 N.Y.2d 228, 445 N.Y.S.2d 87, 429 N.E.2d 765 (1981), certiorari denied 456 U.S. 1006, 102 S.Ct. 2296, 73 L.Ed.2d 1300 (1982). Accord, California v. LaRue, 409 U.S. 109, 93 S.Ct. 390, 34 L.Ed.2d 342 (1972), rehearing denied 410 U.S. 948, 93 S.Ct. 1351, 35 L.Ed.2d 615 (1973).

In *LaRue*, the first case that raised this issue, the Court discussed the facts in some detail. In the licensed liquor establishments, there were both topless and bottomless dancers. "Customers were found engaging in oral copulation with women entertainers; customers engaged in public masturbation; and customers placed rolled currency either directly into the vagina of a female entertainer, or on the bar in order that she might pick it up herself. Numerous other forms of contact between the mouths of male customers and the vaginal areas of female performers were reported to have occurred." Some of the female dancers were involved in prostitution in and around the licensed premises and both rape and attempted rape took place "on or immediately adjacent to such premises." California v. LaRue, 409 U.S. 109, 111, 93 S.Ct. 390, 393, 34 L.Ed.2d 342 (1972), rehearing denied 410 U.S. 948, 93 S.Ct. 1351, 35 L.Ed.2d 615 (1973).

Pursuant to its power to regulate the sale of liquor within its boundaries, [the New York Legislature] has banned topless dancing in establishments granted a license to serve liquor. The State's power to ban the sale of alcoholic beverages entirely includes the lesser power to ban the sale of liquor on premises where topless dancing occurs.[67]

The legislature judged that "mixing alcohol and nude dancing" causes disturbances which the state sought to avoid by a reasonable restriction on places which sell liquor for consumption on the premises. The Court would respect this judgment, to which the twenty-first amendment gave an "added presumption." [68]

In contrast, a statute prohibiting nude entertainment in places that serve no alcohol but only food or nonalcoholic beverages, violates the first amendment. Nudity alone is not obscene in the constitutional sense, and because such a law applies to establishments that do not serve liquor, it is overbroad.[69]

The twenty-first amendment has long been used to grant the states extensive authority over liquor, and to some extent immunize state regulation from commerce clause challenge.[70] However, the twenty-first amendment has never been read to immunize state regulation over liquor from the civil liberties guarantees of the Constitution.[71] Thus,

67. 452 U.S. at 717, 101 S.Ct. at 2601.

There is no constitutional requirement that the governmental unit that grants liquor licenses must be the same one which regulates the conditions under which liquor is sold. Thus, it is irrelevant that a city ordinance bans nude or nearly nude dancing in places licensed to sell liquor although, under state law, only local voters (not the city or the state), pursuant to a popular election, can impose prohibition of alcohol. City of Newport, Ky. v. Iacobucci, 479 U.S. 92, 107 S.Ct. 383, 93 L.Ed.2d 334 (1986), rehearing denied 479 U.S. 1047, 107 S.Ct. 913, 93 L.Ed.2d 862 (1987) (per curiam).

68. 452 U.S. at 718, 101 S.Ct. at 2602, quoting California v. LaRue, 409 U.S. 109, 118, 93 S.Ct. 390, 397, 34 L.Ed.2d 342 (1972), rehearing denied 410 U.S. 948, 93 S.Ct. 1351, 35 L.Ed.2d 615 (1973). Only Stevens, J., dissented. Marshall J., concurred in the judgment but filed no written opinion. Brennan, J., dissented from the summary disposition of the case and would have set it for oral argument.

On remand the New York State Court of Appeals held that the state statute violated the free speech provisions of the state constitution, because the twenty-first amendment does not confer a power on the states

that is superior to, or free from, state constitutional restraints. Bellanca v. New York State Liquor Authority, 54 N.Y.2d 228, 445 N.Y.S.2d 87, 429 N.E.2d 765 (1981), certiorari denied 456 U.S. 1006, 102 S.Ct. 2296, 73 L.Ed.2d 1300 (1982). See also, 54 N.Y.2d at 241, 445 N.Y.S.2d at 93, 429 N.E.2d at 771, citing treatise (Gabrielli, J., dissenting).

69. Chase v. Davelaar, 645 F.2d 735 (9th Cir.1981); Morris v. Municipal Court for San Jose–Milpitas Judicial District of Santa Clara County, 32 Cal.3d 553, 186 Cal.Rptr. 494, 652 P.2d 51 (1982).

70. See, e.g., State Bd. of Equalization v. Young's Market Co., 299 U.S. 59, 57 S.Ct. 77, 81 L.Ed. 38 (1936) (California may impose $500 fee for privilege of importing into that state beer from a sister state even though such a fee would have violated the commerce clause prior to the twenty-first amendment), rehearing denied 299 U.S. 623, 57 S.Ct. 229, 81 L.Ed. 458 (1936).

71. See, e.g., Craig v. Boren, 429 U.S. 190, 97 S.Ct. 451, 50 L.Ed.2d 397 (1976), rehearing denied 429 U.S. 1124, 97 S.Ct. 1161, 51 L.Ed.2d 574 (1977), where the Court invalidated a state statute prohibiting the sale of 3.2% beer to males under 21 and females under 18; the discrimination

Bellanca should be read narrowly: it does *not* stand for the proposition that the first and fourteenth amendments are inapplicable to the states when they regulate liquor. Rather the twenty-first amendment only allows the states greater freedom to regulate "adult" speech in connection with its power to regulate the sale of liquor within its boundaries. This state regulatory power appears to be similar to its zoning power to restrict "adult," non-obscene speech.[72]

(f) Non-pictorial Obscenity

On the same day that *Miller v. California*[73] was decided, the Court

based on gender violated the equal protection guarantees of the fourteenth amendment:

"Once passing beyond consideration of the Commerce Clause, the relevance of the Twenty–First Amendment to other constitutional provisions becomes increasingly doubtful. ... [T]he Court has never recognized sufficient 'strength' in [that] Amendment to defeat an otherwise established claim of invidious discrimination in violation of the Equal Protection Clause." 429 U.S. at 206–07, 97 S.Ct. at 461–62.

324 Liquor Corp. v. Duffy, 479 U.S. 335, 346–48, 107 S.Ct. 720, 726–27, 93 L.Ed.2d 667 (1987) (the power of the states under 21st Amendment is circumscribed by other provisions of the Constitution, such as the establishment clause, equal protection clause, procedural due process, and export-import clauses), on remand 69 N.Y.2d 891, 515 N.Y.S.2d 231, 507 N.E.2d 1087 (1987).

See also, Moose Lodge No. 107 v. Irvis, 407 U.S. 163, 178–79, 92 S.Ct. 1965, 1974, 32 L.Ed.2d 627 (1972). Cf. California Retail Liquor Dealers Ass'n v. Midcal Aluminum, Inc., 445 U.S. 97, 100 S.Ct. 937, 63 L.Ed.2d 233 (1980) (state wine pricing statute violates Sherman Act, notwithstanding twenty-first amendment); Department of Revenue v. James B. Beam Distilling Co., 377 U.S. 341, 84 S.Ct. 1247 12 L.Ed.2d 362 (1964) (state tax on Scotch violates export-import clause, notwithstanding twenty-first amendment).

R. Rotunda, Modern Constitutional Law: Cases and Notes 147–48 (1981).

72. A state law prohibiting cable television systems from retransmitting out-of-state signals containing alcoholic beverage commercials was invalid under the supremacy clause because it conflicted with, and was preempted by, federal regulation of the cable television industry in Capital Cities Cable, Inc. v. Crisp, 467 U.S. 691, 104 S.Ct. 2694, 81 L.Ed.2d 580 (1984). The invalidation of the state law was consistent with the twenty-first amendment because the limited restriction on advertising was not closely related to "exercising control over whether to permit importation or sale of liquor and to structure the liquor distribution system". 467 U.S. at 715, 104 S.Ct. at 2709, 81 L.Ed.2d at 599 (internal quotation and citation omitted). The Court did not reach the question of whether the state law violated the first amendment.

City of Newport, Ky. v. Iacobucci, 479 U.S. 92, 95 & n. 5, 107 S.Ct. 383, 385 & n. 5, 93 L.Ed.2d 334 (1986) (per curiam), rehearing denied 479 U.S. 1047, 107 S.Ct. 913, 93 L.Ed.2d 862 (1987). In that case the Court adopted with approval Justice Stewart's warning that the twenty-first amendment does not allow a state to act with "total irrationality or invidious discrimination in controlling the distribution of liquor within its borders. And it most assuredly is not to say that the Twenty-first Amendment necessarily overrides in its allotted area *any other* relevant provision of the Constitution." (emphasis added). The Court was quoting Stewart, J., concurring in California v. LaRue, 409 U.S. 109, 120 n. *, 93 S.Ct. 390, 398 n. *, 34 L.Ed.2d 342 (1972), rehearing denied 410 U.S. 948, 93 S.Ct. 1351, 35 L.Ed.2d 615 (1973). Stevens, J., dissenting, joined by Brennan, J., complained: The twenty-first amendment "is toothless, except when freedom of speech is involved." City of Newport, Ky. v. Iacobucci, 479 U.S. 92, 98–99, 107 S.Ct. 383, 387, 93 L.Ed.2d 334 (1986) (Stevens, J., dissenting) (footnote omitted), rehearing denied 479 U.S. 1047, 107 S.Ct. 913, 93 L.Ed.2d 862 (1987).

73. 413 U.S. 15, 93 S.Ct. 2607, 37 L.Ed.2d 419 (1973), rehearing denied 414 U.S. 881, 94 S.Ct. 26, 38 L.Ed.2d 128 (1973).

ruled in *Kaplan v. California* [74] that books alone, containing only words and no pictures, may be obscene.[75] The Court recognized that books "have a different and preferred place in our hierarchy of values...." [76] But they nonetheless may be found to be obscene.

(g) Use of Experts

Once the allegedly obscene material is actually placed into evidence the state need not present expert testimony that the material is obscene, lacks serious artistic value, or any other ancillary evidence of obscenity.[77] The defense, however, is free to introduce appropriate expert testimony.[78]

(h) National vs. Local Standards

In *Miller v. California* [79] the Court held, *inter alia,* that obscenity is to be determined by applying contemporary community standards, not national standards. In that case, the trial court instructed the jury to consider state community standards. The following year the Court extended that holding to apply to a federal prosecution:

> Since this case was tried in the Southern District of California, and presumably jurors from throughout that judicial district were available to serve on the panel which tried petitioners, it would be the standards of that "community" upon which the jurors would draw. But this is not to say that a district court would not be at liberty to admit evidence of standards existing in some place outside of this particular district, if it felt such evidence would

74. 413 U.S. 115, 116, 93 S.Ct. 2680, 2682–83, 37 L.Ed.2d 492 (1973), rehearing denied 414 U.S. 883, 94 S.Ct. 28, 38 L.Ed.2d 131 (1973).

75. Only once between *Roth* and *Miller,* in Mishkin v. New York, 383 U.S. 502, 86 S.Ct. 958, 16 L.Ed.2d 56 (1966), rehearing denied 384 U.S. 934, 86 S.Ct. 1440, 16 L.Ed.2d 535 (1966), did the high Court hold books to be obscene, and in that case most if not all of the books were illustrated. 383 U.S. at 505, 86 S.Ct. at 961–62. See also Kaplan v. California, 413 U.S. 115, 118 n. 3, 93 S.Ct. 2680, 2683 n. 3, 37 L.Ed.2d 492 (1973), rehearing denied 414 U.S. 883, 94 S.Ct. 28, 38 L.Ed.2d 131 (1973).

76. 413 U.S. at 119, 93 S.Ct. at 2684.

77. 413 U.S. at 121, 93 S.Ct. at 2685; Paris Adult Theatre I v. Slaton, 413 U.S. 49, 56, 93 S.Ct. 2628, 2634–35, 37 L.Ed.2d 446 (1973), rehearing denied 414 U.S. 881, 94 S.Ct. 27, 38 L.Ed.2d 128 (1973), on remand 231 Ga. 312, 201 S.E.2d 456 (1973), certiorari denied 418 U.S. 939, 94 S.Ct. 3227, 41 L.Ed.2d 1173 (1974).

There might be a case where the allegedly obscene material is directed at such a bizarre deviant group that the experience of the jurors would be inadequate to judge if the material appeals to the particular prurient interest. In such a case, the government may have to use expert testimony. Pinkus v. United States, 436 U.S. 293, 303, 98 S.Ct. 1808, 1814–15, 56 L.Ed.2d 293 (1978), on remand 579 F.2d 1174 (9th Cir.1978), certiorari dismissed 439 U.S. 999, 99 S.Ct. 605, 58 L.Ed.2d 674 (1978).

See generally, Frank, Obscenity and the Use of Expert Testimony, 41 U.Wash. L.Rev. 631 (1966).

78. 413 U.S. at 121, 93 S.Ct. at 2685; Smith v. California, 361 U.S. 147, 164–65, 80 S.Ct. 215, 224–25, 4 L.Ed.2d 205 (1959) (Frankfurter, J., concurring), rehearing denied 361 U.S. 950, 80 S.Ct. 399, 4 L.Ed.2d 383 (1960).

79. 413 U.S. 15, 93 S.Ct. 2607, 37 L.Ed.2d 419 (1973), rehearing denied 414 U.S. 881, 94 S.Ct. 26, 38 L.Ed.2d 128 (1973).

assist the jurors in the resolution of the issues which they were to decide.[80]

The Court has since made clear that *Miller* did not mandate use of a statewide standard; the trial court may use a national standard and it may instruct the jury to apply "community standards" without instructing it what community was specified.[81] It is unclear if such holdings mean that a trial court may instruct the jury to apply national standards even if it could be shown that national standards apply a stricter definition of obscenity than local standards.

In *Smith v. United States*[82] the Court placed some limits on the power of the state to attempt to define legislatively the contemporary community standard of appeal to prurient interest or patent offensiveness. First, in state obscenity proceedings:

> [The state could, if it wished] impose a geographic limit on the determination of community standards by defining the area from which the jury could be selected in an obscenity case, or by legislating with respect to the instructions that must be given to the jurors in such cases.... [However] the question of the community standard to apply, when appeal to prurient interest and patent offensiveness are considered, is not one that can be defined legislatively.[83]

As to federal obscenity proceedings, no state law can regulate distribution of obscene materials and define contemporary standards. Thus, in a federal prosecution for wholly intrastate mailings of allegedly obscene material it is irrelevant that the state in which the mailings took place did not regulate at all obscenity aimed at adults. A state's laissez-faire attitude towards obscenity cannot nullify federal efforts to regulate it. In federal obscenity prosecutions federal jury instructions as to community standards will be given.[84]

In *Pinkus v. United States*,[85] the Court clarified several requirements concerning jury instructions in federal obscenity prosecutions.

---

80. Hamling v. United States, 418 U.S. 87, 105–06, 94 S.Ct. 2887, 2901–02, 41 L.Ed.2d 590 (1974), rehearing denied 419 U.S. 885, 95 S.Ct. 157, 42 L.Ed.2d 129 (1974).

81. Jenkins v. Georgia, 418 U.S. 153, 94 S.Ct. 2750, 41 L.Ed.2d 642 (1974), on remand 232 Ga. 797, 209 S.E.2d 151 (1974).

82. 431 U.S. 291, 97 S.Ct. 1756, 52 L.Ed.2d 324 (1977).

83. 431 U.S. 291 at 303, 97 S.Ct. at 1765 (dictum).

84. 431 U.S. 291 at 304, 97 S.Ct. at 1765–66.

Note that the standards of Miller v. California, 413 U.S. 15, 93 S.Ct. 2607, 37 L.Ed.2d 419 (1973), rehearing denied 414 U.S. 881, 94 S.Ct. 26, 38 L.Ed.2d 128 (1973) are not applied retroactively to the extent that they burden criminal defendants but they are applied retroactively to the extent they benefit criminal defendants. Marks v. United States, 430 U.S. 188, 97 S.Ct. 990, 51 L.Ed.2d 260 (1977).

85. 436 U.S. 293, 98 S.Ct. 1808, 56 L.Ed.2d 293 (1978), on remand 579 F.2d 1174 (9th Cir.1978), certiorari dismissed 439 U.S. 999, 99 S.Ct. 605, 58 L.Ed.2d 674 (1978).

While *Pinkus* was decided under the *Roth*[86] test of obscenity, the court approved of instructions as to what types of people should be included in the community; these instructions still should be law under *Miller*.[87] *Miller* only rejected the national standards definition of "community" in favor of a smaller geographic area: the actual local community.

The *Pinkus* Court overturned Pinkus' conviction for mailing obscene materials based on its statutory interpretation that children had been improperly included in determining community standards. "[C]hildren are not to be included ... as part of the 'community' as that term relates to the 'obscene materials' proscribed by 18 U.S.C.A. § 1461." [88]

The Court went on to state that under the Constitution, it was permissible to include "particularly sensitive persons" when considering community standards, since the "community includes all adults who comprise it." The jury may not be instructed to focus on the most susceptible and sensitive members of the community, but the jury need not exclude such people from the community as a whole for purposes of judging the material's obscenity.[89] Finally, the Constitution allows an instruction on prurient appeal to deviant sexual groups as part of the instruction concerning the appeal of the materials to the average person when the evidence supports such a charge.

The Third Prong of the *Miller* Test and Contemporary Community Standards

In *Pope v. Illinois*,[90] the Court made clear that the "value" of an allegedly obscene work (the third prong of the *Miller* test) is not to be determined by the jury applying local "contemporary community standards" but by the jury being instructed to decide whether a reasonable person would find serious literary, artistic, political, or scientific value in the material taken as a whole.[91] While the "community standards" test applies to the first and second prong of Miller, the danger of a "community standards" instruction is that a juror might consider himself or herself bound to follow prevailing local views "without considering whether a reasonable person would arrive at a different

---

86. 354 U.S. 476, 77 S.Ct. 1304, 1 L.Ed.2d 1498 (1957), rehearing denied 355 U.S. 852, 78 S.Ct. 8, 2 L.Ed.2d 60 (1957).

87. Miller v. California, 413 U.S. 15, 93 S.Ct. 2607, 37 L.Ed.2d 419 (1973), rehearing denied 414 U.S. 881, 94 S.Ct. 26, 38 L.Ed.2d 128 (1973).

88. 436 U.S. at 297, 98 S.Ct. at 1812. Since the Court specifically referred to the federal statute it appears that the decision is based on an interpretation of that stat-

ute. Whether the states, as a matter of constitutional law, must follow this ruling, remains unclear.

89. 436 U.S. at 299–300, 98 S.Ct. at 1812–13.

90. 481 U.S. 497, 107 S.Ct. 1918, 95 L.Ed.2d 439 (1987), on remand 162 Ill. App.3d 299, 113 Ill.Dec. 547, 515 N.E.2d 356 (1987), appeal denied 118 Ill.2d 549, 117 Ill.Dec. 229, 520 N.E.2d 390 (1988).

91. 481 U.S. at 501, 107 S.Ct. at 1921.

conclusion." [92] The value of a work, unlike its prurient appeal or patent offensiveness (the first two elements of *Miller*) does not vary from community to community based on the degree of local acceptance it has won.

(i) Role of the Jury After Miller

While *Miller v. California* [93] talked of the necessity of relying on the jury system and suggested that it might thus have a lesser role for appellate courts in reviewing obscenity convictions, such a rule of law has not come to pass. In *Jenkins v. Georgia*, [94] the Court held that even though "questions of appeal to the 'prurient interest' or of patent offensiveness are 'essentially questions of fact'; it would be a serious misreading of *Miller* to conclude that juries have unbridled discretion in determining what is 'patently offensive.' " [95] The appellate courts can conduct an "independent review" of the constitutional claims where necessary.[96]

In *Jenkins* itself the Court concluded that "Our own viewing of the film satisfies us that ..." it is not obscene.[97] Justice Brennan, concurring in the result and joined by Justices Stevens and Marshall thought that *Miller* and *Jenkins* brought the Court back to the case-by-case approach.[98]

The Court has also held that in civil cases there is no federal constitutional mandate requiring the states to use a jury.[99]

---

92. 481 U.S. at 501 n. 3, 107 S.Ct. at 1921 n. 3.

See also, Smith v. United States, 431 U.S. 291, 301, 97 S.Ct. 1756, 1763, 52 L.Ed.2d 324 (1977).

Justice Scalia, concurring in *Pope,* urged the need to reexamine *Miller:* "in my view it is quite impossible to come to an objective assessment of (at least) literary or artistic value, there being many accomplished people who have found literature in Dada and art in the replication of a soup can." 481 U.S. at 513, 107 S.Ct. at 1923.

Justice Stevens, joined by Marshall, J., dissented and argued that a state may not criminalize the "mere possession or sale of obscene literature, absent some connection to minors, or obtrusive display to unconsenting adults." 481 U.S. at 504, 107 S.Ct. at 1927 (footnote omitted).

Footnote 11 of the Stevens dissent noted that the "insurmountable vagueness problems involved in criminalization are not in my view, implicated with respect to *civil* regulation of sexually explicit material, an area in which the States retain substantial leeway." 481 U.S. at 516–17 n. 11, 107 S.Ct. at 1929 n. 11 (emphasis added). Jus-

tice Brennan joined all but footnote 11 of the Stevens dissent.

93. 413 U.S. 15, 93 S.Ct. 2607, 37 L.Ed.2d 419 (1973), rehearing denied 414 U.S. 881, 94 S.Ct. 26, 38 L.Ed.2d 128 (1973).

94. 418 U.S. 153, 94 S.Ct. 2750, 41 L.Ed.2d 642 (1974), on remand 232 Ga. 797, 209 S.E.2d 151 (1974).

95. 418 U.S. at 160, 94 S.Ct. at 2755.

96. Id.

97. 418 U.S. at 161, 94 S.Ct. at 2755.

98. 418 U.S. at 162–65, 94 S.Ct. at 2755.

See, Note, An Empirical Inquiry Into the Effects of Miller v. California on the Control of Obscenity, 52 N.Y.U.L.Rev. 819 (1977) (arguing that *Miller* has had little effect on the day-to-day regulation of obscenity).

99. Melancon v. McKeithen, 345 F.Supp. 1025, 1035–45, 1048 (E.D.La.1972), affirmed sub nom. Mayes v. Ellis, 409 U.S. 943, 93 S.Ct. 289, 34 L.Ed.2d 214 (1972); Alexander v. Virginia, 413 U.S. 836, 93 S.Ct. 2803, 37 L.Ed.2d 993 (1973) (per curiam), rehearing denied 414 U.S. 881, 94

(j) Burden of Proof

If the government brings a *criminal* prosecution in an obscenity case, then it must prove its charges "beyond a reasonable doubt" because this burden of proof requirement is an element of due process binding on both the state and federal governments.[100] But an obscenity case may be a *civil* proceeding as well, such as a proceeding to abate a public nuisance. In such instances, there is no federal constitutional requirement of proof beyond a reasonable doubt.[101]

(k) Feminism and Pornography

In the late 1970's and the 1980's a new group—using a new argument—objected to obscenity, so-called adult entertainment, and pornography. Feminists focused their support of various types of antiobscenity legislation not on the ground that the state should regulate to protect morality but on the ground that the state should regulate because pornography degrades women.[102]

S.Ct. 29, 38 L.Ed.2d 128 (1973), mandate conformed 214 Va. 539, 203 S.E.2d 441 (1974). Brennan, J., joined by Marshall, J., dissented for the reasons stated in his separate opinion, concurring in part, in McKinney v. Alabama, 424 U.S. 669, 687–89, 96 S.Ct. 1189, 1199–1200, 47 L.Ed.2d 387 (1976).

100. In re Winship, 397 U.S. 358, 364, 90 S.Ct. 1068, 1072–73, 25 L.Ed.2d 368 (1970), mandate conformed 27 N.Y.2d 728, 314 N.Y.S.2d 536, 262 N.E.2d 675 (1970).

101. Cooper v. Mitchell Bros.' Santa Ana Theater, 454 U.S. 90, 102 S.Ct. 172, 70 L.Ed.2d 262 (1981) (per curiam), on remand 128 Cal.App.3d 937, 180 Cal.Rptr. 728 (1982), certiorari denied 459 U.S. 944, 103 S.Ct. 259, 74 L.Ed.2d 202 (1982), rehearing denied 459 U.S. 1093, 103 S.Ct. 581, 74 L.Ed.2d 940 (1982). The Court noted that in some civil areas of great importance it has required the "clear and convincing" standard of proof in civil cases, rather than the "preponderance of the evidence" test normally used. 454 U.S. at 93, 102 S.Ct. at 173. See, e.g., Addington v. Texas, 441 U.S. 418, 431, 99 S.Ct. 1804, 1812, 60 L.Ed.2d 323 (1970) (clear and convincing standard in civil commitment), on remand 588 S.W.2d 569 (Tex.1979); Rosenbloom v. Metromedia, Inc., 403 U.S. 29, 52, 91 S.Ct. 1811, 1824, 29 L.Ed.2d 296 (1971) (clear and convincing standard in libel cases) (opinion of Brennan, J.); Woodby v. INS, 385 U.S. 276, 285–86, 87 S.Ct. 483, 487–88, 17 L.Ed.2d 362 (1966) (deportation); Chaunt v. United States, 364 U.S. 350, 353, 81 S.Ct. 147, 149–50, 5 L.Ed.2d 120 (1960) (deportation); Schneiderman v. United States, 320

U.S. 118, 159, 63 S.Ct. 1333, 1353, 87 L.Ed. 1796 (1943) (denaturalization). But see Vance v. Terrazas, 444 U.S. 252, 100 S.Ct. 540, 62 L.Ed.2d 461 (1980) (constitutional for Congress to establish preponderance of evidence standard in expatriation cases), rehearing denied 445 U.S. 920, 100 S.Ct. 1285, 63 L.Ed.2d 606 (1980), on remand 494 F.Supp. 1017 (N.D.Ill.1980), judgment affirmed 653 F.2d 285 (7th Cir.1981).

The Court in *Cooper* did not decide whether or not the clear and convincing standard was necessary, but rather remanded the case. Brennan, J. joined by Marshall, J., filed a dissenting opinion arguing for the standard of beyond a reasonable doubt, based on Brennan's separate opinion in McKinney v. Alabama, 424 U.S. 669, 683–87, 96 S.Ct. 1189, 1197–99, 47 L.Ed.2d 387 (1976). Stevens, J., also filed a dissenting opinion.

102. The literature on this topic is growing. See e.g., Morgan, How to Run the Pornographers Out of Town (And Preserve the First Amendment), Ms. Magazine (Nov.1978), at 55. L. Lederer, ed., Take Back the Night: Women on Pornography (1980); S. Griffin, Pornography and Silence (1981); A. Dworkin, Pornography: Men Possessing Women (1981); Note, Anti-Pornography Laws and First Amendment Values, 98 Harv.L.Rev. 460 (1984); Jacobs, Patterns of Violence: A Feminist Perspective on the Regulation of Pornography, 7 Harv. Women's L.J. 5 (1984); Comment, Feminism, Pornography, and Law, 133 U.Pa.L.Rev. 497 (1985); Stone, Comment: Anti-Pornography Legislation as View-

Thus feminists have proposed various antipornography ordinances. Under Supreme Court doctrine these laws are tested by the same legal principles which govern other obscenity legislation. It makes no difference that the local supporters of some antipornography laws claim that pornography is a form of sex discrimination and the vocal supporters of similar laws base their arguments on morality. Good motives, or different motives, cannot validate an otherwise invalid law. Therefore, the federal district court in Indiana, after a thorough discussion, invalidated an Indianapolis ordinance which sought to limit the availability of materials which depict the "sexually explicit subordination of women, graphically depicted, whether in pictures or in words ..." [103] The court acknowledged that this definition—and its use of the term "subordination of women"—was different than that often used in anti-obscenity laws; it was also unconstitutionally vague.[104] And while the court noted that the state has a strong interest in prohibiting sex discrimination and in protecting the physical and psychological well-being of women, this interest is not compelling enough to override the first amendment.[105]

point Discrimination, 9 Harv.J. of L. & Publ. Policy 461 (1986). Linda Lovelace & McGrady, Ordeal (1980); MacKinnon, Pornography, Civil Rights and Speech, 20 Harv.Civ.Rts.–Civ.Lib.L.Rev. 1 (1985); Lynn, "Civil Rights" Ordinance and the Attorney General's Commission on Pornography: New Developments in Pornography Regulation, 21 Harv.Civ.Rts.–Civ.Lib. L.Rev. 27 (1986); Layman, Violent Pornography and the Obscenity Doctrine: The Road Not Taken, 75 Georgetown L.J. 1475 (1987); Post, Cultural Heterogeneity and Law: Pornography, Blasphemy, and the First Amendment, 76 Calif.L.Rev. 297 (1988).

103. American Bookseller Ass'n, Inc. v. Hudnut, 598 F.Supp. 1316, 1329 (S.D.Ind. 1984), affirmed 771 F.2d 323 (7th Cir.1985).

104. 598 F.Supp. at 1338. The court added:

"Many, if not all of the other words and phrases challenged by the plaintiff in this lawsuit on the grounds of vagueness are as difficult, indeed mystifying, as is 'the subordination of women.'"

598 F.Supp. at 1339.

105. The court stated, 598 F.Supp. at 1335–37 (footnote omitted):

"If this Court were to accept defendants' argument—that the State's interest in protecting women from the humiliation and degradation which comes from being depicted in a sexually subordinate context is so compelling as to warrant the regulation of otherwise free speech to accomplish that end—one wonders what would prevent the City–County Council (or any other legislative body) from enacting protections for other equally compelling claims against exploitation and discrimination as are presented here. Legislative bodies, finding support here, could also enact legislation prohibiting other unfair expression—the publication and distribution of racist material, for instance, on the grounds that it causes racial discrimination, or legislation prohibiting ethnic or religious slurs on the grounds that they cause discrimination against particular ethnic or religious groups, or legislation barring literary depictions which are uncomplimentary to handicapped persons on the grounds that they cause discrimination against that group of people, and so on. ...

"It ought to be remembered by defendants and all others who would support a legislative initiative that, in terms of altering sociological patterns, much as alteration may be necessary and desirable, free speech, rather than being the enemy, is a long-tested and worthy ally."

In this case one of the arguments used by the proponents of the ordinance was that the ordinance was justified by the same basic theory used by the Supreme Court in New York v. Ferber, 458 U.S. 747, 102 S.Ct. 3348, 73 L.Ed.2d 1113 (1982) (New York law aimed at child pornography up-

(l) Nude Dancing

For many years, the Court has intimated that nonobscene nude dancing is expressive conduct protected under the first amendment.[106] The Court, however, never focused on the degree of first amendment protection afforded nude dancing until *Barnes v. Glen Theatre, Inc.*[107]

Indiana enacted a public indecency law, which prohibited "knowingly or intentionally" appearing nude in "a public place." Two Indiana establishments,[108] and individuals who were employed as nude dancers in those establishments sued to enjoin enforcement of the law, which required that the dancers wear pasties and G-strings. The plaintiffs sued to enjoin enforcement of the law, and the Seventh Circuit, en banc, reversed the trial court and ruled that nonobscene nude dancing, performed for entertainment purposes, is protected by the first amendment. The Seventh Circuit also ruled that the statute was unconstitutional because its purpose was to prevent the message of eroticism and sexuality that the dancers conveyed.

In *Barnes v. Glen Theatre, Inc.*,[109] the Supreme Court, with no majority opinion, reversed. Chief Justice Rehnquist's plurality opinion accepted the notion that nonobscene nude dancing has some first amendment protection. However, he also explained that the government has a substantial governmental interest in protecting societal order and morality.[110] The state's police power has been traditionally

held because of state's interest in safeguarding the physical well-being of minors and protecting minors from child sex abuse), on remand 57 N.Y.2d 256, 455 N.Y.S.2d 582, 441 N.E.2d 1100 (1982). It is ironic, to say the least, that feminists would seek to protect adult women by analogizing them to children in need of the state's care.

106. See, California v. LaRue, 409 U.S. 109, 118, 93 S.Ct. 390, 397, 34 L.Ed.2d 342 (1972), rehearing denied 410 U.S. 948, 93 S.Ct. 1351, 35 L.Ed.2d 615 (1973). Doran v. Salem Inn, Inc., 422 U.S. 922, 932, 95 S.Ct. 2561, 2568, 45 L.Ed.2d 648 (1975) said that "the customary 'barroom' type of nude dancing may involve the barest minimum of protected expression...." Schad v. Borough of Mount Ephraim, 452 U.S. 61, 66, 101 S.Ct. 2176, 2181, 68 L.Ed.2d 671 (1981) noted that "nude dancing is not without its First Amendment protections from official regulation."

107. 501 U.S. ___, 111 S.Ct. 2456, 115 L.Ed.2d 504 (1991). Rehnquist, C.J., announced the judgment of the Court and delivered an opinion in which O'Connor & Kennedy, JJ., joined. Scalia, J., filed an opinion concurring in the judgment. Souter, J., filed another opinion concurring in the judgment. White, J., joined by Marshall, Blackmun, & Stevens, JJ., filed a dissenting opinion.

108. One of the establishments served liquor. The other provided "adult entertainment" in the form of printed materials, movie showings, and live entertainment. The movies were not the subject of this dispute. The live entertainment consisted, inter alia, of nude and seminude performances as well as the showing of nude and seminude female bodies through glass panels. One of the live dancers was also a performer in an "adult" movie, which was being shown at a nearby theatre. Ironically, viewers of the movie could see this dancer perform a nude dance in a nonobscene "adult" film, but could not see her perform the same dance live.

109. 501 U.S. ___, 111 S.Ct. 2456, 115 L.Ed.2d 504 (1991).

110. E.g., Bowers v. Hardwick, 478 U.S. 186, 196, 106 S.Ct. 2841, 2846, 92 L.Ed.2d 140 (1986), rehearing denied 478 U.S. 1039, 107 S.Ct. 29, 92 L.Ed.2d 779 (1986) stated explicitly, the law "is constantly based on morality, and if all laws representing essentially moral choices are to be invalidat-

defined as encompassing the power to regulate for health, safety, and morality.[111]

Rehnquist then analyzed the Indiana restriction as a question of symbolic speech,[112] and concluded that the public indecency statute was justified despite its incidental limitations on some expressive activity. The state's interest in prohibiting nude dancing in places open to the public is unrelated to the suppression of free speech, because the state seeks to prevent public nudity, *whether or not that nudity is combined with expressive activity.* Thus, the law does not ban only nudity that conveys an erotic message; it bans all nudity. Nor does the law ban erotic dances; the dancers are permitted to present erotic dances as long as they wear a scant amount of clothing. Dancing, the Rehnquist plurality said, has a communicative element, but the statute in question did not punish dancing; it punished nudity, a noncommunicative element. In short, the statute is not a means to an end; the banning of public nudity is an end in itself, and the statute is narrowly tailored to meet that end.

Justice Scalia, concurring in the judgment, explained that he would uphold the statute, not because it survives some lower level first amendment scrutiny but because it is a general law regulating conduct and not specifically directed against expression. The Indiana statute does not target nude expression; it targets public nudity. The Indiana law applies to forbid nude beaches as well as nude dancing. Thus, in his view, it was not subject to any first amendment scrutiny.

Justice Scalia also rejected the dissent's argument that the Indiana statute cannot constitutionally be applied to nudity practiced among consenting patrons who pay the price of admission. The Henry David Thoreau philosophy of "you-may-do-what-you-like-so-long-as-it-does-not-injure-someone-else" was not written into our Constitution:

> "The purpose of Indiana's nudity law would be violated, I think, if 60,000 fully consenting adults crowded into the Hoosierdome to display their genitals to one another, even if there were not an offended innocent in the crowd. Our society prohibits, and all human societies have prohibited, certain activities not because they harm others but because they are considered, in the traditional phrase, *'contra bonos mores,'* i.e., immoral." [113]

Such activities, Justice Scalia noted, included sadomasochism, cockfighting, bestiality, suicide, drug use, prostitution, and sodomy.

ed under the Due Process Clause, the courts will be very busy indeed."

111. The Supreme Court recognized the offense of "gross and open indecency" in Winters v. New York, 333 U.S. 507, 515, 68 S.Ct. 665, 670, 92 L.Ed. 840 (1948). The Common Law considered public nudity to be *malum in se.* Le Roy v. Sidley, 1 Sid. 168, 82 Eng.Rep. 1036 (K.B.1664).

112. See, United States v. O'Brien, 391 U.S. 367, 88 S.Ct. 1673, 20 L.Ed.2d 672 (1968), rehearing denied 393 U.S. 900, 89 S.Ct. 63, 21 L.Ed.2d 188 (1968).

113. 501 U.S. at ___, 111 S.Ct. at 2465.

Justice Souter also concurred in the judgment. Not all dancing is protected by the first amendment, he argued. For example, he believed that ballroom dancing or aerobics are outside the first amendment, but the erotic dancing here carries "an endorsement of erotic experience" and so is expressive. He agreed with the plurality that the case should be analyzed as symbolic speech, but he concluded that the statute should be upheld because the Court has, in other cases, upheld zoning laws intended to deal with the harmful secondary effects, such as reduced property values, associated with adult entertainment.[114] Although Indiana had not made factual findings to support this hypothesis, Justice Souter did not think that localized proof should be necessary. Nor did he appear concerned that the Indiana law, unlike the adult zoning cases, did not disperse or concentrate nude dancing; rather, the law flatly forbade it.

Justice White, joined by Justices Marshall, Blackmun, and Stevens, dissented. The Indiana law, in their view, was not truly a general prohibition of nudity, because the law did not prohibit nudity in the home. Hence, they would invalidate the law. They added that it would be unconstitutional for Indiana to prohibit nudity in the home.

---

114. See, e.g., Renton v. Playtime Theatres, Inc., 475 U.S. 41, 106 S.Ct. 925, 89 L.Ed.2d 29 (1986), rehearing denied 475 U.S. 1132, 106 S.Ct. 1663, 90 L.Ed.2d 205 (1986); Young v. American Mini Theatres, Inc., 427 U.S. 50, 71 n. 34, 96 S.Ct. 2440, 2453 n. 34, 49 L.Ed.2d 310 (1976), rehearing denied 429 U.S. 873, 97 S.Ct. 191, 50 L.Ed.2d 155 (1976).

Chapter 21

FREEDOM OF RELIGION

Table of Sections

I. INTRODUCTION

§ 21.1 The Natural Antagonism Between the Two Clauses

There are two clauses of the first amendment which deal with the subject of religion.[1] The amendment mandates that "Congress shall make no law respecting an establishment of religion, or prohibiting the free exercise thereof...." The first clause is referred to as the establishment clause; the second is the free exercise clause. The Supreme Court has held that both of these clauses are made applicable to the states by the due process clause of the fourteenth amendment.[2]

There is a natural antagonism between a command not to establish religion and a command not to inhibit its practice. This tension between the clauses often leaves the Court with having to choose between competing values in religion cases. The general guide here is the concept of "neutrality." The opposing values require that the government act to achieve only secular goals and that it achieve them in a religiously neutral manner. Unfortunately, situations arise where government may have no choice but to incidentally help or hinder religious groups or practices.

Professor Philip Kurland has advanced the theory that government can only remain neutral by prohibiting the use of religion as a standard for government action.[3] So long as a law avoids "classification in terms

---

§ 21.1

1. It should also be noted that art. VI, cl. 3, of the Constitution provides that "no religious Test shall ever be required as a Qualification to any Office of Public Trust under the United States."

2. The free exercise clause was first held applicable to the states in Cantwell v. Connecticut, 310 U.S. 296, 60 S.Ct. 900, 84 L.Ed. 1213 (1940). The establishment clause was held applicable to the states in Everson v. Board of Education, 330 U.S. 1, 67 S.Ct. 504, 91 L.Ed. 711 (1947), rehearing denied 330 U.S. 855, 67 S.Ct. 962, 91 L.Ed. 1297 (1947).

3. P. Kurland, Religion and Law 112 (1962). See generally, Laycock, "Nonpreferential" Aid to Religion: A False Claim About Original Intent, 27 Wm. & Mary L.Rev. 875 (1986); Tushnet, The Constitution of Religion, 18 Conn.L.Rev. 701 (1986). McConnell, Neutrality Under The Religion Clauses, 81 Nw.U.L.Rev. 146 (1986); Stone, The Equal Access Controversy: The Religion Clauses and the Meaning of "Neutrality", 81 Nw.U.L.Rev. 168 (1986); Valavri, The Concept of Neutrality in Establishment Clause Doctrine, 48 U.Pitt.L.Rev. 83 (1986); Garvey, A Comment on Religious Convictions and Lawmaking, 84 Mich. L.Rev. 1288 (1986); McCoy & Kurtz, A

of religion either to confer a benefit or to impose a burden"[4] he would find it in conformity with both clauses. This position has much to recommend it, for insistence on avoiding incidental aid to religion is likely to inhibit its free exercise. Similarly, requiring a great degree of government accommodation of religious practices might result in impermissible aid to religion. However, despite the great theoretical appeal of the Kurland position the Court has never adopted such a theory. Instead the Court has reviewed the claims under the different clauses on independent bases and has developed separate tests for determining whether a law violates either clause.[5] While "neutrality" is still a central principle of both clauses, we have no single standard for determining what is a religiously neutral act. Instead, we must examine the neutrality or permissibility of a law in terms of the challenge to it.

As we will see in other sections in this chapter, the Supreme Court has been sensitive to the concept of neutrality as a central principle of the religion clauses in its refusal to define the nature of the types of beliefs constituting religious beliefs and in its circumscription of governmental authority to either define religion or inquire into the sincerity of religious beliefs in some circumstances.[6]

The Supreme Court's adoption of separate tests for establishment clause and free exercise clause cases may seem to bring the values

---

Unifying Theory for the Religion Clauses of the First Amendment, 39 Vand.L.Rev. 249 (1986). Tushnet, Religion and Theories of Constitutional Interpretation, 33 Loyola L.Rev. 221 (1987); Dent, Religious Children, Secular Schools, 61 So.Cal.L.Rev. 863 (1988); Oakes, Separation, Accommodation and the Future of Church and State, 35 DePaul L.Rev. 1 (1985); Tushnet, The Emerging Principle of Accommodation of Religion (Dubitante), 76 Georgetown L.J. 1691 (1988); G. Bradley, Church–State Relationships in America (1987); Michael J. Perry, The Role of Religion and Morality in American Politics (1991); Smolin, Regulating Religious and Cultural Conflict in a Postmodern America: A Response to Professor Perry, 76 Iowa L.Rev. 1067 (1991).

4. Id. See also note 5, infra.

5. See generally, Kurland, The Origins of the Religion Clauses of the Constitution, 27 Wm. & Mary L.Rev. 839 (1986).

See Choper, The Religion Clauses of the First Amendment: Reconciling the Conflict, 41 U.Pitt.L.Rev. 673 (1980), in which Professor Choper proposes that the conflict can be resolved by only applying the establishment clause to forbid government action undertaken for a religious purpose

and likely to result in coercing, compromising or influencing religious beliefs.

For examinations of the relationship between the establishment and free exercise clause decisions of the Supreme Court and the views of justices regarding the value of religious freedom for our society, Garvey, Freedom and Equality in the Religion Clauses, 1981 Sup.Ct.Rev. 193; Smith, The Special Place of Religion in the Constitution, 1983 Sup.Ct.Rev. 83; Greenawalt, Religion as a Concept in Constitutional Law, 72 Calif.L.Rev. 753 (1984); Johnson, Concepts and Compromise in First Amendment Religious Doctrine, 72 Calif.L.Rev. 817 (1984); Mansfield, The Religion Clauses of the First Amendment and the Philosophy of the Constitution, 72 Calif.L.Rev. 847 (1984).

See generally, Greenawalt, The Limits Of Rationality And The Place Of Religious Conviction: Protecting Animals And The Environment, 27 Wm. & Mary L.Rev. 1011 (1986); Laycock, Equal Access and Moments of Silence: The Equal Status of Religious Speech by Private Speakers, 81 Nw. U.L.Rev. 1 (1986).

6. See §§ 21.8, 21.9(a), 21.11, 21.12, infra.

embodied in those two clauses into conflict. Perhaps the Court's creation of independent tests has put American governmental entities in a position in neutrality towards religion that accommodates the values of both clauses, but that is a value judgment that each reader must make for himself or herself. In the last sections of this chapter a series of problems, under the general title of "Other Establishment—Free Exercise Problems",[7] we examine a series of problems in which the Supreme Court has directly confronted the apparent tension between its establishment clause and free exercise clause rulings. The case descriptions in the sections of this Chapter titled "The Establishment Clause,"[8] and "The Free Exercise Clause,"[9] will also include some examination of whether the Supreme Court's rulings on a specific area created some tension between the establishment clause and free exercise clause values.

When the Supreme Court examines a legislative attempt to accommodate religious activities or organizations, the judicial examination of that legislative action will involve a determination of whether the legislature's promotion of free exercise values aided religion in a manner that violated the establishment clause.[10]

An example of the way in which the judicial definition of values under the religion clauses has created a tension between those two clauses is *Texas Monthly, Inc. v. Bullock.*[11] In this decision, the Supreme Court by a vote of six to three, invalidated a Texas statute that exempted from the state sales tax those "periodicals that are published or distributed by a religious faith and that consists wholly of writings promulgating the teaching of the faith and books that consist wholly of writings sacred to a religious faith." Justice White believed that this statute violated the press clause of the first amendment, and

7. See part IV of this Chapter, §§ 21.10–21.16.

8. See part II of this Chapter, §§ 21.3–21.5. The tension between accommodating and advancing religion is brought out in the variety of problems that the Court has faced regarding "religion and the public schools," see §§ 21.5(a)–21.5(e).

9. See part III of this Chapter, §§ 21.6–21.9.

10. In addition to the case discussed in the closing paragraphs of this section, the Court has examined legislative attempts to accommodate religion when it has reviewed laws regulating employment practices of both nonreligious and religious entities. See §§ 21.3, 21.5, 21.6. Compare, Estate of Thornton v. Caldor, Inc., 472 U.S. 703, 105 S.Ct. 2914, 86 L.Ed.2d 557 (1985) (Supreme Court holds that a statute requir-

ing employers to give every employee released time from work on the employee's Sabbath violates the establishment clause by advancing religion), with Corporation of Presiding Bishop of Church of Jesus Christ of Latter–Day Saints v. Amos, 483 U.S. 327, 107 S.Ct. 2862, 97 L.Ed.2d 273 (1987) (Court upholds exemption in federal civil rights statute that allows religious organizations to discriminate in employment practices on the basis of religion and to make religious beliefs an employment criteria; the accommodation of religion is seen as a permissible governmental purpose and the incidental aid to religion does not violate the establishment clause). These cases are examined in §§ 21.3, 21.6.

11. 489 U.S. 1, 109 S.Ct. 890, 103 L.Ed.2d 1 (1989).

did not reach the problem of whether the statute also violated the establishment clause.[12] Five Justices believed that this legislative attempt to accommodate religious activities violated the establishment clause, but there was no majority opinion explaining why the statute was invalid. Justice Brennan, joined by Justices Marshall and Stevens, found that laws that aid religion, whether or not they are designed to "accommodate" religion, must be reviewed under the standards that the Court has developed in its establishment clause cases.[13] Those establishment clause standards require that any statute that has the incidental effect of aiding religion must: (1) have a secular purpose, (2) have a principle or primary effect that does not advance or inhibit religion, and (3) not give rise to an excessive entanglement between government and religion.[14] In the view of the Brennan plurality, the Supreme Court's earlier decisions approving exemptions from taxes for religious organizations involve statutes that exempted religious organizations together with other organizations that provided nonsectarian public services (such as a tax exemption given to all nonprofit private schools, both religious and nonreligious).[15] In the view of these Justices, a legislative accommodation of religion is permissible only if the statute aids a large group of activities defined in nonreligious terms (of which religious activity could be a part).[16] The Brennan plurality opinion found that the Supreme Court cases from the 1940s that prohibited the imposition of a flat fee license tax on persons who came into a state to engage in preaching and selling of religious books or pamphlets only meant that the free exercise clause would prevent the government from establishing a special tax on religious activities, or from applying a flat fee license tax to religious preachers if the structure of the tax was such that it would effectively prevent persons

---

12. 489 U.S. at 24–26, 109 S.Ct. at 905 (White, J., concurring).

13. Texas Monthly, Inc. v. Bullock, 489 U.S. 1, 109 S.Ct. 890, 103 L.Ed.2d 1 (1989) (Brennan, J., announces the judgment of the Court in an opinion joined by Marshall and Stevens, JJ.).

14. The three part test has been applied by the Supreme Court in virtually all of its establishment clause cases since 1971. The three part test is usually called the "*Lemon* test" because it is often traced to the Supreme Court's decision in Lemon v. Kurtzman, 403 U.S. 602, 91 S.Ct. 2105, 29 L.Ed.2d 745 (1971), rehearing denied 404 U.S. 876, 92 S.Ct. 24, 30 L.Ed.2d 123 (1971). The three part test is examined in §§ 21.3–21.5.

15. The tax exemption case that was the subject of dispute between the Justices was Walz v. Tax Commission, 397 U.S. 664,

90 S.Ct. 1409, 25 L.Ed.2d 697 (1970) (sustaining a property tax exemption that applied to property owned by religious organizations; the real estate tax also provided the tax exemption to a variety of nonprofit organizations).

16. The Supreme Court has upheld the exemption of religious organizations from laws prohibiting employment discrimination on the basis of religion, so that a religious organization could make membership in the religion an employment qualification. Corporation of Presiding Bishop of Church of Jesus of Latter–Day Saints v. Amos, 483 U.S. 327, 107 S.Ct. 2862, 97 L.Ed.2d 273 (1987). The Supreme Court has invalidated a statute that required employers to give every employee a release from work on the employee's Sabbath. Estate of Thornton v. Caldor, Inc., 472 U.S. 703, 105 S.Ct. 2914, 86 L.Ed.2d 557 (1985). See §§ 21.13, 21.15.

from engaging in the religious activity.[17]

Justices Blackmun and O'Connor, in the *Texas Monthly* decision, believed that the Texas statute violated the establishment clause, although they found it "difficult to reconcile in this case the Free Exercise and Establishment Clause values."[18] These two Justices believed that a state could draft a tax exemption statute that would preserve both free exercise and establishment clause values by defining the class of literature that was exempt from the tax laws to include both religious literature and "philosophical literature distributed by nonreligious organizations devoted to such matters of conscience as life and death, good and evil, being and nonbeing, right and wrong."[19] Such a tax exemption might not survive the establishment clause tests espoused by Justice Brennan, because it would involve tax exempt class of activities that were either religious activities or activities that were clearly analogous to religious activities.

Justice Scalia was joined by Chief Justice Rehnquist and Justice Kennedy in dissent.[20] These Justices believed that the Supreme Court holding in the *Texas Monthly* case, and the opinions of both Justice Brennan and Justice Blackmun, subordinated free exercise clause values to values that the majority read into the establishment clause. In the view of the dissent, the accommodation of religion that was required by the free exercise clause meant that a law that was designed to accommodate religion did not endanger the values of the establishment clause.

§ 21.2 The Appeal to History

There is a seemingly irresistible impulse to appeal to history when analyzing issues under the religion clauses. This tendency is unfortunate because there is no clear history as to the meaning of the clauses. It is of course true that many of the colonists fled religious persecution, but in this country the experience differed widely throughout the

---

17. See Murdock v. Pennsylvania, 319 U.S. 105, 117, 63 S.Ct. 870, 876–77, 87 L.Ed. 1292 (1943); Follett v. Town of McCormick, 321 U.S. 573, 64 S.Ct. 717, 88 L.Ed. 938 (1944).

In a case decided one year after the *Texas Monthly* decision, the Justices unanimously found that these decisions from the 1940s did not give religious organizations a right to be exempt from taxes of general applicability. Jimmy Swaggart Ministries v. Board of Equalization, 493 U.S. 378, 110 S.Ct. 688, 107 L.Ed.2d 796 (1990) (religious organization has no constitutional right to an exemption from a general sales and use tax law that would require the religious organization to collect and pay such taxes for the sales of goods

and literature in a state). The taxes invalidated in the 1940s decisions were flat-fee license taxes that the Supreme Court found to be an invalid means of restricting the ability to engage in first amendment activities in a manner similar to an invalid prior restraint on speech.

18. Texas Monthly, Inc. v. Bullock, 489 U.S. 1, 24–26, 109 S.Ct. 890, 905, 103 L.Ed.2d 1 (1989) (Blackmun, J., joined by O'Connor, J., concurring in the judgment).

19. 489 U.S. at 26–27, 109 S.Ct. at 906.

20. Texas Monthly, Inc. v. Bullock, 489 U.S. 1, 28–30, 109 S.Ct. 890, 907, 103 L.Ed.2d 1 (1989) (Scalia, J., joined by Rehnquist, C.J., and Kennedy, J., dissenting).

colonies. It is common to refer to the Virginia experience when arguing for a complete separation of religious matters from secular government. In Virginia, Jefferson and Madison led a continuing battle for total religious freedom and an end of government aid to religion. Their position was most clearly stated by Madison in his "Memorial and Remonstrance" against an assessment bill to aid religion.[1] The first amendment was a product of Madison and the Virginia influence in the first Congress. However, this is not the only history that is relevant to these issues. The clauses were ratified as a part of the Bill of Rights, and the intention of those in the ratifying states should be as important as that of the Virginia representatives. Moreover, because the first amendment was only a limitation on the actions of the federal government,[2] one could read this history as an affirmance of state sovereignty over this subject.

In other states close ties existed between church and state, with a number of states having established churches until well after the time of the revolution.[3] For these states the amendment insured that the federal government could not interfere with their state preferences for certain religions. It also would forbid the federal government from benefiting one religion over another. The close ties between religion and state governments indicate that many states would not have opposed federal government aid to all religions on an equal basis. Indeed, Justice Story was certain that the federal government was barred only from punishing or benefiting specific religions.[4] He thought the amendment allowed for aid to all religions on an equal basis. However, beyond this unclear history, little can be said with any certainty. Even after the established churches had ended in the states, aid to religious entities continued. For example, religious teachers often made use of public schools, and the tax exempt status of churches was guaranteed in many states.[5]

§ 21.2

1. This Madison "Remonstrance" was reprinted in Walz v. Tax Com'n, 397 U.S. 664, 719–27, 90 S.Ct. 1409, 1437–41, 25 L.Ed.2d 697 (1970) (Douglas, J., dissenting, app. II).

2. In Barron v. Mayor and City Council of City of Baltimore, 32 U.S. (7 Pet.) 243, 8 L.Ed. 672 (1833) the Court, per Chief Justice Marshall, held that the Bill of Rights was not applicable to the activities of state or local governments.

See supra § 21.1, note 2, as to the application of these guarantees to the states by the fourteenth amendment.

3. For an excellent presentation of early history of church-state relationship and theories, see C. Antieau, A. Downey, & E. Roberts, Freedom From Federal Establishment (1964).

See generally, Hoskins, The Original Separation of Church and State in America, 2 J.L. & Religion 221 (1984); Greenawalt, Religious Convictions and Lawmaking, 84 Mich.L.Rev. 352 (1985).

4. J. Story, Commentaries on the Constitution of the United States 627–34 (5th ed. 1891).

5. For some examples of this see, Choper, The Establishment Clause and Aid to Parochial Schools, 56 Calif.L.Rev. 260, 263 (1969); C. Antieau, P. Carroll, C. Antieau, P. Carroll, & T. Burke, Religion under the State Constitutions (1965).

The religion clauses were among the first portions of the Bill of Rights incorporated into the fourteenth amendment and made applicable to the states by the Supreme Court. Although the original understanding of the drafters of the first and fourteenth amendments may be unclear, a majority of the justices on the Supreme Court during the past 50 years consistently have held that the values protected by the religion clauses are fundamental aspects of liberty in our society and must be protected from both state and federal interference.[6]

6. See Cantwell v. Connecticut, 310 U.S. 296, 60 S.Ct. 900, 84 L.Ed. 1213 (1940) (free exercise clause made applicable to the states); Everson v. Board of Education, 330 U.S. 1, 67 S.Ct. 504, 91 L.Ed. 711 (1947) (establishment clause held applicable to the states), rehearing denied 330 U.S. 855, 67 S.Ct. 962, 91 L.Ed. 1297 (1947).

Regarding the difficulty of assessing the intentions of the framers of the first and fourteenth amendment regarding the religion clauses and their applicability to the states, see School District v. Schempp, 374 U.S. 203, 230, 83 S.Ct. 1560, 1575, 10 L.Ed.2d 844 (1963) (Brennan, J., concurring). Regarding the difficulty of assessing the intentions of the framers of the fourteenth amendment in particular see generally § 18.7 of this treatise. Regarding the difficulty of determining whether even the "framers" of the Constitution intended that "original intention" should be critical to later interpretations of the meaning and applicability of constitutional principles of the later point in time see Powell, The Original Understanding of Original Intent, 98 Harv.L.Rev. 885 (1985).

In Wallace v. Jaffree, 472 U.S. 38, 105 S.Ct. 2479, 86 L.Ed.2d 29 (1985) the Court invalidated a state law that allowed for a period of silence in public schools "for meditation or voluntary prayer" because the legislature which passed this law did so for the purpose of promoting religious beliefs. Although questions regarding the "moment of silence" present some difficult issues, the Supreme Court has held consistently, since it first considered this issue in the 1960s, that government-endorsed prayer or religious activity in public schools violates the establishment clause of the first amendment. Nevertheless, the Supreme Court in Wallace was called upon to overturn a district court ruling that would have allowed the state not only to have a moment of silence for silent prayer or meditation but also a separate statute that would have authorized teachers to lead "willing students" in a legislatively prescribed prayer. The federal district court

reached this decision by determining that the Supreme Court of the United States had misinterpreted the meaning of the first and fourteenth amendments and that, in the district judge's view, those amendments would not prohibit state sponsored prayer in state schools. Jaffree v. Board of School Com'rs, 554 F.Supp. 1104 (S.D.Ala. 1983), rev'd sub nom. Wallace v. Jaffree, 472 U.S. 38, 105 S.Ct. 2479, 86 L.Ed.2d 29 (1985). The Supreme Court's majority opinion in Wallace merely termed the district judge's opinion regarding the state prescribed prayer as only "remarkable"; the Supreme Court reaffirmed its longstanding view of the applicability of the religion clauses to the states. Regardless of whether historians or lower court judges believe that the Supreme Court has in some abstract or ultimate sense misinterpreted these or any other provisions of the Constitution, lower federal court and state court judges are not free to disregard rulings and majority opinions of the Supreme Court of the United States. See generally §§ 1.3–1.6.

See generally, Laycock, "Nonpreferential Aid to Religion: A False Claim About Original Intent", 27 Wm. & Mary L.Rev. 875 (1986); Developments in the Law—Religion and the State, 100 Harv.L.Rev. 1607 (1987); Bradley, Dogmatomachy—A "Privatization" Theory of the Religion Clause Cases, 30 St. Louis U.L.J. 275 (1986).

For an argument that the Supreme Court has used a distorted view of the history of the establishment clause to justify the modern rulings see Bradley, Imagining the Past and Remembering the Future: The Supreme Court's History of the Establishment Clause, 18 Connecticut L.Rev. 827 (1986). Compare with Professor Bradley's thesis Professor Van Alstyne's view of the danger of using historical evidence regarding government practices to justify government acts that give incidental aid to religion. Van Alstyne, Trends in the Supreme Court: Mr. Jefferson's Crumbling Wall—A Comment on Lynch v. Donnelly, 1984 Duke L.J. 770. See also, Laycock, Text, Intent,

Since assessing history to determine the exact meaning of the religious freedom that was to be guaranteed by the first amendment will not produce clear answers to current issues, we must plunge ahead and study the development of the separate doctrines in the case law. Here we will find that the Court has both found and created certain "historic" principles which are suited to protecting religious freedom— past and present. As almost all of the important Supreme Court decisions in this area have come after 1940, we have only the modern Court's view of history and the justices' current tests to guide us.[7]

II. THE ESTABLISHMENT CLAUSE

§ 21.3 Introduction

The establishment clause applies to both the federal and local governments. It is a prohibition of government sponsorship of religion which requires that government neither aid nor formally establish a religion. While at its inception the clause might not have been intended to prohibit governmental aid to all religions, the accepted view today is that it also prohibits a preference for religion over non-religion. However, the government simply cannot avoid aiding religion in some manner unless it actively opposes religion—something that it is forbidden to do by the free exercise clause. For example, the granting of police or fire protection to churches clearly aids the practice of religion, but the withholding of such services would single out religious activities for a special burden. Thus it is clear that some test is required to determine when such incidental aid is permissible and when it is prohibited.

The Supreme Court applies the three part test (the purpose-effect-entanglement test) in virtually all establishment clause cases.[1] How-

and the Religion Clauses, 4 Notre Dame Journal of Law, Ethics & Public Policy 683 (1990); Smith, Nonpreferentialism in Establishment Clause Analysis: A Response to Professor Laycock, 65 St. John's L.Rev. 245 (1991); G. Bradley, Church–State Relationships in America (1987).

7. The Supreme Court did decide several important cases under the free exercise clause between 1878 and 1940. These are discussed in § 21.7, infra.

State courts were confronted with problems of religious freedom at an earlier time, e.g., Donahoe v. Richards, 38 Me. 379 (1854) (schoolchildren can be forced to participate in religious exercises).

§ 21.3

1. In every case in which a law is challenged as a violation of the establishment

clause, a court must determine whether the law has a secular purpose and a primary secular effect, and does not create excessive entanglement with religion. This three part test will be employed regardless of whether the law at issue is attacked as a direct advancement of religion or a mere accommodation of religion. The cases examined in this section and in § 21.4 ("Aid to Religious Institutions") involve laws that were challenged as governmental attempts to promote religious activities.

A legislative accommodation of religion may or may not survive the three part test, depending on the particular statute. For example, the Supreme Court in Corporation of the Presiding Bishop of the Church of Jesus Christ of Latter–Day Saints v. Amos, 483 U.S. 327, 107 S.Ct. 2862, 97

ever, the Court has ruled that a law that involves a "denominational preference" or a "sect preference" should not be subject to these tests but, instead, should be subject to a more rigorous "compelling interest" test.

If a law creates a denominational preference it will violate the establishment clause unless its distinction between different religious

L.Ed.2d 273 (1987) upheld a statutory exemption for religious organizations from the statutory prohibition against discrimination in employment of the basis on religion. The exemption allowed a religious organization to make employment decisions based on the religious beliefs of job applicants or employees, although a nonreligious organization could not distinguish between its employees on the basis of religion. The majority opinion found that a legislative purpose of avoiding "governmental interference" with the religious organization's activities was a permissible purpose. The Supreme Court also found that the exemption did not aid religion or did not create an entanglement between government and religion. Conversely, in Estate of Thornton v. Caldor, Inc., 472 U.S. 703, 105 S.Ct. 2914, 86 L.Ed.2d 557 (1985) the Supreme Court invalidated a state statute that gave every employee a right to be released from work on the employee's Sabbath. Writing for a majority in *Estate of Thornton,* Chief Justice Burger found that the law had a primary effect that advanced religion because it subjected employers and coworkers of the religious employee to significant costs in order to accommodate the desire of an employee to take actions based upon his religion. These cases are examined in §§ 21.13, 21.15.

The three part test (the purpose, primary effect, and excessive entanglement tests) has been used in most of the majority opinions of the Supreme Court that examined establishment clause issues since the early 1970s. However, there appears to be an increasing division between the Justices regarding the appropriate standard to be used when determining whether a governmental act violates the establishment clause. Justice O'Connor has favored a test that focused on whether the government act at issue "endorsed" religion. See, e.g., Lynch v. Donnelly, 465 U.S. 668, 690, 104 S.Ct. 1355, 1366, 79 L.Ed.2d 604 (1984) (O'Connor, J., concurring), rehearing denied 466 U.S. 994, 104 S.Ct. 2376, 80 L.Ed.2d 848 (1984); Witters v. Washington Department of Services for the Blind, 474 U.S. 481, 493, 106 S.Ct. 748, 755, 88

L.Ed.2d 846 (1986) (O'Connor, J., concurring), rehearing denied 475 U.S. 1091, 106 S.Ct. 1485, 89 L.Ed.2d 737 (1986). See generally, Smith, Symbols, Perceptions, and Doctrinal Illusions: Establishment, Neutrality, and the "No Endorsement Test," 86 Michigan Law Review 266 (1977); Loewy, Rethinking Government Neutrality Towards Religion Under the Establishment Clause: The Untapped Potential of Justice O'Connor's Insight, 64 North Carolina Law Review 1049 (1986).

Justice O'Connor and Justice Blackmun (and, perhaps, a majority of the Justices) see a significant overlap between the endorsement standard used by Justice O'Connor and the primary effect branch of the three-part test. See, County of Allegheny v. American Civil Liberties Union, 492 U.S. 573, 590–93, 109 S.Ct. 3086, 3099–3101, 106 L.Ed.2d 472 (1989) (majority opinion by Justice Blackmun), on remand 887 F.2d 260 (3d Cir.1989); Board of Education of Westside Community Schools v. Mergens, 496 U.S. 226, ___, 110 S.Ct. 2356, 2371–73, 110 L.Ed.2d 191 (1990) (this portion of the opinion is a plurality opinion written by Justice O'Connor and joined by Chief Justice Rehnquist and Justices White and Blackmun).

Justices Kennedy and Scalia appear to favor abandoning the three-part test; they would question only whether the government was directly supporting religious activity or coercing persons to engage in religious activity. The opinions of Justices Kennedy and Scalia are sometimes joined by Chief Justice Rehnquist and Justice White. See, e.g., County of Allegheny v. American Civil Liberties Union, 492 U.S. 573, 655, 109 S.Ct. 3086, 3134, 106 L.Ed.2d 472 (1989) (Kennedy, J., joined by Rehnquist, C.J. and White and Scalia, JJ., concurring in the judgment in part and dissenting in part), on remand 887 F.2d 260 (3d Cir.1989); Board of Education of Westside Community Schools v. Mergens, 496 U.S. 226, ___, 110 S.Ct. 2356, 2376, 110 L.Ed.2d 191 (1990) (Kennedy, J., joined by Scalia, J., concurring in part and concurring in the judgment).

denominations is necessary to promote a compelling interest. It is difficult to imagine the circumstances under which the government would have a compelling need to prefer some religions over others. Because of the stringency of the test used to examine denominational preferences, some cases involve disputes concerning whether a denominational preference was created by a statute. For example, in *Larson v. Valente* [2] the Supreme Court invalidated a state statute that regulated the solicitation of donations by charitable organizations if, but only if, the organization solicited more than 50% of its funds from nonmembers. This law was viewed as creating a denominational preference because the burdens of the regulation, in the view of the Court, clearly discriminated against religious organizations that were significantly involved in fund raising activities aimed at nonmembers. The majority opinion in *Larson* was written by Justice Brennan; he found that the imposition of regulatory burdens only on certain types of charitable and religious fund raising was not "closely fitted" to any compelling interest. Therefore, the law violated the establishment clause, and no further examination of the statute under other types of establishment clause tests was necessary.

The Supreme Court, in *Hernandez v. Commissioner of Internal Revenue*,[3] upheld the denial of a tax deduction to a taxpayer for a contribution to a church that was a "fixed donation" for religious services provided by the church. In *Hernandez*, a member of the Church of Scientology wanted to deduct from his gross income the amount of money he paid for "auditing" and "training" services provided by the Church. The Church had a system of mandatory fixed charges for these religious services; no member would receive the service without paying the fixed price. The Internal Revenue Code was interpreted by both the Internal Revenue Service and the Supreme Court to preclude a deduction for a payment made to a charity that constituted an exchange for a product or service. The Supreme Court ruled that the Internal Revenue Code prohibition of a charitable deduction under such circumstances did not violate the establishment or free exercise clauses of the first amendment. The Court found that the tax classification was not subject to the compelling interest test because the Internal Revenue Code did not on its face create any distinction between different types of religious entities. Because the statute, and the interpretation of it by the Internal Revenue Service, contained no denominational preference, the tax code provision was subject only to the three part establishment clause test (the purpose-effect-entanglement test). First, the Court found that there was no evidence of animus to any religion, or to religion in general, in the

---

2. 456 U.S. 228, 102 S.Ct. 1673, 72 L.Ed.2d 33 (1982), rehearing denied 457 U.S. 1111, 102 S.Ct. 2916, 73 L.Ed.2d 1323 (1982).

3. 490 U.S. 680, 109 S.Ct. 2136, 104 L.Ed.2d 766 (1989), rehearing denied 492 U.S. 933, 110 S.Ct. 16, 106 L.Ed.2d 630 (1989).

purpose of the statute. Second, the Court ruled that the statute's effect of encouraging general gifts to charitable entities that were not in exchange for goods or services neither advanced or inhibited religion. Third, the Court held that the Internal Revenue Code did not create any entanglement between the government and religion, because the minimal regulatory interaction between taxpayers, churches, and the Internal Revenue Service was not the kind of administrative entanglement that endangered religion clause values.[4]

The Court in *Hernandez* also ruled that the denial of the deduction did not violate the free exercise clause for two reasons. First, the Internal Revenue Code did not place a substantial burden on any person who was carrying out a tenet of a religious belief. Second, the public interest in maintaining a tax system free of exemptions tailored to accommodate a wide variety of religions outweighed any burden on persons who were denied deductions under these circumstances.[5]

In *Jimmy Swaggart Ministries v. Board of Equalization*,[6] the Justices unanimously found that a religious organization, and the members of the organization, had no right to refuse to pay general sales and use taxes for the sales of religious goods and literature. Justice O'Connor's opinion for the unanimous Court tracked the reasoning of the *Hernandez* decision. Because sales and use taxes were designed to tax solely at religious activities, the taxes did not have to be justified by a compelling state interest. If a "flat tax" operates as a license fee (a fixed fee) that restricts the ability of persons to engage in religious activities that tax would be analogous to a prior restraint on speech activities. The Court would find that the flat-tax license fee, as applied to religious activity, violated the establishment and free exercise clauses.[7] However, a tax applying to all sales and uses of tangible personal property, like a tax on individual or corporate income, did not raise the concern of whether the tax was a "flat license tax that would act as a

---

4. For an examination of a variety of cases involving regulations of religious organizations or their members that are asserted to violate both the free exercise and establishment clauses, see §§ 21.13, 21.15, 21.16.

5. The Supreme Court's ruling on the free exercise claim was consistent with its earlier decision in United States v. Lee, 455 U.S. 252, 102 S.Ct. 1051, 71 L.Ed.2d 127 (1982) in which the Court found that Amish employers of Amish individuals did not have a constitutional right to an exemption from compulsory participation in the Social Security System. See § 21.8.

6. 493 U.S. 378, 110 S.Ct. 688, 107 L.Ed.2d 796 (1990).

7. Murdock v. Pennsylvania, 319 U.S. 105, 63 S.Ct. 870, 87 L.Ed. 1292 (1943) (invalidating an ordinance requiring persons canvassing or soliciting within a city to pay a flat fee for a license tax as applied to a person distributing religious literature); Follett v. McCormick, 321 U.S. 573, 64 S.Ct. 717, 88 L.Ed. 938 (1944) (invalidating a flat fee tax as applied to a religious minister selling religious literature). These decisions involved rulings regarding the free exercise clause, but the decisions seem to provide constitutional protection of a variety of first amendment activities (such as the activities of sellers of nonreligious books) as well as the specific protection of religiously motivated actions. See §§ 21.6–21.8.

precondition to the free exercise of religious beliefs." [8] Thus, it appears that the Supreme Court would be highly unlikely to find that any tax on its face, or as applied to religious organizations, violates the establishment clause or the free exercise clause unless the tax singled out religious activity for a special tax or created a flat fee that was a precondition to the exercise of religious beliefs.[9]

When a law is challenged under the establishment clause it must pass a three part test. First, it must have a secular purpose. Second, it must have a primary secular effect. Third, it must not involve the government in an excessive entanglement with religion. When the potentiality for excessive entanglement must be determined another three part test is employed. The degree of entanglement is estimated by evaluating: (1) the character and purpose of the religious institution to be benefited, (2) the nature of the aid, and (3) the resulting relationship between the government and religious authorities. Additionally (although this may be considered a part of the entanglement test) the law must not create an excessive degree of political division along religious lines.

An outline of the history of the establishment clause tests may give some added perspective. There were only two significant decisions under the establishment clause prior to 1947. In that year, the Court held the clause applicable to the states, while approving the reimbursement of bus fees for all students, including those attending parochial schools. It did so without a clear standard, for a majority simply found that no prohibited form of aid was involved in that program. In the cases dealing with prayers and Bible reading in the public schools the Court enunciated a "secular purpose and primary effect" test. This two part test was the sole standard for a time and was used in reviewing the permissibility of loaning textbooks to parochial school students. In 1970, the Court upheld property tax exemptions for churches while using for the first time the present purpose-effect-entanglement test.

To withstand analysis under the establishment clause a government act must have not only a secular purpose and a primary effect which neither advances nor inhibits religion, it also must avoid creating the type of entanglement between government and religion which might lead to an erosion of the principle of government neutrality in religious decisionmaking. The government may take action for secular purposes which aid all persons in a religiously neutral manner even

---

8. Jimmy Swaggart Ministries v. Board of Equalization, 493 U.S. 378, 110 S.Ct. 688, 107 L.Ed.2d 796 (1990). "Our concern in *Murdock* and *Follett*—that a flat license tax would act as a *precondition* to the free exercise of religious beliefs—is simply not present where a tax applies to all sales and uses of tangible personal property in the state." 493 U.S. at 387, 110 S.Ct. at 694 (emphasis in original).

9. Id. For an examination of the instances in which the free exercise clause may require a state to grant an exemption from laws of general applicability, see §§ 21.6–21.8.

though there is some incidental aid to religious organizations. Additionally, the Supreme Court in limited circumstances has allowed the government to recognize the historic role of religion in American society.

Direct entanglement with religion—delegation of legislative power. In some instances it is relatively easy to determine that a governmental action violates the establishment clause because it either delegates governmental power to a religious group in a manner that allows for excessive entanglement between the government and religion or it constitutes a preference for certain religions. For example, in *Larkin v. Grendel's Den, Inc.*[10] the Supreme Court found that a zoning law violated the establishment clause by granting to all churches or schools a veto power over the issuance of a liquor license for any premises within a five hundred foot radius of the church or school.

Although the law might have had a secular purpose (the promotion of a quiet atmosphere around certain cultural and educational centers) that purpose alone could not establish the statute's constitutionality. The statute was clearly susceptible to being used for the promotion of religious rather than secular ends. Under the statute each church exercised a governmental power which was subject to no clear secular standard; that power could be used to promote primarily religious goals. Even if one assumed that the statute had both a secular purpose and primary effect, the law clearly failed the excessive entanglement test. The law vested governmental authority in churches; in the words of the Court, the law "enmeshes churches in the exercise of substantial government powers contrary to our consistent interpretation of the establishment clause." [11] The excessive entanglement test was meant to avoid the danger to both secular government and religious autonomy that accompanies a sharing of power between religious and governmental agencies.

The government may regulate the actions of all persons, including actions undertaken by some persons for religiously motivated reasons, without violating the establishment clause or free exercise clause if the regulation is religiously neutral and promotes significant societal interests. A law which regulates the activities of religious organizations or private persons will be invalid if it distinguishes between various types of activities on the basis of the religious belief, or the religious affiliation, of the persons or organizations that engage in the activity.[12] If a

---

10. 459 U.S. 116, 103 S.Ct. 505, 74 L.Ed.2d 297 (1982).

11. 459 U.S. at 127, 103 S.Ct. at 512.

12. See, e.g., Larson v. Valente, 456 U.S. 228, 102 S.Ct. 1673, 72 L.Ed.2d 33 (1982), rehearing denied 457 U.S. 1111, 102 S.Ct. 2916, 73 L.Ed.2d 1323 (1982) finding a violation of the establishment clause when a state statute regarding solicitation of charitable contributions imposed regulations and reporting requirements only on those religious organizations which solicited more than fifty percent of their funds from nonmembers. This law was considered a "denominational preference" that was such a clear violation of the estab-

law regulating private sector activity favors persons with religious beliefs over other persons it may have the primary effect of advancing religion; such a law would violate the establishment clause.[13]

A law which is religiously neutral may have to give way to a claim for exemption from the regulation by persons whose religious beliefs prevent them from complying with the law. The government will not have to grant an exemption from a religiously neutral regulation of activities of all persons if the regulation does not impose a significant burden on the ability of persons seeking the exemption to maintain their religious beliefs. If the regulation does impose such a burden, the government will have to grant the exemption unless the regulation promotes a societal interest which outweighs the burden imposed on those who must follow it despite their religious beliefs.[14]

The use of historical evidence to determine establishment clause violations. In several instances the Court has based a finding that a governmental practice did not violate the establishment clause on a history of that practice which the Court believed showed that the governmental practice involved no significant danger of eroding governmental neutrality regarding religious matters.

In *Walz v. Tax Commission*[15] the Supreme Court upheld a state law exempting from state taxation property and income of religious organizations. The tax exemption survived the three-part purpose-effect-entanglement test primarily because of historical evidence that the federal and state governments since the time of the American Revolution had granted tax exemptions to such property and income as a part of general tax exemptions for nonprofit or socially beneficial organizations. The majority opinion by Chief Justice Burger found

lishment clause that the Court did not have to consider free exercise values. For further examination of this case, see § 21.16, infra.

13. Estate of Thornton v. Caldor, Inc., 472 U.S. 703, 105 S.Ct. 2914, 86 L.Ed.2d 557 (1985) (state legislation which gives workers an absolute right to refuse to engage in employment activities on their sabbath day violates the establishment clause because it has the primary effect of advancing religion through an "unyielding" and inflexible system of giving preferences in employment practice to employees with religious beliefs). This case is examined further in § 21.13.

14. Regarding the free exercise clause basis upon which courts may find that the government must exempt from its regulations persons who seek to take actions, or refrain from taking actions, based on sincerely held religious beliefs see §§ 21.8, 21.9. In Tony & Susan Alamo Foundation v. Secretary of Labor, 471 U.S. 290, 105 S.Ct. 1953, 85 L.Ed.2d 278 (1985) the Court held that a religious organization which engages in commercial activities is properly subject to the requirements of the Fair Labor Standards Act regarding minimum wage and overtime payments to its employees even though the employees themselves do not wish to receive cash wages because of their religious belief. Requiring the employees to receive a minimum wage, but allowing them to receive that wage in a manner other than through cash payments, imposes no burden on the employees' religious beliefs. The requirements the Act imposes on the employer do not violate the establishment clause because they are religiously neutral regulations of secular commercial activity. Regarding the regulation of religious organization activities see §§ 21.15 and 21.16.

15. 397 U.S. 664, 90 S.Ct. 1409, 25 L.Ed.2d 697 (1970).

that this history established that the legislature's purpose in creating the exemption was not one that contravened the principle of separation of church and state; history showed no significant danger that such exemptions would give rise to either a religious effect or an entanglement of government and religion.

In *Marsh v. Chambers* [16] the Court, again in an opinion by Chief Justice Burger, upheld a legislature's practice of employing a religious chaplain whose primary duty was to open each legislative day with a prayer. The Court based its finding that there was no establishment clause violation on the "unambiguous and unbroken history of more than two hundred years" of legislative prayer, although the majority opinion also stated that history "could not justify contemporary violations" of the first amendment. In the majority's view, legislative prayer was a recognition of a belief widely held among the people of the country; its history demonstrated that such activity did not constitute the type of religious purpose, religious effect, or entanglement between government and religion that threatened the first amendment value of religious neutrality on the part of government.

Chief Justice Burger also wrote for the Court in *Lynch v. Donnelley*.[17] In *Lynch* the Court upheld a municipal policy under which a city park was decorated with displays celebrating the Christmas holiday season, including a Christian nativity scene. The majority opinion found that the use of the nativity scene, at least in the context of a Christmas display which included nonreligious as well as religious symbols of the holiday, was not done for any purpose which threatened establishment clause values because there was no governmental purpose to aid religion in general or to aid a particular faith. The Chief Justice found that the history of Christmas celebrations in this country was such that it was unlikely that members of the public, when viewing the scene, would find the practice to be an endorsement of religion; there was no other primary effect of the city's action that would constitute a substantial or impermissible benefit to religion. For these reasons, the majority also found that there was no entanglement between government and religion.[18]

---

16. 463 U.S. 783, 103 S.Ct. 3330, 77 L.Ed.2d 1019 (1983).

17. 465 U.S. 668, 104 S.Ct. 1355, 79 L.Ed.2d 604 (1984), rehearing denied 466 U.S. 994, 104 S.Ct. 2376, 80 L.Ed.2d 848 (1984).

18. If a city allows its park to be used for a variety of speech activities, including nonreligious holiday displays, there is a question as to whether individuals or groups have a right under the free speech clause to place a religious symbol or display on the park premises. In McCreary v. Stone, 739 F.2d 716 (2d Cir.1984) (per cu-

riam), judgment aff'd sub nom. by an equally divided Court, Board of Trustees v. McCreary, 471 U.S. 83, 105 S.Ct. 1859, 85 L.Ed.2d 63 (1985), a village refused to allow religious organizations to place a nativity scene on a public park even though other speech activities were conducted on the park premises and other nonreligious decorations were placed in the park during the Christmas holiday season. The court of appeals ruled that the exclusion of the nativity scene might violate free speech principles if it was based solely on the content of the display, although the nativi-

Although Chief Justice Burger wrote for the Court in *Walz, Marsh* and *Lynch,* it is not clear whether the Chief Justice, and a majority of the justices in these cases, was taking the position that certain practices which have existed throughout our history should be exempted from the three-part test. The Chief Justice instead, appears to have found that the three-part test was met in each case because in each case there was historic proof that there had been no entanglement which had threatened the religious neutrality of government; in addition, there had been no effect of granting a benefit to religion (or any particular religion) flowing from any of these practices, and the legislature's purpose in each case must not have been one which contravened the policies of the first amendment because none of the practices had ever led to any impermissible erosion of religious neutrality on the part of government.[19]

In *County of Allegheny v. American Civil Liberties Union*[20] there was significant disagreement between the Justices concerning both the constitutionality of holiday displays on public property and the method by which the judiciary should determine whether holiday displays with religious connotations violate establishment clause principles. At issue in *County of Allegheny* were two holiday displays located on public property. The first display was a creche on the staircase of a county courthouse which had been set up by a Roman Catholic organization. The creche was accompanied by flowers and a sign stating the display had been donated by the Holy Name Society. There was a fence around the creche display; there were no other holiday decorations on the county courthouse staircase area. The second display was approximately one city block away from the first; the second display was at the entrance to the main office building for the city and county. The dispute regarding the second display related to an 18 foot menorah, which was owned by a Jewish organization but stored, maintained, and erected by the city. The menorah was next to a large (over 40 foot tall)

---

ty scene could be excluded if the exclusion was based on a content neutral form of time, place, or manner regulation. Justice Powell did not participate in the Supreme Court review of this decision and the eight voting justices divided evenly when they reviewed this case. The Supreme Court affirmed the decision without an opinion. The lower court had held only that the village could not rely on the religion clauses of the first amendment as a basis for denying access to the park. Thus, the final resolution of all such "equal access issues" remains in doubt pending future Supreme Court decisions. See generally §§ 21.5(c), 21.5(e).

19. For an analysis of the dangers posed to first amendment values by the Court's use of "historical" evidence to ap-

prove governmental acts which give incidental aid to religion, see Van Alstyne, Trends in the Supreme Court: Mr. Jefferson's Crumbling Wall—A Comment on Lynch v. Donnelly, 1984 Duke L.J. 770.

Contrast the view of Professor Van Alstyne with Conkle, Toward a General Theory of the Establishment Clause, 82 Northwestern University L.Rev. 1113 (1988). See also, Dorsen & Sims, The Nativity Scene Case: An Error in Judgment, 1985 U.Ill.L.Rev. 837. Marshall, "We Know It When We See It" The Supreme Court and Establishment, 59 So.Cal.L.Rev. 495 (1986).

20. 492 U.S. 573, 109 S.Ct. 3086, 106 L.Ed.2d 472 (1989), on remand 887 F.2d 260 (3d Cir.1989).

decorated evergreen (Christmas) tree. The second display also included a sign referring to the display as a "Salute to Liberty."

In *County of Allegheny,* a majority of Justices found that the first display (the creche display), violated the establishment clause but that the second display (the menorah-tree-sign display), did not violate the establishment clause. Justice Kennedy, joined by Chief Justice Rehnquist and Justices White and Scalia, would have found that both displays were consistent with the establishment clause. Those Justices believe that government accommodation of, and acknowledgment of public support for, religion were permissible so long as the government was not providing direct benefits to religion or coercing of religious beliefs.[21]

Justices Brennan, Marshall, and Stevens believed that the three-part (purpose-effect-entanglement) test that had been used for two decades in cases examining incidental aid to religion should be used to review holiday displays. They believed that both displays were unconstitutional forms of aid to religion.[22]

In *County of Allegheny,* only Justices Blackmun and O'Connor believed that there was a constitutional difference between the two displays but, as they were the "swing votes" in the case, their view dictated the outcome of the case. In earlier cases, Justice O'Connor had stated her belief that establishment clause should prohibit government aid to religion if the government action effectively endorsed religion in a way that would send a message to the populace that the government favored certain types of religions and that those persons who were not a part of the religions being aided were disfavored.[23] In her view the display that included only the creche involved a type of government endorsement of religion that was prohibited by the establishment clause. However, the menorah-tree-sign display included a variety of holiday symbols and did not constitute an impermissible

---

21. County of Allegheny v. American Civil Liberties Union, 492 U.S. 573, 655, 109 S.Ct. 3086, 3134, 106 L.Ed.2d 472 (1989) (Kennedy, J., joined by Rehnquist, C.J., and White and Scalia, JJ., concurring in the judgment in part and dissenting in part), on remand 887 F.2d 260 (3d Cir. 1989).

22. County of Allegheny v. American Civil Liberties Union, 492 U.S. 573, 645, 109 S.Ct. 3086, 3129, 106 L.Ed.2d 472 (1989) (Stevens, J., joined by Brennan and Marshall, JJ., concurring in part and dissenting in part), on remand 887 F.2d 260 (3d Cir.1989).

23. See, e.g., Lynch v. Donnelly, 465 U.S. 668, 690, 104 S.Ct. 1355, 1366, 79 L.Ed.2d 604 (1984) (O'Connor, J., concurring), rehearing denied 466 U.S. 994, 104 S.Ct. 2376, 80 L.Ed.2d 848 (1984); Witters v. Washington Department of Services for the Blind, 474 U.S. 481, 493, 106 S.Ct. 748, 755, 88 L.Ed.2d 846 (1986), rehearing denied 475 U.S. 1091, 106 S.Ct. 1485, 89 L.Ed.2d 737 (1986) (O'Connor, J., concurring). See generally, Smith, Symbols, Perceptions, and Doctrinal Illusions: Establishment, Neutrality, and the "No Endorsement Test," 86 Mich.L.Rev. 266 (1987); Loewy, Rethinking Government Neutrality Towards Religion Under the Establishment Clause: The Untapped Potential of Justice O'Connor's Insight, 64 N.C.L.Rev. 1049 (1986).

endorsement of religion.[24]

Justice Blackmun wrote an opinion that was in part a majority opinion, in part a plurality opinion, and in part a opinion expressing only his own views.[25] Justice Blackmun believed that the three-part (purpose-effect-entanglement) test used in establishment clause cases since the early 1970s was the proper test to use in this case. However, Justice Blackmun also believed that Justice O'Connor's endorsement test was consistent with earlier cases applying the three part establishment clause test.[26] Justice Blackmun found that the display that included the menorah, tree, and liberty sign did not violate the three-part test because the symbols had both secular and religious aspects; the message conveyed by the display was a basically secular one that endorsed the values of liberty. The menorah-sign-tree display, in Justice Blackmun's view, had a permissible purpose, did not aid religion, and did not create an excessive entanglement between government and religion. Justice Blackmun believed that the creche display violated the establishment clause because it conveyed religious message that could not be defended as a secular government display.

§ 21.4 Aid to Religious Institutions

(a) Primary and Secondary Schools

There is very little state aid that may go to religious primary and secondary schools without violating the establishment clause. Because the Supreme Court has held that these schools are permeated by religious teaching, any significant aid will have a high potentiality for having the effect of aiding religion. The only way to avoid such an effect would be the imposition of so many procedural checks that the program would result in the excessive entanglement between government and religious entities. Additionally, these programs have a history of causing serious political divisions.[1] For these reasons the Court has been quite strict in applying the purpose-effect-entanglement test to these programs. Because the first amendment principles which govern this area are the product of a series of Supreme Court decisions

---

24. County of Allegheny v. American Civil Liberties Union, 492 U.S. 573, 623, 109 S.Ct. 3086, 3117, 106 L.Ed.2d 472 (1989) (O'Connor concurring in part and concurring in the judgment; Justice O'Connor's opinion is joined in part by Justices Brennan and Stevens), on remand 887 F.2d 260 (3d Cir.1989).

25. County of Allegheny v. American Civil Liberties Union, 492 U.S. 573, 109 S.Ct. 3086, 106 L.Ed.2d 472 (1989) (judgment of the Court announced by Justice Blackmun in an opinion that is in part a majority opinion, in part an opinion joined by Justices O'Connor and Stevens, in part

an opinion joined only by Justice Stevens, in part an opinion (in respect to part VI) that is not joined by any other justice), on remand 887 F.2d 260 (3d Cir.1989).

26. 492 U.S. at 590–94, 109 S.Ct. at 3099–3101 (this language appears in part IIIA of the Blackmun opinion, which was joined by a majority of the Justices).

§ 21.4

1. See § 21.4(d), infra, for further analysis of the "excessive entanglement" principle.

on very specific types of aid to religiously affiliated schools, we must review those decisions to understand these first amendment principles.[2]

Student Transportation. In *Everson v. Board of Education* [3] the Court, by a five to four vote, upheld a program which in effect paid the transportation costs of parochial school students. Pursuant to a state statute, a local school board established a program which reimbursed the parents of students at public and nonprofit private schools for the amounts they spent for bus transportation.[4] The only private nonprofit school in the district was a Catholic school.

A majority of the justices upheld this program even though they took the position that no aid could be given to a religion in accordance with the establishment clause. The majority was of the view that the provision of free bus transportation to all school children on an equal basis constituted only a general service to benefit and safeguard children rather than an aid to religion. The opinion noted that basic governmental services, such as fire and police protection, could be extended to religious institutions along with the rest of the public without aiding religion. Because the majority saw the general provision of free transportation to be akin to such a service, the program was approved.

This position was taken over several vigorous dissents [5] and at a later time one member of the majority in *Everson* indicated that he felt the case was wrongly decided.[6] However, *Everson* remains the law today and the Court has shown no inclination to reverse its position on basic bus fare reimbursement programs, even though, as discussed later in this section, the state cannot pay for parochial school "field trips."

If a similar aid program were limited by statute, to public and parochial school students the Court would come to a different conclusion because of the exclusion of children in private nonprofit schools.

2. Related decisions concerning governmental acts that arguably advance religious goals in a public school system are examined in § 21.5, infra.

See generally, Rotunda, The Constitutional Future of the Bill of Rights: A Closer Look at Commercial Speech and State Aid to Religiously Affiliated Schools, 65 No.Car.L.Rev. 917, 929–34 (1987); Choper, The Establishment Clause and Aid to Parochial Schools—An Update, 75 Calif.L.Rev. 5 (1987).

3. 330 U.S. 1, 67 S.Ct. 504, 91 L.Ed. 711 (1947), rehearing denied 330 U.S. 855, 67 S.Ct. 962, 91 L.Ed. 1297 (1947).

4. There is no serious problem presented by the exclusion of students at private profit making or proprietary schools. To date the legislature is free to classify on the basis of wealth or financial characteris-

tics so long as the classification is not irrational or clearly invidious. Cf., San Antonio Independent School District v. Rodriguez, 411 U.S. 1, 28, 93 S.Ct. 1278, 1293–94, 36 L.Ed.2d 16 (1973), rehearing denied 411 U.S. 959, 93 S.Ct. 1919, 36 L.Ed.2d 418 (1973). See § 18.25, supra.

5. The dissent of Justice Rutledge is worth noting for it contains a history of many of the circumstances that led to the drafting of the amendment. Everson v. Board of Ed., 330 U.S. 1, 33–43, 67 S.Ct. 504, 520–25, 91 L.Ed. 711 (1947) (Rutledge, J., dissenting), rehearing denied 330 U.S. 855, 67 S.Ct. 962, 91 L.Ed. 1297 (1947).

6. Engel v. Vitale, 370 U.S. 421, 443–44, 82 S.Ct. 1261, 1273–74, 8 L.Ed.2d 601 (1962) (Douglas, J., concurring).

Such a statute would have the effect of preferring religious school students over students at other nonprofit schools and this preference should be held to violate the establishment clause.

By the time that the Court was next confronted with a program of aid to parochial school students, it was employing the "purpose and effect" test to resolve establishment clause claims.[7] Under this test the purpose of a state program must be secular in nature. Additionally, the program may not have a primary effect of either advancing or inhibiting religion or religious practices to withstand review under this test.

Textbooks. In *Board of Education v. Allen*[8] the Court upheld a program of providing textbooks to parochial school students under the purpose and effect test. The New York textbook law under review required school boards to loan textbooks to students in all public or private schools. This resulted in books being given to parochial school students for their studies in the religious schools. However, only books for secular studies could be loaned to students and the books had to be either ones used in public schools or approved by the school board as being secular in nature. The opinion found no religious purpose in this law because it accepted the position that the program was designed to aid the secular education of students. This secular purpose—the improvement of the educational opportunities for all children—has sufficed in every case relating to aid for religious schools.[9]

The *Allen* majority also found that the program did not have a primary effect of advancing religion. At this time a majority of the justices refused to assume that the religious schools—including Catholic primary and secondary schools—were so permeated by religion that even classes in secular subjects advanced religion. Thus the majority could find that the books were used only for the secular teaching component of such schools. The local board's insuring that only secular books were loaned, and the absence of proof that secular classes were used to advance religion, were the mainstays of the majority position.[10]

Allen may mark the outermost reaches of permissible aid to parochial school students. Like *Everson,* it remains the law on the basis of *stare decisis,*[11] since the Court has become increasingly strict in the scope of aid that may be afforded to such schools. Additionally, it must

7. This test was developed in the "school prayer" cases, see § 21.5(c), infra.

8. 392 U.S. 236, 88 S.Ct. 1923, 20 L.Ed.2d 1060 (1968).

9. The only cases which center on a finding of religious purpose are Epperson v. Arkansas, 393 U.S. 97, 89 S.Ct. 266, 21 L.Ed.2d 228 (1968) which is discussed in § 21.5, infra, and Stone v. Graham, 449 U.S. 39, 101 S.Ct. 192, 66 L.Ed.2d 199 (1980), which is examined in § 21.5(c), infra.

10. Board of Education v. Allen, 392 U.S. 236, 245–48, 88 S.Ct. 1923, 1927–29, 20 L.Ed.2d 1060 (1968).

11. See notes 29–31 of this section, infra, and accompanying text.

be noted that even these programs would be invalid if they aided schools that discriminated on the basis of race.[12]

Tax Exempt Status for Religious Organizations. In *Walz v. Tax Commission*[13] the Court expanded the establishment clause tests while upholding another form of aid to religious entities. In this case the Court upheld the granting of exemptions from property taxes to churches as a part of a general exception for a wide variety of nonprofit institutions.[14] Presumably this ruling validates the granting of tax exemptions to religious schools so long as the exemption is granted to all nonprofit schools.

The majority opinion by Chief Justice Burger required that the program withstand a three-part test to avoid invalidation under the establishment clause. The program would be invalid unless it: (1) had a secular purpose, (2) had no primary effect of advancing or inhibiting religion, and (3) avoided causing an "excessive entanglement" between government and religion.[15] The general tax exemption was found to have a secular purpose and provide only incidental aid to religion. The majority opinion also found that the taxation of church property would cause at least as much administrative entanglement between government and religious authorities as did the exemption. The Court was clearly persuaded by the long history of such exemptions: more than 200 years of a virtually uniform practice in the states without any further "establishment" effects.[16]

Other Forms of Aid to Religiously Affiliated Schools or Their Students. The Court invalidated two state attempts to subsidize the costs of parochial school education in *Lemon v. Kurtzman.*[17] Rhode

---

12. In Bob Jones University v. United States, 461 U.S. 574, 103 S.Ct. 2017, 76 L.Ed.2d 157 (1983), the Supreme Court upheld the authority of the Internal Revenue Service to deny tax exempt status to private schools which practice racial discrimination in their admission standards or educational policy on the basis of the religious doctrine of the school's administration. Because the Internal Revenue Service had chosen to follow earlier lower federal court rulings prohibiting such tax exempt status for racially discriminatory private schools, the Supreme Court was not required to determine whether a Congressional or administrative decision to grant such status to discriminatory organizations would violate the equal protection component of the fifth amendment due process clause. See §§ 16.4(c), 18.9(a)(2)(b), supra.

Regarding the Supreme Court's ruling that the denial of tax exempt status to such schools did not violate the free exercise clause of the first amendment, see §§ 21.4(c), 21.7, infra.

13. 397 U.S. 664, 90 S.Ct. 1409, 25 L.Ed.2d 697 (1970).

14. It should be noted that the opinion did not approve granting exemptions for church property where no similar exemption existed for other social service or nonprofit activities. Such a preferential exemption would almost certainly constitute a prohibited direct aid to certain religious entities.

15. 397 U.S. at 664, 90 S.Ct. at 1409.

16. 397 U.S. at 676–80, 90 S.Ct. at 1115–17.

17. 403 U.S. 602, 91 S.Ct. 2105, 29 L.Ed.2d 745 (1971), rehearing denied 404 U.S. 876, 92 S.Ct. 24, 30 L.Ed.2d 123 (1971), on remand 348 F.Supp. 300 (E.D.Pa.1972).

At this time the Court also decided Tilton v. Richardson, 403 U.S. 672, 91 S.Ct. 2091, 29 L.Ed.2d 790 (1971), rehearing denied 404 U.S. 874, 92 S.Ct. 25, 30 L.Ed.2d 120 (1971) involving aid to religious col-

Island provided a fifteen percent salary supplement to teachers of secular subjects in private schools where the per-pupil expenditure was below that of the public schools. In the second program, Pennsylvania authorized the reimbursement of nonpublic schools for a fraction of teacher salaries and instructional materials in secular subjects. Under both state systems, Catholic schools were the main beneficiaries of the programs.[18]

Once again, the Court accepted the legislators' position that they were pursuing the secular end of promoting the nonreligious education of young children. The Court did not come to an exact ruling on whether the programs had a primary effect of advancing religion.[19] However, the Court's discussion of the need for avoiding administrative entanglement indicated that such programs could have a prohibited effect. Because the majority assumed that religious elementary and secondary schools were likely to advance religion even in their secular subjects, it would seem that these subsidies would constitute direct aid to religion.

Instead of basing the ruling on the effect of these programs, the opinion in *Lemon* struck down these statutes because it found that they fostered an excessive entanglement between church and state. Chief Justice Burger, writing for the majority, held that, in assessing the degree of entanglement, three factors were to be considered: (1) the character and purpose of the institution benefited; (2) the nature of the aid; (3) the resulting relationship between government and religious authorities.[20]

In applying this three part test the majority opinion first found that Catholic elementary and secondary schools were an integral part of the religious program of that church. The religious atmosphere and control of this type of school showed that religious teaching might be advanced, even inadvertently, in secular courses. Second, the aid here was a subsidy for teacher salaries. The Court noted that, unlike textbooks, teachers could not be checked in advance to insure that they

---

leges. This subject is examined in § 21.4(b), infra.

For an interesting examination of the development of the *Lemon* test see Simson, The Establishment Clause in the Supreme Court: Rethinking the Court's Approach, 72 Cornell L.Rev. 905 (1987).

18. While the majority has noted this fact in several cases it is difficult to see its relevance. It might be used in an attempt to show a religious "purpose" but the Court has never looked into the motives of the legislature in such a manner. The religious effect of administrative entanglements might be quantitatively (but not qualitatively) greater if a large number of

parochial schools were aided. This would not relate to the number or names of the religions involved. The justices may feel that Catholic primary schools are uniquely permeated with religion, but that raises questions as to the basis for such a judicial ruling and why other parochial schools are treated in the same manner by the Court. Finally, the justices might feel that Catholic schools generate greater political division. One might question both the propriety and usefulness of such judicial assumptions.

19. 403 U.S. at 613–14, 91 S.Ct. at 2111–12.

20. 403 U.S. at 615, 91 S.Ct. at 2112.

would not teach religion. Though the teachers could in good faith promise to remain neutral, they might inadvertently advance religion in the classroom. Finally, the majority found that in order to insure that religious activities or teaching were not aided by the program, the state would have to place a great number of restrictions on the schools and engage in a monitoring program which would be little short of ongoing surveillance. Thus, the character of the school and the aid required complex ongoing relationships between secular and religious authorities. This three part analysis showed that the program would result in an excessive entanglement violative of the establishment clause.

The Chief Justice also stressed the fact that these types of programs were politically divisive. The provision of significant ongoing aid to parochial elementary and secondary schools injected an explosive political issue which caused division along religious lines. These programs virtually guarantee that there will be yearly public debate and political conflict between religious factions. The majority opinion stated that this division was to be eliminated by the establishment clause.[21] However, the opinion was not clear as to whether this was merely the reason for strict application of the purpose-effect-entanglement test, a branch of the entanglement test, or a fourth test. Thus, we can only say that where the majority views an aid program as causing an undue amount of political division along religious lines the program is likely to be invalidated.

Since the *Lemon* decision in 1970 the Supreme Court has reviewed a wide variety of government programs of aid to religiously affiliated schools, the students of those schools, or the parents of those students. The Court has used the purpose, primary effect, and excessive entanglement tests for reviewing the validity of those laws. The Court also has used the *Lemon* three part approach to assessing the excessive entanglement issue as it has in each case looked at the character of the institution benefited, the nature of the aid, and the resulting relationship between government and religious authorities. Because many of the Supreme Court cases involve the review of several types of aid to religious schools or students we will review those decisions chronologically rather than in terms of specific types of government aid programs. In most of these cases the Court invalidated the government attempt to aid parochial schools or students. Near the end of this section we will review the recent cases that have approved forms of aid to religious schools beyond the granting of basic student transportation, textbook programs, and tax-exempt status which we have examined previously in this section.[22]

---

21. 403 U.S. at 622, 91 S.Ct. at 2115–16.

22. In the years in which the Court ruled on these forms of aid to grade schools and high schools the Court also examined, and upheld in some cases, aid to religiously affiliated colleges. See, e.g., Hunt v.

The Court held invalid a law granting all private schools a payment for services mandated by state law in *Levitt v. Committee for Public Education*.[23] The lump sum per pupil payment was to cover the cost of keeping certain records, preparation of various reports to the state, and the testing of students on required subjects. The largest amount was for required tests, some of which were prepared by the private school teachers and some by the state. A majority of the justices easily concluded that these grants constituted a prohibited form of aid to religion. Given the nature of religious primary and secondary schools these unrestricted lump sum grants might go to advance the sectarian activities as well as the secular functions of these schools. The fact that these services were required by the state could not furnish a way to avoid the prohibition against subsidizing religious activities.

The Court examined the constitutionality of tuition reimbursement and tax credit programs in *Committee for Public Education v. Nyquist*[24] and *Sloan v. Lemon*.[25] In these cases New York and Pennsylvania had attempted to reimburse the parents of students attending nonpublic schools for a portion of the tuition which they paid to those schools. Once again, the greatest number of these schools were Catholic schools, and both programs were invalidated by the Court. The *Nyquist* case gave rise to the more significant opinion because New York had attempted to insure the secular effect of its program by making the payments and granting the tax credits directly to the parents, limiting the amounts to no more than one-half of the tuition paid, and excluding high income families.[26]

The Court invalidated both programs when it found that the programs had the effect of advancing religion. The state had to insure that these funds did not advance religion and the majority was unwilling to accept statistical guarantees that only the secular function could benefit from this aid.[27] In *Nyquist* and *Sloan*, the Court invalidated statutory grants, tax credits, and tax deductions that reimbursed only private school students for educational costs.

A statute which granted tax deductions to *all* students or parents based upon actual expenditures for attending public *or* private schools

McNair, 413 U.S. 734, 93 S.Ct. 2868, 37 L.Ed.2d 923 (1973). See § 21.4(b), infra.

23. 413 U.S. 472, 93 S.Ct. 2814, 37 L.Ed.2d 376 (1973).

24. 413 U.S. 756, 93 S.Ct. 2955, 37 L.Ed.2d 948 (1973).

25. 413 U.S. 825, 93 S.Ct. 2982, 37 L.Ed.2d 939 (1973), rehearing denied 414 U.S. 881, 94 S.Ct. 30, 38 L.Ed.2d 128 (1973).

26. The law provided for payments to parents with an annual taxable income of under $15,000 and tax credits to those with an adjusted gross income of under $25,000. In no event could the payment exceed the lesser of the statutory limits (set between $50 and $100) or 50 percent of the tuition actually paid. The law, complete with tax tables, is reprinted at 413 U.S. at 761–67, 93 S.Ct. at 2959–63.

27. 413 U.S. at 787–89, 93 S.Ct. at 2972–74.

would appear to have a religiously neutral purpose and effect. Such a statute might not require an excessive entanglement between government and religion in order to limit deductions to secular expenses. Therefore, the Court will uphold a statute granting a tax deduction for educational expenses that is truly neutral in its treatment of public and private school students and their expenses.[28]

In *Meek v. Pittenger*[29] the Court invalidated several new forms of aid to nonpublic schools. Following the rejection of its earlier program, Pennsylvania had adopted three new forms of aid for students at nonpublic schools: (1) a textbook-loan program similar to the one approved in *Allen;* (2) the loaning to nonpublic schools of instructional materials of a secular nature; (3) the provision of auxiliary guidance, testing, remedial and therapeutic services by public school employees who would provide services at the private schools. The Court upheld the textbook program but invalidated the other two forms of aid. The textbook program was upheld on the basis of the *Allen* decision. But, due to the view of parochial schools taken in later cases and the new entanglement test, some justices would even have reconsidered the validity of such programs.[30] However, it appears that *Allen* will not be reexamined and that these textbook programs will be upheld on the basis of *stare decisis.*

The loan of instructional materials, such as recording equipment, laboratory materials or maps was held invalid in *Meek* because such loans had the impermissible effect of aiding religion. Although the majority accepted the lower court characterization of these materials as so secular that they were "self-policing,"[31] the opinion found an impermissible degree of aid to religion in this program. The grant of materials to the schools aided their operation and made the entire religious enterprise a more viable institution. As the function of

28. The Supreme Court later upheld a state statute allowing taxpayers to deduct, when computing their income tax liability, the cost of "tuition, textbooks, and transportation" expenses incurred to send their children to either a public or private school. Because the deduction was available to all students or parents, not just those who attended private or religious schools, five justices found that the law had a nonreligious purpose and effect. Because only neutral, incidental aid was given to students attending religious schools, the majority ruled that the government involvement in audits of deductions to insure proper tax computations, and disallowance of deductions for textbooks used to teach religious doctrines, did not constitute an excessive entanglement between government and religion. Mueller v. Allen, 463 U.S. 388, 103 S.Ct. 3062, 77 L.Ed.2d 721 (1983).

The dissenters believed that there was no meaningful distinction between *Mueller* and *Nyquist.* 463 U.S. at 404–08, 103 S.Ct. at 3053–62 (Marshall, Brennan, Blackmun, & Stevens, JJ., dissenting).

29. 421 U.S. 349, 95 S.Ct. 1753, 44 L.Ed.2d 217 (1975), rehearing denied 422 U.S. 1049, 95 S.Ct. 2668, 45 L.Ed.2d 702 (1975).

30. 421 U.S. at 378–79, 95 S.Ct. at 1769–70 (Brennan, J., concurring in part, dissenting in part).

31. Meek v. Pittenger, 421 U.S. 349, 365, 95 S.Ct. 1753, 1763, 44 L.Ed.2d 217 (1975), rehearing denied 422 U.S. 1049, 95 S.Ct. 2668, 45 L.Ed.2d 702 (1975) quoting Meek v. Pittenger, 374 F.Supp. 639, 660 (E.D.Pa.1974).

parochial primary and secondary schools was inherently religious, this constituted impermissible aid to religion in the majority's view. This "aid-to-the-enterprise" theory is the culmination of the view of parochial schools taken in earlier cases and it eliminates most forms of aid which might help these schools.

The provision of auxiliary services also was invalidated in *Meek*. The state sought to avoid a religious effect by using its own employees to provide assistance in developing purely secular educational skills. In this way the state hoped to also avoid the necessity for a surveillance of the teachers and programs which might constitute an excessive entanglement. Justice Stewart, writing for the majority, found the use of state employees insufficient to guarantee a purely secular program. In the majority's view there remained the possibility that even a public school employee might advance religious ends in such a situation. Consequently, the Court held that it is impossible to avoid all possible religious effect, even in secular programs for remedial students, without supervision of the programs on a scale that would result in a prohibited form of entanglement. Once again the majority was of the view that the politically divisive nature of these programs required their invalidation under the establishment clause. However, it remains unclear whether this question of political divisiveness is a separate test, a part of the entanglement test, or merely the majority's policy reason for the strict application of other tests.

In *Meek* the majority did indicate that certain diagnostic health or speech services might be compatible with the establishment clause. Thus, if a state uses its own employees to go into public schools to make diagnosis of illness or educational disabilities and, perhaps, offer some basic treatment the program may withstand constitutional challenge. As to the diagnosis of speech or other education related skills, it was questionable whether state employees could do more than come into the nonpublic school to make a basic evaluation and diagnosis of students. Treatment which would constitute remedial educational training seemed difficult, if not impossible, to uphold after *Meek*. Thus it was not surprising that the Court later held that these remedial services could only be given to parochial students at a site away from the parochial school.[32]

In *Wolman v. Walter* [33] the Court examined a variety of school and student aid programs. In a complicated statutory program, Ohio attempted to aid private schools, which were primarily Catholic schools. This program consisted of six types of aid for all nonpublic elementary and secondary schools: (1) a textbook program like the ones approved in earlier Supreme Court cases; (2) the provision of funds to distribute and score standardized educational tests; (3) diagnostic services with

32. Wolman v. Walter, 433 U.S. 229, 97 S.Ct. 2593, 53 L.Ed.2d 714 (1977).

33. 433 U.S. 229, 97 S.Ct. 2593, 53 L.Ed.2d 714 (1977).

state personnel testing individual children for specified health and educational problems; (4) therapeutic services for health and educational disabilities provided by state personnel at sites outside of the parochial school; (5) loans to students of instructional materials and equipment; (6) funds for commercial transportation or the use of state school buses for field trips.

The rulings on these provisions were consistent with earlier cases, and basic tests remained the same, but the Court showed itself hopelessly fragmented in *Wolman*. The Court continued to have a majority that formally supports the three part test, though fewer justices may actually wish to employ the test in this school aid area. The *Wolman* opinion by Justice Blackmun was a majority opinion in part and a plurality opinion in part. The opinion applied the standard three part test in a straight forward manner and the results are best understood in the terms of this opinion.

The textbook program (# 1) in *Wolman* was upheld by a vote of six to three on the basis of *Allen*. The testing and test scoring provision (# 2), was upheld by a six to three vote, because, unlike *Levitt*, these were standard educational tests prepared by state employees and designed to insure that private school students are in fact being properly educated. The diagnostic services (# 3) were upheld by a vote of eight to one, because as there was an important secular goal in caring for children and no possible religious effect. The therapeutic services (# 4) were upheld by a vote of seven to two, because the removal of the services from the school eliminated the danger of religious permeation of the program. The instructional materials program (# 5) was held invalid, by a six to three vote, on precisely the same basis as was the similar program in *Meek*. The provision of transportation aid (# 6) was held invalid, by a five to four vote, on an aid to the religious enterprise concept quite similar to *Meek* rationale.

The reason for the differing votes in *Wolman* was that the justices were evenly split between three positions. Chief Justice Burger and Justices White and Rehnquist would allow the state to help the education of all children so long as there is no clear aid to religion. Justices Stewart, Blackmun and Powell believed that an independent application of the three part test will allow the state to promote secular education without impermissibly fostering religion. Justices Brennan, Marshall and Stevens are committed to the position that the first amendment was designed to prohibit any aid to religion, although only Justice Brennan could follow this position when voting on the diagnostic services.

Both before and after Justice Stewart retired from the Court, a majority of justices agreed on the basic three part test established in *Lemon* but the justices held a wide range of views regarding how the tests should be applied. Justice O'Connor, like Justice Stewart before her, would take a case-by-case approach as to the strictness with which she should apply the three part test to allow for the promotion of secular educational goals through aid to religious schools.[34] In two instances the Court, by a five to four vote of the justices, approved limited forms of reimbursement to religious schools for certain administrative expenses or the granting of tuition tax credits. In 1985, however, the justices invalidated a variety of government programs designed to aid the secular portion of a religious school student's education and, in so doing, indicated adherence to the strict approach taken in the *Meek* and *Wolman* rulings.[35] We will now examine the administrative expense and tuition tax credit cases before concluding with an analysis of the 1985 rulings and the continued restriction on student aid programs.

Reimbursement of Parochial Schools for Grading State Tests and Reporting Data to the State. In *Committee for Public Education and Religious Liberty v. Regan,*[36] the Supreme Court upheld, by a five to four vote, a state statute which reimbursed nonpublic schools for expenses incurred in administering and scoring standardized educational achievement tests; recording and reporting data concerning student

34. Regarding Justice O'Connor's independent review of school aid programs, see Grand Rapids School Dist. v. Ball, 473 U.S. 373, 399, 105 S.Ct. 3216, 3231, 87 L.Ed.2d 267 (1985) (O'Connor, J., concurring in the judgment in part and dissenting in part); Aguilar v. Felton, 473 U.S. 402, 421, 105 S.Ct. 3232, 3243, 87 L.Ed.2d 290 (1985) (O'Connor, J., dissenting, joined in part by Rehnquist, J.). See also, Estate of Thornton v. Caldor, Inc., 472 U.S. 703, 710, 105 S.Ct. 2914, 2918, 86 L.Ed.2d 557 (1985) (O'Connor, J., joined by Marshall, J., concurring in a case wherein the Court invalidated a state statute granting employees an absolute right to refuse to work for a private employer on the day they honored as their sabbath).

35. Prior to ruling on the cases described in the remainder of this section, the Court ruled in Wheeler v. Barrera, 417 U.S. 402, 94 S.Ct. 2274, 41 L.Ed.2d 159 (1974), judgment modified 422 U.S. 1004, 95 S.Ct. 2625, 45 L.Ed.2d 667 (1975), appeal after remand 531 F.2d 402 (8th Cir.1976) that Title I of the Federal Elementary and Secondary Education Act of 1965, as amended, 20 U.S.C.A. § 241A et seq. was not on its face unconstitutional because it made money available for services for private as well as public school students. Because no specific program was before the Court, the justices did not rule that these funds could be used to provide services to students on property owned by religious

schools. Later the Supreme Court would indicate that this ruling did not approve the provision of educational services to parochial school students on parochial school premises; the Court invalidated state use of federal money for such programs. See the discussion of Aguilar v. Felton, 473 U.S. 402, 105 S.Ct. 3232, 87 L.Ed.2d 290 (1985) later in this section.

The Supreme Court, in 1986, upheld a program of aid to blind students that involved state payments directly to such students which allowed them to engage in professional or vocational training. A visually handicapped student used the aid to attend a religiously affiliated college for the purpose of pursuing a religious vocation, but this fact did not establish that the program had either a religious purpose or an ultimate effect of aiding religion. Witters v. Washington Department of Services for the Blind, 474 U.S. 481, 106 S.Ct. 748, 88 L.Ed.2d 846 (1986), rehearing denied 475 U.S. 1091, 106 S.Ct. 1485, 89 L.Ed.2d 737 (1986). Although the justices were unanimous in upholding the statute, the majority opinion was written in a way that did not endorse a more lenient attitude towards the review of aid to religious schools or their students than the Court employed in the 1970s and 1980s.

36. 444 U.S. 646, 100 S.Ct. 840, 63 L.Ed.2d 94 (1980).

attendance; and compiling and reporting statistical information about the students, staff, and facilities of each institution.

Writing for the majority, Justice White found that the program had a secular purpose, that its principal or primary effect neither advanced nor inhibited religion, and that it did not foster an excessive government entanglement with religion. The promotion of quality nonreligious education of students in private schools was once again found sufficient to pass the first prong of the three part test.

The Court found that the program did not have a religious effect because, unlike the state law stricken in *Levitt v. Committee for Public Education*,[37] this program involved repayment for administrative costs connected to specific state-required functions and, therefore, had virtually no potential for aiding the propagation of religious beliefs. The Court already had approved the use of state standardized educational achievement tests in private schools in *Wolman v. Walter*. In *Committee for Public Education and Religious Liberty*, the Court held that direct cash reimbursement to nonpublic schools for administering and grading the examinations did not promote sectarian beliefs because the content of the tests was controlled by public authorities and the grading of the objective and essay questions did not provide any realistic opportunity to advance religious beliefs. The other administrative and record-keeping expenses reimbursed by the state involved the collection and reporting of attendance records and information concerning the personnel, facilities, and curriculum of each school. The majority found that state payment of such costs created no appreciable risk of aiding the religious function of the school even though the reimbursement might free other funds within the school's budget for unspecified purposes.

Finally, in *Committee for Public Education and Religious Liberty* the majority concluded that there was no excessive entanglement fostered by this program even though the program required the schools to maintain separate accounts for the reimbursable expenses and to submit the accounts for audits by public authorities. Since the services were "discrete and clearly identifiable" the Court held that the review process did not pose a danger to either government neutrality or religious freedom. In this case Justices Stewart and Powell, who had often voted to apply the three part test very strictly in order to invalidate state programs aiding religious schools, joined with Chief Justice Burger and Justices White and Rehnquist in voting to uphold the reimbursement program.[38]

37. 413 U.S. 472, 93 S.Ct. 2814, 37 L.Ed.2d 736 (1973).

38. Although Justice Stewart has retired, the Court's five to four ruling upholding the reimbursement program at issue in this case does not appear to be in jeopardy. Justice O'Connor, who replaced Justice Stewart, has taken a position similar to that of Justice Stewart and might be expected to vote, as he did, to uphold these programs. See the discussions of Mueller v. Allen, 463 U.S. 388, 103 S.Ct. 3062, 77

Tuition Tax Credits or Deductions. In *Mueller v. Allen*,[39] the Court, by five to four vote, upheld a state tax statute which allowed taxpayers to deduct from their state income tax the expenses incurred in providing "tuition, textbooks and transportation" for their children attending any public or private elementary or secondary school in the state. Justice Rehnquist, who wrote the majority opinion, found that the law was valid under the purpose-effect-entanglement test. The state's secular purpose was to improve the education of all young persons within the state. The majority could rely on earlier Supreme Court recognition that legislators have a nonreligious purpose in aiding the secular education of children regardless of where they attend school.

Justice Rehnquist differentiated this tuition and expense deduction from those which had been stricken down in earlier cases.[40] In the earlier cases states had given tax credits or deductions only to those parents who sent their children to nonpublic schools; this created a governmentally established preference for nonpublic and religious schools. In *Mueller,* Justice Rehnquist stressed that the legislature had attempted to equalize the tax burden of all of its citizens by allowing all parents, whether their children attended public or private schools, to deduct their children's educational expenses. This was religiously neutral help to the students which conferred only the most "attenuated financial benefit" on religious schools.[41] The fact that parents sending

L.Ed.2d 721 (1983), Grand Rapids School Dist. v. Ball, 473 U.S. 373, 105 S.Ct. 3216, 87 L.Ed.2d 267 (1985), and Aguilar v. Felton, 473 U.S. 402, 105 S.Ct. 3232, 87 L.Ed.2d 290 (1985) in the following paragraphs of this section.

39. 463 U.S. 388, 103 S.Ct. 3062, 77 L.Ed.2d 721 (1983). The basic portion of the Minnesota statute at issue was reprinted in footnote 1 of the Court's opinion: Minn.Stat. § 290.09(22) (1982) permits a taxpayer to deduct from his or her computation of gross income the following:

"*Tuition and transportation expense.* The amount he has paid to others, not to exceed $500 for each dependent in grades K to 6 and $700 for each dependent in grades 7 to 12, for tuition, textbooks and transportation of each dependent in attending an elementary or secondary school situated in Minnesota, North Dakota, South Dakota, Iowa, or Wisconsin, wherein a resident of this state may legally fulfill the state's compulsory attendance laws, which is not operated for profit, and which adheres to the provisions of the Civil Rights Act of 1964 and chapter 363. As used in this subdivision, "textbooks" shall mean and include books and other instructional materials and equipment used in elementary and secondary schools in teaching only those subjects legally and commonly taught in public elementary and secondary schools in this state and shall not include instructional books and materials used in the teaching of religious tenets, doctrines or worship, the purpose of which is to inculcate such tenets, doctrines or worship, nor shall it include such books or materials for, or transportation to, extracurricular activities including sporting events, musical or dramatic events, speech activities, driver's education, or programs of a similar nature."

40. See Committee for Public Education v. Nyquist, 413 U.S. 756, 93 S.Ct. 2955, 37 L.Ed.2d 948 (1973); Sloan v. Lemon, 413 U.S. 825, 93 S.Ct. 2982, 37 L.Ed.2d 939 (1973), rehearing denied 414 U.S. 881, 94 S.Ct. 30, 38 L.Ed.2d 128 (1973). See notes 24–28 supra and accompanying text.

41. In his *Mueller* majority opinion, Justice Rehnquist compared the aid in this case to the religiously neutral activity of government in providing a forum open to religious as well as nonreligious speech that was endorsed in Widmar v. Vincent,

their children to nonpublic schools might receive greater tax deductions because they had greater expenses would not constitute an impermissible form of aid to religion since those attending public schools received a direct subsidy. This provision was on its face a neutral attempt by the state to award financial and tax benefits to students and their parents. Similarly, the fact that most private school students in the state attended religiously affiliated schools would not affect the Court's analysis. A law which neutrally helped children would not be upheld or stricken solely upon the fact that in a given year persons who claimed the otherwise nonobjectionable benefit sent their children to a school affiliated with a particular religion.

Finally, these justices found no violation of the entanglement test even though the deduction could not be allowed for "instructional books and materials used in the teaching of religious tenets, doctrines or worship, the purpose of which is to inculcate such tenets, doctrines or worship." The majority found that this determination of the legitimacy of any individual's deduction required no more entanglement between government and religion than would a determination of whether textbooks given or loaned to parents or children attending nonpublic schools were truly secular in nature, a type of administrative entanglement that had been upheld in previous cases.[42] The justices were concerned here only with whether there was such administrative entanglement between the government and religion as to jeopardize the concept of neutrality and the principles that underlie the establishment clause rather than with a concern with whether such programs created political divisiveness.[43]

Secular Instruction or Services for Religious Schools Students—The 1985 Cases. In 1985 the Supreme Court ruled on two cases involving the provision of nonreligious instruction or services for religious school students by government employees on premises owned

454 U.S. 263, 102 S.Ct. 269, 70 L.Ed.2d 440 (1981). *Widmar* is noted in § 21.5(e), infra. See Mueller v. Allen, 463 U.S. 388, 397, 103 S.Ct. 3062, 3068–69, 77 L.Ed.2d 721, 730–31 (1983).

42. See Board of Education v. Allen, 392 U.S. 236, 88 S.Ct. 1923, 20 L.Ed.2d 1060 (1968); see notes 3–12 supra and accompanying text.

43. Although political divisiveness was not at issue in the *Mueller* case, the Court noted that the language of the Supreme Court regarding such a concern "must be regarded as confined to cases where direct financial subsidies are paid to parochial schools or to teachers in parochial schools." Mueller v. Allen, 463 U.S. 388, 403–03 n. 11, 103 S.Ct. 3062, 3071 n. 11, 77 L.Ed.2d 721, 733 n. 11 (1983).

The dissenting justices in *Mueller* would have invalidated the law because the tax benefit that flowed to students and parents made it possible for them to increase their financial support for and payments to the school. These justices believed that this type of aid to the general educational functions of such schools resulted in aid to the sectarian enterprise as a whole. The result of this aid to the enterprise theory was to view the provision of such aid as prohibited by earlier cases as "at odds with the fundamental principle that a State may provide no financial support whatsoever to promote religion." Mueller v. Allen, 463 U.S. 388, 417, 103 S.Ct. 3062, 3078, 77 L.Ed.2d 721, 742 (1983) (Marshall, J., joined by Brennan, Blackmun and Stevens, JJ., dissenting).

by a religious organization. The Court invalidated these programs but, in so doing, broke no new theoretical ground as the justices applied the purpose-effect-entanglement test in the same manner as they had in earlier student aid cases. The Court in the 1985 cases did not reverse any of the earlier decisions allowing limited aid to religious school students that were noted previously in this Chapter.

In *Grand Rapids School District v. Ball* [44] the Court invalidated two programs which it found to have a primary religious effect. The Grand Rapids City School District had adopted two programs to provide nonreligious classes for private school students that were taught by teachers who were hired by the school system and conducted in "leased" classrooms in the private schools, virtually all of which were sectarian schools. The classroom space for both programs was leased at a rate of six dollars per classroom per week; the regulations stated that these rooms were to be considered public school classrooms and had to be free of any religious symbols.

One of the Grand Rapids programs was titled a "community education program"; the second program was titled a "shared time program." The community education program offered classes for both adults and children at private elementary schools at the close of the regular school day. None of the classes offered were available at the regular day sessions of the private schools and were not considered part of their basic curriculum. Similar courses, however, were a regular part of the more extensive curriculum of the Grand Rapids public schools. The community education program teachers were private school teachers who were considered part time public school employees.

Under the shared time program, the Grand Rapids school board financed a program in which full time public employees went into the private schools and moved from classroom to classroom during the course of a school day teaching nonreligious courses. These courses supplemented the core curriculum courses required by the state of Michigan as a part of an accredited school's program. These subjects were labeled "remedial" and "enrichment" courses; they involved subjects such as art, mathematics, and reading. Approximately ten percent of each private school student's time, according to the findings of the lower court, was spent in the shared time program.

Justice Brennan wrote the majority opinion in *Grand Rapids School District* and held that the community education program and the shared time program were both invalid because each had a primary effect of advancing religion. Justice Brennan's majority opinion stated that the establishment clause would absolutely prohibit government financed or government sponsored indoctrination into the beliefs of a particular religious faith. Both programs involved a significant risk of

44. 473 U.S. 373, 105 S.Ct. 3216, 87 L.Ed.2d 267 (1985).

state sponsored indoctrination of religious beliefs. In arriving at this conclusion Justice Brennan employed the approach adopted in *Lemon v. Kurtzman* [45] and previously used in *Wolman v. Walter* [46] to invalidate the use of state paid professional staff to provide remedial and accelerated instruction to nonpublic school students on religious school premises.

The community education program was easily invalidated in *Grand Rapids School District,* as seven justices found that the attempt to use religious school teachers to teach secular subjects on religious school premises had a significant potential for inadvertent, as well as conscious, communication of religious beliefs and attitudes during the secular course.[47]

The shared time program, which involved government employees teaching nonreligious subjects in the religious schools, was invalidated by a five to four vote of the justices in *Grand Rapids School District.*[48] A majority of the justices found that religiously affiliated grade schools and high schools are pervasively sectarian and that any government aid to the educational function of such schools might advance religion.

As to both of the programs in *Grand Rapids School District,* Justice Brennan found an impermissible advancement of religion in three ways. First, the teachers participating in the programs might intentionally or inadvertently advance particular religious tenets or beliefs. Second, the programs provided a crucial symbolic link between government and religion, thereby enlisting—at least in the eyes of impressionable youngsters—the power of government to support the religious denomination operating the school. Third, the programs could have the effect of directly promoting religion by impermissibly providing a subsidy to the primary religious mission of the institutions affected. The shared time program, as well as the community education program, involved aid to the basic educational function of religious schools and thereby freed religious school resources for other purposes, including the teaching of religion classes.

45. 403 U.S. 602, 91 S.Ct. 2105, 29 L.Ed.2d 745 (1971), rehearing denied 404 U.S. 876, 92 S.Ct. 24, 30 L.Ed.2d 123 (1971). See note 17 supra.

46. 433 U.S. 229, 97 S.Ct. 2593, 53 L.Ed.2d 714 (1977). See note 33 supra.

47. In Grand Rapids School District v. Ball, 473 U.S. 373, 105 S.Ct. 3216, 87 L.Ed.2d 267 (1985), Justice Brennan's majority opinion, which invalidated both the community education program and shared time program was joined by Justices Blackmun, Marshall, Powell, and Stevens. Chief Justice Burger and Justice O'Connor concurred in the judgment in *Grand Rapids School District* insofar as the Court invalidated the community education program; they dissented from the invalidation of the shared time program. 473 U.S. at 399, 105 S.Ct. at 3231 (Burger, C.J., concurring in the judgment in part and dissenting in part); id. (O'Connor, J., concurring in the judgment in part and dissenting in part). Justices White and Rehnquist dissented; they would have upheld both programs.

48. See note 47 regarding the division of the justices in this case.

In *Aguilar v. Felton*,[49] the Court, by a five to four vote of the justices, invalidated a program under which New York City used federal funds it received under Title I of the Elementary and Secondary Education Act to pay the salaries of public school district employees who provided nonreligious instruction and services at private schools, including religiously affiliated schools. Justice Brennan again wrote the majority opinion; he found that the New York program violated the excessive entanglement test. The federal law provided funds for local school districts to provide services for both public and private school students. The Supreme Court in *Aguilar* did not invalidate the federal law but prohibited the use of funds for programs wherein the services or courses were provided for students on the grounds of a religiously affiliated school. The majority opinion in *Aguilar* did not overturn the ruling of *Wolman v. Walter*[50] that allowed state-supported testing for health or learning problems on parochial school premises and remedial education and health services for religious school students if those services were offered away from religious school premises.

The New York program at issue in *Aguilar* involved public employees providing courses or programs for remedial reading skills, remedial mathematics, English as a second language, and a variety of guidance services. All the services were provided by public school teachers, counselors, psychologists, psychiatrists or social workers as the particular service or program required. Unlike the programs that the Court had invalidated in *Grand Rapids School District,* the New York program appeared to involve administrative regulations designed to insure that the services offered by the public school teachers at the parochial schools could not involve religious content or the advancement of religious beliefs. The majority opinion in *Aguilar* dispensed with primary effect analysis and invalidated the program because it created an excessive entanglement between church and state. Justice Brennan's majority opinion approached the analysis of the excessive entanglement issue as the Court had in the cases in the 1970s. The majority opinion found that the schools were pervasively sectarian and that the type of aid involved a significant potential for the advancement of religion. Justice Brennan also found that pervasive monitoring would be required to avoid a primary religious effect. The degree of administrative involvement between government and religion required to avoid the advancement of religion as an effect of the program created an excessive entanglement between governmental and religious authorities. That type of entanglement potentially could lead to the exercise of improper governmental authority over a religious organization and an improper influence in government decisionmaking by members of the denomination which the government was regulating. The majority opinion in *Aguilar* also noted, though it did not emphasize this point,

49. 473 U.S. 402, 105 S.Ct. 3232, 87   50. 433 U.S. 229, 97 S.Ct. 2593, 53
L.Ed.2d 290 (1985).   L.Ed.2d 714 (1977).

that the danger of political divisiveness along religious lines increases as the degree of involvement between government decisionmakers and religious authorities increases.

Educational Aid Payments to Handicapped Students. *Witters v. Washington Department of Services for the Blind* [51] unanimously upheld a state program providing physically handicapped students with "vocational rehabilitation assistance" payments which allowed those students to obtain "special education and/or training in the professions, businesses or trades." The state courts had ruled that payment of aid to a blind student attending a Christian college and preparing himself for a career as a religious pastor, missionary, or youth director violated the first amendment establishment clause. Justice Marshall's majority opinion ruled that the aid program, including payment to the blind student engaged in religious studies at a religiously affiliated school, had both a sufficient nonreligious purpose and nonreligious primary effect to withstand scrutiny under the Court's prior decisions.[52] The state courts had not sufficiently analyzed the question of whether there was improper administrative entanglement between government administrators and religious schools under this program. The Supreme Court, for this reason, did not rule on that issue.

None of the justices in *Witters* found that the state had any purpose to endorse religion. Even those persons who attacked the law admitted that it had a nonreligious purpose. The aid program did not have an impermissible primary religious effect because it was a payment made directly to visually handicapped students to provide them with sufficient financial resources for vocational training. Justice Marshall reasoned that a student's decision to use the money at a

---

51. 474 U.S. 481, 106 S.Ct. 748, 88 L.Ed.2d 846 (1986), rehearing denied 475 U.S. 1091, 106 S.Ct. 1485, 89 L.Ed.2d 737 (1986).

52. The *Witters* decision involved a curious alignment of the justices, which might indicate that the case would have a more sweeping impact than the majority opinion indicates. Although Justice Marshall wrote for a majority of the Court, five justices wrote separate opinions. Justice White joined the majority opinion but wrote separately to indicate that he remained in disagreement with the Court's earlier, strict restrictions on aid to religious schools. 474 U.S. at 490, 106 S.Ct. at 753 (White, J., concurring).

Justice O'Connor concurred in the judgment in *Witters* and wrote an opinion concurring in part to indicate her belief that the law should be upheld because it could not be reasonably construed by anyone to constitute an endorsement of religious beliefs or practices. She continues to hold the belief set forth in her concurring opinion in Lynch v. Donnelly, 465 U.S. 668, 690, 104 S.Ct. 1355, 1366, 79 L.Ed.2d 604 (1984) (O'Connor, J., concurring), rehearing denied 466 U.S. 994, 104 S.Ct. 2376, 80 L.Ed.2d 848 (1984) that the primary test under the establishment clause is whether a government program constitutes endorsement of religion. Witters v. Washington Department of Services for the Blind, 474 U.S. 481, 493, 106 S.Ct. 748, 755, 88 L.Ed.2d 846 (1986) (O'Connor, J., concurring), rehearing denied 475 U.S. 1091, 106 S.Ct. 1485, 89 L.Ed.2d 737 (1986).

Justice Powell, joined by Chief Justice Burger and Justice Rehnquist wrote a concurring opinion in *Witters* indicating that the law should be upheld on the basis of the Court's decision regarding the permissibility of tax credits or deductions for students and parents.

religious school or for religious vocational studies was "only as a result of the genuinely independent and private choices of the aid recipient." In this sense, the aid did not differ from generalized aid to segments of society or payments to government employees. Persons who receive any type of monetary payment from the government could always make an independent decision to donate some of their money to a religious organization or to attend a religious school. Interestingly, the majority opinion stated that "nothing in the record indicates that, if petitioner [the blind student and the state] succeeds, any significant portion of the aid expended under the Washington program as a whole will end up flowing to religious education." It is difficult to understand the significance of this statement, since Justice Marshall did not state that the program would become invalid if a higher percent of students receiving the aid attended religious schools.

Justice Powell, joined by Chief Justice Burger and Justice Rehnquist concurred in the opinion and judgment. He wrote separately to state his belief that the amount of aid which might eventually flow to religious schools and the number of handicapped students who use their aid for religious vocational education was not relevant to the result in this case.[53] Justice Powell believed that the case should be upheld on the basis of *Mueller v. Allen.*[54] In *Mueller,* the Court upheld a system of tax credits and deductions to all parents or students for educational expenses regardless of whether the expenses were incurred while attending public, private, or religiously affiliated schools. It would be difficult to find a principled basis for invalidating an otherwise valid program of aid to handicapped persons merely because a large segment of those persons chose to use their increased economic resources to engage in religious activities or attend religious schools.[55]

Conclusion. The justices have, since the early 1970's, used a three-part test to determine whether a government program that aids religiously affiliated schools or their students violates the establishment clause. In order to be valid, a governmental program must have a secular purpose, its primary effect must be one that neither advances nor inhibits religion, and the program must not create an excessive entanglement between government and religion. When assessing the degree of entanglement, the Court is likely to consider the character and purposes of the institution benefited, the nature of the aid given, and the resulting relationship between government and religious authorities. The politically divisive nature of the program may be con-

---

53. 474 U.S. at 490–92, 106 S.Ct. at 753–55 (Powell, J., joined by Burger, C.J., and Rehnquist, J., concurring).

54. 463 U.S. 388, 103 S.Ct. 3062, 77 L.Ed.2d 721 (1983).

55. The alignment of the justices would indicate that there were five justices in this case (Chief Justice Burger, and Justices O'Connor, Powell, Rehnquist, and White) who would have no difficulty in upholding the program even though a large number of students made an independent decision to use their aid at religiously affiliated schools.

sidered by some justices in determining how strictly to apply these tests but political divisiveness has never been a clearly identifiable test for a program's validity.

Despite the concurrence of a majority of the justices on these standards, results in the cases have varied with the views of justices concerning the purpose of the establishment clause. Those justices who believe that the establishment clause was intended to avoid any element of political divisiveness across religious lines and to avoid any aid to pervasively sectarian enterprises will apply these tests in such a manner as to invalidate almost any form of aid to religious schools or their students. Those justices who believe that the purposes of the religion clauses were to protect government neutrality in religious matters and to allow persons to be free to choose educational benefits for themselves or their children without a governmental preference for nonreligious education will apply these tests in a manner that will allow aid to students of religiously affiliated schools, to their parents, or to the schools whenever those justices believe that the aid does not directly promote sectarian activity.

There is no basis apart from one's view of the history and functions of the religion clauses for determining which of these justices are correct in their approach to establishment clause cases but it appears at this time that those justices who would focus on neutrality and allow a wider range of government aid to students in religiously affiliated schools constitute a majority of the Supreme Court. Because of the close division of the justices in the cases throughout the 1970's and 1980's, however, one cannot predict with any certainty how the Court will rule on precise forms of aid to students in religiously affiliated schools that may be challenged in the years ahead.

(b) Aid to Colleges and Universities

Although aid to nonpublic institutions of higher education has been the subject of only a few Supreme Court decisions, it is clear that government programs aiding these schools must be tested under the same tests that have been employed in the primary school cases. The aid must have a secular purpose, its primary effect cannot advance or inhibit religion, and it must avoid creating an excessive entanglement between government and religion.

In determining whether excessive entanglement exists, three factors are examined: (1) the character of the institutions benefited; (2) the nature of the aid provided; (3) the resulting relationship between government and church authorities. Additionally, the program must not be of a type which will cause political division along religious lines. Once again, the Court will accept the legislative purpose of the aid programs as secular in nature. The announced intention of the legislature to assist the secular portion of all students' education has never been challenged by the Court in any school aid case.

These programs also have been held not to have a primary effect of aiding religion where there was at least some formal guarantee by the college authorities that the funds would not be used for religious instruction or other sectarian activities. The Court has refused to assume that religious colleges are so permeated with religion that their secular functions cannot be separated from their religious mission. Thus, a program which is tied to only secular instruction will not have an effect of advancing religion.

However, if the institution to be aided is sectarian to the extent that the advancing of religious beliefs permeated its entire program then this analysis could not apply. Such an institution would be similar to the parochial elementary and secondary schools which the majority of justices have deemed to have a primary function of propagating religious doctrine. In such a situation the secular teaching function could not be sufficiently separated from the religious mission of the school. Thus, any significant aid to the school would have the prohibited effect of advancing religion.

It is unclear whether granting aid to a pervasively sectarian institution is per se unconstitutional. The amount of government regulation that would be necessary to ensure that the aid given to a pervasively sectarian institution was used in a nonreligious manner would certainly give rise to an excessive entanglement between government and religion. However, it is arguable that there might be circumstances under which a pervasively sectarian institution could show that it could administer government funds for a nonreligious program in a manner that did not have the effect of aiding religion and that did not require an excessive entanglement between religion and government.[56]

There is a two part test to determine whether a specific aid program for religiously affiliated colleges and universities has a "primary effect" of advancing religion. To avoid such an effect: (1) the

56. This problem was examined in Bowen v. Kendrick, 487 U.S. 589, 108 S.Ct. 2562, 101 L.Ed.2d 520 (1988). In *Kendrick* the Supreme Court found that the Adolescent Family Life Act [AFLA], which provided aid to public and nonpublic private organizations for services related to the care of pregnant adolescents and the prevention of adolescent sexual relationships, did not violate the establishment clause on its face due to the involvement of religious organizations in the program. The Supreme Court found that the AFLA: (1) was not enacted by Congress for a religious purpose, (2) did not, on its face, have a primary effect of aiding or inhibiting religion, and (3) did not inherently give rise to an excessive entanglement between government and religion. The majority opinion in *Kendrick*, written by Chief Justice Rehnquist, left open the possibility that specific grants under the AFLA might be invalid because they went to pervasively sectarian organizations or were used by religious organizations to teach religious doctrine to young people with whom it dealt in the programs that were funded by the act. The majority opinion was not completely clear as to whether giving aid to a pervasively sectarian institution was a per se violation of the establishment clause. Compare the majority opinion in Bowen v. Kendrick, 487 U.S. 589, 108 S.Ct. 2562, 101 L.Ed.2d 520 (1988) with id. at 623–25, 108 S.Ct. at 2582 (Kennedy, J., joined by Scalia, J., concurring).

institution's secular function must not be permeated with a religious atmosphere, and (2) there must be assurances by the college and the government authority that the aid will not be used for religious teaching or other religious activities.

It is relatively easy for these programs aiding higher education to pass the three factor test for determining the presence of excessive entanglement. First, since the institutions are not "permeated" with religion, there is little need for extensive controls to insure against advancing religion.

Second, the aid is usually granted for a specific secular purpose. If so, it is likely to be only a one-time grant which is easily monitored. However, the Court has also upheld annual general grants to colleges where the college and government authorities would give assurances of their use for secular purposes.

Third, the administrative contacts between government and religious authorities can easily be kept to a minimum in such programs. Because the nature of the institution and aid do not have a high potential for advancing religion, the state need not engage in a program of constant surveillance. As long as the Court is of the impression that the program invokes little more contact between the religious authorities and the state than the normal accreditation procedures, no excessive administrative entanglement will be found.

Finally, these programs have not been found to be politically divisive by the Court. The one-time grants for specific purposes rarely stir emotion concerning government subsidies to religion. Even annual grant programs are not the subject of debate along religious lines. The largely secular atmosphere of these institutions, and the public evaluation of higher education, helps to keep debate on such subjects focused on educational and fiscal policy rather than religion. Additionally, the high percentage of nonsectarian private colleges prevents these programs from becoming religious issues.

Government aid to religiously affiliated institutions of higher education has been the subject of several Supreme Court decisions. In *Tilton v. Richardson* [57] the Court, by a five to four vote, upheld the federal Higher Education Facilities Act. Under this act federal grants were made for the construction of college facilities for other than religious activities or religious instruction.

In accordance with the analysis outlined above, the program was found to be permissible under the purpose-effect-entanglement test.

---

57. 403 U.S. 672, 91 S.Ct. 2091, 29 L.Ed.2d 790 (1971), rehearing denied 404 U.S. 874, 92 S.Ct. 25, 30 L.Ed.2d 120 (1971). Justice White, who does not believe that the excessive entanglement test is required to protect establishment clause values, also voted to uphold the program. Thus the 5 to 4 ruling does not constitute a true application of the three-part test. For a similar voting alignment of the justices in another case see notes 48, 50 to this section, infra.

First, the purpose of the program was to aid secular education. Second, the court found that aid to these religious colleges did not have a primary religious effect. Their dedication to secular educational goals, the policy of academic freedom and the nature of higher education were such that these colleges were not found to be permeated with religion; the program did not have the effect of advancing religion so long as the government was given assurances that the buildings were not to be used for a sectarian purpose. Third, no excessive entanglement was created by these programs. This conclusion followed from three factors: (1) the institution was not permeated with religion, (2) the aid was a one-time grant for specific building, and (3) the resulting contact between church and state could be kept to a minimum. Finally, the majority found that this program was not likely to result in political division.

One section of the federal law was held invalid in *Tilton*. Under the act the government gave up any ability to demand a return of funds after twenty years even if the buildings then were used for religious purposes. A majority of the justices concluded that the limitation of the government's enforcement powers after twenty years would be the equivalent of an unrestricted gift to the college after that time. Since this delayed grant could have the effect of advancing religion, the Court held that both the assurance of secular use and the government power to demand return of money used for religious purposes must continue so long as the facility was of any value.[58]

In *Hunt v. McNair*[59] the Court upheld a state program of issuing revenue bonds for the benefit of private colleges, including religiously affiliated schools. An "Educational Facilities Authority" issued bonds to finance construction of facilities which did not involve sectarian uses and the schools repaid these bonds from their own revenues. Although the state incurred no financial obligation under the program, the state authority issued the bonds, financed the construction with the bond revenues and leased the facilities to the institution. The use of the state bonding system allowed these schools to sell bonds at a reduced interest rate; this saved the schools significant interest payments. The Authority also was authorized to establish regulations and conduct inspections to insure secular use of the buildings which were conveyed to it.

This program easily withstood review under the three part purpose-effect-entanglement test. The Court found no impermissible effect in this case. There would be a primary effect of advancing religion if either (1) the institution was so religious in character that its function was subsumed in the religious mission, or (2) the funded activity was religious in nature. Under this program the institutions aided were

58. 403 U.S. at 682–84, 91 S.Ct. at 2097–99.

59. 413 U.S. 734, 93 S.Ct. 2868, 37 L.Ed.2d 923 (1973).

not subsumed in their religious mission and only secular facilities were financed by the bonds. The Court also found the act permissible under the excessive entanglement test. The three factor entanglement analysis required this result: (1) the institution was not permeated with religion, (2) the aid was not of a general character, and (3) the state authority would not be involved in detailed relationship with the college. While it was possible that the state authority might be involved in such a relationship if it had to help a program which was becoming financially insolvent, no such case was before the Court.[60]

In *Roemer v. Board of Public Works,* [61] the justices approved an annual grant program which benefited religious colleges. Maryland established a program of annual grants which provided for each full time student (excluding those enrolled in seminary or theological programs) a grant of 15% of the per-pupil amount that the state spent in the public college system. Originally this program was subject to virtually no restrictions on the use of the grant money. However, Maryland had amended the act to provide that the Maryland Council of Higher Education screen the institution application to insure that the institution was not pervasively religious and that the institution had given adequate assurance that the funds would be used for a secular purpose. The Court, by a five to four vote, upheld this amended program.[62]

Justice Blackmun, in *Roemer,* wrote an opinion (joined by Chief Justice Burger and Justice Powell) which found that the amended program passed the three part purpose-effect-entanglement test. Justices White and Rehnquist agreed that the program had a secular purpose and effect, but they did not apply an entanglement test because they believed that no such test is mandated by the establishment clause.[63] The plurality opinion of Justice Blackmun accepted the purpose of the act as secular. He found that it did not have a primary effect of aiding religion because it neither aided an institution subsumed in religion nor in a specific religious activity. As these institutions were not "pervasively sectarian," the requirement of assurance of secular use and review by the Council on Higher Education was sufficient guarantee to avoid an effect of advancing religion.

The Blackmun plurality found that using the three factor assessment did not result in a finding of excessive entanglement. First, the

---

60. For this reason the majority specifically refused to consider the degree to which the state could become involved in such a situation. 413 U.S. at 748–49, 93 S.Ct. at 2876–77.

61. 426 U.S. 736, 96 S.Ct. 2337, 49 L.Ed.2d 179 (1976) (plurality opinion by Blackmun, J.).

62. The invalidity of the first program was in effect conceded by the state and the Court did not consider it. The status of the payments under programs which are later held invalid is considered in the next section of this chapter.

63. Roemer v. Board of Public Works, 426 U.S. 736, 767, 96 S.Ct. 2337, 2354–55, 49 L.Ed.2d 179 (1976) (White, J., concurring).

character of the institution was not pervasively sectarian so as to require constant surveillance of the aid. Second, the nature of a specific program was not before the Court and so the justices could only consider the character of an annual grant program in the last part of the test. Third, the resulting relationship was not materially distinguishable from earlier cases. While the aid consisted of annual grants, the justices were of the opinion that this would not involve significantly greater contact between the state and the colleges than did normal accreditation procedures.

Finally, Justice Blackmun noted what may be the key factor that has caused the Court to uphold these programs—the absence of political division resulting from the enactment of such aid programs. Debate on aid to institutions of higher education, Justice Blackmun found, does not involve lobbying by churches and intense divisions among religious sects. Instead, those programs tend to be evaluated on their educational and fiscal merits. A majority of the justices have not been disposed to overturn such programs without a very clear showing of an impermissible purpose, effect or excessive administrative entanglement.[64]

(c) Other Issues in Aid to Religious Institutions

(1) Payments Under Programs Later Held Invalid. Even though a program of aid to religious schools has been held invalid under the establishment clause, payments may have been made to schools under the law prior to its invalidation. The question then arises as to whether the recipient institutions should be ordered to return the funds. This is precisely the situation that was present in *Lemon v. Kurtzman (Lemon II).*[65] Prior to the Supreme Court's decision in *Lemon I*[66] Pennsylvania had made substantial payments to parochial schools under the challenged act. The Court held that two factors were relevant in determining whether to grant a retroactive remedy: (1) the reasonableness and degree of reliance by the institution on the payments, and (2) the necessity of refunds to protect the constitutional right involved.

In *Lemon II* the Court found that reimbursement was not required because reliance had been reasonable. Additionally, the return of

---

64. During the 1977–1978 Term, the Supreme Court summarily affirmed two cases that upheld state programs which provided scholarships, tuition assistance, and financial aid to college students, including some students attending religiously affiliated schools. Smith v. Board of Governors, 434 U.S. 803, 98 S.Ct. 39, 54 L.Ed.2d 65 (1977), affirming 429 F.Supp. 871 (W.D.N.C.1977) (three-judge court); Americans United for Separation of Church and State v. Blanton, 434 U.S. 803, 98 S.Ct. 39, 54 L.Ed.2d 65 (1977) (three-judge court), affirming 433 F.Supp. 97 (M.D.Tenn.1977). Justices Brennan, Marshall, and Stevens voted to review each case.

65. 411 U.S. 192, 93 S.Ct. 1463, 36 L.Ed.2d 151 (1973).

66. Lemon v. Kurtzman, 403 U.S. 602, 91 S.Ct. 2105, 29 L.Ed.2d 745 (1971). In this case the Court invalidated a Pennsylvania program involving payments to religious primary schools. The case is discussed in § 21.4(a), supra.

funds would not be necessary to guard against impermissibly aiding religion as the money had been spent on secular purposes under the supervision of secular authorities.[67]

In *New York v. Cathedral Academy,* [68] the Court invalidated a state statute that would have granted reimbursement to private schools for state mandated record keeping and testing services under a program that previously had been held to violate the first and fourteenth amendments. A federal district court had found the original state act regarding payments for record keeping and testing to be unconstitutional; this had been upheld by the Supreme Court.[69] The district court had enjoined the distribution of funds for this program including distribution of funds for the last half of the 1971–72 school year. In June 1972, the state legislature attempted to limit the impact of the district court injunction by passing a new state statute granting reimbursement for expenses incurred prior to July, 1972, by schools that had attempted to follow the previous record keeping and testing requirements.

In *Cathedral Academy,* the Supreme Court held that this reimbursement act was invalid, and distinguished it from the situation in *Lemon II.* In *Lemon I* the state program violated the first amendment because it created an excessive entanglement between government and religion. The lower court's refusal to grant retroactive injunctive relief in that case was justified because allowing payments for the prior period did not do any further damage to constitutional values; those payments involved no further entanglement between government and religion, and the payments did not serve a religious purpose. In *Cathedral Academy,* the district court had enjoined all payments in the original action; the Supreme Court indicated that it could not allow state legislators to modify the impact of such injunctions.

However, the opinion recognized that the primary issue was whether the new act itself violated the religion clauses of the first amendment, as applied to the states by the fourteenth amendment. The Court found that the reimbursement statute failed the three part establishment test on two bases: (1) the reimbursement payments would have a religious effect because the grant program itself had been

---

67. This reasoning was reaffirmed in Roemer v. Board of Public Works, 426 U.S. 736, 745 n. 11, 767 n. 23, 96 S.Ct. 2337, 2344 n. 11, 2354 n. 23, 49 L.Ed.2d 179 (1976) (plurality opinion by Blackmun, J.). Here the Court did not have to consider the constitutionality of payments made under a superceded statute which was admittedly unconstitutional. However, the opinion indicated that the earlier payments to religious colleges under the invalid program need not be returned to the state as the state's actions were reasonable. It was also noted that the separation of church and state would not be promoted by making the state a judgment creditor of these religious institutions.

68. 434 U.S. 125, 98 S.Ct. 340, 54 L.Ed.2d 346 (1977), on remand 43 N.Y.2d 940, 403 N.Y.S.2d 895, 374 N.E.2d 1246 (1978).

69. Levitt v. Committee for Public Education, 413 U.S. 472, 93 S.Ct. 2814, 37 L.Ed.2d 736 (1973).

a prohibited form of aid to religion; (2) the procedures required by the Act to insure the secular nature of the reimbursement payments would involve an excessive entanglement between state and religious authorities. Thus, there could be no reimbursement payments under the statute even though some religious schools might have relied on the original statute, prior to the first federal court action, when they incurred these expenses. The differences in the original trial court actions in *Lemon I* and *Levitt*,[70] as well as the nature of the aid programs, resulted in the different holdings in *Lemon II* and in *Cathedral Academy*.

(2) **Aid to Schools That Discriminate on the Basis of Race.** Although a program of state aid to a private school may not violate the establishment clause, it cannot aid a school that discriminates on the basis of race. In *Norwood v. Harrison*[71] the Supreme Court held that textbooks could not be loaned to students of a school which discriminated on the basis of race. Such a textbook program may aid religious schools as they represent a value in the free exercise of religion which offsets any slight aid to religion. However, there is no countervailing constitutional value which could justify state aid to a racially discriminatory system. Thus, the aid to these students would violate the equal protection clause of the fourteenth amendment.

A related issue is the question of whether Congress can prohibit a private school from discriminating on the basis of race because it is affiliated with a religion which requires segregation as a tenet of the religious belief.[72] It may well be that the free exercise clause requires

70. Levitt v. Committee for Public Ed. and Religious Liberty, 413 U.S. 472, 93 S.Ct. 2814, 37 L.Ed.2d 736 (1973).

71. 413 U.S. 455, 93 S.Ct. 2804, 37 L.Ed.2d 723 (1973), on remand 382 F.Supp. 921 (N.D.Miss.1974).

72. In Runyon v. McCrary, 427 U.S. 160, 96 S.Ct. 2586, 49 L.Ed.2d 415 (1976), appeal after remand 569 F.2d 1294 (4th Cir.1978), cert. denied 439 U.S. 927, 99 S.Ct. 311, 58 L.Ed.2d 320 (1978), the Supreme Court ruled that federal statute 42 U.S.C.A. § 1981 prohibited racial discrimination in private schools but explicitly reserved the question of whether the statute did or could apply to prohibit racial discrimination by religiously affiliated schools where the discrimination was required by religious doctrine. 427 U.S. at 167 n. 6, 96 S.Ct. at 2953 n. 6. See generally § 18.9(a)(2)(b), supra. The Supreme Court declined to review a decision that might have resolved the issue of whether a religious school could exclude racial minorities. Brown v. Dade Christian Schools, Inc., 556 F.2d 310 (5th Cir.1977) (en banc),

certiorari denied 434 U.S. 1063, 98 S.Ct. 1235, 55 L.Ed.2d 763 (1978). The lower court in *Brown* had found that the school in question was secular and that the school could not base a claim on the religious principles of some of its students. For this reason, the application of 42 U.S.C.A. § 1981 to this school presented no significant free exercise clause problem.

In Bob Jones University v. United States, 461 U.S. 574, 103 S.Ct. 2017, 76 L.Ed.2d 157 (1983), the Supreme Court ruled that a denial of tax exempt status to religiously affiliated racially discriminatory schools violated neither the establishment clause nor the free exercise clause of the first amendment. However, in that case the Internal Revenue Service had chosen to follow lower court opinions finding that the granting of tax exempt status to such schools would be a violation of the equal protection component of the fifth amendment. For that reason the Supreme Court did not have to address the question of whether the granting of tax exempt status to racially discriminatory schools or

only that such religious-segregated schools be accommodated in that their existence is not made illegal. Indeed, it is not clear whether the mere existence of such schools is prohibited by the thirteenth amendment or legislation passed pursuant to it.[73] The Civil War Amendments might be found to establish racial equality as a preeminent goal which overrides the interests of religiously affiliated schools.

At a minimum, the thirteenth and fourteenth amendments represent values that should prevent the government from actively aiding these schools. Because those schools represent values opposed to constitutional rights of racial minorities, only accommodation of their existence and the provision of such general governmental services as police and fire protection might be required.

In *Bob Jones University v. United States,*[74] the Court upheld the authority of the Internal Revenue Service to deny tax exempt status to private schools which practice racially discriminatory admissions standards on the basis of their religious doctrine. The Court noted that the denial "of tax benefits will inevitably have a substantial impact on the operation of private religious schools, but will not prevent those schools from observing their religious tenets." Moreover, "the Government has a fundamental, overriding interest in eradicating racial discrimination in education" and this interest "substantially outweighs whatever burden denial of tax benefits places on petitioners' exercise of their religious beliefs."

The Court found that the compelling governmental interest in avoiding aid to racially discriminatory schools could not be equally served by "less restrictive means," through an accommodation of an exemption for schools that practice such discrimination on the basis of religious doctrines, thus there was no free exercise clause violation.[75]

organizations, whether or not religiously affiliated, would violate the equal protection component of the fifth amendment or the equal protection clause of the fourteenth amendment, if such tax exempt status were granted by a state or local government.

73. The Supreme Court has held that legislation passed pursuant to the thirteenth amendment prohibits the racial discrimination by private schools. Runyon v. McCrary, 427 U.S. 160, 96 S.Ct. 2586, 49 L.Ed.2d 415 (1976), appeal after remand 569 F.2d 1294 (4th Cir.1978), cert. denied 439 U.S. 927, 99 S.Ct. 311, 58 L.Ed.2d 320 (1978), this case is discussed in §§ 19.6–19.10, supra. The Court specifically left open the case where a school discriminated by race due to religious beliefs, 427 U.S. at 167 n. 6, 96 S.Ct. at 2593 n. 6. The Supreme Court has upheld restrictions

on the freedom of associations to discriminate in membership decisions on the basis of sex or race, but, in so doing, has left open the question of whether some associations dedicated to expressive or religious purposes might be immune from such regulation because of first amendment protections. See generally, § 20.41, supra.

74. 461 U.S. 574, 103 S.Ct. 2017, 76 L.Ed.2d 157 (1983).

75. 461 U.S. at 604, 103 S.Ct. at 2035, 76 L.Ed.2d at 181.

Professors Freed and Polsby have criticized the free exercise clause analysis in this case and have put forward a theory of free exercise analysis which would have courts evaluate the extent to which persons or organizations might insincerely claim a religious basis for their actions if the Court were to rule that an exemption

The establishment clause was not violated even though the effect of the requirement that schools not discriminate on the basis of race was to allow some religious schools to receive tax exempt status while those religiously affiliated schools that could not comply with the requirement would fail to receive the exemption. This rule was not a preference of one religion over another but merely the carrying out of a policy founded on a "neutral, secular basis" which was uniformly applied to all schools.

In addition to the nonreligious purpose and primary effect of the Internal Revenue Service position, the denial of exemptions to all schools that practice racial discrimination avoided a potential for excessive entanglement between government and religion by avoiding the necessity of inquiring into the sincerity of those asserting a religious basis for their discriminatory practices.[76]

(3) **State Constitutional Restrictions.** A number of states have constitutional provisions that specifically restrict aid to religious institutions.[77] In such states even such forms of aid as bus fees, textbooks, and tax exemptions might be denied to religious institutions by the state constitution. Because the Supreme Court of the United States has only indicated that such forms of aid are permissible if the state desires to furnish them, there is no violation of the first amendment if a state refuses to aid religious schools.

If a state went so far as to deny basic governmental services such as police and fire protection to religious institutions, there would be a significant issue as to whether the denial of services so inhibited the practice of religion as to amount to a violation of the free exercise clause. However, no state has done this.

(4) **Government Payments of Money "Owned" by Private Individuals.** The government may pay the tuition of students at religious schools if the tuition payment is made with money owned or earned by

from laws was available to persons acting on the basis of religious belief. This strategic behavior analysis would evaluate the economic and other incentives for taking such actions and might give a clearer picture of the competing interests at stake in free exercise clause cases. See Freed and Polsby, Race, Religion, and Public Policy: Bob Jones University v. United States, 1983 Sup.Ct.Rev. 1.

76. 461 U.S. at 604 n. 30, 103 S.Ct. at 2035 n. 30, 76 L.Ed.2d at 181 n. 30. Even though the decision in the particular case might not be objectionable, the "public policy" that was the Court's basis for finding the Internal Revenue Service was authorized to deny a charitable exemption to groups that discriminated on account of

race is subject to criticism because of the uncertain nature of the Court's methodology and the danger that it may be used to justify Internal Revenue Service public policy decisions with less than clear Congressional authority. See Freed and Polsby, Race, Religion, and Public Policy: Bob Jones University v. United States, 1983 Sup.Ct.Rev. 1; Stephan, Bob Jones University v. United States: Public Policy in Search of Tax Policy, 1983 Sup.Ct.Rev. 33.

77. For a review of such provisions see, C. Antieau, P. Carroll & T. Burke, Religion Under the State Constitutions (1965).

See generally, Greenawalt, The Concept of Religion in State Constitutions, 8 Campbell.L.Rev. 437 (1986).

the students. In *Reuben Quick Bear v. Leupp*[78] the Supreme Court upheld a federal government payment to religious organizations on Indian reservations since the money used was owned by the Indian tribes and only held in trust by the federal government. A similar analysis might support the use of tuition payments for veterans of the armed services to religious colleges, or the government loaning money at reduced interest rates to all students regardless of whether they attend religiously affiliated schools.[79]

(5) **Financial Aid to Religiously Affiliated Institutions Other Than Schools.** If the government is granting financial aid to a religiously affiliated institution of any type, the program must be tested under the establishment clause in the same manner as are programs which aid schools. Thus, the program must have a secular purpose, no primary effect which either advances or inhibits religion and no excessive entanglement between government and religious authority. Again, excessive entanglement will be looked at in terms of: (1) the character of the institution, (2) the type of aid, and (3) the resulting administrative relationships. Additionally, the potential of the program for causing political division along religious lines will be an important factor in determining its validity.

The key to analysis of any such program is the determination of the degree of the independent secular function in the institution to be aided. If the institution is pervasively religious, it will be practically impossible to aid the institution without either having the impermissible effect of aiding religion or else having to establish so many procedural safeguards that an excessive entanglement results. However, if the institution has a clearly independent secular function the state should be able to design a program which aids only the secular activities. This type of institution can then be aided with a minimum of administrative entanglement, as the lesser potential for aiding the religious function requires fewer safeguards.

78. 210 U.S. 50, 28 S.Ct. 690, 52 L.Ed. 954 (1908).

79. The Court unanimously upheld a program of state aid to visually handicapped students in Witters v. Washington Department of Services for the Blind, 474 U.S. 481, 106 S.Ct. 748, 88 L.Ed.2d 846 (1986), rehearing denied 475 U.S. 1091, 106 S.Ct. 1485, 89 L.Ed.2d 737 (1986). The program was upheld although the student involved in the individual case had used the aid to attend a religiously affiliated school for the purpose of pursuing a religious vocation. The Court found that the aid to handicapped students had a secular purpose, as the program did not have a religious effect because it merely increased the economic resources of all visually handicapped persons who wished to obtain special education or vocational training. The majority opinion by Justice Marshall stated that any aid that flowed to religious schools from the program "does so only as a result of the genuinely independent and private choices of the aid recipients." Justice Marshall analogized these payments to the payment of government employees' salaries. Government employees could use their economic resources to pursue a religious education or make donations to a religious entity. The case, therefore, seems to support the statement made in this paragraph that the payment of money to persons who are employees or wards of the government does not constitute a violation of the establishment clause even though those persons independently choose to use that money for religious purposes.

During the last century the Supreme Court upheld grants to church affiliated hospitals in *Bradfield v. Roberts*,[80] cited in modern times with approval by the Court.[81] As religious hospitals seem to have an independent secular function, the analysis should be the same as that for religious colleges—the state need only avoid aiding pervasively religious institutions or clearly religious activities. So long as the hospital aided is not so "pervasively sectarian" as to subsume its role as a hospital in its religious mission, its secular medical function may receive state aid.

The Supreme Court relied on *Bradfield* when it upheld a federal statute that granted funds to public and nonprofit organizations to provide services, other than family planning or abortion related services, to pregnant adolescents and to conduct programs to prevent adolescent sexual relations.[82] In *Bowen v. Kendrick*[83] the Supreme Court upheld the constitutionality of the Adolescent Family Life Act [AFLA] against the claim that the AFLA on its face violated the establishment clause of the first amendment. Under the AFLA grants are given to various organizations to give care or counselling to pregnant adolescents and their parents or to counsel adolescents (through prevention services and programs). The AFLA specifically states that religious and charitable organizations, as well as other public and nonprofit organizations, are eligible for these grants; the AFLA requires grant applicants to show how they will involve families of adolescents, and religious and charitable organizations and other associations and groups in the private sector, in the services that the grantee would provide to adolescents and their parents. The AFLA prohibits the use of any grant money for family planning services, abortions, abortion counselling, or the promotion of abortion.

In *Kendrick* the Court, in a majority opinion written by Chief Justice Rehnquist, ruled that the AFLA on its face did not violate the establishment clause, although the Court also found that individual grants made under the AFLA might be invalid under the establishment clause. The AFLA on its face survived the purpose, effect, and entanglement tests that had been developed for determining whether any type of government support for religion violated the establishment clause.[84] Congress had asserted the nonreligious purpose of addressing problems associated with adolescent sexuality; Chief Justice Rehnquist

80. 175 U.S. 291, 20 S.Ct. 121, 44 L.Ed. 168 (1899).

81. Roemer v. Board of Public Works, 426 U.S. 736, 746, 96 S.Ct. 2337, 2344–45, 49 L.Ed.2d 179 (1976) (plurality opinion by Blackmun, J.).

82. Bradfield v. Roberts, 175 U.S. 291, 20 S.Ct. 121, 44 L.Ed. 168 (1899), cited by the Supreme Court with approval in Bowen v. Kendrick, 487 U.S. 589, 608–10, 108

S.Ct. 2562, 2574, 101 L.Ed.2d 520 (1988), on remand 703 F.Supp. 1 (D.D.C.1989).

83. 487 U.S. 589, 108 S.Ct. 2562, 101 L.Ed.2d 520 (1988), on remand 703 F.Supp. 1 (D.D.C.1989).

84. See §§ 21.3–21.5 regarding the development and application of these establishment clause tests in other areas.

found that the AFLA did not have a religious purpose. Congress could not be found to have endorsed religion merely because its views on the subject of abortion coincided with those of religious organizations.[85]

Chief Justice Rehnquist, writing for the majority, ruled that the AFLA on its face did not have an effect that either advanced or inhibited religion in a manner that would violate the establishment clause. The establishment clause did not prevent religious organizations from participating in government funded programs to promote social welfare goals. So long as the government program and the use of government aid did not advance religion, the primary effect test would not be violated. Chief Justice Rehnquist found that the AFLA on its face did not have the effect of advancing religion for four reasons. First, the statute did not indicate that a large proportion of the funds would go to "pervasively sectarian" organizations. Second, the funding of programs under the AFLA did not necessarily result in religious organizations using the funds for religious purposes; nothing in the statute or prior cases justified a presumption that religious organizations could not carry out these grant programs in a secular manner. Third, the statute did not advance religion merely because many religious organizations agreed with the message that Congress intended to promote with AFLA grants. Fourth, the AFLA was designed to promote the social welfare through nonreligious means and it would not be invalidated on the theory that any participation of religious organizations in government programs created a "symbolic link" between government and religion.

The Court in *Kendrick* also ruled that the AFLA did not, on its face, give rise to an excessive government entanglement with religion. The majority opinion found no reason to assume that the religious organizations that were receiving grants were so "pervasively sectarian" that the government would need to engage in such extensive monitoring of their programs, in order to ensure that the grant money was not used for religious purposes, that it would become enmeshed in an excessive entanglement with those religious organizations.[86]

When the Court upholds a statute granting money to religiously affiliated organizations, such as it did in *Kendrick,* it is not ruling that every possible grant given under the authority of the statute will be valid. In *Kendrick* the Supreme Court only upheld the AFLA on its face; the Court did not rule on the question of whether individual grants to religious organizations to provide counselling or services to adolescents violated the establishment clause. The majority opinion by Chief Justice Rehnquist found that taxpayers had standing to challenge

---

85. Bowen v. Kendrick, 487 U.S. 589, 602–04, 108 S.Ct. 2562, 2571, 101 L.Ed.2d 520 (1988), on remand 703 F.Supp. 1 (D.D.C.1989).

86. 487 U.S. at 617 n. 14, 108 S.Ct. at 2578 n. 14 (the discussion of this point is contained in the text of Chief Justice Rehnquist's opinion as well as in footnote 14 of his opinion).

specific grants under the AFLA. Taxpayers could attempt to show that a specific grant violated the establishment clause because it had the effect of advancing religion or because it would give rise to an excessive entanglement between government and religion.[87] Chief Justice Rehnquist's opinion is not clear regarding whether a grant to a "pervasively sectarian" institution is per se unconstitutional, or whether a grant to a pervasively sectarian institution was only presumptively unconstitutional, due to the fact that a grant to a pervasively sectarian organization might need extensive monitoring to ensure that the government funds were not used for religious teaching or other religious activities.[88]

(d) A Comment on the Emergence and Impact of the Excessive Entanglement Test [89]

Prior to the Supreme Court decisions of the 1970's, it appeared that the states would be able to give financial assistance to children who chose to receive their educations away from the public school system. Because the Court had refused to assume that there was no independent secular function in parochial schools, the "purpose and effect" test did not bar general aid to students in all private schools. But one leading scholar, Professor Paul Freund, thought that the incidental aid to religion which resulted from government transportation payments or textbook programs violated the first amendment principles of government neutrality and separation between church and state.[90] However another leading scholar in this area, Professor Jesse Choper, attempted to keep the Court from a more restrictive approach by demonstrating how the government, through the use of vouchers, might aid only the secular function of religiously affiliated schools.[91] Such government aid would encourage alternative school systems.

Economic and statistical analysis shows that it is possible to construct a tuition tax credit or voucher system, which reimburses families for part of the expense of sending their children to private schools, without aiding religion.[92] So long as the amounts would be less than

87. Bowen v. Kendrick, 487 U.S. 589, 617–23, 108 S.Ct. 2562, 2579–81, 101 L.Ed.2d 520 (1988), on remand 703 F.Supp. 1 (D.D.C.1989).

88. Id. At least two justices believe that not all grants to pervasively sectarian religious organizations are per se unconstitutional. Bowen v. Kendrick, 487 U.S. 589, 623–25, 108 S.Ct. 2562, 2582, 101 L.Ed.2d 520 (1988) (Kennedy, J., joined by Scalia, J., concurring), on remand 703 F.Supp. 1 (D.D.C.1989).

89. An earlier version of this comment appeared in Nowak, The Supreme Court, the Religion Clauses and the Nationalization of Education, 70 Nw.U.L.Rev. 883 (1976).

90. Freund, Public Aid to Parochial Schools, 82 Harv.L.Rev. 1680 (1969).

91. Choper, The Establishment Clause and Aid to Parochial Schools, 56 Calif.L.Rev. 260 (1968). This article contains a comprehensive analysis of the history and effect of programs of aid to religious schools.

92. For an economic analysis of these programs and the rulings of the Supreme Court, see Nowak, The Supreme Court, the Religion Clauses and the Nationalization of Education, 70 Nw.U.L.Rev. 883 (1976). The voucher system and economic analysis which follow were first suggested in A. Smith, The Wealth of Nations 736–38 (Mod.Lib. ed. 1937). The concept was fully

the amount expended for the secular courses in these schools, no funds inure to the benefit of religious education. It would be true that more families might be able to opt out of the public school system and send their children to parochial schools if such a refund or voucher program existed. But this decision would not be the result of any government encouragement or aid to religion. Instead these programs merely offer families a choice of receiving their educational benefits "in kind" at the local public school or "in cash" if they chose to send their children to an alternative school system.

The most important effect of a general aid program to students attending alternative systems of education is that such a program provides a more meaningful equality of educational opportunity for children from low-income families. The provision of subsidized education only through a government operated school system imposes very severe hardships on children from low-income families who seek a superior education. If the local public school system seems insufficient for developing the intellectual abilities of their children, higher income parents may move to a place where the public school system is superior or they may simply withdraw their child from the public system and provide the child with a privately financed education. Neither of these options is available to low-income families.

The low-income parents may be equally desirous of improving the education of their children, especially if they perceive that their children have exceptional intellectual abilities or that the local public schools fail to provide even a minimally adequate education. Indeed these parents might well be willing to do without many other "basic necessities" in order to provide their children with a superior education. However, because subsidized education is provided only in kind, they can only change the quality of their child's education with a massive dollar supplement which is beyond their means. If the state would give them the dollar equivalent of the per-pupil cost of the local public school, they could supplement this figure with some of their own resources and use the increased amount to send their child to another school. However, where the subsidized education is provided only in kind, the parents would have to be able to move to a substantially richer neighborhood or to bear the entire cost of private education themselves in order to improve the educational opportunities of their children. These options, of course, will be beyond the means of such families.

Government financial aid to religious schools would provide an alternative to these poorer families, but that aid might require such

developed and the analysis refined by Professor Friedman. M. Friedman, Capitalism & Freedom 85–107 (1962).

The problems of zero tuition and higher education that were explored by Professor Alchian also relate directly to the analysis of the voucher program. Alchian, The Economic and Social Impact of Free Tuition, in H. Manne, The Economics of Legal Relationships 598–613 (1975).

regulation. The administrative regulation of religious activities would pose great danger to the values of government neutrality in religious matters. First, programs which call for a high degree of administrative contact and regulation might leave the impression that those groups which survive regulation are governmentally approved. Such regulation also endangers the freedom of religious societies by requiring them to be responsive to government administrators in order to maintain the flow of benefits. Additionally, this type of involvement may undermine the neutrality of the government itself.

A high degree of regulation will require some formal administration to insure that the day-to-day regulations are followed and that reporting requirements are met. However, in the long run, administrators and those who are being regulated frequently develop a mutuality of interest. It is in the interest of the public administrators to please those who are regulated in order to maintain their position and increase the power of their agency. Similarly, it is in the interest of the regulated entities to accommodate, if not control, those who regulate them so that they will receive favorable rulings in areas where the administrators exercise some discretion. This mutuality of interest can lead to the "capture" of administrative agencies by those whom they are supposed to regulate and make it difficult to determine whether such agencies are acting on behalf of the public or the regulated entity.[93] There is no reason to believe that the regulation of religious activities would follow a different pattern.[94]

Thus, Chief Justice Burger was correct in concluding that the first amendment forbids any program of government aid which would re-

93. K. Davis, Administrative Law Treatise § 1.03 (1958); T. Morgan, Economic Regulation of Business—Cases and Materials 21–23 (1976); Posner, Theories of Economic Regulation, 5 Bell J. of Econ. & Mgt. Science 335 (1974); Stigler, The Theory of Economic Regulation, 2 Bell J. of Econ. & Mgt. Science 3 (1970). See also, L. Kohlmeier, The Regulators—Watchdog Agencies and the Public Interest 69–82 (1969).

94. In Larkin v. Grendel's Den, Inc., 459 U.S. 116, 103 S.Ct. 505, 74 L.Ed.2d 297 (1982), the Court found that a zoning law violated the first amendment establishment clause by granting to all churches or schools a veto power over the issuance of liquor licenses for any premises within a 500 foot radius of the church or the school. The Court applied the three-part test under the establishment clause.

Although the law in *Larkin* might have had a secular purpose, (the promotion of a quiet atmosphere around certain cultural and educational centers) that purpose could not alone sustain the statute's constitutionality. The zoning statute was clearly susceptible to being used to promote religious rather than secular ends. The churches had a power under the statute which was subject to no clear secular standards; that power could be used to promote primarily religious goals.

Even if one assumed that the statute had both a secular purpose and primary effect, the law clearly failed the excessive entanglement test. A law which vested governmental authority in churches "enmeshes churches in the exercise of substantial governmental powers contrary to our consistent interpretation of the establishment clause." 459 U.S. at 127, 103 S.Ct. at 512. The excessive entanglement branch of the establishment clause test was meant to avoid the danger to both secular government and religious autonomy that accompanies a sharing of power and entanglement of administrative agencies.

quire substantial reporting and regulation[95] since it is the first step to agency regulation of religious societies. However, so long as the aid program does not involve a substantial probability that the benefits could be used directly for sectarian functions, there is no need for a reporting and regulation system which would lead to administrative entanglement. For example, vouchers which are computed by a formula which gives statistical assurance that no aid will be provided to sectarian activities should not require further regulation of this type.[96] Similarly, the provision of truly neutral educational materials which are not readily adaptable for religious education requires no further regulation to insure that they are not used for the religious orientation of students.[97]

Economic and statistical analysis should indicate that no danger to the values of the religion clauses results from school aid programs which have statistical assurances against aid to religious teaching. Programs such as those described by Professor Choper cannot aid the religious function of parochial schools because the dollar supplement is less than their cost for the teaching of secular subjects. No principle of voluntarism is endangered by such a program because no tax dollars go to the funding of religious activities. There is no danger to government neutrality, since the programs merely allow low-income families to exercise freedom of choice in educational matters. Such programs offer no incentive or encouragement for parents to send their children to parochial schools, so long as they could receive at least as great a financial benefit by sending their children to the public schools. Finally, the principle of mutual abstention is preserved by providing only services or dollar amounts which are not likely to aid religious activities and which avoid administrative entanglement.

As we saw in the previous sections of this chapter, the Court in the 1970's rejected the use of statistical guarantees to prove that an educational assistance program did not aid religion. Instead, the majority held that any significant aid to children attending religious elementary or secondary schools would be presumed to aid the religious function of those schools. This impermissible effect could only be avoided if administrative systems were designed to prevent any aid to religious teaching. Of course, if a state used such a system, it would give rise to an excessive entanglement between government and religion which would violate the first amendment. To insist that any form of aid, no matter how neutral, continually be reported to insure its

---

95. The administrative entanglement test was added in Walz v. Tax Com'n, 397 U.S. 664, 90 S.Ct. 1409, 25 L.Ed.2d 697 (1970).

96. Choper, The Establishment Clause and Aid to Parochial Schools, 56 Calif.L.Rev. 260, 287–90 (1968).

97. Even the new majority of the Court has admitted that a variety of instructional materials may be "self-policing" in this sense. Meek v. Pittenger, 421 U.S. 349, 365, 95 S.Ct. 1753, 1763, 44 L.Ed.2d 217 (1975), rehearing denied 422 U.S. 1049, 95 S.Ct. 2668, 45 L.Ed.2d 702 (1975).

neutrality, but then to invalidate the program because of the reporting requirement, seems circular. This result is justified, in the view of a majority of the Court, by the political divisiveness principle and the first amendment prohibition of government aid to religion.

The Origin of the Excessive Entanglement–Political Divisiveness Test. The origin of the excessive entanglement-political divisiveness test merits attention. The concept was introduced by Justice Harlan in his concurring opinions in *Board of Education v. Allen*[98] and *Walz v. Tax Commission.*[99] However, he only meant to use the concept to indicate that the Court should be careful not to encourage such political fragmentation. His conclusions as to the validity of the textbook program and the tax exemption show that he did not intend to use the concept as a strict test of constitutional validity.[100]

Similarly, in the *Lemon* and *Tilton* decisions, it appeared that Chief Justice Burger was only using this concept to reinforce the conclusions of the Court. He found that the programs of aid to religious primary, secondary and college level schools all had a secular purpose. However, the challenged forms of aid to primary and secondary schools were found to be extremely susceptible to use for religiously oriented activities, which meant that the government would have to engage in a prohibitive form of day-to-day regulation to insure that no aid was given to religious functions. At the college level, the greatly decreased likelihood that the forms of aid could or would be used for sectarian activities meant that the government could rely on milder forms of reporting and regulation to insure secular use of funds. Thus the real distinction between the two programs was not in the politically divisive nature of each program, but that one form of aid invited excessive administration while the other did not.[101] Chief Justice Burger merely reinforced the Court's conclusions by noting that there was political division over the primary school aid programs, but not the college grant programs.[102]

98. 392 U.S. 236, 249, 88 S.Ct. 1923, 1929, 20 L.Ed.2d 1060 (1968) (Harlan, J., concurring).

99. 397 U.S. 664, 694, 90 S.Ct. 1409, 1424, 25 L.Ed.2d 697 (1970) (Harlan, J., concurring); the concept of entanglement was also used by the majority in *Walz* without defining the principle. 397 U.S. at 670, 674–75, 90 S.Ct. at 1412, 1414–15.

100. Thus, although Justice Harlan cited the Freund article, Public Aid to Parochial Schools, 82 Harv.L.Rev. 1680 (1969), in his *Walz* concurrence, 397 U.S. at 695, 90 S.Ct. at 1424–25, he showed no inclination to reconsider his position in *Allen* because of this concept. Id.

101. Compare Lemon v. Kurtzman, 403 U.S. 602, 618–22, 91 S.Ct. 2105, 2113–16, 29

L.Ed.2d 745 (1971), rehearing denied 404 U.S. 876, 92 S.Ct. 24, 30 L.Ed.2d 123 (1971), on remand 348 F.Supp. 300 (E.D.Pa.1972), with Tilton v. Richardson, 403 U.S. 672, 685–88, 91 S.Ct. 2091, 2099–2101, 29 L.Ed.2d 790 (1971) (Burger, C.J., plurality opinion), rehearing denied 404 U.S. 874, 92 S.Ct. 25, 30 L.Ed.2d 120 (1971).

102. Lemon v. Kurtzman, 403 U.S. 602, 622–25, 91 S.Ct. 2105, 2115–17, 29 L.Ed.2d 745 (1971), rehearing denied 404 U.S. 876, 92 S.Ct. 24, 30 L.Ed.2d 123 (1971), on remand 348 F.Supp. 300 (E.D.Pa.1972); Tilton v. Richardson, 403 U.S. 672, 689, 91 S.Ct. 2091, 2101, 29 L.Ed.2d 790 (1971) (Burger, C.J., plurality opinion), rehearing denied 404 U.S. 874, 92 S.Ct. 25, 30 L.Ed.2d 120 (1971).

The Political Divisiveness Concept. The political divisiveness "test" took on a life of its own in *Nyquist.* Here a form of completely neutral aid—a tuition-voucher plan—was stricken in part because of the belief that any significant aid to students in sectarian schools caused political division.[103] This principle was invoked again in *Meek* to justify the prohibition of furnishing auxiliary educational aids and services to students, a form of aid with little potential for use in sectarian functions.[104] Indeed, three of the justices were so committed to this concept that they favored invoking it to strike down the *Allen* textbook program.[105] They were correct in noting that no significant aid to parochial schools is permissible under the political divisiveness test. There was no principled way to distinguish the textbook program under the test,[106] since any form of aid which would enable children to go to parochial schools will carry with it the seeds for debate cast in religious terms about its merits.

If the political divisiveness test is in fact being used by the majority to ban religious conflict, the attempt would appear to be futile at best. The prohibition of aid to parochial schools cannot end sectarian debate over educational programs and budgets—it can only shift its focus. By prohibiting even neutral aid to parochial schools, the Court has seriously disadvantaged parochial schools in competing with the governmentally operated school system. Instead of religious groups proposing legislation which would benefit the students who would attend their schools, they will be forced to oppose aid to public schools so as to benefit their schools indirectly. Insofar as the proponents of religious education can reduce the amounts spent on public schools, they will decrease the economic incentive for parents to send their children to such schools. Opposition to public school bond referendums by religious groups may occur in the future unless those groups are content to watch increasing student transfers to the better financed systems. It seems unlikely that this will reduce political division.

The shifted focus of the political conflict may well increase political division along religious lines. If inner city school performance continues to decrease, one would expect increased pressure on government to aid private schools so that the residents of the city have an alternative to the public school system.[107] However, it will be in the interest of

103. Committee for Public Education v. Nyquist, 413 U.S. 756, 795–97, 93 S.Ct. 2955, 2976–78, 37 L.Ed.2d 948 (1973).

104. Meek v. Pittenger, 421 U.S. 349, 365 n. 15, 372, 95 S.Ct. 1753, 1763 n. 15, 1766–67, 44 L.Ed.2d 217 (1975), rehearing denied 422 U.S. 1049, 95 S.Ct. 2668, 45 L.Ed.2d 702 (1975).

105. 421 U.S. at 374–78, 95 S.Ct. at 1767–70 (Brennan, J.). This opinion was joined by Justices Douglas and Marshall.

106. 421 U.S. at 377–78, 95 S.Ct. at 1769–70 (Brennan, J.).

107. In fact, this is exactly what has happened in major urban areas. The majority of parochial schools exist in the most populous states and serve urban areas. U.S. Department of Health, Education & Welfare, Digest of Education Statistics 39–41 (1973). In those low-income areas the quality of education can be expected to decline in the presence of increasing prob-

those who favor religiously oriented education to oppose such aid if it is not provided on an equal basis to parochial schools. Those who favor parochial schools will perceive that aid to nonreligious private schools directly threatens their existence by offering an alternative to the public school system which the state has placed in an economically preferred position to their schools.

This scenario would leave religious schools at a dual disadvantage in the market place. Public schools would have the benefit of the highest governmental subsidy, while private nonreligious schools would have a lower subsidy but greater responsiveness to parents and teachers. Those who favor the continued existence of parochial schools would find it beneficial to oppose aid to both the public schools and nonreligious private schools. Thus, new forms of political division along religious lines may result from the Court's ban on aid to parochial schools.

A majority of the justices in the 1970's used the excessive entanglement test and the concept of political divisiveness to strike down any form of aid to religiously affiliated schools, to their students, or to the parents of those students if the aid would have helped such schools to attract students from public school systems. These justices believed that such schools were permeated with religion and that any form of aid allowing students or parents greater freedom to pay tuition to such schools, even for their nonreligious functions, aided the enterprise as a unit and allowed the school to spend additional money on inculcating its students with religious values. Because the justices believed that any aid, whether direct or indirect, to such activity was prohibited, they believed that any form of aid beyond the most generalized services (such as police and fire protection and a few other basic student-oriented services) would require an impermissible involvement between government and religion.

In the early 1980's it appeared that a majority of the justices would not impose strict limitations on religiously neutral aid to religious schools or their students. In *Committee for Public Education and Religious Liberty v. Regan,* [108] the Court upheld, by a five to four vote of

lems of financing and overcrowding. See, President's Panel on Nonpublic Education and the Public Good (1972). The eight most populous states face even greater problems in the years ahead if parochial schools close and the government operated systems are forced to serve additional students who otherwise would have attended these schools. See Swartz, The Estimated Marginal Costs of Absorbing All Nonpublic Students into the Public School System, in President's Commission on School Finance, Economics of Nonpublic Schools, 301, 347 (1972).

For further analysis of the restrictive effect of the current public school system on lower income groups and economic mobility, see Clark, Alternative Public School Systems, in Equal Educational Opportunity (Harv.Educ.Rev. ed. 1969). See generally, J. Coons, W. Clune & S. Sugarman, Private Wealth and Public Education (1970).

108. 444 U.S. 646, 100 S.Ct. 840, 63 L.Ed.2d 94 (1980).

the justices, a state program which reimbursed private schools for the scoring of standardized achievement tests and the reporting of certain data to state authorities. In *Mueller v. Allen,* [109] the justices, again by a five to four vote, upheld a statute granting a state tax deduction for expenses incurred in providing tuition, textbooks, or transportation of children attending any public or private elementary or secondary school. In these cases the Court found that the government programs had a secular purpose because the legislature in each case was attempting to help the nonreligious aspects of every child's education. The Court ruled that it was possible in each case for the program to have a primary effect that neither advanced nor inhibited religion without an administrative monitoring system that would give rise to an excessive entanglement between government and religion.

In *Committee for Public Education and Liberty* and *Mueller* a majority of the justices recognized that religiously affiliated private schools served a nonreligious as well as religious purpose and that the religiously neutral form of aid to students or their parents did not endanger establishment clause values. Although lessening the economic costs of attending a private, religiously affiliated school might make it easier for persons to choose to leave the public school system for religious school systems, this greater freedom of choice was only an incidental aspect of the program; it did not constitute impermissible government advancement of or involvement with religion. In both cases the majority was comprised of Justices Rehnquist and White, who had long opposed invalidation of religiously neutral aid to all students, Chief Justice Burger, who had come to doubt the wisdom of using the excessive entanglement test as a means of invalidating religiously neutral aid, Justice Powell and Justice Stewart or Justice O'Connor, each of whom had taken a case-by-case approach to determining whether specific forms of aid to religious school students involved government advancement of religion.

In 1985 Justice Powell again cast his vote with Justices Blackmun, Brennan, Marshall and Stevens, who consistently had asserted that rigorous enforcement of the purpose, effect, and entanglement tests was necessary to avoid any aid to what they saw as a pervasively sectarian enterprise in religious grade school or high school education. In view of these justices any form of significant aid to such enterprises must involve either a government subsidy for the religious function of the school or must require such an extensive administrative monitoring system to avoid the religious effect that it will give rise to an excessive entanglement between government administrators and religious authorities.

109.   463 U.S. 388, 103 S.Ct. 3062, 77 L.Ed.2d 721 (1983).

In *Grand Rapids School District v. Ball*, [110] the Court invalidated state programs in which public school teachers taught nonreligious courses to religious school students during the school day, and religious school employees taught nonreligious courses after the school day on religious school premises. The majority found that these programs had a primary effect of advancing religion because the programs had the potential for subsidizing religious education and created a symbolic link between government and religion.

In *Aguilar v. Felton*, [111] the Court invalidated a state program which used federal funds, under the authority of a federal statute, to provide remedial education programs and services to children at religious schools. The Court avoided ruling on whether the administrative system the state had set up to avoid the advancement of religious beliefs had been successful in avoiding the impermissible effect of advancing religion. The Court ruled instead that the state's extensive monitoring system gave rise to an excessive entanglement between government and religion. Although the majority opinion noted that such programs might give rise to "political divisiveness," the opinion focused on the administrative entanglement between government and religious authorities. The majority believed that the administrative entanglement endangered both the religious neutrality of government and also the freedom of members of the religious organization whose administrators interacted with the government on a day-to-day basis.

Justice Powell, whose vote was crucial to forming a majority in all of the 1980–1985 cases, wrote separately in 1985.[112] Justice Powell admitted that the majority of which he was a part had created a "difficult dilemma" for a governmental entity attempting to create a system of aid for the nonreligious aspects of private school students' education while trying to avoid an excessive entanglement with religious authorities. According to Justice Powell, the Court's 1985 rulings were justified by its earlier interpretations of the purpose, effect, and entanglement tests. However, he wished to "write to emphasize additional reasons why precedents of this Court require us to invalidate these two educational programs [providing on-site remedial education or guidance services] that concededly have done so much good and little, if any, detectable harm." For Justice Powell, strict application of the purpose, effect, and entanglement tests was necessary because "there remains a considerable risk of continuing political strife over the propriety of direct aid to religious schools and the proper allocation of government resources." Thus it appears that the concept of political divisiveness, rather than an examination of the dangers of administrative entanglement between government and religious administrators,

110. 473 U.S. 373, 105 S.Ct. 3216, 87 L.Ed.2d 267 (1985).

111. 473 U.S. 402, 105 S.Ct. 3232, 87 L.Ed.2d 290 (1985).

112. Aguilar v. Felton, 473 U.S. 402, 414, 105 S.Ct. 3232, 3239, 87 L.Ed.2d 290 (1985) (Powell, J., concurring).

explains why some justices vote for a very strict application of the purpose, effect, and entanglement tests.[113]

The foregoing analysis of the entanglement and political division concepts appears to have been affirmed by the Court's decision in *Bowen v. Kendrick.*[114] In *Kendrick,* the Supreme Court upheld the Adolescent Family Life Act [AFLA], which provided for grants to religious, as well as nonreligious, organizations for the purpose of providing services and counselling to pregnant adolescents and for the purpose of deterring adolescent sexual relationships through counselling and educational programs. The majority opinion by Chief Justice Rehnquist found that the AFLA was valid on its face, although taxpayers could challenge individual grants to religious organizations on the basis that the individual grant had the effect of advancing religion or resulted in an excessive entanglement between government and religion. The Court found that Congress had a secular purpose in enacting the AFLA and that the statute did not inherently have the effect of advancing religion. The Chief Justice's majority opinion found that the statute only involved religious organizations in programs that were intended to be secular in nature and that the resulting relationship between government and religion did not necessarily constitute an excessive entanglement. If the Court ruled that an excessive entanglement arose from the mere fact that government would have to monitor grants to religious organizations to ensure that the governmental grant money was not used for religious purposes, the excessive entanglement concept would make religious organizations ineligible to participate in government funded programs designed to promote secular social goals.

The Chief Justice's majority opinion in *Kendrick* found that the first amendment did not preclude all involvement of religious organizations in social programs.[115] The Chief Justice noted that a government grant of money to a religious organization that was "pervasively sectarian" might inherently give rise to excessive entanglement between

---

113. Witters v. Washington Department of Services for the Blind, 474 U.S. 481, 106 S.Ct. 748, 88 L.Ed.2d 846 (1986), rehearing denied 475 U.S. 1091, 106 S.Ct. 1485, 89 L.Ed.2d 737 (1986), unanimously upheld a program of state payments to blind students designed to allow those students to obtain special education or vocational training. The program was upheld even though the case involved a blind student who used the aid to attend a religiously affiliated school for the purpose of training for a religious vocation. The Court found that there was a secular purpose for the program and that the program did not give rise to a religious effect, because it only increased the economic resources of handicapped students who were then free to use these resources based on their inde-

pendent educational choices. The majority opinion did not address the entanglement question because it had not been clearly raised and analyzed in the state courts. 474 U.S. at 489 n. 5, 106 S.Ct. 753 n. 5. Three of the concurring Justices agreed that the entanglement issue was not properly raised before the Supreme Court. 474 U.S. at 490, 106 S.Ct. at 753 (Powell, J., joined by Burger, C.J., and Rehnquist, J., concurring).

114. 487 U.S. 589, 108 S.Ct. 2562, 101 L.Ed.2d 520 (1988), on remand 703 F.Supp. 1 (D.D.C.1989).

115. For a more complete examination of this case see § 21.4(c)(5). [The addition to this supplement that corresponds to page 375 of the text in the main volume].

government and religion, because the government would need to engage in extensive monitoring of such an organization in order to insure that it would not use grant funds to advance religious goals.

The Court in *Kendrick* refused to find excessive entanglement inherent in the AFLA program on the basis of a political division concept. The Chief Justice stated that the concept of political divisiveness should be confined to cases in which government aid was going to parochial schools.[116] Thus, it appears that political divisiveness should not be used as a separate test to determine the permissibility of government aid to religion. Rather, it appears to be a factor that influences some justice to use the purpose, effect, and entanglement tests to invalidate many types of aid to parochial schools. The excessive entanglement test appears to be only what its name implies, a test that is designed to prevent the types of involvement of government and religious organizations that might, in the long run, threaten independence of both government and organized religion.

§ 21.5 Religion and the Public Schools

(a) Introduction

Questions concerning the introduction of religion into the governmentally operated school system may arise in several ways. Many of the cases examining particular ways in which public schools had become involved with religious activities or beliefs were decided before the emergence of the three-part purpose-effect-entanglement test. It would appear that the Court now will use this three-part test when examining any issue concerning whether public school activities constitute a form of establishment of religion that is prohibited by the first amendment.[1] We will divide this section of the treatise into various subsections based on the problem areas—the particular types of in-

---

116. Bowen v. Kendrick, 487 U.S. 589, 617 n. 14, 108 S.Ct. 2562, 2578 n. 14, 101 L.Ed.2d 520 (1988), on remand 703 F.Supp. 1 (D.D.C.1989). The Court quoted with approval the statement in Mueller v. Allen, 463 U.S. 388, 404 n. 11, 103 S.Ct. 3062, 3071 n. 11, 77 L.Ed.2d 721 (1983) that the political divisiveness concept should be "regarded as confined to cases where direct financial subsidies are paid to parochial schools or to teachers in parochial schools."

§ 21.5

1. See, e.g., Stone v. Graham, 449 U.S. 39, 101 S.Ct. 192, 66 L.Ed.2d 199 (1980), rehearing denied 449 U.S. 1104, 101 S.Ct. 904, 66 L.Ed.2d 832 (1981), on remand 612 S.W.2d 133 (Ky.1981). See § 21.5(c), infra; Widmar v. Vincent, 454 U.S. 263, 102 S.Ct. 269, 70 L.Ed.2d 440 (1981). See § 21.5(e), infra.

In a very limited group of cases the Court has found a historical basis for ruling that an involvement between government and religion did not constitute an establishment of religion and has not employed with any strictness the three part purpose-effect-entanglement test. See Marsh v. Chambers, 463 U.S. 783, 103 S.Ct. 3330, 77 L.Ed.2d 1019 (1983) (upholding legislature's practice of opening of each day of legislature with a prayer by a chaplain); Lynch v. Donnelly, 465 U.S. 668, 104 S.Ct. 1355, 79 L.Ed.2d 604 (1984) (upholding city action of erecting a Christmas display on public property which included a nativity scene), rehearing denied 466 U.S. 994, 104 S.Ct. 2376, 80 L.Ed.2d 848 (1984). See § 21.3, supra.

volvement between religion and public schools—that have been the subject of Supreme Court opinions. One can then evaluate the Court's use of establishment clause tests in terms of specific problem areas.

(b) Released or Shared Time

The Supreme Court has considered public school programs involving the exemption of public school students from class so that they could receive religious instruction. The Court has held that the students could not be given religious instruction on the public school premises because such a program has the direct effect of aiding the establishment of religious beliefs. However, the state may release students from school so that they may attend religious instruction away from the public school. This early release of students is viewed as only an accommodation of individual religious preferences rather than an aid to the religions.

In *Illinois ex rel. McCollum v. Board of Education* [2] the Court held invalid a system whereby religious teachers came into the public school to give instruction to students. The program allowed members of any religious organization to instruct those students who had requested the instruction. Students who did not request instruction remained in the school, as the programs took place during a time when the compulsory attendance laws required all students below the age of 17 to be in school.

The Court found a direct aid to religion as government facilities were being used for the propagation of religious beliefs. While no formal test was employed, the opinion noted that this policy removed any "wall" between church and state as it had the government giving direct help to the advancing of religion. It was irrelevant that all religions might be helped by the program as the first amendment was held to forbid the advancing of religious beliefs over non-religious ones as well as the advancement of a particular sect.

Only four years later, in *Zorach v. Clauson,* [3] the Court upheld a program where students were released from public schools so that they could receive religious instruction at other locations. Although all children were required to be either in school or at religious classes during this period, a majority of the justices found that the program did not constitute government aid to religion. Because no government funds or other support went to the advancing of religious ends, this was considered to be only the accommodation of the desires of individual students and their families to be free of the public school system so that they could receive their religious education. Moreover, there was no religious doctrine taught on public property, in the public schools.

---

2. 333 U.S. 203, 68 S.Ct. 461, 92 L.Ed. 649 (1948).

3. 343 U.S. 306, 72 S.Ct. 679, 96 L.Ed. 954 (1952).

The key concept here is the neutral principle of "accommodation." If there had been proof that the program coerced students into attending religious classes, the state support of those programs would violate both the free exercise and the establishment clauses. However, there was no such proof in *Zorach* and, on this basis, the majority found the program to be a mere accommodation of the desires of individual students to exercise rights whose values are reflected in the free exercise clause.[4]

(c) Prayers or Bible Reading

The use of officially authorized prayers or Bible readings for motivational purpose constitutes a direct violation of the establishment clause. Even though a practice may not be coercive, active support of a particular belief raises the danger of eventual establishment of state approved religious views. Although a given prayer or practice may not favor any one sect, the principle of neutrality in religious matters is violated by any program which places tacit government approval on "religious" views or practices. Under the basic purpose-and-effect test these programs must be found to violate the first amendment. The purpose of the program might be a neutral or secular one of state accommodation of student desires. However, the effect of any such practice is to give government aid and support to the advancing of religious beliefs. Thus the programs were held invalid even prior to the use of the additional entanglement test.

Not all religious references must be banned from the public schools. Religion and religious literature, including the Bible, may be studied in a purely academic manner. So long as the study does not amount to prayer or the advancement of religious beliefs, a teacher may discuss such materials in the secular course of study.[5] Religious references in official ceremonies, including some school exercises, will

---

4. In Board of Education of Westside Community Schools v. Mergens, 496 U.S. 226, 110 S.Ct. 2356, 110 L.Ed.2d 191 (1990) the Supreme Court upheld a federal statute that gave "equal access" to student groups (including religious student groups) to the premises of high schools that received federal financial assistance. The federal statute accomplished this result by prohibiting such high schools from discrimination against student groups, on the basis of the group's beliefs if the school had created a limited open forum for any non-curriculum related student organization. The federal statute allowed the student groups to meet only at times other than the times at which class or other instruction was held; these student meetings would not involve faculty or staff as active participants in the religious meetings. Therefore, the federal statute did not involve the subsidy to or endorsement of religion that was involved in the instruction on school premises cases. 496 U.S. at 250–51, 110 S.Ct. at 2372 (plurality opinion by Justice O'Connor). See § 21.5(e) infra for an examination of equal access issues and cases.

5. School District v. Schempp, 374 U.S. 203, 225, 83 S.Ct. 1560, 1573, 10 L.Ed.2d 844 (1963).

See generally, Leedes, Taking the Bible Seriously, 1987, Am.B.Found.Res.J. 311; Dellinger, The Sound of Silence: An Epistle on Prayer and the Constitution, 95 Yale L.J. 1631 (1986).

be also allowed as a part of our secularized traditions and not an advancement of religion similar to state approved prayer.[6]

In *Engel v. Vitale*[7] the Supreme Court held that the use of a "nondenominational prayer" written by government authorities violated the establishment clause. The decision was easily reached because the government writing of a prayer was sponsorship of religious views similar to the official establishment of religion, which many of the framers of the first amendment had fled from and feared. Moreover, like the program in *Illinois ex rel. McCollum v. Board of Education*, discussed above, the religious exercise was performed on school property.

In a second case, *School District v. Schempp*,[8] the Court examined school programs of voluntary Bible reading or the use of the "Lord's Prayer." Unlike *Engel*, it was not part of the job of any public official to compose a prayer: the prayer came from the Bible. Yet this difference did not save the program from Constitutional attack. In *Schempp* the Court used the purpose and effect test to review the programs under the establishment clause. Although the program was voluntary and did not favor any sect, the effect was to aid the advancement of religion; it constituted a generalized religious ceremony. Thus, it violated the concepts of separation and neutrality between government and religion and there was but one dissent to the invalidation of these practices.[9]

An important part of the *Schempp* decision was the majority's answer to the argument that elimination of voluntary prayers would amount to government sponsorship of an anti-religious position. The Court found that neutrality in religious matters did not constitute the implied teaching of a "religion of secularism."[10] This viewpoint is important to the decisions involving aid to religious schools for it rejects the argument that providing publicly funded education only in secular schools inhibits the free exercise of religion by those who want their children trained in a religious manner. So long as the state does not legally prohibit private, religious schools, its offering of public edu-

---

6. Engel v. Vitale, 370 U.S. 421, 435 n. 21, 82 S.Ct. 1261, 1269 n. 21, 8 L.Ed.2d 601 (1962). The Court has upheld a state legislature's employment of a chaplain and use of an opening prayer. These practices were upheld on the basis of the history of legislative prayer, which dated back to the Congress which drafted the first amendment. The ruling does not modify the principles regarding religious activity in public schools. Marsh v. Chambers, 463 U.S. 783, 103 S.Ct. 3330, 77 L.Ed.2d 1019 (1983); see note 15, infra.

7. 370 U.S. 421, 82 S.Ct. 1261, 8 L.Ed.2d 601 (1962).

8. 374 U.S. 203, 83 S.Ct. 1560, 10 L.Ed.2d 844 (1963).

9. Justice Stewart was the sole dissenter. 374 U.S. at 308, 83 S.Ct. at 1616. It is interesting to note that while these decisions were the subject of intense public debate, there was virtual unanimity among the justices on these issues.

10. 374 U.S. at 225–26, 83 S.Ct. at 1573–74.

cation in this manner is not a violation of the religion clauses.[11]

In *Stone v. Graham*,[12] the Supreme Court held that a Kentucky statute requiring the posting of the Ten Commandments on the wall of each public classroom in the state violated the establishment clause. Any use of prayers or Bible passages in school must be reviewed under the three part test for compatibility with the establishment clause. First, the statute must have a secular legislative purpose. Second, its primary effect must neither advance nor inhibit religion. Third, the statute must not create an excessive entanglement between government and religion.[13] Any use of prayers or religious literature for inspirational purpose would violate the purpose and effect tests for validity.

The Supreme Court's opinion in *Stone* stated that the preeminent purpose of the Kentucky statute was "plainly religious in nature" and had no secular legislative purpose, even though the legislation included a statement of avowed secular purpose.[14] The fact that the Bible verses were to be posted rather than read aloud, and the fact that they were to be financed by voluntary private contributions, had no bearing on the validity of the statute because it had a plainly religious purpose, and "it is no defense to urge that the religious practices here may be relatively minor encroachments on the first amendment."

In a different context, the Supreme Court has upheld governmental involvement with prayer services. In *Marsh v. Chambers*[15] the Court upheld a state legislature's action in employing a chaplain for the primary purpose of opening each legislative day with a prayer. The majority opinion by Chief Justice Burger relied heavily on the history of American legislatures (including the Continental Congress and the first United States Congress) employing legislative chaplains and prayer in the legislative day. The majority opinion stated that history alone "could not justify contemporary violations" of the establishment clause. Yet the Chief Justice found that historical evidence indicated that the Court should not apply the three-part test so strictly as to find

11. The Court's rulings on aid to parochial schools and the refusals to recognize a state interest in enabling students to attend those schools are the subject of § 21.4(a), supra.

12. 449 U.S. 39, 101 S.Ct. 192, 66 L.Ed.2d 199 (1980), rehearing denied 449 U.S. 1104, 101 S.Ct. 904, 66 L.Ed.2d 832 (1981), on remand 612 S.W.2d 133 (Ky. 1981).

13. 449 U.S. at 40, 101 S.Ct. at 193, citing Lemon v. Kurtzman, 403 U.S. 602, 612–13, 91 S.Ct. 2105, 2111, 29 L.Ed.2d 745 (1971), rehearing denied 404 U.S. 876, 92 S.Ct. 24, 30 L.Ed.2d 123 (1971), on remand 348 F.Supp. 300 (E.D.Pa.1972).

14. The Kentucky legislation required the following notation in small print at the bottom of each posted copy of the Ten Commandments: "The secular application of the Ten Commandments is clearly seen in its adoption as the fundamental legal code of Western Civilization and the Common Law of the United States." K.R.S. 158.178 (1980). Stone v. Graham, 449 U.S. 39, 40 n. 1, 101 S.Ct. 192, 193 n. 1, 66 L.Ed.2d 199 (1980), rehearing denied 449 U.S. 1104, 101 S.Ct. 904, 66 L.Ed.2d 832 (1981), on remand 612 S.W.2d 133 (Ky. 1981).

15. 463 U.S. 783, 103 S.Ct. 3330, 77 L.Ed.2d 1019 (1983).

that this practice was a violation of the establishment clause because such activity, in fact, never had resulted in an establishment of religion or encroachment on the separation of religious beliefs from governmental functions. Nothing in the *Marsh v. Chambers* majority opinion, however, shed any light on whether the Court would uphold practices in public schools which might have some incidental religious effect but which do not involve the type of prayers or inspirational use of the Bible which have been found to violate the establishment clause in earlier cases.[16]

Some state governments and school boards, following the school prayer decisions, passed statutes either requiring or allowing a period of silence in each public school day, during which time students would be free to think, meditate, or pray silently. In *Wallace v. Jaffree*,[17] the Court did not have to rule on a true moment of silence statute. The litigation that resulted in the Supreme Court case initially involved constitutional challenges to three Alabama statutes. The first statute, enacted in 1978 by the Alabama legislature, established a "period of silence not to exceed one minute in duration, that should be observed for meditation." The Supreme Court did not have to rule on this statute because the persons who attacked the statute in the lower court, "abandoned any claim" that the statute was unconstitutional in their argument before the Supreme Court of the United States.[18] The second statute passed by Alabama, in 1981, authorized a period of silence "for meditation or voluntary prayer". The third statute was enacted in 1982; it stated that any teacher "in any educational institution within the state of Alabama, recognizing that the Lord God is one, at the beginning of any homeroom or any class" could lead a legislatively prescribed prayer.[19] There was no significant issue regarding the constitutionality of the third statute which was clearly invalid on the basis of the Court's previous rulings regarding government prescribed prayer.[20] Thus, the only significant issue facing the Court in *Wallace*

---

16. See also, Lynch v. Donnelly, 465 U.S. 668, 104 S.Ct. 1355, 79 L.Ed.2d 604 (1984), rehearing denied 466 U.S. 994, 104 S.Ct. 2376, 80 L.Ed.2d 848 (1984), in which the Supreme Court upheld a city policy which called for the erection of a Christmas display in a public park that included a Christian nativity scene in part on the basis that such displays of the nativity scene, through historic use in the country, had come to constitute observance of a general holiday season and not the endorsement of a religious faith or the granting of a benefit to a particular faith. In this case, as in *Marsh*, Chief Justice Burger wrote a majority opinion that focused on the history of this particular practice as he found that there was no violation of the three-part purpose-effect-entanglement

test. The opinion did not indicate that the Court would modify its strict view against the government's use of prayer or inspirational bible readings in public schools.

17. 472 U.S. 38, 105 S.Ct. 2479, 86 L.Ed.2d 29 (1985).

18. 472 U.S. at 40 n. 1, 105 S.Ct. at 2481 n. 1.

19. The statute and prayer are set out at 472 U.S. at 40 n. 3, 105 S.Ct. at 2481 n. 3.

20. The district court upheld the government prescribed prayer and all three of the statutes on the theory that the Supreme Court rulings regarding religious activities were not binding precedent on the states because, according to the district

was the constitutionality of the period of silence for "meditation or voluntary prayer" statute.

The Court found in *Wallace* one of the rare cases in which a piece of legislation passed by a legislative body was unconstitutional because the legislature was motivated only by a religious purpose in enacting the statute. The Court ruled that the "meditation or voluntary prayer" statute violated the establishment clause due to the religious purpose of the legislature. This ruling made it unnecessary to consider whether a similarly worded statute enacted for religiously neutral reasons by another legislature might be upheld or whether such a moment of silence statute could be upheld, if at all, only if it referred to meditation rather than prayer.

Six justices found that the legislative history of the Alabama statute made it clear that the law at issue was passed only for a religious purpose and that this improper motivation required the Court to invalidate the law. Justice Stevens, in a majority opinion for five members of the Court, stated that the legislation would have to be invalidated under the first amendment if it was motivated entirely by a

court, the first amendment religion clauses should never have been made applicable to the states. This ruling of the district court had been reversed by the court of appeals. The Supreme Court, in fact, had earlier summarily affirmed the Court of Appeals ruling overturning the district court. Jaffree v. Board of School Commissioners, 554 F.Supp. 1104 (S.D.Ala.1983) (summary affirmance and notation of probable jurisdiction as to one question in the case), reversed Jaffree v. Wallace, 705 F.2d 1526, 1535 (11th Cir.1983), court of appeals affirmed Wallace v. Jaffree, 466 U.S. 924, 104 S.Ct. 1704, 80 L.Ed.2d 178 (1984). The Supreme Court now took time to explain why it should reverse what the majority opinion kindly referred to only as the "remarkable" ruling of the district court regarding the applicability of the first amendment to the states. The majority opinion by Justice Stevens found, as the Court has in all cases since the 1940's, that the values of the first amendment are a fundamental part of the liberty protected by the fourteenth amendment. The federal government and local governments are prohibited from interfering with principles which the Supreme Court has delineated under the establishment and free exercise clauses of the first amendment. Wallace v. Jaffree, 472 U.S. 38, 49–56, 105 S.Ct. 2479, 2486–2489, 86 L.Ed.2d 29 (1985).

Justice O'Connor's concurring opinion in *Wallace,* 472 U.S. at 68, 105 S.Ct. at 2496,

and the dissenting opinions of Chief Justice Burger, 472 U.S. at 86, 105 S.Ct. at 2505, and Justice White, 472 U.S. at 91, 105 S.Ct. at 2508 questioned the strictness of the court's ruling. These separate opinions were based in part on justices' desire to reassess some earlier decisions of the Court, and in part on a belief that the history of the first and fourteenth amendments did not justify judicial exclusion of all religious activity or aid to religion from state school systems. However, Justice Rehnquist was alone in voting to approve the district court's ruling based on his reexamination of the history of the first amendment. This reexamination led Justice Rehnquist to believe that the first amendment had limited applicability to state and local governmental activities which have an incidental effect of advancing religion through what he described as a "generalized endorsement of prayer." Wallace v. Jaffree, 472 U.S. 38, 91, 105 S.Ct. 2479, 2508, 86 L.Ed.2d 29 (1985) (Rehnquist, J., dissenting).

For an analysis of Justice O'Connor's "No Endorsement" test see Smith, Symbols, Perceptions, and Doctrinal Illusions: Establishment, Neutrality and the "No Endorsement Test" 86 Mich.L.Rev. 266 (1987); Loewy, Rethinking Government Neutrality Towards Religion Under the Establishment Clause: The Untapped Potential of Justice O'Connor's Insight, 64 N.C.L.Rev. 1049 (1986).

purpose to advance religion.[21] Statements of legislators inserted into the legislative record, and testimony of the bill's sponsor before the district court, made it clear that the persons who drafted and passed the amendment had not attempted to justify the statute in terms of any nonreligious purpose. The majority opinion concluded that "the legislative intent to return prayer to the public schools is, of course, quite different from merely protecting every student's right to engage in voluntary prayer during an appropriate moment of silence during the school day." Although the Court did not rule on a true moment of silence statute, it appears that such a statute may be upheld if it was not passed for entirely religious purposes and if it was not used as a means for governmental encouragement of religious beliefs or religious activities on public school property.[22]

(d) Modification of the Curriculum for Religious Purposes

The Supreme Court has ruled that a state may not eliminate the teaching of certain ideas related to normal classroom subjects because they conflict with religious beliefs. In *Epperson v. Arkansas*[23] the Court reviewed a statute which made it unlawful for teachers in state schools to teach a theory of human biological evolution. The Court held that the statute violated the establishment clause because it had a religious purpose—thus failing the secular purpose test. It was an impermissible breach of the principle of government neutrality for the state to eliminate a particular piece of information from a course merely because it conflicted with some religious beliefs.

It should be noted that this case does not, by itself, eliminate the ability of the state to adjust or eliminate the subjects that are taught in its school system. Justice Black, in a concurring opinion, noted that a state should be able to eliminate any given subject matter from its school system without raising a first amendment issue.[24] This principle would seem to be true, for if the state is under no obligation to teach a specific subject there should be nothing wrong with eliminating a given course.

21. Wallace v. Jaffree, 472 U.S. 38, 56, 105 S.Ct. 2479, 2490, 86 L.Ed.2d 29 (1985).

22. Justice Powell concurring in the opinion of the Court, and Justice O'Connor concurring only in the judgment, both stated that they believed that a true moment of silence statute should be upheld. Wallace v. Jaffree, 472 U.S. 38, 62, 105 S.Ct. 2479, 2493, 86 L.Ed.2d 29 (1985) (Powell, J., concurring); 472 U.S. at 68, 105 S.Ct. at 2496 (O'Connor, J., concurring in the judgment). Chief Justice Burger and Justices White and Rehnquist dissented in *Wallace;* see note 20, supra. Thus, five justices appear to be willing to uphold such a statute in a future case.

In Karcher v. May, 484 U.S. 72, 108 S.Ct. 388, 98 L.Ed.2d 327 (1987) the Supreme Court avoided ruling on the constitutionality of a statute providing for a minute of silence at the beginning of a school day. The Court in *Karcher* ruled that the appellants, who were former members of the state legislature, could not appeal from an adverse judgment regarding the minute of silence statute once these individuals had lost their status as officers of the state legislature.

23. 393 U.S. 97, 89 S.Ct. 266, 21 L.Ed.2d 228 (1968).

24. 393 U.S. at 113–14, 89 S.Ct. at 275–76 (Black, J., concurring).

However, there are two bases for making an exception to this deference to state educational authority. First, where the state has eliminated only one element from a course of study for religious reasons it has attempted to help the religious point of view by eliminating ideas which would challenge that view. In *Epperson,* the Court focused extensively on the evidence that the state's motivation for excluding the teaching of evolution was improper. Second, where the state can offer no secular educational reason for altering the curriculum there is no reason to defer to the state's educational policy. It was this unusual case of an open attempt to aid certain religious views that was presented to the Court in *Epperson.* This official attempt to aid a specific religious view openly breached the principle of neutrality, which is the core of the Religion Clauses.

In *Edwards v. Aguillard,*[25] the Supreme Court, by a seven to two vote of the justices, invalidated another legislative attempt to modify the curriculum of the public schools for religious purposes.[26] At issue in *Edwards* was the Louisiana "balanced treatment for creation-science and evolution-science in public school instruction" legislation. Under the legislation, any public school that taught the theory of human biological evolution was required to give equal treatment to "creation science." The majority opinion by Justice Brennan found that the legislative history of the statute, and the language of the statute itself, demonstrated that the legislation was designed to promote religion and, therefore, that it violated the establishment clause.[27]

The state had attempted to show that the law promoted academic freedom and the comprehensiveness of science instruction; but the statute itself, in the majority's view, undercut these arguments by removing the teachers' authority to examine only theories of human biological evolution and discouraging rather than encouraging the teaching of all scientific theories about the origins of the human race

25. 482 U.S. 578, 107 S.Ct. 2573, 96 L.Ed.2d 510 (1987).

26. Justice Scalia, joined by Chief Justice Rehnquist, found that the statute had a non-religious purpose; they also challenged the validity of the secular purpose test. 482 U.S. at 609, 107 S.Ct. 2591 (Scalia, J., dissenting, joined by Rehnquist, C.J.). Justice White concurred only in the judgment of the court, 482 U.S. at 608, 107 S.Ct. at 2590 (White, J., concurring in the judgment). Justices Powell and O'Connor wrote a concurring opinion to emphasize that legislative actions with some religious purpose were not invalid unless the religious purpose predominated the legislative decision and that public school instruction could include references to religion so long as the references did not have the purpose

of advancing religious beliefs. 482 U.S. at 596, 107 S.Ct. at 2584 (Powell, J., joined by O'Connor, J., concurring).

27. Since 1971 the Supreme Court has required that legislation or other government elections which have the effect of advancing religion meet a three-part test: (1) the governmental entity adopting the law or regulation must have a secular purpose; (2) the statute's primary effect must neither advance nor inhibit religion; (3) the statute must not create an excessive entanglement between government and religion. The three-part test was created in a case regarding aid to religious schools; the test and its application in aid to religious institutions cases are examined in §§ 21.3, 21.4.

(by requiring the teaching of creation science when other theories of evolution were taught).

The Court did not attempt to restrict the authority of the legislatures or the school boards to design a curriculum for non-religious reasons. It would appear that all references to religion need not be excised from a public school curriculum. References to religion may be a part of public school instruction in history or literature, or any other subject, so long as the references to religion or a religious text do not have the purpose or effect of advancing religious goals.[28]

(e) Equal Access to School Facilities

In *Widmar v. Vincent*[29] the Supreme Court invalidated a state university regulation which denied access to school facilities to religious student organizations as a violation of the freedom of speech.[30] In so doing the Court provided some insight into the related problem of defining the scope of university involvement with religious organizations.

In 1977 the University of Missouri at Kansas City began to enforce a policy prohibiting the use of university buildings or grounds "for purposes of religious worship or religious teaching." University officials informed a registered student religious group that the University was discontinuing what had been a four-year practice of permitting the group to conduct its meetings in university facilities. The majority opinion in *Widmar* by Justice Powell found that once it had opened its facilities for use by student groups the university had created a public forum. It was then required to justify any content-based exclusions under the applicable standard of review and the regulation would be

---

28. The majority opinion by Justice Brennan noted that the potential for influencing college students' thinking about religion through the introduction of or references to religious documents was less than the potential for influencing the beliefs of grade school and high school students in public school courses. For this reason, state supported colleges and universities had greater authority than state grade schools or high schools to offer courses regarding religion or theology. Edwards v. Aguillard, 482 U.S. 578, 584 n. 5, 107 S.Ct. 2573, 2577 n. 5, 96 L.Ed.2d 510 (1987).

Justices Powell and O'Connor noted that: "As a matter of history, school children can and should properly be informed of all aspects of this Nation's religious heritage. I would see no constitutional problem if school children were taught the nature of the Founding Fathers' religious beliefs and how these beliefs affected the attitudes of the times and the structure of our govern-

ment. Courses in comparative religion are, of course, customary and constitutionally appropriate." 482 U.S. at 605–09, 107 S.Ct. at 2589–90 (Powell, J., joined by O'Connor, J., concurring).

In a case that was decided before the Supreme Court's adoption of the three-part purpose-effect-entanglement test, Justice Brennan, the author of the majority opinion in *Edwards*, stated his belief that a state school would be allowed to make references to the Bible and other religious literature so long as the courses did not constitute governmental aid to or promotion of religion. School District of Abington Tp., Pa. v. Schempp, 374 U.S. 203, 300–302, 83 S.Ct. 1560, 1612–13, 10 L.Ed.2d 844 (1963) (Brennan, J., concurring).

29. 454 U.S. 263, 102 S.Ct. 269, 70 L.Ed.2d 440 (1981).

30. See §§ 20.45–20.47, supra.

upheld only if it was necessary to serve a compelling state interest and if it was narrowly drawn to achieve that end.

Justice Powell's opinion stated that the university's interest in maintaining a strict separation of church and state, as mandated by the establishment clauses of the federal and Missouri constitutions was compelling. However, Justice Powell, applying the three pronged purpose-effect-entanglement test, did not agree that a policy allowing equal access to university facilities to religious groups would violate the establishment clause.

He found that the first and last parts of the test—purpose and entanglement—were clearly met: a policy fostering an open university forum for all registered student groups has a secular purpose. Opening facilities to all students would not involve excessive entanglement between government and religion. In addition, the Court was satisfied that the "primary effect" of allowing student religious groups to share the limited public forum, open to all forms of discourse, was not to benefit religion. Any religious benefits would be merely incidental for two reasons. First, the creation of a limited public forum at the university, and allowing religious groups access to that forum, does not confer state approval on any religious sect or practice. Second, the forum was available to a broad class of non-religious, as well as religious, groups. In the absence of concrete evidence that campus religious groups would dominate the open forum, the Court was unwilling to find that the benefits to religion were to any degree greater than the general benefits such as police and fire protection which were clearly compatible with the establishment clause.

Justice Powell also held that, despite the fact that the Missouri constitution required stricter separation of church and state than the federal Constitution, the State's interest in achieving complete separation of church and state was limited by the free exercise and free speech clauses of the first amendment and was not sufficiently compelling to justify the content-based discrimination against these students' speech activities.

It should be noted that in *Widmar* the Court ruled only that a state university could not engage in content-based discrimination against religious speech. If the university had not created the "public forum" it would not have been required to furnish facilities for use by religious groups. Thus, the case may be of little relevance to determining if high school student religious organizations must be allowed access to some high school facilities, where there may be no "public forum." [31]

31. The Supreme Court faced a related problem in McCreary v. Stone, 739 F.2d 716 (2d Cir.1984) (per curiam), judgment affirmed sub nom. by an evenly divided Court, Board of Trustees v. McCreary, 471 U.S. 83, 105 S.Ct. 1859, 85 L.Ed.2d 63 (1985). In this case, two groups sought to place a Nativity scene in a public park in a business district during the December holiday season. The village had no content-

In *Board of Education of Westside Community Schools v. Mergens* [32] the Supreme Court upheld a federal statute that requires any secondary school receiving federal financial assistance to provide "equal access" to student groups. The statute achieved this result by prohibiting a secondary school from denying equal access to student groups on the basis of the group's religious, political or philosophical beliefs (or the content of their speech) if (1) the school received federal financial assistance and (2) if the school had created a "limited open forum" by providing access to any "noncurriculum related student group." The *Mergens* case presented only the issue of whether the statutory access granted to religiously oriented student groups violated the establishment clause. The Court did not reach the question of whether the free speech principles that it had examined in *Widmar*, would require a high school to provide access to school facilities in a situation where the federal statute did not apply.

Justice O'Connor wrote an opinion in *Mergens* that was, in part, a majority opinion and, in part, a plurality opinion. In the portions of her opinion that were joined by a majority of Justices, Justice O'Connor interpreted and explained the meaning and coverage of the federal statute. The majority concluded that the statutory term "limited open forum" was different from the Supreme Court's definition, in first amendment cases, of a "limited public forum." The statute applied

neutral regulations that precluded the display; the village allowed other types of decorations, displays and speech-related activities in the park. The village denied consent to groups wishing to place a Nativity scene on the park although no content-neutral regulation required the denial. The court of appeals held that the village could not rely on the establishment clause principles set forth in supreme court cases to deny these groups permission to place the Nativity scene in the park. The court of appeals ruled that a content-based denial of access appeared to violate Widmar v. Vincent, 454 U.S. 263, 102 S.Ct. 269, 70 L.Ed.2d 440 (1981), but that the placing of the Nativity scene, or any other speech activities in the park, could be subject to time, place, or manner restrictions. Justice Powell did not take part in the Supreme Court review of the court of appeals decision and the other eight justices divided evenly in this case. The court of appeals thus was affirmed by an evenly divided Court and without an opinion issuing from the United States Supreme Court.

In Bender v. Williamsport Area School District, 475 U.S. 534, 106 S.Ct. 1326, 89 L.Ed.2d 501 (1986), rehearing denied 476 U.S. 1132, 106 S.Ct. 2003, 90 L.Ed.2d 682 (1986), the Supreme Court avoided ruling

on whether students in a student-initiated, nondenominational prayer club had a constitutional right to meet in a public school. The Court in *Bender* ruled that an individual school board member did not have standing to pursue an appeal of a decision against the school board, which would have given the student prayer club access to the school. Because the school board had not appealed, and the individual did not have standing in his individual capacity, the majority opinion did not reach the substantive issue in the case. Three dissenting Justices in the case believed that the individual member of the school board had standing and that the establishment clause did not require a public high school to prevent student initiated groups from meeting during an extra curricular activity period. 475 U.S. at 551, 106 S.Ct. at 1336 (Burger, C.J., joined by White and Rehnquist, JJ., dissenting); 475 U.S. at 555, 106 S.Ct. at 1338 (Powell, J., dissenting).

See generally, Laycock, Equal Access and Moments of Silence: The Equal Status of Religious Speech by Private Speakers, 81 Nw.U.L.Rev. 1 (1986).

32. Board of Education of Westside Community Schools v. Mergens, 496 U.S. 226, 110 S.Ct. 2356, 110 L.Ed.2d 191 (1990).

whenever a "noncurriculum related" student group was given access to school facilities. A "noncurriculum related" student group, according to the majority, was any student group whose activities and purpose did not directly relate to courses offered by the school. Thus, both a chess club and a student organization that provided social services for needy persons in the community were not curriculum related groups, even though math professors and social science professors at the school might strongly encourage participation in those clubs. The equal access requirement of the statute only prohibited the denial of access to school premises at noninstructional times to a group if the denial was based on the religious or political content of the group's speech or beliefs. The Act allowed a faculty member to monitor the student group's activities, but the Act limited participation by school officials at any meeting of religious groups. Persons who were not a part of the faculty, staff, or student body would not be able to direct or regularly attend the activities of student groups at the public school premises.

Although the constitutionality of the Equal Access Act was upheld by an eight to one vote of the Justices, there was no majority opinion explaining why the statute was consistent with the establishment clause.[33] Justice O'Connor wrote an opinion, which was joined by Chief Justice Rehnquist and Justices White and Blackmun, in which she found that the statute complied with the three part test—the purpose, primary effect, excessive entanglement tests—used most commonly by the Supreme Court in establishment clause cases.[34] First, Justice O'Connor found that the legislative purpose of prohibiting discrimina-

---

33. Board of Education of Westside Community Schools v. Mergens, 496 U.S. 226, 246–53, 110 S.Ct. 2356, 2370–73, 110 L.Ed.2d 191 (1990) (Part III of Justice O'Connor's opinion, in which she examined the constitutionality of the statute, was joined by Chief Justice Rehnquist and Justices White and Blackmun). There were two concurring opinions. 496 U.S. at 258, 110 S.Ct. at 2376 (Kennedy, J., joined by Scalia, J., concurring in part and concurring in the judgment); 496 U.S. at 262, 110 S.Ct. at 2378 (Marshall, J., joined by Brennan, J., concurring in the judgment). Justice Stevens was the sole dissenter, his dissent focused on the interpretation of the statute. 496 U.S. at 270, 110 S.Ct. at 2383 (Stevens, J., dissenting).

34. The three pronged test is referred to as the "*Lemon* test" because it was first clearly stated by the Court in Lemon v. Kurtzman, 403 U.S. 602, 91 S.Ct. 2105, 29 L.Ed.2d 745 (1971), rehearing denied 404 U.S. 876, 92 S.Ct. 24, 30 L.Ed.2d 123 (1971). Under this three-part test a law is invalid unless: (1) the law has a secular purpose; (2) the primary effect of the law is neither

the advancement or inhibition of religion; (3) the law does not give rise to an excessive entanglement between government and religion. This test is examined in §§ 21.3, 21.4 of this Treatise. Justice O'Connor has at times advocated replacement of the three-part test with a test which would determine whether the government action at issue involved an unconstitutional "endorsement" of religion. See, e.g., Lynch v. Donnelly, 465 U.S. 668, 690, 104 S.Ct. 1355, 1366, 79 L.Ed.2d 604 (1984) (O'Connor, J., concurring), rehearing denied 466 U.S. 994, 104 S.Ct. 2376, 80 L.Ed.2d 848 (1984). It now appears that the endorsement test used by Justice O'Connor may be blending with the three-part *Lemon* test; the endorsement test may be the way in which the Court determines whether a particular government law or program has a primary effect of advancing or inhibiting religion. See, County of Allegheny v. American Civil Liberties Union, 492 U.S. 573, 590–94, 109 S.Ct. 3086, 3099–3101, 106 L.Ed.2d 472 (1989), on remand 887 F.2d 260 (3d Cir. 1989).

tion on the basis of political, philosophical or religious views was not a legislative purpose that violated the establishment clause.[35] Second, Justice O'Connor found that the law did not have a primary effect of advancing religion, because the law did not involve a subsidy to the teaching of religion that might be seen as the government endorsement of religious beliefs.[36] The law did not involve meetings of religious groups during instructional time, the participation of school officials in the meetings, or any direct or indirect coercion of student participation in such groups.[37] Finally, the plurality found that the law did not create an "excessive entanglement" between government and religion, because any faculty sponsor for the group would be unable to participate actively in the religious group's meetings.

Justices Marshall and Brennan concurred only in the judgment of the Court, even though they did not challenge the use of the three-part test to evaluate the constitutionality of the statute.[38] These Justices wrote separately to state their belief that any school that allowed a religiously oriented student group to meet on its premises would have to take steps to avoid giving any appearance that it was endorsing the views of the religious group. Justice O'Connor's plurality did not explain how an individual school might violate the establishment clause by appearing to endorse a particular religious group's beliefs.

Justices Kennedy and Scalia voted to uphold the Act, but they refused to join Justice O'Connor's use of the three-part establishment clause test.[39] These two Justices believed that only two questions should be asked in determining whether the equal access law was

---

35. Board of Education of Westside Community Schools v. Mergens, 496 U.S. 226, 248–49, 110 S.Ct. 2356, 2371, 110 L.Ed.2d 191 (1990) (O'Connor, J., joined by Rehnquist, C.J., and White and Blackmun, JJ.). The Supreme Court has found in other cases that the legislative "accommodation" of persons with religious beliefs is not a purpose that violates the establishment clause. See, Corporation of Presiding Bishop of Church of Jesus Christ of Latter–Day Saints v. Amos, 483 U.S. 327, 107 S.Ct. 2862, 97 L.Ed.2d 273 (1987), which is examined in § 21.15 of this Treatise.

36. Board of Education of Westside Community Schools v. Mergens, 496 U.S. 226, 249–53, 110 S.Ct. 2356, 2371–73, 110 L.Ed.2d 191 (1990) (O'Connor, J., joined by Rehnquist, C.J., and White and Blackmun, JJ.). The plurality therefore found that this program did not suffer from the constitutional defect in the "release time" programs whereby students were released from regular class sessions, at a portion of

the day in which they were otherwise required to be in school, in order to attend meetings of religious organizations conducted on school premises. Such a program had been invalidated in Illinois ex rel. McCollum v. Board of Education, 333 U.S. 203, 68 S.Ct. 461, 92 L.Ed. 649 (1948). The "release time" decisions of the Supreme Court are examined at the beginning of this section of the Treatise.

37. Board of Education of Westside Community Schools v. Mergens, 496 U.S. 226, 251–52, 110 S.Ct. 2356, 2372–73, 110 L.Ed.2d 191 (1990) (O'Connor, J., joined by Rehnquist, C.J., and White and Blackmun, JJ.).

38. Board of Education of Westside Community Schools v. Mergens, 496 U.S. 226, 262, 110 S.Ct. 2356, 2378, 110 L.Ed.2d 191 (1990) (Marshall, J., joined by Brennan, J., concurring in the judgment).

39. 496 U.S. at 258, 110 S.Ct. at 2376 (Kennedy, J., joined by Scalia, J., concurring in part and concurring in the judgment).

consistent with the establishment clause. First, did the law give direct benefits to religion in such a way as to establish a state religion or to have a clear tendency to establish a state religion? Second, did the government act coerce student participation in religious activities? These two Justices found that both questions should be answered in the negative and, therefore, that the Act was constitutional. They did not believe that the establishment clause requires the Court to determine whether the law could be described as government endorsement of religion. They would not use the purpose, effect, and entanglement tests to place significant restrictions on government accommodation of religion.

III. THE FREE EXERCISE CLAUSE

§ 21.6 Introduction—Overview

The text of the Constitution contains one specific provision regarding religious freedom. Article VI prohibits the use of any religious test as a condition or qualification for holding any office or position in the federal government.[1]

The first amendment provides, in part, that Congress shall make law "prohibiting the free exercise" of religion.[2] The free exercise clause, like all of the guarantees of the first amendment, applies to state and local governments through the fourteenth amendment.[3]

The Supreme Court has invalidated very few government actions on the basis of the free exercise clause. The Court has consistently held that the government may not punish religious beliefs. The government may not impose burdens on, or give benefits to, people solely because of their religious beliefs. Because federal, state and local governmental entities have not engaged in many activities that could

---

§ 21.6

1. "[N]o Religious test shall ever be required as a qualification to any office of public trust under the United States." U.S. Const. art. VI.

2. "Congress shall make no law respecting an establishment of religion or prohibiting the free exercise thereof ..." U.S. Const. amend 1.

For thoughtful discussions of the relationship between the establishment clause and free exercise clause decisions and the views expressed in Supreme Court opinions regarding the value of religious freedom, see, Smith, the special place of religion in the Constitution, 1983 Sup.Ct.Rev. 83; Greenawalt, Religion as a Concept in a Constitutional Law, 72 Calif.L.Rev. 753 (1984); Johnson, Concepts and Compromise in First Amendment Religious Doctrine, 72

Calif.L.Rev. 817 (1984); Mansfield, The Religion Clauses of the First Amendment and the Philosophy of the Constitution, 72 Calif.L.Rev. 847 (1984).

See generally, Lupu, Where Rights Begin: The Problem of Burdens on the Free Exercise of Religion, 102 Harvard L.Rev. 933 (1989); Garvey, Churches and the Free Exercise of Religion, 4 Notre Dame Journal of Law, Ethics & Public Policy 567 (1990); Adams & Gordon, The Doctrine of Accommodation in the Jurisprudence of the Religion Clauses, 37 DePaul L.Rev. 317 (1988).

3. The free exercise clause was first held applicable to the states in Cantwell v. Connecticut, 310 U.S. 296, 60 S.Ct. 900, 84 L.Ed. 1213 (1940).

be described as the punishment of religious beliefs, there are very few Supreme Court decisions explaining the meaning of that constitutional restriction.

Some Supreme Court opinions have indicated that a law would be invalid if the legislature passed the law prohibiting some type of activity only because of the religious belief displayed by the activity or only because the government wished to burden a particular religion. In order to show that a law banning a certain type of activity (such as the killing of a certain animal) violated this prohibition, a person would have to prove that the legislative purpose was the promotion of religious beliefs or the suppression of the religious practices of a religious sect. The Supreme Court has not encountered such a case, presumably because the federal and state governments have not been banning persons from engaging in certain activities merely as a pretext to suppress an activity that is central to the religious beliefs of one sect.

The Supreme Court has wavered in deciding whether the free exercise clause protects religiously motivated actions from a law of general applicability. The Court has usually indicated that a religiously neutral law must be followed by all persons, including persons whose religious beliefs command them to disobey the law. However, in a few cases regarding the granting of unemployment compensation benefits, the Court required an exemption from a requirement for unemployment compensation to be granted to religious persons whose religious beliefs prevented them from meeting the eligibility requirement.

Religious Beliefs. Just as the establishment clause prohibits the government from providing benefits to one religious sect or denomination, the free exercise clause prohibits the government from denying benefits to, or imposing burdens on, persons because of their religious beliefs. The use of religious beliefs as any type of standard for the granting of government benefits and burdens might violate both the establishment and free exercise clauses by violating a religious neutrality principle that is central to both. As a technical matter, it is not clear whether the free exercise clause involves a total prohibition of the government use of religious beliefs as a means of allocating burdens and benefits or whether a government regulation that used religious beliefs in that manner could be justified by a "compelling" government interest. That technical distinction is probably unimportant, because the Court has given us no reason to believe that a government law or regulation that denied a benefit to persons because of their religious beliefs would be upheld by a compelling interest.

There are Supreme Court cases that have invalidated a law on its face because it punished religious beliefs. Just as the federal government is prohibited from using religion as a test for government office, the state and local governments are prohibited from using such tests by the free exercise clause.[4] The Supreme Court, by a unanimous vote but without a majority opinion, invalidated a law that prohibited ministers or members of religious orders from being members of the state legislature.[5] Several of the Justices believed that the exclusion of ministers and clerics from the legislature constituted the imposition of a special disability on someone because of the strength or nature of his religious views.

While the free exercise clause gives no one the right to disregard criminal laws of general applicability, the government may not create a criminal law that is based upon the falsity of a particular religious belief. Such a law would violate the free exercise clause.[6]

When different groups of a religious organization have a dispute over property, the state and federal courts are prohibited from deciding those controversies in any way that would involve a judicial ruling that was based upon the religious beliefs or religious doctrine. The government's use of religious doctrine to solve such a dispute should be held to violate both the establishment clause and the free exercise clause.[7]

Regulations of Actions—Exemptions for Religiously Motivated Actions? A person may be unable to comply with a law because his religious beliefs prohibit him from taking an action that is required by law (such as paying a certain type of tax) or because his religious beliefs require him to do something that is prohibited by the law (such as ingesting a drug that is banned by law). These types of situations raise the question of whether the free exercise clause requires the government to grant an exemption from a law of general applicability to a person who cannot conform his actions to the law due to his religious beliefs.

It is important to keep in mind the type of fact situation and the type of law, that is at issue in the cases regarding religiously motivated actions. The law at issue in such a case will not be a law that includes religious criteria for determining who is benefitted or burdened by the law. If the law made use of religious criteria as a standard for determining the legality of actions, or for the allocation of benefits or burdens from the government, the law would be invalid as the direct punishment of religious beliefs. The law at issue in the case will not be a law that was enacted only for the purpose of harming people of one religion (who could not comply with the law) because proof of such a

---

4. Torcaso v. Watkins, 367 U.S. 488, 81 S.Ct. 1680, 6 L.Ed.2d 982 (1961) (invalidating under the free exercise clause a state constitutional provision requiring a declaration of a belief in God as a prerequisite to taking public office). See footnote 1, supra, for the Article VI restriction on the federal government.

5. McDaniel v. Paty, 435 U.S. 618, 98 S.Ct. 1322, 55 L.Ed.2d 593 (1978). This case is examined in § 21.14.

6. The first amendment problems involved with "government inquiries into religious frauds" are examined in § 21.11.

7. The first amendment problems that arise from "state involvement in ecclesiastical disputes" are examined in § 21.12.

purpose on the part of the legislative entity would make the law invalid.

The law that will be at issue in a religiously motivated action case will be a law of general applicability that requires all persons (or a class of persons defined by criteria that do not include religious criteria) to take an action or refrain from taking a action. The claim of the individual in the case is that she cannot comply with the law and remain faithful to her religious beliefs. The person alleges that she should receive an exemption from the law because of the burden placed upon her religious beliefs by the need to conform her actions to a law that conflicts with her beliefs.

There would be no free exercise issue in a case if the individual seeking the exemption could not demonstrate that complying with the law constituted a burden on her religious beliefs. In some Supreme Court cases, there is dicta describing the burden placed upon the person who cannot comply with a law of general applicability as a "direct" or "indirect" burden. A law would directly burden a religion by making illegal a religious practice. An example of a law that created a direct burden would be a law prohibiting the use of a drug that was a part of the religious ceremony. A law that creates an indirect burden is one that does not regulate a religiously motivated practice, as such, but which makes the practice of a person's religion more difficult, usually by having the effect of imposing additional economic costs. An example of a law that creates an indirect burden is a legal requirement that shops close on Sunday; this law has the effect of imposing a burden on Sabbatarians whose religion requires them to refrain from work on Saturdays. If the Sabbatarians follow both their religious beliefs and the government law, they will have to close their shops on two days a week rather than one. Despite dicta in some cases indicating that a law imposing an indirect burden might be easier to uphold than a law which directly burdens religious activities, the distinction between direct and indirect burdens does not have any legal significance.

The basic free exercise principle regarding requested exemptions from laws of general applicability is easy to state: the free exercise clause does not require that an exemption from laws of general applicability to protect persons with religiously motivated actions. In 1990, a Supreme Court majority opinion stated: "We have never held that an individual's religious beliefs excuse him from compliance with an otherwise valid law prohibiting conduct that the state is free to regulate." [8]

No exemptions from criminal laws of general applicability are required by the free exercise clause. It may also be true that the free

---

8. Employment Division, Dept. of Human Resources v. Smith, 494 U.S. 872, 878–9, 110 S.Ct. 1595, 1602, 108 L.Ed.2d 876 (1990), rehearing denied __ U.S. __, 110 S.Ct. 2605, 110 L.Ed.2d 285 (1990).

exercise clause will not require exemptions from laws regulating conduct of all persons even if the law is not part of the general criminal law. For example, if an individual was granted a license to have a radio station that broadcast at a certain frequency and at a power level that would allow the radio station to be received by persons within a 100 mile area, the individual would not be free to increase the power in his station so that he could be heard throughout the United States, even if he is a religious minister who claims that God has commanded him to disregard the Federal Communications Commission regulations and to send the word of God to all people across the United States. If the radio station license holder violated federal regulations concerning the amount of power used in his station (regulations that are designed to prevent stations from having the effect of "jamming" each other) then the individual would be subject to punishment, which might involve a criminal punishment or simply the revocation of the license to broadcast.

Between 1963 and 1989, the Supreme Court used a two-step balancing process in determining whether an individual had a free exercise right to be exempted from a law of general applicability. First, the person claiming the exemption had to show that the law at issue interfered with the practice of his religion by requiring him to engage in a practice (or to refrain from engaging in a practice) in violation of his religion. The mere fact that the government had adopted a law or policy, that, was inconsistent with a person's religious beliefs would not create the type of burden that would trigger the balancing test. In the first step, it was the duty of the individual to show the burden imposed on her by the law. In the second step of the test, the Court required the government to demonstrate that granting an exemption to the person whose religious beliefs prevented compliance with the law would interfere with a governmental interest that could be described as "compelling". The government would be able to meet the second part of the test if the Court determined that the regulation at issue was tailored to promote an end that was important enough to override the burden on the free exercise of religion by persons who could not comply with the law.

Prior to 1963, the Court had found that the first amendment required an exemption to be granted from certain types of laws for persons who wanted to engage in first amendment activity such as speech or assembly (regardless of whether the first amendment activity involved religion). For example, the Court prohibited the government from punishing children who refused to pledge allegiance to the United States Flag at the start of the school day regardless of whether the child's refusal was based upon a religious belief or a nonreligious opposition to the Pledge of Allegiance.[9] Similarly, the Court exempted

---

9. West Virginia State Board of Education v. Barnette, 319 U.S. 624, 63 S.Ct. 1178, 87 L.Ed. 1628 (1943), overruling Min-ersville School District v. Gobitis, 310 U.S. 586, 60 S.Ct. 1010, 84 L.Ed. 1375 (1940).

both religious and nonreligious speakers from certain types of licensing systems that would have been validly applied to business that did not involve first amendment activity.[10]   The Court's opinions prior to 1963 did not give special protection to religiously motivated activity.

Between 1963 and 1989, the Supreme Court did not require significant governmental accommodation of religion.   Although Court opinions during this era used a balancing test and read as if the Supreme Court would give significant protection to religiously motivated actions, the Court ruled against persons seeking a religiously based exemption from laws of general applicability in every area except two: unemployment eligibility requirements and compulsory school attendance for Amish children of high school age.

First, the Supreme Court held that the government had to waive some types of conditions for the receipt of unemployment compensation by persons who could not comply with the condition because of their religious beliefs.   For example, unemployment compensation statutes often make a person ineligible for benefits if the person left his job voluntarily.   The rationale for an involuntary unemployment requirement is the need to avoid having persons use the unemployment benefit system as a type of paid vacation by working the minimum number of weeks to qualify for unemployment compensation and then resigning in order to receive a paid vacation through receipt of unemployment benefits.   The Supreme Court found that the requirement of involuntary termination from a job had to be waived for a person who resigned from his employment at a factory due to his religious beliefs, when his required duties were changed so as to include making parts for tanks and other weapons.[11]   Unemployment compensation statutes in many states require a person to demonstrate that he is looking for, and willing to accept work by being willing to accept jobs that are referred to him by the unemployment compensation administration.   Some of these unemployment compensation statutes require that a person be available for jobs that would require work from Monday through Saturday of each week.   The Supreme Court found that this type of six-day a week job availability requirement had to be waived for a person who was prohibited from working on Saturday because of his religious beliefs.[12]   In these unemployment compensation cases the Court found that the condition for unemployment benefits imposed a significant

---

10.   See, e.g., Cantwell v. Connecticut, 310 U.S. 296, 60 S.Ct. 900, 84 L.Ed. 1213 (1940).   These cases, which rested on the free speech and free exercise clause, are noted in § 21.7, infra.

11.   Thomas v. Review Board, 450 U.S. 707, 101 S.Ct. 1425, 67 L.Ed.2d 624 (1981), on remand 421 N.E.2d 642 (Ind.1981).   The

unemployment compensation cases are examined in greater detail in § 21.8.

12.   Sherbert v. Verner, 374 U.S. 398, 83 S.Ct. 1790, 10 L.Ed.2d 965 (1963); Hobbie v. Unemployment Appeals Commission of Florida, 480 U.S. 136, 107 S.Ct. 1046, 94 L.Ed.2d 190 (1987).

burden on an individual, in the sense of imposing a monetary deterrent to the exercise of the individual's religious beliefs. The Court found that the government interest in these unemployment compensation qualifications would not be impaired by a limited exemption for persons whose sincerely held religious beliefs prevented them from complying with the eligibility condition.

The Supreme Court held that an individual could be made ineligible for unemployment compensation if the basis for ineligibility was the fact that the individual was fired for job related misconduct that involved violation of a criminal law. When a drug counsellor at a privately owned drug rehabilitation facility was found to have violated criminal laws banning the use of peyote, the Supreme Court found that the individual could be fired for misconduct and denied unemployment compensation benefits. The individual's violation of a criminal law was not excused by the fact that his religious beliefs required him to use peyote for sacramental purposes.[13]

Why did the Supreme Court require the government to grant exemptions from unemployment compensation requirements, other than requirements that were tied to criminal laws? Two reasons may explain the results in these cases. First, the government benefit system required individual decision-making about whether a claimant for unemployment compensation benefits had met criteria that were designed to stop the system from being misused (as a form of government paid vacation time).[14] The government, in a sense, was testing the good faith of persons who applied for unemployment compensation and the system seemed easily suited to determining whether an individual was sincerely asserting a religious belief for failure to comply with a condition for the receipt of the benefits. Second, the government interest in protecting the unemployment system from being misused did not appear to be impaired to any significant degree by accommodating persons who could not comply with one of the technical requirements due to their religious beliefs.[15]

The second area in which the Court, during the 1963–89 balancing era, protected religiously motivated actions involved compulsory edu-

---

13. Employment Division, Dept. of Human Resources v. Smith, 494 U.S. 872, 110 S.Ct. 1595, 108 L.Ed.2d 876 (1990), rehearing denied ___ U.S. ___, 110 S.Ct. 2605, 110 L.Ed.2d 285 (1990).

14. This aspect of the unemployment compensation cases was cited as a key to their validity in the 1990 decision of the Supreme Court that refused to require an exemption to laws prohibiting all use of peyote for persons whose religious beliefs required them to use that substance. Employment Division, Dept. of Human Resources v. Smith, 494 U.S. 872, 884, 110

S.Ct. 1595, 1603, 108 L.Ed.2d 876 (1990), rehearing denied ___ U.S. ___, 110 S.Ct. 2605, 110 L.Ed.2d 285 (1990). "The Sherbert Test [the test used to create the rulings in the unemployment compensation cases], it must be recalled, was developed in a context that lent itself to individualized governmental assessment of the reasons for the relevant conduct."

15. Sherbert v. Verner, 374 U.S. 398, 410, 83 S.Ct. 1790, 1797, 10 L.Ed.2d 965 (1963).

cation laws. In *Wisconsin v. Yoder*[16] the Court held that a state could not require members of the Amish Church to send their children to school after the eighth grade. *Yoder* stands out as the one instance in which the Court required the government to grant an exemption from a general regulatory law (a law regulating the conduct of all persons) to persons who could not comply with the law due to their religious beliefs.

In 1990, the Supreme Court described *Yoder* as a case that involved not only the freedom to exercise religion but also the liberty interest of parents to direct the education of their children that was protected by the due process clauses.[17] If we accept the Supreme Court's 1990 characterization of that 1972 decision, the *Yoder* decision can be seen as a variation of the "flag salute" and "speech licensing" cases, in which the Supreme Court found that certain types of government regulations had to allow exceptions for both religious and nonreligious activity that was protected by a specific provision of the Constitution, such as the free speech clause or the due process clause.[18]

Except for these two areas (unemployment compensation and the *Yoder* decision) the Supreme Court during the 1963–1990 balancing era ruled in favor of the government in every case in which an individual sought a free exercise clause exemption from a government regulation of the actions of persons within its jurisdiction. In some cases, the Court found that the government had not imposed any burden on an individual, so that the government was not required to justify its law. For example, the Court found that the federal government's destruction of trees in a federally owned national forest did not have to be justified by a compelling interest, even though the forested area was sacred to the religion of American Indian tribes who were located near to the forest.[19] In some cases, the Court found that the government law at issue imposed a burden on the ability of some persons to exercise their sincerely held religious beliefs, but found that the government interest was compelling and justified the denial of any exemption from the law. For example, the Court found that the free exercise clause did not require the military to allow a service person to wear a religious symbol together with his military uniform while on duty.[20]

16. Wisconsin v. Yoder, 406 U.S. 205, 92 S.Ct. 1526, 32 L.Ed.2d 15 (1972). This case is examined in greater detail in § 21.8.

17. Employment Division, Dept. of Human Resources v. Smith, 494 U.S. 872, 801 n. 1, 110 S.Ct. 1595, 1601 n. 1, 108 L.Ed.2d 876 (1990), rehearing denied ___ U.S. ___, 110 S.Ct. 2605, 110 L.Ed.2d 285 (1990).

18. See note 10, supra.

19. Lyng v. Northwest Indian Cemetery Protective Association, 485 U.S. 439, 108 S.Ct. 1319, 99 L.Ed.2d 534 (1988).

20. Goldman v. Weinberger, 475 U.S. 503, 106 S.Ct. 1310, 89 L.Ed.2d 478 (1986).

Prisoners' Rights Cases. The balancing test was never used in cases in which the judiciary examines legislation, or a prison regulation, that restricts the ability of prison inmates to take actions based on their religious beliefs. In O'Lone v. Estate of Shabazz, 482 U.S. 342, 107

Taxation Issues. The cases involving taxation issues indicate that, even during the balancing era, the government would be able to win any free exercise case, so long as the government did not punish religious beliefs or use religious criteria in its laws. The Supreme Court in the 1940s had found that a state or city could not make the payment of a license fee a condition to distributing religious literature, even though that type of license fee could be a condition for allowing a person to sell merchandise in a state.[21] This restriction on license fees was viewed by the Court as a part of the first amendment prohibition of prior restraints on the exercise of first amendment freedoms (including both religiously motivated speech and nonreligious speech activities).[22] In the 1970s and 1980s the Supreme Court found that religious groups had no right to a tax deduction or tax exemption that had not been granted by statute, so long as the tax was not designed to burden religious beliefs and it was not a license fee. Thus, the Court found that an Amish employer of Amish workmen had to pay Social Security taxes even though compulsory participation in the Social Security system violated their religious beliefs.[23] The Court found that a sales and use tax that applied to the sales of all goods and services could be constitutionally applied to the sales and use of religious literature.[24] The Court found that the Internal Revenue Service was justified in refusing to allow members of a church to deduct (as payments to a charitable organization) a payment to the church that was a payment for specific products or services.[25] In each of these cases, the Court

---

S.Ct. 2400, 96 L.Ed.2d 282 (1987), on remand 829 F.2d 32 (3d Cir.1987), the Court found that a prison regulation restricting the free exercise rights of prisoners should be upheld if the regulation was reasonably related to a legitimate penological interest. Applying this standard, the Court upheld a regulation regarding prisoner work duties outside of the prison that precluded Muslim prisoners from attending religious services on Friday afternoons, as was required by their faith. The Court in *O'Lone* was applying the standard enunciated in Turner v. Safley, 482 U.S. 78, 107 S.Ct. 2254, 96 L.Ed.2d 64 (1987). In *Turner*, the Court found that a restriction on the fundamental rights of prison inmates should be upheld so long as the restriction was reasonably related to legitimate penological interests. This standard seems to require a case-by-case approach to determining the reasonableness of all prison regulations that restrict fundamental rights. In *Turner*, for example, the Court upheld restrictions on the ability of prison inmates to send mail to each other, but invalidated a prison regulation that virtually prohibited all marriages between prisoners or be-

tween a prisoner and a person outside of the prison facility.

21. Murdock v. Pennsylvania, 319 U.S. 105, 63 S.Ct. 870, 87 L.Ed. 1292 (1943); Follett v. McCormick, 321 U.S. 573, 64 S.Ct. 717, 88 L.Ed. 938 (1944).

22. In Jimmy Swaggart Ministries v. Board of Equalization, 493 U.S. 378, 110 S.Ct. 688, 107 L.Ed.2d 796 (1990), the Justices unanimously upheld the application of a sales and use tax to the sales of religious goods and literature in a state. The Court's opinion, written by Justice O'Connor found that the 1940s decisions had invalidated the license fees (which are also described as flat taxes) "that operated as a prior restraint on the exercise of religious liberty".

23. United States v. Lee, 455 U.S. 252, 102 S.Ct. 1051, 71 L.Ed.2d 127 (1982).

24. Jimmy Swaggart Ministries v. Board of Equalization, 493 U.S. 378, 110 S.Ct. 688, 107 L.Ed.2d 796 (1990).

25. Hernandez v. Commissioner of Internal Revenue, 490 U.S. 680, 109 S.Ct. 2136, 104 L.Ed.2d 766 (1989), rehearing

found that the burden that was placed on the members of the religion by the tax law at issue was not significant. But the Court also found that, even if the burden were considered substantial, the taxes at issue were justified by the societal interest in a fiscally sound tax system.

In the next sections of this chapter, we will examine in greater detail the cases that have been referred to in this overview of the principles used by the Supreme Court in free exercise cases. There are two questions that the reader should consider when reviewing specific decisions of the Supreme Court. First, does the difficulty of defining religion or testing sincerity play a part in the Court's refusal to create free exercise clause exemptions to law of general applicability? Second, can a legislature provide an accommodation of religion, through statutory exemptions for religiously motivated actions, in situations where the free exercise clause would not require an exemption from the regulatory legislation?

Defining Religion—Testing Sincerity. Assume that the Supreme Court ruled that the free exercise clause required the government to create an exemption to a criminal law for persons whose sincerely held religious beliefs made it impossible for them to comply with the law. That ruling would require the judiciary to define religion or to test the sincerity of individuals who claimed that their religious beliefs allowed them to disregard the law. If the Court did not narrow the potential group of persons who could claim the exemption, a ruling finding that the government must create a religious exemption from the criminal law would make compliance with the law optional for every person. For example, let us assume that the Supreme Court ruled that the government could not penalize a person for using a banned substance (e.g., peyote) if that substance was used for religious reasons.[26] Every person who was arrested for using the banned substance might claim that he was using the substance because he was commanded to do so by the tenants of his religion. If the Supreme Court did not define religion or allow lower courts to test the sincerity of a person seeking immunity from the drug law, it would allow the individual to grant himself a religious exemption.

Any attempt to define religion, or to test sincerity, raises concerns under both the establishment and free exercise clauses of the first amendment. It is difficult to see how the Supreme Court could define religion in a manner that would not involve the governmental punishment of beliefs or the granting of a denominational preference. The Supreme court has not attempted to define religion although it has

denied 492 U.S. 933, 110 S.Ct. 16, 106 L.Ed.2d 630 (1989).

26. In fact, the Supreme Court made the opposite ruling and, by denying any right to an exemption from a law banning the use of a specific drug, the Court avoid-

ed problems concerning the definition of religion. Employment Division, Dept. of Human Resources v. Smith, 494 U.S. 872, 110 S.Ct. 1595, 108 L.Ed.2d 876 (1990), rehearing denied ___ U.S. ___, 110 S.Ct. 2605, 110 L.Ed.2d 285 (1990).

noted that any exemptions that the judiciary created under the free exercise clause would be limited to persons asserting a religious belief.[27] The Court has never ruled on whether the beliefs must be theocratic (God centered) to be religious beliefs or whether a system of beliefs could be religious even though it was not based upon the concept of an almighty being.[28] The determination of which beliefs constituted religious beliefs would have to avoid any government declaration (even by the courts) that (1) some beliefs are religious because they are true or reasonable or (2) that certain beliefs do not qualify as religious beliefs because the beliefs are ones that no reasonable person would accept, although the Supreme Court has not been clear on this point.[29] The Court has held that a state court may not limit a group of persons who would be receiving a religiously based exemption from an unemployment compensation law to those persons who were members of an

---

27. "[A]lthough a determination of what is a 'religious' belief or practice entitled to constitutional protection may present a most delicate question, the very concept of ordered liberty precludes allowing every person to make his own standards on matters of conduct in which society as a whole has important interest." Wisconsin v. Yoder, 406 U.S. 205, 215–16, 92 S.Ct. 1526, 1533, 32 L.Ed.2d 15 (1972) (majority opinion by Chief Justice Burger).

28. The Supreme Court interpreted the statutory exemption of conscientious objectors from military service in a manner that allowed persons with nontheocratic beliefs to qualify for the exemption in some circumstances. The Court did not make a determination of the nature of religious beliefs that would qualify for protection by the free exercise clause in these military service cases. See § 21.9(a) Exemptions From Military Service.

29. In Thomas v. Review Board, 450 U.S. 707, 715, 101 S.Ct. 1425, 1430, 67 L.Ed.2d 624 (1981) (finding that a person could not be disqualified from unemployment compensation benefits for the sole reason that he had left his employment on the basis of his sincerely held religious beliefs), on remand 421 N.E.2d 642 (Ind. 1981) the majority opinion stated that some beliefs asserted by individuals as the basis for a religious exemption from a law might be: "so bizarre, so clearly nonreligious in motivation, as not to be entitled to protection under the free exercise clause." This statement would appear to relate to testing of an individual's sincerity. The statement does not create or recognize a government power to determine that some beliefs are not "religious" simply because the beliefs are held only by a very small

number of people. In Thomas, the majority opinion also stated that "courts should not undertake to dissect religious beliefs because the believer admits that he is struggling with his position" and that "the guarantee of free exercise is not limited to beliefs which are shared by all members of a religious sect.... courts are not arbiters of scriptural interpretation" 450 U.S. at 715–16, 101 S.Ct. at 430–31.

In Frazee v. Illinois Department of Employment Security, 489 U.S. 829, 109 S.Ct. 1514, 103 L.Ed.2d 914 (1989) the Court held that a state could not make membership in an organized church, religious sect, or religious denomination a condition of being able to claim a religious exemption to an unemployment insurance statute requirement that claimants be able to work on all seven days of the week. The Court in Frazee, as in Thomas, noted that the government did not claim that the individual's beliefs were not religious in nature or that the individual was not sincere. In Frazee the Court referred to the passages from the Thomas opinion quoted in the previous paragraph and concluded that "claims by Christians that their religion forbids Sunday work cannot be deemed bizarre or incredible." 489 U.S. at 834 n. 2, 109 S.Ct. at 1518 n. 2. This footnote in Frazee reinforces the view that the statements in Thomas concerning "bizarre" beliefs related to the credibility and sincerity of the claimant, rather than to the definition of religion.

---

organized church.[30] Religious beliefs are not limited to the beliefs asserted by persons who have joined a formal religious organization.

It is possible that the Supreme Court might adopt different definitions of religion under the establishment and free exercise clauses, even though the word religion is mentioned only once in the first amendment.[31] One could argue that the Court should use a very narrow concept of religion in establishment clause cases because no significant danger to religious freedom would arise from government aid to persons or institutions that promoted a philosophy that is not God centered and not a part of an organized religion. The Supreme Court made a limited ruling concerning the definition of religion for establishment clause purposes when it found that a public school that could not include prayer or Bible reading would not, as a result of the absence of prayer, be teaching a "religion of secularism." [32] In the free exercise clause cases, one could argue that the Supreme Court should be more lenient in defining religion because the exemption of persons from a law may not raise significant establishment clause concerns. The Supreme Court has limited the role of lower courts in determining whether a person's beliefs are religious in free exercise clause cases.[33]

In free exercise cases, the Court could rule that any asserted belief was religious in nature, but that an individual would only have a claim for exemption from a law if he could show that he was sincere in asserting his religious beliefs prevented him from complying with the law at issue. If the Supreme Court had granted a free exercise clause

---

30. Frazee v. Illinois Department of Employment Security, 489 U.S. 829, 109 S.Ct. 1514, 103 L.Ed.2d 914 (1989).

31. For an analysis of the difficulty of attempting to arrive at a legal definition of religion or religious beliefs, see generally, Bowser, Delimiting Religion in the Constitution: A Classification Problem, 11 Val. U.L.Rev. 163 (1977); Boyan, Defining Religion in Operational and Institutional Terms, 116 U.Pa.L.Rev. 479 (1968); Choper, Defining Religion in the First Amendment, 1982 U.Ill.L.Rev. 579; Clark, Guidelines for the Free Exercise Clause, 83 Harv.L.Rev. 327 (1969); Fernandez, The Free Exercise of Religion, 36 S.Cal.L.Rev. 546 (1963); Freeman, The Misguided Search for the Constitutional Definition of "Religion" 71 Geo.L.J. 1519 (1983); Freund, Public Aid to Parochial Schools, 82 Harv.L.Rev. 1680, 1686–87 n. 14 (1969); Garvey, Freedom and Equality in the Religion Clauses, 1981 Sup.Ct.Rev. 193; Galanter, Religious Freedoms in the United States: A Turning Point?, 1966 Wis.L.Rev. 217; Hollingsworth, Constitutional Religious Protection: Antiquated Oddity or Vi-

tal Reality?, 34 Ohio St.L.J. 15 (1973); Killilea, Standards for Expanding Freedom of Conscience, 34 U.Pitt.L.Rev. 531 (1973); Merel, The Protection of Individual Choice: A Consistent Understanding of Religion Under the First Amendment, 45 U.Chi. L.Rev. 805 (1978); Rabin, When is a Religious Belief Religious; United States v. Seeger and the Scope of Free Exercise, 51 Cornell L.Q. 231 (1966); Note, Toward a Constitutional Definition of Religion, 91 Harv.L.Rev. 1056 (1978); Note, The Sacred and the Profane: A First Amendment Definition of Religion, 61 Tex.L.Rev. 139 (1982); Comment, Defining Religion: Of God, the Constitution and the D.A.R., 32 U.Chi. L.Rev. 533 (1965).

32. School District of Abington Tp. v. Schempp, 374 U.S. 203, 225–26, 83 S.Ct. 1560, 1573–74, 10 L.Ed.2d 844 (1963) (finding that prayers or Bible reading conducted by school officials violates the establishment clause).

33. See note 29, supra.

right to be exempted from laws prohibiting the use of peyote, a person who was charged with the criminal use of peyote would be unchallenged regarding whether his asserted beliefs were "religious," but the government could challenge the person as to whether he was "sincere" in asserting those beliefs. The Supreme Court has indicated that the mere testing of a person's sincerity is not a *per se* violation of the religion clauses. However, in testing the sincerity of an individual, a government agency or a Court could not use a definition of religion or a test for sincerity that would be based upon religious principles.[34] Courts simply are precluded from ruling on the truth of religious principles.

The difficulty of defining religion or testing sincerity may be a reason why the Supreme Court has not created free exercise clause exemptions from laws of general applicability. In other words, the Court would need to consider the danger to establishment clause and free exercise clause values that would be part of the process by which courts or government agencies would determine who was eligible for a free exercise clause exemption. When the Court found that there was no free exercise clause right to use peyote,[35] it avoided the problems inherent in judicial definitions of religion or the testimony of sincerity.

Legislative Accommodation of Religion. In several cases in which the Supreme Court found that the Constitution did not require a religiously based exemption from laws of general applicability, the Court has indicated that the legislature could take steps to accommodate the views of persons whose religious beliefs would not allow them to comply with the law. For example, in *Employment Division v. Smith (Smith II),*[36] the Supreme Court found that a state criminal law that totally prohibited the use of peyote could be applied to someone who used peyote based on a sincerely held religious belief that the drug had to be used in a religious ceremony. Justice Scalia's majority opinion in *Smith II* indicated that a state or federal legislature might create an exemption to drug laws that would accommodate the religious need of some persons to use a banned substance. Justice Scalia said: "Values that are protected against government interference through enshrinement in the Bill of Rights are not thereby banished from the political process.... But to say that a nondiscriminatory religious-practice

---

34. See note 29, supra. The problem of examining the sincerity of a person's assertion of a religious belief is also examined in § 21.11 "Inquiries Into Religious Frauds."

For an explanation of an analytical system that would assess the danger of persons insincerely claiming exemptions as a part of the determination whether the government must grant any exemption from a regulatory statute, see Freed &

Polsby, Race, Religion, and Public Policy: Bob Jones University v. United States, 1983 Sup.Ct.Rev. 1.

35. Employment Division, Dept. of Human Resources v. Smith, 494 U.S. 872, 110 S.Ct. 1595, 108 L.Ed.2d 876 (1990), rehearing denied ___ U.S. ___, 110 S.Ct. 2605, 110 L.Ed.2d 285 (1990).

36. Id.

exemption is permitted, or even that it is desirable, is not to say that it is constitutionally required.... it may fairly be said that leaving accommodation to the political process will place at a relative disadvantage those religious practices that are not widely engaged in; but that unavoidable consequence of democratic government must be preferred to a system in which each conscience is a law unto itself or in which judges weigh the social importance of all laws against the centrality of religious beliefs." [37]

The Supreme Court has never explained the precise limits that the establishment clause may place on the ability of government to accommodate religion. An exemption from law of general applicability (such as a criminal law or a tax law) that only provided an exemption for members of a specific religion, or an exemption only for persons who held religious beliefs, would establish a denominational preference that would violate the establishment clause. For example, a legislature cannot create a tax exemption from the sales tax solely for sales of religious literature, because that preference for religious activity violates the establishment clause.[38] Exemptions to taxes and regulatory laws must not involve a denominational preference or the endorsement of religious beliefs. At several points in this Chapter, we will examine the problem of legislative accommodation of religious practices.[39]

§ 21.7   The Early Decisions

The claims of religious minorities received little serious attention from the Supreme Court through the first part of this century. In *Reynolds v. United States* [1] the Supreme Court upheld the application of a federal law prohibiting polygamy to a Mormon whose religion required him to engage in that practice.[2] The majority opinion indicated that Congress was free to prohibit any action regardless of its religious implications so long as it did not formally prohibit a belief.[3] Thus construed, the clause would give no protection against the proscription

---

37. Employment Division, Dept. of Human Resources v. Smith, 494 U.S. 872, 890, 110 S.Ct. 1595, 1606, 108 L.Ed.2d 876 (1990), rehearing denied __ U.S. __, 110 S.Ct. 2605, 110 L.Ed.2d 285 (1990).

38. Texas Monthly, Inc. v. Bullock, 489 U.S. 1, 109 S.Ct. 890, 103 L.Ed.2d 1 (1989).

39. This problem is examined in §§ 21.1, 21.9(a), 21.13, 21.15, 21.16.

§ 21.7

1. 98 U.S. (8 Otto) 145, 25 L.Ed. 244 (1879).

2. Actually the church required polygamy by male members only "when circum-

stances would admit," but it was conceded that Mr. Reynolds' second marriage was sanctioned by the church as being within the requirement. 98 U.S. (8 Otto) at 161.

3. The majority opinion by Chief Justice Waite stated: "Congress was deprived of all legislative power over mere opinion, but was left free to reach actions which were in violation of social duties or subversive of good order." 98 U.S. (8 Otto) at 164. For an argument that the societal interest in prohibiting polygamy should not have been held to outweigh a claim for an exemption from this law, see Miller, A Critique of the Reynolds Decision, 11 Western State U.L.Rev. 165 (1984).

of actions deemed central to a religion unless the legislature formally outlawed the belief itself.

The cases for some years implicitly supported this view, as the Court upheld other laws which burdened the practice of the Mormon religion by imposing various penalties on polygamy.[4] Similarly, the Court also upheld a government system of compulsory vaccinations as applied to those who objected to vaccinations on a religious basis.[5]

Prior to the application of the religion clauses to the states the Supreme Court decided two cases under the due process clause of the fourteenth amendment which have significant free exercise implications. In *Hamilton v. Regents of the University of California*,[6] the Court held that requiring male students at a state university to take courses in military training was not a denial of liberty which violated due process. This decision is questionable in light of the Court's recent decision in the conscientious objector cases and the demise of the "right-privilege" distinction,[7] but it serves to emphasize the absence of significant judicial protection for religious minorities during this period.

The second major due process case in this area was *Pierce v. Society of Sisters*.[8] In this case the Court struck down a statute which required that children attend only public schools as an undue restriction on the freedom of both parents and students. Today *Pierce* stands for the right of children to attend private (including religious) schools so long as they meet basic educational standards. In this regard it should be noted that the state apparently cannot control the subjects taught in those schools beyond its assurance that children are given competent instruction in specified secular subjects and that they are in a safe and healthy environment; further restrictions on the educational process

---

4. Davis v. Beason, 133 U.S. 333, 10 S.Ct. 299, 33 L.Ed. 637 (1890); Late Corporation of the Church of Jesus Christ of Latter Day Saints v. United States, 136 U.S. 1, 10 S.Ct. 792, 34 L.Ed. 478 (1890), see also State v. Barlow, 107 Utah 292, 153 P.2d 647 (1944) (state bigamy law upheld), appeal dismissed 324 U.S. 829, 65 S.Ct. 916, 89 L.Ed. 1396 (1945), rehearing denied 324 U.S. 891, 65 S.Ct. 1026, 89 L.Ed. 1438 (1945); In re State in Interest of Black, 3 Utah 2d 315, 283 P.2d 887 (1955) (Parents might lose custody of children for teaching polygamy), appeal dismissed, 350 U.S. 923, 76 S.Ct. 211, 100 L.Ed. 807 (1955). If the government totally proscribes an activity, such as bigamy, courts today are still likely to find that the state has a police power interest in promoting the public welfare that is sufficient to justify denying the ability to engage in the practice to those persons who believe that they must do so for religious reasons. See, §§ 21.6, 21.8.

5. Jacobson v. Massachusetts, 197 U.S. 11, 25 S.Ct. 358, 49 L.Ed. 643 (1905); Zucht v. King, 260 U.S. 174, 43 S.Ct. 24, 67 L.Ed. 194 (1922).

6. 293 U.S. 245, 55 S.Ct. 197, 79 L.Ed. 343 (1934), rehearing denied 293 U.S. 633, 55 S.Ct. 197, 79 L.Ed. 717 (1935).

7. The conscientious objector cases are discussed in § 21.9(a), infra.

At an earlier time the Court protected only those interests which could be termed "rights" to which one was entitled rather than a "privilege" which was a benefit (such as a college education) which the government need not provide. This distinction has been eliminated and the Constitution now protects all interests. See § 17.2, supra.

8. 268 U.S. 510, 45 S.Ct. 571, 69 L.Ed. 1070 (1925).

would have to be necessary to promote important secular interests.[9]

During the 1940's and 1950's, the Supreme Court invalidated a number of laws which restricted religious practices primarily on the basis that they interfered with the free speech protection of the first amendment. The most important of these cases was *Cantwell v. Connecticut*,[10] where the Court struck down the conviction of several Jehovah's Witnesses for soliciting funds without a license because they were engaged in the distribution of religious materials. It was in this decision that the Court held the free exercise clause applicable to the states.

The majority in *Cantwell* noted that while the freedom to believe was absolute, the freedom to act was not. A general regulation of solicitation which left no room for official discretion and did not unduly obstruct religious practices would have been permissible. Because this statute allowed a licensing officer discretion to determine whether the solicitation was for a religious cause it was invalid. This law would allow the officer to determine who would be allowed to engage in solicitation based on his view of that religious content of their message. Such a statute would violate both the freedoms of speech and religion.

Cantwell was followed by a number of decisions which overturned statutes regulating the dissemination of religious views because they interfered with both the freedom of speech and religion. In each case, however, it appeared that the free speech claim was central to the decision.

In a series of decisions the Court struck down licensing systems for demonstrations or meetings which gave government officials discretion to deny licenses on the basis of the content of the speech, while upholding ones which had permit requirements based on nondiscriminatory "time, place or manner" factors.[11] In these cases the fact that religious meetings were suppressed under discretionary statutes indicated a violation of free exercise rights, but the statutes were held invalid total because they conflicted with the free speech clause. Similarly, the Court invalidated laws prohibiting the distribution of handbills on city streets or in residential neighborhoods as applied to those

---

9. Even prior to the *Pierce* decision the Court held that a state violated the due process clause when it prohibited the teaching of any language other than English in private (and parochial) schools. Meyer v. Nebraska, 262 U.S. 390, 43 S.Ct. 625, 67 L.Ed. 1042 (1923).

10. 310 U.S. 296, 60 S.Ct. 900, 84 L.Ed. 1213 (1940).

11. See, e.g., Schneider v. Town of Irvington, 308 U.S. 147, 60 S.Ct. 146, 84 L.Ed. 155 (1939); Largent v. Texas, 318 U.S. 418,

63 S.Ct. 667, 87 L.Ed. 873 (1943) (discretionary sales license system invalid); Kunz v. New York, 340 U.S. 290, 71 S.Ct. 312, 95 L.Ed. 280 (1951) (discretionary public meeting licensing system invalid); Cox v. New Hampshire, 312 U.S. 569, 61 S.Ct. 762, 85 L.Ed. 1049 (1941) (non-discretionary parade licensing system upheld); Poulos v. New Hampshire, 345 U.S. 395, 73 S.Ct. 760, 97 L.Ed. 1105 (1953) (non-discretionary system upheld), rehearing denied 345 U.S. 978, 73 S.Ct. 1119, 97 L.Ed. 1392 (1953).

who sought to distribute religious literature.[12] In a decision which focused on religious freedom, the Court held that a license tax on all persons soliciting orders for goods could not be applied to a Jehovah's Witness who went door to door distributing religious literature and asking for contributions.[13]

Cantwell and the other solicitation and licensing cases were decided on the basis of freedom of speech principles. Laws that impose time, place, or manner limitations on literature distribution or funds solicitation can be validly applied to activities conducted by members of religious sects if the laws are compatible with the freedom of speech.[14]

The Flag Salute Cases. One of the most interesting problems concerned the requiring of school children to take part in a flag salute ceremony. The Court overruled a decision rendered only three years

12. Jamison v. Texas, 318 U.S. 413, 63 S.Ct. 669, 87 L.Ed. 869 (1943); see also Martin v. Struthers, 319 U.S. 141, 63 S.Ct. 862, 87 L.Ed. 1313 (1943).

13. Murdock v. Pennsylvania, 319 U.S. 105, 117, 63 S.Ct. 870, 876–77, 87 L.Ed. 1292 (1943), overruling Jones v. Opelika, 316 U.S. 584, 62 S.Ct. 1231, 86 L.Ed. 1691 (1942); see, also, Jones v. Opelika, 319 U.S. 103, 63 S.Ct. 890, 87 L.Ed. 1290 (1943) (per curiam), vacating Jones v. Opelika, 316 U.S. 584, 62 S.Ct. 1231, 86 L.Ed. 1691 (1942); Follett v. Town of McCormick, 321 U.S. 573, 64 S.Ct. 717, 88 L.Ed. 938 (1944).

The *Murdock* and *Follett* decisions focused on religious freedom; these decisions appear to be based upon the establishment and free exercise clauses. However, these cases may best be understood as a part of the series of decisions in which the Supreme Court protected all first amendment activities (activities involving assemblies, association, speech, newspaper distribution, and religious activities) from certain types of licensing systems. The latter view of *Murdock* and *Follett* is supported by the Supreme Court decision in Jimmy Swaggart Ministries v. Board of Equalization, 493 U.S. 378, 110 S.Ct. 688, 107 L.Ed.2d 796 (1990) in which the Supreme Court ruled that a religious organization had no right to refuse to pay general sales and use taxes on the sales and use of religious goods and literature in a state. Justice O'Connor wrote for a unanimous Court in *Jimmy Swaggart Ministries*. Justice O'Connor found that a tax of general applicability on the proceeds of sales of goods and services did not violate the establishment clause when it was applied to the sales of religious literature. The free exercise clause did not require an exemption

from such a general tax for religious activities. Justice O'Connor's opinion found that each of the taxes invalidated in *Murdock* and *Follett* was a flat tax (license fee) "that operated as a prior restraint on the exercise of religious liberty." The sales and use taxes could be applied to religious organizations and religious literature because "our concern in *Murdock* and *Follett*—that a flat license tax would act as a *precondition* to the free exercise of religious beliefs—is simply not present where a tax applies to all sales and uses of tangible personal property in the state." 493 U.S. at 386, 110 S.Ct. at 694 (emphasis in original).

14. In Heffron v. International Society for Krishna Consciousness, Inc., 452 U.S. 640, 101 S.Ct. 2559, 69 L.Ed.2d 298 (1981), on remand 311 N.W.2d 843 (Minn.1981), the Court upheld a state fair rule whereby a non-discretionary licensing system forced all persons to confine distribution or sales of literature and solicitation activities to a fixed location. The rule was upheld on its face and as applied to members of a religious sect. The majority opinion stated:

"None of our cases suggest that the inclusion of peripatetic solicitation as part of a church ritual entitles church members to solicitation rights in a public forum superior to those of members of other religious groups that raise money but do not purport to ritualize the process. Nor for present purposes do religious organizations enjoy rights to communicate, distribute, and solicit on the fairgrounds superior to those of other organizations having social, political, or other ideological messages to proselytize."

452 U.S. at 652, 101 S.Ct. at 2566.

earlier and held that students could not be compelled to salute the flag against their beliefs.[15] Once again basing the decision on the right of free speech, a majority of the justices found that the requirement invaded the sphere of free intellect and belief that was the core of these first amendment principles.

In these cases it was the limitation of freedoms essentially protected by the free speech clause which made the requirements unconstitutional. Although the Jehovah Witnesses brought these cases because of their religious objections to the honoring of "idols," the infringement of religious beliefs was not crucial to the decision. Anyone opposed to saluting the flag had to be excused from the requirement without regard to whether their refusal was based on religious or non-religious grounds.

Despite these seemingly liberal free speech-free exercise decisions, the Supreme Court did not give significant independent protection to the free exercise of religion against police power regulations during this period. Thus, in *Prince v. Massachusetts*,[16] the Court upheld the application of a law prohibiting the selling of merchandise in public places by minors to a nine year old child who was distributing religious literature with her guardian. The majority found that the state's interest in the health and well being of young people was a significant secular end which justified the incidental burden on religion.

As of 1960, no case in the Supreme Court had resulted in the overturning of police power regulations solely on the basis that they had a coercive effect on the free exercise of religion. If the end pursued was a significant secular goal, the Court would uphold incidental restrictions on religiously motivated activity. Only when the law proscribed beliefs or interfered with free speech as well as the exercise of religion would the Court overturn the law. After 1960, the belief-action distinction would be replaced by tests that would place meaningful limits on the government's ability to regulate actions essential to the exercise of religion. Yet the distinction is still of some importance for there is still an absolute prohibition of governmental proscription of beliefs. Incident to this prohibition, the Court has precluded the government from inquiring into the truth of religious teaching or resolving ecclesiastical disputes on the basis of religious doctrine.[17]

§ 21.8 The Modern Cases

Overview. Between 1960 and 1990, Justices of the Supreme Court were sharply divided over the extent to which the free exercise clause

15. West Virginia State Bd. of Education v. Barnette, 319 U.S. 624, 63 S.Ct. 1178, 87 L.Ed. 1628 (1943), overruling Minersville School Distri⸱ v. Gobitis, 310 U.S. 586, 60 S.Ct. 1010, 84 L.Ed. 1375 (1940).

16. 321 U.S. 158, 64 S.Ct. 438, 88 L.Ed. 645 (1944), rehearing denied 321 U.S. 804, 64 S.Ct. 784, 88 L.Ed. 1090 (1944).

17. Both of these problems are reviewed in §§ 21.11, 21.12, infra.

allowed the judiciary to determine whether a law of general applicability, which included no explicitly religious criteria, could be applied to persons whose sincerely held religious beliefs prevented them from complying with the law. In the cases decided by the Court during this period, as in earlier Supreme Court decisions, the Justices clearly endorsed the principle that the government could not punish a person solely because of his religious belief or allocate benefits or burdens on the basis of people's religious beliefs.

In *Torcaso v. Watkins*,[1] the Court invalidated a state constitutional provision that required a declaration of a belief in God as a prerequisite to taking public office. The majority noted that the original Constitution prohibited the use of religious tests for federal government offices.[2] The Court found that the free exercise clause prohibited the government from awarding benefits to, or imposing burdens on, a person due to his religious beliefs or his lack of religious faith.

The division between the Justices arose in cases concerning whether the Court should declare that a law of general applicability could not be applied to a person whose religious beliefs required him to take actions that were contrary to the law. Between 1963 and 1989, it appeared that the Court would balance the importance of the government interest that was furthered by such a law against the burden on persons who could not follow their religious beliefs if they complied with the law. However, even during the era of the balancing test the government won virtually every case which did not involve the punishment of religious beliefs. The government was only required to grant religious exemptions in (1) a few cases involving technical requirements for unemployment compensation and (2) one case involving an exemption from a compulsory school attendance law for Amish children.

In 1990 the Supreme Court, in *Employment Division v. Smith (Smith II)*[3] reviewed and summarized a century of the Court's rulings concerning the free exercise clause. *Smith II* involved two individuals who were disqualified from receiving unemployment compensation benefits under a state law that disqualified anyone who had been fired from his job for job related misconduct. These persons had been fired from their positions as drug and alcohol abuse rehabilitation counsellors at a private clinic after it was found out that they had ingested peyote, which was banned by state law. The former drug counselors claimed that the free exercise clause protected their use of peyote in connection with a religious ceremony.

§ 21.8

1. 367 U.S. 488, 81 S.Ct. 1680, 6 L.Ed.2d 982 (1961).

2. "[No] religious Test shall ever be required as a Qualification to any Office of Public Trust under the United States." U.S. Const. art. VI, cl. 3.

3. 494 U.S. 872, 110 S.Ct. 1595, 108 L.Ed.2d 876 (1990), rehearing denied ___ U.S. ___, 110 S.Ct. 2605, 110 L.Ed.2d 285 (1990).

The Supreme Court of the United States, in *Employment Division v. Smith (Smith I),*[4] had remanded the case to the state court for a determination of whether state law prohibited all use of peyote, including the use of peyote in a religious ceremony. If the state law had provided an exemption for the sacramental use of peyote, the Supreme Court might have avoided the free exercise clause question. The denial of unemployment compensation to individuals who had used the peyote in a lawful manner might have been totally arbitrary. The state supreme court, after the remand of the case, found that state law prohibited any use of peyote, including any religiously motivated or sacramental use. The state court also held that the state's total prohibition of peyote use violated the free exercise clause of the first amendment to the Constitution of the United States and, for that reason, the state court found that the state could not deny unemployment compensation to the former drug counselors.

In *Smith II,* the Supreme Court of the United States ruled: (1) that the free exercise clause did not require an exemption from criminal laws banning the use of peyote; and (2) that unemployment compensation could be denied to persons whose discharge from employment had been based upon their violation of a valid criminal statute.[5]

In *Smith II,* Justice Scalia wrote the majority opinion, which held that the free exercise clause did not require the government to justify its refusal to exempt religiously motivated drug use from its general prohibition of drug use. The majority believed that the judiciary was not authorized by the free exercise clause to balance the societal interest in the drug proscription against the degree to which compliance with the law burdened the sincerely held religious beliefs of the individuals in the case.

Justice Scalia, writing for the majority, recognized two basic free exercise clause principles. First, the government is prohibited from regulating religious beliefs. This principle prohibits the government from compelling the affirmation of religious beliefs, punishing religious

---

4. 485 U.S. 660, 108 S.Ct. 1444, 99 L.Ed.2d 753 (1988), on remand 307 Or. 68, 763 P.2d 146 (1988).

5. Employment Division, Dept. of Human Resources v. Smith, 494 U.S. 872, 110 S.Ct. 1595, 108 L.Ed.2d 876 (1990), rehearing denied ___ U.S. ___, 110 S.Ct. 2605, 110 L.Ed.2d 285 (1990). The denial of the exemption was upheld by a six to three vote of the Justices. Justice Scalia wrote the majority opinion, his opinion was joined by Chief Justice Rehnquist and Justices White, Stevens, and Kennedy. Justice O'Connor believed that a balancing test should be used in this case, but she found that the government interest was sufficiently compelling to justify a denial of an exemption for persons whose religious beliefs required them to use peyote. 494 U.S. at 891, 110 S.Ct. at 1606 (O'Connor, J., concurring in the judgment). Justices Brennan, Marshall, and Blackmun, joined the portion of Justice O'Connor's opinion in which she explained why the government would need a compelling interest to override the request for an exemption by persons whose religious beliefs prevented them from complying with the law. However, these three Justices did not agree with Justice O'Connor's use of that test in this case; these three Justices dissented from the ruling in the case. 494 U.S. at 907, 110 S.Ct. 1595 (1990).

expression thought to be false, or using of religious doctrine as a basis for judicial decisions.[6]

Second, the free exercise clause would invalidate a law that appeared to be religiously neutral on its face, if it could be shown that the purpose of the legislature that passed the law had done so for the sole purpose of prohibiting or regulating an act because of its religious significance. Justice Scalia stated: "It would be true, we think (though no case of ours has involved the point), that a state would be 'prohibiting the free exercise [of religion]' if it sought to ban such acts or abstentions only when they are engaged in for religious reasons, or only because of the religious belief that they display. It would doubtless be unconstitutional, for example, to ban the casting of 'statutes that are to be used for worship purposes,' or to prohibit bowing down before a golden calf."[7]

The free exercise clause does not require exemptions for religious persons who cannot comply with a religiously neutral law. Justice Scalia's majority opinion stated: "The only decisions in which we have held the first amendment bars application of a neutral, generally applicable law to religiously motivated action have involved not the free exercise clause alone, but the free exercise clause in conjunction with other constitutional protections."[8]

According to the majority opinion in *Smith II,* the only cases that were inconsistent with the principle that religiously neutral, generally applicable laws did not have to provide a religious exemption were the cases in which the Court had found that the government was required to waive a condition for unemployment compensation benefits (for persons who could not meet the condition due to their sincerely held religious beliefs).[9] In those unemployment compensation cases, the

---

6. Employment Division v. Smith, 494 U.S. 872, 877, 110 S.Ct. 1595, 1599, 108 L.Ed.2d 876 (1990), rehearing denied ___ U.S. ___, 110 S.Ct. 2605, 110 L.Ed.2d 285 (1990). The problem of punishing false religious statements in fraud prosecutions is examined in § 21.11 of this Treatise. The problems faced by courts in making decisions concerning ecclesiastical disputes is examined in § 21.12 of this Treatise.

7. 494 U.S. at 877–8, 110 S.Ct. at 1599.

8. 494 U.S. at 881, 110 S.Ct. at 1600. The cases in which the Supreme Court found that the free speech and free exercise clauses together prohibited the government from subjecting both religious and nonreligious speakers to certain types of licensing statutes or to other regulations of speech (of both nonreligious and religious content) are examined in § 21.7.

9. Id. All of these cases are examined in later paragraphs of this section. The first important case concerning unemployment compensation was Sherbert v. Verner, 374 U.S. 398, 83 S.Ct. 1790, 10 L.Ed.2d 965 (1963).

Justice Scalia found that the Supreme Court's decision in Wisconsin v. Yoder, 406 U.S. 205, 92 S.Ct. 1526, 32 L.Ed.2d 15 (1972), in which the Court held that Amish parents could not be required to send their children to school after the eighth grade, was not based solely on the free exercise clause but on a combination of the free exercise clause and the liberty of parents to control the education of their children that was protected by the due process clause of the fourteenth amendment. However, the *Yoder* opinion appears to be based upon the free exercise clause alone. The case is examined in later paragraphs in this chapter.

Court had used a two-step balancing test. First, the individual was required to show that complying with the eligibility condition (such as a condition that the individual be available for work on Saturday) imposed a substantial burden on the person's ability to carry out his religious beliefs. If the person made that demonstration, the government, in the second part of the test, was required to demonstrate that granting an exemption from the law at issue would interfere with a compelling or overriding government interest. In *Smith II*, Justice Scalia's majority opinion found that the balancing test had never been used by the Court except to examine certain conditions for unemployment compensation that were unrelated to a general criminal law.

The *Smith II* decision was reminiscent of the Court's decision in *Braunfeld v. Brown*[10] in 1961. The Court in *Braunfeld* upheld the constitutionality of applying laws that required businesses to be closed on Sundays to persons who were required to observe a day other than Sunday as the Sabbath. A majority of the Justices in *Braunfeld*, although without a majority opinion, held that the additional economic burdens placed on a Sabbatarian (who would be required to be closed more days a week than his competitors) did not violate the free exercise clause. Chief Justice Warren, writing for four members of the Court in *Braunfeld*, found that the law placed a real burden on Sabbatarian retailers. The plurality opinion by Chief Justice Warren also found that the state had an overriding nonreligious interest in setting aside a single day for "rest, recreation, and tranquility." Some portions of Chief Justice Warren's plurality opinion appear to involve a balancing of the societal interest in the Sunday closing laws against the burdens placed on Sabbatarians, but the plurality did not require any real justification for the refusal to grant an exemption from the Sunday closing laws to Sabbatarians.

Justices Frankfurter and Harlan, in a concurring opinion in *Braunfeld*,[11] balanced the societal interest in the preservation of the "traditional institution" of a day of rest against the economic disadvantage to the retailer who had to be closed an extra day due to his religious beliefs. Despite the language in the concurring opinion regarding the need to balance the individual retailer's interest against societal interests, Justices Frankfurter and Harlan appeared to uphold the law simply because it imposed only an incidental burden on religious practices. Justices Frankfurter and Harlan found that even if there were no Sunday closing laws, the Sabbatarian retailer would still lose a day of sales opportunities that was available to his nonreligious compet-

---

The relationship of the unemployment compensation cases, and the *Yoder* decision, to all of the decisions in which the Supreme Court had found that there was no free exercise clause right to an exemption from a general regulatory law is examined in § 21.6 of this Chapter.

10. Braunfeld v. Brown, 366 U.S. 599, 81 S.Ct. 1144, 6 L.Ed.2d 563 (1961).

11. 366 U.S. at 521–22, 81 S.Ct. at 1186–87 (Frankfurter, J., concurring, joined by Harlan, J.).

itors, due to his religious need to refrain from working on a certain day of the week.

In 1963, the Court for the first time used a balancing test to require the government to grant unemployment compensation benefits to a person who, due to her religious beliefs, could not meet all of the requirements for those benefits.[12] That decision was applied in several later cases, which required state to waive conditions for unemployment compensation relating to availability for work.[13]

The Court also used a balancing test to find that a state could not require the Amish to send their children to public schools after the eighth grade.[14] When this case was decided, in 1972, it appeared to be consistent with the approach used in the unemployment compensation cases.

The balancing test used in the unemployment benefits and Amish school cases was quoted in many decisions during the 1963–1990 era. However, other than in the unemployment compensation or school attendance cases, the Court did not rule in favor of any free exercise clause claims during this era that did not involve a regulation of religious beliefs.[15]

The remainder of this section will be divided into examinations of the unemployment compensation and school attendance cases and the other topics that came before the Supreme Court during the 1963–1990 time period.

Unemployment Compensation. In *Sherbert v. Verner*[16] a majority of the justices held that state unemployment benefits could not be denied to a Seventh Day Adventist because she refused to work on Saturday due to her religious beliefs. Justice Brennan, writing for a seven member majority, stated that for the denial of benefits to withstand scrutiny under the free exercise clause "it must be either because her disqualification as a beneficiary represents no infringement by the state of her constitutional right of free exercise, or because any incidental burden on the free exercise of appellant's religion may be justified

---

12. Sherbert v. Verner, 374 U.S. 398, 83 S.Ct. 1790, 10 L.Ed.2d 965 (1963) (the Court finds that a state cannot deny unemployment benefit payments to a woman who refused to work on Saturday due to her religious beliefs).

13. Thomas v. Review Board, 450 U.S. 707, 101 S.Ct. 1425, 67 L.Ed.2d 624 (1981), on remand 421 N.E.2d 642 (Ind.1981); Hobbie v. Unemployment Appeals Commission of Florida, 480 U.S. 136, 107 S.Ct. 1046, 94 L.Ed.2d 190 (1987). These cases are examined in later paragraphs of this section.

14. Wisconsin v. Yoder, 406 U.S. 205, 92 S.Ct. 1526, 32 L.Ed.2d 15 (1972). This case is examined in later paragraphs of this section.

15. Supreme Court decisions finding that laws were invalid because of their punishment of religious beliefs are examined in § 21.11 Inquiries into Religious "Frauds", § 21.12 State Involvement of Ecclesiastical Disputes, § 21.14 Prohibiting "Ministers" from Holding Public Office, § 21.16 Direct Regulation of Religious Organizations.

16. 374 U.S. 398, 83 S.Ct. 1790, 10 L.Ed.2d 965 (1963).

by a compelling state interest in the regulation...." [17] The majority employed a two-part balancing test. First, plaintiff had to show a substantial burden on the exercise of her religion from the law under review. Second, such a burden would only be valid if the Court found it necessary to a "compelling state interest" which outweighed the degree of impairment of free exercise rights. The majority opinion implied that the degree of burden on religious activity was balanced against the importance of the state interest and the degree to which it would be impaired by an accommodation for the religious practice. Relevant to such an inquiry is the importance of the state's interest [is it a "compelling" one?] and the degree to which there are alternative means to achieve it which do not burden religious practices [least restrictive means are required].

In *Sherbert* the majority found that the denial of unemployment benefits was invalid under its two part test. First, there was a significant coercive effect on the practice of religion because the Sabbatarian was forced to make a choice between receiving state benefits or following her beliefs. Second, no compelling or overriding interest in the regulation was shown by the state. The state claimed only that this restriction avoided fraudulent claims, but this contention had not been raised in the state courts and was not sustained by the record.[18] Additionally, even if avoidance of false claims to benefits were assumed *arguendo* to be a compelling interest, there had been no demonstration that alternative means of avoiding fraud were not available. Thus there was no demonstration by the state that the denial of benefits was necessary to promote a compelling interest and, therefore, the state was required to exempt workers with religious objections to Saturday work from its requirement that they be available for work on Saturdays.

The majority opinion in *Sherbert* noted that the case was not one where "an employee's religious connections made her a non-productive member of society." [19] This language indicates that the state would not have to give benefits to those who were permanently unemployable because of their religious beliefs since that would interfere with the state's goal of providing benefits to those involuntarily unemployed but available for work. While the state might have to accommodate certain religious practices which it had no real need to burden, it would not be required to abandon the goal of its program in order to accommodate everyone who might be unemployed for religious reasons.

In *Thomas v. Review Board* [20] the Supreme Court was required to determine the validity of an individual's claim that he was acting on the basis of a religious belief when a state asserted that the motivation for his action was nonreligious. Mr. Thomas, a Jehovah's Witness, quit

17. 374 U.S. at 403, 83 S.Ct. at 1793.
18. 374 U.S. at 407, 83 S.Ct. at 1795–96.
19. 374 U.S. at 410, 83 S.Ct. at 1797.

20. 450 U.S. 707, 101 S.Ct. 1425, 67 L.Ed.2d 624 (1981), on remand 421 N.E.2d 642 (Ind.1981).

his job when his employer transferred him from a metal foundry to a factory department that produced parts for military tanks and gave him no opportunity to transfer to another job. Thomas testified that he believed his religion prohibited him from working on war materials although he had been advised by at least one fellow employee who was a friend and a Jehovah's Witness that such work did not violate the principles of the religion. Thomas was denied unemployment compensation because state law precluded the granting of benefits to a person who voluntarily terminated his employment for reasons other than "good cause [arising] in connection with [his] work." The unemployment compensation hearing officer and state review board found that Thomas had left his job for religious reasons but that he did not qualify for benefits under the statute.

The state supreme court found that the denial of benefits for voluntary termination of employment did not violate the free exercise clause for three reasons: (1) Thomas's belief was more a "personal philosophical choice" than a religious belief; (2) the burden on Thomas's religious belief was only "indirect"; and (3) the granting of benefits only to persons who voluntarily left employment for religious reasons would violate the establishment clause. The United States Supreme Court had little difficulty finding that the denial of benefits to Thomas violated the free exercise clause; only Justice Rehnquist would have upheld the state supreme court and denied the claim.[21]

The majority opinion in *Thomas* was written by Chief Justice Burger. The Chief Justice avoided ruling on what type of beliefs were "religious," although the majority opinion indicated that judges had to accept an individual's assertion that his belief or motivation for his actions was religious so long as the person asserts the claim in good faith and so long as the belief could arguably be termed religious:

> Courts should not undertake to dissect religious beliefs because the believer admits that he is "struggling" with his position or because his beliefs are not articulated with the clarity and precision that a more sophisticated person might employ ... one can, of course, imagine an asserted claim so bizarre, so clearly nonreligious in motivation, as not to be entitled to protection under the Free Exercise Clause; but that is not the case here, and the guarantee of free exercise is not limited to beliefs which are shared by all members of a religious sect.... Courts are not arbiters of scriptural interpretation.

The narrow function of a reviewing court in this context is to determine whether there was an appropriate finding that petition-

---

21. 450 U.S. at 720, 101 S.Ct. at 1433 (Rehnquist, J., dissenting). Justice Blackmun joined parts of the majority opinion by Chief Justice Burger and concurred in the result but not the Court's opinion holding that the granting of benefits to religious persons under these circumstances did not constitute an aid to religion. 450 U.S. at 720, 101 S.Ct. at 1433 (Blackmun, J., concurring).

er terminated his work because of an honest conviction that such work was forbidden by his religion. . . . On this record, it is clear that Thomas terminated his employment for religious reasons.[22]

Once Thomas' reasons were found to be religious, the case was easily disposed of under the first amendment. Conditioning a significant benefit upon conduct prohibited by a religious belief places a substantial burden on the individual regardless of whether the burden can be labeled direct or indirect.[23] The state's asserted interests in denying benefits to those leaving employment for religious reasons were the avoidance of large scale unemployment and the avoidance of employer inquiries into religious beliefs. However, the state was unable to prove that granting benefits to such persons would lead to either widespread unemployment or detailed questioning of beliefs by employers. Thus, the Court held that "[n]either of the interests advanced is sufficiently compelling to justify the burden upon Thomas' religious liberty."[24] On the basis of *Sherbert v. Verner* the majority opinion by Chief Justice Burger found that the granting of an exception to the conditions for unemployment compensation based upon religious objectives did not promote the establishment of religion but only moved the government to a position of neutrality toward religious beliefs.[25]

The *Sherbert* and *Thomas* decisions were reaffirmed and applied in *Hobbie v. Unemployment Appeals Commission of Florida.*[26] Ms. Hobbie had worked for an employer for over two years before she became a member of a religion that prohibited work from sundown on Friday until sundown on Saturday. Because of her newly formed religious belief, she informed her employer that she could no longer work on Friday evenings or during the day on Saturday. She was then discharged from her employment because of her refusal to work at those times. State law granted full unemployment compensation benefits only to persons who became "unemployed through no fault of their own." Ms. Hobbie was found by the state to be ineligible for full unemployment compensation benefits because she had been discharged for her refusal to work her scheduled shifts.

---

22. 450 U.S. at 715–16, 101 S.Ct. at 1430–31.

In Frazee v. Illinois Department of Employment Security, 489 U.S. 829, 109 S.Ct. 1514, 103 L.Ed.2d 914 (1989) the Justices unanimously held that a state violated the free exercise clause by refusing to grant an exemption from an unemployment compensation system requirement regarding availability for work on all days of the week to an individual who sincerely claimed that his religious beliefs prohibited him from working on Sunday solely because the individual was not a member of an organized church, sect, or denomination. The Court in Frazee noted that,

in this case, the sincerity and religious nature of the individual's claim for an exemption was admitted by the government. 489 U.S. at 832–35, 109 S.Ct. at 1517.

23. 450 U.S. at 717–18, 101 S.Ct. at 1431–32.

24. 450 U.S. at 719, 101 S.Ct. at 1432.

25. Thomas v. Review Bd., 450 U.S. 707, 719, 101 S.Ct. 1425, 1432–33, 67 L.Ed.2d 624 (1981), on remand 421 N.E.2d 642 (Ind. 1981).

26. 480 U.S. 136, 107 S.Ct. 1046, 94 L.Ed.2d 190 (1987).

The Supreme Court, by an eight to one vote, found that the *Thomas* and *Sherbert* decisions were indistinguishable from this case, even though the woman formed her religious beliefs following her acceptance of the employment and despite the fact that she had accepted work on Fridays and Saturdays before she formulated her current religious beliefs. Justice Brennan, writing for six members of the Court, applied the balancing test that had been used in the *Thomas* and *Sherbert* cases. According to the majority opinion by Justice Brennan, a state law which denied a benefit to an individual because of her sincerely held religious belief imposed a significant burden on the individual's right to free exercise of religion and must be subjected to "strict scrutiny". Once the individual had shown that her free exercise rights were burdened, it was the state's obligation to demonstrate that it had a "compelling interest" that outweighed the burden on the individual's free exercise clause rights.

As in *Sherbert* and *Thomas,* the majority in *Hobbie* found that the state did not have a compelling interest in denying unemployment compensation benefits to persons who had to leave their employment because of religious beliefs. The awarding of unemployment compensation benefits to persons who voluntarily left their jobs for religious reasons, or to persons who were terminated from their employment due to their inability to comply with employment regulations because of their religious beliefs,[27] did not violate establishment clause principles because the granting of benefits merely accommodated religious practices and did not have the primary effect of promoting religion or entangling the state with religious activities or principles.[28]

It should be noted that in *Sherbert, Thomas,* and *Hobbie* the unemployment compensation claimant had not violated any criminal law of general applicability; the claimant in each case was only asking for an exemption from a condition to the receipt of unemployment compensation. If a state had a law that denied a person unemployment

---

27. Justice Brennan's majority opinion found that the government could not inquire into whether the religious beliefs were true or reasonable, but he did not explain whether the government could inquire into whether the beliefs were sincerely held. Hobbie v. Unemployment Appeals Commission of Florida, 480 U.S. 136, 144 n. 9, 107 S.Ct. 1046, 1051 n. 9, 94 L.Ed.2d 190 (1987). The problem of determining whether an individual is sincerely asserting religious beliefs is examined in § 21.11 of this treatise.

28. Justice Brennan's majority opinion in *Hobbie* found that this decision was not inconsistent with Estate of Thornton v. Caldor, Inc., 472 U.S. 703, 105 S.Ct. 2914, 86 L.Ed.2d 557 (1985) in which the Su-

preme Court invalidated a state statute that gave employees an absolute right to refuse to work on their Sabbath. Justice Brennan found that granting the unemployment compensation benefits did not result in an impermissible shifting of burdens to employers and coworkers to enable an individual to exercise her religion. Hobbie v. Unemployment Appeals Commission of Florida, 480 U.S. 136, 145 n. 11, 107 S.Ct. 1046, 1051 n. 11, 94 L.Ed.2d 190 (1987). For an analysis of the establishment clause and free exercise clause problems inherent in regulating employment practices (other than the rulings regarding qualifications for unemployment benefits) see §§ 21.13, 21.15.

compensation if he had lost his employment due to his commission of a crime, the government interest in deterring the criminal activity would justify denying unemployment compensation to that person.[29]

Compulsory Education—The *Yoder* Decision. In *Wisconsin v. Yoder*[30] the Court held Wisconsin could not require members of the Amish Church to send their children to public school after the eighth grade. In 1990, the Supreme Court described *Yoder* as a case that was not based upon the free exercise clause alone, but, rather, upon the free exercise clause and the constitutional "right of parents . . . to direct the education of their children."[31]

Although Chief Justice Burger's majority opinion cited due process rulings concerning parental rights,[32] the majority opinion in *Yoder* focused on the free exercise clause issue and used the two part balancing test. First, a significant burden on the free exercise of religion would have to be shown. Second, this burden would be balanced against the importance of the state's interest and the degree to which it would be impaired by a religious exemption.

In finding that there was a significant burden on the free exercise of religion, the Court had to determine whether the parents' refusal to send their children to school was based on religious beliefs. The Court noted that a claim based on a personal or philosophical rejection of secular values would not be protected by the free exercise clause. Thus, if the Amish refused to send their children to school merely to preserve a "traditional way of life", their claim would be denied. As Chief Justice Burger stated for the majority in *Yoder,* "although a determination of what is a 'religious' belief or practice entitled to constitutional protection may present a most delicate question, the very concept of ordered liberty precludes allowing every person to make his own standards on matters of conduct in which society as a whole has important interests."[33]

The Court found that the Amish lifestyle, educational practices and refusal to submit their children to further secular education were religious. Central to this determination were the following facts: (1) this was a shared belief by an organized group rather than a personal

29. Employment Division, Dept. of Human Resources v. Smith, 494 U.S. 872, 110 S.Ct. 1595, 108 L.Ed.2d 876 (1990).

30. 406 U.S. 205, 92 S.Ct. 1526, 32 L.Ed.2d 15 (1972). The Court was unanimous as to the result in this case, but three justices filed separate opinions. 406 U.S. at 237, 92 S.Ct. at 1544 (Stewart and Brennan, JJ., concurring), 406 U.S. at 241, 92 S.Ct. at 1546 (Douglas, J., concurring). Two Justices (Powell & Rehnquist) did not participate.

31. Employment Division, Dept. of Human Resources v. Smith, 494 U.S. 872, 881 n. 1, 110 S.Ct. 1595, 1601 n. 1, 108 L.Ed.2d 876 (1990), rehearing denied ___ U.S. ___, 110 S.Ct. 2605, 110 L.Ed.2d 285 (1990).

32. Wisconsin v. Yoder, 406 U.S. 205, 233–34, 92 S.Ct. 1526, 1542, 32 L.Ed.2d 15 (1972) citing and discussing Pierce v. Society of Sisters, 268 U.S. 510, 45 S.Ct. 571, 69 L.Ed. 1070 (1925).

33. Wisconsin v. Yoder, 406 U.S. 205, 215–16, 92 S.Ct. 1526, 1533, 32 L.Ed.2d 15 (1972).

preference, (2) the belief related to certain theocratic principles and interpretation of religious literature, (3) the system of beliefs pervaded and regulated their daily lives, (4) the system of belief and lifestyle resulting therefrom had been in existence for a substantial period of time.[34] It is not clear which, if any, of these factors mentioned in the *Yoder* opinion determined the presence of a "religion" or a "religious belief" as the basis for the parents' claim and the Court's ruling.

Because the Amish had shown their refusal to send children to school after the eighth grade was religiously based, the Court in *Yoder* determined the permissibility of applying the compulsory education laws to them under the two part balancing test. The Court did not use the "compelling interest" test, thus suggesting the use of a more open balancing test.[35] The compulsory attendance laws could be applied to the Amish if "the State does not deny the free exercise of religious belief by its requirement, or that there is a state interest of sufficient magnitude to override the interest claiming protection under the Free Exercise Clause." [36]

The first part of the test—the demonstration of a burden on the exercise of religion—was met by the Amish. The education of their children in the public schools beyond the eighth grade was in conflict with their religious principles and threatened the entire religious training of their children. Because there was a burden on the exercise of religion incident to a state regulation of general activity, the Court had to balance the interests of the state against those of the Amish. Here the state would have to show both that it was promoting an interest which was superior to these free exercise rights and that this goal would be unduly impaired by granting an exemption to the Amish.

The state asserted that the attendance of these children at school between the ages of 14 and 16 was necessary to their development as citizens and members of society. However, the Court found that these goals would not be impaired by an exemption for the Amish. The first eight years of formal education and the home training of young people by the Amish parents made the children both able citizens and productive members of society.

The state also argued that its interest in the children's health and well being justified an absolute rule to grant secondary education to all children. The Court recognized that this interest would overcome a claim for religious freedom where the practice was detrimental to the health, training or well being of a child.[37] But since the record showed

34. 406 U.S. at 215–17, 92 S.Ct. at 1533–34.

35. While the word "compelling" appears at several points in the majority opinion, it was not used as part of the statement of the test to be employed in

reviewing claims under the free exercise clause.

36. 406 U.S. at 214, 92 S.Ct. at 1532.

37. 406 U.S. at 229–30, 92 S.Ct. at 1540–41. In this way the Court distinguished the earlier cases relating to child

that the Amish children were well cared for and well trained in their community, the state's goals would not be impaired by an exemption for the Amish children.

The majority did not find it necessary to discuss the interest of Amish children who wished to attend school after the eighth grade against the wishes of their parents. Absent an actual case involving such a parent-child conflict, the Court refused to decide if the state's interest in the child would allow the government to require a parent to send a child to school at the child's request over the religious objections of the parent.

In 1990, the Court ruled that the free exercise clause did not require a religious use exception from law prohibiting the use of peyote and, in dicta, described *Yoder* as a decision that was based on both the free exercise clause and the parental interest in directing the education of their children that was protected by the due process clause of the fourteenth amendment.[38] Thus viewed, *Yoder* appears to create only a very limited exemption from compulsory attendance laws for families who can base their claim for an exemption on shared religious beliefs as well as on a general due process-liberty argument.

Taxation. In the 1940s the Supreme Court held that persons who wished to distribute religious literature could not be prohibited from doing so because they had failed to pay a license fee.[39] Such a fee is often called a "flat tax", because the fee or tax is for a specified amount. These license fees, or flat taxes, had to be paid prior to engaging in the business activity. The 1940s decisions exempting distributors of religious literature from license fees focused on the free exercise clause. However, it appears that those rulings would protect a distributor of any type of literature from a flat tax or license fee because that type of fee-tax may be an unconstitutional prior restraint on first amendment activity.[40]

labor or the protection of their health. See Jacobson v. Massachusetts, 197 U.S. 11, 25 S.Ct. 358, 49 L.Ed. 643 (1905) (vaccinations required); Prince v. Massachusetts, 321 U.S. 158, 64 S.Ct. 438, 88 L.Ed. 645 (1944) (child labor law upheld as applied to child distributing religious materials), rehearing denied 321 U.S. 804, 64 S.Ct. 784, 88 L.Ed. 1090 (1944).

38. Employment Division, Department of Human Resources v. Smith, 494 U.S. 872, 881 n. 1, 110 S.Ct. 1595, 1601 n. 1, 108 L.Ed.2d 876 (1990), rehearing denied __ U.S. __, 110 S.Ct. 2605, 110 L.Ed.2d 285 (1990). This case and its relationship to *Yoder* is examined in § 21.6 and in the introductory paragraphs of this section.

39. Murdock v. Pennsylvania, 319 U.S. 105, 63 S.Ct. 870, 87 L.Ed. 1292 (1943);

Follett v. McCormick, 321 U.S. 573, 64 S.Ct. 717, 88 L.Ed. 938 (1944).

40. In Jimmy Swaggart Ministries v. Board of Equalization, 493 U.S. 378, 110 S.Ct. 688, 107 L.Ed.2d 796 (1990) the Supreme Court ruled that a religious organization had no right to refuse to pay general sales and use taxes on the sales and use of religious goods and literature in a state. Justice O'Connor wrote for a unanimous Court in *Jimmy Swaggart Ministries*. Justice O'Connor found that a tax of general applicability on the proceeds of sales of goods and services did not violate the establishment clause when it was applied to the sales of religious literature. The free exercise clause did not require an exemption from such a general tax for religious activities. Justice O'Connor's opinion

If a tax employs a religious classification, or provides a denominational preference, the tax will violate the establishment clause.[41] To the extent that such a tax constitutes a burden on some persons due to their religious affiliation the law would also violate the free exercise clause.[42] However, the Supreme Court has never ruled that the free exercise clause requires the government to grant any person or organization an exemption from a generally applicable, religiously neutral tax that was not a prior restraint on religious activity.

In *United States v. Lee,*[43] the Court denied an Amish employer of Amish workmen an exemption from compulsory participation in the Social Security System. The majority opinion, written by Chief Justice Burger, first held that the employer could not claim the statutory exemption allowed self-employed individuals who had religious objections to payment of the tax. The Chief Justice first considered whether the payment of social security taxes by an Amish employer or the receipt of benefits by Amish employees from the system interfered with the free exercise of their religious beliefs. The Chief Justice accepted Lee's claim that both payment of taxes and receipt of benefits were forbidden by the Amish faith. Therefore, because compulsory participation in the social security system violated Lee's and his employee's beliefs, such compulsion constituted a burden on the free exercise of their religion.

In the second part of the opinion, the Chief Justice asked if this burden on the free exercise of religion was justified by an overriding governmental interest and, if so, whether the religious belief could be

---

found that each of the taxes invalidated in *Murdock* and *Follett* was a flat tax (license fee) "that operated as a prior restraint on the exercise of religious liberty." The sales and use taxes could be applied to religious organizations and religious literature because "our concern in *Murdock* and *Follett*—that a flat license tax would act as a *precondition* to the free exercise of religious beliefs—is simply not present where a tax applies to all sales and uses of tangible personal property in the state." 493 U.S. at 386, 110 S.Ct. at 694 (emphasis in original).

41. See, e.g., Texas Monthly, Inc. v. Bullock, 489 U.S. 1, 109 S.Ct. 890, 103 L.Ed.2d 1 (1989) (statutory exemption from the state sales tax only for religious literature violates the establishment clause); Larson v. Valente, 456 U.S. 228, 102 S.Ct. 1673, 72 L.Ed.2d 33 (1982) (regulation of solicitations by charitable organizations interpreted to provide a denominational preference and, on that basis, to violate the establishment clause), rehearing denied 457 U.S. 1111, 102 S.Ct. 2916, 73 L.Ed.2d 1323 (1982).

In Employment Division, Dept. of Human Resources v. Smith, 494 U.S. 872, 877, 110 S.Ct. 1595, 1599, 108 L.Ed.2d 876 (1990), rehearing denied __ U.S. __, 110 S.Ct. 2605, 110 L.Ed.2d 285 (1990) Justice Scalia's majority opinion cited *Larson* as authority for the proposition that the free exercise clause would invalidate a government action that attempted to "impose special disabilities on the basis of religious views or religious status."

Taxes that provide a benefit to religious and nonreligious organizations of a certain type (such as nonprofit charitable organizations) do not violate the free exercise or establishment clause. Walz v. Tax Commission, 397 U.S. 664, 90 S.Ct. 1409, 25 L.Ed.2d 697 (1970).

42. Id. For further examination of these establishment clause and free exercise clause principles, see §§ 21.1, 21.3, 21.6.

43. 455 U.S. 252, 102 S.Ct. 1051, 71 L.Ed.2d 127 (1982).

accommodated without unduly interfering with the achievement of that interest. Chief Justice Burger found that the governmental interest in the social security system was compelling. This was a nationwide system of comprehensive insurance providing a variety of benefits and contributed to by both employers and employees. The government viewed compulsory payments as necessary for the vitality of the system because voluntary participation would undermine its soundness and would be difficult to administer.

The Court in *Lee* did not examine whether alternative means were available to achieve this compelling interest that would not burden the Amish. Chief Justice Burger stated that the Social Security taxing system was organized in such a way that it would be difficult to accommodate exceptions which might arise from a large spectrum of religious beliefs, except to the extent such accommodation had already been made by the Congress in the statutory self-employment exemption. The category exempted by statute was narrow (self-employed members of a religious group which made sufficient provision for its dependent members) and readily identifiable.

The Court seemed to be concerned, as Justice Stevens recognized in his concurrence,[44] that granting the exemption in this case would result in numerous other claims that would be difficult to administer. Thus, the government's interest in an efficient Social Security System justified forcing Lee to comply with the law in violation of his faith.

In *Hernandez v. Commissioner of Internal Revenue,*[45] the Supreme Court held that denial of a deduction from gross income for payments made to the Church of Scientology as a "fixed donation" for certain religious services did not violate the free exercise clause. The Internal Revenue Code gives a taxpayer the right to take a deduction from gross income for contributions that are charitable in nature. However, the Code, as interpreted by the Internal Revenue Service, does not allow a taxpayer to deduct a payment to a charitable organization if that payment was a quid pro quo exchange for services or products. The IRS admitted, for purposes of the litigation, that Scientology should be considered a religion. The Church of Scientology required members to take "training" and "auditing" sessions, but the Church would not provide those sessions to any member of the Church who did not pay the fixed price for the training and auditing sessions. The mandatory fixed price system was asserted to be a central tenet of Scientology.

Although the Court in *Hernandez* upheld the denial of the deduction for these payments to the Church, it used a two-step balancing

44. 455 U.S. at 262–64, 102 S.Ct. at 1057–58 (1982) (Stevens, J., concurring).

45. 490 U.S. 680, 109 S.Ct. 2136, 104 L.Ed.2d 766 (1989), rehearing denied 492 U.S. 933, 110 S.Ct. 16, 106 L.Ed.2d 630 (1989).

approach to resolve the free exercise clause problem.[46]　The majority opinion by Justice Marshall stated: "The free exercise inquiry asks whether government has placed a substantial burden on the observation of a central religious belief or practice and, if so, whether a compelling governmental interest justifies the burden."　In other words, the government would be required to show that it has an interest that is sufficiently compelling to outweigh the burden which it has placed on the individual if, but only if, the individual first shows that compliance with the government regulation places a substantial burden on the fulfillment of the individual's religious beliefs.

In determining whether the denial of the tax deduction constituted a substantial burden on the ability of members of the Church of Scientology to practice their religion, the majority opinion stated: "it is not within the judicial ken to question the centrality of particular beliefs or practices to a faith or the validity of a particular litigant's interpretation of those creeds."　Nevertheless, the majority in *Hernandez* found that the burden on the taxpayer was not very substantial. The denial of a deduction for payments to the Church imposed no greater a burden on an individual than any income tax code provision that imposed a tax burden on individuals.　All taxes paid to the government lessen the amount of disposable income that the individual has to give to a church.

The majority opinion, after minimizing the burden on the members of the Church, stated that the Court would not determine whether the burden was a substantial one.　The Court found that, even if the burden were considered substantial, the burden on free exercise of religion in this case was "justified by the broad public interest in maintaining a sound tax system free of myriad exceptions flowing from a variety of religious beliefs." [47]

In *Jimmy Swaggart Ministries v. Board of Equalization*,[48] the Supreme Court ruled that a religious organization, and its members, had no right to refuse to pay a state's general sales and use taxes on the sales and use of religious products and religious literature.　Justice O'Connor's opinion for a unanimous Court in *Jimmy Swaggart Ministries* tracked the reasoning used in the *Hernandez* decision.　The general sales and use taxes did not employ religious criteria and they

---

46. The Court also ruled that the interpretation of the tax code, which disallowed deductions that were made in exchange for services or products, did not constitute a preference for some religious denominations and did not violate the establishment clause. Hernandez v. Commissioner of Internal Revenue, 490 U.S. 680, 695–98, 109 S.Ct. 2136, 2146–48, 104 L.Ed.2d 766 (1989), rehearing denied 492 U.S. 933, 110 S.Ct. 16, 106 L.Ed.2d 630 (1989). See § 21.3.

47. Hernandez v. Commissioner of Internal Review, 490 U.S. 680, 699, 109 S.Ct. 2136, 2149, 104 L.Ed.2d 766 (1989) (internal quotation marks omitted), rehearing denied 493 U.S. 933, 110 S.Ct. 16, 106 L.Ed.2d 630 (1989) in part quoting United States v. Lee, 455 U.S. 252, 260, 102 S.Ct. 1051, 1057, 71 L.Ed.2d 127 (1982).

48. 493 U.S. 378, 110 S.Ct. 688, 107 L.Ed.2d 796 (1990).

did not constitute a special tax on religious goods or activities. Because the taxes were not denominational or religious preferences they did not have to be justified by a compelling interest. The taxes did not violate the establishment clause because the general sales and use taxes had a nonreligious purpose, a primary nonreligious effect, and the collection of taxes from a religious person or organization does not constitute an excessive entanglement between government and religion.

Justice O'Connor's opinion found that the general sales and use taxes did not constitute a prior restraint in the sale of religious literature or the ability to engage in religious activity. For that reason these taxes did not violate the free exercise clause principle, established in the 1940s decisions of the Court, that required an exemption from certain occupational license fees for persons who wanted to distribute religious literature.[49]

In *Jimmy Swaggart Ministries* the individuals, and the religious organization, did not contend that their religious beliefs prohibited them from paying taxes. Justice O'Connor's opinion dismissed their free exercise clause claim but, in so doing, she appeared to endorse the use of a balancing test for free exercise clause cases. The opinion stated:

> "Our cases have established that '[t]he free exercise inquiry asks whether government has placed a substantial burden on the observation of a central religious belief or practice and, if so, whether a compelling governmental interest justifies the burden.' *Hernandez v. Commissioner,* 490 U.S. 680, 698, 109 S.Ct. 2136, 2148, 104 L.Ed.2d 766 (1989) (citations omitted)....

> Appellant [the religious group in this case] has never alleged that the mere act of paying the tax, by itself, violates its sincere religious beliefs.

> We therefore conclude that the collection and payment of the generally applicable tax in this case imposes no constitutionally significant burden on appellant's religious practices or beliefs. The Free Exercise Clause accordingly does not *require* the State to grant appellant an exemption from its generally applicable sales and use tax. Although it is of course possible to imagine that a more onerous tax rate, even if generally applicable, might effectively choke off an adherent's religious practices, cf. *Murdock,* [Murdock v. Pennsylvania] 319 U.S., at 115, 63 S.Ct., at 876 (the burden of a flat tax could render itinerant evangelism "crushed and closed out by the sheer weight of the toll or tribute which is exacted town by town"), we face no such situation in this case. Accordingly, we

49. 493 U.S. at 391–97, 110 S.Ct. at 697–99.

intimate no views as to whether such a generally applicable tax might violate the Free Exercise Clause." [50]

Three months after the decision in *Jimmy Swaggart Ministries,* the Supreme Court issued its decision in *Employment Division v. Smith (Smith II),* [51] in which the majority ruled that the free exercise clause did not require exemptions from generally applicable criminal laws for persons whose religious beliefs prevented them from complying with the law. Justice Scalia's majority opinion in *Smith II* appears to reject the approach taken by the Court in the tax cases. The majority in *Smith II* found that courts should not balance societal interests in a general regulatory law against the burdens the law placed on persons whose religious beliefs prevented their compliance. Justice O'Connor concurred in the result in *Smith II,* but she wrote a separate opinion to express her belief that the free exercise clause required the judiciary to use the balancing approach that was rejected in the majority opinion. [52]

After *Jimmy Swaggart Ministries* and *Smith II,* it appears that the Supreme Court will not require the government to grant tax exemptions to religious organizations or persons who refuse to pay a generally applicable, religiously neutral tax that does not operate as a prior restraint on activity protected by the first amendment.

Military Regulations. In *Goldman v. Weinberger,* [53] the Court held that the free exercise clause did not require the Air Force to allow a serviceman, an orthodox Jew and ordained rabbi, to wear his yarmulke while on duty and in uniform. The Air Force had a regulation which prohibited on-duty and in-uniform personnel from wearing any nonregulation items of clothing. For some years, this officer had worn his yarmulke while on duty and in uniform, without objection from Air Force authorities. Eventually, he was informed that he could not continue to wear the yarmulke while on duty. The majority opinion by Justice Rehnquist appeared to employ a two-step balancing analysis, although Justice Rehnquist's opinion was clouded by a variety of statements concerning the need for the judiciary to defer to military authorities concerning matters of military deportment.

The first step of the inquiry in *Goldman* presented no problem, because the regulation clearly imposed a burden on the officer's ability

---

50. 493 U.S. at 384, 391, 110 S.Ct. at 693, 697.

51. 494 U.S. 872, 110 S.Ct. 1595, 108 L.Ed.2d 876 (1990), rehearing denied __ U.S. __, 110 S.Ct. 2605, 1110 L.Ed.2d 285 (1990). This decision is examined at the start of this section of the Treatise.

52. Employment Division, Dept. of Human Resources v. Smith, 494 U.S. 872, 891, 110 S.Ct. 1595, 1606, 108 L.Ed.2d 876 (1990) (O'Connor, J., concurring in the judgment), rehearing denied __ U.S. __,

110 S.Ct. 2605, 110 L.Ed.2d 285 (1990). Justices Brennan, Marshall and Blackmun joined the parties of Justice O'Connor's opinion in which she advocated the use of the balancing test, but they did not agree with her conclusion regarding the outcome of the case. 494 U.S. at 907, 110 S.Ct. at 1615 (Blackmun, J., joined by Brennan & Marshall, JJ., dissenting).

53. 475 U.S. 503, 106 S.Ct. 1310, 89 L.Ed.2d 478 (1986).

to conform his actions to his sincerely held religious belief. The second stage of the traditional balancing test would have required a determination of whether the government had a sufficiently important or compelling interest that justified denying the requested exemption from the dress code. Justice Rehnquist's majority opinion in part appears to apply this test and to find the interest in military discipline is a sufficiently important reason to outweigh the incidental burden on an individual's religious belief. In part, Justice Rehnquist's opinion appears to require such deference to military authorities that one might question whether there was any meaningful judicial review of the nature of the government interest in this case.

Three concurring justices in *Goldman* noted their belief that the government's interest in requiring uniformity in military dress did outweigh the burden on the individual.[54] The uniform dress requirement avoided the need for the government to engage in a case-by-case and religion-by-religion determination of whether specific types of religious symbols or apparel could be worn by individual members of the military without undermining the military's interest in uniformity and discipline. This fact strengthened the concurring justices' assessment of the military's interest in this case. The four dissenting Justices believed that the government had failed to show any overriding or significant interest that would be undercut by allowing the officer in this case to wear his religious apparel.[55]

In *Johnson v. Robison*,[56] the Supreme Court upheld the granting of educational benefits to veterans who served active duty but denied them to conscientious objectors who performed alternate service. In finding that there was no violation of the free exercise clause, the majority first noted that there was little, if any, real burden on religious practices which resulted from these programs. Second, the government interest in the raising and supporting of armies was of a "kind and weight" sufficient to overcome the alleged burden on the free exercise right of those who did not receive the educational benefits.

Government Administrative Systems—Use of Social Security Numbers. In *Bowen v. Roy*[57] the Supreme Court held that an individual child and her parent did not have a free exercise right to preclude a state agency from using a Social Security number to identify the child. This case involved a challenge to use of Social Security numbers in

---

54. Goldman v. Weinberger, 475 U.S. 503, 510, 106 S.Ct. 1310, 1314, 89 L.Ed.2d 478 (1986) (Stevens, J., joined by White and Powell, JJ., concurring).

55. Goldman v. Weinberger, 475 U.S. 503, 513, 106 S.Ct. 1310, 1316, 89 L.Ed.2d 478 (1986) (Brennan, J., joined by Marshall, J., dissenting); 475 U.S. at 524, 106

S.Ct. at 1322 (Blackmun, J., dissenting); 475 U.S. at 528, 106 S.Ct. at 1324 (O'Connor, J., joined by Marshall, J., dissenting).

56. 415 U.S. 361, 94 S.Ct. 1160, 39 L.Ed.2d 389 (1974).

57. 476 U.S. 693, 106 S.Ct. 2147, 90 L.Ed.2d 735 (1986).

federal Food Stamp and Aid to Families with Dependent Children programs. Federal statutes require state agencies administering these programs to employ Social Security numbers in identifying the recipients of aid. Initially, the parents of the child contended that obtaining a Social Security number violated their Native American religious beliefs. Because the obtaining and submission of a Social Security number was a condition to the receipt of such benefits, the state refused to pay benefits on the child's behalf. At trial, it was learned that a Social Security number for the child (whose name was Little Bird of the Snow) had been issued very near the time of her birth. At that point in the litigation, the child's father sought an injunction to prohibit the government from making any use of her Social Security number. The Supreme Court rejected the father's attempt to prohibit the state agency from using the child's Social Security number in administering aid programs.

Chief Justice Burger announced the judgment of the Court in *Roy* and delivered an opinion which was, in part, an opinion of the Court and, in part, an opinion expressing only the views of himself and Justices Powell and Rehnquist. In the portion of the opinion by Chief Justice Burger that was a majority opinion, the Court held that the government's use of a Social Security number submitted to it, or the assignment of some type of identifying number to an individual's case file in order to efficiently operate a government program, did not violate the free exercise clause. Government administrative practices do not impose a clear burden on an individual's religious belief if the government is not forcing the person to take an action contrary to her religious belief. Additionally, the government's use of the previously submitted number, or the use of a newly assigned number to the case file, promoted a government interest in operating a welfare program in an efficient and honest manner that outweighs the incidental burden on the objecting individual.[58]

The Court in *Roy* did not rule on the question of whether a federal requirement that a person obtain and provide a Social Security number as a condition for receiving aid violated the first amendment free exercise clause insofar as no exemption was granted for persons whose sincerely held religious beliefs prevented them from meeting that condition. If a case arises where persons cannot provide an identifying number to the government because of their sincerely held religious

---

58. Most of the Chief Justice's analysis of this point was summarized in his assertion that "[n]ever to our knowledge has the Court interpreted the First Amendment to require the Government *itself* to behave in ways that the individual believes will further his or her spiritual development or that of his or her family. The Free Exercise Clause simply cannot be understood to require the Government to conduct its own internal affairs in ways that comport with the religious beliefs of particular citizens." 476 U.S. at 699, 106 S.Ct. at 2152 (emphasis in original).

beliefs, the government requirement would be upheld if the Supreme Court refused to use a balancing test.[59] However, in such a case the Supreme Court might use the two-step balancing test in determining whether those individuals should be granted an exemption from the condition.[60] In the first step of the analysis, the Court would determine whether there was a significant burden on the person's sincerely held religious belief. Assuming that such a burden existed, the Court would go on to examine whether the government had a compelling or sufficiently important interest to justify denying the requested religious exemption. In analyzing the government's interest, and the extent to which it would be undercut by the exemption, the Court might consider possible administrative alternatives. It also might consider whether the danger of persons falsely making a religious claim to be free from identification by number might undercut the government's ability to efficiently operate the aid program.[61] Four of the justices voting in *Roy* indicated that they would apply a balancing test to determine whether an individual would have to submit an identifying number to the government as a condition to receiving welfare benefits if such a case were clearly presented to the Court.[62] Justice White dissented in *Roy*

59. The Supreme Court refused to use a balancing test, when it determined that the government did not have to give an exemption from a law banning the use of peyote to persons who used peyote due to their religious beliefs. Employment Division, Dept. of Human Resources v. Smith, 494 U.S. 872, 110 S.Ct. 1595, 108 L.Ed.2d 876 (1990), rehearing denied ___ U.S. ___, 110 S.Ct. 2605, 110 L.Ed.2d 285 (1990). However, in that case the Court did not overrule the cases in which it used a balancing test to determine whether the government had to waive a condition for unemployment compensation cases. These cases were examined in earlier paragraphs of this section of the Treatise.

60. Id.

61. For an explanation of an analytical system that would assess the danger of persons insincerely claiming exemptions as a part of the determination whether the government must grant any exemption from a regulatory statute, see Freed & Polsby, Race, Religion, and Public Policy: Bob Jones University v. United States, 1983 Sup.Ct.Rev. 1.

See Quaring v. Peterson, 728 F.2d 1121 (8th Cir.1984) (per curiam), judgment affirmed by an evenly divided court, Jensen v. Quaring, 472 U.S. 478, 105 S.Ct. 3492, 86 L.Ed.2d 383 (1985). The court of appeals in *Quaring* found that a woman's sincerely

held belief that the Second Commandment prohibited her from possessing a photograph was a religious belief though the woman was not a member of an organized church. The government's requirement that all automobile drivers obtain a driver's license with the individual's photograph on it was a burden on her ability to carry out her sincerely held religious belief. The court of appeals concluded that the state interest was not sufficient to deny the woman a driver's license without her photograph if she otherwise was qualified for the license. Justice Powell did not participate in the Supreme Court review of this decision. The other eight justices split four to four in this case and, therefore, the court of appeals decision was affirmed without opinion by the Supreme Court.

62. Bowen v. Roy, 476 U.S. 693, 712–16, 106 S.Ct. 2147, 2158–60, 90 L.Ed.2d 735 (1986) (Blackmun, J., concurring in part); 476 U.S. at 724–32, 106 S.Ct. at 2164–69 (O'Connor, J., joined by Brennan and Marshall, JJ., concurring in part and dissenting in part). Justice Stevens concurred in part in the majority opinion and did not explain whether he would apply the balancing test to determine whether there should be an exemption from the requirement of obtaining and submitting a social security number. 476 U.S. at 716–23, 106 S.Ct. at 2160–64 (Stevens, J., concurring in part and concurring in the result).

because he believed that prior decisions of the Supreme Court which established and applied the balancing test required granting this family an exemption to the Social Security number requirement.[63]

Government Administrative Systems—Governmental Use or Destruction of Government Property. The government does not have to justify its administrative practices under the free exercise clause, even if its actions are inconsistent with the sincerely held religious beliefs of persons in our society. In *Bowen v. Roy*[64] the Court found that the government would not have to justify its practice of assigning numbers, including social security numbers, to identify the recipients of certain welfare benefits. Although the assigning of numbers to case files might burden the sincerely held religious beliefs of persons who objected to the use of numbers to identify themselves, the government was not requiring those persons to act, or to refrain from acting, in a manner inconsistent with their religion. The government did not have to justify its own practices under the free exercise clause merely because those practices were inconsistent with the religious beliefs of persons that the government regulated.

Similarly, in *Lyng v. Northwest Indian Cemetery Protective Association*[65] the Supreme Court found that the free exercise clause did not restrict the ability of the Federal government to permit timber harvesting, and to engage in road construction, in an area of a federally owned national forest, even though this forested area was sacred to members of American Indian tribes and even though the destruction of the forested area imposed a significant burden on the sincerely held religious beliefs of those persons. The majority opinion in *Lyng,* written by Justice O'Connor, found that *Bowen v. Roy* established the principle that the incidental burden on persons' religious beliefs caused by the government's conduct of its own internal affairs was not subject to free exercise clause restrictions.[66]

63. Justice White's dissenting opinion consisted entirely of the following statement: "Being of the view that Thomas v. Review Board [citation omitted] and Sherbert v. Verner [citation omitted] control this case, I cannot join the Court's opinion and judgment." Bowen v. Roy, 476 U.S. 693, 733, 106 S.Ct. 2147, 2169, 90 L.Ed.2d 735 (1986) (White, J., dissenting).

64. 476 U.S. 693, 106 S.Ct. 2147, 90 L.Ed.2d 735 (1986).

65. 485 U.S. 439, 108 S.Ct. 1319, 99 L.Ed.2d 534 (1988).

66. Id. Justice O'Connor, in her opinion for the Court, stated: "whatever may be the exact line between unconstitutional prohibitions on the free exercise of religion and the legitimate conduct by government of its own affairs, the location of the line cannot depend on measuring the effects of a governmental action on a religious objector's spiritual development. The government does not dispute, and we have no reason to doubt, that the logging and road-building projects at issue in this case could have devastating effects on traditional Indian Religious Practices." Lyng v. Northwest Indian Cemetery Protective Association, 485 U.S. 439, 452, 108 S.Ct. 1319, 1327, 99 L.Ed.2d 534 (1988). Thus, the severe impact of the government's use of its property on the religious beliefs of the members of the Indian Tribe did not establish a basis for using the free exercise clause to test the government action.

Aid to Racially Discriminatory Schools. In *Bob Jones University v. United States,*[67] the Court evidenced little difficulty in finding no violation of the free exercise clause in the denial of tax exempt status under the Internal Revenue Code to all schools that discriminated on the basis of race, including religiously affiliated schools that discriminated because of sincerely held religious beliefs.[68] Because the Court found that the schools which claimed the exemption on the basis of religious beliefs did so sincerely and that the denial of the exemption would have substantial impact on the operation of their schools, the Supreme Court weighed the governmental interest in avoiding aid to racially discriminatory practices against the burden on the free exercise rights of those schools, their students, and the parents of those students.

The governmental interest in ending racial discrimination in education was labeled both a "compelling" and "fundamental, overriding interest." The Court found that the interest of the government did not have to be achieved through "less restrictive means" because the interest asserted by the schools and their students "cannot be accommodated" with the compelling governmental interest in ending racial discrimination in education.

It should be noted, however, that the Court did not rule on the question of whether the government could outlaw the existence of religious schools that discriminated on the basis of race in their admissions or educational policies.[69] The Court ruled only that the governmental interest outweighed "whatever burden denial of tax benefits places on petitioners' exercise of their religious belief" and

---

67. 461 U.S. 574, 103 S.Ct. 2017, 76 L.Ed.2d 157 (1983).

68. Justice Rehnquist, the only dissenter in this case, dissented on the basis that Congress had not authorized the Internal Revenue Service to make such a decision, even though he agreed that Congress could make such an authorization. Bob Jones University v. United States, 461 U.S. 574, 612, 103 S.Ct. 2017, 2039, 76 L.Ed.2d 157, 186 (1983) (Rehnquist, J., dissenting). Justice Powell, concurring, agreed with the Court's constitutional rulings but attempted to limit the Court's ability to allow the Internal Revenue Service to promote "public policy" without clear authorization by Congress. 461 U.S. at 606, 103 S.Ct. at 2036, 76 L.Ed.2d at 182 (Powell, J., concurring in part and concurring in the judgment). Although the Court's ultimate decision in this case has been the subject of little dispute, there are serious questions concerning whether in other settings the Internal Revenue Service should be al-

lowed to define public policy in the nature of its authority as broadly as was done in this case. See Freed and Polsby, Race, Religion, and Public Policy: Bob Jones University v. United States, 1983 Sup.Ct. Rev. 1; Stephan, Bob Jones University v. United States: Public Policy in Search of Tax Policy, 1983 Sup.Ct.Rev. 33.

69. The Supreme Court has held that legislation passed pursuant to the thirteenth amendment prohibits racial discrimination by private schools. Runyon v. McCrary, 427 U.S. 160, 96 S.Ct. 2586, 49 L.Ed.2d 415 (1976), appeal after remand 569 F.2d 1294 (4th Cir.1978), certiorari denied 439 U.S. 927, 99 S.Ct. 311, 58 L.Ed.2d 320 (1978). The Court specifically left open the question of whether a school that discriminated by race due to religious beliefs would be governed by this statute. 427 U.S. at 167 n. 6, 96 S.Ct. at 2593 n. 6, 49 L.Ed.2d at 423 n. 6. See §§ 16.4(c), 18.9(a)(2)(b), 19.6–19.10, 21.4(c)(2), supra.

noted that the denial "will not prevent those schools from observing their religious tenets."

§ 21.9   Recurrent Free Exercise Problems

(a) Exemptions From Military Service

The Supreme Court has never held that the religion clauses require the government to grant an exemption from military service to persons who object to such service on a religious basis. However, it is at least arguable that such an exemption should be required if the interests of those who object to military service were balanced against the government's need for universal conscription in the same manner as other interests are balanced under the modern free exercise clause cases.[1]

While there are early decisions which state that the war powers of the government should not be required to yield for the accommodation of individual beliefs,[2] strong considerations weigh in favor of requiring such an exemption under modern free exercise clause analysis.[3] The individual interest in adhering to religious beliefs which prohibit the use of violence would seem strong and the burden imposed on those beliefs by universal conscription is severe. Additionally, the government's interest in raising armies might be adequately met without the conscription of these persons. The possible lack of suitability for armed combat on the part of these persons and the social problems created by the forced conscription of religious objectors also indicates that no important government interest would in reality be furthered by the drafting of these persons into the armed services.

Yet the government interest in defense, especially in time of war, has been historically deferred to by the Supreme Court.[4] Thus, the Court could find that it was not the proper branch of government to weigh these individual interests against the national interest in defense. Indeed, the Court in 1971 approved the government's refusal to exempt those who objected only to particular wars and indicated that

§ 21.9

1. In assessing the need for a religious exemption from state regulation, the court employs a two part balancing test. First, the claimant must show that the regulation substantially burdens the practice of his religion. Second, the government interest in the regulation is weighed against the burden on free exercise rights. For a more complete discussion of the modern cases see § 21.8, supra.

2. See, The Selective Service Draft Law Cases, 245 U.S. 366, 389–90, 38 S.Ct. 159, 165, 62 L.Ed. 349 (1918); United States v. MacIntosh, 283 U.S. 605, 51 S.Ct. 570, 75 L.Ed. 1302 (1931); Dickinson v. United

States, 346 U.S. 389, 74 S.Ct. 152, 98 L.Ed. 132 (1953).

3. For an excellent discussion of this and other issues raised by conscientious objectors, see Greenawalt, All or Nothing at All; The Defeat of Selective Conscientious Objection, 1971 Supreme Court Rev. 31.

4. See, e.g., United States v. O'Brien, 391 U.S. 367, 88 S.Ct. 1673, 20 L.Ed.2d 672 (1968) (prohibition of destroying draft cards upheld), rehearing denied 393 U.S. 900, 89 S.Ct. 63, 21 L.Ed.2d 188 (1968); Korematsu v. United States, 323 U.S. 214, 65 S.Ct. 193, 89 L.Ed. 194 (1944) (domestic detention of Japanese persons in World War II upheld),

even today no exemption might be required.[5] In short, there are good arguments on both sides of this issue. Absent congressional authorization for universal conscription and a case concerning the need for a religious exemption, the question will remain unresolved.

Despite the lack of certainty regarding the need for any religious exemption, the history of statutory exemptions and their interpretation gives us insights into this clash between religious beliefs and the military powers. Even if no exemption need be granted, if the government grants an exemption to any persons who object to war on a religious basis it must do so in a way which violates neither religion clause.

Any exception must be so broad in nature that it does not benefit particular religions and thereby violate the establishment clause.[6] Thus, any exemption must have a secular purpose, a secular effect and avoid giving rise to an excessive entanglement between government and religion. Establishment clause considerations favor broad exemption from military service for conscientious objectors as narrow definitions are likely to favor a given religion or, at a minimum, common religious beliefs which are theistic (God-centered).

In refusing anyone an exemption under a statute, the government must not violate the free exercise clause. This will require the government to grant the exemption to all whose conscription into military service would not aid the defense effort because their beliefs make them similarly unsuited for service. The government remains free to draft those whose objections to war could be differentiated on a secular basis from those it exempted from service.

The Supreme Court decisions regarding conscientious objectors have followed this analysis. The Court has deferred to the interest in defense and refused to declare a first amendment right to avoid military service. However, the Court has read the statutory exemption from service to apply to all persons who are opposed to war in any form on the basis of beliefs which are the functional equivalent of a theistic religious belief.[7] Thus, any persons who objected to all wars on the basis of sincerely held personal principles which occupied a place in their lives similar to religion would receive an exemption. Problems under the religion clauses were avoided by interpreting the exemption so that all those who objected to participation in any war received an exemption. The only ones who failed to qualify for an exemption were those whose objections to all war were not sincere or whose objections

rehearing denied 324 U.S. 885, 65 S.Ct. 674, 89 L.Ed. 1435 (1945).

5. Gillette v. United States, 401 U.S. 437, 461 n. 23, 91 S.Ct. 828, 842 n. 23, 28 L.Ed.2d 168 (1971), rehearing denied 402 U.S. 934, 91 S.Ct. 1521, 28 L.Ed.2d 869 (1971).

6. Welsh v. United States, 398 U.S. 333, 356, 90 S.Ct. 1792, 1804–05, 26 L.Ed.2d 308 (1970) (Harlan, J., concurring).

7. United States v. Seeger, 380 U.S. 163, 85 S.Ct. 850, 13 L.Ed.2d 733 (1965).

were based "solely upon considerations of policy, pragmatism or expediency." [8]

The history of military conscription and statutory exemptions has avoided clear constitutional rulings beyond these guidelines. Prior to the Civil War, the conscription of men into the armed service was a matter regulated to state law. During this time it was customary to allow a person to avoid service by the payment of a fee. Near the middle of the nineteenth century, some states began to allow those who opposed service on a religious basis to do alternative noncombatant work in lieu of joining the army. [9]

By 1864, after the federal government had taken over the administration of the armed services, the first federal statute considering conscientious objectors was passed, providing for alternate service in military hospitals. The Selective Service Law of 1917 provided an exemption from compulsory combatant service to anyone belonging to a "well-recognized" religious sect or organization whose creed forbade members to participate in war in any form and whose religious convictions were against war or participation in it. This provision was upheld by the Supreme Court but it must be remembered that the Court did not actively protect religious values during this period. [10]

The Selective Training and Service Act of 1940 broadened the classification by exempting those who by "religious training and belief" were opposed to participation in war in any form. Eight years later, in the Selective Service Act of 1948, the exemption section was narrowed with the addition of a clarification of "religious training and belief" as "belief in relation to a Supreme Being" and not "essentially political, sociological, or philosophical views or a merely personal moral code." [11]

The "Supreme Being Clause" of the 1948 Act was interpreted by the Selective Service System, and the Department of Justice, as excluding those whose objections to service were not based on theistic beliefs. But in *United States v. Seeger* [12] the Supreme Court interpreted the statute as granting an exemption to all those whose nontheistic beliefs occupied in their lives the place of a religion.

The Military Service Act of 1967 reflected the *Seeger* decision and deleted the reference to the "Supreme Being." The exemption clause is now phrased thusly:

8. Welsh v. United States, 398 U.S. 333, 342–43, 90 S.Ct. 1792, 1798, 26 L.Ed.2d 308 (1970) (Plurality opinion by Black, J.).

The scope of court authority to inquire into the sincerity of religious beliefs is examined in § 21.11, supra.

9. E.N. Wright, Conscientious Objectors in the Civil War (1931).

10. The Selective Draft Law Cases, 245 U.S. 366, 389–90, 38 S.Ct. 159, 165, 62 L.Ed. 349 (1918). For a discussion of the Court's position on religious issues during this period see § 21.7, supra.

11. 50 U.S.C.A. § 301.

12. 380 U.S. 163, 85 S.Ct. 850, 13 L.Ed.2d 733 (1965).

[Nothing] contained in this Act shall be construed to require any person to be subject to combatant training and service in the land or naval forces of the United States who, by reason of religious training and belief, is conscientiously opposed to participation in war in any form. As used in this subsection, the term religious training and belief does not include essentially political, sociological, or philosophical views, or a merely personal code.[13]

In 1970 the Court interpreted this language to include all those whose sincere beliefs required them to refuse to participate in any war for other than purely pragmatic reasons.[14] Justice Harlan concurred in this result because he was of the opinion that the statute's restriction to only religious beliefs violated the establishment clause.[15] But there was no ruling of the Court on this issue because the new statutory interpretation avoided the question.

Gillette v. United States[16] was a case where the Court was required to address the compatibility of the statutory exemption with the religion clauses. The current statutory exemption is clearly granted only to those who oppose participation in any war and denied to those who object only to some wars. This distinction was challenged by those whose formal religion or religious philosophy required them to refrain only from participation in "unjust" wars.

A majority of the justices found that the narrow definition of the statute was compatible with both religion clauses. The Court held that the granting of exemption only to those whose beliefs opposed all war did not violate the establishment clause. The majority found that the limitation was based on secular reasons relating to the persons involved rather than adherence to accepted beliefs. The Court found a secular purpose in defining the exemption so as to exclude in the most fair way those persons not readily available or suitable for service due to their beliefs. The effect of the statute was not religious because it served only to insure a fair process by avoiding a definition which would complicate the determination of those with such claims. The definition did not have the effect of aiding religion because it did not encourage any belief. Finally, the narrow definition avoided further entanglement between government and religion as there was less need to examine the sincerity and character of individual beliefs.

The claimants in *Gillette* also argued that failure to grant an exemption to those who opposed only unjust wars on a religious basis violated the free exercise clause. The majority opinion found that the burden on these persons was justified by substantial government inter-

---

13. P.L. No. 90–40, June 30, 1967, 81 Stat. 100, 50 U.S.C.A. § 451 et seq.

14. Welsh v. United States, 398 U.S. 333, 90 S.Ct. 1792, 26 L.Ed.2d 308 (1970) (Plurality opinion by Black, J.).

15. 398 U.S. at 344, 90 S.Ct. at 1798 (Harlan, J., concurring).

16. 401 U.S. 437, 91 S.Ct. 828, 28 L.Ed.2d 168 (1971), rehearing denied 402 U.S. 934, 91 S.Ct. 1521, 28 L.Ed.2d 869 (1971).

ests in defense and the power to raise armies. It was clear that the Court reached this result by granting great deference to these governmental interests and without any real weighing of the individual interests. With these important national interests at issue, the Court simply refused to review the legislative determination of who should serve in the armed forces as the justices did not view the law as a penalty against any belief or religion.[17]

Finally, the treatment of those who had done alternative service as conscientious objectors did raise one further issue. The persons who were granted this exemption but required to do alternative service did not receive the same benefits as those who served in normal military operations. In *Johnson v. Robison,*[18] the Court found that this differing treatment did not violate the first amendment. Since the majority found both a secular distinction between the types of service and a minimal burden on the practice of religion resulting from that distinction, the justices had little trouble in ruling that the secular governmental interest was sufficient to overrule the conscientious objector's claim for further benefits.

(b) Health and Medical Regulations

It has been the time honored position of American courts that the government interest in health and medical treatment of the populace will override individual religious objections to such regulation. These brief notes describe the main issues that have arisen in this area and the historic responses of the courts to these issues. However, it should be noted that all of these issues were resolved prior to the development of the modern balancing test under the free exercise clause. It is always possible that the Supreme Court will reverse its position on these questions, so one should evaluate these issues under the modern approach. But, despite the possibility of contrary rulings in the future, it must be remembered that the following notes do reflect the current position of the Court.

(1) **Vaccinations.** The Supreme Court very early in this century held that an individual could be required to receive a vaccination against disease.[19] Although the submission to such a program might violate the individual's religious beliefs, a compulsory vaccination program is a direct method of effectuating the secular interest in public health.

Even when the chance of epidemics have been small, the courts have continually upheld vaccination requirements as a precondition to

17. 401 U.S. at 461–62, 91 S.Ct. at 842–43.

18. 415 U.S. 361, 94 S.Ct. 1160, 39 L.Ed.2d 389 (1974).

19. Jacobson v. Massachusetts, 197 U.S.

a child's attendance at public school.[20]

(2) Treatment of Children. American courts have upheld the right of the state to protect the health and safety of minor children over the religiously based objections of the child or their parent. Thus, courts have appointed guardians to consent to necessary medical treatment (such as blood transfusions) for children even though the treatment violates the child's or parent's religion.[21]

Similarly appropriate action may be taken against parents for the neglect of the health or safety of their children regardless of whether the parent acted on the basis of religious principles.[22]

(3) Blood Transfusions and the "Right to Die". Current developments in medicine have permitted the continuation of a person's life for extended periods of time after it is apparent that the person will never recover from some eventually terminal illness or injury. This scientific advance has raised serious questions as to whether an individual can be required to undergo such treatment or whether that person has a "right to die." This problem, in terms of modern life support techniques, has not yet been finally resolved by the state or federal courts.

There is no issue under the religion clauses unless the individual's desire to forego medical treatment and die a "natural" death is based on religious beliefs.[23] If the individual's preference is not religious in nature there is only a conflict between personal choice relating to health and state medical regulations. Such a conflict would be resolved under the due process clauses.[24]

11, 25 S.Ct. 358, 49 L.Ed. 643 (1905).

20. See, e.g., Wright v. DeWitt School District, 238 Ark. 906, 385 S.W.2d 644 (1965); Vonnegut v. Baun, 206 Ind. 172, 188 N.E. 677 (1934); McCartney v. Austin, 57 Misc.2d 525, 293 N.Y.S.2d 188 (1968), judgment affirmed 31 A.D.2d 370, 298 N.Y.S.2d 26 (1969).

21. See, e.g., In re Sampson, 29 N.Y.2d 900, 328 N.Y.S.2d 686, 278 N.E.2d 918 (1972); People ex rel. Wallace v. Labrenz, 411 Ill. 618, 104 N.E.2d 769 (1952), certiorari denied 344 U.S. 824, 73 S.Ct. 24, 97 L.Ed. 642 (1952); Jehovah's Witnesses v. King County Hosp., 278 F.Supp. 488 (W.D.Wash. 1967), affirmed 390 U.S. 598, 88 S.Ct. 1260, 20 L.Ed.2d 158 (1968), rehearing denied 391 U.S. 961, 88 S.Ct. 1844, 20 L.Ed.2d 874 (1968).

In a few cases a court has refused to order medical treatment which was beneficial but not related to the preservation of the child's life. See, In re Green, 448 Pa. 338, 292 A.2d 387 (1972), appeal after remand 452 Pa. 373, 307 A.2d 279 (1973).

22. See Perricone v. New Jersey, 371 U.S. 890, 83 S.Ct. 189, 9 L.Ed.2d 124 (1962).

23. In Wisconsin v. Yoder, 406 U.S. 205, 92 S.Ct. 1526, 32 L.Ed.2d 15 (1972) the Court made it clear that exemption from regulations on the basis of the free exercise clause required a showing that the regulation interfered with religious beliefs and practices. This decision is noted in § 21.8, supra.

24. In Cruzan by Cruzan v. Director, Missouri Department of Public Health, 497 U.S. ___, 110 S.Ct. 2841, 111 L.Ed.2d 224 (1990) the Court upheld a state requirement that the parents or guardian of a comatose individual prove by "clear and convincing" evidence that the comatose patient would reject life sustaining medical treatment or nutrition if she were competent to make such a decision for herself. The majority opinion, by Chief Justice Rehnquist, assumed, but did not decide, that a mentally competent adult had a right to reject medical treatment that was

When the objection to medical treatment is based on religious principles, however, a serious free exercise clause problem is presented. While the modern life support issue has not been resolved, courts have been confronted with cases in which a person has refused medical treatment (usually a blood transfusion) on the basis of religious beliefs. Where the person who needed treatment was a minor [25] or mentally incompetent,[26] the courts have ordered the treatment, but where the person is a mentally competent adult, there is a split among the cases as to whether the life saving treatment may be ordered.

Those courts who view the state as having an identifiable interest in the life of each person will order the treatment, for this state interest will outweigh the individual's right to freedom of conscience.[27] Some courts have taken the position that the state has no interest in protecting a person's life against his own wishes. These courts have approached the problem in a manner similar to that of John Stuart Mill, whose philosophy mandated the primacy of an individual decision to die unless a contrary state decision could be justified by a very narrow and important social interest.[28] Such an approach has led these courts to take the position that life saving procedures cannot be ordered for a competent adult who refuses treatment on a religious basis.[29] Yet it should be noted that even judges who are philosophically disposed to such a view may in fact order treatment when the patient indicates that they want to live but that they simply will not sign the required consent forms.[30]

Because the Supreme Court has not resolved this issue, no final opinion can be given regarding the propriety of such orders. However, in considering this issue it should be remembered that the balancing test can yield either result—depending on whether the court would or would not accept the legitimacy of the state interest in individual life.

protected by the due process clause. The *Cruzan* decision is examined in § 18.30(c). The *Cruzan* case did not involve any claims or issues under the free exercise clause.

25. See notes 21 and 22 of this section, supra.

26. See, e.g., Application of the President and Directors of Georgetown College, 331 F.2d 1000 (D.C.Cir.1964), rehearing denied 331 F.2d 1010 (1964), certiorari denied 377 U.S. 978, 84 S.Ct. 1883, 12 L.Ed.2d 746 (1964); see also Winters v. Miller, 446 F.2d 65 (2d Cir.1971), certiorari denied 404 U.S. 985, 92 S.Ct. 450, 30 L.Ed.2d 369 (1971).

27. See, e.g., John F. Kennedy Memorial Hosp. v. Heston, 58 N.J. 576, 279 A.2d 670 (1971); United States v. George, 239 F.Supp. 752 (D.Conn.1965).

28. J.S. Mill, On Liberty 9–10 (Crofts Classics ed.).

29. See In re Brooks' Estate, 32 Ill.2d 361, 205 N.E.2d 435 (1965); see also the opinion of Judge (now Chief Justice) Burger in Application of the President and Directors of Georgetown College, 331 F.2d 1010, 1015 (D.C.Cir.1964) (Petition for rehearing en banc—Burger, J., dissenting).

30. Application of the President and Directors of Georgetown College, 331 F.2d 1000, 1010 (D.C.Cir.1964) (Wright, J.), certiorari denied 377 U.S. 978, 84 S.Ct. 1883, 12 L.Ed.2d 746 (1964).

IV. OTHER ESTABLISHMENT— FREE EXERCISE PROBLEMS

§ 21.10 Sunday Closing Laws

In four companion decisions the Supreme Court upheld "Sunday closing laws" over objections based on the establishment clause, the free exercise clause, and the due process and equal protection clauses.[1] These laws prohibited most forms of commercial activity on Sundays. Several forms of retail commercial activities were allowed to operate on Sunday but these classifications were easily upheld.

Absent consideration under the religion clauses, the goal of providing a uniform day of rest must be held to be a legitimate government goal for the purposes of the due process and equal protection clauses. To rule otherwise would involve a return to the position that it is not a lawful end of government to regulate the hours and conditions of labor. The issue under the equal protection clause was whether the exemptions were reasonable in view of the legislative goal. Because the state laws involved purely economic legislation the classification had to be upheld as long as it was arguable that it related to the legitimate state end.[2]

The question of whether these laws violated the establishment clause received the most comprehensive analysis in *McGowan v. Maryland*.[3] Writing for the majority, Chief Justice Warren found that the present "purpose and effect" of these laws was not religious, even though the laws originally had a religious character. Crucial to the majority determination of this question was the history of these laws. Despite their religious origin, such laws had existed in Virginia following the passage of the act for religious freedom that embodied the views of Jefferson and Madison. The existence of such legislation in virtually every one of the original states, including Virginia, detracted from the view that the amendment was necessarily incompatible with all Sunday closing laws.

If those laws had retained their religious character the majority would nevertheless have found them invalid as an attempt to advance religion, but the history of these laws showed that they had become non-religious over the years. Sunday closing laws now appeared in some form in every state and these laws had the support of labor and trade associations as measures for the health and welfare of commercial workers. Modern statutory programs appeared to be designed to insure a uniform day of rest and non-commercial activity.

§ 21.10

1. McGowan v. Maryland, 366 U.S. 420, 81 S.Ct. 1101, 6 L.Ed.2d 393 (1961); Two Guys from Harrison—Allentown, Inc. v. McGinley, 366 U.S. 582, 81 S.Ct. 1135, 6 L.Ed.2d 551 (1961); Braunfeld v. Brown, 366 U.S. 599, 81 S.Ct. 1144, 6 L.Ed.2d 563 (1961); Gallagher v. Crown Kosher Super Market, 366 U.S. 617, 81 S.Ct. 1122, 6 L.Ed.2d 536 (1961).

2. McGowan v. Maryland, 366 U.S. 420, 425–28, 81 S.Ct. 1101, 1104–06, 6 L.Ed.2d 393 (1961).

3. Id.

Undoubtedly Sunday closing laws made attendance at religious services easier for workers of majority Christian sects. However, given the secular purpose of the law, this was seen only as an effect which happened to coincide with certain religious beliefs and not a real aid to those religions. To hold otherwise would be to require the state to pursue its goal of establishing a uniform day of rest by choosing a day when the least number of people might use the time to attend religious services. In the Court's view such a result would be hostile to the public welfare without promoting the separation of church and state.

While a majority of the justices had little trouble in upholding these laws against a general establishment clause challenge,[4] a much more difficult problem was presented by the application of these laws to Sabbatarians. But, as we have seen, the Court held that the state's interest in promoting a uniform day of rest justified the incidental economic burden on these people.[5]

§ 21.11 Inquiries Into Religious "Frauds"

A question may arise in some cases as to whether an individual is seeking to perpetrate a fraud on others through the false representation of religious beliefs. It is clear that the religion clauses forbid an inquiry by any branch of government, including the courts, into the truth or falsity of asserted religious beliefs. However, it is not clear when an inquiry may be made as to whether an individual is sincerely advocating a religious doctrine (regardless of the truth or falsity of that doctrine) or falsely professing such a belief for fraudulent purposes.

In *United States v. Ballard*[1] the defendants were charged with using the mail to obtain money by fraud. The two defendants, Edna and Donald Ballard, claimed that they had been made divine messengers by "Saint Germain" who was Gary Ballard when he (Gary Ballard) was alive. They represented themselves as the divine messengers and teachers of the "I am" movement with powers to heal many diseases, including some classified medically as incurable. The indictment charged that they "well knew" that these representations were false and that they made the representations to fraudulently collect donations from their followers for themselves. The district court had submitted to the jury the question of whether the defendants in good faith believed the representations. The trial judge, however, did not submit to the jury any issue as to the truth or falsity of the representations. The Court of Appeals reversed the defendants' convictions on

---

4. Justice Douglas was the only one who would have held that the laws were invalid under the establishment clause, 366 U.S. at 561, 81 S.Ct. at 1218 (Douglas, J., dissenting).

5. The claims under the free exercise clause are examined in § 21.8, supra.

§ 21.11

1. 322 U.S. 78, 64 S.Ct. 882, 88 L.Ed. 1148 (1944), on remand 152 F.2d 941 (9th Cir.1945).

the basis that it was necessary to prove that the representations were in fact false. The Supreme Court in turn reversed the Court of Appeals decision.

In an opinion by Justice Douglas, a majority of the justices held that the guarantees against the establishment of any creed and the assurance of the free exercise of any religion constituted a prohibition of inquiries into the truth or falsity of an asserted religious belief. To hold otherwise would allow a trial for heresy. The majority noted that any religion could be made the subject of such a trial, but that we are free to believe what we cannot prove. The "falsity" may rest only in the views of more common faiths rather than in any absolute definition of true religion. But while holding that a court could never inquire into the falsity of a religious belief, the Supreme Court did not rule on whether a court could inquire into whether the defendant honestly held the belief. This issue was never ruled on by the Court, for when the case was returned to it a majority of the justices reversed the indictment because of the exclusion of women from the jury.[2]

Justice Jackson dissented from the remanding of the case to the circuit court because he found that any inquiry into religious "fraud" was prohibited by the first amendment.[3] He argued that to allow inquiry into a defendant's good faith in asserting a belief was not materially different from a testing of the belief itself. Unless one proves that the asserted religion is not worthy of belief it is not likely that anyone will be convinced of a defendant's bad faith. Additionally, the possibility that government might begin testing when "preachers" lack true belief is in itself dangerous to religious freedom.

Justice Jackson noted that a purely secular fraud such as using, for private purposes, money solicited for building a church could be prosecuted since the prosecution would not involve the testing of beliefs. But to find that a would-be religious leader was getting money for his general support through fraud because he did not really believe what he preached could endanger, or "chill", every religious teacher of any faith. That people may give their money or, more importantly, their minds and hopes to religions of dubious merit preached by persons with questionable faith is the price we pay for religious freedom.

It is not at all clear whether a majority of the justices would accept the Jackson position that the sincerity of one asserting a religious belief may not be put in issue in a prosecution for fraud. However, two points must be noted in relation to both the *Ballard* opinion and Justice Jackson's dissent. First, the inability to inquire into religious beliefs does not prevent the outlawing of actions based on those beliefs. Thus,

---

2. Ballard v. United States, 329 U.S. 187, 67 S.Ct. 261, 91 L.Ed. 181 (1946).

3. United States v. Ballard, 322 U.S. 78, 92, 64 S.Ct. 882, 889, 88 L.Ed. 1148 (1944)

(Jackson, J., dissenting), on remand 152 F.2d 941 (9th Cir.1945).

the issue of whether the government may ban the taking of money for curing cancer by any means other than accepted medical procedure has no relation to an inquiry into religious beliefs. If the government prohibits the act (regardless of whether it is done on a religious basis) there is no inquiry into the merit of any religious belief. The only issue is whether the prohibition of this activity violates the free exercise rights of those who believe in faith healing.[4]

Second, even if the Court were to adopt the Jackson view, the sincerity of one who requested a religious exemption from some general regulation might still be tested by government agencies or the courts. Justice Jackson only took the position that the government could not prosecute a person for his failure to truly believe in some religious principle. He did not examine the question of whether anyone who seeks a benefit from government because of his religious beliefs must be taken at his word.

For example, if a person claims the right to be exempted from work on Saturday because he is a Sabbatarian, may the unemployment compensation agency inquire as to whether he honestly holds the belief? This question was not answered in *Sherbert v. Verner*[5] where Sabbatarians were exempted from the six-day work requirement as the issue had not been raised in the case. However, in the draft exemption cases the Court assumed that the sincerity of one seeking a conscientious objection exemption could be tested both by the draft boards and the courts.[6] There would seem to be merit in allowing these tests of sincerity when the person seeks to use his religious beliefs in this manner—as a sword rather than a shield.

In this situation the law allows for a special treatment of some individuals in order to accommodate their religious beliefs. This promotion of the values of the free exercise clause is only applicable where the person in fact does want to practice a religion. There is little or no danger of persecuting unorthodox beliefs here as the individual has requested the exemption. Thus, it is possible that the Court might adopt the Jackson view and prohibit inquiries into the sincerity of one asserting a religious belief where the action is one relating to misrepresentation of religious teaching to others, while requiring those seeking a religious exemption from secular regulatory statutes to demonstrate their sincerity in the asserted religious belief.[7] Of course, in neither

---

4. This is a basic issue in all claims raised under the free exercise clause, see §§ 21.6–21.9, supra.

5. 374 U.S. 398, 83 S.Ct. 1790, 10 L.Ed.2d 965 (1963). The majority opinion noted that it was not necessary to decide this issue. 374 U.S. at 407–08, 83 S.Ct. at 1795–96.

6. These cases are examined in § 21.9(a), supra.

7. This position has received support from some legal scholars. See Giannella, Religious Liberty, Nonestablishment and Doctrinal Development—Part I: The Religious Liberty Guarantee, 80 Harv.L.Rev. 1381, 1417–18 (1967); Greenawalt, All or Nothing At All: The Defeat of Selective Conscientious Objection, 1971 Sup.Ct.Rev. 31, 57 n. 92.

case could the agency or the court inquire into the truth or falsity of the belief itself—that is clearly barred by the decision in *Ballard.*

The Court's decisions concerning unemployment compensation appear to assume the validity of testing the sincerity of claimants for religious exemptions from laws of general applicability. In *Thomas v. Review Board*[8] the Supreme Court held that a state could not deny unemployment compensation to an individual who quit his job when his employer transferred him to a department that produced military equipment and gave him no opportunity to transfer to another job. The condition for unemployment compensation that required a claimant not to have voluntarily left his employment could not be applied to this individual, because his resignation was mandated by his religious beliefs. The state court had denied Thomas an exemption (from the statutory denial of benefits to persons who resigned from a job) because it found that his belief was no more than a personal choice. Thomas was a Jehovah's Witness who admitted that he was "struggling" with his beliefs; he admitted that other members of the religion to which he belonged did not believe that working on the production of military equipment was barred by their religion. The Supreme Court, in an opinion by Chief Justice Burger, stated that the Court would assume that the claimant's beliefs were sincere, because the record showed no basis for disputing the individual's sincerity. Although the Chief Justice's majority opinion did not define the types of beliefs that would be "religious," the majority opinion stated that: "one can, of course, imagine an asserted claim so bizarre, so clearly nonreligious in motivation, as not to be entitled to protection under the Free Exercise Clause; but that is not the case here, and the guarantee of free exercise is not limited to beliefs which are shared by all members of a sect.... The narrow function of a review court in this context is to determine whether there was an appropriate finding that petitioner terminated

Professors Freed and Polsby have articulated a theory by which the Supreme Court would take cognizance of the danger of inquiring into the sincerity of religious beliefs in its substantive definition of the scope of protection for religiously motivated activities granted by the free exercise clause. See Freed and Polsby, Race, Religion, and Public Policy: Bob Jones University v. United States, 1983 Sup.Ct.Rev. 1. Under this "strategic behavior" analysis, the Supreme Court (when ruling on claims for religious exemptions from governmental regulatory statutes) would include in its free exercise analysis an assessment of the likelihood that individuals would base a claim of religious exemption on insincere or strategic behavior rather than true religious belief; the Court would also assess the cost and danger of government adjudication of sincerity of religious beliefs when the Court weighs the burden on religious freedom and the importance of the nonreligious interest at stake.

It is also arguable that inquiries into "sincerity" might also be permissible when it is alleged that an individual has been subject to coercive indoctrination into a religion, see Delgado, When Religious Exercise is Not Free: Deprogramming and the Constitutional Status of Coercively Induced Religious Belief, 37 Vand.L.Rev. 1071 (1984).

See also, Noonan, How Sincere Do You Have to Be to Be Religious?, 1988 University of Illinois L.Rev. 713 (1988) (arguing against the judicial testing of sincerity).

8. 450 U.S. 707, 101 S.Ct. 1425, 67 L.Ed.2d 624 (1981), on remand 421 N.E.2d 642 (Ind.1981).

his work because of an honest conviction that such work was forbidden by his religion." [9]

In *Frazee v. Illinois Department of Employment Security* [10] the Supreme Court examined a state court's refusal to grant an exemption to an unemployment compensation requirement that a claimant be available for work on seven days a week to a person who sincerely asserted that he could not work on Sunday due to his beliefs "as a Christian", but who was not a member of an organized church, sect, or denomination. The state courts had ruled that a religious exemption to the work availability requirement would only be given to a person who was a member of an organized church, sect, or denomination. The Justices of the United States Supreme Court unanimously held that requiring membership in a recognized church or sect (as a condition for receiving the exemption) violated the free exercise clause. Justice White's opinion for the Court in *Frazee* stated: "there is no doubt that the only beliefs rooted in religion are protected by the Equal Protection Clause ... purely secular views do not suffice." [11] The Court in *Frazee* did not rule on whether the government could test the sincerity of a person who was claiming a religious exemption to a law of general applicability. However, Justice White's opinion appears to assume that testing the sincerity of persons who are claiming government benefits is permissible. After noting the fact that only religious beliefs were protected by the free exercise clause, Justice White's opinion stated: "nor do we underestimate the difficulty of distinguishing between religious and secular convictions and in determining whether a professed belief is sincerely held. States are clearly entitled to assure themselves that there is an ample predicate for invoking the free exercise clause. We do not face problems about sincerity or about the religious nature of Frazee's conviction, however. The courts below did not question his sincerity, and the state concedes it." [12]

Some testing of sincerity may be compatible with the restrictions of the establishment and free exercise clause. It appears that the Justices believe that it is possible to test the sincerity of an individual who claims a religious exemption in a manner that avoids endangering the values of the free exercise and establishment clauses. [13]

9. 450 U.S. at 715–16, 101 S.Ct. at 1430–31. This case, and other cases regarding unemployment compensation statutes and the need to grant exceptions to persons who cannot comply with the conditions in such statutes on the basis of their religious beliefs are examined in §§ 21.6, 21.8.

10. 489 U.S. 829, 109 S.Ct. 1514, 103 L.Ed.2d 914 (1989).

11. 489 U.S. at 832–34, 109 S.Ct. at 1517 (internal quotations omitted), in part quoting Thomas v. Review Board, 450 U.S.

707, 713, 101 S.Ct. 1425, 1430, 67 L.Ed.2d 624 (1981), on remand 421 N.E.2d 641 (Ind. 1981).

12. Frazee v. Illinois Department of Employment Security, 489 U.S. 829, 833, 109 S.Ct. 1514, 1517, 103 L.Ed.2d 914 (1989).

13. Justice White's opinion for a unanimous Court in *Frazee* quoted the language from Thomas v. Review Board that some asserted religious beliefs might be "so bizarre, so clearly nonreligious" as to not

§ 21.12   State Involvement in Ecclesiastical Disputes

When there is a dispute between factions of a religious organization, one or more of the parties may seek resolution of the dispute by a state court. Of course, the government cannot declare which party is correct in matters of religion, for that would violate the principles of both religion clauses. A judicial declaration of such matters would simultaneously establish one religious view as correct for the organization while inhibiting the free exercise of the opposing belief. Yet when the opposing groups both claim the church property the state will have to make some judgment as to who is entitled to possession. This must be done under carefully circumscribed rules which guarantee the avoidance of civil court rulings on matters of religious belief.

Where the disputed property is subject to some express condition in a deed, a court can rule on the occurrence of the condition if that does not involve a ruling on religious matters. Thus, if a building was deeded to a church for so long as it is used as a place of religious worship, a court could order the return of the property if it were used as a retail sales establishment. But if the condition in the deed was that the general church could keep the property so long as it was true to its doctrine, that condition could not be enforced. Any ruling requiring the return of such property would involve a state ruling on religious beliefs.

Most disputes center around property which is not subject to such a specific condition. In these situations two or more groups present themselves to a court and claim the right to possess and control church property. The permissible basis for court rulings in these situations varies with the type of church involved in the dispute.

Where the church group is an independent congregation, not subject to a general or higher church authority, the will of a majority of the members must control the decision. Because this church group is a self-governing unit, the only secular basis for a ruling between competing groups is based on the preferences of a majority of the members. There might be a separate secular way to determine ownership if the deed or incorporation documents specified some other form of resolving disputes which did not require the court to review religious doctrine. As it is highly unlikely that such a neutral, secular rule for dispute

receive the protection of the free exercise clause. Justice White noted that "claims by Christians that their religion forbids Sunday work cannot be deemed bizarre or incredible." 489 U.S. at 834 n. 2, 109 S.Ct. at 1518 n. 2. This footnote in *Frazee* would appear to give credence to the view that the reference in *Thomas* to "bizarre" beliefs only reflected a view that the assertion of such beliefs might reflect adversely on the credibility of the persons asserting them. There might be a finding that the individual who asserted "bizarre" beliefs was not sincerely asserting a religious belief. The establishment clause might prohibit a state agency or court from determining that a belief was not religious merely because it was held by very few people or was considered to be "bizarre" by a majority of the populace.

572

resolution could be found, it is only safe to assume that the majority rule principle must prevail in these cases.

Most commonly, disputes arise between a local congregation and a general church with which it has been affiliated in the past. Where the dispute involves a hierarchical church, or organized body of churches of a similar faith and subject to a common ecclesiastical authority, different principles apply. Here there are only two questions for state court resolution: (1) whether this is a hierarchical church, (2) whether the local group in the past affiliated itself and its property with the hierarchical church. If either of these questions were answered in the negative, the local group would be an independent congregation. However, when these questions are answered affirmatively the courts must defer to the hierarchical authority. The rulings of the highest ecclesiastical authority must be enforced by the civil courts. Only in the case of clear fraud by persons in that authority could the court question the judgment of ecclesiastical authority—and even this possible exception is subject to dispute. The highest ecclesiastical authority—an assembly in some religions or a clerical superior in others—is the final arbiter of the church doctrine and authority.

Because the few decisions in this area deal with widely varying fact situations, it is important to review the individual rulings of the Supreme Court.

Watson v. Jones,[1] the first case involving internal ecclesiastical dissension,[2] was decided on common law principles rather than a constitutional basis. With jurisdiction based on diversity of citizenship, the federal courts were required to determine which of two contesting groups would be deemed to lawfully control the property of the Walnut Street Presbyterian Church of Louisville. In this case the local elders and trustees had been decreed by a state court to control the church property, even though they had been replaced by the edict of the highest council of the "Presbyterian Church in the United States of America."

The Supreme Court held that in this situation the state courts were required to follow the edicts of the highest ecclesiastical tribunal. Although the first amendment had not yet been made applicable to the States, the decision is now recognized as reflecting the values of the religion clauses.

The majority in *Watson* found three general rules applicable to civil court resolution of internal ecclesiastical disputes. First, if proper-

§ 21.12

1. 80 U.S. (13 Wall.) 679, 20 L.Ed. 666 (1872).

2. There was an earlier decision concerning property held by religious organizations but it did not examine the issues discussed in this section. Terrett v. Taylor, 13 U.S. (9 Cranch) 43, 3 L.Ed. 650 (1815).

ty is given to a congregation with an express condition in the terms of the grant that it shall be used only to support a specific purpose, the civil courts could order a return of the property if the property is no longer used for that purpose. Second, where property has been given to the general use of an independent religious group the property must be used as determined by a majority of the society or by another manner that the group has previously established for this purpose. Third, where property has been acquired by a society or group which constitutes a part of a general religious organization, the established tribunals of that organization must be deferred to by civil courts. The right to church property insofar as it is dependent on questions of religious doctrine or ecclesiastical law must be settled by the highest tribunal or authority of the religious organization.

Since the time of the *Watson* decision the ability of a civil court to resolve questions of "departure from purpose" has been limited in light of the principles of the first amendment. However, the principles of deference to a congregational polity or hierarchical authority has been strengthened by later decisions.

Two other decisions relating to church disputes were rendered by the Supreme Court prior to the application of the first amendment to the States. In *Bouldin v. Alexander* [3] the Court held that a civil court could declare who was entitled to control the property of an independent congregational church. In this case a minority of the congregation had met and expelled the majority of the members and the trustees in whom the title to the church property was formally vested. The Court found that civil courts must follow the will of the majority of this congregational church to decide the question of legal title. While it is not clear that this decision was based on first amendment principles, it is the only case in which the Supreme Court has been presented with a dispute over the property of a clearly independent local congregation and it follows the principle stated in *Watson.*

In *Gonzalez v. Roman Catholic Archbishop of Manila,* [4] the Court refused to allow a civil court to determine the qualification of a chaplain of the Roman Catholic Church. A testatrix had given funds to the Church to establish a "chaplaincy" to which her nearest male relative was to be appointed whenever possible. One of her descendants sought the post, and the income from the fund, but was refused appointment by the church authorities due to his failure to qualify under ecclesiastical law.

The Supreme Court held that a civil court could not award the fund or the position to the heir as it could not disturb the judgment of the church authorities. Because the chaplaincy was a part of a hierarchical church, the rulings on ecclesiastical matters by the church

---

3. 82 U.S. (15 Wall.) 131, 21 L.Ed. 69 (1872).

4. 280 U.S. 1, 50 S.Ct. 5, 74 L.Ed. 131 (1929).

organization could not be reviewed. However, the Court noted that this conclusion was true in the absence of "fraud, collusion or arbitrariness." [5] In later years this statement has been regarded as dicta and there is no general ability of courts to review church decisions to determine if they are arbitrary.

Following the application of the religion clauses to the states, the Supreme Court was confronted with legislative and judicial attempts to grant sole control of the property held by the Russian Orthodox Church to American members of that Church. But in both instances the Court refused to allow the government to interfere with the authority of the hierarchical church even though the highest authority of that church resided in a country hostile to the interests of the United States.

New York passed legislation which would have placed control of the church property of the Russian Orthodox Church in an autonomous part of that church in New York. This was challenged by an archbishop of the church who had been appointed by the ecclesiastical authority of the central church in Moscow. The Russian Orthodox Church was admittedly a hierarchical church to which the American groups had been joined in the past. However, formal title was in a corporation with officers who were citizens of the United States. At issue was whether the American churches could renounce their affiliation to the central church and retain the church property.

In *Kedroff v. St. Nicholas Cathedral* [6] the Supreme Court invalidated the New York legislation which would have given control to the American controlled sect. In the majority's view, this legislation violated the principles of the free exercise clause by interfering with the control and decisions of the ecclesiastical authority. A hierarchical church is one which is "organized as a body with other churches having a similar faith and doctrine with a common ruling convocation or ecclesiastical head." [7] If state law allowed one group to take control of the property of such a church against the will of the formal ecclesiastical authority, the state would be determining the status of one faction as the "true" church. As a contrary ruling would prevent the free operation of the hierarchical church, the state must accept the decisions of the highest formal authority in the church when it resolves such disputes. This principle remains true even in the absence of legislation, for civil courts have no more power to review the decisions of a church than does the legislature. [8]

5. 280 U.S. at 16, 50 S.Ct. at 7.

6. 344 U.S. 94, 73 S.Ct. 143, 97 L.Ed. 120 (1952).

7. 344 U.S. at 110, 73 S.Ct. at 151.

8. After this decision, the New York courts held that the American controlled faction of the Russian Church was entitled to the property even though the statute had been held invalid. In Kreshik v. Saint Nicholas Cathedral, 363 U.S. 190, 80 S.Ct. 1037, 4 L.Ed.2d 1140 (1960), rehearing denied 364 U.S. 855, 81 S.Ct. 35, 5 L.Ed.2d 79 (1960) the Supreme Court overruled the decision of the New York court. The Supreme Court held that civil courts had to defer to the ecclesiastical authorities and

It is now clear that civil courts may not make any inquiry into the correctness of decisions concerning religious doctrine. In *Presbyterian Church v. Mary Elizabeth Blue Hull Memorial Presbyterian Church* [9] the state courts were confronted with a withdrawal of two local churches from the general Presbyterian Church. The state courts applied a rule of law which granted a trust of church property to a general church on the sole condition that it adhere to the faith and doctrine which existed when the local churches affiliated with it. The Supreme Court of the United States ruled that no inquiry could be made into whether the general church had deviated from its doctrine. This question was undeniably a decision that belonged to the hierarchical church authority, because only that authority could decide the true faith of the church. Thus, the local churches could not retain their property as they had subjected themselves and their property to church control and there was no basis for granting them the property without an inquiry into religious matters.

The state courts can resolve these conflicting claims for property so long as they do not rule on religious matters. These decisions might occur in several ways. For example, a donor might grant property to a church with the provision that the property will revert to the donor on the happening of a specific condition. This condition could be enforced so long as the happening of the event could be determined without a court ruling on religious doctrine. Similarly, state law could establish a purely secular or non-religious basis for finding title in a local church unless title had been formally granted to the general church. This law would be proper as long as the question of whether control over the property had been given to the general church could be determined without a judicial inquiry into religious doctrine. Thus, even though a local group belonged to a hierarchical church, they could withdraw from the church and retain their property when the state property law, and the deeds for the property, made it clear that the property had never been given over to the control of the general church.[10]

Courts can never question a church's rulings on matters of religious doctrine or even authority. When a church is truly local or congregational the will of a majority controls the decision. Once it is found that a group has submitted itself and its property to the control

that there could be no judicial review of those decisions—regardless of whether the review was based on statute or "common law."

9. 393 U.S. 440, 89 S.Ct. 601, 21 L.Ed.2d 658 (1969), on remand 225 Ga. 259, 167 S.E.2d 658 (1969), certiorari denied 396 U.S. 1041, 90 S.Ct. 680, 24 L.Ed.2d 685 (1970).

10. Such a situation was presented in Maryland & Virginia Eldership of the Churches of God v. Church of God, 396 U.S.

367, 90 S.Ct. 499, 24 L.Ed.2d 582 (1970). A discussion of the secular basis for ruling on such conditions is contained in the concurring opinion of Justice Brennan. 396 U.S. at 368, 90 S.Ct. at 500. See also, First Presbyterian Church v. United Presbyterian Church, 62 N.Y.2d 110, 476 N.Y.S.2d 86, 464 N.E.2d 454, 458, 459 (1984), certiorari denied 469 U.S. 1037, 105 S.Ct. 514, 83 L.Ed.2d 404 (1984) (citing an earlier edition of this treatise).

of a hierarchical church, the rulings of the highest formal authority in that church must be accepted by the civil courts.

There is the possibility that the Supreme Court may allow a further inquiry into whether the general church has replaced local authority over the property for reasons of "fraud or collusiveness." However, if such an inquiry can be made at all, the civil court could only prevent a clear theft of local church property for the personal benefit of members of the hierarchical organization.

The Court has made it clear that the hierarchical authority cannot have its decisions overturned because they are "arbitrary" or contrary to the church's own rules. In a case concerning this issue, a hierarchical church replaced one of its higher clerics and granted control of the church property to a new officer seemingly in violation of its own rules of procedure. But in *Serbian Eastern Orthodox Diocese v. Milivojevich*,[11] the Court ruled that any review of the jurisdiction of the general church authorities or whether they acted in conformity with the church laws would result in undue interference with the freedom of religion. Any review of such principles would require a state judgment on the meaning and applicability of religious rules and doctrine. This review can only be avoided by accepting the judgment of the highest formal authority of the hierarchical organization. Therefore, state courts must refrain from ruling contrary to such authorities unless their decision is clearly based on principles which have no reference to religious doctrines or rulings.

The justices were closely divided by the application of these principles to the resolution of a complex dispute between some members of a local religious group and the church with which they had been affiliated in *Jones v. Wolf*[12]. In that case the Court examined a dispute between members of the Vineville Presbyterian Church of Macon, Georgia and between some members of that local church group and the Augusta–Macon Presbytery of the Presbyterian Church in the United States. Approximately 40 years earlier, a local group in Macon, Georgia had founded a congregation and property had been acquired in the name of the trustees of the Vineville Presbyterian Church. When it

11. 426 U.S. 696, 96 S.Ct. 2372, 49 L.Ed.2d 151 (1976), rehearing denied 429 U.S. 873, 97 S.Ct. 191, 50 L.Ed.2d 155 (1976), on remand 66 Ill.2d 469, 6 Ill.Dec. 792, 363 N.E.2d 606 (1977), appeal after remand 74 Ill.2d 574, 25 Ill.Dec. 629, 387 N.E.2d 285 (1979), certiorari denied 443 U.S. 904, 99 S.Ct. 3096, 61 L.Ed.2d 872 (1979).

12. 443 U.S. 595, 99 S.Ct. 3020, 61 L.Ed.2d 775 (1979), on remand 244 Ga. 388, 260 S.E.2d 84 (1979), certiorari denied 444 U.S. 1080, 100 S.Ct. 1031, 62 L.Ed.2d 763 (1980). The majority opinion in this case

was written by Justice Blackmun and joined by Justices Brennan, Marshall, Rehnquist and Stevens.

See generally, Adams & Hanlon, *Jones v. Wolf*: Church Autonomy and the Religion Clauses of the First Amendment, 128 U.Pa. L.Rev. 1291 (1980) (proposing for courts a mode of decision which would recognize the freedom of churches to determine the limits of their association and encourage them to comply with their obligation to avoid requiring civil courts to resolve ecclesiastical questions).

was organized the Vineville Church group became a member church of the Presbyterian Church in the United States (PCUS). PCUS has a higher hierarchical form of government, as contrasted with a congregational form, but the local church property was never formally deeded over to the general church or subjected to the control of the general church according to any identifiable document.

In 1973 a congregational meeting of the local Vineville Church, at which a quorum of its members were present, voted to separate from PCUS and to unite with another Presbyterian denomination, the Presbyterian Church in America (PCA). A minority of the local church wished to stay with PCUS and in response to the schism in the local congregation PCUS appointed a commission to resolve the dispute and found that the minority faction was the "true congregation" of the Vineville Church. There then ensued a dispute brought to state court over whether the PCUS and the local minority controlled title to the property or whether the majority which had disaffiliated itself from PCUS, controlled title.

By a five to four vote the Supreme Court found that the Georgia courts could apply "neutral principles" of property law to determine that title remained in the local congregation and was to be controlled by a majority vote of that congregation. The majority opinion appears to be consistent with earlier Court decisions. The majority held only that state courts may examine the language of real and personal property deeds, the terms of church charters or state statutes relating to the control of property, and documents affiliating the local group with the general church and the constitution of the general church in order to determine technically if the local group had become a member of an hierarchical church and subjected its property to control of that church.

The majority opinion noted that the "neutral principles approach" was to rely only on "objective, well established concepts of trust and property law" and that any examination of the instruments of ownership that were religious documents must be examined in a strictly secular manner to determine whether those documents technically place property ownership in the local group or the general church. The majority refused to adopt a rule of compulsory deference to the higher church authority in all instances because it felt that the neutral principles approach would involve less entanglement with religious doctrine by requiring judges to abstain from a determination as to what authority is the highest in a church organization and simply to examine the documents in a secular manner to determine where title to the property had been formally placed.

Applying this rule to the specific case before it, the majority found that the Georgia courts could have found that the deeds, contracts of conveyance and trust, and church charters left title to the property in the local church. However, the Georgia courts had not explained how they had determined that the local church was represented by the majority rather than the minority. In determining which group would control the use of property by the local congregation the state was still required to adopt rules that did not involve an examination of religious doctrine. The state could adopt a presumptive rule of majority representation, which could be changed by a showing that the local church group had chosen another means for property control through contract or deed terms. In fact the state could adopt any method of overcoming the majoritarian presumption so long as the civil courts did not entangle themselves in religious controversy or impair free exercise rights.

It was unclear whether the Georgia courts had applied a truly neutral rule of majority ownership or a neutral examination of property and contract terms to determine if majority rule was to control under the terms of the property contracts and deeds of the Vineville Church. Thus, the Supreme Court remanded the case to the Georgia courts to determine if Georgia had a rule requiring deference to a majority of the local congregation or whether state law provided that the identity of the controlling local group was to be determined on the basis of religious principles. The latter position would require a granting of automatic deference to the general church (PCUS) because otherwise the civil court would be involved in questions of religious doctrine rather than the following of neutral principles of contract and property law.

The dissenting justices would have required automatic deference to the general church councils (PCUS) because they believed that only such deference could avoid impermissible entanglement between the state and religious authorities.[13] Whenever a local group affiliates technically with a hierarchical church, the dissent would subject the local group to the control of the higher church authorities with no recourse to civil courts. These justices felt that it would be impossible to apply the Court's neutral principles approach without examining religious documents and effectively making decisions on questions of religious doctrine.

If the majority in *Jones* is correct and the state courts can be kept to a purely secular examination of documents relating to formal control of property, then its neutral principles approach does not deviate from the analysis employed in earlier Supreme Court decisions. But if ruling on these property disputes involves government agents or judges in examining religious charters in a manner that calls for some evaluation of religious principles or doctrine, the neutral principles approach

---

13. Jones v. Wolf, 443 U.S. 595, 610, 99 S.Ct. 3020, 3029, 61 L.Ed.2d 775 (1979) (Powell, J., dissenting, joined by Burger, C.J., and Stewart and White, JJ.), on re- mand 244 Ga. 388, 260 S.E.2d 84 (1979), cert. denied 444 U.S. 1080, 100 S.Ct. 1031, 62 L.Ed.2d 763 (1980).

will lead to what should be deemed an unconstitutional entanglement between government and religion.[14]

§ 21.13 Legislative Action to End Religious Discrimination in Private Employment

Although a governmental unit may attempt to prohibit discrimination against employees based upon an employee's religious beliefs, the establishment clause places limitations on the extent to which the government may force an employer to make accommodations for the religious views and practices of employees.[1] In *Estate of Thornton v. Caldor, Inc.*[2] the Court, by an eight to one vote of the justices, invalidated a state statute which required private employers to honor every employee's desire to refuse to work on "his Sabbath." The majority opinion, by Chief Justice Burger, found that, although the law was an attempt to accommodate the free exercise of religion, the law was subject to the establishment clause tests. Such legislation must have a secular purpose and a primary effect that does not advance or inhibit religion; it must not give rise to an excessive entanglement between government and religion. The Court was not required to focus on the purpose or entanglement tests, as the Chief Justice found that the law was invalid because it had a primary effect that advanced religion.

The law at issue in *Estate of Thornton* gave every employee an absolute right to refrain from work on her or his sabbath. It thus subjected employers and other workers to significant costs in order to

---

14. For an examination of whether courts should define and protect a contractual right to academic freedom for theology professors at sectarian universities, see Curran, Academic Freedom and Catholic Universities, 66 Texas L.Rev. 1441 (1988); Laycock & Waelbroeck, Academic Freedom and the Free Exercise of Religion, 66 Texas L.Rev. 1455 (1988).

§ 21.13

1. In this section we will examine the problem of requiring private employers to accommodate the religious practices of their employees. The regulation, or the absence of regulation, of the employment practices of religious organizations is examined in § 21.15.

Legislative accommodations of religion that do not involve employment practices, and the direct regulation of religious organizations, are discussed in §§ 21.1 and 21.3.

Issues regarding the accommodation of student religious organizations that seek "equal access" to school facilities are examined in § 21.5.

2. 472 U.S. 703, 105 S.Ct. 2914, 86 L.Ed.2d 557 (1985).

The Connecticut statute at issue read as follows: "No person who states that a particular day of the week is observed as his Sabbath may be required by his employer to work on such day. And employee's refusal to work on his Sabbath shall not constitute grounds for his dismissal." Conn.Gen.Stat.   § 53–303e(b)   (Supp. 1962–1984) quoted in 472 U.S. at 706, 105 S.Ct. at 2916. Only Justice Rehnquist dissented in this case, and he did so without opinion. 472 U.S. at 710, 105 S.Ct. at 2918 (Rehnquist, J., dissenting). Justices O'Connor and Marshall concurred in the Court's judgment and opinion but wrote separately to state their belief that the opinion in *Estate of Thornton* would not require invalidation of the accommodation of employee's religious beliefs and practices mandated by Title VII of the federal Civil Rights Act, which is discussed later in this section. 472 U.S. at 710, 105 S.Ct. at 2918 (O'Connor, J., joined by Marshall, J., concurring).

accommodate the desire of an employee to take actions based upon religious beliefs. The statute did not require only reasonable accommodation of an employee's religious activities, or a mere prohibition of discrimination on the basis of religious beliefs; the statute did not provide any exception for employers who were subject to special circumstances or who were presented by employee's claims that would impose a significant shifting of costs and burdens to other employees. The majority opinion quoting Judge Learned Hand, held that a "fundamental principle of the religion clauses" was that no individual had "the right to insist that in pursuit of their own interests others must conform their conduct to his own religious necessities." [3]

Title VII of the Civil Rights Act of 1964 [4] prohibits employers covered by the Act from discriminating against persons because of their religion. This statute has a great impact on the employment market because it applies to most forms of private, as well as governmental, employment and the activities of labor unions.[5]

The Act itself is fairly straightforward in its approach to this problem. It prohibits an employer from discriminating in the hiring, payment or treatment of employees on the basis of their religion.[6] Similarly, the statute makes it unlawful for a labor organization to exclude or burden a worker on the basis of their religion.[7]

In 1972, the Act was amended to include a definition of religion which also defines an employer's duties in this area. The Act now reads:

3. Estate of Thornton v. Caldor, Inc., 472 U.S. 703, 710, 105 S.Ct. 2914, 2918, 86 L.Ed.2d 557 (1985) in part quoting Otten v. Baltimore and Ohio R. Co., 205 F.2d 58, 61 (2d Cir.1953).

See generally, Lieberman, The Future of the Establishment Clause in the Wake of Estate of Thornton v. Caldor, Inc. 18 Conn. L.Rev. 845 (1986).

4. 42 U.S.C.A. § 2000e et seq. (Civil Rights Act of 1964, Pub.L. No. 88-352, title VII, §§ 701 et seq., 78 Stat. 253).

5. Employers with over 15 employees, most forms of government employment and most labor unions are covered by the Act. For the exact coverage see 42 U.S.C.A. §§ 2000e & 2000e-1 (as amended).

6. 42 U.S.C.A. § 2000e-2(a) provides in part:

"It shall be an unlawful employment practice for an employer—(1) to fail or refuse to hire or to discharge any individual or otherwise to discriminate against any individual with respect to his compensation, terms, conditions, or privileges of employment, because of such individual's race, color, religion, sex, or national origin; . . . ."

7. 42 U.S.C.A. § 2000e-2(c) provides:

"It shall be an unlawful employment practice of a labor organization—(1) to exclude or to expel from its membership, or otherwise to discriminate against, any individual because of his race, color, religion, sex, or national origin; (2) to limit, segregate, or classify its membership or applicants for membership, or to classify or fail or refuse to refer for employment any individual, in any way which would deprive or tend to deprive any individual of employment opportunities, or would limit such employment opportunities or otherwise adversely affect his status as an employee or as an applicant for employment, because of such individual's race, color, religion, sex, or national origin; or (3) to cause or attempt to cause an employer to discriminate against an individual in violation of this section."

The term "religion" includes all aspects of religious observance and practice, as well as belief, unless an employer demonstrates that he is unable to reasonably accommodate to an employee's or prospective employee's religious observance or practice without undue hardship on the conduct of the employer's business.[8]

This amendment to the Act confirmed some of the previous rulings of the Equal Employment Opportunity Commission (EEOC), which is the agency empowered to promulgate regulation to implement Title VII.[9] Employers now are required not only to refrain from discriminating against persons because of their religion but also to accommodate a wide variety of religious practices.[10]

Whether this statute, as it had been applied by the EEOC and lower courts, would withstand attack under the first amendment remains an open question. Twice the Justices of the Supreme Court have split four to four in cases which presented this issue.[11] In its third attempt at resolving the issue the Court interpreted the statute in a manner that avoided a constitutional ruling.

In *Trans World Airlines, Inc. v. Hardison*,[12] the Court held that the statute did not require the employer to alter Saturday work schedules in violation of a seniority system established by collective bargaining. By a vote of seven to two the Court held that requiring the employer to bear more than *de minimis* costs was not required by the act. Thus the Court recognized that further congressional action of this type raises most serious issues under the religion clauses.[13]

---

8. Act of March 24, 1972, Pub.L. No. 92–261, § 2, 86 Stat. 103, codified at 42 U.S.C.A. § 2000e, amending 42 U.S.C.A. § 2000e.

9. At first the EEOC interpreted the statute as only prohibiting discriminatory practices and allowing the application of a uniform work week even though it burdened some religions. 29 C.F.R. § 1605.1(a)(3), 31 Fed.Reg. 8370. In 1967 the EEOC required reasonable accommodation such as granting Sabbatarians exemptions from Saturday work requirements. 29 C.F.R. § 1605.1(b), 32 Fed.Reg. 10298.

10. By far the most common issue is the exemption of employees from work on their Sabbath. However, there may be claims for exemption from religious services at business meetings, Young v. Southwestern Savings and Loan Ass'n, 509 F.2d 140 (5th Cir.1975), or exemption from dress or hair style regulations, EEOC Dec. No. 71–2620, 1973 C.C.H. EEOC Dec. 4500 (June 25, 1971).

11. In each of these cases one justice did not participate in the decision or the remaining eight Justices were evenly divided. In such instances the lower court ruling is affirmed, normally without opinion. Dewey v. Reynolds Metals Co., 402 U.S. 689, 91 S.Ct. 2186, 29 L.Ed.2d 267 (1971), affirming Dewey v. Reynolds Metals, 429 F.2d 324 (6th Cir.1970); Parker Seal Co. v. Cummins, 429 U.S. 65, 97 S.Ct. 342, 50 L.Ed.2d 223 (1976), affirming Cummins v. Parker Seal Co., 516 F.2d 544 (6th Cir. 1975).

12. 432 U.S. 63, 97 S.Ct. 2264, 53 L.Ed.2d 113 (1977).

13. In the case in which the Court invalidated a state statute because it gave an absolute right to employees to observe their Sabbath and thereby always shift certain cause to fellow employees, Justices O'Connor and Marshall wrote a concurring opinion to express their view that Title VII could be interpreted to require reasonable accommodation of religious beliefs without involving an endorsement of religion or advancement of religious practices in a way that would violate the first amendment. Estate of Thornton v. Caldor, Inc.,

If an employer claims that it cannot offer any reasonable accommodation to an employee who must deviate from employment rules due to the employee's religious belief, the court must determine whether requiring the employer to provide some accommodation to the employee would result in undue hardship on the employer or on other employees. When an employer offers a plan to an employee that would reasonably accommodate the employee's religious beliefs and practices, the employer has met its obligation under Title VII; the employer is not required to adopt a specific method of accommodation that is preferred by the employee.[14] This interpretation of the employer's statutory obligation to accommodate the religious beliefs and practices of its employees has allowed the Supreme Court to avoid the question of whether a federal statute requiring a wide degree of accommodation of employee religious beliefs would violate the establishment clause.

§ 21.14   Prohibiting "Ministers" From Holding Public Office

Early in the country's history, several states by statute or constitutional provision, had prohibited members of religious orders or ministers from holding public office. By the turn of this century it was generally recognized that these laws conflict with the free exercise and establishment clauses, and—although the Court had not held them to be *per se* invalid—these laws were repealed or annulled in almost every state that had adopted them. Tennessee had, by statute, barred "ministers of the gospel, or priest[s] of any denomination whatever," from serving as delegates to the state's constitutional convention; this statute mirrored a provision of the state constitution barring such persons from membership in the state legislature. The Supreme Court unanimously found that the statute was unconstitutional in *McDaniel v. Paty.*[1] There was no majority opinion in *McDaniel,* however, because the justices could not agree on exactly why the statute was unconstitutional. The Court had previously held, in *Torcaso v. Watkins,*[2] that the states could not require persons to take a religious oath before accepting public employment or office. This holding was based on the

---

472 U.S. 703, —, 105 S.Ct. 2914, 2918, 86 L.Ed.2d 557 (1985) (O'Connor, J., joined by Marshall, J., concurring). Justice Marshall had previously expressed the view that Title VII could be interpreted to mandate a wide degree of accommodation of employee religious beliefs without violating the Establishment Clause. See Trans World Airlines, Inc. v. Hardison, 432 U.S. 63, 90 n. 4, 97 S.Ct. 2264, 2280, n. 4, 53 L.Ed.2d 113 (1977) (Marshall, J., dissenting).

14. Ansonia Board of Education v. Philbrook, 479 U.S. 60, 107 S.Ct. 367, 93 L.Ed.2d 305 (1986), appeal after remand 925 F.2d 47 (2d Cir.1991), cert. denied — U.S. —, 111 S.Ct. 2828, 115 L.Ed.2d 998 (1991).

§ 21.14

1. 435 U.S. 618, 98 S.Ct. 1322, 55 L.Ed.2d 593 (1978) (Justice Blackmun did not participate in the decision). A history of the use and repeal of disqualification statutes appears in the plurality opinion written by the Chief Justice. 435 U.S. at 622–25, 98 S.Ct. at 1325–27 (Burger, C.J.).

2. 367 U.S. 488, 81 S.Ct. 1680, 6 L.Ed.2d 982 (1961).

principle that no individual can be punished for his religious beliefs. The relevance of *Torcaso* to the Tennessee disqualification laws divided the Court.

In *McDaniel*, Chief Justice Burger wrote an opinion, joined by Justices Powell, Rehnquist and Stevens. Burger concluded that the disqualification statute violated the free exercise clause. The opinion by the Chief Justice found that the law was not one that infringed the "freedom to believe," and, therefore, was not automatically invalid under *Torcaso.*[3] The Chief Justice noted that the history of such disqualification clauses in the original states indicated that such laws had been aimed merely at restricting acts of religious groups that would have further entangled the states with religion. The Tennessee law, however, regulated actions that related to the individual's religion, and, therefore, it was to be tested by the free exercise clause balancing test. Under this test, the state's failure to demonstrate that participation by clergy in the political process would bring about further "establishment" problems indicated that this law in fact did not promote a strong state interest. Thus, the law was invalid because it burdened religious practices without advancing overriding state interests. Burger found no reason to examine whether the state's asserted interest in furthering separation of church and state under other circumstances, might constitute a permissible legislative goal.

Justice Brennan, joined by Justice Marshall, found that the statute violated both the free exercise and establishment clauses of the first amendment, which applied to the states through the fourteenth amendment. Unlike the Chief Justice, Justice Brennan found that this law disadvantaged the person because of his religious belief. So construed, the law was a *per se* violation of the free exercise clause; there was no reason to employ the balancing test in such a case. Brennan noted that requiring a minister to forego either his ministry or public office constituted a sufficient burden to invoke the free exercise prohibition against burdening religious beliefs.[4]

Justice Brennan also found that the law violated the establishment clause. He agreed that a purpose of the establishment clause was to eliminate religious divisiveness, but believed that the state could not pursue that goal through the use of religious classifications. Justice Brennan noted that this law might fail the secular purpose test, because it was at least possible that it was based on the religious beliefs of a dominant sect within the jurisdiction; but he found it unnecessary to resolve this issue.[5] The statute was invalid in Justice Brennan's view because it failed the primary secular effect test. He believed that

3. McDaniel v. Paty, 435 U.S. 618, 98 S.Ct. 1322, 55 L.Ed.2d 593 (1978) (Burger, C.J., plurality opinion).

4. 435 U.S. at 632, 98 S.Ct. at 1330–31 (Brennan, J., concurring in the judgment).

5. 435 U.S. at 636 n. 9, 98 S.Ct. at 1333 n. 9 (Brennan, J., concurring in the judgment).

a primary effect of this statute was the inhibition of the practice of religion.

Justice Stewart concurred in the judgment because he believed, as did Justice Brennan, that the law constituted a restriction on religious beliefs. In his opinion, such restrictions were prohibited by *Torcaso*.[6]

Justice White was the only justice who did not believe that the disqualification law was invalid under the free exercise clause; he did not believe that the law, in any meaningful way, compelled a person to abandon the ministry. However, he found that it was a significant limitation on the right to seek elective office; many ministers would be deterred from running for office by the law, even though they would not feel compelled to abandon their ministries. For this reason, he found the law to be unconstitutional as a violation of the equal protection clause of the fourteenth amendment. In support of his position, Justice White noted that the Court had held that the right to vote and the right to be a candidate were of sufficient constitutional magnitude to require the states "to provide substantial justification for any requirement that prevents a class of citizens" from exercising these rights. He found that, while the state's interest in separating church and state might be legitimate, "close scrutiny reveals that the challenged law is not 'reasonably necessary to the accomplishment of ...' that objective."[7]

§ 21.15 Regulation of the Employment Practices of Religious Organizations

When the members of a religious organization take any action in society, they may be subject to religiously neutral regulations. When they claim that religiously neutral regulations of their commercial or noncommercial activities impose a burden on their ability to carry out the religious beliefs, the claim for an exemption from those regulations will be tested under the free exercise clause principles we have examined earlier in this chapter.[1] If employees or employers can show that a governmental employment regulation imposes a burden on their religious faith, a court must determine whether the government has an overriding interest in denying the employee or employer an exemption from the regulation. When a religious organization employs persons in commercial activities that duplicate and compete with nonreligious

---

6. 435 U.S. 642–43, 98 S.Ct. at 1336 (Stewart, J., concurring in the judgment).

7. 435 U.S. at 645, 98 S.Ct. at 1337–38 (White, J., concurring in the judgment), quoting from Bullock v. Carter, 405 U.S. 134, 92 S.Ct. 849, 31 L.Ed.2d 92 (1972).

§ 21.15

1. The free exercise clause principles that restrict governmental actions are ex-

amined in § 21.8. When considering the regulation of the employment practices of religious organizations, a court must be cognizant of the limitations that the establishment clause may place on the ability of government to accommodate religion. Government accommodation of religion is examined at several points in this chapter. See §§ 21.1, 21.3, 21.13.

businesses, it should not be surprising if the organization is subjected to religiously neutral business, labor, and taxation statutes.

In *Tony and Susan Alamo Foundation v. Secretary of Labor,*[2] the justices unanimously upheld the application of the federal Fair Labor Standards Act minimum wage, overtime, and recordkeeping requirements to commercial businesses operated by a nonprofit religious organization even though it was claimed that those businesses were "churches in disguise" that were means of "spreading the gospel" and used, in lieu of employees, only members of the religious group who did not wish to receive cash wages or overtime payments. This case presented no significant free exercise clause problem because the "employees" suffered no burden whatsoever from having to receive the minimum wage. The Court found that the employees, under the federal statutes, were free to accept the minimum wage in living arrangements and services and that they were free to return voluntarily any payments that they received from the religious employer back to that employer.

In *United States v. Lee,*[3] an Amish employer and his employees were required to pay social security taxes. Congress had granted a statutory exemption to self-employed individuals who objected on religious grounds to making payments for government-operated retirement and welfare systems. The Court found that the requirement that the employer pay the social security tax on the work of the employees operated as a burden on the employer's Amish faith but found that that burden was outweighed by the government interest in the efficient operation of the Social Security system. The Court in *Lee* stated a principle that is likely to be a guide for the Court in many of the free exercise clause cases.

> Congress and the courts have been sensitive to the needs flowing from the free exercise clause, but every person cannot be shielded from all the burdens incident to exercising every aspect of the right to practice religious beliefs. When followers of a particular sect enter into commercial activity as a matter of choice, the limits they accept on their own conduct as a matter of conscience and faith are not to be superimposed on the statutory schemes which are binding on others in that activity.[4]

When the government regulates the practices of a religious organization, including commercial practices, questions may arise as to whether the regulation violates the establishment clause of the first amendment. A court, in such cases, should apply the establishment

2. 471 U.S. 290, 105 S.Ct. 1953, 85 L.Ed.2d 278 (1985).

3. 455 U.S. 252, 102 S.Ct. 1051, 71 L.Ed.2d 127 (1982).

4. 455 U.S. at 261, 102 S.Ct. at 1057.

clause tests which we examined earlier in this chapter.[5] Such a regulation must have a secular purpose and a primary effect which neither advances nor inhibits religion. In addition, the regulation must not create an excessive entanglement between government and religion. When a religious organization is engaging in a business activity that mirrors nonreligious commercial enterprises, one can expect that the three-part purpose-effect-entanglement test may be easily met and the government regulation upheld. Business regulations are virtually certain to have a secular purpose; it is difficult to imagine what types of general business regulatory actions would not have a primary effect that was religiously neutral. The excessive entanglement test also should not present a significant barrier to most types of regulations of commercial enterprises owned and operated by religious organizations. The involvement between the government and religiously operated business incident to the enforcement of religious neutral commercial regulations should not endanger governmental neutrality or religious organizational autonomy.

In *Tony and Susan Alamo Foundation v. Secretary of Labor,*[6] the Court upheld the application of the Fair Labor Standards Act wage requirements to the commercial activities of a religious organization, which alleged that the seemingly commercial enterprises were an integral part of its religious mission and that the recordkeeping provisions of the Act led to an excessive entanglement between government and religion. Justice White, writing for a unanimous Court, found that the regulations applied only to "commercial activities undertaken with a 'business purpose' and would therefore have no impact on [the religious organization's] own evangelical activities or on individuals engaged in volunteer work for other religious organizations." The Court ruled that the recordkeeping, and government monitoring, required by the Act did not give rise to an excessive entanglement between government and religion because the law did not give rise to governmental intrusion into religious activities. Justice White's opinion stated: "The establishment clause does not exempt religious organizations from such secular government activity as fire inspections and building and zoning regulations ... the record-keeping requirements of the Fair Labor Standards Act, while perhaps more burdensome in terms of paperwork, are not significantly more intrusive into religious affairs."

If the government sought to regulate the evangelical activities of religious organizations, or activities that involved a combination of religious and secular activities, there would be a question as to whether the law violated the establishment clause. If the law was designed to interfere with the operation of specific religions, it might be held

5. See §§ 21.3–21.5.

6. 471 U.S. 290, 105 S.Ct. 1953, 85 L.Ed.2d 278 (1985).

invalid as giving a preference to some religious organizations or sects over others.[7] A religiously neutral regulation of either commercial or noncommercial activity is likely to have a secular purpose. However, if such a law involves extensive monitoring of religious activities, it is possible that a particular law, or its application to religious organizations through a particular administrative system, might be held invalid under the establishment clause because it had a primary effect that inhibited religion or it created an excessive entanglement between government administrators and religious authorities.

The Supreme Court faced a difficult question regarding the constitutionality of the actions of the National Labor Relations Board in attempting to regulate the relationship between faculty members at religiously affiliated schools and the churches that operated those schools. However, the Court managed to avoid ruling on this issue through its interpretation of federal statutes.

In *National Labor Relations Bd. v. Catholic Bishop of Chicago* [8] the Supreme Court, by a five to four vote, held that the National Labor Relations Board (N.L.R.B.) was not authorized by the National Labor Relations Act to regulate the unionization of lay faculty members at schools affiliated with the Roman Catholic Church. In so doing, the majority opinion by Chief Justice Burger indicated that it was unlikely that the Court would allow secular authorities to engage in detailed regulation of the conditions of labor or the employer-employee relationship at church affiliated schools.

The N.L.R.B. had asserted jurisdiction to resolve questions regarding elections for union representation and union representatives at Catholic schools in Chicago and Indiana.[9] The majority stated that it would have to determine if this extension of jurisdiction gave rise to "serious constitutional questions" and, if so, whether those questions could be avoided by construing the statute to avoid jurisdiction.[10]

---

7. See § 21.16 regarding the invalidity of direct regulations of religious organization activities that grant a preference to some religions over others.

8. 440 U.S. 490, 99 S.Ct. 1313, 59 L.Ed.2d 533 (1979).

9. The Chicago parochial schools involved in the case were related to the training of young men for the Roman Catholic priesthood; the Indiana schools were more traditional high schools. This distinction, however, played no part in the decision. Both sets of schools were certified by their respective states as meeting the basic requirements for private educational institutions.

10. 440 U.S. at 501, 99 S.Ct. at 1319. See also St. Martin Evangelical Lutheran Church v. South Dakota, 451 U.S. 772, 101 S.Ct. 2142, 68 L.Ed.2d 612 (1981) in which the Supreme Court construed the Federal Unemployment Tax Act (FUTA) and the Unemployment Compensation Amendments of 1976 so that non-profit church-related schools were not subject to FUTA's unemployment tax on school personnel. The Court thus avoided ruling on the first amendment objections to the tax, and related regulations, raised by the church.

In Ohio Civil Rights Commission v. Dayton Christian Schools, Inc., 477 U.S. 619, 106 S.Ct. 2718, 91 L.Ed.2d 512 (1986), on remand 802 F.2d 457 (6th Cir.1986), the Supreme Court avoided ruling on the government's power to subject religious entities to laws prohibiting sex discrimination in employment. In this case, the

Chief Justice Burger noted that the Court had stressed in past decisions the important role of a teacher in a church affiliated school. Indeed, this fact has formed the basis for the invalidation of some state laws that would have allowed for government subsidies to parochial schools to offset the cost of teachers for subjects that were not sectarian in nature.[11] The N.L.R.B. claimed that its jurisdiction would only require it to resolve factual issues in disputes between union groups and the church employer and that it could avoid religious issues when ruling on teacher disputes. But the majority opinion found that a significant risk of greater and unconstitutional entanglement between the government agency and church authority would be created if the Board were to regulate this important component of religious education. The Court noted that the resolution of many disputes concerning "terms and conditions of employment" might involve inquiries into the good faith of positions asserted on a religious basis by administrators of these school systems. Indeed, the majority added an appendix to its opinion which was an excerpt of an inquiry by the Board's hearing officer regarding prayers at Catholic schools that involved the questioning of a member of the Catholic clergy concerning the nature of Catholic liturgy and its use at such schools; the majority opinion noted that this type of involvement between secular and religious authorities presented significant dangers to the values protected by the first

Court held that the district court should have abstained from ruling on whether a charge of illegal sex discrimination by a religious school, then pending before a state's civil rights commission, violated the free exercise and establishment clauses of the first amendment. The Court found a sufficient reason for abstention in the fact that the constitutional claims of the school could be considered by the state's civil rights commission or "may be raised in state court judicial review of the administrative proceeding."

In so ruling, the majority opinion by Justice Rehnquist stated that, "[e]ven religious schools cannot claim to be wholly free from some state regulation.... [w]e therefore think that however Dayton's constitutional claim should be decided on the merits, the Commission violates no constitutional rights by merely investigating the circumstances of Hoskinson's [the person who filed the civil rights complaint] discharge in this case, if only to ascertain whether the ascribed religious-based reason was in fact the reason for the discharge." The effect of the ruling is to allow some inquiry into the employment practices of religious schools, although the ruling gives no guidance on whether the free exercise and establishment clauses restrict the scope of that inquiry.

In Roberts v. United States Jaycees, 468 U.S. 609, 104 S.Ct. 3244, 82 L.Ed.2d 462 (1984), the Court held that a state antidiscrimination law could prohibit a commercially-oriented association from discriminating in its membership practices on the basis of gender. However, Roberts did not explain the extent to which the rights of more intimate associations or religious associations could be restricted in order to end gender or race discrimination. See also § 20.41 of the treatise regarding "the freedom to associate and not to associate."

The Court in Bob Jones University v. United States, 461 U.S. 574, 103 S.Ct. 2017, 76 L.Ed.2d 157 (1983) upheld the denial of tax exempt status to schools discriminating on the basis of race, but the Court did not rule on whether schools not receiving government aid or tax exemptions could be prohibited from engaging in forms of race or gender discrimination that were based upon sincerely held religious beliefs.

11. 440 U.S. at 501–02, 99 S.Ct. at 1319–20.

amendment.[12]

The majority opinion then went on to examine whether there was a clear congressional authorization of N.L.R.B. jurisdiction over parochial schools, so as to require the Court to face the issue of whether the asserted jurisdiction violated the first amendment. The majority found the statutes might have been interpreted to allow for such jurisdiction and the necessary conflict with church operated schools, but that Congress had not clearly demonstrated an intent to bring teachers at such schools within the jurisdiction of the N.L.R.B. Therefore, the congressional act would be construed so as to avoid the constitutional question.

The dissenting justices found that the history of the National Labor Relations Act demonstrated a clear intent to allow the Board to assert jurisdiction over all non-profit institutions that affected commerce, including private schools affiliated with religious organizations.[13] But the dissent did not express a view on the ultimate constitutional issue because the majority opinion had avoided the issue.[14]

Title VII of the Civil Rights Act of 1964, as amended, exempts religious organizations from the statutory prohibition against discrimination in employment on the basis of religion. Under the statute a religious entity is allowed to make employment determinations based upon religious affiliation in its nonprofit activities.

Although regulation of the employment practices of religious organizations may present significant establishment clause and free exercise clause problems, the Supreme Court had little difficulty in finding that the absence of regulation regarding such practices did not violate the establishment clause. In *Corporation of Presiding Bishop of Church of Jesus Christ of Latter–Day Saints v. Amos* [15] the Court found that this exemption of religious organizations from the prohibition against religious discrimination did not violate the establishment clause. The Court applied the three-part purpose-effect-entanglement test to determine the validity of this law.[16]

---

12. Chief Justice Burger has provided the leadership in defining the concept of excessive entanglement so as to protect both the autonomy of religious organizations and to avoid providing aid to religious entities.

See § 21.4(d), supra, for a critique of the history and usefulness of the excessive entanglement concept.

13. National Labor Relations Bd. v. Catholic Bishop of Chicago, 440 U.S. 490, 508, 99 S.Ct. 1313, 1323, 59 L.Ed.2d 533 (1979) (Brennan, J., dissenting, joined by White, Marshall & Blackmun, JJ.).

14. See D. Laycock, Towards a General Theory of the Religion Clauses: The Case

of Church Labor Relations and the Right to Church Autonomy, 81 Colo.L.Rev. 1373 (1981), for the view that a constitutional right to church autonomy exists based on the free exercise clause, so that any regulation of churches must be justified by a compelling governmental interest.

15. 483 U.S. 327, 107 S.Ct. 2862, 97 L.Ed.2d 273 (1987).

16. This three-part test has been applied by the Supreme Court in almost all establishment cases since 1971. The three-part test is usually traced to the Supreme Court's decision in Lemon v. Kurtzman, 403 U.S. 602, 91 S.Ct. 2105, 29 L.Ed.2d 745 (1971), rehearing denied 404 U.S. 876, 92

Justice White, who wrote the majority opinion, first found that a legislative purpose to "alleviate significant governmental interference" with the actions of religious organizations was a permissible purpose. Although the purpose might be related to religion, there was no legislative intent to promote a particular religion or religious activity in general. Second, Justice White's opinion ruled that the law did not have a primary effect which advanced or inhibited religion, even though the statute allowed the religious organizations to act upon their religious beliefs. The law did not require a private employer to favor religious employees; it did not provide a special benefit for employees with certain religious beliefs or impose a burden on nonreligious persons.[17] Any advancement of religion was accomplished as a result of a religious organization's decision to employ only members of its own religion in its nonprofit activities. The Court found that "the government itself" had not advanced religion through this statute. Finally, Justice White's majority opinion found that the law could not create an excessive entanglement between government and religion because exemption reduced the administrative entanglement between government and religion.

§ 21.16　Direct Regulation of Religious Organizations

The activities of religious organizations and their members are subject to religiously neutral regulation. Members of a religious organization who seek to take actions that are prohibited by regulatory statutes, or who claim an inability to conform their conduct to regulatory statutes, because of religious beliefs, must show that the government regulations impose some burden on their ability to carry out their faith. If the regulatory statute at issue does impose a burden on the members of the religious organization, those individuals may have a right to an exemption from the statute under the free exercise clause unless the judiciary finds that the government has an overriding interest in denying an exemption from the regulatory system to the members of the religious group.[1]

S.Ct. 24, 30 L.Ed.2d 123 (1971). The test was developed in cases regarding aid to religious institutions; it is examined in §§ 21.3–21.5.

17. Corporation of Presiding Bishop of Church of Jesus Christ of Latter–Day Saints v. Amos, 483 U.S. 327, 337 n. 15, 107 S.Ct. 2862, 2869 n. 15, 97 L.Ed.2d 273 (1987). In this way the Court distinguished Estate of Thornton v. Caldor, Inc., 472 U.S. 703, 105 S.Ct. 2914, 86 L.Ed.2d 557 (1985) in which the Supreme Court invalidated a state statute that required employers to give every employee release from work time on the employee's Sabbath.

The *Estate of Thornton* decision is examined in § 21.13 of this Treatise.

§ 21.16

1. See § 21.8 regarding the free exercise clause standards used by the Court. Religiously neutral regulations of the time, place, or manner of speech that are consistent with the free speech principles may be applied to the speech and evangelical activities of religious organizations. See Heffron v. International Society for Krishna Consciousness, Inc., 452 U.S. 640, 652–53, 101 S.Ct. 2559, 2566, 69 L.Ed.2d 298 (1981), on remand 311 N.W.2d 843 (Minn.1981).

Additionally, a law which directly regulates religious organizations may be susceptible to attack under the establishment clause. Government interference in the internal organization of a religious group may be held invalid if it has a primary effect of inhibiting religious activity or if it creates an excessive entanglement between government and religion.[2] A religiously neutral law may be applied to religious orga-

Although it may be a rare problem, government statutes that delegate power over other members of society to religious organizations should be found to violate the basic establishment clause principle prohibiting the government from enacting laws that have a primary effect of advancing religion over nonreligion. See Larkin v. Grendel's Den, Inc., 459 U.S. 116, 103 S.Ct. 505, 74 L.Ed.2d 297 (1982) (zoning law which gives churches and schools a veto power over the issuance of liquor licenses for any premises within a 500 foot radius of the church or school violates the establishment clause by delegating governmental power to a religious organization). This case is noted in connection with the establishment clause principles examined in §§ 21.13–21.15.

Zoning Laws and Religious Activities. A zoning ordinance which restricts a portion of a community for residential use might be challenged by a religious organization which seeks to use a structure or land in the area for religious activities. Similarly, a zoning ordinance which restricts the number of persons who may use or inhabit a dwelling may restrict religious activity. Though less common, a zoning ordinance that sets aside a portion of a community for business purposes may exclude religious activities from the permitted uses of property in that area. In any case wherein a zoning ordinance denies permission to persons to use property for religious activities a court will have to use the free exercise clause principles and standards examined in § 21.8 to determine whether the zoning authority is constitutionally required to grant a special use permit or exemption for the religious activities. The Supreme Court has not ruled on this issue although it has, in dicta, indicated that religious activity may be subject to religiously neutral laws restricting property use. Lemon v. Kurtzman, 403 U.S. 602, 614, 91 S.Ct. 2105, 2112, 29 L.Ed.2d 745 (1971) (Court invalidates state aid to religious schools as creating an excessive entanglement between government and religion but states that "building and zoning regulations are examples of necessary and permissible contacts" between government

and religion), rehearing denied 404 U.S. 876, 92 S.Ct. 24, 30 L.Ed.2d 123 (1971); Tony and Susan Alamo Found. v. Secretary of Labor, 471 U.S. 290, 306, 105 S.Ct. 1953, 1964, 85 L.Ed.2d 278 (1985) (upholding application of Fair Labor Standards Act to commercial activities of a religious organization).

Building safety ordinances and zoning laws may be enforced without creating the type of excessive entanglement between government and religion that violates the establishment clause. However, the precise terms of each zoning ordinance, the interest the ordinance seeks to protect, the burden on the ability of persons to carry out their religious beliefs, and the nature of the religious activities that the group seeks to perform on the land or in the dwelling (and the impact of those activities on surrounding dwellings, persons, or property) are all factors that a court would have to assess in analyzing a religious organization's free exercise clause claim for an exemption from the zoning ordinance. Lower federal courts and state courts have not adopted a uniform approach to this issue. This lack of uniformity is in part attributable to the fact that state courts are free to alter or invalidate zoning regulations under provisions of a state constitution (such as state constitutional provisions regarding due process protection for property or freedom of religion) even though a court might not be required by federal constitutional principles to invalidate the zoning regulation. See generally § 1.6(c) regarding state court review of state laws.

For analysis of the lower federal court and state court decisions analyzing religious organization claims for exemption from zoning ordinances see Reynolds, Zoning the Church: The Police Power Versus the First Amendment, 64 Boston Univ. L.Rev. 767 (1984); Comment, Justice Douglas' Sanctuary: May Churches be Excluded From Suburban Residential Areas?, 45 Ohio St.L.J. 1018 (1984).

2. No branch of the government, including the judiciary, may undertake a di-

nizations without violation of the establishment clause in most instances. Such a law must have a secular purpose and a primary effect that neither advances nor inhibits religion. Additionally, the type of interaction between government administrators and religious organizations that results from religiously neutral regulation must not constitute an excessive entanglement of government and religion.[3]

When a religious organization receives funds from the government, a court must determine whether the governmental monitoring of the religious organization, which will be necessary to ensure that the religious organization does not use the aid to advance religion, constitutes an excessive entanglement of government and religion.[4]

Although it may be expected that religious organizations can be subject to many forms of religiously neutral regulation, the judiciary should invalidate under the establishment clause any regulation of religious organizations that is found to include on its face or in its purpose a preference for some religious organizations over others. In

rect inquiry into the truth or falsity of religious beliefs although a governmental entity, including the judiciary, may settle disputes between the government and members of religious organizations, or disputes between persons within a religious organization, on a religiously neutral basis. See § 21.12 regarding state involvement in ecclesiastical disputes.

3. Regulations of business activities that conflict with the religious beliefs of members of religious organizations which engage in those activities are examined in §§ 21.8, 21.15.

4. The tests for determining whether government aid to religion constitutes a violation of the establishment clause are examined in §§ 21.3, 21.4 of this Treatise. The governmental monitoring of the use of government funds by a religious organization, at least if the organization is not pervasively sectarian, does not constitute a per se violation of the establishment clause. Each government program that involves granting funds to, and monitoring the use of funds by, a religious organization must be examined under the three-pronged purpose-effect-excessive entanglement test used by the judiciary to determine whether such aid violates the establishment clause. See generally, Bowen v. Kendrick, 487 U.S. 589, 108 S.Ct. 2562, 101 L.Ed.2d 520 (1988) (finding that the establishment clause did not prohibit religious organizations from participating in programs giving grants to nonprofit organiza-

tions to promote social welfare goals; the monitoring of the use of government funds by such organizations, at least if they are not pervasively sectarian, does not automatically give rise to an excessive entanglement between government and religion), on remand 703 F.Supp. 1 (D.D.C.1989); Hernandez v. Commissioner of Internal Revenue, 490 U.S. 680, 695, 109 S.Ct. 2136, 2147–48, 104 L.Ed.2d 766 (1989) (Internal Revenue Code provision that denies charitable deduction for money given to a charitable organization, including a religious organization, in a quid pro quo transaction does not violate the establishment clause; the routine regulatory interaction between the Internal Revenue Service and taxpayers in determining whether an asserted contribution involved a quid pro quo transaction does not constitute excessive entanglement), rehearing denied 492 U.S. 933, 110 S.Ct. 16, 106 L.Ed.2d 630 (1989).

In Jimmy Swaggart Ministries v. Board of Equalization, 493 U.S. 378, 110 S.Ct. 688, 107 L.Ed.2d 796 (1990), the Justices unanimously upheld the application of general sales and use taxes to the sales and use of religious goods and literature. Justice O'Connor's opinion for a unanimous Court followed the reasoning used in the majority opinion used in *Hernandez*. Justice O'Connor found that these general taxes, which involved no use of religious criteria to define the transactions or persons subject to the tax, violated neither the establishment clause nor the free exercise clause.

Larson v. Valente, [5] the Court held that a section of the Minnesota Charitable Solicitation Act, which imposed registration and reporting requirements upon only those religious organizations which solicit more than 50% of their funds from non-members, discriminated against those organizations in violation of the establishment clause of the first amendment. The Unification Church, a religious organization heavily involved in fund-raising activities aimed at non-members, sought a declaration that statute denied its members free exercise of their religion and that it favored some religious organizations over others, contrary to the establishment clause.

Before addressing the establishment clause issue, the Supreme Court, in an opinion by Justice Brennan, noted that the Unification Church was a religious organization within the meaning of the statutory section in question. The State of Minnesota had attempted to force the Church to comply with a rule which applied only to religious organizations and so the state could not now claim that the Church was not a religion. The Court then went on to hold that the denominational preference inherent in the "fifty percent" classification, the statute must be invalidated unless it was justified by a compelling government interest, and unless it was "closely fitted" to further that interest: "The clearest command of the establishment clause is that one religious denomination cannot be officially preferred over another." [6]

5. 456 U.S. 228, 102 S.Ct. 1673, 72 L.Ed.2d 33 (1982), rehearing denied 457 U.S. 1111, 102 S.Ct. 2916, 73 L.Ed.2d 1323 (1982).

6. 456 U.S. at 244–45, 102 S.Ct. at 1683.

Strict judicial scrutiny of laws regulating religious organizations is only required when there is an apparent interference with the religious freedom of such organizations or an apparent preference for some religious organizations under the legislation or regulation at issue. If the government chooses to refrain from regulating all religious organizations, it need not always justify its decision under a compelling interest test.

In Corporation of Presiding Bishop of Church of Jesus Christ of Latter–Day Saints v. Amos, 483 U.S. 327, 337–41, 107 S.Ct. 2862, 2869–70, 97 L.Ed.2d 273 (1987) the Supreme Court upheld federal legislation which exempted religious organizations from federal civil rights statutes prohibiting employment discrimination on the basis of religion insofar as the religious organization was making religiously-based employment decisions regarding its non-profit activity. In *Amos,* the majority opinion by Justice White found that the *Larson* decision discussed in this para-

graph "indicates that laws discriminating among religions are subject to strict scrutiny ... and that laws affording a uniform benefit to *all* religions should be analyzed under *Lemon* [the case establishing the commonly used-purpose effect-entanglement tests under the establishment clause]" 483 U.S. at 337–41, 107 S.Ct. at 2869–70 (internal quotations omitted).

In Hernandez v. Commissioner of Internal Revenue, 490 U.S. 680, 109 S.Ct. 2136, 104 L.Ed.2d 766 (1989), rehearing denied 492 U.S. 933, 110 S.Ct. 16, 106 L.Ed.2d 630 (1989) the Supreme Court upheld a provision of the Internal Revenue Code that, as interpreted by the Internal Revenue Service, denied a charitable deduction for any payment to a charitable organization, including a religious organization, that was a quid pro quo exchange for goods or services. The Supreme Court ruled that this tax code provision violated neither the establishment clause nor the free exercise clause. The majority opinion by Justice Marshall found that the law did not on its face involve a preference for some denominations or sects and, therefore, it need not be subject to the strict scrutiny test that had been employed in Larson v. Valente, 456 U.S. 228, 102 S.Ct. 1673, 72 L.Ed.2d 33

Justice Brennan acknowledged Minnesota's significant interest in protecting its citizens from abusive practices in the solicitation of funds for religious organizations. However, the majority found that the fifty percent classification was not tailored to advance this purpose. There was no factual support for the state's claim that members can and will effectively control an organization if they contribute more than half of its solicited income or that religious organizations are any less able to regulate themselves than other charitable organizations. The Court also found it more plausible that the need for public disclosure rose in proportion to the absolute amount, as opposed to the percentage, of non-member contributions.

Although he deemed it "unnecessary" (because the classification was invalid under the compelling interest test that must be applied to denominational classifications), Justice Brennan also applied the three-pronged purpose-effect-entanglement test. Brennan found that the law violated all three parts of the test. This type of law created a danger of "politicizing religion," because it imposed selective legislative burdens and advantages on particular denominations. This risk was made clear by this law's legislative history, which indicated that the legislature's

(1982). Because the statute did not make a distinction between different types of religions, it was only subject to the three part (purpose-effect-entanglement) test to determine whether it complied with the establishment clause. See § 21.3. After finding that the law did not violate the establishment clause, the Court found that any incidental interference with the free exercise of religion that resulted from denying a tax deduction for payments to a religious organization that were a part of a quid pro quo transaction was justified by the government interests in the tax system; the denial of the deduction did not violate the free exercise clause. See § 21.8.

In Jimmy Swaggart Ministries v. Board of Equalization, 493 U.S. 378, 110 S.Ct. 688, 107 L.Ed.2d 796 (1990), the Justices unanimously upheld the application of general sales and use taxes to the sales and use of religious goods and literature. Justice O'Connor's opinion for a unanimous Court followed the reasoning used in the majority opinion used in *Hernandez*. Justice O'Connor found that these general taxes, which involved no use of religious criteria to define the transactions or persons subject to the tax, violated neither the establishment clause nor the free exercise clause.

In United States Catholic Conference v. Abortion Rights Mobilization, Inc., 487 U.S. 72, 108 S.Ct. 2268, 101 L.Ed.2d 69 (1988), on remand 885 F.2d 1020 (2d Cir. 1989), the Supreme Court avoided ruling on whether a federal court could require a church to submit its records to the court when another organization sought, through judicial action, to have the tax exempt status of the church revoked. In this case the Abortion Rights Mobilization organization, and others, brought suit in federal court against government officials for the purpose of revoking the tax exempt status of the Roman Catholic Church in the United States. The parties seeking to revoke the tax exempt status of the Catholic Church alleged that it persistently intervened in elections to support of candidates who supported the Church's position on abortion and that it had violated the antielectioneering requirement for tax exempt organizations [26 U.S.C.A. § 501(c)(3)]. The Supreme Court of the United States held that the Catholic Church, although it was not a party to the court action, could assert lack of subject matter jurisdiction in defense of its refusal to comply with the lower court order to produce records and its defense against a civil contempt citation. Because the Catholic Church had not been given the opportunity to challenge the subject matter jurisdiction of the court in the lower court proceedings, the case was remanded without a ruling as to whether the court order requiring the Church to turn over its records would violate either the establishment clause or free exercise clause of the first amendment.

intention was to include certain religious groups within the regulatory requirements and to exclude others.

Chapter 22

NATURALIZATION AND CITIZENSHIP

Table of Sections

I. INTRODUCTION

§ 22.1 Generally

In Sections 18.11 through 18.13 we considered the constitutionality of laws that classify on the basis of alienage. In this Chapter we will analyze other constitutional guarantees relating to alienage—congressional power over admission, immigration and naturalization; voluntary and involuntary expatriation or repudiation of citizenship; and deportation. In considering the cases that follow, it is important to remember that Congress enjoys "broad power over immigration and naturalization...."[1]

Consequently, courts have no general equitable power to confer

---

§ 22.1

1. Fiallo v. Bell, 430 U.S. 787, 792, 97 S.Ct. 1473, 1478, 52 L.Ed.2d 50 (1977); see also Galvan v. Press, 347 U.S. 522, 530–32, 74 S.Ct. 737, 742–43, 98 L.Ed. 911 (1954), rehearing denied 348 U.S. 852, 75 S.Ct. 17, 99 L.Ed. 671 (1954). In Nyquist v. Mauclet, 432 U.S. 1, 7 n. 8, 97 S.Ct. 2120, 2124 n. 8, 53 L.Ed.2d 63 (1977), appeal dismissed 433 U.S. 901, 97 S.Ct. 2962, 53 L.Ed.2d 1086 (1977), rehearing denied 434 U.S. 881, 98 S.Ct. 242, 54 L.Ed.2d 164 (1977), the Court said that because of this broad power it would apply "relaxed scrutiny" in judicial review of such statutes.

citizenship on grounds of, for example, estoppel [2] or equity.[3] As the Court stated in *United States v. Ginsberg*.[4]

> An alien who seeks political rights as a member of this Nation can rightfully obtain them only upon terms and conditions specified by Congress. Courts are without authority to sanction changes or modifications; their duty is rigidly to enforce the legislative will in respect of a matter so vital to the public welfare.[5]

Thus in *Immigration & Naturalization Service v. Pangilinan* [6] the Court rejected the claims of Filipino nationals who served with the United States Armed Forces during World War II. These Filipinos claimed that they were entitled to apply for and receive American citizenship under a special immigration statute that had expired over 40 years ago. The Court in this case ruled that the Attorney General's withdrawal of naturalization authority from the vice counsel station in the Philippines in 1945 and 1946 did not violate the fifth amendment or equal protection rights of these persons.

II. ADMISSION, IMMIGRATION, AND ACQUISITION OF CITIZENSHIP

§ 22.2 Admission

In a long line of cases the Supreme Court has stated that the power of Congress over the admission of aliens to this country is absolute.

The Chinese Exclusion Case. This principle is illustrated in *The Chinese Exclusion Case*.[1] A federal statute prohibited Chinese nation-

---

2. U.S. Immigration & Naturalization Service v. Hibi, 414 U.S. 5, 8, 94 S.Ct. 19, 21–22, 38 L.Ed.2d 7 (1973), rehearing denied 414 U.S. 1104, 94 S.Ct. 738, 38 L.Ed.2d 559 (1973).

3. Cf. Hedges v. Dixon County, 150 U.S. 182, 192, 14 S.Ct. 71, 74–75, 37 L.Ed. 1044 (1893).

4. 243 U.S. 472, 37 S.Ct. 422, 61 L.Ed. 853 (1917).

5. 243 U.S. at 474, 37 S.Ct. at 425.

6. 486 U.S. 875, 108 S.Ct. 2210, 100 L.Ed.2d 882 (1988), rehearing denied 487 U.S. 1264, 109 S.Ct. 27, 101 L.Ed.2d 977 (1988).

§ 22.2

1. 130 U.S. 581, 9 S.Ct. 623, 32 L.Ed. 1068 (1889). The case is also titled Chae Chan Ping v. United States.

Though this principle is well-settled, it has been subject to well-taken and thoughtful criticism. See Martin, Due Process and Membership in the National

Community: Political Asylum and Beyond, 44 U.Pitt.L.Rev. 165 (1983); Note, Constitutional Limits on the Power to Exclude Aliens, 82 Colum.L.Rev. 957 (1982); Note, The Constitutional Rights of Excluded Aliens: Proposed Limitations on the Indefinite Detention of the Cuban Refugees, 70 Georgetown L.J. 1303 (1982); Developments in the Law: Immigration and Nationality, 66 Harv.L.Rev. 643, 674–76 (1953). See also, Note, Filling the Immigration Void: Rodriguez–Fernandez v. Wilkinson—An Excludable Alien's Right to Be Free from Indefinite Detention, 31 Cath. L.Rev. 335 (1982); Note, The Indefinite Detention of Excluded Aliens: Statutory and Constitutional Justifications and Limitations, 82 Mich.L.Rev. 61 (1983).

Excludable versus Deportable Aliens. In general one should distinguish excludable aliens from deportable aliens. A *deportable* alien is one who has made an "entry" into the United States, even an illegal, secret clandestine border crossing. See, e.g., Cheng v. Immigration and Naturalization Service, 534 F.2d 1018 (2d Cir. 1976).

The *excludable* alien (who has fewer rights than the deportable alien) usually stands at the border, trying to be admitted. See 1A C. Gordon & H. Rosenfield, Immigration Law and Procedure § 5.6c (1981). Such an alien, detained at the border, may be taken physically into the United States pending determination of his admissibility. And, rather than face imprisonment while his status is being determined, the Attorney General may decide to parole him. But such an alien's physical entry into the United States is not treated as being "within the United States." Even a parole does not change that status. As a legal fiction the alien in detention (or on parole) who was seized at the border is treated as not having made an "entry" in the United States. Therefore he only has the limited rights of an excludable alien. Leng May Ma v. Barber, 357 U.S. 185, 78 S.Ct. 1072, 2 L.Ed.2d 1246 (1958).

One of the leading cases illustrating the minimal rights of an excludable alien is United States ex rel. Knauff v. Shaughnessy, 338 U.S. 537, 70 S.Ct. 309, 94 L.Ed. 317 (1950). The United States sought to exclude—without a hearing—the alien wife (war bride) of a citizen who had served honorably in the U.S. armed forces during World War II. She was excluded solely upon a finding by the Attorney General that her admission would be prejudicial to the interests of the United States. The Court, per Minton, J., found that the Congressional statutory scheme authorized such action, and excluded judicial review. The American citizen not only could not bring his wife into the country, he could not find out why she was excluded. "Whatever the rule may be concerning deportation of persons who have gained entry into the United States, it is not within the province of any court, unless expressly authorized by law, to review the determination of the political branch of the Government to exclude a given alien.... Whatever the procedure authorized by Congress is, it is due process as far as an alien denied entry is concerned." 338 U.S. at 544, 70 S.Ct. at 313.

Subsequently, in Shaughnessy v. United States ex rel. Mezei, 345 U.S. 206, 73 S.Ct. 625, 97 L.Ed. 956 (1953), Mezei, an alien immigrant, was permanently excluded from the United States on security grounds. Because no other nation could take him, he was stranded on Ellis Island. The alien lawfully lived in the United States from 1923–1948 and then left for Hungary to visit his dying mother. On his return, armed with a visa issued by the American Consul in Budapest, he was denied entry on the "basis of information of a confidential nature, the disclosure of which would be prejudicial to the public interest." 345 U.S. at 208, 73 S.Ct. at 627. The Attorney General argued that his continued exclusion of the alien without a hearing was constitutional. The Supreme Court, per Clark, J., agreed: "It is true that aliens who have once passed through our gates, even illegally, may be expelled only after proceedings conforming to traditional notions of due process of law. But an alien on the threshold of initial entry stands on a different footing." 345 U.S. at 212, 73 S.Ct. at 629. Then the Court quoted with approval Justice Minton's comment in *Knauff* that any process to an excludable alien is due process. Mezei could find no other country to take him, so he simply "sat on Ellis Island...." 345 U.S. at 209, 73 S.Ct. at 627. A few months after the adverse Supreme Court decision, the Justice Department granted a parole to Mezei, "until his departure from the United States could be effected." Otherwise he would have faced indefinite detention. New York Times, Aug. 10, 1954, at 10 col. 2.

It should not be correct to consider these cases as holding that an excludable alien has no due process rights. The degree of process due should be less for an excludable alien because he has not developed the same ties to this country as a deportable alien, who already is a resident. However, lessened due process does not mean no due process.

In Jean v. Nelson, 472 U.S. 846, 105 S.Ct. 2992, 86 L.Ed.2d 664 (1985) the Court interpreted INS regulations to deny the INS discretion to consider race or national origin in deciding whether to grant parole to excludable aliens. The Solicitor General, while agreeing with this interpretation of the regulations, also argued that the Constitution itself does not prohibit racial or any other discrimination against excludable aliens.

Justice Marshall, joined by Justice Brennan, dissented. They would have interpreted the regulations differently and reached the constitutional question. Then, after interpreting *Mezei* and *Knauff* narrowly, they would have ruled that the Government, in deciding which aliens to parole pending the determination of their admissibility, may not discriminate on the

als from entering the United States. The Supreme Court applied that statute to persons who had departed before that statute's enactment; these persons, who now were excluded from entering the United States, had a certificate issued under an earlier Act granting them permission to return.

The later Act was attacked as a violation of existing treaties between the United States and China and in violation of rights vested in Chinese laborers by the previous law. As to the conflict of the later statute with the earlier treaty, Justice Field, speaking for a unanimous Court, held that the "last expression of the sovereign must control." [2] Turning to congressional power to exclude aliens, the Court emphasized Congress' absolute power:

> [These Chinese laborers who seek to return to the United States] are not citizens of the United States; they are aliens. That the government of the United States, through the action of the legislative department, can exclude aliens from its territory is a proposition which we do not think open to controversy. Jurisdiction over its own territory to that extent is an incident of every independent nation.[3]
>
> The power of the government to exclude foreigners from the country whenever, in its judgment, the public interest requires such exclusion, has been asserted in repeated instances, and never denied by the executive or legislative departments.[4]

Congress, in "broad terms," may also authorize the executive to exercise this power to exclude aliens.[5]

Early Federal Statutes. Notwithstanding the fact that the case law has long recognized a broad federal power over the admission of aliens, Congress enacted no laws regulating immigration for about a century,[6] though in 1798 it did pass the short-lived and ill-fated Alien Act[7] as part of its Alien and Sedition Laws.[8] In 1875, it enacted a statute barring convicts and prostitutes; there followed a series of other

basis of race or national origin, in the absence of any reasons closely related to immigration concerns. 472 U.S. at 858–82, 105 S.Ct. at 2998–3011.

2. 130 U.S. at 600, 9 S.Ct. at 628.

3. 130 U.S. at 603, 9 S.Ct. at 628–29. Cf. § 22.7, infra.

4. 130 U.S. at 606–07, 9 S.Ct. at 630.

See also, e.g., The Japanese Immigrant Case (Yamataya v. Fisher), 189 U.S. 86, 23 S.Ct. 611, 47 L.Ed. 721 (1903); Oceanic Steam Navigation Co. v. Stranahan, 214 U.S. 320, 339, 29 S.Ct. 671, 676, 53 L.Ed. 1013 (1909); Bugajewitz v. Adams, 228 U.S.

585, 33 S.Ct. 607, 57 L.Ed. 978 (1913), Hines v. Davidowitz, 312 U.S. 52, 61 S.Ct. 399, 85 L.Ed. 581 (1941).

5. United States ex rel. Knauff v. Shaughnessy, 338 U.S. 537, 543, 70 S.Ct. 309, 313, 94 L.Ed. 317 (1950); Shaughnessy v. United States ex rel. Mezei, 345 U.S. 206, 73 S.Ct. 625, 97 L.Ed. 956 (1953).

6. See generally, Higham, American Immigration Policy in Historical Perspective, 21 L. & Contemp.Prob. 213 (1956).

7. Act of June 25, 1798, 1 Stat. 570.

8. See § 20.4, supra.

acts,[9] and in 1924 it enacted a national origins quota system that was not repealed until 1965.[10]

Admission and Free Speech. The broad power to exclude aliens has not been weakened by more recent Supreme Court decisions, though several justices have occasionally dissented from this position.

In *Kleindienst v. Mandel*[11] the Supreme Court upheld a decision of the Attorney General refusing to grant a temporary nonimmigrant visa to an alien scholar and a self-proclaimed "revolutionary Marxist" who also claimed not to be a member of the Communist Party. This alien scholar, Mandel, had entered the country twice before to accept invitations to speak; at those times the Attorney General had exercised his statutory discretion, under the Immigration and Nationality Act of 1952,[12] to admit Mandel temporarily despite the fact that Mandel was otherwise ineligible under section 212(a)(28) as an alien who is, or at any time has been, advocating economic doctrines of world communism or writing or publishing the economic doctrines of world communism. But this time the Attorney General denied application for a temporary visa.

The Court declined to reach the issue of whether the first amendment rights of the listeners in this country (who are citizens) should prevail when the Attorney General advanced no reason for his denial of a waiver.[13] The Attorney General had in fact written the alien's counsel that the reason he (Mandel) was denied a waiver was that Mandel had engaged in previous abuses by violating the terms of his earlier waivers. But Mandel apparently was not made aware of the

---

9. 18 Stat. 477; see Kleindienst v. Mandel, 408 U.S. 753, 761, 92 S.Ct. 2576, 2581, 33 L.Ed.2d 683 (1972). The Constitution of the United States: Analysis and Interpretation, 92d Cong.2d Sess. Document 92–82 (1973), at 295–96. See, e.g., id. at 295, n. 4, citing 22 Stat. 214 (exclusion of idiots, lunatics, convicts, and persons likely to become public charges); 26 Stat. 1084 (exclusion of persons suffering from certain diseases, those convicted of crimes involving moral turpitude, paupers, and polygamists); 32 Stat. 1213 (exclusion of epileptics, insane persons, professional beggars, and anarchists); 34 Stat. 898 (exclusion of feeble minded, children unaccompanied by parents, tuberculosis sufferers, women entering for prostitution and other immoral purposes).

10. Act of May 26, 1924, § 11, 43 Stat. 153, 159; Act of Oct. 3, 1965, § 2, 79 Stat. 911 (repealing legislation).

11. 408 U.S. 753, 92 S.Ct. 2576, 33 L.Ed.2d 683 (1972).

But see, Reagan v. Abourezk, 484 U.S. 1, 108 S.Ct. 252, 98 L.Ed.2d 1 (1987) (per curiam) where an equally divided Supreme Court affirmed the judgment below; in the judgment below, 785 F.2d 1043 (D.C.Cir. 1986), a divided Court of Appeals had ruled that the Government's mandatory duty under 8 U.S.C.A. § 1182(a)(27) to exclude an alien whose activities would be prejudicial to, or endanger, the interests of the United States could not be exercised to exclude an alien merely because the alien is a member of the Communist Party; the threat to the United States must be independent of Communist Party membership.

See also, Judge Enslen, citing Treatise in Ben–Issa v. Reagan, 645 F.Supp. 1556, 1563 (W.D.Mich.1986).

12. 66 Stat. 182, 8 U.S.C.A. § 1101 et seq.

13. 408 U.S. at 766–69, 92 S.Ct. at 2583–85.

conditions attached to his previous waivers,[14] and the Government chose not to rely on the Attorney General's letter to Mandel's counsel, either at the district court or at the Supreme Court.[15]

The Court quoted many of the earlier cases which had said that the legistative power of Congress to exclude aliens or prescribe the conditions for their entry is plenary. Then it held:

> The fact remains, however, that the official empowered to make the decision stated that he denied a waiver because he concluded that previous abuse by Mandel made it inappropriate to grant a waiver again. With this, we think the Attorney General validly exercised the plenary power that Congress delegated to the Executive. . . . We hold that when the Executive exercises this power negatively on the basis of a facially legitimate and bona fide reason, the courts will look neither behind the exercise of that discretion, nor test it by balancing its justification against the First Amendment interests of those who seek personal communication with the applicant.[16]

The Court distinguished an earlier case, *Lamont v. Postmaster General*,[17] where the Court had held that a statute permitting the Government to hold "communist political propaganda" arriving in the mails from abroad unless the addressee affirmatively requested in writing that it be delivered to him placed an unjustifiable burden on the addressee's first amendment rights. *Lamont* was simply inapplicable because that case did not involve the Government's plenary power over admission of aliens.

In *Mandel* two justices, Marshall and Brennan, dissented on constitutional grounds. Justice Douglas dissented on statutory grounds.[18]

Admission and the Rights of Illegitimates. More recently, the Supreme Court upheld other sections of the Immigration and Nationality Act which had the effect of excluding the relationship between an illegitimate child and his natural father—but not his natural mother—from the special preference immigration status given to a "child" or "parent" of a United States citizen or lawful permanent resident.[19] The Court again reviewed the relevant line of cases and said it was "no more inclined to reconsider this line of cases today than we were five

---

14. 408 U.S. at 758 n. 5, 759, 92 S.Ct. at 2579 n. 5, 2580.

15. 408 U.S. at 769, 92 S.Ct. at 2585. See also, § 22.7, infra.

16. 408 U.S. at 769–70, 92 S.Ct. at 2585.

17. 381 U.S. 301, 85 S.Ct. 1493, 14 L.Ed.2d 398 (1965).

18. Justice Douglas dissented on statutory grounds, 408 U.S. at 770–74, 92 S.Ct. at 2585–87. Justice Marshall, joined by Justice Brennan, dissented on constitutional grounds. 408 U.S. at 774–85, 92 S.Ct. at 2587–93.

19. Fiallo v. Bell, 430 U.S. 787, 97 S.Ct. 1473, 52 L.Ed.2d 50 (1977).

years ago...." [20] Justices Marshall, Brennan, and White again dissented on constitutional grounds.

The same day the Court upheld the federal law, the Supreme Court did strike a state law which allowed illegitimate children to inherit by intestate succession only from their mothers while legitimates were allowed in such cases to inherit from both parents.[21] The federal law which discriminated against certain types of illegitimates, unlike the state law, was apparently saved from unconstitutionality because it was based on Congress' plenary power over the admission of aliens.

§ 22.3 Immigration and Acquisition of Citizenship

Born in the United States. One method of acquiring United States citizenship is to be born in the United States. One born in the United States and subject to the jurisdiction thereof is a citizen of the United States by virtue of the first sentence of the first section of the fourteenth amendment. "Subject to the jurisdiction thereof" means that the person is not born of parents who are employed in a diplomatic or official capacity of a foreign government.

For example, in *United States v. Wong Kim Ark*,[1] the Supreme Court held that a child born in the United States of alien parents of Chinese descent became, at the time of his birth, a citizen of the United States by virtue of the first clause of the fourteenth amendment. The alien parents were subjects of the Emperor of China, but the parents had a permanent domicile and residence in the United States. They were carrying on business in the United States and were not employed in any diplomatic or official capacity under the Emperor of China. Thus, even the child of illegal immigrants is a United States citizen if he or she is born in the United States, even though the illegal immigrant parents are not, and never become, United States citizens.[2]

Naturalization. The other means of obtaining citizenship is through naturalization.

20. 430 U.S. at 793 n. 4, 97 S.Ct. at 1478 n. 4 (1977).

21. Trimble v. Gordon, 430 U.S. 762, 97 S.Ct. 1459, 52 L.Ed.2d 31 (1977).

§ 22.3

1. 169 U.S. 649, 18 S.Ct. 456, 42 L.Ed. 890 (1898).

The Wong Family

The Wong family, it may be interesting to note, has a long history. There are approximately 60 million Wongs in the world today. They trace their family clan back 4,000 years (circa 2637 B.C.) when Huang Ti conquered a vast area along the lower Yellow River and then granted land to his various aides, including one Nom Look, who became the first Wong, a name meaning "of earth or yellow color." Members of this family include Anna May Wong, the first Chinese to become a Hollywood star, cinematographer James Wong Howe, who won two Oscars, and Willy "Woo Woo" Wong (of the University of San Francisco Dons) who was the first Chinese–American to play basketball in Madison Square Garden. See, Wong, "Of 60 Million Wongs, 500 Are in S.F. for Family Hopla," S.F. Sunday Examiner & Chronicle, Aug. 15, 1982, at A7.

2. See Immigration and Naturalization Service v. Rios–Pineda, 471 U.S. 444, 445, 105 S.Ct. 2098, 2100, 85 L.Ed.2d 452 (1985).

Article I, Section 8, Clause 4, gives Congress the power to "establish an uniform Rule of Naturalization...." Like the power of admission, the initial Congressional decision as to whom is eligible for naturalization may be virtually unchecked by the due process clause of the fifth amendment and other constitutional restrictions. However, once naturalization is conferred, due process and other restrictions limit Congress' power to involuntarily expatriate a citizen, as discussed in the next subsection.

As the Supreme Court stated in *United States v. MacIntosh:*[3]

Naturalization is a privilege, to be given, qualified or withheld as Congress may determine, and which the alien may claim as of right only upon compliance with the terms which Congress imposes.

Throughout the years Congress has by statute imposed various qualifications on those seeking naturalization, such as those based on race and beliefs. In 1790 only a "free white person" was eligible for naturalization pursuant to an act of the First Congress.[4] It was not until after the Civil War that those of "African" birth or descent were eligible to be naturalized.[5] In 1882, Congress excluded Orientals.[6] Belief in doctrines such as anarchy or belief in or advocacy of the overthrow by force or violence of the Government of the United States made one ineligible as of 1903.[7]

The Distinction Between Naturalization Inside of the United States and Naturalization Outside of the United States. In the next subsection we consider the main Supreme Court cases dealing with the involuntary expatriation of naturalized citizens. In this section it is important to note that Congress' power over naturalization differs when the person who is naturalized becomes so while in this country. The first sentence of the first clause of the fourteenth amendment provides: "All persons born or naturalized in the United States and subject to the jurisdiction thereof, are citizens of the United States and of the State wherein they reside." The purpose of this sentence was "to make citizenship of Negroes permanent and secure" and not subject to loss by any statutory change.[8] But this sentence of the fourteenth

---

3. 283 U.S. 605, 615, 51 S.Ct. 570, 572, 75 L.Ed. 1302 (1931).

See generally, Burr, Immigration and the First Amendment, 73 Calif.L.Rev. 1889 (1985).

4. Act of Mar. 26, 1790, 1 Stat. 103.

5. Act of July 14, 1870, § 7, 16 Stat. 254, 256.

6. Act of May 6, 1882, § 1, 22 Stat. 58. See Hidemitsu Toyota v. United States, 268 U.S. 402, 45 S.Ct. 563, 69 L.Ed. 1016 (1925); Kharaiti Ram Samras v. United States,

125 F.2d 879 (9th Cir.1942), certiorari denied 317 U.S. 634, 63 S.Ct. 34, 87 L.Ed. 511 (1942).

7. Act of March 3, 1903, 32 Stat. 1213. The constitutionality of this act was upheld in United States ex rel. Turner v. Williams, 194 U.S. 279, 24 S.Ct. 719, 48 L.Ed. 979 (1904). Aliens now excludable are listed in 8 U.S.C.A. § 1182.

8. Afroyim v. Rusk, 387 U.S. 253, 263, 268, 87 S.Ct. 1660, 1665, 1668, 18 L.Ed.2d 757 (1967); H. Flack, Adoption of the Fourteenth Amendment 88–94 (1908).

amendment "has not touched the acquisition of citizenship by being born abroad of American parents; and has left that subject to be regulated, as it had always been, by Congress, in the exercise of the power conferred by the Constitution to establish an uniform rule of naturalization." [9]   A person naturalized in the United States cannot have his or her citizenship taken away, as discussed below.[10]   A person naturalized outside of the United States does not have such protections, as also discussed below.[11]

Thus, as to persons naturalized in the United States, Congress may only establish conditions precedent to naturalization.[12]   But, if the person has been naturalized abroad—as is one who has the benefit of a federal statute granting United States citizenship by virtue of having been born abroad to parents, one of whom is an American citizen—Congress may also impose conditions subsequent. In *Rogers v. Bellei,* [13] also discussed in the subsection below, the majority noted:

> The central fact, in our weighing of the plaintiff's claim to continuing and therefore current United States citizenship, is that he was born abroad. He was not born in the United States. He was not naturalized in the United States. And he has not been subject to the jurisdiction of the United States. All this being so, it seems indisputable that the first sentence of the Fourteenth Amendment has no application. . . .   He simply is not a Four-teenth-Amendment-first-sentence citizen.[14]

The restriction on Congress' power to take away citizenship conferred by the use of conditions subsequent over such persons is not governed by the specific guarantees of the first sentence of the fourteenth amendment but rather by the more generalized restrictions of the due process clause and other constitutional safeguards. It is to this power of involuntary expatriation we now turn.

III. VOLUNTARY AND INVOLUNTARY EXPATRIATION

§ 22.4 Voluntary Expatriation

Early in our history Justice Story for the Court argued that the "general doctrine is, that no persons can, by any act of their own, without the consent of the government, put off their allegiance, and

---

9. United States v. Wong Kim Ark, 169 U.S. 649, 688, 18 S.Ct. 456, 472, 42 L.Ed. 890 (1898).

10. See § 22.5, infra.

11. See § 22.6, infra.

12. Schneider v. Rusk, 377 U.S. 163, 84 S.Ct. 1187, 12 L.Ed.2d 218 (1964).

13. 401 U.S. 815, 91 S.Ct. 1060, 28 L.Ed.2d 499 (1971).

14. 401 U.S. at 827, 91 S.Ct. at 1067.

become aliens." [1] But now it is agreed that an American citizen may voluntarily relinquish, repudiate, or renounce his or her citizenship.[2] "Voluntary" in this sense is used literally: a free giving up of a known right.

Rules of Evidence. Sometimes it is not clear whether a U.S. citizen had earlier relinquished his or her citizenship voluntarily. The leading case on the constitutional power of Congress to prescribe rules of evidence and burdens of proof on this question is *Vance v. Terrazas.*[3] In that case, the Court construed and ruled on the constitutionality of various sections of the Immigration and Nationality Act.

One section of that Act provides: "a person who is a national of the United States ... shall lose his nationality by ... taking an oath or making an affirmation or other formal declaration of allegiance to a foreign state...." [4] The party claiming such loss of U.S. citizenship must "establish such claim by a preponderance of the evidence," and the voluntary nature of the expatriating conduct is rebuttably presumed.[5] In *Vance* the United States claimed that Laurence Terrazas, a dual United States and Mexican citizen by birth, had lost his American citizenship at age 22 when in his application for a certificate of Mexican nationality—swore allegiance to Mexico and "expressly renounced" his "submission, obedience, and loyalty to any foreign government, especially to that of the United States of America...." [6]

The Court first held that the mere taking of an oath of allegiance to a foreign power or other expatriating acts as defined by Congress do not per se amount to a loss of citizenship. Congress may not simply specify those acts which cause a renunciation of citizenship. The Government therefore must prove not only the voluntary commission of an expatriating act specified in the statute but also the citizen's specific intent to renounce U.S. citizenship. "In the last analysis, expatriation

---

§ 22.4

1. Shanks v. Dupont, 28 U.S. (3 Pet.) 242, 246, 7 L.Ed. 666 (1830); Inglis v. Trustees of Sailor's Snug Harbour, 28 U.S. (3 Pet.) 99, 7 L.Ed. 617 (1830); cf. Talbot v. Jansen, 3 U.S. (3 Dall.) 133, 153–54, 1 L.Ed. 540 (1795) (opinion of Paterson, J.); 3 U.S. (3 Dall.) at 161–66 (opinion of Iredell, J.); See also 4 Annals of Cong. 1005, 1027–1030 (1794) (view of some Congressmen also accepting this doctrine of perpetual allegiance); 7 Annals of Cong. 349 et seq. (1797) (same); 31 Annals of Cong. 495 (1817) (introduction of bill to allow for voluntary repudiation of citizenship).

2. Perkins v. Elg, 307 U.S. 325, 334, 59 S.Ct. 884, 889, 83 L.Ed. 1320 (1939); Kennedy v. Mendoza–Martinez, 372 U.S. 144,

159 n. 11, 83 S.Ct. 554, 563, n. 11, 9 L.Ed.2d 644 (1963); Perez v. Brownell, 356 U.S. 44, 66, 78 S.Ct. 568, 580, 2 L.Ed.2d 603 (1958) (Warren, C.J., dissenting). See also 8 U.S.C.A. §§ 1482, 1483.

3. 444 U.S. 252, 100 S.Ct. 540, 62 L.Ed.2d 461 (1980), rehearing denied 445 U.S. 920, 100 S.Ct. 1285, 63 L.Ed.2d 606 (1980), on remand 494 F.Supp. 1017 (N.D.Ill.1980), judgment affirmed 653 F.2d 285 (7th Cir.1981).

See generally, Note, Evidence in Deportation Proceedings, 63 Tex.L.Rev. 1537 (1985).

4. 8 U.S.C.A. § 1481(a)(2).

5. 8 U.S.C.A. § 1481(c).

6. 444 U.S. at 256–58, 100 S.Ct. at 542.

depends on the will of the citizen rather than on the will of Congress and the assessment of his conduct." [7]

However, it is constitutional for Congress to provide, by statute, evidentiary rules to govern what the Government must prove, pursuant to Congress' traditional powers to establish rules of evidence and standards of proof in federal courts. In *Vance* the Court held that the particular evidentiary standards which Congress had prescribed to determine expatriation violated neither the due process nor citizenship clauses of the fourteenth amendment.

The statute in question provided that the party claiming voluntary expatriation must prove one of the expatriating acts by a preponderance of the evidence. If proved, it is presumed to have been committed voluntarily, but this presumption of voluntariness could be rebutted, also by a preponderance of the evidence. In addition the party claiming expatriation must also prove, also by a preponderance of the evidence (and without the benefit of any presumption), that the act had been performed with the specific intent to relinquish American citizenship.[8] Although this statutory rule of evidence rule reversed a previous Supreme Court decision,[9] the previous case had not been based on the Constitution.

§ 22.5 Involuntary Expatriation of One Born or Naturalized in the United States

More difficult than the question of voluntary expatriation is the question of involuntary expatriation; that is, does Congress have the power to take away someone's citizenship by providing that the doing of a certain act forfeits citizenship or implies its repudiation? A brief history of the case law is necessary to answer this question and illuminate the various distinctions.

7. 444 U.S. at 262, 100 S.Ct. at 546. Relying on Afroyim v. Rusk, 387 U.S. 253, 87 S.Ct. 1660, 18 L.Ed.2d 757 (1967). Accord, 42 Op.Atty.Gen. 397 (1969).

8. But see, Woodby v. INS, 385 U.S. 276, 285–86, 87 S.Ct. 483, 487–88, 17 L.Ed.2d 362 (1966) (clear and convincing standard in deportation proceedings); Schneiderman v. United States, 320 U.S. 118, 159, 63 S.Ct. 1333, 1353, 87 L.Ed. 1796 (1943) (clear and convincing standard in denaturalization proceedings), rehearing denied 320 U.S. 807, 64 S.Ct. 24, 88 L.Ed. 488 (1943).

9. The statutory rule of evidence upheld in *Vance* reversed a previous Supreme Court decision, Mitsugi Nishikawa v. Dulles, 356 U.S. 129, 78 S.Ct. 612, 2 L.Ed.2d 659 (1958) (requiring Government to prove voluntary expatriating act by clear and convincing evidence, without any benefit of a presumption), but that previous case had not been based on the Constitution.

In *Vance* Marshall, J. and Stevens, J., each concurring in part, and Brennan, J., joined in part by Stewart, J., dissenting, believed that a citizen should not lose his

In *Perez v. Brownell*[1] a five to four majority of the Supreme Court upheld the constitutionality of a federal statute which deprived the plaintiff, a national of the United States by birth, of his American citizenship for voting in a Mexican political election. Justice Frankfurter for the bare majority reviewed the earlier case law and concluded that the statute was within Congress' foreign affairs power.

The statute was upheld because there was a "rational nexus" between the withdrawal of citizenship and the regulation of foreign affairs.[2] In a footnote Frankfurter dismissed in one sentence the argument that the fourteenth amendment restricted Congressional power.[3] He declined to decide whether it was constitutional for Congress to strip away citizenship of a person who remains outside of the United States to avoid military service.[4]

Chief Justice Warren and Justices Black and Douglas dissented on broad constitutional grounds,[5] and Justice Whittaker also dissented, though on narrower constitutional grounds, for he agreed with the "major premise" of the majority.[6]

The same day that the Court decided *Perez* it decided *Trop v. Dulles*.[7] A fragmented Court, with no majority opinion, found unconstitutional on various grounds a federal statute providing that a citizen loses "his nationality" if he deserts the United States military or naval forces in time of war provided that he is convicted for that offense by court martial and, as a result, "is dismissed or dishonorably discharged from the service."

Chief Justice Warren, (again joined by Justices Black and Douglas) and also Justice Whittaker adhered to their views in their *Perez* dissents and in addition found that the statute in question violated the

citizenship unless there was clear and convincing evidence that he so intended.

§ 22.5

1. 356 U.S. 44, 78 S.Ct. 568, 2 L.Ed.2d 603 (1958).

In *Perez*, Warren dissented. He also wrote what was to have been the opinion of the Court in Trop v. Dulles, 356 U.S. 86, 78 S.Ct. 590, 2 L.Ed.2d 630 (1958), decided the same day as *Perez*. When *Perez* and *Trop* "were finally decided, the two decisions appeared inconsistent, leaving the extent of Congressional power to declare citizenship forfeit uncertain, despite the Court's lengthy consideration of the subject. All this would have been avoided had the draft opinions of the Court originally prepared by Chief Justice Warren" been adopted by the Court. B. Schwartz, The Unpublished Opinions of the Warren Court 77 (1985).

The original drafts of these two opinions are found in Schwartz, id. at 81–104.

See generally, Harry Kalven, Jr. (ed. by Jamie Kalven), A Worthy Tradition: Freedom of Speech in America 423–36 (1988).

2. 356 U.S. at 58, 78 S.Ct. at 576.

3. 356 U.S. at 58 n. 3, 78 S.Ct. at 576 n. 3.

4. 356 U.S. at 62, 78 S.Ct. at 578.

5. 356 U.S. at 62, 78 S.Ct. at 578 (Warren, C.J., dissenting, joined by Black and Douglas, JJ.); 356 U.S. at 79, 78 S.Ct. at 586 (Douglas, J., dissenting, joined by Black, J.).

6. 356 U.S. at 84, 78 S.Ct. at 590 (Memorandum of Whittaker, J.).

7. 356 U.S. 86, 78 S.Ct. 590, 2 L.Ed.2d 630 (1958).

eighth amendment because it was penal and "cruel and unusual." [8]
Justice Black, joined by Douglas, also wrote a separate opinion arguing
that even if citizenship could be involuntarily divested, the authority to
do so could not be placed in the hands of the military.[9] And Justice
Brennan also concurred in *Trop,* though still agreeing with the majority
he had joined in *Perez.*[10] Justices Frankfurter, Burton, Clark, and
Harlan all dissented.[11]

Five years later a majority of the Court answered the question
reserved in *Perez* and held that Congress could *not* constitutionally strip
someone of his citizenship because he remained outside the jurisdiction
of the United States in time of war or national emergency to avoid
military service.[12] Justice Goldberg was now on the Court and he
wrote the opinion for the five to four majority. *Perez* was distinguished, and Justice Brennan who joined the majority, stated in a
concurring opinion that the "instant cases do not require me to resolve
some felt doubts of the correctness of *Perez,* which I joined." [13]

A year later, in a short opinion, Justice Douglas for the majority
struck a federal statute which sought to divest citizenship from a
German born woman who came to this country as a child and acquired
derivative American citizenship. The invalidated statute provided that
a naturalized citizen (with certan exceptions not applicable here) loses
her citizenship by continuous residence for three years in the country of
origin.[14] Justice Douglas noted, in an understatement, that the "[v]iews
of the Justices have varied when it comes to the problem of expatriation." [15]

Then, in 1967 a five to four majority of the Supreme Court in
Afroyim v. Rusk [16] explicitly overruled the already eroded doctrine of
Perez. Justice Black now wrote for the majority. He upheld the
citizenship claims of a naturalized American of Polish birth who, nearly
a quarter of a century after naturalization, went to Israel and voted in
an Israeli legislative election in 1951.

First Black argued Congress has no general power, express or
implied, to strip people of their citizenship without their assent. The
power to take away citizenship cannot be sustained as an implied

8. 356 U.S. at 87–104, 78 S.Ct. at
591–600.

9. 356 U.S. at 104–05, 78 S.Ct. at
599–600.

10. 356 U.S. at 105–14, 78 S.Ct. at
600–05.

11. 356 U.S. at 114–28, 78 S.Ct. at
605–12.

12. Kennedy v. Mendoza–Martinez, 372
U.S. 144, 83 S.Ct. 554, 9 L.Ed.2d 644 (1963).

The original draft of this case is reprinted in B. Schwartz, The Unpublished Opinions of the Warren Court 113–38 (1985).

13. 372 U.S. at 187, 83 S.Ct. at 577
(Brennan, J., concurring).

14. Schneider v. Rusk, 377 U.S. 163, 84
S.Ct. 1187, 12 L.Ed.2d 218 (1964).

15. 377 U.S. at 166, 84 S.Ct. at 1189.

16. 387 U.S. 253, 87 S.Ct. 1660, 18
L.Ed.2d 757 (1967), overruling Perez v.
Brownell, 356 U.S. 44, 78 S.Ct. 568, 2
L.Ed.2d 603 (1958).

attribute of sovereignty possessed by all nations: "Other nations are governed by their own constitutions, if any, and we can draw no support from theirs." [17]

Then, unlike the other majority opinions in the previous cases, Justice Black specifically relied on the first sentence of the first section of the fourteenth amendment: "All persons born or naturalized in the United States . . . are citizens of the United States. . . ."

Black explained that this sentence granted permanence and security of citizenship in order to protect the freed black slaves. Just a few years before the ratification of the fourteenth amendment, the *Dred Scott v. Sandford* [18] case had denied any power of Congress to grant citizenship to blacks. The Civil Rights Act of 1866 [19] had attempted to confer citizenship on all persons born or naturalized in the United States, but the Senate sponsors of the soon to be enacted fourteenth amendment were afraid that this statutory right might later be taken away by another Congress.

"[I]t was to provide an insuperable obstacle against every governmental effort to strip Negroes of their newly acquired citizenship that the first clause was added to the Fourteenth Amendment." [20] This purpose "would be frustrated by holding that the Government can rob a citizen of his citizenship without his consent by simply proceeding to act under an implied general power to regulate foreign affairs or some other power generally granted." [21]

The general state of the law now appears to be as follows. If a person is born in the United States and subject to the jurisdiction thereof, he or she is a citizen by virtue of the first sentence of the first section of the fourteenth amendment. Such citizenship cannot be taken away. If a person is naturalized in the United States and subject to the jurisdiction thereof, the same clause confers the same rights. However, Congress may confer preconditions to achieving such naturalization. Once those preconditions are filled, the recipient is within the protection of the fourteenth amendment and the full force of the *Afroyim* rule applies. However, as Justice Black specifically noted in

---

17. 387 U.S. at 257, 87 S.Ct. at 1662. Justice Black also relied on some frequently quoted dictum by Chief Justice Marshall in Osborn v. Bank of United States, 22 U.S. (9 Wheat.) 738, 827, 6 L.Ed. 204 (1824):

"[The naturalized citizen] becomes a member of the society, possessing all the rights of a native citizen, and standing, in the view of the constitution, on the footing of a native. The constitution does not authorize Congress to enlarge or abridge those rights. The simple power

of the national Legislature, is to prescribe a uniform rule of naturalization, and the exercise of this power exhausts it, so far as respects the individual."

See 387 U.S. at 261, 87 S.Ct. at 1664–65.

18. 60 U.S. (19 How.) 393, 15 L.Ed. 691 (1857).

19. 14 Stat. 27.

20. 387 U.S. at 262–63, 87 S.Ct. at 1665 (footnote omitted).

21. 387 U.S. at 263, 87 S.Ct. at 1665.

Afroyim, "naturalization unlawfully procured can be set aside." [22] Thus, if the person engages in fraud or misrepresentation in the naturalization process, later discovery will annul the grant. [23]

A proposed exception that has been suggested to this irrevocable grant of citizenship to those who are born or properly naturalized in the United States and subject to the jurisdiction thereof is one offered by some justices in the older cases. They argued that Congress, by statute, may require a person to reject one's citizenship for an act totally opposed to that status, such as service in the armed forces of a nation at war with the United States. [24] However, the Court definitely rejected

22. 387 U.S. at 267 n. 23, 87 S.Ct. at 1667 n. 23. Cf. Luria v. United States, 231 U.S. 9, 34 S.Ct. 10, 58 L.Ed. 101 (1913).

23. 8 U.S.C.A. § 1451(a); e.g., Costello v. United States, 365 U.S. 265, 81 S.Ct. 534, 5 L.Ed.2d 551 (1961). See also, Fedorenko v. United States, 449 U.S. 490, 101 S.Ct. 737, 66 L.Ed.2d 686 (1981) (after the Government proves that a naturalized citizen has procured citizenship illegally or by wilful misrepresentation, the federal courts lack equitable discretion to refrain from entering a judgment of naturalization).

The Test To Determine Whether Naturalization Was "Illegally Procured" or Procured by "Concealment of a Material Fact." Section 1451(a) of title 8 provides that the Government may institute a denaturalization proceeding on the ground that the order and certificate of naturalization "were illegally procured or were procured by concealment of a material fact or by willful misrepresentation." In Kungys v. United States, 485 U.S. 759, 108 S.Ct. 1537, 99 L.Ed.2d 839 (1988), a splintered Court was able to create a majority on two issues—what materiality standard applies to the "concealment or representation" clause, and the "illegally procured" clause. The Court thereby shed some light on the statutory requirements in a denaturalization proceeding.

The "concealment or misrepresentation" clause has four independent elements: "[1] the naturalized citizen must have misrepresented or concealed some fact, [2] the misrepresentation or concealment must have been willful, [3] the fact must have been material, and [4] the naturalized citizen must have procured citizenship as a result of the misrepresentation or concealment." 485 U.S. at 767, 108 S.Ct. at 1545. Turning to the third and fourth elements, relating to "materiality," the Court concluded that the test is whether the mis-

representation or concealment "was predictably capable of affecting, i.e., had a natural tendency to affect," or to "produce the conclusion that the applicant was qualified" for admission to citizenship. This test must be met by "clear, unequivocal, and convincing" evidence. Materiality, the Court added, is an issue of law, for the courts, and not a question of fact for the trier of fact. 485 U.S. at 771, 108 S.Ct. at 1547.

The Court treated the "procurement" clause differently. Under 8 U.S.C.A. § 1101(f)(6), a person is not deemed to be of "good moral character" if he or she "has given false testimony for the purpose of obtaining" naturalization or immigration benefits. Another issue in *Kungys* was whether naturalization was "illegally procured" under 8 U.S.C.A. § 1451(a), and other sections of the Immigration law, because the applicant lacked good moral character because he or she had given false testimony. The Court ruled that § 1101(f)(6) does *not* contain a materiality requirement. Lack of good moral character appears "to some degree whenever there is a subjective intent to deceive, no matter how immaterial the deception." 485 U.S. at 779, 108 S.Ct. at 1551. However, the "testimony" that is the subject of this clause is limited to oral statements under oath, made with the subjective intent to obtain immigration benefits, and—in order to support denaturalization—there must be " 'clear, unequivocal, and convincing' evidence which does not leave the 'issue in doubt.' " 485 U.S. at 779–81, 108 S.Ct. at 1551–52.

24. See, e.g., Warren, C.J., dissenting (joined by Black and Douglas, JJ.), in Perez v. Brownell, 356 U.S. 44, 68, 78 S.Ct. 568, 581, 2 L.Ed.2d 603 (1958): "Any action by which he manifests allegiance to a foreign state may be so inconsistent with the retention of citizenship as to result in loss of that status." (footnote omitted).

this position in *Vance v. Terrazas*,[25] which stated that the fourteenth amendment constitutional definition of citizenship "cannot coexist with a congressional power to specify acts that work a renunciation of citizenship even absent an intent to renounce. In the last analysis, expatriation depends on the will of the citizen rather than on the will of Congress and its assessment of the citizen's conduct."[26]

§ 22.6 Involuntary Expatriation of One Born and Naturalized Outside of the United States

Thus far we have only considered the involuntary expatriation of one born or naturalized in the United States. The case of one born outside of the United States and naturalized outside of the United States is subject to different considerations. The leading case in this area is *Rogers v. Bellei*.[1]

Bellei was born abroad to parents, one of whom was an American citizen. By statute he, therefore, acquired United States citizenship. But the statute also imposed a condition subsequent: One who so acquires United States citizenship loses it unless he resides in this country continuously for five years between the ages of 14 and 28. A five to four majority upheld the constitutionality of this statute on the grounds that Congress has the power to impose the condition of subsequent residence in this country on one who does not come within the fourteenth amendment's definition of citizens as those "born or naturalized in the United States...." These conditions subsequent are only subject to the general requirements of due process and other such restrictions.

To determine, in a *Bellei* type of problem whether the condition subsequent causing the involuntary expatriation is valid, one must use the *Perez*[2] line of cases concerning due process which, it would appear, are still good law as to a *Bellei* issue.

IV. DEPORTATION

§ 22.7 Generally

Congress has the power to regulate the behavior of aliens in this

---

25. 444 U.S. 252, 100 S.Ct. 540, 62 L.Ed.2d 461 (1980), rehearing denied 445 U.S. 920, 100 S.Ct. 1285, 63 L.Ed.2d 606 (1980), on remand 494 F.Supp. 1017 (N.D.Ill.1980), judgment affirmed 653 F.2d 285 (7th Cir.1981).

26. 444 U.S. at 262, 100 S.Ct. at 545.

§ 22.6

1. 401 U.S. 815, 91 S.Ct. 1060, 28 L.Ed.2d 499 (1971).

See generally, Harry Kalven, Jr. (ed. by Jamie Kalven), A Worthy Tradition: Freedom of Speech in America 423–36 (1988).

2. § 22.5, supra.

country.[1] To enforce these restrictions, Congress may deport aliens for a wide variety of activities Congress deems harmful.[2] In interpreting the constitutional restraints on this substantive power, the Court has exercised very little review. So long "as aliens fail to obtain and maintain citizenship by naturalization, they remain subject to the plenary power of Congress to expel them under the sovereign right to determine what noncitizens shall be permitted to remain within our borders."[3]

Procedural Due Process. Important procedural guarantees do exist for the alien to be deported, in sharp contrast to the absence of similar procedures for the alien seeking admission.[4] The excludable alien typically is one who stands at the border, trying to be admitted.

The resident alien has a right to procedural due process, including a hearing prior to deportation;[5] at this hearing it is determined if he is

§ 22.7

1. See, e.g., Justice Rehnquist dissenting in Hampton v. Mow Sun Wong, 426 U.S. 88, 117, 96 S.Ct. 1895, 1912, 48 L.Ed.2d 495 (1976), on remand 435 F.Supp. 37 (N.D.Cal.1977).

See generally, Harry Kalven, Jr. (ed. by Jamie Kalven), A Worthy Tradition: Freedom of Speech in America 403–23, 437–48 (1988).

2. 8 U.S.C.A. § 1251.

3. Carlson v. Landon, 342 U.S. 524, 534, 72 S.Ct. 525, 531, 96 L.Ed. 547 (1952) (footnote omitted), rehearing denied 343 U.S. 988, 72 S.Ct. 1069, 96 L.Ed. 1375 (1952). See also Ludecke v. Watkins, 335 U.S. 160, 68 S.Ct. 1429, 92 L.Ed. 1881 (1948) (Congressional power to deport enemy alien after cessation of actual hostilities), rehearing denied 335 U.S. 837, 69 S.Ct. 14, 93 L.Ed. 389 (1948); Harisiades v. Shaughnessy, 342 U.S. 580, 72 S.Ct. 512, 96 L.Ed. 586 (1952) (Congressional power to deport a legally resident alien because of membership in the Communist Party, which membership terminated before the enactment of the Alien Registration Act of 1940), rehearing denied 343 U.S. 936, 72 S.Ct. 767, 96 L.Ed. 1344 (1952). See also Galvan v. Press, 347 U.S. 522, 74 S.Ct. 737, 98 L.Ed. 911 (1954), rehearing denied 348 U.S. 852, 75 S.Ct. 17, 99 L.Ed. 671 (1954); Rowoldt v. Perfetto, 355 U.S. 115, 78 S.Ct. 180, 2 L.Ed.2d 140 (1957); Berenyi v. District Director, 385 U.S. 630, 87 S.Ct. 666, 17 L.Ed.2d 656 (1967).

4. See § 22.2, supra. "[I]f an alien is a lawful permanent resident of the United States *and remains physically present there,* he is a person within the protection of the Fifth Amendment. He may not be deprived of his life, liberty or property with out due process of law." Kwong Hai Chew v. Colding, 344 U.S. 590, 596, 73 S.Ct. 472, 477, 97 L.Ed. 576 (1953) (Emphasis added) (footnote omitted).

See generally, 1A C. Gordon & H. Rosenfield, Immigration Law and Practice § 5.6c (1981).

5. See 8 U.S.C.A. § 1252(b); Ng Fung Ho v. White, 259 U.S. 276, 281, 42 S.Ct. 492, 494, 66 L.Ed. 938 (1922) (Habeas corpus proceeding; Court holds that Ng Fung Ho entitled to trial de novo and an independent judicial judgment on the issue of citizenship); see also, Kwong Hai Chew v. Colding, 344 U.S. 590, 73 S.Ct. 472, 97 L.Ed. 576 (1953); Wong Yang Sung v. McGrath, 339 U.S. 33, 48–51, 70 S.Ct. 445, 453–55, 94 L.Ed. 616 (1950), judgment modified 339 U.S. 908, 70 S.Ct. 564, 94 L.Ed. 1336 (1950); Heikkila v. Barber, 345 U.S. 229, 73 S.Ct. 603, 97 L.Ed. 972 (1953), rehearing denied 345 U.S. 946, 73 S.Ct. 828, 97 L.Ed. 1371 (1953).

See generally, H. Hart & H. Wechsler's, The Federal Courts and the Federal System 351–354 nn. 40–44 (2d ed. 1973).

The Supreme Court has held, as a matter of statutory interpretation, that 8 U.S.C.A. § 1105a(a)(5) requires that persons who claim to be U.S. citizens, and who seek review of a deportation order, be given a de novo judicial review of the order whenever there is any "genuine issue of material fact" regarding the nationality claim. Agosto v. INS, 436 U.S. 748, 98 S.Ct. 2081, 56 L.Ed.2d 677 (1978).

an alien and if the conditions for continuing residence have been met.[6]

An alien who is criminally prosecuted for illegal entry following an earlier deportation may assert in the criminal proceeding the invalidity of the underlying deportation order.[7] The fact of the original deportation may be used to convert the misdemeanor of unlawful entry into the felony of unlawful entry after deportation, yet Congress had precluded judicial review of that hearing. Hence due process requires that a means of judicial review must be available before the administrative order may be used to establish conclusively an element of a criminal offense. The Court presented this test: "If the violation of respondents' right that took place in this [the original deportation hearing] amounted to complete deprivation of judicial review of the determination [of the validity of the original deportation order], that determination may not be used to enhance the penalty for unlawful entry of § 1326 [of title 8]."[8]

However, the congressional delegation of discretion to the Attorney General to detain aliens without bail—that is, to deny parole—pending

6. A person who is deported is entitled not only to a fundamentally fair hearing but to a procedure which follows the dictates of federal statutes. The question of whether the Immigration and Naturalization Service has properly followed statutory requirements is one of statutory interpretation rather than an analysis of due process principles. See Immigration and Naturalization Service v. Miranda, 459 U.S. 14, 103 S.Ct. 281, 74 L.Ed.2d 12 (1982).

Burden of Proof of Prosecution. An alien who is deportable under statute but who seeks exemption on the statutory ground that he would be subject to persecution in the country to which he would be returned must establish a "clear probability of persecution" to avoid deportation on this basis. Immigration & Naturalization Service v. Stevic, 467 U.S. 407, 104 S.Ct. 2489, 81 L.Ed.2d 321 (1984).

On the other hand, if the alien is a "refugee" who is unable or unwilling to return to his or her home country because of "a well grounded fear of persecution on account of race, religion, nationality, membership in a particular social group, or political opinion," the refugee seeking asylum need only show past persecution or "good reason" to fear further persecution. Immigration & Naturalization Service v. Cardoza–Fonseca, 480 U.S. 421, 107 S.Ct. 1207, 94 L.Ed.2d 434 (1987).

Reopening of Deportation Proceedings. Pursuant to regulations promulgated by the Attorney General, a deportable alien, on the basis of newly discovered evidence, may file a motion to request asylum. The alien may seek judicial review, in the courts of appeals, of the denial of such a motion by the Board of Immigration Appeals. In such a case, the courts should review the denials under an abuse of discretion standard. Immigration and Naturalization Service v. Abudu, 485 U.S. 94, 108 S.Ct. 904, 99 L.Ed.2d 90 (1988).

7. United States v. Mendoza–Lopez, 481 U.S. 828, 107 S.Ct. 2148, 95 L.Ed.2d 772 (1987).

See generally, Note, Collaterally Attacking Deportation Orders in Criminal Prosecutions for Illegal Entry Under Section 276 of the Immigration and Nationality Act of 1952, 56 Notre Dame Lawyer 677 (1981); Comment, Collateral Attacks on Deportation Orders in Prosecutions for Illegal Entry, 48 U.Chi.L.Rev. 83 (1981).

8. 481 U.S. at 840, 107 S.Ct. at 2156.

Contrast, Lewis v. United States, 445 U.S. 55, 67, 100 S.Ct. 915, 922, 63 L.Ed.2d 198 (1980), where there was available effective judicial review. In Mendoza–Lopez, in contrast, there was no effective judicial review of the administrative determination. "The fundamental procedural defects of the deportation hearing in this case rendered direct review of the immigration judge's determination unavailable to respondents." 481 U.S. at 841, 107 S.Ct. at 2156.

deportation hearings does not constitute an unlawful delegation nor violate the due process clause because the statute contains definite legislative standards. Moreover, according to the Court, there is no denial of due process in the detention of alien communists without bail in such cases where there is reasonable cause to believe that their release on bail would endanger the safety and welfare of the United States.[9]

Under federal statutes, the Attorney General or his or her delegates may suspend for reasons of "extreme hardship" the deportation

---

9. See § 22.2. Carlson v. Landon, 342 U.S. 524, 72 S.Ct. 525, 96 L.Ed. 547 (1952), rehearing denied 343 U.S. 988, 72 S.Ct. 1069, 96 L.Ed. 1375 (1952).

Limits on the Power to Detain Aliens Subject to Exclusion. The Supreme Court's position should not be read too broadly. Commentators have raised serious questions regarding the extent of the power to detain aliens subject to exclusion. See generally, Note, Constitutional Limits on the Power to Exclude Aliens, 82 Colum.L.Rev. 957 (1982); Note, The Constitutional Rights of Excluded Aliens: Proposed Limitations on the Indefinite Detention of the Cuban Refugees, 70 Georgetown L.J. 1303 (1982); Note, Filling the Immigration Void: Rodriguez–Fernandez v. Wilkinson—An Excludable Alien's Right to Be Free from Indefinite Detention, 31 Cath.L.Rev. 335 (1982); Note, The Indefinite Detention of Excluded Aliens: Statutory and Constitutional Justifications and Limitations, 82 Mich.L.Rev. 61 (1983); Developments in the Law—Immigration Policy and the Rights of Aliens, 96 Harv.L.Rev. 1286, 1311–33 (1983).

See also the careful analysis in Martin, Due Process and Membership in the National Community: Political Asylum and Beyond, 44 U.Pitt.L.Rev. 165 (1983); Schuck, The Transformation of Immigration Law, 84 Colum.L.Rev. 1 (1984).

Combination of Functions. For a discussion of the extent to which an administrator may combine in himself the functions of a prosecutor and judge in the context of deportation cases, see Rotunda, The Combination of Functions in Administrative Actions: An Examination of European Alternatives, 40 Ford.L.Rev. 101, 102–03 (1971).

Relationship to the Fourth Amendment Exclusionary Rule. In Immigration & Naturalization Service v. Lopez–Mendoza, 468 U.S. 1032, 104 S.Ct. 3479, 82 L.Ed.2d 778 (1984), on remand 738 F.2d 1067 (9th Cir.1984), the Supreme Court found that in a civil deportation hearing the fourth amendment "exclusionary rule" should not be applied so as to exclude from evidence an alien's admission, after an unlawful arrest, of illegal entry and presence in the country. The majority opinion by Justice O'Connor noted, at the conclusion of the opinion, that the Court's decision regarding applicability of the exclusionary rule might change "if there developed good reason to believe that Fourth Amendment violations by INS officers were widespread," and that the Court was not ruling on "egregious violations of Fourth Amendment or other liberties that might transgress notions of fundamental fairness and undermine the probative value of the evidence obtained."

The Decision to Parole and Discrimination on the Basis of Race or National Origin. In Jean v. Nelson, 472 U.S. 846, 105 S.Ct. 2992, 86 L.Ed.2d 664 (1985), the Court accepted the interpretation of the agency, the court below, and all parties to the proceeding, before it, that INS discretion to parole to undocumented aliens in this country seeking admission does not extend to considerations of race or national origin. The alternative to parole is to remain in detention pending a decision on the alien's admission or exclusion.

Constitutionally, the Solicitor General at oral argument in the *Jean* case contended that discrimination on the basis of race or national origin was not prohibited, but that the regulations forbade such discrimination. See 472 U.S. at 856, 105 S.Ct. at 2998.

In dissent, Marshall, J., joined by Brennan, J., interpreted the INS regulations differently; in their view it would be unconstitutional ("in the absence of any reasons closely related to immigration concerns") to discriminate on the basis of national origin or race in deciding whether to grant or deny parole. 472 U.S. 858–82, 105 S.Ct. at 2998–3011.

of an otherwise deportable alien who has resided in the United States for seven years and is of "good moral character." The statute does not grant such a deportable alien a right to a hearing as to whether the Attorney General should use this authority to suspend the deportation. And under this provision federal courts may not substitute a judicial determination of extreme hardship for that made by the Attorney General or his or her delegates.[10] Also under this statutory scheme the executive department may not grant a hardship exemption from deportation to an alien who had failed to be in continual physical presence in the United States for the seven year period required by statute.[11]

The distinction between the rights of deportees versus the rights of aliens seeking admission should not be overdrawn, for the deportees' substantive rights and rights of judicial review are narrow, and the Immigration and Naturalization Service's discretion not to seek deportation is narrowly exercised even in cases of extreme hardship.[12]

Deportation Versus Exclusion for a Permanent Alien. Under the statutory scheme, which has been upheld as constitutional, if a permanent resident alien leaves this country's borders for an "innocent, casual, and brief excursion," then the government—if it desires to determine his or her admissibility and deny him or her entry back into the United States, must proceed by way of a deportation hearing rather than an exclusion hearing.[13]

The deportation hearing is the usual way that the government must use to proceed against an alien already physically within this country. The exclusion hearing is, in contrast, the usual method of proceeding against an alien who is physically outside of the United States and seeking entry.[14] The distinction, as noted above, is not only in name, for a deportation hearing carries with it important procedural

---

10. Immigration and Naturalization Service v. Jong Ha Wang, 450 U.S. 139, 101 S.Ct. 1027, 67 L.Ed.2d 123 (1981) (per curiam), rehearing denied 451 U.S. 964, 101 S.Ct. 2037, 68 L.Ed.2d 342 (1981).

Abuse of Discretion. The Attorney General does not abuse discretion in refusing to reopen a decision denying aliens' request to suspend deportation where seven years of residence of the aliens accrued because of baseless appeals from adverse decision of the Board of Immigration Appeals. Immigration and Naturalization Service v. Rios–Pineda, 471 U.S. 444, 105 S.Ct. 2098, 85 L.Ed.2d 452 (1985). In this case, aliens argued that their deportation would result in extreme hardship to their two children, born in the United States during that seven year period. The Court acknowledged that the two children were

therefore U.S. citizens, but rejected the hardship argument.

11. Immigration and Naturalization Service v. Phinpathya, 464 U.S. 183, 104 S.Ct. 584, 78 L.Ed.2d 401 (1984), on remand 758 F.2d 656 (9th Cir.1985).

12. See, e.g., Dunn v. INS, 419 U.S. 919, 95 S.Ct. 197, 42 L.Ed.2d 156 (1974) (Stewart, J., joined by Douglas, J., dissenting from denial of certiorari); Bufalino v. Holland, 277 F.2d 270 (3d Cir.1960), certiorari denied 364 U.S. 863, 81 S.Ct. 103, 5 L.Ed.2d 85 (1960).

13. Rosenberg v. Fleuti, 374 U.S. 449, 462, 83 S.Ct. 1804, 1812, 10 L.Ed.2d 1000 (1963).

14. Landon v. Plasencia, 459 U.S. 21, 25, 103 S.Ct. 321, 325, 74 L.Ed.2d 21 (1982), on remand 719 F.2d 1425 (9th Cir.1983).

and substantive rights that do not exist for exclusion hearings.[15]

When a Resident Alien Becomes Subject to Exclusion. If a resident alien leaves the United States, the effort to return may be treated as a new "entry." The basic issue is whether the departure was a meaningful interruption in the alien's permanent residence. If the permanent resident alien's purpose for leaving the United States is in order to "accomplish some object which is itself contrary to some policy reflected in our immigration laws, it would appear that the interruption of residence thereby occurring would properly be regarded as meaningful,"[16] requiring the alien to submit to an exclusion hearing. Therefore when a permanent resident alien sought to return to this country after a brief visit to Mexico, and the government charged that the purpose of her trip had been to smuggle aliens for gain, then her departure was "meaningfully interruptive" of her residence here, and under the statute, she was subject to an exclusion hearing.[17] Even though a *resident* alien returning from a brief trip out of United States has a right to due process, it is not the same due process rights to which a *continuously present* resident alien is entitled.[18]

15. See generally, 1A C. Gordon & H. Rosenfield, Immigration Law and Procedure § 3.18.

See generally, Maldonado–Sandoval v. United States INS, 518 F.2d 278, 280 n. 3 (9th Cir.1975); Landon v. Plasencia, 459 U.S. 21, 25–6, 103 S.Ct. 321, 325–26, 74 L.Ed.2d 21 (1982) (permanent resident alien, after brief visit to Tijuana, Mexico, treated as subject to exclusion hearing because it was alleged that she had attempted to smuggle other aliens for gain), on remand 719 F.2d 1425 (9th Cir.1983); Cheng v. Immigration and Naturalization Service, 534 F.2d 1018 (2d Cir.1976).

See generally, Martin, Due Process and Membership in the National Community:

Political Asylum and Beyond, 44 U.Pitt. L.Rev. 165 (1983).

16. Rosenberg v. Fleuti, 374 U.S. 449, 462, 83 S.Ct. 1804, 1812, 10 L.Ed.2d 1000 (1963) (afternoon trip across border by resident alien does not cause the return to be designated an "entry").

17. Landon v. Plasencia, 459 U.S. 21, 31, 103 S.Ct. 321, 328, 74 L.Ed.2d 21 (1982), on remand 719 F.2d 1425 (9th Cir.1983).

18. Compare Kwong Hai Chew v. Colding, 344 U.S. 590, 596, 73 S.Ct. 472, 477, 97 L.Ed. 576 (1953), with Landon v. Plasencia, 459 U.S. 21, 31, 103 S.Ct. 321, 328, 74 L.Ed.2d 21 (1982), on remand 719 F.2d 1425 (9th Cir.1983).

Chapter 23

THEORIES AND METHODS OF CONSTITUTIONAL CONSTRUCTION AND INTERPRETATION IN THE CASE LAW AND THE LITERATURE

Table of Sections

I. INTRODUCTION

§ 23.1   Generally

Should judges apply the words of the Constitution "strictly" in the manner they were understood at the time the constitutional provision was adopted? Should the judge independently determine the core societal values to be protected by the provision and disregard historical limitations so that the values may be fully protected? Such questions are not definitively answerable because they turn on one's view of the proper role of the judiciary in our democracy—a subject of continuing debate since the Supreme Court first established the judiciary's claim to being the ultimate interpreter of the Constitution. Nevertheless, when litigating new constitutional issues not decided on the basis of doctrine clearly settled by prior decisions of the Supreme Court, attorneys and judges sometimes must address the issue of how a Constitution is to be interpreted.

There are probably as many ways of interpreting the Constitution as there are ways of interpreting the Bible. The various legal schools of thought give different emphasis to each of several factors: the intent of the framers, the relevance of history, the "plain language" of the provision, and changed circumstances, to name a few. Court decisions, in turn, reflect the scholarly thought of the various schools of interpretation, such as the strict constructionists and the legal realists.

We offer this chapter as an aid to the attorneys and judges who must confront such issues. The attorney who must argue for a "narrow" or "liberal" construction of a constitutional provision should consult the table of contents to this chapter and read those sections which might be useful in arguing for such a construction. In these sections the reader will find a selection of Supreme Court decisions which support various theories of constitutional construction.

Sections 23.2 through 23.5 discuss the literature which analyzes the proper role of the judiciary in a constitutional democracy. Although space limitations prevent us from citing every book or law journal article on this subject, our discussion of, and references to, the literature should offer the attorney or judge an entry into the vast commentary on this subject. No single work advances a demonstratively "correct" theory; these works advance or criticize particular theories of judicial review. We leave it to the reader to evaluate and utilize those works which refer to a theory useful to the reader's purposes. This introductory analysis regarding the nature of scholarly debate on theories of judicial review may also be helpful to those who consult the sources and caselaw cited later in this chapter. Our assessment of debate in the literature, though not an entirely neutral or dispassionate analysis, provides a framework for evaluating the caselaw presented later in this chapter.

Following these sections, which analyze the various theories and methods of interpretation which have been advanced in the scholarly literature, we turn to the caselaw in sections 23.6 through 23.36. These sections collect many of the Supreme Court opinions which demonstrate the Court's changing approaches toward constitutional interpretation. The Court's approach varies depending on when the opinion was written, which justice wrote the opinion, and what the subject matter of the opinion is. Sections 23.6 through 23.36 focus on the case law and a collection of the various—often inconsistent—rules and viewpoints which the Court has developed over the years.

II. THE SCHOOLS OF THOUGHT REGARDING CONSTITUTIONAL CONSTRUCTION AND INTERPRETATION

§ 23.2 The Movement Away From Natural Law and Contractual Theorists

In the latter part of the nineteenth century formal jurisprudence was popular among judges and scholars alike.[1] There were jurisprudential debates over the nature of the correct legal rules that should govern society; we might label various segments of this turn of the century jurisprudential debate as natural law theorist and others as contractarian theorists. But a premise common to virtually all parties to this jurisprudential debate was the belief that "law" existed apart from those who decreed it. Judges were seen as discovering law; legislators were seen as bound by principles of higher law beyond their control. The law was truly neutral in that it did not favor particular classes of persons; the law was seen as a set of principles to be discovered by judges and applied to cases before them.

In the late nineteenth and early twentieth centuries, some lawyers and scholars realized that a theory of law as separate from the men who made it could not withstand analysis. This realization mirrored the growth of the progressive political movement. That political movement demanded that legal institutions respond to the plight of persons who had been victimized by the American economic system.[2] Legal theorists who recognized the essential truth of this economic claim could not help but realize that judge-made law, of both the nonconstitutional and constitutional type, involved an exercise of power by a ruling class against the interest of the working class. Elegant theories of proximate cause developed by judges who were supposedly applying previously established and discoverable legal principles really boiled down to one fact: railroads would not have to pay for the damage they

---

§ 23.2

1. For a critique of this formal jurisprudence, see Pound, Mechanical Jurisprudence, 8 Colum.L.Rev. 605 (1908). For an excellent examination of this formal jurisprudence and the development of the sociological and realist jurisprudential schools see, White, The Evolution of Reasoned Elaboration: Jurisprudential Criticism and Social Change, 59 Va.L.Rev. 279 (1973); White, From Sociological Jurisprudence to Realism: Jurisprudence and Social Change in Early Twentieth–Century America, 58 Va.L.Rev. 999 (1972). Both articles are reprinted in G. White, Patterns of American Legal Thought (1978).

See generally, E. Purcell, The Crisis of Democratic Theory (1973); Mensch, The History of Mainstream Legal Thought, in D. Kairys (ed.), The Politics of Law: A Progressive Critique, 18–39 (1982); Valauri, Constitutional Theodicy: The Antimony of Finality and Fallibility in Judicial Review, 29 St. Louis U.L.J. 245 (1985); Kaplin, The Process of Constitutional Interpretation: A Synthesis of the Present and a Guide to the Future, 4 Rutgers L.Rev. 983 (1990) (describing and analyzing the modern debate). Rudolph & Rudolph, The

Evolving Role of the Supreme Court in Constitutional Contexts, 21 Memphis State U.L.Rev. 291 (1991); William Kaplin, The Concepts and Methods of Constitutional Law (Carolina Academic Press, 1991); Redish & Cisar, "If Angels Were to Govern": The Need for Pragmatic Formalism in Separation of Powers Theory, 41 Duke L.J. 449 (1991).

2. Cf. B. Cardozo, The Nature of the Judicial Process 112–13 (Yale U. Press 1921, Copyright renewed 1949): "My analysis of the judicial process comes then to this, and little more: logic, and history, and custom, and utility, and the accepted standards of right conduct, are the forces which singly or in combination shape the progress of the law. . . . The social interest served by symmetry or certainty must then be balanced against the social interest served by equity and fairness or other elements of social welfare."

B. Cardozo, The Growth of the Law 20 (Yale U. Press 1924): "The Law, like the traveler, must be ready for the morrow. It must have a principle of growth."

did to the person or property of the average man who stood in the way of their and the nation's economic growth.[3] Statutes such as antitrust laws passed by political reformers to control the economic abuses of the capitalist system were subjected to "unprejudiced" judicial interpretation and used more strictly against labor organizations than manufacturing monopolies.[4] Judges examined the language and history of the Constitution and discovered principles to protect individual liberty. But the liberty protected was the liberty of the poor to send their children to work at as early an age as the marketplace would have them,[5] or to work a day upon which there could be no legal time limits [6] and no guaranteed wage.[7] According to formal jurisprudence, legal principles were discovered by judges as they interpreted "the law" without favoritism to the parties before them. Progressives could not help but note that those neutral legal rules almost always favored the economically and politically powerful segment of society.

Oliver Wendell Holmes was one of the most astute observers of the failings of formal jurisprudence. Holmes leveled two types of criticisms at that formalism which eventually were mirrored in two new jurisprudential schools.[8] First, Holmes found that it was unrealistic to expect the judicially or legislatively created law to develop principles that would be neutral in their application to all classes of persons who might come before courts since conflict between segments of society would inevitably result in legal principles being developed that would favor

---

3. The lawyer-hallowed decision in Palsgraf v. Long Island R. Co., 248 N.Y. 339, 162 N.E. 99 (1928) can best be understood as one of hundreds of decisions which shaped legal theories to protect economic interests of railroads. See, J. Noonan, Persons & Masks of the Law (1976) at 129, 151. See generally, L. Friedman, A History of American Law, 409–27 (1973). See also, M. Horwitz, The Transformation of American Law, 1780–1860 (1977). For a contrasting view, based on a study of tort cases decided in nineteenth century California and New Hampshire, see, Schwartz, Tort Law and the Economy in Nineteenth–Century America, 90 Yale L.J. 1717 (1981).

4. See, e.g., Loewe v. Lawlor (The Danbury Hatters Case), 208 U.S. 274, 28 S.Ct. 301, 52 L.Ed. 488 (1908); Duplex Printing Press Co. v. Deering, 254 U.S. 443, 41 S.Ct. 172, 65 L.Ed. 349 (1920). Congress eventually passed the Norris–LaGuardia Act restriction of federal court jurisdiction over labor disputes in order to stop judicial interference with labor organization practices. The restriction is contained in 29 U.S.C.A. §§ 101–115; the statute was upheld in Lauf v. E.G. Shinner & Co., 303 U.S. 323, 58 S.Ct. 578, 82 L.Ed. 872 (1938).

5. Hammer v. Dagenhart, 247 U.S. 251, 38 S.Ct. 529, 62 L.Ed. 1101 (1918) (federal statute prohibiting interstate shipment of products made with child labor held to violate tenth amendment restriction on federal commerce power).

6. Lochner v. New York, 198 U.S. 45, 25 S.Ct. 539, 49 L.Ed. 937 (1905).

7. Morehead v. New York ex rel. Tipaldo, 298 U.S. 587, 56 S.Ct. 918, 80 L.Ed. 1347 (1936).

8. Holmes' criticisms and their relevance to modern legal theory are analyzed in Tushnet, The Logic of Experience: Oliver Wendell Holmes on the Supreme Judicial Court, 63 Va.L.Rev. 975 (1977); Tushnet, Truth, Justice, and the American Way: An Interpretation of Public Law Scholarship in the Seventies, 57 Texas L.Rev. 1307 (1979); J. Noonan, Persons & Masks of the Law 4 (1976); Posner, Book Review, 53 Geo.Wash.L.Rev. 879 (1985). Sheldon M. Novick, Honorable Justice: The Life of Oliver Wendell Holmes (1989); Liva Baker, The Justice from Beacon Hill: The Life and Times of Oliver Wendell Holmes (1991); Conrad, L'Esprit de Holmes, 67 Ind.L.J. 753 (1992).

one segment over another.[9] Second, in his now famous dissents from Supreme Court invalidations of economic reform legislation, Holmes challenged the majority of Supreme Court justices to demonstrate that their formal jurisprudence, which resulted in the selection of libertarian principles that would favor the economically powerful, involved anything more than the use of judicial power to enforce the justices' personal views of the proper political, economic and social order for the country.[10]

In modern times, judges and lawyers, in interpreting our Constitution, rely on at least five different types of argument.[11] They reason: (1) from the text of the Constitution; (2) from the framers' intent; (3) from constitutional theory (some of which can be quite abstract); (4) from precedent; and (5) from moral and policy values. The use of any argument does not, of course, preclude the use of other arguments—either simultaneously or subsequently. The validity of any, or all, of these approaches is the subject of much debate in the literature and the caselaw.

§ 23.3 Sociological Jurisprudence

The first jurisprudential movement that arose in the twentieth century, as a response to the formal jurisprudence is known as sociological jurisprudence.[1] Roscoe Pound was the leading figure, if not the founder, of this movement. Pound and the sociological jurisprudents responded to the second of Holmes' critiques of formal jurisprudence, accusing current judges of misusing the judicial power, but disregarded the first critique, that the law reflects divisions and conflicts between classes of society.

The sociological jurisprudents believed that law could be derived from basic principles which were discoverable from moral philosophy, history, and a societal concensus that could be observed and verified by judges. They rejected the formal jurisprudence by admitting that judicial rulings involved judge-made rather than judicially discovered

---

9. See Comment, The Gas–Stoker's Strike, 7 Am.L.Rev. 582 (1873). Holmes believed that this use of power by a ruling class was inevitable under any legal system: "It [legislation] is necessarily made a means by which a body, having the power, put burdens which are disagreeable to them on the shoulders of somebody else. Communism would no more get rid of the difficulty than any other system...." Id. at 584. Holmes was the editor of the American Law Review at this time and wrote this unsigned case note.

10. See, e.g., Lochner v. New York, 198 U.S. 45, 75, 25 S.Ct. 539, 546–47, 49 L.Ed. 937 (1905) (Holmes, J., dissenting).

See, Graglia, Judicial Activism: Even on the Right, It's Wrong, The Public Interest 57 (Spring, 1989).

11. See generally, Fallon, A Constructivist Coherence Theory of Constitutional Interpretation, 100 Harv.L.Rev. 1189 (1987).

§ 23.3

1. See Pound, The Scope and Purpose of Sociological Jurisprudence, 24 Harv.L.Rev. 591 (1911) (pt. 1), 25 Harv.L.Rev. 489 (1912) (pt. 2). See also Pound, The Theory of Judicial Decision, 36 Harv.L.Rev. 641, 802, 940 (1923–24) (3 parts).

law. The sociological jurisprudents believed that judges should make law by adjusting legal principles to changing social conditions. Court decisions were to be evaluated in terms of the values shared by a majority of the public and the effect of judicial decisions on social progress.

This jurisprudential movement dovetailed nicely with the progressive movement in the political arena. The sociological jurisprudents believed that there was a societal concensus on social progress and that judges should help to reform social and economic conditions just as legislators were being asked to do by the progressives.

Yet sociological jurisprudence must be seen as an outgrowth of, rather than a rejection of, formal jurisprudence. Both schools believed that law was a set of principles that could be devised by judges who did not merely exercise power to enforce their personal views of moral, political or economic philosophy.[2]

§ 23.4 Realist Jurisprudence

Realist jurisprudence involves the first of Holmes' critiques of formal jurisprudence, the recognition that law must inevitably reflect divisions within society. Writers such as Frank,[1] Hutcheson,[2] Llewellyn,[3] Oliphant,[4] and Rodell[5] called for a change in jurisprudential focus from an examination of correct principles, whether defined through formalist or sociological jurisprudence, to the exercise of power by the individuals who made the law. The realists believed that the rulings of judges were personal to those judges and reflected only the views of individual judges with the power to decree the outcome of a case before them. They went beyond the sociological jurisprudence by claiming not only that judges made law but that there was no law that existed apart from governmental decisionmakers. In other words, the judges not only made the law, they were the law. Legislators and executive branch officials also were the law. The law was simply what govern-

---

2. See G. White, Patterns of American Legal Thought 103–15 (1978).

§ 23.4

1. J. Frank, Law and the Modern Mind (1930).

See also, G. White, Patterns of American Legal Thought (1978); Nowak, Resurrecting Realist Jurisprudence: The Political Bias of Burger Court Justice, 17 Suffolk U.L.Rev. 551 (1983); Nagel, Rationalism in Constitutional Law, 4 Const. Commentary 9 (1987).

2. J. Hutcheson, Judgment Intuitive (1938); Hutcheson, The Judgment Intuitive: The Function of the "Hunch" in Judicial Decision, 14 Cornell L.Q. 274 (1929).

3. Llewellyn, A Realistic Jurisprudence—The Next Step, 30 Colum.L.Rev. 431 (1930); Llewellyn, Some Realism about Realism—Responding to Dean Pound, 44 Harv.L.Rev. 1222 (1931). See generally, K. Llewellyn, Jurisprudence: Realism in Theory and Practice (1962); K. Llewellyn, The Common Law Tradition: Deciding Appeals (1960).

4. Oliphant, A Return to Stare Decisis, 14 A.B.A.J. 71, 159 (1928) (two parts); Oliphant, Facts, Opinions, and Value–Judgments, 10 Tex.L.Rev. 127 (1932).

5. F. Rodell, Woe Unto You Lawyers! (1939).

mental officials decided to do in resolving disputes between individuals or economic forces.

While denying the existence of "law", the realists admitted that there were many laws written down on paper by judges or legislators. That fact did not mean that there was something called "law" which existed apart from persons exercising political power. The legal rules that were written by judges or legislators were only expressions by persons in power as to how they would exercise that power. Legislation was a communication to judges as to how the legislators wished private or social disputes to be resolved and notice to the citizenry regarding that fact. Written decisions of courts were only the exercise of power in individual cases and the notification to the public, and other persons in power, as to how judges would resolve certain public or private disputes.

Case decisions could be explained, according to the realists, but they could not be proven right or wrong since the realists denied the existence of any set of normative principles which could be proven to be true and a measure for the correctness of judicial rulings. By recognizing that a certain class of persons would be likely to dominate all three branches of government, the realists invited the legal profession to explain the worth of judicial decisions in terms of which classes were benefited or harmed by judicial rulings, rather than in terms of legal principles defined by either formal or sociological jurisprudence.

The legal realists were attacked both by advocates of a formal or natural law jurisprudence and by the sociological jurisprudents. The primary attack leveled at these realists, as evidenced by the writings of Roscoe Pound, was that legal realism left society without a means for evaluating judicial rulings or protecting fundamental societal values.[6] Decried as a "jurisprudence of despair", legal realism was said to leave society without a basis upon which to protect individual liberty or social values.[7] This basic attack on legal realism, that it leaves us without a value system for the operation of our society, has led realism's opponents to label legal realists as "nihilists." [8]

The charge that legal realism leads to nihilism is critical to an understanding of the use of the legal realism label today. A true legal realist must be a nihilist. That is, a realist believes that there is no way to demonstrate the correctness of any moral or philosophical position and that legal rules are simply a set of principles established by those persons who have the power to get away with it. A realist or nihilist takes the position that from time to time a specific class of

---

6. See, e.g., Pound, The Call for a Realist Jurisprudence, 44 Harv.L.Rev. 697 (1931); Lucey, Natural Law and American Legal Realism: Their Respective Contributions to a Theory of Law in a Democratic Society, 30 Georgetown L.J. 493 (1942).

7. Mechem, The Jurisprudence of Despair, 21 Iowa L.Rev. 669 (1936).

8. Tushnet, Truth, Justice, and the American Way: An Interpretation of Public Law Scholarship in the Seventies, 57 Tex.L.Rev. 1307, 1342 (1979).

persons will tend to dominate the legal decision-making apparatus, whether judicial, legislative or executive. Those persons will exercise their power to benefit themselves and to establish legal principles which match their political philosophy. Persons who would oppose prevailing political philosophy as "wrong" may appeal to competing moral or political philosophies but realists believe that such persons are without the ability to demonstrate that one philosophy is correct and the other erroneous. Instead, the worth of positions taken by persons in power, or the claims of those who would challenge them must be evaluated in terms of the practical benefits or burdens allocated to members of society.

The classical realist seeks only to explain the exercise of governmental power, rather than the correctness of the principles established by persons who are exercising power. The worth of competing philosophies is left to the realm of the philosopher; the legal analyst must be content, in the realist world, with an explanation of how governmental power is used. One who is a realist may go from this analysis of political power to a condemnation of the use of power by a particular ruling class, but when he does so he goes from being a legal analyst to being a progressive or Marxist political philosopher.[9]

Legal realism in its classic form has been in hiding for almost a half century. The disappearance of legal realism as an open force in modern American jurisprudential debates can be traced to three reasons. First, the leading legal realists of the 1930's in fact backed down in the face of the attacks on their jurisprudence. Realists were accused of providing the basis for judges to arbitrarily protect their economic class by striking down progressive legislation and by removing from society the jurisprudential argument for a rejection of authoritarian doctrines.[10]

By the close of the 1930's legal realists modified their position to meet the objections of those who said that their theories justified the actions of Supreme Court justices who had invalidated New Deal legislation, or that their theories removed a sense of shared societal values which could form a jurisprudential basis for objecting to the rise of fascism and the loss of freedom in certain European states.[11] Llewel-

---

9. See generally, D. Kairys (ed.), The Politics of Law: A Progressive Critique (1982).

For a nonMarxist, economic analysis, cf., e.g., Posner, Economics, Politics, and the Reading of Statutes and the Constitution, 49 U.Chi.L.Rev. 263 (1982) (considers the judicial interpretation of statutes as an intrinsic part of a complete economic theory of legislation).

10. See Mechem, The Jurisprudence of Despair, 21 Iowa L.Rev. 669 (1936); Pound,

The Call for a Realist Jurisprudence, 44 Harv.L.Rev. 697 (1931); Lucey, Natural Law and American Legal Realism: Their Respective Contributions to Law in a Democratic Society, 30 Georgetown L.J. 493 (1942). See generally, E. Purcell, The Crisis of Democratic Theory (1973).

11. For an examination of the rise and fall of legal realism see G. White, Patterns of American Legal Thought (1978), and E. Purcell, The Crisis of Democratic Theory (1973).

lyn, by 1940, found that realism allowed for an examination of shared societal values as a basis for normative judgment regarding legal decisions.[12]

The second reason that legal realism disappeared from the jurisprudential debate relates to changes in the private law system in America. Much of the legal realist critique had focused on the way that judges had created arbitrary common law rules in areas such as contract, property or torts. Writing in 1961, the late Professor Grant Gilmore declared that legal realism had permanently passed from the jurisprudential scene because the conditions which had called for it had also disappeared.[13] In so doing, Professor Gilmore noted that he was focusing only on the realist attack on private law rulings, rather than on public law issues such as those which came under the label of constitutional law. Gilmore recognized that the system of common law adjudication was breaking down in the early 1900's in the face of rapid population and economic growth. There were simply too many cases and too many variants of economic and social problems for judges to develop unifying, neutral legal principles in the common law system.

The legal realist movement demonstrated that judges were arbitrarily exercising power and that unifying legal rules had to be developed outside of the judicial system. Those rules, Professor Gilmore correctly noted, had been formulated by codes and legislation on the state and federal level, the development of uniform laws, and the quasi-codification of some areas such as torts or property law through the development of restatements by the American Law Institute.

Legislatively and administratively established rules and the clarification of common law principles through restatements had narrowed the scope of judicial power over private law. Some scholars believed this clarification of the law had eliminated the need for a legal realist philosophy. As Professor Gilmore noted:

"[Legal] realism was the academic formulation of a crisis through which our legal system passed during the first half of this century ... legal realism was essentially a demonstration that the system of law which had evolved in this country had become intolerably burdened and unworkably complex. Realism in this century had been an American exclusive: It has no counterpart in England or

---

12. Llewellyn, On Reading and Using the Newer Jurisprudence, 40 Colum.L.Rev. 581 (1940). See also J. Frank, Law and The Modern Mind (1939 ed.). Judge Frank's conversion was so complete that in his introduction to the 1959 edition of Fred Rodell's 1939 realist text, Woe Unto You, Lawyers!, Judge Frank doubted that Rodell would still hold to his "excessive" condemnation of lawyers and judges. To his credit, Rodell was unwilling to compromise. Compare, F. Rodell, Woe Unto You, Law-

yers! xi–xiv (introduction by Jerome Frank) (1959 ed., reprinted as Berbely Paperbook ed. 1980) with id. at xvii (Foreword to the Second Edition by Fred Rodell). The late Professor Rodell made no change to the 1939 edition of his book except to add this foreword. The 1980 reprinting includes both forewords.

13. Gilmore, Legal Realism: Its Causes and Cure, 70 Yale L.J. 1037 (1961).

the European countries whose legal systems are closely related to our own. It was a response to an American crisis—a crisis which was precipitated by our phenomenally rapid growth in population, in wealth, in diversity of economic organization and cultural circumstance." [14]

Because the focus of legal realism in the 1930's had been private law adjudication, changes in our private law system led scholars such as Gilmore to believe that legal realism no longer had a place in jurisprudential debate.

The third reason why legal realism has faded is discussed in the next section.

§ 23.5   Neutral Principles or Process Oriented Jurisprudence

(a) Legal Realism Versus Neutral Principles

Legal realists have disappeared for the most part from modern legal debate. As discussed in the prior section, realists modified their position in reaction to strong attacks. Secondly, the private law system (which the realists had attacked) had changed. The third reason why legal realism seemed to disappear is that the realist label was taken over in the constitutional law arena by a decidedly nonrealist form of jurisprudence.[1] In 1936 and 1937 legal realism appeared to have won total victory in the constitutional law arena. Principles that had been

---

14. Gilmore, 70 Yale L.J. at 1047. See Schauer, Does Doctrine Matter?, 82 Mich. L.Rev. 655 (1984).

Whether one is a realist or not, it must be remembered that judges are human beings, and the justices of the Supreme Court "are products of their environment just as all men and women are.... [N]o theory of judicial review can prevent a member of the Court from acting upon his or her own predilections. No matter which theory a justice adopts, substantive beliefs are likely to be expressed in the end.... [A]nd recent empirical evidence seems to indicate that the justices have transformed at least some of their preferences of society's elites into law. Nonetheless, they have broken the bounds of their backgrounds from time to time and rendered unexpected decisions—most notably on busing." Rosen, Democracy and Demographics: The Inevitability of a Class–Bound Interpretation, 10 U.Dayton L.Rev. 37, 93 (1984).

While legal realism is no longer at the forefront, it still has its forceful advocates. See, e.g., Miller, Myth and Reality in American Constitutionalism (Book Review), 63 Tex.L.Rev. 181, 191 (1984) (" 'the law' is a fraud in that no obviously correct body of principles exists by which constitutional issues can be decided.") (footnote omitted). Miller, Pretense and Our Two Constitutions, 54 Geo.Wash.L.Rev. 375 (1986); Nowak, Resurrecting Realist Jurisprudence: The Political Bias of Burger Court Justice, 17 Suffolk U.L.Rev. 551 (1983).

§ 23.5

1. Professor Tushnet previously has noted this development. See Tushnet, Truth, Justice, and the American Way: An Interpretation of Public Law Scholarship in the Seventies, 57 Tex.L.Rev. 1307, 1314 (1979). Tushnet chooses to attack realist jurisprudence in terms of the writings of these pseudo-realists and in terms of the writings of modern "nihilists". It would appear that Professor Tushnet may not reject realist jurisprudence but only finds it incomplete, given his adoption of a progressive-Marxist position. See 57 Tex. L.Rev. at 1345–59.

discoverable from the nature of the Constitution in 1936 were rejected a year later.[2] Yet, a majority of the justices and the public appeared to have rejected earlier Supreme Court actions without rejecting Supreme Court authority.[3] Political power as great as that held by Supreme Court justices could not be left unexercised for long. A new group of justices would soon find areas of adjudication in which they could exercise their power more in keeping with the political sentiments of the public.

The path that the Court would take in exercising this power was first laid out in a casual footnote in an otherwise not very important decision. In the now famous "*Carolene Products* Footnote 4", the Court noted that an active judicial role might be justified when the Court was enforcing textual guarantees of the Constitution, defining and protecting rights of the political process, or protecting discrete and insular minorities.[4] The *Carolene Products* approach to constitutional adjudication does no more than select three areas for independent judicial activity which seemed to some justices and theorists to involve proper defenses of values that cannot be entrusted to the democratic process. A realist would find these values to be no more or less defensible limits on legislative power than were values protected by the Court prior to 1937. At the same time that the Court was expanding its power in these areas, however, there arose a school of constitutional law scholars who claimed to justify many of these rulings without the arbitrary selection of values and use of judicial power based upon the personal political philosophy of justices. This school of jurisprudence has come to be labeled the "neutral principles" or "process oriented" theory of constitutional law.

2. Compare West Coast Hotel Co. v. Parrish, 300 U.S. 379, 57 S.Ct. 578, 81 L.Ed. 703 (1937) (upholding minimum wage law) with, Morehead v. New York ex rel. Tipaldo, 298 U.S. 587, 56 S.Ct. 918, 80 L.Ed. 1347 (1936) (invalidating minimum wage law as a violation of due process), rehearing denied 299 U.S. 619, 57 S.Ct. 4, 81 L.Ed. 456 (1936). Compare, Carter v. Carter Coal Co., 298 U.S. 238, 56 S.Ct. 855, 80 L.Ed. 1160 (1936) (invalidating federal legislation under Tenth Amendment as exceeding the federal commerce power) with N.L.R.B. v. Jones & Laughlin Steel Corp., 301 U.S. 1, 57 S.Ct. 615, 81 L.Ed. 893 (1937) (upholding federal regulation of labor dispute resolution).

3. For an insightful analysis of the ability of the American public to favor simultaneously the inconsistent principles of popular sovereignty and fundamental or natural law, and the relationship of these contradictory beliefs to the Supreme Court battle with President Roosevelt, see R.

McCloskey, The American Supreme Court, 3–25, 136–80 (1960).

4. United States v. Carolene Products Co., 304 U.S. 144, 152–53 n. 4, 58 S.Ct. 778, 783–84 n. 4, 82 L.Ed. 1234 (1938). See L. Lusky, By What Right?, 110 (1975) (discussing origins of this footnote).

Footnote 4 of *Carolene Products*. Powell, Carolene Products Revisited, 82 Colum.L.Rev. 1087 (1982); Lusky, Footnote Redux: A Carolene Products Reminiscence, 82 Colum.L.Rev. 1093 (1982); Cover, The Origins of Judicial Activism in the Protection of Minorities, 91 Yale L.J. 1287 (1982); Ackerman, Beyond Carolene Products, 98 Harv.L.Rev. 713 (1985); Balkin, The Footnote, 83 Nw.U.L.Rev. 275 (1989); Farber & Frickey, Is Carolene Products Dead? Reflections on Affirmative Action and the Dynamics of Civil Rights Legislation, 79 Calif.L.Rev. 685 (1991).

Professors Bickel,[5] Ely,[6] Choper,[7] and Wechsler[8] typify neutral principles theorists. These scholars and others of their school of thought require justices to detail the reasons which identify the judicial choice of a particular constitutional principle on a "neutral basis" that is not dependent on the parties to the litigation; they also require justices to judicially protect values which are based on an open political process. Alexander Bickel eventually recognized the weakness of the premise of this argument due to its failure to substantively justify the judicial selection of democratic process values rather than other substantive values. Nevertheless, the neutral principles theory sidestepped the legal realist attack.

Those persons who demand that the Court justify its rulings in terms of "neutral principles" seem at first glance to be legal realists. After all, this neutral principle argument would allow judges to select almost any value to defend against the majority so long as they openly stated why they believed the value could not be entrusted to the democratic process and so long as the reason for ruling in a given case was something more than a preference for one particular party in the litigation. But neutral principles theorists have been unable to accept this "anything goes" aspect of their theory, just as legal realists of the 1940's could not accept the total absence of normative values that was dictated by strict adherence to a realist philosophy.[9] As Professor

---

5. Professor Bickel began as a neutral principles theorist but eventually came to endorse a role for the Supreme Court much more limited than that of even the neutral principles or process-oriented scholars. Perhaps to a greater degree than any other American scholar, Bickel sought to honestly and openly confront the realist challenge. For a listing of Professor Bickel's publications, see Writings of Alexander M. Bickel, 84 Yale L.J. 201 (1974). For a representative sample of the scholarship of Alexander Bickel, see Bickel & Wellington, Legislative Purpose and the Judicial Process: The Lincoln Mills Case, 71 Harv. L.Rev. 1 (1957); A. Bickel, The Least Dangerous Branch (1962); A. Bickel, The Supreme Court and the Idea of Progress (Yale Press ed., 1978); A. Bickel, The Morality of Consent (1975).

For commentaries on Bickel's theories and writings, see Holland, American Liberals and Judicial Activism: Alexander Bickel's Appeal from the New to the Old, 51 Ind.L.J. 1025 (1976); Purcell, Alexander M. Bickel and the Post–Realist Constitution, 11 Harv.C.R.–C.L.L.Rev. 521 (1976); Nowak, Foreword: Evaluating the Work of the New Libertarian Supreme Court, 7 Hastings Const.L.Q. 263, 266–72 (1980); Kronman, Alexander Bickel's Philosophy

of Prudence, 94 Yale L.J. 1567 (1985); Kronman, Alexander Bickel's Philosophy of Prudence, 94 Yale L.J. 1567 (1985).

6. J. Ely, Democracy and Distrust (1980).

7. J. Choper, Judicial Review and the National Political Process: A Functional Reconsideration of the Role of the Supreme Court (1980). There is some question whether Professor Choper should be placed in the neutral principles school. Although he may object to having his work categorized in this manner, his study of the institutional role of the Supreme Court justifies such a classification of his work. See Nowak, Book Review, 68 Calif.L.Rev. 1223 (1980).

8. Wechsler, Toward Neutral Principles of Constitutional Law, 73 Harv.L.Rev. 1 (1959).

9. See, e.g., Newman, Between Legal Realism and Neutral Principles: The Legitimacy of Institutional Values, 72 Calif.L.Rev. 200 (1984). See also, Greenawalt, The Enduring Significance of Neutral Principles, 78 Colum.L.Rev. 982 (1978); Henkin, Some Reflections on Current Constitutional Controversy, 109 U.Pa.L.Rev. 637 (1961).

Tushnet has noted, the legal realist label has been taken over by neutral principles theorists who believed that they could evaluate the correctness of Supreme Court decisions in terms of the institutional role of the Court in the democratic process.[10]

A recent and perhaps best example of this philosophy is the work of Professor, now Dean, John Hart Ely.[11] Dean Ely's scholarly defense of a *Carolene Products* theory in which the Court protects the openness of the political process and discrete minorities whose interests cannot be trusted to that process is claimed to be justified by values specified in the Constitution rather than the personal preference of judges.[12] This institutional role argument is merely a way of protecting values which are favored by what most Americans call "liberal" political factions.

Neutral principles or democratic process theory has been attacked as a return to the formalism of the turn of the century. Judges are told to examine the words of the Constitution, its amendments, and the governmental structure to find that there are values established therein which are not dependent on their personal political philosophy and which can be defended under a claim of neutrality against contrary value choices made by the democratic process. Alexander Bickel argued that there is no basis for choosing majoritarian theories of government over other theories of the workings of a democracy as the basis for defining a judicial role in the governmental process. As the late Professor Bickel noted, any claim that the Supreme Court enhances the democratic process by striking down legislation is "question begging."[13] Neutral principles and democratic process theorists assert as their premise that democratic process values are neutrally derived from an examination of the Constitution and are not the arbitrary exercise of political power by judges. They are not realists; they find

See also, Bruce Ackerman, We the People: Foundations (1991); Klarman, Constitutional Fact/Constitutional Fiction: A Critique of Bruce Ackerman's Theory of Constitutional Moments, 44 Stan.L.Rev. 759 (1991).

10. See Tushnet, Truth, Justice, and the American Way: An Interpretation of Public Law Scholarship in the Seventies, 57 Tex.L.Rev. 1307, 1345–59 (1979). See also, Tushnet, Following the Rules Laid Down: A Critique of Interpretivism and Neutral Principles, 96 Harv.L.Rev. 781 (1983).

11. See J. Ely, Democracy and Distrust (1980). While believing the challenge posed to the selection of democratic values by Alexander Bickel was not answered fully by Ely, "Professor Ely's analysis is the most important attempt in several years to deal with the problem of Supreme Court

values as it was analyzed by Alexander Bickel...." Nowak, Foreword: Evaluating the Work of the New Libertarian Supreme Court, 7 Hastings Const.L.Q. 263, 271 (1980). For a different view of Professor Ely's work, see Tushnet, Darkness on the Edge of Town: The Contributions of John Hart Ely to Constitutional Theory, 89 Yale L.J. 1037 (1980). See also, Kronman, Alexander Bickel's Philosophy of Prudence, 94 Yale L.J. 1567 (1985).

12. J. Ely, Democracy and Distrust 75 n.* (1980).

13. A. Bickel, The Supreme Court and the Idea of Progress 34–5, 83, 108–15, 166–67 (Yale Press ed. 1978).

For an overview of competing theories of representation, see R. Dahl, A Preface to Democratic Theory (1956); Nomos X: Representation (J. Pennock & J. Chapman, eds. 1968).

"law" in a formal jurisprudence based upon their view of the proper functioning of a democracy.

(b) The Interpretivist School

The modern jurisprudential competition to the neutral principles school has come from two sides. First, there is the "interpretivist" school of scholars and judges who believe that courts should apply only the words of the Constitution as they were understood by the persons who wrote them.[14] Courts, according to the interpretivists, are not to

---

14. See, e.g., R. Berger, Government by Judiciary: The Transformation of the Fourteenth Amendment (1977); Bork, Neutral Principles and Some First Amendment Problems, 47 Ind.L.J. 1 (1971).

Justice Black is the most obvious example of a justice who claimed to be an interpretivist. See, e.g., In re Winship, 397 U.S. 358, 377, 90 S.Ct. 1068, 1079, 25 L.Ed.2d 368 (1970) (Black, J., dissenting), mandate conformed 27 N.Y.2d 728, 314 N.Y.S.2d 536, 262 N.E.2d 675 (1970); Konigsberg v. State Bar of California, 366 U.S. 36, 56, 81 S.Ct. 997, 1009, 6 L.Ed.2d 105 (1961) (Black, J., dissenting), rehearing denied 368 U.S. 869, 82 S.Ct. 21, 7 L.Ed.2d 69 (1961).

Cf. Rehnquist, The Notion of a Living Constitution, 54 Tex.L.Rev. 693 (1976).

The scholarship literature that relates to this issue includes: P. Bobbit, Constitutional Fate (1982); Tushnet, A Note on the Revival of Textualism in Constitutional Theory, 58 So.Calif.L.Rev. 683 (1985); Simon, The Authority of the Constitution and Its Meaning: A Preface to a Theory of Constitutional Interpretation, 58 So.Calif.L.Rev. 603 (1985); Simson, The Role of History in Constitutional Interpretation: A Case Study, 70 Cornell L.Rev. 253 (1985) (State of Nevada v. Hall, 440 U.S. 410, 99 S.Ct. 1182, 59 L.Ed.2d 416 (1979), rehearing denied 441 U.S. 917, 99 S.Ct. 2018, 60 L.Ed.2d 389 (1979)).

See also McArthur, Abandoning the Constitution: The New Wave in Constitutional Theory, 59 Tulane L.Rev. 280 (1984) (discussing interpretative and structural arguments); Carter, Constitutional Adjudication and the Indeterminate Text: A Preliminary Defense of an Imperfect Muddle, 94 Yale L.J. 821 (1985); Sherry, Selective Judicial Activism in the Equal Protection Context: Democracy, Distrust and Deconstruction, 73 Georgetown L.J. 89 (1985). Monaghan, Our Perfect Constitution, 56 N.Y.U.L.Rev. 353 (1981); Monaghan, Constitutional Fact Review, 85 Colum.L.Rev. 229 (1985); Van Alstyne, Interpreting This

Constitution: The Unhelpful Contributions of Special Theories of Judicial Review, 35 U.Fla.L.Rev. 209 (1983); Saphire, Constitutional Theory in Perspective: A Response to Professor Van Alstyne, 78 Nw.U.L.Rev. 1435 (1984); Powell, Rules for Originalists, 73 Va.L.Rev. 659 (1987); Berger, Some Reflections on Interpretivism, 55 Geo.Wash. L.Rev. 1 (1986); Conkle, Non-originalist Constitutional Rights and the Problem of Judicial Finality, 13 Hastings Const.L.Q. 9 (1985); Powell, The Original Understanding of Original Intent, 98 Harv.L.Rev. 885 (1985); Rotunda, Original Intent, the View of the Framers, and the Role of the Ratifiers, 41 Vand.L.Rev. 507 (1988); Nagel, The Formulaic Constitution, 84 Mich. L.Rev. 165 (1985); Schlag, Rules and Standards, 33 U.C.L.A.L.Rev. 379 (1985); Wilson, The Morality of Formalism, 33 U.C.L.A.L.Rev. 431 (1985); Dickerson, Toward a Legal Dialectic, 61 Indiana L.J. 315 (1986); Goodrich, Historical Aspects of Legal Interpretation, 61 Indiana L.J. 331 (1986); Kevelson, Semiotics and Methods of Legal Inquiry: Interpretation and Discovery in Law from the Perspective of Pierce's Speculative Reasoning, 61 Indiana L.J. 355 (1986); Sinclair, The Semantics of Common Law Predicates, 61 Indiana L.J. 373 (1986); Jaffa, What Were the "Original Intentions" of the Framers of the Constitution of the United States?, 10 U.Puget Sound L.Rev. 351 (1987); Gerard, A Restrained Perspective on Activism, 64 Chicago–Kent L.Rev. 605 (1988); Wroth, The Constitution and the Common Law: The Original Intent About the Original Intent, 22 Suffolk U.L.Rev. 553 (1988); Graglia, The "Remedy" Rationale For Requiring Or Permitting Otherwise Prohibited Discrimination: How the Court Overcame the Constitution and the 1964 Civil Rights Act, 22 Suffolk U.L.Rev. 569 (1988); Shane, Rights, Remedies and the Community, 64 Chicago–Kent L.Rev. 531 (1989).

As one thoughtful commentator has noted:

inject their personal political philosophy in the constitutional rulings.

"The 'intent of the framers' [does not compensate] fully for the shortcomings of the textual approach to constitutional interpretation. However, it sometimes suggests general thematic directions which, when supplemented by the other modes of constitutional interpretation ... significantly assist in crystallizing the 'great purposes' [of the Constitution]." K. Ripple, Constitutional Litigation 14 (1984).

Originalism. Attorney General Edwin Meese popularized the term "Originalism" with his call for a return to a "jurisprudence of original intention." This term, instead of "interpretivism," is "found more frequently in current writings on the subject because it emphasizes that the issue is the role of original intent in constitutional interpretation." Farber, The Originalism Debate: A Guide for the Perplexed, 49 Ohio State L.J. 1085 (1989).

Constitutional Language. See J. Brigham, Constitutional Language: An Interpretation of Judicial Decision (1978); Levinson, Law as Literature, 60 Tex.L.Rev. 373 (1982); Schauer, An Essay on Constitutional Language, 29 U.C.L.A.L.Rev. 797 (1982).

Original Intent. See generally, Monaghan, The Constitution Goes to Harvard, 13 Harv.Civ.Rts.–Civ.Lib.L.Rev. 117 (1978); Berger, The Scope of Judicial Review: A Continuing Dialogue, 31 S.Cal.L.Rev. 171 (1980); Bennett, Objectivity in Constitutional Law, 132 U.Pa.L.Rev. 445 (1984); Grey, The Constitution as Scripture, 37 Stan.L.Rev. 1 (1984); Richards, Interpretation and Historiography, 58 So.Cal.L.Rev. 489 (1985); Powell, The Original Understanding of Original Intent, 98 Harv.L.Rev. 885 (1985); Simon, The Authority of the Framers of the Constitution: Can Originalist Interpretation Be Justified?, 73 Calif.L.Rev. 1482 (1985); Nelson, History and Neutrality in Constitutional Adjudication, 72 Va.L.Rev. 1237 (1986); Bork, The Constitution, Original Intent, and Economic Rights, 23 San Diego L.Rev. 823 (1986); Meese, The Supreme Court of the United States: Bulwark of a Limited Constitution, 27 S.Tex.L.J. 455 (1986); Sherry, The Founders' Unwritten Constitution, 54 U.Chi.L.Rev. 1127 (1987); Conkle, Nonoriginalist Constitutional Rights and the Problem of Finality, 13 Hastings Const. L.Q. 9 (1985); Symposium: Framers' Intent: An Exchange, 10 U.Puget Sound L.Rev. 343–569 (1987); Gralia, Democracy and Original Intent, The Public Interest 97 (Fall, 1989). Fried, Sonnet LXV and the "Black Ink" of the Framers' Intention, 100 Harv.L.Rev. 751 (1987); M. Curtis, No State Shall Abridge: The Fourteenth Amendment and the Bill of Rights (1987); Raoul Berger, Federalism: The Founder's Design (1987); Gangi, On Raoul Berger's Federalism: The Founder's Design, 13 Law & Social Inquiry 801 (1988); Lofgren, The Original Understanding of Original Intent?, 5 Const.Commentary 77 (1988); Belz, The Civil War Amendments to the Constitution: The Relevance of Original Intent, 5 Const.Commentary 115 (1988); Berger, Originalist Theories of Constitutional Interpretation, 73 Cornell L.Rev. 350 (1988); Bennett, Originalist Theories of Constitutional Interpretation, 73 Cornell L.Rev. 355 (1988); Smith, The Search for Original Intent: Curtis on the Fourteenth Amendment and the Bill of Rights, 13 L. & Social Inquiry 583 (1988); Monaghan, Stare Decisis and Constitutional Interpretation, 88 Colum.L.Rev. 723 (1988); Hirshman, Bronte, Bloom, and Bork: An Essay on the Moral Education of Judges, 137 U.Pa. L.Rev. 177 (1988); Curtis, Privileges and Immunities, Individual Rights, and Federalism, 12 Harv.J. of Law & Pub.Policy 53 (1989); Scalia, Is There An Unwritten Constitution?, 12 Harv.J. of Law & Pub.Policy 1 (1989); Moore, The Written Constitution and Interpretivism, 12 Harv.J. of Law & Pub.Policy 3 (1989); Rotunda, Interpreting an Unwritten Constitution, 12 Harv.J. of Law & Pub.Policy 15 (1989); Graglia, Do We Have an Unwritten Constitution?, 12 Harv.J. of Law & Pub.Policy 83 (1989); Friedlander, Judicial Selection and the Constitution: What Did the Framers Originally Intend?, 8 St.L.U.Pub.L.Rev. 1 (1989); Farber, The Originalism Debate: A Guide for the Perplexed, 49 Ohio State L.J. 1085 (1989); Robert Bork, The Tempting of America: The Political Seduction of the Law (1989); Smith, Establishment Clause Analysis: A Liberty Maximizing Proposal, 4 Notre Dame J. of L., Ethics & Public Policy 463 (1990); Baade, "Original Intent" in Historical Perspective: Some Critical Glosses, 69 Tex.L.Rev. 1001 (1991).

The Second Amendment

See Halbrook, What the Framers Intended: A Linguistic Analysis of the Right to "Bear Arms," 49 Law & Contemp.Prob. 151 (1986).

Rather, judges are to determine correct constitutional principles by an examination of the wording and history of the Constitution. Interpretivist theory can involve a return to the turn of the century formal jurisprudence.[15] The use of interpretivist theory does not, however, require that the judge ignore the policies or history behind a law, or the costs and benefits of any given interpretation. Interpretivist theory is an effort to cabin the judge, to place some limits on judicial review.

Justice Story was an interpretivist. In his *Constitutional Commentaries,* he argued, "The first and fundamental rule in the interpretation of all instruments is, to construe them according to the sense of the terms and the intention of the parties." [16] Yet, Story did not focus on abstractions. He argued further, "Upon subjects of government it has always appeared to me that metaphysical refinements are out of place. A constitution of government is addressed to the common sense of the people; and was never designed for trials of logical skill, or visionary speculation." [17] As Judge Bork has noted, "For Story, Kent, Cooley, and Thayer, the source was the intent of the framers and ratifiers, and that was to be discerned from text, history, structure, and precedent. What is important about the non-interpretivists is not that they added moral philosophy but that moral philosophy displaces such traditional sources as text and history and renders them unimportant." [18]

(c) Value–Oriented Jurisprudence

The second attack on neutral principles theory has come from value-oriented scholars, who demand that the Court promote the social good by requiring all branches of government to comply with principles of moral philosophy which these scholars believe are evidenced by the provisions of the Constitution and a current societal concensus on

15. One need not be a die hard realist to appreciate that the interpretivist argument can be misleading. See Brest, The Misconceived Quest for the Original Understanding, 69 B.U.L.Rev. 204 (1980); Ely, Constitutional Interpretivism: Its Allure and Impossibility, 53 Ind.L.J. 399 (1978); Sandalow, Constitutional Interpretation, 79 Mich.L.Rev. 1033 (1981). See Dworkin, The Forum of Principle, 56 N.Y.U.L.Rev. 469, 477 (1981): "[T]here is no such thing as the intention of the Framers waiting to be discovered, even in principle."

See also, Tushnet, Following the Rules Laid Down: A Critique of Interpretivism and Neutral Principles, 96 Harv.L.Rev. 781 (1983).

Older constitutional interpretivists include Justice Story, see 1 J. Story, Commentaries on the Constitution of the United States, at viii (3d ed. 1858), and Thayer.

See, Thayer, The Origin and Scope of the American Doctrine of Constitutional Law, 7 Harv.L.Rev. 129, 150 (1893).

For an extensive argument that the framers intended the judiciary to protect individuals to determine the uses of their land, labor, and capital, and that the courts should restore the protection of economic liberties, see, J. Dorn & H. Manne, eds., Economic Liberties and the Judiciary (1987).

16. 1 J. Story, Commentaries on the Constitution of the United States, § 400 (1833). See also, R. Rotunda & J. Nowak, eds., Joseph Story's Commentaries on the Constitution of the United States (1987, originally published 1833).

17. 1 J. Story, Commentaries on the Constitution vi (1833).

18. Bork, Styles in Constitutional Theory, 26 So.Tex.L.J. 383, 394 (1985).

fundamental values.[19] Although there are differences in methodology

19. There are too many scholars who advocate a value oriented jurisprudence to list them all here. See, e.g., Brest, The Fundamental Rights Controversy: The Essential Contradictions of Normative Constitutional Scholarship, 90 Yale L.J. 1063 (1981) (considers the judiciary's activity in the area of fundamental rights such as privacy and sexual choice and the criticism of those who argue that shared social values do not exist or in any event, courts cannot ascertain them); Brest, The Misconceived Quest for the Original Understanding, 60 B.U.L.Rev. 204 (1980); Brest, Foreword: In Defense of the Antidiscrimination Principle, 90 Harv.L.Rev. 1 (1976); L. Tribe, The Puzzling Persistence of Process–Based Constitutional Theories, 89 Yale L.J. 1063 (1980); Wellington, Common Law Rules and Constitutional Double Standards: Some Notes on Adjudication, 83 Yale L.J. 221 (1978); Wellington, The Nature of Judicial Review, 91 Yale L.J. 486 (1982); Privacy and Social Contract: A Defense of Judicial Activism in Privacy Cases, 33 Ariz.L.Rev. 811 (1991).

The Search for Legislative Control of the Court. Some have argued that as a limit on possible judicial excesses, Congress has plenary power to limit the Court's jurisdiction to hear certain disputes. E.g., M. Perry, The Constitution, The Courts, and Human Rights 128–37 (1982); Perry, Moral Knowledge, Moral Reasoning, Moral Relativism: A "Naturalist" Perspective, 20 Ga.L.Rev. 995 (1986); Perry, A Critique of the "Liberal" Political–Philosophical Project, 28 Wm. & Mary L.Rev. 205 (1987); M. Perry, Morality, Politics and Law (1988). This book was reviewed by, Farber, The Man Who Mistook His Life for a Plant, 63 Tulane L.Rev. 1445 (1989) (part of a Symposium on Professor Michael Perry's book Morality, Politics, and Law (1988).)

Others have suggested that federal judicial rulings on Constitutional matters perhaps should be subject to direct reversal by ordinary statute. Congress would then not have to use the back door of limiting jurisdiction. "[T]he Court's decisions interpreting the Constitution may be viewed as provisional judgments ultimately subject to reversal through an ongoing adjudication without *stare decisis* or by simple statute if Congress can ever muster the necessary dialogue. This vision of the Court as initiator of a dialogue certainly makes judicial review more consistent with traditional

theory of democracy." Dimond, Provisional Review: An Exploratory Essay on an Alternative Form of Judicial Review, 12 Hastings Constitutional L.Q. 201, 208–09 (1985) (footnotes omitted). See also, Wellington, The Nature of Judicial Review, 91 Yale L.J. 486 (1982); Sandalow, Judicial Protection of Minorities, 75 Mich.L.Rev. 1162 (1977).

Morris, Interpretive and Noninterpretive Constitutional Theory, 94 Ethics 501 (April 1984) (review of M. Perry, The Constitution, the Courts, and Human Rights (1982) and P. Bobbitt, Constitutional Fate: Theory of the Constitution (1982)); Symposium: Judicial Review and the Constitution—the Text and Beyond, 8 U.Dayton L.Rev. 443 et seq. (1983); Sedler, The Legitimacy Debate in Constitutional Adjudication: An Assessment and a Different Perspective, 44 Ohio St.L.J. 93 (1983) (concluding, id. at 137, that "noninterpretive review is not only legitimate, but is also a necessary postulate for constitutional adjudication under our constitutional system ... to ensure that the overriding principle in the structure of constitutional governance established by our Constitution—that the power of the government must be limited to protect individual rights—will have full force and effect in each succeeding generation."); Ackerman, Beyond Carolene Products, 98 Harv.L.Rev. 713 (1985).

Grey, The Constitution as Scripture, 37 Stan.L.Rev. 1 (1985); Perry, The Authority of Text, Tradition, and Reason: A Theory of Constitutional "Interpretation," 58 So.Calif.L.Rev. 551 (1985); Bennett, The Mission of Moral Reasoning in Constitutional Law, 58 So.Calif.L.Rev. 647 (1985); Brest, Who Decides?, 58 So.Calif.L.Rev. 661 (1985); Simon, The Authority of the Constitution and Its Meaning: A Preface to a Theory of Constitutional Interpretation, 58 So.Calif.L.Rev. 603 (1985); Michaels, Response to Perry and Simon, 58 So.Calif.L.Rev. 673 (1985); McArthur, Abandoning the Constitution: The New Wave in Constitutional Theory, 59 Tulane L.Rev. 280 (1984); Graglia, Was the Constitution a Good Idea, National Review 34 (July 13, 1984).

Conkle, The Legitimacy of Judicial Review in Individual Rights Cases: Michael Perry's Constitutional Theory and Beyond, 69 Minn.L.Rev. 587 (1985) (a thorough discussion of Professor Perry's thesis and much of the commentary it has spawned;

by judges and scholars in the value-oriented jurisprudential school as a whole, they mark a return to a formal jurisprudence. One may debate whether they are properly labeled natural law theorists or sociological jurisprudents. However, because they believe in "law" apart from the exercise of political power, they are not realists.[20]

Although the value oriented legal philosophers purport to believe in law even though they would not cabin the judge to the Constitution, they have not built an accepted, logical structure that uses agreed premises to answer questions not answered by the written Constitution. As Judge Bork has argued:

> The groves of legal academe are thick with young philosophers who propose various systems of morality that judges must use to create new constitutional rights. An important feature of these systems is that they not only control democratic choice but that they purport to have sufficient rigor so that they can control the judge. The judge is, the theorists claim, prevented by their systems from simply imposing his own views of policy and morality. [Yet the] nature of non-interpretive enterprise is such that its theories must end in constitutional nihilism and the imposition of the judge's merely personal values on the rest of us. The reason is that none of these theorists has been able—and I venture to suggest none will ever be able—to build a philosophical structure that starts from accepted premises and logically demonstrates the answers, or the range of allowable answers, to questions not answered by the written Constitution.... Nothing less than this power and rigor is required if we are to accept government by judges who are not applying the Constitution.... This failure will become apparent— indeed it is already apparent as each of the non-interpretive theorists convincingly destroys all the others' systems—and that is why the inevitable end to non-interpretivist, value-choosing theory is constitutional nihilism.[21]

Conkle is in the camp of those unpersuaded by Perry's argument).

Miller, Social Justice and the Warren Court: A Preliminary Examination, 11 Pepperdine L.Rev. 473 (1984); Miller, Myth and Reality in American Constitutionalism (Book Review), 63 Tex.L.Rev. 181 (1984).

S. Barber, On What the Constitution Means (1984); J. Agresto, The Supreme Court and Constitutional Democracy (1984). Both of these books are thoughtfully reviewed in Graglia, Constitutional Mysticism: The Aspirational Defense of Judicial Review, 98 Harv.L.Rev. 1331 (1985).

Compare, Clor, Judicial Statesmanship and Constitutional Interpretation, 26 S.Tex.L.J. 397 (1985), with, Graglia, Judi-

cial Review on the Basis of "Regime Principles": A Prescription for Government by Judges, 26 S.Tex.L.J. 435 (1985).

See also, Conkle, Nonoriginalist Constitutional Rights and the Problem of Judicial Finality, 13 Hastings Const.L.Q. 9 (1985).

20. See generally, Nowak, Realism, Nihilism and The Supreme Court: Do the Emperors Have Nothing but Robes?, 22 Washburn U.L.Rev. 901 (1982).

21. Bork, Styles in Constitutional Theory, 26 South Tex.L.Rev. 383, 387 (1985). See also, Graglia, Judicial Review on the Basis of "Regime Principles": A Prescription for Government by Judges, 26 South Tex.L.Rev. 435 (1985).

(d) Neutral Principles as Related to Legal Realism

In opposition to the interpretivist and value-oriented schools, the democratic process or neutral principles theory of constitutional law appears to be the closest to legal realism. It recognizes that the selection of values by judges cannot be defended as correct or incorrect in any absolute sense. Thus, there is a rejection of the judicial ability to define a higher law that must lie at the basis of all value-oriented or natural law theories. Democratic process theories also deny the ability of judges to apply the words of the Constitution without defining values to protect against the prevailing political philosophy. Neutral principles theorists claim to recognize the arbitrary nature of the exercise of judicial power and to have found a way to circumscribe the use of that power by protecting only democratic process values. The fact that neutral principles or democratic process theory accepts one set of values—the value of democracy—and rejects others, means that neutral principles theorists accept a nonneutral principle and make a value judgment.[22] Yet, this democratic process theory retains vitality because it offers an answer to the realist critique of judicial power. The popularity of process oriented theories is not surprising to legal realists, who claim that scholars know that judicial power is political power, even if they refuse to admit to the consequences of that knowledge.[23]

All three camps of judicial scholars—the interpretivists, the neutral principles scholars, and the value-oriented scholars—are advancing formal theories of constitutional law jurisprudence. All believe that constitutional law is something other than the exercise of power and that judges can define legal principles which are not dependent upon the personal political philosophy of the justices. Because all three camps of scholars believe in a law apart from the judges who exercise power, all three jurisprudential schools oppose legal realism. The interpretivists find legal realists guilty of encouraging Supreme Court justices to impose their personal views upon the country.[24] Value-

---

22. See, e.g., Tribe, The Puzzling Persistence of Process–Based Constitutional Theories, 89 Yale L.J. 1063 (1980) (who argues that this value judgment is made without a philosophical justification of the choice).

Interpretivists reject Tribe's argument. The Constitution itself places value on democracy, and "there is neither a constitutional nor an extra-constitutional basis for making the Constitution more democratic than the Constitution is." Bork, Styles in Constitutional Theory, 26 South Tex.L.Rev. 383, 390 (1985). See, Weiler, Eurocracy and Distrust: Some Questions Concerning The Role of the European Court of Justice in the Protection of Fundamental Human Rights within the Legal Order of the Euro-

pean Communities, 61 Wash.L.Rev. 1103 (1986).

23. This point is the central thesis of the late Professor Rodell's scholarship. F. Rodell, Nine Men (1955).

24. A publication of the proceedings of an American Enterprise Institute Conference is replete with references to legal realism providing a basis for a "legislative model" for judicial decision making. See, e.g., Mishkin, The Reforming Judiciary, reprinted in American Enterprise Institute, Judicial Power in the United States: What are the Appropriate Restraints? See generally Berger, Government by Judiciary: John Hart Ely's "Invitation", 54 Ind.L.J. 277 (1979).

oriented scholars accuse legal realists of denying the existence of fundamental values which must be protected by the Court and promoting a philosophy of nihilism.[25] Members of the neutral principles camp, who defend the Court as the protector of the political process, accuse legal realists of "trashing" the only institution that can protect democracy and minorities.[26] All three camps are united in their desire to protect the Supreme Court from the accusation that constitutional law does not exist apart from the persons who are currently in power on the Court.

25. See Tushnet, Truth, Justice, and the American Way: An Interpretation of Public Law Scholarship in the Seventies, 57 Tex.L.Rev. 1307, 1342 (1979). See also, Tushnet, Legal Scholarship: Its Causes and Cure, 90 Yale L.J. 1205 (1981).

Critical Legal Studies. On the critical legal studies (CLS) movement, see, e.g., R. Unger, Knowledge and Politics (1975); Leff, Memorandum, 29 Stan.L.Rev. 879 (1977); Delgado, The Ethereal Scholar: Does Critical Studies Have What Minorities Want?, 22 Harv.Civ.Rts.Civ.Lib.L.Rev. 301 (1987); Symposium, Minority Critiques of the Critical Legal Studies Movement, 22 Harv.Civ.Rts.Civ.Lib.L.Rev. 297 (1987); Symposium, Critical Legal Studies, 36 Stan.L.Rev. 1 (1984); M. Kelman, A Guide to Critical Legal Studies (1988).

As Hutchinson & Monaghan, Law, Politics, and the Critical Legal Scholars: The Unfolding Drama of American Legal Thought, 36 Stan.L.Rev. 199, 206–07 (1984) (footnotes omitted) point out:

"Like traditional jurists, the Critical scholars are obsessed with the judicial function and its alleged central importance for an understanding of law in society. Yet, while they share this infatuation, they adopt a radically different view of the judicial process: All the Critical scholars unite in denying the rational determinacy of legal reasoning. Their basic credo is that no distinctive mode of legal reasoning exists to be contrasted with political dialogue. Law is simply politics dressed in different garb; it neither operates in a historical vacuum nor does it exist independently of ideological struggles in society. Legal doctrine not only does not, but also cannot, generate determinant results in concrete cases.

Law is not so much a rational enterprise as a vast exercise in rationalization. Legal doctrine can be manipulated to justify an almost infinite spectrum of possible outcomes.... CLSers claim [that] lawyers establish a *fake* rationalistic discourse out of the chaos of political and social life.... [T]he difference between Critical and mainstream legal thought is that, although the latter rejects formalism, it persists in the view that *some* viable distinction can be drawn between legal reasoning and vulgar political debate. CLSers, on the other hand, refuse to hedge on the indeterminancy of the legal order."

CLSers tend to be self-described Marxists or neo-Marxists; the expositors tend to be utopian and theoretical who believe in exposing the "incoherence" and "contradictions" of liberal philosophy; they are hostile to formalism, legalism, and rules and instead prefer broad, flexible "standards"; law and politics, in their view, are the same and there is no neutral justice; compromise is not favored, and contracts and bargains are thought to be a mask for domination; "illegitimate hierarchies" such as bar associations are the masks and bastions of special privilege. Schwartz, With Gun and Camera Through Darkest CLS–Land, 36 Stand.L.Rev. 413, 422–23 (1984); Hegland, Goodbye to Deconstruction, 58 So.Calif.L.Rev. 1203 (1985).

26. See Freeman, Truth and Mystification in Legal Scholarship, 90 Yale L.J. 1229 (1981) (discussing the "trashing" attack). Some members of the judiciary seem to think attacking the justices has become an end in itself. See Wright, Professor Bickel, The Scholarly Tradition, and the Supreme Court, 84 Harv.L.Rev. 769 (1971).

III. THE HISTORICAL BACKGROUND BEHIND THE CONSTITUTION

§ 23.6 The Historical Conditions and Circumstances [1]

(a) Introduction

The Supreme Court has stated that courts may turn to the historical origins of the U.S. Constitution, and to historical evidence, for aid in construing and applying words and provisions of the Constitution.[2]

Events that occurred before the Constitution's adoption also throw light on its provisions.[3] One judicially acceptable method of interpreting a constitutional provision of doubtful meaning is to read the provision's language in the context of the known condition of affairs existing at the time the provision was adopted, and then to construe the provision in a way, so far as is reasonably possible, to forward the known purpose or object for which it was adopted.[4]

§ 23.6

1. Sections 23.6 through 23.36 are derived, in part, with permission from U.S.C.A., Constitution (West Pub. Co., St. Paul, Minn., 1968).

2. Twining v. New Jersey, 211 U.S. 78, 29 S.Ct. 14, 53 L.Ed. 97 (1908); Williamson v. United States, 207 U.S. 425, 28 S.Ct. 163, 52 L.Ed. 278 (1908); Appleyard v. Massachusetts, 203 U.S. 222, 27 S.Ct. 122, 51 L.Ed. 161 (1906); Missouri v. Illinois, 180 U.S. 208, 21 S.Ct. 331, 45 L.Ed. 497 (1901); Veazie Bank v. Fenno, 75 U.S. (8 Wall.) 533, 19 L.Ed. 482 (1869); Weeks v. United States, 216 Fed. 292 (2d Cir.1914), certiorari denied 235 U.S. 697, 35 S.Ct. 199, 59 L.Ed. 431 (1914).

"The necessities which gave birth to the Constitution, the controversies which preceded its formation, and the conflicts of opinion which were settled by its adoption, may properly be taken into view for the purpose of tracing to its source any particular provision of the Constitution, in order thereby to be enabled to correctly interpret its meaning." Knowlton v. Moore, 178 U.S. 41, 95, 20 S.Ct. 747, 768, 44 L.Ed. 969, 991 (1900).

See generally, Rotunda, Life Under the Articles of Confederation, 75 Ill.B.J. 544 (1987); Hutson, The Creation of the Constitution: The Integrity of the Documentary Record, 65 Tex.L.Rev. 1 (1986).

See also McGautha v. California, 402 U.S. 183, 91 S.Ct. 1454, 28 L.Ed.2d 711 (1971) (taking history into account when evaluating the constitutionality of the death penalty), rehearing denied 406 U.S. 978, 92 S.Ct. 2407, 32 L.Ed.2d 677 (1972).

"In order to see petitioners' claim in perspective, it is useful to call to mind the salient features of the history of capital punishments for homicides under the common law in England and subsequent statutory developments." 402 U.S. at 197, 91 S.Ct. at 1462, 28 L.Ed.2d at 720.

3. Marshall v. Gordon, 243 U.S. 521, 37 S.Ct. 448, 61 L.Ed. 881 (1917).

4. South Carolina v. United States, 199 U.S. 437, 26 S.Ct. 110, 50 L.Ed. 261, 4 Ann.Cas. 737 (1905); Maxwell v. Dow, 176 U.S. 581, 20 S.Ct. 448, 44 L.Ed. 597 (1900); Legal Tender Cases, 79 U.S. (12 Wall.) 457, 20 L.Ed. 287 (1871); Prigg v. Pennsylvania, 41 U.S. (16 Pet.) 539, 10 L.Ed. 1060 (1842); Rhode Island v. Massachusetts, 37 U.S. (12 Pet.) 657, 9 L.Ed. 1233 (1838); Kendall v. United States, 37 U.S. (12 Pet.) 524, 9 L.Ed. 1181 (1838); Adams v. Storey, 1 Fed.Cas. 141 (C.C.D.N.Y.1817) (No. 66); State v. Gibson, 36 Ind. 389 (1871); Campbell v. Morris, 3 H. & McH. 535 (Md.1797).

"Before coming, however, to the text of the [Sixteenth] Amendment, to the end that its significance may be determined in the light of the previous legislative and judicial history of the subject with which the Amendment is concerned, and with a knowledge of the conditions which presumptively led up to its adoption, and hence of the purpose it was intended to accomplish, we make a brief statement on those subjects." Brushaber v. Union Pacific R. Co., 240 U.S. 1, 12, 36 S.Ct. 236, 239, 60 L.Ed. 493, 499 (1916).

See also Tom v. Sutton, 533 F.2d 1101, 1105 (9th Cir.1976).

(b) The Union Before the Constitution of 1787

Like the Greek City States, the American colonies, during and after the Revolutionary War, had several important common purposes, but many local differences, and no central unifying force. Under the Articles of Confederation of 1777 the state legislatures decided how the delegates to the Congress were to be appointed annually.[5] Each state was represented by no less than two and no more than seven members,[6] and the states could recall and replace one or more of their representatives at any time.[7] Each state had only one vote, regardless of population.[8] The representatives were of necessity responsive to the states qua states, and not to the persons within each state.

The central government at that time could not exercise many powers—e.g., the power to engage in a war, enter into a treaty, coin money, borrow or appropriate money, appoint a commander in chief—unless nine of the thirteen states agreed.[9] It had no power to make a treaty of commerce "whereby the legislative powers of the respective states would be restrained from imposing such imports and duties on foreigners, as their own people are subjected to, or from prohibiting the exportation or importation of any species of goods or commodities whatsoever." [10] Congress also had no power of direct taxation but had to rely on the individual states to levy taxes in proportion to the value of all the land within a state.[11]

Commercial Rivalries. The states' rivalries caused laws to be passed in the commercial area which had unfortunate economic effects. In fact one of the major incentives for a more unified nation was to eliminate "the mutual jealousies and aggressions of the States, taking form in customs barriers and other economic retaliation." [12]

Foreign Affairs. In foreign relations as well, the states purported to exercise a power over foreign affairs in a manner inconsistent with the central government's purpose. South Carolina's constitution empowered its government "to make war, conclude a peace, enter into treaties, lay embargoes, and provide an army and navy." [13] Other

---

5. Articles of Confederation art. V, cl. 1. See Appendix B, where the Articles are reproduced. Landever, Those Indispensable Articles of Confederation—Stage in Constitutionalism, Passage for the Framers, and Clue to the Nature of the Constitution, 31 Ariz.L.Rev. 79 (1989). Cf. O'Fallon, Marbury, 44 Stan.L.Rev. 219 (1992).

6. Articles of Confederation art. V at cl. 2.

7. Id. at cl. 1.

8. Id. at cl. 4.

9. Id. at art. VII, cls. 1 & 2.

10. Id. at art. IX, cl. 6.

11. Id. at art. IX, cl. 1.

12. Baldwin v. G.A.F. Seelig, Inc., 294 U.S. 511, 522, 55 S.Ct. 497, 500, 79 L.Ed. 1032 (1935), citing inter alia, 2 Farrand, Records of the Federal Convention, at 308; 3 Farrand, id., at 478, 547, 548; The Federalist, No. 42.

13. C.H. Van Tyne, Sovereignty in the American Revolution: An Historical Study, 12 Am.Historical Rev. 529, 539–40 (Oct.–July, 1906–07) (footnote omitted).

states implicitly or explicitly purported to exercise one or more such powers.[14]

> Patrick Henry, who has talked of all America being "thrown into one mass" and who was not a Virginian but an American— ... this same eloquent Henry actively negotiated with Spain in 1778 for a loan and for the approval of Spain to the erection of a fort on Virginia's border, promising in return "the gratitude of this free and independent country, the trade in any or all of its valuable productions, and the friendship of its warlike inhabitants." [15]

Congress, under the Articles of Confederation, was only "a political gelding, and its resolves were puissant only as the states might make them so." [16] The trade wars and other mutual jealousies led to the establishment of an economic and political union. The move to a federal political union occurred at the same time as the economic union.

(c) The Central Government's Role Under the Constitution of 1787

The Constitutional Convention was the response to these events. The framers chose a federal rather than a unitary system of government. Their product, the Constitution of 1787, differed in several important respects from the Articles of Confederation. First, the central government was given the power to act directly on individuals, not just on the states. The central government now could tax directly; [17] the members of its House of Representatives were to be elected "by the people;" [18] there was representation in the House in proportion

---

14. Van Tyne at 540.

15. Id. Mr. Justice Sutherland, in United States v. Curtiss–Wright Export Corp., 299 U.S. 304, 57 S.Ct. 216, 81 L.Ed. 255 (1936), argued that the foreign relations power was never possessed by the states and that under the Constitution of 1787 the central government received such powers directly from the Crown.

> "[T]he powers of external sovereignty passed from the Crown not to the colonies severally, but to the colonies in their collective and corporate capacity as the United States of America.... When, therefore, the external sovereignty of Great Britain in respect of the colonies ceased, it immediately passed to the Union."

299 U.S. at 315–20, 57 S.Ct. at 218–21. However useful this theory may be in an analytic sense, it is historically inaccurate. See generally Van Tyne, Sovereignty in the American Revolution: An Historical Study, 12 Am. Historical Rev. 529 (Oct.–July 1906–07). Levitan, The Foreign Rela-

tions Power: An Analysis of Mr. Justice Sutherland's Theory, 55 Yale L.J. 467 (1946).

16. J. Goebel, Volume 1, The Oliver Wendell Holmes Devise History of the Supreme Court of the United States: Antecedents and Beginnings to 1801, at 197 (P. Freund, ed., 1971).

17. U.S. Const. art. I, § 8, cl. 1.

On the events leading to the Constitutional Convention and the Convention itself, see generally, e.g., Warren, The Making of the Constitution (1937); Crosskey, Politics and the Constitution in the History of the United States (1953); McDonald, E Pluribus Unam: The Formation of the American Republic, 1776–1790 (1965); Rossiter, 1787: The Grand Convention (1966); Wood, The Creation of the American Republic (1969).

18. U.S. Const. art. I, § 2, cl. 1. The Senators were elected by the state legislators, art. I, § 3, cl. 1, but in 1913 this

to population; [19] and the states as well as federal legislative, executive, and judicial officials, were bound by oath or affirmation to support the Constitution,[20] which included what has become known as the supremacy clause:

> This Constitution, and the Laws of the United States which shall be made in Pursuance thereof; and all Treaties made, or which shall be made, under the Authority of the United States, shall be the supreme law of the Land; and the Judges in every State shall be bound thereby, any Thing in the Constitution or Laws of any State to the Contrary notwithstanding.[21]

Enumerated powers. The Constitution explicitly delegates to the central government certain powers. Most of these delegated powers are found in section 8 of the first article, which provides:

> [1] The Congress shall have Power to lay and collect Taxes, Duties, Imposts and Excises, to pay the Debts and provide for the common Defence and general Welfare of the United States; but all Duties, Imposts and Excises shall be uniform throughout the United States;

> [2] To borrow money on the credit of the United States;

> [3] To regulate Commerce with foreign Nations, and among the several States, and with the Indian Tribes;

> [4] To establish an uniform Rule of Naturalization, and uniform Laws on the subject of Bankruptcies throughout the United States;

> [5] To coin Money, regulate the Value thereof, and of foreign Coin, and fix the Standard of Weights and Measures;

> [6] To provide for the Punishment of counterfeiting the Securities and current Coin of the United States;

> [7] To Establish Post Offices and Post Roads;

> [8] To promote the Progress of Science and useful Arts, by securing for limited Times to Authors and Inventors the Exclusive Right to their respective Writings and Discoveries;

> [9] To constitute Tribunals inferior to the Supreme Court;

> [10] To define and punish Piracies and Felonies committed on the high Seas, and Offenses against the Law of Nations;

> [11] To declare War, grant Letters of Marque and Reprisal, and make Rules concerning Captures on Land and Water;

provision was repealed; with the adoption of the 17th Amendment the Senators are also elected by the people.

19. Id., art. I, § 2, cl. 3. The Senators number two from each state, without regard to the population of the state. Art. I, § 3, cl. 1.

20. Id., art. VI, cl. 3.

21. Id., art. VI, cl. 2.

[12] To raise and support Armies, but no Appropriation of Money to that Use shall be for a longer Term than two Years;

[13] To provide and maintain a Navy;

[14] To make Rules for the Government and Regulation of the land and naval Forces;

[15] To provide for calling forth the Militia to execute the Laws of the Union, suppress Insurrections and repel Invasions;

[16] To provide for organizing, arming, and disciplining, the Militia, and for governing such Part of them as may be employed in the Service of the United States, reserving to the States respectively, the Appointment of the Officers, and the Authority of training the Militia according to the discipline prescribed by Congress;

[17] To exercise exclusive Legislation in all Cases whatsoever, over such District (not exceeding ten Miles square) as may, by Cession of particular States, and the Acceptance of Congress, become the Seat of the Government of the United States, and to exercise like Authority over all Places purchased by the Consent of the Legislature of the State in which the Same shall be, for the Erection of Forts, Magazines, Arsenals, dock-Yards, and other needful Buildings;—And

[18] To make all Laws which shall be necessary and proper for carrying into Execution the foregoing Powers, and all other Powers vested by this Constitution in the Government of the United States, or in any Department or Officer thereof.

In addition other clauses of the Constitution explicitly grant other powers to the President, Congress, or the federal courts. For example, Article II, section 2, clause 1, gives the President the power to grant pardons for offenses against the United States, and section 3 of that Article gives him the power to receive Ambassadors, from which is implied the power to recognize foreign governments. Article III creates the federal judicial power and also grants to Congress the power to establish federal courts inferior to the U.S. Supreme Court. Article IV, section 3, clause 2, grants Congress the power to dispose of and regulate the territory or other property of the United States, and section 4 of that same article provides that the United States shall guarantee to every state in the union a republican form of government.

Later, various Amendments provided that Congress should have the power to enforce those Amendments by appropriate legislation.[22]

These enumerated powers, particularly the commerce power,[23] and

---

22. Amend. 13, § 2; Amend. 14, § 5; Amend. 15, § 2; Amend. 19, § 2; Amend. 23, § 2; Amend. 24, § 2; Amend. 26, § 2. See generally, Chapter 19.

23. U.S. Const. art. I, § 8, cl. 3. See generally, Chapter 4, supra.

the "necessary and proper" power [24] have undergone significant evolution over the years, as discussed earlier in this Treatise.

The important point to bear in mind here is that the central government only has those powers which were expressly delegated to it; all other powers were reserved to and retained by the people, who could choose to delegate as much of that power as they wished to the states [25] except to the extent to which the Constitution explicitly placed restraints on the states. Thus, only limited powers are delegated to the federal government; it can only exercise these powers—as well as implied powers necessary and proper to the exercise of those powers— unless the exercise violates a specific restraint on the federal government embodied in the Constitution.

To illustrate, Congress has the explicit power to "define and punish Piracies and Felonies committed on the high Seas, and Offenses against the Law of Nations." [26] In the exercise of that power, Congress could also "make all Laws which shall be necessary and proper for carrying into Execution...." [27] this power, but all of this power is limited by the fact that Congress cannot validly enact a Bill of Attainder or an ex post facto law.[28] Similarly Congress has the power to "lay and collect Taxes, Duties, Imposts and Excises," [29] and also has all powers "necessary and proper" to effectuate the taxing power, but this power is nonetheless limited by the requirement that "[n]o Tax or Duty shall be laid on Articles exported from any state." [30]

---

24. Id., art. I, § 8, cl. 18. See generally, § 3.2.

25. The tenth amendment, enacted in 1791, explicitly provides: "The powers not delegated to the United States by the Constitution, nor prohibited by it to the states, are reserved to the States respectively, or to the people." This amendment is usually thought of as declaratory of existing law. That is, it simply states that the federal government, being a government of limited powers, is limited to those powers.

"[The Tenth Amendment] states but a truism that all is retained which has not been surrendered. There is nothing in the history of its adoption to suggest that it was more than declaratory of the relationship between the national and state governments as it had been established by the Constitution before the amendment or that its purpose was other than to allay fears that the new national government might seek to exercise powers not granted, and that the states might not be able to exercise fully their reserved powers."

United States v. Darby, 312 U.S. 100, 117, 61 S.Ct. 451, 458, 85 L.Ed. 609 (1941).

But see National League of Cities v. Usery, 426 U.S. 833, 96 S.Ct. 2465, 49 L.Ed.2d 245 (1976), wherein Justice Rehnquist argues for the Court that the tenth amendment also means that Congress cannot pass laws under the Commerce power that impair the "integrity" of the states or their "ability to function effectively in a federal system." *National League of Cities* was subsequently overruled in Garcia v. San Antonio Metropolitan Transit Authority, 469 U.S. 528, 105 S.Ct. 1005, 83 L.Ed.2d 1016 (1985), rehearing denied 471 U.S. 1049, 105 S.Ct. 2041, 85 L.Ed.2d 340 (1985).

26. U.S. Const. art. I, § 8, cl. 10.

27. Id., art. I, § 8, cl. 18.

28. Id., art. I, § 9, cl. 3.

29. Id., art. I, § 8, cl. 1.

30. Id., art. I, § 9, cl. 5. See, e.g., William E. Peck & Co. v. Lowe, 247 U.S. 165, 38 S.Ct. 432, 62 L.Ed. 1049 (1918); National Paper & Type Co. v. Bowers, 266 U.S. 373, 45 S.Ct. 133, 69 L.Ed. 331 (1925); Fairbank v. United States, 181 U.S. 283, 21 S.Ct. 648, 45 L.Ed. 862 (1901); United States v. Hvoslef, 237 U.S. 1, 35 S.Ct. 459, 59 L.Ed. 813 (1915); Thames & Mersey

State powers. The states may also exercise various powers, if those powers do not violate certain explicit provisions of the Federal Constitution, and are allowed by that state's own constitution. To find out what those reserved powers are, we do not look to the federal but to the state constitution. If the state can, under its own law, exercise a power—and that decision is up to the state, not the central government—then we only look to the federal constitution to see if that power is restricted. For example, a state cannot grant a "Letter of Marque and Reprisal" or "enter into any treaty...."[31] As a result, a state law—or state constitutional provision—must fall if it is in conflict with a valid federal law or treaty because they are also the "supreme Law of the Land."[32]

The federal government then is supreme within the areas of its delegated authority, if not restricted by the Federal Constitution itself. The states are supreme within all other areas of authority unless restricted by the Federal Constitution or valid federal law or treaties.

§ 23.7　The Debates in the Constitutional Convention and in Congress

Over the years, courts have used the history of the Constitutional Convention to help determine the meaning of particular clauses in the Constitution. The views of particular members of the Constitutional Convention, however, and the course of proceedings in the Convention, should not control the fair meaning and general scope of the Constitution as it was finally framed.[1] Similarly, what *individual* Senators or Representatives may have urged in debate regarding the meaning to be given to a proposed amendment does not necessarily furnish a firm ground for its construction, nor should such an individual view conclusively explain why the whole body adopted the amendment.[2] However, because speeches given by those who took part in enacting a constitu-

---

Marine Ins. Co. v. United States, 237 U.S. 19, 35 S.Ct. 496, 59 L.Ed. 821 (1915).

31. U.S. Const. art. I, § 10, cl. 1.

32. Id., art. VI, cl. 2.

§ 23.7

1. Legal Tender Cases, 79 U.S. (12 Wall.) 457, 20 L.Ed. 287 (1871); The Huntress, 12 Fed.Cas. 984 (D.C.D.Me.1840) (No. 6,914).

"As an illustration of the danger of giving too much weight, upon such a question, to the debates and the votes in the convention, it may also be observed that propositions to authorize congress to grant charters of incorporation for national objects were strongly opposed, especially as regarded banks, and defeated. [5 Elliot, Deb.] 440, 543, 544. The power of congress to emit bills of credit, as well

as to incorporate national banks, is now clearly established...." Juilliard v. Greenman ("The Legal Tender Cases"), 110 U.S. 421, 444, 4 S.Ct. 122, 128, 28 L.Ed. 204, 213 (1884).

See also Loving v. Virginia, 388 U.S. 1, 87 S.Ct. 1817, 18 L.Ed.2d 1010 (1967).

"As for the various statements directly concerning the Fourteenth Amendment, we have said in connection with a related problem, that although these historical sources 'cast some light' they are not sufficient to resolve the problem; '[a]t best they are inconclusive.' " 388 U.S. at 9, 87 S.Ct. at 1822, 18 L.Ed.2d at 1016.

2. "In the case of a constitutional amendment it is of less materiality than in that of an ordinary bill or resolution. A constitutional amendment must be agreed

tional provision are relevant, courts may take such speeches into account in order to determine why Congress enacted the constitutional clauses in question.[3]

§ 23.8 Principles of the Common Law

The Supreme Court has sometimes stated, particularly in cases near the turn of the twentieth century, that interpretation of the Constitution is necessarily influenced by the fact that its provisions are framed in the language of the common law.[1] The range of a constitutional provision phrased in terms of the common law may sometimes be

to, not only by Senators and Representatives, but it must be ratified by the legislatures, or by conventions in three fourths of the states before such amendment can take effect. The safe way is to read its language in connection with the known condition of affairs out of which the occasion for its adoption may have arisen, and then to construe it, if there be therein any doubtful expressions, in a way so far as is reasonably possible, to forward the known purpose or object for which the amendment was adopted. This rule could not, of course, be so used as to limit the force and effect of an amendment in a manner which the plain and unambiguous language used therein would not justify or permit." Maxwell v. Dow, 176 U.S. 581, 602, 20 S.Ct. 448, 456–57, 44 L.Ed. 597, 605 (1900).

"Doubtless the intention of the congress which framed, and of the states which adopted, this [Fourteenth] amendment of the constitution, must be sought in the words of the amendment, and the debates in congress are not admissible as evidence to control the meaning of those words. But the statements above quoted [from debates in Congress] are valuable as contemporaneous opinions of jurists and statesmen upon the legal meaning of the words themselves, and are, at the least, interesting as showing that the application of the amendment to the Chinese race was considered and not overlooked." United States v. Wong Kim Ark, 169 U.S. 649, 699, 18 S.Ct. 456, 476, 42 L.Ed. 890, 908 (1898).

"It is unnecessary to enter into the details of this debate. The arguments of individual legislators are no proper subject for judicial comment. They are so often influenced by personal or political considerations, or by the assumed necessities of the situation, that they can hardly be considered even as the deliberate views of the persons who make them,

much less as dictating the construction to be put upon the Constitution by the courts." Downes v. Bidwell, 182 U.S. 244, 254, 21 S.Ct. 770, 774, 45 L.Ed. 1088, 1093–94 (1901).

3. United States v. Cornell, 36 F.Supp. 81 (D.Idaho 1940).

§ 23.8

1. Ex parte Grossman, 267 U.S. 87, 45 S.Ct. 332, 69 L.Ed. 527, 38 A.L.R. 131 (1925); South Carolina v. United States, 199 U.S. 437, 26 S.Ct. 110, 50 L.Ed. 261, 4 Ann.Cas. 737 (1905); Schick v. United States, 195 U.S. 65, 24 S.Ct. 826, 49 L.Ed. 99, 1 Ann.Cas. 585 (1904); United States v. Wong Kim Ark, 169 U.S. 649, 18 S.Ct. 456, 42 L.Ed. 890 (1898); United States v. Sanges, 144 U.S. 310, 12 S.Ct. 609, 36 L.Ed. 445 (1892); Smith v. Alabama, 124 U.S. 465, 8 S.Ct. 564, 31 L.Ed. 508 (1888); Dickinson v. United States, 159 Fed. 801 (1st Cir.1908), certiorari dismissed 213 U.S. 92, 29 S.Ct. 485, 53 L.Ed. 711 (1909).

Existence and Authority of the Common Law. Before the Constitution was adopted, the colonies recognized the rules of the common law. These rules were used to the extent that they were applicable to the conditions existing in the colonies, and were subject to modification dictated by the needs of the people. The colonists could enforce their common law rights in the existing tribunals. The adoption of the Constitution did not deprive the people in the colonies of the protection and advantages of the common law. The Constitution itself recognizes the fact of the continued existence of the common law. Indeed, the Constitution is based on common law principles, and its correct interpretation requires that its provisions shall be read and construed in the light of the common law. Murray v. Chicago & N.W.R. Co., 62 Fed. 24, 27 (C.C.Iowa 1894), affirmed 92 Fed. 868 (8th Cir.1899).

fixed by looking to the common law, provided that the common law rule invoked was not rejected by the framers as unsuited to their civil or political conditions.[2]

By adopting common law phrases such as "pardon," "impeachment," "trial by jury," "felony," "ex post facto," "bill of attainder,"

"The Constitution of the United States, like those of all the original states (and in fact, of all the states now forming the Union, with the exception of Louisiana), presupposed the existence and authority of the common law. The principles of that law were the basis of our institutions. In adopting the state and national constitutions; those fundamental laws which were to govern their political action and relations in the new circumstances arising from the assumption of sovereignty, both local and national; our ancestors rejected so much of the common law as was then inapplicable to their situation, and prescribed new rules for their regulation and government. But in so doing, they did not reject the body of the common law. They founded their respective state constitutions and the great national compact, upon its existing principles, so far as they were consistent and harmonious with the provisions of those constitutions. A brief reference to the Constitution of the United States will illustrate this idea. It gives the sole power of impeachment to the House of Representatives, and the sole power of trying an *impeachment* to the Senate. *Impeachment* is thus treated as a well known, defined and established proceeding. Yet it was only known to the common law, and could be understood only by reference to the principles of that law. The Congress was authorized to provide for the punishment of *felonies* committed on the high seas, and for punishing certain other crimes. The common law furnished the only definition of *felonies*. The trial of all crimes, except in cases of impeachment, was to be by jury; and the Constitution speaks of *treason, bribery, indictment, cases in equity, a uniform system of bankruptcy, attainder, and the writ of habeas corpus;* all of which were unknown, even by name, to any other system of jurisprudence than the common law. In like manner, the amendments to the Constitution make provisions in reference to the *right of petition, search warrants, capital crimes, grand jury, trial by jury, bail, fines, and the rules of the common law.* In these instances, no legislative definition or exposition, was apparently deemed necessary by the framers of the Constitution. They are spoken of as substantial things, already existing and established, and which will continue to exist." Lynch v. Clarke, 1 Sand.Ch. 583, 652–53 (N.Y.Ch.1844).

Blackstone's Commentaries are accepted as a satisfactory exposition of the common law of England. At the time of the adoption of the United States Constitution, Blackstone's Commentaries had been in print for about twenty years. It has been said that more copies of the work had been sold in this country than in England. Undoubtedly, the framers of the Constitution were familiar with Blackstone's work. Schick v. United States, 195 U.S. 65, 69, 24 S.Ct. 826, 49 L.Ed. 99, 102, 1 Ann.Cas. 585, 586 (1904).

"I have cited Blackstone's Commentaries because that work was contemporaneous with our Constitutions, and brought the law of England down to that day, and then, as now, was the authoritative textbook on its subject, familiar not only to the profession, but to all men of the general education of the founders of our Constitution. Mr. Burke, in his speech 'On conciliation with America,' delivered in March, 1775, referring to information derived from 'an eminent bookseller,' as to the great exportation of law-books to this country, says: 'The colonists have now fallen into the way of printing them for themselves. I hear that they have sold nearly as many of Blackstone's Commentaries in America as in England.' That book, therefore, thus belongs to the precise time to which our question relates, and is especially authoritative on its subject, and therefore I shall continue to cite it." Knote v. United States ("Knote's Case"), 10 Ct.Cl. 397, 399–400 (1874), affirmed 95 U.S. (5 Otto) 149, 24 L.Ed. 442 (1877).

See also, M. Eisenberg, The Nature of the Common Law (1988); Bainbridge, Social Propositions and Common Law Adjudication, 1990 U.Ill.L.Rev. 231 (1990).

2. Grosjean v. American Press Co., 297 U.S. 233, 56 S.Ct. 444, 80 L.Ed. 660 (1936).

"habeas corpus," "unreasonable searches and seizures," "presentment,"
"indictment," "infamous crime," "right to be informed of the nature of
the accusation," and "twice put in jeopardy," the framers recognized
the maxims and essential principles of the common law. Courts should
resort to common law principles in order to ascertain the true meaning
of words and phrases, if the framers adopted these words and phrases
from the common law.[3] The common law meaning of such words and
phrases is not, however, necessarily conclusive of the constitutional
meaning of the same words. The clause in the Constitution may have a
different purpose than the phrase had in the common law; therefore,
the phrase may have a different interpretation. For example, in
holding that an indictment or presentment is not essential to "due

---

3. Callan v. Wilson, 127 U.S. 540, 8
S.Ct. 1301, 32 L.Ed. 223 (1888); Ex parte
Bain, 121 U.S. 1, 7 S.Ct. 781, 30 L.Ed. 849
(1887); Locke v. New Orleans, 71 U.S. (4
Wall.) 172, 18 L.Ed. 334 (1867); Low v.
United States, 169 Fed. 86 (6th Cir.1909);
West v. Gammon, 98 Fed. 426 (6th Cir.
1899); United States v. Potter, 56 Fed. 83
(C.C.Mass.1892), reargued in part 56 Fed.
97 (1892), reversed on other grounds 155
U.S. 438, 15 S.Ct. 144, 39 L.Ed. 214 (1894);
United States v. Three Copper Stills, 47
Fed. 495 (D.C.Ky.1890); United States v.
Ayres, 46 Fed. 651 (D.C.S.C.1891); United
States v. Harris, 26 Fed.Cas. 174 (C.C.D.Ky.
1866) (No. 15,312); United States v. Gibert,
25 Fed.Cas. 1287 (C.C.D.Mass.1834) (No.
15,204); United States v. Block, 24 Fed.
Cas. 1174 (C.C.D.Or.1877) (No. 14,609).

Pardoning Power. Pardoning Power
of President, 5 Op.Att'y Gen. 532, 535
(1852); Hopkins v. United States, 4 App.
D.C. 430, 436 (D.C.Cir.1839).

"As this power had been exercised from
time immemorial by the executive of
that nation whose language is our language, and to whose judicial institutions
ours bear a close resemblance, we adopt
their principles respecting the operation
and effect of a pardon, and look into
their books for the rules prescribing the
manner in which it is to be used by the
person who would avail himself of it."
United States v. Wilson, 32 U.S. (7 Pet.)
150, 160, 8 L.Ed. 640, 643–44 (1833).

But as to the extent of the pardoning power, the Attorney General said:

"The powers of the President, in this
respect, cannot be enlarged by analogy
to the powers of an English king, because the powers of the two have their
origin and mode of existence in different

and opposite principles. (See Bl.Com.,
Book 4, c. 31.) 'His (the king's) power of
pardoning was said by our Saxon ancestors to be derived *a lege suae dignitatis;*
and it is declared in Parliament, by Stat.
27, Hen. 8, that no other person hath
power to pardon or remit any treason or
felonies whatsoever; but that the king
hath the whole and sole power thereof,
united and knit to the imperial crown of
this realm.' And hence, in a former
opinion, (of July 5, 1861,) speaking of the
pardoning power and some others of that
nature, I said: 'These belong to that
class which, in England, are called *prerogative powers,* inherent in the crown.
And yet the framers of our Constitution
thought proper to preserve them, and to
vest them on the President, as necessary
to the good government of the country.'
As far as they are so preserved and vested they are legitimate powers in the
hand of the President. But they are not
prerogatives—they are legal powers vested in, and duties imposed upon the President by the letter of the Constitution;
and they are to be exercised and judged
of as other granted powers and imposed
duties are.

"The power to grant reprieves and pardons, is given, in terms, to the President;
but the power to remit forfeitures, fines,
and penalties (as distinct from the pardon of crimes) is not given. Yet the kind
had both powers. And necessarily so, in
the theory of the English government, in
which the king is the only person offended by the commission of crimes, and the
only owner of things forfeited, unless
expressly provided otherwise by statute."
Pardoning Power of the President, 10
Op.Att'y Gen. 452, 454–55 (1863).

process of law" under the fourteenth amendment, when applied to prosecutions for felonies in state courts, the Supreme Court noted:

> In this country written constitutions were deemed essential to protect the rights and liberties of the people against the encroachments of power delegated to their governments, and the provisions of *Magna Charta* were incorporated into bills of rights. They were limitations upon all the powers of government, legislative as well as executive and judicial. It necessarily happened, therefore, that as these broad and general maxims of liberty and justice held in our system a different place and performed a different function from their position and office in English constitutional history and law, they would receive and justify a corresponding and more comprehensive interpretation. Applied in England only as guards against executive usurpation and tyranny, here they have become bulwarks also against arbitrary legislation; but in that application, as it would be incongruous to measure and restrict them by the ancient customary English law, they must be held to guaranty, not particular forms of procedure, but the very substance of individual rights to life, liberty, and property. Restraints that could be fastened upon executive authority with precision and detail might prove obstructive and injurious when imposed on the just and necessary discretion of legislative power; and while, in every instance laws that violated express and specific injunctions and prohibitions might without embarrassment be judicially declared to be void, yet any general principle or maxim founded on the essential nature of law, as a just and reasonable expression of the public will, and of government as instituted by popular consent and for the general good, can only be applied to cases coming clearly within the scope of its spirit and purpose, and not to legislative provisions merely establishing forms and modes of attainment.[4]

Thus, the purpose of a particular clause determines whether the interpretation must be consistent with the rules of English law existing when the Constitution was adopted.[5]

§ 23.9 Principles of Existing Law

As a part of a historical interpretative method of construing constitutional provisions, the Supreme Court has sometimes taken the position that the scope and effect of many of the provisions of the Constitution are best ascertained by bearing in mind what the law was at the time the Constitution and its amendments were adopted and

---

4. Hurtado v. California, 110 U.S. 516, 531–32, 4 S.Ct. 111, 119, 28 L.Ed. 232, 237 (1884).

5. United States v. Wood, 299 U.S. 123, 57 S.Ct. 177, 81 L.Ed. 78 (1936), rehearing denied 299 U.S. 624, 57 S.Ct. 319, 81 L.Ed. 459 (1937); Continental Ill. Nat. Bank & Trust Co. of Chicago v. Chicago, R.I. & P. Ry. Co., 294 U.S. 648, 55 S.Ct. 595, 79 L.Ed. 1110 (1935).

ratified.[1] The opinions taking this position have stated that, in general, the Constitution did not reach out for new guarantees, but sought to secure guarantees already recognized by law.[2] For instance, the requirement of "full faith and credit" was never intended to modify or override well-established principles of justice protected by other constitutional provisions.[3] The provision that an accused person shall "be confronted with the witnesses against him" is not infringed by permitting the testimony of a deceased witness who had been under oath at a former trial to be read against the accused. The advantage of seeing the witness at the former trial, and of subjecting him to the ordeal of cross-examination, preserves the defendant's constitutional protection. The Constitution also recognizes certain exceptions to the confrontation rules because the exceptions were well established at the time the Constitution was adopted. Thus, one may infer that the framers did not intend to abrogate these exceptions.[4] For example, the admission of a dying declaration was a well established exception to the confrontation rule.

A further example of this method of interpretation may be found in article I, section 10. That section provides that no state shall, without the consent of Congress, lay any imposts or duties on imports or exports, except such imposts or duties that may be absolutely necessary for executing the state's inspection laws. The meaning of "inspection laws" was well understood at the time the Constitution was adopted.[5]

IV. GENERAL RULES AND PRINCIPLES OF INTERPRETATION

§ 23.10 The Duty to Avoid Constitutional Issues

The Supreme Court, reaffirms with some frequency, the principle that it has a duty to avoid deciding a constitutional issue if a nonconsti-

§ 23.9

1. Ex parte Wilson, 114 U.S. 417, 5 S.Ct. 935, 29 L.Ed. 89 (1885); Turner v. Maryland, 107 U.S. 38, 2 S.Ct. 44, 27 L.Ed. 370 (1883).

An amendment should be construed in the light of conditions existing at the time of its adoption. For example, at the time the fourteenth amendment was adopted, several states had made provision for prosecuting public offenses by information. Several states had practically dispensed with the grand jury system, yet the courts of those states had affirmed the validity of such constitutional and statutory provisions for prosecuting crime. If an indictment or presentment of a grand jury is essential to "due process of law," within the meaning of that phrase as used in the fourteenth amendment, then all of the states would be required to proceed in that manner against persons charged with vio-

lations of state law. Nonetheless, 25 years after the adoption of the fourteenth amendment, no court had interpreted the amendment to prohibit laws providing for prosecution by information. In re Humason, 46 Fed. 388 (D.Wash.1891).

2. Mattox v. United States, 156 U.S. 237, 15 S.Ct. 337, 39 L.Ed. 409 (1895).

3. Bigelow v. Old Dominion Copper Mining & Smelting Co., 225 U.S. 111, 32 S.Ct. 641, 56 L.Ed. 1009, 30 Ann.Cas. 875 (1912); Darling & Co. v. Burchard, 69 N.D. 212, 284 N.W. 856 (1939).

4. Kirby v. United States, 174 U.S. 47, 19 S.Ct. 574, 43 L.Ed. 890 (1899); Mattox v. United States, 156 U.S. 237, 15 S.Ct. 337, 39 L.Ed. 409 (1895).

5. New York v. Compagnie Generale Transatlantique, 10 Fed. 357, 361 (C.C.S.N.Y.1882), affirmed 107 U.S. 59, 2 S.Ct. 87, 27 L.Ed. 383 (1883).

tutional ground will dispose of the case.[1] These other grounds may be creatures of the judiciary's own making, such as the nonconstitutional rules regarding standing, or they may be statutory grounds. The rationale for this general reluctance to decide constitutional issues—a reluctance articulated even by activist Courts—has been discussed earlier in this Treatise and that discussion will not be repeated here.[2] That earlier discussion also analyzes the tools created by the judiciary to avoid constitutional decisions.[3]

The main point for purposes of this chapter is that Supreme Court justices, through the years, have announced (and sometimes, though not always, followed) various rules to avoid constitutional issues.[4] Thus the Supreme Court will not determine the constitutionality of legislation in a friendly, nonadversary proceeding.[5] The Court will not anticipate and decide a constitutional issue before it necessarily must reach the question;[6] it will not formulate a constitutional rule broader than necessary to decide the facts before it;[7] it will not decide a properly presented constitutional issue if nonconstitutional grounds exist, such as a statutory construction, or a state law ground.[8]

§ 23.10

1. See, e.g., Ashwander v. TVA, 297 U.S. 288, 347, 56 S.Ct. 466, 483, 80 L.Ed. 688, 711 (1936) (Brandeis, J., concurring), rehearing denied 297 U.S. 728, 56 S.Ct. 588, 80 L.Ed. 1011 (1936); Rescue Army v. Municipal Court, 331 U.S. 549, 67 S.Ct. 1409, 91 L.Ed. 1666 (1947).

2. See § 2.13(g), supra.

3. See §§ 2.13–2.16, supra.

4. See generally, Brandeis, J., concurring in Ashwander v. TVA, 297 U.S. 288, 347–49, 56 S.Ct. 466, 483–84, 80 L.Ed. 688, 710–12 (1936), rehearing denied 297 U.S. 728, 56 S.Ct. 588, 80 L.Ed. 1011 (1936), for a discussion of these various rules and a list of citations.

5. E.g., Chicago & G.T.R. Co. v. Wellman, 143 U.S. 339, 345, 12 S.Ct. 400, 402, 36 L.Ed. 176, 179 (1892): "It never was the thought that, by means of a friendly suit, a party beaten in the legislature could transfer to the courts an inquiry as to the constitutionality of legislation."

6. E.g., Burton v. United States, 196 U.S. 283, 295, 25 S.Ct. 243, 245, 49 L.Ed. 482, 485 (1905): "It is not the habit of the Court to decide questions of a constitutional nature unless absolutely necessary to a decision of the case."

Brockett v. Spokane Arcades, Inc., 472 U.S. 491, 502, 105 S.Ct. 2794, 2801, 86 L.Ed.2d 394 (1985).

7. E.g., Liverpool, N.Y. & P.S.S. Co. v. Commissioners of Emigration, 113 U.S. 33, 39, 5 S.Ct. 352, 355, 28 L.Ed. 899, 901 (1885): The Court has "rigidly adhered" to the rule that it is "never to formulate a rule of constitutional law broader than is required by the precise facts to which it is to be applied."

See also, Brockett v. Spokane Arcades, Inc., 472 U.S. 491, 502, 105 S.Ct. 2794, 2801, 86 L.Ed.2d 394 (1985).

8. Escambia County v. McMillan, 466 U.S. 48, 49–53, 104 S.Ct. 1577, 1578–79, 80 L.Ed.2d 36, 39 (1984) (per curiam), on remand 748 F.2d 1037 (11th Cir.1984): "Affirmance of the statutory ground would moot the constitutional issues presented by the case. It is a well established principle governing the prudent exercise of this Court's jurisdiction that normally the Court will not decide a constitutional question if there is some other ground upon which to dispose the case."

See also Paulussen v. Herion, 475 U.S. 557, 106 S.Ct. 1339, 89 L.Ed.2d 521 (1986) (per curiam) (avoiding ruling on the constitutionality of a state law governing support payments to illegitimate children on the basis that there was uncertainty re-

The Court will not hear a complaint as to the alleged constitutionality of a statute by one who is not in fact injured by the statute's operation.[9] The Court will not decide the validity of a statute if the complainant has voluntarily accepted the provisions of the statute and availed himself of the statute's benefits.[10]

If a federal statute or federal regulation is challenged, the Court will try to construe the law to avoid the constitutional issue *if* such a construction is fairly possible,[11] because the Court assumes that Congress, which has always sworn to protect the Constitution, would "err on the side of fundamental constitutional liberties when its legislation

garding the effect of a new state law and a new statute of limitations; the Court stated that "we are reluctant to address a federal constitutional question until it is clearly necessary to do so"), on remand 359 Pa.Super. 520, 519 A.2d 473 (1986), appeal denied 515 Pa. 614, 530 A.2d 868 (1987).

9. E.g., New York ex rel. Hatch v. Reardon, 204 U.S. 152, 160–61, 27 S.Ct. 188, 190–91, 51 L.Ed. 415, 422–23 (1907).

10. E.g., Great Falls Manufacturing Co. v. Garland, 124 U.S. 581, 599, 8 S.Ct. 631, 638, 31 L.Ed. 527, 533 (1888) (Harlan, J., for the Court).

11. Crowell v. Benson, 285 U.S. 22, 62, 52 S.Ct. 285, 296–97, 76 L.Ed. 598, 619 (1932): "When the validity of an act of Congress is drawn in question, and even if a serious doubt of constitutionality is raised, it is a cardinal principle that this Court will first ascertain whether a construction of the statute is fairly possible by which the question may be avoided."

Gulf Oil Co. v. Bernard, 452 U.S. 89, 99, 101 S.Ct. 2193, 2199, 68 L.Ed.2d 693 (1981): "[P]rior to reaching any constitutional questions, federal courts must consider nonconstitutional grounds for decision."

The constitutional question must be "unavoidable." Spector Motor Service v. McLaughlin, 323 U.S. 101, 105, 65 S.Ct. 152, 154, 89 L.Ed. 101 (1944).

See also, United States v. Gerlach Live Stock Co., 339 U.S. 725, 737, 70 S.Ct. 955, 961, 94 L.Ed. 1231 (1950); Mobile v. Bolden, 446 U.S. 55, 60, 100 S.Ct. 1490, 1495, 64 L.Ed.2d 47 (1980); Larson v. Valente, 456 U.S. 228, 257, 102 S.Ct. 1673, 1690, 72 L.Ed.2d 33 (1982) (Stevens, J., concurring), rehearing denied 457 U.S. 1111, 102 S.Ct. 2916, 73 L.Ed.2d 1323 (1982); Kolender v. Lawson, 461 U.S. 352, 361 n. 10, 103 S.Ct. 1855, 1860 n. 10, 75 L.Ed.2d 903 (1983); Three Affiliated Tribes of Fort Berthold

Reservation v. Wold Engineering, 467 U.S. 138, 104 S.Ct. 2267, 81 L.Ed.2d 113 (1984), on remand 364 N.W.2d 98 (N.D.1985), certiorari granted 474 U.S. 900, 106 S.Ct. 270, 88 L.Ed.2d 224 (1985); Jean v. Nelson, 472 U.S. 846, 854–57, 105 S.Ct. 2992, 2997–98, 86 L.Ed.2d 664 (1985); Escambia County v. McMillan, 466 U.S. 48, 51, 104 S.Ct. 1577, 1579, 80 L.Ed.2d 36 (1984) (per curiam), on remand 748 F.2d 1037 (5th Cir.1984); Atkins v. Parker, 472 U.S. 115, 123 n. 22, 105 S.Ct. 2520, 2526 n. 22, 86 L.Ed.2d 81 (1985); Lowe v. SEC, 472 U.S. 181, 190, 105 S.Ct. 2557, 2563, 86 L.Ed.2d 130 (1985); In re Snyder, 472 U.S. 634, 643, 105 S.Ct. 2874, 2880, 86 L.Ed.2d 504 (1985), on remand 770 F.2d 743 (8th Cir.1985).

No Disingenuous Evasion. However, as Justice Cardozo recognized, the Court cannot press the interpretation of a statute "to the point of disingenuous evasion" even to avoid deciding a constitutional question. George Moore Ice Cream Co. v. Rose, 289 U.S. 373, 379, 53 S.Ct. 620, 622, 77 L.Ed. 1265 (1933) (Cardozo, J.); Yu Cong Eng v. Trinidad, 271 U.S. 500, 518, 46 S.Ct. 619, 623, 70 L.Ed. 1059 (1926) ("amendment may not be substituted for construction"); Heckler v. Mathews, 465 U.S. 728, 740, 104 S.Ct. 1387, 1396, 79 L.Ed.2d 646 (1984); United States v. Locke, 471 U.S. 84, 95, 105 S.Ct. 1785, 1793, 85 L.Ed.2d 64 (1985); United States v. Albertini, 472 U.S. 675, 680, 105 S.Ct. 2897, 2902, 86 L.Ed.2d 536 (1985), on remand 783 F.2d 1484 (9th Cir. 1986): "Statutes should be construed to avoid constitutional questions, but this interpretative canon is not a license to rewrite language written by the judiciary." Commodity Futures Trading Commission v. Schor, 478 U.S. 833, 842, 106 S.Ct. 3245, 3252, 92 L.Ed.2d 675 (1986) (Court does not have prerogative to ignore legislative will in order to avoid constitutional adjudication).

implicates those liberties." [12]

The Court will not decide issues if the record before it is thought to be too "inadequate," or too "abstract".[13]

On the other hand, the justices have been ambivalent. While Chief Justice Marshall described the power of judicial review as a reluctant power exercised only because the Court has to decide cases brought before it in conformity with the Constitution,[14] that same Chief Justice Marshall also said:

> It is most true that this Court will not take jurisdiction if it should not; but it is equally true that it must take jurisdiction if it should. The judiciary cannot, as the legislature may, avoid a measure, because it approaches the confines of the constitution.... We have no more rights to decline the exercise of jurisdiction which is given, than to usurp that which is not given. The one or the other would be treason to the Constitution.[15]

§ 23.11 Reasonable Interpretation of the Constitution's Intent and Meaning

In order to interpret the Constitution according to its true intent and meaning,[1] one must constantly keep in view the purposes behind the various clauses.[2] Where the courts consider a constitutional provi-

---

12. Regan v. Time, Inc., 468 U.S. 641, 696, 104 S.Ct. 3262, 3292, 82 L.Ed.2d 487 (1984) (Stevens, J., concurring in part and dissenting in part).

13. Rescue Army v. Municipal Court, 331 U.S. 549, 67 S.Ct. 1409, 91 L.Ed. 1666 (1947); Socialist Labor Party v. Gilligan, 406 U.S. 583, 92 S.Ct. 1716, 32 L.Ed.2d 317 (1972), judgment affirmed 409 U.S. 942, 93 S.Ct. 282, 34 L.Ed.2d 214 (1972); Simmons v. West Haven Housing Authority, 399 U.S. 510, 511, 90 S.Ct. 1960, 26 L.Ed.2d 764 (1970), rehearing denied 400 U.S. 856, 91 S.Ct. 23, 27 L.Ed.2d 94 (1970): "Because of an ambiguity in the record ... we now conclude that this appeal should be dismissed."

See also, Naim v. Naim, 350 U.S. 891, 76 S.Ct. 151, 100 L.Ed. 784 (1955), motion denied, 350 U.S. 985, 76 S.Ct. 472, 100 L.Ed. 852 (1956).

Compare A. Bickel, The Least Dangerous Branch: The Supreme Court at the Bar of Politics 174 (1962), with Wechster, Towards Neutral Principles of Constitutional Law, 73 Harv.L.Rev. 1, 34 (1959) (discussing *Naim* cases).

14. Marbury v. Madison, 5 U.S. (1 Cranch) 137, 2 L.Ed. 60 (1803).

15. Cohens v. Virginia, 19 U.S. (6 Wheat.) 264, 404, 5 L.Ed. 257 (1821).

§ 23.11

1. Ex parte Yerger, 75 U.S. (8 Wall.) 85, 19 L.Ed. 332 (1869).

2. United States v. Wong Kim Ark, 169 U.S. 649, 18 S.Ct. 456, 42 L.Ed. 890 (1898); Rhode Island v. Massachusetts, 37 U.S. (12 Pet.) 657, 9 L.Ed. 1233 (1838); M'Culloch v. Maryland, 17 U.S. (4 Wheat.) 316, 4 L.Ed. 579 (1819).

"[A]n adherence to the letter and a violation of the spirit of the instrument ought not to be tolerated or supposed possible." Landry v. Klopman, 13 La.Ann. 345, 345–46 (1858).

A clause "is not to be frittered away by doubtful construction, but like every clause in every constitution it must have a reasonable interpretation, and be held to express the intention of its framers." Woodson v. Murdock, 89 U.S. (22 Wall.) 351, 369, 22 L.Ed. 716, 720 (1874).

"The solution of this question [of the jurisdiction of the Supreme Court over a controversy between two states on a question of boundary] must necessarily

sion to be unambiguous, and its meaning to be entirely free from doubt, the courts often say that there is no need to inquire into the intention of the framers; in such a case, the Supreme Court says that it will give the unambiguous meaning of the constitutional provision full operation.[3]

The Constitution must, however, be given a reasonable interpretation, according to the import of its terms.[4] Construction of a provision should not differ from its obvious or necessarily implied sense.[5]

§ 23.12 Other Laws and Instruments

In deciding issues of constitutional interpretation, the courts may resort to the same rules of interpretation and sources of judicial information that the courts use in constructing statutes[1] and other instruments granting power.[2] The Constitution should be expounded according to those general principles which usually govern the construction of other fundamental laws.[3]

§ 23.13 Construction as Single Instrument

The Constitution of the United States, as amended, must be regarded as one instrument. Every provision has equal weight.[1] The Constitution must be construed as a whole, within its four corners,[2] by

depend on the words of the constitution; the meaning and intention of the convention which framed and proposed it for adoption and ratification to the conventions of the people of and in the several states; together with a reference to such sources of judicial information as are resorted to by all courts in construing statutes...." Rhode Island v. Massachusetts, 37 U.S. (12 Pet.) 657, 721, 9 L.Ed. 1233, 1259 (1838).

See generally, Shane, Conventionalism In Constitutional Interpretation and the Place of Administrative Agencies, 36 Am. U.L.Rev. 573 (1987).

3. Ogden v. Saunders, 25 U.S. (12 Wheat.) 213, 316–17, 6 L.Ed. 606, 641–46 (1827) (Trimble, J.).

4. Martin v. Hunter's Lessee, 14 U.S. (1 Wheat.) 304, 4 L.Ed. 97 (1816); Woodson v. Murdock, 89 U.S. (22 Wall.) 351, 369, 22 L.Ed. 716, 720 (1874).

5. Rhode Island v. Massachusetts, 37 U.S. (12 Pet.) 657, 9 L.Ed. 1233 (1838); Gibbons v. Ogden, 22 U.S. (9 Wheat.) 1, 6 L.Ed. 23 (1824); Cohens v. Virginia, 19 U.S. (6 Wheat.) 264, 5 L.Ed. 257 (1821).

See generally, Laycock, Constitutional Theory Matters, 65 Tex.L.Rev. 767 (1987).

§ 23.12

1. Adams v. Storey, 1 Fed.Cas. 141 (C.C.N.Y.1817) (No. 66); Landry v. Klopman, 13 La.Ann. 345 (1858).

2. Rhode Island v. Massachusetts, 37 U.S. (12 Pet.) 657, 9 L.Ed. 1233 (1838).

3. Bank of United States v. Deveaux, 9 U.S. (5 Cranch) 61, 3 L.Ed. 38 (1809).

§ 23.13

1. Prout v. Starr, 188 U.S. 537, 23 S.Ct. 398, 47 L.Ed. 584 (1903). See also Tom v. Sutton, 533 F.2d 1101 (9th Cir.1976) (discussing principles of constitutional construction when interpreting the constitution of an Indian Tribe): "Every provision in a constitution must be interpreted in the light of the entire document ... and all constitutional provisions are of equal dignity and, if possible, should be construed in harmony with each other. (Citations omitted.) 533 F.2d at 1105–06.

2. Town of Concord v. Portsmouth Sav. Bank, 92 U.S. (2 Otto) 625, 23 L.Ed. 628 (1876); Kneedler v. Lane, 45 Pa. 238 (1863).

"There is no sounder rule of interpretation than that which requires us to look at the whole of an instrument, before we

considering each clause together with the other parts.[3]   One cannot presume that a clause in the Constitution has no effect.[4]

The Preamble to the Constitution.   Justice Joseph Story argued in his influential Treatise, that the "preamble never can be resorted to, to enlarge the powers confided to the general government, or any of its departments."[5]   The words are too vague and the principles articulated are too open ended.   Moreover, the preamble does not suggest which branch is to receive the alleged powers that the preamble confers. However, the courts, in Story's view, should not adopt a restrictive view of a power that is enumerated in the body of the Constitution if the enumerated power admits of a more liberal construction and that more liberal construction is in accord with the preamble: "Are we at liberty,"—Story asks rhetorically—"upon any principles of reason, or common sense, to adopt a restrictive meaning, which will defeat an avowed object of the Constitution, when another, equally natural, and more appropriate to the object, is before us?"[6]

In *Jacobson v. Massachusetts,*[7] Justice Holmes, for the Court, rejected the argument that a state law requiring vaccinations violated rights secured by the Preamble of the Constitution:

> Although [the Constitution's] preamble indicates the general purpose for which the people ordained and established the Constitution, it has never been regarded as the source of any substantive power conferred on the government of the United States, or on any of its departments.   Such powers embrace only those expressly

determine a question of construction of any particular part; and this rule is of the utmost importance, when applied to an instrument, the object of which was to create a government for a great country, working harmoniously and efficiently through its several executive, legislative, and judicial departments." United States v. Morris, 26 Fed.Cas. 1323, 1332 (C.C.D.Mass.1851) (No. 15,815).

"If the different parts of the same instrument ought to be so expounded as to give meaning to every part which will bear it, shall one part of the same sentence be excluded altogether from a share in the meaning; and shall the more doubtful and indefinite terms be retained in their full extent, and the clear and precise expressions be denied any signification whatsoever?   For what purpose could the enumeration of particular powers be inserted, if these and all others were meant to be included in the preceding general power?   Nothing is more natural nor common than first to use a general phrase, and then to explain and qualify it by a recital of particulars.   But the

idea of an enumeration of particulars which neither explain nor qualify the general meaning, and can have no other effect than to confound and mislead, is an absurdity, which, as we are reduced to the dilemma of charging either on the authors of the objection or on the authors of the Constitution, we must take the liberty of supposing, had not its origin with the latter." J. Madison, The Federalist, No. XLI.

3.   Campbell v. Morris, 3 Har. & McH. 535 (Md.1797).

4.   Marbury v. Madison, 5 U.S. (1 Cranch) 137, 2 L.Ed. 60 (1803).   United States v. Isaacs, 493 F.2d 1124 (7th Cir. 1974), certiorari denied 417 U.S. 976, 94 S.Ct. 3184, 41 L.Ed.2d 1146 (1974).

5.   R. Rotunda & J. Nowak, eds., Joseph Story's Commentaries on the Constitution § 221 (Originally published, 1833; reprinted, Carolina Academic Press 1987).

6.   Id.

7.   Jacobson v. Massachusetts, 197 U.S. 11, 22, 25 S.Ct. 358, 359, 49 L.Ed. 643 (1905).

granted in the body of the Constitution, and such as may be implied from those so granted. Although, therefore, one of the declared objects of the Constitution was to secure the blessings of liberty to all under the sovereign jurisdiction and authority of the United States, no power can be exerted to that end by the United States, unless apart from the preamble, it be found in some express delegation of power, or in some power to be properly implied therefrom.[8]

The case law[9] and the commentators[10] are generally in agreement regarding the use of the preamble in Constitutional interpretation, though the words of the preamble should not be ignored, and may be useful to set the tone of Constitutional interpretation.[11]

§ 23.14 Furtherance of Objects and Purpose

When investigating the nature and extent of the powers conferred by the Constitution upon the general government, one must necessarily consider the objects for which these powers were granted.[1] The lan-

8. 197 U.S. at 22, 25 S.Ct. at 359.

9. E.g., United States v. Boyer, 85 Fed. 425, 430–32 (W.D.Mo.1898); Hart Coal Corp. v. Sparks, 7 F.Supp. 16, 27 (W.D.Ky. 1934); Amazon Petroleum Corp. v. Railroad Commission, 5 F.Supp. 639, 647–48 (E.D.Tex.1934), reversed sub nom., Ryan v. Amazon Petroleum Corp., 71 F.2d 1 (5th Cir.1934), reversed sub nom., Panama Refining Co. v. Ryan, 293 U.S. 388, 55 S.Ct. 241, 70 L.Ed. 446 (1935).

10. E.g., Monaghan, Our Perfect Constitution, 56 N.Y.U.L.Rev. 353, 371 & n. 109 (1981); Rubin, Due Process and the Administrative State, 72 Calif.L.Rev. 1044, 1089 n. 233 (1984).

11. E.g., 1 W. Crosskey, Politics and the Constitution in the History of the United States 365–66, 374–79 (1953); S. Barber, On What the Constitution Means 51–53 (1984). A recent and thoughtful discussion on these issues is: Handler, Leiter, & Handler, A Reconsideration of the Relevance and Materiality of the Preamble in Constitutional Interpretation, 12 Cardozo L.Rev. 117 (1990).

§ 23.14

1. Virginia v. Tennessee, 148 U.S. 503, 13 S.Ct. 728, 37 L.Ed. 537 (1893); Legal Tender Cases, 79 U.S. (12 Wall.) 457, 20 L.Ed. 287 (1871); Brown v. Maryland, 25 U.S. (12 Wheat.) 419, 6 L.Ed. 678 (1827); Gibbons v. Ogden, 22 U.S. (9 Wheat.) 1, 6 L.Ed. 23 (1824); Williams v. The Lizzie Henderson, 29 Fed.Cas. 1373 (D.C.S.D.Fla.

1880) (No. 17,726a); President's Power to Fill Vacancies in Recess of the Senate, 12 Op.Att'y.Gen. 32 (1866); Executive Authority to Fill Vacancies, 1 Op.Att'y.Gen. 631 (1823).

No distinction between nature of power and nature of subject:

"[T]he power to regulate commerce, embraces a vest field, containing not only many, but exceedingly various subjects, quite unlike in their nature; some imperatively demanding a single uniform rule, operating equally on the commerce of the United States in every port; and some, like the subject now in question, as imperatively demanding that diversity, which alone can meet the local necessities of navigation.

"Either absolutely to affirm, or deny that the nature of this power requires exclusive legislation by Congress, is to lose sight of the nature of the subjects of this power, and to assert concerning all of them, what is really applicable but to a part. Whatever subjects of this power are in their nature national, or admit only of one uniform system, or plan of regulation, may justly be said to be of such a nature as to require exclusive legislation by Congress. That this cannot be affirmed of laws for the regulation of pilots and pilotage is plain. The act of 1789 contains a clear and authoritative declaration by the first Congress, that the nature of this subject is such, that

guage of constitutional provisions must be construed to further the instrument's general purpose.[2] Where there are several possible mean-

until Congress should find it necessary to exert its power, it should be left to the legislation of the States; that it is local and not national; that it is likely to be the best provided for, not by one system, or plan of regulations, but by as many as the legislative discretion of the several States should deem applicable to the local peculiarities of the ports within their limits.

"Viewed in this light, so much of this act of 1789 as declares that pilots shall continue to be regulated 'by such laws as the States may respectively hereafter enact for that purpose,' instead of being held to be inoperative, as an attempt to confer on the States a power to legislate, of which the Constitution had deprived them, is allowed an appropriate and important signification. It manifests the understanding of Congress, at the outset of the government, that the nature of this subject is not such as to require its exclusive legislation. The practice of the States, and of the national government, has been in conformity with this declaration, from the origin of the national government to this time; and the nature of the subject when examined, is such as to leave no doubt of the superior fitness and propriety, not to say the absolute necessity, of different systems of regulation, drawn from local knowledge and experience, and conformed to local wants. How then can we say, that by the mere grant of power to regulate commerce, the States are deprived of all the power to legislate on this subject, because from the nature of the power the legislation of Congress must be exclusive. This would be to affirm that the nature of the power is in any case something different from the nature of the subject to which, in such case, the power extends, and that the nature of the power necessarily demands, in all cases, exclusive legislation by Congress, while the nature of one of the subjects of that power, not only does not require such exclusive legislation, but may be best provided for by many different systems enacted by the States, in conformity with the circumstances of the ports within their limits. In construing an instrument designed for the formation of a government, and in determining the ex-

tent of one of its important grants of power to legislate, we can make no such distinction between the nature of the power and the nature of the subject on which that power was intended practically to operate, nor consider the grant more extensive by affirming of the power, what is not true of its subject now in question." Cooley v. Board of Wardens, 53 U.S. (12 How.) 299, 319–20, 13 L.Ed. 996, 1005 (1851).

2. Maxwell v. Dow, 176 U.S. 581, 20 S.Ct. 448, 44 L.Ed. 597 (1900); Keokuk Northern Line Packet Co. v. Keokuk, 95 U.S. (5 Otto) 80, 24 L.Ed. 377 (1877); Legal Tender Cases, 79 U.S. (12 Wall.) 457, 20 L.Ed. 287 (1871).

Construction to favor obvious ends.

"It will, indeed, probably, be found, when we look to the character of the Constitution itself, the objects which it seeks to attain, the powers which it confers, the duties which it enjoins, and the rights which it secures, as well as the known historical fact that many of its provisions were matters of compromise of opposing interests and opinions, that no uniform rule of interpretation can be applied to it, which may not allow, even if it does not positively demand, many modifications in its actual application to particular clauses. And, perhaps, the safest rule of interpretation after all will be found to be to look to the nature and objects of the particular powers, duties, and rights, with all the lights and aids of contemporary history; and to give to the words of each just such operation and force, consistent with their legitimate meaning, as may fairly secure and attain the ends proposed. . . . If by one mode of interpretation the right must become shadowy and unsubstantial, and without any remedial power adequate to the end, and by another mode it will attain its just end and secure its manifest purpose, it would seem, upon principles of reasoning, absolutely irresistible, that the latter ought to prevail." Prigg v. Pennsylvania, 41 U.S. (16 Pet.) 539, 610–12, 10 L.Ed. 1060, 1987–88 (1842).

See also Kendall v. United States, 37 U.S. (12 Pet.) 524, 9 L.Ed. 1181 (1838); State v. Gibson, 36 Ind. 389 (1871).

ings of the words of the Constitution, courts prefer that meaning which will effectuate rather than defeat the constitutional purpose.[3]

§ 23.15 Effect of Purposes of Adoption

Courts, however, need not limit the construction and application of a provision to the purposes leading to its adoption. For instance, the fourteenth amendment is not limited to legislation affecting blacks. Similarly, the general prohibitions of the thirteenth amendment, which originated in response to the existence of African slavery, apply to the slavery of whites as well as blacks, and also to serfage, vassalage, villenage, peonage, and every other form of compulsory labor.[1] The constitutional provision which prohibits legislation by states impairing the obligation of contracts originated in response to problems surrounding the existence of tender laws, appraisement laws, stay laws, and installment laws passed by the states soon after the Revolution.[2] At that time, the states had financial problems and their people felt overwhelmed by debts. The framers intended the prohibition against impairing contracts to nullify those state laws which affected all private credit to favor debtors. Yet, in its construction, courts have not limited the contract provision to mere private, commercial contracts.[3]

§ 23.16 Adaptability to New Conditions

The framers designed the Constitution to meet new conditions and circumstances.[1] Thus, in determining whether a provision of the Constitution applies to a new subject matter, the courts should give little

Construction not to defeat object of grant.

"It has, I know, been contended that, in order to enable the President to make the appointment, the vacancy must take place during the recess; in other words, that the office must be full at the time of the adjournment of the Senate, and become vacant afterwards.

"I cannot think that this is the true interpretation of the article in question. The constitution was formed for practical purposes, and a construction that defeats the very object of the grant of power cannot be the true one." Power of President to Fill Vacancies, 2 Op. Att'y.Gen. 525, 526–27 (1832).

3. United States v. Classic, 313 U.S. 299, 61 S.Ct. 1031, 85 L.Ed. 1368 (1941), rehearing denied 314 U.S. 707, 62 S.Ct. 51, 86 L.Ed. 565 (1941).

§ 23.15

1. Such was the implicit holding of McDonald v. Santa Fe Trail Transp. Co., 427 U.S. 273, 96 S.Ct. 2574, 49 L.Ed.2d 493 (1976), on remand 540 F.2d 219 (5th Cir.

1976), which applied 42 U.S.C.A. § 1981 to prohibit discrimination in employment against any racial group, minority or majority. Implicitly the court held that such an interpretation of § 1981—based on the thirteenth amendment—is constitutional. See also Hodges v. United States, 203 U.S. 1, 16–17, 27 S.Ct. 6, 8–9, 51 L.Ed. 65, 68–69 (1906) (Congress authorized under enforcement clause of thirteenth amendment to legislate for "every race and individual"); Jones v. Alfred H. Mayer Co., 392 U.S. 409, 441 n. 78, 88 S.Ct. 2186, 2204 n. 78, 20 L.Ed.2d 1189, 1208 n. 78 (1968).

2. B. Wright, The Growth of American Constitutional Law 64 (1967); Home Building & Loan Ass'n v. Blaisdell, 290 U.S. 398, 427–28, 54 S.Ct. 231, 236, 78 L.Ed. 413, 423 (1934).

3. County of San Mateo v. Southern Pac. R.R. Co. ("Railroad Tax Cases"), 13 Fed. 722 (C.C.D.Cal.1882), error dismissed 116 U.S. 138, 6 S.Ct. 317, 29 L.Ed. 589 (1885).

§ 23.16

1. United States v. Smith, 68 F.Supp. 737 (D.D.C.1946).

weight to the fact that the framers were not familiar with the subject. The Supreme Court does not read the Constitution's words as legislative codes which are subject to continuous revision with the changing course of events, but rather the court reads them as the revelation of the purposes which the framers intended the Constitution to achieve as a continuing instrument of government.[2] The Supreme Court is, in a sense, a continual Constitutional Convention.

Justice Story cautioned, nearly two centuries ago:

> The Constitution unavoidably deals in general language. It did not suit the purposes of the people, in framing this great charter of our liberties, to provide for minute specifications of its powers, or to declare the means by which those powers should be carried into execution. It was foreseen, that this would be perilous and difficult, if not an impracticable, task. The instrument was not intended to provide merely for the exigencies of a few years, but was to endure through a long lapse of ages, the events of which were locked up in the inscrutable purposes of Providence. It could not be foreseen, what new changes and modifications of power might be indispensable to effectuate the general objects of the charter; and restrictions and specifications, which, at the present, might seem salutary, might, in the end, prove the overthrow of the system itself. Hence, its powers are expressed in general terms, leaving to the legislature, from time to time, to adopt its own means to effectuate legitimate objects, and to mould and model the exercise of its powers, as its own wisdom, and the public interests, should require.[3]

2. United States v. Classic, 313 U.S. 299, 61 S.Ct. 1031, 85 L.Ed. 1368 (1941), rehearing denied 314 U.S. 707, 62 S.Ct. 51, 86 L.Ed. 565 (1941). See also Harper v. Virginia Bd. of Electors, 383 U.S. 663, 86 S.Ct. 1079, 16 L.Ed.2d 169 (1966) where the Court discussed equal protection:

"[T]he Equal Protection Clause is not shackled to the political theory of a particular era. In determining what lines are unconstitutionally discriminatory, we have never been confined to historic notions of equality, any more than we have restricted due process to a fixed catalogue of what was at a given time deemed to be the limits of fundamental rights. Notions of what constitutes equal treatment of the purposes of the Equal Protection Clause *do* change." 383 U.S. at 669, 86 S.Ct. at 1083, 16 L.Ed.2d at 174 (emphasis in original).

3. Martin v. Hunter's Lessee, 14 U.S. (1 Wheat.) 304, 326, 4 L.Ed. 97, 102 (1816).

"The powers thus granted are not confined to the instrumentalities of com-merce, or the postal service known or in use when the Constitution was adopted, but they keep pace with the progress of the country, and adapt themselves to the new developments of time and circumstances. They extend from the horse with its rider to the stage-coach, from the sailing vessel to the steamboat, from the coach and the steamboat to the railroad, and from the railroad to the telegraph, as these new agencies are successively brought into use to meet the demands of increasing population and wealth. They were intended for the government of the business to which they relate, at all times and under all circumstances." Pensacola Tel. Co. v. Western Union Tel. Co., 96 U.S. (6 Otto) 1, 9, 24 L.Ed. 708, 710 (1878).

"Constitutional provisions do not change, but their operation extends to new matters as the modes of business and the habits of life of the people vary with each succeeding generation. The law of the common carrier is the same today as

As the Supreme Court has tried to explain, even a "changeless" Constitution is adaptable:

> The Constitution is a written instrument. As such its meaning does not alter. That which it meant when adopted it means now. Being a grant of powers to a government its language is general, and as changes come in social and political life it embraces in its grasp all new conditions which are within the scope of the powers in terms conferred. In other words, while the powers granted do not change, they apply from generation to generation to all things to which they are in their nature applicable. This in no manner abridges the fact of its changeless nature and meaning. Those things which are within its grants of power, as those grants were understood when made, are still within them, and those things not within them remain still excluded.[4]

Under this theory, the meaning of constitutional guaranties never varies, but the scope of their application may expand or contract to meet new and different conditions.[5]

§ 23.17 Conflicting or Inconsistent Provisions

If there is any conflict between an amendment and a provision in the original Constitution, the amendment obviously must control; the governing rule is that the last expression of the will of the lawmaker prevails over an earlier expression.[1] However, the original Constitution and the first ten amendments were substantially contemporaneous, and thus should be construed *in pari materia.*[2]

when transportation on land was by coach and wagon, and on water by canal boat and sailing vessel, yet in its actual operation it touches and regulates transportation by modes then unknown, the railroad train and the steamship. Just so is it with the grant to the national government of power over interstate commerce. The Constitution has not changed. The power is the same. But it operates to-day upon modes of interstate commerce unknown to the fathers, and it will operate with equal force upon any new modes of such commerce which the future may develop." In re Debs, 158 U.S. 564, 591, 15 S.Ct. 900, 909, 39 L.Ed. 1092, 1105 (1895).

4. South Carolina v. United States, 199 U.S. 437, 448–49, 26 S.Ct. 110, 111, 50 L.Ed. 261, 264, 4 Ann.Cas. 737, 738 (1905).

5. Michigan v. Wisconsin, 272 U.S. 398, 47 S.Ct. 114, 71 L.Ed. 315 (1926).

§ 23.17

1. Schick v. United States, 195 U.S. 65, 24 S.Ct. 826, 49 L.Ed. 99, 1 Ann.Cas. 585 (1904).

Construction to avoid conflict. Of section 3 of the fourteenth amendment, the court said:

"Of two constructions, either of which is warranted by the words of an amendment of a public act, that is to be preferred which best harmonizes the amendment with the general terms and spirit of the act amended. This principle forbids a construction of the amendment, not clearly required by its terms, which will bring it into conflict or disaccord with the other provisions of the constitution." Griffin's Case, 11 Fed.Cas. 7, 25 (C.C.D.Va.1869) (No. 5,815).

2. Patton v. United States, 281 U.S. 276, 50 S.Ct. 253, 74 L.Ed. 854, 70 A.L.R. 263 (1930).

Whenever possible, conflicting provisions should be reconciled and construed so as to give effect to both.[3] In construing clauses which involve conflicting powers of state and federal governments, the Supreme Court thus can consider, not only a literal meaning of the words to be expounded, but also their connection with other words, and the general objects to be accomplished by the clauses.[4]

§ 23.18 The Remedy for Mischief

Certain clauses of the Constitution were designed to address specific problems or "mischief" existing at the time of adoption. Thus, any questioned clause, or part of a clause, should be construed to afford a remedy for the mischief existing under the old law or conditions.[1] For example, the clause of section 2 of article III, providing that the judicial power shall extend "to controversies between two or more states," gives the federal tribunals jurisdiction over controversies between states involving boundary disputes. Jurisdiction exists over all such boundary disputes, irrespective of whether the boundaries were drawn at the time of, or prior to, the adoption of the Constitution.[2]

3. Cohens v. Virginia, 19 U.S. (6 Wheat.) 264, 5 L.Ed. 257 (1821).

4. Brown v. Maryland, 25 U.S. (12 Wheat.) 419, 6 L.Ed. 678 (1827).

§ 23.18

1. Jarrolt v. Moberly, 103 U.S. (13 Otto) 580, 26 L.Ed. 492 (1881); Prigg v. Pennsylvania, 41 U.S. (16 Pet.) 539, 10 L.Ed. 1060 (1842); Kendall v. United States, 37 U.S. (12 Pet.) 524, 9 L.Ed. 1181 (1838); Dartmouth College v. Woodward, 17 U.S. (4 Wheat.) 518, 4 L.Ed. 629 (1819); State v. Gibson, 36 Ind. 389 (1871).

The grant of power to regulate commerce should be as extensive as is necessary to deal with the mischief. Leisy v. Hardin, 135 U.S. 100, 10 S.Ct. 681, 34 L.Ed. 128 (1890).

The fourteenth amendment, the purpose of which was to secure to newly made citizens the enjoyment of their freedom, is not to be restricted in its application. County of Santa Clara v. Southern Pac. R. Co., 18 Fed. 385, 397 (C.C.Cal.1883), affirmed 118 U.S. 394, 6 S.Ct. 1132, 30 L.Ed. 118 (1886).

2. Controversies between states respecting boundaries.

"It is a part of the public history of the United States, of which we cannot be judicially ignorant, that at the adoption of the constitution, there were existing controversies between eleven states respecting their boundaries, which arose under their respective charters, and had continued from the first settlement of the colonies. New Hampshire and New York contended for the territory which is now Vermont, until the people of the latter assumed by their own power the position of a state, and settled the controversy by taking to themselves the disputed territory, as the rightful sovereign thereof. Massachusetts and Rhode Island are now before us; Connecticut claimed part of New York and Pennsylvania. She submitted to the decree of the council of Trenton, acting pursuant to the authority of the confederation which decided that Connecticut had not the jurisdiction; but she claimed the right of soil till 1800. New Jersey had a controversy with New York, which was before this court in 1832; and one yet subsists between New Jersey and Delaware. Maryland and Virginia were contending about boundaries in 1835, when a suit was pending in this Court; and the dispute is yet an open one. Virginia and North Carolina contended for boundary till 1802; and the remaining states, South Carolina and Georgia, settled their boundary in the April preceding the meeting of the general convention, which framed and proposed the constitution." Rhode Island v. Massachusetts, 37 U.S. (12 Pet.) 657, 723, 9 L.Ed. 1233, 1260 (1838).

During the Revolution, the states issued bills to circulate as money on the credit of the issuing state. Problems arose because the states lacked any real and substantial fund for payment and redemption, as well as any method to enforce payment. This problem underlies the constitutional provision that "no state shall ... emit bills of credit." [3]

V. LIBERAL OR STRICT CONSTRUCTION

§ 23.19 In General

The case law is quite clear that the Constitution, whose purposes were to establish a government, declare fundamental principles, and create a national sovereignty, is not to be interpreted with the strictness of a code of laws or of a private contract.[1]

3. Briscoe v. Bank of Kentucky, 36 U.S. (11 Pet.) 257, 9 L.Ed. 709 (1837); Craig v. Missouri, 29 U.S. (4 Pet.) 410, 7 L.Ed. 903 (1830).

Alexander Hamilton and the Bank of the United States. When Hamilton was appointed Secretary of the Treasury, the United States had a federal currency that was virtually worthless, and a national debt that—measured in relation to federal revenues—was nearly four times what the total national debt is today! Hamilton persuaded Washington to create the first Bank of the United States, and then did much to put the new Government on a sound financial footing. Later, in M'Culloch v. Maryland, 17 U.S. (4 Wheat.) 316, 4 L.Ed. 579 (1819), Chief Justice Marshall, for the Court, upheld the constitutionality of the creation of the Second Bank of the United States.

In 1795, when Hamilton left office, he left his country a sound financial legacy. The new United States had a higher credit rating than any country in Europe. The United States bonds, paying 4.5% or 5% interest, were selling at about ten percent over par. See, Hendrickson, A Monument for Hamilton ... Finally, Wall St. Jr., Nov. 17, 1990, at A14, col. 3–5; Robert Hendrickson, The Rise and Fall of Alexander Hamilton (1981).

§ 23.19

1. Fairbank v. United States, 181 U.S. 283, 287, 21 S.Ct. 648, 650, 45 L.Ed. 862, 864–65 (1901); Legal Tender Cases, 79 U.S. (12 Wall.) 457, 531–32, 20 L.Ed. 287, 306 (1870).

Marks merely the outlines of the powers granted.

"The constitution of the United States, by apt words of designation or general description, marks the outlines of the powers granted to the national legislature; but it does not undertake, with the precision and detail of a code of laws, to enumerate the subdivisions of those powers, or to specify all the means by which they may be carried into execution." Juilliard v. Greenman ("The Legal Tender Cases"), 110 U.S. 421, 439, 4 S.Ct. 122, 125, 28 L.Ed. 204, 211 (1884).

"A constitution, to contain an accurate detail of all the subdivisions of which its great powers will admit, and of all the means by which they may be carried into execution, would partake of a prolixity of a legal code, and could scarcely be embraced by the human mind. It would probably never be understood by the public. Its nature, therefore, requires, that only its great outlines should be marked, its important objects designated, and the minor ingredients which compose those objects be deduced from the nature of the objects themselves. That this idea was entertained by the framers of the American constitution, is not only to be inferred from the nature of the instrument, but from the language. Why else were some of the limitations, found in the ninth section of the first article, introduced? It is also, in some degree, warranted by their having omitted to use any restrictive term which might prevent its receiving a fair and just interpretation. In considering this question, then, we must never forget that it is *a constitution* we are expounding." M'Culloch v. Maryland, 17 U.S. (4 Wheat.) 316, 407, 4 L.Ed. 579, 601–02 (1819) (emphasis in original).

§ 23.20   Provisions for Protection of Life, Liberty and Property

The provisions for the protection of life, liberty, and property are largely and liberally construed in favor of the citizen.[1] The protections concerning persons charged with crime should receive a similar construction.[2]

The fourteenth amendment has also been liberally construed to carry out the purpose of its framers.[3] Courts have not, especially in

---

§ 23.20

1. Dorman v. State, 34 Ala. 216, 238 (1859).

Searches and seizures.

"Though the proceeding in question is divested of many of the aggravating incidents of actual search and seizure, yet, as before said, it contains their substance and essence, and effects their substantial purpose. It may be that it is the obnoxious thing in its mildest and least repulsive form; but illegitimate and unconstitutional practices get their first footing in that way, namely, by silent approaches and slight deviations from legal modes of procedure. This can only be obviated by adhering to *the rule that constitutional provisions for the security of person and property should be liberally construed. A close and literal construction deprives them of half their efficacy, and leads to gradual depreciation of the right, as if it consisted more in sound than in substance.*" Boyd v. United States, 116 U.S. 616, 635, 6 S.Ct. 524, 535, 29 L.Ed. 746, 752 (1886) (Harlan, J.) (emphasis added).

Constitutional provisions protecting the security of persons and property should be liberally construed. United States v. Smith, 23 F.Supp. 528, 529 (E.D.Mo.1938).

Deprivation of property. The fourteenth amendment, which prohibits state action depriving an individual of his property, is to be liberally construed. It is not to be confined to a legislative act specifically appropriating private property to some public use. "A state acts by agents, and the inhibition runs against all who are in fact such agents, acting within the scope of an authority conferred upon them by the statute." Huntington v. City of New York, 118 Fed. 683, 686 (S.D.N.Y.1902), affirmed 193 U.S. 441, 24 S.Ct. 505, 48 L.Ed. 741 (1904).

Putting twice in jeopardy. "The fifth amendment of the constitution declares 'nor shall any person be subject for the same offense to be twice put in jeopardy of life or limb.' This constitutional guaranty by a liberal construction is held to apply to misdemeanors as well as to treason and felony." Berkowitz v. United States, 93 Fed. 452, 454 (3d Cir.1899).

2. Ex parte Lange, 85 U.S. (18 Wall.) 163, 21 L.Ed. 872 (1874).

3. Strauder v. West Virginia, 100 U.S. (10 Otto) 303, 307, 25 L.Ed. 664, 665 (1880).

The circuit court, in holding that persons in office by lawful appointment or election before the promulgation of the fourteenth amendment were not removed from those offices by the direct and immediate effect of the prohibition contained in the third section of the fourteenth amendment, said:

"In the examination of questions of this sort, great attention is properly paid to the argument from inconvenience. This argument, it is true, can not prevail over plain words or clear reason. But, on the other hand, a construction which must necessarily occasion great public and private mischief, must never be preferred to a construction which will occasion neither, or neither in so great degree, unless the terms of the instrument absolutely require such preference. Let it then be considered what consequences would spring from the literal interpretation contended for in behalf of the petition." Griffin's Case, 11 Fed.Cas. 7, 24 (C.C.D.Va.1869) (No. 5,815).

Fourteenth Amendment as restricting methods of taxation.

"[I]t is important ... to avoid extracting from the very general language of the fourteenth amendment a system of delusive exactness in order to destroy methods of taxation which were well known when that amendment was adopted, and which it is safe to say that no one then supposed would be disturbed." Louis-

---

modern times, restricted the application of the amendment merely because its framers designed it originally to rectify an existing wrong. The amendment was adopted soon after the close of the civil war in order to protect the rights of the newly made citizens to fully enjoy their new freedom. But the fourteenth amendment's present operation is in no respect limited to blacks. Courts apply it universally, extending its protective force over all men and women, of every race and color, who come within the jurisdiction of the states throughout the United States.[4]

Likewise, it has been said that a literal construction of the fifth amendment, which provides that no person shall be compelled to be a witness against himself, would deprive the amendment of much of its efficacy. The privilege against self-incrimination has long been regarded as one of the safeguards of civil liberty. Courts should apply the amendment in a broad spirit, to secure to the citizen immunity from every kind of self-accusation.[5]

§ 23.21   Powers Granted to the Federal Government

Courts should regard the powers confided in the federal government as broadly granted and should not construe them strictly.[1] Such powers should be interpreted as conferring upon the federal government the authority to exercise those powers and to pass those acts

ville & Nashville R. Co. v. Barber Asphalt Paving Co., 197 U.S. 430, 434, 25 S.Ct. 466, 467, 49 L.Ed. 819, 821 (1905).

"The counsel for the state of Maryland insist, with great reason, that if the words of the prohibition be taken in their utmost latitude, they will abridge the power of taxation, which all admit to be essential to the states, to an extent which has never yet been suspected, and will deprive them of resources which are necessary to supply revenue, and which they have heretofore been admitted to possess. These words must therefore be construed with some limitation; and, if this be admitted, they insist, that entering the country is the point of time when the prohibition ceases, and the power of the state to tax commences.

"It may be conceded that the words of the prohibition ought not to be pressed to their utmost extent; that in our complex system, the object of the powers conferred on the government of the Union, and the nature of the often conflicting powers which remain in the states, must always be taken into view, and may aid in expounding the words of any

particular clause. But, while we admit that sound principles of construction ought to restrain all courts from carrying the words of the prohibition beyond the object the constitution is intended to secure, that there must be a point of time when the prohibition ceases, and the power of the state to tax commences; we cannot admit that this point of time is the instant that the articles enter the country. It is, we think, obvious, that this construction would defeat the prohibition." Brown v. Maryland, 25 U.S. (12 Wheat.) 419, 440–41, 6 L.Ed. 678, 686 (1827).

4. Santa Clara County v. Southern Pac. R. Co., 18 Fed. 385 (C.C.Cal.1883), affirmed 118 U.S. 394, 6 S.Ct. 1132, 30 L.Ed. 118 (1886).

5. Counselman v. Hitchcock, 142 U.S. 547, 562, 12 S.Ct. 195, 198, 35 L.Ed. 1110, 1114 (1892); In re Nachman, 114 Fed. 995 (D.C.S.C.1902).

§ 23.21

1. Gibbons v. Ogden, 22 U.S. (9 Wheat.) 1, 6 L.Ed. 23 (1824).

which may be reasonably necessary to carry the powers into full execution. Courts are not to nullify those constitutional powers by astute verbal criticism, without regard to the grand aim and object of the instrument.[2] A remedial power, such as that which extends the judicial power "to controversies between a state and citizens of another state," should also be liberally construed.[3]

The Supreme Court has given the broadest construction to the clause which grants Congress exclusive legislative power over all lands purchased for the erection of forts, magazines, arsenals, dockyards, and other needful buildings. Although such lands are within the territorial boundaries of the states, the Court has construed the clause to cover all structures and all places necessary to carry on the business of the national government.[4]

§ 23.22   Prohibitions and Limitations

Courts should apply the same rule of liberal construction where the Constitution places a prohibition or limitation upon the power of Congress. The prohibition or limitation should be enforced in its spirit

2. Fairbank v. United States, 181 U.S. 283, 289, 21 S.Ct. 648, 650, 45 L.Ed. 862, 865 (1901); Williams v. The Lizzie Henderson, 29 Fed.Cas. 1373 (D.C.S.D.Fla. 1880) (No. 17,726a).

Statute incidentally extending beyond limitation of power.

"It will not do to say that the exercise of an admitted power of congress conferred by the constitution is to be withheld, if it appears, or can be shown, that the effect and operation of the law may incidentally extend beyond the limitation of the power. Upon any such interpretation, the principal object of the framers of the instrument in conferring the power would be sacrificed to the subordinate consequences resulting from its exercise. These consequences and incidents are very proper considerations to be urged upon congress for the purpose of dissuading that body from its exercise, but afford no ground for denying the power itself, or the right to exercise it." Pennsylvania v. Wheeling & Belmont Bridge Co., 59 U.S. (18 How.) 421, 433–34, 15 L.Ed. 435, 438 (1856).

"In the last of the enumerated powers, that which grants, expressly, the means of carrying all others into execution, Congress is authorized 'to make all laws which shall be necessary and proper' for the purpose. But this limitation on the means which may be used, is not extended to the powers which are conferred...." Gibbons v. Ogden, 22 U.S. (9 Wheat.) 1, 187, 6 L.Ed. 23, 68 (1824).

That which is reasonably appropriate and relevant to the exercise of a granted power is to be considered as accompanying the grant. Marshall v. Gordon, 243 U.S. 521, 37 S.Ct. 448, 61 L.Ed. 881 (1917); M'Culloch v. Maryland, 17 U.S. (4 Wheat.) 316, 4 L.Ed. 579 (1819).

See generally, Amar, Of Sovereignty and Federalism, 96 Yale L.J. 1425 (1987).

3. See U.S. Const. art. III, § 2, cl. 1. In 1793, the Supreme Court held that a state could be made a party defendant in any case in the courts of the United States, if the state is sued by a private person who is a citizen of another state. Chisholm v. Georgia, 2 U.S. (2 Dall.) 419, 476, 1 L.Ed. 440, 464, 465 (1793). The next Congress proposed, and the states promptly adopted, the eleventh amendment providing that "the judicial power of the United States shall not be construed to extend to any suit in law or equity commenced or prosecuted against one of the United States by Citizens of another State, or by Citizens or Subjects of any Foreign State."

4. See U.S. Const. art. I, § 8, cl. 17. United States v. Tucker, 122 Fed. 518, 522 (W.D.Ky.1903).

and to its entirety.[1] The limitations on the powers of the states should receive a like interpretation.[2] A court charged with construing the true grants, or the prohibitions and limitations, of a power, must give a full, liberal construction to the language of the Constitution, and aim to show fidelity to the spirit and purpose of the constitutional provision concerning the power.

§ 23.23 Practical Construction Required

Above all, courts should give provisions of the Constitution a practical construction.[1] For example, the protection against self-incrimination was not necessarily designed to protect witnesses from every prejudicial effect resulting from their own testimony; the protection was designed to limit the coercive power of the government. Therefore, the clause should not be construed in a way that unduly impedes, hinders, or obstructs the administration of criminal justice.[2] Courts should not extend the limitations and ample provisions of the Constitution so far as to destroy the necessary powers of the states or prevent the efficient exercise of state power.[3] As Justice Holmes said: "Great constitutional provisions must be administered with caution. Some play must be allowed for the joints of the machine, and it must be

§ 23.22

1. Fairbank v. United States, 181 U.S. 283, 289, 21 S.Ct. 648, 650, 45 L.Ed. 862, 865 (1901).

2. Keokuk Northern Line Packet Co. v. City of Keokuk, 95 U.S. (5 Otto) 80, 87, 24 L.Ed. 377, 381 (1877); Brown v. Maryland, 25 U.S. (12 Wheat.) 419, 438, 6 L.Ed. 678, 685 (1827).

§ 23.23

1. "There are many provisions in the Constitution itself which require the application of the same principle. For instance, it says that 'the citizens of each State shall be entitled to all privileges and immunities of citizens in the several States.' Negroes are citizens of some States, and have the right of suffrage. By a literal construction of the Constitution, any number of negroes may be brought from Massachusetts into Pennsylvania, and control the elections of the latter state; but this is one of the privileges which have never yet been claimed for the African race. In all of these cases, a literal construction would be less absurd than a similar construction of the laws under consideration." Compensation of Laborers in Executive Departments, 9 Op.Att'y.Gen. 117, 120 (1857).

2. Compelling a person to be a witness against himself.
"The clause of the constitution in question is obviously susceptible of two interpretations. If it be construed literally, as authorizing the witness to refuse to disclose any fact which might tend to incriminate, disgrace, or expose him to unfavorable comments, then, as he must necessarily, to a large extent, determine, upon his own conscience and responsibility, whether his answer to the proposed question will have that tendency ..., the practical result would be that no one could be compelled to testify to a material fact in a criminal case, unless he chose to do so, or unless it was entirely clear that the privilege was not set up in good faith. If, upon the other hand, the object of the provision be to secure the witness against a criminal prosecution, which might be aided directly or indirectly by his disclosure, then, if no such prosecution be possible, in other words, if his testimony operate as a complete pardon for the offense to which it relates, a statute absolutely securing to him such immunity from prosecution would satisfy the demands of the clause in question." Brown v. Walker, 161 U.S. 591, 595, 16 S.Ct. 644, 646, 40 L.Ed. 819, 820 (1896).

3. Union Pac. R. Co. v. Peniston, 85 U.S. (18 Wall.) 5, 31, 21 L.Ed. 787, 791 (1873).

remembered that legislatures are ultimate guardians of the liberties and welfare of the people in quite as great a degree as the courts."[4]

VI. THE CONSTRUCTION OF WORDS AND PHRASES IN THE CASE LAW

§ 23.24 Introduction

Words in the Constitution, like words in a statute, presumably retain their common usage meaning, unless persuasive reasons exist to the contrary.[1] Courts should give words their natural and obvious meaning, and not a meaning unreasonably restricted or enlarged.[2] When interpreting the Constitution, courts normally do not reject words or clauses as superfluous or having no meaning. Rather, courts

---

4. Missouri, Kansas & Texas R. Co. v. May, 194 U.S. 267, 270, 24 S.Ct. 638, 639, 48 L.Ed. 971, 973 (1904). In construing the fourteenth amendment, the Court held that a Texas statute directed solely against railroad companies for permitting Johnson grass or Russian thistle to go to seed upon their right of way was not a clear violation of the equal protection clause. 194 U.S. at 270, 24 S.Ct. at 639, 48 L.Ed. at 973.

§ 23.24

1. Tennessee v. Whitworth, 117 U.S. 139, 147, 6 S.Ct. 649, 652, 29 L.Ed. 833, 835 (1886).

Regarding the printing and form of the Constitution see Amar, Our Forgotten Constitution: A Bicentennial Comment, 97 Yale L.J. 281 (1987).

The spirit of the Constitution affects the interpretation of its words.

To construe the language of the Constitution, a court may weigh arguments drawn from the nature of government and the general spirit of the instrument urging narrow construction against arguments drawn from the same sources which urge a broader natural construction. In Cohens v. Virginia, 19 U.S. (6 Wheat.) 264, 5 L.Ed. 257 (1821), the plaintiff in error argued that the judicial power of the government must be coextensive with the legislative power. The Court termed this argument a political axiom and reasoned:

"We do not mean to say, that the jurisdiction of the courts of the Union should be construed to be co-extensive with the legislative, merely because it is fit that it should be so; but we mean to say that this fitness furnishes an argument in construing the constitution, which ought

never to be overlooked, and which is most especially entitled to consideration, when we are inquiring, whether the words of the instrument which purport to establish this principle, shall be contracted for the purpose of destroying it." Cohens v. Virginia, 19 U.S. (6 Wheat.) 264, 384, 5 L.Ed. 257, 286 (1821).

The spirit of an instrument and its words deserve equal weight. The words of an instrument, however, are often the best evidence of its spirit. In one case the Court, faced with a challenge to a plain, uncontradicted provision of the Constitution, concluded that for such a challenge to succeed, the situation must be one "in which the absurdity and injustice of applying the provision to the case, would be so monstrous, that all mankind would, without hesitation, unite in rejecting the application." Sturges v. Crowninshield, 17 U.S. (4 Wheat.) 122, 202–03, 4 L.Ed. 529, 550 (1819). See also Jacobson v. Massachusetts, 197 U.S. 11, 22, 25 S.Ct. 358, 359, 49 L.Ed. 643, 648 (1905).

2. Pollock v. Farmers' Loan & Trust Co., 158 U.S. 601, 618, 15 S.Ct. 912, 913, 39 L.Ed. 1108, 1109 (1895); Martin v. Hunter's Lessee, 14 U.S. (1 Wheat.) 304, 326, 4 L.Ed. 97, 102 (1816).

The words expressing the various grants in the Constitution are words of general import. Courts should construe them as such, and as granting the powers named to their full extent. Fairbank v. United States, 181 U.S. 283, 287, 21 S.Ct. 648, 650, 45 L.Ed. 862, 864 (1901).

give each word or clause its due force and appropriate meaning.[3]
Words should receive the same construction as that given to them at
common law and at the adoption of the Constitution and the amendments.[4] At that time, the framers presumably used the normal or
ordinary, as distinguished from the technical, meaning of the words.[5]
Where any particular word or sentence standing alone is obscure or of
doubtful meaning, the obscurity of the word or sentence may be
removed by comparing it with the words and sentences which surround
it.[6]

3. Wright v. United States, 302 U.S.
583, 58 S.Ct. 395, 82 L.Ed. 439 (1938);
Knowlton v. Moore, 178 U.S. 41, 87, 20
S.Ct. 747, 765, 44 L.Ed. 969, 987 (1900).

The plain, obvious meaning of the words
should control. Jacobson v. Massachusetts, 197 U.S. 11, 22, 25 S.Ct. 358, 359, 49
L.Ed. 643, 648 (1905).

Agreement and compact

"When, therefore, the second clause declares that no state shall enter into 'any
agreement or compact' with a foreign
power without the assent of Congress,
the words 'agreement' and 'compact' cannot be construed as synonymous with
one another; and still less can either of
them be held to mean the same thing
with the word 'treaty' in the preceding
clause, into which the states are positively and unconditionally forbidden to enter; and which even the consent of Congress could not authorize." Holmes v.
Jennison, 39 U.S. (14 Pet.) 540, 571, 10
L.Ed. 579, 595 (1840).

See also Virginia v. Tennessee, 148 U.S.
503, 519, 13 S.Ct. 728, 734, 37 L.Ed. 537,
543 (1893) ("agreement" and "compact"
construed as any combination tending to
increase power in the states while en-
croaching on political supremacy of the
United States).

Due process of law

"According to a recognized canon of interpretation, especially applicable to formal and solemn instruments of constitutional law, we are forbidden to assume,
without clear reason to the contrary,
that any part of this most important
amendment is superfluous. The natural
and obvious inference is, that in the
sense of the Constitution, 'due process of
law' was not meant or intended to include, *ex vi termini,* the institution and
procedure of a grand jury in any case.
The conclusion is equally irresistible
that when the same phrase was employed in the Fourteenth Amendment to

restrain the action of the States, it was
used in the same sense and with no
greater extent; and that if in the adoption of that amendment it had been part
of its purpose to perpetuate the institution of the grand jury in all the States, it
would have embodied, as did the Fifth
Amendment, express declarations to that
effect." Hurtado v. California, 110 U.S.
516, 534–35, 4 S.Ct. 111, 120–21, 28 L.Ed.
232, 238 (1884).

4. South Carolina v. United States, 199
U.S. 437, 450, 26 S.Ct. 110, 111, 50 L.Ed.
261, 265 (1905) (extent of grants of power
construed as Framers understood the scope
of those grants); Veazie Bank v. Fenno, 75
U.S. (8 Wall.) 533, 542, 19 L.Ed. 482, 486
(1869); Locke v. New Orleans, 71 U.S. (4
Wall.) 172, 174, 18 L.Ed. 334, 335 (1866);
Gibbons v. Ogden, 22 U.S. (9 Wheat.) 1,
11–13, 6 L.Ed. 23, 25–26 (1824); United
States v. Block, 24 Fed.Cas. 1174, 1175
(D.C.Or.1877) (No. 14,609); United States v.
Harris, 26 Fed.Cas. 174, 175 (D.C.Ky.1866)
(No. 15,312); Pardoning Power of Presi-
dent, 5 Op.Atty.Gen. 532, 536 (1852).

5. United States v. Sprague, 282 U.S.
716, 731, 51 S.Ct. 220, 222, 75 L.Ed. 640,
644 (1931).

6. Rhode Island v. Massachusetts, 37
U.S. (12 Pet.) 657, 722, 9 L.Ed. 1233, 1259
(1838); Wheaton v. Peters, 33 U.S. (8 Pet.)
591, 661, 8 L.Ed. 1055, 1080 (1834); Beck-
with v. United States, 16 Ct.Cl. 250, 261
(1880).

The Court has recognized that the word
necessary does not have a unique, fixed
character; rather the words surrounding it
color its meaning.

"It is, we think, impossible to compare
the sentence which prohibits a state
from laying 'impost, or duties on imports
or exports, except what may be *absolutely* necessary for executing its inspection
laws,' with that which authorizes con-

§ 23.25 Interpretation at the Time of Adoption

The Constitution should be construed in the sense in which those who adopted it understood its words and terms.[1] Courts do not ordinarily give words narrower meanings than the words had in common parlance at the time when the clauses to be construed were written.[2] For example, the term *"ex post "* facto, literally construed, would describe any act operating upon a previous fact. Yet the term was understood at the time the Constitution was adopted, both in this country and in England, to embrace only criminal laws and laws providing for the recovery of penalties or forfeitures.[3]

gress 'to make all laws which shall be necessary and proper for carrying into execution' the powers of the general government, without feeling a conviction, that the convention understood itself to change materially the meaning of the word 'necessary,' by prefixing the word 'absolutely.' " M'Culloch v. Maryland, 17 U.S. (4 Wheat.) 316, 413, 4 L.Ed. 579, 603 (1819).

The subject, the context, and the intention of the person using the words are relevant to the construction of words which may be used in various senses. Id.

In view of the combination of the two words "just" and "compensation" in the Fifth Amendment, "[t]here ... can be no doubt that the compensation must be a full and perfect equivalent for the property taken." Monongahela Navigation Co. v. United States, 148 U.S. 312, 326, 13 S.Ct. 622, 626, 37 L.Ed. 463, 468 (1893).

See also Campbell v. Morris, 3 H. & McH. 535, 554 (Md.1797) ("The way to expound a clause in the general government or Constitution of the *United States,* is by comparing it with other parts, and considering them together....").

See also Richardson v. Ramirez, 418 U.S. 24, 94 S.Ct. 2655, 41 L.Ed.2d 551 (1974), certiorari denied 418 U.S. 904, 94 S.Ct. 3194, 41 L.Ed.2d 1152 (1974). The issue in this case was whether the disenfranchisement of ex-felons was an equal protection violation. The Court construed section 1 of the fourteenth amendment in light of the express exemption for citizens disenfranchised by the commission of crimes from the sanction of lesser representation in Congress. The Court concluded:

"[W]e may rest on the demonstrably sound proposition that § 1, in dealing with voting rights as it does, could not have been meant to bar outright a form of disenfranchisement which was expressly exempted from the less drastic sanction of reduced representation which § 2 imposed for other forms of disenfranchisement. Nor can we accept respondents' argument that because § 2 was made part of the amendment largely through the accident of political exigency rather than through the relation which it bore to the other Sections of the Amendment, we must not look to for guidance in interpreting § 1. It is as much a part of the amendment as any of the other Sections, and how it became part of the amendment is less important than what it says and what it means." 418 U.S. at 55, 94 S.Ct. at 2671, 41 L.Ed.2d at 571.

§ 23.25

1. The Huntress, 12 Fed.Cas. 984, 988–89 (D.Me.1840) (No. 6,914); Padelford, Fay & Co. v. Mayor and Aldermen of Savannah, 14 Ga. 438, 445–46 (1854).

When construing the language of the Constitution, the courts should put themselves as nearly as possible in the position of the men who framed that instrument. Ex parte Bain, 121 U.S. 1, 12, 7 S.Ct. 781, 787, 30 L.Ed. 849, 853 (1887).

2. United States v. South–Eastern Underwriters Ass'n, 322 U.S. 533, 539, 64 S.Ct. 1162, 1166, 88 L.Ed. 1440, 1449 (1944), rehearing denied 323 U.S. 811, 65 S.Ct. 26, 89 L.Ed. 646 (1944).

3. Locke v. New Orleans, 71 U.S. (4 Wall.) 172, 174, 18 L.Ed. 334, 335 (1866); Carpenter v. Pennsylvania, 58 U.S. (17 How.) 456, 463, 15 L.Ed. 127, 129 (1854).

§ 23.26 Particular Powers, Duties, and Rights

Courts often consider the nature and objects of the particular powers, duties, and rights they are interpreting in the light of, and with the aid of, contemporary history; they should give the words to be construed just such operation and force, consistent with the words' legitimate meaning, as may fairly secure and attain the ends proposed.[1] Where the Constitution expressly confers a power in general terms, courts should not restrict the power unless that restrictive construction grows out of the historical context either expressly or by necessary implication.[2]

§ 23.27 Liberal Construction

Courts should generally construe words and sentences liberally, and avoid technical constructions.[1] Where the text is clear and dis-

§ 23.26

1. Virginia v. Tennessee, 148 U.S. 503, 519, 13 S.Ct. 728, 734, 37 L.Ed. 537, 543 (1893); Prigg v. Pennsylvania, 41 U.S. (16 Pet.) 539, 610–11, 10 L.Ed. 1060, 1087 (1842); Kendall v. United States, 37 U.S. (12 Pet.) 524, 609, 9 L.Ed. 1181, 1214 (1838); State v. Gibson, 36 Ind. 389, 391 (1871).

2. Martin v. Hunter's Lessee, 14 U.S. (1 Wheat.) 304, 332, 4 L.Ed. 97, 104 (1816) (noting that the mode of judicial power is not limited in the Constitution, and thus it may extend to all cases in which judicial power may be exercised).

§ 23.27

1. Lane County v. Oregon, 74 U.S. (7 Wall.) 71, 79, 19 L.Ed. 101, 105 (1868); President's Power to Fill Vacancies in Recess of Senate, 12 Op.Atty.Gen. 32, 35 (1866).

"In performing the delicate and important duty of construing clauses in the constitution of our country, which involve conflicting powers of the government of the Union, and of the respective states, it is proper to take a view of the literal meaning of the words to be expounded, of their connection with other words, and of the general objects to be accomplished by the prohibitory clause, or by the grant of power." Brown v. Maryland, 25 U.S. (12 Wheat.) 419, 436, 6 L.Ed. 678, 684 (1827).

Writings. The word "writings" in article I, section 8, clause 8 gives Congress the power to grant to authors exclusive rights over their respective writings. "Writings" should be liberally construed to include original designs for engravings, prints, and so forth, but only as they are original and

are founded in the creative powers of the mind. See In re Trade–Mark Cases, 100 U.S. (10 Otto) 82, 94, 25 L.Ed. 550, 552 (1879).

Appointment to "vacancies that may happen." The President may fill by temporary commission, during a recess of the Senate, a vacancy that occurred during a previous Senate session. The issue arises whether the word "happen" should be interpreted as being equivalent to "happen to exist." Arguably, the relevant language could be construed to limit the President's power to fill vacancies to those vacancies that "happen" during the actual Senate recess. The United States Attorney General has recognized that this construction, although perhaps more consonant with the language—

"... overlooks the spirit, reason, and purpose; and, like all constructions merely literal, its tendency is to defeat the substantial meaning of the instrument, and to produce the most embarrassing inconveniences." Executive Authority to Fill Vacancies, 1 Op.Atty.Gen. 631, 633 (1823).

The Attorney General advocated the "happen to exist" construction. He reasoned that such a construction acknowledges both the high responsibility and brief tenure of the presidency and the policy objective that vacancies be regularly and expeditiously filled. Id.

Similarly, the Supreme Court gave the word "charged," as it appears in the phrase "fugitive from justice charged with a crime," a broad meaning. "... [O]rdinarily words [in the Constitution] do not receive a narrow, contracted meaning, but

tinct, no restriction on its plain and obvious meaning should be admitted unless the inference is irresistible.[2]

§ 23.28 Transposition of Words and Sentences

Often, in considering ordinary legislation, the court may transpose the words and sentences of a law in order to achieve what the court views as the intent of the legislature, as gathered from other parts of the law or from the entire scope. Yet the Supreme Court has held that it should not ordinarily transpose language when construing the Constitution, because the language of the Constitution was so maturely considered by its framers, and so severely examined and criticized by its opponents.[1]

§ 23.29 Affirmative and Negative Words

A court can imply a negative operation from affirmative words only where the implication promotes, and does not defeat, the obvious intention of an article. The Court must consider every part of the article, and adopt that construction which will promote the article's general intention most consistently with its words. Thus, in the case of the grant to the Supreme Court of original jurisdiction in certain cases, a court must imply a negative or exclusive operation or the grant has no effect.[1] But in the grant of appellate jurisdiction, jurisdiction may be exercised in every case cognizable under article III of the Constitution in the federal courts, which cannot exercise original jurisdiction. The extent of this judicial power is measured, not by giving the affirmative words of the distributive clause a negative operation in

are presumed to have been used in a broad sense, with a view of covering all contingencies." Matter of Strauss, 197 U.S. 324, 330, 25 S.Ct. 535, 536, 49 L.Ed. 774, 778 (1905).

The Court has said that the "taking" provision in the Constitution "has received the commendation of jurists, statesmen and commentators as placing the just principles of the common law on that subject beyond the power of ordinary legislation to change or control them." Pumpelly v. Green Bay & Mississippi Canal Co., 80 U.S. (13 Wall.) 166, 177–78, 20 L.Ed. 557, 560 (1871). The Court declined to hold that only absolute conversion of real property to public use constituted a "taking." A narrow construction of "taking" would permit the Government to destroy the value of real property entirely without making compensation if such property was not "taken" in its narrow sense, for public use:

"Such a construction would pervert the constitutional provision into a restriction upon the rights of the citizen, as those rights stood at the common law, instead of the government, and make it an authority for invasion of private right under the pretext of the public good, which had no warrant in the laws or practices of our ancestors." Id.

Thus, a clause that would otherwise be given a broad interpretation may be limited by the more specific requirements of another clause.

2. Martin v. Hunter's Lessee, 14 U.S. (1 Wheat.) 304, 4 L.Ed. 97 (1816).

§ 23.28

1. Ogden v. Saunders, 25 U.S. (12 Wheat.) 213, 267–68, 6 L.Ed. 606, 624 (1827).

§ 23.29

1. Ex parte Vallandigham, 68 U.S. (1 Wall.) 243, 252, 17 L.Ed. 589, 593 (1863); Marbury v. Madison, 5 U.S. (1 Cranch) 137, 174, 2 L.Ed. 60, 72 (1803).

every possible case, but by giving the words which define its extent their natural meaning.[2]

VII.   THE VIEWS OF THE CASE LAW ON CONTEMPORANEOUS AND SUBSEQUENT PRACTICAL CONSTRUCTION

§ 23.30   Ambiguity or Doubt

Where a court considers the meaning of the word "plain" and "clear," to the extent any words can be said to be either, courts typically state that the words leave no room for construction and provide no excuse for interpolation.[1] In such cases, courts also say that collateral aids to interpretation are unnecessary and impermissible, and the court will not use them to narrow or enlarge the text. But where there is ambiguity or doubt, or where two views are equally reasonable, contemporaneous and subsequent practical construction of the text is entitled to the greatest weight.[2] The correct meaning of a constitutional provision must be unclear, however, before courts can apply practical construction.[3]

2. The affirmative grant of original jurisdiction to the Supreme Court of the United States "in all cases . . . in which a state shall be a party" does not prevent the Court from constitutionally exercising appellate jurisdiction in a case in which a state is a party and in which a federal question is involved. Cohens v. Virginia, 19 U.S. (6 Wheat.) 264, 394, 5 L.Ed. 257, 288–89 (1821).

§ 23.30

1. United States v. Sprague, 282 U.S. 716, 731, 51 S.Ct. 220, 221, 75 L.Ed. 640, 643 (1931). Munn v. Illinois, 94 U.S. (4 Otto) 113, 123, 24 L.Ed. 77, 83 (1876) (saying that in order to determine the significance of the word "deprive" as used in the fourteenth amendment, a court must determine its meaning when used in similar circumstances).

Under the constitutional provision that a bill not returned by the President to the House where it originated within 10 days shall become a law, "unless the Congress by their Adjournment prevent its Return, in which Case it shall not be a Law," the quoted words are entirely free from ambiguity, so that there is no occasion for construction. Wright v. United States, 302 U.S. 583, 587, 58 S.Ct. 395, 396, 82 L.Ed. 439, 442 (1938).

2. McPherson v. Blacker, 146 U.S. 1, 27, 13 S.Ct. 3, 7, 36 L.Ed. 869, 874 (1892). See

also Oneida Indian Nation v. New York, 691 F.2d 1070 (2d Cir.1982), appeal after remand 732 F.2d 259 (2d Cir.1984), on remand 102 F.R.D. 450 (N.D.N.Y.1984), case remanded 757 F.2d 19 (2d Cir.1985) where the court said:

"Thus, in ruling upon the motion to dismiss, the district court was faced with the difficult task of interpreting pertinent provisions of the Articles [of Confederation], some of which appeared on their face to be ambiguous, with possible internal inconsistencies. It is the court's duty in such circumstances to make every effort give [sic] effect to every word of a constitution, [citations omitted], to resolve ambiguities, and to reconcile inconsistencies. The starting point. Of course, is the language of the pertinent Articles of Confederation. [Citation omitted]. Where, as here, the language is ambiguous, contemporary construction and Congress' own interpretation are entitled to weight. [Cites omitted]. The surrounding circumstances, including custom, usage, and the factual context in which the words were used, may also be of importance in resolving a facial ambiguity or inconsistency." 691 F.2d at 1085–86.

3. Fairbank v. United States, 181 U.S. 283, 307, 21 S.Ct. 648, 657, 45 L.Ed. 862, 872 (1901); McPherson v. Blacker, 146 U.S.

§ 23.31   Stare Decisis

Especially in cases of unclear meaning, courts ought to decide issues of interpretation in favor of a well-established construction, even though the present judges would have decided the issue differently if it had come to them as an issue of first impression.[1] The solemn, deliberate, well-considered, and long-settled decisions of the judiciary, and the quiet assent of the people to an unbroken and unvarying practice, weigh heavily in favor of the established construction.[2]

§ 23.32   Contemporaneous Construction of the Constitution

The general rule is that courts should use a contemporaneous construction of a statute by those charged with executing the statute. Courts should adopt this rule for constitutional construction, unless cogent reasons compel the opposite result.[1] This rule applies with even greater force to a court construing a well-settled provision of the Constitution, unless the court finds the construction clearly erroneous.[2] Contemporary construction of the Constitution is very relevant[3] and courts should give it great weight.[4] Acquiescence to such construction,

1, 27, 13 S.Ct. 3, 7, 36 L.Ed. 869, 874 (1892); M'Culloch v. Maryland, 17 U.S. (4 Wheat.) 316, 401, 4 L.Ed. 579, 600 (1819).

§ 23.31

1. Missouri v. Illinois, 180 U.S. 208, 219, 21 S.Ct. 331, 335, 45 L.Ed. 497, 504 (1901); Provident Institution v. Massachusetts, 73 U.S. (6 Wall.) 611, 626, 18 L.Ed. 907, 912 (1867); Martin v. Hunter's Lessee, 14 U.S. (1 Wheat.) 304, 351, 4 L.Ed. 97, 109 (1816); The Huntress, 12 Fed.Cas. 984, 994 (D.C.Me.1840) (No. 6,914); Ferris v. Coover, 11 Cal. 175, 179 (1858); Thayer v. Hedges, 23 Ind. 141, 147 (1864).

2. Findley v. Satterfield, 9 Fed.Cas. 67, 68 (C.C.Ga.1877) (No. 4,792); Ex rel. Gist, 26 Ala. 156, 164 (1855); Ferris v. Coover, 11 Cal. 175, 178–79 (1858); State v. Davis, 12 S.C. 528, 534 (1879). But see Edelman v. Jordan, 415 U.S. 651, 671, 94 S.Ct. 1347, 39 L.Ed.2d 662, 677 (1974), (stating that when dealing with a constitutional question, a court is less constrained by the principles of *stare decisis* than in other areas of the law), on remand 551 F.2d 152 (7th Cir.1977)

§ 23.32

1. Stuart v. Laird, 5 U.S. (1 Cranch) 299, 309, 2 L.Ed. 115, 118 (1803).

However, creation of after-the-fact legislative history through the *post hoc* declara-

tions of interested onlookers, is entitled to no weight. Western Air Lines, Inc. v. Board of Equalization of State of South Dakota, 480 U.S. 123, 131 n. *, 107 S.Ct. 1038, 1043 n. **, 94 L.Ed.2d 112 (1987).

2. United States v. Midwest Oil Co., 236 U.S. 459, 474, 35 S.Ct. 309, 313, 59 L.Ed. 673, 681 (1915); Field v. Clark, 143 U.S. 649, 691, 12 S.Ct. 495, 504, 36 L.Ed. 294, 309 (1892); M'Culloch v. Maryland, 17 U.S. (4 Wheat.) 316, 4 L.Ed. 579 (1819); Adams v. Storey, 1 Fed.Cas. 141 (C.C.N.Y.1817) (No. 66); James v. United States, 38 Ct.Cl. 615, 631 (1902), reversed on other grounds 202 U.S. 401, 26 S.Ct. 685, 50 L.Ed. 1079 (1906).

See generally, The Role of Precedent in Constitutional Decisionmaking and Theory, 60 Geo.Wash.L.Rev. 67 (1991).

3. Myers v. United States, 272 U.S. 52, 175, 47 S.Ct. 21, 45, 71 L.Ed. 160, 190 (1926); The Laura, 114 U.S. 411, 416, 5 S.Ct. 881, 883, 29 L.Ed. 147, 148 (1885); M'Culloch v. Maryland, 17 U.S. (4 Wheat.) 316, 4 L.Ed. 579 (1819).

4. United States v. Moore, 95 U.S. (5 Otto) 760, 763, 24 L.Ed. 588, 589 (1877); Murray v. Hoboken Land & Improvement Co., 59 U.S. (18 How.) 272, 279–80, 15 L.Ed. 372, 375 (1856); The Propeller Genesee Chief v. Fitzhugh, 53 U.S. (12 How.) 443,

in practice, for a period of years, may afford an irresistible answer to objection and thus fix the proper construction.[5] For example, when the

458, 13 L.Ed. 1058, 1065 (1851); Cooley v. Board of Wardens, 53 U.S. (12 How.) 299, 315, 13 L.Ed. 996, 1003 (1851). State v. Keyes, 8 Vt. 57, 64 (1836) (refusing to adopt a construction of the fifth amendment that would extend its protections to trials in state courts as wholly at variance with contemporaneous construction and subsequent practice).

A distress warrant, issued by the Solicitor of the Treasury under an Act of Congress, was upheld against a due process challenge:

> "This legislative construction of the constitution, commencing so early in the government, when the first occasion for this manner of proceeding arose, continued throughout its existence, and repeatedly acted on by the judiciary and the executive, is entitled to no inconsiderable weight upon the question whether the proceeding adopted by it was 'due process of law.' " Murray v. Hoboken Land & Improvement Co., 59 U.S. (18 How.) 272, 279–80, 15 L.Ed. 372, 375 (1856).

5. J.W. Hampton, Jr. & Co. v. United States, 276 U.S. 394, 48 S.Ct. 348, 72 L.Ed. 624 (1928).

Congress' interpretation of the Constitution, that it has the right to invest the Secretary of the Treasury with power to remit penalties, proved "too strong and obstinate to be shaken or controlled." The Laura, 114 U.S. 411, 416, 5 S.Ct. 881, 883, 29 L.Ed. 147, 148 (1885).

See also Burrow–Giles Lithographic Co. v. Sarony, 111 U.S. 53, 57, 4 S.Ct. 279, 280, 28 L.Ed. 349, 351 (1884) (long-standing interpretation of the Constitution "almost conclusive"); Postal Conventions with Foreign Countries, 19 Op.Att'y Gen. 513, 514 (1890); Ex rel. Gist, 26 Ala. 156 (1855); Lick v. Faulkner, 25 Cal. 404, 407 (1864); Ferris v. Coover, 11 Cal. 175, 178 (1858) (enduring interpretation entitled to "controlling weight").

The Supreme Court responded to objections about justices of the Supreme Court sitting as circuit judges without holding distinct commissions for that purpose by saying:

> "To this objection, which is of recent date, it is sufficient to observe, that practice, and acquiescence under it, for a period of several years, commencing with the organization of the judicial system, affords an irresistible answer, and has indeed fixed the construction. It is a contemporary interpretation of the most forcible nature. This practical exposition is too strong and obstinate to be shaken or controlled. Of course, the question is at rest, and ought not now to be disturbed." Stuart v. Laird, 5 U.S. (1 Cranch) 299, 308, 2 L.Ed. 115, 118 (1803).

The Court has noted that the grant of appellate jurisdiction over state courts is well-settled.

> "This weight of contemporaneous exposition by all parties, this acquiescence of enlightened state courts, and these judicial decisions of the supreme court, through so long a period, do, as we think, place the doctrine upon a foundation of authority which cannot be shaken, without delivering over the subject to perpetual and irremediable doubts." Martin v. Hunter's Lessee, 14 U.S. (1 Wheat.) 304, 351–52, 4 L.Ed. 97, 109 (1816).

The Court has also recognized that the power of Congress to delegate to the states the authority to make regulations respecting mining claims is well established by usage.

> "It has been acted upon as valid through all the mining regions of the country. Property rights have been built up on the faith of it. To now strike it down would unsettle countless titles and work manifold injury to the great mining interests of the Far West. While, of course, consequences may not determine a decision, yet in a doubtful case the court may well pause before thereby it unsettles interests so many and so vast— interests which have been built up on the faith not merely of Congressional action, but also of judicial decisions of many state courts sustaining it, and of a frequent recognition of its validity by this court." Butte City Water Co. v. Baker, 196 U.S. 119, 127, 25 S.Ct. 211, 213, 49 L.Ed. 409, 412 (1905).

See also Ray v. Blair, 343 U.S. 214, 72 S.Ct. 654, 96 L.Ed. 894 (1952) (looking at past practice in order to determine whether an elector could constitutionally be required to pledge his vote in the electoral college for his party's candidate). The Court said:

> "This long-continued practical interpretation of the constitutional propriety of

text is unclear, powers of execution granted by the Constitution may be established by usage.[6]

§ 23.33 Congressional Interpretation and the Uses of History

A congressional construction of the Constitution that has prevailed since the founding of the federal government is also entitled to great respect.[1] The weight courts should give the congressional legislation in determining how to construe the Constitution depends on the nature of the question, the attitude of the executive and judicial branches, and the number of instances in the execution of the law affording opportunity for objection.[2]

Long acquiescence of Congress and the Executive, however, does not make constitutional that which is unconstitutional.[3] Statutes or

an implied or oral pledge of his ballot by a candidate for elector as to his vote in the electoral college weighs heavily in considering the constitutionality of a pledge such as the one here required in the primary." 343 U.S. at 229–30, 72 S.Ct. at 662, 96 L.Ed. at 169.

6. Inland Waterways Corp. v. Young, 309 U.S. 517, 524, 60 S.Ct. 646, 650, 84 L.Ed. 901, 906 (1940), rehearing denied 309 U.S. 698, 60 S.Ct. 884, 84 L.Ed. 1037 (1940); United States v. Midwest Oil Co., 236 U.S. 459, 473, 35 S.Ct. 309, 313, 59 L.Ed. 673, 681 (1915); Indiana v. Killigrew, 117 F.2d 863, 868 (7th Cir.1941).

§ 23.33

1. Ex Parte Quirin, 317 U.S. 1, 41, 63 S.Ct. 2, 17, 87 L.Ed. 3, 19 (1942), order modified ___ U.S. ___, 63 S.Ct. 22, ___ L.Ed. ___ (1942). See also Dames & Moore v. Regan, 453 U.S. 654, 101 S.Ct. 2972, 69 L.Ed.2d 918 (1981). The Court discussed the effect of past practice on constitutional interpretation regarding the power of the executive branch.

"Past practice does not, by itself, create power but 'long-continued practice, known to and acquiesced in by Congress, would raise a presumption that the [action] has been [taken] in pursuance of its consent.'" 453 U.S. at 686, 101 S.Ct. at 2990, 69 L.Ed.2d at 944.

Similarly, in Haig v. Agee, 453 U.S. 280, 101 S.Ct. 2766, 69 L.Ed.2d 640 (1981), the Court gave great weight to past practice when determining the extent of the Secretary of State's authority to revoke passports. The Court explained:

"The history of passport controls since the earliest days of the Republic shows Congressional recognition of Executive authority to withhold passports on the basis of substantial reasons of national security and foreign policy. Prior to 1856, when there was no statute on the subject, the common perception was that the issuance of a passport was committed to the sole discretion of the Executive and that the Executive would exercise this power in the interests of the national security and foreign policy of the United States." 453 U.S. at 293, 101 S.Ct. at 2775, 69 L.Ed.2d at 653.

2. Myers v. United States, 272 U.S. 52, 170, 47 S.Ct. 21, 43, 71 L.Ed. 160, 188 (1926).

On the other hand, a party to litigation should not be able to create legislative history for a statute or for a constitutional provision merely by providing after-the-fact statements or purported history subsequently supplied by interested onlookers. See, Western Air Lines, Inc. v. Board of Equalization of State of South Dakota, 480 U.S. 123, 130 n. **, 107 S.Ct. 1038, 1043 n. **, 94 L.Ed.2d 112 (1987).

3. James v. United States, 38 Ct.Cl. 615, 631 (1902), reversed on other grounds 202 U.S. 401, 26 S.Ct. 685, 50 L.Ed. 1079 (1906). See also Immigration and Naturalization Service v. Chadha, 462 U.S. 919, 103 S.Ct. 2764, 77 L.Ed.2d 317 (1983). In Chadha, the Court rejected past practice as a justification for a legislative veto that did not include both houses of Congress:

"[T]he fact that a given law or procedure is efficient, convenient, and useful in fa-

practices inconsistent with the Constitution, however numerous, cannot create a power that the Constitution does not bestow nor furnish a construction that the Constitution does not warrant.[4] Yet, as Justice Holmes has noted: "If a thing has been practiced for two hundred years by common consent, it will need a strong case for the Fourteenth Amendment to affect it...."[5]

cilitating functions of government, standing alone, will not save it if it is contrary to the Constitution. Convenience and efficiency are not the primary objectives—or the hallmarks—of democratic government and our inquiry is sharpened rather than blunted by the fact that congressional veto provisions are appearing with increasing frequency in statutes which delegate authority to executive and independent agencies...." 462 U.S. at 944, 103 S.Ct. at 2780, 77 L.Ed.2d at 340.

The Court in Nixon v. Administrator of General Services, 433 U.S. 425, 97 S.Ct. 2777, 53 L.Ed.2d 867 (1977) also rejected past practice as a justification for an absolute privilege of confidentiality for presidential records.

4. Field v. Clark, 143 U.S. 649, 691, 12 S.Ct. 495, 504, 36 L.Ed. 294, 309 (1892); United States v. Boyer, 85 Fed. 425 (W.D.Mo.1898).

5. Jackman v. Rosenbaum Co., 260 U.S. 22, 31, 43 S.Ct. 9, 10, 67 L.Ed. 107, 112 (1922).

In Marsh v. Chambers, 463 U.S. 783, 103 S.Ct. 3330, 77 L.Ed.2d 1019 (1983), the Supreme Court upheld, against a challenge claiming a violation of the establishment clause, the practice of the Nebraska legislature of opening each session with a prayer by a chaplain paid by public funds:

"From colonial times through the founding of the Republic and ever since, the practice of legislative prayer has coexisted with the principles of disestablishment and religious freedom. In the very courtroom in which the United States District Judge and later three Circuit Judges heard and decided this case, the proceedings opened with an announcement that concluded, 'God save the United States and this Honorable Court.' The same invocation occurs at all sessions of this Court.

"The tradition in many of the colonies was, of course, linked to an established church, but the Continental Congress, beginning in 1774, adopted the traditional procedure of opening its sessions with

a prayer offered by a paid chaplain.... Although prayers were not offered during the Constitutional Convention, the First Congress, as one of its early items of business, adopted the policy of selecting a chaplain to open each session with prayer.... On April 25, 1789, the Senate elected its first chaplain, J. of the Sen. 16; the House followed suit on May 1, 1789, J. of the H.R. 26. A statute providing for the payment of these chaplains was enacted into law on Sept. 22, 1789. 2 Annals of Cong. 2180; 1 Stat. 71.

"On Sept. 25, 1789, three days after Congress authorized the appointment of paid chaplains, final agreement was reached on the language of the Bill of Rights, J. of the Sen. 88; J. of the H.R. 121. Clearly the men who wrote the First Amendment Religion Clause did not view paid legislative chaplains and opening prayers as a violation of that Amendment, for the practice of opening sessions with prayer has continued without interruption ever since that early session of Congress. It has also been followed consistently in most of the states....

"Standing alone, historical patterns cannot justify contemporary violations of constitutional guarantees, but there is far more here than simply historical patterns. In this context, historical evidence sheds light not only on what the draftsmen intended the Establishment clause to mean, but also on how they thought that Clause applied to the practice authorized by the First Congress—their actions reveal their intent." 463 U.S. at 786–90, 103 S.Ct. at 3333–34, 77 L.Ed.2d at 1024–26 (footnotes omitted).

In Walz v. Tax Com'n, 397 U.S. 664, 678, 90 S.Ct. 1409, 1416, 25 L.Ed.2d 697, 706 (1970), the Court upheld a state law granting property tax exemptions to religious organizations used solely for religious worship and said:

"It is obviously correct that no one acquires a vested or protected right in violation of the Constitution by long use,

§ 23.34 Legislation Enacted Soon After the Adoption of the Constitutional Provision Subject to Interpretation

Congressional legislation enacted immediately following the adoption of the Constitution, legislation enacted at the time Congress proposed an amendment, or legislation enacted immediately following the proposal or adoption of an amendment, is significant in determining the scope of a constitutional provision.[1] Such legislation is thus entitled to great weight.[2] For example, the first Congress of the United States proposed the Bill of Rights, the first ten amendments to the Constitution, at its first session, on September 25, 1789. At the same

even when that span of time covers our entire national existence and indeed predates it. Yet an unbroken practice ... is not something to be lightly cast aside."

§ 23.34

1. An Act "passed by the first Congress assembled under the Constitution, many of whose members had taken part in framing that instrument, ... is contemporaneous and weighty evidence of its true meaning." Wisconsin v. Pelican Ins. Co., 127 U.S. 265, 297, 8 S.Ct. 1370, 1377, 32 L.Ed. 239 (1888).

J.W. Hampton Jr., & Co. v. United States, 276 U.S. 394, 48 S.Ct. 348, 72 L.Ed. 624 (1928); Myers v. United States, 272 U.S. 52, 47 S.Ct. 21, 71 L.Ed. 160 (1926); Waring v. Clarke, 46 U.S. (5 How.) 441, 456, 12 L.Ed. 226, 233 (1847); Ogden v. Saunders, 25 U.S. (12 Wheat.) 213, 6 L.Ed. 606 (1827); Stuart v. Laird, 5 U.S. (1 Cranch) 299, 2 L.Ed. 115 (1803).

2. The opinions of the early Congress are entitled to at least as much authority as the opinions of the authors of the Federalist. Cohens v. Virginia, 19 U.S. (6 Wheat.) 264, 420, 5 L.Ed. 257, 295 (1821).

The practical construction put upon a provision of the Constitution by Congress at the time of the organization of the government is very persuasive, particularly where no court of the United States has ever adjudicated to the contrary. Ames v. Kansas, 111 U.S. 449, 469, 4 S.Ct. 437, 446, 28 L.Ed. 482, 490 (1884).

See also, United States v. Villamonte–Marquez, 462 U.S. 579, 103 S.Ct. 2573, 77 L.Ed.2d 22 (1983), on remand 714 F.2d 428 (5th Cir.1983). The Court upheld 19 U.S.C.A. § 1581(a), rejecting a claim that it violated the fourth amendment search and seizure protections. Section 1581(a) provides that "[a]ny officer of the customs may at any time go on board of any vessel

... at any place in the United States ... and examine the manifest and other documents and papers ... and to this end may hail and stop such vessel ... and use all necessary force to compel compliance." The defendants asserted that this statute violated the fourth amendment because it authorized customs officials, without any suspicion of wrongdoing, to board, for inspection of documents, a vessel locateed in waters providing ready access to the open sea. The Supreme Court disagreed, and reasoned:

"In 1790 the First Congress enacted a comprehensive statute to provide more effectually for the collection of the duties imposed by law on goods, wares and merchandise imported into the United States, and on the tonnage of ships or vessels. Act of Aug. 4, 1790, ch. 35, 1 Stat. 145.... This statute appears to be the lineal ancestor of the provision of present law upon which the government relies to sustain the boarding of the vessel in this case.... We of course agree with respondents' argument that 'no Act of Congress can authorize a violation of the Constitution,' Almedia Sanchez v. United States, 413 U.S. 266, 272, 93 S.Ct. 2535, 2539, 37 L.Ed.2d 596 (1973). But we also agree with the Government's contention that the enactment of this statute by the same Congress that promulgated the constitutional amendments that ultimately became the Bill of Rights gives the statute an impressive historical pedigree." 462 U.S. at 584–85, 103 S.Ct. at 2577–78, 77 L.Ed.2d at 28 (footnote omitted).

See also Boyd v. United States, 116 U.S. 616, 623, 6 S.Ct. 524, 528, 29 L.Ed. 746, 750 (1886); United States v. Ramsey, 431 U.S. 606, 97 S.Ct. 1972, 52 L.Ed.2d 617 (1977).

session, Congress passed a law "to regulate the collection of the duties imposed by law on the tonnage of ships or vessels, and on goods, wares, and merchandise imported into the United States." This statute authorized customs officials to search for and seize goods which the officials suspected were concealed or fraudulently entered. The same Congress which proposed the fourth and fifth amendments most probably did not consider these amendments to forbid the enactment of the statute.[3]

At this same session, Congress passed the Judiciary Act of 1789. In section 25 of this statute, Congress gave the Supreme Court of the United States jurisdiction to hear appeals from final judgments in the highest courts of states where federal treaties, statutes, or rights were challenged.[4] In an opinion sustaining the constitutional right of the Supreme Court, under article III, section 2, to review the judgments and decrees of the supreme courts of the several states involving federal questions, Chief Justice Marshall said:

> We know, that in the Congress which passed that act were many eminent members of the convention which formed the constitution. Not a single individual, so far as is known, supposed that part of the act which gives the supreme court appellate jurisdiction over the judgments of the state courts, in the cases therein specified, to be unauthorized by the constitution.[5]

As a further example, Congress passed the Civil Rights Bill of April 9, 1866, after it had passed the bill that proposed the thirteenth amendment. Courts have given weight and significance to this fact in determining whether that amendment gave Congress the power to enact the statute.[6]

Similarly, in holding that a state practice of placing on a criminal murder defendant the burden of proving that she was acting in self defense did not violate due process. The Court noted that it was relevant that the common law rule, when both the fifth and fourteenth amendments were adopted, was that affirmative defenses were for the defendant to prove.[7]

The alleged existence of a power or right granted by the Constitution is not conclusively defeated merely because that power has only recently been exercised or that right was not previously asserted. Congress did not enact the Sherman Act until 1890; the Act is nevertheless constitutional because Congress, given its power over interstate

---

3. In re Platt, 19 Fed.Cas. 815 (D.N.Y. 1874) (No. 11,212).

4. Act of Sept. 24, 1789, 1 Stat. 73.

See Appendix D, which reprints the Judiciary Act of 1789.

5. Cohens v. Virginia, 19 U.S. (6 Wheat.) 264, 420, 5 L.Ed. 257, 295 (1821).

6. United States v. Rhodes, 27 F.Cas. 785 (C.C.Ky.1866) (No. 16,151).

7. Patterson v. New York, 432 U.S. 197, 202, 97 S.Ct. 2319, 2322, 53 L.Ed.2d 281 (1977); Martin v. Ohio, 480 U.S. 228, 236, 107 S.Ct. 1098, 1103, 94 L.Ed.2d 267 (1987), rehearing denied 481 U.S. 1024, 107 S.Ct. 1913, 95 L.Ed.2d 519 (1987).

commerce, could have passed such a law at any time after the Constitution was adopted.[8] Thus, many powers granted by the Constitution to the legislature lie dormant until the need arises to invoke them.[9]

§ 23.35   The Role of the Federalist Papers in the Courts

The Federalist is a collection of eighty-five essays which appeared in the newspapers immediately after the framers submitted the Constitution to the conventions of the several states. Alexander Hamilton, James Madison, and John Jay wrote the essays, which discussed the defects existing under the Confederation, and advocated the adoption of the Constitution. Like similar contemporaneous exposition, the construction given to the Constitution by the authors of the Federalist is entitled to great weight.[1] Thus, Thomas Jefferson believed that The Federalist Papers are "evidence of the general opinion of those who framed and those who accepted the Constitution of the United States, on questions as to its genuine meaning."[2] And James Madison, one of the prime authors of our Constitution, believed that The Federalist

8. The Sherman Act prohibits among other things, any contract, combination, or conspiracy in restraint of commerce among the several states, or with foreign nations. It also grants to the federal courts the jurisdiction to enforce the law. Act of Congress of July 2, 1890, 26 Stat. 209, c. 647 (15 U.S.C.A. §§ 1–7).

9. Pensacola Telegraph Co. v. Western Union Telegraph Co., 96 U.S. (6 Otto) 1, 9, 24 L.Ed. 708, 710 (1877); Martin v. Hunter's Lessee, 14 U.S. (1 Wheat.) 304, 4 L.Ed. 97 (1816); United States v. Elliott, 64 Fed. 27 (C.C.Mo.1894).

The practice of prosecution by criminal information existed at common law and is clearly implicated in the fifth amendment. A federal court has held that—

"[E]ven though such right has been in abeyance for eighty years, there has been no abrogation of the power of the government to assert that right, particularly as the courts do not seem to have refused, by any well considered case, the exercise of such right, though we find some intimations by the courts adverse to its exercise." United States v. Shepard, 27 Fed.Cas. 1056, 1059 (E.D.Mich. 1870) (No. 16,273).

§ 23.35

1. Wheeling, Parkersburg & Cincinnati Transportation Co. v. Wheeling, 99 U.S. (9 Otto) 273, 25 L.Ed. 412 (1878); M'Culloch v. Maryland, 17 U.S. (4 Wheat.) 316, 433, 4 L.Ed. 579, 608 (1819).

"The opinion of the Federalist has always been considered as of great authority. It is a complete commentary on our constitution; and is appealed to by all parties, in the question to which that instrument has given birth. Its intrinsic merit entitles it to this high rank; and the part two of its authors performed in framing the constitution, put it very much in their power to explain the views with which it was framed. These essays having been published, while the constitution was before the nation for adoption or rejection, and having been written in answer to objections founded entirely on the extent of its powers, and on its diminution of state sovereignty, *are entitled to the more consideration, where they frankly avow that the power objected to is given, and defend it.*" Cohens v. Virginia, 19 U.S. (6 Wheat.) 264, 418–19, 5 L.Ed. 257, 294 (1821) (emphasis added).

The construction the authors of the Federalist gave to the Constitution should not and cannot be disregarded. Pollock v. Farmers' Loan & Trust Co., 158 U.S. 601, 627, 15 S.Ct. 912, 961, 39 L.Ed. 1108, 1122 (1895). See also Nixon v. Administrator of General Services, 433 U.S. 425, 442–43, 97 S.Ct. 2777, 2789–90, 53 L.Ed.2d 867, 890–91 (1977) (citing the Federalist Papers as demonstrating the "more pragmatic, flexible approach").

2. See, Diamond, Democracy and the Federalist: A Reconsideration of the Framer's Intent, 50 Am.Pol.Sci.Rev. 53 (Mar. 1959).

Papers "may fairly enough be regarded as the most authentic exposition of the text of the federal Constitution, as understood by the Body which prepared and the Authority which accepted it."[3] In fact, turning to The Federalist Papers was one of Justice Story's techniques of interpretation.[4]

But in applying the authors' opinions to cases which may arise, courts retain the power to evaluate the proper weight that they should give to a specific opinion expressed in a Federalist essay.[5]

VIII. THE EFFECT OF EXCEPTIONS AS REFLECTED IN THE CASE LAW

§ 23.36 Generally

If the Constitution enumerates exceptions from a power, those exceptions can serve to mark its extent.[1] As it is often said, the exceptions prove the rule. When the Constitution excepts any particular case, a court may presuppose that similar cases, that are not excepted, are within the relevant grant or prohibition.[2]

3. Letter from James Madison to Thomas Jefferson, Feb. 8, 1825, quoted in H. Long, The American Ideal of 1776, at 148 (1976).

4. R. Rotunda & J. Nowak, eds., Joseph Story's Commentaries on the Constitution of the United States 148–51 (originally published, 1833; reprinted, Carolina Academic Press, 1987).

5. M'Culloch v. Maryland, 17 U.S. (4 Wheat.) 316, 433, 4 L.Ed. 579, 608 (1819). Thus, one state court has opined:

"[A]ble as were the authors of the work referred to [the Federalist Papers] their opinions cannot be received as authority in judicial investigations. The purpose of that work was to reconcile a divided community to the adoption of the Constitution; and in accomplishing this object, it can hardly be denied that they sometimes exaggerated its advantages, and spread over the objectionable features the gloss of plausible construction." State v. McBride, 24 S.C.L. 400, 409–10 (1839).

On the Federalist Papers, see generally, H. Storing, What the Anti–Federalists Were For (1981); D. Epstein, The Political Theory of the Federalist (1984); G. Wills,

Explaining America: The Federalist (1981).

§ 23.36

1. "If, then, there are in the constitution plain exceptions from the power over navigation ... it is a proof that those who made these exceptions ... understood the power to which they applied as being granted." Gibbons v. Ogden, 22 U.S. (9 Wheat.) 1, 191, 6 L.Ed. 23, 69 (1824).

The general rule of interpretation, that exception of an item from a general clause proves the drafter's belief that but for the exception, the item would be within the general clause, applies to the Constitution. The Court has held that the exception in article I, § 10, cl. 2, which excepts duties supporting inspection laws from the general prohibition of import and export duties, proves that the framers classed taxes similar to inspection duties within the general prohibition. Brown v. Maryland, 25 U.S. (12 Wheat.) 419, 436, 6 L.Ed. 678, 685 (1827).

2. Township of Pine Grove v. Talcott, 86 U.S. (19 Wall.) 666, 675, 22 L.Ed. 227, 232–33 (1873); Rhode Island v. Massachusetts, 37 U.S. (12 Pet.) 657, 722, 9 L.Ed. 1233, 1259–60 (1838).

However, if no exception exists expressly, court should not invent exceptions by mere implication or construction.[3]

3. Rhode Island v. Massachusetts, 37 U.S. (12 Pet.) 657, 722, 9 L.Ed. 1233, 1259–60 (1838); Cohens v. Virginia, 19 U.S. (6 Wheat.) 264, 378, 5 L.Ed. 257, 284–85 (1821).

*

APPENDICES

Apps.

Appendix A

THE DECLARATION OF INDEPENDENCE
(1776)

In Congress, July 4, 1776.[1]

1. The delegates of the United Colonies of New Hampshire; Massachusetts Bay; Rhode Island and Providence Plantations; Connecticut; New York; New Jersey; Pennsylvania; New Castle, Kent, and Sussex, in Delaware; Maryland; Virginia; North Carolina, and South Carolina, in Congress assembled at Philadelphia, Resolved on the 10th of May, 1776, to recommend to the respective assemblies and conventions of the United Colonies, where no government sufficient to the exigencies of their affairs had been established, to adopt such a government as should, in the opinion of the representatives of the people, best conduce to the happiness and safety of their constituents in particular, and of America in general. A preamble to this resolution, agreed to on the 15th of May, stated the intention to be totally to suppress the exercise of every kind of authority under the British crown. On the 7th of June, certain resolutions respecting independency were moved and seconded. On the 10th of June it was resolved, that a committee should be appointed to prepare a declaration to the following effect: "That the United Colonies are, and of right ought to be, free and independent States; that they are absolved from all allegiance to the British crown; and that all political connection between them and the State of Great Britain is, and ought to be, totally dissolved." On the preceding day it was determined that the committee for preparing the declaration should consist of five, and they were chosen accordingly, in the following order: Mr. Jefferson, Mr. J. Adams, Mr. Franklin, Mr. Sherman, Mr. R.R. Livingston. On the 11th of June a resolution was passed to appoint a committee to prepare and digest the form of a confederation to be entered into between the colonies, and another committee to pre- pare a plan of treaties to be proposed to foreign powers. On the 12th of June, it was resolved, that a committee of Congress should be appointed by the name of a board of war and ordinance, to consist of five members. On the 25th of June, a declaration of the deputies of Pennsylvania, met in provincial conference, expressing their willingness to concur in a vote declaring the United Colonies free and independent States, was laid before Congress and read. On the 28th of June, the committee appointed to prepare a declaration of independence brought in a draught, which was read, and ordered to lie on the table. On the 1st of July, a resolution of the convention of Maryland, passed the 28th of June, authorizing the deputies of that colony to concur in declaring the United Colonies free and independent States, was laid before Congress and read. On the same day Congress resolved itself into a committee of the whole, to take into consideration the resolution respecting independency. On the 2d of July, a resolution declaring the colonies free and independent States, was adopted. A declaration to that effect was, on the same and the following days, taken into further consideration. Finally, on the 4th of July, the Declaration of Independence was agreed to, engrossed on paper, signed by John Hancock as president, and directed to be sent to the several assemblies, conventions, and committees, or councils of safety, and to the several commanding officers of the continental troops, and to be proclaimed in each of the United States, and at the head of the Army. It was also ordered to be entered upon the Journals of Congress, and on the 2d of August, a copy engrossed on parchment was signed by all but one of the fifty-six signers whose names are appended to it. That one was Matthew Thornton, of

The unanimous Declaration of the thirteen united States of America

When in the Course of human events it becomes necessary for one people to dissolve the political bands which have connected them with another, and to assume among the Powers of the earth, the separate and equal station to which the Laws of Nature and of Nature's God entitle them, a decent respect to the opinions of mankind requires that they should declare the causes which impel them to the separation.

We hold these truths to be self-evident, that all men are created equal, that they are endowed by their Creator with certain unalienable Rights, that among these are Life, Liberty and the pursuit of Happiness. That to secure these rights, Governments are instituted among Men, deriving their just powers from the consent of the governed, That whenever any Form of Government becomes destructive of these ends, it is the Right of the People to alter or to abolish it, and to institute new Government, laying its foundation on such principles and organizing its powers in such form, as to them shall seem most likely to effect their Safety and Happiness. Prudence, indeed, will dictate that Governments long established should not be changed for light and transient causes; and accordingly all experience hath shown, that mankind are more disposed to suffer, while evils are sufferable, than to right themselves by abolishing the forms to which they are accustomed. But when a long train of abuses and usurpations, pursuing invariably the same Object evinces a design to reduce them under absolute Despotism, it is their right, it is their duty, to throw off such Government, and to provide new Guards for their future security.—Such has been the patient sufferance of these Colonies; and such is now the necessity which constrains them to alter their former Systems of Government. The history of the present King of Great Britain is a history of repeated injuries and usurpations, all having in direct object the establishment of an absolute Tyranny over these States. To prove this, let Facts be submitted to a candid world.

He has refused his Assent to Laws, the most wholesome and necessary for the public good.

New Hampshire, who on taking his seat in November asked and obtained the privilege of signing it. Several who signed it on the 2d of August were absent when it was adopted on the 4th of July, but, approving of it, they thus signified their approbation.

NOTE.—The proof of this document as published above, was read by Mr. Ferdinand Jefferson, the Keeper of the Rolls at the Department of State, at Washington, who compared it with the fac-simile of the original in his custody. He says: "In the fac-simile, as in the original, the whole instrument runs on without a break, but dashes are mostly inserted. I have, in this copy, followed the arrangement of paragraphs adopted in the publication of the Declaration in the newspaper of John Dunlap, and as printed by him for the Congress, which printed copy is inserted in the original Journal of the old Congress. The same paragraphs are also made by the author, in the original draught preserved in the Department of State."

N.B. Adapted, with permission, from United States Code Annotated, Constitution of the United States, Annotated (West Publishing Co.)

He has forbidden his Governors to pass Laws of immediate and pressing importance, unless suspended in their operation till his Assent should be obtained; and when so suspended, he has utterly neglected to attend to them.

He has refused to pass other Laws for the accommodation of large districts of people, unless those people would relinquish the right of Representation in the Legislature, a right inestimable to them and formidable to tyrants only.

He has called together legislative bodies at places unusual, uncomfortable, and distant from the depository of their Public Records, for the sole purpose of fatiguing them into compliance with his measures.

He has dissolved Representative Houses repeatedly, for opposing with manly firmness his invasions on the rights of the people.

He has refused for a long time, after such dissolutions, to cause others to be elected; whereby the Legislative Powers, incapable of Annihilation, have returned to the People at large for their exercise; the State remaining in the mean time exposed to all the dangers of invasion from without, and convulsions within.

He has endeavored to prevent the population of these States; for that purpose obstructing the Laws for Naturalization of Foreigners; refusing to pass others to encourage their migration hither, and raising the conditions of new Appropriations of Lands.

He has obstructed the Administration of Justice, by refusing his Assent to Laws for establishing Judiciary Powers.

He has made Judges dependent on his Will alone, for the tenure of their offices, and the amount and payment of their salaries.

He has erected a multitude of New Offices, and sent hither swarms of Officers to harass our People, and eat out their substance.

He has kept among us, in times of peace, Standing Armies without the Consent of our Legislature.

He has affected to render the Military independent of and superior to the Civil Power.

He has combined with others to subject us to a jurisdiction foreign to our constitution, and unacknowledged by our laws; giving his Assent to their acts of pretended Legislation:

For quartering large bodies of armed troops among us:

For protecting them, by a mock Trial, from Punishment for any Murders which they should commit on the Inhabitants of these States;

For cutting off our Trade with all parts of the world:

For imposing taxes on us without our Consent:

For depriving us in many cases, of the benefits of Trial by Jury:

For transporting us beyond Seas to be tried for pretened offenses:

For abolishing the free System of English Laws in a neighboring Province, establishing therein an Arbitrary government, and enlarging its Boundaries so as to render it at once an example and fit instrument for introducing the same absolute rule into these Colonies:

For taking away our Charters, abolishing our most valuable Laws, and altering fundamentally the Forms of our Government:

For suspending our own Legislature, and declaring themselves invested with Power to legislate for us in all cases whatsoever.

He has abdicated Government here, by declaring us out of his Protection and waging War against us.

He has plundered our seas, ravaged our Coasts, burnt our towns, and destroyed the lives of our people.

He is at this time transporting large armies of foreign mercenaries to compleat the works of death, desolation and tyranny, already begun with circumstances of Cruelty & perfidy scarcely paralleled in the most barbarous ages, and totally unworthy the Head of a civilized nation.

He has constrained our fellow Citizens taken Captive on the high Seas to bear Arms against their Country, to become the executioners of their friends and Brethren, or to fall themselves by their Hands.

He has excited domestic insurrections amongst us, and has endeavored to bring on the inhabitants of our frontiers, the merciless Indian Savages, whose known rule of warfare, is an undistinguished destruction of all ages, sexes and conditions.

In every stage of these Oppressions We have Petitioned for Redress in the most humble terms: Our repeated Petitions have been answered only by repeated injury. A Prince, whose character is thus marked by every act which may define a Tyrant, is unfit to be the ruler of a free People.

Nor have We been wanting in attention to our British brethren. We have warned them from time to time of attempts by their legislature to extend an unwarrantable jurisdiction over us. We have reminded them of the circumstances of our emigration and settlement here. We have appealed to their native justice and magnanimity, and we have conjured them by the ties of our common kindred to disavow these usurpations, which, would inevitably interrupt our connections and correspondence. They too have been deaf to the voice of justice and consanguinity. We must, therefore, acquiesce in the necessity, which denounces our Separation, and hold them, as we hold the rest of mankind, Enemies in War, in Peace Friends.

We, therefore, the Representatives of the united States of America, in General Congress, Assembled, appealing to the Supreme Judge of the world for the rectitude of our intentions, do, in the Name, and by

Authority of the good People of these Colonies, solemnly publish and declare, That these United Colonies are, and of Right ought to be Free and Independent States; that they are Absolved from all Allegiance to the British Crown, and that all political connection between them and the State of Great Britain, is and ought to be totally dissolved; and that as Free and Independent States, they have full Power to levy War, conclude Peace, contract Alliances, establish Commerce, and to do all other Acts and Things which Independent States may of right do. And for the support of this Declaration, with a firm reliance on the Protection of Divine Providence, we mutually pledge to each other our Lives, our Fortunes and our sacred Honor.

JOHN HANCOCK

New Hampshire [2]

JOSIAH BARTLETT,
WM. WHIPPLE,
MATTHEW THORNTON.

Massachusetts Bay

SAML. ADAMS,
JOHN ADAMS,
ROBT. TREAT PAINE,
ELBRIDGE GERRY.

Rhode Island

STEP. HOPKINS,
WILLIAM ELLERY.

Connecticut

ROGER SHERMAN,
SAM'EL HUNTINGTON,
WM. WILLIAMS,
OLIVER WOLCOTT.

New York

WM. FLOYD,
PHIL. LIVINGSTON,
FRANS. LEWIS,
LEWIS MORRIS.

2. Mr. Ferdinand Jefferson, Keeper of the Rolls in the Department of State, at Washington, says: "The names of the signers are spelt above as in the fac-simile of the original, but the punctuation of them is not always the same; neither do the names of the States appear in the fac-simile of the original. The names of the signers of each State are grouped together in the fac-simile of the original, except the name of Matthew Thornton, which follows that of Oliver Wolcott."

New Jersey

RICHD. STOCKTON,
JNO. WITHERSPOON,
FRAS. HOPKINSON,
JOHN HART,
ABRA. CLARK.

Pennsylvania

ROBT. MORRIS,
BENJAMIN RUSH,
BENJA. FRANKLIN,
JOHN MORTON,
GEO. CLYMER,
JAS. SMITH,
GEO. TAYLOR,
JAMES WILSON,
GEO. ROSS.

Delaware

CAESAR RODNEY,
GEO. READ,
THO. M'KEAN.

Maryland

SAMUEL CHASE,
WM. PACA,
THOS. STONE,
CHARLES CARROLL
of Carrollton.

Virginia

GEORGE WYTHE,
RICHARD HENRY LEE,
TH. JEFFERSON,
BENJA. HARRISON,
THOS. NELSON, jr.,
FRANCIS LIGHTFOOT LEE,
CARTER BRAXTON.

North Carolina

WM. HOOPER,
JOSEPH HEWES,
JOHN PENN.

South Carolina

EDWARD RUTLEDGE,
THOS. HEYWARD, Junr.,
THOMAS LYNCH, Junr.,
ARTHUR MIDDLETON.

Georgia

BUTTON GWINNETT,
LYMAN HALL,
GEO. WALTON.

Appendix B

THE ARTICLES OF CONFEDERATION
(1777)

To all to whom these Presents shall come, we the undersigned Delegates of the States affixed to our Names send greeting [1]

1. Congress Resolved, on the 11th of June, 1776, that a committee should be appointed to prepare and digest the form of a confederation to be entered into between the Colonies; and on the day following, after it had been determined that the committee should consist of a member from each Colony, the following persons were appointed to perform that duty, to wit: Mr. Bartlett, Mr. S. Adams, Mr. Hopkins, Mr. Sherman, Mr. R.R. Livingston, Mr. Dickinson, Mr. M'Kean, Mr. Stone, Mr. Nelson, Mr. Hewes, Mr. E. Rutledge, and Mr. Gwinnett. Upon the report of this committee, the subject was, from time to time, debated, until the 15th of November, 1777, when a copy of the confederation being made out, and sundry amendments made in the diction, without altering the sense, the same was finally agreed to. Congress, at the same time, directed that the articles should be proposed to the legislatures of all the United States, to be considered, and if approved of by them, they were advised to authorize their delegates to ratify the same in the Congress of the United States; which being done, the same should become conclusive. Three hundred copies of the Articles of Confederation were ordered to be printed for the use of Congress; and on the 17th of November, the form of a circular letter to accompany them was brought in by a committee appointed to prepare it, and being agreed to, thirteen copies of it were ordered to be made out, to be signed by the president and forwarded to the several States, with copies of the confederation. On the 29th of November ensuing, a committee of three was appointed, to procure a translation of the articles to be made into the French language, and to report an address to the inhabitants of Canada, & c. On the 26th of June, 1778, the form of a ratification of the Articles of Confederation was adopted, and, it having been engrossed on parchment, it was signed on the 9th of July on the part and in behalf of their respective States, by the delegates of New Hampshire, Massachusetts Bay, Rhode Island and Providence Plantations, Connecticut, New York, Pennsylvania, Virginia, and South Carolina, agreeably to the powers vested in them. The delegates of North Carolina signed on the 21st of July, those of Georgia, on the 24th of July, and those of New Jersey on the 26th of November following. On the 5th of May, 1779, Mr. Dickinson and Mr. Van Dyke signed in behalf of the State of Delaware, Mr. M'Kean having previously signed in February, at which time he produced a power to that effect. Maryland did not ratify until the year 1781. She had instructed her delegates, on the 15th of December, 1778, not to agree to the confederation until matters respecting the western lands should be settled on principles of equity and sound policy; but, on the 30th of January, 1781, finding that the enemies of the country took advantage of the circumstance to disseminate opinions of an ultimate dissolution of the Union, the legislature of the State passed an act to empower their delegates to subscribe and ratify the articles, which was accordingly done by Mr. Hanson and Mr. Carroll, on the 1st of March of that year, which completed the ratifications of the act; and Congress assembled on the 2d of March under the new powers.

NOTE.—The proof of this document, as published above, was read by Mr. Ferdinand Jefferson, the Keeper of the Rolls of the Department of State, at Washington, who compared it with the original in his custody. He says: "The initial letters of many of the words in the original of this instrument are capitals, but as no system appears to have been observed, the same words sometimes beginning with a capital and sometimes with a small letter, I have

App. B THE ARTICLES OF CONFEDERATION (1777)

Whereas the Delegates of the United States of America in Congress assembled did on the fifteenth day of November in the Year of our Lord One Thousand Seven Hundred and Seventyseven, and in the Second Year of the Independence of America agree to certain articles of Confederation and perpetual Union between the States of New Hampshire, Massachusetts-bay, Rhodeisland and Providence Plantations, Connecticut, New York, New Jersey, Pennsylvania, Delaware, Maryland, Virginia, North–Carolina, South–Carolina and Georgia in the Words following, viz.

Articles of Confederation and perpetual Union Between the States of Newhampshire, Massachusetts-bay, Rhodeisland and Providence Plantations, Connecticut, New–York, New–Jersey, Pennsylvania, Delaware, Maryland, Virginia, North–Carolina, South–Carolina and Georgia

Article I. The stile of this confederacy shall be "The United States of America."

Article II. Each State retains its sovereignty, freedom and independence, and every power, jurisdiction and right, which is not by this confederation expressly delegated to the United States, in Congress assembled.

Article III. The said States hereby severally enter into a firm league of friendship with each other, for their common defence, the security of their liberties, and their mutual and general welfare, binding themselves to assist each other, against all force offered to, or attacks made upon them, or any of them, on account of religion, sovereignty, trade, or any other pretence whatever.

Article IV. The better to secure and perpetuate mutual friendship and intercourse among the people of the different States in this Union, the free inhabitants of each of these States, paupers, vagabonds and fugitives from justice expected, shall be entitled to all privileges and immunities of free citizens in the several States; and the people of each State shall have free ingress and regress to and from any other State, and shall enjoy therein all the privileges of trade and commerce, subject to the same duties, impositions and restrictions as the inhabitants thereof respectively, provided that such restrictions shall not extend so far as to prevent the removal of property imported into any State, to any other State of which the owner is an inhabitant; provided also that no imposition, duties or restriction shall be laid by any State, on the property of the United States, or either of them.

thought it best not to undertake to follow the original in this particular. Moreover, there are three forms of the letter s: the capital s, the small s, and the long f, the last being used indiscriminately to words that should begin with a capital and those that should begin with a small s."

N.B. Adapted, with permission, from United States Code Annotated, Constitution of the United States, Annotated (West Publishing Co.)

If any person guilty of, or charged with treason, felony, or other high misdemeanor in any State, shall flee from justice, and be found in any of the United States, he shall upon demand of the Governor or Executive power, of the State from which he fled, be delivered up and removed to the State having jurisdiction of his offense.

Full faith and credit shall be given in each of these States to the records, acts and judicial proceedings of the courts and magistrates of every other State.

Article V. For the more convenient management of the general interests of the United States, delegates shall be annually appointed in such manner as the legislature of each State shall direct, to meet in Congress on the first Monday in November, in every year, with a power reserved to each State, to recall its delegates, or any of them, at any time within the year, and to send others in their stead, for the remainder of the year.

No State shall be represented in Congress by less than two, nor by more than seven members; and no person shall be capable of being a delegate for more than three years in any term of six years; nor shall any person, being a delegate, be capable of holding any office under the United States, for which he, or another for his benefit receives any salary, fees or emolument of any kind.

Each State shall maintain its own delegates in a meeting of the States, and while they act as members of the committee of the States.

In determining questions in the United States, in Congress assembled, each State shall have one vote.

Freedom of speech and debate in Congress shall not be impeached or questioned in any court, or place out of Congress, and the members of Congress shall be protected in their persons from arrests and imprisonments, during the time of their going to and from, and attendance on Congress, except for treason, felony, or breach of the peace.

Article VI. No State without the consent of the United States in Congress assembled, shall send any embassy to, or receive any embassy from, or enter into any conference, agreement, alliance or treaty with any king, prince or state; nor shall any person holding any office of profit or trust under the United States, or any of them, accept of any present, emolument, office or title of any kind whatever from any king, prince or foreign state; nor shall the United States in Congress assembled, or any of them, grant any title of nobility.

No two or more States shall enter into any treaty, confederation or alliance whatever between them, without the consent of the United States in Congress assembled, specifying accurately the purposes for which the same is to be entered into, and how long it shall continue.

No State shall lay any imposts or duties, which may interfere with any stipulations in treaties, entered into by the United States in

Congress assembled, with any king, prince or state, in pursuance of any treaties already proposed by Congress, to the courts of France and Spain.

No vessels of war shall be kept up in time of peace by any State, except such number only, as shall be deemed necessary by the United States in Congress assembled, for the defence of such State, or its trade; nor shall any body of forces be kept up by any State, in time of peace, except such number only, as in the judgment of the United States, in Congress assembled, shall be deemed requisite to garrison the forts necessary for the defence of such State; but every State shall always keep up a well regulated and disciplined militia, sufficiently armed and accoutered, and shall provide and constantly have ready for use, in public stores, a due number of field pieces and tents, and a proper quantity of arms, ammunition and camp equipage.

No State shall engage in any war without the consent of the United States in Congress assembled, unless such State be actually invaded by enemies, or shall have received certain advice of a resolution being formed by some nation of Indians to invade such State, and the danger is so imminent as not to admit of a delay, till the United States in Congress assembled can be consulted; nor shall any State grant commissions to any ships or vessels of war, nor letters of marque or reprisal, except it be after a declaration of war by the United States in Congress assembled, and then only against the kingdom or state and the subjects thereof, against which war has been so declared, and under such regulations as shall be established by the United States in Congress assembled, unless such State be infested by pirates, in which case vessels of war may be fitted out for that occasion, and kept so long as the danger shall continue, or until the United States in Congress assembled shall determine otherwise.

Article VII. When land-forces are raised by any State for the common defence, all officers of or under the rank of colonel, shall be appointed by the Legislature of each State respectively by whom such forces shall be raised, or in such manner as such State shall direct, and all vacancies shall be filled up by the State which first made the appointment.

Article VIII. All charges of war, and all other expenses that shall be incurred for the common defence or general welfare, and allowed by the United States in Congress assembled, shall be defrayed out of a common treasury, which shall be supplied by the several States, in proportion to the value of all land within each State, granted to or surveyed for any person, as such land and the buildings and improvements thereon shall be estimated according to such mode as the United States in Congress assembled, shall from time to time direct and appoint.

The taxes for paying that proportion shall be laid and levied by the authority and direction of the Legislatures of the several States within the time agreed upon by the United States in Congress assembled.

Article IX. The United States in Congress assembled, shall have the sole and exclusive right and power of determining on peace and war, except in the cases mentioned in the sixth article—of sending and receiving ambassadors—entering into treaties and alliances, provided that no treaty of commerce shall be made whereby the legislative power of the respective States shall be restrained from imposing such imposts and duties on foreigners, as their own people are subjected to, or from prohibiting the exportation or importation of any species of goods or commodities whatsoever—of establishing rules for deciding in all cases, what captures on land or water shall be legal, and in what manner prizes taken by land or naval forces in the service of the United States shall be divided or appropriated—of granting letters of marque and reprisal in times of peace—appointing courts for the trial of piracies and felonies committed on the high seas and establishing courts for receiving and determining finally appeals in all cases of captures, provided that no member of Congress shall be appointed a judge of any of the said courts.

The United States in Congress assembled shall also be the last resort on appeal in all disputes and differences now subsisting or that hereafter may arise between two or more States concerning boundary, jurisdiction or any other cause whatever; which authority shall always be exercised in the manner following. Whenever the legislative or executive authority or lawful agent of any State in controversy with another shall present a petition to Congress, stating the matter in question and praying for a hearing, notice thereof shall be given by order of Congress to the legislative or executive authority of the other State in controversy, and a day assigned for the appearance of the parties by their lawful agents, who shall then be directed to appoint by joint consent, commissioners or judges to constitute a court for hearing and determining the matter in question: but if they cannot agree, Congress shall name three persons out of each of the United States, and from the list of such persons each party shall alternately strike out one, the petitioners beginning, until the number shall be reduced to thirteen; and from that number not less than seven, nor more than nine names as Congress shall direct, shall, in the presence of Congress be drawn out by lot, and the persons whose names shall be so drawn or any five of them, shall be commissioners or judges, to hear and finally determine the controversy, so always as a major part of the judges who shall hear the cause shall agree in the determination: and if either party shall neglect to attend at the day appointed, without showing reasons, which Congress shall judge sufficient, or being present shall refuse to strike, the Congress shall proceed to nominate three persons out of each State, and the Secretary of Congress shall strike in behalf of such party absent or refusing; and the judgment and sentence of the court to be appointed, in the manner before prescribed, shall be final and conclusive; and if any of the parties shall refuse to submit to the authority of such court, or to appear or defend their claim or cause, the court shall nevertheless proceed to pronounce sentence, or judgment, which shall in like manner be final and decisive, the judgment or sentence and other proceedings being in either case transmitted to Congress, and lodged among the acts of Congress for the security of the parties concerned: provided that every commissioner, before he sits in judgment, shall take an oath to be administered by one of the judges of the supreme or superior court of the State where the cause shall be tried, "well and truly to hear and determine the matter in question, according to the best of his judgment, without favour, affection or hope of reward:" provided also that no State shall be deprived of territory for the benefit of the United States.

All controversies concerning the private right of soil claimed under different grants of two or more States, whose jurisdiction as they may respect such lands, and the States which passed such grants are adjusted, the said grants or either of them being at the same time claimed to have originated antecedent to such settlement of jurisdiction, shall on the petition of either party to the Congress of the United States, be finally determined as near as may be in the same manner as is before prescribed for deciding disputes respecting territorial jurisdiction between different States.

The United States in Congress assembled shall also have the sole and exclusive right and power of regulating the alloy and value of coin struck by their own authority, or by that of the respective States.—fixing the standard of weights and measures throughout the United States.—regulating the trade and managing all affairs with the Indians, not members of any of the States, provided that the legislative right of any State within its own limits be not infringed or violated—establishing and regulating post-offices from one State to another, throughout all the United States, and exacting such postage on the papers passing thro' the same as may be requisite to defray the expenses of the said office—appointing all officers of the land forces, in the service of the United States, excepting regimental officers—appointing all the officers of the naval forces, and commissioning all officers whatever in the service of the United States—making rules for the government and regulation of the said land and naval forces, and directing their operations.

The United States in Congress assembled shall have authority to appoint a committee, to sit in the recess of Congress, to be denominated "a Committee of the States," and to consist of one delegate from each State; and to appoint such other committees and civil officers as may be necessary for managing the general affairs of the United States under their direction—to appoint one of their number to preside, provided that no person be allowed to serve in the office of president more than one year in any term of three years; to ascertain the necessary sums of money to be raised for the service of the United States, and to appropriate and apply the same for defraying the public expenses—to borrow money or emit bills on the credit of the United States transmitting every half year to the respective States an account of the sums of money so borrowed or emitted,—to build and equip a navy—to agree upon the number of land forces, and to make requisitions from each State for its quota, in proportion to the number of white inhabitants in such State; which requisition shall be binding, and thereupon the Legislature of each State shall appoint the regimental officers, raise the men and cloath, arm and equip them in a soldier like manner, at the expense of the United States; and the officers and men so cloathed, armed and equipped shall march to the place appointed, and within the time agreed on by the United States in Congress assembled; but if the United States in Congress assembled shall, on consideration of circumstances judge proper that any State should not raise men, or should raise a smaller number than its quota, and that any other State should raise a greater number of men than the quota thereof, such extra number shall be raised, officered, cloathed, armed and equipped in the same manner as the quota of such State, unless the legislature of such State shall judge that such extra number cannot be safely spared out of the same, in which case they shall raise officer, cloath, arm and equip as many of such extra number as they judge can be safely spared. And the officers and men so cloathed, armed and equipped, shall march to the place appointed, and within the time agreed on by the United States in Congress assembled.

The United States in Congress assembled shall never engage in a war, nor grant letters of marque and reprisal in time of peace, nor enter into any treaties or alliances, nor coin money, nor regulate the value thereof, nor ascertain the sums and expenses necessary for the defence and welfare of the United States, or any of them, nor emit bills, nor borrow money on the credit of the United States, nor appropriate money, nor agree upon the number of vessels of war, to be built or purchased, or the number of land or sea forces to be raised, nor appoint a commander in chief of the army or navy, unless nine States assent to the same: nor shall a question on any other point, except for adjourning from day to day be determined, unless by the votes of a majority of the United States in Congress assembled.

The Congress of the United States shall have power to adjourn to any time within the year, and to any place within the United States, so that no period of adjournment be for a longer duration than the space of six months, and shall publish the journal of their proceedings monthly, except such parts thereof relating to treaties, alliances or military operations, as in their judgment require secresy; and the yeas and nays of the delegates of each State on any question shall be entered on the journal, when it is desired by any delegate; and the delegates of a State, or any of them, at his or their request shall be furnished with a transcript of the said journal, except such parts as are above excepted, to lay before the Legislatures of the several States.

Article X. The committee of the States, or any nine of them, shall be authorized to execute in the recess of Congress, such of the powers of Congress as the United States in Congress assembled, by the consent of nine States, shall from time to time think expedient to vest them with; provided that no power be delegated to the said committee, for the exercise of which, by the articles of confederation, the voice of nine States in the Congress of the United States assembled is requisite.

Article XI. Canada acceding to this confederation, and joining in the measures of the United States, shall be admitted into, and entitled to all the advantages of this Union: but no other colony shall be admitted into the same, unless such admission be agreed to by nine States.

Article XII. All bills of credit emitted, monies borrowed and debts contracted by, or under the authority of Congress, before the assembling of the United States, in pursuance of the present confederation, shall be deemed and considered as a charge against the United States, for payment and satisfaction whereof the said United States, and the public faith are hereby solemnly pledged.

Article XIII. Every State shall abide by the determinations of the United States in Congress assembled, on all questions which by this confederation are submitted to them. And the articles of this confederation shall be inviolably observed by every State, and the Union shall be perpetual; nor shall any alteration at any time hereafter be made in any of them; unless such alteration be agreed to in a Congress of the United States, and be afterwards confirmed by the Legislatures of every State.

And whereas it has pleased the Great Governor of the world to incline the hearts of the Legislatures we respectively represent in Congress, to approve of, and to authorize us to ratify the said articles of confederation and perpetual union. Know ye that we the undersigned delegates, by virtue of the power and authority to us given for that purpose, do by these presents, in the name and in behalf of our respective constituents, fully and entirely ratify and confirm each and every of the said articles of confederation and perpetual union, and all and singular the matters and things therein contained: and we do further solemnly plight and engage the faith of our respective constituents, that they shall abide by the determinations of the United States in Congress assembled, on all questions, which by the said confederation are submitted to them. And that the articles thereof shall be inviolably observed by the States we re[s]pectively represent, and that the Union shall be perpetual.

In witness whereof we have hereunto set our hands in Congress. Done at Philadelphia in the State of Pennsylvania the ninth day of July in the year of our Lord one thousand seven hundred and seventy-eight, and in the third year of the independence of America.[2]

On the part and behalf of the State of New Hampshire

JOSIAH BARTLETT,

JOHN WENTWORTH, Junr.,

August 8th, 1778.

On the part and behalf of the State of Massachusetts Bay

JOHN HANCOCK,

SAMUEL ADAMS,

ELBRIDGE GERRY,

FRANCIS DANA,

JAMES LOVELL,

SAMUEL HOLTEN.

On the part and behalf of the State of Rhode Island and Providence Plantations

WILLIAM ELLERY,

HENRY MARCHANT,

JOHN COLLINS.

On the part and behalf of the State of Connecticut

ROGER SHERMAN,

SAMUEL HUNTINGTON,

OLIVER WOLCOTT,

TITUS HOSMER,

ANDREW ADAMS.

On the part and behalf of the State of New York

JAS. DUANE,

FRA. LEWIS,

WM. DUER,

GOUV. MORRIS.

On the part and in behalf of the State of New Jersey, Novr. 26, 1778

JNO. WITHERSPOON,

NATHL. SCUDDER.

2. From the circumstances of delegates from the same State having signed the Articles of Confederation at different times, as appears by the dates, it is probable they affixed their names as they happened to be present in Congress, after they had been authorized by their constituents.

On the part and behalf of the State of Pennsylvania
ROBT. MORRIS,
DANIEL ROBERDEAU,
JONA. BAYARD SMITH,
WILLIAM CLINGAN,
JOSEPH REED,
22d July, 1778.

On the part & behalf of the State of Delaware
THO. M'KEAN, Feby. 12, 1779.
JOHN DICKINSON, May 5th, 1779
NICHOLAS VAN DYKE.

On the part and behalf of the State of Maryland
JOHN HANSON,
March 1, 1781.
DANIEL CARROLL,
Mar. 1, 1781.

On the part and behalf of the State of Virginia
RICHARD HENRY LEE,
JOHN BANISTER,
THOMAS ADAMS,
JNO. HARVIE,
FRANCIS LIGHTFOOT LEE.

On the part and behalf of the State of No. Carolina
JOHN PENN, July 21st, 1778.
CORNS. HARNETT,
JNO. WILLIAMS.

On the part & behalf of the State of South Carolina
HENRY LAURENS,
WILLIAM HENRY DRAYTON,
JNO. MATHEWS,
RICHD. HUTSON,
THOS. HEYWARD, Junr.

On the part & behalf of the State of Georgia
JNO. WALTON, 24th July, 1778.
EDWD. TELFAIR,
EDWD. LANGWORTHY.

Appendix C

THE ORDINANCE OF 1787: THE NORTHWEST TERRITORIAL GOVERNMENT

[The Confederate Congress, July 13, 1787]

An Ordinance for the government of the territory of the United States northwest of the river Ohio

Section 1. Be it ordained by the United States in Congress assembled, That the said territory, for the purpose of temporary government, be one district, subject, however, to be divided into two districts, as future circumstances may, in the opinion of Congress, make it expedient.

Sec. 2. Be it ordained by the authority aforesaid, That the estates both of resident and non-resident proprietors in the said territory, dying intestate, shall descend to, and be distributed among, their children and the descendants of a deceased child in equal parts, the descendants of a deceased child or grandchild to take the share of their deceased parent in equal parts among them; and where there shall be no children or descendants, then in equal parts to the next of kin, in equal degree; and among collaterals, the children of a deceased brother or sister of the intestate shall have, in equal parts among them, their deceased parent's share; and there shall, in no case, be a distinction between kindred of the whole and half blood; saving in all cases to the widow of the intestate, her third part of the real estate for life, and one-third part of the personal estate; and this law relative to descents and dower, shall remain in full force until altered by the legislature of the district. And until the governor and judges shall adopt laws as hereinafter mentioned, estates in the said territory may be devised or bequeathed by wills in writing, signed and sealed by him or her in whom the estate may be, (being of full age,) and attested by three witnesses; and real estates may be conveyed by lease and release, or bargain and sale, signed, sealed, and delivered by the person, being of full age, in whom the estate may be, and attested by two witnesses, provided such wills be duly proved, and such conveyances be acknowledged, or the execution thereof duly proved, and be recorded within one year after proper magistrates, courts, and registers, shall be appointed for that purpose; and personal property may be transferred by delivery, saving, however, to the French and Canadian inhabitants, and other settlers of the Kaskaskies, Saint Vincents, and the neighboring villages, who have heretofore professed themselves citizens of Virginia, their laws and

701

customs now in force among them, relative to the descent and conveyance of property.

Sec. 3.   Be it ordained by the authority aforesaid, That there shall be appointed, from time to time, by Congress, a governor, whose commission shall continue in force for the term of three years, unless sooner revoked by Congress; he shall reside in the district, and have a freehold estate therein, in one thousand acres of land, while in the exercise of his office.

Sec. 4.   There shall be appointed from time to time, by Congress, a secretary, whose commission shall continue in force for four years, unless sooner revoked; he shall reside in the district, and have a freehold estate therein, in five hundred acres of land, while in the exercise of his office.   It shall be his duty to keep and preserve the acts and laws passed by the legislature, and the public records of the district, and the proceedings of the governor in his executive department, and transmit authentic copies of such acts and proceedings every six months to the Secretary of Congress.   There shall also be appointed a court, to consist of three judges, any two of whom to form a court, who shall have a common-law jurisdiction, and reside in the district, and have each therein a freehold estate, in five hundred acres of land, while in the exercise of their offices; and their commissions shall continue in force during good behavior.

Sec. 5.   The governor and judges, or a majority of them, shall adopt and publish in the district such laws of the original States, criminal and civil, as may be necessary, and best suited to the circumstances of the district, and report them to Congress from time to time, which laws shall be in force in the district until the organization of the general assembly therein, unless disapproved of by Congress; but afterwards the legislature shall have authority to alter them as they shall think fit.

Sec. 6.   The governor, for the time being, shall be commander-in-chief of the militia, appoint and commission all officers in the same below the rank of general officers; all general officers shall be appointed and commissioned by Congress.

Sec. 7.   Previous to the organization of the general assembly the governor shall appoint such magistrates, and other civil officers, in each county or township, as he shall find necessary for the preservation of the peace and good order in the same.   After the general assembly shall be organized the powers and duties of magistrates and other civil officers shall be regulated and defined by the said assembly; but all magistrates and other civil officers, not herein otherwise directed, shall, during the continuance of this temporary government, be appointed by the governor.

Sec. 8.   For the prevention of crimes and injuries, the laws to be adopted or made shall have force in all parts of the district, and for the execution of process, criminal and civil, the governor shall make proper divisions thereof; and he shall proceed, from time to time, as circumstances may require to lay out the parts of the district in which the Indian titles shall have been extinguished, into counties and townships, subject, however, to such alterations as may thereafter be made by the legislature.

Sec. 9. So soon as there shall be five thousand free male inhabitants, of full age, in the district, upon giving proof thereof to the governor, they shall receive authority, with time and place, to elect representatives from their counties or townships, to represent them in the general assembly: Provided, That for every five hundred free male inhabitants there shall be one representative, and so on, progressively, with the number of free male inhabitants, shall the right of representation increase, until the number of representatives shall amount to twenty-five; after which the number and proportion of representatives shall be regulated by the legislature: Provided, That no person be eligible or qualified to act as a representative, unless he shall have been a citizen of one of the United States three years, and be a resident in the district, or unless he shall have resided in the district three years; and, in either case, shall likewise hold in his own right, in fee-simple, two hundred acres of land within the same: Provided also, That a freehold in fifty acres of land in the district, having been a citizen of one of the States, and being resident in the district, or the like freehold and two years' residence in the district, shall be necessary to qualify a man as an elector of a representative.

Sec. 10. The representatives thus elected shall serve for the term of two years; and in case of the death of a representative, or removal from office, the governor shall issue a writ to the county or township, for which he was a member, to elect another in his stead, to serve for the residue of the term.

Sec. 11. The general assembly, or legislature, shall consist of the governor, legislative council, and a house of representatives. The legislative council shall consist of five members, to continue in office five years, unless sooner removed by Congress; any three of whom to be a quorum; and the members of the council shall be nominated and appointed in the following manner, to wit: As soon as representatives shall be elected the governor shall appoint a time and place for them to meet together, and when met they shall nominate ten persons, resident in the district, and each possessed of a freehold in five hundred acres of land, and return their names to Congress, five of whom Congress shall appoint and commission to serve as aforesaid; and whenever a vacancy shall happen in the council, by death or removal from office, the house of representatives shall nominate two persons, qualified as aforesaid, for each vacancy, and return their names to Congress, one of whom Congress shall appoint and commission for the residue of the term; and every five years, four months at least before the expiration of the time of service of the members of the council, the said house shall nominate ten persons, qualified as aforesaid, and return their names to Congress, five of whom Congress shall appoint and commission to serve as members of the council five years, unless sooner removed. And the governor, legislative council, and house of representatives shall have authority to make laws in all cases for the good government of the district, not repugnant to the principles and articles in this ordinance established and declared. And all bills, having passed by a majority in the house, and by a majority in the council, shall be referred to the governor for his assent; but no bill, or legislative act whatever, shall be of any force without his assent. The governor shall have power to convene, prorogue, and dissolve the general assembly when, in his opinion, it shall be expedient.

Sec. 12. The governor, judges, legislative council, secretary, and such other officers as Congress shall appoint in the district, shall take an oath or affirmation of fidelity, and of office; the governor before the President of Congress, and all other officers before the governor. As soon as a legislature shall be formed in the district, the council and house assembled, in one room, shall have authority, by joint ballot, to elect a delegate to Congress, who shall have a seat in Congress with a right of debating, but not of voting, during this temporary government.

Sec. 13. And for extending the fundamental principles of civil and religious liberty, which form the basis whereon these republics, their laws and constitutions, are erected; to fix and establish those principles as the basis of all laws, constitutions, and governments, which forever hereafter shall be formed in the said territory; to provide, also, for the establishment of States, and permanent government therein, and for their admission to a share in the Federal councils on an equal footing with the original States, at as early periods as may be consistent with the general interest:

Sec. 14. It is hereby ordained and declared, by the authority aforesaid, that the following articles shall be considered as articles of compact, between the original States and the people and States in the said territory, and forever remain unalterable, unless by common consent, to wit:

ARTICLE I

No person, demeaning himself in a peaceable and orderly manner, shall ever be molested on account of his mode of worship, or religious sentiments, in the said territories.

ARTICLE II

The inhabitants of the said territory shall always be entitled to the benefits of the writs of habeas corpus, and of the trial by jury; of a proportionate representation of the people in the legislature, and of judicial proceedings according to the course of the common law. All persons shall be bailable, unless for capital offenses, where the proof shall be evident, or the presumption great. All fines shall be moderate; and no cruel or unusual punishments shall be inflicted. No man shall be deprived of his liberty or property, but by the judgment of his peers, or the law of the land, and should the public exigencies make it necessary, for the common preservation, to take any person's property, or to demand his particular services, full compensation shall be made for the same. And, in the just preservation of rights and property, it is understood and declared, that no law ought ever to be made or have force in the said territory, that shall, in any manner whatever, interfere with or affect private contracts, or engagements, bona fide, and without fraud previously formed.

ARTICLE III

Religion, morality, and knowledge being necessary to good government and the happiness of mankind, schools and the means of education shall forever be encouraged. The utmost good faith shall always be observed towards the Indians; their lands and property shall never be taken from them without their consent; and in their property, rights, and liberty they never shall be invaded or disturbed, unless in just and lawful wars authorized by Congress; but laws founded in justice and humanity shall, from time to time, be made, for preventing wrongs being done to them, and for preserving peace and friendship with them.

ARTICLE IV

The said territory, and the States which may be formed therein, shall forever remain a part of this confederacy of the United States of America, subject to the Articles of Confederation, and to such alterations therein as shall be constitutionally made; and to all the acts and ordinances of the United States in Congress assembled, conformable thereto. The inhabitants and settlers in the said territory shall be subject to pay a part of the Federal debts, contracted, or to be contracted, and a proportional part of the expenses of government to be apportioned on them by Congress, according to the same common rule and measure by which apportionments thereof shall be made on the other States; and the taxes for paying their proportion shall be laid and levied by the authority and direction of the legislatures of the district, or districts, or new States, as in the original States, within the time agreed upon by the United States in Congress assembled. The legislatures of those districts, or new States, shall never interfere with the primary disposal of the soil by the United States in Congress assembled, nor with any regulations Congress may find necessary for securing the title in such soil to the bona fide purchasers. No tax shall be imposed on lands the property of the United States; and in no case shall nonresident proprietors be taxed higher than residents. The navigable waters leading into the Mississippi and Saint Lawrence, and the carrying places between the same, shall be common highways, and forever free, as well to the inhabitants of the said territory as to the citizens of the United States, and those of any other States that may be admitted into the confederacy, without any tax, impost, or duty therefor.

ARTICLE V

There shall be formed in the said territory not less than three nor more than five States; and the boundaries of the States, as soon as Virginia shall alter her act of cession and consent to the same, shall become fixed and established as follows, to wit: The western State, in the said territory, shall be bounded by the Mississippi, the Ohio, and the Wabash Rivers; a direct line drawn from the Wabash and Post Vincents, due north, to the territorial line between the United States and Canada; and by the said territorial line to the Lake of the Woods and Mississippi. The middle State shall be bounded by the said direct line, the Wabash from Post Vincents to the Ohio, by the Ohio, by a direct line drawn due north from the mouth of the Great Miami to the said territorial line, and by the said territorial line. The eastern State shall be bounded by the last-mentioned direct line, the Ohio, Pennsylvania, and the said territorial line: Provided, however, And it is further understood and declared, that the boundaries of these three States shall be subject so far to be altered, that, if Congress shall hereafter find it expedient, they shall have authority to form one or two States in that part of the said territory which lies north of an east and west line drawn through the southerly bend or extreme of Lake Michigan. And whenever any of the said States shall have sixty thousand free inhabitants therein, such State shall be admitted, by its delegates, into the Congress of the United States, on an equal footing with the original States, in all respects whatever; and shall be at liberty to form a permanent constitution and State government: Provided, The constitution and government, so to be formed, shall be republican, and in conformity to the principles contained in these articles, and, so far as it can be consistent with the general interest of the confederacy, such admission shall be allowed at an earlier period, and when there may be a less number of free inhabitants in the State than sixty thousand.

ARTICLE VI

There shall be neither slavery nor involuntary servitude in the said territory, otherwise than in the punishment of crimes, whereof the party shall have been duly convicted: Provided always, That any person escaping into the same, from whom labor or service is lawfully claimed in any one of the original States, such fugitive may be lawfully reclaimed, and conveyed to the person claiming his or her labor or service as aforesaid.

Be it ordained by the authority aforesaid, That the resolutions of the 23d of April, 1784, relative to the subject of this ordinance, be, and the same are hereby, repealed, and declared null and void.

Done by the United States, in Congress assembled, the 13th day of July, in the year of our Lord 1787, and of their sovereignty and independence the twelfth.

Appendix D

THE JUDICIARY ACT OF 1789

1 Statutes at Large 73

Chap. XX.—*An act to establish the Judicial Courts of the United States.*

Section 1.   Be it enacted by the Senate and House of Representatives of the United States of America in Congress assembled, That the supreme court of the United States shall consist of a chief justice and five associate justices, any four of whom shall be a quorum, and shall hold annually at the seat of government two sessions, the one commencing the first Monday of February, and the other the first Monday of August. That the associate justices shall have precedence according to the date of their commissions, or when the commissions of two or more of them bear date on the same day, according to their respective ages.

Sec. 2.   And be it further enacted, That the United States shall be, and they hereby are divided into thirteen districts, to be limited and called as follows, to wit: one to consist of that part of the State of Massachusetts which lies easterly of the State of New Hampshire, and to be called Maine District; one to consist of the State of New Hampshire, and to be called New Hampshire District; one to consist of the remaining part of the State of Massachusetts, and to be called Massachusetts District; one to consist of the State of Connecticut, and to be called Connecticut District; one to consist of the State of New York, and to be called New York District; one to consist of the State of New Jersey, and to be called New Jersey District; one to consist of the State of Pennsylvania, and to be called Pennsylvania District; one to consist of the State of Delaware, and to be called Delaware District; one to consist of the State of Maryland, and to be called Maryland District; one to consist of the State of Virginia, except that part called the District of Kentucky, and to be called Virginia District; one to consist of the remaining part of the State of Virginia, and to be called Kentucky District; one to consist of the State of South Carolina, and to be called South Carolina District; and one to consist of the State of Georgia, and to be called Georgia District.

Sec. 3.   And be it further enacted, That there be a court called a District Court, in each of the aforementioned districts, to consist of one judge, who shall reside in the district for which he is appointed, and shall be called a District Judge, and shall hold annually four sessions, the first of which to commence as follows, to wit: in the districts of New York and of New Jersey on the first, in the district of Pennsylvania on the second, in the district of Connecticut on the third, and in the district of Delaware on the fourth, Tuesdays of November next; in the districts of Massachusetts, of Maine, and of Maryland, on the first, in the district of Georgia on the second, and in the districts of New Hampshire, of Virginia, and of Kentucky, on the Third Tuesdays of December next; and the other three sessions progressively in the respective districts on the like Tuesdays of every third calendar month afterwards, and in the district of South Carolina, on the third Monday in March and September, the first Monday in July, and the second Monday in December of each and every year, commencing in December next; and that the District Judge shall have power to hold special courts at his discretion. That the stated District Court shall be held at the places following, to wit: in the district of Maine, at Portland and Pownalsborough alternately, beginning at the first; in the district of New Hampshire, at Exeter and Portsmouth alternately, beginning at the first; in the district of Massachusetts, at Boston and Salem alternately, beginning at the first; in the district of Connecticut, alternately at Hartford and New Haven, beginning at the first; in the district of New York, at New York; in the district of New Jersey, alternately at New Brunswick and Burlington, beginning at the first; in the district of Pennsylvania, at Philadelphia and York Town alternately, beginning at the first; in the district of Delaware, alternately at Newcastle and Dover, beginning at the first; in the district of Maryland, alternately at Baltimore and Easton, beginning at the first; in the district of Virginia, alternately at Richmond and Williamsburgh, beginning at the first; in the district of Kentucky, at Harrodsburgh; in the district of South Carolina, at Charleston; and in the district of Georgia, alternately at Savannah and Augusta, beginning at the first; and that the special courts shall be held at the same place in each district as the stated courts, or in districts that have two, at either of them, in the discretion of the judge, or at such other place in the district, as the nature of the business and his discretion shall direct. And that in the districts that have but one place for holding the District Court, the records thereof shall be kept at that place; and in districts that have two, at that place in each district which the judge shall appoint.

Sec. 4. And be it further enacted, That the before mentioned districts, except those of Maine and Kentucky, shall be divided into three circuits, and be called the eastern, the middle, and the southern circuit. That the eastern circuit shall consist of the districts of New Hampshire, Massachusetts, Connecticut and New York; that the middle circuit shall consist of the districts of New Jersey, Pennsylvania, Delaware, Maryland and Virginia; and that the southern circuit shall consist of the districts of South Carolina and Georgia, and that there shall be held annually in each district of said circuits, two courts, which shall be called Circuit Courts, and shall consist of any two justices of the Supreme Court, and the district judge of such districts, any two of whom shall constitute a quorum: *Provided,* That no district judge shall give a vote in any case of appeal or error from his own decision; but may assign the reasons of such his decision.

Sec. 5. And be it further enacted, That the first session of the said circuit court in the several districts shall commence at the times following, to wit: in New Jersey on the second, in New York on the fourth, in Pennsylvania on the eleventh, in Connecticut on the twenty-second, and in Delaware on the twenty-seventh, days of April next; in Massachusetts on the third, in Maryland on the seventh, in South Carolina on the twelfth, in New Hampshire on the twentieth, in Virginia on the twenty-second, and in Georgia on the twenty-eighth, days of May next, and the subsequent sessions in the respective districts on the like days of every sixth calendar month afterwards, except in South Carolina, where the session of the said court shall commence on the first, and in Georgia where it shall commence on the seventeenth day of October, and except when any of those days shall happen on a Sunday, and then the session shall commence on the next day following. And the sessions of the said circuit court shall be held in the district of New Hampshire, at Portsmouth and Exeter alternately, beginning at the first; in the district of Massachusetts, at Boston; in the district of Connecticut, alternately at Hartford and New Haven, beginning at the last; in the district of New York, alternately at New York and Albany, beginning at the first; in the district of New Jersey, at Trenton; in the district of Pennsylvania, alternately at Philadelphia and Yorktown, beginning at the first; in the district of Delaware, alternately at New Castle and Dover, beginning at the first; in the district of Maryland, alternately at Annapolis and Easton, beginning at the first; in the district of Virginia, alternately at Charlottesville and Williamsburgh, beginning at the first; in the district of South Carolina, alternately at Columbia and Charleston, beginning at the first; and in the district of Georgia, alternately at Savannah and Augusta, beginning at the first. And the circuit courts shall have power to hold special sessions for the trial of criminal causes at any other time at their discretion, or at the discretion of the Supreme Court.

Sec. 6. And be it further enacted, That the Supreme Court may, by any one or more of its justices being present, be adjourned from day to day until a quorum be convened; and that a circuit court may also be adjourned from day to day by any one of its judges, or if none are present, by the marshal of the district until a quorum be convened; and that a district court, in case of the inability of the judge to attend at the commencement of a session, may by virtue of a written order from the said judge, directed to the marshal of the district, be adjourned by the said marshal to such day, antecedent to the next stated session of the said court, as in the said order shall be appointed; and in case of the death of the said judge, and his vacancy not being supplied, all process, pleadings and proceedings of what nature soever, pending before the

709

said court, shall be continued of course until the next stated session after the appointment and acceptance of the office by his successor.

Sec. 7. And be it [further] enacted, That the Supreme Court, and the district courts shall have power to appoint clerks for their respective courts, and that the clerk for each district court shall be clerk also of the circuit court in such district, and each of the said clerks shall, before he enters upon the execution of his office, take the following oath or affirmation, to wit: "I, A.B., being appointed clerk of _____, do solemnly swear, or affirm, that I will truly and faithfully enter and record all the orders, decrees, judgments and proceedings of the said court, and that I will faithfully and impartially discharge and perform all the duties of my said office, according to the best of my abilities and understanding. So help me God." Which words, so help me God, shall be omitted in all cases where an affirmation is admitted instead of an oath. And the said clerks shall also severally give bond, with sufficient sureties, (to be approved of by the Supreme and District Courts respectively) to the United States, in the sum of two thousand dollars, faithfully to discharge the duties of his office, and seasonably to record the decrees, judgments and determinations of the court of which he is clerk.

Sec. 8. And be it further enacted, That the justices of the Supreme Court, and the district judges, before they proceed to execute the duties of their respective offices, shall take the following oath or affirmation, to wit: "I, A.B., do solemnly swear or affirm, that I will administer justice without respect to persons, and do equal right to the poor and to the rich, and that I will faithfully and impartially discharge and perform all the duties incumbent on me as _____ according to the best of my abilities and understanding, aggreeably to the constitution and laws of the United States. So help me God."

Sec. 9. And be it further enacted, That the district courts shall have, exclusively of the courts of the several States, cognizance of all crimes and offences that shall be cognizable under the authority of the United States, committed within their respective districts, or upon the high seas; where no other punishment than whipping, not exceeding thirty stripes, a fine not exceeding one hundred dollars, or a term of imprisonment not exceeding six months, is to be inflicted; and shall also have exclusive original cognizance of all civil causes of admiralty and maritime jurisdiction, including all seizures under laws of impost, navigation or trade of the United States, where the seizures are made, on waters which are navigable from the sea by vessels of ten or more tons burthen, within their respective districts as well as upon the high seas; saving to suitors, in all cases, the right of a common law remedy, where the common law is competent to give it; and shall also have exclusive original cognizance of all seizures on land, or other waters than as aforesaid, made, and of all suits for penalties and forfeitures incurred, under the laws of the United States. And shall also have cognizance, concurrent with the courts of the several States, or the circuit courts, as the case may be, of all causes where an alien sues for a tort only in violation of the law of nations or a treaty of the United States. And shall also have cognizance, concurrent as last mentioned, of all suits at common law where the United States sue, and the matter in dispute amounts, exclusive of costs, to the sum or value of one hundred dollars. And shall also have jurisdiction exclusively of the courts of the several States, of all suits against consuls or vice-consuls, except for offences above the description aforesaid. And the trial of issues in fact, in the district courts, in all causes except civil causes of admiralty and maritime jurisdiction, shall be by jury.

Sec. 10. And be it further enacted, That the district court in Kentucky district shall, besides the jurisdiction aforesaid, have jurisdiction of all other causes, except of appeals and writs of error, hereinafter made cognizable in a circuit court, and shall proceed therein in the same manner as a circuit court, and writs of error and appeals shall lie from decisions therein to the Supreme Court in the same causes, as from a circuit court to the Supreme Court, and under the same regulations. And the district court in Maine district shall, besides the jurisdiction hereinbefore granted, have jurisdiction of all causes, except of appeals and writs of error herein after made cognizable in a circuit court, and shall proceed therein in the same manner as a circuit court: And writs of error shall lie from decisions therein to the circuit court in the district of Massachusetts in the same manner as from other district courts to their respective circuit courts.

Sec. 11. And be it further enacted, That the circuit courts shall have original cognizance, concurrent with the courts of the several States, of all suits of a civil nature at common law or in equity, where the matter in dispute exceeds, exclusive of costs, the sum or value of five hundred dollars, and the United States are plaintiffs, or petitioner; or an alien is a party, or the suit is between a citizen of the State where the suit is brought, and a citizen of another State. And shall have exclusive cognizance of all crimes and offences cognizable under the authority of the United States, except where this act otherwise provides, or the laws of the United States shall otherwise direct, and concurrent jurisdiction with the district courts of the crimes and offences cognizable therein. But no person shall be arrested in one district for trial in another, in any civil action before a circuit or district court. And no civil suit shall be brought before either of said courts against an inhabitant of the United States, by any original process in any other district than that whereof he is an inhabitant, or in which he shall be found at the time of serving the writ, nor shall any district or circuit court have cognizance of any suit to recover the contents of any promissory note or other chose in action in favour of an assignee, unless a suit might have been prosecuted in such court to recover the said contents if no assignment had been made, except in cases of foreign bills of exchange. And the circuit courts shall also have appellate jurisdiction from the district courts under the regulations and restrictions herein after provided.

Sec. 12. And be it further enacted, That if a suit be commenced in any state court against an alien, or by a citizen of the state in which the suit is brought against a citizen of another state, and the matter in dispute exceeds the aforesaid sum or value of five hundred dollars, exclusive of costs, to be made to appear to the satisfaction of the court; and the defendant shall, at the time of entering his appearance in such state court, file a petition for the removal of the cause for trial into the next circuit court, to be held in the district where the suit is pending, or if in the district of Maine to the district court next to be holden therein, or if in Kentucky district to the district court next to be holden therein, and offer good and sufficient surety for his entering in such court, on the first day of its session, copies of said process against him, and also for his there appearing and entering special bail in the cause, if special bail was originally requisite therein, it shall then be the duty of the state court to accept the surety, and proceed no further in the cause, and any bail that may have been originally taken shall be discharged, and the said copies being entered as aforesaid, in such court of the United States, the cause shall there proceed in the same manner as if it had been brought there by original process. And any attachment of the goods or estate of the defendant by the original process, shall hold the goods or estate so attached, to answer the final judgment in the same manner as by the laws of such state they would have been holden to answer final judgment had it been rendered by the court in which the suit commenced. And if in any action commenced in a state court, the title of land be concerned, and the parties are citizens of the same state, and the matter in dispute exceeds the sum or value of five hundred dollars, exclusive of costs, the sum or value being made to appear to the satisfaction of the court, either party, before the trial, shall state to the court and make affidavit if they require it, that he claims and shall rely upon a right or title to the land, under a grant from a state other than that in which the suit is pending, and produce the original grant or an exemplification of it, except where the loss of public records shall put it out of his power, and shall move that the adverse party inform the court, whether he claims a right or title to the land under a grant from the state in which the suit is pending; the said adverse [party] shall give such information, or otherwise not be allowed to plead such grant, or give it in evidence upon the trial, and if he informs that he does claim under such grant, the party claiming under the grant first mentioned may then, on motion, remove the cause for trial to the next circuit court to be holden in such district, or if in the district of Maine, to the court next to be holden therein; or if in Kentucky district, to the district court next to be holden therein; but if he is the defendant, shall do it under the same regulations as in the beforementioned case of the removal of a cause into such court by an alien; and neither party removing the cause, shall be allowed to plead or give evidence of any other title than that by him stated as aforesaid, as the ground of his claim; and the trial of issues in fact in the circuit courts shall, in all suits, except those of equity, and of admiralty, and maritime jurisdiction, be by jury.

Sec. 13. And be it further enacted, That the Supreme Court shall have exclusive jurisdiction of all controversies of a civil nature, where a state is a party, except between a state and its citizens; and except also between a state and citizens of other states, or aliens, in which latter case it shall have original but not exclusive jurisdiction. And shall have exclusively all such jurisdiction of suits or proceedings against ambassadors, or other public ministers, or their domestics, or domestic servants, as a court of law can have or exercise consistently with the law of nations; and original, but not exclusive jurisdiction of all suits brought by ambassadors, or other public ministers, or in which a consul, or vice consul, shall be a party. And the trial of issues in fact in the Supreme Court, in all actions at law against citizens of the United States, shall be by jury. The Supreme Court shall also have appellate jurisdiction from the circuit courts and courts of the several states, in the cases herein after specially provided for; and shall have power to issue writs of prohibition to the district courts, when proceeding as courts of admiralty and maritime jurisdiction, and writs of *mandamus,* in cases warranted by the principles and usages of law, to any courts appointed, or persons holding office, under the authority of the United States.

Sec. 14. And be it further enacted, That all the before-mentioned courts of the United States, shall have power to issue writs of *scire facias, habeas corpus,* and all other writs not specially provided for by statute, which may be necessary for the exercise of their respective jurisdictions, and agreeable to the principles and usages of law. And that either of the justice of the supreme court, as well as judges of the district courts, shall have power to grant writs of *habeas corpus* for the purpose of an inquiry into the cause of commitment.—*Provided,* That writs of *habeas corpus* shall in no case extend to prisoners in gaol, unless where they are in custody, under or by colour of the authority of the United States, or are committed for trial before some court of the same, or are necessary to be brought into court to testify.

Sec. 15. And be it further enacted, That all the said courts of the United States, shall have power in the trial of actions at law, on motion and due notice thereof being given, to require the parties to produce books or writings in their possession or power, which contain evidence pertinent to the issue, in cases and under circumstances where they might be compelled to produce the same by the ordinary rules of proceeding in chancery; and if a plaintiff shall fail to comply with such order, to produce books or writings, it shall be lawful for the courts respectively, on motion, to give the like judgment for the defendant as in cases of nonsuit; and if a defendant shall fail to comply with such order, to produce books or writings, it shall be lawful for the courts respectively on motion as aforesaid, to give judgment against him or her by default.

Sec. 16. And be it further enacted, That suits in equity shall not be sustained in either of the courts of the United States, in any case where plain, adequate and complete remedy may be had at law.

Sec. 17. And be it further enacted, That all the said courts of the United States shall have power to grant new trials, in cases where there has been a trial by jury for reasons for which new trials have usually been granted in the courts of law; and shall have power to impose and administer all necessary oaths or affirmations, and to punish by fine or imprisonment, at the discretion of said courts, all contempts of authority in any cause or hearing before the same; and to make and establish all necessary rules for the orderly conducting business in the said courts, provided such rules are not repugnant to the laws of the United States.

Sec. 18. And be it further enacted, That when in a circuit court, judgment upon a verdict in a civil action shall be entered, execution may on motion of either party, at the discretion of the court, and on such conditions for the security of the adverse party as they may judge proper, be stayed forty-two days from the time of entering judgment, to give time to file in the clerk's office of said court, a petition for a new trial. And if such petition be there filed within said term of forty-two days, with a certificate thereon from either of the judges of such court, that he allows the same to be filed, which certificate he may make or refuse at his discretion, execution shall of course be further stayed to the next session of said court. And if a new trial be granted, the former judgment shall be thereby rendered void.

Sec. 19. And be it further enacted, That it shall be the duty of circuit courts, in causes in equity and of admiralty and maritime jurisdiction, to cause the facts on which they found their sentence or decree, fully to appear upon the record either from the pleadings and decree itself, or a state of the case agreed by the parties, or their counsel, or if they disagree by a stating of the case by the court.

Sec. 20. And be it further enacted, That where in a circuit court, a plaintiff in an action, originally brought there, or a petitioner in equity, other than the United States, recovers less than the sum or value of five hundred dollars, or a libellant, upon his own appeal, less than the sum or value of three hundred dollars, he shall not be allowed, but at the discretion of the court, may be adjudged to pay costs.

Sec. 21. And be it further enacted, That from final decrees in a district court in causes of admiralty and maritime jurisdiction, where the matter in dispute exceeds the sum or value of three hundred dollars, exclusive of costs, an appeal shall be allowed to the next circuit court, to be held in such district. *Provided nevertheless,* That all such appeals from final decrees as aforesaid, from the district court of Maine, shall be made to the circuit court, next to be holden after each appeal in the district of Massachusetts.

Sec. 22. And be it further enacted, That final decrees and judgments in civil actions in a district court, where the matter in dispute exceeds the sum or value of fifty dollars, exclusive of costs, may be reexamined, and reversed or affirmed in a circuit court, holden in the same district, upon a writ of error, whereto shall be annexed and returned therewith at the day and place therein mentioned, and authenticated transcript of the record, and assignment of errors, and prayer for reversal, with a citation to the adverse party, signed by the judge of such district court, or a justice of the Supreme Court, the adverse party having at least twenty days' notice. And upon a like process, may final judgments and decrees in civil actions, and suits in equity in a circuit court, brought there by original process, or removed there from courts of the several States, or removed there by appeal from a district court where the matter in dispute exceeds the sum or value of two thousand dollars, exclusive of costs, be re-examined and reversed or affirmed in the Supreme Court, the citation being in such case signed by a judge of such circuit court, or justice of the Supreme Court, and the adverse party having at least thirty days' notice. But there shall be no reversal in either court on such writ of error for error in ruling any plea in abatement, other than a plea to the jurisdiction of the court, or such plea to a petition or bill in equity, as is in the nature of a demurrer, or for any error in fact. And writs of error shall not be brought but within five years after rendering or passing the judgment or decree complained of, or in case the person entitled to such writ of error be an infant, *feme covert, non compos mentis,* or imprisoned, then within five years as aforesaid, exclusive of the time of such disability. And every justice or judge signing a citation on any writ of error as aforesaid, shall take good and sufficient security, that the plaintiff in error shall prosecute his writ to effect, and answer all damages and costs if he fail to make his plea good.

Sec. 23. And be it further enacted, That a writ of error as aforesaid shall be a supersedeas and stay execution in cases only where the writ of error is served, by a copy thereof being lodged for the adverse party in the clerk's office where the record remains, within ten days, Sundays exclusive, after rendering the judgment or passing the decree complained of. Until the expiration of which term of ten days, executions shall not issue in any case where a writ of error may be a supersedeas; and whereupon such writ of error the Supreme or a circuit court shall affirm a judgment or decree, they shall adjudge or decree to the respondent in error just damages for his delay, and single or double costs at their discretion.

715

Sec. 24. And be it further enacted, That when a judgment or decree shall be reversed in a circuit court, such court shall proceed to render such judgment or pass such decree as the district court should have rendered or passed; and the Supreme Court shall do the same on reversals therein, except where the reversal is in favour of the plaintiff, or petitioner in the original suit, and the damages to be assessed, or matter to be decreed, are uncertain, in which case they shall remand the cause for a final decision. And the Supreme Court shall not issue execution in causes that are removed before them by writs of error, but shall send a special mandate to the circuit court to award execution thereupon.

Sec. 25. And be it further enacted, That a final judgment or decree in any suit, in the highest court of law or equity of a State in which a decision in the suit could be had, where is drawn in question the validity of a treaty or statute of, or an authority exercised under the United States, and the decision is against their validity; or where is drawn in question the validity of a statute of, or an authority exercised under any State, on the ground of their being repugnant to the constitution, treaties or laws of the United States, and the decision is in favour of such their validity, or where is drawn in question the construction of any clause of the constitution or of a treaty, or statute of, or commission held under the United States, and the decision is against the title, right, privilege or exemption specially set up or claimed by either party, under such clause of the said Constitution, treaty, statute or commission, may be re-examined and reversed or affirmed in the Supreme Court of the United States upon a writ of error, the citation being signed by the chief justice, or judge or chancellor of the court rendering or passing the judgment or decree complained of, or by a justice of the Supreme Court of the United States, in the same manner and under the same regulations, and the writ shall have the same effect, as if the judgment or decree complained of had been rendered or passed in a circuit court, and the proceeding upon the reversal shall also be the same, except that the Supreme Court, instead of remanding the cause for a final decision as before provided, may at their discretion, if the cause shall have been once remanded before, proceed to a final decision of the same, and award execution. But no other error shall be assigned or regarded as a ground of reversal in any such case as aforesaid, than such as appears on the face of the record, and immediately respects the before mentioned questions of validity or construction of the said constitution, treaties, statutes, commissions, or authorities in dispute.

Sec. 26. And be it further enacted, That in all causes brought before either of the courts of the United States to recover the forfeiture annexed to any articles of agreement, covenant, bond, or other speciality, where the forfeiture, breach or non-performance shall appear, by the default or confession of the defendant, or upon demurrer, the court before whom the action is, shall render judgment therein for the plaintiff to recover so much as is due according to equity. And when the sum for which judgment should be rendered is uncertain, the same shall, if either of the parties request it, be assessed by a jury.

Sec. 27. And be it further enacted, That a marshal shall be appointed in and for each district for the term of four years, but shall be removable from office at pleasure, whose duty it shall be to attend the district and circuit courts when sitting therein, and also the Supreme Court in the district in which that court shall sit. And to execute throughout the district, all lawful precepts directed to him, and issued under the authority of the United States, and he shall have power to command all necessary assistance in the execution of his duty, and to appoint as there shall be occasion, one or more deputies, who shall be removable from office by the judge of the district court, or the circuit court sitting within the district, at the pleasure of either; and before he enters on the duties of his office, he shall become bound for the faithful performance of the same, by himself and by his deputies before the judge of the district court to the United States, jointly and severally, with two good and sufficient sureties, inhabitants and free-holders of such district, to be approved by the district judge, in the sum of twenty thousand dollars, and shall take before said judge, as shall also his deputies, before they enter on the duties of their appointment, the following oath of office: "I, A.B., do solemnly swear or affirm, that I will faithfully execute all lawful precepts directed to the marshal of the district of ＿＿＿ under the authority of the United States, and true returns make, and in all things well and truly, and without malice or partiality, perform the duties of the office of marshal (or marshal's deputy, as the case may be) of the district of ＿＿＿, during my continuance in said office, and take only my lawful fees. So help me God."

Sec. 28. And be it further enacted, That in all causes wherein the marshal or his deputy shall be a party, the writs and precepts therein shall be directed to such disinterested person as the court, or any justice or judge thereof may appoint, and the person so appointed, is hereby authorized to execute and return the same. And in case of the death of any marshal, his deputy or deputies shall continue in office, unless otherwise specially removed; and shall execute the same in the name of the deceased, until another marshal shall be appointed and sworn: and the defaults or misfeasances in office of such deputy or deputies in the mean time, as well as before, shall be adjudged a breach of the condition of the bond given, as before directed, by the marshal who appointed them; and the executor or administrator of the deceased marshal shall have like remedy for the defaults and misfeasances in office of such deputy or deputies during such interval, as they would be entitled to if the marshal had continued in life and in the exercise of his said office, until his successor was appointed, and sworn or affirmed:

And every marshal or his deputy when removed from office, or when the term for which the marshal is appointed shall expire, shall have power notwithstanding to execute all such precepts as may be in their hands respectively at the time of such removal or expiration of office; and the marshal shall be held answerable for the delivery to his successor of all prisoners which may be in his custody at the time of his removal, or when the term for which he is appointed shall expire, and for that purpose may retain such prisoners in his custody until his successor shall be appointed and qualified as the law directs.

Sec. 29. And be it further enacted, That in cases punishable with death, the trial shall be had in the county where the offence was committed, or where that cannot be done without great inconvenience, twelve petit jurors at least shall be summoned from thence. And jurors in all cases to serve in the courts of the United States shall be designated by lot or otherwise in each State respectively according to the mode of forming juries therein now practised, so far as the laws of the same shall render such designation practicable by the courts or marshals of the United States; and the jurors shall have the same qualifications as are requisite for jurors by the laws of the State of which they are citizens, to serve in the highest courts of law of such State, and shall be returned as there shall be occasion for them, from such parts of the district from time to time as the court shall direct, so as shall be most favourable to an impartial trial, and so as not to incur an unnecessary expense, or unduly to burthen the citizens of any part of the district with such services. And writs of *venire facias* when directed by the court shall issue from the clerk's office, and shall be served and returned by the marshal in his proper person, or by his deputy, or in case the marshal or his deputy is not an indifferent person, or is interested in the event of the cause, by such fit person as the court shall specially appoint for that purpose, to whom they shall administer an oath or affirmation that he will truly and impartially serve and return such writ. And when from challenges or otherwise there shall not be a jury to determine any civil or criminal cause, the marshal or his deputy shall, by order of the court where such defect of jurors shall happen, return jurymen *de talibus circumstantibus* sufficient to complete the panel; and when the marshal or his deputy are disqualified as aforesaid, jurors may be returned by such disinterested person as the court shall appoint.

Sec. 30. And be it further enacted, That the mode of proof by oral testimony and examination of witnesses in open court shall be the same in all the courts of the United States, as well in the trial of causes in equity and of admiralty and maritime jurisdiction, as of actions at common law. And when the testimony of any person shall be necessary in any civil cause depending in any district in any court of the United States, who shall live at a greater distance from the place of trial than one hundred miles, or is bound on a voyage to sea, or is about

718

to go out of the United States, or out of such district, and to a greater distance from the place of trial than as aforesaid, before the time of trial, or is ancient or very infirm, the deposition of such person may be taken *de bene esse* before any justice or judge of any of the courts of the United States, or before any chancellor, justice or judge of a supreme or superior court, mayor or chief magistrate of a city, or judge of a county court or court of common pleas of any of the United States, not being of counsel or attorney to either of the parties, or interested in the event of the cause, provided that a notification from the magistrate before whom the deposition is to be taken to the adverse party, to be present at the taking of the same, and to put interrogatories, if he think fit, be first made out and served on the adverse party or his attorney as either may be nearest, if either is within one hundred miles of the place of such caption, allowing time for their attendance after notified, not less than at the rate of one day, Sundays exclusive, for every twenty miles travel. And in causes of admiralty and maritime jurisdiction, or other cases of seizure when a libel shall be filed, in which an adverse party is not named, and depositions of persons circumstanced as aforesaid shall be taken before a claim be put in, the like notification as aforesaid shall be given to the person having the agency or possession of the property libelled at the time of the capture or seizure of the same, if known to the libellant. And every person deposing as aforesaid shall be carefully examined and cautioned, and sworn or affirmed to testify the whole truth, and shall subscribe the testimony by him or her given after the same shall be reduced to writing, which shall be done only by the magistrate taking the deposition, or by the deponent in his presence. And the depositions so taken shall be retained by such magistrate until he deliver the same with his own hand into the court for which they are taken, or shall, together with a certificate of the reasons as aforesaid of their being taken, and of the notice if any given to the adverse party, be by him the said magistrate sealed up and directed to such court, and remain under his seal until opened in court. And any person may be compelled to appear and depose as aforesaid in the same manner as to appear and testify in court. And in the trial of any cause of admiralty or maritime jurisdiction in a district court, the decree in which may be appealed from, if either party shall suggest to and satisfy the court that probably it will not be in his power to produce the witnesses there testifying before the circuit court should an appeal be had, and shall move that their testimony be taken down in writing, it shall be so done by the clerk of the court. And if an appeal be had, such testimony may be used on the trial of the same, if it shall appear to the satisfaction of the court which shall try the appeal, that the witnesses are then dead or gone out of the United States, or to a greater distance than as aforesaid from the place where the court is sitting, or that by reason of age, sickness, bodily infirmity or imprisonment, they are unable to travel and appear at court, but not otherwise. And unless the same shall be made to appear on the trial of any cause, with respect to witnesses whose depositions may have been taken therein, such depositions shall not be admitted or used in the cause. *Provided*, That nothing herein shall be construed to prevent any court of the United States from granting a *dedimus potestatem* to take depositions according to common usage, when it may be necessary to prevent a failure or delay of justice, which power they shall severally possess, nor to extend to depositions taken in *perpetuam rei memoriam*, which if they relate to matters that may be cognizable in any court of the United States, a circuit court on application thereto made as a court of equity, may, according to the usages in chancery direct to be taken.

Sec. 31. And be it [further] enacted, That where any suit shall be depending in any court of the United States, and either of the parties shall die before final judgment, the executor or administrator of such deceased party who was plaintiff, petitioner, or defendant, in case the cause of action doth by law survive, shall have full power to prosecute or defend any such suit or action until final judgment; and the defendant or defendants are hereby obliged to answer thereto accordingly; and the court before whom such cause may be depending, is hereby empowered and directed to hear and determine the same, and to render judgment for or against the executor or administrator, as the case may require. And if such executor or administrator having been duly served with a *scire facias* from the office of the clerk of the court where such suit is depending, twenty days beforehand, shall neglect or refuse to become a party to the suit, the court may render judgment against the estate of the deceased party, in the same manner as if the executor or administrator had voluntarily made himself a party to the suit. And the executor or administrator who shall become a party as aforesaid, shall, upon motion to the court where the suit is depending, be entitled to a continuance of the same until the next term of the said court. And if there be two or more plaintiffs or defendants, and one or more of them shall die, if the cause of action shall survive to the surviving plaintiff or plaintiffs, or against the surviving defendant or defendants, the writ or action shall not be thereby abated; but such death being suggested upon the record, the action shall proceed at the suit of the surviving plaintiff or plaintiffs against the surviving defendant or defendants.

Sec. 32. And be it further enacted, That no summons, writ, declaration, return, process, judgment, or other proceedings in civil causes in any of the courts of the United States, shall be abated, arrested, quashed or reversed, for any defect or want of form, but the said courts respectively shall proceed and give judgment according as the right of the cause and matter in law shall appear unto them, without regarding any imperfections, defects, or want of form in such writ, declaration, or other pleading, return, process, judgment, or course of proceeding whatsoever, except those only in cases of demurrer, which the party demurring shall specially set down and express together with his demurrer as the cause thereof. And the said courts respectively shall and may, by virtue of this act, from time to time, amend all and every such imperfections, defects and wants of form, other than those only which the party demurring shall express as aforesaid, and may at any time permit either of the parties to amend any defect in the process or pleadings, upon such conditions as the said courts respectively shall in their discretion, and by their rules prescribe.

Sec. 33. And be it further enacted, That for any crime or offence against the United States, the offender may, by any justice or judge of the United States, or by any justice of the peace, or other magistrate of any of the United States where he may be found agreeably to the usual mode of process against offenders in such state, and at the expense of the United States, be arrested, and imprisoned or bailed, as the case may be, for trial before such court of the United States as by this act has cognizance of the offence. And copies of the process shall be returned as speedily as may be into the clerk's office of such court, together with the recognizances of the witnesses for their appearance to testify in the case; which recognizances the magistrate before whom the examination shall be, may require on pain of imprisonment. And if such commitment of the offender, or the witnesses shall be in a district other than that in which the offence is to be tried, it shall be the duty of the judge of that district where the delinquent is imprisoned, seasonably to issue, and of the marshal of the same district to execute, a warrant for the removal of the offender, and the witnesses, or either of them, as the case may be, to the district in which the trial is to be had. And upon all arrests in criminal cases, bail shall be admitted, except where the punishment may be death, in which cases it shall not be admitted but by the supreme or a circuit court, or by a justice of the supreme court, or a jduge of a district court, who shall exercise their discretion therein, regarding the nature and circumstances of the offence, and of the evidence, and the usages of law. And if a person committed by a justice of the supreme or a judge of a district court for an offence not punishable with death, shall afterwards procure bail, and there be no judge of the United States in the district to take the same, it may be taken by any judge of the supreme or superior court of law of such state.

Sec. 34. And be it further enacted, That the laws of the several states, except where the constitution, treaties or statutes of the United States shall otherwise require or provide, shall be regarded as rules of decision in trials at common law in the courts of the United States in cases where they apply.

Sec. 35. And be it further enacted, That in all the courts of the United States, the parties may plead and manage their own causes personally or by the assistance of such counsel or attorneys at law as by rules of the said courts respectively shall be permitted to manage and conduct causes therein. And there shall be appointed in each district a meet person learned in the law to act as attorney for the United States in such district, who shall be sworn or affirmed to the faithful execution of his office, whose duty it shall be to prosecute in such district all delinquents for crimes and offences, cognizable under the authority of the United States, and all civil actions in which the United States shall be concerned, except before the supreme court in the district in which that court shall be holden. And he shall receive as a compensation for his services such fees as shall be taxed therefor in the respective courts before which the suits or prosecutions shall be. And there shall also be appointed a meet person, learned in the law, to act as attorney-general for the United States, who shall be sworn or affirmed to a faithful execution of his office; whose duty it shall be to prosecute and conduct all suits in the Supreme Court in which the United States shall be concerned, and to give his advice and opinion upon questions of law when required by the President of the United States, or when requested by the heads of any of the departments, touching any matters that may concern their departments, and shall receive such compensation for his services as shall by law be provided.

Approved September 24, 1789.

Appendix E

THE CIVIL RIGHTS STATUTES OF THE POST CIVIL WAR RECONSTRUCTION

1. **The Civil Rights Act of 1866, An Act to protect all Persons in the United States in their Civil Rights, and furnish the Means of their Vindication, 14 Statutes at Large 27 (April 9, 1866)**

Be it enacted by the Senate and House of Representatives of the United States of America in Congress assembled. That all persons born in the United States and not subject to any foreign power, excluding Indians not taxed, are hereby declared to be citizens of the United States; and such citizens, of every race and color, without regard to any previous condition of slavery or involuntary servitude, except as a punishment for crime whereof the party shall have been duly convicted, shall have the same right, in every State and Territory in the United States, to make and enforce contracts, to sue, be parties, and give evidence, to inherit, purchase, lease, sell, hold, and convey real and personal property, and to full and equal benefit of all laws and proceedings for the security of person and property, as is enjoyed by white citizens, and shall be subject to like punishment, pains, and penalties, and to none other, any law, statute, ordinance, regulation, or custom, to the contrary notwithstanding.

Sec. 2. And be it further enacted, That any person who, under color of any law, statute, ordinance, regulation, or custom, shall subject, or cause to be subjected, any inhabitant of any State or Territory to the deprivation of any right secured or protected by this act, or to different punishment, pains, or penalties on account of such person having at any time been held in a condition of slavery or involuntary servitude, except as a punishment for crime whereof the party shall have been duly convicted, or by reason of his color or race, than is prescribed for the punishment of white persons, shall be deemed guilty of a misdemeanor, and, on conviction, shall be punished by fine not exceeding one thousand dollars, or imprisonment not exceeding one year, or both, in the discretion of the court.

Sec. 3. And be it further enacted, That the district courts of the United States, within their respective districts, shall have, exclusively of the courts of the several States, cognizance of all crimes and offences committed against the provisions of this act, and also, concurrently with the circuit courts of the United States, of all causes, civil and criminal, affecting persons who are denied or cannot enforce in the courts or judicial tribunals of the State or locality where they may be any of the rights secured to them by the first section of this act; and if any suit or prosecution, civil or criminal, has been or shall be commenced in any State court, against any such person, for any cause whatsoever, or against any officer, civil or military, or other person, for any arrest or imprisonment, trespasses, or wrongs done or committed by virtue or under color of authority derived from this act or the act establishing a Bureau for the relief of Freedmen and Refugees, and all acts amendatory thereof, or for refusing to do any act upon the ground that it would be inconsistent with this act, such defendants shall have the right to remove such cause for trial to the proper district or circuit court in the manner prescribed by the "Act relating to habeas corpus and regulating judicial proceedings in certain cases," approved March three, eighteen hundred and sixty-three, and all acts amendatory thereof. The jurisdiction in civil and criminal matters hereby conferred on the district and circuit courts of the United States shall be exercised and enforced in conformity with the laws of the United States, so far as such laws are suitable to carry the same into effect; but in all cases where such laws are not adapted to the object, or are deficient in the provisions necessary to furnish suitable remedies and punish offences against law, the common law, as modified and changed by the constitution and statutes of the State wherein the court having jurisdiction of the cause, civil or criminal, is held, so far as the same is not inconsistent with the Constitution and laws of the United States, shall be extended to and govern said courts in the trial and disposition of such cause, and, if of a criminal nature, in the infliction of punishment on the party found guilty.

Sec. 4. And be it further enacted, That the district attorneys, marshals, and deputy marshals of the United States, the commissioners appointed by the circuit and territorial courts of the United States, with powers of arresting, imprisoning, or bailing offenders against the laws of the United States, the officers and agents of the Freedmen's Bureau, and every other officer who may be specially empowered by the President of the United States, shall be, and they are hereby, specially authorized and required, at the expense of the United States, to institute proceedings against all and every person who shall violate the provisions of this act, and cause him or them to be arrested and imprisoned, or bailed, as the case may be, for trial before such court of the United States or territorial court as by this act has cognizance of the offence. And with a view to affording reasonable protection to all persons in their constitutional rights of equality before the law, without distinction of race or color, or previous condition of slavery or involuntary servitude, except as a punishment for crime, whereof the party shall have been duly convicted, and to the prompt discharge of the duties of this act, it shall be the duty of the circuit courts of the United States and the superior courts of the Territories of the United States, from time to time, to increase the number of commissioners, so as to afford a speedy and convenient means for the arrest and examination of persons charged with a violation of this act; and such commissioners are hereby authorized and required to exercise and discharge all the powers and duties conferred on them by this act, and the same duties with regard to offences created by this act, as they are authorized by law to exercise with regard to other offences against the laws of the United States.

Sec. 5. And be it further enacted, That it shall be the duty of all marshals and deputy marshals to obey and execute all warrants and precepts issued under the provisions of this act, when to them directed; and should any marshal or deputy marshal refuse to receive such warrant or other process when tendered, or to use all proper means diligently to execute the same, he shall, on conviction thereof, be fined in the sum of one thousand dollars, to the use of the person upon whom the accused is alleged to have committed the offence. And the better to enable the said commissioners to execute their duties faithfully and efficiently, in conformity with the Constitution of the United States and the requirements of this act, they are hereby authorized and empowered, within their counties respectively, to appoint, in writing, under their hands, any one or more suitable persons, from time to time, to execute all such warrants and other process as may be issued by them in the lawful performance of their respective duties; and the persons so appointed to execute any warrant or process as aforesaid shall have authority to summon and call to their aid the bystanders or *posse comitatus* of the proper county, or such portion of the land or naval forces of the United States, or of the militia, as may be necessary to the performance of the duty with which they are charged, and to insure a faithful observance of the clause of the Constitution which prohibits slavery, in conformity with the provisions of this act; and said warrants shall run and be executed by said officers anywhere in the State or Territory within which they are issued.

Sec. 6. And be it further enacted, That any person who shall knowingly and wilfully obstruct, hinder, or prevent any officer, or other person charged with the execution of any warrant or process issued under the provisions of this act, or any person or persons lawfully assisting him or them, from arresting any person for whose apprehension such warrant or process may have been issued, or shall rescue or attempt to rescue such person from the custody of the officer, other person or persons, or those lawfully assisting as aforesaid, when so arrested pursuant to the authority herein given and declared, or shall aid, abet, or assist any person so arrested as aforesaid, directly or indirectly, to escape from the custody of the officer or other person legally authorized as aforesaid, or shall harbor or conceal any person for whose arrest a warrant or process shall have been issued as aforesaid, so as to prevent his discovery and arrest after notice or knowledge of the fact that a warrant has been issued for the apprehension of such person, shall, for either of said offences, be subject to a fine not exceeding one thousand dollars, and imprisonment not exceeding six months, by indictment and conviction before the district court of the United States for the district in which said offence may have been committed, or before the proper court of criminal jurisdiction, if committed within any one of the organized Territories of the United States.

Sec. 7. And be it further enacted, That the district attorneys, the marshals, their deputies, and the clerks of the said district and territorial courts shall be paid for their services the like fees as may be allowed to them for similar services in other cases; and in all cases where the proceedings are before a commissioner, he shall be entitled to a fee of ten dollars in full for his services in each case, inclusive of all services incident to such arrest and examination. The person or persons authorized to execute the process to be issued by such commissioners for the arrest of offenders against the provisions of this act shall be entitled to a fee of five dollars for each person he or they *may* arrest and take before any such commissioner as aforesaid, with such other fees as may be deemed reasonable by such commissioner for such other additional services as may be necessarily performed by him or them, such as attending at the examination, keeping the prisoner in custody, and providing him with food and lodging during his detention, and until the final determination of such commissioner, and in general for performing such other duties as may be required in the premises; such fees to be made up in conformity with the fees usually charged by the officers of the courts of justice within the proper district or county, as near as may be practicable, and paid out of the Treasury of the United States on the certificate of the judge of the district within which the arrest is made, and to be recoverable from the defendant as part of the judgment in case of conviction.

Sec. 8. And be it further enacted, That whenever the President of the United States shall have reason to believe that offences have been or are likely to be committed against the provisions of this act within any judicial district, it shall be lawful for him, in his discretion, to direct the judge, marshal, and district attorney of such district to attend at such place within the district, and for such time as he may designate, for the purpose of the more speedy arrest and trial of persons charged with a violation of this act; and it shall be the duty of every judge or other officer, when any such requisition shall be received by him, to attend at the place and for the time therein designated.

Sec. 9. And be it further enacted, That it shall be lawful for the President of the United States, or such person as he may empower for that purpose, to employ such part of the land or naval forces of the United States, or of the militia, as shall be necessary to prevent the violation and enforce the due execution of this act.

Sec. 10. And be it further enacted, That upon all questions of law arising in any cause under the provisions of this act a final appeal may be taken to the Supreme Court of the United States.

SCHUYLER COLFAX,

Speaker of the House of Representatives.

LA FAYETTE S. FOSTER,

President of the Senate, *pro tempore.*

In the Senate of the United States, April 6, 1866.

The President of the United States having returned to the Senate, in which it originated, the bill entitled "An act to protect all persons in the United States in their civil rights, and furnish the means of their vindication," with his objections thereto, the Senate proceeded, in pursuance of the Constitution, to reconsider the same; and,

Resolved, That the said bill do pass, two-thirds of the Senate agreeing to pass the same.

> Attest: J.W. Forney,
> Secretary of the Senate.

In the House of Representatives U.S. April 9th, 1866.

The House of Representatives having proceeded, in pursuance of the Constitution, to reconsider the bill entitled "An act to protect all persons in the United States in their civil rights, and furnish the means of their vindication," returned to the Senate by the President of the United States, with his objections, and sent by the Senate to the House of Representatives, with the message of the President returning the bill:

Resolved, That the bill do pass, two-thirds of the House of Representatives agreeing to pass the same.

> Attest: Edward McPherson, Clerk,
> by Clinton Lloyd, Chief Clerk.

2. The Enforcement Act, the Civil Rights Act of 1870, An Act to enforce the Right of Citizens of the United States to vote in the several States of this Union, and for other Purposes, 16 Statutes at Large 140 (May 31, 1870)

Be it enacted by the Senate and House of Representatives of the United States of America in Congress assembled, That all citizens of the United States who are or shall be otherwise qualified by law to vote at any election by the people in any State, Territory, district, county, city, parish, township, school district, municipality, or other territorial subdivision, shall be entitled and allowed to vote at all such elections, without distinction of race, color, or previous condition of servitude;

any constitution, law, custom, usage, or regulation of any State or Territory, or by or under its authority, to the contrary notwithstanding.

Sec. 2. And be it further enacted, That if by or under the authority of the constitution or laws of any State, or the laws of any Territory, any act is or shall be required to be done as a prerequisite or qualification for voting, and by such constitution or laws persons or officers are or shall be charged with the performance of duties in furnishing to citizens an opportunity to perform such prerequisite, or to become qualified to vote, it shall be the duty of every such person and officer to give to all citizens of the United States the same and equal opportunity to perform such prerequisite, and to become qualified to vote without distinction of race, color, or previous condition of servitude; and if any such person or officer shall refuse or knowingly omit to give full effect to this section, he shall, for every such offence, forfeit and pay the sum of five hundred dollars to the person aggrieved thereby, to be recovered by an action on the case, with full costs, and such allowance for counsel fees as the court shall deem just, and shall also, for every such offence, be deemed guilty of a misdemeanor, and shall, on conviction thereof, be fined not less than five hundred dollars, or be imprisoned not less than one month and not more than one year, or both, at the discretion of the court.

Sec. 3. And be it further enacted, That whenever, by or under the authority of the constitution or laws of any State, or the laws of any Territory, any act is or shall be required to [be] done by any citizen as a prerequisite to qualify or entitle him to vote, the offer of any such citizen to perform the act required to be done as aforesaid shall, if it fail to be carried into execution by reason of the wrongful act or omission aforesaid of the person or officer charged with the duty of receiving or permitting such performance or offer to perform, or acting thereon, be deemed and held as a performance in law of such act; and the person so offering and failing as aforesaid, and being otherwise qualified, shall be entitled to vote in the same manner and to the same extent as if he had in fact performed such act; and any judge, inspector, or other officer of election whose duty it is or shall be to receive, count, certify, register, report, or give effect to the vote of any such citizen who shall wrongfully refuse or omit to receive, count, certify, register, report, or give effect to the vote of such citizen upon the presentation by him of his affidavit stating such offer and the time and place thereof, and the name of the officer or person whose duty it was to act thereon, and that he was wrongfully prevented by such person or officer from performing such act, shall for every such offence forfeit and pay the sum of five hundred dollars to the person aggrieved thereby, to be recovered by an action on the case, with full costs, and such allowance for counsel fees as the court shall deem just, and shall also for every such offence be guilty of a misdemeanor, and shall, on conviction thereof, be fined not less than five hundred dollars, or be imprisoned not less than one month and not more than one year, or both, at the discretion of the court.

Sec. 4. And be it further enacted, That if any person, by force, bribery, threats, intimidation, or other unlawful means, shall hinder, delay, prevent, or obstruct, or shall combine and confederate with others to hinder, delay, prevent, or obstruct, any citizen from doing any act required to be done to qualify him to vote or from voting at any election as aforesaid, such person shall for every such offence forfeit and pay the sum of five hundred dollars to the person aggrieved thereby, to be recovered by an action on the case, with full costs, and such allowance for counsel fees as the court shall deem just, and shall also for every such offence be guilty of a misdemeanor, and shall, on conviction thereof, be fined not less than five hundred dollars, or be imprisoned not less than one month and not more than one year, or both, at the discretion of the court.

Sec. 5. And be it further enacted, That if any person shall prevent, hinder, control, or intimidate, or shall attempt to prevent, hinder, control, or intimidate, any person from exercising or in exercising the right of suffrage, to whom the right of suffrage is secured or guaranteed by the fifteenth amendment to the Constitution of the United States, by means of bribery, threats, or threats of depriving such person of employment or occupation, or of ejecting such person from rented house, lands, or other property, or by threats of refusing to renew leases or contracts for labor, or by threats of violence to himself or family, such person so offending shall be deemed guilty of a misdemeanor, and shall, on conviction thereof, be fined not less than five hundred dollars, or be imprisoned not less than one month and not more than one year, or both, at the discretion of the court.

Sec. 6. And be it further enacted, That if two or more persons shall band or conspire together, or go in disguise upon the public highway, or upon the premises of another, with intent to violate any provision of this act, or to injure, oppress, threaten, or intimidate any citizen with intent to prevent or hinder his free exercise and enjoyment of any right or privilege granted or secured to him by the Constitution or laws of the United States, or because of his having exercised the same, such persons shall be held guilty of felony, and, on conviction thereof, shall be fined or imprisoned, or both, at the discretion of the court,—the fine not to exceed five thousand dollars, and the imprisonment not to exceed ten years,—and shall, moreover, be thereafter ineligible to, and disabled from holding, any office or place of honor, profit, or trust created by the Constitution or laws of the United States.

Sec. 7. And be it further enacted, That if in the act of violating any provision in either of the two preceding sections, any other felony, crime, or misdemeanor shall be committed, the offender, on conviction of such violation of said sections, shall be punished for the same with such punishments as are attached to the said felonies, crimes, and misdemeanors by the laws of the State in which the offence may be committed.

Sec. 8. And be it further enacted, That the district courts of the United States, within their respective districts, shall have, exclusively of the courts of the several States, cognizance of all crimes and offences committed against the provisions of this act, and also, concurrently with the circuit courts of the United States, of all causes, civil and criminal, arising under this act, except as herein otherwise provided, and the jurisdiction hereby conferred shall be exercised in conformity with the laws and practice governing United States courts; and all crimes and offences committed against the provisions of this act may be prosecuted by the indictment of a grand jury, or, in cases of crimes and offences not infamous, the prosecution may be either by indictment or information filed by the district attorney in a court having jurisdiction.

Sec. 9. And be it further enacted, That the district attorneys, marshals, and deputy marshals of the United States, the commissioners appointed by the circuit and territorial courts of the United States, with powers of arresting, imprisoning, or bailing offenders against the laws of the United States, and every other officer who may be specially empowered by the President of the United States, shall be, and they are hereby, specially authorized and required, at the expense of the United States, to institute proceedings against all and every person who shall violate the provisions of this act, and cause him or them to be arrested and imprisoned, or bailed, as the case may be, for trial before such court of the United States or territorial court as has cognizance of the offense. And with a view to afford reasonable protection to all persons in their constitutional right to vote without distinction of race, color, or previous condition of servitude, and to the prompt discharge of the duties of this act, it shall be the duty of the circuit courts of the United States, and the superior courts of the Territories of the United States, from time to time, to increase the number of commissioners, so as to afford a speedy and convenient means for the arrest and examination of persons charged with a violation of this act; and such commissioners are hereby authorized and required to exercise and discharge all the powers and duties conferred on them by this act, and the same duties with regard to offences created by this act as they are authorized by law to exercise with regard to other offences against the laws of the United States.

Sec. 10. And be it further enacted, That it shall be the duty of all marshals and deputy marshals to obey and execute all warrants and precepts issued under the provisions of this act, when to them directed; and should any marshal or deputy marshal refuse to receive such warrant or other process when tendered, or to use all proper means diligently to execute the same, he shall, on conviction thereof, be fined in the sum of one thousand dollars, to the use of the person deprived of the rights conferred by this act. And the better to enable the said commissioners to execute their duties faithfully and efficiently, in conformity with the Constitution of the United States and the requirements of this act, they are hereby authorized and empowered, within their districts respectively, to appoint, in writing, under their hands, any one or more suitable persons, from time to time, to execute all such warrants and other process as may be issued by them in the lawful performance of their respective duties, and the persons so appointed to execute any warrant or process as aforesaid shall have authority to summon and call to their aid the bystanders or *posse comitatus* of the proper county, or such portion of the land or naval forces of the United States, or of the militia, as may be necessary to the performance of the duty with which they are charged, and to insure a faithful observance of the fifteenth amendment to the Constitution of the United States; and such warrants shall run and be executed by said officers anywhere in the State or Territory within which they are issued.

Sec. 11. And be it further enacted, That any person who shall knowingly and wilfully obstruct, hinder, or prevent any officer or other person charged with the execution of any warrant or process issued under the provisions of this act, or any person or persons lawfully assisting him or them from arresting any person for whose apprehension such warrant or process may have been issued, or shall rescue or attempt to rescue such person from the custody of the officer or other person or persons, or those lawfully assisting as aforesaid, when so arrested pursuant to the authority herein given and declared, or shall aid, abet, or assist any person so arrested as aforesaid, directly or indirectly, to escape from the custody of the officer or other person legally authorized as aforesaid, or shall harbor or conceal any person for whose arrest a warrant or process shall have been issued as aforesaid, so as to prevent his discovery and arrest after notice or knowledge of the fact that a warrant has been issued for the apprehension of such person, shall, for either of said offences, be subject to a fine not exceeding one thousand dollars, or imprisonment not exceeding six months, or both, at the discretion of the court, on conviction before the district or circuit court of the United States for the district or circuit in which said offence may have been committed, or before the proper court of criminal jurisdiction, if committed within any one of the organized Territories of the United States.

Sec. 12. And be it further enacted, That the commissioners, district attorneys, the marshals, their deputies, and the clerks of the said district, circuit, and territorial courts shall be paid for their services the like fees as may be allowed to them for similar services in other cases. The person or persons authorized to execute the process to be issued by such commissioners for the arrest of offenders against the provisions of this act shall be entitled to the usual fees allowed to the marshal for an arrest for each person he or they may arrest and take before any such commissioner as aforesaid, with such other fees as may be deemed reasonable by such commissioner for such other additional services as may be necessarily performed by him or them, such as attending at the examination, keeping the prisoner in custody, and providing him with food and lodging during his detention and until the final determination of such commissioner, and in general for performing such other duties as may be required in the premises; such fees to be made up in conformity with the fees usually charged by the officers of the courts of justice within the proper district or county as near as may be practicable, and paid out of the treasury of the United States on the certificate of the judge of the district within which the arrest is made, and to be recoverable from the defendant as part of the judgment in case of conviction.

Sec. 13. And be it further enacted, That it shall be lawful for the President of the United States to employ such part of the land or naval forces of the United States, or of the militia, as shall be necessary to aid in the execution of judicial process issued under this act.

Sec. 14. And be it further enacted, That whenever any person shall hold office, except as a member of Congress or of some State legislature, contrary to the provisions of the third section of the fourteenth article of amendment of the Constitution of the United States, it shall be the duty of the district attorney of the United States for the district in which such person shall hold office, as aforesaid, to proceed against such person, by writ of *quo warranto* returnable to the circuit or district court of the United States in such district, and to prosecute the same to the removal of such person from office; and any writ of *quo warranto* so brought, as aforesaid, shall take precedence of all other cases on the docket of the court to which it is made returnable, and shall not be continued unless for cause proved to the satisfaction of the court.

Sec. 15. And be it further enacted, That any person who shall hereafter knowingly accept or hold any office under the United States, or any State to which he is ineligible under the third section of the fourteenth article of amendment of the Constitution of the United States, or who shall attempt to hold or exercise the duties of any such office, shall be deemed guilty of a misdemeanor against the United States, and, upon conviction thereof before the circuit or district court of the United States, shall be imprisoned not more than one year, or fined not exceeding one thousand dollars, or both, at the discretion of the court.

Sec. 16. And be it further enacted, That all persons within the jurisdiction of the United States shall have the same right in every State and Territory in the United States to make and enforce contracts, to sue, be parties, give evidence, and to the full and equal benefit of all laws and proceedings for the security of person and property as is enjoyed by white citizens, and shall be subject to like punishment, pains, penalties, taxes, licenses, and exactions of every kind, and none other, any law, statute, ordinance, regulation, or custom to the contrary notwithstanding. No tax or charge shall be imposed or enforced by any State upon any person immigrating thereto from a foreign country which is not equally imposed and enforced upon every person immigrating to such State from any other foreign country; and any law of any State in conflict with this provision is hereby declared null and void.

Sec. 17. And be it further enacted, That any person who, under color of any law, statute, ordinance, regulation, or custom, shall subject, or cause to be subjected, any inhabitant of any State or Territory to the deprivation of any right secured or protected by the last preceding section of this act, or to different punishment, pains, or penalties on account of such person being an alien, or by reason of his color or race, than is prescribed for the punishment of citizens, shall be deemed guilty of a misdemeanor, and, on conviction, shall be punished by fine not exceeding one thousand dollars, or imprisonment not exceeding one year, or both, in the discretion of the court.

Sec. 18. And be it further enacted, That the act to protect all persons in the United States in their civil rights, and furnish the means of their vindication, passed April nine, eighteen hundred and sixty-six, is hereby re-enacted; and sections sixteen and seventeen hereof shall be enforced according to the provisions of said act.

Sec. 19. And be it further enacted, That if at any election for representative or delegate in the Congress of the United States any person shall knowingly personate and vote, or attempt to vote, in the name of any other person, whether living, dead, or fictitious; or vote more than once at the same election for any candidate for the same office; or vote at a place where he may not be lawfully entitled to vote; or vote without having a lawful right to vote; or do any unlawful act to secure a right or an opportunity to vote for himself or any other person; or by force, threat, menace, intimidation, bribery, reward, or offer, or promise thereof, or otherwise unlawfully prevent any qualified voter of any State of the United States of America, or of any Territory thereof, from freely exercising the right of suffrage, or by any such means induce any voter to refuse to exercise such right; or compel or induce by any such means, or otherwise, any officer of an election in any such State or Territory to receive a vote from a person not legally qualified or entitled to vote; or interfere in any manner with any officer of said elections in the discharge of his duties; or by any of such means, or other unlawful means, induce any officer of an election, or officer whose duty it is to ascertain, announce, or declare the result of any such election, or give or make any certificate, document, or evidence in relation thereto, to violate or refuse to comply with his duty, or any law regulating the same; or knowingly and wilfully receive the vote of any person not entitled to vote, or refuse to receive the vote of any person entitled to vote; or aid, counsel, procure, or advise any such voter, person, or officer to do any act hereby made a crime, or to omit to do any duty the omission of which is hereby made a crime, or attempt to do so, every such person shall be deemed guilty of a crime, and shall for such crime be liable to prosecution in any court of the United States of competent jurisdiction, and, on conviction thereof, shall be punished by a fine not exceeding five hundred dollars, or by imprisonment for a term not exceeding three years, or both, in the discretion of the court, and shall pay the costs of prosecution.

Sec. 20. And be it further enacted, That if, at any registration of voters for an election for representative or delegate in the Congress of the United States, any person shall knowingly personate and register, or attempt to register, in the name of any other person, whether living, dead, or fictitious, or fraudulently register, or fraudulently attempt to register, not having a lawful right so to do; or do any unlawful act to secure registration for himself or any other person; or by force, threat, menace, intimidation, bribery, reward, or offer, or promise thereof, or other unlawful means, prevent or hinder any person having a lawful right to register from duly exercising such right; or compel or induce, by any of such means, or other unlawful means, any officer of registration to admit to registration any person not legally entitled thereto, or interfere in any manner with any officer of registration in the discharge of his duties, or by any such means, or other unlawful means, induce any officer of registration to violate or refuse to comply with his duty, or any law regulating the same; or knowingly and wilfully receive the vote of any person not entitled to vote, or refuse to receive the vote of any person entitled to vote, or aid, counsel, procure, or advise any such voter, person, or officer to do any act hereby made a crime, or to omit any act, the omission of which is hereby made a crime, every such person shall be deemed guilty of a crime, and shall be liable to prosecution and punishment therefor, as provided in section nineteen of this act for persons guilty of any of the crimes therein specified: *Provided,* That every registration made under the laws of any State or Territory, for any State or other election at which such representative or delegate in Congress shall be chosen, shall be deemed to be a registration within the meaning of this act, notwithstanding the same shall also be made for the purposes of any State, territorial, or municipal election.

Sec. 21. And be it further enacted, That whenever, by the laws of any State or Territory, the name of any candidate or person to be voted for as representative or delegate in Congress shall be required to be printed, written, or contained in any ticket or ballot with other candidates or persons to be voted for at the same election for State, territorial, municipal, or local officers, it shall be sufficient prima facie evidence, either for the purpose of indicting or convicting any person charged with voting, or attempting or offering to vote, unlawfully under the provisions of the preceding sections, or for committing either of the offenses thereby created, to prove that the person so charged or indicted, voted, or attempted or offered to vote, such ballot or ticket, or committed either of the offenses named in the preceding sections of this act with reference to such ballot. And the proof and establishment of such facts shall be taken, held, and deemed to be presumptive evidence that such person voted, or attempted or offered to vote, for such representative or delegate, as the case may be, or that such offense was committed with reference to the election of such representative or delegate, and shall be sufficient to warrant his conviction, unless it shall be shown that any such ballot, when cast, or attempted or offered to be cast, by him, did not contain the name of any candidate for the office of representative or delegate in the Congress of the United States, or that such offense was not committed with reference to the election of such representative or delegate.

Sec. 22. And be it further enacted, That any officer of any election at which any representative or delegate in the Congress of the United States shall be voted for, whether such officer of election be appointed or created by or under any law or authority of the United States, or by or under any State, territorial, district, or municipal law or authority, who shall neglect or refuse to perform any duty in regard to such election required of him by any law of the United States, or of any State or Territory thereof; or violate any duty so imposed, or knowingly do any act thereby unauthorized, with intent to affect any such election, or the result thereof; or fraudulently make any false certificate of the result of such election in regard to such representative or delegate; or withhold, conceal, or destroy any certificate of record so required by law respecting, concerning, or pertaining to the election of any such representative or delegate; or neglect or refuse to make and return the same as so required by law; or aid, counsel, procure, or advise any voter, person, or officer to do any act by this or any of the preceding sections made a crime; or to omit to do any duty the omission of which is by this or any of said sections made a crime, or attempt to do so, shall be deemed guilty of a crime and shall be liable to prosecution and punishment therefor, as provided in the nineteenth section of this act for persons guilty of any of the crimes therein specified.

Sec. 23. And be it further enacted, That whenever any person shall be defeated or deprived of his election to any office, except elector of President or Vice–President, representative or delegate in Congress, or member of a State legislature, by reason of the denial to any citizen or citizens who shall offer to vote, of the right to vote, on account of race, color, or previous condition of servitude, his right to hold and enjoy such office, and the emoluments thereof, shall not be impaired by such denial; and such person may bring any appropriate suit or proceeding to recover possession of such office, and in cases where it shall appear that the sole question touching the title to such office arises out of the denial of the right to vote to citizens who so offered to vote, on account of race, color, or previous condition of servitude, such suit or proceeding may be instituted in the circuit or district court of the United States of the circuit or district in which such person resides. And said circuit or district court shall have, concurrently with the State courts, jurisdiction thereof so far as to determine the rights of the parties to such office by reason of the denial of the right guaranteed by the fifteenth article of amendment to the Constitution of the United States, and secured by this act.

3. **The Force Act of 1871, An Act to amend an Act approved May thirty-one, eighteen hundred and seventy, entitled "An Act to enforce the Rights of Citizens of the United States to vote in the several States of this Union, and for other Purposes," 16 Statutes at Large 433 (Feb. 28, 1871)**

Be it enacted by the Senate and House of Representatives of the United States of America in Congress assembled, That section twenty of the "Act to enforce the rights of citizens of the United States to vote in the several States of this Union, and for other purposes," approved May thirty-one, eighteen hundred and seventy, shall be, and hereby is, amended so as to read as follows:

"Sec. 20. And be it further enacted, That if, [at] any registration of voters for an election for representative or delegate in the Congress of the United States, any person shall knowingly personate and register, or attempt to register, in the name of any other person, whether living, dead, or fictitious, or fraudulently register, or fraudulently attempt to register, not having a lawful right so to do; or do any unlawful act to secure registration for himself or any other person; or by force, threat, menace, intimidation, bribery, reward, or offer, or promise thereof, or other unlawful means, prevent or hinder any person having a lawful right to register from duly exercising such right; or compel or induce, by any of such means, or other unlawful means, any officer of registration to admit to registration any person not legally entitled thereto, or interfere in any manner with any officer of registration in the discharge of his duties, or by any such means, or other unlawful means, induce any officer of registration to violate or refuse to comply with his duty or any law regulating the same; or if any such officer shall knowingly and wilfully register as a voter any person not entitled to be registered, or refuse to so register any person entitled to be registered: or if any such officer or other person whose duty it is to perform any duty in relation to such registration or election, or to ascertain, announce, or declare the result thereof, or give or make any certificate, document, or evidence in relation thereto, shall knowingly neglect or refuse to perform any duty required by law, or violate any duty imposed by law, or do any act unauthorized by law relating to or affecting such registration or election, or the result thereof, or any

certificate, document, or evidence in relation thereto, or if any person shall aid, counsel, procure, or advise any such voter, person, or officer to do any act hereby made a crime, or to omit any act the omission of which is hereby made a crime, every such person shall be deemed guilty of a crime, and shall be liable to prosecution and punishment therefor as provided in section nineteen of said act of May thirty-one, eighteen hundred and seventy, for persons guilty of any of the crimes therein specified: *Provided,* That every registration made under the laws of any State or Territory for any State or other election at which such representative or delegate in Congress shall be chosen, shall be deemed to be a registration within the meaning of this act, notwithstanding the same shall also be made for the purposes of any State, territorial, or municipal election."

Sec. 2. And be it further enacted, That whenever in any city or town having upward of twenty thousand inhabitants, there shall be two citizens thereof who, prior to any registration of voters for an election for representative or delegate in the Congress of the United States, or prior to any election at which a representative or delegate in Congress is to be voted for, shall make known, in writing, to the judge of the circuit court of the United States for the circuit wherein such city or town shall be, their desire to have said registration, or said election, or both, guarded and scrutinized, it shall be the duty of the said judge of the circuit court, within not less than ten days prior to said registration, if one there be, or, if no registration be required, within not less than ten days prior to said election, to open the said circuit court at the most convenient point in said circuit. And the said court, when so opened by said judge, shall proceed to appoint and commission, from day to day and from time to time, and under the hand of the said circuit judge, and under the seal of said court, for each election district or voting precinct in each and every such city or town as shall, in the manner herein prescribed, have applied therefor, and to revoke, change, or renew said appointment from time to time, two citizens, residents of said city or town, who shall be of different political parties, and able to read and write the English language, and who shall be known and designated as supervisors of election. And the said circuit court, when opened by the said circuit judge as required herein, shall therefrom and thereafter, and up to and including the day following the day of election, be always open for the transaction of business under this act, and the powers and jurisdiction hereby granted and conferred shall be exercised as well in vacation as in term time; and a judge sitting at chambers shall have the same powers and jurisdiction, including the power of keeping order and of punishing any contempt of his authority, as when sitting in court.

Sec. 3. And be it further enacted, That whenever, from sickness, injury, or otherwise, the judge of the circuit court of the United States in any judicial circuit shall be unable to perform and discharge the duties by this act imposed, it shall be his duty, and he is hereby required, to select and to direct and assign to the performance thereof, in his place and stead, such one of the judges of the district courts of the United States within his circuit as he shall deem vest; and upon such selection and assignment being made, it shall be lawful for, and shall be the duty of, the district judge so designated to perform and discharge, in the place and stead of the said circuit judge, all the duties, powers, and obligations imposed and conferred upon the said circuit judge by the provisions of this act.

Sec. 4. And be it further enacted, That it shall be the duty of the supervisors of election, appointed under this act, and they and each of them are hereby authorized and required, to attend at all times and places fixed for the registration of voters, who, being registered, would be entitled to vote for a representative or delegate in Congress, and to challenge any person offering to register; to attend at all times and places when the names of registered voters may be marked for challenge, and to cause such names registered as they shall deem proper to be so marked; to make, when required, the lists, or either of them, provided for in section thirteen of this act, and verify the same; and upon any occasion, and at any time when in attendance under the provisions of this act, to personally inspect and scrutinize such registry, and for purposes of identification to affix their or his signature to each and every page of the original list, and of each and every copy of any such list of registered voters, at such times, upon each day when any name may or shall be received, entered, or registered, and in such manner as will, in their or his judgment, detect and expose the improper or wrongful removal therefrom, or addition thereto, in any way, of any name or names.

Sec. 5. And be it further enacted, That it shall also be the duty of the said supervisors of election, and they, and each of them, are hereby authorized and required, to attend at all times and places for holding elections of representatives or delegates in Congress, and for counting the votes cast at said elections; to challenge any vote offered by any person whose legal qualifications the supervisors, or either of them, shall doubt; to be and remain where the ballot-boxes are kept at all times after the polls are open until each and every vote cast at said time and place shall be counted, the canvass of all votes polled be wholly completed, and the proper and requisite certificates or returns made, whether said certificates or returns be required under any law of the United States, or any State, territorial, or municipal law, and to personally inspect and scrutinize, from time to time, and at all times, on the day of election, the manner in which the voting is done, and the way and method in which the poll-books, registry-lists, and tallies or check-books, whether the same are required by any law of the United States, or any State, territorial, or municipal law, are kept; and to the end that each candidate for the office of representative or delegate in

Congress shall obtain the benefit of every vote for him cast, the said supervisors of election are, and each of them is, hereby required, in their or his respective election districts or voting precincts, to personally scrutinize, count, and canvass each and every ballot in their or his election district or voting precinct cast, whatever may be the indorsement on said ballot, or in whatever box it may have been placed or be found; to make and forward to the officer who, in accordance with the provisions of section thirteen of this act, shall have been designated as the chief supervisor of the judicial district in which the city or town wherein they or he shall serve shall be, such certificates and returns of all such ballots as said officer may direct and require, and to attach to the registry list, and any and all copies thereof, and to any certificate, statement, or return, whether the same, or any part or portion thereof, be required by any law of the United States, or of any State, territorial, or municipal law, any statement touching the truth or accuracy of the registry, or the truth or fairness of the election and canvass, which the said supervisors of election, or either of them, may desire to make or attach, or which should properly and honestly be made or attached, in order that the facts may become known, any law of any State or Territory to the contrary notwithstanding.

Sec. 6. And be it further enacted, That the better to enable the said supervisors of election to discharge their duties, they are, and each of them is, hereby authorized and directed, in their or his respective election districts or voting precincts, on the day or days of registration, on the day or days when registered voters may be marked to be challenged, and on the day or days of election, to take, occupy, and remain in such position or positions, from time to time, whether before or behind the ballot-boxes, as will, in their judgment, best enable them or him to see each person offering himself for registration or offering to vote, and as will best conduce to their or his scrutinizing the manner in which the registration or voting is being conducted; and at the closing of the polls for the reception of votes, they are, and each of them is, hereby required to place themselves or himself in such position in relation to the ballot-boxes for the purpose of engaging in the work of canvassing the ballots in said boxes contained as will enable them or him to fully perform the duties in respect to such canvass provided in this act, and shall there remain until every duty in respect to such canvass, certificates, returns, and statements shall have been wholly completed, any law of any State or Territory to the contrary notwithstanding.

Sec. 7. And be it further enacted, That if any election district or voting precinct in any city, town, or village, for which there shall have been appointed supervisors of election for any election at which a representative or delegate in Congress shall be voted for, the said supervisors of election, or either of them, shall not be allowed to exercise and discharge, fully and freely, and without bribery, solicitation, interference, hinderance, molestation, violence, or threats thereof, on the part of or from any person or persons, each and every of the duties, obligations, and powers conferred upon them by this act and the act hereby amended, it shall be the duty of the supervisors of election, and each of them, to make prompt report, under oath, within ten days after the day of election, to the officer who, in accordance with the provisions of section thirteen of this act, shall have been designated as the chief supervisor of the judicial district in which the city or town wherein they or he served shall be, of the manner and means by which they were, or he was, not so allowed to fully and freely exercise and discharge the duties and obligations required and imposed by this act. And upon receiving any such report, it shall be the duty of the said chief supervisor, acting both in such capacity and officially as a commissioner of the circuit court, to forthwith examine into all the facts thereof; to subpoena and compel the attendance before him of any witnesses; administer oaths and take testimony in respect to the charges made; and prior to the assembling of the Congress for which any such representative or delegate was voted for, to have filed with the clerk of the House of Representatives of the Congress of the United States all the evidence by him taken, all information by him obtained, and all reports to him made.

Sec. 8. And be it further enacted, That whenever an election at which representatives or delegates in Congress are to be chosen shall be held in any city or town of twenty thousand inhabitants or upward, the marshal of the United States for the district in which said city or town is situated shall have power, and it shall be his duty, on the application, in writing, of at least two citizens residing in any such city or town, to appoint special deputy marshals, whose duty it shall be, when required as provided in this act, to aid and assist the supervisors of election in the verification of any list of persons made under the provisions of this act, who may have registered, or voted, or either; to attend in each election district or voting precinct at the times and places fixed for the registration of voters, and at all times and places when and where said registration may by law be scrutinized, and the names of registered voters be marked for challenge; and also to attend, at all times for holding such elections, the polls of the election in such district or precinct. And the marshal and his general deputies, and such special deputies, shall have power, and it shall be the duty of such special deputies, to keep the peace, and support and protect the supervisors of elections in the discharge of their duties, preserve order at such places of registration and at such polls, prevent fraudulent registration and fraudulent voting thereat, or fraudulent conduct on the part of any officer of election, and immediately, either at said place of registration or polling-place, or elsewhere, and either before or after registering or voting, to arrest and take into custody, with or without process, any person who shall commit, or attempt or offer to commit, any of the acts or offences prohibited by this act, or the act hereby amended, or who shall commit any offence against the laws of the United States: *Provided,* That no person shall be arrested without process for any offence not committed in the presence of the marshal or his general or special deputies, or either of them, or of the supervisors of election, or either of them, and, for the purposes of arrest or the preservation of the peace, the supervisors of election, and each of them, shall, in the absence of the marshal's deputies, or if required to assist said deputies, have the same duties and powers as deputy marshals: *And provided further,* That no person shall, on the day or days of any such election, be arrested without process for any offence committed on the day or days of registration.

Sec. 9. And be it further enacted, That whenever any arrest is made under any provision of this act, the person so arrested shall forthwith be brought before a commissioner, judge, or court of the United States for examination of the offences alleged against him; and such commissioner, judge, or court shall proceed in respect thereto as authorized by law in case of crimes against the United States.

Sec. 10. And be it further enacted, That whoever, with or without any authority, power, or process, or pretended authority, power, or process, of any State, territorial, or municipal authority, shall obstruct, hinder, assault, or by bribery, solicitation, or otherwise, interfere with or prevent the supervisors of election, or either of them, or the marshal or his general or special deputies, or either of them, in the performance of any duty required of them, or either of them, or which he or they, or either of them, may be authorized to perform by any law of the United States, whether in the execution of process or otherwise, or shall by any of the means before mentioned hinder or prevent the free attendance and presence at such places of registration or at such polls of election, or full and free access and egress to and from any such place of registration or poll of election, or in going to and from any such place of registration or poll of election, or to and from any room where any such registration or election or canvass of votes, or of making any returns or certificates thereof, may be had, or shall molest, interfere with, remove, or eject from any such place of registration or poll of election, or of canvassing votes cast thereat, or of making returns or certificates thereof, any supervisor of election, the marshal, or his general or special deputies, or either of them, or shall threaten, or attempt, or offer so to do, or shall refuse or neglect to aid and assist any supervisor of election, or the marshal or his general or special deputies, or either of them, in the performance of his or their duties when required by him or them, or either of them, to give such aid and assistance, he shall be guilty of a misdemeanor, and liable to instant arrest without process, and on conviction thereof shall be punished by imprisonment not more than two years, or by fine not more than three thousand dollars, or by both such fine and imprisonment, and shall pay the costs of the prosecution. Whoever shall, during the progress of any verification of any list of the persons who may have registered or voted, and which shall be had or made under any of the provisions of this act, refuse to answer, or refrain from answering, or answering shall knowingly give false information in respect to any inquiry lawfully made, such person shall be liable to arrest and imprisonment as for a misdemeanor, and on conviction thereof shall be punished by imprisonment not to exceed thirty days, or by fine not to exceed one hundred dollars, or by both such fine and imprisonment, and shall pay the costs of the prosecution.

Sec. 11. And be it further enacted, That whoever shall be appointed a supervisor of election or a special deputy marshal under the provisions of this act, and shall take the oath of office as such supervisor of election or such special deputy marshal, who shall thereafter neglect or refuse, without good and lawful excuse, to perform and discharge fully the duties, obligations, and requirements of such office until the expiration of the term for which he was appointed, shall not only be subject to removal from office with loss of all pay or emoluments, but shall be guilty of a misdemeanor, and on conviction shall be punished by imprisonment for not less than six months nor more than one year, or by fine not less than two hundred dollars and not exceeding five hundred dollars, or by both fine and imprisonment, and shall pay the costs of prosecution.

Sec. 12. And be it further enacted, That the marshal, or his general deputies, or such special deputies as shall be thereto specially empowered by him, in writing, and under his hand and seal, whenever he or his said general deputies or his special deputies, or either or any of them, shall be forcibly resisted in executing their duties under this act, or the act hereby amended, or shall, by violence, threats, or menaces, be prevented from executing such duties, or from arresting any person or persons who shall commit any offence for which said marshal or his general or his special deputies are authorized to make such arrest, are, and each of them is hereby, empowered to summon and call to his or their aid the bystanders or posse comitatus of his district.

Sec. 13. And be it further enacted, That it shall be the duty of each of the circuit courts of the United States in and for each judicial circuit, upon the recommendation in writing of the judge thereof, to name and appoint, on or before the first day of May, in the year eighteen hundred and seventy-one, and thereafter as vacancies may from any cause arise, from among the circuit court commissioners in and for each judicial district in each of said judicial circuits, one of such officers, who shall be known for the duties required of him under this act as the chief supervisor of elections of the judicial district in and for which he shall be a commissioner, and shall, so long as faithful and capable, discharge the duties in this act imposed, and whose duty it shall be to prepare and furnish all necessary books, forms, blanks, and instructions for the use and direction of the supervisors of election in the several cities and towns in their respective districts; to receive the applications of all parties for appointment to such positions; and upon the opening, as contemplated in this act, of the circuit court for the judicial circuit in which the commissioner so designated shall act, to present such applications to the judge thereof, and furnish information to said judge in respect to the appointment by the said court of such supervisors of election; to require of the supervisors of election, where necessary, lists of the persons who may register and vote, or either, in their respective election districts or voting precincts, and to cause the names of those upon any such list whose right to register or vote shall be honestly doubted to be verified by proper inquiry and examination at the respective places by them assigned as their residences; and to receive, preserve, and file all oaths of office of said supervisors of election, and of all special deputy marshals appointed under the provisions of this act, and all certificates, returns, reports, and records of every kind and nature contemplated or made requisite under and by the provisions of this act, save where otherwise herein specially directed. And it is hereby made the duty of all United States marshals and commissioners who shall in any judicial district perform any duties under the provisions of this act, or the act hereby amended, relating to, concerning, or affecting the election of representatives or delegates in the Congress of the United States, to, from time to time, and with all due diligence, forward to the chief supervisor in and for their judicial district all complaints, examinations, and records pertaining thereto, and all oaths of office by them administered to any supervisor of election or special deputy marshal, in order that the same may be properly preserved and filed.

Sec. 14. And be it further enacted, That there shall be allowed and paid to each chief supervisor, for his services as such officer, the following compensation, apart from and in excess of all fees allowed by law for the performance of any duty as circuit court commissioner: For filing and caring for every return, report, record, document, or other paper required to be filed by him under any of the provisions of this act, ten cents; for affixing a seal to any paper, record, report, or instrument, twenty cents; for entering and indexing the records of his office, fifteen cents per folio; and for arranging and transmitting to Congress, as provided for in section seven of this act, any report, statement, record, return, or examination, for each folio, fifteen cents; and for any copy thereof, or of any paper on file, a like sum. And there shall be allowed and paid to each and every supervisor of election, and each and every special deputy marshal who shall be appointed and shall perform his duty under the provisions of this act, compensation at the rate of five dollars per day for each and every day he shall have actually been on duty, not exceeding ten days. And the fees of the said chief supervisors shall be paid at the treasury of the United States, such accounts to be made out, verified, examined, and certified as in the case of accounts of commissioners, save that the examination or certificate required may be made by either the circuit or district judge.

Sec. 15. And be it further enacted, That the jurisdiction of the circuit court of the United States shall extend to all cases in law or equity arising under the provisions of this act or the act hereby amended; and if any person shall receive any injury to his person or property for or on account of any act by him done under any of the provisions of this act or the act hereby amended, he shall be entitled to maintain suit for damages therefor in the circuit court of the United States in the district wherein the party doing the injury may reside or shall be found.

Sec. 16. And be it further enacted, That in any case where suit or prosecution, civil or criminal, shall be commenced in a court of any State against any officer of the United States, or other person, for or on account of any act done under the provisions of this act, or under color thereof, or for or on account of any right, authority, or title set up or claimed by such officer or other person under any of said provisions, it shall be lawful for the defendant in such suit or prosecution, at any time before trial, upon a petition to the circuit court of the United States in and for the district in which the defendant shall have been served with process, setting forth the nature of said suit or prosecution, and verifying the said petition by affidavit, together with a certificate signed by an attorney or counsellor at law of some court of record of the State in which such suit shall have been commenced, or of the United States, setting forth that as counsel for the petition[er] he has examined the proceedings against him, and has carefully inquired into all the matters set forth in the petition, and that he believes the same to be true, which petition, affidavit, and certificate shall be presented to the said circuit court, if in session, and, if not, to the clerk thereof at his office, and shall be filed in said office, and the cause shall thereupon be entered on the docket of said court, and shall be thereafter proceeded in as a cause originally commenced in that court; and it shall be the duty of the clerk of said court, if the suit was commenced in the court below by summons, to issue a writ of certiorari to the State court, requiring said court to send to the said circuit court the record and proceedings in said cause; or if it was commenced by capias, he shall issue a writ of habeas corpus cum causa, a duplicate of which said writ shall be delivered to the clerk of the State court, or left at his office by the marshal of the district, or his deputy, or some person duly authorized thereto; and thereupon it shall be the duty of the said State court to stay all further proceedings in such cause, and the said suit or prosecution, upon delivery of such process, or leaving the same as aforesaid, shall be deemed and taken to be moved to the said circuit court, and any further proceedings, trial, or judgment therein in the State court shall be wholly null and void; and any person, whether an attorney or officer of any State court, or otherwise, who shall thereafter take any steps, or in any manner proceed in the State court in any action so removed, shall be guilty of a misdemeanor, and liable to trial and punishment in the court to which the action shall have been removed, and upon conviction thereof shall be punished by imprisonment for not less than six months nor more than one year, or by fine not less than five hundred nor more than one thousand dollars, or by both such fine and imprisonment, and shall in addition thereto be amenable to the said court to which said action shall have been removed as for a contempt; and if the defendant in any such suit be in actual custody on mesne process therein, it shall be the duty of the marshal, by virtue of the writ of habeas corpus cum causa, to take the body of the defendant into his custody, to be dealt with in the said cause according to the rules of law and the order of the circuit court, or of any judge thereof in vacation. And all attachments made and all bail or other security given upon such suit or prosecution shall be and continue in like force and effect as if the same suit or prosecution had proceeded to final judgment and execution in the State court. And if upon the removal of any such suit or prosecution it shall be made to appear to the said circuit court that no copy of the record and proceedings therein in the State court can be obtained, it shall be lawful for said circuit court to allow and require the plaintiff to proceed de novo, and to file a declaration of his cause of action, and the parties may thereupon proceed as in actions originally brought in said circuit court; and on failure of so proceeding judgment of non prosequitur may be rendered against the plaintiff, with costs for the defendant.

Sec. 17. And be it further enacted, That in any case in which any party is or may be by law entitled to copies of the record and proceedings in any suit or prosecution in any State court, to be used in any court of the United States, if the clerk of said State court shall, upon demand and the payment or tender of the legal fees, refuse or neglect to deliver to such party certified copies of such record and proceedings, the court of the United States in which such record and proceedings may be needed, on proof by affidavit that the clerk of such State court has refused or neglected to deliver copies thereof on demand as aforesaid, may direct and allow such record to be supplied by affidavit or otherwise, as the circumstances of the case may require and allow; and thereupon such proceeding, trial, and judgment may be had in the said court of the United States, and all such processes awarded, as if certified copies of such records and proceedings had been regularly before the said court; and hereafter in all civil actions in the courts of the United States either party thereto may notice the same for trial.

Sec. 18. And be it further enacted, That sections five and six of the act of the Congress of the United States approved July fourteen, eighteen hundred and seventy, and entitled "An act to amend the naturalization laws, and to punish crimes against the same," be, and the same are hereby, repealed; but this repeal shall not affect any proceeding or prosecution now pending for any offence under the said sections, or either of them, or any question which may arise therein respecting the appointment of the persons in said sections, or either of them, provided for, or the powers, duties, or obligations of such persons.

Sec. 19. And be it further enacted, That all votes for representatives in Congress shall hereafter be by written or printed ballot, any law of any State to the contrary notwithstanding; and all votes received or recorded contrary to the provisions of this section shall be of none effect.

4. The Ku Klux Klan Act, The Civil Rights Act of 1871, An Act to enforce the Provisions of the Fourteenth Amendment to the Constitution of the United States, and for other Purposes, 17 Statutes at Large 13 (April 20, 1871)

Be it enacted by the Senate and House of Representatives of the United States of America in Congress assembled, That any person who, under color of any law, statute, ordinance, regulation, custom, or usage of any State, shall subject, or cause to be subjected, any person within the jurisdiction of the United States to the deprivation of any rights, privileges, or immunities secured by the Constitution of the United States, shall, any such law, statute, ordinance, regulation, custom, or usage of the State to the contrary notwithstanding, be liable to the party injured in any action at law, suit in equity, or other proper proceeding for redress; such proceeding to be prosecuted in the several district or circuit courts of the United States, with and subject to the same rights of appeal, review upon error, and other remedies provided in like cases in such courts, under the provisions of the act of the ninth of April, eighteen hundred and sixty-six, entitled "An act to protect all persons in the United States in their civil rights, and to furnish the means of their vindication"; and the other remedial laws of the United States which are in their nature applicable in such cases.

Sec. 2. That if two or more persons within any State or Territory of the United States shall conspire together to overthrow, or to put down, or to destroy by force the government of the United States, or to levy war against the United States, or to oppose by force the authority of the government of the United States, or by force, intimidation, or threat to prevent, hinder, or delay the execution of any law of the United States, or by force to seize, take, or possess any property of the United States contrary to the authority thereof, or by force, intimidation, or threat to prevent any person from accepting or holding any office or trust or place of confidence under the United States, or from discharging the duties thereof, or by force, intimidation, or threat to induce any officer of the United States to leave any State, district, or place where his duties as such officer might lawfully be performed, or to injure him in his person or property on account of his lawful discharge of the duties of his office, or to injure his person while engaged in the lawful discharge of the duties of his office, or to injure his property so as to molest, interrupt, hinder, or impede him in the discharge of his official duty, or by force, intimidation, or threat to deter any party or witness in any court of the United States from attending such court, or from testifying in any matter pending in such court fully, freely, and truthfully, or to injure any such party or witness in his person or property on account of his having so attended or testified, or by force, intimidation, or threat to influence the verdict, presentment, or indictment, of any jury or grand juror in any court of the United States, or to injure such juror in his person or property on account of any verdict, presentment, or indictment lawfully assented to by him, or on account of his being or having been such juror, or shall conspire together, or go in disguise upon the public highway or upon the premises of another for the purpose, either directly or indirectly, of depriving any person or any class of persons of the equal protection of the laws, or of equal privileges or immunities under the laws, or for the purpose of preventing or hindering the constituted authorities of any State from giving or securing to all persons within such State the equal protection of the laws, or shall conspire together for the purpose of in any manner impeding, hindering, obstructing, or defeating the due course of justice in any State or Territory, with intent to deny to any citizen of the United States the due and equal protection of the laws, or to injure any person in his person or his property for lawfully enforcing the right of any person or class of persons to the equal protection of the laws, or by force, intimidation, or threat to prevent any citizen of the United States lawfully entitled to vote from giving his support or advocacy in a lawful manner towards or in favor of the election of any lawfully qualified person as an elector of President or Vice-President of the United States, or as a member of the Congress of the United States, or to injure any such citizen in his person or property on account of such support or advocacy, each and every person so offending shall be deemed guilty of a high crime, and, upon conviction thereof in any district or circuit court of the United States or district or supreme court of any Territory of the United States having jurisdiction of similar offences, shall be punished by a fine not less than five hundred nor more than five thousand dollars, or by imprisonment, with or without hard labor, as the court may determine, for a period of not less than six months nor more than six years, as the court may determine, or by both such fine and imprisonment as the court shall determine. And if any one or more persons engaged in any such conspiracy shall do, or cause to be done, any act in furtherance of the object of such conspiracy, whereby any person shall be injured in his person or property, or deprived of having and exercising any right or privilege of a citizen of the United States, the person so injured or deprived of such rights and privileges may have and maintain an action for the recovery of damages occasioned by such injury or deprivation of rights and privileges against any one or more of the persons engaged in such conspiracy, such action to be prosecuted in the proper district or circuit court of the United States, with and subject to the same rights of appeal, review upon error, and other remedies provided in like cases in such courts under the provisions of the act of April ninth, eighteen hundred and sixty-six, entitled "An act to protect all persons in the United States in their civil rights, and to furnish the means of their vindication."

Sec. 3. That in all cases where insurrection, domestic violence, unlawful combinations, or conspiracies in any State shall so obstruct or hinder the execution of the laws thereof, and of the United States, as to deprive any portion or class of the people of such State of any of the rights, privileges, or immunities, or protection, named in the Constitution and secured by this act, and the constituted authorities of such State shall either be unable to protect, or shall, from any cause, fail in or refuse protection of the people in such rights, such facts shall be deemed a denial by such State of the equal protection of the laws to which they are entitled under the Constitution of the United States; and in all such cases, or whenever any such insurrection, violence, unlawful combination, or conspiracy shall oppose or obstruct the laws of the United States or the due execution thereof, or impede or obstruct the due course of justice under the same, it shall be lawful for the President, and it shall be his duty to take such measures, by the employment of the militia or the land and naval forces of the United States, or of either, or by other means, as he may deem necessary for the suppression of such insurrection, domestic violence, or combinations; and any person who shall be arrested under the provisions of this and the preceding section shall be delivered to the marshal of the proper district, to be dealt with according to law.

Sec. 4. That whenever in any State or part of a State the unlawful combinations named in the preceding section of this act shall be organized and armed, and so numerous and powerful as to be able, by violence, to either overthrow or set at defiance the constituted authorities of such State, and of the United States within such State, or when the constituted authorities are in complicity with, or shall connive at the unlawful purposes of, such powerful and armed combinations; and whenever, by reason of either or all of the causes aforesaid, the conviction of such offenders and the preservation of the public safety shall become in such district impracticable, in every such case such combinations shall be deemed a rebellion against the government of the United States, and during the continuance of such rebellion, and within the limits of the district which shall be so under the sway thereof, such limits to be prescribed by proclamation, it shall be lawful for the President of the United States, when in his judgment the public safety shall require it, to suspend the privileges of the writ of habeas corpus, to the end that such rebellion may be overthrown: *Provided,* That all the provisions of the second section of an act entitled "An act relating to habeas corpus, and regulating judicial proceedings in certain cases," approved March third, eighteen hundred and sixty-three, which relate to the discharge of prisoners other than prisoners of war, and to the penalty for refusing to obey the order of the court, shall be in full force so far as the same are applicable to the provisions of this section: *Provided further,* That the President shall first have made proclamation, as now provided by law, commanding such insurgents to disperse: *And provided also,* That the provisions of this section shall not be in force after the end of the next regular session of Congress.

Sec. 5. That no person shall be a grand or petit juror in any court of the United States upon any inquiry, hearing, or trial of any suit, proceeding, or prosecution based upon or arising under the provisions of this act who shall, in the judgment of the court, be in complicity with any such combination or conspiracy; and every such juror shall, before entering upon any such inquiry, hearing, or trial, take and subscribe an oath in open court that he has never, directly or indirectly, counselled, advised, or voluntarily aided any such combination or conspiracy; and each and every person who shall take this oath, and shall therein swear falsely, shall be guilty of perjury, and shall be subject to the plans and penalties declared against that crime, and the first section of the act entitled "An act defining additional causes of challenge and prescribing an additional oath for grand and petit jurors in the United States courts," approved June seventeenth, eighteen hundred and sixty-two, be, and the same is hereby, repealed.

Sec. 6. That any person or persons, having knowledge that any of the wrongs conspired to be done and mentioned in the second section of this act are about to be committed, and having power to prevent or aid in preventing the same, shall neglect or refuse so to do, and such wrongful act shall be committed, such person or persons shall be liable to the person injured, or his legal representatives, for all damages caused by any such wrongful act which such first-named person or persons by reasonable diligence could have prevented; and such damages may be recovered in an action on the case in the proper circuit court of the United States, and any number of persons guilty of such wrongful neglect or refusal may be joined as defendants in such action: *Provided,* That such action shall be commenced within one year after such cause of action shall have accrued; and if the death of any person shall be caused by any such wrongful act and neglect, the legal representatives of such deceased person shall have such action therefor, and may recover not exceeding five thousand dollars damages therein, for the benefit of the widow of such deceased person, if any there be, or if there be no widow, for the benefit of the next of kin of such deceased person.

Sec. 7. That nothing herein contained shall be construed to supersede or repeal any former act or law except so far as the same may be repugnant thereto; and any offences heretofore committed against the tenor of any former act shall be prosecuted, and any proceeding already commenced for the prosecution thereof shall be continued and completed, the same as if this act had not been passed, except so far as the provisions of this act may go to sustain and validate such proceedings.

5. **The Civil Rights Act of 1875, An Act to protect all citizens in their civil and legal rights, 18 Statutes at Large, Part 3, 335 (March 1, 1875)**

Whereas, it is essential to just government we recognize the equality of all men before the law, and hold that it is the duty of government in its dealings with the people to mete out equal and exact justice to all, of whatever nativity, race, color, or persuasion, religious or political; and it being the appropriate object of legislation to enact great fundamental principles into law: Therefore,

Be it enacted by the Senate and House of Representatives of the United States of America in Congress assembled, That all persons within the jurisdiction of the United States shall be entitled to the full and equal enjoyment of the accommodations, advantages, facilities, and privileges of inns, public conveyances on land or water, theaters, and other places of public amusement; subject only to the conditions and limitations established by law, and applicable alike to citizens of every race and color, regardless of any previous condition of servitude.

Sec. 2. That any person who shall violate the foregoing section by denying to any citizen, except for reasons by law applicable to citizens of every race and color, and regardless of any previous condition of servitude, the full enjoyment of any of the accommodations, advantages, facilities, or privileges in said section enumerated, or by aiding or inciting such denial, shall, for every such offense, forfeit and pay the sum of five hundred dollars to the person aggrieved thereby, to be recovered in an action of debt, with full costs; and shall also, for every such offense, be deemed guilty of a misdemeanor, and, upon conviction thereof, shall be fined not less than five hundred nor more than one thousand dollars, or shall be imprisoned not less than thirty days nor more than one year: *Provided,* That all persons may elect to sue for the penalty aforesaid or to proceed under their rights at common law and by State statutes; and having so elected to proceed in the one mode or the other, their right to proceed in the other jurisdiction shall be barred. But this proviso shall not apply to criminal proceedings, either under this act or the criminal law of any State: *And provided further,* That a judgment for the penalty in favor of the party aggrieved, or a judgment upon an indictment, shall be a bar to either prosecution respectively.

Sec. 3. That the district and circuit courts of the United States shall have, exclusively of the courts of the several States, cognizance of all crimes and offenses against, and violations of, the provisions of this act; and actions for the penalty given by the preceding section may be prosecuted in the territorial, district, or circuit courts of the United States wherever the defendant may be found, without regard to the other party; and the district attorneys, marshals, and deputy marshals of the United States, and commissioners appointed by the circuit and territorial courts of the United States, with powers of arresting and imprisoning or bailing offenders against the laws of the United States, are hereby specially authorized and required to institute proceedings against every person who shall violate the provisions of this act, and cause him to be arrested and imprisoned or bailed, as the case may be, for trial before such court of the United States, or territorial court, as by law has cognizance of the offense, except in respect of the right of action accruing to the person aggrieved; and such district attorneys shall cause such proceedings to be prosecuted to their termination as in other cases: *Provided,* That nothing contained in this section shall be construed to deny or defeat any right of civil action accruing to any person, whether by reason of this act or otherwise; and any district attorney who shall willfully fail to institute and prosecute the proceedings herein required, shall, for every such offense, forfeit and pay the sum of five hundred dollars to the person aggrieved thereby, to be recovered by an action of debt, with full costs, and shall, on conviction thereof, be deemed guilty of a misdemeanor, and be fined not less than one thousand nor more than five thousand dollars: *And provided further,* That a judgment for the penalty in favor of the party aggrieved against any such district attorney, or a judgment upon an indictment against any such district attorney, shall be a bar to either prosecution respectively.

Sec. 4. That no citizen possessing all other qualifications which are or may be prescribed by law shall be disqualified for service as grand or petit juror in any court of the United States, or of any State, on account of race, color, or previous condition of servitude; and any officer or other person charged with any duty in the selection of summoning of jurors who shall exclude or fail to summon any citizen for the cause aforesaid shall, on conviction thereof, be deemed guilty of a misdemeanor, and be fined not more than five thousand dollars.

Sec. 5. That all cases arising under the provisions of this act in the courts of the United States shall be reviewable by the Supreme Court of the United States, without regard to the sum in controversy, under the same provisions and regulations as are now provided by law for the review of other causes in said court.

Appendix F

THE MODERN CIVIL RIGHTS STATUTES

42 U.S.C.A.

§ 1981. Equal rights under the law

(a) All persons within the jurisdiction of the United States shall have the same right in every State and Territory to make and enforce contracts, to sue, be parties, give evidence, and to the full and equal benefit of all laws and proceedings for the security of persons and property as is enjoyed by white citizens, and shall be subject to like punishment, pains, penalties, taxes, licenses, and exactions of every kind, and to no other.

(b) For purposes of this section, the term "make and enforce contracts" includes the making, performance, modification, and termination of contracts, and the enjoyment of all benefits, privileges, terms, and conditions of the contractual relationship.

(c) The rights protected by this section are protected against impairment by nongovernmental discrimination and impairment under color of State law.

R.S. § 1977.

Historical Note

Short Title of 1970 Amendment. Pub.L. 94–559, § 1, Oct. 19, 1976, 90 Stat. 2641, provided: "That this Act [amending section 1988 of this title] may be cited as 'The Civil Rights Attorney's Fees Awards Act of 1976'." The Civil Rights Act of 1991, Public Law 102–166 (Nov. 21, 1991), added subsections (b) and (c), and retitled the original law as subsection (a).

Codification. R.S. § 1977 is from Act May 31, 1870, c. 114, § 16, 16 Stat. 144.

Section was formerly classified to section 41 of Title 8, Aliens and Nationality.

Code of Federal Regulations

Banking provisions, see 12 CFR 528.1 et seq., 531.1 et seq., 701.1 et seq.

§ 1982. Property rights of citizens

All citizens of the United States shall have the same right, in every State and Territory, as is enjoyed by white citizens thereof to inherit, purchase, lease, sell, hold, and convey real and personal property.

R.S. § 1978.

Historical Note

Codification. R.S. § 1978 is from Act Apr. 9, 1866, c. 31, § 1, 14 Stat. 27.

Section was formerly classified to section 42 of Title 8, Aliens and Nationality.

§ 1983. Civil action for deprivation of rights

Every person who, under color of any statute, ordinance, regulation, custom, or usage, of any State or Territory or the District of Columbia, subjects, or causes to be subjected, any citizen of the United States or other person within the jurisdiction thereof to the deprivation of any rights, privileges, or immunities secured by the Constitution and laws, shall be liable to the party injured in an action at law, suit in equity, or other proper proceeding for redress. For the purposes of this section, any Act of Congress applicable exclusively to the District of Columbia shall be considered to be a statute of the District of Columbia.

R.S. § 1979; Pub.L. 96–170, § 1, Dec. 29, 1979, 93 Stat. 1284.

Historical Note

Codification. R.S. § 1979 is from Act Apr. 20, 1871, c. 22, § 1, 17 Stat. 13.

Section was formerly classified to section 43 of Title 8, Aliens and Nationality.

1979 Amendment. Pub.L. 96–170 added "or the District of Columbia" following "Territory," and provisions relating to Acts of Congress applicable solely to the District of Columbia.

Effective Date of 1979 Amendment. Amendment by Pub.L. 96–170 applicable with respect to any deprivation of rights, privileges, or immunities secured by the Constitution and laws occurring after Dec. 29, 1979, see section 3 of Pub.L. 96–170, set out as an Effective Date of 1979 Amendment note under section 1343 of Title 28, Judiciary and Judicial Procedure.

Legislative History. For legislative history and purpose of Pub.L. 96–170, see 1979 U.S.Code Cong. and Adm.News, p. 2609.

§ 1985. Conspiracy to interfere with civil rights

Preventing officer from performing duties

(1) If two or more persons in any State or Territory conspire to prevent, by force, intimidation, or threat, any person from accepting or holding any office, trust, or place of confidence under the United States, or from discharging any duties thereof; or to induce by like means any officer of the United States to leave any State, district, or place, where his duties as an officer are required to be performed, or to injure him in his person or property on account of his lawful discharge of the duties of his office, or while engaged in the lawful discharge thereof, or to injure his property so as to molest, interrupt, hinder, or impede him in the discharge of his official duties;

753

Obstructing justice; intimidating party, witness, or juror

(2) If two or more persons in any State or Territory conspire to deter, by force, intimidation, or threat, any party or witness in any court of the United States from attending such court, or from testifying to any matter pending therein, freely, fully, and truthfully, or to injure such party or witness in his person or property on account of his having so attended or testified, or to influence the verdict, presentment, or indictment of any grand or petit juror in any such court, or to injure such juror in his person or property on account of any verdict, presentment, or indictment lawfully assented to by him, or of his being or having been such juror; or if two or more persons conspire for the purpose of impeding, hindering, obstructing, or defeating, in any manner, the due course of justice in any State or Territory, with intent to deny to any citizen the equal protection of the laws, or to injure him or his property for lawfully enforcing, or attempting to enforce, the right of any person, or class of persons, to the equal protection of the laws;

Depriving persons of rights or privileges

(3) If two or more persons in any State or Territory conspire or go in disguise on the highway or on the premises of another, for the purpose of depriving, either directly or indirectly, any person or class of persons of the equal protection of the laws, or of equal privileges and immunities under the laws; or for the purpose of preventing or hindering the constituted authorities of any State or Territory from giving or securing to all persons within such State or Territory the equal protection of the laws; or if two or more persons conspire to prevent by force, intimidation, or threat, any citizen who is lawfully entitled to vote, from giving his support or advocacy in a legal manner, toward or in favor of the election of any lawfully qualified person as an elector for President or Vice President, or as a Member of Congress of the United States; or to injure any citizen in person or property on account of such support or advocacy; in any case of conspiracy set forth in this section, if one or more persons engaged therein do, or cause to be done, any act in furtherance of the object of such conspiracy, whereby another is injured in his person or property, or deprived of having and exercising any right or privilege of a citizen of the United States, the party so injured or deprived may have an action for the recovery of damages occasioned by such injury or deprivation, against any one or more of the conspirators.

R.S. § 1980.

Historical Note

Codification. R.S. § 1980 is from Acts July 31, 1861, c. 33, 12 Stat. 284; Apr. 20, 1871, c. 22, § 2, 17 Stat. 13.

Section was formerly classified to section 47 of Title 8, Aliens and Nationality.

§ 1986. Action for neglect to prevent

Every person who, having knowledge that any of the wrongs conspired to be done, and mentioned in section 1985 of this title, are about to be committed, and having power to prevent or aid in preventing the commission of the same, neglects or refuses so to do, if such wrongful act be committed, shall be liable to the party injured, or his legal representatives, for all damages caused by such wrongful act, which such person by reasonable diligence could have prevented; and such damages may be recovered in an action on the case; and any number of persons guilty of such wrongful neglect or refusal may be joined as defendants in the action; and if the death of any party be caused by any such wrongful act and neglect, the legal representatives of the deceased shall have such action therefor, and may recover not exceeding $5,000 damages therein, for the benefit of the widow of the deceased, if there be one, and if there be no widow, then for the benefit of the next of kin of the deceased. But no action under the provisions of this section shall be sustained which is not commenced within one year after the cause of action has accrued.

R.S. § 1981.

Historical Note

Codification. R.S. § 1981 is from Act Apr. 20, 1871, c. 22, § 6, 17 Stat. 15.

Section was formerly classified to section 48 of Title 8, Aliens and Nationality.

§ 1987. Prosecution of violation of certain laws

The United States attorneys, marshals, and deputy marshals, the magistrates appointed by the district and territorial courts, with power to arrest, imprison, or bail offenders, and every other officer who is especially empowered by the President, are authorized and required, at the expense of the United States, to institute prosecutions against all persons violating any of the provisions of section 1990 of this title or of sections 5506 to 5516 and 5518 to 5532 of the Revised Statutes, and to cause such persons to be arrested, and imprisoned or bailed, for trial before the court of the United States or the territorial court having cognizance of the offense.

R.S. § 1982; Mar. 3, 1911, c. 231, § 291, 36 Stat. 1167; June 25, 1948, c. 646, § 1, 62 Stat. 909; Oct. 17, 1968, Pub.L. 90–578, Title IV, § 402(b)(2), 82 Stat. 1118.

Historical Note

References in Text. Sections 5506 to 5516 and 5518 to 5532 of the Revised Statutes, referred to in text, which related to crimes against the elective franchise and civil rights of citizens, were all repealed by Acts Mar. 4, 1909, c. 321, § 341, 35 Stat. 1153, or Feb. 8, 1894, c. 25, § 1, 28 Stat. 37. However, the provisions of sections 5508, 5510, 5516, 5518, and 5524 to 5532 were substantially reenacted by Act Mar. 4, 1909, and were classified to sections 51, 52, 54 to 59, 246, 428, and 443 to 445 of former Title 18, Criminal Code and Criminal Procedure. Such sections of former Title 18 were repealed by Act June 25, 1948, c. 645, § 21, 62 Stat. 862, and are now covered by sections 241, 242, 372, 592, 593, 752, 1071, 1581, 1583 and 1588 of Title 18, Crimes and Criminal Procedure.

Codification. R.S. § 1982 is from Acts Apr. 9, 1866, c. 31, § 4, 14 Stat. 28; May 31, 1870, c. 114, § 9, 16 Stat. 142.

Section was formerly classified to section 49 of Title 8, Aliens and Nationality.

Change of Name. "Magistrates" was substituted for "commissioners" pursuant to Pub.L. 90–578, Title IV, § 402(b)(2), Oct. 17, 1968, 82 Stat. 1118. See chapter 43 (§ 631 et seq.) of Title 28, Judiciary and Judicial Procedure.

Act June 25, 1948, eff. Sept. 1, 1948, substituted "United States attorneys" for "district attorneys." See section 541 of Title 28, Judiciary and Judicial Procedure, and Historical and Revision Note thereunder.

Reference to the district courts was substituted for reference to the circuit courts on authority of section 291 of Act Mar. 3, 1911.

§ 1988. Proceedings in vindication of civil rights; attorney's fees

The jurisdiction in civil and criminal matters conferred on the district courts by the provisions of this Title, and of Title "CIVIL RIGHTS," and of Title "CRIMES," for the protection of all persons in the United States in their civil rights, and for their vindication, shall be exercised and enforced in conformity with the laws of the United States, so far as such laws are suitable to carry the same into effect; but in all cases where they are not adapted to the object, or are deficient in the provisions necessary to furnish suitable remedies and punish offenses against law, the common law, as modified and changed by the constitution and statutes of the State wherein the court having jurisdiction of such civil or criminal cause is held, so far as the same is not inconsistent with the Constitution and laws of the United States, shall be extended to and govern the said courts in the trial and disposition of the cause, and, if it is of a criminal nature, in the infliction of punishment on the party found guilty. In any action or proceeding to enforce a provision of sections 1981, 1982, 1983, 1985, and 1986 of this title, title IX of Public Law 92–318, or title VI of the Civil Rights Act of 1964, the court, in its discretion, may allow the prevailing party, other than the United States, a reasonable attorney's fee as part of the costs.

R.S. § 722; Pub.L. 94–559, § 2, Oct. 19, 1976, 90 Stat. 2641; Pub.L. 96–481, Title II, § 205(c), Oct. 21, 1980, 94 Stat. 2330.

Historical Note

References in Text. This Title, and of Title "CIVIL RIGHTS," and of Title "CRIMES," referred to in text, mean titles XIII, XXIV, and LXX of the Revised

Statutes, which comprise sections 530 to 1093, 1977 to 1991, and 5323 to 5550, respectively. For complete classification of these titles to the Code, see Tables volume.

Title IX of Public Law 92–318, referred to in text, is Title IX of Pub.L. 92–318, June 23, 1972, 86 Stat. 373, popularly known as the Education Amendments of 1972, which is classified principally to chapter 38 (section 1681 et seq.) of Title 20, Education. For complete classification of this Act to the Code, see Tables volume.

The United States Internal Revenue Code, referred to in text, is classified, generally to Title 26, Internal Revenue Code.

The Civil Rights Act of 1964, referred to in text, is Pub.L. 88–352, July 2, 1964, 78 Stat. 241. Title VI of the Civil Rights Act of 1964 is classified generally to subchapter V (section 2000d et seq.) of this chapter. For complete classification of this Act to the Code, see Short Title note set out under section 2000a of this title and Tables volume.

Codification. R.S. § 722 is from Acts Apr. 9, 1866, c. 31, § 3, 14 Stat. 27; May 31, 1870, c. 114, § 18, 16 Stat. 144.

Section was formerly classified to section 729 of Title 28 prior to the general revision and enactment of Title 28, Judiciary and Judicial Procedure, by Act June 25, 1948, c. 646, § 1, 62 Stat. 869.

1980 Amendment. Pub.L. 96–481 substituted "Pub.L. 92–318, or title VI of the Civil Rights Act of 1964" for "Pub.L. 92–318, or in any civil action or proceeding, by or on behalf of the United States of America, to enforce, or charging a violation of, a provision of the United States Internal Revenue Code, or title VI of the Civil Rights Act of 1964".

1976 Amendment. Pub.L. 94–559 authorized the court, in its discretion, to allow a reasonable attorney's fee as part of the prevailing party's costs.

Effective Date of 1980 Amendment. Amendment by Pub.L. 96–481 effective Oct. 1, 1981, and applicable to adversary adjudication as defined in section 504(b)(1)(C) of Title 5, Government Organization and Employees, and to civil actions and adversary adjudications described in section 2412 of Title 28, Judiciary and Judicial Procedure, which are pending on, or commenced on or after Oct. 1, 1981, see section 208 of Pub.L. 96–481, set out as an Effective Date of 1980 Amendment note under section 504 of Title 5.

Legislative History. For legislative history and purpose of Pub.L. 94–559, see 1976 U.S.Code Cong. and Adm.News, p. 5908.

Appendix G

THE JUSTICES OF THE SUPREME COURT IN HISTORICAL PERSPECTIVE *

Prepared by JOHN J. COUND

Professor of Law, University of Minnesota

The data which follow, summarizing the prior public careers of the many individuals who have served upon the Supreme Court of the United States, are not presented with any notion that they did presage or now explain their judicial performance or constitutional philosophy. The experience which the justices have at any one time brought to bear upon the issues before the Court, however, seem worthy of interest, and may serve as a consideration in assessing charges that the Court has in particular cases rendered "ivory tower" decisions, unaware or heedless of "the realities."

Two conclusions are manifest. First, the diversity of distinguished experience which the bench of the Court has at all times reflected, always among its members and frequently in a single justice, is startling. William Howard Taft is unique, but surely few Americans have lived lives of diversified public service so rich as John Jay, Levi Woodbury, Lucius Q.C. Lamar, Charles Evans Hughes and Fred M. Vinson. Second, a broad background in public service has not assured prominence upon the Court, nor has its absence precluded it. Gabriel Duvall, with prior executive, legislative and judicial experience, was forgotten in the first edition of the Dictionary of American Biography. Samuel F. Miller and Joseph P. Bradley, with no prior public offices, surely stand among the front rank of the justices. (The interested student will find stimulation in Frankfurter, The Supreme Court in the Mirror of Justice, 105 U.Pa.L.Rev. 781 (1957), which treats particularly of the relevance of prior judicial office).

* Adapted, with permission, from W. Lockhart, Y. Kamisar, and J. Choper, Constitutional Law: Cases—Comments—Questions, Appendix A (4th ed. 1975), with the addition of information relating to the more recent appointments and retirements.

758

The accompanying Table of Justices has been planned so that the composition of the Court at any time can be readily ascertained.

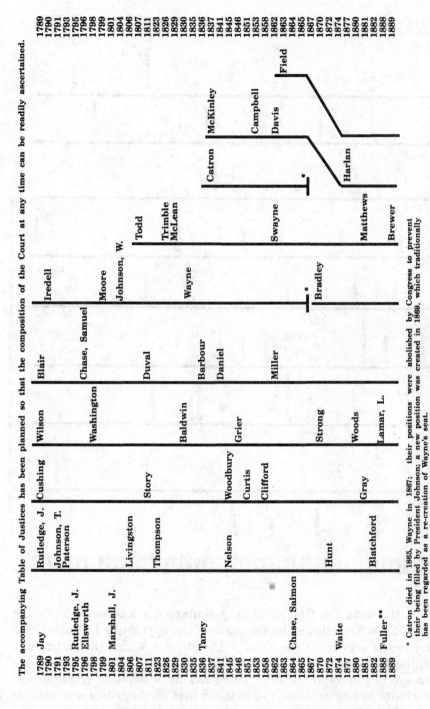

[18A]

1789 1790 1791 1793 1795 1796 1798 1799 1801 1804 1806 1807 1811 1823 1826 1829 1830 1835 1836 1837 1841 1845 1846 1851 1853 1858 1862 1863 1864 1865 1867 1870 1872 1874 1877 1880 1881 1882 1888 1889

Jay — Rutledge, J. — Cushing — Blair — Iredell — Todd — Field

Johnson, T.

Paterson

Rutledge, J. — Ellsworth — Washington — Chase, Samuel — Moore

Marshall, J.

Johnson, W.

Livingston — Story — Duval — Trimble / McLean — Catron — McKinley

Thompson — Baldwin — Barbour — Daniel — Campbell / Davis

Taney — Nelson — Grier — Wayne

Woodbury — Curtis — Clifford

Chase, Salmon — Hunt — Strong — Woods — Miller — Swayne — Harlan — Bradley

Waite — Blatchford — Gray — Lamar, L. — Matthews — Brewer

Fuller**

* Catron died in 1865, Wayne in 1867; their positions were abolished by Congress to prevent their being filled by President Johnson; a new position was created in 1869, which traditionally has been regarded as a re-creation of Wayne's seat.

** Fuller died in 1910, and White was named Chief Justice. Hughes resigned in 1941, and Stone was named Chief Justice. Burger resigned in 1986 and Rehnquist was named Chief Justice.

759

[19A]

1890 1892 1893 1894 1895 1898 1902 1903 1906 1909 1910 1912 1914 1916 1921 1922 1923 1925 1930 1932 1937 1938 1939 1940 1941 1943 1945 1946 1949 1953 1955 1956 1957 1958 1962 1965 1966 1967 1968 1969 1970 1972 1975 1976 1977 1978 1979 1980 1981 1982 1983 1986 1987 1988 1989 1990 1991

McKenna

Jackson, R.

Stone

Rehnquist

Scalia

Pitney Sanford Roberts Burton Stewart O'Connor

Hughes Clarke Sutherland Reed Whittaker White, B.

Shiras Day Butler Murphy Clark Marshall, T. Thomas, C.

Brown Moody Lamar, J. Brandeis Douglas Stevens

Jackson, H. Peckham Lurton McReynolds Byrnes Rutledge Minton Brennan Souter

Holmes Cardozo Frankfurter Goldberg Fortas Blackmun

White, E. Van Devanter Black Powell *** Kennedy

White, E. Taft Hughes Stone Vinson Warren Burger Rehnquist

** Justice Powell resigned in 1987; the Senate confirmed Anthony Kennedy in 1988.

1890 1892 1893 1894 1895 1898 1902 1903 1906 1909 1910 1912 1914 1916 1921 1922 1923 1925 1930 1932 1937 1938 1939 1940 1941 1943 1945 1946 1949 1953 1955 1956 1957 1958 1962 1965 1966 1967 1968 1969 1970 1972 1975 1976 1977 1978 1979 1980 1981 1982 1983 1986 1987 1988 1989 1990 1991

In the data, the first dates in parentheses are those of birth and death; these are followed by the name of the appointing President, and the dates of service on the Court. The state in which the justice was residing when appointed and his political affiliation at that time are then given. In detailing prior careers, I have followed chronological order, with two exceptions: I have listed first that a justice was a signer of the Declaration of Independence or the Federal Constitution, and I have indicated state legislative experience only once for each justice. I have not distinguished between different bodies in the state legislature,

760

and I have omitted service in the Continental Congresses. Private practice, except where deemed especially significant, and law teaching have been omitted, except where the justice was primarily engaged therein upon his or her appointment. (Blackmun, Burger, Douglas, Fortas, Holmes, Hughes, L.Q.C. Lamar, Lurton, McReynolds, Murphy, Roberts, W. Rutledge, Stevens, Stone and Van Devanter, in addition to Taft and Frankfurter, had all taught before going on the Court; Story, Strong and Wilson taught while on the Court or after leaving it). The activity in which a justice was engaged upon appointment has been italicized. Figures in parentheses indicate years of service in the position. In only a few cases, a justice's extra-Court or post-Court activity has been indicated, or some other note made. *An asterisk designates the Chief Justices.*

For detailed information on the individuals who have served as members of the Supreme Court, see L. Friedman & F. Israel, eds., The Justices of the United States Supreme Court 1789–1969: Their Lives and Major Opinions (Chelsea House, 1969), and the bibliographical references collected therein.

(This material has been compiled from a great number of sources, but special acknowledgment must be made to the Dictionary of American Biography (Charles Scribner's Sons), the A.N. Marquis Company works, and Ewing, The Judges of the Supreme Court, 1789–1937 (University of Minnesota Press, 1938).)

BALDWIN, HENRY (1780–1844; Jackson, 1830–1844). Pa.Dem.— U.S., House of Representatives (5). *Private practice.*

BARBOUR, PHILIP P. (1783–1841; Jackson, 1836–1841). Va. Dem.—Va., Legislature (2). U.S., House of Representatives (14). Va., Judge, General Court (2); President, State Constitutional Convention, 1829–30. *U.S., Judge, District Court (5).*

BLACK, HUGO L. (1886–1971; F.D. Roosevelt, 1937–1971). Ala. Dem.—Captain, Field Artillery, World War I. Ala., Judge, Police Court (1); County Solicitor (2). *U.S., Senate (10).*

BLACKMUN, HARRY A. (1908–___; Nixon, 1970–___). Minn. Rep.—Resident Counsel, Mayo Clinic, (10). *U.S., Judge, Court of Appeals (11).*

BLAIR, JOHN (1732–1800; Washington, 1789–1796). Va.Fed.— Signer, U.S. Constitution, 1787. Va., Legislature (9); Judge and Chief Justice, General Court (2), *Court of Appeals (9).* His opinion in *Commonwealth v. Caton,* 4 Call 5, 20 (Va.1782), is one of the earliest expressions of the doctrine of judicial review.

BLATCHFORD, SAMUEL (1820–1893; Arthur, 1882–1893). N.Y.Rep.—U.S., Judge, District Court (5); *Circuit Court (10).*

BRADLEY, JOSEPH P. (1803–1892; Grant, 1870–1892). N.J.Rep.—Actuary. *Private practice.*

BRANDEIS, LOUIS D. (1856–1941; Wilson, 1916–1939). Mass. Dem.—*Private practice.* Counsel, variously for the government, for industry, and "for the people", in numerous administrative and judicial proceedings, both state and federal.

BRENNAN, WILLIAM J. (1906–___; Eisenhower, 1956–___). N.J.Dem.—U.S. Army, World War II. N.J., Judge, Superior Court (1); Appellate Division (2); *Supreme Court (4).*

BREWER, DAVID J. (1837–1910; B. Harrison, 1889–1910). Kans. Rep.—Kans., Judge, County Criminal and Probate Court (1), District Court (4); County Attorney (1); Judge, Supreme Court (14), *U.S., Judge, Circuit Court (5).*

BROWN, HENRY B. (1836–1913; B. Harrison, 1890–1906). Mich. Rep.—U.S., Assistant U.S. Attorney (5). Mich., Judge, Circuit Court (1). *U.S., Judge, District Court (15).*

* BURGER, WARREN E. (1907–___; Nixon, 1969–86). Va.Rep.— U.S., Assistant Attorney General, Civil Division (3), *Judge, Court of Appeals (13).*

BURTON, HAROLD H. (1888–1964; Truman, 1945–1958). Ohio Rep.—Capt., U.S.A., World War I. Ohio, Legislature (2). Mayor, Cleveland, O. (5). *U.S., Senate (4).*

BUTLER, PIERCE (1866–1939; Harding, 1922–1939). Minn. Dem.—Minn., County Attorney (4). *Private practice.*

BYRNES, JAMES F. (1879–1972; F.D. Roosevelt, 1941–1942). S.C.Dem.—S.C., Solicitor, Circuit Court (2). U.S., House of Representatives (14); *Senate (12).* Resigned from the Court to become U.S. Director of Economic Stabilization.

CAMPBELL, JOHN A. (1811–1889; Pierce, 1853–1861). Ala. Dem.—*Private practice.* After his resignation, he became Assistant Secretary of War, C.S.A.

CARDOZO, BENJAMIN N. (1870–1938; Hoover, 1932–1938). N.Y.Dem.—N.Y., Judge, Supreme Court (6 weeks); Associate Judge and *Chief Judge, Court of Appeals (18).*

CATRON, JOHN (1778–1865; Van Buren, 1837–1865). Tenn. Dem.—Tenn., Judge and Chief Justice, Supreme Court of Errors and Appeals (10). *Private practice.*

* CHASE, SALMON P. (1808–1873; Lincoln, 1864–1873). Ohio Rep.—U.S., Senate (6). Ohio, Governor (4). *U.S., Secretary of the Treasury (3).*

CHASE, SAMUEL (1741–1811; Washington, 1796–1811). Md. Fed.—Signer, U.S., Declaration of Independence, 1776. Md., Legisla-

* The Chief Justices' names are preceded by an asterisk.

ture (20); Chief Judge, Court of Oyer and Terminer (2), *General Court (5)*. Impeached and acquitted, 1804–05.

CLARK, TOM C. (1899–1977; Truman, 1949–1967). Tex.Dem.— U.S. Army, World War I. Tex., Civil District Attorney (5). U.S., Assistant Attorney General (2), *Attorney General (4)*.

CLARKE, JOHN H. (1857–1945; Wilson, 1916–1922). Ohio Dem.— *U.S., Judge, District Court (2)*.

CLIFFORD, NATHAN (1803–1881; Buchanan, 1858–1881). Me. Dem.—Me., Legislature (4); Attorney General (4). U.S., House of Representatives (4); Attorney General (2); Minister Plenipotentiary to Mexico, 1848. *Private practice.*

CURTIS, BENJAMIN R. (1809–1874; Fillmore, 1851–1857). Mass. Whig.—Mass., Legislature (1). *Private practice.*

CUSHING, WILLIAM (1732–1810; Washington, 1789–1810). Mass. Fed.—Mass., Judge, Superior Court (3); Justice and *Chief Justice, Supreme Judicial Court (14)*.

DANIEL, PETER V. (1784–1860; Van Buren, 1841–1860). Va. Dem.—Va., Legislature (3); Member, Privy Council (23). *U.S., Judge, District Court (5)*.

DAVIS, DAVID (1815–1886; Lincoln, 1862–1877). Ill.Rep.—Ill., Legislature (2); *Judge, Circuit Court (14)*. His resignation to become U.S. Senator upset the agreed-upon composition of the Hayes–Tilden Electoral Commission.

DAY, WILLIAM R. (1849–1923; T. Roosevelt, 1903–1922). Ohio Rep.—Ohio, Judge, Court of Common Pleas (4). U.S., Assistant Secretary of State (1), Secretary of State (½); Chairman, U.S. Peace Commissioners, 1898; *Judge, Circuit Court of Appeals (4)*.

DOUGLAS, WILLIAM O. (1898–1980; F.D. Roosevelt, 1939–1975). Conn.Dem.—Pvt., U.S. Army, World War I. *U.S., Chairman, Securities and Exchange Commission (3)*. His was the longest tenure in the history of the Court.

DUVAL(L), GABRIEL (1752–1844; Madison, 1811–1835). Md. Rep.—Declined to serve as delegate, U.S. Constitutional Convention, 1787. Md., State Council (3). U.S., House of Representatives (2). Md., Judge, General Court (6). *U.S., Comptroller of the Treasury (9)*.

* ELLSWORTH, OLIVER (1745–1807; Washington, 1796–1800). Conn.Fed.—Delegate, U.S. Constitutional Convention, 1787. Conn., Legislature (2); Member, Governor's Council (4); Judge, Superior Court (5). *U.S., Senate (7)*.

FIELD, STEPHEN J. (1816–1899; Lincoln, 1863–1897). Calif.Dem.—*Calif., Justice, and Chief Justice, Supreme Court (6)*.

FORTAS, ABE (1910–1982; L.B. Johnson, 1965–1969). Tenn. Dem.—U.S. Government attorney and consultant (A.A.A., S.E.C., P.W.A., Dep't of Interior (9); Undersecretary of Interior (4). *Private practice in Washington, D.C.* Nominated as Chief Justice; nomination withdrawn, 1968. Resigned.

FRANKFURTER, FELIX (1882–1965; F.D. Roosevelt, 1939–1962). Mass. Independent.—U.S., Assistant U.S. Attorney (4); Law Officer, War Department, Bureau of Insular Affairs (3); Assistant to Secretary of War (1). *Professor of Law (25).*

* FULLER, MELVILLE W. (1833–1910; Cleveland, 1888–1910). Ill. Dem.—Ill., Legislature (2). *Private practice.*

GOLDBERG, ARTHUR J. (1908–1990; Kennedy, 1962–1965). Ill. Dem.—Major, U.S.A., World War II. General Counsel, USW–AFL–CIO (13). *U.S., Secretary of Labor (1).* Resigned to become Ambassador to U.N.

GRAY, HORACE (1828–1902; Arthur, 1881–1902). Mass.Rep.— *Mass.,* Associate Justice and *Chief Justice, Supreme Judicial Court (18).*

GRIER, ROBERT O. (1794–1870; Polk, 1846–1870). Pa.Dem.—*Pa., Presiding Judge, District Court (13).*

HARLAN, JOHN M. (1833–1911; Hayes, 1877–1911). Ky.Rep.— Ky., Judge, County Court (1). Col., Union Army, 1861–63. Ky., Attorney General (4). U.S., Member, President's Louisiana Commission, 1877. *Private practice.* Grandfather of:

HARLAN, JOHN M. (1899–1971; Eisenhower, 1955–1971). N.Y.Rep.—Col., U.S.A.A.F., World War II. N.Y. Chief Counsel, State Crime Commission (2). *U.S., Judge, Court of Appeals (1).*

HOLMES, OLIVER W., JR. (1841–1935; T. Roosevelt, 1902–1932). Mass.Rep.—Lt. Col., Mass. Volunteers, Civil War. *Mass.,* Associate Justice, and *Chief Justice, Supreme Judicial Court (20).*

* HUGHES, CHARLES E. (1862–1948; Taft, 1910–1916, and Hoover, 1930–1941). N.Y.Rep.—N.Y., Counsel, legislative committees investigating gas and insurance industries, 1905–06. U.S., Special Assistant to Attorney General for Coal Investigation, 1906. *N.Y., Governor (3).* [Between appointments to the Supreme Court: Presidential Nominee, Republican Party, 1916. U.S., Secretary of State (4). *Member, Permanent Court of Arbitration, The Hague (4). Judge, Permanent Court of International Justice (2).*] Chief Justice on second appointment.

HUNT, WARD (1810–1886; Grant, 1872–1882). N.Y.Rep.—N.Y., Legislature (2). Mayor of Utica, N.Y. (1). N.Y. Associate Judge, and Chief Judge, Court of Appeals (4); *Commissioner of Appeals (4).* He did not sit from 1879 to his retirement in 1882.

IREDELL, JAMES (1750–1799; Washington, 1790–1799). N.C.Fed.—Comptroller of Customs (6), Collector of Port (2), Edenton, N.C., N.C., Judge, Superior Court (½); Attorney General (2); Member, Council of State, 1787; *Reviser of Statutes* (3).

JACKSON, HOWELL E. (1832–1895; B. Harrison, 1893–1895). Tenn.Dem.—Tenn., Judge, Court of Arbitration (4); Legislature (1). U.S. Senate (5); *Judge, Circuit Court of Appeals (7).*

JACKSON, ROBERT H. (1892–1954; F.D. Roosevelt, 1941–1954). N.Y.Dem.—U.S., General Counsel, Bureau of Internal Revenue (2); Assistant Attorney General (2); Solicitor General (2); *Attorney General (1).*

* JAY, JOHN (1745–1829; Washington, 1789–1795). N.Y.Fed.— N.Y., Chief Justice, Supreme Court (2). U.S., Envoy to Spain (2); Commissioner, Treaty of Paris, 1782–83; Secretary for Foreign Affairs (6). Co-author, The Federalist.

JOHNSON, THOMAS (1732–1819; Washington, 1791–1793). Md. Fed.—Md., Brigadier–General, Militia (1); Legislature (5); Governor (2); *Chief Judge, General Court (1).*

JOHNSON, WILLIAM (1771–1834; Jefferson, 1804–1834). S.C.Rep.—S.C., Legislature (4); *Judge, Court of Common Pleas (6).*

KENNEDY, ANTHONY M. (1936–___, Reagan, 1988–___). Calif.- Rep.—*U.S. Judge, Court of Appeals (12).*

LAMAR, JOSEPH R. (1857–1916; Taft, 1910–1916). Ga.Dem.— Ga., Legislature (3); Commissioner to Codify Laws (3); Associate Justice, Supreme Court (4). *Private practice.*

LAMAR, LUCIUS Q.C. (1825–1893; Cleveland, 1888–1893). Miss. Dem.—Ga., Legislature (2). U.S., House of Representatives (4). Draftsman, Mississippi Ordinance of Secession, 1861. C.S.A., Lt. Col. (1); Commissioner to Russia (1); Judge–Advocate, III Corps, Army of No. Va. (1). U.S., House of Representatives (4); Senate (8); *Secretary of the Interior (3).*

LIVINGSTON, (HENRY) BROCKHOLST (1757–1823; Jefferson, 1806–1823). N.Y.Rep.—Lt. Col., Continental Army. *N.Y., Judge, Supreme Court (4).*

LURTON, HORACE H. (1844–1914; Taft, 1909–1914). Tenn. Dem.—Sgt. Major, C.S.A. Tenn., Chancellor (3); Associate Justice and Chief Justice, Supreme Court (7). *U.S., Judge, Circuit Court of Appeals (16).*

McKENNA, JOSEPH (1843–1926; McKinley, 1898–1925). Calif.Rep.—Calif., District Attorney (2); Legislature (2). U.S., House of Representatives (7); *Judge, Circuit Court of Appeals (5); Attorney General (1).*

McKINLEY, JOHN (1780–1852; Van Buren, 1837–1852). Ala. Dem.—Ala., Legislature (4). U.S., Senate (5); House of Representatives (2); *re-elected to Senate,* but appointed to Court before taking seat.

McLEAN, JOHN (1785–1861; Jackson, 1829–1861). Ohio Dem.— U.S., House of Representatives (4). Ohio, Judge, Supreme Court (6). U.S., Commissioner, General Land Office (1); *Postmaster–General (6).*

McREYNOLDS, JAMES C. (1862–1946; Wilson, 1914–1941). Tenn. Dem.—U.S., Assistant Attorney General (4); *Attorney General (1).*

* MARSHALL, JOHN (1755–1835; J. Adams, 1801–1835). Va. Fed.—Va., Legislature (7); U.S., Envoy to France (1); House of Representatives (1); *Secretary of State (1).*

MARSHALL, THURGOOD (1908–___; L.B. Johnson, 1967–___). N.Y.Dem.—Counsel, Legal Defense and Educational Fund, NAACP (21). U.S., Judge, Court of Appeals (4); *Solicitor General (2).*

MATTHEWS, STANLEY (1824–1889; Garfield, 1881–1889). Ohio Rep.—Ohio, Judge, Court of Common Pleas (2); Legislature (3). U.S., District Attorney (3). Col., Ohio Volunteers. Ohio, Judge, Superior Court (2). Counsel before Hayes–Tilden Electoral Commission, 1877. U.S., Senate (2). *Private practice.* His first appointment to the Court by Hayes in 1881 was not acted upon by the Senate.

MILLER, SAMUEL F. (1816–1890; Lincoln, 1862–1890). Iowa Rep.—Physician. *Private practice.*

MINTON, SHERMAN (1890–1965; Truman, 1949–1956). Ind. Dem.—Capt., Inf., World War I. U.S., Senate (6); *Judge, Court of Appeals (8).*

MOODY, WILLIAM H. (1853–1917; T. Roosevelt, 1906–1910). Mass.Rep.—U.S., District Attorney (5); House of Representatives (7); Secretary of the Navy (2); *Attorney General (2).*

MOORE, ALFRED (1755–1810; J. Adams, 1799–1804). N.C.Fed.— N.C., Col. of Militia; Legislature (2); Attorney General (9). U.S., Commissioner, Treaty with Cherokee Nation (1); *N.C., Judge, Superior Court (1).*

MURPHY, FRANK (1893–1949; F.D. Roosevelt, 1940–1949). Mich. Dem.—Capt., Inf., World War I. U.S., Assistant U.S. Attorney (1). Mich., Judge, Recorder's Court (7). Mayor, Detroit, Mich. (3). U.S., Governor–General, and High Commissioner, P.I. (3). Mich., Governor (2). *U.S., Attorney General (1).*

NELSON, SAMUEL (1792–1873; Tyler, 1845–1872). N.Y.Dem.— N.Y., Judge, Circuit Court (8); Associate Justice, and *Chief Justice, Supreme Court (14).*

O'CONNOR, SANDRA DAY (1930–___; Reagan, 1981–___). Ariz.—Rep. Private practice & Assistant Ariz. State Atty. Gen.; Ariz.

State Senate (5); Judge, Superior Court (trial court) Maricopa County, Ariz. (5); *Judge, Ariz. Appellate Court (2).*

PATERSON, WILLIAM (1745–1806; Washington, 1793–1806). N.J.Fed.—Signer, U.S. Constitution, 1787. N.J., Legislature (2); Attorney General (7). U.S., Senate (1). *N.J., Governor (3).* Reviser of English Pre–Revolutionary Statutes in Force in N.J.

PECKHAM, RUFUS W. (1838–1909; Cleveland, 1895–1909). N.Y.Dem.—N.Y., District Attorney (1); Justice, Supreme Court (3); *Associate Judge, Court of Appeals (9).*

PITNEY, MAHLON (1858–1924; Taft, 1912–1922). N.J.Rep.—U.S., House of Representatives (4). N.J., Legislature (2); Associate Justice, Supreme Court (7); Chancellor (4).

POWELL, LEWIS F. (1907–___; Nixon, 1972–87). Va.Dem.—Col., U.S.A.A.F., World War II. *Private practice.*

REED, STANLEY F. (1884–1980; F.D. Roosevelt, 1938–1957). Ky. Dem.—Ky., Legislature (4). 1st Lt., U.S.A., World War I. U.S., General Counsel, Federal Farm Board (3); General Counsel, Reconstruction Finance Corporation (3); *Solicitor General (3).*

REHNQUIST, WILLIAM H. (1924–___; Nixon, later Reagan 1972–___ Chief Justice, 1986–___). Ariz.Rep.—U.S.A.F., World War II. Law Clerk, Justice Jackson, 1952–53. *U.S., Assistant Attorney General (3).*

ROBERTS, OWEN J. (1875–1955; Hoover, 1930–1945). Pa.Rep.— Pa., Assistant District Attorney (3). U.S., Special Deputy Attorney General in Espionage Act Cases, World War I; Special Prosecutor, Oil Cases, 1924. *Private practice.*

* RUTLEDGE, JOHN (1739–1800; Washington, 1789–1791, and Washington, 1795). S.C.Fed.—Signer, U.S. Constitution, 1787. S.C., Legislature (18); Attorney General (1); President and Governor (6); *Chancellor (7).* [Between appointments to the Supreme Court: *S.C., Chief Justice, Court of Common Pleas and Sessions (4).*] He did not sit under his first appointment; he sat with a recess appointment as Chief Justice, but his regular appointment was rejected by the Senate.

RUTLEDGE, WILEY B. (1894–1949; F.D. Roosevelt, 1943–1949). Iowa Dem.—Mo., then Iowa, Member, National Conference of Commissioners on Uniform State Laws (10). *U.S., Judge, Court of Appeals (4).*

SANFORD, EDWARD T. (1865–1930; Harding, 1923–1930). Tenn. Rep.—U.S., Assistant Attorney General (1); *Judge, District Court (15).*

SCALIA, ANTONIN (1936–___; Reagan, 1986–). Washington, D.C.Rep.—Assistant Atty. Gen. (3); *U.S. Judge, Court of Appeals (5).* The first Italian–American to be appointed to the Court.

SHIRAS, GEORGE (1832–1924; B. Harrison, 1892–1903). Pa.Rep. *Private practice.*

SOUTER, DAVID H. (1939–___; Bush, 1990–___). Mass.Rep.—Assistant N.H. Atty. Gen. (3); Deputy N.H. Atty. Gen. (5); N.H. Atty. Gen. (2); Associate Justice, N.H. Superior Court (5); Judge, N.H. Supreme Court (7); *Judge, Court of Appeals (5 months)*.

STEWART, POTTER (1915–1985; Eisenhower, 1958–1981). Ohio Rep.—Lt., U.S.N.R., World War II. *U.S., Judge, Court of Appeals (4)*.

STEVENS, JOHN PAUL (1920–___; Ford, 1975–___). Ill.Rep.—U.S. Navy, 1942–1945. Law Clerk, Justice Wiley Rutledge, 1947–1948. Associate Counsel, House Judiciary Committee's Subcommittee on Study of Monopoly Power, 1951–52; member of Attorney General's National Committee to Study Antitrust Laws, 1953–1955; Counsel to special commission to investigate allegations of misconduct on Illinois Supreme Court, 1969. *U.S. Court of Appeals (5)*.

* STONE, HARLAN F. (1872–1946; Coolidge, later F.D. Roosevelt, 1925–1946). N.Y.Rep.—*U.S., Attorney General (1)*. Chief Justice, 1941–1946.

STORY, JOSEPH (1779–1845; Madison, 1811–1845). Mass.Rep.—Mass., Legislature (5). U.S., House of Representatives (2). *Private practice.*

STRONG, WILLIAM (1808–1895; Grant, 1870–1880). Pa.Rep.—U.S., House of Representatives (4). Pa., Justice, Supreme Court (11). *Private practice.*

SUTHERLAND, GEORGE (1862–1942; Harding, 1922–1938). Utah Rep.—Utah, Legislature (4). U.S., House of Representatives (2); Senate (12). *Private practice.*

SWAYNE, NOAH H. (1804–1884; Lincoln, 1862–1881). Ohio Rep.—Ohio, County Attorney (4); Legislature (2). U.S., District Attorney (9). *Private practice.*

* TAFT, WILLIAM H. (1857–1930; Harding, 1921–1930). Conn. Rep.—U.S., Collector of Internal Revenue (1). Ohio Judge, Superior Court (3). U.S., Solicitor General (2); Judge, Circuit Court of Appeals (8); Governor–General, P.I. (3); Secretary of War (4); President (4). *Professor of Law.*

* TANEY, ROGER B. (1777–1864; Jackson, 1836–1864). Md. Dem.—Md., Legislature (7); Attorney General (2). U.S., Attorney General (2), Secretary of the Treasury (3/4; rejected by the Senate). *Private practice.*

THOMAS, CLARENCE (1948–___; Bush, 1991–___). Va.Rep.—Assistant Mo. Atty. Gen. (3); Legis. Assistant, Senator Danforth (2); Assistant Secretary for Civil Rights, U.S. Department of Education (1); Chairman, Equal Employment Opportunity Commission (8); Judge, U.S., Court of Appeals (one year, eight months).

THOMPSON, SMITH (1768–1843; Monroe, 1823–1843). N.Y.Rep.—N.Y., Legislature (2); Associate Justice, and Chief Justice, Supreme Court (16). *U.S., Secretary of the Navy (4).*

TODD, THOMAS (1765–1826; Jefferson, 1807–1826). Ky.Rep.— Ky., Judge, and *Chief Justice, Court of Appeals (6).*

TRIMBLE, ROBERT (1777–1828; J.Q. Adams, 1826–1828). Ky. Rep.—Ky., Legislature (2). Judge, Court of Appeals (2). U.S., District Attorney (4); *Judge, District Court (9).*

VAN DEVANTER, WILLIS (1859–1941; Taft, 1910–1937). Wyo. Rep.—Wyo., Legislature (2); Chief Justice, Supreme Court (1). U.S., Assistant Attorney General (Interior Department) (6); Judge, Circuit Court of Appeals (7).

* VINSON, FRED M. (1890–1953; Truman, 1946–1953). Ky. Dem.—Ky., Commonwealth Attorney (3). U.S., House of Representatives (14); Judge, Court of Appeals (5); Director, Office of Economic Stabilization (2); Federal Loan Administrator (1 mo.); Director, Office of War Mobilization and Reconversion (3 mo.); *Secretary of the Treasury (1).*

* WAITE, MORRISON R. (1816–1888; Grant, 1874–1888). Ohio Rep.—Ohio, Legislature (2). Counsel for United States, U.S.–Gr.Brit. Arbitration ("Alabama" Claims), 1871–72. *Private practice.*

* WARREN, EARL (1891–1974; Eisenhower, 1953–1969). Calif.Rep.—1st Lt., Inf., World War I. Deputy City Attorney (1); Deputy District Attorney (5); District Attorney (14); Attorney General (4); *Governor (10).*

WASHINGTON, BUSHROD (1762–1829; J. Adams, 1798–1829). Pa.Fed.—Va., Legislature (1). *Private practice.*

WAYNE, JAMES M. (1790–1867; Jackson, 1835–1867). Ga.Dem.— Ga., Officer, Hussars, War of 1812; Legislature (2). Mayor of Savannah, Ga. (2). Ga., Judge, Superior Court (5). *U.S., House of Representatives (6).*

WHITE, BYRON R. (1917–___; Kennedy, 1962–___). Colo.Dem.— U.S. N.R., World War II. Law Clerk, Chief Justice Vinson, 1946–47. *U.S., Deputy Attorney General (1).*

* WHITE, EDWARD D. (1845–1921; Cleveland, later Taft, 1894–1921). La.Dem.—La., Legislature (4); Justice, Supreme Court (2). *U.S., Senate (3).* Chief Justice, 1910–1921.

WHITTAKER, CHARLES E. (1901–1973; Eisenhower, 1957–1962). Mo.Rep.—U.S., Judge, District Court (2); *Court of Appeals (1).*

WILSON, JAMES (1724–1798; Washington, 1789–1798). Pa.Fed.— Signer, U.S. Declaration of Independence, 1776, and U.S. Constitution, 1787. Although he was strongly interested in western-land development companies for several years prior to his appointment, his primary activity in the period immediately preceding his appointment was in obtaining ratification of the Federal and Pennsylvania Constitutions.

WOODBURY, LEVI (1789–1851; Polk, 1845–1851). N.H.Dem.— N.H., Associate Justice, Superior Court (6); Governor (2); Legislature (1). U.S., Senate (6); Secretary of the Navy (3); Secretary of the Treasury (7); *Senate (4)*.

WOODS, WILLIAM B. (1824–1887; Hayes, 1880–1887). Ga.Rep.— Mayor, Newark, O. (1). Ohio, Legislature (4). Brevet Major General, U.S. Vol., Civil War. Ala., Chancellor (1). *U.S., Judge, Circuit Court (11)*.

Appendix H

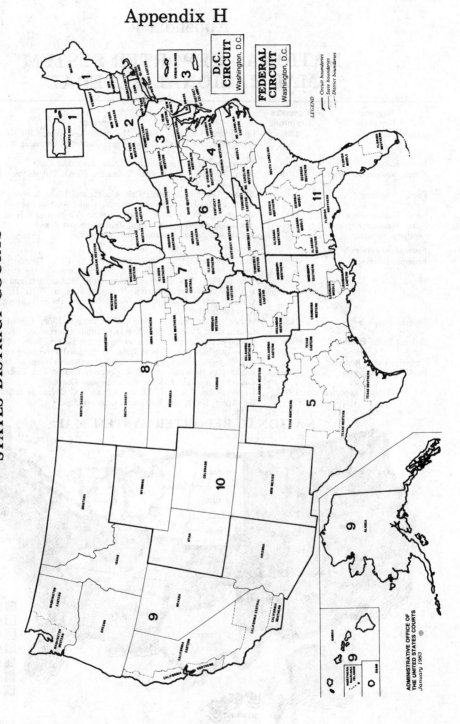

UNITED STATES COURTS OF APPEALS AND UNITED STATES DISTRICT COURTS

Appendix I

NATIONAL REPORTER SYSTEM
MAP REGIONAL/FEDERAL

Regional Reporters	Coverage Beginning	Coverage
Atlantic Reporter	1885	Connecticut, Delaware, Maine, Maryland, New Hampshire, New Jersey, Pennsylvania, Rhode Island, Vermont, and District of Columbia Municipal Court of Appeals
North Eastern Reporter	1885	Illinois, Indiana, Massachusetts, New York and Ohio
North Western Reporter	1879	Iowa, Michigan, Minnesota, Nebraska, North Dakota, South Dakota and Wisconsin
Pacific Reporter	1883	Alaska, Arizona, California, Colorado, Hawaii, Idaho, Kansas, Montana, Nevada, New Mexico, Oklahoma, Oregon, Utah, Washington and Wyoming
South Eastern Reporter	1887	Georgia, North Carolina, South Carolina, Virginia and West Virginia
South Western Reporter	1886	Arkansas, Kentucky, Missouri, Tennessee and Texas
Southern Reporter	1887	Alabama, Florida, Louisiana and Mississippi
Federal Reporters		
Federal Reporter	1880	United States Circuit Court from 1880 to 1912; Commerce Court of the United States from 1911 to 1913; District Courts of the United States from 1880 to 1932; U.S. Court of Claims from 1929 to 1932 and since 1960; the U.S. Court of Appeals from its organization in 1891; the U.S. Court of Customs and Patent Appeals from 1929; and the U.S. Emergency Court of Appeals from 1943.
Federal Supplement	1932	United States Court of Claims from 1932 to 1960; United States District Courts since 1932; United States Customs Court since 1956.
Federal Rules Decisions	1939	United States District Courts involving the Federal Rules of Civil Procedure since 1939 and the Federal Rules of Criminal Procedure since 1946.
Supreme Court Reporter	1882	U.S. Supreme Court beginning with the October term of 1882.
Bankruptcy Reporter	1980	Bankruptcy decisions of U.S. Bankruptcy Courts, U.S. District Courts, U.S. Courts of Appeals and the U.S. Supreme Court.
Military Justice Reporter	1978	United States Court of Military Appeals and Courts of Military Review for the Army, Navy, Air Force and Coast Guard.

NATIONAL REPORTER SYSTEM MAP

Pacific
North Western
South Western
North Eastern
Atlantic
South Eastern
Southern

772

Appendix J

AN ORGANIZATIONAL CHART OF THE GOVERNMENT OF THE UNITED STATES

AN ORGANIZATIONAL CHART OF THE GOVERNMENT OF THE UNITED STATES

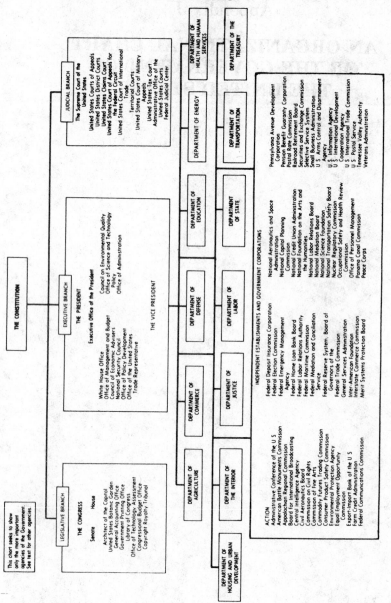

Source: United States Government Manual 1983–84

Appendix K

THE PRESIDENTS AND VICE PRESIDENTS OF THE UNITED STATES IN HISTORICAL PERSPECTIVE

(As of June 1, 1992)

Order	President	Vice President	Service
1.	George Washington	John Adams	1789–1797
2.	John Adams	Thomas Jefferson	1797–1801
3.	Thomas Jefferson	Aaron Burr	1801–1805
	Thomas Jefferson	George Clinton	1805–1809
4.	James Madison	George Clinton [1]	1809–1813
	James Madison	Elbridge Gerry [2]	1813–1817
5.	James Monroe	Daniel D. Tompkins	1817–1825
6.	John Quincy Adams	John C. Calhoun	1825–1829
7.	Andrew Jackson	John C. Calhoun [3]	1829–1833
	Andrew Jackson	Martin Van Buren	1833–1837
8.	Martin Van Buren	Richard M. Johnson	1837–1841
9.	William Henry Harrison [4]	John Tyler	1841
10.	John Tyler		1841–1845
11.	James K. Polk	George M. Dallas	1845–1849
12.	Zachary Taylor [5]	Millard Fillmore	1849–1850
13.	Millard Fillmore		1850–1853
14.	Franklin Pierce	William R. King [6]	1853–1857
15.	James Buchanan	John C. Breckinridge	1857–1861
16.	Abraham Lincoln	Hannibal Hamlin	1861–1865
	Abraham Lincoln [7]	Andrew Johnson	1865
17.	Andrew Johnson		1865–1869
18.	Ulysses S. Grant	Schuyler Colfax	1869–1873
	Ulysses S. Grant	Henry Wilson [8]	1873–1877
19.	Rutherford B. Hayes	William A. Wheeler	1877–1881
20.	James A. Garfield [9]	Chester A. Arthur	1881
21.	Chester A. Arthur		1881–1885

1. Died in office, April 20, 1812.
2. Died in office, November 23, 1814.
3. Resigned December 28, 1832 to become U.S. Senator.
4. Died in office, April 4, 1841.
5. Died in office, July 9, 1850.
6. Died in office, April 18, 1853.
7. Died in office, April 15, 1865.
8. Died in office, November 22, 1875.
9. Died in office, September 19, 1881.

Order	President	Vice President	Service
22.	Grover Cleveland	Thomas A. Hendricks [10]	1885–1889
23.	Benjamin Harrison	Levi P. Morton	1889–1893
24.	Grover Cleveland	Adlai E. Stevenson	1893–1897
25.	William McKinley	Garret A. Hobart [11]	1897–1901
	William McKinley [12]	Theodore Roosevelt	1901
26.	Theodore Roosevelt		1901–1905
	Theodore Roosevelt	Charles W. Fairbanks	1905–1909
27.	William H. Taft	James S. Sherman [13]	1909–1913
28.	Woodrow Wilson	Thomas R. Marshall	1913–1921
29.	Warren G. Harding [14]	Calvin Coolidge	1921–1923
30.	Calvin Coolidge		1923–1925
	Calvin Coolidge	Charles G. Dawes	1925–1929
31.	Herbert C. Hoover	Charles Curtis	1929–1933
32.	Franklin D. Roosevelt	John N. Garner	1933–1941
	Franklin D. Roosevelt	Henry A. Wallace	1941–1945
	Franklin D. Roosevelt [15]	Harry S Truman	1945
33.	Harry S Truman		1945–1949
	Harry S Truman	Alben W. Barkley	1949–1953
34.	Dwight D. Eisenhower	Richard M. Nixon	1953–1961
35.	John F. Kennedy [16]	Lyndon B. Johnson	1961–1963
36.	Lyndon B. Johnson		1963–1965
	Lyndon B. Johnson	Hubert H. Humphrey	1965–1969
37.	Richard M. Nixon	Spiro T. Agnew [17]	1969–1973
	Richard M. Nixon [18]	Gerald R. Ford [19]	1973–1974
38.	Gerald R. Ford [20]	Nelson A. Rockefeller [21]	1974–1977
39.	Jimmy Carter	Walter F. Mondale	1977–1981
40.	Ronald W. Reagan	George H.W. Bush	1981–1989
41.	George H.W. Bush	James Danforth Quale	1989–

10. Died in office, November 25, 1885.
11. Died in office, November 21, 1899.
12. Died in office, September 14, 1901.
13. Died in office, October 30, 1912.
14. Died in office, August 2, 1923.
15. Died in office, April 12, 1945.
16. Died in office, November 22, 1963.
17. Resigned October 12, 1973.

18. Resigned August 9, 1974.
19. Appointed and confirmed as Vice President under the 25th Amendment.
20. Succeeded to the Presidency on resignation of the President, August 9, 1974.
21. Appointed and confirmed as Vice President under the 25th Amendment.

Appendix L

THE STATES OF THE UNION—
HISTORICAL DATA

State or other jurisdiction	Capital	Source of state lands	Date organized as Territory	Date admitted to Union	Chronological order of admission to Union
ALABAMA	Montgomery	Mississippi Territory, 1798 a	March 3, 1817	Dec. 14, 1819	22
ALASKA	Juneau	Purchased from Russia, 1867	Aug. 24, 1912	Jan. 3, 1959	49
ARIZONA	Phoenix	Ceded by Mexico, 1848 b	Feb. 24, 1863	Feb. 14, 1912	48
ARKANSAS	Little Rock	Louisiana Purchase, 1803	March 2, 1819	June 15, 1836	25
CALIFORNIA	Sacramento	Ceded by Mexico, 1848	c	Sept. 9, 1850	31
COLORADO	Denver	Louisiana Purchase, 1803 d	Feb. 28, 1861	Aug. 1, 1876	38
CONNECTICUT	Hartford	Fundamental Orders, Jan. 14, 1638; Royal charter, April 23, 1662 e	—	Jan. 9, 1788 f	5
DELAWARE	Dover	Swedish charter, 1638; English charter, 1683 e	—	Dec. 7, 1787 f	1
FLORIDA	Tallahassee	Ceded by Spain, 1819	March 30, 1822	March 3, 1845	27
GEORGIA	Atlanta	Charter, 1732, from George II to Trustees for Establishing the Colony of Georgia e	—	Jan. 2, 1788 f	4
HAWAII	Honolulu	Annexed, 1898	June 14, 1900	Aug. 21, 1959	50
IDAHO	Boise	Treaty with Britain, 1846	March 4, 1863	July 3, 1890	43
ILLINOIS	Springfield	Northwest Territory, 1787	Feb. 3, 1809	Dec. 3, 1818	21
INDIANA	Indianapolis	Northwest Territory, 1787	May 7, 1800	Dec. 11, 1816	19
IOWA	Des Moines	Louisiana Purchase, 1803	June 12, 1838	Dec. 28, 1846	29
KANSAS	Topeka	Louisiana Purchase, 1803 d	May 30, 1854	Jan. 29, 1861	34
KENTUCKY	Frankfort	Part of Virginia until admitted as State	c	June 1, 1792	15
LOUISIANA	Baton Rouge	Louisiana Purchase, 1803 g	March 26, 1804	April 30, 1812	18
MAINE	Augusta	Part of Massachusetts until admitted as State	c	March 15, 1820	23
MARYLAND	Annapolis	Charter, 1632, from Charles I to Calvert e	—	April 28, 1788 f	7
MASSACHUSETTS	Boston	Charter to Massachusetts Bay Company, 1629 e	—	Feb. 6, 1788 f	6
MICHIGAN	Lansing	Northwest Territory, 1787	Jan. 11, 1805	Jan. 26, 1837	26
MINNESOTA	St. Paul	Northwest Territory, 1787 h	March 3, 1849	May 11, 1858	32
MISSISSIPPI	Jackson	Mississippi Territory i	April 7, 1798	Dec. 10, 1817	20
MISSOURI	Jefferson City	Louisiana Purchase, 1803	June 4, 1812	Aug. 10, 1821	24
MONTANA	Helena	Louisiana Purchase, 1803 j	May 26, 1864	Nov. 8, 1889	41
NEBRASKA	Lincoln	Louisiana Purchase, 1803	May 30, 1854	March 1, 1867	37
NEVADA	Carson City	Ceded by Mexico, 1848	March 2, 1861	Oct. 31, 1864	36
NEW HAMPSHIRE	Concord	Grants from Council for New England, 1622 and 1629. Made Royal province, 1679 e	—	June 21, 1788 f	9
NEW JERSEY	Trenton	Dutch settlement, 1618; English charter, 1664 e	—	Dec. 18, 1787 f	3
NEW MEXICO	Santa Fe	Ceded by Mexico, 1848 b	Sept. 9, 1850	Jan. 6, 1912	47
NEW YORK	Albany	Dutch settlement, 1623; English control, 1664 e	—	July 26, 1788 f	11
NORTH CAROLINA	Raleigh	Charter, 1663, from Charles II e	—	Nov. 21, 1789 f	12
NORTH DAKOTA	Bismarck	Louisiana Purchase, 1803 k	March 2, 1861	Nov. 2, 1889	39
OHIO	Columbus	Northwest Territory, 1787	May 7, 1800	March 1, 1803	17
OKLAHOMA	Oklahoma City	Louisiana Purchase, 1803	May 2, 1890	Nov. 16, 1907	46
OREGON	Salem	Settlement and treaty with Britain, 1846	Aug. 14, 1848	Feb. 14, 1859	33
PENNSYLVANIA	Harrisburg	Grant from Charles II to William Penn, 1681 e	—	Dec. 12, 1787 f	2
RHODE ISLAND	Providence	Charter, 1663, from Charles II e	—	May 29, 1790 f	13
SOUTH CAROLINA	Columbia	Charter, 1663, from Charles II e	—	May 23, 1788 f	8
SOUTH DAKOTA	Pierre	Louisiana Purchase, 1803	March 2, 1861	Nov. 2, 1889	40
TENNESSEE	Nashville	Part of North Carolina until land ceded to U.S. in 1789	June 8, 1790 l	June 1, 1796	16
TEXAS	Austin	Republic of Texas, 1845	c	Dec. 29, 1845	28
UTAH	Salt Lake City	Ceded by Mexico, 1848	Sept. 9, 1850	Jan. 4, 1896	45
VERMONT	Montpelier	From lands of New Hampshire and New York	c	March 4, 1791	14

STATES OF THE UNION

State or other jurisdiction	Capital	Source of state lands	Date organized as Territory	Date admitted to Union	Chronological order of admission to Union
VIRGINIA . . . . Richmond		Charter, 1609, from James I to London Company e	—	June 25, 1788 f	10
WASHINGTON . . . . Olympia		Oregon Territory, 1848	March 2, 1853	Nov. 11, 1889	42
WEST VIRGINIA . . . . . . Charleston		Part of Virginia until admitted as State	c	June 20, 1863	35
WISCONSIN . . . . Madison		Northwest Territory, 1787	April 20, 1836	May 29, 1848	30
WYOMING . . . . Cheyenne		Louisiana Purchase, 1803 dj	July 25, 1868	July 10, 1890	44
D.C. . . . . —		Maryland m	—	—	—
AMERICAN SAMOA . . . Pago Pago		—	Became a Territory, 1900		—
GUAM . . . . Agana		Ceded by Spain, 1898	Aug. 1, 1950	—	—
PUERTO RICO . . . . San Juan		Ceded by Spain, 1898	—	July 25, 1952 n	—
TTPI . . . . Saipan		Administered as trusteeship for the United Nations, July 18, 1947 o			—
VIRGIN ISLANDS . . . . . Charlotte Amalie		Purchased from Denmark, March 31, 1917			—

a. By the Treaty of Paris 1783, England gave up claim to the thirteen original Colonies, and to all land within an area extending along the present Canadian border to the Lake of the Woods, down the Mississippi River to the 31st parallel, east to the Chattahoochie, down that river to the mouth of the Flint, east to the source of the St. Mary's, down that river to the ocean. Territory west of the Alleghenies was claimed by various States, but was eventually all ceded to the Nation. Thus, the major part of Alabama was acquired by the Treaty of Paris, but the lower portion from Spain in 1813.

b. Portion of land obtained by Gadsden Purchase, 1853.

c. No territorial status before admission to Union.

d. Portion of land ceded by Mexico, 1848.

e. One of the original thirteen Colonies.

f. Date of ratification of U.S. Constitution.

g. West Feliciana District (Baton Rouge) acquired from Spain, 1810, added to Louisiana, 1812.

h. Portion of land obtained by Louisiana Purchase, 1803.

i. See footnote (a). The lower portion of Mississippi was also acquired from Spain in 1813.

j. Portion of land obtained from Oregon Territory, 1848.

k. The northern portion and the Red River Valley were acquired by treaty with Great Britain in 1818.

l. Date Southwest Territory (identical boundary as Tennessee) was created.

m. Area was originally 100 square miles, taken from Virginia and Maryland. Virginia's portion south of the Potomac was given back to that State in 1846. Site chosen in 1790, city incorporated 1802.

n. On this date Puerto Rico became a self-governing Commonwealth by compact approved by the United States Congress and the voters of Puerto Rico as provided in U.S. Public Law–600 of 1950.

o. In March 1976, the Mariana Islands separated themselves from the rest of TTPI and became a self-governing Commonwealth.

Source: The book of the States 1982–83 is published biennially by The Council of State Governments, Lexington, Ky.

Appendix M

PROPOSED AMENDMENTS NOT RATIFIED BY THE STATES *

During the course of our history, in addition to the 26 amendments which have been ratified by the required three-fourths of the States, six other amendments have been submitted to the States but have not been ratified by them.

Beginning with the proposed Eighteenth Amendment, Congress has customarily included a provision requiring ratification within seven years from the time of the submission to the States. The Supreme Court in Coleman v. Miller, 307 U.S. 433, 59 S.Ct. 972, 83 L.Ed. 1385 (1939), declared that the question of the reasonableness of the time within which a sufficient number of States must act is a political question to be determined by the Congress. See generally § 2.16(c)(2).

In 1789, at the time of the submission of the Bill of Rights, twelve proposed amendments were submitted to the States. Of these, Articles III–XII were ratified and became the first ten amendments to the Constitution. Proposed Articles I and II were not ratified. The following is the text of those articles:

ARTICLE I. After the first enumeration required by the first article of the Constitution, there shall be one Representative for every thirty thousand, until the number shall amount to one hundred, after which the proportion shall be so regulated by Congress, that there shall be not less than one hundred Representatives, nor less than one Representative for every forty thousand persons, until the number of Representatives shall amount to two hundred; after which the proportion shall be so regulated by Congress, that there shall not be less than two hundred Representatives, nor more than one Representative for every fifty thousand persons.

ARTICLE II. No law varying the compensation for the services of the Senators and Representatives shall take effect, until an election of Representatives shall have intervened.**

* Adapted from, The Constitution of the United States of America: Analysis and Interpretation, Senate Document No. 92–82, 92d Cong., 2d Sess., 51–52 (1973).

** Michigan became the 38th state to ratify this amendment on May 7, 1992.

The Archivist of the United States later announced that he would accept this amendment as valid, making it the 27th Amendment. On May 18th this amendment became part of our Constitution.

Thereafter, in the 2d session of the 11th Congress, the Congress proposed the following amendment to the Constitution relating to acceptance by citizens of the United States of titles of nobility from any foreign government.

The proposed amendment which was not ratified by three-fourths of the States reads as follows:

Resolved by the Senate and House of Representatives of the United States of America in Congress assembled (two-thirds of both Houses concurring), That the following section be submitted to the legislatures of the several states, which, when ratified by the legislatures of three fourths of the states, shall be valid and binding, as a part of the constitution of the United States.

If any citizen of the United States shall accept, claim, receive or retain any title of nobility or honour, or shall, without the consent of Congress, accept and retain any present, pension, office or emolument of any kind whatever, from any emperor, king, prince or foreign power, such person shall cease to be a citizen of the United States, and shall be incapable of holding any office of trust or profit under them, or either of them.

During the second session of the 36th Congress on March 2, 1861, the following proposed amendment to the Constitution relating to slavery was signed by the President. It is interesting to note in this connection that this is the only proposed amendment to the Constitution ever signed by the President. The President's signature is considered unnecessary because of Article V, which provides that upon the concurrence of two-thirds of both Houses of Congress the proposal shall be submitted to the States and shall be ratified by three-fourths of the States. Hollingsworth v. Virginia, 3 U.S. (3 Dall.) 378, 381 n. 1, 1 L.Ed. 644, 646 n. 1 (1798).

Resolved by the Senate and House of Representatives of the United States of America in Congress assembled, That the following article be proposed to the Legislatures of the several States as an amendment to the Constitution of the United States, which, when ratified by three-fourths of said Legislatures, shall be valid, to all intents and purposes, as part of the said Constitution, viz:

"ARTICLE THIRTEEN

"No amendment shall be made to the Constitution which will authorize or give to Congress the power to abolish or interfere, within any State, with the domestic institutions thereof, including that of persons held to labor or service by the laws of said State."

In more recent times a proposed amendment that has not been ratified by three-fourths of the States is the proposed child-labor amendment, which was submitted to the States during the 1st session of the 68th Congress in June 1924, as follows:

JOINT RESOLUTION PROPOSING AN AMENDMENT TO
THE CONSTITUTION OF THE UNITED STATES

Resolved by the Senate and House of Representatives of the United States of America in Congress assembled (two-thirds of each House concurring therein), That the following article is proposed as an amendment to the Constitution of the United States, which when ratified by the legislatures of three-fourths of the several States, shall be valid to all intents and purposes as a part of the Constitution:

ARTICLE—

SECTION 1. The Congress shall have power to limit, regulate, and prohibit the labor of persons under 18 years of age.

SECTION 2. The power of several States is unimpaired by this article except that the operation of State laws shall be suspended to the extent necessary to give effect to legislation enacted by the Congress.

On March 22, 1972, Congress submitted to the States for ratification the proposed Equal Rights Amendment. The resolution accompanying this proposed amendment states that "[t]his article shall be valid to all intents and purposes as part of the Constitution of the United States when ratified by the legislatures of three-fourths of the several States within seven years from the date of its submission by the Congress." When it appeared that a sufficient number of the States would not ratify within the required period of time, Congress extended the period for ratification until June 30, 1982. H.J.Res. 638, 92 Stat. 3799 (1978). However, no new States ratified, and the proposed amendment therefore died. It would have provided:

ARTICLE—

SECTION 1. Equality of rights under the law shall not be denied or abridged by the United States or by any State on account of sex.

SECTION 2. The Congress shall have the power to enforce, by appropriate legislation, the provisions of this article.

SECTION 3. This amendment shall take effect two years after the date of ratification.

The House of Representatives on March 2, 1978, and the Senate on March 6, 1978, passed a proposed amendment to provide for representation of the District of Columbia in Congress. It was then sent to the States for ratification. The proposed amendment provides:

ARTICLE—

SECTION 1. For purposes of representation in the Congress, election of the President and Vice President, and article V of this

Constitution, the District constituting the seat of government of the United States shall be treated as though it were a State.

SECTION 2. The exercise of the rights and powers conferred under this article shall be by the people of the District constituting the seat of government, and as shall be provided by Congress.

SECTION 3. The twenty-third article of amendment to the Constitution of the United States is hereby repealed.

SECTION 4. This article shall be inoperative, unless it shall have been ratified as an amendment to the Constitution by the legislatures of three-fourths of the several States within seven years from the date of its submission.

Appendix N

THE CONSTITUTION OF THE UNITED STATES *

1787 [1]

Preamble

We the People of the United States, in Order to form a more perfect Union, establish Justice, insure domestic Tranquility, provide for the common defence, promote the general Welfare, and secure the

* Adapted, with permission, from United States Code Annotated, Constitution of the United States, Annotated (West Publishing Co. 1958).

1. In May, 1785, a committee of Congress made a report recommending an alteration in the Articles of Confederation, but no action was taken on it, and it was left to the State Legislatures to proceed in the matter. In January, 1786, the Legislature of Virginia passed a resolution providing for the appointment of five commissioners, who, or any three of them, should meet such commissioners as might be appointed in the other States of the Union, at a time and place to be agreed upon, to take into consideration the trade of the United States; to consider how far a uniform system in their commercial regulations may be necessary to their common interest and their permanent harmony; and to report to the several States such an act, relative to this great object, as, when ratified by them, will enable the United States in Congress effectually to provide for the same. The Virginia commissioners, after some correspondence, fixed the first Monday in September as the time, and the city of Annapolis as the place for the meeting, but only four other States were represented, viz.: Delaware, New York, New Jersey, and Pennsylvania; the commissioners appointed by Massachusetts, New Hampshire, North Carolina, and Rhode Island failed to attend. Under the circumstances of so partial a representation, the commissioners present agreed upon a report, (drawn by Mr. Hamilton of New York,) expressing their unanimous conviction that it might essentially tend to advance the interests of the Union if the States by which they were respectively delegated would concur, and use their endeavors to

procure the concurrence of the other States, in the appointment of commissioners to meet at Philadelphia on the second Monday of May following, to take into consideration the situation of the United States; to devise such further provisions as should appear to them necessary to render the Constitution of the Federal Government adequate to the exigencies of the Union; and to report such an act for that purpose to the United States in Congress assembled as, when agreed to by them, and afterwards confirmed by the Legislatures of every State, would effectually provide for the same.

Congress, on the 21st of February, 1787, adopted a resolution in favor of a convention, and the Legislatures of those States which had not already done so (with the exception of Rhode Island) promptly appointed delegates. On the 25th of May, seven States having convened, George Washington, of Virginia, was unanimously elected President, and the consideration of the proposed constitution was commenced. On the 17th of September, 1787, the Constitution as engrossed and agreed upon was signed by all the members present, except Mr. Gerry, of Massachusetts, and Messrs. Mason and Randolph, of Virginia. The president of the convention transmitted it to Congress, with a resolution stating how the proposed Federal Government should be put in operation, and an explanatory letter. Congress, on the 28th of September, 1787, directed the Constitution so framed, with the resolutions and letter concerning the same, to "be transmitted to the several Legislatures in order to be submitted to a convention of delegates chosen in each State by the people thereof, in conformity to the resolves of the convention."

Blessings of Liberty to ourselves and our Posterity, do ordain and establish this Constitution for the United States of America.

Article I

Section 1. All legislative Powers herein granted shall be vested in a Congress of the United States, which shall consist of a Senate and House of Representatives.

Section 2. [1] The House of Representatives shall be composed of Members chosen every second Year by the People of the several States, and the Electors in each State shall have the Qualifications requisite for Electors of the most numerous Branch of the State Legislature.

[2] No Person shall be a Representative who shall not have attained to the Age of twenty five Years, and been seven Years a Citizen of the United States, and who shall not, when elected, be an Inhabitant of that State in which he shall be chosen.

[3] [Representatives and direct Taxes shall be apportioned among the several States which may be included within this Union, according to their respective Numbers, which shall be determined by adding to the whole Number of free Persons, including those bound to Service for a Term of Years, and excluding Indians not taxed, three fifths of all other Persons.] The actual Enumeration shall be made within three Years after the first Meeting of the Congress of the United States, and within every subsequent Term of ten Years, in such Manner as they shall by Law direct. The Number of Representatives shall not exceed one for every thirty Thousand, but each State shall have at Least one Representative; and until such enumeration shall be made, the State of New Hampshire shall be entitled to chuse three, Massachusetts eight, Rhode Island and Providence Plantations one, Connecticut five, New York six, New Jersey four, Pennsylvania eight, Delaware one, Maryland six, Virginia ten, North Carolina five, South Carolina five, and Georgia three.

The clause of this paragraph inclosed in brackets was amended, as to the mode of apportionment of representatives among the several states, by the

On the 4th of March, 1789, the day which had been fixed for commencing the operations of Government under the new Constitution, it had been ratified by the conventions chosen in each State to consider it, as follows: Delaware, December 7, 1787; Pennsylvania, December 12, 1787; New Jersey, December 18, 1787; Georgia, January 2, 1788; Connecticut, January 9, 1788; Massachusetts, February 6, 1788; Maryland, April 28, 1788; South Carolina, May 23, 1788; New Hampshire, June 21, 1788; Virginia, June 26, 1788; and New York, July 26, 1788.

The President informed Congress, on the 28th of January, 1790, that North Carolina had ratified the Constitution November 21, 1789; and he informed Congress on the 1st of June, 1790, that Rhode Island had ratified the Constitution May 29, 1790. Vermont, in convention, ratified the Constitution January 10, 1791, and was on March 4, 1791, by an act of Congress approved February 18, 1791, "received and admitted into this Union as a new and entire member of the United States".

Fourteenth Amendment, § 2, and as to taxes on incomes without apportionment, by the Sixteenth Amendment.

[4] When vacancies happen in the Representation from any State, the Executive Authority thereof shall issue Writs of Election to fill such Vacancies.

[5] The House of Representatives shall chuse their Speaker and other Officers; and shall have the sole Power of Impeachment.

Section 3. [1] [The Senate of the United States shall be composed of two Senators from each State, chosen by the Legislature thereof, for six Years; and each Senator shall have one Vote.]

This paragraph and the clause of following paragraph inclosed in brackets were superseded by the Seventeenth Amendment.

[2] Immediately after they shall be assembled in Consequence of the first Election, they shall be divided as equally as may be into three Classes. The Seats of the Senators of the first Class shall be vacated at the Expiration of the Second Year, of the second Class at the Expiration of the fourth Year, and of the third Class at the Expiration of the sixth Year, so that one third may be chosen every second Year; [and if Vacancies happen by Resignation, or otherwise, during the Recess of the Legislature of any State, the Executive thereof may make temporary Appointments until the next Meeting of the Legislature, which shall then fill such Vacancies.]

See note to preceding paragraph of this section.

[3] No Person shall be a Senator who shall not have attained to the Age of thirty Years, and been nine Years a Citizen of the United States, and who shall not, when elected, be an Inhabitant of that State for which he shall be chosen.

[4] The Vice President of the United States shall be President of the Senate, but shall have no Vote, unless they be equally divided.

[5] The Senate shall chuse their other Officers, and also a President pro tempore, in the Absence of the Vice President, or when he shall exercise the Office of President of the United States.

[6] The Senate shall have the sole Power to try all Impeachments. When sitting for that Purpose, they shall be on Oath or Affirmation. When the President of the United States is tried, the Chief Justice shall preside: And no Person shall be convicted without the Concurrence of two thirds of the Members present.

[7] Judgment in Cases of Impeachment shall not extend further than to removal from Office, and disqualification to hold and enjoy any Office of honor, Trust, or Profit under the United States: but the Party convicted shall nevertheless be liable and subject to Indictment, Trial, Judgment, and Punishment, according to Law.

Section 4. [1] The Times, Places and Manner of holding Elections for Senators and Representatives, shall be prescribed in each State by the Legislature thereof; but the Congress may at any time by Law make or alter such Regulations, except as to the Places of chusing Senators.

[2] The Congress shall assemble at least once in every Year, and such Meeting shall be on the first Monday in December, unless they shall by Law appoint a different Day.

Section 5. [1] Each House shall be the Judge of the Elections, Returns, and Qualifications of its own Members, and a Majority of each shall constitute a Quorum to do Business; but a smaller Number may adjourn from day to day, and may be authorized to compel the Attendance of absent Members, in such Manner, and under such Penalties as each House may provide.

[2] Each House may determine the Rules of its Proceedings, punish its Members for disorderly Behavior, and, with the Concurrence of two thirds, expel a Member.

[3] Each House shall keep a Journal of its Proceedings, and from time to time publish the same, excepting such Parts as may in their Judgment require Secrecy; and the Yeas and Nays of the Members of either House on any question shall, at the Desire of one fifth of those Present, be entered on the Journal.

[4] Neither House, during the Session of Congress, shall, without the Consent of the other, adjourn for more than three days, nor to any other Place than that in which the two Houses shall be sitting.

Section 6. [1] The Senators and Representatives shall receive a Compensation for their Services, to be ascertained by Law, and paid out of the Treasury of the United States. They shall in all Cases, except Treason, Felony and Breach of the Peace, be privileged from Arrest during their Attendance at the Session of their respective Houses, and in going to and returning from the same; and for any Speech or Debate in either House, they shall not be questioned in any other Place.

[2] No Senator or Representative shall, during the Time for which he was elected, be appointed to any civil Office under the Authority of the United States, which shall have been created, or the Emoluments whereof shall have been increased during such time; and no Person holding any Office under the United States, shall be a Member of either House during his Continuance in Office.

Section 7. [1] All Bills for raising Revenue shall originate in the House of Representatives; but the Senate may propose or concur with Amendments as on other Bills.

[2] Every Bill which shall have passed the House of Representatives and the Senate, shall, before it become a Law, be presented to the President of the United States; If he approve he shall sign it, but if not he shall return it, with his Objections to the House in which it shall have originated, who shall enter the Objections at large on their

Journal, and proceed to reconsider it. If after such Reconsideration two thirds of that House shall agree to pass the Bill, it shall be sent together with the Objections, to the other House, by which it shall likewise be reconsidered, and if approved by two thirds of that House, it shall become a Law. But in all such Cases the Votes of both Houses shall be determined by Yeas and Nays, and the Names of the Persons voting for and against the Bill shall be entered on the Journal of each House respectively. If any Bill shall not be returned by the President within ten Days (Sundays excepted) after it shall have been presented to him, the Same shall be a Law, in like Manner as if he had signed it, unless the Congress by their Adjournment prevent its Return in which Case it shall not be a Law.

[3] Every Order, Resolution, or Vote, to Which the Concurrence of the Senate and House of Representatives may be necessary (except on a question of Adjournment) shall be presented to the President of the United States; and before the Same shall take Effect, shall be approved by him, or being disapproved by him, shall be repassed by two thirds of the Senate and House of Representatives, according to the Rules and Limitations prescribed in the Case of a Bill.

Section 8. [1] The Congress shall have Power to lay and collect Taxes, Duties, Imposts and Excises, to pay the Debts and provide for the common Defence and general Welfare of the United States; but all Duties, Imposts and Excises shall be uniform throughout the United States;

[2] To borrow money on the credit of the United States;

[3] To regulate Commerce with foreign Nations, and among the several States, and with the Indian Tribes;

[4] To establish an uniform Rule of Naturalization, and uniform Laws on the subject of Bankruptcies throughout the United States;

[5] To coin Money, regulate the Value thereof, and of foreign Coin, and fix the Standard of Weights and Measures;

[6] To provide for the Punishment of counterfeiting the Securities and current Coin of the United States;

[7] To Establish Post Offices and Post Roads;

[8] To promote the Progress of Science and useful Arts, by securing for limited Times to Authors and Inventors the exclusive Right to their respective Writings and Discoveries;

[9] To constitute Tribunals inferior to the supreme Court;

[10] To define and punish Piracies and Felonies committed on the high Seas, and Offenses against the Law of Nations;

[11] To declare War, grant Letters of Marque and Reprisal, and make Rules concerning Captures on Land and Water;

[12] To raise and support Armies, but no Appropriation of Money to that Use shall be for a longer Term than two Years;

[13] To provide and maintain a Navy;

[14] To make Rules for the Government and Regulation of the land and naval Forces;

[15] To provide for calling forth the Militia to execute the Laws of the Union, suppress Insurrections and repel Invasions;

[16] To provide for organizing, arming, and disciplining, the Militia, and for governing such Part of them as may be employed in the Service of the United States, reserving to the States respectively, the Appointment of the Officers, and the Authority of training the Militia according to the discipline prescribed by Congress;

[17] To exercise exclusive Legislation in all Cases whatsoever, over such District (not exceeding ten Miles square) as may, by Cession of particular States and the Acceptance of Congress, become the Seat of the Government of the United States, and to exercise like Authority over all Places purchased by the Consent of the Legislature of the State in which the Same shall be, for the Erection of Forts, Magazines, Arsenals, dock-Yards, and other needful Buildings;—And

[18] To make all Laws which shall be necessary and proper for carrying into Execution the foregoing Powers, and all other Powers vested by this Constitution in the Government of the United States, or in any Department or Officer thereof.

Section 9. [1] The Migration or Importation of Such Persons as any of the States now existing shall think proper to admit, shall not be prohibited by the Congress prior to the Year one thousand eight hundred and eight, but a Tax or duty may be imposed on such Importation, not exceeding ten dollars for each Person.

[2] The privilege of the Writ of Habeas Corpus shall not be suspended, unless when in Cases of Rebellion or Invasion the public Safety may require it.

[3] No Bill of Attainder or ex post facto Law shall be passed.

[4] No Capitation, or other direct, Tax shall be laid, unless in Proportion to the Census or Enumeration herein before directed to be taken.

[5] No Tax or Duty shall be laid on Articles exported from any State.

[6] No Preference shall be given by any Regulation of Commerce or Revenue to the Ports of one State over those of another: nor shall Vessels bound to, or from, one State be obliged to enter, clear, or pay Duties in another.

788

[7] No money shall be drawn from the Treasury, but in Consequence of Appropriations made by Law; and a regular Statement and Account of the Receipts and Expenditures of all public Money shall be published from time to time.

[8] No Title of Nobility shall be granted by the United States: And no Person holding any Office of Profit or Trust under them, shall, without the Consent of the Congress, accept of any present, Emolument, Office, or Title, of any kind whatever, from any King, Prince, or foreign State.

Section 10. [1] No State shall enter into any Treaty, Alliance, or Confederation; grant Letters of Marque and Reprisal; coin Money; emit Bills of Credit; make any Thing but gold and silver Coin a Tender in Payment of Debts; pass any Bill of Attainder, ex post facto Law, or Law impairing the Obligation of Contracts, or grant any Title of Nobility.

[2] No State shall, without the Consent of the Congress, lay any Imposts or Duties on Imports or Exports, except what may be absolutely necessary for executing it's inspection Laws: and the net Produce of all Duties and Imposts, laid by any State on Imports or Exports, shall be for the Use of the Treasury of the United States; and all such Laws shall be subject to the Revision and Control of the Congress.

[3] No State shall, without the Consent of Congress, lay any Duty of Tonnage, keep Troops, or Ships of War in time of Peace, enter into any Agreement or Compact with another State, or with a foreign Power or engage in War, unless actually invaded, or in such imminent Danger as will not admit of delay.

Article II

Section 1. [1] The executive Power shall be vested in a President of the United States of America. He shall hold his Office during the Term of four Years, and, together with the Vice President, chosen for the same Term, be elected, as follows:

[2] Each State shall appoint, in such Manner as the Legislature thereof may direct, a Number of Electors, equal to the whole Number of Senators and Representatives to which the State may be entitled in the Congress; but no Senator or Representative, or Person holding an Office of Trust or Profit under the United States, shall be appointed an Elector.

[3] [The Electors shall meet in their respective States, and vote by Ballot for two Persons, of whom one at least shall not be an Inhabitant of the same State with themselves. And they shall make a List of all the Persons voted for, and of the Number of Votes for each; which List they shall sign and certify, and transmit sealed to the Seat of the Government of the United States, directed to the President of the Senate. The President of the Senate shall, in the Presence of the

Senate and House of Representatives, open all the Certificates, and the Votes shall then be counted. The Person having the greatest Number of Votes shall be the President, if such Number be a Majority of the whole Number of Electors appointed; and if there be more than one who have such Majority, and have an equal Number of Votes, then the House of Representatives shall immediately chuse by Ballot one of them for President; and if no Person have a Majority, then from the five highest on the List the said House shall in like Manner chuse the President. But in chusing the President, the Votes shall be taken by States the Representation from each State having one Vote; A quorum for this Purpose shall consist of a Member or Members from two thirds of the States, and a Majority of all the States shall be necessary to a Choice. In every Case, after the Choice of the President, the Person having the greater Number of Votes of the Electors shall be the Vice President. But if there should remain two or more who have equal Votes, the Senate shall choose from them by Ballot the Vice President.]

> This paragraph, inclosed in brackets, was superseded by the Twelfth Amendment, post.

[4] The Congress may determine the Time of chusing the Electors, and the Day on which they shall give their Votes; which Day shall be the same throughout the United States.

[5] No person except a natural born Citizen, or a Citizen of the United States, at the time of the Adoption of this Constitution, shall be eligible to the Office of President; neither shall any Person be eligible to that Office who shall not have attained to the Age of thirty five Years, and been fourteen Years a Resident within the United States.

[6] In case of the removal of the President from Office, or of his Death, Resignation or Inability to discharge the Powers and Duties of the said Office, the Same shall devolve on the Vice President and the Congress may by Law provide for the Case of Removal, Death, Resignation or Inability, both of the President and Vice President, declaring what Officer shall then act as President, and such Officer shall act accordingly, until the Disability be removed, or a President shall be elected.

[7] The President shall, at stated Times, receive for his Services, a Compensation, which shall neither be increased nor diminished during the Period for which he shall have been elected, and he shall not receive within that Period any other Emolument from the United States, or any of them.

[8] Before he enter on the Execution of his Office, he shall take the following Oath or Affirmation: "I do solemnly swear (or affirm) that I will faithfully execute the Office of President of the United States, and will to the best of my Ability, preserve, protect and defend the Constitution of the United States."

Section 2. [1] The President shall be Commander in Chief of the Army and Navy of the United States, and of the militia of the several States, when called into the actual Service of the United States; he may require the Opinion, in writing, of the principal Officer in each of the Executive Departments, upon any Subject relating to the Duties of their respective Offices and he shall have Power to grant Reprieves and Pardons for Offenses against the United States, except in Cases of Impeachment.

[2] He shall have Power, by and with the Advice and Consent of the Senate to make Treaties, provided two thirds of the Senators present concur; and he shall nominate, and by and with the Advice and Consent of the Senate, shall appoint Ambassadors, other public Ministers and Consuls, Judges of the supreme Court, and all other Officers of the United States, whose Appointments are not herein otherwise provided for, and which shall be established by Law; but the Congress may by Law vest the Appointment of such inferior Officers, as they think proper, in the President alone, in the Courts of Law, or in the Heads of Departments.

[3] The President shall have Power to fill up all Vacancies that may happen during the Recess of the Senate, by granting Commissions which shall expire at the End of their next Session.

Section 3. He shall from time to time give to the Congress Information of the State of the Union, and recommend to their Consideration such Measures as he shall judge necessary and expedient; he may, on extraordinary Occasions, convene both Houses, or either of them, and in Case of Disagreement between them, with Respect to the Time of Adjournment, he may adjourn them to such Time as he shall think proper; he shall receive Ambassadors and other public Ministers; he shall take Care that the Laws be faithfully executed, and shall Commission all the Officers of the United States.

Section 4. The President, Vice President and all civil Officers of the United States, shall be removed from Office on Impeachment for, and Conviction of, Treason, Bribery, or other high Crimes and Misdemeanors.

Article III

Section 1. The judicial Power of the United States, shall be vested in one supreme Court, and in such inferior Courts as the Congress may from time to time ordain and establish. The Judges, both of the supreme and inferior Courts, shall hold their Offices during good Behaviour, and shall, at stated Times, receive for their Services a Compensation, which shall not be diminished during their Continuance in Office.

Section 2. [1] The judicial Power shall extend to all Cases, in Law and Equity, arising under this Constitution, the Laws of the United

States, and Treaties made, or which shall be made, under their Authority;—to all Cases affecting Ambassadors, other public Ministers and Consuls;—to all Cases of admiralty and maritime Jurisdiction;—to Controversies to which the United States shall be a Party;—to Controversies between two or more States;—between a State and Citizens of another State;—between Citizens of different States;—between Citizens of the same State claiming Lands under the Grants of different States, and between a State, or the Citizens thereof, and foreign States, Citizens or Subjects.

[2] In all Cases affecting Ambassadors, other public Ministers and Consuls, and those in which a State shall be a Party, the supreme Court shall have original Jurisdiction. In all the other Cases before mentioned, the supreme Court shall have appellate Jurisdiction, both as to Law and Fact, with such Exceptions, and under such Regulations as the Congress shall make.

[3] The trial of all Crimes, except in Cases of Impeachment, shall be by Jury; and such Trial shall be held in the State where the said Crimes shall have been committed; but when not committed within any State, the Trial shall be at such Place or Places as the Congress may by Law have directed.

Section 3. [1] Treason against the United States, shall consist only in levying War against them, or, in adhering to their Enemies, giving them Aid and Comfort. No Person shall be convicted of Treason unless on the Testimony of two Witnesses to the same overt Act, or on Confession in open Court.

[2] The Congress shall have Power to declare the Punishment of Treason, but no Attainder of Treason shall work Corruption of Blood, or Forfeiture except during the Life of the Person attainted.

Article IV

Section 1. Full Faith and Credit shall be given in each State to the public Acts, Records, and judicial Proceedings of every other State. And the Congress may by general Laws prescribe the Manner in which such Acts, Records and Proceedings shall be proved, and the Effect thereof.

Section 2. [1] The Citizens of each State shall be entitled to all Privileges and Immunities of Citizens in the several States.

[2] A Person charged in any State with Treason, Felony, or other Crime, who shall flee from Justice, and be found in another State, shall on demand of the executive Authority of the State from which he fled, be delivered up, to be removed to the State having Jurisdiction of the Crime.

[3] No Person held to Service or Labour in one State, under the Laws thereof, escaping into another, shall, in Consequence of any Law

or Regulation therein, be discharged from such Service or Labour, but shall be delivered up on Claim of the Party to whom such Service or Labour may be due.

Section 3. [1] New States may be admitted by the Congress into this Union; but no new State shall be formed or erected within the Jurisdiction of any other State; nor any State be formed by the Junction of two or more States, or Parts of States, without the Consent of the Legislatures of the States concerned as well as of the Congress.

[2] The Congress shall have Power to dispose of and make all needful Rules and Regulations respecting the Territory or other Property belonging to the United States; and nothing in this Constitution shall be so construed as to Prejudice any Claims of the United States, or of any particular State.

Section 4. The United States shall guarantee to every State in this Union a Republican Form of Government, and shall protect each of them against Invasion; and on Application of the Legislature, or of the Executive (when the Legislature cannot be convened) against domestic Violence.

Article V

The Congress, whenever two thirds of both Houses shall deem it necessary, shall propose Amendments to this Constitution, or, on the Application of the Legislatures of two thirds of the several States, shall call a Convention for proposing Amendments, which, in either Case, shall be valid to all Intents and Purposes, as part of this Constitution, when ratified by the Legislatures of three fourths of the several States, or by Conventions in three fourths thereof, as the one or the other Mode of Ratification may be proposed by the Congress; Provided that no Amendment which may be made prior to the Year One thousand eight hundred and eight shall in any Manner affect the first and fourth Clauses in the Ninth Section of the first Article; and that no State, without its Consent, shall be deprived of its equal Suffrage in the Senate.

Article VI

[1] All Debts contracted and Engagements entered into, before the Adoption of this Constitution shall be as valid against the United States under this Constitution, as under the Confederation.

[2] This Constitution, and the Laws of the United States which shall be made in Pursuance thereof; and all Treaties made, or which shall be made, under the Authority of the United States, shall be the supreme Law of the Land; and the Judges in every State shall be bound thereby, any Thing in the Constitution or Laws of any State to the Contrary notwithstanding.

[3] The Senators and Representatives before mentioned, and the Members of the several State Legislatures, and all executive and judicial Officers, both of the United States and of the several States, shall be bound by Oath or Affirmation, to support this Constitution; but no religious Test shall ever be required as a Qualification to any Office or public Trust under the United States.

Article VII

The Ratification of the Conventions of nine States shall be sufficient for the Establishment of this Constitution between the States so ratifying the Same.

DONE in Convention by the Unanimous Consent of the States present the Seventeenth Day of September in the Year of Our Lord one thousand seven hundred and Eighty seven and of the Independence of the United States of America the Twelfth. IN WITNESS whereof We have hereunto subscribed our Names,

Go. WASHINGTON—*Presidt.*
and deputy from Virginia

New Hampshire

JOHN LANGDON	NICHOLAS GILMAN

Massachusetts

NATHANIEL GORHAM	RUFUS KING

Connecticut

WM. SAML. JOHNSON	ROGER SHERMAN

New York

ALEXANDER HAMILTON

New Jersey

WIL: LIVINGSTON	WM. PATERSON
DAVID BREARLEY	JONA: DAYTON

Pennsylvania

B. FRANKLIN	THOS. FITZSIMONS
THOMAS MIFFLIN	JARED INGERSOLL
ROBT. MORRIS	JAMES WILSON
GEO. CLYMER	GOUV MORRIS

Delaware

GEO: READ	RICHARD BASSETT
GUNNING BEDFORD JUN	JACO: BROOM
JOHN DICKINSON	

Maryland

JAMES MCHENRY	DANL. CARROLL
DAN OF ST. THOS. JENIFER	

Virginia

JOHN BLAIR	JAMES MADISON, JR.

North Carolina

WM. BLOUNT	HU WILLIAMSON
RICHD. DOBBS SPAIGHT	

South Carolina

J. RUTLEDGE

CHARLES COTESWORTH PINCKNEY

CHARLES PINCKNEY

PIERCE BUTLER

Georgia

WILLIAM FEW

ABR BALDWIN

Attest

WILLIAM JACKSON
Secretary

ARTICLES IN ADDITION TO, AND AMENDMENT OF, THE CONSTITUTION OF THE UNITED STATES OF AMERICA, PROPOSED BY CONGRESS, AND RATIFIED BY THE LEGISLATURES OF THE SEVERAL STATES PURSUANT TO THE FIFTH ARTICLE OF THE ORIGINAL CONSTITUTION.[1]

Amendment [I] [1791] [2]

Congress shall make no law respecting an establishment of religion, or prohibiting the free exercise thereof; or abridging the freedom of speech, or of the press; or the right of the people peaceably to assemble, and to petition the Government for a redress of grievances.

Amendment [II] [1791]

A well regulated Militia, being necessary to the security of a free State, the right of the people to keep and bear Arms, shall not be infringed.

Amendment [III] [1791]

No Soldier shall, in time of peace be quartered in any house, without the consent of the Owner, nor in time of war, but in a manner to be prescribed by law.

Amendment [IV] [1791]

The right of the people to be secure in their persons, houses, papers, and effects, against unreasonable searches and seizures, shall

1. All of the Amendments except the 13th, 14th, 15th, and 16th, were not specifically assigned a number in the resolution proposing the Amendment. Brackets enclose the number for such Amendments. The 13th, 14th, 15th, and 16th Amendments were ratified by number and thus no brackets enclose such Amendment numbers.

2. The first ten amendments to the Constitution of the United States were proposed to the legislatures of the several States by the First Congress, on the 25th of September 1789. They were ratified by the following States, and the notifications of ratification by the governors thereof were successively communicated by the President to Congress: New Jersey, November 20, 1789; Maryland, December 19, 1789; North Carolina, December 22, 1789; South Carolina, January 19, 1790; New Hampshire, January 25, 1790; Delaware, January 28, 1790; Pennsylvania, March 10, 1790; New York, March 27, 1790; Rhode Island, June 15, 1790; Vermont, November 3, 1791, and Virginia, December 15, 1791. The legislatures of Connecticut, Georgia, and Massachusetts ratified them on April 19, 1939, March 24, 1939, and March 2, 1939, respectively.

Note: other amendments have also been ratified by states after the amendment has been announced as ratified; these other, after-the-fact ratifications are not usually noted in this appendix.

not be violated, and no Warrants shall issue, but upon probable cause, supported by Oath or affirmation, and particularly describing the place to be searched, and the persons or things to be seized.

Amendment [V] [1791]

No person shall be held to answer for a capital, or otherwise infamous crime, unless on a presentment or indictment of a Grand Jury, except in cases arising in the land or naval forces, or in the Militia, when in actual service in time of War or public danger; nor shall any person be subject for the same offence to be twice put in jeopardy of life or limb; nor shall be compelled in any criminal case to be a witness against himself, nor be deprived of life, liberty, or property, without due process of law; nor shall private property be taken for public use, without just compensation.

Amendment [VI] [1791]

In all criminal prosecutions, the accused shall enjoy the right to a speedy and public trial, by an impartial jury of the State and district wherein the crime shall have been committed, which district shall have been previously ascertained by law, and to be informed of the nature and cause of the accusation; to be confronted with the witnesses against him; to have compulsory process for obtaining witnesses in his favor, and to have the Assistance of Counsel for his defence.

Amendment [VII] [1791]

In Suits at common law, where the value in controversy shall exceed twenty dollars, the right of trial by jury shall be preserved, and no fact tried by jury, shall be otherwise re-examined in any Court of the United States, than according to the rules of the common law.

Amendment [VIII] [1791]

Excessive bail shall not be required, nor excessive fines imposed, nor cruel and unusual punishments inflicted.

Amendment [IX] [1791]

The enumeration in the Constitution, of certain rights, shall not be construed to deny or disparage others retained by the people.

Amendment [X] [1791]

The powers not delegated to the United States by the Constitution, nor prohibited by it to the States, are reserved to the States respectively, or to the people.

Amendment [XI] [1798]

The Judicial power of the United States shall not be construed to extend to any suit in law or equity, commenced or prosecuted against one of the United States by Citizens of another State, or by Citizens or Subjects of any Foreign State.

Historical Note

This amendment was proposed to the legislatures of the several States by the Third Congress, on the 5th September, 1794, and was declared in a message from the President to Congress, dated the 8th of January, 1798, to have been ratified by the legislatures of three-fourths of the States.

Amendment [XII] [1804]

The Electors shall meet in their respective states and vote by ballot for President and Vice–President, one of whom, at least, shall not be an inhabitant of the same state with themselves; they shall name in their ballots the person voted for as President, and in distinct ballots the person voted for as Vice–President, and they shall make distinct lists of all persons voted for as President, and of all persons voted for as Vice–President, and of the number of votes for each, which lists they shall sign and certify, and transmit sealed to the seat of the government of the United States, directed to the President of the Senate;—The President of the Senate shall, in the presence of the Senate and House of Representatives, open all the certificates and the votes shall then be counted;—The person having the greatest number of votes for President, shall be the President, if such number be a majority of the whole number of Electors appointed; and if no person have such majority, then from the persons having the highest numbers not exceeding three on the list of those voted for as President, the House of Representatives shall choose immediately, by ballot, the President. But in choosing the President, the votes shall be taken by states, the representation from each state having one vote; a quorum for this purpose shall consist of a member or members from two-thirds of the states, and a majority of all the states shall be necessary to a choice. And if the House of Representatives shall not choose a President whenever the right of choice shall devolve upon them before the fourth day of March next following, then the Vice–President shall act as President, as in the case of the death or other constitutional disability of the President.—The person having the greatest number of votes as Vice–President, shall be the Vice–President, if such number be a majority of the whole number of Electors appointed, and if no person have a majority, then from the two highest numbers on the list, the Senate shall choose the Vice–President; a quorum for the purpose shall consist of two-thirds of the whole number of Senators, and a majority of the whole number shall be necessary to a choice. But no person constitutionally ineligible to the office of President shall be eligible to that of Vice–President of the United States.

Historical Note

This amendment was proposed to the legislatures of the several States by the Eighth Congress, on the 12th of December, 1803, in lieu of the original third paragraph of the first section of the second article, and was declared in a proclamation of the Secretary of State, dated the 25th of September, 1804, to have been ratified by the legislatures of three-fourths of the States.

Amendment XIII [1865] *

Section 1. Neither slavery nor involuntary servitude, except as a punishment for crime whereof the party shall have been duly convicted, shall exist within the United States, or any place subject to their jurisdiction.

Section 2. Congress shall have power to enforce this article by appropriate legislation.

Historical Note

This amendment was proposed to the legislatures of the several States by the Thirty-eighth Congress, on the 1st of February, 1865, and was declared, in a proclamation of the Secretary of State, dated the 18th of December, 1865, to have been ratified by the legislatures of twenty-seven of the thirty-six States, viz: Illinois, Rhode Island, Michigan, Maryland, New York, West Virginia, Maine, Kansas, Massachusetts, Pennsylvania, Virginia, Ohio, Missouri, Nevada, Indiana, Louisiana, Minnesota, Wisconsin, Vermont, Tennessee, Arkansas, Connecticut, New Hampshire, South Carolina, Alabama, North Carolina, and Georgia.

Amendment XIV [1868] *

Section 1. All persons born or naturalized in the United States, and subject to the jurisdiction thereof, are citizens of the United States and of the State wherein they reside. No State shall make or enforce any law which shall abridge the privileges or immunities of citizens of the United States; nor shall any State deprive any person of life, liberty, or property, without due process of law; nor deny to any person within its jurisdiction the equal protection of the laws.

Section 2. Representatives shall be apportioned among the several States according to their respective numbers, counting the whole number of persons in each State, excluding Indians not taxed. But when the right to vote at any election for the choice of electors for President and Vice President of the United States, Representatives in Congress, the Executive and Judicial officers of a State, or the members of the Legislature thereof, is denied to any of the male inhabitants of such State, being twenty-one years of age, and citizens of the United States, or in any way abridged, except for participation in rebellion, or other crime, the basis of representation therein shall be reduced in the proportion which the number of such male citizens shall bear to the whole number of male citizens twenty-one years of age in such State.

Section 3. No person shall be a Senator or Representative in Congress, or elector of President and Vice President, or hold any office, civil or military, under the United States, or under any State, who having previously taken an oath, as a member of Congress, or as an officer of the United States, or as a member of any State legislature, or as an executive or judicial officer of any State, to support the Constitu-

* See note 1, supra.

tion of the United States, shall have engaged in insurrection or rebellion against the same, or given aid or comfort to the enemies thereof. But Congress may by a vote of two-thirds of each House, remove such disability.

Section 4. The validity of the public debt of the United States, authorized by law, including debts incurred for payment of pensions and bounties for services in suppressing insurrection or rebellion, shall not be questioned. But neither the United States nor any State shall assume or pay any debt or obligation incurred in aid of insurrection or rebellion against the United States, or any claim for the loss or emancipation of any slave; but all such debts, obligations and claims shall be held illegal and void.

Section 5. The Congress shall have power to enforce, by appropriate legislation, the provisions of this article.

Historical Note

This amendment was proposed to the legislatures of the several States by the Thirty-ninth Congress, on the 16th of June, 1866. On the 21st of July, 1868, Congress adopted and transmitted to the Department of State a concurrent resolution, declaring that "the legislatures of the States of Connecticut, Tennessee, New Jersey, Oregon, Vermont, New York, Ohio, Illinois, West Virginia, Kansas, Maine, Nevada, Missouri, Indiana, Minnesota, New Hampshire, Massachusetts, Nebraska, Iowa, Arkansas, Florida, North Carolina, Alabama, South Carolina, and Louisiana, being three-fourths and more of the several States of the Union, have ratified the fourteenth article of amendment to the Constitution of the United States, duly proposed by two-thirds of each House of the Thirty-ninth Congress: Therefore, Resolved, That said fourteenth article is hereby declared to be a part of the Constitution of the United States, and it shall be duly promulgated as such by the Secretary of State." The Secretary of State accordingly issued a proclamation, dated the 28th of July, 1868, declaring that the proposed fourteenth amendment had been ratified, in the manner hereafter mentioned by the legislatures of thirty of the thirty-six States, viz: Connecticut, June 30, 1866; New Hampshire, July 7, 1866; Tennessee, July 19, 1866; New Jersey, September 11, 1866, (and the legislature of the same State passed a resolution in April, 1868, to withdraw its consent to it); Oregon, September 19, 1866; Vermont, November 9, 1866; Georgia rejected it November 13, 1866, and ratified it July 21, 1868; North Carolina rejected it December 4, 1866, and ratified it July 4, 1868; South Carolina rejected it December 20, 1866, and ratified it July 9, 1868; New York ratified it January 10, 1867; Ohio ratified it January 11, 1867, (and the legislature of the same State passed a resolution in January, 1868, to withdraw its consent to it); Illinois ratified it January 15, 1867; West Virginia, January 16, 1867; Kansas, January 18, 1867; Maine, January 19, 1867; Nevada, January 22, 1867; Missouri, January 26, 1867; Indiana, January 29, 1867; Minnesota, February 1, 1867; Rhode Island, February 7, 1867; Wisconsin, February 13, 1867; Pennsylvania, February 13, 1867; Michigan, February 15, 1867; Massachusetts, March 20, 1867; Nebraska, June 15, 1867; Iowa, April 3, 1868; Arkansas, April 6, 1868; Florida, June 9, 1868; Louisiana, July 9, 1868; and Alabama, July 13, 1868. Georgia again ratified the amendment February 2, 1870. Texas rejected it November 1, 1866, and ratified it February 18, 1870. Virginia rejected it January 19, 1867, and ratified October 8, 1869. The amendment was rejected by Kentucky January 10, 1867; by Delaware February 8, 1867; by Maryland March 23, 1867.

Amendment XV [1870] *

Section 1. The right of citizens of the United States to vote shall not be denied or abridged by the United States or by any State on account of race, color, or previous condition of servitude.

Section 2. The Congress shall have power to enforce this article by appropriate legislation.

Historical Note

This amendment was proposed to the legislatures of the several States by the Fortieth Congress, on the 27th of February, 1869, and was declared, in a proclamation of the Secretary of State, dated March 30, 1870, to have been ratified by the legislatures of twenty-nine of the thirty-seven States. The dates of these ratifications (arranged in the order of their reception at the Department of State) were: from North Carolina, March 5, 1869; West Virginia, March 3, 1869; Massachusetts, March 9–12, 1869; Wisconsin, March 9, 1869; Maine, March 12, 1869; Louisiana, March 5, 1869; Michigan, March 8, 1869; South Carolina, March 16, 1869; Pennsylvania, March 26, 1869; Arkansas, March 30, 1869; Connecticut, May 19, 1869; Florida, June 15, 1869; Illinois, March 5, 1869; Indiana, May 13–14, 1869; New York, March 17–April 14, 1869, (and the legislature of the same State passed a resolution January 5, 1870, to withdraw its consent to it); New Hampshire, July 7, 1869; Nevada, March 1, 1869; Vermont, October 21, 1869; Virginia, October 8, 1869; Missouri, January 10, 1870; Mississippi, January 15–17, 1870; Ohio, January 27, 1870; Iowa, February 3, 1870; Kansas, January 18–19, 1870; Minnesota, February 19, 1870; Rhode Island, January 18, 1870; Nebraska, February 17, 1870; Texas, February 18, 1870. The State of Georgia also ratified the amendment February 2, 1870.

Amendment XVI [1913] *

The Congress shall have power to lay and collect taxes on incomes, from whatever source derived, without apportionment among the several States, and without regard to any census or enumeration.

Historical Note

This Amendment was proposed to the legislatures of the several states by the Sixty–First Congress, on the 31st of July, 1909, and was declared, in a proclamation by the Secretary of State, dated the 25th of February, 1913, to have been ratified by the legislatures of the states of Alabama, Kentucky, South Carolina, Illinois, Mississippi, Oklahoma, Maryland, Georgia, Texas, Ohio, Idaho, Oregon, Washington, California, Montana, Indiana, Nevada, North Carolina, Nebraska, Kansas, Colorado, North Dakota, Michigan, Iowa, Missouri, Maine, Tennessee, Arkansas, Wisconsin, New York, South Dakota, Arizona, Minnesota, Louisiana, Delaware, and Wyoming, in all, thirty-six. The legislatures of New Jersey and New Mexico also passed resolutions ratifying the said proposed amendment.

Amendment [XVII] [1913] *

[1] The Senate of the United States shall be composed of two Senators from each State, elected by the people thereof, for six years; and each Senator shall have one vote. The electors in each State shall have the qualifications requisite for electors of the most numerous branch of the State legislatures.

* See note 1, supra.

[2] When vacancies happen in the representation of any State in the Senate, the executive authority of such State shall issue writs of election to fill such vacancies: *Provided,* that the legislature of any State may empower the executive thereof to make temporary appointments until the people fill the vacancies by election as the legislature may direct.

[3] This amendment shall not be so construed as to affect the election or term of any Senator chosen before it becomes valid as part of the Constitution.

Historical Note

This amendment was proposed to the legislatures of the several states by the Sixty–Second Congress, on the 16th of May, 1912, in lieu of the original first paragraph of section 3 of article I, and in lieu of so much of paragraph 2 of the same section as related to the filling of vacancies, and was declared, in a proclamation by the Secretary of State, dated the 31st of May, 1913, to have been ratified by the legislatures of the states of Massachusetts, Arizona, Minnesota, New York, Kansas, Oregon, North Carolina, California, Michigan, Idaho, West Virginia, Nebraska, Iowa, Montana, Texas, Washington, Wyoming, Colorado, Illinois, North Dakota, Nevada, Vermont, Maine, New Hampshire, Oklahoma, Ohio, South Dakota, Indiana, Missouri, New Mexico, New Jersey, Tennessee, Arkansas, Connecticut, Pennsylvania, and Wisconsin, said states constituting three-fourths of the whole number of states.

Amendment [XVIII] [1919]

Section 1. After one year from the ratification of this article the manufacture, sale, or transportation of intoxicating liquors within, the importation thereof into, or the exportation thereof from the United States and all territory subject to the jurisdiction thereof for beverage purposes is hereby prohibited.

Section 2. The Congress and the several States shall have concurrent power to enforce this article by appropriate legislation.

Section 3. This article shall be inoperative unless it shall have been ratified as an amendment to the Constitution by the legislatures of the several States, as provided in the Constitution, within seven years from the date of the submission hereof to the States by the Congress.

Historical Note

This amendment was proposed to the legislatures of the several states by the Sixty–Fifth Congress, on the 19th day of December, 1917, and was declared, in a proclamation by the Acting Secretary of State, dated on the 29th day of January, 1919, to have been ratified by the legislatures of the states of Alabama, Arizona, California, Colorado, Delaware, Florida, Georgia, Idaho, Illinois, Indiana, Kansas, Kentucky, Louisiana, Maine, Maryland, Massachusetts, Michigan, Minnesota, Mississippi, Montana, Nebraska, New Hampshire, North Carolina, North Dakota, Ohio, Oklahoma, Oregon, South Dakota, South Carolina, Texas, Utah, Virginia, Washington, West Virginia, Wisconsin, and Wyoming.

Amendment [XIX] [1920]

[1] The right of citizens of the United States to vote shall not be denied or abridged by the United States or by any State on account of sex.

[2] Congress shall have power to enforce this article by appropriate legislation.

Historical Note

This amendment was proposed to the legislatures of the several states by the Sixty–Sixth Congress, on the 5th day of June, 1919, and was declared, in a proclamation by the Secretary of State, dated on the 26th day of August, 1920, to have been ratified by the legislatures of the states of Arizona, Arkansas, California, Colorado, Idaho, Illinois, Indiana, Iowa, Kansas, Kentucky, Maine, Massachusetts, Michigan, Minnesota, Missouri, Montana, Nebraska, Nevada, New Hampshire, New Jersey, New Mexico, North Dakota, New York, Ohio, Oklahoma, Oregon, Pennsylvania, Rhode Island, South Dakota, Tennessee, Texas, Utah, Washington, West Virginia, Wisconsin and Wyoming.

Amendment [XX] [1933]

Section 1. The terms of the President and Vice President shall end at noon on the 20th day of January, and the terms of Senators and Representatives at noon on the 3d day of January, of the years in which such terms would have ended if this article had not been ratified; and the terms of their successors shall then begin.

Section 2. The Congress shall assemble at least once in every year, and such meeting shall begin at noon on the 3d day of January, unless they shall by law appoint a different day.

Section 3. If, at the time fixed for the beginning of the term of the President, the President elect shall have died, the Vice President elect shall become President. If the President shall not have been chosen before the time fixed for the beginning of his term, or if the President elect shall have failed to qualify, then the Vice President elect shall act as President until a President shall have qualified; and the Congress may by law provide for the case wherein neither a President elect nor a Vice President elect shall have qualified, declaring who shall then act as President, or the manner in which one who is to act shall be selected, and such person shall act accordingly until a President or Vice President shall have qualified.

Section 4. The Congress may by law provide for the case of the death of any of the persons from whom the House of Representatives may choose a President whenever the right of choice shall have devolved upon them, and for the case of the death of any of the persons from whom the Senate may choose a Vice President whenever the right of choice shall have devolved upon them.

Section 5. Sections 1 and 2 shall take effect on the 15th day of October following the ratification of this article.

Section 6. This article shall be inoperative unless it shall have been ratified as an amendment to the Constitution by the legislatures of three-fourths of the several States within seven years from the date of its submission.

Historical Note

This amendment was proposed to the legislatures of the several states by the Seventy–Second Congress, on March 3, 1932, and was declared, in a proclamation by the Secretary of State, dated Feb. 6, 1933, to have been ratified by the legislatures of the states of Alabama, Arizona, Arkansas, California, Colorado, Connecticut, Delaware, Georgia, Idaho, Illinois, Indiana, Kansas, Kentucky, Louisiana, Maine, Massachusetts, Michigan, Minnesota, Mississippi, Missouri, Montana, Nebraska, New Jersey, New York, North Carolina, North Dakota, Ohio, Oklahoma, Pennsylvania, Rhode Island, South Carolina, South Dakota, Texas, Utah, Virginia, Washington, West Virginia, Wisconsin, and Wyoming.

Amendment [XXI] [1933]

Section 1. The eighteenth article of amendment to the Constitution of the United States is hereby repealed.

Section 2. The transportation or importation into any State, Territory, or possession of the United States for delivery or use therein of intoxicating liquors, in violation of the laws thereof, is hereby prohibited.

Section 3. This article shall be inoperative unless it shall have been ratified as an amendment to the Constitution by conventions in the several States, as provided in the Constitution, within seven years from the date of the submission hereof to the States by the Congress.

Historical Note

This amendment was proposed to the several states by the Seventy–Second Congress, on Feb. 20, 1933, and was declared, in a proclamation by the Secretary of State, dated Dec. 5, 1933, to have been ratified by conventions in the States of Arizona, Alabama, Arkansas, California, Colorado, Connecticut, Delaware, Florida, Idaho, Illinois, Indiana, Iowa, Kentucky, Maryland, Massachusetts, Michigan, Minnesota, Missouri, Nevada, New Hampshire, New Jersey, New Mexico, New York, Ohio, Oregon, Pennsylvania, Rhode Island, Tennessee, Texas, Utah, Vermont, Virginia, Washington, West Virginia, Wisconsin and Wyoming.

Amendment [XXII] [1951]

Section 1. No person shall be elected to the office of the President more than twice, and no person who has held the office of President, or acted as President, for more than two years of a term to which some other person was elected President shall be elected to the office of President more than once. But this Article shall not apply to any person holding the office of President when this Article was proposed by the Congress, and shall not prevent any person who may be holding the office of President, or acting as President, during the term within which this Article becomes operative from holding the office of President or acting as President during the remainder of such term.

Section 2. This article shall be inoperative unless it shall have been ratified as an amendment to the Constitution by the legislatures of three-fourths of the several States within seven years from the date of its submission to the States by the Congress.

Historical Note

Proposal and Ratification. This amendment was proposed to the legislatures of the several States by the Eightieth Congress on Mar. 24, 1947 by House Joint Res. No. 27, and was declared by the Administrator of General Services on Mar. 1, 1951, to have been ratified. The legislatures ratified this Amendment on the following dates: Maine, Mar. 31, 1947; Michigan, Mar. 31, 1947; Iowa, Apr. 1, 1947; Kansas, Apr. 1, 1947; New Hampshire, Apr. 1, 1947; Delaware, Apr. 2,

1947; Illinois, Apr. 3, 1947; Oregon, Apr. 3, 1947; Colorado, Apr. 12, 1947; California, Apr. 15, 1947; New Jersey, Apr. 15, 1947; Vermont, Apr. 15, 1947; Ohio, Apr. 16, 1947; Wisconsin, Apr. 16, 1947; Pennsylvania, Apr. 29, 1947; Connecticut, May 21, 1947; Missouri, May 22, 1947; Nebraska, May 23, 1947; Virginia, Jan. 28, 1948; Mississippi, Feb. 12, 1948; New York, Mar. 9, 1948; South Dakota, Jan. 21, 1949; North Dakota, Feb. 25, 1949; Louisiana, May 17, 1950; Montana, Jan. 25, 1951; Indiana, Jan. 29, 1951; Idaho, Jan. 30, 1951; New Mexico, Feb. 12, 1951; Wyoming, Feb. 12, 1951; Arkansas, Feb. 15, 1951; Georgia, Feb. 17, 1951; Tennessee, Feb. 20, 1951; Texas, Feb. 22, 1951; Utah, Feb. 26, 1951; Nevada, Feb. 26, 1951; Minnesota, Feb. 27, 1951, and North Carolina, Feb. 28, 1951.

Subsequent to the proclamation, Amendment XXII was ratified by South Carolina on Mar. 13, 1951; Maryland, Mar. 14, 1951; Florida, Apr. 16, 1951, and Alabama, May 4, 1951.

Certification of Validity. Publication of the certifying statement of the Administrator of General Services that the Amendment had become valid was made on Mar. 1, 1951, F.R.Doc. 51–2940, 16 F.R. 2019.

Amendment [XXIII] [1961]

Section 1. The District constituting the seat of Government of the United States shall appoint in such manner as the Congress may direct:

A number of electors of President and Vice President equal to the whole number of Senators and Representatives in Congress to which the District would be entitled if it were a State, but in no event more than the least populous state; they shall be in addition to those appointed by the states, but they shall be considered, for the purposes of the election of President and Vice President, to be electors appointed by a state; and they shall meet in the District and perform such duties as provided by the twelfth article of amendment.

Section 2. The Congress shall have power to enforce this article by appropriate legislation.

Historical Note

Proposal and Ratification. This amendment was proposed by the Eighty-sixth Congress on June 16, 1960 and was declared by the Administrator of General Services on Apr. 3, 1961, to have been ratified.

The amendment was ratified by the following States: Hawaii, June 23, 1960; Massachusetts, Aug. 22, 1960; New Jersey, Dec. 19, 1960; New York, Jan. 17, 1961; California, Jan. 19, 1961; Oregon, Jan. 27, 1961; Maryland, Jan. 30, 1961; Idaho, Jan. 31, 1961; Maine, Jan. 31, 1961; Minnesota, Jan. 31, 1961; New Mexico, Feb. 1, 1961; Nevada, Feb. 2, 1961; Montana, Feb. 6, 1961; Colorado, Feb. 8, 1961; Washington, Feb. 9, 1961; West Virginia, Feb. 9, 1961; Alaska, Feb. 10, 1961; Wyoming, Feb. 13, 1961; South Dakota, Feb. 14, 1961; Delaware, Feb. 20, 1961; Utah, Feb. 21, 1961; Wisconsin, Feb. 21, 1961; Pennsylvania, Feb. 28, 1961; Indiana, Mar. 3, 1961; North Dakota, Mar. 3, 1961; Tennessee, Mar. 6, 1961; Michigan, Mar. 8, 1961; Connecticut, Mar. 9, 1961; Arizona, Mar. 10, 1961; Illinois, Mar. 14, 1961; Nebraska, Mar. 15, 1961; Vermont, Mar. 15, 1961; Iowa, Mar. 16, 1961; Missouri, Mar. 20, 1961; Oklahoma, Mar. 21, 1961; Rhode Island, Mar. 22, 1961; Kansas, Mar. 29, 1961; Ohio, Mar. 29, 1961, and New Hampshire, Mar. 30, 1961.

Certification of Validity. Publication of the certifying statement of the Administrator of General Services that the amendment had become valid was made on Apr. 3, 1961, F.R.Doc. 61–3017, 26 F.R. 2808.

Amendment [XXIV] [1964]

Section 1. The right of citizens of the United States to vote in any primary or other election for President or Vice President, for electors for President or Vice President, or for Senator or Representative in Congress, shall not be denied or abridged by the United States or any State by reason of failure to pay any poll tax or other tax.

Section 2. The Congress shall have power to enforce this article by appropriate legislation.

Historical Note

Proposal and Ratification. This amendment was proposed by the Eighty-seventh Congress by Senate Joint Resolution No. 29, which was approved by the Senate on Mar. 27, 1962, and by the House of Representatives on Aug. 27, 1962. It was declared by the Administrator of General Services on Feb. 4, 1964, to have been ratified.

This amendment was ratified by the following States: Illinois, Nov. 14, 1962; New Jersey, Dec. 3, 1962; Oregon, Jan. 25, 1963; Montana, Jan. 28, 1963; West Virginia, Feb. 1, 1963; New York, Feb. 4, 1963; Maryland, Feb. 6, 1963; California, Feb. 7, 1963; Alaska, Feb. 11, 1963; Rhode Island, Feb. 14, 1963; Indiana, Feb. 19, 1963; Utah, Feb. 20, 1963; Michigan, Feb. 20, 1963; Colorado, Feb. 21, 1963; Ohio, Feb. 27, 1963; Minnesota, Feb. 27, 1963; New Mexico, Mar. 5, 1963; Hawaii, Mar. 6, 1963; North Dakota, Mar. 7, 1963; Idaho, Mar. 8, 1963; Washington, Mar. 14, 1963; Vermont, Mar. 15, 1963; Nevada, Mar. 19, 1963; Connecticut, Mar. 20, 1963; Tennessee, Mar. 21, 1963; Pennsylvania, Mar. 25, 1963; Wisconsin, Mar. 26, 1963; Kansas, Mar. 28, 1963; Massachusetts, Mar. 28, 1963; Nebraska, Apr. 4, 1963; Florida, Apr. 18, 1963; Iowa, Apr. 24, 1963; Delaware, May 1, 1963; Missouri, May 13, 1963; New Hampshire, June 12, 1963; Kentucky, June 27, 1963; Maine, Jan. 16, 1964; South Dakota, Jan. 23, 1964.

Certification of Validity. Publication of the certifying statement of the Administrator of General Services that the amendment had become valid was made on Feb. 5, 1964, F.R.Doc. 64–1229, 29 F.R. 1715. President Johnson and the Administrator signed this certificate on Feb. 4, 1964.

Amendment [XXV] [1967]

Section 1. In the case of the removal of the President from office or of his death or resignation, the Vice President shall become President.

Section 2. Whenever there is a vacancy in the office of the Vice President, the President shall nominate a Vice President who shall take office upon confirmation by a majority vote of both Houses of Congress.

Section 3. Whenever the President transmits to the President pro tempore of the Senate and the Speaker of the House of Representatives his written declaration that he is unable to discharge the powers and duties of his office, and until he transmits to them a written declaration to the contrary, such powers and duties shall be discharged by the Vice President as Acting President.

Section 4. Whenever the Vice President and a majority of either the principal officers of the executive departments or of such other body as Congress may by law provide, transmit to the President pro tempore of the Senate and the Speaker of the House of Representatives, their written declaration that the President is unable to discharge the powers and duties of his office, the Vice President shall immediately assume the powers and duties of the office as Acting President.

Thereafter, when the President transmits to the President pro tempore of the Senate and the Speaker of the House of Representatives his written declaration that no inability exists, he shall resume the powers and duties of his office unless the Vice President and a majority of either the principal officers of the executive department or of such other body as Congress may by law provide, transmit within four days to the President pro tempore of the Senate and the Speaker of the House of Representatives their written declaration and the President is unable to discharge the powers and duties of his office. Thereupon Congress shall decide the issue, assembling within forty-eight hours for that purpose if not in session. If the Congress, within twenty-one days after receipt of the latter written declaration, or, if Congress is not in session, within twenty-one days after Congress is required to assemble, determines by two-thirds vote of both Houses that the President is unable to discharge the powers and duties of his office, the Vice President shall continue to discharge the same as Acting President; otherwise, the President shall resume the powers and duties of his office.

Historical Note

Proposal and Ratification. This amendment was proposed by the Eighty-Ninth Congress by Senate Joint Resolution No. 1, which was approved by the Senate on Feb. 19, 1965, and by the House of Representatives, in amended form, on Apr. 13, 1965. The House of Representatives agreed to a Conference Report on June 30, 1965, and the Senate agreed to the Conference Report on July 6, 1965. It was declared by the Administrator of General Services, on Feb. 23, 1967, to have been ratified.

This amendment was ratified by the following States: Nebraska, July 12, 1965; Wisconsin, July 13, 1965; Oklahoma, July 16, 1965; Massachusetts, Aug. 9, 1965; Pennsylvania, Aug. 18, 1965; Kentucky, Sept. 15, 1965; Arizona, Sept. 22, 1965; Michigan, Oct. 5, 1965; Indiana, Oct. 20, 1965; California, Oct. 21, 1965; Arkansas, Nov. 4, 1965; New Jersey, Nov. 29, 1965; Delaware, Dec. 7, 1965; Utah, Jan. 17, 1966; West Virginia, Jan. 20, 1966; Maine, Jan. 24, 1966; Rhode Island, Jan. 28, 1966; Colorado, Feb. 3, 1966; New Mexico, Feb. 3, 1966; Kansas, Feb. 8, 1966; Vermont, Feb. 10, 1966; Alaska, Feb. 18, 1966; Idaho, Mar. 2, 1966; Hawaii, Mar. 3, 1966; Virginia, Mar. 8, 1966; Mississippi, Mar. 10, 1966; New York, Mar. 14, 1966; Maryland, Mar. 23, 1966; Missouri, Mar. 30, 1966; New Hampshire, June 13, 1966; Louisiana, July 5, 1966; Tennessee, Jan. 12, 1967; Wyoming, Jan. 25, 1967; Washington, Jan. 26, 1967; Iowa, Jan. 26, 1967; Oregon, Feb. 2, 1967; Minnesota, Feb. 10, 1967; Nevada, Feb. 10, 1967; Connecticut, Feb. 14, 1967; Montana, Feb. 15, 1967; South Dakota, Mar. 6, 1967; Ohio, Mar. 7, 1967; Alabama, Mar. 14, 1967; North Carolina, Mar. 22, 1967; Illinois, Mar. 22, 1967; Texas, Apr. 25, 1967; Florida, May 25, 1967.

Certification of Validity. Publication of the certifying statement of the Administrator of General Services that the amendment had become valid was made on Feb. 25, 1967, F.R.Doc. 67–2208, 32 F.R. 3287, and signed on July 23, 1967.

Amendment [XXVI] [1971]

Section 1. The right of citizens of the United States, who are eighteen years of age or older, to vote shall not be denied or abridged by the United States or by any State on account of age.

Section 2. The Congress shall have power to enforce this article by appropriate legislation.

Historical Note

Proposal and Ratification. This amendment was proposed by the Ninety-second Congress by Senate Joint Resolution No. 7, which was approved by the Senate on Mar. 10, 1971, and by the House of Representatives on Mar. 23, 1971. It was declared by the Administrator of General Services on July 5, 1971, to have been ratified.

This amendment was ratified by the following States: Connecticut, Mar. 23, 1971; Delaware, Mar. 23, 1971; Minnesota, Mar. 23, 1971; Tennessee, Mar. 23, 1971; Washington, Mar. 23, 1971; Hawaii, Mar. 24, 1971; Massachusetts, Mar. 24, 1971; Idaho, Mar. 30, 1971; Montana, Mar. 31, 1971; Arkansas, Apr. 1, 1971; Iowa, Apr. 1, 1971; Nebraska, Apr. 2, 1971; Kansas, Apr. 7, 1971; Michigan, Apr. 7, 1971; Indiana, Apr. 8, 1971; Maine, Apr. 9, 1971; Vermont, Apr. 16, 1971; California, Apr. 19, 1971; South Carolina, Apr. 28, 1971; West Virginia, Apr. 28, 1971; Pennsylvania, May 3, 1971; New Jersey, May 4, 1971; Texas, May 5, 1971; Maryland, May 6, 1971; New Hampshire, May 13, 1971; Arizona, May 17, 1971; Colorado, May 24, 1971; Louisiana, May 27, 1971; Rhode Island, May 27, 1971; New York, June 2, 1971; Oregon, June 5, 1971; Missouri, June 14, 1971; Wisconsin, June 18, 1971; Illinois, June 29, 1971; Alabama, June 30, 1971; Ohio, June 30, 1971; North Carolina, July 1, 1971; Oklahoma, July 1, 1971.

Certification of Validity. Publication of the certifying statement of the Administrator of General Services that the amendment had become valid was made on July 7, 1971, F.R.Doc. 71–9691, 36 F.R. 12725, and signed on July 5, 1971.

Amendment [XXVII] [1992]

No law varying the compensation for the services of the Senators and Representatives shall take effect, until an election of Representatives shall have intervened.

Historical Note

Proposal and Ratification. This amendment was one of twelve that the first Congress proposed on September 25, 1789. Ten of these twelve became the first ten amendments, often called the Bill of Rights. A sufficient number of states did not ratify until 203 years later.

This amendment was ratified by the following States: Maryland, Dec. 19, 1789; North Carolina, Dec. 22, 1789; South Carolina, Jan. 19, 1790; Delaware, Jan. 28, 1790; Vermont, Nov. 3, 1791; Virginia, Dec. 15, 1791; Ohio, May 6, 1873; Wyoming, Mar. 3, 1978; Maine, Apr. 2, 1983; Colorado, Apr. 18, 1984; South Dakota, Feb. 21, 1985; New Hampshire, Mar. 7, 1985; Arizona, Apr. 3, 1985; Tennessee, May 23, 1985; Oklahoma, July 10, 1985; New Mexico, Feb. 14, 1986; Indiana, Feb. 24, 1986; Utah, Feb. 26, 1986; Arkansas, Mar. 5, 1987; Montana, Mar. 17, 1987; Connecticut, May 13, 1987; Wisconsin, June 30, 1987; Georgia, Feb. 2, 1988; West Virginia, Mar. 10, 1988; Louisiana, July 6,

1988; Iowa, Feb. 7, 1989; Idaho, Mar. 23, 1989; Nevada, Apr. 26, 1989; Alaska, May 5, 1989; Oregon, May 19, 1989; Minnesota, May 22, 1989; Texas, May 25, 1989; Kansas, Apr. 4, 1990; Florida, May 31, 1990; North Dakota, Mar. 25, 1991; Missouri, May 5, 1992; Alabama, May 5, 1992; Michigan, May 7, 1992; New Jersey, May 7, 1992; Illinois, May 12, 1992.

Certification of Validity. On May 13, 1992, the Archivist of the United States announced that he would accept this amendment as valid once he received formal notice pursuant to 1 U.S.C.A. § 106b.

Appendix O

CONSTITUTIONAL LAW RESEARCH
ON WESTLAW

Analysis

Section 1. Introduction

The discussion in this text provides a strong base for analyzing constitutional law questions. Analyzing a constitutional law question can be a complex task, requiring the examination of case law, statutes, administrative materials and commentary in addition to the applicable constitutional text. Along with West books, WESTLAW® is an excellent source of research materials.

In the area of constitutional law, WESTLAW expands your library by giving you access to documents issued by state and federal courts, legislatures and agencies. To assist you in keeping up-to-date with the activities of these government bodies, WESTLAW provides topical highlights databases such as the WESTLAW Bulletin databases covering developments at the U.S. Supreme Court and activities affecting state law. The following databases may also assist you with your constitutional law research: Constitutional Commentary (CONSTCOM), Texts & Periodicals—All Law Reviews, Texts & Bar Journals (TP–ALL), Congressional Quarterly's Washington Alert (CQ–ALERT), State Net Bill Tracking—All States & Congress (BILLTRK), State Net Regulation Tracking—All States & Congress (REGTRK), and Billcast (BC). With WESTLAW, unparalleled resources are at your fingertips. The West

Reference Attorneys are trained, licensed attorneys, available throughout the work day and on weekends to answer your WESTLAW or West book research questions.

Additional Resources: If you have not used WESTLAW or have questions not addressed in this appendix, see the *WESTLAW Reference Manual* or contact the West Reference Attorneys at 1–800–688–6363.

Section 2. Menu–Driven WESTLAW: EZ ACCESS™

EZ ACCESS is West Publishing Company's menu-driven research system. It is ideal for new or infrequent WESTLAW users because it requires no experience or training on WESTLAW.

To access EZ ACCESS, type **ez.** Whenever you are unsure of the next step, or if the choice you want is not listed, simply type **ez;** additional choices will be displayed. Once you retrieve documents with EZ ACCESS, use standard WESTLAW commands to browse your documents. For more information on browsing documents, see the *WESTLAW Reference Manual.*

Section 3. Retrieving a Document With a Citation: Find

Find is a WESTLAW service that allows you to retrieve a document by entering its citation. Find allows you to retrieve documents from anywhere in WESTLAW without accessing or changing databases or losing your search result. Find is available for many documents, including case law (federal and state), state statutes, *United States Code Annotated,*® *Code of Federal Regulations* and *Federal Register.*

To use FIND, type **fi** followed by the document citation. Below is a list of examples.

To Find This Document	Type
Young v. Klutznick, 652 F.2d 617 (6th Cir.1981)	**fi 652 f2d 617**
Zobel v. Williams, 102 S.Ct. 2309 (1982)	**fi 102 sct 2309**
Freeman v. Pitts, 1992 WL 59190 (U.S.)	**fi 1992 wl 59190**
U.S.C.A. Const. Art. 1 § 2, clause 5	**fi usca const art 1 s 2 cl 5**

Section 4. Query Formulation

Overview: A query is a request you make to WESTLAW specifying the information you wish to retrieve. The terms in a query are words or numbers that you include in your request so that WESTLAW will retrieve documents containing those words or numbers. These terms are linked together by connectors, which specify the relationship in which the terms must appear.

4.1 Terms

Plurals and Possessives: Plurals are automatically retrieved when you enter the singular form of a term. This is true for both regular and irregular plurals (e.g., **child** retrieves *children*). If you enter the plural form of a term, you will not retrieve the singular form.

If you enter the non-possessive form of a term, WESTLAW automatically retrieves the possessive form as well. If you enter the possessive form, however, only the possessive form is retrieved.

Automatic Equivalencies: Some terms have alternate forms or equivalencies; for example, *5* and *five* are equivalent terms. WEST-LAW automatically retrieves equivalent terms. The *WESTLAW Reference Manual* contains a list of equivalent terms.

Compound Words and Acronyms: When a compound word is one of your search terms, use a hyphen to retrieve all forms of the word. For example, the term **long-term** retrieves *long-term, long term* and *longterm.*

When using an acronym as a search term, place a period after each of the letters in the acronym to retrieve any of its forms. For example, the term **u.s.c.a.** retrieves *usca, u.s.c.a., u s c a* and *u. s. c. a.*

Root Expander and Universal Character: Placing a root expander (!) at the end of a root term retrieves ALL other terms with that root. For example, adding the ! symbol to the root *constru* in the query

constru! /s statute

instructs WESTLAW to retrieve such words as *construe, construes, construed, construing,* and *construction.*

The universal character (*) stands for one character and can be inserted in the middle or at the end of a term. For example, the term

s****holder

will retrieve *shareholder* and *stockholder*. But adding only two asterisks to the root *jur* in the query

jur**

instructs WESTLAW to retrieve all forms of the root with up to two additional characters. Terms like *jury* or *juror* are retrieved by this query. However, terms with more than two letters following the root, such as *jurisdiction,* are not retrieved. Plurals are always retrieved, even if more than two letters follow the root.

Phrase Searching: To search for a phrase on WESTLAW, place it within quotation marks. For example, to search for references to the establishment of a prima facie case, type **"prima facie"**. You should use phrase searching only when you are certain that the phrase will not appear in any other form.

4.2 Alternative Terms

After selecting the terms for your query, consider which alternative terms are necessary. For example, if you are searching for the

811

term *contract,* you might also want to search for the term *agreement.* You should consider both synonyms and antonyms as alternative terms.

4.3 Connectors

After selecting terms and alternative terms for your query, use connectors to specify the relationship that should exist between search terms in your retrieved documents. The connectors you can use are described below:

Use:	To retrieve documents with:	Example:
& (and)	search terms in the same document	**establishment & entanglement**
or (space)	one search term or the other	**controversial unorthodox**
/p	search terms in the same paragraph	**establishment /p entanglement**
/s	search terms in the same sentence	**privacy /s inva!**
+s	one search term preceding the other within the same sentence	**subject +s lease**
/n	search terms within "n" words of each other (where "n" is a number)	**police /3 power**
+n	one search term preceding the other by "n" words (where "n" is a number)	**yee +3 escondido**

Use:	To exclude documents with:	Example:
% (but not)	search terms following the % symbol	**42 +5 1988 % to(110)**

4.4 Restricting Your Search by Field

Overview: Documents in each WESTLAW database consist of several segments, or fields. One field may contain the citation, another the title, another the synopsis, and so forth. A query can be formulated to retrieve only those documents that contain search terms in a specified field. Not all databases contain the same fields. Also, depending on the database, fields of the same name may contain different types of information.

To view the fields and field content for a specific database, type **f** while in the database. Note that in some databases, not every field is available for every document. To search in a specific field, type the field name or abbreviation followed by the search terms enclosed in parentheses. For example, to retrieve a case entitled *Young v. Klutznick,* restrict your search to the title field

ti(young   &   klutznick)

The following fields are available in WESTLAW databases you might use for constitutional law research:

Digest and Synopsis Fields: The digest and synopsis fields, provided in case law databases by West Publishing Company's editors, summarize the main points of a case. A search in these fields is useful because it retrieves only cases in which a search term was significant enough to be included in a summary.

Consider searching for terms in one or both of these fields if

☐ you are searching for common terms or terms with more than one meaning and you need to narrow your search; or

☐ you cannot narrow your search by moving to a smaller data-base.

For example, to retrieve cases decided after 1988 that discuss compensation for taking, access the U.S. Supreme Court Cases database (SCT) and type

sy,di(taking /p compensat!) & da(aft 1988)

Headnote Field: The headnote field is a part of the digest field, but does not contain the topic number, the key number, the case citation or the title. The headnote field contains only the one-sentence summary of the point of law and any supporting statutory citations given by the author of the opinion. A headnote field search is useful when you are searching for specific code sections or rule numbers. For example, to retrieve headnotes that cite 15 U.S.C.A. 3314, type the following query:

he(15 +5 3314)

Topic Field: The topic field is also a part of the digest field. It contains the West digest topic name and number, the key number, and the key line text. You should restrict search terms to the topic field in a case law database if

☐ a digest field search retrieves too many documents; or

☐ you want to retrieve cases with digest paragraphs classified under more than one topic.

An example of the first type of topic field search is the following. The topic number for Taxation is 371. To retrieve Supreme Court cases that discuss taxation issues associated with interstate commerce, access the U.S. Supreme Court Cases database (SCT) and type a query like the following:

to(371) /p interstate /5 commerce

The second type of topic field search allows you to retrieve cases with West headnotes classified under more than one topic and key number. Search for the topic name in the topic field; for example, to retrieve other headnotes discussing taxation issues associated with interstate commerce, modify the above query to read as follows:

to(tax!) /p interstate /5 commerce

The TOPIC database contains a complete list of West Digest topics and their corresponding topic numbers.

813

> Be aware that slip opinions and cases from looseleaf services do not contain the digest, synopsis, headnote or topic fields.

Prelim and Caption Fields: When searching in a database containing statutes or regulations, restrict your search to the prelim and caption fields to retrieve documents in which your terms are important enough to appear in a section name or heading. For example, to retrieve *United States Code Annotated* sections relating to survivors' benefits under federal employee retirement programs, access the United States Code Annotated database (USCA) and type

pr,ca(retirement & survivor)

4.5 Restricting Your Search by Date

You can instruct WESTLAW to retrieve documents *decided* or *issued* before, after or on a specified date, as well as within a range of dates. The following are examples of queries that contain date restrictions:

da(bef 1992 & aft 1986) & strict! /5 scrutin!

da(1990) & strict! /5 scrutin!

da(7/3/89) & strict! /5 scrutin!

You can also instruct WESTLAW to retrieve documents *added to a database* on or after a specified date, or within a range of dates. The following are examples of queries that contain added date restrictions:

ad(aft 1–1–91) & strict! /5 scrutin!

ad(1–92) & strict! /5 scrutin!

ad(aft 2–1–91 & bef 3–1–91) & strict! /5 scrutin!

Section 5. Insta–Cite®

Overview: Insta–Cite is West Publishing Company's case history and citation verification service. It is the most current case history service available. Insta–Cite provides the following types of information about a citation:

Direct History. In addition to reversals and affirmances, Insta–Cite gives you the complete reported history of a litigated matter including any related cases. Insta–Cite provides the federal direct history of a case from 1754, and the state direct history from 1879.

Related References. Related references are cases that involve the same parties and facts as your case, but deal with different legal issues. Insta–Cite provides related references from 1983 to date.

Negative Indirect History. Insta–Cite lists subsequent cases that have a substantial negative impact on your case, including cases overruling your case or calling it into question. Cases affected by decisions from 1972 to date will be displayed on Insta–Cite. To retrieve negative indirect history prior to 1972, use Shepard's Citations (discussed in Section 6).

Secondary Source References. Insta–Cite also provides references to secondary sources that cite your case. These secondary sources presently include legal encyclopedias, such as *Corpus Juris Secundum.*®

Parallel Citations. Insta–Cite provides parallel citations for cases, including citations to *U.S. Law Week* and many other looseleaf reporters.

Citation Verification. Insta–Cite confirms that you have the correct volume and page number for a case. Citation verification information is available from 1754 for federal cases and from 1920 for state cases.

Commands

The following commands can be used in Insta–Cite:

ic xxx or **ic**	Retrieves an Insta–Cite result when followed by a case citation (where **xxx** is the citation), or when entered from a displayed case, Shepard's result or Shepard's PreView result.
pubs	Displays a list of publications and publication abbreviations available in Insta–Cite.
sc	Displays the scope of Insta–Cite coverage.
expand	Displays the Insta–Cite result in chronological order, including cases that affect negative indirect history cases.
loc xxx	Restricts an Insta–Cite result (where xxx is *dir, indir, hist* or *sec*).
xloc	Cancels your Locate request.
loc auto xxx	Automatically restricts subsequent Insta–Cite results according to your Locate request (where xxx is a Locate request).
xloc auto	Cancels your Locate Auto request.
gb or **map2**	Returns you to your previous service or search result, if one exists.

Section 6. Shepard's® Citations

Overview: Shepard's provides you with a comprehensive list of cases and publications that have cited a particular case. Shepard's also includes explanatory analysis to indicate how the citing cases have treated the case, e.g., "followed," "explained."

Commands

The following commands can be used in Shepard's:

sh xxx or **sh**	Retrieves a Shepard's result when followed by a case citation (where **xxx** is the citation), or when entered

	from a displayed case, Insta–Cite or Shepard's Pre-View result.
pubs	Displays a list of publications that can be Shepardiz-ed® and their publication abbreviations.
sc xxx	Displays the scope of coverage for a specific publication in Shepard's, where **xxx** is the publication abbreviation (e.g., **scope sw2d**).
cmds	Displays a list of Shepard's commands.
loc	Restricts a Shepard's result to a specific category when followed by the analysis code, headnote number, state/circuit or publication abbreviation to which you want the display restricted. For example, **loc 5** restricts the Shepard's result to cases discussing the point of law contained in headnote number five of the cited case. Type **xloc** to cancel Locate.
gb or **map2**	Leaves Shepard's and returns you to your previous service or search result, if one exists.

Section 7. Shepard's PreView™

Overview: Shepard's PreView gives you a preview of citing references from West's® National Reporter System® that will appear in Shepard's Citations. Depending on the citation, Shepard's PreView provides citing information days, weeks or even months before the same information appears in Shepard's online. Use Shepard's PreView to update your Shepard's results.

Commands

The following commands can be used in Shepard's PreView:

sp xxx or **sp**	Retrieves a Shepard's PreView result when followed by a case citation (where **xxx** is the citation), or when entered from a displayed case, Insta–Cite or Shepard's result.
pubs	Displays a list of publications and publication abbreviations that are available in Shepard's PreView.
sc xxx	Displays the scope of citing references.
cmds	Displays a list of Shepard's PreView commands.
loc xxx	Restricts a Shepard's PreView result to a specific publication, where **xxx** is the publication abbreviation.
gb or **map2**	Leaves Shepard's PreView and returns you to your previous service or search result, if one exists.

Section 8. Quick*Cite* ™

Using Quick*Cite*, you can retrieve the most recent citing cases on WESTLAW in one step. Quick*Cite* formulates a query for the case citation you enter and automatically runs the query for you in an appropriate database.

To retrieve citing references for *Village of Arlington Heights v. Metropolitan Housing Development Corp.,* 97 S.Ct. 555 (1977), type:

qc 97 sct 555

Quick *Cite* also allows you to choose a different date range and database for your query, so you can tailor it to your specific research needs.

Section 9. WESTLAW as a Citator

Using WESTLAW as a citator, you can search for documents citing a specific statute, regulation, rule or agency decision.

To retrieve documents citing 42 U.S.C.A. 2000e, access the U.S. Supreme Court Cases database (SCT) and search for the citation, adding an appropriate date restriction:

42 +5 2000e & da(aft 1989)

If the citation is not a unique term, add descriptive terms. For example, to retrieve cases citing N.Y. Real Prop. Law 231, access the New York Real Property Cases database (NYRP–CS) and type:

231 /p void! /p lease

Section 10. Research Examples

1. Nowak and Rotunda are authors of the following law review article: *Sales and Use Tax Credits, Discrimination Against Interstate Commerce, and the Useless Multiple Tax Concept,* 20 U.C. Davis L.Rev. 273 (1987). If your library does not subscribe to the *U.C. Davis Law Review,* how can you retrieve the article on WESTLAW?

Solution

☐ Access the University of California at Davis Law Review database (UCDLR). Restricting your search to the citation field, type the following query:

ci(20 + 5 273)

2. You are researching Establishment Clause issues related to U.S. Supreme Court case discussion of the three-pronged Lemon test, set forth in *Lemon v. Kurtzman,* 92 S.Ct. 2105 (1971). How do you retrieve cases that discuss the Lemon test?

Solution

☐ Access the U.S. Supreme Court Cases database (SCT) and type the following query:

lemon /s test

☐ After browsing your search result, you decide to check for cases that cite *Bowen v. Kendrick,* 108 S.Ct. 2562 (1988). Go to the first case of your search result and type **loc kendrick**.

☐ After entering the Locate request above, you want to view a list of Locate documents. The List Locate command allows you to list the retrieved documents that contain your Locate terms. To display a list of only Locate documents, type **lloc**.

☐ To cancel Locate, type **xloc**.

3. Your civil rights research leads you to 18 U.S.C.A. § 242. When you have the citation for a specific statute section, use Find to retrieve the statute. (Note: For more information on Find, see Section 3 of this appendix.)

Solution

☐ Type **fi 18 usca s 242**.

☐ To look at code sections surrounding § 242, use the Documents in Sequence command. To retrieve the section preceding § 242, type **d-**. To retrieve the section immediately following § 242, type **d**.

☐ To see if a statute has been amended or repealed, use the Update service. Simply type **update** while viewing the statute to display any session law that amends or repeals the statute.

Because slip laws are added to WESTLAW before they contain full editorial enhancements, they are not retrieved with Update. To retrieve slip laws, access the United States Public Laws database by typing **db us-pl** and then type **ci(slip)   &   18 +5   242**. Update does not contain material that has no prior counterpart in existing law. To ensure that you retrieve all relevant documents, run a descriptive word search in the legislative service database for the state desired.

4. Your client was threatened with eviction from his apartment shortly after his partner died of AIDS complications. Is it a denial of equal protection when a city denies a surviving homosexual partner protected status in housing?

Solution

☐ Access the ALLSTATES database and type the following query:

gay lesbian homosexual /s rent apartment

housing /p "equal protection"

☐ You are browsing one of the cases in your search result and want to view the text of footnote 2 in the opinion. Use the Locate command: type **loc fn2**.

5. The WESTLAW Bulletin—U.S. Supreme Court database (WLB–SCT) alerts you to recent Supreme Court news. Updated on a daily basis if material is available, WLB–SCT contains cases, rules and

orders. Your firm concentrates on employment law; how do you target developments in this area?

Solution

☐ Access the WESTLAW Bulletin—U.S. Supreme Court database (WLB–SCT). You automatically retrieve a citations list of documents added to the database in the past two weeks. To see where employment law is discussed, type **loc employment labor**.

*

TABLE OF CASES

A

Aaron v. Cooper, 156 F.Supp. 220 (D.C.Ark. 1957)—§ **18.9, n. 10.**

Abate v. Mundt, 403 U.S. 182, 91 S.Ct. 1904, 29 L.Ed.2d 399 (1971)—§ **18.36;** § **18.36, n. 43, 49.**

Abbott Laboratories v. Gardner, 387 U.S. 136, 87 S.Ct. 1507, 18 L.Ed.2d 681 (1967)—§ **2.11, n. 23.**

Abbott Laboratories, United States v., 369 F.Supp. 1396 (D.C.N.C.1973)—§ **20.25, n. 40.**

Ableman v. Booth, 62 U.S. 506, 16 L.Ed. 169 (1858)—§ **12.7, n. 5;** § **18.6, n. 7.**

Abood v. Detroit Bd. of Educ., 431 U.S. 209, 97 S.Ct. 1782, 52 L.Ed.2d 261 (1977)— § **20.11, n. 5;** § **20.41;** § **20.41, n. 61.**

A Book Named 'John Cleland's Memoirs of a Woman of Pleasure' v. Attorney General of Com. of Mass., 383 U.S. 413, 86 S.Ct. 975, 16 L.Ed.2d 1 (1966)—§ **20.59;** § **20.59, n. 3, 12, 19;** § **20.60.**

Abrams v. United States, 250 U.S. 616, 40 S.Ct. 17, 63 L.Ed. 1173 (1919)—§ **20.6, n. 8;** § **20.13;** § **20.13, n. 7, 14, 17.**

Accardi, United States ex rel. v. Shaughnessy, 347 U.S. 260, 74 S.Ct. 499, 98 L.Ed. 681 (1954)—§ **9.10, n. 52;** § **17.9, n. 101.**

ACF Industries, Inc., Commonwealth v., 441 Pa. 129, 271 A.2d 273 (Pa.1970)— § **13.4, n. 98.**

Acree v. County Bd. of Ed. of Richmond County, Ga., 458 F.2d 486 (5th Cir. 1972)—§ **18.9, n. 103.**

Adair v. United States, 208 U.S. 161, 28 S.Ct. 277, 52 L.Ed. 436 (1908)—§ **2.11, n. 34;** § **4.6, n. 29;** § **15.3, n. 36.**

Adam v. Saenger, 303 U.S. 59, 58 S.Ct. 454, 82 L.Ed. 649 (1938)—§ **17.8, n. 10.**

Adamo Wrecking Co. v. United States, 434 U.S. 275, 98 S.Ct. 566, 54 L.Ed.2d 538 (1978)—§ **2.11;** § **2.11, n. 71.**

Adams v. McIlhany, 593 F.Supp. 1025 (D.C.Tex.1984)—§ **19.23, n. 34.**

Adams v. Storey, 1 Fed.Cas. 141 (C.C.N.Y. 1817)—§ **23.6, n. 4;** § **23.12, n. 1;** § **23.32, n. 2.**

Adams v. Texas, 448 U.S. 38, 100 S.Ct. 2521, 65 L.Ed.2d 581 (1980)—§ **17.3, n. 11.**

Adams v. Williams, 407 U.S. 143, 92 S.Ct. 1921, 32 L.Ed.2d 612 (1972)—§ **14.2, n. 4.**

Adams Exp. Co. v. Croninger, 226 U.S. 491, 33 S.Ct. 148, 57 L.Ed. 314 (1913)— § **12.1, n. 10.**

Adamson v. California, 332 U.S. 46, 67 S.Ct. 1672, 91 L.Ed. 1903 (1947)—§ **15.6, n. 11, 15, 16, 17;** § **15.7, n. 2;** § **19.14, n. 18.**

Adderley v. Florida, 385 U.S. 39, 87 S.Ct. 242, 17 L.Ed.2d 149 (1966)—§ **20.45, n. 2;** § **20.47;** § **20.47, n. 27, 36, 43;** § **20.54, n. 52.**

Addington v. Texas, 441 U.S. 418, 99 S.Ct. 1804, 60 L.Ed.2d 323 (1979)—§ **17.4;** § **17.4, n. 14;** § **17.8, n. 34;** § **17.9;** § **17.9, n. 52;** § **20.61, n. 101.**

Addyston Pipe & Steel Co. v. United States, 175 U.S. 211, 20 S.Ct. 96, 44 L.Ed. 136 (1899)—§ **4.6, n. 13.**

Adickes v. Kress & Co., 398 U.S. 144, 90 S.Ct. 1598, 26 L.Ed.2d 142 (1970)— § **2.13, n. 263;** § **19.17, n. 2, 10, 11;** § **19.18;** § **19.18, n. 1;** § **19.28, n. 15.**

Adkins v. Children's Hospital, 261 U.S. 525, 43 S.Ct. 394, 67 L.Ed. 785 (1923)— § **2.7, n. 16, 17;** § **4.6, n. 28;** § **15.3, n. 51;** § **15.4;** § **15.4, n. 22, 24;** § **18.21;** § **18.21, n. 18, 19.**

Adler v. Board of Education, 342 U.S. 485, 72 S.Ct. 380, 96 L.Ed. 517 (1952)— § **2.13;** § **2.13, n. 121, 122;** § **20.24, n. 37;** § **20.42;** § **20.42, n. 2.**

Advance–Wilson Industries, Inc., Commonwealth v., 456 Pa. 200, 317 A.2d 642 (Pa.1974)—§ **13.4, n. 109.**

Aero Mayflower Transit Co. v. Board of Railroad Com'rs, 332 U.S. 495, 68 S.Ct. 167, 92 L.Ed. 99 (1947)—§ **13.2, n. 98.**

Aero Mayflower Transit Co. v. Georgia Public Serv. Com'n, 295 U.S. 285, 55 S.Ct. 709, 79 L.Ed. 1439 (1935)—§ **13.2, n. 98.**

Aetna Life Ins. Co. v. Lavoie, 475 U.S. 813, 106 S.Ct. 1580, 89 L.Ed.2d 823 (1986)— § **17.8, n. 14;** § **17.9, n. 3.**

Aetna Life Ins. Co. of Hartford, Conn. v. Haworth, 300 U.S. 227, 57 S.Ct. 461, 81 L.Ed. 617 (1937)—§ **2.13, n. 1, 21, 22, 48.**

Affleck, United States v., 765 F.2d 944 (10th Cir.1985)—§ **15.9, n. 49.**

TABLE OF CASES

C

TABLE OF CASES

846

TABLE OF CASES

TABLE OF CASES

F

861

G

H

871

K

TABLE OF CASES

884

888

N

905

O

918

S

T

937

938

TABLE OF CASES

TABLE OF AUTHORITIES

A

A.A.L.S., Selected Essay on Constitutional Law (D. Maggs, Ed., 1938)—§ **1.4, n. 16;** § **11.1, n. 4.**

A.B.A., Special Constitutional Convention Study Committee, Amendment to the Constitution by the Convention Method Under Article V (1974)—§ **10.10, n. 1.**

ABA Standards Relating to Judicial Discipline and Disability Retirement, Part 10 (1977)—§ **8.13, n. 11.**

Abascal & Kramer, Presidential Impoundments, Part II: Judicial and Legislative Responses, 63 Georgetown L.J. 149 (1974)—§ **7.4, n. 29.**

Abernathy, C., Civil Rights: Cases and Materials (1980)—§ **19.13, n. 1;** § **19.35, n. 12;** § **19.17, n. 1.**

Abernathy, T., The Burr Conspiracy (1968)—§ **7.1, n. 26.**

Abinger, E., Forty Years at the Bar (1930)—§ **7.1, n. 51.**

Abourezk, The Congressional Veto: A Contemporary Response to Executive Encroachment on Legislative Prerogatives, 52 Ind.L.Rev. 323 (1977)—§ **10.8, n. 3, 5.**

Abraham, H., Justices and Presidents: A Political History of Appointments to the Supreme Court (1985)—§ **2.7, n. 18, 21.**

Abraham, Limiting Federal Court Jurisdiction: A "Self–Inflicted Wound?", 65 Judicature 179 (1981)—§ **2.11, n. 20.**

Abramowitz and Jackson, Desegregation: Where Do We Go From Here?, 19 How.L.J. 92 (1975)—§ **18.9, n. 28.**

Abrams, Book Review, 86 Yale L.J. 361 (1976)—§ **20.18, n. 91.**

Abrams, The Pentagon Papers Case a Decade Later, New York Times Magazine, June 7, 1981—§ **20.17, n. 12.**

Abrams, What are the Rights Guaranteed by the Ninth Amendment?, 53 A.B.A.J. 1033 (1967)—§ **15.7, n. 10.**

Abrams & Dimond, Toward a Constitutional Framework for the Control of State Court Jurisdiction, 69 Minn.L.Rev. 75 (1984)—§ **12.7, n. 4;** § **17.8, n. 11.**

Abramson, Equal Protection and Administrative Convenience, 52 Tennessee L.Rev. 1 (1984)—§ **18.3, n. 25.**

Abramson, House Votes 413–3 to Impeach Judge On Charge He Conspired to Take Bribe, Wall St. Journal, Aug. 4, 1988— § **2.9, n. 21, 22;** § **8.10, n. 1.**

Abramson, Oliver North Wins Dismissal of U.S. Case, Wall St.Jrl., Sept. 17, 1991 (Midwest ed.)—§ **9.6, n. 48.**

Ackerman, Beyond Carolene Products, 98 Harv.L.Rev. 713 (1985)—§ **15.7, n. 17;** § **18.3, n. 25;** § **23.5, n. 4, 19.**

Ackerman, Bruce, We the People: Foundations (1991)—§ **23.5, n. 9.**

Ackerman, Discovering the Cosntitution, 93 Yale L.J. 1013 (1984)—§ **1.1, n. 119.**

Ackerman, Transformative Appointments, 101 Harv.L.Rev. 1164 (1988)—§ **2.7, n. 18.**

Adams, C., Works of John Adams (C.Adams ed.1850)—§ **1.1, n. 16.**

Adams & Gordon, The Doctrine of Accommodation in the Jurisprudence of the Religion Clauses, 37 DePaul L.Rev. 317 (1988)—§ **21.6, n. 2.**

Adams & Hanlon, Jones v. Wolf: Church Autonomy and the Religion Clauses of the First Amendment, 128 U.Pa.L.Rev. 1291 (1980)—§ **21.12, n. 12.**

Adler, R. Reckless Disregard (1986)— § **20.33, n. 12.**

Adler & Pollock, Rose Pact is One More Trade–Off, Wall St. Jrl., Aug. 25, 1989— § **20.17, n. 13.**

Adye, S., A Treatise on Courts Martial (1786)—§ **6.13, n. 15.**

Aeschylus, Plays (Loeb Classical Library, 1922–1926)—§ **20.13, n. 9.**

Agresto, J., The Supreme Court and Constitutional Democracy (1984)—§ **23.5, n. 19.**

Albert, Justiciability and Theories of Judicial Review: A Remote Relationship, 50 So.Calif.L.Rev. 1139 (1977)—§ **2.13, n. 196.**

Alchian, The Economic and Social Impact of Free Tuition, in H. Manne, The Economics of Legal Relationships (1975)— § **21.4, n. 92.**

Alderman, Commercial Entities' Noncommercial Speech: A Contradiction in Terms, 1982 Utah L.Rev. 731—§ **20.31, n. 100.**

Aldisert, Judicial Expansion of Federal Jurisdiction: A Federal Judge's Thoughts on Section 1983, Comity and the Federal Caseload, 1973 Ariz.St.U.L.J. 557— § **19.39, n. 3.**

Aldisert, R., The Judicial Process (1976)— § **2.6, n. 1.**

TABLE OF AUTHORITIES

TABLE OF AUTHORITIES

TABLE OF AUTHORITIES

TABLE OF AUTHORITIES

TABLE OF AUTHORITIES

966

TABLE OF AUTHORITIES

TABLE OF AUTHORITIES

D

TABLE OF AUTHORITIES

TABLE OF AUTHORITIES

TABLE OF AUTHORITIES

G

TABLE OF AUTHORITIES

TABLE OF AUTHORITIES

987

TABLE OF AUTHORITIES

988

TABLE OF AUTHORITIES

TABLE OF AUTHORITIES

TABLE OF AUTHORITIES

K

TABLE OF AUTHORITIES

TABLE OF AUTHORITIES

TABLE OF AUTHORITIES

TABLE OF AUTHORITIES

TABLE OF AUTHORITIES

TABLE OF AUTHORITIES

TABLE OF AUTHORITIES

TABLE OF AUTHORITIES

TABLE OF AUTHORITIES

TABLE OF AUTHORITIES

TABLE OF AUTHORITIES

TABLE OF AUTHORITIES

TABLE OF AUTHORITIES

TABLE OF AUTHORITIES

TABLE OF AUTHORITIES

TABLE OF AUTHORITIES

TABLE OF AUTHORITIES

TABLE OF AUTHORITIES

TABLE OF AUTHORITIES

TABLE OF AUTHORITIES

TABLE OF AUTHORITIES

TABLE OF AUTHORITIES

TABLE OF AUTHORITIES

INDEX

A

F

INDEX

1081

†